FROMMER'S

COMPREHENSIVE TRAVEL GUIDE

FRANCE '94-'95

by Darwin Porter
Assisted by Danforth Prince

MACMILLAN • USA

NEW YORK • LONDON • TORONTO • SYDNEY • TOKYO • SINGAPORE

MACMILLAN TRAVEL
A Prentice Hall Macmillan Company
15 Columbus Circle
New York, NY 10023

ISBN 0-671-86612-5
ISSN 0899-3351

Design by Robert Bull Design
Maps by Geografix Inc.

SPECIAL SALES
Bulk purchases (10+ copies) of Frommer's Travel Guides are available to corporations at special discounts. The Special Sales Department can produce custom editions to be used as premiums and/or for sales promotion to suit individual needs. Existing editions can be produced with custom cover imprints such as corporate logos. For more information write to: Special Sales, Macmillan, 15 Columbus Circle, New York, NY 10023.

Manufactured in the United States of America

CONTENTS

LIST OF MAPS

INVITATION TO THE READERS

In researching this book, I have come across many fine establishments, the best of which I have included here. I'm sure that many of you will also come across recommendable hotels, inns, restaurants, guesthouses, shops, and attractions. Please don't keep them to yourself. Share your experiences, especially if you want to comment on places that I have covered in this edition that have changed for the worse. You can address your letters to me:

Darwin Porter
Frommer's France '94–'95
c/o Prentice Hall Travel
15 Columbus Circle
New York, NY 10023

A DISCLAIMER

Readers are advised that prices fluctuate in the course of time and travel information changes under the impact of the varied and volatile factors that affect the travel industry. The author and publisher cannot be held responsible for the experiences of readers while traveling. Readers are invited to write to the publisher with ideas, comments, and suggestions for future editions.

SAFETY ADVISORY

Whenever you're traveling in an unfamiliar city or country, stay alert. Be aware of your immediate surroundings. Wear a moneybelt and keep a close eye on your possessions. Be particularly careful with cameras, purses, and wallets, all favorite targets of thieves and pickpockets.

GETTING TO KNOW FRANCE

France is a nation of contrasts, united by love of country . . . and a loaf of bread. Wherever you go, from the streets of Marseille to the fishing hamlets of Brittany, from the provincial capitals to the "capital of capitals," you'll see the French, the matronly and the chic, carry home their daily bread.

Of course, even this time-honored ritual is changing. Many modern homemakers in France buy their bread wrapped in waxpaper at supermarkets. Gaul is not entirely trapped by its traditions. You may find some elderly wives of fishermen in Brittany wearing the starched-lace headdresses their grandmothers' mothers did before them. But at the next table you might meet their daughters, exquisitely attired in the latest Parisian fashions, discussing the state of the theater in New York.

Some things in France never change, however. Priests still walk the streets of provincial towns greeting aging women in black, lovers with their arms wrapped around each other still stroll along the banks of the Seine, and Left Bank students still spend an evening arguing philosophy over a bottle of wine. The *agent pivot* still directs traffic with a white baton, waving speeding motorists around the Arc de Triomphe; French people still spend hours in their favorite cafés; and little old winemakers practice the same basic techniques they have for generations. The nation, then, is a land rich in tradition, and it is that quality I'll search for in exploring—

THE BEST OF FRANCE I have set myself the formidable task of seeking out France at its finest and condensing that between the covers of this book. The best towns, villages, cities, and sightseeing attractions; the best hotels, restaurants, bars, cafés, and nightspots.

But the best need not be the most expensive. My ultimate aim—beyond that of familiarizing you with the offerings of France—is to stretch your dollar power . . . to reveal to you that you need not always pay scalpers' prices for charm, top-grade comfort, and gourmet-level food.

In this guide I'll devote a great deal of attention to those old tourist meccas—Paris, Cannes, Monaco, Biarritz—focusing on both their obvious and hidden treasures. But they are not the full "reason why" of this book. Important as they are, they simply do not reflect fully the widely diverse and complicated country that France is. To discover that, you must venture deep into the provinces.

1. GEOGRAPHY & HISTORY

GEOGRAPHY

Many of the differences between the provinces of France are based on geographical variations. The highly publicized area where blue sea waters lap the Côte d'Azur of the Mediterranean, known as the French Riviera, is totally unlike the northwestern corner of the country, Brittany, although both are coastal areas. Blessed with long, dry summers and inviting beaches, the international playground of the south was a drawing card in the slower-paced days of aristocratic and royal visitors, and it is still so for a lively crowd today.

The sea and tides have long governed the lives of the people in coastal provinces. In Brittany, and elsewhere to a lesser degree, the products of the sea are still a means of livelihood. In the southwest and south, this has given way to other sea-going enterprises, such as operation of yachts and other pleasure vessels, as well as cruise ships, all of which ply the waters and keep the economy healthy there.

France faces the Mediterranean on the south, the Bay of Biscay and the Atlantic Ocean on the west, and the English Channel and the Strait of Dover on the northwest. It is bordered on the north by Belgium and Luxembourg, on the northeast by Germany, on the east by Switzerland, on the southeast by Italy, and it is divided from Spain on the south by the rugged Pyrénées Mountains. Besides the Pyrénées, other mountain ranges of the country are the Alps and the Jura. Scattered plains make up more than half of the country. All these geographical definitions have brought about the development of France into a rich and fertile land.

Farming, wine and brandy production, and cheese making are only some of the pursuits of the country people in the interior, with modern factories, scientists, and laboratories bringing their own coloration to the cities, towns, and villages.

The Grand Tour of France

To be blunt and in contradiction of our headline, a "grand tour" of France is almost impossible for the average visitor. It takes at least two weeks to tour each major province, and France has a lot of provinces—all of tourist interest either major or limited—and few people have months in which to see the country, as delectable an idea as that might be. Some strong choices about where to go have to be made. The answer of where to go depends entirely on your time, whim, inclination, and often, your pocketbook. I'll give you what I hope are helpful suggestions to get you across at least some of the highlights of a constantly changing but ever-fascinating countryside.

Covering 212,741 square miles, France is slightly smaller than Texas. But no other patch on the globe concentrates such a fabulous diversity of sights and scenery in so compact an area. Within her borders, France houses each of the natural characteristics that make up Europe: the flat, fertile north, the rolling green hills of the central Loire valley, the snowcapped alpine ranges of the east, the towering Pyrénées in the south, and the lushly semitropical Mediterranean coast of the southeast.

Name your taste and France has a spot for you: The châteaux country around Orléans for castles and vineyards. Normandy and Brittany for rugged seashores and apple orchards. The Mont Blanc area for mountain climbing and skiing. The Champagne for sun-warmed valleys and the greatest of all wines. Languedoc for Spanish flavor, olive groves, and Mediterranean cookery. The Riviera for golden sands, palm-fringed beaches, and bodies beautiful.

Because the country is—by American standards—not very large, all these contrasts beckon within easy traveling range. By train from Paris, it's just four hours to Alsace, five hours to the Alps, seven hours to the Pyrénées, and eight hours to the Côte d'Azur. France's National Railroads (SNCF) actually *want* passengers and operate one of the finest services in the world. They're also impressively fast to and from Paris, but more inclined to crawl on routes unconnected with the capital.

There are some 44,000 miles of roadway at your disposal, most in good condition for fast, long-distance driving. But take a tip and don't stick to the Route Nationale network all the time. Nearly all the scenic splendors lie alongside the secondary roads, and what you lose in mileage you more than make up for in enjoyment.

Regions in Brief

Ile de France Versailles, Fontainebleau, and Chartres all fall in this region encircling Paris. Once called the "garden of kings," much of it has been destroyed by urban sprawl, but some delightful spots remain, such as the forest of Fontainebleau.

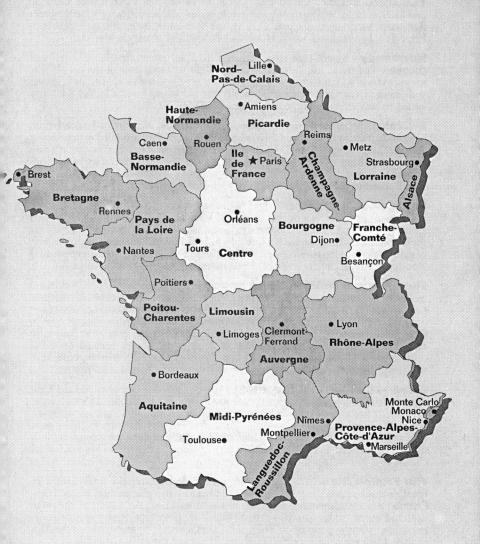

Nord–
Pas-de-Calais

Lille●

●Amiens

Haute-
Normandie

Picardie

Reims●

●Metz

Caen●

Rouen●

Ile
de
France

★ Paris

Champagne-
Ardenne

Strasbourg●

Lorraine

Brest

Basse-
Normandie

Alsace

Bretagne

Rennes●

Orléans●

Bourgogne

Franche-
Comté

Pays de
la Loire

Dijon●

●Nantes

Tours●

Centre

Besançon●

Poitiers●

Poitou-
Charentes

Limousin

●Lyon

●Limoges

Clermont-
Ferrand●

Rhône-Alpes

Auvergne

●Bordeaux

Aquitaine

Midi-Pyrénées

Nîmes●

Monte Carlo
Monaco
Nice●

Montpellier●

Provence-Alpes-
Côte-d'Azur

Toulouse●

Languedoc-
Roussillon

●Marseille

THE FRENCH METROPOLITAN REGIONS

Corse
(Corsica)

Ajaccio●

The Loire Valley Called the "garden of France" in a country of beautiful provinces, it is one of the most beautiful. It is explored primarily for its magnificent Renaissance-style châteaux that were visited or lived in by such august figures as François I, Leonardo da Vinci, Honoré de Balzac, and Marie de Medici.

Normandy Blond, blue-eyed Vikings settled this region that has 372 miles of coastline. The sea is still very much part of the traditional lives of the people. For summer chic it's Deauville in August, but most people come to see the great abbeys and châteaux, such as Rouen cathedral and the "city of one hundred spires." It's also visited by war veterans who come to view the D-Day beaches.

Brittany Some locals might tell you that Brittany is not part of France but an independent duchy, and indeed this traditional corner of France is filled with seafaring individualists. Facing the English Channel, the westernmost point of France, it's best visited from May to September. Many of its churches hold religious processions known as *pardons*. A popular vacation area, after the Côte d'Azur, it is the most visited coastline in France for its sandy beaches and high cliffs.

Reims and Champagne The 78-mile road from Reims to Vertus takes in a trio of wine-growing regions that produce 80% of the bubbly used for celebrations around the world. Clovis was baptized in the cathedral at Reims in A.D. 496, and later the dauphin was also crowned here, thanks to Joan of Arc. Lying directly in the path of any invader wishing to occupy Paris, both Reims and Champagne have experienced bloody warfare, including some of the worst trench warfare during World War I.

The Ardennes and Northern Beaches This is a region often neglected by North American visitors. The French come to visit such Channel beach resorts as Le Touquet–Paris-Plage. Among the many famous French personalities associated with the region, Henri Matisse from St-Quentin and poet Arthur Rimbaud from Chareville stand out. The cathedral of Notre-Dame at Amiens is its most impressive cathedral, but its most intriguing town is Laon, which stands isolated on a hill overlooking the Champagne plain. The last offensive of the Nazi army was fought in the heavily forested Ardennes. Dunkirk and Calais are its two best-known ports.

Alsace-Lorraine and the Vosges Lying between Germany and the great forests of the Vosges, Alsace, with its capital at Strasbourg, is celebrated for its cuisine, particularly foie gras and choucroute (sauerkraut). It is the most German of all French provinces. Travel the wine road—the *Route de Vin*—and visit historic old towns, such as Colmar. Lorraine, birthplace of Joan of Arc, saw some of the worst fighting in the two world wars. Even though it's a center of industry, this region has much rural charm, too. The Vosges forest is great for hiking.

The French Alps The region that includes Savoy (Savoie) contains some of France's most striking scenery—snowcapped peaks and glaciers and alpine lakes. Chamonix is a world-famous ski resort facing Mont Blanc, the highest mountain in western Europe. Today Courcheval and Megève are more chic. Summers are equally rewarding, when you can enjoy Evian and Lake Geneva. The area between the Alps and the Mediterranean is called Dauphine. Its ancient capital is Grenoble.

Burgundy Great wines and vineyards and splendid old cities, such as Dijon, make this a visitor's mecca. Besides the renowned cuisine (boeuf bourguignon, remember) it also contains some of the finest Romanesque architecture in Europe—

IMPRESSIONS

The country seems to me as beautiful as Japan for clarity of atmosphere and gay color effects. Water forms patches of lovely emerald or rich blue in the landscape, just as we see it in the crêpe prints. The pale orange of the sunsets make the fields appear blue.
—VAN GOGH, LETTERS, 1888

for example, at Vézelay, which UNESCO declared an "international treasure." Few trips will prove as rewarding as a five-day trek through Burgundy.

The Rhône Valley Only two hours by fast train from Paris, Lyon is the "second city" of France. It's famous for its chefs (Paul Bocuse, for example). North of here, visitors travel the Beaujolais trail or head for the ancient capital of Bresse, Bourg-en-Bresse, a gastronomic center said to produce the finest poultry in the world. The Rhône Valley can be explored en route to Provence and the south. Try to visit the little medieval villages of Pérouges and Vienne, 17 miles south of Lyon, the latter known for its Roman ruins.

The Massif Central The rugged agricultural heartland of France, it contains ancient cities and unspoiled scenery. It's provincial with a vengeance—and the locals want to keep it that way. Explore the old capital of the Auvergne, Clermont-Ferrand, or Limoges, the capital of Limousin. Bourges, a gateway to the region and once the capital of Aquitaine, has a beautiful Gothic cathedral. Take the waters at Vichy on the northern edge of the Auvergne or follow the trail of George Sand. Visit, too, Le Puy, which is built in the center of a natural amphitheater encircled by volcanic mountains.

Dordogne and Périgord The land of foie gras and truffles. In Périgord traces of Cro-Magnon are evidenced by the cave paintings at Les Eyzies. Dordogne is the second-largest *département* in the country and includes parts of the old provinces of Limousin and Quercy. It is, unfortunately, no longer undiscovered.

Bordeaux and the Atlantic Coast While you travel along the wine routes tasting the bordeaux, you can also visit some ancient cities like Angoulême, 72 miles north of Bordeaux and associated with Balzac; Saintes, the old Roman capital of southwest France; and Poitiers, the ancient capital of Poitou, the northern part of Aquitaine.

The Basque Country and the Pyrénées Famous resorts like Biarritz and St-Jean-de-Luz and the Parc National des Pyrénées make this a vacationer's paradise. Much of the region has a Spanish flavor, and you can even attend a bullfight. The pilgrimage city of Lourdes draws four million visitors a year. The old traditions live on in the villages and towns of the Pyrénées.

Languedoc, Roussillon and the Camargue Lying between the Pyrénées and the Mediterranean, Languedoc-Roussillon is a wine-growing region that has a Spanish flavor. Roussillon is the French answer to Catalonia, and the Camargue is the name given to the marshy delta between two arms of the Rhône River. Visit such old towns as Auch, the ancient capital of Gascony; Toulouse, the old capital of Languedoc; and the "red city" of Albi, birthplace of Toulouse-Lautrec. Carcassonne, a marvelously preserved medieval walled city, is the region's sightseeing highlight. The university city of Montpellier is the capital of Lower Languedoc, and 31 miles away lies Nîmes, famous for its Roman relics.

Provence This region offers visitors a host of options. Premier targets are Aix-en-Provence, associated with Paul Cézanne; Arles, "the soul of Provence" (captured so brilliantly by van Gogh); Avignon, the 14th-century capital of Christendom during the schism; and Marseille, more North African than French. But the special gems are the small villages, such as Les Baux and St-Rémy-de-Provence, birthplace of Nostradamus.

The French Riviera The fabled gold-plated Côte d'Azur is now hideously overbuilt and spoiled by tourism. Even so, the names of its resorts still evoke glamour and excitement around the world: Cannes, Monaco, St-Tropez. July and August are the most crowded months to visit, but spring and fall can be a delight. There are some sandy beaches, but many are rocky or pebbly. Topless bathing is common, especially in St-Tropez. It's not just a place for sun and fun, though—there are many galleries and museums worth visiting.

Corsica The third-largest island in the Mediterranean, more Italian than French, it's the birthplace of Napoléon. Few North Americans visit it. The largest port on the island is Bastia; Ajaccio, Napoléon's birthplace, is the capital. The real charm, though, lies in its mountains and coastal villages.

DATELINE	HISTORY

Early Gaul and the Ancient Romans The political unit that the world knows today as France resulted from an often-bloody series of conflicts among fiercely competitive personalities and factions. When the ancient Romans considered it a part of their empire, their boundaries extended deep into the forests of the Paris basin and up to the edges of the Rhine. As it declined, Rome retreated to the flourishing colonies it had established along a strip of the Mediterranean coastline. Rome colonized them with what were reputed to be the best traders of the era, Greeks and Syrians, who intermarried with local residents and blond-haired, blue-eyed northerners. Centuries later their ancestors contributed their offspring to the racial melting pot that became modern France.

Grateful for Rome's protection from the barbaric northerners, the residents of this coastal strip became the most cultivated and cultured inhabitants of Gaul. In the north, however, a cluster of tribal kingdoms was already established. Each of these was strengthened and became bolder after the retreat of Rome. The Visigoths, Burgundians, Franks, Ripuarians, Salians, and, in Brittany, the Celts, controlled regions whose boundaries sometimes overlapped those of modern Germany and Spain. Borders and alliances shifted according to an unrecorded array of skirmishes.

The Roman armies left as their legacy the Catholic church, which, for all its abuses, was probably the only real guardian of civilization. A form of low Latin was the common language, and it slowly evolved into the archaic French that both delights and confuses today's medieval scholars.

In this semi-barbaric political vacuum, the form of Christianity adopted by many of the chieftains was considered heretical by Rome. Consequently, when Clovis, king of northeastern Gaul's Salian Franks, astutely converted to Catholicism, he won the approval of the pope, the political support of the powerful archbishop of Reims, and the loyalty of the many Gallic tribes who had grown disenchanted with anarchy. At the battle of Soissons in 486, the armies of Clovis defeated the last vestiges of Roman power in Gaul. Other conquests that followed included expansions first westward to the Seine, then to the Loire. After a battle in Dijon in 500, he became the nominal overlord of the king of Burgundy. Seven years later, after the battle of Vouillé, his armies drove the Visigoths into Spain, giving most of Aquitaine, in western France, to his newly founded Merovingian dynasty. Trying to make the best of an earlier humiliation, Anastasius, the Byzantium-based emperor of the Eastern Roman Empire, finally gave the kingdom of the Franks his legal sanction.

After the death of Clovis in 511, his kingdom was split

- **121 B.C.** The Romans establish the province of Gallia Narbonensis to guard the overland routes between Spain and Italy; its borders correspond roughly to today's Provence.
- **58–51 B.C.** Julius Caesar conquers Gaul (central and northern France).
- **52 B.C.** The Roman city of Lutetia, later Paris, is built on a defensible island in the Seine.
- **2nd century A.D.** Christianity arrives in Gaul.
- **451** Romans (with Visigoths and Franks) vanquish Attila the Hun near Troyes.
- **485–511** Under Clovis I, Franks defeat the Roman armies and establish the Merovingian dynasty.
- **511 on** Confusion and disorder; feudalism and the power of the Catholic church grows.
- **768** Charlemagne (768–814) becomes Frankish king and establishes the Carolingian dynasty; from Aix-la-Chapelle (Aachen) he rules lands from north-

(continues)

among his squabbling heirs. The Merovingian dynasty, however, managed to survive in fragmented form for another 250 years. During this period, the power of the bishops and the great lords grew, firmly entrenching the complex rules and preoccupations of what we today know as feudalism.

The Coming of Charlemagne From the wreckage of a Merovingian court swathed in intrigue, the Carolingian dynasty produced the first strong leader in centuries, Charlemagne. Crowned emperor in Rome on Christmas Day of the year 800, he returned to his capital at Aix-la-Chapelle (Aachen) to found the Holy Roman Empire. Distinct cultural differences were already visible within this sprawling empire, most of which was eventually divided between two of Charlemagne's three squabbling heirs. Charles of Aquitaine agreed to accept the western region, while Louis of Bavaria took the east. Historians credit this official division with the development of modern France and Germany as separate nations.

Shortly afterward the Vikings began plundering from the north, while the Muslim Saracens launched raids in the south. When the Merovingian dynasty died out in 987, Hugh Capet, Count of Paris and Duke of France, officially began the Middle Ages. In 1154, Eleanor of Aquitaine's marriage to Henry II of England placed the entire western half of France under English control, where vestiges of their power would remain for centuries. Meanwhile, vast forests and swamps were cleared for harvesting, the population grew, and monastic life contributed heavily to every level of a rapidly developing social order. Louis IX (Saint Louis) emerged as the 13th century's most memorable king, even though he ceded most of the hard-earned military conquests of his predecessors back to the English. He died of disease along with most of his army in 1270 during the Eighth Crusade in Tunis. Notre-Dame Cathedral and the Sainte-Chapelle in Paris had been completed, and the arts of tapestry-making and stonecutting flourished.

The Middle Ages and French Kings During the 1300s the struggle of French sovereignty against the claims of a rapacious Roman pope tempted Philip the Fair to encourage support for a pope based in Avignon. (The Roman pope, Boniface VIII, is said to have died of the shock.) Two popes ruled simultaneously, competing fiercely for the financial and spiritual loyalty of Christendom, until the French pope stepped down in 1378. The centuries saw an increase in the wealth and power of the French kings, an increase in the general prosperity, and a decrease in the power of the feudal lords. The death of Louis X without an heir in 1316 prompted more than a decade of intrigue before the eventual accession of the Valois dynasty. The Black Death began in the summer of 1348, killing an estimated 33% of the population. A financial crisis coupled with a ruinous series of harvests almost bankrupted the nation.

During the Hundred Years' War, the English made sweeping inroads into France in an attempt to grab the throne. At their most powerful, they controlled almost all of the north (Picardy and Normandy), Champagne, and

DATELINE

ern Italy to Bavaria to Paris.
- **800** Charlemagne is crowned Holy Roman Emperor in Rome.
- **814** Death of Charlemagne; empire breaks up.
- **1066** William of Normandy (the Conqueror) invades England; Conquest completed by 1087.
- **1140** St-Denis Cathedral built, the first example of Gothic architecture.
- **1270** Louis IX (St. Louis), along with most of his army, dies in Tunis on the Eighth Crusade.
- **1309** Schism—Philip the Fair establishes the Avignon Papacy, which lasts nearly 70 years; two popes struggle for domination.
- **1347–51** Bubonic plague (the Black Death) kills 33% of the population; peasant disturbances.
- **1431** English burn Joan of Arc at the stake in Rouen for resisting their occupation of France.
- **1434** Johannes Gutenberg invents the printing press.
- **1453** The French drive the English out of all of France except Calais; Hundred Years' War ends.
- **1515–47** Fran-
(continues)

DATELINE

çois I, patron of Leonardo da Vinci, lays the foundation of monarchy and nation.

• **1558** France captures Calais.

• **1562–98** Wars of Religion: Catholics fight Protestants; Henri IV converts to Catholicism and issues the Edict of Nantes, granting limited rights to Protestants.

• **1643–1715** Reign of Louis XIV, the Sun King; France develops the most powerful army in Europe, but wars in Flanders and court extravagance sow seeds of decline.

• **1763** Treaty of Paris effectively ends French power in North America.

• **1789–94** Storming of the Bastille, July 14, 1789; the Reign of Terror follows.

• **1793** Louis XVI and Marie Antoinette guillotined.

• **1794** Robespierre and the leaders of the Terror guillotined.

• **1799** Napoléon enters Paris and unites factions; military victories in northern Italy solidify his power in Paris.

• **1804** Napoléon crowns himself emperor in the cathedral at Paris.

• **1805–11** Napo-

(continues)

most of the Loire Valley. They also ruled the huge western region of France called Guyenne. The peasant-born Joan of Arc, with her visions and enthusiasm, rallied the French troops as well as the timid dauphin, Charles VII, until she was burned at the stake in Rouen by the English in 1431. A barely cohesive France, led by the newly crowned king, initiated internal reforms which strengthened its finances and its vigor. After compromises among the quarreling factions, the French army drove the increasingly discontented English out of France, leaving them only the port of Calais.

In the late 1400s Charles VIII married Brittany's last duchess, Anne, for a unification of France with its Celtic-speaking western outpost. In the early 1500s the endlessly fascinating François I, through war and diplomacy, strengthened the monarchy, rid it of its dependence on Italian bankers, coped with the intricate policies of the Renaissance, and husbanded the arts into a form of patronage which French monarchs would continue for centuries.

Meanwhile, the allure of Protestantism and the unwillingness of the Catholic church to tolerate it led to some of the most intense civil strife in French history. In 1572 Catherine de Médicis reversed her policy of religious tolerance and ordered the St. Bartholomew's Day Massacre of hundreds of Protestants throughout France. The very urbane Henri IV, fearing that a fanatically Catholic Spain would meddle in France's religious conflicts, and tired of the bloodshed, converted to Catholicism as a compromise gesture in 1593. Just before being fatally stabbed by a half-crazed monk, he issued the Edict of Nantes in 1598. This granted freedom of religion to Protestants in France, as well as safeguarding their "places of security," notably La Rochelle.

The Passing of Feudalism By now France was a modern state, finally rid of all but a few of the vestiges of feudalism. In 1624 Louis XIII appointed a Catholic cardinal, the Duke of Richelieu, as his chief minister. Richelieu virtually ruled the country until his death in 1642. Under Richelieu, the Protestants lost their stronghold at La Rochelle but were then assimilated into French society, and the power of France, with a minimum of bloodshed, was greatly increased within Europe. Richelieu's one focused objective, the total power of the monarchy, paved the way for the eventual absolutism of Louis XIV.

Although he ascended the French throne when he was only nine years old, with the help of his Sicilian-born chief minister Mazarin, Louis XIV was probably the most powerful monarch Europe had seen since the fall of the Roman emperors. Through first a brilliant military campaign against Spain, and then a judicious marriage to one of its royal daughters, he expanded France to include the southern provinces of Artois and Roussillon. Later, a series of diplomatic and military victories along the Flemish border expanded France toward the north and east as well. The estimated population of France at this time was 20 million, as opposed to eight million in England and six million in Spain. French colonies in Canada, the West Indies, and Louisiana flourished. The mercantilism which

Louis' brilliant finance minister, Colbert, was able to implement is regarded as one of the most important fiscal policies of the era, one that hugely increased the power and wealth of France. The arts flourished. The palace of Versailles is probably the most visible monument to the most flamboyantly consumptive era of French history.

Louis's territorial ambitions so deeply threatened the other nations of Europe that, led by William of Orange (the Dutch-born English king), they united to hold him in check. France entered a series of expensive and demoralizing wars which, coupled with high taxes and years of bad harvests, engendered much civil discontent. England was now viewed as a threat both within Europe and in the global rush for lucrative colonies. The great Atlantic ports of the west, especially Bordeaux, grew and prospered because of France's success in the West Indian slave and sugar trade. Despite France's power, the total number of French colonies diminished thanks to the naval power of the English. The rise of Prussia as a militaristic neighbor posed an additional problem.

The Revolution Meanwhile, the Enlightenment was training a new generation of thinkers for the struggle against absolutism, religious fanaticism, and superstition. Europe was never again the same after the Revolution of 1789, although the ideas that engendered it had been brewing for more than 50 years. On August 10, 1792, troops from Marseille, aided by a Parisian mob, threw Louis XVI and his Austrian-born queen, Marie Antoinette, into prison. After bloodshed and bickering among violently competing factions, the two were executed. France's problems got worse before they got better. In the bloodbaths that followed, both moderates and radicals were guillotined within full view of the bloodthirsty crowd. It usually included voyeurs such as Dickens's Madame Defarge, who brought her knitting every day to the place de la Révolution (later renamed the place de la Concorde) to watch the beheadings.

The Rise of Napoléon It required the militaristic fervor of Napoléon to unite France once again. Possessed of genius and unlimited ambition, he restored to France a national pride which had been diminished during the horror of the Revolution. In 1799, at the age of 30, he entered Paris and was crowned First Consul and Master of France. Soon after, a decisive victory in his northern Italian campaign solidified his power at home. A brilliant politician, he made peace through a compromise with the Vatican, moderating the atheistic rigidity of the earliest days of the Revolution.

Napoléon's victories made him the envy of Europe. Beethoven dedicated one of his symphonies to him (*Eroica*), but later retracted the dedication when Napoléon committed what Beethoven considered atrocities. Napoléon's famous retreat from Moscow during the winter of 1812 reduced his formerly invincible army to tatters, as 400,000 Frenchmen died in the Russian snows. After a complicated series of ebbings and wanings of his almost mystical good luck, Napoléon was defeated at Waterloo by the combined armies of the English, the Dutch, and the Prussians. Exiled to the British-held island of St. Helena in

DATELINE

léon and his armies successfully invade most of Europe.

- **1814–15** Napoléon abdicates after failure of Russian campaign; exiled to Elba but returns; June 18, 1815, he is finally defeated at Waterloo; exiled to St. Helena, where he dies in 1821.
- **1830–48** Reign of Louis-Philippe.
- **1848** Revolution topples Louis-Philippe; Napoléon III (nephew of Napoléon Bonaparte) elected president.
- **1851–71** Napoléon III declares himself emperor.
- **1863** An exhibition of paintings marks the birth of impressionism.
- **1870–71** The Franco-Prussian War: Paris falls; France cedes Alsace-Lorraine but aggressively colonizes North Africa and Southeast Asia.
- **1873** France loses Suez to the British; financial scandal wrecks attempt to dredge canal.
- **1889** Eiffel Tower built for Paris Exhibition and Revolution's centennial; architectural critics howl with disgust.
- **1914–18** World War I; French casu-

(continues)

DATELINE

alties exceed five million.

- **1923** France occupies the Ruhr, Germany's industrial zone, and demands (and collects) enormous war reparations.
- **1929** France retreats from the Ruhr and the Rhineland; constructs the Maginot Line, dubbed "impregnable."
- **1934** Depression; political crisis as left and right clash.
- **1936** Germans march into demilitarized Rhineland; France takes no action.
- **1939** France and Britain guarantee protection to Poland, Romania, and Greece from aggressors; Germany invades Poland; France declares war.
- **1940** Paris falls, June 14; Marshal Pétain's Vichy government collaborates with Nazis; General de Gaulle forms government-in-exile in London directing the *maquis* (French resistance fighters).
- **1944** June 6, the Allies invade Normandy beaches; other Allied troops invade from the south; Paris liberated in August.
- **1946–54** War in Indochina; the *(continues)*

the south Atlantic, he died in 1821, probably the victim of an unknown poisoner.

The Return of the Bourbons In 1814 the Bourbon monarchy was reestablished, with reduced powers and a changing array of leaders, including the Prince of Polignac and, later, Charles X. In 1830 the regime was thrown out after it imposed censorship on newspapers and dissolved Parliament. Louis-Philippe, Duke of Orléans, the son of a duke who had voted in 1793 for the death of Louis XIV, was elected king of the French under a liberalized constitution. His reign lasted for 18 years of calm prosperity during which England and France more or less collaborated on matters of foreign policy. The establishment of an independent Belgium and the French conquest of Algeria (1840–47) were to have resounding effects on French politics a century later. It was a time of wealth, grace, and the expansion of the arts for most French people, although the industrialization of the north and the east produced some of the most horrible poverty of the 19th century.

The Second Empire A revolution in 1848, encouraged by a financial crash and fueled by disgruntled workers in Paris, forced Louis-Philippe out of office. That year, on the dawn of the Second Republic, Emperor Napoléon's nephew, Napoléon III, was elected president by moderate and conservative elements. Appealing to the property-protecting instinct of a nation that had not forgotten the violent upheaval of less than a century before, he initiated a right-wing government where he was eventually able to gain complete power—as emperor—in 1851. Unlike those of the First Empire, the clergy of the Second Empire enjoyed great power, especially in the countryside. Steel production, a railway system, and Indochinese colonies were established and expanded.

By 1866 an industrialized France began to see the Second Empire as more of a hindrance to its continued development than as an encouragement. The dismal failure at colonizing Mexico and the increasing power of Austria and Prussia were setbacks to the empire's prestige. In 1870 the Prussians defeated Napoléon III at Sedan and held him prisoner with 100,000 of his soldiers. Paris was besieged by an enemy who only just failed to march their vastly superior armies through the streets of the capital. After the Prussians withdrew, a violent revolt ushered in the Third Republic and its elected president, Marshal MacMahon, in 1873. Peace and prosperity slowly returned, France regained its glamour, the Eiffel Tower was built, and the impressionists made their visual statements. French influence in North Africa, Southeast Asia, and Madagascar was greatly increased. However, France in humiliation lost Suez to the British.

The World Wars International rivalries and conflicting alliances led to World War I, which, after decisive German victories for two years, degenerated into the mud-slogged horror of trench warfare. In 1917 the United States broke the European deadlock by entering the war. Immediately after the Allied victory, grave economic problems, coupled with a populace demoralized from years of fighting, offered fertile ground for the rise of socialism and an active Communist party. The French government, led by a vindictive Clemenceau, demanded every centime of reparations it could wring from a crushed Germany. That is said to have increased the Germans' passionate determination to rise from the ashes of 1918 to a place in the sun.

That sun cast its shadow over France again on June 14, 1940, when German armies, under the control of Hitler, marched arrogantly down the Champs-Elysées in Paris, and newsreel cameras recorded Frenchmen openly weeping at their humiliating defeat. Marshal Henri Pétain agreed to form a ministry. Under terms of the armistice, the north of France was occupied by the Nazis and the puppet French government was established at Vichy. Free-French forces, however, continued to fight with the Allies on such battlegrounds as North Africa.

A Committee of National Liberation was set up in Algeria in 1943, declaring itself the legitimate government of the Republic. Under Gen. Dwight Eisenhower, the D-Day landings in Normandy in June of 1944 launched the reconquest of France. The invasion troops were aided by French resistance forces. Paris rose in rebellion even before the Allied armies arrived, and on August 26 Charles de Gaulle entered the capital as head of the government. The Fourth Republic was begun as Nazi occupation forces retreated.

The Postwar Years The postwar years were rough for France, and many French soldiers died on the battlefield as former colonies rebelled. It took 80,000 lives, for example, to put down a revolt in Madagascar. French industry was greatly aided by the Marshall Plan in 1948. France associated itself more and more with the United States in foreign affairs, and in 1949 it joined NATO. After suffering a bitter defeat in 1954, France ended the war in Indochina and freed its former colony. It also granted internal self-rule to Tunisia, and Morocco also became independent.

Algeria was to remain a greater problem. War in Algeria dragged on. The situation worsened in 1958, and De Gaulle was called back to form a new government. The Fifth Republic was launched. The Algerian war came to an end in 1962, and the sun had set on most of France's far-flung colonial empire.

In 1960, in the Sahara desert, France exploded its first atomic bomb. In 1968 major social unrest centered among Paris students led to the collapse of the government. Additional social unrest continues to this day in Corsica and by Muslim fundamentalists residing in France, usually in Paris and Marseille. In 1981 François Mitterand was elected the first Socialist president of France (with a very close vote of 51%) since World War II. The flight of capital by French millionaires slowed somewhat after some jitters, but many wealthy French chose to remove their investments from the country (and its increased taxation). Although much feared by the rich, Mitterrand was elected again in 1988.

Today In 1989 France celebrated the Bicentennial of the French Revolution with much fanfare. In the winter of 1990–91 France joined with the United States, Great Britain, and other Allies in a successful war against Iraq, in response to that country's invasion of Kuwait.

In April 1993, French voters dumped the long-ruling Socialists from office and installed a new conservative government, with a huge parliamentary majority. Polls cited corruption scandals, rising unemployment, and urban insecurity as reasons for

DATELINE

French withdraw from Southeast Asia; North and South Vietnam created.

• **1954–58** Algerian revolution and subsequent independence from France; refugees flood France; Fourth Republic collapses.

• **1958** De Gaulle initiates the Fifth Republic, calling for a France independent from the U.S. and Europe.

• **1960** France tests its first atomic bomb.

• **1968** Students riot in Paris; de Gaulle resigns.

• **1981** François Mitterrand becomes first socialist president since World War II; reelected in 1988.

• **1989** French Revolution Bicentennial; Eiffel Tower Centennial.

• **1991** France joins allies in war against Iraq.

• **1993** Conservatives topple Socialists, as Edouard Balladur becomes premier of France.

❓ DID YOU KNOW . . . ?

- More tourists visit France than any other country in Europe.
- Between the Rhône River and the Pyrénées lies the largest single tract of vineyards in the world.
- France has 265 *spécialités de fromages* (kinds of cheese)—this according to Gen. Charles de Gaulle, who presumably sampled each one.
- More gold is secretly held in private hands in France than in any other country.
- Louis Henri Jean Farigoule (writing under the nom de plume of Jules Romains) wrote the longest important novel in the world: *Les hommes de bonne volonté* was published in 27 volumes between 1932 and 1946.
- France is probably the European country most dependent on atomic energy.

the defeat of the Socialists. The conservative primier, Edouard Balladur, virtually has to "cohabit" the government with Mitterrand until the Socialist president's term ends in 1995.

GOVERNMENT   There may still be pretenders to the "throne" of France, but that kingdom is long gone. As everybody knows, France is a republic. Its Parliament, chosen through free elections, consists of a National Assembly and the Senate. The National Assembly makes the laws. The president of the Republic is elected by a clear majority and serves a term of seven years. After that, he or she can be elected only one more time. The president represents France in international negotiations, as he is considered the representative of the most "permanent and immutable interests of the state." Political parties are not always well organized in France on a national level. Their political opinions range from the far right to socialist to the extreme left, as exemplified by the most militant of the Communists. Sometimes loose and temporary coalitions among some of the political parties are formed, but these alliances tend to be weak and can easily divide over one issue.

---

2. FRANCE'S FAMOUS PEOPLE

Eleanor of Aquitaine   (ca. 1122–1204) The most famous woman of the Middle Ages, she unwittingly sowed the seeds of hundreds of years of future conflicts between the English and the French. Married first to Louis VII of France, and later to Henry II of England, she brought huge regions of western France (Aquitaine) to the English as part of her dowry. The English were thrown out 300 years later.

Honoré de Balzac   (1799–1850) French novelist who dropped out of law school and became the greatest portrayer of the mores and values of 19th-century French society. Always in debt, he produced more than 350 lengthy works. He built his elaborate fictional universe by amassing details about interiors, fashions, objects, settings, and personal foibles. Among his most famous works—collectively called *La comédie humaine*—are *Eugénie Grandet* and *La cousine Bette*. *Père Goriot* is required reading for all social-climbing young men.

Charles Baudelaire   (1821–67) French impressionistic poet whose work was condemned by mainstream critics as obscene and decadent. Considered one of the world's first modern poets, he ended his life in abject poverty, hopelessly addicted to opiates. His most famous work is *Les fleurs de mal* (Flowers of Evil, 1857).

Simone de Beauvoir   (1908–86) French essayist and novelist. She was the leading female writer of the existentialist movement and the on-again, off-again lover of Jean-Paul Sartre. Awarded the Prix Goncourt in 1945 for her novel *The Mandarins*, she was also one of the most articulate spokespersons for the postwar feminist movement. Her most influential feminist books are *All Men Are Mortal* and *The Second Sex*. *Memoirs of a Dutiful Daughter* amounts to an autobiography.

Louis Braille   (1809–52) French musician and educator of the blind who invented a reading and writing system for the blind using a system of embossed dots. Himself blind from the age of 3, Braille became a noted organist and cellist and was far more famous as a musician during his lifetime than as the inventor of braille. Braille died impoverished and alone.

Anthelme Brillat-Savarin (1755–1826) French politician and gastronome. A provincial lawyer and the mayor and representative of King Louis XVI for the town of Belley, he was banished during the French Revolution and fled first to Switzerland and then to America. He returned to France and became a prominent lawyer, but he is remembered for his work on gastronomy, *La physiologie du goût* (The Physiology of Taste), published shortly before his death.

Albert Camus (1913–60) French existentialist, born in Algeria. The leading proponent of post–World War II existentialist nihilism, Camus was a folk hero for his brutally denuded views of the anguish and loneliness of humankind. His most popular works include *The Stranger* (1942) and *The Myth of Sisyphus* (1942). Camus won the 1957 Nobel Prize for literature.

Jacques Cartier (1494–1557) French explorer, navigator, and colonizer who explored Canada's St. Lawrence River in 1536. Although he failed to find the Northwest Passage, which he sought, he carved out the territory of what is now Québec, claiming it for France.

Gabrielle ["Coco"] Chanel (1883–1971) French image-maker and designer, who created chic and simple women's clothing whose classic lines have endured longer than those of any other designer in the world. Establishing her career from a shop on the boardwalk of Deauville, she promoted small and pert hats to replace the garlands of fruit, swaths of veils, and masses of straw or linen that were fashionable in the Edwardian age. In the 1920s and '30s, she was the first to popularize suntans, knit suits, and simplified accessories. In the 1950s she introduced her famous "little black dress."

François René, vicomte de Chateaubriand (1768–1848) French writer and statesman, generally credited with launching the Romantic movement in France. The archetype of the melancholy, romantic hero comes from Chateaubriand's novel *Atala et René,* a model quickly emulated by many other writers. Most people remember him today for the thick and juicy cut of grilled center-cut filet steak (*"un chateaubriand"*), which was originally prepared for the statesman by his chef, Montmireil.

Chrétien de Troyes (fl. 1170) French poet who developed the legend of King Arthur in verse. His poems, later used and adapted by countless artists, include *Lancelot, Le chevalier de la charette, Yvain, Perceval,* and *Erec et Enid.*

Georges Clemenceau (1841–1929) French statesman who worked as a newspaper correspondent and a French teacher during a three-year residence in the United States. When he returned to France, he became leader of a far-left radical political group that advocated the full pardon of Dreyfus, a total separation of church and state, and full military preparedness against the "German menace." He was the premier of France from 1906 to 1909 and from 1917 to 1920. Many blame him for the unrealistically brutal peace terms imposed on Germany.

Jean Cocteau (1889–1963) Multimedia French artist, style setter, and *enfant terrible.* After experimenting in the surrealistic and avant-garde movements of the 1910s and '20s, Cocteau wrote novels, poems, film scripts, essays, and scenarios for plays; painted church murals; designed restaurant menus; invented costumes; choreographed parties; and directed films. *Blood of a Poet, Beauty and the Beast,* and *Orphée* are three of his best-known films. His important writings include *Les enfants terribles, Journal d'un inconnu,* and *La difficulté d'être.* Cocteau's addiction to drugs contributed to his death. He was buried, with full honors from the Académie Française, near his country home at Milly-en-Fleurs, in the Ile de France.

Georges-Jacques Danton (1759–94) French revolutionary and political philosopher. At his most powerful, he served as minister of justice and president of the Committee of Public Safety shortly after the fall of Louis XVI. His policies of relative moderation evoked the rage of more radical factions, who had him guillotined.

Honoré Daumier (1808–79) Cartoonist, caricaturist, and painter. Daumier was the most acerbic cartoonist of the 19th century, exposing in his more than 4,000 cartoons the smugness, corruption, arrogance, and silliness of the 19th-century French bourgeoisie.

Claude Debussy (1862–1918) French composer, widely credited with drawing the guidelines for the Impressionist School of music. He introduced new tonal colors and freer harmonics, doing for music what his contemporaries Monet and Manet were doing for painting. His most famous symphonic works are *La mer* (The Sea), *Prélude à l'après-midi d'un faune* (Prelude to the Afternoon of a Faun), and *Clair de Lune.* His most famous opera is *Pelléas et Mélisande.*

Christian Dior (1905–57) Fashion designer who helped to revolutionize the French fashion industry with the "New Look" after establishing his own couture business in 1947. The recognition, the prestige, and the money his work brought to a France ravaged by the traumas of World War II eventually earned him membership in the French Legion of Honor.

Jean-Honoré Fragonard (1732–1806) Artist whose paintings capture the illusionary sweetness of upper-class life during the *ancien régime.* His best-known work, *The Swing,* is an unabashedly rococo portrayal full of ribbons, flowers, and blue satin, of fey and perhaps fickle young lovers joyously appreciating the airborne rhythms of a swing in a highly idealized garden.

Eugene Henry Paul Gauguin (1848–1903) French painter. Hating his work in a bank, which his family had pressured him to do, he emigrated first to Guadeloupe, then to Tahiti, where he produced some of his best work. Obsessed by guilt for the abandonment of his family in France, ridden with venereal disease, and always desperately poor, his life was anything but the idyllic fantasy that the flat and bright designs of his paintings suggest. His works strongly influenced the Fauvists.

Henri Matisse (1869–1954) Celebrated painter known for his flattened perspectives and bright colors. His most famous paintings include *Odalisque, The Dance,* and *The Blue Window.* Don't miss the murals he painted and the windows he designed for the chapel at Vence, in Provence.

Blaise Pascal (1623–62) Mathematician, scientist, and philosopher, best remembered for his widely popular *Pensées,* which praised mystical revelation and criticized pure reason. Despite his disbelief in the powers of reason, he founded much of his career on logic and its conclusions. He was the founder of the modern theory of probability and he contributed greatly to a modern understanding of the differential calculus. He defined Pascal's law, which declares that pressure applied to a fluid is transmitted equally in all directions, acting at right angles against the walls of the vessel that contains it.

Edith Piaf (1915–63) The quintessential Parisian singer, who could move listeners to tears. Born Edith Gassion, the daughter of a circus acrobat, she was raised by her grandmother, who owned and operated a brothel. Piaf began singing in the streets at age 15 and later began appearing in cafés. Beautiful only when her plain features were illuminated while singing, Piaf was nicknamed "The Little Sparrow" by her ardent admirers. Companion of pimps, thieves, prostitutes, and drug addicts, she led a life filled with tragedy, illness, despair, and lost love. Best-loved songs include "Milord," "A quoi ça sert?", "L'amour," "La foule," and "La vie en rose."

François Rabelais (ca. 1494–1553) French author and failed monk who realized early that celibacy and piety were inconsistent with his lusty and irreverent temperament. He wrote two medieval masterpieces of satire and comedy, *Gargantua* and *Pantagruel,* poking fun at the clerical, the pompous, the vain, and the intellectually arrogant.

Cardinal Richelieu (Armand Jean du Plessis, duc de Richelieu; 1585–1642) French financier and prelate. After the death of Louis XIII's mother, Catherine de Médici, Richelieu effectively controlled France. He consolidated French wealth, centralized power in Paris, and laid the foundations of modern France. Merciless in his hatred and persecution of Protestants, Richelieu starved and destroyed the Huguenot strongholds of France, most notably La Rochelle. He founded the Académie Française to impose linguistic and grammatical rules upon the then loosely defined language that we now know as French.

Madame de Staël (Anne-Louise-Germaine Necker, baronne de Staël-

---

IMPRESSIONS

Frivolity and lightheartedness are proverbial characteristics of the French.
—HENRY WADSWORTH LONGFELLOW

Holstein; 1766–1817) French writer who maintained the most sought-after salon in Paris prior to, during, and after the French Revolution. She popularized and praised German romanticism in her most widely read book, *De l'Allemagne*, which, although at first suppressed by Napoléon, later encouraged the Romantic movement in France.

Bernadette Soubirous/Sainte Bernadette (1844–79) Canonized French shepherd who received visions of the Virgin Mary, the first in 1858 in the Pyrenean city of Lourdes. At first condemned, and then embraced, by the church, she helped to create a Catholic cult whose traditions now almost completely dominate the city. Bernadette died in a French convent in 1879. She was beatified in 1925 and canonized in 1933.

3. ARCHITECTURE & ART

During the heyday of Rome, only the southernmost region of France was considered of any commercial or artistic merit. This region, through trade with the architecturally sophisticated Mediterranean, was quick to adopt the building techniques that were common in the Roman world. As it applies to architecture, it has been said that the Romans' triumphal arches, their rhythmically massive aqueducts, and their mausoleums fixed themselves in the French aesthetic for all time.

Romanesque As Christianity made inroads toward the Celtic tribes of the northern edges of Gaul, an abbreviated and naïve kind of naturalism permeated the old Roman ideals, resulting in a crude aesthetic of geometric carvings and primitive architectural masses of which only a few remain today. Those that do are occasionally influenced slightly with eastern motifs from Byzantium, which flourished at the time.

The architectural form called Romanesque developed from these trials. Its rise is sometimes attributed to the growing spiritual power of the 11th- and 12th-century church which in many areas was the only constant factor in a region of shifting political alliances. The earliest manifestations appear more like thick-walled fortresses, and often served as refuges during times of invasion. At first they were unembellished with sculpture of any kind, relying on rounded arches and occasional windows for ornamentation.

Many critics consider the echoing simplicity of the Cistercians—a reform-minded offshoot of the Benedictines—to be among the more spiritually alluring styles of the era. (Clairvaux and Fontenay are the best remaining examples.)

By the 1100s, notably in Poitou, the facades and sections of the interiors of some Romanesque churches were almost completely covered with sculptures whose forms were designed to emphasize the architecture, rather than serve as separate works of art. Although many more visible Romanesque sculptures are solid, rigid, unyielding, and lifeless, the capitals above the massive columns are often charming, the most natural representations that can be found. These are studied today with great interest by art historians who are sometimes able to assign almost forgotten biblical allegories to some of them.

The first French Romanesque church was built around 1002 in Dijon (the Monastery of St. Bénigne). The flowering of the style appeared ·in the vast ecclesiastical complex of Cluny in Burgundy, which was begun in 1089 and destroyed by zealous townspeople just after the French Revolution.

Contemporaneously with the 10th- and 11th-century construction of churches, the era also produced secular fortresses whose crenellations and thick walls often concealed dank, drafty, cramped quarters where cooped-up occupants barely managed to stay sane during times of war. Often, when a fortress was destroyed during a pillage, the survivors rebuilt it into a more fashionable form. In this way, some of the greatest châteaux of France were built, altered, upgraded, and transformed into the sometimes elegant domiciles that are preserved today as symbols of the Renaissance.

Gothic About 400 years before the great châteaux of the Loire reached their present form, the hard-working architects of the royal abbey of Saint-Denis, outside

Paris, completed the first section of a radically new architectural style—Gothic. The cathedrals of Noyon, begun a year later in 1145, and Laon, launched in 1155, almost immediately exemplified the new principles, as did Notre-Dame of Paris when construction on it was undertaken in 1163. Gothic churches usually, but not always, included a choir, a ring-around ambulatory, radiating chapels, pointed arches, clustered (rather than monolithic) columns, and ribbed ceilings. Probably most important is the presence of wide, soaring windows occupying the space which, in a Romanesque church, would have been devoted to thick stone walls. This new design usually required the addition of exterior flying buttresses to support the weight of the very heavy roof and ceiling.

It was at Chartres, 60 miles southwest of Paris, that an adaptation of earlier Gothic principles was developed for the first time into a flamboyant High Gothic style when a section of the existing cathedral was destroyed in a fire. The tendency toward increased altitude was more and more fully developed until the cathedrals of Reims and Amiens reached heights so dizzying that medieval man couldn't help but be awed by the might and majesty of God.

Meanwhile, the ecclesiastical sculpture that ornamented the portals and facades of Gothic churches progressed from an early, very static kind of stern rigidity to a more fluid, more relaxed, sometimes coquettish kind of naturalism. By the 14th century, ecclesiastical and especially secular carvings attained a kind of international refinement and courtliness that was appreciated and copied in aristocratic circles throughout Europe.

Renaissance It wasn't long, however, before the Renaissance helped Frenchmen realize that the glass and stone marvels erected to the glory of God were also examples of the sophisticated building techniques of the time. When the 14th-century papal schism encouraged a portion of Europe's bishops to recognize that Avignon, not Rome, was the legitimate seat of the papacy, a fortress was required that would also be a palace. New political and social conditions encouraged aristocratic residences filled with sunlight, tapestries, paintings, and music. Adaptations of Gothic architecture, mingled with strong doses of the Italian Renaissance, were applied to secular residences more suited to peace than the times of war. (Chambord, the hunting château of François I, is a good example.) Architectural motifs as well as paintings abandoned religious themes. French painting modeled itself first after Flemish, then after the northern Italian examples. It began to distance itself increasingly from the dictates of the church.

Baroque The early 17th century witnessed the architectural burgeoning of Paris, whose skyline bristled with domes in the restrained baroque of the Italianate style. Louis XIV employed Le Vau, Perrault, both Mansarts, and Bruand for his buildings, and Le Nôtre for the rigidly intelligent layouts of his gardens at Versailles. Meanwhile, court painters such as Boucher depicted allegorical shepherdesses and cherubs at play, while Georges de la Tour used techniques of light and shadow garnered from Caravaggio during a sojourn in Italy. The châteaux designed in this era included the lavishly expensive Vaux-le-Vicomte, and the even more lavishly expensive royal residence of Versailles.

Neo-Classicism By the 18th century French architects returned to a restrained and dignified form of classicism. Public parks in Metz, Bordeaux, Nancy, and Paris were laid out, sometimes requiring the demolition of acres of twisted medieval sections of cities. Roman styles in painting, sculpture, and dress became the rage, although a brief fling with Egyptology followed the discovery of the Rosetta Stone during Napoléon's campaign in Egypt. The revolutionary school of David came and went and, within the new order, Ingres strove for a kind of classical calm.

The 19th Century Around 1850 a new school of eclecticism combined elements from scattered eras of the past into new, sometimes inharmonious wholes. Between 1855 and 1869 Napoléon III and his chief architect, Baron Haussmann, demolished much of the crumbling medieval Paris to lay out the wide avenues that today connect the various monuments in broad, well-proportioned vistas. New building techniques were developed, including the use of iron as the structural support of bridges, viaducts, and buildings such as the National Library, completed in 1860. Naturally, this opened the way for Alexandre Gustave Eiffel to design and erect the most frequently slurred building of its day, the Eiffel Tower, for the Paris exposition of 1889.

Among sculptors, the only authentic giant to emerge from the 19th century was Auguste Rodin, born in 1840. He brought new energy and vision to sculpture. His human figures were vital and lifelike, and he became known for such works as *The Thinker* and *The Kiss*.

Eugène Delacroix, born in 1798, became the greatest name in French Romantic painting, showing great skill as a colorist. In the second quarter of the 19th century landscape painting rose in prominence, and none was better at this form than Jean-Baptiste Corot, the French painter of the Barbizon school. To many critics, the first modern painter in France was Edouard Manet, born in 1832. He painted portraits and scenes of everyday life, but could also create a scandal (*Picnic on the Grass*) by depicting nudes among dressed figures. Manet is not to be confused with Monet, born in 1840. Claude Monet was a great innovator, known for his series of paintings of water lilies and of Rouen Cathedral. Pierre Augustine Renoir, born 1841, became celebrated for his sensuously rounded nudes in pearl white, and Edgar Degas, born 1834, turned to ballet dancers and scenes of racing and the theater for his inspiration.

Outside all movements, but equally important, was Henri de Toulouse-Lautrec, born in 1864. Satiric but amused, his style was exemplified by the posters and sketches of music hall life he depicted. His interest was in the demimonde of his day.

The 20th Century   In the early part of the 20th century, the Fauves or "wild beasts" attracted the most attention, and the greatest of their lot was Henri Matisse, born 1869. He became known for his bright colors and flattened perspective.

Throughout the 20th century exquisite beaux-arts buildings continued to be erected throughout Paris, most of them at roughly the same height, giving the city an evenly spaced skyline and rhythmically ornate facades which have caused it to be deemed again and again the most beautiful city in the world. The art nouveau movement added garlands of laurel and olive branches to the gray-white stone of elegant apartment buildings and hotels throughout France. In the 1920s and '30s art deco's simplified elegance captivated sophisticated sensibilities throughout the world. Braque defined cubism, and Picasso worked at his mission of turning the art world upside down. Le Corbusier developed his jutting, gently curved planes of concrete, opening the door for a new, but often less talented school of modern French architects. As for recent years, critics have not been kind to the exposed, rapidly rusting structural elements of Paris's notorious Centre Beaubourg. The new Opera House has also stirred controversy. The most recent controversial structure is without a doubt I.M. Pei's glass pyramid outside the Louvre.

4. LANGUAGE, LITERATURE & FILM

LANGUAGE

The nation has always been so varied that at times it seems that the main link which unites France is its mellifluous language. For centuries it was associated with diplomacy, fine literature, and romance. Even today a proficiency in reading it is viewed both as a glittering social ornament and a psychological tool for plumbing the depths of the human spirit.

Like any language, its evolution into what you'll hear today on the streets of Paris was a function both of popular usage and concerted efforts by scholastic bodies to standardize its syntax and spelling. Its origins came from the mingling of Latin, the language of the ancient Roman conquerors, with the now forgotten languages of the native Celts. During the early Middle Ages, two main divisions developed, the sides being the "langue d'Oil" in the north (particularly Paris), and the "langue d'Oc" of the south. (The ancient district of Languedoc derived its name from the language that was originally spoken there.) Eventually the dictates of the academic and political stronghold of Paris acquired a supremacy in both the spoken vernacular and the written languages.

The Académie Française   The potential of civil discord, provoked and encouraged by the era's linguistic differences, had always terrified French monarchs. It was Richelieu in 1635 who finally established a governing body to sometimes legally enforce the linguistic purity of the French language. Called the Académie Française and composed of the most notable men (and recently, women) of French letters, it was recognized as the world's official arbiter and judge of which phrases and forms of French grammar would or would not be accepted into the official linguistic canon

Dialects   In spite of the sometimes heroic efforts of the Académie Française, a wealth of dialectical differences is still heard, but to a decreasing degree. It required the homogenizing influence of media—especially television—to blur the ancient linguistic divisions of France. Even until the end of World War II, Provencale (a variation of the ancient langue d'Oc) was widely spoken in the south. A Celtic language, called Breton, was spoken in Brittany, the linguistically baffling Basque tongue in the southwest, and even Catalán, the language of Barcelona, was heard along sections of the Spanish border. German dialects were used in Alsace and Lorraine, and the adaptation of Flemish was spoken near the Belgian border.

Delight in Exactitude and Elegance   Although each of these languages was spoken within homes and cottages of the rural areas, the mainstream of French society has always prided itself on the exactitude of the phrases and nuances of grammar that are at first such a torment and later such a delight to foreigners who study them. Perhaps the greatest celebration of the language occurred in the literary forms of the 19th and early 20th century, when novelists and poets (especially Flaubert, Proust, and Baudelaire) toyed, tinkered, and reveled in paragraphs that are sometimes overwhelmingly evocative. Flaubert, while writing in his Norman garden, would compose the same paragraph as many as 20 times before achieving an elegance of phrasing and a precision of emotional states which an increasingly telegraphic world may never see again.

Some French-speaking people staunchly defend the purity of their tongue, while others have become increasingly vocal about the inability of their rigidly structured language to remain scientifically competitive with the vastly more flexible English language. The computer boom and developments in almost every form of scientific research have tended to be expressed in what has become the second language of educated people throughout the world—English. This is of enormous concern to French leaders who, despite their qualms, have sometimes levied fines on manufacturers whose advertisements include phrases from English or other languages. (The French translation for "computer software" is hopelessly convoluted, even for a person who speaks French fluently.)

In spite of its drawbacks as a scientific language, French is arguably the best vehicle for expressing subtle variations of feeling which never sound quite as meaningful when translated into another language. Cynics have claimed that no other language in Europe is as well suited to irony, skepticism, or sarcasm. But, as anyone who's ever fallen in love with a French-speaking person knows, affairs of the heart are always best expressed *en français.*

LITERATURE

Early Poetry and Troubadours   The development of a body of French literature is intricately tied with the emergence of French as a workaday vernacular language. Some historians consider the body of French literature to have existed only since the Renaissance, although a strong body of work, very definitely produced by the ancestors of the culture which is today called France, was popular as early as the 11th century. The langue d'Oc, spoken as a well-defined language of the south, especially in Provence in the 11th century, produced an evocative and unique kind of poetry that the world had never seen before. Usually sung by wandering adventurers called troubadours, it praised the virtues of courtly love, perhaps laying the foundation of the legends that have always enveloped the supposedly exalted romantic powers of the French.

The crusade by the northern French against the Albigensian Heresy in the 1400s virtually destroyed both the political independence and the literary forms of Provence, although those that had already been recorded are still regarded as examples of the boldest and most charming literary form to emerge from the Middle Ages.

In the north, around 1007 an unknown writer composed the heroic poem *Chanson de Roland* (Song of Roland), which consists of 4,002 unrhymed 10-syllable lines describing the heroic death of a warrior at Roncesvalles in the Pyrénées. Other contemporary works involved the *Breton Cycle,* a French adaptation of the legend of England's King Arthur and his Knights of the Round Table, and an Anglo-Norman version of the story of Tristan and his love for Isolde.

For the next 200 years literature struggled to be recorded and encompassed everything from didactic essays meant to instruct to political satires, morality plays, and buffoonish dialogues between righteous men and wily foxes (who usually won). François Villon, born in 1431 of poor parents, educated by a helpful priest, and later attracted to a life of vice and crime, left a handful of genuinely evocative poems.

The Renaissance During the Renaissance, French poetry flowered in the hands of Clément Marot. Du Bellay, in his 1549 *Defense and Illustration of the French Language,* elaborated upon new poetic theories without apology to his wish to express them in the vernacular. Later Rabelais (1494–1553), a man well versed in classical literature, wrote graphically amusing tales loaded with the kind of political implications that both vastly amused his readers and later forced him into exile in Rome. Pierre de Ronsard (1524–85) was a nobleman destined for an important military career. Faced with deafness and drawn to his writing, he produced some of the most elegant poetry of his era. Later, Montaigne, for a time the mayor of Bordeaux, delighted in exploring his own psyche, recording in his *Essays* his belief in the absolute negation of all knowledge not gained from personal experience. He is credited today with leaving to France what might be the most remarkable distillation of Renaissance values ever recorded.

The Age of Enlightenment By the 17th century a new appreciation of the rational powers of man, partially sparked by the Age of Enlightenment's scientific discoveries, produced a literature filled with lofty language and heroic struggles of conscience versus the dictates of society. Pierre Corneille and his contemporary, Racine, produced both tragedies and comedies which sometimes touched on the delicate balance of the era's religious passions. Later, Blaise Pascal wrote a piquant and brilliant text defending the Jansenists against an attack led by the Jesuits. Despite its popularity at the time, Pascal is much better remembered today for his *Pensées* and its exploration of the relationship of a suffering man and an all-powerful God.

The late 17th century was one of violent conflicts of religion and philosophy, and much of the urbane polish of its writers probably came from their success at negotiating the era's politics. Madame de Sévigné perfected the art of letter writing. La Fontaine wrote his charmingly insightful *Fables,* and François de la Rochefoucauld created his *Maxims.* The battle-scarred poet, the Duke of Saint-Simon (1675–1755), recorded his urbane memoirs, one of the best insights into the era of Louis XIV. One of France's most performed playwrights, Molière, left a still-vivid portrayal of the foibles of human nature in his dryly entertaining comedies whose incidents almost always show a love of ostentatious show and ceremony. Despite his humor and the favor he enjoyed from Louis XIV, his satirical jabs at the established tenets of his day embroiled him in the undying enmity of several religious factions.

By the early 1700s the novel took its first form in Prévost's great (and only) novel of love, *Manon Lescaut,* thus launching a literary tradition which in France would reach dizzying heights of expression a century and a half later. Prévost, as did earlier writers, accepted the social order with resignation and stoic calm, although with the advent of Voltaire, a new sarcasm and irreverence permeated the literary air, particularly as it applied to both religious pomposity and fanaticism. Rousseau preached the nobility of both animals and savages untouched by social teachings, and Montesquieu established a new field of study, the philosophy of history. Diderot compiled an encyclopedia in 17 volumes filled with essays whose conclusions were based on the scientific discoveries of the era. A few years later the Marquis de Sade (1740–1814) both practiced and wrote about cruelties which made him a social untouchable at the time, but which influenced the Romanticism of later generations of writers.

Romanticism   In the early 1800s, Romanticism allied itself with the political and social preoccupations of the times. Probably weary of the heroic militarism of the Napoleonic wars, it celebrated a sentimental lyricism and a sometimes personal outpouring of emotion. Victor Hugo, who envisioned himself as "the embodiment of the French soul," became the movement's leader. His *Hunchback of Notre Dame* is the most famous to North American audiences, although *Les Misérables*, a novel of social injustice, has been called one of the greatest works of popular literature ever written. On his 80th birthday in 1882, more than 600,000 French people came to pay their respects.

By the mid-1800s both the literary salon and a handful of literary journals disseminated new ideas to a wider group of readers than ever before in French history. Benjamin Constant's dry and cerebral recitation of the blistering emotions of his semi-autobiographical hero in *Adolphe* ushered in a new generation of novelists. Stendhal led a life of revolt and adventure, and later wrote both *The Red and the Black* and *The Charterhouse of Parma*, where his appreciation of Italy was expressed through the aristocratic bravado of its hero.

A man who had failed in virtually every business he ever tried except writing, Balzac produced a voluminous collection of novels which were entitled *The Human Comedy*. Balzac was very much a product of the bourgeois age of industrialization that swept across France. His sometimes verbose novels were created almost as serials, where characters and plots were interwoven from novel to novel. Never before had French society been so insightfully analyzed on such a large scale. Sometimes riveting, Balzac's novels give deep insights into the commercial envy and social competition of the age of Napoléon III.

Realism and Naturalism   By now, a yearning for realism and naturalism was enveloping literary tastes. A new generation of writers shunned both sentimentality and frivolous romanticism, returning to a sometimes rigorous precision and almost scientific objectivity. Flaubert, who produced some of the most emotionally satisfying novels ever written, believed in concealing his own thoughts and feelings as completely as possible, bringing a vigor and depth to his characters—especially in *Madame Bovary,* which is almost pure joy to read. Flaubert was as concerned about the way he expressed an idea as he was with the idea itself. His prose in the original French is as highly polished, elegant, and emotionally precise as anything else from its era. Emile Zola, who probably understood the commercial value of media attention better than any other writer who preceded him, believed that a human personality is the product of the environment in which it developed. Almost constantly the target of obscenity suits, he described graphically the brutality of life in the lowest class of French urban society.

Impressionism   Meanwhile, clusters of impressionistic poets (Verlaine, Mallarmé, and Valéry) experimented with new forms of poetry. Baudelaire conveyed with symbols and images his own passions and despair. Rimbaud wrote stunning and highly influential verse before abandoning poetry for a life of action at the ripe age of 19. Apollinaire produced elegant surrealistic writing considered decadent because of its divorce from the trials of everyday people.

The 20th Century   Marcel Proust, considered by many critics to be the finest 20th-century writer in any language, tried to illuminate the recesses of his mind where memories lay hidden, sometimes devoting page after page to the childhood feelings that lay behind the odor of a freshly baked madeleine. His *Remembrance of Things Past* is sometimes viewed as an artful, very fertile effort to bring to light the emotions that only years of the very best and most dedicated psychoanalysis might bring out. Later, André Gide, in his sustained and painful self-investigation, explored his relationship to his innermost thoughts and to society.

The disturbing events leading up to World War II provoked the existentialist movement. It stressed the absurdity of life and the meaninglessness of any attempt to establish a real communication among people. Sartre and Camus are the movement's best-remembered advocates. The movement quickly split into Christian and atheistic branches, each loaded with implications that have influenced theologists and philosophers ever since.

FILM

The World's First Movie   Although the Americans understood—and very quickly, too—the commercial wealth to be made from films, the French are credited with the scientific and technical inventions that made them possible. Although groups of French physicists had laid the groundwork for a movie camera as early as the mid-1880s, the world's first movie was shown in Paris on December 28, 1895. Its makers were the Lumière brothers, who considered filmmaking a scientific oddity and stubbornly confined its use to the production of international newsreels. Later, a vaudevillian actor and illusionist, Georges Méliès, used film to convey plot and drama.

Charles Pathé and Leon Gaumont were the first to exploit filmmaking on a grand scale. Beginning in 1896, they produced and distributed their own films, building their company into a giant before World War I. When Gaumont made his first film, he enlisted his secretary, Alice Guy-Blaché, to create the plot, design the scenery, and direct it. She proved so successful that she was eventually promoted to the head of Paris's largest studio and became the world's first female director.

Before World War I the many talented actors arriving *en scène* included Max Linder, a popular French comic, whose style influenced Charlie Chaplin and helped him develop his keen sense of timing. After World War I a flood of film imports from the United States and an economic depression slowed down the growth of French filmmaking.

Avant-Garde   By the 1920s the French began to view filmmaking as an art form, and infused it with surreal and dada themes. These were eventually named "Avant-Garde" and included experimentations viewed (sometimes skeptically, sometimes encouragingly) in Hollywood and around the world. Examples include Man Ray's *Le retour à la raison* (1923), Fernand Léger's *Le ballet mécanique* (1924), and Jean Cocteau's *Le sang d'un poète* (1930).

The Golden Age   The golden age of the silent screen in France (and Hollywood, too) was probably 1927–29. Actors were directed with more sophistication and technical abilities reached an all-time high. One of my favorite films—despite its mind-numbing length—is Abel Gance's sweepingly evocative masterpiece *Napoléon* (1927); its grisly battle scenes are easily as chilling as any war film made today. Other highlights from this era include René Clair's *Un chapeau de paille d'Italie* (An Italian Straw Hat; 1927), Carl Dreyer's *La passion de Jeanne d'Arc* (1928), and an adaptation of Emile Zola's *Thérèse Raquin* (1928) by Jacques Feyder.

Experiments with the early productions of "talkies" were less successful. One popular film director, Pagnol, declared outright that the role of films was to publicize to the masses the benefits of the theatrical stage. During this period, many of the counterculture's most gifted directors either left France altogether (as did René Clair, who emigrated to England in 1934) or died (Jean Vigo, *Zéro de conduite*).

In 1936 the Cinémathèque Française was established to find and preserve old (usually silent) French films. By that time, French cinematographers had divorced themselves completely from the value systems of the stage and had found a style of their own. An average of 130 films a year were made in France, by (among others) Jean Renoir, Charles Spaak, and Marcel Carne. This was also the era that brought such French luminaries as Claudette Colbert and Maurice Chevalier to Hollywood.

During World War II, the best known (to Americans) of the French directors fled to Hollywood. Those who remained were heavily censored by the Vichy government. Despite that, more than 350 French films, many relating to long-past (and therefore uncontroversial) events were produced. Exceptions were Carne's *Les enfants du paradis* (Children of Paradise; 1945).

In 1946 France slapped a heavy quota system onto the importation of foreign (especially American) films. A semigovernmental film authority (Le Centre National du Cinéma Français) financed independent French film companies and encouraged liaisons between the French and Italian film industries. Many directors who had supported the Vichy government's Nazi collaboration were soon accepted back into the cinematic community.

Film Noir and Literary Traditions Two strong traditions—Le Film Noir and a return to literary traditions—grew strong. Film noir included such existentially inspired nihilistic themes as André Cayatte's *Nous sommes tous des assassins* (We Are All Assassins; 1952) and Yves Allegret's *Dedée d'Anvers* (1948). Examples of the literary tradition include Bresson's *Journal d'un curé de campagne* (Diary of a Country Priest; 1951) and a film rendition of Stendahl's *Le rouge et le noir* (The Red and the Black; 1954) by Autant-Lara.

By the 1950s comedy adopted a new kind of genre with Jacques Tati's *Les vacances de Monsieur Hulot* (Mr. Hulot's Holiday). By the mid-1950s French filmmaking ushered in the era of enormous budgets, à la Hollywood, and the creation of such frothy potboilers as *And God Created Woman*, which helped make Brigitte Bardot a penthouse name around the world, contributing greatly to the image in America of France as the kingdom of sexual liberation.

The New Wave (La Nouvelle Vague) By the late 1950s François Truffaut, widely publicizing his *auteur* theories, rebelled with a series of short films (most famous of which was *The 400 Blows;* 1959), which were partly financed by government funds, partly by wealthy benefactors. With Jean-Luc Godard (*A bout de souffle;* Breathless; 1959) and Claude Chabrol (*Le beau Serge;* 1959), they pioneered one of the most publicized movements in 20th-century French art, *La Nouvelle Vague*. In the early 1960s dozens of new directors joined the movement, furiously making films, some of which are considered classics, others of which have been thrown into the collective dustbin of forgotten artistic endeavors. Enthusiastically endorsed by the counterculture on both sides of the Atlantic, these directors included Resnais (*Muriel*), Roger Vadim, Agnès Varda (*Le bonheur*), Jacques Demy (*Les parapluies de Cherbourg*), Godard (*Pierrot-le-Fou*), Louis Malle, Chris Marker, and Marguerite Duras (*Detruire, dit-elle*).

After a switch to political themes (Costa-Gavras's *Z*) during the 1968 rebellions (and a politically motivated abandonment of the film festival at Cannes by at least a dozen prominent French directors), French cinema turned to comedy in the early 1970s. Examples include Bunuel's *Le charme discret de la bourgeoisie* (1972) and Yanne's *Tout le monde il est beau, tout le monde il est gentil* (1972).

Today The transatlantic movie deal is a relatively common occurrence, and movie executives from California, New York, and Paris regularly collaborate and compete on films suitable for both cultures.

In the 1990s French films gained an audience in North America. Agnieszka Holland, who wrote and directed *Europa, Europa,* followed it with *Olivier, Olivier,* a perverse idyll set in the Ile de France. *Les amants du Pont Neuf,* written and directed by Léos Carax, tells the story of a sad young wino who lives on the Pont Neuf, the oldest and most beautiful bridge in Paris.

Touts les matins du monde (1991) is Alain Corneau's film about a minor baroque composer during the reign of Louis XIV. Jean-Jacques Annaud's *The Lover* (1992) is an adaptation of Marguerite Duras's novel about a young French girl in Indochina and an older, rich Chinese man. With a budget of $20 million, *Indochine* is the most expensive French film ever made. Honored with an Oscar for best foreign film, *Indochine* stars Catherine Deneuve and was directed by Régis Wargnier; this love story is set amid the fall of French rule in Asia.

5. FOOD & DRINK

Volumes have been written about French gastronomy, and I will not attempt to do so here, but a few general comments may be in order. First, as any French person will tell you, French food is the best in the world. That is as true today as it was in the days of the great Escoffier. More than ever, chefs de cuisine, especially the younger ones, are making creative statements in the kitchen, and never in the history of the country has there been such an emphasis on super-fresh ingredients. One chef I know in Bordeaux has been known to shut down his restaurant for the day if he didn't find exactly what he wanted in the marketplace that morning. There are certain rules to observe when dining in France, and I'll review a few of them.

Of course, the first question you may ask is, What will it cost? France, especially Paris, has gained a reputation as being a damnably expensive place in the food department. True, its star-studded, internationally famous establishments are very expensive indeed. Places like Tour d'Argent and Maxim's are not so much restaurants as temples of gastronomy, living memorials to the glory of French cuisine. Tour d'Argent, for example, boasts what is widely regarded as the finest wine cellar in the world. In these culinary cathedrals, you pay not only for superb decor and regal service, but also for the art of celebrated chefs on ministerial salaries.

There is also a vast array of expensive dineries—not only in Paris but increasingly throughout the country—that exist almost exclusively for the tourist trade. Their food may be indifferent or downright bad, but they'll have ice water and ketchup to anesthetize your tastebuds, trilingual waiters, and quadrilingual menus. Luckily, there are others. Hundreds of others. Even Paris, which is said to have more restaurants than any other city on earth, has many good, reasonably priced ones. And they don't take much finding. I've counted 18 of them in a single, narrow Left Bank street.

DINING TIPS French restaurants by law add a service charge of 12%–15% to your bill (*service compris*) which means you don't have to leave a tip, but it's customary always to leave something extra.

In many of the less expensive places I'll be taking you to in this guide, the menu will be handwritten in French only. Don't let that intimidate you. You needn't be timid either about ordering dishes without knowing precisely what they are. You'll get some delightful surprises. I know a woman who wouldn't have dreamed of asking for escargots if she'd realized they were snails cooked in garlic sauce. As it was, she ate this appetizer in a spirit of thrift rather than adventure—and has been addicted to it ever since. As for vegetables, the French regard them as a separate course and eat them apart from the meat or poultry dishes. But I wouldn't advise you to order them specially, unless you're an exceptionally hearty eater. Most main courses come with a small helping of *garni* of vegetables anyway.

You'll find a large number of specific dishes explained in the restaurant descriptions. No one, however, can explain the subtle nuances of flavor that distinguish them. Those you have to taste for yourself.

As a rule, it's better to order an apéritif—often the house will have a specialty—rather than a heavy drink such as a martini before a classic French dinner. Vodka or scotch can assault your palate, destroying your tastebuds for the festive repast to come. Allow plenty of time for a gourmet dinner. Orders are often prepared individually, and it takes time to absorb the wine and the flavors. Sometimes sorbet (a sherbet) is served midway in your meal to cleanse your palate.

Making reservations is important, and please try to show up on time. Too many Americans make reservations and then become a "no-show," and this creates ill-will, especially since many nine-table restaurants must be filled completely every night in order to make a profit. If you're window-shopping for a restaurant, you'll find the menu most often displayed outside. French people read it like a book. It's there for you to study and ponder over—so read it in anticipation. Most French people have their main meal during the day, and when in France you, too, may want to follow that custom, dining lighter in the evening.

Most French meals consist of several small courses. You can begin, for example, with hors d'oeuvres or a light potage, or soup, although chefs don't serve soups as frequently as they used to. The classic restaurant used to serve fish, a small order, after the appetizer, then the meat or poultry course. But nowadays it's likely to be either fish or meat. A salad follows the main course, then a selection of cheese (there are 365 registered ones alone), and dessert, often a fruit concoction or a sorbet.

If you find the food "too rich, too many sauces," that may be because you've been ordering wrong. Elaborately prepared gourmet banquets should not be consumed for both lunch and dinner, or even every day. The French don't. Sometimes an omelet or a roast chicken can make a delightful light meal, and you can "save up" for your big dining experience.

CUISINE MODERNE   The revolution against Escoffier has been raging for so long that many of the early rebels are now returning to the old style of cookery, as exemplified by boeuf bourguignon, blanquette de veau, and pot-au-feu. Nevertheless, the unfashionable expression, La Nouvelle Cuisine, even if it isn't that "new," remains a viable part of the French dining scene. Unlike another revolution, the battle between haute cuisine and La Nouvelle Cuisine didn't begin in Paris. Romantically, one would like to think it started when Michel Guérard's beautiful Christine murmured in his ear, "Vous savez, Michel, if you would lose some weight, you'd look *great*."

For a man who loved food as much as Guérard, that was a formidable challenge. But he set to work and, ultimately, invented the "cuisine minceur," which is a way to cook good French food without the calories. The world now makes its way to Guérard's restaurant, at Eugénie-les-Bains in the Landes, just east of the Basque country. His *Cuisine Minceur* became a bestseller in North America, and Gael Greene, the food critic, hailed Guérard as "the brilliant man who is France's most creative chef." The cuisine minceur is more of a diet cuisine than La Nouvelle Cuisine. However, the "new cuisine," like cuisine minceur, represents a major break with haute cuisine, yet it is still based on the classic principles of French cookery. Rich sauces, for example, are eliminated. Cooking times that can destroy the best of fresh ingredients are considerably shortened. The aim is to release the natural flavor of food without covering it with heavy layers of butter and cream. New flavor combinations in this widely expanding repertoire are often inspired.

Many chefs, and these include some of the finest in France, dislike the word "nouvelle" when applied to cuisine. They call theirs "moderne," which blends the finest dishes of the classic repertory with that of the nouvelle kitchen. Although widely defined, moderne basically means paying homage to the integrity of ingredients, certainly fresh ones, and working in the kitchen to bring out natural flavors and aromas.

PROVINCE BY PROVINCE   What exactly is "French food"? That's a hard question to answer. Even cities have their own specialties: **Toulouse,** for example, is known for its cassoulet, a shell-bean stew made with pork, mutton, and goose or duck.

Gastronomy would be good enough reason for going to the **Loire** even if it didn't have châteaux. From Nantes to Orléans, the specialties are many, including, for example, shad cooked with sorrel, Loire salmon, chitterling sausage, lark pâté, goats'-milk cheese, partridge, rillettes (shredded and potted pork), herb-flavored black pudding, plus good Loire wines, including rosés.

The Normans are known not only as good soldiers but as hearty eaters. Their gastronomic table enjoys world renown. Many Parisians drive to **Normandy** for *le weekend* just to sample the rich Norman cuisine, which uses a lot of fresh butter and thick cream. Harvested along the seacoast are sole, brill, mackerel, and turbot. Shellfish are also common, especially those fat black mussels, the prawns of Cherbourg, the demoiselles of Dieppe. Try also Madame Poulard's featherweight omelet, sole normande (stewed in rich cream), tripe à la mode de Caen, chicken from the Auge Valley, and duckling from Rouen. Normandy apples, especially those from the Auge Valley, produce a most potent cider. Matured in oaken casks, the apples also are turned into Calvados, a sort of applejack, a distillation of cider flavored with hazelnuts. A true Norman drinks this cider spirit at breakfast. Bénédictine, the liqueur made at Féchamp, also enjoys acclaim. The rich Norman camembert is imitated but never equaled. Pont l'Évêque cheese has been known here since the 13th century. The Livarot is just fine for those who can get past the smell.

The province of **Brittany** is rich in seafood, the mainstay of its diet, including Aulne salmon, pike (best with white butter), scallops, trout, winkles, cockles, spiny lobsters, and Lorient sardines. Of course, the pré-salé (salt-meadow lamb) is the best meat course, traditionally served with white beans. The finest artichokes come from Roscoff, the most succulent strawberries from Plougastel. Nearly every village has its own crêperie, specializing in those paper-thin pancakes with an infinite variety of fillings. Buckwheat griddlecakes are another popular item. The food is washed down with Breton cider (admittedly inferior to the Norman variety, but quite good nevertheless). Unlike much of France, the province lacks wine, except for muscadet, a light white wine produced from the vineyards around the old Breton capital of Nantes in the lower Loire Valley.

Alsace-Lorraine has a strong Germanic flavor in its cuisine, as reflected by its sauerkraut garni, its most popular dish. It is also the home of foie gras, an expensively delicious treat. The **Savoy**, taking in the French Alps, also has many specialties, especially in its use of rich cream and milk. Game such as woodcock is common. The cuisine is heavy but tasty.

The best food and best wines are found in **Burgundy.** You'll also see à la Bourgogne (bourguignon) after a dish (that means cooked in a red wine sauce and often garnished with buttonhole mushrooms and pearl onions). Lyon is regarded as the gastronomic capital of France. For example, tripe lyonnaise is known around the world. Lyonnais sausage is also well known, and the city's many famous dishes include quenelles (fish balls, often made with pike).

The **Périgord** and **Dordogne** regions are known for their foie gras and truffles. Many farmers' wives sell foie gras directly from their kitchen door. Foie gras, naturally, comes from either a goose or a duck. The rose-hued goose liver is considered the greater delicacy. But the poor goose has a rough time of it in life, and it's a distasteful business to many sensitive souls. The goose is force-fed about one kilogram of corn every day: the French call this *gavage*. In about 22 days the liver is swollen to about 25 ounces (in many cases, far more than that). The foie gras is most often served with truffles. Otherwise, it's called *au naturel*. Even if you don't like foie gras, you'll surely want to try the fish from the rivers of the Dordogne, along with morels, strawberries, and flap mushrooms—called cèpes—from the field.

Gourmets, not just beach lovers, go to the **Riviera** too. The food, especially fish, tends to be exceptionally good. It also tends to be expensive. Bouillabaisse, said to have been invented by Venus, is the area's best-known dish. Each chef has his or her own ideas on the subject. Rascasse (hogfish), a fish found only in the Mediterranean, is invariably put in. One of the best seafood selections, rouget (red mullet) sometimes appears on fancy menus as bécasse de mer (sea woodcock). Yet another is loup (bass) de mer, cooked with fennel. Aïoli, mayonnaise with a garlic and olive-oil base, is usually served with hors d'oeuvres or boiled fish. Other specialties include soupe au pistou (vegetable soup with basil), salade niçoise (likely to include everything, but traditionally made with tomatoes, green beans, olives, tuna, anchovies, and radishes), pan bagnat (bread doused in olive oil and served with olives, anchovies, and tomatoes), and ravioli, which needs no explanation.

THE DRINKING OF WINE French cookery only achieves palate perfection when lubricated by wine, which is not considered a luxury or even an addition, but an integral part of every meal. Certain rules about wine drinking have been long established in France, but no one except traditionalists seems to follow them anymore. For example, if you're having a roast, steak, or game, a good burgundy might be your choice. If it's chicken, lamb, or veal, perhaps you might choose a red from the Bordeaux country, certainly a full-bodied red with cheese such as camembert, and a blanc de blanc with oysters. A light rosé can go with almost anything, especially if enjoyed on a summer terrace overlooking a willow-fringed riverbank.

Let your own good taste—and sometimes almost equally as important, your pocketbook—determine your choice of wine. Most wine stewards, called somme-liers, are there to help you in your choice, and only in the most dishonest of restaurants will they push you toward the most expensive selections. Of course, if you prefer only bottled water or perhaps a beer, then be firm and order either without embarrassment. In fact, bottled water might be a good idea at lunch if you're planning to drive on the roads of France later. Some restaurants include a beverage in their menu rates (*boisson compris*), but that is only in the cheaper places. Nevertheless, some of the most satisfying wines I've drunk in France came from unlabeled house bottles or carafes, called a *vin de la maison*. Unless you're a real connoisseur, you can, for the most part, not worry about labels and vintages.

When in doubt, you can rarely go wrong with a good burgundy or bordeaux, but you may want to be more experimental than that. That's when the sommelier (who today is likely to be a woman) can help you, particularly if you tell him or her your taste in wine (semidry or very dry, for example). State frankly how much you're willing to pay and what you plan to order for your meal. If you're dining with others, you may want to order two or three bottles with an entire dinner, selecting a wine to suit each course. However, even the French at most informal meals, and especially if there are only two people dining, select only one wine to go with all their platters from hors d'oeuvres to cheese. As a rule of thumb, it is estimated that a French person dining out expects to spend about one-third of the restaurant tab for wine.

LABELS OF WINE Since the latter part of the 19th century French wine has been labeled (that is, French wine served in France; outside of France, who knows?). The general label is known as *Appellations Contrôlées*. These controls, for the most part, are by regions such as Bordeaux or the Loire. These are the simple, honest wines of the district. They can be blended from grapes grown at any place in the region. Some are composed of the vintages of different years.

The more specific the label, the greater the wine (in most cases). For example, instead of a bordeaux, the wine might be labeled a Médoc (pronounced maydawk), which is a triangle of land extending some 50 miles north from Bordeaux. Wine labels can be narrowed down to a particular vine-growing property, such as a Château Haut-Brion, one of the most famous and greatest of red wines of Bordeaux (this château produces only about 10,000 cases a year).

On some burgundies, you are likely to see the word *clos* (pronounced clo). Originally, that meant a walled or otherwise enclosed vineyard, as in Clos de Beze, which is a celebrated Burgundian vineyard producing a superb red wine. *Cru* (pronounced crew and meaning "growth") suggests a wine of superior quality when it appears on a label as a *vin de cru*. Wines and vineyards are often divided into crus. A Grand Cru or Premier Cru should, by implication, be an even superior wine.

Labels are only part of the story. It's the vintage that counts. Essentially vintage is the annual grape harvest and the wine made from those grapes. Therefore, any wine can be a vintage wine unless it was blended. Like people, there are good vintages and bad. The variation between wine produced in a "good year" and wine produced in a "bad year" can be major, even to the neophyte palate.

Finally, champagne is the only wine that can be correctly served through all courses of a meal, but only to those who can afford its astronomical prices.

6. RECOMMENDED BOOKS

Becoming more familiar with France before you go can greatly enhance your trip. There are numerous books on all aspects of French history and society—ranging from the very general, such as the section on France in the *Encyclopedia Americana*, International Edition (Grolier, 1989), which presents an excellent, illustrated overview of the French people and their way of life, to the very specific, such as Judi Culbertson and Tom Randall's *Permanent Parisians: An Illustrated Guide to the Cemeteries of Paris* (Chelsea Green, 1986), which vividly depicts the lives of many famous French and foreign people who are buried in Paris. The books that I have selected are grouped into five categories below: history, biography, art, travel, and fiction.

HISTORY

In addition to the encyclopedia reference above, a broad overview of French history can be found in other encyclopedias and general history books. One very good one is *History of France* by Guillaume de Bertier de Sauvigny and David H. Pinkney (Forum Press, 1983), a comprehensive history with illustrations and lots of obscure but interesting facts.

For a glimpse of the Middle Ages, try *Mont-Saint-Michel and Chartres* by Henry Adams (W. H. Smith, 1980). This abridged version has an introduction by Lord Briggs, a historian at Oxford University, and many examples of the art of the period. These both contribute to our understanding of the religious feelings surrounding the production of these two monuments.

Two books that present French life and society in the 17th century are Warren Lewis's *The Splendid Century* (William Morrow, 1978) and *Madame de Sévigné: Selected Letters,* edited by Leonard W. Tancock (Penguin, 1982), which contains imaginative and witty letters written to her daughter during the reign of Louis XIV.

Simon Schama's *Citizens* (Alfred A. Knopf, 1989) is "a magnificent and electrifyingly new history of the French Revolution"—long, but very enjoyable.

Moving into the 20th century, *Pleasures of the Belle Epoque: Entertainment and Festivity in Turn-of-the-Century France* by Charles Rearick (Yale University Press, 1985) depicts public diversions in the changing and troubled times of the Third Republic. *Paris Was Yesterday, 1925–1939* (Viking 1972) is a fascinating collection of excerpts from Janet Flanner's "Letters from Paris" column of *The New Yorker.* Larry Collins and Dominique Lapierre have written a popular history of the liberation of Paris in 1944 called *Is Paris Burning?* (Warner Books, 1991).

Finally, two unusual approaches to French history are Rudolph Chleminski's *The French at Table* (William Morrow, 1985), a funny and honest history of why the French know how to eat better than any people on earth and how they go about it; and *Paris: A Century of Change, 1878–1978* by Norman Evenson (Yale University Press, 1979), a notable study of the urban development of Paris.

The Fall of Paris: June 1940, by Herbert R. Lottman (Harper Collins, 1992), was written by the biographer of Colette, Flaubert, and Pétain. It's a riveting account of one of the saddest events of World War II.

BIOGRAPHY

You can get a different perspective on history by reading biographies of historical figures, such as *Eleanor of Aquitaine and the Four Kings* by Amy Ruth Kelly (Harvard University Press, 1950). This is a beautifully told story of one of the great women of the Middle Ages, wife of two kings and mother of two others. Hugh Ross Williamson also brings to life Catherine de Medici in his *Catherine de Medici* (Viking Press, 1973), by combining text and magnificent illustrations from the art of the 16th century. This queen of France was the dominant personality during her nation's religious wars and mother of three kings of France, a queen of Spain, and a queen of Navarre.

Representing a very different era is *A Moveable Feast* (Collier Books, 1987), Ernest Hemingway's recollections of Paris during the 1920s. Another interesting read is *The Autobiography of Alice B. Toklas* (Vintage Books, 1990), by Gertrude Stein. It's not only the account of 30 years in Paris, but also the biography of Gertrude Stein.

Simone de Beauvoir by Deirdre Bair (Summit Books, 1990) was described by one critic as a biography "à l'Américaine—that is to say, long, with all the warts of its subject unsparingly described." The story of the great feminist intellectual was based in part on tape-recorded conversations and unpublished letters. *Colette: A Life,* by Herbert R. Lottman (Little Brown & Company, 1991), is a painstakingly researched biography of the celebrated French writer and her strange life—which included not only writing novels and appearing in cabarets but also dabbling in lesbianism and perhaps even collaborating with the enemy during the Nazi occupation of France.

You See, I Haven't Forgotten, by Yves Montand, with Hervé Hamon and Patrick Rotman (Alfred A. Knopf, 1992), is a fine biography of one of France's most beloved showmen. Montand may not have been the actual author, but he cooperated fully on the biography, granting 200 hours of interviews.

In *Madame Du Barry: The Wages of Beauty* (Grove Weidenfeld, 1992), Joan Haslip tells the saga of the convent-educated prostitute who at the age of 25 became the last mistress of Louis XV. Surviving the king and going on to other lovers, Madame du Barry met her fate at the guillotine in the Reign of Terror.

The Divine Sarah: A Life of Sarah Bernhardt, by Arthur Gold and Robert

Fizdale (Knopf, 1991), is the life story of the woman still acclaimed as the world's greatest actress—her triumphs and tragedies, her love affairs, her friends and foes, all enlivened by journals, letters, and comments from contemporaries.

ART

Much of France's beauty can be found in its art. Three excellent books that approach France from this perspective are *The History of Impressionism,* by John Rewald (Museum of Modern Art, 1973), which is a collection of documents, both writings and quotations of the artists, clearly illuminating this valuable period in the history of art; *The French Through Their Films,* by Robin Buss (Ungar, 1988), an exploration of the history and themes of more than 100 widely circulated films; and *The Studios of Paris: The Capital of Art in the Late Nineteenth Century,* by John Milner (Yale University Press, 1988). In the last, Milner presents the dynamic forces that made Paris one of the most complex centers of the art world in the early modern era.

Henri Matisse: A Retrospective, by John Elderfield (Museum of Modern Art, 1992), reproduces more than 400 artworks, most in color, the largest Matisse retrospective ever assembled.

French Painting, by Charles Stuckey (Macmillian, 1991), is a large-format book with 300 color plates. From prehistoric Lascaux cave paintings to Renoir and Dufy, it moves across the panorama of French art.

TRAVEL

In Robert Daly's vibrant *Portraits of France* (Little Brown & Company, 1991), it's all here: landscapes, villages, graveyards, wines, and portraits of such great figures as Lafayette.

The Lost Upland, by W. S. Merwin (Knopf, 1992), is a collection of stories from southwestern France. *New York* magazine called it "a lyrical evocation of a vanishing world."

FICTION

The *Chanson de Roland* (edited by F. Whitehead, 2nd ed.; Basil Blackwell, 1942) written between the 11th and 14th centuries, is the earliest and most celebrated of the "songs of heroic exploits." *The Misanthrope* and *Tartuffe* are two masterful satires on the frivolity of the 17th century by the great comic dramatist Molière (Harcourt, Brace and World, 1965). François-Marie Arouet Voltaire's *Candide* (Bantam Classics, 1981) is a classic satire attacking both the philosophy of optimism and the abuses of the Ancien Régime.

A few of the masterpieces of the 19th century are *Madame Bovary* by Gustave Flaubert (Random House, 1982), in which the carefully wrought characters, setting, and plot attest to the genius of Flaubert in presenting the tragedy of Emma Bovary; Victor Hugo's *Les Misérables* (Modern Library, 1983), a classic tale of social oppression and human courage set in the era of the first Napoléon; and the collection *Selected Stories* by the master of short stories, Guy de Maupassant (New American Library, 1984).

Honoré de Balzac's *La comédie humaine* (1830–50) (actually a series of novels which includes *Père Goriot* and *Eugénie Grandet*) depicts life in France from the fall of Napoléon to 1848. Henry James's *The Ambassadors* (Oxford University Press, 1985) and *The American* (Houghton, Mifflin and Company, 1985) both take place in Paris. *The Vagabond,* by Colette (1910, translated 1955), evokes the colorful life of a French music-hall performer (Ballantine, 1982).

Tropic of Cancer (1934) is the semi-autobiographical story of Henry Miller's early years in Paris (Modern Library, 1983). One of France's leading thinkers, Jean-Paul Sartre, shows individuals struggling against their freedom in *No Exit and Three Other Plays* (Random House, 1955). Finally, writer Georges Simenon and illustrator Frederick Franck combined to create *Simenon's Paris* (Dial Press, 1970), a beautifully illustrated book of Simenon's Paris stories.

PLANNING YOUR TRIP

This chapter and the next are devoted to the where, the when, and the how of your trip to France—all those issues required to get your trip together and take it on the road.

In this chapter, I concentrate on what you need to do *before* you go. (See Chapter 3 for information on getting to and around France.) In addition to helping you decide when to take your vacation, I answer questions you might have about what to take, where to gather information, and what documents you need to obtain. I also cover various alternative and specialty travel options, such as educational and wilderness travel, and include tips for special travelers.

1. INFORMATION, DOCUMENTS & MONEY

SOURCES OF INFORMATION

In the U.S. Your best source of information before you go—besides this guide—is the **French Government Tourist Office,** at the following addresses in the U.S.: 628 Fifth Ave., New York, NY 10020; 645 N. Michigan Ave., Suite 630, Chicago, IL 60611; 2305 Cedar Springs Rd., Dallas, TX 75201; 9454 Wilshire Blvd., Beverly Hills, CA 90212-2967. To request information at any of these offices, call the **France on Call** hotline (tel. 900/990-0040); each call costs 50¢ per minute.

In Canada Write to Maison de la France/French Government Tourist Office, at either 1981, av. McGill College, Tour Esso, Suite 490, Montréal, PQ H3A 2W9 (tel. 514/288-4264); or 30 St. Patricks St., Suite 700, Toronto, ON M5T 3A3 (tel. 416/593-4723).

In Great Britain Write to Maison de la France/French Government Tourist Office, 178 Piccadilly, London, W1V 0AL (tel. 071/491-7622).

In Australia Write to the French Tourist Office, in the B.N.P. Building, 12th Floor, 12 Castlereagh St., Sydney, N.S.W. 2000 (tel. 02/231-5244).

In Ireland Write to the Maison de la France/French Government Tourist Office, 35 Lower Abbey St., Dublin 1, Ireland (tel. 01/771871).

In New Zealand Currently there is no representative in New Zealand, so citizens should contact the representative in Australia.

INFORMATION ON TRAVEL TO MONACO

Information on travel to Monaco (which retains some degree of autonomy from the rest of France) is available from the **Monaco Government Tourist and Convention Bureau,** 845 Third Ave., New York, NY 10022 (tel. 212/759-5227, or toll free 800/753-9696). Although most of its facilities (along with its consulate) are in New York at the above-listed address, Monaco maintains a branch office at 542 S. Dearborn Ave., Chicago, IL 60605 (tel. 312/939-7863). Visa requirements for travel to Monaco are exactly the same as those for travel to France, and there are virtually no border patrols or passport formalities at the Monegasque frontier.

DOCUMENTS

PASSPORTS   All foreign (i.e., non-French) nationals need a valid passport to enter France (check its expiration date).

VISAS For U.S. Citizens   As of July 1, 1989, the French government no longer requires visas for U.S. visitors to France, providing they are staying for less than 90 days. For longer stays, visitors must apply for a long-term visa, a residence card, or a temporary-stay visa. Each requires proof of income or a viable means of support within France, and a legitimate purpose for remaining within the country. Applications are available from the French Embassy, 4001 Reservoir Rd. NW, Washington, DC 20007 (tel. 202/944-6015), or from the visa section of the French Consulate at 935 Fifth Ave., New York, NY 10021 (tel. 212/606-3653).

For Other Nationals   Canadian, Swiss, and Japanese citizens and citizens of E.C. countries are exempt from the visa requirement, but check with your nearest French consulate, as the situation can change overnight.

MONEY

CASH/CURRENCY   The basic unit of French currency is the **franc (F),** worth about 18¢ U.S. (about 5.55 francs to $1 U.S.). One franc breaks down into 100 **centimes.** Coins are issued in units of 5, 10, 20, and 50 centimes, plus 1, 2, 5, and 10 francs. Bills come in 10, 20, 50, and 100 francs. The franc and the dollar, like all world currencies, fluctuate on the market. That means that the franc-to-dollar conversions appearing in parentheses throughout the upcoming chapters cannot possibly be exact. Currency conversions are presented only to give you a rough idea of the price you'll pay in U.S. dollars. There is no way to predict exactly what the rate of exchange will be when you visit France. Check with your bank for up-to-the-minute quotations.

When converting your home currency into French francs, know that rates vary. Your hotel will offer the worst rate of exchange. In general, banks offer the best rate, but even banks charge a commission for the service, often $2 or $3, depending on the transaction. Whenever you can, stick to the big banks of France, like Crédit Lyonnais, which offer the best exchange rates and charge the lowest commission for exchanging money or traveler's checks.

Always make sure you have enough francs for the weekend, especially when you're going to off-the-beaten-track places in the countryside of France.

Note: For U.S. citizens, I recommend bringing about $200 in U.S. dollars in cash; and before leaving home, I'd exchange another $50 in francs so as to avoid waiting in long lines at the airport's currency-exchange offices.

TRAVELER'S CHECKS   Before leaving home, you should also purchase traveler's checks.

American Express (tel. toll free 800/221-7282 in the U.S. and Canada) charges a 1% commission. Checks are free to members of the American Automobile Association.

Barclay's Bank/Bank of America (tel. toll free 800/221-2426 in the U.S. and Canada). Through Barclay's subsidiary, Interpayment Services, VISA traveler's checks are sold denominated in either U.S. dollars or British pounds.

Citicorp (tel. toll free 800/645-6556 in the U.S. and Canada) issues checks in U.S. dollars, British pounds, or German marks.

MasterCard International/Thomas Cook International (tel. toll free 800/223-9920 in the U.S., or 212/974-5695, collect, from the rest of the world), issues checks in about a dozen currencies.

Each of these agencies will refund your checks if they're lost or stolen, provided you can produce sufficient documentation. Of course, your documentation should be carried in a safe place—never along with your checks. When purchasing checks from one of the banks listed, ask about refund hotlines; American Express and Bank of America have the most offices around the world. Purchase checks in a variety of denominations—$20, $50, and $100.

Sometimes you can purchase traveler's checks in the currency of the country you're planning to visit, thereby avoiding a conversion fee. American Express, for example, issues checks in French francs. Foreign banks may ask up to 5% to convert your checks into French francs. Note, also, that you always get a better rate if you cash traveler's checks at the banks issuing them: VISA at Barclays or Bank of America, American Express at American Express, and so forth.

CREDIT & CHARGE CARDS   Credit cards are useful in France. Both **American Express** and **Diners Club** are widely recognized. The French equivalent for VISA is **Carte Bleue.** If you see the **Eurocard** sign on an establishment, it means it accepts MasterCard.

Credit and charge cards can save your life when you're abroad. With American Express and VISA, for example, not only can you charge purchases in shops and restaurants that take the card, but also you can withdraw francs from bank cash machines at many locations in France. Check with your credit-card company before leaving home.

Of course, you may make a purchase with a credit card thinking it will be at a certain rate, only to find that the U.S. dollar or British pound has declined by the time your bill arrives, and you're actually paying more for an item than you bargained for. But those are the rules of the game. It also can work in your favor if the dollar or pound should unexpectedly rise after you make a purchase.

CONVERSION-RELATED FINANCIAL TRANSACTIONS   Many hotels in France will simply not accept a dollar-denominated check, and if they do, they'll certainly charge for the conversion. In some cases they'll accept countersigned traveler's checks, or a credit card, but if you're prepaying a deposit on hotel reservations it's cheaper and easier to pay with a check drawn on a French bank.

This can be arranged by a large commercial bank or by a currency specialist like **Ruesch International,** 1350 Eye St. NW, Washington, DC 20005 (tel. 202/408-1200, or toll free 800/424-2923), which can perform a wide variety of conversion-related financial transactions for individual travelers.

To place an order, call them and tell them the type and amount of the franc-denominated check you need. Ruesch will quote a U.S. dollar equivalent, adding a $2 fee per check as their service fee. After receiving your dollar-denominated personal check for the agreed-upon amount, Ruesch will mail you a franc-denominated bank draft, drawn on a French bank and payable to whichever party you specified, for the agreed-upon amount. Ruesch will also convert checks expressed in foreign currency into U.S. dollars, provide foreign currencies in cash from more than 120 countries, and sell traveler's checks payable in either dollars or any of six foreign currencies, including French francs.

In addition to its Washington, D.C. headquarters, Ruesch maintains offices in New York, Los Angeles, Chicago, Atlanta, and Boston, although the Washington, D.C., office can supply, through phone orders, any of the bank draft and traveler's check services mentioned above. Ruesch will mail brochures and information packets upon request.

WHAT WILL IT COST?

France, frankly, is one of the world's most expensive destinations. But, to compensate, it often offers top-value food and lodging. Part of the problem is the Value-Added Tax (VAT), which tacks on about 6%–33% on top of everything. It's expensive to rent and drive a car in France (gasoline is costly, too), and flying in France is costly compared to flying in the U.S. Train travel is relatively inexpensive, though, especially if you purchase a rail pass. The good news is that in the early 1990s inflation stayed low, about 2%–3% per year.

A Wide Range of Living and Eating Styles

You can live on $25 a day or $3,000 a day in France—the amount will depend on your own budget and tastes. You can stay at super-deluxe palaces in Paris and continue your tour through Relais & Châteaux (castle-hotels; see "Special Accommodations in France" in this chapter) all the way to the posh palaces along the Rivera, or you can live inexpensively in low-cost hotels in Paris or *auberges* (small inns) or *logis* (budget hotels) throughout France. *Frommer's France* documents a wide range of living and eating styles.

As a general rule of thumb, two people dining in medium-price restaurants and/or in medium-price hotels will spend $200–$300 a day for food and lodging in France—that's per couple. That's an average—it will be higher in Paris, lower in the country. Transportation is extra, of course. But the figure does include three meals, a glass or two of wine in a café, and basic sightseeing costs. Of course, if you're on a strict budget, you can find hotels in Paris charging about $75 a night for a double room. Likewise, many $50 double rooms exist in rural France. If your budget allows for first-class or deluxe travel, then in France the sky's the limit.

Prices by Region   Remember that prices in Paris and on the Riviera are higher than in the provinces. If budget is paramount, cut short your visit to these fabled places and spend more time in the country. You'll still enjoy *tout confort* (every comfort), but you'll pay half or a third the price you might be charged in Paris or on the Riviera.

Meals in Paris in deluxe restaurants will cost $250 and up for two people. In first-class restaurants expect to pay $160–$200 for two. In the medium-priced range, you can dine for $100–$150 for two people. Anytime two people dine for less than $80 in Paris, the bill is considered cheap. Of course, these are real restaurants and bistros, not fast-food take-outs.

Three of the most touristy parts of France—Brittany, Normandy, and the Loire Valley—have reasonably priced hotels and scads of restaurants offering superb food at medium-priced tabs.

In Rouen, Normandy, first-class double rooms cost about $85 and up a night. You can live less expensively in medium-priced hotels for about $60–$85 a night, and inexpensively in double rooms for under $60 a night (in the latter you may have only a sink and toilet in your room).

In expensive restaurants, sampling the famous duck of Rouen, two diners will pay from $90, excluding wine. Moderate usually means $55–$90 for two people, and anytime two diners get a check for under $55 in a restaurant, they've scored a coup.

Restaurant Costs   I've provided the cost of fixed-price *menus* (meals) if featured, and you may want to stick to them if you're afraid of getting a shocker of a bill. I've also indicated the price range of appetizers and main dishes. If you're an average eater, double the price of your main dish and you'll get a fair idea of what a typical meal will cost. The cost of your wine will be extra in many cases, or sometimes a carafe of the local wine is included; it depends on the restaurant.

Caveat: Please realize that the price range I've cited for restaurants indicates only an average cost. In France, many menus, particularly those specializing in *cuisine du marché* (fresh-from-the-market ingredients), will vary from day to day, the dishes being inspired by the seasonal produce, and the restaurateur will sometimes charge

DRIVING IN EUROPE

Driver's License U.S. and Canadian driver's licenses are valid in France, but if you're touring Europe by car, you may want to invest in an International Driver's License just to be on the safe side. Apply at a branch of the American Automobile Association (AAA). You must be 18 years old and include two two- by two-inch photographs, a $10 fee, and your valid U.S. driver's license with your application. If AAA doesn't have a branch in your hometown, send a photograph of your driver's license (both the front and the back) with the fee and photos to AAA, 1000 AAA Dr. (P.O. Box 28), Heathrow, FL 32746-5063 (tel. 407/444-4240). You should always carry your original license with you to Europe, however.

In Canada, you pay $10 Canadian and apply to the Canadian Automobile Association (CAA), 2 Carlton St., Toronto, ON M5B 1S3 (tel. 416/593-6119).

Insurance In Europe, you must have an international insurance certificate, called a green card (*carte verte* in French). The car-rental agency will provide one if you're renting.

more. For example, if the chef suddenly decides to buy some lobster and other seafood ingredients on any particular night, he may throw my main-dish "highs" into a tailspin. You can, of course, stick to the less expensive sole meunière and stay more within my price guidelines. Therefore, consider the price range for appetizers and main dishes a general guideline only.

THE FRENCH FRANC

For American Readers At this writing $1 = approximately 5.50 francs (or 1 franc = 18¢), and this was the rate of exchange used to calculate the dollar values given in this book (rounded to the nearest nickel).

For British Readers At this writing £1 = approximately 8.3 francs (or 1 franc = 12p), and this was the rate of exchange used to calculate the pound values in the table below.

Note The exchange rate fluctuates from time to time depending on a complicated series of fiscal and political factors, and may not be the same when you travel to France. Therefore this table should be used only as a guide:

F	U.S.$	U.K.£	F	U.S.$	U.K.£
1	.18	.12	75	13.64	9.04
2	.36	.24	100	18.18	12.05
3	.55	.36	125	22.73	15.06
4	.73	.48	150	27.27	18.07
5	.91	.60	175	31.82	21.08
6	1.09	.72	200	36.36	24.10
7	1.27	.84	225	40.91	27.11
8	1.45	.96	250	45.45	30.12
9	1.64	1.08	275	50.00	33.13
10	1.82	1.20	300	54.55	36.14
15	2.73	1.81	350	63.64	42.17
20	3.64	2.41	400	72.73	48.19
25	4.55	3.01	450	81.82	54.22
50	9.09	6.02	500	90.91	60.24

WHAT THINGS COST IN PARIS   U.S. $

Taxi from Charles de Gaulle Airport to the city center	46.00
Taxi from Orly Airport to the city center	38.00
Public transportation for an average trip within the city (from a Métro carnet of 10)	.65
Local telephone call	.20
Double room at Le Ritz (very expensive)	747.00
Double room at the Lord Byron (moderate)	162.00
Double room at the Family (budget)	122.40
Lunch for one, without wine, at Chez Georges (moderate)	31.50
Lunch for one, without wine, at Le Drouot (budget)	15.00
Dinner for one, without wine, at Le Grand Véfour (very expensive)	108.00
Dinner for one, without wine, at Brasserie Flo (moderate)	36.00
Dinner for one, without wine, at La Petit Chaise (budget)	30.00
Glass of wine	3.80
Coca-Cola	3.80
Cup of coffee	3.50
Roll of ASA 100 film, 36 exposures	7.00
Admission to the Louvre	6.00
Movie ticket	8.00
Theater ticket (at the Comédie-Française)	25.00

2. WHEN TO GO

France is a country for all seasons. Travel-wise visitors who have a choice of when to visit France cite late spring (June) or early autumn (September) as ideal. I think that's good advice for most people (although I personally find France a delight at any time).

July and August are considered the worst months by most people—that's when there are the most tourists. Parisians desert their city in August, leaving it to the tourists and the businesses that cater to them.

Paris has an uncommonly long springtime, lasting through April, May, and June, and an equally extended fall, September through November. The climate, however, is temperate throughout the year.

The best time to come to Paris is off-season, in the early spring or late autumn, when the tourist trade has trickled to a manageable flow and everything is easier to come by—hotel rooms, Métro seats, even good-tempered waiters.

Don't come to Paris in the first two weeks of October without a confirmed hotel reservation. The weather's fine, but the place is jammed for the annual motor show when the French indulge their passion for cars.

CLIMATE

In France, the weather varies considerably from region to region and sometimes from town to town as little as 12 miles apart.

Although global warming seems to have made weather forecasting very inaccurate, here are a few tentative predictions—enough to give you some idea of what to pack.

Despite its northerly latitude, Paris never gets very cold. Snow is a rarity.

The hands-down winner for wetness is Brittany, where Brest (known for the mold that adds flavor to its blue cheeses—probably a function of the constant rainfall) receives a staggering amount of rain between October and December. The rain usually falls in a kind of steady, foggy drizzle and rarely lasts more than a day. May is considered the driest month.

The Mediterranean coast of the south of France has the driest climate. When it does rain, it's usually heaviest in spring and autumn. (Surprisingly, Cannes sometimes receives more annual rainfall than Paris.) Summers are comfortably dry—beneficial to humans but deadly to much of the vegetation, which (unless it's irrigated) often dries and burns up in the parched months.

Provence dreads *le mistral* (an unrelenting, hot, dry, dusty wind from North Africa), which most often blows in winter for a few days, but which can blow for up to two weeks.

Regional Rain- and Snowfall An alpine climate, with heavy snowfall, prevails in the French Alps; a mild Atlantic climate prevails in the southwest near the delta of the Garonne. In the east of France, when it does rain it's likely to cascade down in heavy thundershowers, although rarely strong enough to do any serious damage to riverbanks or houses. On France's central plateau, the elevated altitude causes more snow to remain on the ground than you'll find in most of the rest of the country, and traffic is sometimes slowed down by snow blockage.

Weather Forecasts For up-to-the-minute weather forecasts in the U.S., dial 900/WEATHER, at a cost of 95¢ per minute. This weather report comes from the cable television station, Weather Channel. Punch in the first four letters of the city name. That is, PARI for Paris, after dialing the 900 number given above. The service is 24 hours a day.

HOLIDAYS (JOURS FERIES)

In France, holidays are known as *jours fériés*. Shops and many businesses—banks and some museums and restaurants—close on holidays, but hotels and emergency services remain open.

The main holidays—a mix of both secular and religious ones—include: New Year's Day (Jan 1), Shrove Tuesday (the Tuesday before Ash Wednesday), Good Friday, Easter Sunday, Ascension Day (40 days after Easter), Pentecost Sunday (seventh Sunday after Easter), Whit Monday, Labor Day (May 1), V-E Day in Europe (May 8), Bastille Day (July 14), Assumption of the Blessed Virgin (August 15), All Saints' Day (November 1), Armistice Day (November 11), and Christmas (December 25).

FRANCE
CALENDAR OF EVENTS

JANUARY

☐ **Monte Carlo Motor Rally.** The world's most venerable car race. Usually mid-January.

FEBRUARY

✪ *CARNIVAL OF NICE* *Float processions, parades, confetti battles, boat races, street music and food, masked balls, and fireworks are all part of this ancient celebration. The climax is the burning in effigy of King Carnival, preceded by the Batailles des Fleurs (Battles of the Flowers), during which members of opposing teams pelt one another with flowers.*

Where: Nice, especially on the Promenade des Anglais. When: Late February to early March. How: Come with proof of a hotel reservation. For information, contact the Comité des fêtes, 5, promenade des Anglais, 06000 Nice (tel. 93-87-16-28).

APRIL

☐ **Son-et-Lumière (Sound-and-Light) Shows.** Loire Valley. April to September.

MAY

☐ **Mai Musicale.** Bordeaux. Music festival with operas, recitals, and concerts. May 8–27.

✪ *CANNES FILM FESTIVAL* *The population swells during the movie madness that transforms this city into the kingdom of the media-related "deal," with daily melodramas acted out in cafés, on sidewalks, in hotel lobbies, and in suites by stars of all ages, nations, and sexes. Great for voyeurs.*
Where: Cannes. When: Mid-May. How: Reserve early and make a deposit. Getting a table on the terrace at the Carlton Hotel is even more difficult. Admission to some of the prestigious films is by invitation only. There are box-office tickets for the less important films, which play 24 hours a day. For information, contact Direction du Festival International du Film, 71, rue du Faubourg St-Honoré, 75008 Paris (tel. 1/42-66-92-20).

☐ **Monaco Grand Prix.** Monaco. Cars race through the medieval streets. May 11–12.
☐ **Grand Pélerinage de Mai.** Les Saintes-Maries-de-la-Mer. Held in the historic horse-breeding lowlands of the Camargue. Gypsies from throughout Europe congregate for a reunion. Late May.

JUNE

☐ **Strasbourg International Music Festival.** Strasbourg. Different musical concerts in various public buildings. Mid-June.
☐ **Spectacle de Puy du Fou.** *Son et lumière* at the Château du Puy du Fou. Les Epesses (Vendée). With a cast of 300 actors and a soundtrack by famous actors. Mid-June to early September.
☐ **The 24-Hour Le Mans Car Race.** Late June.

JULY

☐ **Grand Prix de France.** Le Castellet. Formula One car races. Early July.
☐ **Le Tour de France.** The world's most famous (and most difficult) bicycle race. Early July.
☐ **Les Chorégies d'Orange.** Orange. One of southern France's most important music and opera festivals. Mid-July to early August.
☐ **Bastille Day.** Dances, drinking, and fireworks, throughout France. This holiday celebrates the storming of the Bastille and the start of the French Revolution in 1789. July 14.

✪ *FESTIVAL D'AVIGNON* *The weather is warm enough to sit out in sight of the 14th-century papal palace. One of France's most prestigious theater events, featuring groups from around the world performing in many different languages. Mime, too.*
Where: Avignon. When: Mid-July to early August. How: Make hotel reservations early. For information, contact L'Office de Tourisme, 41, cours Jean-Jaurès, Avignon 84000 (tel. 90-82-65-11).

✪ *FESTIVAL D'AIX-EN-PROVENCE* *A musical event par excellence, featuring everything from Gregorian chant to melodies composed on computerized synthesizers. Operas are performed in three different* locations, and local recitals are performed in the cloister of the Cathédrale St-Sauveur. **Where:** Aix-en Provence, Bouches-du-Rhône. **When:** July 13–31. **How:** Make advance hotel reservations and take a written confirmation with you when you arrive. Expect heat, crowds, and traffic. For information, contact the festival International d'Art Lyrique et de Musique, Palais de l'Ancien Archévêche, 13100 Aix-en-Provence (tel. 42-23-11-20).

✪ **GRAND PARADE DU JAZZ (Nice Jazz Festival)** The biggest, flashiest, and most prestigious jazz festival in Europe. World-class entertainers. Concerts begin in early afternoon and go until late at night (sometimes all night in the clubs) on a hill above the city. **Where:** Nice. **When:** 10 days in July. **How:** Reserve hotel space way in advance. For information, contact the Grand Parade du Jazz, Opéra de Nice, 4, rue St-François-de-Paule, 06300 Nice (tel. 93-85-67-31); or Office de Tourisme, avenue Thiers, 06000 Nice (tel. 93-87-07-07).

SEPTEMBER

✪ **FESTIVAL INTERNATIONAL DE FOLKLORE ET FETE DE LA VIGNE (International Festival of Folklore and Wine)** Dijon. Dance troupes from around the world help to celebrate the famous wines of Burgundy. **Where:** Dijon and many villages nearby. **When:** Early September. **How:** For information, contact the Festival de Musique et Danse Populares, boulevard de la Tremouille, 21025 Dijon (tel. 80-30-37-95).

☐ **Festival de Musique de Besançon et de Franche-Comté.** Besançon. First two weeks of September.

NOVEMBER

✪ **LES TROIS GLORIEUSES** The country's most important wine festival is celebrated in three Burgundian towns. Although you may not gain access to many of the gatherings, there are enough wine tastings and other amusements to keep you occupied. **Where:** Clos-de-Vougeot, Beaune, and Meursault. **When:** Third week in November. A wine auction in Beaune at Hospices de Beaune is held on the third Sunday. The termination (which is more accessible) is held on the third Monday in Meursault. **How:** Reserve early or visit from a nearby village. Confirm information by contacting Comité Régional du Tourisme, B.P. 1602, 21035 Dijon (tel. 80-50-10-20), or Office de Tourisme, rue de l'Hôtel-Dieu, 21200 Beaune (tel. 80-22-24-51).

DECEMBER

☐ **Christmas Fair.** Strasbourg. Late December.

PARIS
CALENDAR OF EVENTS

JANUARY

☐ **The Boat Fair** (Le Salon International de la Navigation de Plaisance). One of Europe's largest boat shows. Parc des Expositions, Porte de Versailles, Paris 15e (Métro: Porte de Versailles).
☐ **International Ready-to-Wear Fashion Shows** (Le Salon International de Prêt-à-Porter). Parc des Expositions, Porte de Versailles, Paris 15e (Métro: Porte de

Versailles). Various couture houses, such as Lanvin and Courrèges, have their own shows at their respective headquarters. Mid-January to mid-February.

MARCH

☐ **Foire du Trone,** Neuilly Lawn of the Bois de Vincennes. A mammoth amusement park. Operates daily from 2pm to midnight from end of March through May.

MAY

☐ **French Open Tennis Championship,** Stade Roland-Garros. May 24–June 6.
☐ **Paris Marathon.** Runners compete from around the world. Second weekend.
☐ **Illuminated fountains at Versailles.** May to September.
☐ **Festival de Versailles.** Features opera, concerts, theater, and ballet. Call 30-21-20-20 for information. Late May to late June.
☐ **Festival de Musique de St-Denis.** Music in the church. Call 42-43-72-72 for information. Late May through late June.
☐ **Festival de Paris,** 38 rue des Blancs-Manteaux, 4e. An assemblage of some of the world's leading orchestras and choruses. Tickets cost 50–500 F ($9–$90). Call 40-26-45-34 for information. Mid-May to late June.

JUNE

☐ **Paris Air Show,** Le Bourget Airport. Early June in alternate years only (next Air Show in 1995).
☐ **Grand Steeplechase de Paris,** Auteuil Racetrack, in the Bois de Boulogne. Mid-June.
☐ **Festival du Marais.** Many events—theater, exhibitions, classical and jazz music—are presented in renovated Renaissance buildings and courtyards. For details, contact the Festival du Marais, 68, rue François Minon, 75004 Paris (tel. 1/48-87-60-08). Mid-June to mid-July.
☐ **Grand Prix de Paris,** Longchamp Raceway. Late June.

JULY

✪ **BASTILLE DAY** *The nation's festivities reach their peak in Paris with street fairs, pageants, fireworks, and feasts. The day begins with a parade down the Champs-Elysées and ends with fireworks at Montmartre. Wherever you are, before the end of the day you'll hear Piaf warbling "La Foule" ("The Crowd"), the song that celebrated her passion for the stranger whom she met and later lost in a crowd on Bastille Day.*

__When:__ July 14. __Where:__ Bars, restaurants, streets, and private homes throughout Paris. __How:__ Hum the Marseillaise; outfit yourself with a beret, a pack of Gauloises, and a bottle of cheap wine; leave your hotel; and stamp around the neighborhood.

☐ **Festival Estival (Summertime Festival).** Music in churches and concert halls throughout Paris. For details, contact the Festival Estival de Paris, 20, rue Geoffrey-l'Asnier, 75004 Paris (tel. 48-04-98-01). Mid-July to late September.
☐ **Le Grand Tour de France.** Europe's most visible bicycle race decides its winner at a finish line drawn across the Champs-Elysées. Late July.

SEPTEMBER

☐ **Festival d'Automne.** Concentrating mainly on modern music, ballet, theater, and modern art, it's the most eclectic of the festivals. For details, contact the Festival d'Automne, 156, rue de Rivoli, 75001 Paris (tel. 42-96-12-27). Late September until just before Christmas.

OCTOBER

☼ **PARIS AUTO SHOW** *Glistening metal, glitzy women, lots of hype, and the latest models from world auto makers—this is the showcase for European car design.*
Where: Parc des Expositions, near the Porte de Versailles in western Paris. *When:* 10 days in early October. *How:* Check Pariscope for details or contact the French Government Tourist Office.

☐ **Prix de l'Arc de Triomphe.** The country's most prestigious horse race. Bois de Boulogne. Early October.

☐ **International Fair of Contemporary Artists,** at the Grand Palais. Late October to early November.

NOVEMBER

☐ **Armistice Day.** Celebrated with a military parade from the Arc de Triomphe to the Hôtel des Invalides. November 11.

DECEMBER

☐ **Fête de St-Sylvestre (New Year's Eve).** It's best celebrated in the Quartier Latin around the Sorbonne. At midnight, the city explodes—strangers kiss strangers. Boulevard St-Michel becomes a virtual pedestrian mall, as does the Champs-Elysées. December 31.

3. HEALTH & INSURANCE

HEALTH

France should not pose any major health hazards, although many travelers suffer from diarrhea. This is generally caused by the overly rich cuisine—heavy cream sauces, butter, olive oil (in the south), and wine. Take along some antidiarrhea medicine, moderate your eating habits, and, even though the water in France is considered safe, consume mineral water only.

Sometimes travelers find that a change of diet in France leads to constipation. If this occurs, eat a high-fiber diet and drink plenty of mineral water. Avoid large lunches and dinners with wine. Consult your pharmacist about taking an over-the-counter drug such as Colace, a stool softener, or Metamucil.

Take along an adequate supply of any prescription drugs that you need and a prescription that gives the generic name of the drug as well—not the brand name.

You aren't required to have any particular inoculations to enter France (except for yellow fever, and then only if you're arriving from an infected area).

If you need a doctor, your hotel will locate one for you. You can also obtain a list of English-speaking doctors in France from the **International Association for Medical Assistance to Travelers (IAMAT):** in the U.S., at 417 Center St., Lewiston, NY 14092 (tel. 716/754-4883); in Canada, at 40 Regal Rd., Guelph, ON N1K 1B5 (tel. 519/836-0102). Getting medical help in France is relatively easy. Don't be unduly alarmed, even in rural areas. Competent doctors are found in every part of the country.

If you're subject to motion sickness on a plane or train, remember to bring along motion-sickness medicine as well.

If your medical condition is chronic, always talk to your doctor before taking an international trip. He or she may have specific advice to give you, depending on your condition. For conditions such as epilepsy, a heart condition, and diabetes, wear a **Medic Alert Identification Tag,** which will immediately alert any doctor to the nature of your trouble. It also provides the number of Medic Alert's 24-hour hotline so that a foreign doctor can obtain medical records for you. A lifetime membership is a well-spent $35. Contact the Medic Alert Foundation, P.O. Box 1009, Turlock, CA 95381-1009 (tel. 800/432-5378).

Of course, carry all your vital medicine and drugs (the legal kind) with you in your carry-on luggage, in case your checked luggage is lost.

INSURANCE

Insurance needs for the traveler abroad fall into three categories: (1) health and accident, (2) trip cancellation, and (3) lost luggage.

First, review your present policies before traveling internationally—you may already have adequate coverage between them and what is offered by credit-card companies.

Many credit-card companies insure their users in case of a travel accident, providing a ticket was purchased with their card. Sometimes fraternal organizations have policies that protect members in case of sickness or accidents aboard.

Incidentally, don't assume that Medicare is the answer to illness in France. It covers U.S. citizens who travel south of the border to Mexico or north of the border to Canada.

Many homeowners' insurance policies cover theft of luggage during foreign travel and loss of documents—your Eurailpass, your passport, or your airline ticket, for instance. Coverage is usually limited to about $500 U.S. To submit a claim on your insurance, remember that you'll need police reports or a statement from a medical authority that you did in fact suffer the loss or experience the illness for which you are seeking compensation. Such claims, by their very nature, can be filed only when you return from France.

Some policies (and this is the type you should have) provide advances in cash or else transferrals of funds so that you won't have to dip into your precious travel funds to settle medical bills.

If you've booked a charter fare, you will probably have to pay a cancellation fee if you cancel a trip suddenly, even if it is due to an unforeseen crisis. It's possible to get insurance against such a possibility. Some travel agencies provide such coverage, and often flight insurance against a cancelled trip is written into tickets paid for by credit cards from such companies as VISA and American Express. Many tour operators or insurance agents provide this type of insurance.

Among the companies offering such policies are the following:

Access America, 6600 W. Broad St., Richmond, VA 23230 (tel. 804/285-3300, or toll free 800/284-8300), offers a comprehensive travel insurance and assistance package, including medical expenses, on-the-spot hospital payments, medical transportation, baggage insurance, trip cancellation/interruption insurance, and collision-damage insurance for a car rental. Their 24-hour hotline connects you to multilingual coordinators who can offer advice and help on medical, legal, and travel problems. Packages begin at $27.

Healthcare Abroad (MEDEX) This company offers coverage for 10–90 days at $3 per day; the policy includes accident and sickness coverage to the tune of $100,000. Medical evacuation is also included, along with $25,000 dismemberment and/or death compensation. Provisions for trip cancellation and lost or stolen luggage can also be written into the policy at a nominal cost. They can be contacted at Wallach & Co., 107 W. Federal St. (P.O. Box 480), Middleburg, VA 22117-0480 (tel. 703/687-3166, or toll free 800/237-6615).

Mutual of Omaha (Tele-Trip), Mutual of Omaha Plaza, Omaha, NE 68175, offers insurance packages priced from $113 for a three-week trip. Included in the packages are travel-assistance services, and financial protection against trip cancellation, trip interruption, flight and baggage delays, accident-related medical costs, accidental death and dismemberment, and medical evacuation coverages. Application for insurance can be taken over the phone for major credit card holders (tel. toll free 800/228-9792).

Travel Guard International, 1145 Clark St., Stevens Point, WI 54481 (tel. toll free 800/826-1300), offers a comprehensive seven-day policy that covers basically everything, including lost luggage. It costs $52, including emergency assistance, accidental death, trip cancellation and interruption, medical coverage abroad, and lost luggage. There are restrictions, however, which you should understand before you accept the coverage.

Travelers Insurance Company, Travel Insurance Division, One Tower Square, 10 NB, Hartford, CT 06183-5040 (tel. toll free 800/243-3174). Travel accident and illness coverage starts at $10 for 6–10 days; $500 worth of coverage for lost, damaged, or delayed baggage costs $20 for 6–10 days; and trip cancellation costs $5.50 for $100 worth of coverage. Written approval is necessary for cancellation coverage above $10,000.

4. WHAT TO PACK

For Paris   Parisians are both stylish and conservative. Big-city clothes are in order here. Men will feel comfortable in suits or sports jackets of a weight appropriate to the season. While ties for men are advisable in the poshest places, they are seldom required in more moderate restaurants.

Women will fit in wearing suits, skirts and sweaters, simple dresses, and good pants. Parisian women go to work, restaurants, and the theater wearing beautifully cut and tailored pants suits. Follow their lead and you won't be turned away at the door by some disapproving manager. In a student café on the Left Bank, your designer jeans are very much in place, but you can't wear them everywhere.

Whatever the season, bring a raincoat and umbrella to Paris—just to be on the safe side.

For Elsewhere in France   What to pack depends on where you're going and at what time of year. Here are some general guidelines:

Don't plan to tour France in a pair of shorts. Churches are prime attractions and you could be denied entry if you're attired in shorts—even if it's the hottest day of the year. (Sometimes you can sneak past, especially if there's no guard at the door, but it's considered disrespectful by the French.) Women are not required to wear head coverings in churches.

If you're sunning on the beach along the Côte d'Azur, always wear a cover-up (and this is true for men and women) when you leave the beach and start promenading along boulevards. Along the Côte d'Azur, winter days sometimes can be warm and mild, but chilly nights call for a sweater and maybe even a jacket.

If you plan to visit casinos or posh nightclubs, dress up—casual chic, perhaps a little black dress for women.

If your summer visit will take you across different regions, take at least one outfit for chilly weather and one outfit for warm weather. Along the rainy coasts of Normandy and Brittany, or in the Alps and Pyrénées, you may experience suddenly chilly weather. And yet, on a February day in Provence, you may feel you're overdressed in your woolens.

Always take two pairs of comfortable shoes for walking the streets during the day—you may get your shoes soaked and need that extra pair.

5. SPECIAL ACCOMMODATIONS IN FRANCE

France accommodates tourists on most budgets, housing them in everything from vine-covered old auberges (inns) to luxurious château-hotels, some of which were

GENERAL PACKING TIPS

Always pack as light as possible. Sometimes it's hard to get a porter or a baggage cart in rail and air terminals. Also, airlines are increasingly strict about how much luggage you can bring aboard, not only carry-on items, but checked suitcases as well. This is particularly true when flights are fully booked (or overbooked, as the case may be). Checked baggage should not be more than 62 inches (width plus length plus height). Bags shouldn't weigh more than 70 pounds. Carry-on luggage shouldn't be more than 45 inches (width plus length plus height). Carry-on pieces must fit under your seat or in the bin above.

It almost goes without saying that you should wear a wardrobe that "travels well." Sometimes it's possible to get pressing done at hotels, but don't count on it. Be prepared to wash your lightweights, such as underwear, in your bathroom and hang them up to dry overnight.

The general rule of packing is to bring four of everything. For men, that means four pairs of socks, four pairs of slacks, four shirts, and four sets of underwear. At least two of these will always be either dirty or in the process of drying. Often you'll have to wrap semi-wet clothes in a plastic bag as you head for your next destination. Women could follow the same rule, four of each of the "basics," such as undergarments and stockings.

once inhabited by a parade of the grand personalities of France. For the greatest concentration of deluxe accommodations, it's Paris or the Riviera. The largest concentration of budget hotels is also either in Paris or the Riviera.

RESERVATIONS

Reservations are advised, even in the so-called slow hotel-booking months from November to March. Slow periods for the hotels of Paris are July and August (at the peak of the tourist season), when many regular French clients are on vacation. On the Riviera, July and August are most crowded because the French are holidaying there.

Paris hotels report their peak business in February, June, and September. Tourist travel to Paris peaks during the months of May to October. Convention travel can also fill up the hotel rooms in small provincial cities even in the coldest, rainiest months. So book rooms in advance. Only the adventurous show up without a reservation. The French, incidentally, are their own best tourists, so visitors from all over the world have to compete with the locals for choice hotel accommodations.

You can reserve yourself or use a reputable travel agent. It's easiest to reserve with a chain via their representatives in North America (and toll-free numbers), but they may not be the type of accommodations you're seeking.

For hotels without representatives in North America, write or call (be prepared for the person at the other end to speak no English). If you write, send an International Reply Coupon, available at post offices. When seeking reservations, give alternative dates if possible. If the hotel accepts your request, you may be asked to send one night's deposit. At smaller inns in France, many readers reported great difficulty or even complete failure in getting their deposit returned if they were forced to cancel their reservations suddenly.

If you call a hotel right before your arrival, you may be lucky enough to secure a room because of a last-minute cancellation. If you arrive in Paris without a reservation, go to the reservations desks at Charles de Gaulle or Orly Airport; they have connections to more than 300 hotels in nearly all price categories.

Like airlines, hotels traditionally overbook, counting on last-minute cancellations. When everybody shows up, however, they face irate customers shouting at the desk, waving a confirmed reservation. But, alas, these are the hazards of travel. To avoid this, give the hotel your credit-card number and authorize the management to add the cost to your bill even if you don't show up.

Faced with an overbooked hotel, and knowing that some rooms are always available, many travelers do as the travel-wise French do. They slip a suitable bribe to a desk clerk.

CLASSIFICATIONS

French hotels are rated by stars: from four-star luxury and four-star deluxe, down through three-star (first class), two-star (good-quality tourist hotel), and one-star (budget). In some of the lower categories, the rooms may not have private baths; instead, many rooms each have what the French call a *cabinet de toilette* (hot and cold running water and a bidet), while others have only sinks. In such hotels, bathrooms are down the hall. Nearly all hotels in France today have central heating, which, in some cases, you might wish the owners would turn up a little on a cold winter's night.

Most hotel rates quoted in France are for double occupancy, since most rooms are doubles. Some of these rooms each contain twin beds, but most of them have double beds, suitable for one or two. France offers more than one million beds to tourists.

Relais & Châteaux

Now known around the world, this coterie of deluxe and first-class properties began in France. It is for the well-heeled visitor seeking the ultimate in French hotel living and dining, most often in a traditional atmosphere. Numbering some 150 establishments, Relais & Châteaux hotels are found throughout the country. Former castles, abbeys, and manor houses have been converted into hostelries or small inns and very elegant hotels. They always have a limited number of rooms, so reservations are imperative. Sometimes these owner-run establishments have swimming pools and tennis courts. The Relais part of the organization refers to inns which are called *relais* in French, meaning posthouse. These tend to be less luxurious than the châteaux, but they are often quite charming for those seeking a traditional atmosphere. Top-quality restaurants are designated *relais gourmand*.

For an illustrated catalog of these establishments, send $10 to Relais & Châteaux, 11 E. 44th St., Suite 707, New York, NY 10017 (for information about and descriptions of individual Relais & Châteaux, call 212/856-0115; for reservations, contact each establishment directly).

Bed and Breakfasts

Called *gîtes-chambres d'hôte* in France, these accommodations may be one or several bedrooms on a farm or in a village home. Many of them offer one main meal of the day as well (lunch or dinner).

There are at least 6,000 of these accommodations listed with **La Maison du Tourisme Vert Fédération Nationale des Gîtes Ruraux-de-France,** 35, rue Godet-de-Mauroy, 75009 Paris (tel. 1/47-42-25-43). Sometimes these B&B accommodations aren't as simple as you might think. Instead of a barebone farm room, you might be housed in a mansion deep in the countryside of France.

In the United States, a good source for this type of accommodation is **The French Experience,** 370 Lexington Ave., New York, NY 10017 (tel. 212/986-3800). The French Experience also rents fully furnished houses with swimming pools for as short a period as one week. Many of these are on scenic hills overlooking the French Riviera.

Listings of more than 300 homes and apartments in Paris ranging from $30 to $55 can be secured from **Bed & Breakfast 1,** located at 73, rue Notre-Dame-des-Champs, 75006 Paris (tel. 1/43-25-42-97).

Condos, Villas, Houses, and Apartments

If you can stay for at least a week and don't mind cooking your own meals and cleaning house, you might want to rent a long-term accommodation. The local French Tourist Board might help you obtain a list of real estate agencies that represent this type of rental (which tends to be especially popular at ski resorts). In France, the best agency for this is the **Fédération Nationale des Agents Immobiliers,** 129, rue du Faubourg St-Honoré, 75008 Paris (tel. 1/44-20-77-00).

In the U.S., **At Home Abroad,** 405 E. 56th St., Apt. 6H, New York, NY 10022-2466 (tel. 212/421-9165), specializes in villas on the French Riviera and in the Dordogne, and also has places in the Provençal hill towns. Rentals are usually two weeks or one month. For a $50 registration fee (applicable to any rental), photographs of the various properties and a newsletter will be sent to you.

HOTEL ASSOCIATIONS

Hometours International, Inc., 1170 Broadway, New York, NY 10001 (tel. 212/689-0851, or toll free 800/367-4668), offers apartments more moderately priced than most others in Paris. Apartment hotels are also offered, along with B&B accommodations. On the French Riviera, beautiful villas, all with private swimming pools, are offered at rates more reasonable than you might expect.

For budget travelers to France, the organization offers a prepaid voucher program for the Campanile hotels, a chain of about 300 two-star, family-run hotels throughout France. Rates begin as low as $60 per night in a double. This is an excellent alternative to B&B hotels in France, since all members of the chain provide a buffet breakfast for only 30F ($5.40) per person.

Others wanting to keep costs trimmed might want to familiarize themselves with the **Mercure** hotel chain, hardly a household word in America, but an organization of simple but clean and modern hotels offering attractive values throughout France. Even at the peak of the tourist season, a room at a Mercure in the heart of Paris rents for about $100 a night. For more information on Mercure hotels and a copy of their 100-page directory, call RESINTER toll free in the U.S. (tel. 800/221-4542).

Travelers to France on a budget might also want to know about a chain of hotels called **Formule 1,** which are bonebare and basic, but clean and safe, offering rooms for up to three guests at the rate of around $25 a night. Built from prefabricated units, the air-conditioned, soundproof hotels are shipped to a site and reassembled, often on the outskirts of such cities as Paris (27 in the suburbs alone). In addition, there's a coterie of 150 of these low-budget hotels throughout the rest of France. (Formule 1, a member of the French hotel giant Accor, recently purchased the Motel 6 chain in the United States, to which Formule 1 bears a resemblance.)

A brochure listing the location and phone contact of each of these rock-bottom chain members in France is available by writing Chaîne des Hôtels Formule 1, B.P. 159, 93163 Noisy-le-Grand, France. VISA is the only credit card accepted.

If you want economy but also want to be assured of strict comfort and cleanliness, write **Fédération Nationale des Logis et Auberges de France,** 83, av. d'Italie, 75013 Paris (tel. 1/44-24-08-74). This is an association of more than 5,000 hotels, most of them rated one to two stars. They are usually simple country inns that are especially convenient for motorists.

The association publishes an annual directory. Many travel bookstores in America and Canada also carry this catalog, including the **Traveller's Bookstore,** 22 W. 52nd St., New York, NY 10019 (tel. 212/664-0995). The cost is $21.95, plus shipping and handling.

HOME EXCHANGES

If you're willing to spend all your time in one area of France, consider exchanging your home with a family somewhere in France. Sometimes you'll be granted use of the family car if you reciprocate with your own buggy back home. You can make your own arrangements, but it's best to make the initial contact via an agency specializing in such exchanges.

Intervac U.S., P.O. Box 590504, San Francisco, CA 94119 (tel. 415/435-3497, or toll free 800/756-HOME), is part of the largest worldwide home-exchange network. It publishes three catalogs a year, containing more than 8,000 homes in more than 36 countries. Members contact each other directly. The $62 cost, plus postage, includes the purchase of all three of the company's catalogs (which will be mailed to you), plus the inclusion of your own listing in whichever one of the three catalogs you select. If you want to publish a photograph of your home, it costs $11 extra. Hospitality and youth exchanges are also available.

The Invented City, 41 Sutter St., Suite 1090, San Francisco, CA 94104 (tel. 415/673-0347, or toll free 800/638-CITY), publishes home listings in February, May, and November each year. For a $50 fee, they'll list your home with your preferred time for an exchange, your occupation, and a description of your hobbies.

Vacation Exchange Club, P.O. Box 650, Key West, FL 33041 (tel. 305/294-3720, or toll free 800/638-3841), will send you four directories a year—in one of which you're listed—for $60.

6. TIPS FOR SPECIAL TRAVELERS

FOR THE DISABLED

If you are disabled, you can still travel to France, as facilities for the disabled are certainly above the world average in Europe. Each year the French government does more and more to improve public facilities to ease life for the disabled.

Nearly all modern hotels in France now provide rooms designed for the disabled. Older hotels, unless they have been renovated, may not provide such important features as elevators, special toilet facilities, or ramps for wheelchair access.

High-speed trains are wheelchair accessible. Older trains have special compartments for wheelchair boarding. On the Paris Métro, handicapped persons are able to sit in wider seats provided for their comfort. Guide dogs ride free. Some stations don't have escalators or elevators, and these obviously present problems.

Before you go on your trip, there are agencies in the United States and France that can provide advance-planning information. Knowing in advance which hotels, restaurants, and attractions are wheelchair accessible can save you a lot of frustration—firsthand accounts by other disabled travelers are the best.

Touriste Quand Même, a publication provided by the French Tourist Office (see "Information," above, in this chapter), gives an overview of facilities for the disabled in the French transportation system and at monuments and museums. The publication is updated on a regular basis. One volume covers Paris alone.

Association des Paralysés de France, 17 bd. Auguste-Blanqui, 75013 Paris (tel. 1/40-78-69-00), operates more than 90 tourist boards in France in nearly all the major cities. They can help you find accessible hotels, transportation, sightseeing, house rentals, and even houseboating.

Travel Information Service, Moss Rehab Hospital, 1200 W. Tabor Rd., Philadelphia, PA 19141 (tel. 215/456-9600), can give you an overview of facilities in Paris and provide toll-free numbers for airlines that have special lines for the hearing impaired.

"Air Transportation of Handicapped Persons," a free publication prepared by the U.S. Department of Transportation, can be obtained by writing to Free Advisory Circular No. AC12032, Distribution Unit, U.S. Department of Transportation, Publications Division, M-4332, Washington, DC 20590.

The **Society for the Advancement of Travel for the Handicapped,** 347 Fifth Ave., New York, NY 10016 (tel. 212/447-7284), can provide a list of companies that operate tours for disabled travelers. Yearly membership dues are $45, $25 for senior citizens and students.

The **Federation of the Handicapped,** 211 W. 14th St., New York, NY 10011 (tel. 212/727-4268), operates summer tours for members, who pay a yearly fee of $45, $25 for senior citizens and students.

FOR SENIORS

Many discounts are available in France for seniors, that is, men and women who have reached the "third age," as the French say. For more information, contact a French

Government Tourist Office (see "Information, Documents, and Money," above, in this chapter).

DISCOUNT RAIL CARD   At any railway station in the country, senior citizens (men and women age 60 and older—with proof of age) can obtain a *Carte Vermeil* (silver-gilt card). (See also "Getting Around: By Train," in Chapter 3.) There are two types of Carte Vermeil: The Carte Vermeil Quatre Temps costs 140 F ($25.20) and allows a 50% discount on four rail trips per year. A Carte Vermeil Plein Temps costs 250 F ($45) and is good for a 50% discount on unlimited rail travel throughout the course of a year.

There are some restrictions on Carte Vermeil travel, such as between 3pm Sunday and noon on Monday; or from noon on Friday until noon on Saturday. There is no Carte Vermeil discount on the Paris network of commuter trains.

Holders of the Plein Temps card sometimes receive discounts of up to 30% on rail trips to many other countries of western Europe.

Other Discounts   Carte Vermeil also delivers reduced prices on certain regional bus lines, as well as theater tickets in Paris, and half-price admission at state-owned museums.

DISCOUNTS ON AIRFARE   The French domestic airline, Air Inter, honors "third agers" by offering a 25%–50% reduction on its regular, nonexcursion tariffs. Restrictions do apply. Senior discounts are available on about 20 Air France flights a week from Paris to Nice.

Organizations for Seniors

AARP (American Association of Retired Persons) 601 E. St. NW, Washington, DC 20049 (tel. 202/434-2277), is the best organization in the United States for seniors; members are offered discounts on car rentals, hotels, and airfares. The association's group travel is provided by the AARP Travel Experience from American Express. Tours may be purchased through any American Express office or travel agent, or by calling toll free 800/927-AARP. Cruises may be purchased only by telephone (tel. toll free 800/745-4567). Flights to the various destinations are handled by either of these toll-free numbers as part of land arrangements or cruise bookings.

Elderhostel, P.O. Box 1959, Wakefield, MA 01880-5959 (tel. 617/426-7788), established in 1975, operates an array of university-based summer educational programs for seniors in France and other parts of the world. Most courses last around three weeks and are remarkable values—airfare, accommodations in student dormitories or modest inns, all meals, and tuition are included. Courses emphasize the liberal arts and include field trips—best of all there's no homework or grades.

Participants must be age 60 or older, but may take an under-60 companion. Meals are of the no-frills fare, typical of educational institutions worldwide. The program provides a safe and congenial environment for single "golden girls," who make up some 67% of the enrollment.

Mature Outlook, 6001 N. Clark St., Chicago, IL 60660 (tel. toll free 800/336-6330), a travel club for people age 50 and older (operated by Sears Roebuck & Co.), provides a bimonthly newsletter featuring discounts at hotels. There's an annual membership fee of $9.95.

SAGA International Holidays, 222 Berkeley St., Boston, MA 02116 (tel. toll free 800/343-0273), is well-known for its all-inclusive tours for seniors, those age 60 and older. Insurance is included in the net price of their tours. Membership is $5 a year.

National Council of Senior Citizens, 1331 F. St. NW, Washington, DC 20005 (tel. 202/347-8800), a nonprofit organization, offers a monthly newsletter (part of which is devoted to travel tips) and discounts on hotel and auto rentals; annual dues are $12 per person or couple.

Publications

For a copy of **"Travel Tips for Senior Citizens"** (publication no. 8970, cost $1), contact the Superintendent of Documents, U.S. Government Printing Office, Washington, DC 20402 (tel. 202/783-5238). Another booklet—this one is free—**"101 Tips for the Mature Traveler,"** is available from Grand Circle Travel, 347 Congress St., Suite 3A, Boston, MA 02210 (tel. 617/350-7500, or toll free 800/221-2610); this travel agency also offers escorted tours and cruises for seniors.

FOR SINGLE TRAVELERS

Unfortunately for the 85 million single Americans, the travel industry is far more geared to duos, and those adventuring about solo often wind up paying the penalty. It pays to travel with someone and split accommodations costs, which for those traveling solo can add up to more than half the price of a double room. There are, of course, dynamic and action-packed tours and vacations designed for the unattached, as well as companies that will match you with a compatible traveling partner.

Travel Companion, Jens Jurgen, P.O. Box P-833, Amityville, NY 11701 (tel. 516/454-0880), matches single travelers with like-minded companions. People seeking travel companions fill out a survey of their preferences and needs and receive a mini-listing of potential travel partners. Companions of the same or opposite sex can be requested. Individuals are then listed for six months on the company's well-publicized records; there's a charge of between $36 and $66. A bimonthly newsletter averaging 34 large pages also gives numerous money-saving travel tips of special interest to solo travelers; a sample copy is available for $4.

Singleworld, 401 Theodore Fremd Ave., Rye, NY 10580 (tel. 914/967-3334, or toll free 800/223-6490), operates tours for solo travelers; some—but not all—are for people under 35. Annual dues are $25.

Cosmos Tourama, 9525 Queens Blvd., Rego Park, NY 11374 (tel. toll free 800/228-0211), offers single travelers on tours a "guaranteed-share plan" on accommodations.

FOR FAMILIES

If you're planning to take your family abroad, you'll need to do some advance planning. If you have very small children, you may want to discuss your vacation plans with your family doctor and take along whatever you think the child will need, along with such standard supplies as children's aspirin, a thermometer, Band-Aids, and the like.

On airlines, you must request a special menu for children at least 24 hours in advance. If baby food is required, however, bring your own and ask a flight attendant to warm it to the right temperature.

Take along a "security blanket" for your child. This might be a pacifier, a favorite toy or book, or, for older children, something to make him or her feel at home in different surroundings—a baseball cap, a favorite T-shirt (even though there'll be plenty to buy in France), or some special trinket or good-luck charm.

Take protection against the sun, especially in summer if you're visiting Mediterranean France. For tiny tots, this might include a sun umbrella, while the whole family will need sunscreen and sunglasses.

Arrange ahead of time for such necessities as a crib, bottle warmer, and car seat if you're driving anywhere. Remember that in France small children aren't allowed to ride in the front seat. Find out if the place you're staying stocks baby food, and, if not, take some with you and plan to buy some abroad in French supermarkets.

Draw up rules for your family to follow during your holiday. These should be flexible, of course—after all, this is a trip for fun. But guidelines on bedtime, eating, keeping tidy, being in the sun if you're at one of the beach resorts, even shopping and spending, can help make everyone's vacation more enjoyable.

Babysitters can be found for you at most hotels, but you should always insist, if possible, that you secure a babysitter with at least a rudimentary knowledge of English in order to avoid traumatic experiences for young children.

Family Travel Times is published 10 times a year by TWYCH, Travel With Your Children, and includes a weekly call-in service for subscribers. Subscriptions cost $55 a year and can be ordered by writing to TWYCH, 45 W. 18th St., 7th Floor, New York, NY 10011 (tel. 212/206-0688). An information packet describing TWYCH's publications, including a recent sample issue, is available by sending $3.50 to the above address.

FOR STUDENTS

Research is the key for students who want to take advantage of budget travel and study abroad. There are organizations and publications that will provide you with all the details of programs available specifically for students; see also "Educational/Study Travel," below in this chapter. Of course, you will want to carry an International Student Identity Card (ISIC)—good for discounts on travel fares and attractions. Youth hostels provide an inexpensive network of accommodations while trekking through the country.

Council Travel This is the largest travel service for students and provides details about budget travel, study abroad, working permits, and insurance. The organization (a subsidiary of the Council on International Education Exchange) issues an International Student Identity Card to bonafide students for $15. Their *Student Travel Catalogue* is available free.

Discounted international and domestic air tickets are available from Council Travel with special prices for student and youth travelers. Eurotrain rail passes, YHA passes, weekend packages, overland safaris, and hostel/hotel accommodations are all bookable from Council Travel.

Council Travel also sells a number of publications that include *Work, Study, Travel Abroad: The Whole World Handbook; Volunteer: The Comprehensive Guide to Voluntary Service in the U.S.A. and Abroad;* and *The Teenager's Guide to Study, Travel, and Adventure Abroad.*

Council Travel has offices throughout the United States. Call toll free 800/GET-AN-ID to find the location nearest you. Their main office is at 205 E. 42nd St., New York, NY 10017 (tel. 212/661-1414).

IYHF (International Youth Hostel Federation) This organization was designed to provide bare-bones overnight accommodations for serious budget-conscious travelers. Membership costs $25 annually, except for those under 18 who pay $10, and those who over 54 who pay $15. For information, contact American Youth Hostels (AYH)/Hostelling International, 733 15th St. NW, Suite 840, Washington, DC 20005 (tel. 202/783-6161).

7. ALTERNATIVE/SPECIALTY TRAVEL

Caveat: Under no circumstances is the inclusion of an organization in this section to be interpreted as a guarantee either of its credit-worthiness or its competency. Information about the organizations listed below is intended only as a preliminary preview, to be followed up by your own investigation should you be interested.

EDUCATION/STUDY TRAVEL

LEARNING THE LANGUAGE The **Alliance Française,** 101, bd. Raspail, 75270 Paris (tel. 1/45-44-38-28)—a state-approved, nonprofit organization that has a network of 1,200 establishments in 107 countries—offers French-language courses to some 350,000 students. The international school in Paris is open all year, and you can enroll for a minimum of a monthly session. Fees tend to be reasonable, and the school offers numerous activities and services. Write for information and application forms at least one month before your departure to Paris.

The **National Registration Center for Studies Abroad (NRCSA),** 823 N. 2nd St. (P.O. Box 1393), Milwaukee, WI 53201 (tel. 414/278-0631), has a catalog ($2) of schools in France. They will register you at the school of your choice, arrange for room and board, and make your airline reservations—all for no extra fee. Contact them and ask for a copy (free) of their newsletter.

COOKING LESSONS If you've always wanted to learn to cook *à la française,* you can take those all-important lessons from **Maxime and Eliane Rochereau** at their hotel-restaurant, Le Castel de Bray-et-Monts, Brehemont, 37130 Langeais (tel. 47-96-70-47).

Before settling on the banks of the Loire, the Rochereaus spent 15 years living and working in the United States—Maxime as chef de cuisine at the Ritz Carlton in Chicago and the Breakers in Palm Beach, Eliane as a caterer for the Palm Beach jet set. In the charming vineyard village of Brehemont now Maxime teaches classic French cooking—scallop mousse pâté and canapés à la française, among other delicacies—in an 18th-century seignorial manor surrounded by a magnificent garden and stream. Assisted by a well-selected staff, they also offer sightseeing tours in the area. One week costs from 6,500F ($1,170). Classes are conducted from February 15 through November 20.

PAINTING WORKSHOPS Amateur watercolor enthusiasts can join an "Arts in the South of France" trip, sponsored by **Art Trek,** P.O. Box 807, Bolinas, CA 94924 (tel. 415/868-1836). Tours, which are led by art instructors familiar with both the techniques and traditions of French art, take you to medieval hill towns, the stylish Mediterranean port of Antibes, such legendary artists' refuges as Arles and St-Remy, and Paris. Tours always take place in June and July, when the Mediterranean sunlight is at its most intense and impressionistic best. The average cost, including airfare from the West Coast, is $3,600 per person. Each tour lasts 15 days, with half board included in accommodations based on double occupancy.

MEETING THE FRENCH

Several organizations offer opportunities to get to know the French at international parties and get-togethers.

One of the most prominent of these is **Accents,** 75, av. Parmentier, 75011 Paris (tel. 1/43-64-71-73). Although most of its activities are for members of the semipermanent expatriate community of Paris, many of their wine-and-cheese soirées and weekend get-togethers are open to tourists and short-term visitors as well.

Accents publishes a newsletter six times a year and a 100-page information booklet (revised annually) that offers advice and information on everyday life in Paris. Accents conducts guided excursions to sites of artistic or historical interest, seminars in both French and English, cooking lessons, and cross-cultural workshops designed to ease a foreigner's sometimes jolting immersion into French life. An annual membership costs 350 F ($63) for first-timers and 100 F ($18) for renewals.

HOME STAYS

The **Friendship Force,** 575 South Tower, 1 CNN Center, Atlanta, GA 30303 (tel. 404/522-9490), is a nonprofit organization existing for the sole purpose of fostering and encouraging friendship among disparate people worldwide.

Dozens of branch offices throughout North America arrange en masse visits, usually once a year. Because of group bookings, the airfare to the host country is usually less than you'd pay if you bought an individual APEX ticket. Each participant is required to spend two weeks in the host country, one full week as a guest in the home of a family. Most volunteers spend the second week traveling in the host country.

Servas ("to serve" in Esperanto), 11 John St., New York, NY 10038 (tel. 212/267-0252), is a nonprofit, nongovernmental, international, interfaith network of travelers and hosts whose goal is to help build world peace, goodwill, and understanding. They do this by providing opportunities for deeper, more personal contacts among people of diverse cultural and political backgrounds.

Servas travelers are invited to share living space in a home in a community, normally staying without charge for visits lasting a maximum of two days. Visitors pay a $55 annual membership fee, fill out an application, and are interviewed for suitability by one of more than 200 Servas interviewers throughout the country. They then receive a Servas directory listing the names and addresses of Servas hosts who welcome visitors into their homes.

SPA STAYS

To restore the well-being of mind and body, **Spa Trek Travel,** 475 Park Ave. S., New York, NY 10016 (tel. 212/779-3480, or toll free 800/272-3480), offers spa programs at such sites in France as Evian, Thalasso Dinard, and La Baule. You can sign up for a week's deluxe accommodations, with medical consultation, two or three treatments a day (depending on your personalized program), and exercise.

OPERA TOURS

On a cultural note, **Dailey-Thorp Travel,** 330 W. 58th St., Suite 610, New York, NY 10019-1817 (tel. 212/307-1555), is probably the best-regarded organizer of music and opera tours operating in America. Because of its "favored" relations with European box offices, the company can purchase blocks of otherwise unavailable tickets to Paris operas and other events and festivals all across Europe. Tours range from 7 to 21 days and include first-class or deluxe accommodations and meals in top-rated European restaurants.

ADVENTURE/WILDERNESS
Bike Tours

Bike Tour France, 5523 Wedgewood Dr., Charlotte, NC 28210-2432 (tel. 704/527-0955, or toll free 800/597-6952), established in 1972, is the oldest American organization offering bicycle tours in France.

Such excursions as a two-week tour of the Loire Valley include the use of an excellent bicycle individually fitted to the user, a knowledgeable and experienced tour leader, and overnight stops at pleasant hotels. Clients are provided with informal lessons in French history and practical lessons in conversational French. If you're interested in a particular region (except Picardy, the Côte d'Azur, or the Alps), Jerry H. Simpson, Jr., head of the organization, will design and arrange an independent tour for you.

Hot Air Ballooning

Hot air balloon flights in Burgurndy are a specialty of Air Escargot, 71150 Chagny (tel. 85-87-12-30), during the flying season from April to the end of November. In a location near Beaune, Christiane and Pierre Bonnet offer two daily departures in a balloon they call *Montgolfier*. The one-hour flights cost 1,200 F ($216) per person. Participants are picked up at their hotel in the area and taken to the departure site. A light truck follows the route of the balloon and returns guests to their hotels at the end of the flight over the region's vineyards. You'll be given a *certificat d'ascension* and a glass of wine to toast your successful journey.

In addition, Air Escargot also offers a four-hour cruise of the Canal de Bourgogne, with the pilot commenting on the scenery. For the flight, cruise, and transfers, the cost is 1,500 F ($270) per person.

Canoeing

Journeys Beyond, P.O. Box 7511-FF, Jackson, WY 83001 (tel. 307/733-9615, or toll free 800/223-6833), offers guided "inn to inn" canoe tours, which include paddling a canoe through some of the most beautiful parts of the château country, along the rivers of Dordogne, and on at least two other rivers. The program includes stops for well-prepared picnic lunches, dinners in fine restaurants (some in castles), and nights spent in good hotels and châteaux. One canoe tour includes hot-air ballooning as an added attraction.

Barge Tours

In addition to its network of superhighways, France contains an intricate network of canals which link its great rivers into a coherent network. An especially alluring way to sample the countryside's pleasures is to ride on a luxuriously converted barge through the locks and channels of France's rivers, past vineyards and fields.

One company well suited to organizing such waterborne jaunts is **Première**

Selections, a division of the Kemwell Company, 106 Calvert St., Harrison, NY 10528 (tel. toll free 800/234-4000). Prices begin at around $1,350 per person, double occupancy, with meals and most costs included, for four-day/three-night excursion. (A seven-day/six-night excursion costs from around $2,000 per person.)

Most itineraries lead through either Burgundy, the Champagne country, Languedoc, or Alsace. Time is allocated for sightseeing visits to monuments which include the cathedral city of Reims, the culinary heart of Burgundy (Dijon), Fontainebleau, the mysterious and mystical city of Vézelay, and the medieval fortress of Carcassonne.

Bicycles, which figure among the cargo of each barge, are readily available without charge for cycling along riverbanks and for local touring. All meals, guide fees, museum entrances, afternoon tea, and a 24-hour open bar are included as part of the price. Many cruises include private visits, with a driver/guide, in minivans to some of the stately homes, châteaux, and manor houses along the way.

Alpine Excursions

Travelers who prefer the high alpine grandeur of France's southeast can contact **Wilderness Travel,** 801 Allston Way, Berkeley, CA 94710 (tel. 510/548-0420, or toll free 800/368-2794). One of the most spectacular offerings is a 16-day hike between Chamonix (France) and Zermatt (Switzerland), through the region where the modern sports of mountaineering and alpinism were first developed during the 19th century. Accommodations in alpine dormitories and family-run inns, as well as most meals and guide fees are included in prices which begin around $2,100, double occupancy.

Equally challenging is the company's "Tour du Mont Blanc," a 14-day circumnavigation of one of the most geologically distinctive granite massifs in the world, complete with visits to seven of the outwardly radiating valleys whose charm and unique history has made Mont Blanc the most famous mountain in Europe. The tour traverses rugged territory belonging to France, Switzerland, and Italy, and achieves a high-altitude maximum of no more than 9,000 feet above sea level.

Tours are recommended only for participants in good physical condition, and camera enthusiasts are welcomed. The company also offers 12-day tours through the lush, historic valley of western France's Dordogne and the ancient and richly evocative landscapes of Provence.

CHAPTER 3

GETTING TO & AROUND FRANCE

1. GETTING THERE
- **FROMMER'S SMART TRAVELER: AIRFARES**
- **SUGGESTED ITINERARIES**

2. GETTING AROUND
- **FAST FACTS: FRANCE**

A holiday in France, for most of the readers of this book, must first begin with a transatlantic trip to France. That requires a brief examination of the available transportation—especially the question of air transportation.

Of equal importance, of course, is the matter of getting around in the country after you arrive. There's so much to see that it pays to have in mind before you go just how you will seek out that little village in Provence and what means of transportation is best to take you to the attractions of the French Riviera, to the imposing châteaux of the Loire Valley, and through the miles of vineyards in the wine country.

As I have traveled extensively and frequently in France, I will seek in this chapter to give you the benefit of my experiences and to share with you my "Suggested Itineraries" to follow on a "grand tour" of the country.

"Fast Facts: France" caps off this chapter and is a quick reference guide to France.

1. GETTING THERE

BY PLANE FROM THE U.S.

Until recently, France-bound passengers from across the United States had to fly from their hometowns to New York, then transfer onto a transatlantic flight to Paris. Changing air routes and regulations, however, have encouraged the development of many nonstop flights to Paris (sometimes on airlines you might not have automatically thought of) from North American hubs such as Atlanta, Cincinnati, Houston, Chicago, Miami, and St. Louis.

Flying time to Paris from New York is about 7 hours; from Chicago, 9 hours; from Los Angeles, 11 hours; from Atlanta, 8 hours; from Miami, 8½ hours; and from Washington, D.C., 7½ hours.

Plane Economics

Seasonal Slots Most airlines divide their year roughly into seasonal slots with the lowest fares offered between November 1 and March 14. Shoulder season, the period between the high and low seasons, is only slightly more expensive and includes all of October, which many veteran tourists consider the ideal time to visit France. Shoulder season also extends from mid-March to mid-June.

APEX All the carriers listed below offer a consistently popular advance-purchase excursion (APEX) fare that requires a 30-day advance payment and a minimum stay of 7–21 days. In most cases this ticket—although reasonably priced—is *not* completely refundable if you change flight dates or destinations.

American Airlines, for example, has a "30-Day Advance Purchase" fare from New York to Paris for $844 on weekdays in high season (summer) and $622 on weekdays in low season. (Flights on Friday through Sunday require a supplement of $30 each way.) Delta offers the same type of ticket from Atlanta to Paris, charging, depending on the day of travel, $764–$824 round-trip in winter and about $100 more in the peak summer months. The above-mentioned fares do not include last-minute promotional fares or special discounts that the major carriers sometimes promote and can save travelers money if their timing is right.

Economy Class With an economy-class ticket, you can literally catch any flight, pending available space, without regard to advance bookings and without penalty for last-minute changes in your itinerary.

A regular economy-class ticket on American Airlines, for example, is priced year-round at $1,197, plus tax, for a round-trip between New York and Paris (subject to change, of course).

Business Class Many passengers opt for the wider seats, increased leg room, and greater comfort of business-class travel, which offers many (but not all) of the comforts of first-class travel.

Currently, Delta's year-round fares from Atlanta to Paris are $3,470 round-trip in business class and $5,684 round-trip in first class. Year-round fares from Cincinnati are $3,462 in business class and $5,928 in first class. These fares carry a $28 surcharge for taxes and security fees.

Major U.S. Carriers

Several U.S.–based airlines make the popular run between North America and the "City of Light."

American Airlines (tel. toll free 800/433-7300) offers daily flights to Paris (Orly Airport) from Dallas/Fort Worth, Raleigh/Durham, Chicago, and New York's JFK. Just before press time, American Airlines developed a new semi-automated way to confirm fares and scheduled flights between most cities in the U.S. and their destinations worldwide. The new "dial a flight" system (tel. toll free 800/223-5436) works from any Touch-Tone phone and gives specific instructions on obtaining information about arrival and departure times, gates, and flight status. You can, if you choose, also be connected to an American Airlines representative at any time during your call.

Delta Airlines (tel. toll free 800/221-1212) is one of the best choices for passengers flying to Paris from both the southeastern United States and the Middle West. In fact, Delta offers the greatest number of flights to Paris from the U.S. From such cities as New Orleans, Savannah, Phoenix, Columbia (S.C.), Birmingham (Ala.), and Nashville, Delta flies to Atlanta, connecting every evening with a nonstop flight to Orly Airport in Paris. Delta also operates a daily nonstop flight to Paris from New York's JFK and Cincinnati, leaving late enough in the afternoon to permit easy transfers from much of its North American network. Delta has good feeder service to Cincinnati from such cities as St. Louis, Kansas City, Denver, Cleveland, Portland (Ore.), and Pittsburgh.

TWA (tel. toll free 800/221-2000) operates frequent daily service to Paris from Boston, St. Louis, Los Angeles, New York's JFK, and Washington, D.C.'s Dulles.

United Airlines (tel. toll free 800/241-6522) is another excellent choice for Paris-bound passengers; this carrier flies from Chicago and Washington, D.C., nonstop every evening to Paris's Charles de Gaulle Airport. United flies into London's Heathrow from New York's JFK twice a night in the summer months, and from Washington, D.C.'s Dulles Airport, Newark International, Seattle-Tacoma, San Francisco International, and Los Angeles. From London it's an easy connection via United, an arrangement that can sometimes (but not always, depending on special promotions) save money for passengers whose timing is right.

USAir (tel. toll free 800/622-1015) offers transatlantic service from Philadelphia to Paris (Charles de Gaulle), a nonstop flight. USAir, of course, operates flights into Philadelphia from many parts of North America.

The French National Carriers

Aircraft belonging to the **Air France Group** (tel. toll free 800/237-2747) fly frequently across the Atlantic. Formed from a recent merger combining three of

France's largest (and completely nationalized) airlines, the conglomerate offers routes that until the merger were maintained separately by Air France, UTA (Union des Transports Aériens), and France's internal domestic airline, Air Inter. In the process, many transatlantic routes that previously flew nonstop into France's provincial capitals were abandoned.

At press time, aircraft fly nonstop from San Francisco to Paris, and from both Newark (N.J.) and New York's JFK to both Charles de Gaulle (Roissy) and Orly in Paris. Members of the group also fly to Paris from about 10 U.S. cities (including Los Angeles), as well as from Mexico City (via Houston), Montréal, Toronto, Chicago, Miami, Washington, D.C., and Boston.

Air France also has an associated partner, **A.O.M. French Airlines** (tel. toll free 800/568-3266), which offers nonstop service between Miami and Paris. (It also flies from Paris to Guadeloupe and Martinique in the French Antilles.)

Other Good-Value Choices

BUCKET SHOPS In the 1960s, mainstream airlines gave this pejorative name to resellers of blocks of unsold tickets consigned to them by major transatlantic carriers; it might be more polite to refer to them as consolidators. They act as clearinghouses for blocks of tickets that airlines discount and consign during normally slow periods of air travel.

Tickets are usually priced 20%–35% below the full fare. Terms of payment vary—from 45 days before departure to last-minute sales. Tickets can be purchased through regular travel agents, who usually mark up the ticket 8%–10%, maybe even more, thereby greatly reducing your discount.

A survey conducted of flyers who use consolidators voiced only one major complaint. Use of such a ticket doesn't qualify you for an advance seat assignment, and you are therefore likely to be assigned a "poor seat" on the plane at the last minute.

The survey revealed that most flyers estimated their savings at around $200 per ticket off the regular price. Nearly a third of the passengers reported savings of up to $300 off the regular price. But—and here's the hitch—many people who booked consolidator tickets reported no savings at all, as the airlines will sometimes match the consolidator ticket by announcing a promotional fare. The situation is a bit tricky and

---

 FROMMER'S SMART TRAVELER: AIRFARES

1. Shop all the airlines that fly to your destination.
2. Always ask for the lowest fare, not just a discount fare.
3. Keep calling the airline—availability of cheap seats changes daily. Airline managers would rather sell a seat than have it fly empty. As the departure date nears, additional low-cost seats become available.
4. Ask about frequent-flyer programs to gain bonus miles when you book a flight.
5. Check "bucket shops" for last-minute discount fares that are even cheaper than their advertised slashed fares.
6. Ask about air/land packages. Land arrangements are often cheaper when booked with an air ticket.
7. Check "standby" fares and "instant purchase" fares offered to London on Virgin Atlantic Airways, and consider whether a detour through London will add or detract from your vacation plans.
8. Fly at a heavy discount as a "courier."
9. Look for special promotions offered by major carriers, each of which is flying new routes and struggling to strengthen its foothold in the transatlantic markets.

calls for some careful investigation on your part to determine just how much you're saving.

Bucket shops abound from coast to coast. Look for their ads in your local newspaper's travel section; they're usually very small and a single column in width. (*Note:* Since dealing with unknown bucket shops might be a little risky, it's wise to call the Better Business Bureau in your area to see if complaints have been filed against the company from which you plan to purchase a ticket.)

Here are some recommendations:

TFI Tours International, 34 W. 32nd St., 12th Floor, New York, NY 10001 (tel. 212/736-1140, or toll free 800/825-3834 outside New York State).

25 West Tours, 2490 Coral Way, Miami, FL 33145 (tel. 305/856-0810, or toll free 800/225-2582, 800/423-6954 in Florida).

Sunline Express Holiday, Inc., 607 Market St., San Francisco, CA 94105 (tel. 415/541-7800, or toll free 800/786-5463).

Travel Management International, 18 Prescott St., Suite 4, Cambridge, MA 02138 (tel. toll free 800/245-3672), offers a wide variety of discount fares, including youth fares. Often, its contract fares are lower than those offered by some rebators (see below).

CHARTER FLIGHTS For reasons of economy (never for convenience), some travelers opt for charter flights to France or to one of the countries bordering France.

Strictly speaking, a charter flight occurs on an aircraft reserved months in advance for a one-time-only transit to some predetermined point. Before paying for a charter, check the restriction on your ticket or contract. You may be asked to purchase a tour package and pay far in advance. You'll pay a stiff penalty—or forfeit the ticket entirely—if you cancel. Charters are sometimes canceled when the plane doesn't fill up. In some cases, the charter-ticket seller will offer you an insurance policy for your own legitimate cancellation (hospital confinement or death in the family, for example).

There's no way to predict whether a charter flight or a bucket shop will cost less—you have to investigate at the time of your trip. My own investigation at press time showed charters to Paris selling for a bit less—perhaps no more than $25 round-trip—than bucket shops.

Note: Some charter companies have proved unreliable in the past, leaving passengers stranded. I prefer to deal with subsidiaries (or at least affiliates) of major international carriers. Some of these include the following:

DER Tours, Inc., 9501 W. Devon Ave., Rosemont, IL 60018-4832 (tel. toll free 800/782-2424). This marketing organization sells seats on flights to Paris at discounted prices—usually from the unsold inventories of United, American, and Northwest Airlines.

Connections from a network of North American cities are available, always with connections through Minneapolis, Boston, Detroit, or Chicago, and almost always with the added inconvenience of requiring an additional change of aircraft in London.

Jet Vacations, 1775 Broadway, New York, NY 10019 (tel. 212/247-0999, or toll free 800/538-0999). This wholly owned subsidiary of Air France is an obvious choice for a charter to Paris. It offers both charter flights and discounted transatlantic tickets from many airlines—not just Air France. Jet Vacations requires a deposit when you reserve your space and full payment 30 days before takeoff. Jet Vacations also arranges hotels, car rentals, châteaux living, and sightseeing.

Europa Travel Service, 911 E. 185th St., Cleveland, OH 44119 (tel. 216/481-3513, or toll free 800/677-1313). This company maintains an inventory of discounted seats on Air Canada's flights from Toronto to Paris, with many restrictions attached. They also offer, depending on market conditions, flights from Cleveland to Frankfurt.

Council on International Educational Exchange (Council Charter), 205 E. 42nd St., New York, NY 10017 (tel. 212/661-0311, or toll free 800/800-8222). This is America's oldest charter company, offering charter and scheduled flights from many U.S. cities to major European capitals such as Paris or London. Council Charter offers both one-way and round-trip fares, allowing passengers to fly into one city and out of another.

Travac, 989 Sixth Ave., New York, NY 10018 (tel. 212/563-3303, or toll free 800/TRAV-800). Other Travac offices include 6151 W. Century Blvd., Los Angeles, CA 90045 (tel. 310/670-9692); 166 Geary St., San Francisco, CA 94108 (tel. 415/392-4610); and 2601 Jefferson St., Orlando, FL 32803 (tel. 407/896-0014).

REBATORS To confuse the situation even more, rebators also compete in the low-airfare market. Rebators pass along to the passenger part of their commission, although many of them assess a fee for their services. Most rebators offer discounts that range from 10% to 25% (but this could vary from place to place), plus a $20 handling charge.

Rebators are not the same as travel agents, although they sometimes offer similar services, including discounted land arrangements and car rentals.

Two rebators are listed below:

Travel Avenue, 641 W. Lake St., Suite 201, Chicago, IL 60606 (tel. 312/876-1116, or toll free 800/333-3335).

The Smart Traveller, 3111 SW 27th Ave., Miami, FL 33133 (tel. 305/448-3338, or toll free 800/448-3338).

STANDBYS A favorite of spontaneous travelers with absolutely no scheduled demands on their time, standby fares leave your departure to the whims of fortune and the hopes that a seat will remain open for you to claim it at the last minute. Not all airlines offer standbys (Air France does not), but a few carriers occasionally do.

You could fly standby to London via Virgin Atlantic Airways (tel. toll free 800/862-8621), and then catch a train or connecting flight to France. (In choosing this route, you'll have to add on the cost of your connection to Paris and factor in both the benefits and inconveniences of a transfer through London.) Virgin Atlantic offers a day-of-departure and day-prior-to-departure standby fare to London from JFK in New York, Newark, Orlando, Miami, and Boston—but only between mid-October to late March.

GOING AS A COURIER This cost-cutting technique may not be for everybody. You travel as a passenger and courier, and for this service you'll secure a greatly discounted airfare or sometimes even a free ticket.

You're allowed one piece of carry-on luggage only; your baggage allowance is used by the courier firm to transport its cargo (which, by the way, is perfectly legitimate). As a courier, you don't actually handle the merchandise you're transporting to Europe, you just carry a manifest to present to Customs. Upon arrival, an employee of the courier service will reclaim the company's cargo.

Incidentally, you fly alone, so don't plan to travel with anybody. (A friend may be able to arrange a flight as a courier on a consecutive day.) Most courier services operate from Los Angeles or New York, but some operate out of other cities, such as Chicago or Miami.

Here are some courier companies to call:

Halbart Express, 147-05 176th St., Jamaica, NY 11434 (tel. 718/656-8189 daily from 10am to 3pm).

Now Voyager, 74 Varick St., Suite 307, New York, NY 10013 (tel. 212/431-1616). Now Voyager has a 24-hour phone system and offers more courier flights to more destinations—including many to Paris.

International Association of Air Travel Couriers, P.O. Box 1349, Lake Worth, FL 33460 (tel. 407/582-8320). For a $35 annual membership fee, this company will send you six issues of its newsletter, *Shoestring Traveler,* and about six issues of a directory of air courier bargains around the world, the *Air Courier Bulletin.* Membership also offers photo-identification cards; and should a courier run into difficulty, the organization acts as a troubleshooter.

BY PLANE FROM THE U.K.

From London, **Air France** (tel. 081/742-6600), **British Airways** (tel. 081/897-4000), and **Caledonian Airways** (tel. 0293/36321), a charter division of BA, fly regularly and frequently from London to Paris (trip time is only one hour). Air France and British Airways alone operate up to 17 flights daily from Heathrow, one of the busiest air routes in Europe. Air France also flies four or five times a day from Gatwick to Charles de Gaulle, the main airport outside Paris. Many commercial travelers also use regular flights originating from the London City Airport in the Docklands.

In addition, there are direct flights to Paris from many regional British airports, departing from such major cities as Manchester, Birmingham, Glasgow, Edinburgh, and Southampton. Some flights in the U.K. (and it's best to check this with a travel agent) will take you to a regional city in France, if that's where you're going—thus letting you avoid a change-over in Paris. Destinations in France include such cities as Lyon, Nice, Bordeaux, Caen, Quimper, Nantes, Toulouse, Montpellier, and Clermont-Ferrand, as well as Marseille.

Flying from England to France is often very expensive, even though the distance is short. That's why most Brits depend on a good travel agent to get them the lowest possible transportation costs. Good values are offered by a number of companies, including **Nouvelles Frontières,** 1-2 Hanover St., London W14 9WB (tel. 071/629-7772). One of the least expensive tickets offered by this company, among others, is a flight aboard Caledonian Airways, taking you from Gatwick to the town of Beauvais, north of Paris, where rail connections can be made south to the French capital, a distance of 46 miles.

BY TRAIN

Paris is one of Europe's most densely concentrated railway junctions, with trains arriving at and departing from its many stations every few minutes. If you're already in Europe, you may want to go to Paris by train, particularly if you have a Eurailpass. Even if you don't, the cost is relatively low—especially in comparison to renting a car.

Fares The one-way fare from London to Paris by train (including the sea crossing between Folkestone and Boulogne) is $113 in second class and $148 in first class. (If you want a reserved seat on the ferry, it will cost an additional $10).

From Rome to Paris (on the night train via Pisa and Genoa), the one-way fare is $224 in first class and $140 in second class. (You'll probably want to rent a sleeper bed for an additional cost ranging from $24 to $196 per person, depending on the accommodation.)

The one-way fare from Madrid to Paris is $205 in first class and $128 in second class, with an additional charge of $24–$278 for a sleeper compartment, depending on the train, the time of travel, and the size of the accommodation.

From the U.K. Visitors from London may want to consider a British/French joint rail pass, linking the two most popular vacation spots on the continent, Britain and France. Called **BritFrance Railpass,** it is available to North Americans, providing unlimited train travel in Britain and France, plus a round-trip ticket for travel across the English Channel via hovercraft. (More rail passes will be previewed in "Getting Around," below.) You may choose a total of any 5 days of unlimited rail travel during a 15-day consecutive period or 10 days during a single month—on both British and French rail networks.

Adult first-class fares (any 5 days in 15) are $359; adult standard fares are $269. There's also a youth standard (ages 12–25) costing $229 for any 5 days in 15. Obtain the pass at RailEurope, Inc. (tel. toll free 800/848-7245) or at BritRail Travel International, 1500 Broadway, New York, NY 10036-4015 (tel. 212/575-2667).

Incidentally, you don't have to go to Paris from London. For example, there are direct trains from London to such places as the Côte d'Azur (French Riviera), the Alps, Strasbourg (capital of Alsace), Lyon (in wine-rich Burgundy), and the Pyrénées bordering Spain.

BY BUS

Bus travel to Paris is available not only from London but also from most major cities on the continent.

One of the largest bus operators in Europe is **Eurolines France,** 5, av. de la Porte-de-la-Villette, 75019 Paris (tel. 1/40-38-93-93), which sends buses among more than 3,000 destinations in France and the rest of Europe. The hub of the company's

---

ADVANCE-PURCHASE RAIL PASSES IN THE U.S.

Tickets for individual train rides or special rail passes can be purchased in advance from **RailEurope**, 226-230 Westchester Ave., White Plains, NY 10604 (tel. toll free 800/848-7245). See also "Getting Around France: By Train," later in this chapter.

---

network is, as you'd expect, Paris, which services these routes from the enormous bus terminal (la Gare Routière) at the Porte de la Villette, on the city's northern perimeter.

Buses on long-haul journeys are equipped with toilets and stop every four hours for rest and refreshment. At press time, the price of a round-trip ticket between Paris and London was 530 F ($95.40); between Paris and Rome, 820 F ($147.60); between Paris and Stockholm, 1,400 F ($252) for a trip taking two days in each direction. A ticket for the bus trip between Paris and Frankfurt was offered at a promotional giveaway of 395 F ($71.10) round-trip, a low price not likely to be in effect by the time of your visit.

At press time, because Eurolines did not maintain a U.S.-based sales agent, most clients wait until they reach Europe to buy their tickets. Any European travel agent can arrange for these purchases. If you're traveling to Paris from London, you can contact Eurolines U.K., Victoria Coach Station (the continental check-in desk) or call 0582/40-45-11 for information. In Frankfurt, contact L'Agence Wasteels, Am Hauptbahnhof 18, 6000 Frankfurt (tel. 069/232385).

BY OCEAN LINER FROM THE U.S.

The era of sailing to Paris in the 1950s style of Marilyn Monroe and Jane Russell is long gone. The only ocean liner now making scheduled transatlantic crossings is the *Queen Elizabeth 2* (QE2), the star and flagship of the British Cunard line.

The *QE2*'s most frequent itinerary is between New York and England's Channel port of Southampton. From Southampton, you can go by ferryboat or hovercraft to France; or you can take a train to London—perhaps taking in some plays, museums, and shopping before flying to Paris.

Cruise hopefuls should remember that Cunard offers greater numbers of eastbound routes into England than it does into France, but that several of its westbound crossings depart for North America directly from the northern French coast rather than from England. This policy makes it especially convenient for travelers to fly directly from their home airports to Paris, then to return to North America by ship directly from Cherbourg. Many passengers appreciate the time and leisure this gives them to relax and "decompress" at the end of their voyage through France.

On board, you'll find four swimming pools, a sauna, nightclubs, a movie theater, boutiques (including the world's only seagoing branch of Harrods), four restaurants, paddle-tennis courts, and a children's playroom staffed with English nannies. There's also an on-board branch of California's Golden Door Health Spa, a computer learning center with a battery of IBM personal computers, seminars by experts on everything from astrology to French cuisine, and meetings with an array of visiting celebrities.

Fares are extremely high, depending on your cabin and season of sailing. Call your travel agent or a Cunard representative (tel. 212/880-7500 in New York City, or toll free 800/221-4770).

BY FERRY FROM THE U.K.

About a dozen companies run hydrofoils, ferries, and hovercraft across La Manche ("the sleeve," as the French call the Channel)—all of which will change once the Channel Tunnel is opened.

Services operate day and night. Most ferries carry cars, but some hydrofoils carry passengers only. Hovercraft or hydrofoils make the trip in just 40 minutes, while slow-moving ferries might take hours, depending on conditions.

The major routes are between Dover or Folkestone and Calais or Boulogne (about 12 trips a day). It's important to make reservations, as vessels are always crowded. Prices and timetables can vary depending on weather conditions.

The major carriers are P&O Channel Lines, Sealink, and Hoverspeed.

P&O maintains a North American sales agency at Scots-American Travel, 26 Rugen Dr., Harrington Park, NJ 07640 (tel. 201/7678-1187), which can reserve passage on any of the P&O ferryboats. It will also issue ironclad reservations for portage of autos. (Advance reservations, particularly in summertime, are usually necessary for cars.)

P&O operates jetfoil service between Dover and Ostende, Belgium (for passengers only), and car and passenger ferries between Portsmouth and Cherbourg, France (three sailings a day, 4¾ hours each way); between Portsmouth and Le Havre (three sailings a day, 5¾ hours each way); between Dover and Calais (sailings every 90 minutes throughout the day, 75 minutes each way); between Dover and Ostende (between six and eight sailings a day, 4 hours each way); and a somewhat less popular passage from Felixstowe to Zeebrugge (twice daily, 5¾ hours each way).

P&O's major competitors include Sealink and Hoverspeed Ltd., either of which can carry both passengers and vehicles on all their routings. Both companies are represented in North America by BritRail (tel. 212/595-2667 in New York City).

By far the most popular routing across the Channel is between Calais, France, and Dover, England. Hoverspeed operates 35-minute hovercraft crossings, at least 12 a day, as well as slightly longer crossings via Seacat (a kind of double-hulled catamaran propelled by jet engines) between Boulogne and Folkestone. Seacats cross about four times a day and require 55 minutes.

Sealink operates conventional ferryboat service between Cherbourg and Southampton (usually one or two a day for a crossing of six to eight hours); and between Dieppe and Newhaven (four times a day for a crossing of four hours). Most popular of all are Sealink's conventional car-ferries between Calais and Dover. Departing 20 times a day in either direction, they require 90 minutes for the crossing, cost $42 each way for a passenger without a car, and $123–$300 for a car—depending on its size and the season—including up to five occupants.

If you plan to take a rented car across the Channel, check carefully about license and insurance requirements with the rental company before you leave.

BY LE SHUTTLE FROM THE U.K.

Expected to open in May 1994, Le Shuttle is a train that will transport motorists beneath the English Channel, completing the 31-mile journey between France and Great Britain in just 35 minutes. At time of press, prices have not been determined but will be comparable to the cross-Channel ferry and Hovercraft, said representatives of Le Shuttle.

Le Shuttle will accommodate passenger cars, charter buses, taxis, and motorcycles through a tunnel under the English Channel from Folkestone, England to Calais, France. Le Shuttle will operate 24 hours a day, 365 days a year, running every 15 minutes during peak travel times and at least once an hour during the night. Tickets will be available in advance or at the toll booth. With Le Shuttle, gone are weather-related delays, seasickness, and the need for reservations.

Motorists will drive onto a half-mile long train and travel through an underground tunnel built beneath the seabed through a layer of impermeable chalk marl and sealed within a reinforced concrete lining.

Before boarding Le Shuttle, motorists will stop at a toll booth and then pass through immigration for both countries at one time. During the ride, motorists will stay in bright, air-conditioned carriages, remaining inside their cars or stepping outside to stretch their legs. When the trip is completed, motorists simply drive off toward their destinations. Total travel time between the French and English highway system will be about one hour.

Stores selling duty-free goods, restaurants, and service stations will be available to travelers on both sides of the Channel. A bilingual staff will be on hand to assist travelers at both the British and French terminals.

PACKAGE TOURS

Some people prefer that a tour operator take care of all the travel arrangements. There are many companies operating tours to France, each offering transportation to and within France, prearranged hotel space, and such extras as a bilingual tour guide and lectures geared more or less to your general interests.

Some operate special-interest tours arranging meetings with local aristocracy, "famous" artists, or leaders of the resistance. Many of these celebrities are legitimate and can contribute much to your tour. Others are not, so beware of any undue sales pressure from a tour operator trying to clinch the deal, especially if the list of guest lecturers reads like the "A-list" from a social event in the *ancien régime* of Pre-Revolutionary France.

Here are some tour operators to contact:

Travel Concepts, 62 Commonwealth Ave., Suite 3, Boston, MA 02116-3029 (tel. 617/266-8450), specializes in art-history and cultural tours through less-traveled regions, such as the Dordogne (with side trips to the prehistoric caves at Lascaux), lesser-known wineries in Burgundy and Chablis, and distilleries in Cognac and Armagnac.

Since tours are usually custom-designed for groups of 10 or more, this company is a favorite of alumni(ae) groups and special-interest groups whose members are traveling together. If butterfly collecting in Provence, birdwatching in Brittany, or following in the footsteps of Nostradamus in southern France interest you, then get a group of like-minded people together. In rare instances, individuals or individual couples can latch onto some other group's prearranged tour, but this company is best used as a vehicle for groups with common interest arranging a tour.

The French Experience, 370 Lexington Ave., New York, NY 10017 (tel. 212/986-3800), offers several fly-drive programs using different types and price levels of hotels. The packages cover different regions of France and can be altered to suit individual needs.

American Express Vacations, P.O. Box 5014, Atlanta, GA 30302 (tel. toll free 800/241-1700), is perhaps the most instantly recognizable tour operator in the world. Their offerings in France and the rest of Europe are probably more comprehensive than those of any other company. If they don't offer what you want, and if you're clear enough in your vision, they'll package a tour for you.

SUGGESTED ITINERARIES

If You Have 4 Days [Normandy and Brittany]

Day 1: Strike out for Normandy and Brittany, the two old provinces of France that North Americans generally find the most intriguing (see Chapters 13 and 14). Head first for Rouen, 84 miles northwest of Paris, to view the site of Joan of Arc's death in 1431 and the famous Rouen Cathedral.

Day 2: Head east toward Caen, the seat of the government of William the Conqueror, 150 miles from Paris. You can overnight there or else travel 17 miles west to Bayeux to see the cathedral and the Bayeux Tapestry.

Day 3: Based either in Bayeux or in Caen, spend the day exploring the D-Day beaches, of great interest to Americans and Canadians. The highlights are described in Chapter 13.

Day 4: Continue west, heading toward Le Mont-St-Michel, one of the great sightseeing attractions of Europe, lying at the border of Normandy and Brittany, 209 miles from Paris. For an overnight stopover in the area, consider those enchanting resort towns in Brittany, St-Malo and Dinard, on the northwest coast, facing each other across an estuary. St-Malo, an ancient pirates' stronghold and walled fishing village, lies 53 miles from Le Mont-St-Michel. Dinard has a gambling casino and sheltered beach, along with golf and tennis courses.

Those with the time will want to explore the entire peninsula of Brittany, with its 600 miles of coast and chains of beaches, rustic fishing ports, and some of the greatest seafood you'll ever taste.

If You Have 6 Days [The Loire Valley]

Day 1: From Paris, take the autoroute to Chartres, 60 miles south. See the fabulous cathedral and stay overnight.

Day 2: Drive to Tours, the capital of the Loire Valley, 144 miles southwest of Paris. It's your best all-around base in the châteaux country because it has a more diversified selection of hotels. Tours is a big city though, and many people prefer to stay in Amboise, 15 miles east of Tours, which is also a good center for exploring.

Day 3: Based in either Tours or Amboise, head for the major attractions in the southwest: Azay-le-Rideau, 17 miles from Tours (a private residence during the Renaissance), and Chinon, 30 miles from Tours, one of the oldest fortress-châteaux in France.

Day 4: Again based in Tours, head for Amboise, with its memories of Leonardo da Vinci, and Chenonceaux, 21 miles southeast of Tours. Chenonceaux is the chef-d'oeuvre of the Renaissance, forever linked to the legend of the dames de Chenonceaux.

Day 5: Leave Tours or Amboise, heading east along the autoroute to Blois, seat of the counts of Blois. Spend the morning sightseeing at Chaumont, with its memories of Diane de Poitiers. Spend the night in Blois.

Day 6: Leave the next morning, heading east to Orléans, but stop first at Chambord, former seat of François I, the Chevalier King. Stay overnight in Orléans, forever associated with the legend of the Maid of Orléans.

If You Have 7 Days [The French Riviera]

Days 1–3: Head for Nice, 577 miles south of Paris, for three nights (fly there to save time and, incidentally, money). Day 1 will be spent getting there and settling into your hotel. I suggest that you spend Day 2 exploring St-Paul-de-Vence, with its Maeght Foundation, and Vence, with its Matisse Chapel. Nice has many attractions of its own (and you'll also want some sun), so spend Day 3 on home ground.

Day 4: Drive to Monte Carlo, at least for a night, going along to St-Jean and Cap Ferrat on the same day if you have time. This is one of the poshest parts of southern France. Monaco is 12 miles from Nice along the Moyenne Corniche.

Days 5 and 6: Head for Cannes, 20 miles east of Nice. Spend Day 5 enjoying Cannes itself and Day 6 exploring at least some of the attractions in its environs, including the Lerins Islands off its shoreline (linked to the legend of *The Man in the Iron Mask*).

Day 7: Visit chic St-Tropez, 46 miles east of Cannes, our last stopover. St-Tropez is strictly for fun and won't dazzle you with a lot of attractions.

If You Have 7 Days [Languedoc and Provence]

Days 1 and 2: From Paris, fly to Marseille (482 miles). If you're already in Nice, it's 117 miles west. Spend Day 1 settling in and Day 2 exploring the attractions of the second-largest city of France, one of the world's major seaports, and the most colorful, turbulent, and exotic place in the country. Part of the day should be spent visiting Château d'If, an island used as a setting for *The Count of Monte Cristo*.

Day 3: It's an easy 19-mile drive to Aix-en-Provence, northeast of Marseille. Aix-en-Provence, the old capital city of Provence, linked with Paul Cézanne, makes a good overnight stopover, and you can spend the day sightseeing there.

Day 4: Leaving Aix-en-Provence in the morning, go to Les Baux, 54 miles from Marseille. Spend part of the day exploring this "nesting place for eagles," then go to Arles, 47 miles west of Aix-en-Provence, to discover why it cast a spell over van Gogh. Spend the night in romantic old Arles.

Day 5: It's on to Avignon, surrounded by ancient ramparts and the seat of the popes during the 14th century, 24 miles from Arles. Arrive early because you'll have a busy day of sightseeing.

Day 6: Two of the most charming cities in the region are Nîmes and Montpellier. Nîmes contains the most impressive Roman remains in France, including an arena and the Temple of Diana. Montpellier is the center of southern wine production and lies in a scenic setting of unsurpassed beauty. They are only 31 miles apart and can be visited in one busy, busy day. Nîmes should be viewed first, as it lies 27 miles west of Avignon. Stay overnight in Montpellier.

Day 7: For a wrap-up, head for one of the major attractions of France, Carcassonne, the greatest fortress city of Europe, 57 miles southeast of Toulouse. It's linked to Montpellier by autoroute. Overnight in Carcassonne after enjoying a platter of cassoulet.

2. GETTING AROUND

BY PLANE

The French domestic airline, **Air Inter,** flies to 30 major French centers, operating an average of 300 flights a day that crisscross the country in an average flight time of one hour.

Air Inter flies in and out of both Paris airports—Orly and Charles de Gaulle—servicing such major cities as Nice, Marseille, Toulouse, Bordeaux, Lyon, Strasbourg, Mulhouse and Basel (Switzerland), Montpellier, and Nantes.

The **Aer Inter Air Pass** offers 7 days of flying within the borders of France (including flights to and from Corsica), which must be used in a 30-day period, for $250 per person. These passes must be reserved and purchased in North America.

For information and reservations in North America, call toll free 800/AF-PARIS; in France, 45-39-25-25.

BY TRAIN

With some 50 cities in France linked by trains, the world's fastest, Paris is connected to many areas of the country by a trip of just a few hours. With 24,000 miles of track and about 3,000 stations, SNCF (French National Railroads) is fabled throughout the world for its on-time performance. You can travel either first or second class by day, and in couchette or sleeper by night. Many trains in France carry dining facilities, which range from cafeteria to formal dinners.

Information

Timetables If you plan to travel on trains a lot, secure the latest copy of the **Thomas Cook European Timetable of Railroads.** This comprehensive 500-plus page timetable details all of Europe's passenger rail and ferry schedules with accuracy. It's available in North America exclusively from Forsyth Travel Library, 9154 W. 57th St. (P.O. Box 2975), Shawnee Mission, KS 66201, at a cost of $24.95 plus $4 shipping. Call toll free 800/FORSYTH to order by VISA or MasterCard.

In the United States For more information and to purchase rail passes (see below) before you leave for France, contact RailEurope at 226-230 Westchester Ave., White Plains, NY 10604 (tel. toll free 800/848-7245); 360 Post St., San Francisco, CA 94102 (tel. 415/982-1993); 110 Wilshire Blvd., Santa Monica, CA 90401 (tel. 213/451-5150); 11 E. Adams St., Chicago, IL 60603 (tel. 312/427-8691); 800 Corporate Dr., Suite 108, Fort Lauderdale, FL 33334 (tel. 305/776-2729); and 6060 N. Central Expressway, Suite 220, Dallas, TX 75206 (tel. 214/691-5573).

In Canada RailEurope, Inc., offices are at 2087 Dundas East, Suite 204, Mississauga, ON L4X 1M2 (tel. 416/602-4195); 643 Notre Dame Ouest, Suite 200, Montréal, PQ H3C 1HB (tel. 514/392-1311); and 409 Granville St., Suite 452, Vancouver, BC V6C 1T2 (tel. 604/688-6707).

In London SNCF has offices at 170 Piccadilly, W1 OBA (tel. 071/493-9731).
In Paris The SNCF offices are at 10, place de Budapest, 75436 Paris (tel. 1/42-85-60-00). For information about train departures, go to the Gare de l'Est, the Gare du Nord, the Gare Saint-Lazare, the Gare Montparnasse, the Gare d'Austerlitz, or the Gare de Lyon.

Rail Passes

Working cooperatively with SNCF, RailEurope offers three economical and flexible rail passes that reduce costs considerably.

The **France Railpass** provides unlimited rail transportation throughout France for three days to be used within a period of one month. It costs $175 in first class and $125 in second class (up to six additional days can be purchased for an additional fee).

The **France Rail 'n Drive Pass,** available only to North Americans, combines good value on rail travel with the possibility of discounted car rentals. It includes the rail pass mentioned above, along with unlimited mileage on a car rental, but only on the condition that two or more people travel together. It can be used during seven nonconsecutive days within a period of one month, and will include four days on the train and three in a rented car. The cost is $229 per person in first class.

The **France Fly Rail 'n Drive Pass** is an arrangement whereby air, rail, and car transportation within France are combined into one discounted purchase. Fly one day (during any 24-hour period) on Air Inter, the French domestic airline; travel any four days by train, and any three days by car—all within any 15-day period at a low, all-inclusive second-class rate of $249 per person. (To qualify, two or more people must travel together.)

Eurailpasses

For years, many in-the-know travelers have been taking advantage of one of the greatest travel bargains in Europe—the **Eurailpass,** which permits unlimited first-class rail travel in any country in western Europe except the British Isles (good in Ireland). Passes are purchased for periods as short as 15 days or as long as three months and are strictly nontransferable.

Here's how it works: The pass is sold only outside Europe and North Africa, and only to residents of countries outside those areas. Vacationers may purchase a 15-day Eurailpass for $460, a 21-day pass for $598, a one-month pass for $728, a two-month pass for $998, and a three-month pass for $1,260. Children under 4 travel free, and children under 12 pay only half fare if they are accompanied by an adult holding a Eurailpass.

The advantages are tempting—no tickets, no supplements (simply show the pass to the ticket collector, then settle back to enjoy the European scenery). Seat reservations are required on some trains. Some trains have couchettes (sleeping cars), for which an additional fee is charged.

Obviously, the two- or three-month visitor gets the greatest economic advantages; he or she can visit all of France's major sights, from the Alps to Brittany, then end the vacation in Norway—all on the same ticket. Eurailpass holders are entitled to considerable reductions on ferry steamers and some buses.

Eurail Saverpass is a good money-saving ticket offering discount 15-day travel, but only if groups of three people travel continuously together between April and September, or of two people travel continuously together between October and March. The price of a Saverpass, valid all over Europe and good in first class only, is $390 per person.

Eurail Youthpass is a single, convenient card designed for people under 26 years. It gives you one or two months of unlimited second-class (coach) rail travel in Eurailpass countries. Rates are $508 for one month, $698 for two months.

Eurail Flexipass allow passengers to visit Europe with more flexibility. It's valid in first class and offers the same privileges as the Eurailpass. However, it provides a number of individual travel days that can be used over a much longer period of consecutive days. That makes it possible to stay in one city and yet not lose a single day of discounted travel. There are three passes: $298 for 5 days of travel within two months, $496 for 10 days of travel within two months, and $676 for 15 days of travel within two months.

Eurail Youth Flexipass is a discounted version of the Flexipass for travelers under 26. Three passes are available: $200 for 5 days of travel within two months, $348 for 10 days of travel within two months, and $474 for 15 days of travel within two months. Children 4–11 years pay 50% of the above fares.

Eurailpasses can be purchased through the offices of RailEurope (see "Information," above).

BY SHIP

Several different cruise lines offer waterborne excursions through the Mediterranean, and many of them make stops at the legendary ports of France. One of the most interesting of the cruise operators is a relative newcomer, **Renaissance Cruises,** P.O. Box 350307, Fort Lauderdale, FL 33335-0307 (tel. toll free 800/525-5350), whose eight-ship fleet is streamlined, seaworthy, intimate, and luxurious. Vessels are small enough to berth at infrequently visited ports that are otherwise inaccessible to larger ships. Each of the vessels offers only "outside" suites (with windows and outside views) for accommodations, thereby freeing cruise participants from the space restrictions so often imposed by other lines. Each ship contains space for only 114 passengers, who are entertained with "destination-oriented" experiences whose attractions are enhanced by the running commentaries of on-board lecturers and cruise directors. Some guests compare the company's "Dine When and With Whom" policy to the sophisticated, loosely structured open seating at a privately hosted dinner party.

Although the line offers sailings through Asia, the Caribbean, Scandinavia, and the Seychelles Islands, many readers of this guidebook might be interested in the company's Mediterranean cruises. One of Renaissance's most popular outings is a one- or two-week sailing from Rome to Barcelona. In addition to stops in Sardinia and Ibiza, with ample time ashore for sightseeing, the ship stops in Monte Carlo and the rarely visited southern French ports of Mahon, Port Vendres, and Port St-Louis. Although prices begin at around $3,000 per person per week, double occupancy, several promotional arrangements were in effect at press time which somewhat reduced these prices. For additional information and reservations, call the toll-free number listed above.

BY CAR

Francophiles maintain that the best way to see France is by car, and I hearily concur The most charming châteaux and the best country hotels always seem to lie away from the main cities and far away from train stations. For that and other reasons, you'll find that renting a car is usually the best way to travel once you get to France, especially if you plan to explore in depth and not just stick to the standard route, such as the Paris–Nice run.

Driving time in Europe is largely a matter of conjecture, urgency, and how much sightseeing you do along the way. Driving time from Geneva to Paris is 5½ hours minimum. Rouen to Paris requires 2½ hours; Nantes to Paris, 3½ hours; Lyon to Paris, 4 hours. The driving time from Marseille to Paris is largely a matter of national pride, and tall tales abound about how rapidly the French can do it. With the accelerator pressed to the floor, you might conceivably make it in 7 hours, but I always make a two-day journey of it.

Frankly, the rail networks of Europe are so well developed, and—compared to the cost and anxiety of driving—so inexpensive that I usually recommend renting a car only for exploring rural areas little serviced by rail lines, such as Brittany, rural Burgundy, and the Dordogne.

CAR RENTALS Renting a car in France is easy. You'll need to present a valid driver's license and be at least 23 years old for the cheaper models and at least 25 for the more expensive vehicles. Renters must also present a valid passport and a valid credit card unless payment is arranged in North America before leaving home. It usually isn't obligatory, but certain companies, perhaps the smaller ones, have at times asked for the presentation of an international driver's license.

Note: The best deal is usually a weekly rental with unlimited mileage. All car-rental bills in France are subject to a 22% government tax, among the highest in Europe.

Budget Rent-a-Car (tel. toll free 800/527-0700) has 24 locations in Paris and dozens of others throughout France, including branches at most of the country's airports. Cars can usually be picked up in one French city and dropped off in another in France for no additional charge if you notify the company in advance. Otherwise, there's an extra charge of 600 F ($108).

The least expensive car will probably be a two-door Peugeot with manual transmission and few frills. Prices vary with the season, but Budget is usually on the cheaper side. Discounts are usually granted for rentals of two weeks or more. Automatic transmission is regarded as a luxury in Europe, so if you need it, you'll pay dearly for it.

Clients who want to protect themselves against international currency-exchange fluctuations can ask Budget to "lock in" the exchange rate in effect at the time of booking. In such cases, a reservation must be made and paid for in North America at least 14 days before the anticipated pickup of the car.

The collision-damage waiver (CDW)—costing 71–101 F ($12.80–$18.20) extra per day, depending on the value of the car—will eliminate most (or all, depending on the company) of your financial responsibility in the event of theft or accidental damage to your car. It's a good idea to take it, although certain credit-card issuers will agree—if the imprint of their credit card appears on the original rental contract—to pay for any accident-related liability. (This varies broadly from company to company and must be confirmed individually with your credit-card issuer.)

National Car Rental (tel. toll free 800/227-3876) is represented in Paris by Europcar, with headquarters at 145, av. Malakoff, 16e (tel. 1/45-00-08-06). It also has offices at each of the Paris airports and at another dozen or so locations within the city. Its headquarters can rent you a car on the spot, but to qualify for the cheaper weekly rental you must reserve at least two days in advance by calling the number above.

Hertz (tel. toll free 800/654-3001) has about 17 locations as well as offices at Orly and Charles de Gaulle Airports. The main office in Paris is at 27, rue St-Ferdinand, 17e (tel. 1/45-74-97-39). A discounted weekly rental must be reserved at least two days in advance. Be sure to ask about any promotional discounts the company might be offering.

Avis (tel. toll free 800/331-2112) has offices in Paris at both Orly and Charles de Gaulle Airports, as well as headquarters at 5, rue Bixio, 7e (tel. 1/44-18-10-50), near the Eiffel Tower. The best rates are given to drivers who reserve a car at least 14 business days before leaving North America.

Kemwell, 106 Calvert St., Harrison, NY 10528 (tel. toll free 800/678-0678). Don't overlook the services of this small but well-recommended company. Kemwell works with Citer, a France-based car-rental company, and offers attractive rental opportunities to clients who are able to pay in full in advance. After payment, a voucher is issued, which clients use to retrieve their car at airports or several city locations. Promotions are also offered on a seasonal basis; discounts are available to clients who book their air and car-rental arrangements simultaneously.

GASOLINE Known in France as *essence,* gasoline is extraordinarily expensive for the visitor used to North American prices. All but the least expensive cars usually require an octane rating that the French classify as *essence super,* which is the most expensive variety offered. At press time, *essence super* sold for about 5.75 F ($1) per liter, which works out to around 21 F ($3.80) per gallon. (Certain smaller engines might get by on *essence ordinaire,* which costs a fraction less than *super.*) Depending on your car, you'll need either leaded (*avec plomb*) or unleaded (*sans plomb*). To fill a tank of a medium-sized car will cost between $40 and $60.

Beware of the mixture of gasoline and oil sold in certain rural communities called *mélange* or *gasoil;* this mixture is for very old two-cycle engines.

Note: Sometimes you can drive for miles in rural France without encountering a gas station, so don't let your tank get dangerously low.

DRIVING RULES Everyone in the car, in both the front and back seats, must wear seatbelts. Children under 12 must ride in the back seat. Drivers are supposed to yield to the car on their right, except where signs indicate otherwise, as at traffic circles. If you violate the speed limits, expect a big fine. Those limits are about 130 kmph (80 m.p.h.) on expressways, about 100 kmph (60 m.p.h.) on major national highways, and 90 kmph (56 m.p.h.) on small country roads. In towns, don't exceed 60 kmph (37 m.p.h.).

MAPS Before setting out on a country tour of France, pick up a good regional map of the district you plan to explore. If you're visiting a town, ask at the local tourist office for a town plan. They are usually given away free.

For France as a whole, most motorists opt for the Michelin map 989. For regions, Michelin publishes a series of yellow maps that are quite good. Big travel-book stores in North America carry these maps, and they are commonly available in France, and at lower prices. One useful feature of the Michelin map (in this age of congested traffic) is its designations of alternative *routes de dégagement,* which let you skirt big cities and avoid traffic-clogged highways.

BREAKDOWNS/ASSISTANCE A breakdown is called *une panne* in France, and it's just as frustrating there as anywhere else. Call the police at 17 anywhere in France and they will put you in touch with the nearest garage. Most local garages have towing services. If your breakdown should occur on an expressway, find the nearest roadside emergency phone box, pick up the phone, and put a call through. You'll be immediately connected to the nearest breakdown service facility.

FAST FACTS FRANCE

The following information applies to the country as a whole. For information specifically about Paris, see "Fast Facts: Paris" in Chapter 4.

Auto Clubs The Association Française des Auto Clubs, 9, rue Anatole-de-la-Forge, 75017 Paris (tel. 1/42-27-82-00), provides some limited information to members of U.S. auto clubs such as the AAA.

Business Hours French business hours are erratic, as befits a nation of individualists. Most **banks** are open Monday through Friday from 9:30am to 4:30pm. Many, particularly in smaller towns or villages, take a lunch break at varying times. Hours are usually posted on the door. Most **museums** close one day a week (often Tuesday). They are generally closed on national holidays. Usual hours are 9:30am to 5pm. Some museums, particularly the smaller and less-staffed ones, close for lunch from noon to 2pm. Most French museums are open on Saturday; many are closed Sunday morning but are open Sunday afternoon. Again, refer to the individual museum listings. Generally, **offices** are open Monday through Friday from 9am to 5pm, but don't count on it. Always call first. In Paris or other big French cities, **stores** are open from 9 or 9:30am (often 10am) to 6 or 7pm without a break for lunch. Some shops, particularly those operated by foreigners, open at 8am and close at 8 or 9pm. In some small stores the lunch break can last three hours, beginning at 1pm. This is more common in the south than in the north.

Camera/Film Take along at least one roll of film for each day of your stay. It's cheaper to process your film at home.

Cigarettes Bring in as many as Customs will allow if you're addicted to a particular brand, as American cigarettes are very expensive in France. Otherwise, learn to smoke French cigarettes, like Gauloise Bleu.

Currency and Exchange See "Information, Documents, and Money" in Chapter 2.

Customs Customs restrictions differ for citizens of the European Community and for citizens of non-E.C. countries.

Non-E.C. nationals can bring in duty free 200 cigarettes or 100 cigarillos or 50 cigars or 250 grams of smoking tobacco. This amount is doubled if you live outside Europe. You can, as well, bring in two liters of wine and one liter of alcohol over 22 proof and two liters of wine 22 proof or under. In addition, you can bring 50 grams of perfume, a quarter liter of toilet water, 500 grams of coffee, and 200 grams of tea. Those over 14 years old can, as well, bring in 300 F ($54) of other goods; for those under 15 the limit is 150 F ($27).

Visitors from E.C. countries can bring in 300 cigarettes or 150 cigarillos or 75 cigars or 400 grams of smoking tobacco. The limit for "spirits" is 5 liters of table wine, 1½ liters of alcohol over 22 proof, and 3 liters of alcohol 22 proof or under. In addition, visitors can bring in 75 grams of perfume, three-eighths of a liter of toilet water, 1,000 grams of coffee, and 80 grams of tea. Passengers 15 years old and over can bring in 4,200 F ($756) of merchandise duty free; passengers under 15 can bring in 1,000 F ($180) worth.

Items destined for personal use, including bicycles and sports equipment, already in use, whether or not contained in personal luggage, are admitted without formality providing the quantity or the type of goods imported does not indicate the owner's intention to carry out a commercial transaction. They cannot be sold or given away in France and must be reexported.

Documents Required See "Information, Documents, and Money" in Chapter 2.

Driving Rules See "Getting Around: By Car," above, in this chapter.

Drug Laws A word of warning: Penalties for illegal drug possession in France are more severe than those in the United States or Canada. You could go to jail or be deported immediately. According to French law, the police can stop you and search you at will. *Caveat:* Drug pushers often turn in their customers to the police.

Drugstores If you need one during off-hours, have your concierge get in touch with the nearest Commissariat de Police. An agent there will have the address of a nearby pharmacy open 24 hours a day. French law requires that the pharmacies in any given neighborhood display the name and location of the one that will remain open all night.

Electricity In general expect 200 volts and 50 cycles, although you'll encounter 110 and 115 volts in some older establishments. Adapters are needed to fit sockets. Many hotels have two-pin (in some cases, three-pin) sockets for electric razors. It's best to ask your hotel concierge before plugging in any electrical appliance.

Embassies and Consulates I hope you'll not need such services. But in case you lose your passport or have some other emergency, here's a list of addresses and phone numbers:

- **Australia** The embassy is at 4, rue Jean-Rey, 75015 Paris (tel. 1/40-59-33-00), open Monday through Thursday from 9:15am to noon and 2 to 5pm. Métro: Bir-Hakeim.
- **Canada** The embassy is at 35, av. Montaigne, 75008 Paris (tel. 1/44-43-32-00), open Monday through Friday from 9am to noon and 2 to 5pm. The Canadian Consulate is at the same address and is open Monday through Friday from 9am to 11:30am and 2 to 4pm (same phone).
- **United Kingdom** The embassy is at 35, rue du Faubourg St-Honoré, 75383 Paris Cedex (tel. 1/42-66-91-42), open Monday through Friday from 9:30am to 1pm and 2:30 to 6pm.
- **United States** The embassy is at 2, av. Gabriel, 75008 Paris (tel. 1/42-96-12-02), open Monday through Friday from 9am to 4pm. Passports are issued at its annex at 2, rue St-Florentin (tel. 1/42-96-12-02, ext. 2613), which lies off the northeast section of place de la Concorde. Métro: Concorde. To get a passport replaced costs about $42.
  In addition to its embassy and consulate in Paris, the United States also maintains the following consulates: 22, cours du Maréchal-Foch, 33080 Bordeaux (tel. 56-52-65-95); 12, bd. Paul-Peytral, 13286 Marseille (tel. 91-54-92-00); and 15, av. d'Alsace, 67082 Strasbourg (tel. 88-35-31-04).

- **New Zealand** The embassy is at 7 ter, rue Léonard-de-Vinci, 75116 Paris (tel. 1/45-00-24-11), open Monday through Friday 9am to 1pm and 2 to 5:30pm. Métro: Victor-Hugo.

Emergencies For specific emergencies when visiting Paris, refer to "Fast Facts: Paris" in Chapter 4. In an emergency while at a hotel, contact the front desk. Most staffs are trained in dealing with a crisis and will call the police, summon an ambulance, or do whatever is necessary. But if it's something like a stolen wallet, you should go to the police station in person. Otherwise, you can get help anywhere in France by calling 17 for police, 18 for the fire department (*pompiers*). For roadside emergencies, see "Getting Around: By Car," above, in this chapter.

Etiquette If you make a reservation at a restaurant, keep it or call in good time to cancel. Always refer to your waiter as *"monsieur,"* not *"garçon."* When entering a shop or café, nod and greet strangers with a "Monsieur" or "Madame." Be aware of your voice level in public places—the French are. Refrain from smoking between courses in restaurants. Avoid discussing money, salaries, size of houses, and horsepower of U.S. cars compared with French cars. Discussions about immigration into France from North Africa, religion, the Algerian revolution, anything to do with World War II, or leftist politics can sometimes spark violent controversy, especially at gatherings of extended families.

Gasoline See "Getting Around: By Car," above, in this chapter.

Hitchhiking Those who travel by thumb rate France low on their list. Look as neat and respectable as possible and you may have some luck. Service stations and toll-booth areas are the best bets for rides. Hitchhiking is not a good idea unless you're traveling with a friend, and even that can be extremely dangerous. Hitchhiking today in France is viewed as something one undertakes at great personal risk.

Holidays See "When to Go" in Chapter 2.

Information See "Information, Documents, and Money" in Chapter 2.

Language The world's best-selling phrase books are published by Berlitz—*French for Travellers* has everything you'll need.

Laundry Many hotels provide laundry service, but it's likely to be expensive. To cut costs, search the phone directory for a *laverie automatique* near your hotel. Watch for Sunday and Monday closings.

Legal Aid This may be hard to come by in France. The French government advises foreigners to consult their embassy or consulate (see "Embassies and Consulates," above) in case of a dire emergency, such as an arrest. Even if a consulate or embassy declines to offer financial or legal help, they will generally offer advice as to how you can obtain help locally. For example, they can furnish a list of attorneys who might represent you. Most arrests are for illegal possession of drugs, and the U.S. embassy and consulate officials cannot interfere with the French judicial system in any way on your behalf. A consulate can only advise you of your rights.

Liquor Laws Visitors will find it easier to get a drink—wine, beer, or other spirits—in France than in England or some other countries. Supermarkets, grocery stores, and cafés sell alcoholic beverages. The legal drinking age is 16. Persons under that age can be served an alcoholic drink in a bar or restaurant if accompanied by a parent or legal guardian. Wine and liquor are sold every day of the week all year round.

Hours of cafés vary throughout the country and with various local restrictions. Some open at 6am, serving drinks until 3am; others are open 24 hours a day. Bars and nightclubs may stay open as they wish.

The Breathalyzer test is in use in France, and a motorist is considered "legally intoxicated" with 0.8 grams of alcohol per liter of blood. (The more liberal U.S. law is 1 gram per liter.) If convicted, a motorist faces a stiff fine and a possible prison term of two months to two years. If bodily injury results, the judge might throw the book at a convicted person.

Mail Most post offices in France are open Monday through Friday from 8am to 7pm and on Saturday from 8am to noon. Allow five to eight days to send or receive mail from your home. To send airmail letters to the U.S. or Canada, it costs 4.20 F

(80¢) for 20 grams or 6.90 F ($1.20) for 30 grams. Letters to the U.K. cost 2.50 F (50¢) for up to 20 grams. To send an airmail postcard to North America or Europe (outside France) costs 3.70 F (70¢).

If you don't have a hotel address in France, you can receive mail c/o American Express (see "Fast Facts: Paris" in Chapter 4). However, you may be asked to show an American Express card or traveler's check when you go to pick up your mail.

Another option is to send your mail *poste restante* (general delivery) in care of the major postal office in whatever town you plan to visit. You'll need to produce a passport to pick up mail, and you may be charged a small fee for the service.

You can also exchange money at post offices.

Many hotels sell stamps, as do local post offices and cafés displaying a red TABAC sign outside. Mailboxes are clearly marked.

Maps See "Getting Around: By Car," above, in this chapter.

Medical Emergencies If you have an emergency in Paris, refer to "Fast Facts: Paris" in Chapter 4. If you are ill and need medicine, go to a *pharmacie* (drugstore). At night and on Sunday, the local Commissariat de Police will tell you the location of the nearest drugstore that's open or the address of the nearest doctor on duty. The police will also summon an ambulance if you need to be rushed to a hospital. Seek assistance first at your hotel desk if language is a problem.

Newspapers/Magazines Most major cities carry copies of the *International Herald/Tribune*, *USA Today*, and usually a major London paper or two. Nearly all big-city newsstands—at least in areas that cater to tourists—also sell copies of *Time* and *Newsweek*.

Passports See "Information, Documents, and Money" in Chapter 2.

Police Call 17 anywhere in France.

Post See "Mail," above.

Radio/TV The major TV channels in France are Antenne 2, TF1, FR3, La Cinq, and M6. All programs are broadcast in French. However, after a day of sightseeing, you might be able to catch a foreign film late at night in English with French subtitles. In the summer months, the domestic radio France-Inter broadcasts daily news and important traffic conditions in English. Broadcast times are (usually) 8am and 1 and 7pm. Short- or medium-wave radios allow you to tune in to BBC programs.

Restrooms If you're in dire need, duck into a café or brasserie to use the lavatory. It's customary to make some small purchase if you do so. Paris Métro stations and underground garages usually contain public lavatories, but the degree of cleanliness varies. France still has many "hole-in-the-ground" toilets, so be forewarned.

Safety Much of France, particularly central France, the northeast, Normandy, and Brittany, remains relatively safe, although no place in the world is crime-free. Visitors contemplating a visit to the south of France, especially the French Riviera, should exercise extreme caution—robberies and muggings are commonplace. It's best to check your baggage into a hotel and then go sightseeing instead of leaving it unguarded in the trunk of a car, which can easily be broken into. Marseille is among the most dangerous cities of Europe, and visitors should keep this in mind. For safety in Paris, see "Fast Facts: Paris" in Chapter 4.

Taxes Watch it: You could get burned. As a member of the European Community France routinely imposes a "Value-Added Tax" (VAT) on many goods and services—currently 6%-33.3%.

Telephone All phone numbers in France require eight digits; these eight digits include the area code. For example, the telephone number for the Carlton Hôtel (93-68-91-68) contains the area code for Cannes. If you were anywhere in France, to call the Carlton Hôtel all you would have to dial is this eight-digit number. When calling the Carlton Hôtel from outside France, all you would have to dial is the country code for France and then the eight-digit number.

This system is complicated by only one factor: Calls destined for Paris or the *région parisienne* from outside the *région parisienne* require the addition of a "1" before the eight digits.

Note that if you are in Paris or in the *région parisienne,* to call the Hôtel de Crillon in Paris, all you would do is dial the eight digit number 42-65-24-24.

If you are in France but outside Paris or the *région parisienne,* dial 1/42-65-24-24 to call the Hôtel de Crillon in Paris.

If you are calling the Hôtel de Crillon from outside France, dial the country code and then 1/42-65-24-24.

Public phone booths are found in cafés, restaurants, Métro stations, post offices, airports, and train stations and occasionally on the streets. Some of these booths work with tokens called *jetons,* which can be purchased at the post office or from the cashier at any café. (It's usually customary to give a small tip if you buy them at a café.)

Pay telephones accept coins of ½, 1, 2, and 5 F; the minimum charge is 1 F (18¢). Pick up the receiver, insert the *jeton* or coin(s), and dial when you hear the tone, pushing the button when there's an answer.

The French also use a *télécarte,* a telephone debit card, which can be purchased at rail stations, post offices, and other places. Sold in two versions, it allows callers to use either 50 or 120 charge units (depending on the card) by inserting the card into the slot of most public telephones. Depending on the type of card you buy, they cost 40–96 F ($7.20–$17.30).

If possible, avoid making calls from your hotel, as some French establishments double or triple the charges on you.

When you're calling long distance within France, dial 16, wait for the dial tone, and then dial the eight-digit number of the person or place you're calling. To call the U.S. or Canada, first dial 19, listen for the tone, then slowly dial 1, the area code, and the seven-digit number. To place a collect call to North America, dial 19-33-11, and an English-speaking operator will assist you. Dial 19-00-11 for an American AT&T operator.

For information, dial 12.

Telex and Fax   Telex and fax messages can be sent from your hotel for a fee. Few budget hotels have Telex or fax machines.

Time   The French equivalent of daylight saving time lasts from around April to September, which puts it one hour ahead of French winter time. Depending on the time of year, France is six or seven hours ahead of eastern standard time in the U.S.

Tipping   This is practiced with flourish and style in France, and as a visitor you are expected to play the game. All bills, as required by law, are supposed to say *service compris,* which means that the tip has been included.

Here are some general guidelines on how much to tip: For, **hotel staff,** tip 5–10 F (90¢–$1.80) for every item of baggage the hotel porter carries on arrival and departure. You are not obligated to tip the concierge (hall porter), doorman, or anyone else—unless you use his or her service. In cafés, **waiter** service is usually included. **Porters** have an official scale of charges. It's usual to give about 5 F (90¢) per bag, depending on the number of bags. Tip **taxi drivers** about 10%–15% of the amount shown on the meter. In theaters and restaurants, give **cloakroom attendants** at least 5 F (90¢) per item. Give **restroom attendants** about 2 F (40¢) in nightclubs and such places. Give **cinema and theater ushers** about 2 F (40¢). Tip the **hairdresser** about 10%, and don't forget also to tip the person who gives you either a shampoo or a manicure 10 F ($1.80). For **guides** for group visits to museums and monuments, 5 F (90¢) is a reasonable tip.

Toilets   See "Restrooms," above.

Visas   See "Information, Documents, and Money" in Chapter 2.

Water   Drinking water is generally safe, although it has been known to cause diarrhea. If you ask for water in a restaurant, it will be served bottled (for which you'll pay) unless you specifically request tap water (*l'eau du robinet*).

Yellow Pages   As in North America, the *Yellow Pages* are immensely useful. Your hotel will almost certainly have a copy, but you'll need the help of a French-speaking resident before tackling the French Telephone Company's (P.T.T.'s) *Yellow Pages.*

Some words aren't too different from the English. *Pharmacie* (pharmacy), *antiquités* (antiques), *théâtres* (theaters), and *objets d'art* may be easy to decipher. But other words, such as *cordonniers* (shoemakers and shoe-repair shops) and *horlogerie* (watch-repair shop), might be less obvious. Ask someone at the reception desk of your hotel for translations if needed.

Don't ever assume that someone on the other end of the phone speaks English. You may have to ask a French-speaking person to make the call for you.

CHAPTER 4

GETTING TO KNOW PARIS

1. ORIENTATION
2. GETTING AROUND
• FAST FACTS: PARIS

If you visit only one city in the world, make it Paris. Stroll along the broad, tree-lined boulevards stopping at the sidewalk cafés, visit the world-renowned art museums and Gothic cathedrals, and sample the meticulously prepared cuisine. From the smoky cafés to the river Seine, Paris always manages to live up to its reputation as one of the world's most beautiful and romantic cities.

Ernest Hemingway referred to the many splendors of Paris as a "moveable feast" and wrote, "There is never any ending to Paris, and the memory of each person who has lived in it differs from that of any other." It is this personal discovery of the city that has always been the most compelling reason for coming to Paris. And perhaps that's why France has been called *le deuxième pays de tout le monde*—everyone's second country.

1. ORIENTATION

ARRIVING

BY PLANE

Paris has two major international airports: Orly, 8½ miles south of Paris, and Charles de Gaulle (also called Roissy), 14¼ miles northeast of the city.

A shuttle operates between the two airports about every 30 minutes, taking 50–75 minutes to make the journey. At Orly catch this bus at Exit B.

The least expensive way to reach the center of the city from either airport is aboard an Air France bus, which runs about every 12 minutes between 5:45am and 11pm.

For information about transportation to Charles de Gaulle Airport or Orly, call 43-46-14-14. For airport flight information, call Charles de Gaulle at 48-62-12-12 and Orly at 49-75-52-52.

Charles de Gaulle Airport

At Charles de Gaulle Airport, foreign carriers use Aérogate 1, and Air France uses Aérogare 2. From Aérogare 1, you take a moving walkway to the passport checkpoint and the Customs area. The two terminals are linked by a shuttle bus (*navette*).

The shuttle bus connecting Aérogare 1 with Aérogare 2 also transports passengers to the Roissy rail station, from which fast RER trains leave every 15 minutes to such Métro stations as Gare du Nord, Châtelet, Luxembourg, Port-Royal, and Denfert-Rochereau. A typical fare is 31 F ($5.50). You can also take an Air France shuttle bus—to the Arc de Triomphe, for example—for 39 F ($7). That ride, depending on traffic, takes less than 45 minutes.

Taxis into the city will cost, about 200 F ($36). At night (from 8pm to 7am), fares more than double.

Buses to Charles de Gaulle Airport leave from the terminal in the basement of the

Palais des Congrès at Porte Maillot every 15 minutes to Aérogare 2 and every 20 minutes to Aérogare 1. The trip takes about 30 minutes, but during rush hours allow another half hour.

Orly Airport

Orly also has two terminals—Orly Sud (south) for international flights and Orly Ouest (west) for domestic flights. They are linked by a shuttle bus.

Air France buses leave Orly Sud every 12 minutes from Exit 1, heading for Gare des Invalides. At Exit D, you can board bus no. 215 for place Denfert-Rochereau in the south of Paris. Don't take a meterless taxi from Orly Sud—it's much safer to get a metered cab from the line, which is under the scrutiny of a police officer.

A shuttle bus leaves Orly about every 15 minutes for the RER train station, Pont-de-Rungis/Aéroport-d'Orly, from which RER trains take 30 minutes into the city center. A typical fare is 25 F ($4.50).

You can also take a shuttle bus from Orly Sud to the Orly train station, where high-speed RER trains leaving every 15 minutes will take you to all the central stops along the Seine. En route you can transfer to any Métro line.

Orlyval, a shuttle train introduced in 1991, runs between Orly and the Antony RER station every seven minutes. The shuttle goes directly to the airport, a ticket from Paris costing 55 F ($9.90). To get to the Orlyval train from the center of Paris, passengers can board the RER B (direction: St-Rémy-les-Chevreuse) to Antony station in the south of the city. The Orlyval then goes directly to the airport. Orlyval operates daily in both directions from 5:30am to 11:48pm.

A taxi from Orly to the center of Paris costs about 160 F ($28.80), more at night, and buses to Orly Airport leave from the Invalides terminal to either Orly Sud or Orly Ouest every 15 minutes, taking about 30 minutes.

BY TRAIN

There are six major train stations in Paris: **Gare d'Austerlitz,** 55, quai d'Austerlitz, 13e (servicing the southwest with trains to the Loire Valley, the Bordeaux country, and the Pyrénées); **Gare de l'Est,** place du 11 Novembre 1918, 10e (servicing the east, with trains to Strasbourg, Nancy, Reims, and beyond to Zurich, Basel, Luxembourg, and Austria); **Gare de Lyon,** 20, bd. Diderot, 12e (servicing the southeast with trains to the Côte d'Azur, Provence, and beyond to Geneva, Lausanne, and Italy); **Gare Montparnasse,** 17, bd. Vaugirard, 15e (servicing the west, with trains to Brittany); **Gare du Nord,** 18, rue de Dunkerque, 15e (servicing the north with trains to Holland, Denmark, Belgium, and the north of Germany); and **Gare St-Lazare,** 13, rue d'Amsterdam, 8e (servicing the northwest, with trains to Normandy).

For general train information from any of these stations, call 45-82-50-50 from 7am to 10pm daily. To make reservations, call 45-65-60-60 daily from 8am to 8pm. Buses operate between stations.

Note: The stations and the surrounding areas are usually seedy and frequented by pickpockets, hustlers, hookers, and drug addicts. Be alert, especially at night.

Each of these stations also has a Métro stop, making the whole city easily accessible. Taxis are also available at every station at designated stands. Look for the sign that says TETE DE STATION.

BY BUS

Most buses arrive at La Gare Routière Internationale, 3, av. Porte-de-la-Villette, 19e (tel. 40-38-93-93; Métro: Stalingrad).

BY CAR

Driving a car in Paris is definitely not recommended. Parking is difficult and traffic is dense. If you do drive, remember that Paris is encircled by a ring road called the

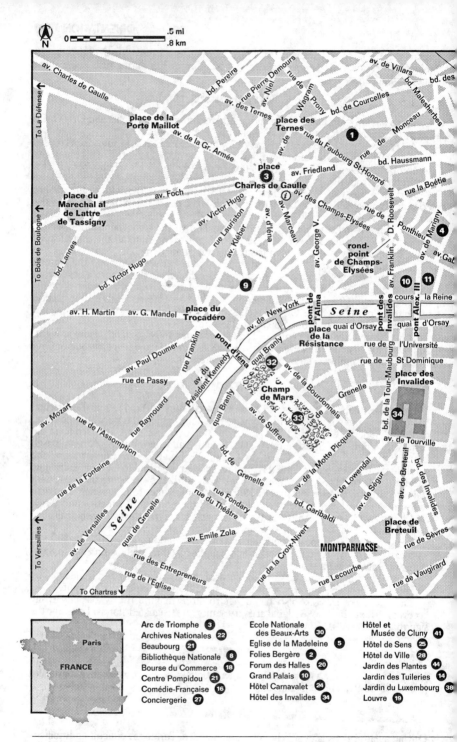

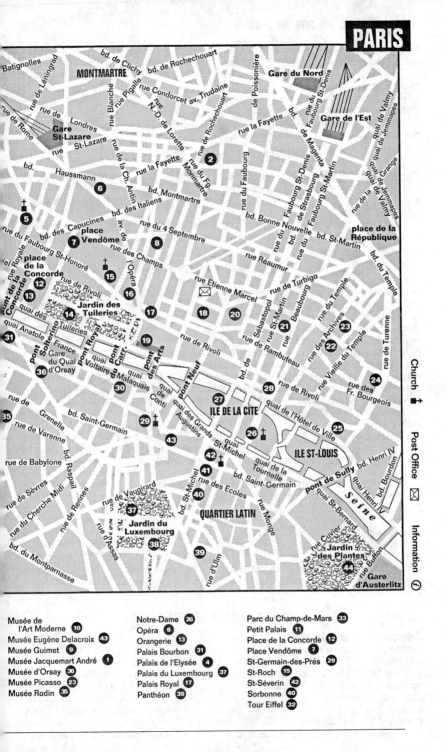

PARIS

MONTMARTRE

bd. de Clichy
bd. de Rochechouart

Batignolles

Gare du Nord

Gare de l'Est

rue de Leningrad
rue de Rome

rue de Londres
Gare St-Lazare
rue St-Lazare

rue Blanche
rue Pigalle
rue Condorcet
av. Trudaine

rue N. D. de Lorette
rue Fontaine

rue du Faubourg Montmartre

rue la Fayette
rue du Faubourg

de Poissonière
Faubourg St-Denis
Faubourg St-Denis
de Strasbourg
rue du Faubourg St-Martin
de Magenta

quai de Valmy
quai de Jemmapes
quai de Grange
rue de la Grange
quai de Valmy

bd. Haussmann

rue de la Ch. Antin

bd. Montmartre

bd. des Italiens

bd. Bonne Nouvelle
bd. St-Martin

place de la République

rue du Temple
bd. du Temple

† 5

bd. des Capucines

place Vendôme 7

rue de la Paix
av. de l'Opéra

rue du 4 Septembre

8

rue Réaumur

rue du Faubourg St-Honoré
rue Royale

place de la Concorde

2

† 15

rue de Rivoli
16

rue Etienne Marcel

17
Jardin des Tuileries
14
quai des Tuileries

18   20

rue de Turbigo

rue de Rambuteau
Sébastopol
rue St-Martin
Beaubourg
21

rue des Archives
23

rue du Temple
22

rue de Turenne

pont de la Concorde
12
13

31
quai Anatole France
quai Voltaire
Gare du Quai d'Orsay
36

Solferino
pont Royal
19
quai du Louvre
pont du Carr.
pont des Arts
30
quai Malaquais
pont Neuf
quai de Conti

rue de Rivoli
rue de la Vieille du Temple
24
rue des Fr. Bourgeois

35
rue de Grenelle
rue de Varenne

bd. Saint-Germain

29
43

27
ILE DE LA CITE
quai de l'Hôtel de Ville
28
quai des Grands Augustins
26 †
quai St-Michel
42 †
ILE ST-LOUIS
25

rue de Babylone

rue de Sèvres

rue du Cherche Midi
bd. Raspail
rue de Rennes
rue de Vaugirard

41
rue des Ecoles
40
bd. St-Michel
quai de la Tournelle
bd. Saint-Germain
rue Monge

pont de Sully
bd. Henri IV
quai Henri IV
bd. Bourdon

Seine

37
Jardin du Luxembourg
38

QUARTIER LATIN

39
rue d'Ulm

rue de Vaugirard
rue d'Assas

bd. du Montparnasse

rue Cuvier
Jardin des Plantes
rue Buffon
44
Gare d'Austerlitz

quai St-Bernard

Church ∎†

Post Office ⊠

Information ⑦

Musée de l'Art Moderne 10	Notre-Dame 26	Parc du Champ-de-Mars 33
Musée Eugène Delacroix 43	Opéra 6	Petit Palais 11
Musée Guimet 9	Orangerie 13	Place de la Concorde 12
Musée Jacquemart André 1	Palais Bourbon 31	Place Vendôme 7
Musée d'Orsay 36	Palais de l'Elysée 4	St-Germain-des-Prés 29
Musée Picasso 23	Palais du Luxembourg 37	St-Roch 15
Musée Rodin 35	Palais Royal 17	St-Séverin 42
	Panthéon 39	Sorbonne 40
		Tour Eiffel 32

périphérique. Always obtain detailed directions to your destination, including the name of the exit on the périphérique (exits are not numbered). Avoid rush hours.

Few hotels, except the luxury ones, have garages, but the staff will usually be able to direct you to one nearby.

The major highways into Paris are the A1 from the north (Great Britain and Benelux); the A13 from Rouen, Normandy, and other points of northwest France; the A109 from Spain, the Pyrénées, and the southwest; the A7 from the French Alps, the Riviera, and Italy; and the A4 from eastern France.

TOURIST INFORMATION

The main **tourist information office** is at 127, av. des Champs-Elysées, 8e (tel. 1/49-52-53-54), where you can secure information about both Paris and the provinces. The office is open daily from 9am to 8pm. For information 24 hours a day, call 1/47-80-88-98.

Welcome Offices in the city center will also give you free maps, brochures, and *Paris Monthly Information,* an English-language listing of all current events and performances.

CITY LAYOUT

In the north-central section of France, Paris is France's largest city, and its industrial and commercial hub, that grew up in the fertile farmland of the Seine Valley. The river Seine divides Paris into the **Right Bank** (Rive Droite) to the north and the **Left Bank** (Rive Gauche) to the south. These designations make sense when you stand on a bridge and face downstream, watching the waters flow out toward the sea—to your right is the north bank; the south is on your left. Thirty-two bridges link the Right and Left Banks, some providing access to the two small islands at the heart of the city, **Ile de la Cité**—the city's birthplace and site of Notre-Dame—and **Ile St-Louis,** a moat-guarded oasis of sober 17th-century mansions. These islands can cause some confusion to walkers who think they've just crossed a bridge from one bank to the other, only to find themselves caught up in an almost medieval maze of narrow streets and old buildings.

The best way to orient yourself is to climb the Eiffel Tower or the Arc de Triomphe and look around. From the top of the Eiffel Tower you can see the whole of Paris in one giant panorama. The view from the top of the Arc de Triomphe is more detailed. Twelve avenues radiate from place de l'Etoile (renamed place Charles-de-Gaulle), sweeping across the city streets, linking the arch, like giant wheel spokes, with place de la Concorde down the Champs-Elysées, the Bois de Boulogne to the west, and the Palais de Chaillot to the south.

For further orientation, take a boat ride on the Seine, preferably on a sunny day when you can sit out on deck. Tune out the babble around you and the recorded guide in four languages. Specific buildings aren't the point—and, besides, you can hardly mistake the luminous towers of Notre-Dame. Just sit back and take in Paris: the quay where Voltaire worked and died, the gargoyles, the golden horses on the stanchions of Pont Alexandre III, the clusters of students on the riverbanks—all essential pieces of a Parisian landscape.

MAIN ARTERIES & STREETS

Between 1860 and 1870 Baron Haussmann forever changed the look of Paris by creating the legendary **boulevards:** boulevards St-Michel, St-Germain, Haussmann, Malesherbes, Sébastopol, Magenta, Voltaire, and Strasbourg.

The "main street" on the Right Bank is, of course, the **Champs-Elysées,** beginning at the Arc de Triomphe and running to place de la Concorde. Haussmann also created avenue de l'Opéra (as well as the Opéra), and the 12 avenues that radiate starlike from the Arc de Triomphe giving it its original name, place de l'Etoile (renamed place Charles-de-Gaulle following the general's death).

Haussmann also cleared Ile de la Cité of its medieval buildings, transforming it into a showcase for Notre-Dame Cathedral. Finally, he laid out the two elegant parks on the western and southeastern fringes of the city: **Bois de Boulogne** and **Bois de Vincennes.**

MAPS If you're staying more than two or three days, purchase a pocket-size "bible" to the streets of Paris, *Plan de Paris par Arrondissement,* available at all major newsstands and bookshops. It not only has a detailed map of each arrondissement, but also gives bus lines, an alphabetized index of Paris streets, and the nearest Métro stops.

ARRONDISSEMENTS IN BRIEF

Paris is divided into 20 districts, or *arrondissements,* each possessing a unique style and flavor. One of your first tasks will be deciding which district appeals most to you and finding accommodations there. Then try and visit as many areas as you can.

City maps show arrondissements, and all addresses include the arrondissement number (written in Roman or Arabic numerals followed by "e" or "er"). Paris also has its own version of a ZIP Code. The proper mailing address for a hotel or restaurant is written, for example, "75014 Paris." The last two digits, the 1 and 4, indicate that the address is in the 14th arrondissement (Montparnasse).

You won't spend time in every arrondissement, but here's a brief rundown of each one:

1st Arr. Located on the Right Bank, the 1st has the most popular attractions, including the Louvre, the Forum des Halles (now transformed into a modern shopping mall), Sainte Chapelle, Conciergerie, and the Jardin des Tuileries. Two of the most prestigious addresses are place Vendôme (site of the Ritz Hotel) and Palais Royal, a section of elegant buildings and galleries surrounding the gardens to the north.

2nd Arr. Home to the Bourse, or stock exchange, the 2nd is in fact primarily a working-class district. Highlights include rue de la Paix, a traditional street of goldsmiths and furriers, and the Bibliothèque Nationale. The district lies mainly between the Grands Boulevards and rue Etienne-Marcel.

3rd Arr. This embraces much of Le Marais ("the marsh"), one of the best-loved neighborhoods of Paris. Many of the buildings date from the Middle Ages, and much of the old has been saved and restored. Highlights include the Picasso Museum.

4th Arr. This area contains the Hôtel de Ville (city hall) and such major attractions as Notre-Dame, the Centre Pompidou, and place des Vosges, site of the Victor Hugo Museum. It also includes Ile Saint-Louis with its aristocratic town houses, courtyards, and antique shops.

5th Arr. Known as the Latin Quarter, its attractions include the Sorbonne, the Panthéon, the Musée de Cluny, and the Jardin des Plantes. When people refer to the Left Bank they usually mean the 5th and 6th arrondissements—an area filled with students, cafés, bistros, and street life.

6th Arr. This is the heartland of Paris publishing and, for some, the most colorful part of the Left Bank. Waves of earnest young artists can be seen emerging from the Ecole des Beaux-Arts. This is one of the best areas for good budget hotels and restaurants. Highlights include the Jardin du Luxembourg and place Saint-Germain-des-Prés.

7th Arr. The home of the Eiffel Tower is primarily an upscale residential and government-diplomatic area. Other highlights include Napoléon's Tomb and the Invalides Army Museum. Next to the Invalides is the city air terminal.

8th Arr. The 8th is the heart of the Right Bank and its prime showcase is the Champs-Elysées, linking the Arc de Triomphe and place de la Concorde. Here you'll find the fashion houses, the most elegant hotels, expensive restaurants and shops, and the most fashionably attired Parisians. Other landmarks include the Palais de l'Elysée, home of the French president; the Church of the Madeleine; the Faubourg Saint-Honoré; and the Parc de Monceau.

9th Arr. Visited primarily because of its Grands Boulevards, such as boulevard des Capucines and boulevard des Italiens, the 9th also includes the Quartier de l'Opéra and the strip joints of Pigalle (the infamous "pig alley" for the G.I.s of World

War II). Other major attractions are the Musée Grevin (the major waxworks of Paris) and the Folies Bergère.

10th Arr. The Gare du Nord and Gare de l'Est are both in this commercial district. Movie theaters and porno houses dot some of this area.

11th Arr. Increasingly fashionable, this is the site of place de la Bastille and the new Bastille opera house. For many decades, it has been a working-class district, attracting new immigrants from all over the world.

12th Arr. Very few tourists come here, but when a famous French chef opened the restaurant Au Trou Gascon, *tout le monde* showed up (see Chapter 6, "Paris Dining"). Its major attraction is the Bois de Vincennes, a popular patch of woodland with boating lakes, a racecourse, and a zoo. The Gare de Lyon is located here, too.

13th Arr. This primarily working-class district grew up around the famous Gobelin tapestries works, which can still be visited today (see the listing for Les Gobelins in "More Museums" in Chapter 7). The Gare d'Austerlitz is a landmark.

14th Arr. Montparnasse, home of the "lost generation," is well known to tourists. Stein, Toklas, Hemingway, and other American expatriates gathered here in the 1920s. After World War II it ceased to be the center of intellectual life in Paris, but the memory lingers on in its cafés.

15th Arr. Beginning at Gare Montparnasse, the 15th stretches all the way to the Seine. In land mass and population, it's the largest *quartier* of Paris, but it attracts few tourists and has few attractions, except for the Parc des Expositions and the Institut Pasteur. In the early 20th century, many artists—Chagall, Léger, and Modigliani—lived in this arrondissement in "The Beehive."

16th Arr. Originally the village of Passy, where Benjamin Franklin lived most of his years in Paris, this district is still reminiscent of Proust's world. Highlights include the Bois de Boulogne, the Jardin du Trocadéro, the Musée de Balzac, the Musée Guimet (famous for its Oriental collections), and the Cimetiére de Passy, resting place of Manet, Talleyrand, Giraudoux, and Debussy.

17th Arr. Although partly in the 8th, Parc Monceau flows into the 17th. This is the home of the Palais des Congrès and Porte Maillot Air Terminal.

18th Arr. The 18th is the most famous outer *quartier* of Paris, embracing Montmartre, associated with such legendary names as the Moulin Rouge, Basilica of Sacré-Coeur, and place du Tertre. Originally a village, Montmartre became the Parisian symbol for art at the turn of the century. Utrillo was its native son, Renoir lived here, and Toulouse-Lautrec adopted the area as his own. The most famous enclave of artists in Paris, Le Bateau-Lavoir, of Picasso fame, gathered here. Max Jacob, Matisse, and Braque all came and went from here. Today place Blanche is known for its prostitutes, and Montmartre is filled with honky tonks and terrible restaurants. Go for the attractions and the *mémoires*. The most famous flea market, Marché aux Puces de Saint-Ouen, is another landmark.

19th Arr. Today visitors come to what was once the village of La Villette to see the new Cité des Sciences et de l'Industrie, a spectacular science museum and park. The district also includes Les Buttes-Chaumont, a park where kids can enjoy puppet shows and donkey rides.

20th Arr. Its greatest landmark is Père Lachaise Cemetery, resting place of Edith Piaf, Marcel Proust, Oscar Wilde, Isadora Duncan, Sarah Bernhardt, Gertrude Stein, Colette, and many, many others.

2. GETTING AROUND

BY METRO

Easy to use, the Métro (tel. 43-46-14-14 for information) is the most efficient and fastest means of transportation in Paris. Each line is numbered, and the final destination of line is clearly marked on subway maps, in the underground passageways, and on the train cars, themselves.

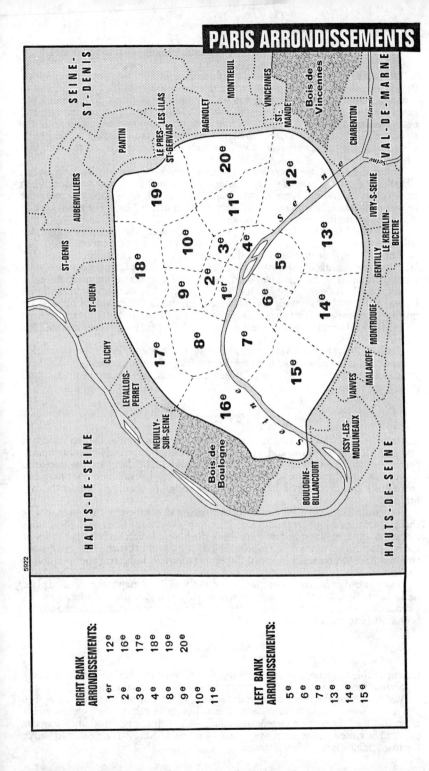

PARIS ARRONDISSEMENTS

RIGHT BANK ARRONDISSEMENTS:

1er	12e
2e	16e
3e	17e
4e	18e
8e	19e
9e	20e
10e	
11e	

LEFT BANK ARRONDISSEMENTS:

5e
6e
7e
13e
14e
15e

5922

The Métro runs daily from 5:30am to around 1:15am. It's reasonably safe at any hour, but beware of pickpockets.

Métro Maps Most stations display a map of the métro system at the entrance. By studying the map, figure out the route to your destination; it's very important to note the station (or stations) where you will have to change trains. To make sure you catch the correct train, find your destination, then follow the rail line it's on to the end of the route, and note the name of the final destination—this final stop is the *direction*. To find your train in the station, you follow the signs labeled with your *direction* in the passageways and you'll see your *direction* labeled on the train that you'll take, too.

Transfer stations are known as *correspondances*—some require long walks, Châtelet is the most difficult—but most trips will require only one transfer. When transferring, follow the bright-orange CORRESPONDANCE signs until you reach the proper platform. Don't follow a SORTIE sign (which means "Exit") or you'll have to pay another fare to resume your journey.

Many of the larger stations have easy-to-use maps with pushbutton indicators that will light up your route when you press the button for your destination.

Fares On the urban lines, it costs the same to any point. One ticket costs 5.50 F ($1). On the Sceaux, the Boissy-Saint-Léger, and the Saint-Germain-en-Laye lines serving the suburbs, fares are based on distance. When purchasing métro tickets, a *carnet* is the best buy—10 tickets for 34.50 F ($6.20). You can also purchase a pass known as *Formule 1* allowing unlimited travel on the city's network of subways for one day; the cost of a *Formule 1* pass depends on the number of zones ranging from 23 F ($4.10) for zones 1 and 2 all the way up to 70 F ($12.60) for all zones and the Paris airports.

Ticket Protocol At the turnstile entrances to the station, insert your ticket in the turnstile and pass through. At some exits tickets are also checked, so hold on to your ticket. There are occasional ticket checks on the trains, platforms, and passageways, too.

BY BUS

Bus travel is much slower than the subway. Most buses run from 6:30am to 9:15pm (a few operate until 12:30am, and a handful operate during the early-morning hours). Service is limited on Sunday and holidays. Bus and Métro fares are the same and you can use the same *carnet* tickets on both. Most bus rides require one ticket, but there are some destinations requiring two (never more than two within the city limits).

At certain bus stops signs list the destinations and numbers of the buses serving that point. Destinations are usually listed north to south, and east to west. Most stops along the way are also posted on the sides of the buses. To catch a bus, wait in line at the bus stop. Signal to the driver to stop the bus and board in order. During rush hour you may have to take a ticket from a dispensing machine, indicating your position in the line.

If you intend to use the buses a lot, pick up an RATP bus map at the office on place de la Madeleine, 8e; at the tourist offices at RATP headquarters, 53 bis, quai des Grands Augustins, 75006 Paris; or write ahead of time. For detailed information on bus and Métro routes, call 43-46-14-14.

BY TAXI

It's impossible to secure one at rush hour, so don't even try. Taxi drivers are strongly organized into an effective lobby to keep their number limited to 14,300.

Watch out for the common rip-offs. Always check out the meter to make sure you're not paying the previous passenger's fare. Beware of cabs without meters, which often wait for tipsy patrons outside nightclubs—or settle the tab in advance. Regular cabs can be hailed on the street when their signs read LIBRE. Taxis are easier to find at the many stands near Métro stations.

DISCOUNT PASSES

If you're staying in Paris for a week or longer, purchase one of several long-term passes, which allows unlimited travel on the city's Métro and buses within Paris city limits. A six-day pass (*coupon jaune*) costs 54 F ($9.70); a monthly pass (*carte orange*) costs 190 F ($34.20). These passes are available at any Métro ticket counter; you must have a photo ID to apply for the passes.

Another possibility is to purchase a *Le Paris-Visite* pass, a tourist pass valid for three or five days on the public transportation system—including the Métro, city buses, even RER trains. (The RER trains have both first- and second-class compartments, and the pass allows you to travel in first class.)

Prices of *Le Paris-Visite* passes vary according to the number of zones. The pass for all zones costs 150 F ($27) for three days or 185 F ($33.30) for five days. *Le Paris-Visite* passes are sold at all major métro stations, as well as at the Tourism Office of the RATP, 53 bis, quai des Grands-Augustins, 6e; and the Paris Convention and Visitors Bureau, 127, av. des Champs-Elysées, 8e.

The flag drops at 10 F ($1.80), and you pay 2.80 F (50¢) per kilometer from 7am to 7:30pm. At night, expect to pay 4.20 F (80¢) per kilometer.

On airport trips you're not required to pay for the driver's empty return ride, but you'll pay 4 F (70¢) extra to be delivered to railroad stations.

You are allowed several small pieces of luggage free if they're transported inside and don't weigh more than 5kg (12 lb.). Heavier suitcases carried in the trunk cost 4 F (70¢) per piece. Tip 12%–15%—the latter usually elicits a *merci*.

BY CAR

Don't even consider driving a car in Paris. Streets are narrow and parking is next to impossible. Besides, most visitors don't have the nerve, skill, and ruthlessness required.

If you insist on ignoring my advice, here are a few tips: Get an excellent street map and ride with a co-pilot because there's no time to think at intersections. "Zone Bleue" means that you can't park without a parking disc, obtainable from garages, police stations, and hotels. Parking is unlimited in these zones on Sunday and holidays. Attach the disc to your windshield, setting its clock to show the time of arrival. Between 9am and noon and from 2:30 to 5pm you may park for 1 hour, from noon to 2:30pm for 2½ hours.

The driver and all passengers (front and back) must wear seatbelts. Children under 12 years old must ride in the back seat. Drivers are supposed to yield to the car on the right, except where signs indicate otherwise, as at traffic circles.

Watch for the gendarmes, who lack patience and consistently countermand the lights. Horn-blowing is absolutely forbidden except in dire emergencies.

To take advantage of the discounts offered by the major U.S.–based firms, rent your car before your trip. See "Getting Around" in Chapter 3 for details.

BY BICYCLE

It's tough to negotiate the narrow, traffic-clogged streets filled with mean-spirited motorists who don't look kindly upon tourists on bikes. Save your cycling for the Bois de Boulogne or another park.

Paris-Vélo, 2, rue du Fer-à-Moulin, 5e (tel. 43-37-59-22; Métro: St-Marcel), rents bicycles for 90–140 F ($16.20–$25.20) a day, but you must post a deposit of 1,000 F ($180), which includes accident insurance.

Bicyclub, 8, place de la Porte-Champerret, 17e (tel. 47-66-55-92; Métro: Porte-de-Champerret), also rents bicycles by the hour, charging from 25 F ($4.50) per hour depending on the bike. A deposit of 1,000 F ($180) is required.

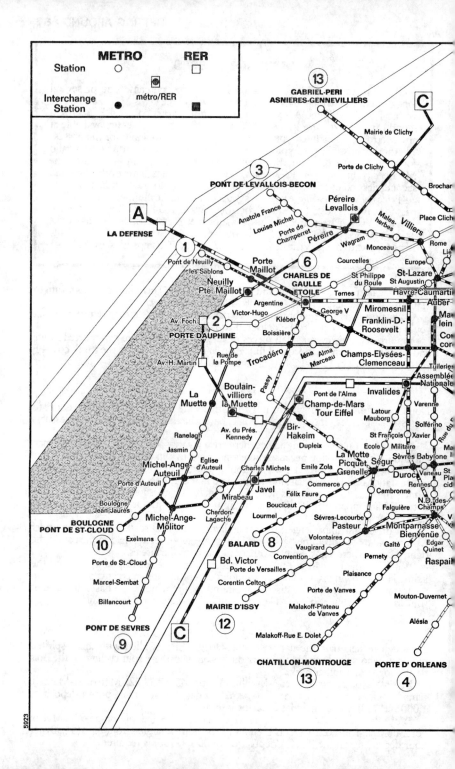

PARIS METRO AND RER

ON FOOT

Walking is absolutely the best way to explore and get to know the city intimately. Paris is a walker's paradise; and in Chapter 8, I've outlined several tours to get you started.

FAST FACTS *PARIS*

For additional practical information see "Fast Facts: France" in Chapter **3**.

American Express   With a grand Paris office, American Express, **11**, rue Scribe, 9e (tel. 47-77-77-07; Métro: Opéra, Chaussée-d'Antin, or Havre-Caumartin; RER: Auber), is extremely busy with customers buying and cashing traveler's checks (not the best rates for exchange transactions), picking up mail, and solving travel problems. They are open Monday through Friday from 9am to 5:30pm; the bank is also open on Saturday (same hours), but the mail pickup window is closed. Other, less busy American Express offices are located at 5, rue de Chaillot, 16e (tel. 47-23-61-20; Métro: Alma-Marceau or Iéna); 83 bis, rue de Courcelles, 17e (tel. 47-66-03-00; Métro: Courcelles); and 38, av. de Wagram, 8e (tel. 42-27-58-80; Métro: Ternes).

Area Code   Paris's telephone area code is 01, followed by an eight-digit number.

Babysitters   There are several agencies available, but first verify that the sitter and your child speak the same language before you commit yourself. Institut Catholique, 21, rue d'Assas, 6e (tel. 44-39-52-35), runs a service staffed by students. The price is 30 F ($5.40) an hour. The main office is open Monday through Friday from 9am to noon and 2 to 6pm.

Bookstores   Paris has several English-language bookstores carrying American and English books and maps and guides to the city and other destinations. Try Brentano's, 37, av. de l'Opéra, 2e (tel. 42-61-52-50; Métro: Opéra), open Monday through Saturday 10am to 7pm; or Galignani, 224, rue de Rivoli, 1e (tel. 42-60-76-07; Métro: Tuileries), open Monday through Saturday from 10am to 7pm. Galignani has French and English books of general interest and an especially fine international fine arts department. Most famous of all is Shakespeare and Company, 37, rue de la Bûcherie, 5e (no phone; Métro or RER: St-Michel). It's open daily from 11am to midnight.

Car Rentals   See "Getting Around" in Chapter 3.

Climate   See "When to Go" in Chapter 2.

Currency Exchange   American Express can fill most of your banking needs. Most banks in Paris are open Monday through Friday from 9am to 4:30pm, but only a few are open on Saturday; ask at your hotel for the location of the one nearest you. For the best exchange rate, cash your traveler's checks at banks or foreign-exchange offices, not at shops and hotels. Most post offices will also change traveler's checks or convert currency. Currency exchanges are also found at Paris airports and train stations. One of the most central currency-exchange branches in Paris is 154, av. des Champs-Elysées, 8e (tel. 42-25-93-33; Métro: George-V or Place-de-l'Etoile). It's open Monday through Friday from 9am to 5pm and on Saturday and Sunday from 10:30am to 6pm. A small commission is charged.

Dentist   For emergency dental service, call 43-37-51-00 Monday through Friday from 8pm to 8am. On holidays and weekends you can call this number 24 hours. The American Hospital, 63, bd. Victor-Hugo, Neuilly (tel. 46-41-25-25; Métro: Pont de Levallois or Pont de Neuilly), operates a bilingual (English-French) dental clinic, open 24 hours a day.

Doctors   Some large hotels have a doctor on staff. If yours doesn't, try the American Hospital, 63, bd. Victor-Hugo, Neuilly (tel. 46-41-25-25; Métro: Pont de Levallois or Pont de Neuilly), which operates a 24-hour emergency service. Blue Cross and other American insurance are accepted by their bilingual staff.

Drugstores   To locate one after regular hours, have your concierge contact the Commissariat de Police for the nearest 24-hour pharmacy. French law requires that one pharmacy in any given neighborhood stay open 24 hours. You'll find the address posted on the doors or windows of all other drugstores. One of the most centrally located all-night pharmacies is Pharmacy Dhery, 84, av. des Champs-Elysées, 8e (tel. 45-62-02-41; Métro: George-V).

Embassies and Consulates   See "Fast Facts: France" in Chapter 3.

Emergencies   For the **police,** call 17; to **report a fire,** 18. For an **ambulance,** call the fire department at 45-78-74-52; a fire vehicle rushes cases to the nearest emergency room. S.A.M.U. (tel. 45-67-50-50) is an independently operated, privately owned ambulance company. You can reach the police at 9, bd. du Palais, 4e (tel. 42-60-33-22; Métro: Cité).

Eyeglasses   Lissac Brothers (Frères Lissac) is one of the city's largest chains, with at least 18 branches in greater Paris. On the Right Bank, go to 112-114, rue de Rivoli, 1e (tel. 42-33-44-77; Métro: Louvre), and on the Left, to 51, bd. St-Michel, 5e (tel. 43-54-24-07; Métro: St-Michel). There's a surcharge for same-day service. Always carry an extra pair.

Hairdressers/Barbers   In France, they're known as *coiffeurs.* One of the best is Alexandre de Paris, 3, av. Matignon, 8e (tel. 42-25-57-90; Métro: F-D-Roosevelt). Everybody from crowned heads to French film stars comes here for that elegant look. Always call for an appointment. Harlow, 24, rue St-Denis, 1er (tel. 42-33-61-36; Métro: Châtelet), is also good. As one satisfied customer put it, "Harlow is with it and yet not too far out." The team specializes in coiffures calling for minimum care. An appointment is needed.

Holidays   See "When to Go" in Chapter 2.

Hospitals   The American Hospital, 63, bd. Victor-Hugo, Neuilly (tel. 46-41-25-25), operates 24-hour emergency service.

Information   See "Tourist Information" in "Orientation," above, in this chapter.

Laundry/Dry Cleaning   Ask at your hotel for the nearest laundry or dry-cleaning establishment. Expensive hotels provide this service, but it costs. Instead, consult the *Yellow Pages* under *laveries automatiques;* for dry cleaning, look under *nettoyage à sec.* If you're staying in the Latin Quarter, take your clothes for cleaning to St-Germain Lav' Club, 9, rue Lobineau, 6e (Métro: Mabillon). Don't call—just show up, dirty laundry in hand. It's open daily from 7am to 10pm.

Libraries   There are many. The American Library, 10, rue du Général-Camou, 7e (tel. 45-51-46-82; Métro: Alma-Marceau), founded in 1920, allows nonmembers to read for 50 F ($9) per day. Hours are Tuesday through Saturday from 10am to 7pm. Bibliothèque Publique Information, 19, rue Beaubourg, 3e (tel. 44-78-12-33; Métro: Rambuteau), has books in English. There's also a video and listening room. You can read on the premises, but you can't check out books. It's open Monday through Friday from noon to 10pm and on Saturday and Sunday from 10am to 10pm.

Lost Property   Frankly, there isn't much chance of retrieving lost property in Paris. Go to (don't call) the Bureau des Objets Trouvés, 36, rue des Morillons, 15e (tel. 45-31-14-80; Métro: Convention). Open in summer Friday through Monday from 8:30am to 5pm and Tuesday through Thursday from 8am to 8pm. In July and August and from December 20 through 31, the longer hours on Tuesday and Thursday are not observed.

Luggage Storage/Lockers   Your best bet is your hotel, especially if you plan to return to Paris after a tour of the provinces. Most hotels will store luggage for you.

Mail   See "Post Office," below.

Newspapers/Magazines   English-language newspapers, including the latest editions of *Time, Newsweek, USA Today,* and the *International Herald Tribune* (published Monday through Saturday) are available at nearly every kiosk/newsstand. Kiosks are generally open daily from 8am to 9pm.

Photographic Needs   All types of film are available in Paris at fairly modest prices. Unless you're going to be in France for an extended period, I don't recommend that you process your film here, for it takes time. Ask at your hotel for the nearest camera and photographic accessory store.

Police   Call 17. The principal Prefecture is at 7, bd. du Palais, 4e (tel. 42-60-33-22; Métro: Cité).

Post Office   The main post office (P.T.T.) for Paris is Bureau de Poste, 52, rue du Louvre, 75001 Paris (tel. 40-28-20-00; Métro: Louvre). Your mail can be sent here *poste restante* (general delivery) for a small fee. Take an ID, such as a passport, if you plan to pick up mail. It's open daily from 8am to 7pm for most services, 24 hours a day for telegrams and phone calls. For postage rates, see "Fast Facts: France" in Chapter 3.

Radio/TV   See "Fast Facts: France" in Chapter 3.

Religious Services   France is a predominantly Roman Catholic country, and churches of this faith are found in every city and town. Many churches in Paris conduct services in English: the nondenominational American Church in Paris, 65, quai d'Orsay, 7e (tel. 47-05-07-99; Métro: Invalides); the First Church of Christ Scientist, 36, bd. St-Jacques, 14e (tel. 47-07-26-60; Métro: St-Jacques); Second Church of Christ Scientist, 58, bd. Flandrin, 16e (tel. 45-04-37-74; Métro: Dauphine); and the Third Church of Christ Scientist, 36, rue La Bruyère, 9e (tel. 45-62-19-85; Métro: St-Georges). The Great Synagogue is at 44, rue de la Victoire, 9e (tel. 42-85-71-09; Métro: La Peletier). An English-speaking Roman Catholic church is St. Joseph's, 50, av. Hoche, 8e (tel. 42-27-28-56; Métro: Charles-de-Gaulle).

Restrooms   See "Fast Facts: France" in Chapter 3.

Safety   Beware of child pickpockets. They roam the French capital, preying on tourists around such sites as the Louvre, Eiffel Tower, Notre-Dame, and Montmartre, and they especially like to pick pockets in the Métro, sometimes blocking the entrance and exit to the escalator. A band of these young thieves can clean out your pockets even while you try to fend them off. They'll get very close to you, sometimes ask for a handout, and deftly help themselves to your money, passport, or whatever. Women should hang on to their purses with both hands. Gendarmes advise tourists to carry umbrellas and to keep anyone who looks like a pickpocket an umbrella's length away.

Shoe Repairs   Ask at your hotel for a nearby repair shop or try Central Crepins, 48, rue de Turbigo, 3e (tel. 42-72-68-64; Métro: Etienne-Marcel), which performs at least some of its sewing by hand and does very competent repair work. It's open Monday through Friday. Or try La Cordonnerie Pulin, 5, rue Chaveau-Lagarde, 8e (tel. 42-65-08-57; Métro: Madeleine), open Monday through Saturday; closed August.

Taxes   France's VAT (Value-Added Tax) should already be included in the cost of items you buy. The rate varies depending on the item—it can be as high as 33.33%. You can get a tax refund on purchases of more than 2,000 F ($360) in a single store. Ask the shopkeeper to make out an export sales invoice (*bordereau*), which you show to the French Customs officer when you leave the country (at the airport, on the train, at the highway border post). In a number of weeks the shop will send you a check for the amount of the refund. Not all shops participate in the program. Ask before you buy.

Telegrams/Telex   Telegrams may be sent from any Paris post office during the day (see "Post Office," above) and anytime from the 24-hour central post office. In telegrams to the United States, the address is counted in the price, there are no special rates for a certain number of words, and night telegrams cost less. If you're in Paris and wish to send a telegram in English, call 42-33-44-11. The 24-hour public Telex office in Paris is at 103, rue de Grenelle, 7e (tel. 45-50-34-34; Métro: rue-du-Bac). By phone, you can dictate a Telex by calling 42-47-12-12. You can also send Telex and fax messages at the main post office in each arrondissement of Paris.

Transit Information   For information on the city's public transportation, stop in at either of the two offices of the Services Touristiques de la RATP—at 53 bis, quai des Grands-Augustins, 6e (Métro: St-Michel), or at place de la Madeleine, 8e (Métro: Madeleine)—or call 43-46-14-14.

Weather   Call 36-69-00-00.

CHAPTER 5

PARIS ACCOMMODATIONS

1. **VERY EXPENSIVE**
- **FROMMER'S SMART TRAVELER: HOTELS**
2. **8TH ARR.**
3. **16TH & 17TH ARR.**
- **FROMMER'S COOL FOR KIDS: HOTELS**
4. **1ST ARR.**
5. **2ND & 9TH ARR.**
6. **5TH ARR.**
7. **6TH ARR.**
8. **7TH & 15TH ARR.**
9. **14TH ARR.**
10. **3RD & 4TH ARR.**
11. **18TH ARR.**
12. **AT ORLY AIRPORT**
13. **AT CHARLES DE GAULLE AIRPORT**

There are 1,400 hotels in Paris to choose from, including several that are world famous. If you're willing to pay the price, you can rent some of the finest rooms in Europe. There are many quality hotels at a reasonable price, but most of these are likely to be full, especially in summer. Reserve rooms at least a month in advance at any time of the year; you can send a one-night deposit just to be sure. Another problem you may face is noise: Traffic sounds seem to be amplified by the narrow streets. Late-night revels and early-morning markets may also disturb you. If you're sensitive to noise, request a room in the back, away from the street.

Most hotels offer a continental breakfast, which includes coffee, tea, or hot chocolate; a freshly baked croissant and roll; plus limited quantities of butter and jam or jelly. It's nowhere near as filling as a traditional English or American breakfast, but it has the advantage of being quick to prepare—it'll be at your door moments after you call down for it, and it can be served at almost any hour requested. The word "breakfast" in the following writeups refers to this continental version.

The French word *hôtel* has many meanings. It means a lodging house for transients, of course. But it also means a large mansion or town house, such as the Hôtel des Invalides, originally a home for disabled soldiers (and now a war museum). Hôtel de Ville means town hall. Hôtel des Postes is the general post office, and Hôtel-Dieu is a hospital.

In my list of hotels, I have grouped those following the "Very Expensive" accommodations first by arrondissement and then by price category, from most expensive to least expensive. Service and tax (Value-Added Tax) are included in the rates quoted unless otherwise specified. A continental breakfast often is included in the room tariff, but increasingly you are charged extra, especially in the more expensive hotels. When a breakfast charge is given for an individual listing, it is always a continental breakfast. Breakfasts with eggs, bacon, ham, or other items will have to be ordered from the à la carte menu. For a charge, larger hotels serve the full breakfast—called "English breakfast"—but smaller hotels often serve only the continental variety.

1. VERY EXPENSIVE

LE BRISTOL, 112, rue du Faubourg St-Honoré, 75008 Paris. Tel. 1/42-66-91-45. Fax 1/42-66-68-68. 150 rms (all with bath), 45 suites. A/C MINIBAR TV TEL **Métro:** Miromesnil.

$ Rates: 2,450–2,900 F ($441–$522) single; 3,500–4,150 F ($630–$747) double; 6,250 F ($1,125) suite. Breakfast 140 F ($25.20) extra. AE, DC, MC, V. **Parking:** Free.

⭐ This medium-size palace is near the Palais de l'Elysée (home of the French president) on the shopping street that runs parallel to the Champs-Elysées. Personalized old-world service is rigidly and meticulously maintained. The classic 18th-century Parisian facade has a glass-and-wrought-iron entryway, where guests are greeted by attendants wearing green and red. Hippolyte Jammet founded the Bristol in 1924, installing many valuable antiques and furnishings from the Louis XV and Louis XVI periods. Bedrooms are opulently furnished with showcase antiques or well-made reproductions, inlaid wood, bronze and crystal, Oriental rugs, and original oil paintings. Bathrooms are sumptuously marbled, with separate stall showers, large towels, and lighted magnifying mirrors for makeup or shaving.

Dining/Entertainment: The Restaurant d'Eté (Summer Restaurant) is open from April through October, and the Restaurant d'Hiver (Winter Restaurant) is open the rest of the year. Tea and drinks are served in a large, landscaped, quiet garden in summer.

Services: 24-hour room service, Telex simultaneous translation, audiovisual equipment rental, laundry, valet.

Facilities: Hairdressing salon, massage parlor, sauna, conference rooms, lobby cocktail lounge, heated indoor swimming pool, rooftop solarium with view of Sacré-Coeur (open daily 7am–10pm).

GEORGE V, 31, av. George-V, 75008 Paris. Tel. 1/47-23-54-00. Fax 1/47-20-40-00. 245 rms (all with bath), 53 suites. A/C MINIBAR TV TEL **Métro:** George-V.

$ Rates: 2,600–3,300 F ($468–$594) single; 2,850–3,800 F ($513–$684) double; from 5,500 F ($990) suite. Breakfast 120 F ($21.60) extra. AE, DC, MC, V.

This hotel offers grandiose luxury in a semimodern building on a tree-lined avenue between the Champs-Elysées and the Seine. J. Paul Getty, Darryl Zanuck, and many "simpler folks" from New York and Beverly Hills have felt at home here. In 1944 it was the headquarters for General Eisenhower during the Liberation. At present, it seems to have regained popularity with its "show-biz" atmosphere. According to legend, the George V keeps a secret file of the preferences of its most-favored guests. Perhaps this is the reason that the hotel offers some of the best service in Europe: Every guest has virtually his or her own personal servant.

The public rooms feel like a museum, with rich old tapestries, paintings from the 18th and 19th centuries, and Pompeian inlaid-marble walls. Try to get a room or suite overlooking the courtyard; these rooms have terrace balconies with summer furniture plus urns and boxes overflowing with geraniums.

Dining/Entertainment: In good weather, haute cuisine luncheons are served in the courtyard's garden-style outdoor café/restaurant. The two more formal restaurants of the hotel are Les Princes and Le Grill. Meals average 300–450 F ($54–$81).

Services: Concierge, 24-hour room service, CBS news service, video movies in guest rooms, laundry, valet.

Facilities: Beauty salon, seven conference rooms, tearooms, florist, gift shop.

L'HOTEL, 13, rue des Beaux-Arts, 75006 Paris. Tel. 1/43-25-27-22. Fax 1/43-25-64-81. 24 rms (all with bath), 3 suites. A/C MINIBAR TV TEL **Métro:** St-Germain-des-Prés.

$ Rates: 900–1,100 F ($162–$198) small double, 1,600–2,100 F ($288–$378) large double; from 3,300 F ($594) suite. Breakfast 90 F ($16.20) extra. AE, DC, MC, V.

In the 19th century, the Hôtel d'Alsace was a "flea-bag," attracting down-and-out artists. Oscar Wilde scrawled his last letter here, beseeching Frank Harris to send him the money he owed him, and he gave the hotel a certain reputation by dying here. Today, called l'Hôtel, it attracts well-heeled show-business and fashion personalities. It's on the Left Bank (out-of-bounds for most deluxe Parisian hotels).

Guy-Louis Duboucheron, one of France's favorite actors, opened the hotel because he wanted an intimate, super-sophisticated place of jewel-box proportions. He said, "I wanted it to be like raiding the icebox at home in the middle of the night." Texas architect Robin Westbrook designed the building and supervised much of the decor, gutting the core of the old hotel to make a miniature circular courtyard. Two of the large bedrooms have fireplaces and open onto the garden. Two rooms are conversation pieces: One, facing the rear garden, is where Wilde died; the other holds the original furnishings and memorabilia of Mistinguett, France's legendary stage star. Her pedestal bed is set in the middle of the room, and all her furnishings, including the bed, are covered with mirrors.

Dining/Entertainment: In the enclosed courtyard, site of the bar and restaurant Le Belier, meals are served from silver dishes on a mahogany pedestal. There are travertine bistro tables with bentwood chairs, flowers, brass street lanterns, a waterfall, even caged monkeys and pigeons. In the reception area there's a drinking lounge with paintings and 18th- and 19th-century furniture. Drinks are also served in a vaulted stone cellar, where fine antiques are set in nooks and crannies. There's also a piano bar.

Services: Concierge, 24-hour room service, babysitting.

HOTEL DE CRILLON, 10, place de la Concorde, 75008 Paris. Tel. 1/44-71-15-00. Fax 2/44-71-15-02. 117 rms (all with bath), 46 suites. A/C MINIBAR TV TEL **Métro:** Concorde.

$ Rates: 2,500 F ($450) single; 3,300–3,900 F ($594–$702) double; from 4,750 F ($855) suite. Breakfast 140 F ($25.20) extra. AE, DC, MC, V.

One of the great hotels of Paris, the Crillon is right on place de la Concorde, across from the American Embassy. The 200-year-old building, designed by Gabriel, was once the palace of the duc de Crillon. It has been a hotel since the first decade of this century. Its most famous guest was Woodrow Wilson. Today the Crillon is owned by Jean Taittinger of the Taittinger Champagne family.

The exterior has a long row of classic fluted columns. Inside there are many well-preserved architectural details and both authentic antiques and reproductions. Salons have paneled walls, parquet floors, 17th- and 18th-century tapestries, gilt moldings, gilt-and-brocade furniture, glittering chandeliers, niches with fine sculpture, inlaid desks, and Louis XVI chests and chairs. The hotel surrounds a formal 18th-century courtyard, ideal for drinks or tea. The large courtyard is ringed by flowers. Rooms are large and classically furnished, and bathrooms are lined with travertine or pink marble.

Dining/Entertainment: Les Ambassadeurs serves quality meals in elegant surroundings. An à la carte dinner costs 700 F ($126). The less formal L'Obelisque costs about the same.

Services: 24-hour room service, secretarial and translation service, laundry and valet.

Facilities: Meeting and conference rooms, garden-style courtyard with restaurant service, elevators, shops.

HOTEL MEURICE, 228, rue de Rivoli, 75001 Paris. Tel. 1/44-58-10-10. Fax 1/44-58-10-15. 148 rms (all with bath), 36 suites. A/C MINIBAR TV TEL **Métro:** Tuileries or Concorde.

$ Rates: 2,200–2,500 F ($396–$450) single; 2,500–3,600 F ($450–$648) double; from 5,500 F ($990) suite. Breakfast 120 F ($21.60) extra. AE, DC, MC, V.

The Meurice offers romantic 18th-century surroundings with a French aura. Its gilded salons were copied from those at the château at Versailles, complete with monumental crystal chandeliers, ornate tapestries, and furnishings from the periods of Louis XIV, XV, and XVI. Built in 1907, the hotel is just off rue de Rivoli and the Tuileries Gardens, within walking distance of the Louvre (you can see the Louvre from the upper floors). The lounge has a circular "star"-studded ceiling.

Rooms are soundproof and richly furnished with some period and modern pieces. Fit for a king, they are more likely to house diplomats, industrialists, and successful authors. The self-proclaimed "mad genius" Salvador Dalí made the Meurice his headquarters, occupying Suite 108, which was once used by the deposed and exiled

FROMMER'S SMART TRAVELER: HOTELS

VALUE-CONSCIOUS TRAVELERS SHOULD
CONSIDER THE FOLLOWING:

1. The price you pay in inexpensive hotels depends on the plumbing. Rooms with showers are cheaper than rooms with private baths. Even cheaper is a room with a sink and a *cabinette de toilet* (toilet and bidet). For a bath, you'll have to use the corridor bathroom, but you'll save a lot of money.
2. Take a package tour (or book land arrangements with your air ticket). You'll often pay at least 30% less than individual "rack" rates (off-the-street, independent bookings).
3. Try bargaining. If Paris hotels are full, forget it. But if they're not, a little on-the-spot bargaining can bring down the cost of a hotel room. Be polite. Ask if there's a "businessperson's rate" or if schoolteachers get a discount. This is a face-saving technique. Sometimes it works; sometimes it doesn't. But you can try. The technique is best at night, when the hotel faces up to 40% vacancy and wants to fill some of those empty rooms.
4. At cheaper hotels that take credit cards, ask if payment by cash will get you a reduction.
5. If you're going to spend at least a week in Paris, ask about long-term discounts.

QUESTIONS TO ASK IF YOU'RE ON A BUDGET

1. Is there a garage? What's the charge?
2. Is there a surcharge on either local or long-distance calls? There usually is. In some places, it might be an astonishing 40%. Make your calls at the nearest post office.
3. Is *service compris*? This means, Does the hotel include service in the rates quoted, or will a service charge be added on at the end of your stay?
4. Are all hotel and city taxes included in the price, or will they be added on?
5. Is continental breakfast included in the rates?

king of Spain, Alfonso XIII. Suite 108 also was used as the office of German General von Choltitz, who was in charge of Paris during the Nazi occupation.

Dining/Entertainment: The Meurice Restaurant serves true French haute cuisine. The Pompadour cocktail lounge is ideal for cocktails and tea, and the elegantly renovated Meurice Bar offers drinks in a warm atmosphere.

Services: 24-hour room service, Telex, fax, "solve-everything" concierge.

Facilities: Six meeting rooms, summer outdoor patio.

PARIS INTER-CONTINENTAL, 3, rue de Castiglione, 75001 Paris. Tel. 1/44-77-11-11, or toll free 800/327-0200 in the U.S. and Canada. Fax 1/44-77-14-60. 424 rms (all with bath), 16 suites. A/C MINIBAR TV TEL **Métro:** Concorde.

$ Rates: 1,750–2,300 F ($315–$414) single; 2,500–3,100 F ($450–$558) double; from 4,100 F ($738) suite. Breakfast 95 F ($17.10) extra. AE, DC, MC, V.

The Inter-Continental is a mixture of French tradition, Gallic know-how, and 20th-century modernism. This Belle Epoque hotel is along rue de Rivoli, across from the Tuileries Gardens. Opened in 1878 as "The Continental," it has welcomed many famous guests, including the Empress Eugénie of France and Jean Giraudoux. In 1883 Victor Hugo was the guest of honor at a luncheon. The great inner courtyard, known as "La Cour d'Honneur," is paved with white marble, with a splashing circular fountain and an 1864 statue by Cunny.

The main lounge has Persian carpets, period furnishings, bronze sconces, and marble cocktail tables. The colonnaded front entrance has a pair of bronze candelabra from a palace in St. Petersburg. The rooms and suites are among the finest in Paris. The decor is classic French with many antiques, including Louis XVI reproductions. Each chamber has paneled walls, crystal, fine fruitwoods, bronze hardware, desks, and tables. A radio and in-room movies also are provided. A one-color theme creates a salon effect.

Dining/Entertainment: There is no main dining room, as a survey indicated that guests prefer more intimate character rooms. The Terrasse Fleurie is an elegant gourmet restaurant in the interior courtyard. It's landscaped to depict the four seasons. The Belle Epoque Café Tuileries serves breakfasts, snacks, light meals, informal suppers, cocktails, and French pastries (open until midnight). In fair weather, luncheon, tea, and drinks are served in the courtyard under a canopy. There's also a coffee shop. Estrela, a green-and-gold disco with mirrored walls is open from 10pm to 4am.

Services: 24-hour room service, concierge, secretarial service, fax, CBS news service.

Facilities: Conference rooms, underground parking, Jacuzzis in some suites, health club.

PLAZA ATHENEE, 25, av. Montaigne, 75008 Paris. Tel. 1/47-23-78-33.
Fax 1/47-20-20-70. 169 rms (all with bath), 42 suites. A/C MINIBAR TV TEL **Métro:** F-D-Roosevelt.
$ Rates: 2,660 F ($478.80) single; 2,920 F ($525.60) double; from 4,610 F ($829.80) suite. Breakfast 120 F ($21.60) extra. AE, DC, MC, V.

About half of all the celebrities visiting Paris have been pampered in this palatial hotel; in the old days Mata Hari used to frequent the place. The hotel is halfway between the Champs-Elysées and the Seine on a shady avenue. Arched windows and ornate balconies give it a distinctive pre–World War I style. Liveried attendants greet guests at the formal entrance below a glass shelter. Many guests come from the nearby embassies and centers of haute couture. It is said that there are two employees for each guest in this citadel dedicated to the good life.

You check in at a Louis XVI desk, facing a rare Flemish tapestry. The finest public room is the Montaigne Salon, paneled in rich grained wood and dominated by a marble fireplace. The best rooms overlook a courtyard, with awnings and parasol-shaded tables. Vines climb over inner balconies, and there are formally laid flowerbeds. The well-maintained rooms have ample closet space. The large, tiled bathrooms have double basins and shower.

Dining/Entertainment: Le Régence is a room of handsome period furniture and delicate pink, peach, and gold colors. The food is superb; try the lobster soufflé. For lunch, the Grill Relais Plaza is the meeting place of dress designers and personalities from the worlds of publishing, cinema, and art.

Services: 24-hour room service, sophisticated concierge, laundry, Reuters Telex with international stock quotes.

Facilities: Conference rooms, beauty parlor and hairdresser, massage parlor.

PRINCE DE GALLES, 33, av. George-V, 75008 Paris. Tel. 1/47-23-55-11, or toll free 800/325-3535 in the U.S. and Canada. Fax 1/47-20-96-92. 171 rms (all with bath), 30 suites. A/C MINIBAR TV TEL **Métro:** George-V.
$ Rates: 2,200–2,600 F ($396–$468) single; 2,400–2,800 F ($432–$504) double; from 3,000 F ($540) suite. Breakfast 110 F ($19.80) extra. AE, DC, MC, V.

When this hotel opened in 1927, the art deco/Neo-Byzantine courtyard was the meeting place for the highest level of Paris social life. The courtyard walls are covered with elaborate mosaics that glisten like the background of a painting by Gustave Klimt. In the 1950s, diarist and composer Ned Rorem described the trysts and trials of the "unapproachable innermost snob-life of Paris" that transpired here. The hotel continues to attract high-class patrons. Recently acquired and restored by ITT Sheraton, the palace maintains its impeccable Parisian standards with a hint of American efficiency.

The "Prince of Wales" is a short promenade from the Champs-Elysées, the Arc de Triomphe, and the boutiques of avenue Montaigne. Guests are greeted by uniformed attendants. In the six-sided Regency lobby, French sofas and armchairs are clustered around bouquets of flowers. Rooms are elegantly furnished, spacious, and sunny—with radios and in-room movies provided. The quietest ones overlook the famous courtyard. The comfortable bathrooms have Edwardian/art deco tilework patterned after the hotel's facade. A well-trained staff is eager to respond to requests, including the need for complete privacy.

Dining/Entertainment: The paneled bar, with its leather replicas of 18th-century armchairs, is one of the great hotel bars of Paris. The paneled dining room overlooks the garden-style courtyard with restaurant service.

Services: 24-hour room service, concierge.

Facilities: Conference rooms, elevator, video movies in the guest rooms.

LE RITZ, 15, place Vendôme, 75001 Paris. Tel. 1/42-60-38-30, or toll free 800/223-6800 in the U.S. Fax 1/42-60-23-71. 187 rms (all with bath), 45 suites. A/C MINIBAR TV TEL **Métro:** Opéra.

$ Rates: 2,450–4,150 F ($441–$747) single; 3,350–4,150 F ($603–$747) double; from 5,500 F ($990) suite. Breakfast 170 F ($30.60) extra. AE, DC, MC, V. **Parking:** 150 F ($27).

⭐ The Ritz is the greatest hotel in Europe. This enduring symbol of elegance and chic is located on one of the most beautiful and historic squares in Paris. César Ritz, the "little shepherd boy from Niederwald," converted the Lazun Mansion into a luxury hotel that opened in 1898. With the help of culinary master Escoffier, the Ritz became a miracle of luxury living, attracting some of the great names of the world, including Edward VII of England.

In 1979 the Ritz family sold the hotel to Egyptian businessman Mohamed Al Fayed, who refurbished the hotel and added a cooking school. The Ritz broke tradition by providing a bath with every guest room. Two town houses were annexed, joined by a long arcade lined with miniature display cases representing 125 of the leading boutiques of Paris. The hotel's drawing rooms, salons, three gardens, and courtyards were preserved. The salons are furnished with museum-caliber antiques: gilt pieces, ornate mirrors, Louis XV and Louis XVI furniture, hand-woven tapestries, and 10-foot-high bronze candelabra. The decor of the bathrooms is impeccably French, with wood and marble, antique chests, desks with bronze hardware, and crystal lighting. Every convenience imaginable has been installed in the elaborate bathrooms.

Dining/Entertainment: The Espadon grill room is one of the finest in Paris. The Ritz Club includes a bar, a salon with a fireplace, a restaurant, and a dance floor. Drinks can be ordered in either Bar Vendôme or Bar Hemingway.

Services: Concierge, 24-hour room service, laundry, valet.

Facilities: Luxury health club with swimming pool and massage parlor, florist, shops, three meeting rooms.

ROYAL MONCEAU, 35-39, av. Hoche, 75008 Paris. Tel. 1/45-61-98-00. Fax 1/45-63-28-93. 180 rms (all with bath), 39 suites. A/C MINIBAR TV TEL **Métro:** Charles-de-Gaulle (Etoile).

$ Rates: 1,950–2,550 F ($351–$405) single; 2,350–3,150 F ($423–$567) double; from 4,500 F ($810) suite. Breakfast 130 F ($23.40) extra. AE, DC, MC, V.

This graceful hotel combines the best of French restraint with Gallic flair. Since it was built in 1928, the hotel has had many famous guests, including occupying Nazi officers, Golda Meir, King Farouk, and Ho Chi Minh. General Eisenhower used it as his base in 1944 for planning his final assault on Germany. It's in an upscale neighborhood, with a view of the Arc de Triomphe. The facade is intricately carved, and the entrance is below a translucent art nouveau canopy. In the center of the airy lobby is an oval dome covered with murals of heavenly skies and fluffy clouds creating a canopy over huge bouquets of flowers. The grand scale of the bedrooms was maintained in a sympathetic restoration completed in 1992. Some of the accommodations are the largest hotel bedrooms in Paris. Sometimes an elegant four-poster bed will be set in an alcove; at other times the walls will be hung with moiré silk, with carved bedheads and a marble chimneypiece. Bathrooms are done in marble.

Dining/Entertainment: Le Jardin restaurant is a glassed-in gazebo with rounded walls combining space-age construction with French neoclassicism. In the surrounding courtyard are double tiers of plants, including a 20-foot magnolia and dozens of flowering shrubs. In addition, guests can dine at Le Carpaccio, one of the best restaurants of Paris, with one of the most acclaimed chefs. It's a very chic place for a dinner rendezvous.

Services: Concierge, secretarial service, 24-hour room service, laundry, valet.

Facilities: State-of-the-art health club/gym with sauna, swimming pool, balneotherapy (hydrotherapy), and massage parlor; solarium; golf practice room; hairdressing salon; conference rooms.

2. 8TH ARR.

EXPENSIVE

HOTEL BALZAC, 6, rue Balzac, 75008 Paris. Tel. 1/45-61-97-22. Fax 1/42-25-24-82. 56 rms (all with bath), 14 suites. A/C MINIBAR TV TEL **Métro:** George-V.

$ Rates: 1,380–1,600 F ($248.40–$288) single; 1,800–2,100 F ($324–$378) double; from 3,000 F ($540) suite. Breakfast 90 F ($16.20) extra. AE, DC, MC, V. **Parking:** 140 F ($25.20).

The Belle Epoque Balzac is a fine addition to the 19th-century grandeur of the neighborhood. Popular with the cognoscenti, it's located a few steps from the Champs-Elysées, near the Arc de Triomphe. The decor blends the best of England, Italy, and France. A team of French and Lebanese designers have created sophisticated public rooms that include elements of art deco, Palladian revival, and Neo-Byzantine. The lobby has a sunny atrium with an alcove covered with hand-painted tendrils and vines. Decorations include kilim carpets, plum-colored upholstery, paneling, and antique oil portraits. A glass-walled elevator transports guests to the upper levels past yards of Turkish-patterned carpeting.

The soundproof rooms were recently restored, with marble bathrooms and radios. For dining, I recommend the Bice restaurant (see "Specialty Dining" in Chapter 6). The breakfast room has the same art deco styling as the Bice. Laundry and 24-hour room service are available.

HOTEL ROYAL ALMA, 35, rue Jean-Goujon, 75008 Paris. Tel. 1/42-25-83-30. Fax 1/45-63-68-64. 68 rms (all with bath), 9 suites. MINIBAR TV TEL **Métro:** Alma-Marceau.

$ Rates: 1,155–1,365 F ($207.90–$245.70) single; 1,365–1,600 F ($245.70–$288) double; from 2,000 F ($360) suite. Breakfast 90 F ($16.20) extra. AE, DC, MC, V.

Just a whisker away from the Seine and eight minutes from the Champs-Elysées, this hotel is in the heart of some of the most expensive real estate in Paris. The newly renovated rooms are comfortable but compact, with carpeting and such nice touches as radios and hairdryers. There is a view of Notre-Dame and the Eiffel Tower from the seventh and eighth floors. Near the lobby is a first-class restaurant with an adjoining bar. There is access to nearby parking.

HOTEL VERNET, 25, rue Vernet, 75008 Paris. Tel. 1/47-23-43-10, or toll free 800/832-2791 in the U.S. Fax 1/40-70-10-14. 54 rms (all with bath), 3 suites. A/C MINIBAR TV TEL **Métro:** George-V or Charles-de-Gaulle (Etoile).

$ Rates: 1,450 F ($261) single; 1,800–2,100 F ($324–$378) double; 3,200 F ($576) suite. Continental breakfast 100 F ($18) extra. AE, DC, MC, V. **Parking:** 70 F ($12.60).

Discreet and elegant, and associated with one of Paris's most legendary (and more expensive) hotels, the nearby Royal Monceau, the Vernet was originally built in the beaux arts style around 1890. About a century later it was radically renovated and upgraded. Today its lobby shimmers with beige and pink-toned marble, and its

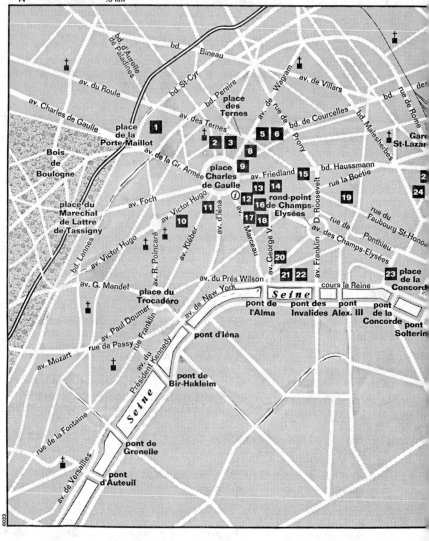

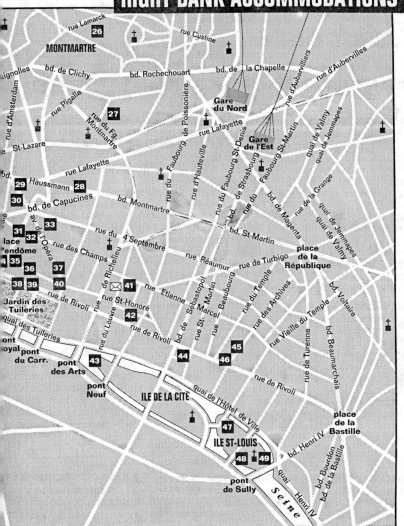

RIGHT BANK ACCOMMODATIONS

MONTMARTRE

rue Lamarck
26

rue Custine

bd. de Clichy
bd. Rochechouart
bd. de la Chapelle

rue Pigalle

27

rue du Fg.
Montmartre

St-Lazare

rue Lafayette

29 Haussmann 28

30

bd. de Capucines

33

31
32

place
vendôme

rue des Champs

rue du 4 Septembre

35

36

37

38 39

40

rue de Rivoli

Jardin des
Tuileries

quai des Tuileries

pont
royal pont
du Carr.

pont des Arts

pont
Neuf

41

rue St-Honoré

42

rue de Rivoli

43

ILE DE LA CITE

44

45

46

Gare
du Nord

Gare
de l'Est

bd. St-Martin

place
de la
République

rue Réaumur
rue de Turbigo

bd. Voltaire

bd. Beaumarchais

rue de Rivoli

quai de l'Hôtel de Ville

47

ILE ST-LOUIS

48   49

pont
de Sully

place
de la
Bastille

bd. Henri IV

Seine

Church ⛪   Post Office ⊠   Information ⓘ

Hotel Regina **40**
Hotel Richmond **28**
Hotel Royal Alma **22**
Hotel Saint-Louis **49**
Hotel de Sèze **29**
Hotel Vernet **12**
Hotel du Vieux Marais **46**
Hotel le Warwick **15**

Hotel Westminster **33**
Lord Byron **14**
Madeleine-Plaza **30**
Le Méridien Paris Etoile **1**
Novotel Paris les Halles **41**
Paris Inter-Continental **36**
Plaza Athénée **5**
Prince de Galles **16**

Raphael **11**
La Regence Etoile **3**
Le Ritz **35**
Royal Monceau **9**
San Regis **21**
Le Stendhal **32**
Tivoli-Etoile **8**

larger-than-you-expected bedrooms are conservatively comfortable mixtures of international inspiration and pastel color schemes.

On the premises is a cozy and secluded bar favored by the neighborhood's cognoscenti, and a sophisticated restaurant, Les Elysées, whose stained-glass dome was designed by Gustave Eiffel himself. Guests of the Vernet enjoy complimentary admission to the spa and beauty facilities at the Royal Monceau.

HOTEL LE WARWICK, 5, rue de Berri, 75008 Paris. Tel. 1/45-63-14-11. Fax 1/45-63-75-81. 137 rms (all with bath), 21 suites. A/C MINIBAR TV TEL **Métro:** George-V.

$ Rates: 1,730–2,030 F ($311.40–$365.40) single; 2,160–2,560 F ($388.80–$460.80) double; from 3,020 F ($543.60) suite. Breakfast 105 F ($18.90) extra. Children under 12 stay free in parents' room. AE, DC, MC, V. **Parking:** 150 F ($27)

This comfortable and elegant modern hotel, built in 1981 at the upper end of the Champs-Elysées, is owned by Hong Kong investors and it shows: Many of the lacquered public rooms are of deep Chinese red, alternating with mirrors and lots of plants. The facade is maroon. It's the favorite of many businesspeople and celebrities, including Boy George, David Bowie, and Grace Jones. The staff is alert and helpful.

About a third of the rooms have evergreen-covered terraces with a view of the Eiffel Tower and the 18th-century buildings across the street. Rooms have soundproof windows, marble bathrooms, in-room movies, and bronze and peach accents. The Swann Bar (after Marcel Proust) offers live piano music and views into the hotel's elegant restaurant (see the listing for La Couronne in "Specialty Dining" in Chapter 6). The hotel has 24-hour room service and laundry and valet service.

SAN REGIS, 12, rue Jean-Goujon, 75008 Paris. Tel. 1/43-59-41-90. Fax 1/45-61-05-48. 44 rms (all with bath), 10 suites. A/C MINIBAR TV TEL **Métro:** Champs-Elysées or F-D-Roosevelt.

$ Rates: 1,325–1,465 F ($238.50–$265.50) single; 1,950–2,200 F ($351–$396) double; from 2,800 F ($504) suite. Breakfast 100 F ($18) extra. AE, DC, MC, V.

Once a fashionable town house, this hotel stands in the midst of embassies and exclusive boutiques (Christian Dior is across the street), near the Champs-Elysées and a short walk from the Seine. One of the best hotels in Paris in its price bracket, it feels like a private club. There is a small but attentive staff who will quickly learn your personal whims and make you feel at home. Each room is uniquely and tastefully decorated, with a radio. A few have a separate sitting room, and many overlook a side garden. The hotel has a lounge, bar, and restaurant.

MODERATE

GALILEO HOTEL, 54, rue Galilée, 75008 Paris. Tel. 1/47-20-66-06. Fax 1/47-20-67-17. 27 rms (all with bath). A/C MINIBAR TV TEL. **Métro:** George-V.

$ Rates: 800 F ($144) single; 950–980 F ($171–$176.40) double. Breakfast 50 F ($9) extra. AE, MC, V

Set about two blocks from the Arc de Triomphe and a block from the Champs-Elysées, this is a streamlined, modern, and very comfortable 1992 restoration of a gracefully elegant older building. Its facade has all the neoclassical carved-stone details and ornate wrought iron you'd expect in this neighborhood, but the inside is well lit, warmly decorated, and comfortably modern. There's a small garden on the premises, and a soothing color scheme inside of neutral ambers and beiges. Breakfast, served in the basement-level breakfast room, is the only meal served.

LORD BYRON, 5, rue de Chateaubriand, 75008 Paris. Tel. 1/43-59-89-98. Fax 1/42-89-46-04. 31 rms (all with bath), 6 suites. TV TEL **Métro:** George-V.

$ Rates: 650–800 F ($117–$144) single; 800–900 F ($144–$162) double; from 1,250 F ($225) suite. Breakfast 50 F ($9) extra. MC, V.

You can feel proud to stay here and recommend it to your friends. It's just off the Champs-Elysées, on a quiet, gently curving street characterized by distinguished buildings. The owner, Mme Françoise Coisne, who moved to Paris from the Ile de France, has added many personal touches. Throughout the hotel are framed prints of butterflies and historic French scenes. The furnishings are usually good reproductions of antiques or else restrained modern. Breakfast is served in the dining room or, in fair weather, in a shaded inner garden.

BUDGET

HOTEL OPAL, 19, rue Tronchet, 75008 Paris. Tel. 1/42-65-77-97. Fax 1/49-24-06-58. 36 rms. MINIBAR TV TEL **Métro:** Madeleine.

$ Rates: 465 F ($83.70) single; 575 F ($103.50) double. Breakfast 40 F ($7.20) extra. AE, MC, V. **Parking:** 120 F ($21.60).

This rejuvenated hotel is a real find. It's in the heart of Paris, in back of the Madeleine Church and an easy walk from the Opéra. Rooms are small but clean and comfortable. The bedrooms on the top floor are reached by a narrow staircase; some have skylights. The reception desk will make arrangements for parking at a nearby garage.

MADELEINE-PLAZA, 33, place de la Madeleine, 75008 Paris. Tel. 1/42-65-20-63. Fax 1/42-65-22-30. 54 rms, including 5 large rooms considered triples, quads, or suites (all with bath). MINIBAR TV TEL **Métro:** Madeleine.

$ Rates: 400–470 F ($72–$84.60) single or double; 620 F ($11.60) triple, quad, or suite. Breakfast 40 F ($7.20) extra. AE, MC, V.

Located on the Right Bank between the Tuileries and the Opéra, the Madeleine-Plaza is in the best district for shopping. There is a view of the rear of the Madeleine Church from the front windows. Rooms are contemporary, with shiny brown Formica headboards and breakfast tables and black leather chairs. For those who don't want breakfast in bed, there's a sunlit breakfast room overlooking the church.

3. 16TH & 17TH ARR.

EXPENSIVE

LE MERIDIEN PARIS ETOILE, 81, bd. Gouvion-Saint-Cyr, 75017 Paris. Tel. 1/40-68-34-34. Fax 1/40-68-31-31. 989 rooms (all with bath), 17 suites. A/C MINIBAR TV TEL **Métro:** Porte-Maillot.

$ Rates: 1,700 F ($306) single; 1,950 F ($351) double; from 3,800 F ($684) suite. Breakfast 95 F ($17.10) extra. AE, DC, MC, V. **Parking:** 100 F ($18).

This contemporary French hotel is the largest in France and the first of its kind in Paris. It's under the aegis of Air France and is across from the Air Terminal. There are separate check-in counters for individuals and groups. The overscale chandelier in the lobby is an eye-catcher. The comfortable bedrooms have many built-in pieces and textured colored fabrics. Bathrooms are partitioned.

There are four restaurants, featuring everything from traditional French cuisine (Le Clos Longchamp) to Japanese specialties (Le Yamato). A musical apéritif begins at 6pm, and there's a jazz session at 10pm in the Lionel Hampton Jazz Club. The most festive brunch in Paris is offered in the lobby every Sunday at noon.

RAPHAEL, 17 av. Kléber, 75016 Paris. Tel. 1/44-28-00-28, or toll free 800/223-5695 in the U.S. Fax 1/45-01-21-50. 52 rms (all with bath), 35 suites. MINIBAR TV TEL **Métro:** Kléber.

$ Rates: 1,600–2,200 F ($288–$396) single; 2,700–3,800 F ($486–$684) double; from 3,800 F ($684) suite. Breakfast 100 F ($18) extra. AE, DC, MC, V.

The luxury of Parisian elegance is on display here. The location is just a block from the Arc de Triumphe in the heart of Paris. The main hallway has walnut-paneled walls, with ornate bronze candelabra and gilt-framed oil paintings. The music salon is also paneled, with fine carving, a marble fireplace, and Turkey-red carpeting. Celebrities enjoy the drinking lounge, furnished with claret velour sofas, carved oak chairs, and fluted columns. Behind the cashier is a gold-and-orange original Turner painting. A mahogany-and-brass elevator takes you to the upper floors. Rooms are large, with silk draperies, gilt- and brass-trimmed chests, tables, inlaid wood, and armoires. The furniture is a mix of Directoire, Louis XVI, and Regency. The hotel is known for its distinguished gourmet restaurant. Services include babysitting, 24-hour room service, and laundry and valet service.

MODERATE

HOTEL ALEXANDER, 102, av. Victor-Hugo, 75016 Paris. Tel. 1/45-53-64-65. Fax 1/45-53-12-51. 59 rms (all with bath), 3 suites. MINIBAR TV TEL **Métro:** Victor-Hugo.
$ Rates: 830–1,090 F ($149.40–$196.20) single; 1,300 F ($234) double; from 1,870 F ($336.60) suite. Breakfast 65 F ($11.70) extra. AE, DC, MC, V.

This is really the perfect bourgeois hotel, the kind you might send an elderly relative to on a first trip to Paris. It was built as a family-run pension late in the 19th century. It's correct and conservative with a few elegant touches, such as chandeliers in each room. A wrought-iron stairwell winds around the elevator. Rooms are carpeted and rather frilly. Half of them face a well-planted and quiet courtyard. One-day laundry service is provided, and room service is available daily from 7am to 9pm.

HOTEL DE NEUVILLE, 3, place Verniquet, 75017 Paris. Tel. 1/43-80-26-30. Fax 1/43-80-38-55. 28 rms (all with bath). **Métro:** Pereire.
$ Rates: 580 F ($104.40) single; 700 F ($126) double. Extra bed 100 F ($18). Breakfast 45 F ($8.10) extra. AE, DC, MC, V.

Built in the 19th century as a private house, the Hôtel de Neuville has retained its symmetrical facade, with wrought-iron balconies adorned with potted plants in the summer. It's located in a prosperous neighborhood just 10 minutes from the Arc de Triomphe. The lobby has Ionic columns and warm tones and textures. Rooms are small with pink-and-beige decor. The owner, Monsieur Bigeard, was formerly a chef at Quai d'Orsay, France's diplomatic headquarters. He runs the hotel restaurant, Les Tartines.

FROMMER'S COOL FOR KIDS: HOTELS

Hôtel le Warwick (see p. 96) For the affluent family seeking a smart Right Bank address, this first-class hotel is inviting. Management welcomes children (in English) and lets those under 12 stay free in their parents' room.

Madeleine-Plaza (see p. 97) Between the Tuileries and the Opéra, this Right Bank choice offers many rooms suitable as triples or quads, ideal for small families. Many major Paris attractions are within walking distance.

Hôtel de Neuville (see p. 98) This former private house, in a quiet neighborhood near the Arc de Triomphe, has a policy of providing an extra bed for children sharing a room with their parents—a great way to save money if you don't mind a little crowding.

Novotel Paris les Halles (see p. 100) Long a family favorite, this hotel stands near what was once the site of the legendary fruit and vegetable market. Rooms offer couches that convert to beds, and breakfast is an all-you-can-eat buffet affair.

HOTEL PLAZA ETOILE, 21, av. de Wagram, 75017 Paris. Tel. 1/43-80-42-24. Fax 1/47-64-00-84. 40 rms (all with shower or bath and toilet). MINIBAR TV TEL **Métro:** Charles-de-Gaulle (Etoile).
$ Rates (including continental breakfast): 500–700 F ($90–$126) single; 600–800 F ($108–$144) double. AE, DC, MC, V.
The Plaza Etoile is near the Tivoli-Etoile (see below) and under the same management. The well-kept rooms have modern furnishings, and each has a radio, safe, hairdryer, and in-room movies. Best of all, breakfast is served on a lovely terrace overlooking avenue de Wagram. There is also a pleasant bar called Le Tiffany.

HOTEL REGENT'S GARDEN, 6, rue Pierre-Demours, 75017 Paris. Tel. 1/45-74-07-30. Fax 1/40-55-01-42. 39 rms (all with bath). MINIBAR TV TEL **Métro:** Ternes or Charles-de-Gaulle (Etoile).
$ Rates: 640–830 F ($115.20–$149.40) single; 690–930 F ($124.20–$167.40) double. Breakfast 38 F ($6.80) extra. AE, DC, MC, V. **Parking:** 50 F ($9).
The Regent's Garden has a proud heritage: Napoléon III built this stately château for his physician. It's near the convention center and minutes from the Arc de Triomphe. There are two gardens, one with ivy-covered walls and umbrella tables—a perfect place to meet other guests. The interior resembles a country house with classic touches. The entryway has fluted columns, and the living room is a casual mixture of comfortable furniture. Rooms have French flower prints on the walls and bedspreads; furniture is mostly traditional French. The tall French windows are soundproof and have light, airy curtains. Hairdryers are thoughtfully provided.

LA REGENCE ETOILE, 24, av. Carnot, 75017 Paris. Tel. 1/43-80-75-60. Fax 1/47-66-78-86. 38 rms (all with bath). TV TEL **Métro:** Charles-de-Gaulle (Etoile).
$ Rates (including breakfast): 480–520 F ($86.40–$93.60) single; 650–700 F ($117–$126) double. AE, MC, V.
This attractive hotel of white stone, shutters, and trim is on a shady street two minutes from the Arc de Triomphe. Inside, a tiny reception area and three small salons are furnished with several antiques, augmented by murals of Paris. A small elevator takes you to the beautiful bedrooms, furnished with reproductions of fine French furniture. The tiled bathrooms often have showers as well as tubs. Laundry service is available.

TIVOLI-ETOILE, 7, rue Brey, 75017 Paris. Tel. 1/42-67-12-68, or toll free 800/528-1234 in the U.S. and Canada. Fax 1/47-64-01-21. 30 rms (all with bath). MINIBAR TV TEL **Métro:** Charles-de-Gaulle (Etoile).
$ Rates (including continental breakfast): 500–700 F ($90–$126) single; 550–800 F ($99–$144) double. AE, DC, MC, V.
Rue Brey is a side street branching off avenue de Wagram, one of the spokelike avenues from the Etoile. This street has a number of moderately priced hotels (all of which seem to be full all year), but the Tivoli-Etoile offers the best value for its mid-city location. It's a member of the Best Western reservations system. The hotel has a contemporary lobby with a mural and a quiet inner patio. The small rooms, all with radios, have modern furnishings.

BUDGET

DES DEUX ACACIAS [Hotel of the Two Locust Trees], 28, rue de l'Arc-de-Triomphe, 75017 Paris. Tel. 1/43-80-01-85. Fax 1/40-53-94-62. 31 rms (all with shower or bath). TEL **Métro:** Charles-de-Gaulle (Etoile).
$ Rates (including breakfast): 335 F ($60.30) single; 400 F ($72) double. MC, V. **Parking:** 80 F ($14.40).
I recommend this semimodern hotel for its cleanliness and location a block from the Arc de Triomphe. It's also a good bargain, one of many in this district of budget hotels. Behind the white marble facade are a small public lounge and neat rooms frequented by visitors seeking to avoid the bustling "student" hotels on the Left Bank.

4. 1ST ARR.

EXPENSIVE

HOTEL DE FRANCE ET CHOISEUL, 239-241, rue St-Honoré, 75001 Paris. Tel. 1/42-61-54-60. Fax 1/40-20-96-32. 120 rms (all with bath), 16 suites. MINIBAR TV TEL **Métro:** Concorde, Tuileries, Opéra, Madeleine, or Palais-Royale.

$ Rates: 900 F ($162) single; 1,490 F ($268.20) double; from 1,900 F ($342) suite. Breakfast 90 F ($16.20) extra. AE, DC, MC, V. **Parking:** 70 F ($12.60).

This remake of a gracious 1720 town house near place Vendôme has been a hotel since the 1870s. A popular haven at the turn of the century, today it has been completely remodeled. The rooms are small but attractively decorated. Most open onto the inner courtyard. Color-coordinated rooms include a dressing table, tile bath, and many accessories. Each room is furnished in a classic style. Suites have twin beds on a balcony. The breakfast room, opening onto the inner courtyard, includes the historic salon where Lafayette received the subsidies to participate in the American War of Independence. Room service is available from noon to 11pm, and laundry and dry cleaning also are offered.

HOTEL LOTTI, 7-9, rue Castiglione, 75001 Paris. Tel. 1/42-60-37-34. Fax 1/42-60-37-34. 121 rms (all with bath), 12 suites. A/C MINIBAR TV TEL **Métro:** Opéra.

$ Rates: 1,400–1,900 F ($252–$342) single; 1,900–2,600 F ($342–$468) double; from 3,300 F ($594) suite. Breakfast 120 F ($21.60) extra. AE, DC, MC, V. **Parking:** 150 F ($27).

Originally built as a 19th-century convent, this hotel has sometimes been compared to a less pretentious and less expensive version of its neighbor, the Ritz. A well-respected hotel since 1910, it is today one of the most luxurious members of the Jolly hotel group, an Italy-based chain whose other hotels are for the most part relatively modern. The Lotti's quiet and elegant atmosphere is enhanced by a traditional (18th-century) French decor and high ceilings. The public rooms contain fine old tapestries, marble-and-gilt tables, and occasional bouquets of fresh flowers. Bedrooms evoke a well-maintained antique flair, with mahogany desks, rosewood chests, gilt chairs, silk-damask draperies, and tufted slipper chairs.

HOTEL REGINA, 2, place des Pyramides (also 192, rue de Rivoli), 75001 Paris. Tel. 1/42-60-31-10. Fax 1/40-15-95-16. 116 rms (all with bath), 14 suites. MINIBAR TV TEL **Métro:** Pyramides or Tuileries.

$ Rates: 1,450 F ($261) single; 1,650–2,600 F ($297–$468) double; from 2,900 F ($522) suite. Breakfast 85 F ($15.30) extra. AE, DC, MC, V.

The flagstone courtyard provides a rural atmosphere in the heart of Paris, near the Tuileries, place Vendôme, the Opéra, and the Louvre. The courtyard has a dolphin fountain, large pots of geraniums, and white wrought-iron furniture. The gracious public rooms have many Louis XV and Louis XVI furnishings. The long corridor lounge links spacious drawing rooms and salons. Throughout are Oriental rugs, bronze statues, 18th-century paintings, bowls of fresh seasonal flowers, and inlaid marquetry desks and tables. Breakfast is pleasant in the morning room, overlooking the garden.

NOVOTEL PARIS LES HALLES, place Marguerite-de-Navarre, 75001 Paris. Tel. 1/42-21-31-31. Fax 1/40-26-05-79. 275 rms (all with bath), 10 suites. MINIBAR TV TEL **Métro:** Les Halles.

$ Rates: 830 F ($149.40) single; 900 F ($162) double; from 1,500 F ($270) suite. Breakfast 58 F ($10.40) extra. AE, DC, MC, V. **Parking:** Nearby for 105 F ($18.90).

Set beside the beaux-arts lattices of place des Halles, this hotel is considered one of the best Novotels in its worldwide network. Built in 1986, the futuristic hotel has a mirrored facade and sloping skylights. The lobby has a small-scale copy of the Statue of Liberty and a stylish bar on a dais. Rooms contain no-nonsense but comfortable decor, each with one double bed and one sofa (which can serve as a single bed); in-room movies are provided. The best rooms overlook Les Halles with its fountains, shrubbery, and carousel. The greenhouse restaurant, the Sun Deck Grill, overlooks the ancient church of St. Eustache on the opposite side of the square. A public parking lot is near the hotel's entrance.

MODERATE

HOTEL BRIGHTON, 218, rue de Rivoli, 75001 Paris. Tel. 1/42-60-30-03.
   Fax 1/42-60-41-78. 70 rms (all with bath), 1 suite. MINIBAR TV TEL **Métro:** Tuileries.
$ Rates (including breakfast): 420–820 F ($75.60–$147.60) single; 550–850 F ($99–$153) double; from 1,260 F ($226.80) suite. AE, DC, MC, V.
Despite its English-sounding name, this is a very French hotel, located on one of the major shopping streets of Paris, across from the Louvre. Front rooms have a view of the world-famous art museum and the Tuileries Gardens. A few rooms have tiny balconies, which offer views of the Seine and the Eiffel Tower. The clean and comfortable rooms are furnished in a traditional style, often with brass beds. Breakfast is the only meal served, but salads and sandwiches can be ordered in a tea salon.

HOTEL DE CASTILLE, 37, rue Cambon, 75001 Paris. Tel. 1/44-58-44-58. Fax 1/44-58-44-00. 66 rms (all with bath), 18 suites. A/C MINIBAR TV TEL **Métro:** Madeleine.
$ Rates: 1,950 F ($351) single; 2,200 F ($396) double; from 2,800 F ($504) suite. Breakfast 115 F ($20.70) extra. Prices much higher during fashion shows. AE, DC, MC, V.
This quiet hotel, near the Paris headquarters of Chanel and across the street from the "back door" of the Ritz, is close to major shops, museums, and busy boulevards, just a few minutes' walk from place Vendôme, place de la Concorde, and the Madeleine. It has been restored in a Venetian style. The black-and-white facade has ornate stonework and 19th-century wrought-iron detailing on the upper floors. The entrance has a double arch. Beige marble panels and big mirrors adorn the low-ceilinged lobby. The sunny streamlined art deco rooms are done in pastels. Bathrooms are white with gray marble sinks. In-room movies are provided. The restaurant, Le Relais Castille, is decorated in flame and rust and serves Italian meals beginning at 150 F ($27); closed Saturday and Sunday.

HOTEL MAYFAIR, 3, rue Rouget-de-Lisle, 75001 Paris. Tel. 1/42-60-38-14. Fax 1/40-15-04-78. 53 rms (all with bath). MINIBAR TV TEL **Métro:** Concorde.
$ Rates: 900 F ($162) single; 1,630 F ($293.40) double. Breakfast 75 F ($13.50) extra. AE, DC, MC, V. **Parking:** 150 F ($27).
This strategically located hotel is a safe oasis near the Tuileries Gardens. It's between the chic place Vendôme and the bustling place de la Concorde, just off rue de Rivoli. The Mayfair offers 19th-century tradition with many modern conveniences, and was renovated in 1993. Rooms are well furnished and modernized.

BUDGET

BRITANNIQUE, 20, av. Victoria, 75001 Paris. Tel. 1/42-33-74-59, or toll free 800/366-1510 in the U.S. Fax 1/42-33-82-65. 40 rms (all with bath). MINIBAR TV TEL **Métro:** Châtelet.

$ Rates: 510 F ($91.80) single; 620–710 F ($111.60–$127.80) double. Breakfast 45 F ($8.10) extra. AE, DC, MC, V. **Parking:** 80 F ($14.40).

After complete renovation, the Britannique has been rated three stars by the government. It's in the heart of Paris, within easy reach of Les Halles, the cultural center Georges Pompidou, and Notre-Dame. Rooms are small but clean, comfortable, and adequately equipped. The TV satellite receiver picks up programs from the U.S. and U.K. The hotel was a Quaker mission in World War I, offering shelter to 1,000 U.S. and British volunteers from 1914 to 1918.

HOTEL HENRI IV, 25, place Dauphine, 75001 Paris. Tel. 1/43-54-44-53.
    22 rms (none with bath). **Métro:** Pont-Neuf.
$ Rates (including continental breakfast): 95 F ($17.10) single; 120–150 F ($21.60–$27) double; 190 F ($34.20) triple. No credit cards.

Four hundred years ago, this narrow building housed the printing presses used for the edicts of Henri IV. Today a budget hotel sits at this dramatic location, with orderly rows of trees out front. The loyal clientele is mostly budget-conscious academicians, journalists, and francophiles. The low-ceilinged lobby, one flight above street level, is cramped and a bit bleak, but the friendly owners make up for it. Rooms, considered romantically threadbare by many, are reached via a winding stairwell; all contain water basins.

5. 2ND & 9TH ARR.

VERY EXPENSIVE

LE GRAND HOTEL, 2, rue Scribe, 75009 Paris. Tel. 1/40-07-32-32, or toll free 800/327-0200 in the U.S. and Canada. Fax 1/42-66-12-51. 514 rms (all with bath), 23 suites. A/C MINIBAR TV TEL **Métro:** Opéra.
$ Rates: 2,300 F ($414) single; 3,400 F ($612) double; from 4,000 F ($720) suite. Breakfast 150 F ($27) extra. AE, DC, MC, V.

Thanks to a successful $58-million renovation by the Inter-Continental group, the Grand retains the original splendor of its architecture, the creation of Charles Garnier (who also designed the Opéra). This five-story, triangular hotel—inaugurated by the Empress Eugénie—is once again one of the leading first-class Parisian hotels. Rooms are refurbished and fully equipped. As part of the Second Empire splendor, a huge former courtyard has been turned into a glass-roofed atrium. The prestige dining choice of the hotel, Le Restaurant Opéra, has received many awards. La Verrière is the second restaurant of the restored hotel. Here you can enjoy Le Grand Hotel's breakfast buffet from 7 to 10:30am. Be sure to view Paris from the world-famous Café de la Paix.

EXPENSIVE

HOTEL WESTMINSTER, 13, rue de la Paix, 75002 Paris. Tel. 1/42-61-57-46. Fax 1/42-60-30-66. 84 rms (all with bath), 18 suites. A/C MINIBAR TV TEL **Métro:** Opéra.
$ Rates: 1,650–1,950 F ($297–$351) single; 2,050–2,450 F ($297–$351) double; 2,500–4,300 F ($450–$774) suite. Breakfast 110 F ($19.80) extra. AE, DC, MC, V.

This traditional hotel is between the Opéra and place Vendôme, a prestigious address near the cultural centers and shops. The hotel was built during Baron Haussmann's reorganization of Paris in 1846, and it incorporated an old convent. It was declared a national monument in 1907. At the turn of the century the hotel was purchased and renovated by Monsieur Bruchon, who brought his famous collection of clocks, which is still on display (in the lobby). In 1981 it was acquired by Warwick International Hotels, which added all the modern comforts. Its cousin hotel is the contemporary Le Warwick in the 8th arrondissement.

Rooms, each with a radio, are uniquely decorated in pastel colors, with rich paneling, molded ceilings, and marble-top fireplaces. Many rooms have Louis XIV antiques. I recommend the bar and gourmet restaurant, Le Celadon (see "Specialty Dining" in Chapter 6). Room service is available around the clock.

LE STENDHAL, 22, rue Danielle-Casanova, 75002 Paris. Tel. 1/44-58-52-52. Fax 1/44-58-52-00. 19 rms (all with bath), 2 suites. A/C MINIBAR TV TEL **Métro:** Opéra.

$ Rates: 1,400–1,500 F ($252–$270) single or double; from 1,800 F ($324) suite. Breakfast 80 F ($14.40) extra. AE, DC, MC, V. **Closed:** Aug.

Set in a six-story white building best known as the site of the death in 1842 of the French novelist Marie-Henri Beyle (alias Stendhal), this hotel was established in 1992. Its decor mingles a sophisticated medley of styles into a youthful, hip, and deliberately iconoclastic mix of old and new. Its location, close to the glamorous jewelry stores and perfect proportions of place Vendôme, couldn't be more grand. Bedrooms, accessible via a tiny elevator, are outfitted in one of three vivid color schemes, with the exception of the red-and-black Stendhal Suite, whose hues pay nostalgic homage to its namesake's classic, *Le rouge et le noir*. Breakfast (the only meal served) is presented in the stone-sided cellar, beneath a charming and cozy vaulted ceiling.

MODERATE

HOTEL RICHMOND, 11, rue du Helder, 75009 Paris. Tel. 1/47-70-53-20. Fax 1/48-00-02-10. 63 rms (all with bath). MINIBAR TV TEL **Métro:** Opéra.

$ Rates (including continental breakfast): 580 F ($104.40) single; 720 F ($129.60) double. AE, DC, MC, V.

This three-star hotel is a short walk from the Opéra, near American Express, the Café de la Paix, and many fine shops. Behind the attractive facade is a pleasant lounge with sofas, marble columns, and a Roman-style fountain—all contributing to an old-world feel. Rooms are comfortably, traditionally furnished.

BUDGET

HOTEL DE NAVARIN ET D'ANGLETERRE, 8, rue de Navarin, 75009 Paris. Tel. 1/48-78-31-80. Fax 1/48-74-14-09. 27 rms (all with shower). TV TEL **Métro:** St-Georges.

$ Rates: 340 F ($61.20) single; 360–390 F ($64.80–$70.20) double. Breakfast 30 F ($5.40) extra. MC, V.

Although it's centrally located, and within trekking distance of many of the city's attractions, the neighborhood that contains this hotel is rarely visited by tourists. Despite that, it contains unusual charms and many buildings which, when they were originally built around 1830, were the height of fashion. This two-star hotel is one of those buildings, graced with a small private garden in back where breakfast is served during clement weather. Renovated and upgraded in 1991, it has simply decorated but clean and comfortable bedrooms with richly textured curtains and the feel of a business run by an on-site family. There is no elevator.

HOTEL DE SEZE, 16, rue de Sèze, 75009 Paris. Tel. 1/47-42-69-12. Fax 1/40-07-10-95. 25 rms (all with bath). TV TEL **Métro:** Madeleine.

$ Rates: 350–430 F ($63–$77.40) single or double. Breakfast 30 F ($5.40) extra. No credit cards.

Here's a bargain, considering its central location—right off avenue de l'Opéra and within sight of the Madeleine. The tiny lobby is elegantly paneled with chunky brass hardware and graced with some Louis XVI–style furniture. The quality of the rooms is hit-or-miss; some are furnished with well-chosen antiques, while others are modern. The hotel doesn't have a restaurant, but a bar is open until midnight. English is spoken.

6. 5TH ARR.

MODERATE

HOTEL AGORA ST-GERMAIN, 42, rue des Bernardins, 75005 Paris. Tel. 1/46-34-13-00. Fax 1/46-34-75-05. 39 rms (all with bath). MINIBAR TV TEL **Métro:** Maubert-Mutualité.

$ Rates: 550–600 F ($99–$108) single; 660 F ($118.80) double. Breakfast 40 F ($7.20) extra. AE, DC, MC, V. **Parking:** 90 F ($16.20).

Recently renovated, this three-star hotel is one of the best values in this artistic and historic part of Paris. Rooms are well furnished and soundproof, each with a clock, hairdryer, and safe. Breakfast is the only meal served.

HOTEL ELYSA-LUXEMBOURG, 6, rue Gay-Lussac, 75005 Paris. Tel. 1/43-25-31-74. Fax 1/46-34-56-27. 30 rms (all with bath). MINIBAR TV TEL **Métro:** Luxembourg.

$ Rates: 450–595 F ($81–$107.10) single; 560–695 F ($100.80–$125.10) double. Breakfast 35 F ($6.30) extra. AE, DC, MC, V. **Parking:** 90 F ($16.20).

One of the best choices in the heart of the Latin Quarter is near the Luxembourg Gardens. The completely renovated rooms here are charming, spacious, and soundproof. Some accommodations are reserved for nonsmokers. Guests may use the sauna.

HOTEL RESIDENCE SAINT-CHRISTOPHE, 17, rue Lacépède, 75005 Paris. Tel. 1/43-31-81-54. Fax 1/43-31-12-54. 31 rms (all with bath). MINIBAR TV TEL **Métro:** Place Monge.

$ Rates: 650 F ($117) single or double. Breakfast 40 F ($7.20) extra. AE, DC, MC, V.

Warmly accommodating and comfortable, this hotel has a gracious, English-speaking staff and a location in one of the least publicized but very charming districts of the Quartier Latin, a short walk east of the Botanical Gardens (Jardin des Plantes). It was created in 1987 when a derelict hotel was interconnected to an adjacent butcher shop. The combination, after millions of francs' worth of restoration, is clean, charming, friendly, and well upholstered, with traditional furniture and wall-to-wall carpeting.

The hotel, which derives its name from the first-born child of a long-ago owner, serves only breakfast, although the staff offers well-advised information about the virtues of neighborhood restaurants. Each room contains a hairdryer, a radio, and tall, sunny windows.

SELECT, 1, place de la Sorbonne, 75005 Paris. Tel. 1/46-34-14-80. Fax 1/46-34-51-79. 69 rms (all with bath). TV TEL **Métro:** St-Michel.

$ Rates (including breakfast buffet): 650 F ($117) single; 690–750 F ($124.20–$135) double. AE, DC, MC, V.

Built by Le Mercier between 1635 and 1642, this hotel is the only one that stands directly on this square dominated by the Church of the Sorbonne. Try to get a room overlooking the fountain in this plaza. Nearby there are cafés on the busy "boul Mich." The modernized hotel's rooms are comfortably furnished, and the style is generally art deco.

BUDGET

GRAND HOTEL MODERNE, 33, rue des Ecoles, 75005 Paris. Tel. 1/43-54-37-78. Fax 1/43-29-74-42. 45 rms (each with bath). TV TEL **Métro:** Maubert-Mutalité or St-Michel.

$ Rates (including continental breakfast): 500–700 F ($90–$126) single; 590–840 F ($106.20–$151.20) double. AE, DC, MC, V.
Located on the tranquil rue des Ecoles, the Grand Hôtel Moderne lies in the heart of the Latin Quarter, near both Notre-Dame and the Panthéon. The charming owner, Madame Gibon, provides a warm atmosphere and immaculate accommodations. The Moderne was renovated in 1991, and a hotel bar was added, along with a sauna and Jacuzzi. Laundry service and a helpful concierge are available.

HOTEL D'ALBE, 1, rue de la Harpe (off place St-Michel), 75005 Paris. Tel. 1/46-34-09-70. Fax 1/40-46-85-70. 45 rms (all with bath). TV TEL **Métro:** St-Michel.
$ Rates (including continental breakfast): 538 F ($96.80) single; 614–653 F ($110.50–$117.50) double; 795 F ($143.10) triple. AE, MC, V. **Parking:** 80 F ($14.40).
This recently modernized, six-story building is well situated for tourists who want to take advantage of the Latin Quarter's street life. The style of the hotel is warm and inviting. The hotel has a lounge with a breakfast salon, an elevator, and comfortable rooms with such amenities as individual safes and hairdryers.

HOTEL DU BRESIL, 10, rue Le Goff, 75005 Paris. Tel. 1/46-33-45-78. Fax 1/46-33-45-78. 30 rms (26 with bath or shower). TEL **Métro:** Luxembourg.
$ Rates (including continental breakfast): 250–280 F ($45–$50.40) single without bath, 305–330 F ($54.90–$59.40) single with bath or shower; 270–310 F ($48.60–$55.80) double without bath, 360–380 F ($64.80–$68.40) double with bath or shower. MC, V.
Although Sigmund Freud lived here in 1885, today this quiet hotel is relatively unknown. Situated on a small back street, the hotel offers renovated rooms, the least expensive of which require you to use the hallway toilet and shower. The styling is traditional.

HOTEL LE JARDIN DES PLANTES, 5, rue Linne, 75005 Paris. Tel. 1/47-07-06-20. Fax 1/47-07-62-74. 33 rms (all with bath). MINIBAR TV TEL **Métro:** Jussieu. **Bus:** 67 or 89.
$ Rates: 390–590 F ($70.20–$106.20) single; 440–640 F ($79.20–$115.20) double. Breakfast 40 F ($7.20) extra. AE, DC, MC, V.
Opened in 1986, the Hôtel Le Jardin des Plantes lies in the academic section of Paris, near the Panthéon and across from the Jardin des Plantes. The hotel offers well-equipped bedrooms, some with flowered terraces, as well as a vaulted lounge in the basement, a sauna, ironing facilities, and an elevator. The hotel has a small roof terrace, and a brasserie and snack bar where breakfast is served.

HOTEL DU LEVANT, 18, rue de la Harpe, 75005 Paris. Tel. 1/46-34-11-00. Fax 1/46-34-25-87. 46 rms (all with bath). TV TEL **Métro:** St-Michel.
$ Rates (including continental breakfast): 310–500 F ($55.80–$90) single; 510–580 F ($91.80–$104.40) double; 780 F ($140.40) quad. AE, MC, V.
The Hôtel du Levant is located on a street of budget restaurants in the center of the St-Michel district. The walls of the lounge are covered with posters advertising concerts, openings, and art shows. Guests have use of an elevator, taking them to a series of modernized bedrooms, each with bath or shower and accommodating one to four guests.

HOTEL SEROTEL LUTECE, 2, rue Bertholet, 75005 Paris. Tel. 1/43-36-26-30. Fax 1/43-31-08-21. 49 rms (all with bath), 1 suite. MINIBAR TV TEL **Métro:** Censier-Daubenton.
$ Rates: 440 F ($79.20) single; 620–690 F ($111.60–$124.20) double; 1,200 F ($216) suite. Breakfast 50 F ($9) extra. AE, MC, V.
Set near the Pont-Royal, in a quiet residential neighborhood of discreet charm, this hotel was built late in the 19th century in a style similar to that of many of its neighbors. A complete renovation in the early 1990s modernized many of the bedrooms, equipping them with wall-to-wall carpeting, pastel color schemes, comfortable beds, and simple furniture. Bathrooms contain adequate (but slightly

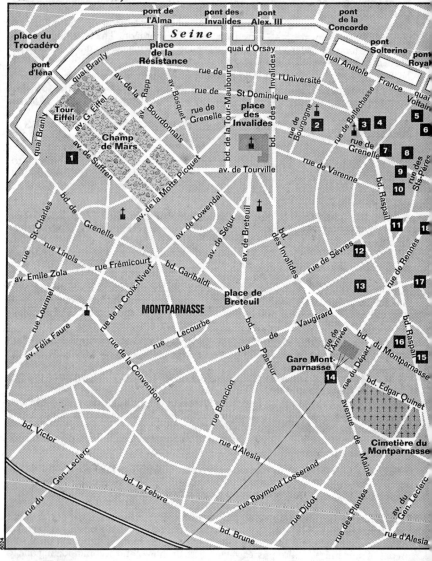

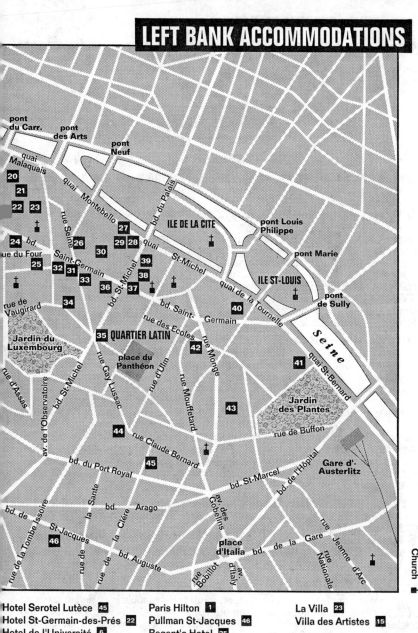

LEFT BANK ACCOMMODATIONS

Hotel Serotel Lutèce **45**
Hotel St-Germain-des-Prés **22**
Hotel de l'Université **6**
Hotel Verneuil St-Germain **10**
L'Hotel **24**
The Lindberg **11**
Lutetia **12**
Michelet-Odéon **37**
Odéon-Hotel **33**

Paris Hilton **1**
Pullman St-Jacques **46**
Regent's Hotel **25**
Relais Christine **27**
Relais-Hotel du Vieux Paris **36**
Le Relais Saint-Germain **32**
La Residence du Globe **29**
Select **38**
St-Thomas-d'Aquin **8**

La Villa **23**
Villa des Artistes **15**

cramped) shower stalls and a handful of pleasant amenities and extras. Breakfast (the only meal served) is presented in the basement-level room which resembles a clean and well-illuminated cave. Some of the bedrooms overlook a quiet courtyard dotted with *jardinières* and potted flowers.

7. 6TH ARR.

EXPENSIVE

HOTEL RELAIS MEDICIS, 23, rue Racine, 75006 Paris. Tel. 1/43-26-00-60. Fax 1/40-46-83-39. 16 rms (all with bath). A/C MINIBAR TV TEL **Métro:** Odéon.

$ Rates (including breakfast): 1,380 F ($248.40) single; 1,480 F ($266.40) double. AE, DC, MC, V.

Until its radical overhaul in 1991, this place was a well-worn two-star hotel favored by students, indigent artists, and visiting professors from abroad. Today, the establishment is a lavishly decorated and romantic hideaway set adjacent to the Théâtre de l'Odéon, near the Luxembourg Gardens. Bedrooms are small (sometimes even cramped) but richly upholstered, and include fabric-covered walls, private safes, cable TVs, and a stylishly cluttered and old-fashioned patina you'd otherwise find in a family homestead in Provence. There's a small bar near the antique oil portraits and lithographs of the public rooms, but other than breakfast, no meals are served.

LUTETIA, 45, bd. Raspail, 75006 Paris. Tel. 1/49-54-46-46. Fax 1/49-54-46-00. 258 rms (all with bath), 27 suites. A/C TV TEL **Métro:** Sèvres-Babylon.

$ Rates: 1,500–2,200 F ($270–$396) single or double; 3,500 F ($630) suite. Breakfast 115 F ($20.70) extra. AE, DC, MC, V.

The largest hotel on the Left Bank, the Lutetia was radically renovated around 1990 to restore its original art deco style. Popular with executives and a wide range of Americans and Europeans, the hotel has better-than-expected copies of 18th-century French furniture, and always seems to have an available room. Amenities include the elegantly decorated Brasserie Lutetia, the upscale restaurant Le Paris, a comfortable watering hole known as the Lutèce Bar, about 20 reception areas for private parties, and an indispensable porter who is able to provide theater tickets and other special items. Most of the bedrooms are fully but conservatively renovated, traditional in style, and very comfortable.

LE RELAIS CHRISTINE, 3, rue Christine, 75006 Paris. Tel. 1/43-26-71-80. Fax 1/43-26-89-38. 51 rms (all with bath), 13 suites. A/C MINIBAR TV TEL **Métro:** St-Michel.

$ Rates: 1,430 F ($257.40) single; 1,430–1,550 F ($257.40–$279) double; from 2,300 F ($414) suite. Breakfast 90 F ($16.20) extra. AE, DC, MC, V. **Parking:** Free.

The Relais Christine welcomes an international clientele into a truly unusual, 16th-century former Augustinian cloister. From a narrow cobblestone street you enter an elegant reception area with baroque sculpture, plush upholsteries, and a scattering of Renaissance antiques. A bar area and sitting room, with 19th-century portraits and leather chairs, are right next door. You won't fully experience the hotel, however, until you go into the vaulted breakfast room on the lower level, with its ancient well and massive central stone column. Each of the bedrooms is individually decorated with antiques or antique reproductions and lots of flair. Accessories include massively beamed ceilings and wall-to-wall carpeting.

LE RELAIS SAINT-GERMAIN, 9, carrefour de l'Odéon, 75006 Paris. Tel. 1/43-29-12-05. Fax 1/46-33-45-30. 10 rms (all with bath), 1 suite. A/C TV TEL **Métro:** Odéon.

$ Rates (including continental breakfast): 1,190 F ($214.20) single; 1,380 F ($248.40) double; 1,790 F ($322.20) suite. AE, DC, MC, V.

This charming 17th-century building is one of the Left Bank's best-kept secrets. Combining tradition with modern elements, the Relais Saint-Germain provides each room with soundproofing, videos, and a private safe. The interior is acclaimed for its beautiful decor.

MODERATE

AVIATIC, 105, rue de Vaugirard, 75006 Paris. Tel. 1/45-44-38-21. Fax 1/45-49-35-83. 43 rms (all with bath). MINIBAR TV TEL **Métro:** Montparnasse-Bienvenue.

$ Rates (including continental breakfast): 640–790 F ($115.20–$142.20) single; 780–830 F ($140.40–$149.40) double. AE, DC, MC, V. **Parking:** 120 F ($21.60).

This small Montparnasse hotel has been family-run for over a century, and it's one of my favorites. The entrance is impressive, with marble columns, brass chandeliers, and vintage furniture. There's an inner courtyard with ivy-covered lattice on the walls, and the guests, ranging from unpublished novelists to jazz musicians, add to the hotel's charm. Each well-furnished bedroom has its own distinct style. The staff speaks English.

GRAND HOTEL DE L'UNIVERS, 6, rue Grégoire-de-Tours, 75006 Paris. Tel. 1/43-29-37-00. Fax 1/40-51-06-45. 34 rms (all with bath). MINIBAR TV TEL **Métro:** Odéon.

$ Rates: 590 F ($106.20) single; 680–750 F ($122.40–$135) double. Breakfast 35 F ($6.30) extra. AE, DC, MC, V.

This venerable and historic building was originally built in the 1400s as the Paris home of a member of the then-emerging bourgeoisie, who probably chose its location because of its nearness to the Luxembourg Palace. Today, the massive ceiling beams, thick stone walls, and the facade's incised "logo" of a loincloth-clad barbarian with a club have been carefully retained by the present owners. Some of the pleasantly renovated rooms enjoy a panoramic view over the crooked rooftops of the surrounding neighborhood, and all contain satellite TV reception and a hairdryer. One of the most amusing rooms is "La Bonbonnière," an all-pink concoction whose name translates as "the candy box." Breakfast, the only meal served, is presented beneath the 500-year-old stone vaults of a well-decorated cellar.

HOTEL BUCI LATIN, 34, rue de Buci, 75006 Paris. Tel. 1/43-29-07-20. Fax 1/43-29-67-44. 25 rms (all with bath), 2 suites. A/C MINIBAR TV TEL **Métro:** St-Germain-des-Prés.

$ Rates (including continental breakfast): 800–1,100 F ($144–$198) single or double; 1,500 F ($270) suite. AE, DC, MC, V.

Set in the heart of the Quartier Latin, this hotel reopened after a complete architectural overhaul in 1992. Two elevators lead from a postmodern lobby whose furnishings, although comfortable, might remind you of wares from a trendy Left Bank art gallery. Upstairs, each of the doors leading into the bedrooms was whimsically and humorously covered with neo-surrealist images by a team of local artists. Inside, you'll find a combination of hi-tech accessories, charming and old-fashioned ceiling beams, platform beds, and warmly textured earth colors. On the premises is a coffee shop, serving drinks and light snacks every day from breakfast time till 6pm.

HOTEL D'ANGLETERRE, 44, rue Jacob, 75006 Paris. Tel. 1/42-60-34-72. Fax 1/42-60-16-93. 29 rms (all with bath). TV TEL **Métro:** St-Germain-des-Prés.

$ Rates: 600–750 F ($108–$135) single; 900–1,100 F ($162–$198) double. Breakfast 40 F ($7.20) extra. AE, DC, V.

Situated amid antique shops and art galleries, this quaint building, constructed in 1650, once housed the British Embassy. Ben Franklin refused to enter this building to sign the Treaty of Paris. Despite the antiquated plumbing, the d'Angleterre has long been favored by such illustrious guests as Anne Morrow Lindbergh and Ernest Hemingway, who stayed here once while he was ill. It still attracts faithful devotees. Shut off from street traffic, most of its rooms open onto an exposed courtyard and garden, where tables are set for breakfast.

HOTEL DE FLEURIE, 32, rue Grégoire-de-Tours, 75006 Paris. Tel. 1/43-29-59-81. Fax 1/43-29-68-44. 29 rms (all with bath). MINIBAR TV TEL **Métro:** Odéon.

$ Rates: 590–780 F ($106.20–$140.40) single; 780–1,150 F ($140.40–$207) double or twin. Breakfast 50 F ($9) extra. AE, DC, MC, V.

The Hôtel de Fleurie, located on a side street off boulevard St-Germain, is one of the best of the "new" old hotels. It has been restored to its 17th-century elegance, complete with statuary, exposed stone walls and beams, latticework, ivy, a spiral staircase, and a refectory desk where guests check in. The hotel also has a TV/breakfast room, an elevator, and safety-deposit boxes in all of the bedrooms. The twin-bedded units are air-conditioned.

HOTEL DES SAINTS-PERES, 65, rue des Sts-Pères, 75006. Tel. 1/45-44-50-00. Fax 1/45-44-90-83. 37 rms (all with bath), 3 suites. MINIBAR TV TEL **Métro:** St-Germain-des-Prés or Sèvres-Babylone.

$ Rates: 450 F ($81) single; 1,200 F ($216) double; 1,600 F ($288) suite. Breakfast 50 F ($9) extra. AE, DC, MC, V.

The best recommendation for this old favorite just off boulevard St-Germain is the long list of habitués, including Edna St. Vincent Millay, who enjoyed the camellia-trimmed garden. The hotel, designed by Louis XIV's architect, is decorated in part with antique paintings, tapestries, and mirrors. The most-sought room is the chambre à la fresque, which has a 17th-century painted ceiling. The modernized bedrooms face the courtyard, where breakfast is served, weather permitting.

HOTEL DU PAS DE CALAIS, 59, rue des Sts-Pères, 75006 Paris. Tel. 1/45-48-78-74. Fax 1/45-44-94-57. 41 rms (all with bath). TV TEL **Métro:** St-Germain-des-Prés.

$ Rates (including continental breakfast): 600 F ($108) single; 760 F ($136.80) double. AE, MC, V.

This 17th-century building has housed many celebrities since it was converted into a hotel in 1815. Beginning with Chateaubriand (who actually lived here before it became a hotel) and later, Maurice Béjart, the dancer–choreographer–stage designer, the hotel has also played host to Sartre as well as many singers, actors, and writers. Guests may enjoy afternoon drinks or breakfast on the small patio. Rooms are well maintained and comfortable, and each accommodation has been modernized.

HOTEL ST-GERMAIN-DES-PRES, 36, rue Bonaparte, 75008 Paris. Tel. 1/43-26-00-19. Fax 1/40-46-83-63. 28 rms (all with bath), 2 suites. MINIBAR TV TEL **Métro:** St-Germain-des-Prés.

$ Rates (including continental breakfast): 750–950 F ($135–$171) single; 800–1,000 F ($144–$180) double; 1,100–1,500 F ($198–$270) suite. V. **Parking:** 95 F ($17.10).

Located on a well-known shopping street in the Latin Quarter, this hotel has 18th-century–inspired paneling, wall niches, and sitting rooms decorated with flowery curtains and wallpaper. The bedrooms are small and charming, some with exposed ceiling beams. Legendary *New Yorker* correspondent Janet Flanner lived here in the 1920s.

HOTEL LE SAINT-GREGORIE, 43, rue de l'Abbé-Grégoire, 75006 Paris. Tel. 1/45-48-23-23. Fax 1/45-48-33-95. 20 rms (all with bath), 1 suite. TV TEL **Métro:** St-Placide.

$ Rates: 720–860 F ($129.60–$154.80) single or double; from 1,200 F ($216) suite. Breakfast 60 F ($10.80) extra. AE, DC, MC, V. **Parking:** 60 F ($10.80).

This modern three-star hotel in a restored town house has a vaulted breakfast room and a fireplace in the sitting room. Bedrooms are well furnished; some have private terraces. The top two floors are air-conditioned.

Lucie Agaud and Michel Bouvier, who operate the hotel, also run a famous Left Bank bistro, Le Marlotte, which is around the corner, serving a traditional French cuisine. Both the restaurant and their hotel attract photographers, actors, and fashion journalists.

HOTEL LE SAINTE-BEUVE, 9, rue Ste-Beuve, 75006 Paris. Tel. 1/45-48-20-07. Fax 1/45-48-67-52. 23 rms (all with bath), 1 suite. MINIBAR TV TEL **Métro:** Vavin.

$ Rates: 650–950 F ($117–$171) double; from 1,600 F ($288) suite. Breakfast 70 F ($12.60) extra. AE, MC, V.

Located around the corner from Rodin's sculpture of Balzac, this small, tastefully restored Montparnasse hotel has a cozy interior of rose-colored chintz and provincial furniture, with fireside drinks available in the lobby bar. All the well-furnished bedrooms are doubles. Breakfast in bed is available.

ODEON-HOTEL, 3, rue de l'Odéon, 75006 Paris. Tel. 1/43-25-90-67. Fax 1/43-25-55-98. 34 rms (all with bath). TV TEL **Métro:** Odéon.

$ Rates: 700–750 F ($126–$135) single; 950–1,100 F ($171–$198) double. Breakfast 60 F ($10.80) extra. AE, DC, MC, V.

Conveniently located near both the Théâtre de l'Odéon and boulevard St-Germain, the hotel stands on what was, in 1779, the first street in Paris to have pavements and gutters. By the turn of the century this area, which at no. 12 housed the bookshop Shakespeare and Co., began attracting such writers as André Gide, Paul Valéry, James Joyce, T. S. Eliot, F. Scott Fitzgerald, Ernest Hemingway, and Gertrude Stein. Today, with its exposed beams, rough stone walls, high crooked ceilings, tapestries, oak-and-bookbinder wallpaper mixed in with bright, contemporary fabrics, mirrored ceilings, and black leather furnishings, the Odéon-Hôtel is reminiscent of a modernized Norman country inn. After modern plumbing was installed, each room was individually designed.

RELAIS-HOTEL DU VIEUX PARIS, 9, rue Gît-le-Coeur, 75006 Paris. Tel. 1/43-54-41-66. Fax 1/43-26-00-15. 13 rms (all with bath), 7 suites. MINIBAR TV TEL **Métro:** St-Michel.

$ Rates: 990–1,270F ($178.20–$228.60) single or double. 1,270–1,470 F ($228.60–$264.60) suite. Breakfast 50 F ($9) extra. AE, MC, V.

Tucked away within a maze of medieval streets in the heart of Paris, this stone-and-timbered building was built in 1480 as the home of the ducs de Luynes. Later, it was the elegantly appointed home of Pierre Seguier—the *real* Marquis d'O—one of Richelieu's advisers. In the 1600s, it was notorious as a hideaway for Henri IV and one of his mistresses. In the 1950s, such members of the Beat Generation as Allen Ginsberg, W. S. Burroughs, and Jack Kerouac made it their Paris headquarters when it was a simple (relatively battered) two-star hotel.

None of them would recognize the place today. In 1991 it was upgraded and restored, and now, though defined as a three-star hotel, it offers some of the amenities and comforts of some of Paris's more expensive four-star properties. Rooms are elegantly furnished with upholstered walls and copies of 19th-century antiques, and about 15 contain the massive beams and timbers of the building's original construction. Each accommodation has a "massage shower," hairdryer, individual safe, and trouser press. Two of the suites have a mezzanine overlooking the rooftops of Paris, and some of the rooms offer views of the Conciergerie.

LA VILLA, 29, rue Jacob, 75006 Paris. Tel. 1/43-26-60-00. Fax 1/46-34-63-63. 28 rms (all with bath), 4 suites. A/C MINIBAR TV TEL **Métro:** St-Germain-des Prés.

$ Rates: 800–1,600 F ($144–$288) single or double; 1,950 F ($351) suite. Breakfast 80 F ($14.40) extra. AE, MC, V.

This four-star hotel was radically renovated and upgraded in the mid-1980s. (Before then, it had been a somewhat run-down hotel, the Hotel Isly.) It lies a few steps from the building where Richard Wagner lived in 1841–42. The soundproof bedrooms, each elegantly decorated in a futuristic and minimalist style, were designed by the well-known French decorator Marie-Christine Dorner. Each contains a hairdryer and ample use of color. No meals are served other than breakfast.

BUDGET

HOTEL LOUIS II, 2, rue St-Sulpice, 75006 Paris. Tel. 1/46-33-13-80. Fax 1/46-33-17-29. 22 rms (all with bath). MINIBAR TV TEL **Métro:** Odéon.
$ Rates: 520–680 F ($93.60–$122.40) single or double; 820 F ($147.60) triple. Breakfast 41 F ($7.30) extra. AE, DC, MC, V.

Housed in what was once a neglected 18th-century building, the Hôtel Louis II today provides rustic, well-decorated accommodations. Afternoon drinks and morning coffee are served in an elegant reception salon, where gilt-framed mirrors, bouquets of fresh flowers, and well-oiled antiques add a provincial feeling. Upstairs, cozy bedrooms contain exposed beams and wide expanses of mellowed patina contrasting with chintz coverings and plush carpeting. Many repeat visitors request the romantic attic rooms. TVs are available upon request.

MICHELET-ODEON, 6, place de l'Odéon, 75006 Paris. Tel. 1/46-34-27-80. Fax 1/46-34-55-35. 42 rms (all with bath). TV TEL **Métro:** Odéon.
$ Rates: 380–430 F ($68.40–$77.40) single; 450–510 F ($81–$91.80) double. Breakfast 40 F ($7.20) extra. AE, MC, V.

With an enviable location between one of Paris's most famous squares and two narrow but bustling streets, this hotel prefers to retain its two-star government status rather than upgrading itself into a more glamorous (but more expensive) category. A much-restored older building set behind a white facade, it contains classic columns, a cozy lounge, and the possibility of breakfast served either in the public areas or in any of its simple, pastel-colored bedrooms.

REGENT'S HOTEL, 44, rue Madame, 75006 Paris. Tel. 1/45-48-02-81. Fax 1/45-44-85-73. 37 rms (all with bath). MINIBAR TEL **Métro:** St-Sulpice or Rennes.
$ Rates (including continental breakfast): 435 F ($78.30) single; 530 F ($95.40) double. MC, V.

Visitors will find the Regent's Hôtel one block from the Luxembourg Gardens on the Left Bank. The hotel has a patio with beds of flowers, shrubbery, and white wrought-iron furniture. The bedroom furnishings are a mixture of modified modern, antiques, and reproductions.

LA RESIDENCE DU GLOBE, 15, rue des Quatre-Vents, 75006 Paris. Tel. 1/46-33-62-69. 15 rms (all with bath). TEL **Métro:** Odéon.
$ Rates: 260–345 F ($46.80–$62.10) single or double. Breakfast 40 F ($7.20) extra. No credit cards. **Closed:** Aug.

This renovation of a 17th-century town house, off carrefour de l'Odéon, revealed rugged stone walls and twisted old oak beams. Modern decorations include an eclectic collection of items—ornate wrought-iron gates, an old chest, a bishop's chair, gilt mirrors, and a bronze chandelier. Guests will find simple and clean accommodations, along with interesting shopping in the surrounding area.

VILLA DES ARTISTES, 9, rue de la Grande-Chaumière, 75006 Paris. Tel. 1/43-26-60-86. Fax 1/43-54-73-70. 60 rms (all with bath). TV TEL **Métro:** Vavin.
$ Rates (including continental breakfast): 600–800 F ($108–$144) single or double. AE, DC, MC, V.

This older hotel derived its name from the dozens of art students who lodged here while pursuing their art at the nearby schools of painting. White-fronted, five-storied, and simple, it offers clean but much-modernized bedrooms, each of which was renovated in 1990. Only breakfast is served, although coffee and snacks can usually be procured throughout the day beneath the greenhouse-style roof of the breakfast area. Adjacent to the breakfast area is an outdoor courtyard with a basin, a fountain, and trompe l'oeil lattices which imbue the area with the feeling of a country garden.

8. 7TH & 15TH ARR.

EXPENSIVE

HOTEL MONTALEMBERT, 3, rue de Montalembert, 75007 Paris. Tel. 1/45-48-68-11. Fax 1/42-22-58-19. 46 rms (all with bath), 5 suites. A/C MINIBAR TV TEL **Métro:** Rue-du-Bac

$ **Rates:** 1,520–1,950 F ($273.60–$351) single or double. 2,500–3,300 F ($450–$594) suite. Breakfast 95 F ($17.10) extra. AE, DC, MC, V. **Parking:** 110 F ($19.80).

✪ Unusually elegant for a Left Bank hotel, the Montalembert was erected in 1926 in a venerable beaux arts style which for many years made it the darling of France's intellectual *crème de la crème.* In 1989, the hotel, much in need of renovation, was bought by a Hong Kong–based chain, the Leo group, whose directors immediately hired one of France's premier architectural designers, Christian Liaigre, for a well-publicized remake. In 1992, after millions of dollars' worth of discreet improvements, the hotel was reopened and immediately hailed as one of the capital's most successful and imaginative restorations.

Inside, you'll find a sophisticated modern interpretation which borrows elements of Bauhaus design and postmodernism in a palette of honey-beiges, creams, and golds. Half the bedrooms follow the architectural patterns established in the public rooms; the other half are stylishly but conservatively decorated in a staid but dignified Louis-Philippe (French Victorian) style. Regardless of their style, bedrooms contain bathrooms sheathed in gray Portuguese marble, safes, and private video players. The in-house restaurant, Restaurant Montalembert, is appropriately savvy and elegant.

PARIS HILTON, 18, av. Suffren, 75015 Paris. Tel. 1/42-73-92-00, or toll free 800/445-8667 in the U.S. and Canada. Fax 1/47-83-62-66. 456 rms (all with bath), 28 suites. A/C MINIBAR TV TEL **Métro:** Champs-de-Mars (RER) or Bir-Hakeim.

$ **Rates:** 1,500–2,150 F ($270–$387) single; 1,700–2,300 F ($306–$414) double; from 3,500 F ($630) suite. Breakfast 130 F ($23.40) extra. AE, DC, MC, V. **Parking:** 120 F ($21.60).

The Hilton, one of Paris's best-established deluxe hotels, is the first to shatter the Right Bank's monopoly on luxury accommodations. It has also become a focal point of social life in this part of the city, with 45% of its income coming from local clientele.

The hotel maintains a Parisian flair and incorporates every modern convenience, from a state-of-the-art security system to daily feature films on TV. Each of the well-furnished bedrooms has a large bathroom covered with tinted marble, an oversize sink, huge towels, terry-cloth bathrobes, and lots of toilet articles. The soundproof bedrooms are decorated with contemporary French-style furniture.

Dining/Entertainment: La Terrasse serves one of the best breakfasts in Paris. Also on the premises are a coffee shop, three bars, and Le Western, a steakhouse. The hotel serves one of the most popular Sunday brunches in Paris from 11am to 3pm, costing 250 F ($45) per person.

Services: 24-hour room service, babysitting service, same-day laundry and dry cleaning, secretarial service, Telex, fax, major airline and car-rental company representatives.

Facilities: Nearby underground garage, beauty parlor, boutiques, 15 TV networks (including CNN).

MODERATE

DUC DE SAINT-SIMON, 14, rue de St-Simon, 75007 Paris. Tel. 1/45-48-35-66. Fax 1/45-48-68-25. 34 rms (all with bath), 5 suites. TEL **Métro:** Rue-du-Bac.

$ Rates: 1,000–1,400 F ($180–$252) single; 1,100–1,500 F ($198–$270) double; from 1,600 F ($288) suite. Breakfast 70 F ($12.60) extra. No credit cards.

Set on a quiet residential street on the Left Bank, this small villa has a tiny front garden and an 1830s decor with *faux-marbre* trompe-l'oeil panels and a frescoed elevator. The vaulted cellar, formerly reserved for coal storage, contains an intimate bar with an adjacent Louis XIII–style breakfast room. Each bedroom is unique, though sure to include at least one antique. The service, perhaps the best reflection of the owner's extensive training, is helpful but reserved.

HOTEL DE L'ACADEMIE, 32, rue des Sts-Peres, 75007 Paris. Tel. 1/45-48-36-22. Fax 1/45-44-75-24. 34 rms (all with bath or shower). MINIBAR TV TEL **Métro:** St-Germain-des-Prés.

$ Rates: 670 F ($120.60) single; 780 F ($140.40) double. Breakfast 45 F ($8.10) extra. AE, DC, MC, V. **Parking:** 50 F ($9).

The exterior walls and the old ceiling beams are all that remain of this 17th-century former residence of the private guards of the duc de Rohan. In 1983, the hotel took on an English-speaking staff and was completely renovated to include an elegant reception area of marble and light-grained oak, with Second Empire–style chairs. The comfortably up-to-date rooms have Directoire beds, an Ile-de-France decor upholstered in soft colors, and views over the 18th- and 19th-century buildings in the immediate neighborhood.

HOTEL DE BOURGOGNE ET MONTANA, 3, rue de Bourgogne, 75007 Paris. Tel. 1/45-51-20-22. Fax 1/45-56-11-98. 35 rms (all with bath), 5 suites. TV TEL **Métro:** Invalides or Chambre des Députés.

$ Rates: (including continental breakfast): 770 F ($138.60) single; 860 F ($154.80) double; from 1,100 F ($198) suite. AE, DC, MC, V.

Located across the river from place de la Concorde and opposite the official residence of the president of the National Assembly, this hotel sits at the edge of the quiet, elegant, and dignified place du Palais-Bourbon. Originally built in the 17th century as a private *maison bourgeoise,* it's warm, cozy, and homey, with an intimate circular writing room, neoclassical columns, and a salon. A small elevator takes you upstairs to rooms decorated with floral chintz and comfortable beds and armchairs.

HOTEL DE L'UNIVERSITE, 22, rue de l'Université, 75007 Paris. Tel. 1/42-61-09-39. Fax 1/42-60-40-84. 28 rms (all with bath), 1 suite. TV TEL **Métro:** Rue-du-Bac or St-Germain-des-Prés.

$ Rates: 450–650 F ($81–$117) single; 750–1,100 F ($135–$198) double. Breakfast 60 F ($10.80) extra. MC, V.

Located within walking distance of boulevard St-Germain, the Hôtel de l'Université is a small, attractive place on the Left Bank near the Seine. The 300-year-old town house has been reconstructed by Monsieur and Madame Bergmann, who have added modern conveniences to the original architectural features. The bedrooms, many with antiques and courtyard views, are sophisticated and one of a kind. Room 54, the only suite, is a favorite for its combination of period pieces and rattan and the marble bath. Twelve rooms contain a minibar. Drinks and light food are served in the lounge in the evening.

HOTEL DU QUAI-VOLTAIRE, 19, quai Voltaire, 75007 Paris. Tel. 1/42-61-50-91. Fax 1/42-61-62-26. 33 rms (all with bath). TEL **Métro:** Rue-du-Bac.

$ Rates: 450 F ($81) single; 550–650 F ($99–$117) double; 790 F ($142.20) triple. Breakfast 40 F ($7.20) extra. AE, DC, MC, V.

Originally built in the 1600s as an abbey, then transformed into a hotel in 1856, the Hôtel du Quai-Voltaire is best known for its list of illustrious guests. They have included Oscar Wilde, Baudelaire, and Richard Wagner, who occupied Rooms 47, 56, and 55, respectively. Most of the rooms—many of them renovated—of this charming if modest inn directly overlook the bookstalls and boats of the Seine. Guests can have drinks in the bar or in the small salon, and simple meals such as omelets or salads can be prepared on request for guests who prefer to eat in.

ST-THOMAS-D'AQUIN, 3, rue de Pré-aux-Clercs, 75007 Paris. Tel.

1/42-61-01-22. Fax 1/42-61-41-43. 21 rms (all with bath). TV TEL **Métro:** St-Germain-des-Prés or Rue-du-Bac.

$ Rates: (including continental breakfast): 500–580 F ($90–$104.40) single; 620 F ($111.60) double. AE, DC, MC, V.

This newly renovated and redecorated hotel stands on a relatively traffic-free street between the busy boulevard St-Germain and rue de l'Université. The staff speaks English, and guests are well attended to. Bedrooms, which are serviced by an elevator, are fresh and modern, with flowered wallpaper.

BUDGET

HOTEL LENOX, 9, rue de l'Université, 75007 Paris. Tel. 1/42-96-10-95. Fax 1/42-61-52-83. 32 rms (all with bath). TV TEL **Métro:** Rue-du-Bac.

$ Rates: 530–750 F ($95.40–$135) double, 870 F ($156.60) double with private salon. AE, DC, MC, V.

The Hôtel Lenox is a favorite for tourists seeking reasonably priced, attractive accommodations in St-Germain-des-Prés. In 1910 the writer T. S. Eliot spent a summer here when the hotel was just a basic little pension. Today this much-improved hotel offers a helpful staff and small but comfortable bedrooms, some with elaborate ceiling molding. Each unit is a double. Many returning guests request the attic duplex with its tiny balcony and skylight. The hotel bar, considered to be *the* watering hole for members of the fashion industry, is open daily from 5pm to 2am.

HOTEL VERNEUIL ST-GERMAIN, 8, rue de Verneuil, 75007 Paris. Tel. 1/42-60-82-14. Fax 1/42-61-40-38. 26 rms (all with bath). TV TEL **Métro:** Rue-du-Bac or St-Germain-des-Prés.

$ Rates: 700 F ($126) single; 800–1,100 F ($144–$198) double; 1,300 F ($234) triple. Breakfast 50 F ($9) extra. AE, DC, MC, V.

A three-star hostelry set a few steps from the Seine, on a street loaded with antique dealers, this hotel was originally built in the 1700s as a private house. Completely renovated in 1992, the hotel offers rustically elegant bedrooms, usually with fabric-upholstered walls and the building's very old structural beams exposed to view. Each contains a marble-tiled bathroom and a hairdryer. Guests may order their breakfast in the stone-walled basement-level breakfast room, and have drinks in the French provincial bar.

LINDBERGH, 5, rue Chomel, 75007 Paris. Tel. 1/45-48-35-53. Fax 1/45-49-31-48. 26 rms (all with bath). TV TEL **Métro:** Sèvres-Babylone or St-Sulpice.

$ Rates: 400–510 F ($72–$91.80) single or double; 630 F ($113.40) triple; 700 F ($126) quad. Breakfast 35 F ($6.30) extra. AE, DC, MC, V. **Parking:** 120 F ($21.60) nearby.

Set in a prosperous and conservative neighborhood rich with bourgeois traditions, this hotel is named after the American aviator who made the historic solo transatlantic flight from New York to Paris in 1927. Tucked away off boulevard Raspail, a short walk from St-Germain-des-Prés, the hotel was originally built early in the 19th century. It has been frequently modernized since then, most recently in the early 1990s, and contains conservatively streamlined and comfortable bedrooms. There's a TV salon and a lounge on the premises.

9. 14TH ARR.

EXPENSIVE

HOTEL MERIDIEN MONTPARNASSE, 19, rue du Commandant-Mouchotte, 75014 Paris. Tel. 1/44-36-44-36. Fax 1/44-36-49-00. 918

rms (all with bath), 33 suites. A/C MINIBAR TV TEL **Métro:** Monparnasse-Bienvenue.

$ Rates: 1,550 F ($279) single; 1,950 F ($351) double; from 3,000 F ($540) suite. Breakfast 115 F ($20.70) extra. AE, DC, MC, V. **Parking:** 10 F ($1.80) per hour.

With its 25-story tower dominating Montparnasse, the Hôtel Meridien is the largest hotel on the Left Bank, thus providing each room with a view of Paris.

The hotel offers three restaurants: Montparnasse '25 serves haute cuisine in art nouveau decor, including reproductions of works by Modigliani and van Dongen. The glass-enclosed Restaurant Justine overlooking the gardens has both a buffet and à la carte specialties. And the Café Atlantic is in the lobby. The Platinum Bar, decorated in gray, black, and pearl, is open for drinks.

PULLMAN ST-JACQUES, 17, bd. St-Jacques, 75014 Paris. Tel. 1/40-78-79-80. Fax 1/45-88-43-93. 783 rms (all with bath), 14 suites. A/C MINIBAR TV TEL **Métro:** St-Jacques.

$ Rates: 1,230 F ($221.40) single; 1,360 F ($244.80) double; from 2,040 F ($367.20) suite. AE, DC, MC, V. **Parking:** 50 F ($9).

Affiliated with Pullman International Hotels, this massive, refreshingly stylish 14-story glass-and-steel structure offers guests a truly French experience. The main lobby has been upgraded, with a marble fountain in the middle. Bedrooms are decorated in color-coordinated fabrics, and each bathroom has both bath and shower. Le Français is the Pullman's bistro, a re-creation of a turn-of-the-century brasserie, with bentwood chairs, 1890s posters, potted palms, and Belle Epoque light fixtures. Meals here begin at 189 F ($34).

10. 3RD & 4TH ARR.

MODERATE

HOTEL BASTILLE SPERIA, 1, rue de la Bastille, 75004 Paris. Tel. 1/42-72-04-01. Fax 1/42-72-56-38. 42 rms (all with bath). MINIBAR TV TEL **Métro:** Bastille.

$ Rates: 580 F ($104.40) single; 630 F ($113.40) double. Breakfast 45 F ($8.10) extra. AE, DC, MC, V.

The seven-story cream-colored Bastille Speria occupies a corner near the Bastille, the Bastille Opéra, and Le Marais. The hotel was completely overhauled in 1980, leaving a modern interior and up-to-date accommodations that belie its mansard exterior. All bedrooms have high ceilings and simple but comfortable furniture and private baths.

HOTEL DE LA BRETONNERIE, 22, rue Ste-Croix-de-la-Bretonnerie, 75004 Paris. Tel. 1/48-87-77-63. Fax 1/42-77-26-78. 29 rms (all with bath), 1 suite. MINIBAR TV TEL **Métro:** Hôtel-de-Ville.

$ Rates: 400 F ($72) single; 530–730 F ($95.40–$131.40) double; 800 F ($144) suite. Breakfast 45 F ($8.10) extra. DC, MC, V.

Located just a short walk from the Pompidou Center in Le Marais, this 17th-century mansion, once occupied by French aristocrats, was modernized in 1987, with a healthy respect for tradition: Freestone walls, exposed beams, and Louis XIII–style furniture provide an intimate atmosphere. Rooms are located under the eaves.

HOTEL DE LUTECE, 65, rue St-Louis-en-I'Ile, 75004 Paris. Tel. 1/43-26-23-52. Fax 1/43-29-60-25. 23 rms (all with bath). TV TEL **Métro:** Pont-Marie.

$ Rates: 620 F ($111.60) single; 750 F ($135) double; 970 F ($174.60) triple. Breakfast 45 F ($8.10) extra. No credit cards.

Walking into this hotel is much like walking into a country house in Brittany. The lounge is graciously furnished with antiques, original tile floors, an old fireplace, and contemporary paintings. Each of the individualized rooms comes furnished with antiques, adding to the sort of refined atmosphere that attracts many famous guests, including the Duke and Duchess of Bedford.

HOTEL DES DEUX-ILES, 59, rue St-Louis-en l'Ile, 75004 Paris. Tel. 1/43-26-13-35. Fax 1/43-29-60-25. 17 rms (all with bath). TV TEL **Métro:** Pont-Marie.

$ Rates: 675 F ($121.50) single; 775 F ($139.50) double. Breakfast 45 F ($8.10) extra. No credit cards.

The Hôtel des Deux-Iles was impeccably restored by Roland Buffat, the same designer who worked on the Hôtel St-Louis and the Hôtel de Lutèce. This 17th-century building is the largest and most glamorous of his creations. There is an eclectic collection of furnishings, mostly bamboo and reed, blended with period pieces and the occasional cage of white doves or antique painting. Downstairs is a rustic tavern with an open fireplace. A lounge has a central garden of plants and flowers. Like the public rooms, the bedrooms are decorated with bamboo and reed.

HOTEL DU VIEUX MARAIS, 8, rue du Plâtre, 75004 Paris. Tel. 1/42-78-47-22. Fax 1/42-78-34-32. 30 rms (all with bath). TV TEL **Métro:** Hôtel-de-Ville.

$ Rates (including breakfast): 390–450 F ($70.20–$81) single; 550–570 F ($99–$102.60) double; 700 F ($126) triple. MC, V.

The Hôtel du Vieux Marais is a good choice for visitors who want to be near the underground culture of Le Marais. Located on a small street just off rue des Archives is this simple, fully renovated hotel hidden behind an ornate beaux-arts exterior. The lobby has marble floors, wood accents, and an enlarged engraving of place des Vosges centuries ago.

HOTEL SAINT-LOUIS, 75, rue St-Louis-en-l'Ile, 75004 Paris. Tel. 1/46-34-04-80. Fax 1/46-34-02-13. 21 rms (all with bath). TEL **Métro:** Pont-Marie.

$ Rates: 665 F ($119.70) single; 765 F ($137.70) double. Breakfast 45 F ($8.10) extra. No credit cards.

The Hôtel Saint-Louis, fashionably situated on the Ile St-Louis, offers travelers a hard-to-find family atmosphere and rooftop views in some of its upper-level accommodations. I prefer the rooms on the fifth floor, which have the most atmosphere and are decorated with old wood and attractive furniture. The breakfast room is in the cellar beneath 17th-century stone vaulting.

LE PAVILLON DE LA REINE, 28, place des Vosges, 75003 Paris. Tel. 1/42-77-96-40. Fax 1/42-77-63-06. 30 rms (all with bath), 23 suites. A/C MINIBAR TV TEL **Métro:** Bastille.

$ Rates: 1,100–2,500 F ($198–$450) single or double; 2,950 F ($531) suite for four. Breakfast 85 F ($15.30) extra. AE, DC, MC, V. **Parking:** 120 F ($21.60).

⭐ Built in 1986, this cream-colored neoclassical villa blends in perfectly in an area that was once home to Victor Hugo. Guests enter the hotel through a tunnel that opens onto a small formal garden. Inside, the Louis XIII decor evokes the heyday of place des Vosges. Wing chairs with flame-stitched upholstery combined with iron-banded Spanish antiques create a rustic feel. Each bedroom is different; some are duplexes with sleeping lofts set above cozy salons. All rooms have a warm decor of weathered beams, reproductions of famous oil paintings, and marble bathrooms. Guests also have use of the 25 underground parking spaces.

11. 18TH ARR.

BUDGET

HOTEL NEW MONTMARTRE, 7, rue Paul-Albert, 75018 Paris. Tel. 1/46-06-03-03. Fax 1/46-06-73-28. 32 rms (all with bath). TV TEL **Métro:** Anvers or Château-Rouge.

$ Prices: 390 F ($70.20) single; 420–480 F ($75.60–$86.40) double; 580 F ($104.40) triple; 680 F ($122.40) quad. Breakfast 37 F ($6.70) extra. MC, V.

Renovated in 1992, this hotel offers good value and a location closer to the Basilica of Sacré-Coeur (about a two-minute walk away) than any other hotel in Paris. A remake of a white-fronted, 19th-century building, it offers an elevator, both smoking and no-smoking breakfast rooms, a café/bar, and a simple lobby sheathed with beige marble and dotted with potted plants. Bedrooms are clean but simple, outfitted with pastel color schemes and views out over a quiet neighborhood.

12. AT ORLY AIRPORT

HILTON INTERNATIONAL ORLY, Aéroport Orly, 267, Orly Sud, 94544 Val-de-Marne. Tel. 1/46-87-33-88. 359 rms (all with bath). A/C MINIBAR TV TEL **Directions:** Free shuttle bus to and from Orly terminal; 30 minutes from Paris by taxi, except during rush hours.

$ Rates: 1,000 F ($180) single; 1,500 F ($270) double. Breakfast 80 F ($14.40) extra. Children stay free in parents' room. AE, DC, MC, V. **Parking:** Free.

The Orly Hilton, located midway between the two terminals, is one of the most contemporary airport hotels in Europe. Catering mostly to international executives, the hotel is efficient, sophisticated, and convenient for travelers who need to be near the airport. Each of the bedrooms contains soundproof walls, multilanguage radio, and TV with in-house movies.

Dining/Entertainment: The hotel has two restaurants, one of them in the Louisiana plantation style, and a bar area.

Services: 24-hour room service, laundry.

Facilities: Swimming pool, ice skating, tennis courts.

13. AT CHARLES DE GAULLE AIRPORT

HOTEL SOFITEL, Aéroport Charles-de-Gaulle, Zone Centrale, 95713 Roissey/Charles-de-Gaulle. Tel. 1/48-62-23-23, or toll free 800/221-4542 in the U.S. Fax 1/48-62-78-49. 344 rms (all with bath), 8 suites. A/C MINIBAR TV TEL **Directions:** Free bus service to and from the airport.

$ Rates: 850 F ($153) single or double, 950 F ($171) "Exclusive Plus" single or double, 500 F ($90) day use single or double; from 1,500 F ($270) suite. Breakfast 80 F ($14.40) extra. AE, DC, MC, V. **Parking:** Free.

The Hotel Sofitel provides attractive, soundproof accommodations. There are enough bars and restaurants to save you from making a difficult trip into Paris—including Les Valois, a gourmet restaurant, and Le Jardin, a grill. Facilities include a swimming pool and sauna and a business center. Laundry and valet service and 24-hour room service are provided.

PARIS DINING

In the gastronomic capital of the world, with more than 12,000 restaurants to choose from, it's tough to list all the noteworthy ones. I have opted to include many favorites, listed in a wide range of prices. Some of the restaurants are famous throughout the world; others are lesser known but still deserve the visitor's attention.

Brasserie and bistro customers beware: Granted Lasserre and Taillevent are fine French restaurants that serve haute cuisine, but there are also restaurants that serve very average food under the guise of haute cuisine and get away with it because of the city's culinary reputation. Don't be wooed by fancy atmosphere or intimidated by haughty maître d's. Use your traveler's common sense: If the locals flock to a particular restaurant, it's probably a sound choice.

1. HAUTE CUISINE

There are several restaurants in Paris that serve truly exceptional—and very expensive—cuisine. Below you'll find the best. Restaurants in this section are not divided into arrondissements.

VERY EXPENSIVE

ALAIN SENDERENS'S LUCAS-CARTON, 9, place de la Madeleine, 8e. Tel. 42-65-22-90.

Cuisine: FRENCH. **Reservations:** Required several days ahead for lunch and several weeks ahead for dinner. **Métro:** Madeleine.

$ Prices: Appetizers 200–400 F ($36–$72); main dishes 250–600 F ($45–$108); fixed-price lunch 375 F ($67.50); *menu dégustation* 1,400 F ($252). MC, V.

Open: Lunch Mon–Fri noon–2:30pm; dinner Mon–Sat 8–10:15pm. **Closed:** Three weeks in Aug (dates vary).

This landmark restaurant, dating from the Belle Epoque, was designed by an Englishman named Lucas and a talented French chef, Francis Carton. Since Senderens has taken over as restauranteur, he has added some welcome modern touches to the historic restaurant. The two dining rooms downstairs and the private rooms upstairs are decorated with mirrors and fragrant bouquets of spring flowers.

Senderens, who bakes his own bread, creates such tasty dishes as fresh cod with eggplant, caviar, and fried zucchini; ravioli filled with scallops and served with thyme-flavored zucchini; and mild smoked salmon with a sprinkling of salmon eggs; plus other delicacies from his own smoker or from the rôtisserie. For dessert, I suggest hot pineapple fritters, beignets d'ananas Eventhia (named for his wife) if they're available. However, Senderens is constantly searching for new culinary creations, so by the time you visit there will probably be a fresh addition to his innovative menu. His *menu dégustation,* although lethally priced, includes a selection of major and very grand French wines—hence the high tab.

LE GRAND VEFOUR, 17, rue de Beaujolais, 1er. Tel. 42-96-56-27.
   Cuisine: FRENCH. **Reservations:** Recommended. **Métro:** Palais-Royal.
$ Prices: Appetizers 150–320 F ($27–$57.60); main dishes 230–380 F ($41.40–$68.40); fixed-price lunch 305 F ($54.90). AE, DC, MC, V.
   Open: Lunch Mon–Fri 12:30–2:15pm; dinner Mon–Fri 7:30–10:15pm. **Closed:** Aug.

Since the reign of Louis XV this has been a restaurant, though not always under the same name. Although the exact date of its opening as the Café de Chartres is not definitely known, it's more than 200 years old and is a historical treasure. It was named after owner Jean Véfour, a former chef to a member of the royal family in 1812.

Since then, Napoléon, Danton, and a host of writers and artists, including Victor Hugo, Colette, and Jean Cocteau, have dined here—as the brass plaques on the tables testify. Jean Taittinger of the Taittinger Champagne family (who also own the Crillon) purchased the restaurant, and the meticulous restoration, overseen by the Department of Historical Monuments, has improved its former glories even more.

Dining here is an experience. Specialties, served on Limoges china, include terrine of half-cooked roe salmon served with "smoked milk" (you heard that right), a bouillon of asparagus with truffles, and a deboned poached filet of sole Grand Véfour (stuffed with a duxelle of mushrooms and served with a mustard-flavored mousseline sauce), or perhaps a parmentier of oxtail with truffles and truffle-studded mashed potatoes. Desserts are often grand occasions, as exemplified by the gourmandises au chocolate, served with a chocolate sorbet. The dining room is under the watchful eye of maître d'hôtel Christian David, one of the finest men in his profession in competitive Paris.

 FROMMER'S SMART TRAVELER: RESTAURANTS

1. Select the prix-fixe (fixed-price) menu. Most restaurants offer both fixed-price and à la carte menus. The latter is more adventurous but at least 30% more expensive.
2. Take advantage of the fixed-price lunch at top restaurants; at dinner, you'll pay three or four times the price on an à la carte menu.
3. If you have a big appetite but don't want to pay the prices for multicourse dinners in typical Paris restaurants, head for one of those all-you-can-eat places, like La Taverne du Sergent Recruteur (see page 148) or L'Espace Cardin (see page 127).
4. Look for the *plats du jour* (daily specials) on any à la carte menu. They're invariably fresh and often carry a lower price tag than regular à la carte listings.
5. Drink *vin ordinaire* (table wine served in a carafe). It costs only a fraction of the price of bottled wine.
6. Remember that anything consumed standing up at a counter in Paris or sitting on a stool at the bar is invariably cheaper than if consumed at a table.
7. To keep costs really low, patronize rue de la Huchette on the Left Bank (Métro: St-Michel). It has some of the cheapest restaurants in Paris, serving mainly Greek cuisine. Or turn onto rue Zavier-Privas, where couscous (the most famous dish of North Africa, made with semolina, stewed vegetables, and stewed meat) is found in many establishments.

JAMIN, 32, rue du Longchamp, 16e. Tel. 47-27-12-27.
Cuisine: FRENCH. **Reservations:** Required two or three months in advance.
Métro: Trocadéro.
$ **Prices:** Appetizers 250–450 F ($45–$81); main dishes 250–500 F ($45–$90); fixed-price menus 890–1,100 F ($160.20–$198). AE, DC, MC, V.
Open: Lunch Mon–Fri 12:30–2:30pm; dinner Mon–Fri 7:30–10:30pm. **Closed:** July.

★ Chef and proprietor Joël Robuchon has a reputation as the country's most innovative cook. Some critics say his restaurant is *la première table de France*. He is a master of *cuisine actuelle* (what is being cooked right now). The food here is light and delicate, with outstanding flavors. And the capable and courteous staff serves dishes that are as pleasing to the eye as they are tempting to the palate. Robuchon bakes his own bread, fresh every day. He is also known to spend long hours in the kitchen testing (or inventing) new recipes. The fish and shellfish are shipped fresh from Brittany.

Among the delectable dishes are kidneys and sweetbreads diced and sautéed with mushrooms, canette rosée (roasted and braised duckling, flavored with ginger, nutmeg, and cinnamon), crayfish-filled ravioli with a sauce of truffles and duck liver, and chicken for two, poached in pig's bladder. His mashed potatoes, once labeled "the silliest dish in the world," are hailed here as a masterpiece—and they are. The chef also confides that the other dish that makes the greatest impression in his restaurant is his salad—only the freshest of greens, the best oil and vinegar, and a dash of natural juices from the meat being served.

LASSERRE, 17, av. Franklin-D-Roosevelt, 8e. Tel. 43-59-53-43.
Cuisine: FRENCH. **Reservations:** Required. **Métro:** F-D-Roosevelt.
$ **Prices:** Appetizers 170–220 F ($30.60–$39.60); main dishes 200–250 F ($36–$45). AE, MC, V.
Open: Lunch Tues–Sat 12:30–2:30pm; dinner Mon–Sat 7:30–10:30pm.
Closed: Aug.

★ This elegant, deluxe restaurant was a simple bistro before World War II. Then along came René Lasserre, who bought it and set out to create a culinary paradise, attracting gourmets from around the world.

Behind the front doors are two private ground-floor dining rooms with a "disappearing wall," plus a reception lounge with Louis XVI furnishings and brocaded walls. You ascend to the second landing in a little elevator lined with brocaded silk. The main dining room is elegantly appointed with a mezzanine on two sides. Tall, arched windows are draped softly with silk. You will be seated on a Louis XV salon chair at an exquisite table set with the finest porcelain, gold-edged crystal glasses, a silver bird, a ceramic dove, and a silver candelabrum.

The ceiling, painted blue with fleecy-white clouds, is pulled back in fair weather to reveal the sky. Monsieur Lasserre has been known to bring white doves from his country place and release them in the main dining room.

I suggest that you begin with the blanc de sandre (zander) à la nage d'estrilles. Among the fish dishes, try a rissolles of crayfish with an essence of green tomatoes. Or try the steak de charolais au Bourgueil. For dessert, try a parfait aux noisettes (hazelnuts) grillées, with a honey-flavored sabayon.

The wine cellar, containing some 180,000 bottles, is one of the most remarkable in Paris. The red wine is decanted into silver or ornate crystal pitchers.

MAXIM'S, 3, rue Royale, 8e. Tel. 42-65-27-94.
Cuisine: FRENCH. **Reservations:** Required. **Métro:** Concorde.
$ **Prices:** Appetizers 90–790 F ($16.20–$142.20); main dishes 200–400 F ($36–$72). AE, DC, MC, V.
Open: Lunch daily 12:30–2pm; dinner daily 7:30–11:30pm. **Closed:** Sun July–Aug.

Maxim's is no longer the pocket of chic it once was, its grandeur and culinary finesse long ago surpassed by other restaurants. Nonetheless, the legend lives on, at least for first-timers to Paris. When Edward VII was the Prince of Wales, he used to revel in his freedom here from his austere mother, Queen Victoria. Perhaps the most legendary restaurant in the world, Maxim's extravagant Belle Epoque decor recalls the days of the Opéra Comique and Gay '90s when it was frequented by elegant cocottes beplumed with ostrich feathers and diamonds.

Because of the richness of its art nouveau interior, it has often been used as a film location. It was the setting for *The Merry Widow,* and Louis Jourdan took Leslie Caron to Maxim's "the night they invented champagne" in *Gigi.* In its heyday, all of society gathered here: grand dukes, royals, famous courtesans, the Aga Khan, Callas, Onassis, Prince Rainier, and Princess Grace.

There are several dining rooms, and the intricacy of which table is best escapes most first-time diners. The background is dazzling—paneled walls, gilt and colored vines, leafy cut-out overlays, and a stained-glass ceiling.

In 1981 clothing industry giant Pierre Cardin took over the restaurant.

You might begin your dinner with Billi-By soup, made with mussels, white wine, cream, chopped onions, celery, parsley, and coarsely ground pepper. Another favorite is the sole Albert, named after the late famous maître d'hôtel, flavored with chopped herbs and breadcrumbs, plus a large glass of vermouth. Also recommended is the Challons duckling in a foie gras sauce. For dessert, try the mousse made with three types of chocolate.

TAILLEVENT, 15, rue Lamennais, 8e. Tel. 45-63-39-94.

Cuisine: FRENCH. **Reservations:** Required, weeks, even months, in advance for both lunch and dinner. **Métro:** George-V.

$ Prices: Appetizers 170–300 F ($30.60–$54); main dishes 250–380 F ($45–$68.40). MC, V.

Open: Lunch Mon–Fri noon–2:30pm; dinner Mon–Fri 7–10pm. **Closed:** Aug.

★ Dine in grand 18th-century style in this town house just off the Champs-Elysées. In 1946, when owner Jean Claude Vrinat's father opened the doors of Taillevent (named after the celebrated 14th-century chef who wrote one of the oldest books on French cuisine), he established one of the outstanding restaurants in all of Paris. The wines are superb, and the service is impeccable. Under the direction of chef Philippe Legendre, menus are deftly balanced between traditional and modern cuisine.

You might begin with aspic de foie gras (dices of liver and veal sweetbreads in aspic jelly with very fine slivers of carrots and truffles). Main-dish specialties (subject to change, of course) include cassolette de langoustines, agneau aux trois cuissons (three cuts of lamb—feet, breast, and tenderloin—with various sauces), followed by fondant aux deux parfumes (an almond-toffee Bavarian cream covered with chocolate).

Taillevent's wine list is one of the best in the city. Monsieur and Madame Vrinat make the selections carefully and knowledgeably, providing bottles pleasing to the palate and complementary to the fine cuisine.

LA TOUR D'ARGENT, 15–17, quai de la Tournelle, 5e. Tel. 43-54-23-31.

Cuisine: FRENCH. **Reservations:** Required. **Métro:** Maubert-Mutualité or Sully-Morland.

$ Prices: Appetizers 215–580 F ($38.70–$104.40); main dishes 330–580 F ($59.40–$104.40); fixed-price lunch (Tues–Sat) 375 F ($67.50). AE, DC, MC, V.

Open: Lunch Tues–Sun 12:30–2:30pm; dinner Tues–Sun 8–11:30pm.

★ Since the 16th century there has always been a restaurant on this spot. The restaurant became famous, though, when it was owned by Frédéric Delair, who purchased the wine cellar of the Café Anglais and began issuing certificates to diners who ordered the house specialty, pressed duck (caneton).

Now this legendary restaurant is under the direction of the debonair restaurateur Claude Terrail, who has catered to celebrities and world figures for years: Truman, Eisenhower, and Churchill all dined here.

A gastronomic museum now surrounds the restaurant. From the top floor, facing the Left Bank and the Seine, the glass enclosure provides a panoramic view of the 17th-century houses along the quays of the Ile-St-Louis. At night, you can see the illuminated flying buttresses of Notre-Dame. So many well-heeled Americans flock here that at times the only French accents heard are those of the staff.

Nonetheless, the cuisine remains classically French. New diners often order the duck—and it's sensational. There are numerous ways to have it prepared. Other selections to choose from include filets de sole cardinal and filet Tour d'Argent. Begin with the potage Claudius Burdel made with sorrel, egg yolks, fresh cream, chicken broth, and butter whipped together. For dessert, the pêches flambées is everything you'd expect it to be.

2. 8TH ARR.

EXPENSIVE

AU PETIT MONTMORENCY, 5, rue Jean-Mermoz, 8e. Tel. 42-25-11-19.
   Cuisine: FRENCH. **Reservations:** Required. **Métro:** F-D-Roosevelt.
$ Prices: Appetizers 110–350 F ($19.80–$63); main dishes 180–270 F ($32.40–$48.60). MC, V.
   Open: Lunch Mon–Fri noon–2:15pm; dinner Mon–Fri 7:30–10:30pm. **Closed:** Aug.

Before Daniel Bouche and his wife, Nicole, opened this place, Bouche trained at a number of restaurants, including Maxim's in Chicago. But he seems to have discarded much of what he learned, preferring to chart his own culinary course and turning out a delicate and subtle cuisine: hot oysters with a Pomerol sauce and wild-mushroom toast, haddock and watercress with fresh salmon toast, canard Lucifer (roast duck with a hot sauce, semolina, vegetables, and chutney), and, in season, such game as hare, venison, partridge, and pheasant. Of course, menu items are always changing, based on the season and the market.

For dessert, I recommend le grand dessert au chocolate (bitter chocolate) or one of an assortment of different chocolate cakes served with a small, hot pistachio soufflé and a coffee sauce.

The French wines are well selected, including some choice but little-publicized ones.

CHIBERTA, 3, rue Arsene-Houssaye, 8e. Tel. 45-63-77-90.
   Cuisine: FRENCH. **Reservations:** Required. **Métro:** Charles-de-Gaulle (Etoile).
$ Prices: Appetizers 125–310 F ($22.50–$55.80); main dishes 200–360 F ($36–$64.80). AE, DC, V.
   Open: Lunch Mon–Fri noon–2:30pm; dinner Mon–Fri 7:30–11pm. **Closed:** Aug.

In an elegantly modern setting, chef Philippe Da Silva has stunned some of the gastronomic circles of Paris, turning out one inventive dish after another. The director of this restaurant is Louis-Noël Richard, who has turned Chiberta into one of the most attractive restaurants in Paris. The restaurant was named for a region of the Pays Basque known for its culinary excellence.

Each dish is admirably presented and described by the maître d'. The menu changes twice a year, but typical opening courses might include pigeon salad with lobster, ravioli with truffles, and salmon tartare. For a main course, try crayfish and leeks in a sweet-and-sour sauce, or filet of sea bass in a truffle sauce. Top it off with wild strawberries and honey ice cream drizzled with raspberry sauce. The wine list is well chosen. Expect a culinary masterpiece and excellent service.

RESTAURANT COPENHAGUE/FLORA DANICA, 143, av. des Champs-Elysées, 8e. Tel. 43-59-20-41.
   Cuisine: DANISH. **Reservations:** Recommended. **Métro:** George-V.
$ Prices: Appetizers 70–190 F ($12.60–$34.20); main dishes 130–280 F ($23.40–$50.40). AE, DC, MC, V.
   Open: Restaurant Copenhague, lunch Mon–Sat noon–2pm; dinner Mon–Sat

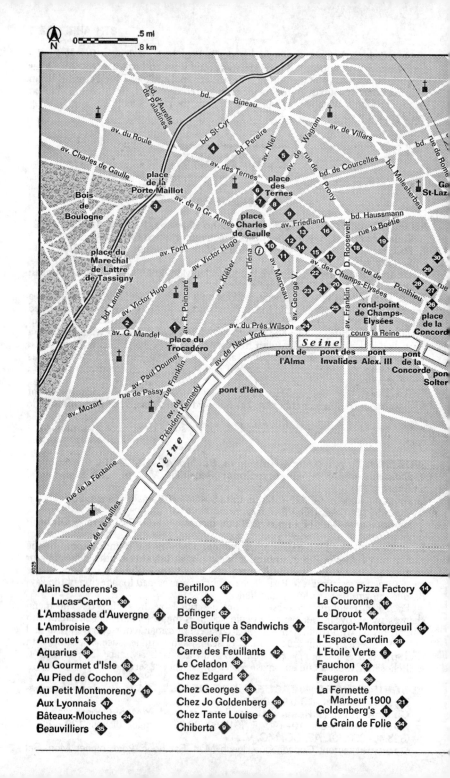

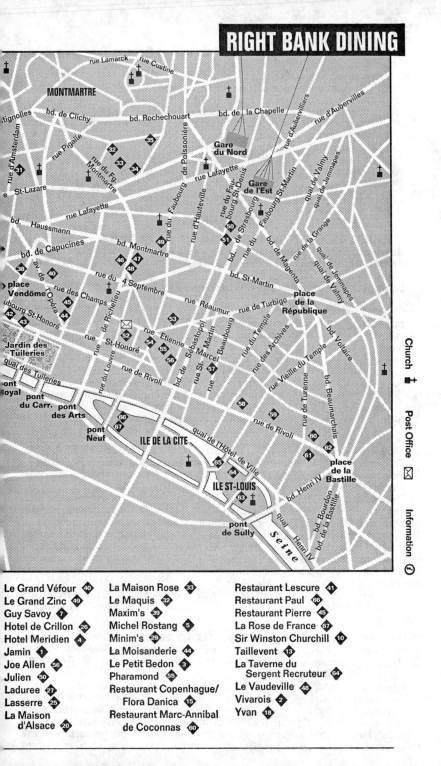

MONTMARTRE

rue Lamarck
rue Custine
bd. de Clichy
bd. Rochechouart
bd. de la Chapelle
rue d'Auberville
rue d'Aubervilliers
Gare du Nord
Gare de l'Est
tignolles
bd. Pigalle
rue du Fg. Montmartre
rue du Faubourg de Poissonnière
rue Lafayette
rue du Faubourg St-Denis
Faubourg St-Martin
quai de Valmy
quai de Jemmapes
rue d'Amsterdam
St-Lazare
rue Lafayette
rue du Faubourg St-Strasbourg
rue du Faubourg St-Martin
rue de la Grange
quai de Jemmapes
quai de Valmy
bd. Haussmann
bd. de Capucines
bd. Montmartre
rue du 4 Septembre
rue Réaumur
rue de Turbigo
bd. de Magenta
bd. St-Martin
place de la République
bd. Voltaire
place Vendôme
av. de l'Opéra
rue des Champs
ubourg St-Honoré
Jardin des Tuileries
quai des Tuileries
rue de Richelieu
rue St-Honoré
rue Etienne Marcel
rue de Sébastopol
rue de Rivoli
rue du Louvre
rue St-Martin
rue Réaumur
rue du Temple
rue des Archives
rue Vieille du Temple
rue de Turenne
bd. Beaumarchais
bd. Voltaire
pont Royal
pont du Carr.
pont des Arts
pont Neuf
ILE DE LA CITÉ
quai de l'Hôtel de Ville
rue de Rivoli
place de la Bastille
ILE ST-LOUIS
bd. Henri IV
bd. Bourdon
bd. de la Bastille
pont de Sully
quai Henri IV
Seine

Church ✝ Post Office ⊠ Information ⓘ

Le Grand Véfour 40
Le Grand Zinc 49
Guy Savoy 7
Hotel de Crillon 26
Hotel Meridien 4
Jamin 1
Joe Allen 56
Julien 50
Laduree 27
Lasserre 25
La Maison d'Alsace 20

La Maison Rose 33
Le Maquis 32
Maxim's 39
Michel Rostang 5
Minim's 29
La Moisanderie 44
Le Petit Bedon 3
Pharamond 55
Restaurant Copenhague/ Flora Danica 15
Restaurant Marc-Annibal de Coconnas 60

Restaurant Lescure 41
Restaurant Paul 66
Restaurant Pierre 45
La Rose de France 67
Sir Winston Churchill 10
Taillevent 13
La Taverne du Sergent Recruteur 64
Le Vaudeville 48
Vivarois 2
Yvan 18

7:15–10:30pm (closed Aug). Flora Danica, lunch daily noon–2pm; dinner daily 7:15–11pm.

The specialties of Denmark are served with style and flair at the "Maison du Danemark," which functions as a quasi-official ambassador of goodwill for Denmark within France. In many ways, it's probably the best restaurant along the Champs-Elysées, with an outside terrace for midsummer dining. There are two dining areas to choose from, the Flora Danica, on the street level, and the somewhat more formal Restaurant Copenhague, upstairs.

To be thoroughly Danish, order an apéritif of aquavit and ignore the wine list in favor of Carlsberg or Tuborg. Menu items include a terrine of foie gras, smoked salmon, a selection of fresh shrimp, or any of an elegant array of open-face sandwiches. The house specialty is a platter of "délices Scandinaves," composed of the many seafood and dairy specialties that the Danes prepare exceptionally well.

MODERATE

ANDROUET, 41, rue d'Amsterdam, 8e. Tel. 48-74-26-93.
Cuisine: FRENCH. **Reservations:** Required. **Métro:** St-Lazare or Liège.
$ Prices: Appetizers 53–70 F ($9.50–$12.60); main dishes 85–270 F ($15.30–$48.60). AE, DC, MC, V.
Open: Lunch Mon–Sat noon–2:30pm; dinner Mon–Sat 7–10pm.

Brightly lit and decorated in pastels, this is one of the most unusual restaurants in the world, because cheese is the basic ingredient in most of the dishes. It all began in World War I, when founder Monsieur Androuet started inviting favored guests down to his cellar to sample cheese and good wine. The idea caught on, and at one time it was considered one of the most fashionable things to do in Paris. Nowadays Androuet isn't merely chic—it's an institution. Cheese experts, of course, flock here; I heard one claim that he could tell what the goat ate by the cheese made from its milk.

For a first course, the ravioles de chèvre frais (ravioli stuffed with fresh goat cheese) is a fine choice. A good main dish is filet de boeuf cotentin (beef filet with roquefort sauce flambé with Calvados). Cheese-lovers come here to order a dégustation de fromages affinés dans nos caves (a sampling of cheese from our cellars). There are as many as 120 varieties of cheese.

LA BOUTIQUE A SANDWICHS, 12, rue du Colisée, 8e. Tel. 43-59-56-69.
Cuisine: FRENCH. **Reservations:** Recommended. **Métro:** F-D-Roosevelt.
$ Prices: Appetizers 22–42 F ($4–$7.60); sandwiches from 15 F ($2.70); main dishes 30–65 F ($5.40–$11.70). MC, V.
Open: Mon–Sat 11:45am–1am. **Closed:** Aug.

Run by two Alsatian brothers, Hubert and Claude Schick, La Boutique is a good place to order absolutely delectable sandwiches in many unusual and imaginative varieties. You'll find this marriage of American and French tastes a quarter of a block from the Champs-Elysées, upstairs, with bare wooden tables and colored mats. There are at least two dozen different sandwich concoctions on the menu, as well as light snacks or "plate meals," some with distinctly Swiss and Alsatian overtones. Special hot plates include pickelfleisch raclette valaisanne à gogo; a wheel of cheese—part of it melted—is taken to your table and scraped right onto your plate; accompanying it are pickles and boiled potatoes. For a delectable conclusion to your meal, try the apple strudel.

CHEZ EDGARD, 4, rue Marbeuf, 8e. Tel. 47-20-51-15.
Cuisine: FRENCH. **Reservations:** Required. **Métro:** F-D-Roosevelt.
$ Prices: Appetizers 45–95 F ($8.10–$17.10); main dishes 85–180 F ($15.30–$32.40). AE, DC, MC, V.
Open: Lunch Mon–Sat noon–3pm; dinner Mon–Sat 7pm–12:30am.

A chic coterie of neighborhood residents regard this Belle Epoque eating place as their favorite neighborhood restaurant, and ebullient owner Paul Benmussa makes it a point to welcome them during their frequent visits as if they were members of his extended family. Chez Edgard is one of the consistently best restaurants in the fashionable 8th arrondissement. Customers include politicians, such as Giscard d'Estaing; members of the press; and such show-business personalities as Roman Polanski, Catherine Deneuve, and Sydney Pollack. Conversation in this scarlet-and-black restaurant can be noisier here than in less expensive restaurants.

Specialties include breast of duckling, rouget with basil in puff pastry, salmon tartare, and several terrines, including one made from scallops. There's also a range of well-prepared meat dishes. In winter, seafood and oysters are shipped in from Brittany. The ice-cream sundaes (listed with other desserts on a special menu) are particularly delectable. There's a small outdoor terrace, but most guests prefer to eat inside on one of the semiprivate banquettes. The service is attentive.

CHEZ TANTE LOUISE, 41, rue Boissy-d'Anglas, 8e. Tel. 42-65-06-85.

Cuisine: FRENCH. **Reservations:** Required. **Métro:** Madeleine.
$ Prices: Appetizers 50–200 F ($9–$36); main dishes 200–220 F ($36–$39.60). AE, DC, MC, V.
Open: Lunch Mon–Fri noon–2:30pm; dinner Mon–Fri 7–10:30pm. **Closed:** Aug.

In this intimate little place with a tiny mezzanine, just off place de la Madeleine and place de la Concorde, an oil painting on the wall and a bronze plaque on the brown marble facade pay homage to the restaurant's originator, who owned it from the mid-1920s to the mid-1950s. Today Eleane and Bernard Lhiabastres carry on in Aunt Louise's worthy tradition; they've inherited her secrets, and the menu includes such specialties as foie gras, seafood platter, duck with orange sauce, and game in season. The turn-of-the-century decor of red curtains and yellow walls has changed very little since the original tenure of Tante Louise.

L'ESPACE CARDIN, 1, av. Gabriel, 8e. Tel. 42-66-11-70.

Cuisine: FRENCH. **Reservations:** Recommended. **Métro:** Champs-Elysées.
$ Prices: Appetizers 85–130 F ($15.30–$23.40); main dishes 135–285 F ($24.30–$51.30); fixed-price meal 230 F ($41.40). AE, DC, MC, V.
Open: Apr–Oct, lunch Sun–Fri noon–2:30pm; dinner Tues–Sat 8:30pm–1am. Nov–Mar, lunch daily noon–2:30pm. **Closed:** Dinner Nov–Mar.

What's probably the most lavish buffet in Paris is served daily in a California-beachside decor of plastic chairs, oilcloth table coverings, and decorative parasols. But nothing could be more French or more centrally located for the flocks of office workers who come here at lunchtime and dine inside or on the terrace overlooking the gardens of the Champs-Elysées. Midway between the American Embassy and the Champs-Elysées, this consciously informal spot was established by Pierre Cardin.

More than 70 hors d'oeuvres—salads, vegetables, cold roast meats, and authentic Italian antipasti—fill the tables. The main course is served by a waiter who brings you your choice of a *plat du jour*. This is followed by a selection from a dessert buffet. Service and drinks are extra (champagne is sold by the glass).

LA FERMETTE MARBEUF 1900, 5, rue Marbeuf, 8e. Tel. 47-20-63-53.

Cuisine: FRENCH. **Reservations:** Required. **Métro:** F-D-Roosevelt.
$ Prices: Appetizers 40–95 F ($7.20–$17.10); main dishes 95–150 F ($17.10–$27); fixed-price menu 160 F ($28.80). AE, DC, MC, V.
Open: Lunch daily 12:30–3pm; dinner daily 7:30–11:30pm.

Turn-of-the-century decor, reasonable prices, and fine cuisine are what you can expect here. The hand-painted tiles and stained-glass windows of the twin dining rooms contribute to its having been designated a historic landmark. Guests come here for the fun of it all, as well as for the well-prepared and flavorful cuisine. Specialties include sweetbreads with a ragoût of wild mushrooms, basil-flavored filet of sole with fresh noodles, a bavarois of salmon, and several beef dishes.

LE 30 [CHEZ FAUCHON], 30, place de la Madeleine, 8e. Tel. 47-42-56-58.

Cuisine: FRENCH. **Reservations:** Recommended, especially at lunch. **Métro:** Madeleine.
$ Prices: Appetizers 70–200 F ($12.60–$36); main dishes 140–200 F ($25.20–$36). AE, DC, MC, V.

Open: Lunch Mon–Sat 12:15–2:30pm; dinner Mon–Sat 7:30–10:30pm.

In 1990, one of Europe's most legendary delicatessens (Fauchon) transformed one of its upper rooms into an airy and elegant pastel-colored showplace dotted with Neo-Grecian columns and accessories. It caught on immediately as the preferred luncheon restaurant for many of the bankers, stockbrokers, and merchants in the neighborhood of place de la Madeleine. Menu items are prepared with the freshest ingredients available from the display racks downstairs, and might include a cassoulet of lobster served with a basil-flavored shellfish sauce, a curried version of fried sweetbreads, suprême of sea bass with fennel, and a luscious assortment of cheeses and pastries.

If you're in the mood for Italian food, Fauchon also operates a somewhat less expensive restaurant, **La Trattoria,** next door at 26, place de la Madeleine (tel. 47-42-60-11), where main courses tend to run 70–100 F ($12.60–$18).

YVAN, 1 bis, rue Jean-Mermoz, 8e. Tel. 43-59-18-40.
   Cuisine: FRENCH. **Reservations:** Required. **Métro:** F-D-Roosevelt.
$ Prices: Lunch, appetizers 70–115 F ($12.60–$20.70), main dishes 85–115 F ($15.30–$20.70); fixed-price menu 178 F ($32) at lunch, 178–278 F ($32–$50) at dinner. AE, DC, MC, V.
   Open: Lunch Mon–Fri noon–2:30pm; dinner Mon–Sat 8pm–midnight.

Hip, fashionable, and in vogue, Yvan opened in 1987 in a stylishly international neighborhood near the Champs-Elysées. Masses of flowers, salmon-colored walls, pink marble floors, and hints of 1930s splendor greet diners as they enter. A convivial apéritif bar near the door sometimes tempts diners with a before-dinner glass of champagne. Menu specialties change with the season, but are likely to include turbot infused with vanilla, filet of beef simmered in red wine, a duet of sole served with a beer-flavored mousseline sauce, chicken ravioli with a lobster-cream sauce, and veal kidneys served with a confit of lemons.

INEXPENSIVE

MINIM'S, 76, rue du Faubourg St-Honoré, 8e. Tel. 42-66-10-09.
   Cuisine: FRENCH. **Reservations:** Recommended. **Métro:** Concorde.
$ Prices: Appetizers 40–70 F ($7.20–$12.60); main dishes 80–90 F ($14.40–$16.20). AE, DC, MC, V.
   Open: Mon–Sat 9am–3pm and 3–6:30pm.

Pierre Cardin created what he calls an "alimentary boutique" on this fashionable street near the Elysée Palace. It's really an ideal breakfast or luncheon restaurant for rich suburbanites spending their day shopping, but it's also a good choice for midafternoon tea or a quick, well-prepared snack. The name, of course, is an amusing adaptation of Maxim's, and like that restaurant, it is filled with art nouveau lighting fixtures and stained glass.

You eat at small tables near a collection of turn-of-the-century silver maidens that are said to hail from Cardin's own collection. It's totally appropriate here to order a *plat du jour.* These change daily, but might include eggplant caviar, carpaccio with salad, and confit de canard. You can also order sandwiches, as well as pastries. A deluxe delicatessen fills an adjoining room. A cup of tea, selected from various types and brews, costs 25 F ($4.50), and sandwiches and pastries, served *à l'anglaise* are priced as additional items.

3. 16TH ARR.

VERY EXPENSIVE

FAUGERON, 52, rue de Longchamp, 16e. Tel. 47-04-24-53.
   Cuisine: FRENCH. **Reservations:** Required. **Métro:** Iéna or Trocadéro.

$ **Prices:** Fixed-price meal 290–340 F ($52.20–$61.20) at lunch, 550 F ($99) at dinner. MC, V.

Open: Lunch Mon–Fri noon–2pm; dinner Mon–Fri 7:30–10pm. **Closed:** Aug.

Chef Henri Faugeron is the inspired master of French cooking in the classic style. He and his Austrian wife, Gerlinde, entertain a faithful list of gourmets, including artists, diplomats, and business executives. Faugeron established this restaurant many years ago in the Trocadéro district, which is at once elegant, yet not an obtrusive backdrop for his superb cuisine.

Calling his cuisine "revolutionary," he is somewhat of a culinary researcher, and his menu always has one or two platters from the classic French table, such as a leg of lamb baked seven hours or rack of hare in traditional French style.

Much of his cooking depends on the season and whatever is fresh at the market. Whether it be game dishes, frogs' legs, oysters, or scallops, Monsieur Faugeron prepares the platters with style.

EXPENSIVE

LA GRANDE CASCADE, allée de Longchamp, Bois de Boulogne, 16e. Tel. 45-27-33-51.

Cuisine: FRENCH. **Reservations:** Required.

$ **Prices:** Appetizers 145–310 F ($26.10–$55.80); main dishes 210–390 F ($37.80–$70.20). AE, DC, MC, V.

Open: Mid-Apr to late Oct, lunch daily noon–3pm; dinner daily 7:30–10:30pm. Nov to mid-Dec and mid-Jan to mid-Apr, lunch only, daily noon–3pm. **Closed:** Mid-Dec to mid-Jan.

In the 17th century this indoor-outdoor restaurant was a hunting lodge for Napoléon III, but its fame as a restaurant dates from the early 20th century. Once it was attended by the theatrical chic—Mistinguett, the French stage star, used to make her entrance in a wide hat as she emerged from a grand carriage.

Just opposite the Longchamp racecourse, this restaurant serves the best food in this fashionable park, but you'll need to take a taxi or drive here. Named after the waterfall of the Bois de Boulogne, the restaurant is a Belle Epoque shrine, the perfect spot for a long, lingering afternoon lunch or a fashionable tea. If the sun is shining, most guests ask for a table on the front terrace with a view. Inside, you'll dine to the soft sounds of the nearby cascade in a room lit by tall frosted lamps.

The restaurant features such à la carte selections as duckling foie gras, fish poached in seaweed and basil, filet of red snapper in truffle sauce, and veal sweetbreads in truffle-flavored butter. The crêpes soufflés à l'orange make for a stunning finish.

VIVAROIS, 192, av. Victor-Hugo, 16e. Tel. 45-04-04-31.

Cuisine: FRENCH. **Reservations:** Required. **Métro:** Pompe.

$ **Prices:** Appetizers 100–430 F ($18–$77.40); main dishes 215–280 F ($38.70–$50.40); fixed-price lunch 345 F ($62.10). AE, DC, MC, V.

Open: Lunch Mon–Fri noon–2pm; dinner Mon–Fri 8–10pm. **Closed:** Aug.

Gourmet magazine once hailed this popular restaurant as "a restaurant of our time . . . the most exciting, audacious, and important restaurant in Paris today." Opened in 1966, it still retains its original standards thanks to the supremely talented owner-chef, Claude Peyrot. He does a most recommendable coquilles St-Jacques (scallops) en crème and a pourpre de turbot Vivarais. His winning dish is rognons de veau (veal kidneys).

Madame Peyrot is one of the finest maîtres d's in Paris. She will guide you beautifully through wine selections to perfectly complement her husband's sublime cuisine.

MODERATE

LE PETIT BEDON, 38, rue Pergolèse, 16e. Tel. 45-00-23-66.

Cuisine: FRENCH. **Reservations:** Required. **Métro:** Argentine.

$ Prices: Appetizers 70–135 F ($12.60–$24.30); main dishes 100–150 F ($18–$27); fixed-price meal 150 F ($27) at lunch, 250 F ($45) at dinner. AE, DC, MC, V. **Open:** Lunch Mon–Fri 12:15–2pm; dinner Mon–Fri 7:15–10:15pm. **Closed:** Aug.

The 14-table dining room is decorated simply but is warm and inviting. The cuisine is traditional yet innovative, and the menu changes frequently. For an appetizer, you might begin with cured and smoked salmon, thinly sliced and seasoned with a South American black pepper. If you visit in early spring, you can order milk-fed lamb from the Dordogne region. The lamb is delicate and tender and prepared to perfection. The kitchen is also known to do marvelous twists with Challons duckling. A masterpiece of desserts is a plate of mixed sorbets. Not only is it a work of art, but also you can guess the flavors.

4. 17TH ARR.

EXPENSIVE

GUY SAVOY, 18, rue Troyon, 17e. Tel. 43-80-40-61.
   Cuisine: FRENCH. **Reservations:** Required, as far in advance as possible.
   Métro: Charles-de-Gaulle (Etoile).
$ Prices: Appetizers 170–350 F ($30.60–$63); main dishes 190–300 F ($34.20–$54); fixed-price meal 680 F ($122.40). V.
   Open: Lunch Mon–Fri 12:30–1:30pm; dinner Mon–Sat 7:30–10:30pm.
   Closed: Last three weeks of July.

⭐ Whenever the names of the five or six hottest chefs in Europe are mentioned, Guy Savoy's will inevitably be among them. Both the restaurant and the cuisine bear Monsieur Savoy's signature style. His cooking almost always takes its inspiration from the market.

Save your appetite and then order his nine-course *menu dégustation*. (Don't worry—the portions are small.) What do you get? Maybe red mullet and wild asparagus, perhaps a cassolette of snails flavored with tarragon (no garlic, for a change) or chicken quenelles with chicken livers and cream, sprinkled with strips of delectable black truffles.

Depending on when you visit, you may have the pleasure of tasting his masterfully prepared mallard, venison, or game birds. He is fascinated with the champignon (mushroom) in all its varieties and has been known to serve as many as a dozen different types, especially in the autumn.

MICHEL ROSTANG, 20, rue Rennequin, 17e. Tel. 47-63-40-77.
   Cuisine: FRENCH. **Reservations:** Required, one week in advance. **Métro:** Ternes.
$ Prices: Appetizers 139–295 F ($25–$53.10); main dishes 195–290 F ($35.10–$52.20); fixed-price meal 285 F ($51.30) at lunch, 495–680 F ($89.10–$122.40) at dinner. AE, MC, V.
   Open: Lunch Mon–Fri noon–2pm; dinner Mon–Sat 7:30–10pm. **Closed:** First two weeks in Aug.

⭐ Monsieur Rostang is a creative fifth-generation chef from one of the most distinguished "cooking families" of France. His family has been connected with the famed Bonne Auberge at Antibes on the French Riviera. Originally from Grenoble, Rostang eventually came to the 17th arrondissement, where the world soon came to dine at what he modestly calls his "boutique restaurant."

Seating up to 70 diners, the restaurant has a menu that changes constantly. Rostang's specialties may include ravioli filled with goat cheese and coated with a sprinkling of chervil bought fresh from the morning market. His Bresse chicken is considered the finest in France. From October to March, he prepares quail eggs with a coque of sea urchins. On occasion he also prepares a delicate fricassée of sole, or another specialty, duckling cooked in its own blood. Wines from the Rhône are available, including Châteauneuf du Pape and Hermitage.

MODERATE

GOLDENBERG'S, 69, av. de Wagram, 17e. Tel. 42-27-34-79.
  Cuisine: KOSHER. **Reservations:** Recommended. **Métro:** Ternes or Charles-de-Gaulle (Etoile).
$ **Prices:** Appetizers 30–40 F ($5.40–$7.20); main dishes 72–112 F ($13–$20.20); fixed-price menu 98 F ($17.60). V.
  Open: Daily 9am–midnight.

This is the best place around the Champs-Elysées for Jewish-deli food. Albert Goldenberg opened his first delicatessen in Montmartre in 1936, and the restaurant has been tempting Parisians ever since with his cabbage borscht, blinis, stuffed carp, and pastrami. Naturally, Jewish rye bread comes with almost everything. The menu even offers Israeli wines.

The front half of the deli is for take-out, the rear half for proper in-house dining. There's also a large room downstairs for guests.

INEXPENSIVE

L'ETOILE VERTE, 13, rue Brey, 17e. Tel. 43-80-69-34.
  Cuisine: FRENCH. **Reservations:** Recommended. **Métro:** Charles-de-Gaulle (Etoile).
$ **Prices:** Appetizers 20–60 F ($3.60–$10.80); main dishes 44–80 F ($7.90–$14.40); three-course fixed-price meal with a quarter carafe of wine 69 F ($12.40). AE, DC, MC, V.
  Open: Lunch daily 11am–3pm; dinner daily 6:30–11pm.

Eat more for less here at the "Green Star." The type of cooking is more typically from an old French bistro menu: rabbit pâté, veal marengo, fresh oysters, excellent escargots, coq au vin in wine from Cahors, stuffed mussels, sole meunière, roast haunch of veal, and beef in madeira sauce. The staff is friendly and helpful.

5. 1ST ARR.

EXPENSIVE

CARRE DES FEUILLANTS, 14, rue de Castiglione, 1er. Tel. 42-86-82-82.
  Cuisine: FRENCH. **Reservations:** Recommended. **Métro:** Tuileries, Concorde, Opéra, or Madeleine.
$ **Prices:** Appetizers 128–220 F ($23–$39.60); main dishes 188–260 F ($33.80–$46.80); fixed-price meal 260 F ($46.80) at lunch, 550 F ($99) at dinner. AE, DC, MC, V.
  Open: Lunch Mon–Fri noon–2pm; dinner Mon–Sat 7:30–10:30pm. **Closed:** Sat lunch and Sun Sept–June; Sat–Sun July–Aug.

When leading chef Alain Dutournier converted this 17th-century convent into a restaurant, in the platinum location near place Vendôme and the Tuileries, it was an overnight success. The interior is like a turn-of-the-century bourgeois house with several small salons that open onto a skylit interior courtyard, across from which is a glass-encased kitchen where you can watch the chefs perform magic.

Monsieur Dutournier launched his career in Gascony, cooking with his mother and grandmother, where he claims he learned cooking as an act of love. He likes to call his brand of French cooking *cuisine du moment,* the product of a wild, experimental imaginative mind that makes it impossible to describe a typical menu—specialties are likely to include cream of pheasant with fresh chestnuts or roasted red mullet with an oyster dressing.

Uninterested in rich sauces, he leans toward a lighter, healthier cuisine, working with farmers who supply him with the freshest produce possible. He also serves beef butchered from one of the oldest breeds of cattle in France, the *race bazadaise,* and his lamb is raised in Pauillac.

The owner has also distinguished himself with his exciting wine cellar containing several little-known wines and a fabulous collection of armagnacs. There's a bar where guests without reservations can wait.

MODERATE

ESCARGOT-MONTORGEUIL, 38, rue Montorgueil, 1er. Tel. 42-36-83-51.

Cuisine: FRENCH. **Reservations:** Recommended. **Métro:** Les Halles.
$ Prices: Appetizers 60–138 F ($10.80–$24.80); main dishes 108–160 F ($19.40–$28.80); fixed-price lunch 130 F ($23.40). AE, DC, MC, V.
Open: Lunch daily noon–2:30pm; dinner daily 7:30–11pm. **Closed:** Part of Aug.

No wonder Sarah Bernhardt took many of her meals here. That ceiling mural of cherubic chefs, by the way, is said to have come from her summer home on an island off the southern coast of Brittany. The actual building dates from the reign of Henri II and Catherine de Medici, but it was not a restaurant until the early 19th century.

Owner Madame Saladin-Terrail, known as Kouikette, has improved the style without disturbing the atmosphere. The original Louis-Philippe decor is carefully preserved; two dining rooms on the ground floor have starched Breton lace curtains and gaslight fixtures on sepia walls.

The Escargot (Snail) of Les Halles reigns supreme. I also recommend the pieds de porcs and the feathery turbot soufflé. For dessert the specialty is crêpes flambés.

JOE ALLEN, 30, rue Pierre-Lescot, 1er. Tel. 42-36-70-13.

Cuisine: AMERICAN. **Reservations:** Recommended. **Métro:** Châtelet or Les Halles.
$ Prices: Appetizers 33–65 F ($5.90–$11.70); main dishes 56–134 F ($10.10–$24.10). MC, V.
Open: Daily noon–2am.

Joe Allen long ago invaded Les Halles with his American hamburger. Even though the New York restaurateur admits "it's a silly idea," it works. After setting up, most of the work went into creating the American burger, which is easily the best in Paris.

While listening to the jukebox, you can order the savory black-bean soup, spicy chili, a juicy sirloin steak, barbecued spareribs, or apple pie. And try the spinach salad topped with creamy roquefort dressing and sprinkled with little crunchy bits of bacon and fresh mushrooms.

Joe claims that his saloon is the only place in Paris that serves an authentic New York cheesecake or a real pecan pie. Thanks to French chocolate, the brownies are better than those made in the States, Joe claims. Giving the brownies tough competition is the California chocolate-mousse pie, along with the strawberry Romanoff and the coconut-cream pie.

Thanksgiving dinner at Joe Allen's is becoming a Paris tradition (you'll need a reservation way in advance). On a regular night, if you haven't made a reservation for dinner, expect to wait at the New York bar for at least 30 minutes.

PHARAMOND, 24, rue de la Grande-Truanderie, 1er. Tel. 42-33-06-72.

Cuisine: FRENCH. **Reservations:** Required. **Métro:** Les Halles.
$ Prices: Appetizers 75–115 F ($13.50–$20.70); main dishes 85–145 F ($15.30–$26.10). AE, DC, MC, V.
Open: Lunch Tues–Sat 12:30–2:30pm; dinner Mon–Sat 7:30–10:45pm.

The restaurant, part of a Neo-Norman structure founded in 1832, sits on a street in Les Halles that was once frequented by the vagabonds of Paris.

For an appetizer (available between October and April), work your way through

1ST ARR. • **133**

half a dozen Breton oysters. But the dish to order here is tripes à la mode de Caen, served over a charcoal burner. Tripe is a delicacy, and if you're at all experimental you'll find no better introduction to it anywhere. Try the coquilles St-Jacques au cidre (scallops in cider) if you're not up to tripe. Other main-dish specialties include grillade du feu de bois for two diners, as well as filets of veal Petit Normande.

RESTAURANT PIERRE, 10, rue de Richelieu, 1er. Tel. 42-96-09-17.
Cuisine: FRENCH. **Reservations:** Required two or three days in advance.
Métro: Palais Royal–Musée du Louvre.
$ Prices: Appetizers 60–145 F ($10.80–$26.10); main dishes 98–170 F ($17.60–$30.60); fixed-price menu 260 F ($46.80). DC, MC, V.
Open: Lunch Mon–Fri noon–2:15pm; dinner Mon–Fri 7–10pm. **Closed:** Aug.

You'll find traditional French cooking here, the kind of flavorful cuisine bourgeoise for which France is famous. Under the direction of owners Nicole and Daniel Dez, the chef prepares updated versions of time-tested recipes. A repeat visitor can take a gastronomic tour of France without ever leaving the restaurant, because so many different regions of the country are represented on the menu.

You might begin with a terrine of foie gras, followed by grilled turbot in a choron sauce or delectably prepared beef. Wild duck is occasionally featured. The menu changes twice a week. Restaurant Pierre is located behind the Comédie Française.

LA ROSE DE FRANCE, 24, place Dauphine, 1er. Tel. 43-54-10-12.
Cuisine: FRENCH. **Reservations:** Recommended. **Métro:** Cité or Pont-Neuf.
$ Prices: Appetizers 55–87 F ($9.90–$15.70); main dishes 82–115 F ($14.80–$20.70); three-course fixed-price lunch or dinner 198 F ($35.60); *menu gastronomique* 300 F ($54). V.
Open: Lunch Mon–Fri noon–2pm; dinner Mon–Fri 7–10pm.

You'll find this restaurant in the old section of the Ile de la Cité near Notre-Dame, just around the corner from the old Pont Neuf. You'll dine with a sophisticated crowd of young Parisians who know that they can expect a good menu at reasonable prices. In warm weather the sidewalk tables overlooking the Palace of Justice are the most popular.

Main dishes include deviled steak, spring lamb chops, a Norman-style veal chop with cooked apples, and a soufflé of scallops with muscadet. For dessert, try the fruit tart of the day, a sorbet, or iced melon (in summer only).

INEXPENSIVE

LA MOISANDERIE, 52, rue de Richelieu, 1er. Tel. 42-96-92-93.
Cuisine: FRENCH. **Reservations:** Recommended. **Métro:** Musée du Louvre.
$ Prices: Appetizers 53–68 F ($9.50–$12.20); main dishes 95–130 F ($17.10–$23.40); fixed-price menus 110–220 F ($19.80–$39.60). AE, DC, MC, V
Open: Lunch Mon–Sat noon–3pm; dinner Mon–Sat 7–10:30pm.

This conveniently located bistro, though relatively unknown, has good, reasonably priced food. It's just off the Palais Royal arcades, opening onto a passageway leading to the 18th-century Théâtre du Palais Royal. (Diderot, editor of the great 28-volume *Encyclopédie*, died at no. 39 on this street on July 31, 1781, and no. 40 is where Molière lived and died, in 1673.)

Though La Moisanderie is small, with tables just big enough for sparrows, everything goes smoothly. It has a homey, rustic French decor: wood paneling covered with 16th-century tapestries, a brick fireplace, a basket of crusty bread, and a counter of mouth-watering homemade pastries.

Fancier dishes include steak with cognac and orange duck. To begin, you are offered eight different hors d'oeuvres, a soup, or marinated herring. Next comes a meat or fowl course—perhaps stuffed chicken, pork with mushrooms, grilled liver, or a veal cutlet in a cream sauce with mushrooms. For dessert, help yourself from a large glass bowl of fresh fruit salad, unless you prefer a wedge of green-apple tart. It gets crowded, so go early.

RESTAURANT LESCURE, 7, rue de Mondovi, 1er. Tel. 42-60-18-91.
Cuisine: FRENCH. **Reservations:** Not accepted. **Métro:** Concorde.

$ Prices: Appetizers 20–40 F ($3.60–$7.20); main dishes 30–100 F ($5.40–$18); fixed-price meal 98 F ($17.60). MC, V.
Open: Lunch Mon–Fri noon–2:15pm; dinner Mon–Fri 7–10pm. **Closed:** Two weeks in Aug.

This miniature bistro, operating since 1919, is a real discovery because reasonably priced restaurants near place de la Concorde are difficult to find. Off rue de Rivoli, it's right around the corner from the 18th-century mansion where Talleyrand died. The tables on the sidewalk are tiny, and there isn't much room inside. What it does have is rustic charm. The kitchen is wide open, and the aroma of drying bay leaves, salami, and garlic pigtails hanging to dry from the ceiling fills the room.

Expect *cuisine bourgeoise* here. Perhaps you'll begin with a pâté en croûte. Main-course house specialties include confit de canard and salmon in a green sauce. My favorite dessert is one of the chef's fruit tarts.

RESTAURANT PAUL, 15, place Dauphine, 1er. Tel. 43-54-21-48.
   Cuisine: FRENCH. **Reservations:** Required. **Métro:** Pont-Neuf.
$ Prices: Appetizers 40–90 F ($7.20–$16.20); main dishes 90–140 F ($16.20–$25.20). MC, V.
   Open: Lunch Wed–Sun noon–2:30pm; dinner Wed–Sun 7:30–10:15pm.
   Closed: Aug.
When this century was young this address used to be given with strictest confidence to first-time visitors to Paris. Over the decades it has become a virtual cliché for the hidden little bistro, and it still serves the same good food it always did. Chez Paul has another entrance bordering the Seine on quai des Orfevres.

Try the filet mignon en papillote (cooked in parchment). For a beginning, why not sample the chicken liver grandmother style? The dessert specialty is baba à la confiture flambé au rhum.

6. 2ND & 9TH ARR.

MODERATE

CHEZ GEORGES, 1, rue du Mail, 2e. Tel. 42-60-07-11.
   Cuisine: FRENCH. **Reservations:** Required. **Métro:** Sentier.
$ Prices: Appetizers 50–110 F ($9–$19.80); main dishes 115–150 F ($20.70–$27). AE, MC, V.
   Open: Lunch Mon–Sat 12:30–2pm; dinner Mon–Sat 7:30–10pm.
This bistro is something of a local landmark, established in 1964 in the then-grimy neighborhood of the stock exchange. At lunch it's heavily patronized by members of the Bourse (the stock exchange), which is about a block away. The owner serves what he calls *"la cuisine typiquement bourgeoise,"* or "food from our grandmère in the provinces."

Waiters bring around bowls of appetizers, such as celery remoulade, to get you started. Then you can follow with such favorites as pot-au-feu (beef simmered with vegetables), a classic cassoulet, or beef braised in red wine. Beaujolais goes great with this hearty food.

INEXPENSIVE

AUX LYONNAIS, 32, rue St-Marc, 2e. Tel. 42-96-65-04.
   Cuisine: FRENCH. **Reservations:** Recommended. **Métro:** Richelieu-Drouot.
$ Prices: Appetizers 40–50 F ($7.20–$9); main dishes 70–100 F ($12.60–$18); fixed-price menu 87 F ($15.70). AE, DC, MC, V.
   Open: Lunch Mon–Fri noon–3pm; dinner Mon–Sat 6pm–midnight.
Set behind a burgundy-colored facade, this is one of the most consistently reliable

bistros in its neighborhood, close to the heart of Paris but far enough removed to offer insightful views of a nontouristy neighborhood. Inside, amid a time-worn decor which has changed very little since the place was established after World War II, you'll find dining rooms on two floors, and a hardworking staff of professional waiters.

Menu specialties include many of the classic dishes of the French bistro regime, including quenelles of brochet, des petits pâtés chauds, chicken baked in a salt crust, steak au poivre, and several kinds of sausages.

LE VAUDEVILLE, 29, rue Vivienne, 2e. Tel. 40-20-04-62.

Cuisine: FRENCH. **Reservations:** Recommended in the evenings. **Métro:** Bourse.

$ Prices: Appetizers 35–80 F ($6.30–$14.40); main dishes 85–120 F ($15.30–$21.60); fixed-price meal 109 F ($19.60) at lunch, 185 F ($33.30) with wine included at dinner. AE, DC, MC, V.

Open: Lunch daily 11:30am–3pm; dinner daily 7pm–2am.

Although a bistro had occupied this spot since 1918, its business began to flourish after 1980 when it was acquired by the same chain that owned such other landmark bistros as Julien and La Coupole. Set adjacent to the Paris stock exchange (La Bourse), it retains its original marble walls and art deco carvings. In summer, tables are placed on a terrace in front amid banks of geraniums. Any time of year, the place is boisterous, informal, and colloquial, often welcoming groups of six or eight diners at a time at its closely spaced tables. A bar near the entrance provides a place to perch if your table reservation is delayed.

Menu items include a bountiful roster of bistro-style platters, including snails in garlic butter, smoked salmon, steak au poivre, sole meunière, sauerkraut, and several kinds of grilled meats.

BUDGET

LE DROUOT, 103, rue Richelieu, 2e. Tel. 42-96-68-23.

Cuisine: FRENCH. **Reservations:** Accepted only for groups of 20 or more. **Métro:** Richelieu-Drouot.

$ Prices: Appetizers 18–35 F ($3.20–$6.30); main dishes 48–72 F ($8.60–$13). MC, V.

Open: Lunch daily 11:45am–3pm; dinner daily 6:30–10pm.

One of the best budget restaurants in the 2nd arrondissement, Le Drouot is usually packed with economy-minded Parisians who know where to go for well-prepared, filling food.

Almost in the tradition of the famous *bouillons* at the turn of the century, a breadman comes around to see that your plate is full. For an appetizer, you might select ham from the Ardennes or perhaps artichoke bottom vinaigrette. Among the main courses offered, I'd recommend pepper steak with french fries or the filet of turbot in hollandaise sauce. Chocolate mousse is the favored dessert.

LE GRAND ZINC, 5, rue du Faubourg-Montmarte, 9e. Tel. 47-70-88-64.

Cuisine: FRENCH. **Reservations:** Not required. **Métro:** Rue Montmarte.

$ Prices: Appetizers 45–55 F ($8.10–$9.90); main dishes 80–120 F ($14.40–$21.60); fixed-price menu 160 F ($28.80). AE, DC, MC, V.

Open: Lunch Mon–Sat noon–3pm; dinner Mon–Sat 7pm–12:45am.

Though this restaurant is in a relatively unfashionable quarter by Parisian standards, at Le Grand Zinc the spirit of 1907 Paris lives on. It's the oldest restaurant in the neighborhood. As you walk in, you pass aisles lined with baskets of seafood—from belons to brown-fleshed oysters from Brittany (a traditional favorite, available year-round).

Well flavored, time-tested, and traditional, the establishment's specialties include steak au poivre, magrêt de canard with grilled peppers, côte de boeuf (prepared only for two diners), confit de canard (duck) prepared in the style of Toulouse and served with ratatouille, and a grilled filet of turbot with beurre blanc (white butter sauce).

7. 10TH ARR.

MODERATE

BRASSERIE FLO, 7, cour des Petites-Ecuries, 10e. Tel. 47-70-13-59.
 Cuisine: FRENCH. **Reservations:** Recommended. **Métro:** Château-d'Eau or Strasbourg-St. Denis.
$ Prices: Appetizers 35–80 F ($6.30–$14.40); main dishes 64–150 F ($11.50–$27); fixed-price menu (lunch or dinner) 196 F ($35.30); late-night supper (available after 11pm) 119 F ($21.40). AE, DC, MC, V.
 Open: Lunch daily noon–2:45pm; dinner daily 7pm–1:30am.

This restaurant is in a remote area and is a little hard to find, but once you arrive (after walking through passageway after passageway), you'll see that fin-de-siècle Paris lives on. The restaurant was originally established in 1860 and has changed its decor very little since its founding date. You may expect high prices, but you'll be pleasantly surprised.

The house specialty is la formidable choucroute (a heaping mound of sauerkraut surrounded by boiled ham, bacon, and sausage) for two. Look for the *plats du jour,* ranging from roast pigeon to fricassée of veal with sorrel. Escargots (snails) are a traditional appetizer. Other specialties include fricassée of chicken with morels and a main course of foie gras served with apples in the Normandy style.

JULIEN, 16, rue du Faubourg St-Denis, 10e. Tel. 47-70-12-06.
 Cuisine: FRENCH. **Reservations:** Required. **Métro:** Strasbourg-St. Denis.
$ Prices: Appetizers 32–109 F ($5.80–$19.60); main dishes 69–169 F ($12.40–$30.40); fixed-price menu 109 F ($19.60). AE, DC, MC, V.
 Open: Lunch daily noon–3pm; dinner daily 7pm–1:30am.

Dine at one of the most sumptuous Belle Epoque restaurants in Paris (not far from Les Halles). The building was originally conceived in 1889 for the Universal Exposition, although it opened only in 1903. Until 1976, it was the most famous cheap working-class eatery in Paris. Today, as you can see, it has been restored to its former elegance.

The food served here is *cuisine bourgeoise,* but without the heavy sauces once used. Excellently prepared dishes include rillettes of smoked salmon, duckling foie gras, or snails in the style of Bourgogne. Mussels also make a savory beginning, poached in Riesling. For your main course, select such dishes as grilled lobster flambéed with whiskey, a cassoulet, or even a fricassée of capon with morels.

8. 5TH & 6TH ARR.

EXPENSIVE

CLOSERIE DES LILAS [Pleasure Garden of the Lilacs], 171, bd. Montparnasse, 6e. Tel. 43-26-70-50.
 Cuisine: FRENCH. **Reservations:** Required. **Métro:** Port-Royal or Vavin.
$ Prices: Restaurant, appetizers 65–200 F ($11.70–$36); main dishes 120–180 F ($21.60–$32.40). Brasserie, appetizers 45–120 F ($8.10–$21.60); main dishes 72–85 F ($13–$15.30). AE, DC, MC, V.
 Open: Restaurant, lunch daily 12:30–2:30pm; dinner daily 7:30pm–12:30am. Brasserie, daily noon–1am.

The number of famous people who have sat in the Closerie watching the falling leaves blow along the streets of Montparnasse, is almost countless: Gertrude Stein, Ingres, Henry James, Chateaubriand, Apollinaire, Lenin and Trotsky at the chess board, Proust, André Gide, Sartre, Simone de Beauvoir, Verlaine, Braque, Valéry, and James Abbot McNeill Whistler, who would sit here expounding the "gentle art" of making enemies. We come here for the memories and the food.

To get a seat in what is called the "bateau" or brasserie section is difficult. However, you may enjoy waiting for a seat at the bar and ordering the best champagne julep in the world. In the bateau, you can order such rustic dishes as poached haddock or beef with a salad or even steak tartare. In the chic restaurant inside the Closerie, the cooking is classic. Try the escargots façon Closerie for openers. Of the main-course selections, the rognons de veau à la moutarde (veal kidneys with mustard) and ribs of veal in a cider sauce are highly recommended. Both sections are on street level—the brasserie faces boulevard Montparnasse, while the restaurant looks out onto boulevard du Port-Royal.

DOMINIQUE, 19, rue Brea, 6e. Tel. 43-27-08-80.
   Cuisine: RUSSIAN. **Reservations:** Required. **Métro:** Vavin.
$ Prices: Appetizers 29–115 F ($5.20–$20.70); main dishes 73–152 F ($13.10–$27.40); fixed-price menu 153 F ($27.50). AE, DC, MC, V.
   Open: Lunch daily 12:15–2:15pm; dinner daily 7:15–10:15pm. **Closed:** Mid-July to mid-Aug.

You'll find shades of imperial Russia right here in Montparnasse, but don't be carried away by the fin-de-siècle St. Petersburg atmosphere in the upstairs room; you might be tempted to order a "tin" of Sevruga caviar before you know it. If you're on a budget and still determined to eat fine Russian food, you can sample the restaurant's delicacies at lower prices by sitting at a counter downstairs.

   All the familiar dishes are offered: borscht, blinis with cream, and a Russian salad. For a main course I recommend cotelette de volaille (poultry) Dominique, and for dessert, the house specialty, kasha Gourieff flambé. And no Russian meal is complete without vodka (try a glass of Zubrovka, imported from Poland and made with a special herb).

JACQUES CAGNA, 14, rue des Grands-Augustins, 6e. Tel. 43-26-49-39.
   Cuisine: FRENCH. **Reservations:** Recommended. **Métro:** St-Michel or Odéon.
$ Prices: Appetizers 130–320 F ($23.40–$57.60); main dishes 200–380 F ($36–$68.40); fixed-price meal 260 F ($46.80) at lunch, 490 F ($88.20) at dinner. AE, DC, MC, V.
   Open: Lunch Mon–Sat noon–2pm; dinner Mon–Sat 7:30–10:30pm. **Closed:** Aug.

In a 17th-century town house, Jacques Cagna is a place where both the clientele and the victuals are considered among the grandest in all of Paris. Its interior is filled with massive timbers and a pleasing color scheme of pinkish beige, plus a series of 17th-century Dutch paintings. The main dining room lies one flight above street level.

   A specialty is the Aberdeen Angus beef, aged for a full three weeks, which chef Cagna imbues with a shallot-flavored sauce rich with herbs and seasonings. You might begin with a salad of prawn fritters and artichoke chips flavored with a gazpacho sauce, or a scallop-and-lobster puff pastry in a sea urchin–cream sauce. Other specialties include milk-fed veal with a ginger-and-lime sauce or Challans duck roasted in a burgundy wine sauce. Desserts are overwhelmingly tempting.

MODERATE

AUBERGE DES DEUX SIGNES, 46, rue Galande, 5e. Tel. 43-25-46-56.
   Cuisine: FRENCH. **Reservations:** Required for dinner. **Métro:** Maubert-Mutualité.
$ Prices: Appetizers 60–190 F ($10.80–$34.20); main dishes 120–210 F ($21.60–$37.80); fixed-price meal 140 F ($25.20) at lunch, 230 F ($41.40) at dinner. AE, DC, MC, V.
   Open: Lunch Sun–Fri 12:30–2pm; dinner Mon–Sat 7:30–10:30pm.

The medieval building containing this restaurant once served as the chapel of St. Blaise. Auvergne-born Georges Dhulster has this place well under control, and many visitors prefer to come here in the evening to enjoy the view of floodlit Notre-Dame

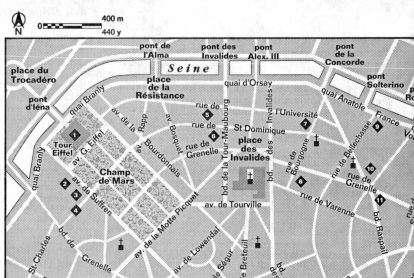

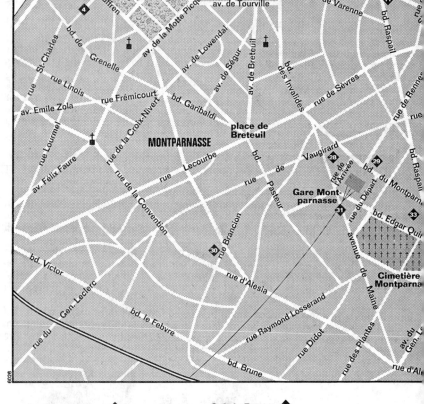

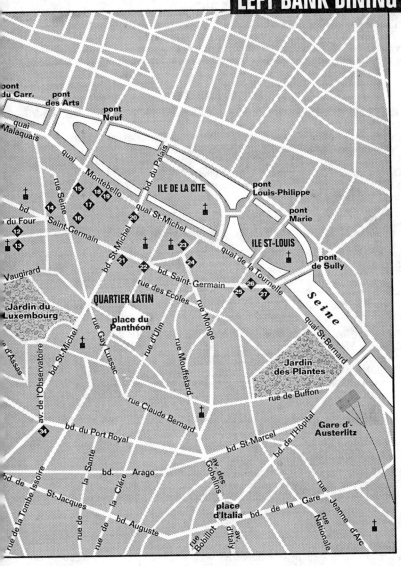

Dominique 32
Le Drug Store 22
La Gauloise 4
Jacques Cagna 18
Le Jules Verne 1
Moissonnier 27
Nuit de Saint Jean 5
Paris Hilton 2
La Petit France 30

La Petit Chaise 11
Le Procope 12
Pub Saint-Germain-des-Prés 14
La Rôtisserie d'en Face 19
The Tea Caddy 24
Tour d'Argent 26
Le Western 3

(without having to pay the prices charged by Tour d'Argent) and the Church of St-Julien-le-Pauvre. Try for a table upstairs, with a view of the garden.

The cuisine of the old province of Auvergne is given a *moderne* twist here. Fresh ingredients go into dishes. Be prepared, at times, for a wait. Try the veal medallions with morels, beef from the Aurillac region of central France, or confit of goose with flap mushrooms.

INEXPENSIVE

LA CABANE D'AUVERGNE, 44, rue Grégoire-de-Tours, 6e. Tel. 43-25-14-75.
  Cuisine: FRENCH. **Reservations:** Recommended. **Métro:** Odéon.
$ Prices: Appetizers 20–55 F ($3.60–$9.90); main dishes 69–80 F ($12.40–$14.40). No credit cards.
  Open: Lunch Tues–Sat noon–2pm; dinner Mon–Sat 7:30–11pm.
This tiny restaurant on a Left Bank street is a self-proclaimed "rabbit hutch," much like a rustic tavern from the Auvergne (a fertile ancient province of France now divided into départements). Under beamed ceilings, you are served typical regional meals on bare plank tables with wooden stools. It gets very crowded, so come early if you want a seat. The owner, Gilbert Guibert, is the hearty patron of the place, and he keeps the breezy chitchat going.

The kitchen specializes in terrines. One is made from marcassin (young boar), another from fricandeau (larded veal loin). Main courses are generous and well cooked. Traditional Auvernat specialties include potée Auvernat (a stewpot simmering with pork, white beans, turnips, and cabbage leaves). Also prominent is a tasty, filling cassoulet. The place has a rich supply of the many processed meats (sausages, pâtés, terrines) for which the Auvergne is famous. You'll find it an effort to order dessert.

LA CAFETIERE, 21, rue Mazarine, 6e. Tel. 46-33-76-90.
  Cuisine: FRENCH. **Reservations:** Recommended. **Métro:** Odéon.
$ Prices: Appetizers 50–60 F ($9–$10.80); main dishes 90–138 F ($16.20–$24.80). No credit cards.
  Open: Lunch Mon–Sat 12:15–2:30pm; dinner Mon–Sat 7:15–10:30pm.
In the heart of the Odéon district is this tiny neighborhood bistro that serves good food at reasonable prices. Dining is on two levels, and the restaurant serves both lunch and dinner. A coffee-pot theme forms the decor, and the service is always laudable.

Founder and owner Louis Diet, a former merchant seaman, sees to it that his kitchen turns out tenderloin of beef in mustard sauce, rack of lamb, salt pork with lentils, and a delectable pot-au-feu.

CHEZ RENE, 14, bd. St-Germain, 5e. Tel. 43-54-30-23.
  Cuisine: FRENCH. **Reservations:** Recommended. **Métro:** Cardinal-Lemoine.
$ Prices: Appetizers 33–85 F ($5.90–$15.30); main dishes 90–160 F ($16.20–$28.80). V.
  Open: Lunch daily noon–2:30pm; dinner daily 7–10pm.
Skip the greasy Middle Eastern eateries and the rarely good Oriental restaurants of the 5th arrondissement and head here for an old-fashioned corner bistro, the kind that Paris used to have so many of before they became pizzerias. The dining room isn't fancy, but a steady clientele frequents the place, knowing that they can order good, reliable food, especially *plats du jour*. At mealtimes, service is rushed and a little hysterical.

For an appetizer, if featured, try fresh wild mushrooms laced with butter and garlic and perhaps a platter of country-style sausages. You'll find such reliable old-time French fare as boeuf bourguignon and a dish of the day that might be pot-au-feu or blanquette de veau (veal in white sauce). Enjoy it all with a bottle of beaujolais.

MOISSONNIER, 28, rue des Fosses St-Bernard, 5e. Tel. 43-29-87-65.
  Cuisine: FRENCH. **Reservations:** Required for dinner. **Métro:** Jussieu or Cardinal-Lemoine.
$ Prices: Appetizers 40–80 F ($7.20–$14.40); main dishes 85–135 F ($15.30–$24.30). V.

Open: Lunch Tues–Sun noon–2:30pm; dinner Tues–Sat 7–10pm. **Closed:** Aug. Come here for real French country cooking, the kind many discriminating palates visit Paris just to sample. Big portions of solid old-fashioned food are served here, beginning with saladiers, large glass salad bowls filled with a selection of charcuterie. You might also select some excellent terrines, perhaps Lyonnais sausages. The specialties, from Burgundy and Lyon, include such main dishes as duck with turnips and rack of herb-flavored lamb.

LE PROCOPE, 13, rue de l'Ancienne-Comédie, 6e. Tel. 43-26-99-20.
   Cuisine: FRENCH. **Reservations:** Required several days in advance. **Métro:** Odéon.
$ **Prices:** Appetizers 37.50–112 F ($6.80–$20.20); main dishes 80–150 F ($14.40–$27); fixed-price menu 289 F ($52). AE, DC, MC, V.
   Open: Daily 8am–2am.
The oldest café in Paris, Le Procope opened in 1686 and was run by a Sicilian named Francesco Procopio dei Coltelli. The art of coffee drinking was popularized here, probably brought to Paris from Italy. The café today is more of a restaurant than it was originally. Along the walls are portraits of former clients—including La Fontaine, Voltaire, Benjamin Franklin, Rousseau, Anatole France, Robespierre, Danton, Marat, Bonaparte (as a youth), Balzac (who drank endless cups of very strong coffee), and Verlaine (who preferred the now-illegal absinthe).
   There are two levels for dining: the spacious upstairs section and the more intimate street-level room. Fresh oysters and shellfish are served from a refrigerated display. Well-chosen classic French dishes include baby duckling with spices and "green coffee" or "drunken chicken."

LA ROTISSERIE D'EN FACE, 2, rue Christine, 6e. Tel. 43-26-40-98.
   Cuisine: FRENCH. **Reservations:** Recommended. **Métro:** St-Michel.
$ **Prices:** Fixed-price menus 175 F ($31.50). MC, V.
   Open: Lunch Mon–Fri noon–2:30pm; dinner daily 7–11pm.
This is a so-called baby bistro operated under the direction and approval of the vastly more expensive (and also-recommended) Jacques Cagna, across the street. Decorated in a crowded, postmodern design of honey-colored walls, hi-tech lighting, and black lacquer chairs, the place is informal, popular, and at times, very very busy.
   Menu items include several sophisticated types of ravioli, a pâté of duckling en croûte with foie gras, an artichoke with leek salad in walnut-oil vinaigrette, a friture de perlan (mixed fish fry of tiny freshwater fish), smoked Scottish salmon with spinach, and several different types of fresh fish and grilled meats. Dessert might be profiteroles stuffed with pistachio ice cream.

BUDGET

LE BISTRO DE LA GARE, 59, bd. du Montparnasse, 6e. Tel. 45-48-38-01.
   Cuisine: FRENCH. **Reservations:** Not accepted. **Métro:** Montparnasse-Bienvenue.
$ **Prices:** Appetizers 17–69 F ($3.10–$12.40); main dishes 59–99 F ($10.60–$17.80). MC, V.
   Open: Daily 11:30am–1am.
   This unusual, popular eatery, offering low cost, well-prepared meals, has an art nouveau decor that is classified as a national treasure by the government. Its hand-painted tiles were installed in 1903 across a busy boulevard from the Montparnasse railway station.
   Today the crowds who elbow in wait for a table at the bar, where a free glass of kir is offered to anyone who waits more than a few minutes. Menu items are straightforward but flavorful, including several kinds of grilled steak, duck, and terrines. A wide assortment of desserts is offered, as well as house wine, sold in carafes. This popular chain is located at strategic locations throughout Paris.

CREMERIE-RESTAURANT POLIDOR, 41, rue Monsieur-le-Prince, 6e. Tel. 43-26-95-34.
   Cuisine: FRENCH. **Reservations:** Recommended. **Métro:** Odéon.

$ Prices: Appetizers 14–48 F ($2.50–$8.60); main dishes 60–80 F ($10.80–$14.40); fixed-price menu 100 F ($18). No credit cards.
Open: Lunch Mon–Sat noon–2:30pm; dinner Mon–Sat 7pm–12:30am, Sun 7–11pm.

This little bistro serves *cuisine familiale*. Frequented by students and artists (who seem to gravitate toward the rear), it opened in 1930 and has changed little since then. The restaurant's name still contains the word *crémerie*, referring to its specialty, frosted crème desserts. It has become one of the Left Bank's most established literary bistros; it was André Gide's favorite, and many other famous people—including Hemingway, Paul Valéry, Artaud, Charles Boyer, and Jack Kerouac—also dined here.

Lace curtains and brass hat racks, drawers in the back where repeat customers lock up their cloth napkins, and clay water pitchers on the tables create an old-fashioned atmosphere. Overworked but smiling waitresses serve dishes like pumpkin soup, snails from Burgundy, rib of beef with onions, rabbit with mustard sauce, and veal in white sauce. Desserts include raspberry or lemon tarts. The menu changes daily.

9. 7TH ARR.

EXPENSIVE

L'ARPEGE, 84, rue de Varenne, 7e. Tel. 47-05-09-06.
Cuisine: FRENCH. **Reservations:** Required. **Métro:** Varenne.
$ Prices: Appetizers 200–360 F ($36–$64.80); main dishes 200–400 F ($36–$72); fixed-price meal 320–820 F ($57.60–$147.60) at lunch, 820 F ($147.60) at dinner. AE, DC, MC, V.
Open: Lunch Sun–Fri 12:30–2pm; dinner Mon–Fri 7:30–10:30pm.

One of the most talked-about restaurants in Paris is L'Arpège, where chef Alain Passard prepares many of his youthful and charming culinary specialties. The restaurant is in a prosperous residential neighborhood, across from the Rodin Museum on the site of what for years was the world-famous l'Archestrate, where Passard once worked in the kitchens.

Amid an intensely cultivated modern decor of etched glass, burnished steel, monochromatic oil paintings, and pearwood paneling, you can enjoy specialties which have been heralded as among the most innovative in recent culinary history. These might include, for example, cabbage stuffed with crabmeat or game cock with chicken livers and herb-flavored onions. Or try the sweetbreads prepared with exotic mushrooms and truffle juice, or the John Dory with celery juice and asparagus flavored with sage. For dessert, try the chocolate beignets or a sugared tomato with a vanilla stuffing. The wine list is something to write home about.

LE BISTROT DE PARIS, 33, rue de Lille, 7e. Tel. 42-61-16-83.
Cuisine: FRENCH. **Reservations:** Required. **Métro:** Solferino.
$ Prices: Appetizers 42–135 F ($7.60–$24.30); main dishes 85–120 F ($15.30–$21.60). MC, V.
Open: Lunch Mon–Fri noon–2pm; dinner Mon–Sat 7:15–10:30pm.

Chef Michel Oliver knows the secret to make discriminating diners zero in on his little chic, sophisticated, and elegant bistro. He is the son of Raymond Oliver, one of the great restaurateurs of France, who ruled supreme for a long time at the prestigious Grand Véfour at the Palais Royal. I will never forget the sweetbreads flavored with orange that Michel served me. The various specialties have changed over the years, but the cooking has consistently remained superb, and the wine list is altogether impressive. Specialties include "three herb" lamb, which is a slow-cooked shoulder of lamb that has been marinated with three herbs (rosemary, thyme, and garlic). Another delight is a brochette of Bresse chicken marinated with lime, coriander, and cumin, and served with artichokes.

LE DIVELLEC CUISINE DE LA MER, 107, rue de l'Université, 7e. Tel. 45-51-91-96.

Cuisine: FRENCH. **Reservations:** Required. **Métro:** Invalides.

$ Prices: Appetizers 170–310 F ($30.60–$55.80); main dishes 210–400 F ($37.80–$72); fixed-price lunch 270–370 F ($48.60–$66.60). AE, DC, MC, V.

Open: Lunch Tues–Sat noon–2pm; dinner Tues–Sat 7–10pm.

This is one of the great seafood restaurants in all of France. In a long, narrow, modern room, you can select some of the most unusual combinations of seafood of *cuisine moderne*. Brittany-born chef Jacques Le Divellec makes dining here like dining at the captain's table on a private yacht.

Many of the most sophisticated diners of Paris consider the simplest dishes here the best. The more experimental try the filet of stingray with truffles, a terrine of foie gras studded with crayfish, a gratin of codfish, a mousseline of shellfish with filet of John Dory, and turbot with noodles tinted with squid ink. Two of the latest specialties include tournedos of tuna with goose liver and truffled toast and red mullet with lettuce sauce and black tagliatelle. Most diners prefer to begin with half a dozen oysters.

LE JULES VERNE, Tour Eiffel, Champ-de-Mars, 7e. Tel. 45-55-61-44.

Cuisine: FRENCH. **Reservations:** Required. **Métro:** Trocadéro, Ecole-Militaire, or Bir-Hakeim.

$ Prices: Appetizers 175–310 F ($31.50–$55.80); main dishes 190–350 F ($34.20–$63); fixed-price lunch 290 F ($52.20); *menu dégustation* 660 F ($118.80). AE, DC, MC, V.

Open: Lunch daily noon–2:30pm; dinner daily 7:30–10:30pm.

Only a handful of other restaurants enjoy so sweeping a view of the City of Light. Set on the second platform of the Eiffel Tower, it's reached by a private elevator which ascends upward from the south foundation (*"le pilier sud"*) of the famous monument. (If you're driving, a valet will whisk your car away and park it for you.) A piano bar offers a relaxing setting for a before-dinner drink, after which you'll be ushered to a table in a darkened room whose indirect lighting shows the glitter of Paris to its maximum advantage.

The menu, which changes with the seasons, might include a chartreuse of asparagus with red snapper and a brandade of codfish, a carpaccio of raw marinated tuna and salmon served with a slice of warm foie gras, baked turbot with herbs and an olive-oil béarnaise sauce, a ravioli of sweetbreads with lobster sauce, or a cassolette of fresh hot oysters with cucumbers. The *menu dégustation* is available at night and at lunch on Saturday and Sunday.

MODERATE

L'AUBERGE BASQUE, 51, rue de Verneuil, 7e. Tel. 45-48-51-98.

Cuisine: FRENCH. **Reservations:** Recommended. **Métro:** Rue-du-Bac.

$ Prices: Appetizers 40–100 F ($7.20–$18); main dishes 90–100 F ($16.20–$18); fixed-price menu 140 F ($25.20). MC, V.

Open: Lunch Mon–Sat noon–2:30pm; dinner Mon–Sat 7:30–11pm.

The fixed-price meal of the day offered here depends on the *cuisine du marché*. Owners M. and Mm Rourre come from Basque country near the Spanish border, and their meals reflect the rich cuisine of that region. Among their satisfied diners are some famous sports figures and French television stars.

You might begin with their Basque pâté, then follow with a piperade, a regionally famous omelet. They also prepare both magrêt and confit of canard (duck). Various fresh fish dishes also are served, along with a selection of cheese and fresh-fruit tarts. Wines are well chosen.

CHEZ LES ANGES, 54, bd. de Latour-Maubourg, 7e. Tel. 47-05-89-86.

Cuisine: FRENCH. **Reservations:** Recommended at lunch. **Métro:** Latour-Maubourg.

$ Prices: Appetizers 98–169 F ($17.60–$30.40); main dishes 142–178 F ($25.60–$32); fixed-price menu 230 F ($41.40). AE, DC, MC, V.

Open: Lunch daily noon–2pm; dinner Mon–Sat 7–11pm.

According to *Larousse Gastronomique,* the best foods and the best wines of France come from Burgundy. The "House of Angels" bistro indeed serves some of the finest Burgundian meals in Paris. It's located on the Left Bank, almost opposite Les Invalides.

Before dinner, try a refreshing apéritif: badule, made with champagne spiked with fresh raspberry juice. As an appetizer, try a charlotte of red peppers with a lemon and olive-oil vinaigrette. Among the main dishes, the classics are boeuf bourguignon and fricassée of veal kidneys. One of the best dishes is la tranche epaisse de foie de veau (thickly sliced calves' liver) cooked very rare, for two. Be sure to order a fluffy light gratin dauphinois, an excellent accompaniment to most dishes. For dessert, you can choose from what is certainly the widest assortment of cow cheese in any Parisian restaurant. Or perhaps a fresh strawberry sorbet with Cassis liqueur from Dijon will tempt you. The burgundy wines in the cellar are above reproach.

INEXPENSIVE

NUIT DE SAINT JEAN, 29, rue Surcouf, 7e. Tel. 45-51-61-49.
  Cuisine: FRENCH. **Reservations:** Required. **Métro:** Invalides.
$ Prices: Appetizers 35–40 F ($6.30–$7.20); main dishes 80–90 F ($14.40–$16.20); fixed-price menu 120 F ($21.60). AE, DC, MC, V.
  Open: Lunch Mon–Fri noon–2pm; dinner Mon–Sat 7:30–10:30pm.

⑤ One of the smallest and most charming restaurants in the well-heeled residential neighborhood of Les Invalides is this enclave of cuisine from France's southwest. Containing only 30 seats, and warmly decorated with ceiling beams and a conservative modern design, it features such dishes as cassoulet, smoked haddock in ginger sauce, tripe andouillette, lamb curry with rice, lime-marinated chicken, and rascasse (scorpion fish) in a champagne-cream sauce. Desserts are tempting, freshly made concoctions which include a fondant au chocolat à la crème anglaise. Although the restaurant has been in place since the early 1950s, it was given new life when owners from Toulouse took it over in the mid-1980s.

LA PETITE CHAISE, 36-38, rue de Grenelle, 7e. Tel. 42-22-13-35.
  Cuisine: FRENCH. **Reservations:** Recommended. **Métro:** Sèvres-Babylone.
$ Prices: Appetizers 50–60 F ($9–$10.80); main dishes 100–120 F ($18–$21.60); fixed-price meal 170 F ($30.60). MC, V.
  Open: Lunch daily noon–2:15pm; dinner daily 7–11pm.

⑤ This very Parisian spot is one of the oldest restaurants in Paris, dating from 1680. Its most reasonable (and most famous) meal is likely to include such specialties as chicken Pojarski (minced, breaded, and sautéed), noisettes of lamb with green beans, pepper steak, trout meunière, escalope of de veau normand, and pavé steak with roquefort sauce. Desserts are good and rich.

10. 15TH ARR.

EXPENSIVE

LA GAULOISE, 59, av. de la Motte-Picquet, 15e. Tel. 47-34-11-64.
  Cuisine: FRENCH. **Reservations:** Required. **Métro:** La Motte-Picquet-Grenelle.
$ Prices: Appetizers 55–133 F ($9.90–$23.90); main dishes 115–165 F ($20.70–$29.70); fixed-price menu 180 F ($32.40). AE, DC, MC, V.
  Open: Lunch daily noon–2:30pm; dinner daily 7–11pm.

With its fire-engine-red canopy that may remind you of a Parisian bistro of the 1930s, La Gauloise has long been an outstanding favorite in the area. Politicians and athletes in particular love its tobacco-tinged walls—in fact, no one wants to see anything changed around here. A member of the staff goes to local markets every morning to seek only the freshest of ingredients, and from the collected bounty the chef composes his *suggestions du marché* (market selections) to tempt hungry diners. Cuisine is traditional and French, and might include such dishes as bouillabaisse, an aiguillette of tuna and marinated salmon served with a warm vinaigrette, veal kidneys with mustard sauce, a rack of lamb roasted with mustard and parsley, and filet of beef béarnaise. During the summer, you can eat on the pavement in front, near a collection of potted conifers and parasols, below the roar of an elevated subway track.

MODERATE

LE WESTERN, in the Hilton Hotel, 18, av. de Suffren, 15e. Tel. 42-73-92-00.
  Cuisine: STEAKS. **Reservations:** Required. **Métro:** Bir-Hakeim.
$ Prices: Appetizers 55–110 F ($9.90–$19.80); main dishes 110–180 F ($19.80–$32.40); fixed-price menu 150 F ($27). AE, DC, MC, V.
  Open: Lunch daily noon–3pm; dinner daily 7–11pm.

The American steak meets French wine at the Hilton's re-creation of the Old West in Paris. The steaks are the best American cuts of beef imported from Kansas and Nebraska, and the service is impeccably French. Servers are dressed western style. This has become one of those chic Parisian places where many of the French go to rubberneck.

You might begin your meal with a crab cocktail, jumbo shrimp, or a Caesar salad, to be followed by a grilled steak, or a roquefort-stuffed chopped sirloin, or a saddle chop of salt-marsh lamb with mint jelly. The portions are large, but if you're still hungry, your meal might be followed by a selection of French cheeses or pastries. At trail's end (according to the menu), you might want a steaming cup of "outlaw's coffee" (made with Kentucky bourbon instead of Irish whiskey).

INEXPENSIVE

LA PETITE FRANCE, 77, rue Brancion, 15e. Tel. 42-50-55-71.
  Cuisine: ALSATIAN. **Reservations:** Recommended. **Métro:** Port de Vanves or Convention. **Bus:** 48.
$ Prices: Appetizers 24–66 F ($4.30–$11.90); main dishes 85–120 F ($15.30–$21.60); fixed-price menus 75–82 F ($13.50–$14.80). AE, DC, MC, V.
  Open: Lunch Tues–Sun 12:30–2:30pm; dinner Tues–Sat 7–10pm. **Closed:** Aug.

Closely linked to its neighborhood clientele, but frequently the host of French-speaking actors, comedians, and television stars, this is a warm and homey tribute to the cuisine and aesthetics of Alsace. Named after a medieval neighborhood in Strasbourg (La Petite France), the place is run by two Alsatian-born sisters, Mmes Kaelbel and Joseph, who prepare conservative and flavorful platters from their native region. Amid half-paneled walls and traditional red napery, you can order such dishes as *choucroute garni* (sauerkraut with sausage, hamhock, and pork chops), *jambon en croûte,* and, if it's ordered in advance, a succulent version of Alsace's native dish, *baeckeoffe* (a long-simmered stew of pork, veal, and lamb with onions and potatoes). Wines, as you'd expect, include a goodly percentage of Alsatian Rieslings.

11. 14TH ARR.

MODERATE

LE BOURBONNAIS, 29, rue Delambre, 14e. Tel. 43-20-61-73.
  Cuisine: FRENCH. **Reservations:** Required. **Métro:** Edgar-Quinet or Vavin.
$ Prices: Appetizers 75–98 F ($13.50–$17.60); main dishes 90–180 F ($16.20–$32.40); fixed-price menus 125–160 F ($22.50–$28.80). AE, DC, MC, V.

Open: Lunch Mon–Fri 12:30–2pm; dinner Mon–Sat 7:30–11pm. **Closed:** Aug 1–15.

In the heart of Montparnasse, the talents of Roger Le Meur are showcased at one of the best dining bargains on this street. Le Meur, a grand chef, receives some of his culinary inspiration from the oldest of his grandmother's recipes. He originally lived in the provinces of Brittany and Périgord, and has added a country zest to the restaurant scene of Paris. For example, you might enjoy codfish peasant style or coq au vin with fresh noodles. Or try his foie gras maison or veal kidneys in a mustard sauce. Much of the food is updated bistro style, however. There is also an array of petits vins at very reasonable prices.

LA CAGOUILLE, 10-12, place Constantin-Brancusi, 14e. Tel. 43-22-09-01.

    Cuisine: FRENCH/SEAFOOD. **Reservations:** Required. **Métro:** Montparnasse-Bienvenue.

$ Prices: Appetizers 60–150 F ($10.80–$27); main dishes 110–220 F ($19.80–$39.60). V.

    Open: Lunch daily noon–2pm; dinner daily 8–10:30pm.

In the landmark area of Tour du Montparnasse, chef Gérard Allemandou, a native of the Cognac region, creates his specialties in this thriving restaurant named for a shellfish delicacy in the local dialect of southwestern France. Here you can sample one of the most splendid selections of cognacs from smaller properties ever amassed in Paris.

But that's not why everyone comes here. They come for some of the freshest and most reasonably priced fish in Paris. Fresh from Rungis, the huge red mullet is grilled to perfection. The fish, such as salmon steak, is usually slightly underdone and served without a sauce (a dieter's dream come true). Ungarnished barnacles, grilled snapper, mussels sautéed in cast-iron pans—it's all here. All the fish is natural and pure, and peppered butter and sea salt are trademarks of the place. Two specialties are escabeche de petits poissons (a stewpot of fresh fish), and effilochée de raie avec sauce gribiche (a filet of stingray with a vinaigrette, capers, and fines herbes sauce). A "teardrop" of butter accompanies perfectly steamed vegetables.

12. 3RD & 4TH ARR.

EXPENSIVE

L'AMBROISIE, 9, place des Vosges, 4e. Tel. 42-78-51-45.

    Cuisine: FRENCH. **Reservations:** Required in advance. **Métro:** St-Paul-le-Marais.

$ Prices: Appetizers 160–380 F ($28.80–$68.40); main dishes 210–380 F ($37.80–$68.40). MC, V.

    Open: Lunch Tues–Sat noon–1:45pm; dinner Tues–Sat 8–9:45pm.

For good dining in a good location, head for L'Ambroisie. Chef Bernard Pacaud is one of the most talented in Paris. He trained at the prestigious Vivarois before deciding to strike out on his own, first at a Left Bank restaurant and now at this location in Le Marais on its square.

His cooking is simple yet elegant, the flavors subtle yet natural. He has the ability to enhance what's already there. His favored dishes include a delectable red-pepper mousse (perhaps the finest you're likely to be served in Paris), skate with the mild pungency of warm wilted cabbage, wild salmon breaded and pan-fried (and served with a thin potato pancake), and a salad of mâche with a ballotine of duck. Several preparations of Brittany lobster are also offered. For dessert, try the velvety-smooth chocolate mousse or anything in puff pastry. Try for a garden table.

RESTAURANT MARC-ANNIBAL DE COCONNAS, 2 bis, place des Vosges, 4e. Tel. 42-78-58-16.

    Cuisine: FRENCH. **Reservations:** Required. **Métro:** Bastille or St-Paul.

IMPRESSIONS

Paris is still monumental and handsome. Along the rivers where its splendours are, there's no denying its man-made beauty. The poor, pale little Seine runs rapidly north to the sea, the sky is pale, pale jade overhead, greenish and Parisian, the trees of black wire stand in rows, and flourish their black wire brushes against a low sky of jade-pale cobwebs, and the huge dark-grey palaces rear up their masses of stone and slope off towards the sky still with a massive, satisfying suggestion of pyramids. There is something noble and man-made about it all.
—D. H. LAWRENCE

Where shall I begin with the endless delights
Of this Eden of milliners, monkies and sights—
This dear busy place, where there's nothing transacting
But dressing and dinnering, dancing and acting?
—THOMAS MOORE, 1818

$ Prices: Appetizers 65–140 F ($11.70–$25.20); main dishes 100–120 F ($18–$21.60); fixed-price lunch 105–130 F ($18.90–$23.40). AE, DC, MC, V.
Open: Lunch Wed–Sun noon–2pm; dinner Wed–Sun 7:45–10:15pm.

Chef Claude Terrail (who also owns La Tour d'Argent) serves superb cuisine in this restaurant, located in a historic neighborhood. (Henri II lost his life on place des Vosges, and Victor Hugo lived in an apartment near here.)

You might begin with Greek-style artichokes with prawns or a cassolette of snails, then follow that with sole flavored with ginger or petit sale de canard (duck). In summer, guests enjoy dining outside.

MODERATE

L'AMBASSADE D'AUVERGNE, 22, rue de Grenier St-Lazare, 3e. Tel. 42-72-31-22.

Cuisine: FRENCH. **Reservations:** Recommended. **Métro:** Rambuteau.
$ Prices: Appetizers 46–130 F ($8.30–$23.40); main dishes 78–108 F ($14–$19.40). AE, MC, V.
Open: Lunch daily noon–2pm; dinner daily 7:30–11pm.

In an obscure district of Paris, this rustic tavern serves the hearty cuisine bourgeoise of Auvergne, the heartland of France. You enter through a busy bar, with heavy oak beams, hanging hams, and ceramic plates. At the entrance is a display of the chef's specialties: jellied meats and fowls, pâté cakes, plus an assortment of regional cheeses and fresh fruits of the season. Rough wheat bread is stacked in baskets, and rush-seated ladderback chairs are placed at tables covered with bright cloths. Stem glassware, mills to grind your own salt and pepper, and a jug of mustard are on each table.

Specialties include cassoulet with lentils, pot-au-feu, confit de canard, and codfish casserole and stuffed cabbage. Some of these specials are featured on one day of the week only. For a side dish, I recommend aligot, a medley of fresh potatoes, garlic, and Cantal cheese.

BOFINGER, 5, rue de la Bastille, 4e. Tel. 42-72-87-82.

Cuisine: FRENCH. **Reservations:** Recommended. **Métro:** Bastille.
$ Prices: Appetizers 45–97 F ($8.10–$17.50); main dishes 68–146 F ($12.20–$26.30); fixed-price menu 166 F ($29.90). AE, DC, MC, V.
Open: Lunch Mon–Fri noon–3pm; dinner Mon–Fri 6:30pm–1am, Sat–Sun noon–1am.

This is the oldest Alsatian brasserie in Paris, tracing its origins back to 1864. It successfully retains the palace style of the Victorian era; fully restored, it looks better than ever. Its decor is such a part of the Paris landscape that it has been classified a historic landmark. At night, many Parisian opera-goers venture here for beer and sauerkraut at Bofinger.

The brasserie offers not only excellent Alsatian fare but also hearty portions served by waiters in floor-length white aprons. The chef prepares a different main dish every day; one Wednesday night the special was savory stew in casserole (cassoulet toulousain). Most guests order the choucroute formidable (sauerkraut), complete with sausages, smoked bacon, and pork chops. The fixed-price menu is the most appealing in the neighborhood, containing such menu choices as foie gras and magrêt de canard. For dessert, if you have room, try the apple tart or the fresh berries of spring.

CHEZ JO GOLDENBERG, 7, rue des Rosiers, 4e. Tel. 48-87-20-16.
   Cuisine: FRENCH. **Reservations:** Recommended. **Métro:** St-Paul.
$ Prices: Appetizers 18–115 F ($3.20–$20.70); main dishes 70–80 F ($12.60–$14.40). AE, DC, MC, V.
   Open: Daily noon–11:30pm.

On this "Street of the Rose Bushes" this is the best-known restaurant. Albert Goldenberg, the doyen of Jewish restaurateurs in Paris, long ago moved to another restaurant in choicer surroundings at 69, av. de Wagram, 17e. But his brother Joseph has remained at the original establishment, which opened in 1936.

Dining here is on two levels, one reserved for nonsmokers. Look for the collection of samovars and the white fantail pigeon in a wicker cage. Interesting paintings and strolling musicians add to the ambience.

On rue des Rosiers, the carpe farcie (stuffed carp) is a preferred selection, but the beef goulash is also good. I also like the eggplant moussaka, and pastrami is one of the most popular items. The menu also offers Israeli wines, but Monsieur Goldenberg admits that they're not as good as French wine.

LA TAVERNE DU SERGENT RECRUTEUR, 41, rue St-Louis-en-l'Ile, 4e. Tel. 43-54-75-42.
   Cuisine: FRENCH. **Reservations:** Required. **Métro:** Pont-Marie.
$ Prices: Fixed-price meal 190 F ($34.20). MC, V.
   Open: Dinner only, Mon–Sat 7pm–2am.

Located on the main street of the Ile Saint-Louis is this 17th-century-style restaurant, where you'll get enough to eat to last you through the next day. The placemats are reproductions of old French engravings, and the chairs are ladderback country style. Pronged iron racks suspended from the ceiling hold everything from round loaves of crusty bread to pigtails of garlic, a horse collar, and oil lamps.

First, the makings of a salad are placed before you: carrots, radishes (red and black), fennel, celery, cucumbers, green peppers, and hard-boiled eggs. Next comes a huge basket of sausages—you slice off as much as you wish. A bottle of wine (rosé, red, or white) is set on your table, along with a crock of homemade pâté. Then the waiter asks you for your selection of a main dish—perhaps steak, chicken, or veal. A big cheese board follows. But that's not the end of it—you can select chocolate mousse or ice cream for dessert.

INEXPENSIVE

AU GOURMET DE L'ISLE, 42, rue St-Louis-en-l'Ile, 4e. Tel. 43-26-79-27.
   Cuisine: FRENCH. **Reservations:** Required. **Métro:** Pont-Marie.
$ Prices: Appetizers 32–90 F ($5.80–$16.20); main dishes 65–85 F ($11.70–$15.30); fixed-price meal 125 F ($22.50). MC, V.
   Open: Lunch Wed–Sun noon–2pm; dinner Wed–Sun 7–10pm.

A good restaurant is hard to find on the Ile Saint-Louis; many just look good, but this is an excellent choice in the 4th arrondissement. It looks good too, with flickering candlelight and heavy dark beams overhead, but in addition it serves fine food. A sign, A.A.A.A.A., is posted outside, signifying that the restaurant is a meeting place for a society of gastronomes—the Association of Amateur Devotees of the Authentic Andouillette.

Andouillettes (chitterling sausages grilled on a low fire) are to the French what clam chowder is to a Cape Cod resident. Accompanied by mashed potatoes, it makes a good, hearty meal. Another well-recommended dish is charbonnée de l'Ile, a savory pork dish. I also recommend the stuffed mussels in shallot butter.

BUDGET

AQUARIUS, 54, rue Ste-Croix-de-la-Bretonnerie, 4e. Tel. 48-87-48-71.
   Cuisine: VEGETARIAN. **Reservations:** Not required. **Métro:** Hôtel-de-Ville.
$ **Prices:** Appetizers 16–29 F ($2.90–$5.20); main dishes 29–47 F ($5.20–$8.50); fixed-price meal 53 F ($9.50). No credit cards.
   Open: Mon–Sat noon–9:45pm. **Closed:** Aug.

Aquarius is one of the best-known vegetarian restaurants in Le Marais, a district that has a lot of health-conscious residents who insist on no smoking. Neither wines nor spirits are sold here, but you can enjoy a fruit-flavored beverage. Meals, regardless of what you order, seem to overflow with raw or steamed vegetables.

13. 18TH & 19TH ARR.

EXPENSIVE

BEAUVILLIERS, 52, rue Lamarck, 18e. Tel. 42-54-54-42.
   Cuisine: FRENCH. **Reservations:** Required. **Métro:** Lamarck-Caulaincourt.
$ **Prices:** Appetizers 110–160 F ($19.80–$28.80); main dishes 180–240 F ($32.40–$43.20); fixed-price menus 320–700 F ($57.60–$126). AE, MC, V.
   Open: Lunch Tues–Sat noon–2pm; dinner Mon–Sat 7:15–10:30pm.

This Montmartre hideaway is reputed to be the favorite Parisian restaurant of master chef Paul Bocuse, who drops in whenever he's visiting from Lyon. The decor is unabashedly romantic, dripping with art nouveau touches that the owners have accumulated since the restaurant was converted from a bakery years ago. Chef Edouard Carlier is the secret behind the success of this restaurant.

   Amid 19th-century statues, old engravings, and massive bouquets of flowers, you can enjoy subtle transformations of traditional French dishes. Specialties include a flan of mussels with zucchini, duckling en cocotte with a confit of lemons, and a succulent leg of lamb with tarragon. During the summer the restaurant moves outside near a wide stairway leading up to the famous Butte.

COCHON D'OR [Golden Pig], 192, av. Jean-Jaurès, 19e. Tel. 42-45-46-46.
   Cuisine: FRENCH. **Reservations:** Required. **Métro:** Porte-de-Pantin.
$ **Prices:** Appetizers 46–200 F ($8.30–$36); main dishes 66–260 F ($11.90–$46.80); fixed-price meal 240 F ($43.20). AE, DC, MC, V.
   Open: Lunch daily noon–2:30pm; dinner daily 7:30–10:30pm.

The slumming chic come here for some of the best beef in the city, even though it means journeying out to the remote Porte de Pantin in the 19th arrondissement. The restaurant's history goes back to the turn of the century, when it was created as a bistro for butchers in skullcaps. Nowadays it's run by René Ayral, who extends personal greetings. You get hefty portions at high prices, but good value nonetheless, considering the quality of the produce and the care that goes into the preparation.

   One dish I'd recommend is the charcoal-grilled côte de boeuf with moelle (marrow) sauce, for two. It's usually accompanied by a potato soufflé. Known mainly by gastronomes, an especially satisfying choice is the onglet grillé, one of the best beef cuts I've ever sampled in Paris.

INEXPENSIVE

LE MAQUIS [Underbrush], 69, rue Caulaincourt, 18e. Tel. 42-59-76-07.
   Cuisine: FRENCH. **Reservations:** Required. **Métro:** Lamarck-Caulaincourt.

$ Prices: Appetizers 45–70 F ($8.10–$12.60); main dishes 80–100 F ($14.40–$18); fixed-price lunch 63 F ($11.30). V.

Open: Lunch Mon–Sat noon–2pm; dinner Mon–Sat 8–10pm.

Named not after the resistance movement of World War II (as many Parisians think) but after the neighborhood (le Maquis) it occupies, this restaurant is lively, inexpensive, and fun. If you don't mind leaving place du Tertre and heading on a 12-minute walk down the Butte, you'll be richly rewarded at this attractive and popular restaurant, which has a tiny terrace in front for fair-weather dining. The menu changes with the seasons, but is personally supervised and adapted by owner-chef Claude Lesage. In winter, menu items might include a sauerkraut of fish, fricassée of rabbit, stuffed mussels, filet of sole cooked in two types of butter, and pheasant with cabbage. In summer, the menu might include a fricassée of chicken with wild mushrooms, a navarin of lamb with baby vegetables, grilled tuna steak in the style of Provence, and grilled filets of the ugliest fish in the Mediterranean, rascasse.

BUDGET

LE GRAIN DE FOLIE, 24, rue de la Vieuville, 18e. Tel. 42-58-15-57.
Cuisine: VEGETARIAN. **Reservations:** Recommended. **Métro:** Abbesses.
$ Prices: Appetizers 20–32 F ($3.60–$5.80); main dishes 48–65 F ($8.60–$11.70). No credit cards.
Open: Lunch Tues–Sun 12:30–2:30pm; dinner daily 6–11:30pm.

Run by a young Frenchwoman, this restaurant has two rooms offering a pleasant ambience. You can take out or eat in at this relaxing restaurant. The culinary inspiration for the all-vegetarian dishes comes from France, Greece, India, and Mexico. The menu includes a full array of salads, cereal products, vegetable tarts, and vegetable terrines. Desserts include an old-fashioned apple crumble and fruit salad. Accompany your meal with either the house beaujolais or a frothy glass of vegetable juice. On Saturday and Sunday the establishment offers a vegetarian brunch in its annex across the street, for which reservations are strongly recommended. From 9:30am to 2:30pm, you can order a breakfast for 35 F ($6.30), or a more elaborate *brunch campagnard* for 45 F ($8.10).

LA MAISON ROSE, 2, rue de l'Abreuvoir, 18e. Tel. 42-57-66-75.
Cuisine: FRENCH. **Reservations:** Recommended. **Métro:** Blanche or Lamarck-Caulaincourt.
$ Prices: Appetizers 20–40 F ($3.60–$7.20); main dishes 42–92 F ($7.60–$16.60); two-course fixed-price menus 69–98 F ($12.40–$17.60). MC, V.
Open: Nov–Mar, daily 11:30am–10pm; Apr–Oct, daily 11:30am–midnight.

In this rosy building (now a historical monument) was the atelier of Utrillo. Legend says that Utrillo's friends used to lock him in during his periods of greatest emotional upsets and financial crises so that he could produce something to sell.

During the summer, the terrace fills up quickly. Meals might include fish soup, confit de magrêt de canard (duck), foie gras, salmon with sorrel sauce, boeuf bourguignon, and paupiettes of sole à la mousseline.

14. 12TH ARR.

EXPENSIVE

AU TROU GASCON, 40, rue Taine, 12e. Tel. 43-44-34-26.
Cuisine: FRENCH. **Reservations:** Recommended. **Métro:** Daumesnil.
$ Prices: Appetizers 88–140 F ($15.80–$25.20); main dishes 148–220 F

($26.60–$39.60); three-course "Diner Gascon" menu 200 F ($36); six-course "Idées de la Saison" menu 450 F ($81). AE, DC, MC, V.

Open: Lunch Mon–Fri noon–2pm; dinner Mon–Fri 7:30–10pm. **Closed:** Aug.

This popular spot has a chef who has an interesting story. One of the most acclaimed chefs in Paris today, Alain Dutournier launched his cooking career in the southwestern Gascony region, working in the kitchen with his mother and grandmother. His parents owned an inn, and they mortgaged it to allow Dutournier to open a turn-of-the-century bistro in a rather unchic part of the 12th arrondissement that had been a rendezvous for chauffeurs. Soon word spread that this man was a true artisan in the kitchen who practiced authentic modern French cooking.

Today, he has opened another restaurant in Paris. The owner's wife, Nicole, is there to greet you, and Monsieur Dutournier has distinguished himself for his extensive cellar containing several little-known wines along with an array of armagnacs. It's estimated that the cellar has some 700 varieties of wine.

Here you get the true cuisine of Gascony—cassoulet, wild salmon with smoked bacon, foie gras (offered all year), and Gascon ham cooked farmer's style.

15. SPECIALTY DINING

HOTEL DINING

BICE, in the Hôtel Balzac, 6, rue Balzac, 8e. Tel. 42-89-86-34.
   Cuisine: ITALIAN. **Reservations:** Required. **Métro:** George-V.
$ Prices: Appetizers 80–120 F ($14.40–$21.60); main dishes 130–160 F ($23.40–$28.80); fixed-price menus 250–350 F ($45–$63). AE, DC, MC, V.
   Open: Lunch Mon–Fri noon–3pm; dinner Mon–Sat 7pm–midnight. **Closed:** First three weeks in Aug.

This is the exclusive restaurant of one of the most elegant four-star hotels of Paris, lying just off the Champs-Elysées. From around the world the rich and famous flock to this classically refined establishment. It's an offshoot of the restaurant Bice, which opened in Milan in 1936—under the direction of "Mama Bice"—and has since gone international with branches in New York and Los Angeles, among other cities. The well-prepared (and well-received) cuisine features many specialties from northern Italy, mainly pastas. Try tagliolini with shrimp or ossobuco of veal with risotto alla milanese. Begin with a Caprese salad with mozzarella and tomato or a vegetable carpaccio with a vinaigrette sauce.

LE CELADON, in the Hôtel Westminster, 13, rue de la Paix, 2e. Tel. 42-61-57-46.
   Cuisine: FRENCH. **Reservations:** Recommended. **Métro:** Opéra.
$ Prices: Appetizers 80–195 F ($14.40–$35.10); main dishes 160–210 F ($28.80–$37.80); fixed-price menus 200 F ($36). AE, DC, MC, V.
   Open: Lunch Mon–Fri noon–2:15pm; dinner Mon–Fri 7:30–10:30pm.

This very fine restaurant near the Opéra and the prestigious place Vendôme takes its name from its outstanding celadon porcelain collection, which you can see on display. Lunch bustles with businesspeople from the 2nd arrondissement; getting a table in the evening is not a problem if you reserve.

You might begin your evening in the bar, Les Chenets, where drinks are served daily from 11am until midnight and there is a cocktail of the day. Light snacks are offered. You can also visit in the afternoon for tea or coffee accompanied by homemade cakes and pastries. During apéritif hours this cozy bar is turned into a piano bar. Its paneling and fireplace are replicas of those in the Gothic Hall at Westminster Abbey.

Chef Joël Boilleaut used to be at the two-star Le Duc d'Enghien in the Paris suburb Enghien-les-Bains. He offers seasonal specialties and traditional but light cuisine. The varied and imaginative menu is embellished by professional service. You might begin with one of the chef's creative appetizers, such as a light medley of red snapper with basil or a salad of sweetbreads with truffle oil. Another intriguing appetizer is roasted crayfish tails served with an infusion of laurel leaves. Main courses are likely to include such specialties as freshwater zander flavored with Dutch cumin and fennel, or roast pigeon served with bacon and its own juices. A dessert delight is vanilla macaroons with vanilla sauce and raspberry seeds.

LA COURONNE, in the Hôtel Le Warwick, 5, rue de Berri, 8e. Tel. 45-63-14-11.
 Cuisine: FRENCH. **Reservations:** Recommended. **Métro:** George-V.
$ Prices: Appetizers 90–360 F ($16.20–$64.80); main dishes 130–225 F ($23.40–$40.50); fixed-price meal 270 F ($48.60). AE, DC, MC, V.
 Open: Lunch Mon–Fri noon–2:30pm; dinner Mon–Sat 8–10pm.

Even if you're not staying in this four-star hotel, consider eating here. Following a trend in hotel dining in Paris of serving substantial and serious food, La Couronne offers not only superb food, but also an elegant setting. Chef Paul Van Gessel makes use of only the freshest ingredients, which he deftly handles with care and finesse.

You might begin with his wild-rabbit salad with sweet corn and follow it with baked salmon in sea salt or stuffed pig's trotters. The wild duck in pepper sauce with turnips, for two, is delectable. Some of his newer specialties include lobster salad, a mosaic of sweetbreads, daurade baked in a mustard sauce, and a paysanne of wild hare flavored with rosemary.

DINING WITH A VIEW
Expensive

BATEAUX-MOUCHES, pont de l'Alma, place de l'Alma, 8e. Tel. 42-25-96-10 for reservations.
 Cuisine: FRENCH. **Reservations:** Required. **Métro:** Alma-Marceau.
$ Prices: Fixed-price cruise and lunch 300 F ($54) Mon–Sat, 350 F ($63) Sun; fixed-price cruise and dinner 500 F ($90). AE, DC, MC, V.
 Open: Lunch cruise Tues–Sun 1pm; dinner cruise daily 8:30pm.

Nothing comes close to the combination of sightseeing and dining you find here. For dinner, men are required to wear jackets and ties. No jeans are allowed. The lunch tour returns at 2:45pm; the dinner tour, at 10:45pm. During the dinner cruise, live music is featured.

LE JULES VERNE, Tour Eiffel, Champ-de-Mars, 7e. Tel. 45-55-61-44.
 Cuisine: FRENCH. **Reservations:** Required. **Métro:** Trocadéro, Ecole-Militaire, or Bir-Hakeim.
$ Prices: Appetizers 175–310 F ($31.50–$55.80); main dishes 190–350 F ($34.20–$63); fixed-price lunch 290 F ($52.20); menu dégustation 660 F ($118.80). AE, DC, MC, V.
 Open: Lunch daily noon–2:30pm; dinner daily 7:30–11pm.

This restaurant is reached by taking an elevator ride up to the second level. It's best at night, where you can dine and survey the lights of the city of lights. For complete details, see "7th Arrondissement," above.

LE CIEL DE PARIS [MAINE-MONTPARNASSE TOWER], 33, av. du Maine, 15e. Tel. 45-38-52-35.
 Cuisine: FRENCH. **Reservations:** Required. **Métro:** Montparnasse-Bienvenue.
$ Prices: Fixed-price menu 250 F ($45). AE, DC, MC, V.
 Open: Lunch daily noon–3pm; dinner daily 7pm–midnight.

Overshadowing the Left Bank quarter of Montparnasse, the tower, completed in 1973, covers an entire block and houses some 80 shops, including Galeries Lafayette, and more than 200 offices. Its floors are serviced by rapid elevators that speed visitors from the lobby to the top floor in less than 40 seconds. The charge for the elevator is 35.50 F ($6.40) for adults and 28 F ($5) for children. It's open April to October, daily from 9:30am to 11pm; off-season, daily from 10am to 10pm.

Sightseers go to Montparnasse 56, the covered, glassed-in observation deck on the

56th floor, where a panoramic view of Paris opens from every side. Your ticket includes an audiovisual presentation of the glamour of Paris, expositions of how the tower was built, and highlights of the Paris skyline far below. The Belvedere bar/café, good for lunch, a quick snack, or a drink, is also in the Montparnasse 56 complex. Le Ciel de Paris is the highest restaurant in the city, where you can enjoy a full dinner—fixed-price menu only—at a reasonable price. When you have finished your meal, you may ask the waiter to give you a ticket for entrance into Montparnasse 56. There's no charge to take the elevator going directly to the restaurant from the lobby.

TOUR D'ARGENT, 15-17, quai de la Tournelle, 5e. Tel. 43-54-23-31.
  Cuisine: FRENCH. **Reservations:** Required. **Métro:** Maubert-Mutualité or Sully-Morland.
$ Prices: Appetizers 215–580 F ($38.70–$104.40); main dishes 330–580 F ($59.40–$104.40); fixed-price lunch 375 F ($67.50), Tues–Sat. AE, DC, MC, V.
  Open: Lunch Tues–Sun 12:30–2:30pm; dinner Tues–Sun 8–11:30pm.
This is one of the most spectacular dining views in all of Paris, despite its lethal prices. Nothing equals its view of the illuminated flying buttresses of Notre-Dame at night. For details, see "Haute Cuisine," above.

FOR BREAKFAST
Expensive

HOTEL DE CRILLON, 10, place de la Concorde, 8e. Tel. 44-71-15-00.
  Cuisine: FRENCH. **Reservations:** Required far in advance. **Métro:** Concorde.
$ Prices: *Petit déjeuner continental* (continental breakfast) 145 F ($26.10); *buffet des gourmets* 200 F ($36). AE, DC, MC, V.
  Open: Breakfast only, daily 7–10:30am.
To experience a luxurious French breakfast, dress the part and head for the Hôtel de Crillon. Along with the international diplomatic and business elite, enjoy your breakfast in style amid the marble and crystal of the Restaurant des Ambassadeurs. Sausages are from England, but the cheese in several varieties is pure French. Fresh fruit is also served. This is a chic place for power breakfasts *à la française*. The 145-F ($26.10) breakfast is called *petit déjeuner des affairs* (businessperson's breakfast). The *buffet des gourmets* is an English-inspired breakfast buffet. Open bottles of champagne are part of the buffet.

Moderate

SIR WINSTON CHURCHILL, 5, rue de Presbourg, 16e. Tel. 40-67-17-37.
  Cuisine: FRENCH. **Reservations:** Required for lunch or dinner, but not breakfast. **Métro:** Charles-de-Gaulle (Etoile).
$ Prices: English breakfast 100–150 F ($18–$27); dinner 200–250 F ($36–$45). AE, MC, V.
  Open: Mon–Sat 9am–2am (breakfast Mon–Sat 9am–noon).
If you like a rib-sticking breakfast as opposed to café au lait and croissants, go to a corner of "ye olde England in Paris." You can order orange juice, porridge, eggs, bacon, grilled tomato, toast, butter, marmalade, and tea or coffee. You might come back for lunch or even dinner, when the chef prepares English dishes, such as roast beef with Yorkshire pudding.

Budget

CAFE DE CLUNY, 20, bd. St-Michel, or 102, bd. St-Germain, 5e. Tel. 43-26-68-24.
  Cuisine: FRENCH. **Reservations:** Not required. **Métro:** St-Michel.
$ Prices: Continental breakfast 40 F ($7.20); café au lait (coffee with milk) 20 F ($3.60); *plats du jour* 45–70 F ($8.10–$12.60). MC, V.
  Open: Daily 4am–2am.
Among the hundreds of Left Bank cafés, this one, located strategically at the intersection of these two famous avenues, overlooks the hub of the Left Bank and the Musée de Cluny. The long hours will enable you to begin the day here at 4am with a

morning omelet and come back for a final brandy at 2am. The café closes from 2 to 4am for cleaning. Breakfast is served at any time, day or night. In the afternoon and until closing you can order various grillades and salads, including steak with pommes frites (french-fried potatoes) and roast loin of pork.

FOR BRUNCH
Expensive

L'ESPACE CARDIN, 1, av. Gabriel, 8e. Tel. 42-66-11-70.
Cuisine: FRENCH. **Reservations:** Required. **Métro:** Champs-Elysées.
$ Prices: Breakfast buffet 230 F ($41.40); glass of champagne 50 F ($9). AE, DC, MC, V.
Open: Sun only, noon–3pm.

Under the ownership of Pierre Cardin, the informal Espace presents 70–100 delicacies, including cold roasts and ample antipasti. The champagne is extra, but you can order it by the glass. If it's a nice day, ask for a garden table.

HOTEL MERIDIEN, 81, bd. Gouvion-Saint-Cyr, 17e. Tel. 40-68-34-34.
Cuisine: FRENCH. **Reservations:** Recommended. **Métro:** Maillot.
$ Prices: 300 F ($54) adults, 150 F ($27) children under 12. AE, DC, MC, V.
Open: Oct–June, Sun only, 12:30–3:30pm.

In my opinion, the greatest place for brunch in Paris is "Le Sunday Jazz Brunch" which takes place in the lobby of the Hôtel Meridien. Jazz artists entertain while you eat smoked salmon and enjoy excellent roasts and various hot and cold dishes. For details on the Jazz Club Lionel Hampton, see "The Club and Music Scene" in Chapter 10.

PARIS HILTON, 18, av. de Suffren, 15e. Tel. 42-73-92-00.
Cuisine: FRENCH. **Reservations:** Not required. **Métro:** Bir-Hakeim.
$ Prices: Brunch from 280 F ($50.40). AE, DC, MC, V.
Open: Sun only, 11:30am–2:30pm.

Of the big hotels, the Hilton still serves an all-you-can devour brunch menu. You can enjoy an abundance of rib-sticking food at this buffet-style brunch, including spareribs, roast beef, and lavish desserts.

LIGHT MEALS & FAST FOOD

Of course, if you're really on the run, do as the French on the go do and grab a quick snack from a street vendor. You'll see them at most intersections, offering such snacks as marrons (roasted chestnuts), crêpes (pancakes), and gaufres (waffles).

Moderate

CHICAGO PIZZA FACTORY, 5, rue de Berri, 8e. Tel. 45-62-50-23.
Cuisine: AMERICAN. **Reservations:** Accepted only for lunch. **Métro:** Champs-Elysées–Clemenceau.
$ Prices: Salads 20–53 F ($3.60–$9.50); pizzas 82–151 F ($14.80–$27.20) for two people; express menu 71 F ($12.80). AE, MC, V.
Open: Daily 11:45am–1am.

Sometimes you get a craving for pizza that nothing else will satisfy. If so, head for the Chicago Pizza Factory, right off the Champs-Elysées, in what was once a garage but is now a "Cheers"–style bar. While music or sports broadcasts are aired from the States, you can order deep-dish pizza and other hometown favorites, like garlic bread, salad, pecan pie, and cheesecake—but no burgers.

Inexpensive

FAUCHON, 26, place de la Madeleine, 8e. Tel. 47-42-60-11.
Cuisine: FRENCH. **Reservations:** Not required. **Métro:** Madeleine.
$ Prices: Lunch from 100 F ($18). AE, DC, MC, V.
Open: Mon–Sat 9:40am–7pm.

For epicureans this has always been the *haut* grocery store of Paris, sort of a Parisian version of Fortnum and Mason. In fact, it's such a symbol of the Establishment that French Maoists once launched what the press called "a daring caviar and foie gras heist in broad daylight" at this exclusive store.

What many people don't know about Fauchon is that it offers a reasonably priced cafeteria-style lunch. First, place your order at the counter, then pay at the cashier's desk and receive a ticket to give to the clerk behind the counter. The only hitch is that you have to stand at the fast-food counter while you eat. Try the Fauchon's club sandwich and a scoop of ice cream. In the afternoon, Fauchon's cakes and pastries make tea a delight. In addition, Fauchon also operates a trattoria, open Monday through Saturday from noon to 4pm, serving homemade pastas and pizza, costing 35 F ($6.30) and up.

Budget

LE DRUG STORE, 149, bd. St-Germain-des-Prés, 6e. Tel. 42-22-92-50.
  Cuisine: FRENCH. **Reservations:** Not required. **Métro:** St-Germain-des-Prés.
  $ Prices: Appetizers 29–79 F ($5.20–$14.20); main dishes 65–130 F ($11.70–$23.40). AE, DC, MC, V.
  Open: Daily 10am–2am.

This is the most popular of a chain of bustling coffee-shop/soda-fountain/snack bar/newsstand/boutiques. When they were opened, these establishments were dismissed by many French as American vulgarisms, but they are, in fact, very Parisian today. Les Drug Stores sell everything from mustache cups to hearts of palm. The most popular item to order is a hamburger on a toasted bun. Some of the desserts are smothered in enough whipped cream to make them immoral.

There's another Drug Store at Publicis Champs-Elysées, 133, av. des Champs-Elysées, 8e (tel. 47-20-94-40).

TEAROOMS & PATISSERIES

London is not the only city that has tearooms. The *salon de thé* has had a surprising revival in Paris. As a rule, expect them to be more sophisticated than cafés with menus that are not as limited. Here you can order a full lunch or expect fantastic, rich desserts for delectable snacks.

Budget

LADUREE, 16, rue Royale, 8e. Tel. 42-60-21-79.
  Cuisine: FRENCH. **Reservations:** Recommended for lunch. **Métro:** Concorde.
  $ Prices: Café au lait 20 F ($3.60); tea 30 F ($5.40). MC, V.
  Open: Mon–Sat 8:30am–7pm. **Closed:** Aug.

Here, more than at any other *salon de thé* in Paris, the clientele look important and affluent. In turn-of-the-century grandeur, you can sip tea or coffee at tables barely big enough to hold a napkin. Diners order light lunches or just-baked pastries while talking quietly beneath the ceiling frescoes of the main salon. Visit for lunch from noon to 3pm to order from a limited menu of traditional French dishes, such as boeuf bourguignon.

THE TEA CADDY, 14, rue St-Julien-le-Pauvre, 5e. Tel. 43-54-15-56.
  Cuisine: FRENCH. **Reservations:** Not required. **Métro:** St-Michel.
  $ Prices: Pot of tea 25 F ($4.50); homemade pastries 28–32 F ($5–$5.80). No credit cards.
  Open: Wed–Mon noon–7pm. **Closed:** July 25–Aug 31.

This just might be the best spot in Paris for a pot of tea. You'll recognize it by the stained-glass windows set into the oak door of what was probably once a stable. Their "ensemble" of furniture, fabrics, flowers, and darkened paneling would remind tea-lovers of a little corner of London except for a view of Notre-Dame, which rises across the river. Set next to the park of what might be "the most famous lesser-known church of Paris" (St. Julien le Pauvre), Tea Caddy is famous for its homemade marmalade, which accompanies the scones; its homemade pastries; and its half-dozen kinds of tea. These include Indian, Chinese, and Russian teas, plus varieties infused with jasmine and mango.

LATE-NIGHT / 24-HOUR DINING
Expensive

AU PIED DE COCHON, 6, rue Coquillière, 1er. Tel. 42-36-11-75.
   Cuisine: FRENCH. **Reservations:** Recommended for lunch but not accepted for dinner after 8:30pm. **Métro:** Les Halles.
$ Prices: Appetizers 45–115 F ($8.10–$20.70); main dishes 75–130 F ($13.50–$23.40); fixed-price menu 119 F ($21.40) after 11pm. AE, DC, MC, V.
   Open: Daily 24 hours.
Near the contemporary buildings that have replaced Les Halles market and near the famous 16th-century church of St-Eustache, this Belle Epoque restaurant specializes in pork. It is also one of the last in Paris to be open all day and night year-round.

The famous onion soup is a standard of the house as a start to your meal. Then enjoy pigs' feet grilled with béarnaise sauce or stuffed with goose liver and mustard sauce. Another specialty is suckling pig St-Eustache (sliced pork filet and chops, roasted and cooked with mustard sauce). Andouillette (chitterling sausage with béarnaise sauce) is also served here. Try one of the trays of shellfish. Oysters, clams, mussels, and sea urchins are brought every day directly from the sea. I'd suggest La Vie en Rose for dessert.

LA MAISON D'ALSACE, 39, av. des Champs-Elysées, 8e. Tel. 43-59-44-24.
   Cuisine: FRENCH. **Reservations:** Not required. **Métro:** Champs-Elysées.
$ Prices: Appetizers 40–90 F ($7.20–$16.20); main dishes 90–140 F ($16.20–$25.20). AE, DC, MC, V.
   Open: Daily 24 hours.
This is one of the largest, busiest, and most visible cafés along the Champs-Elysées, with a bustling business throughout the day and night by all aspects of Parisian society. In place since the end of World War II, with many subsequent owners, it was originally established by Alsatians. This is a convenient late-night stopover on the Right Bank for revelers who want to tuck in some food before going back to their hotels.

Inexpensive

CAFE LE DEPART, 1, place St-Michel, 5e. Tel. 43-54-24-55.
   Cuisine: FRENCH. **Reservations:** Not required. **Métro:** St-Michel.
$ Prices: Beer at the bar 9 F ($1.60), beer at a table 22 F ($4); sandwiches 17 F ($3.10); burgers 54 F ($9.70); grills 57–60 F ($10.30–$10.80). AE, DC, MC, V.
   Open: Daily 24 hours.
One of the most popular cafés on the Left Bank is open 24 hours a day. On the banks of the Seine, within view of both the steeple of the Sainte-Chapelle and the dragon statue of place St-Michel, it is conveniently located for most visitors.

The decor is warmly modern, with lots of shades of brown and etched mirrors reflecting the faces of a diversified clientele. House cocktails include a "Saint-Michel" (Polish vodka, grapefruit juice, and cream of banana), costing 49 F ($8.80). If you're hungry, select from warm and cold snacks, including sandwiches. The most popular late-night order is a grilled entrecôte with french-fried potatoes.

PUB SAINT-GERMAIN-DES-PRES, 17, rue de l'Ancienne-Comédie, 6e. Tel. 43-29-38-70.
   Cuisine: FRENCH. **Reservations:** Accepted for dinner, but not required. **Métro:** Odéon.
$ Prices: Beer 19–74 F ($3.40–$13.30); food plates 70–100 F ($12.60–$18). AE, DC, MC, V.
   Open: Daily 24 hours.
For late-night drinking, this is one of the most popular spots on the Left Bank. In the evening, there's both rock and variety band entertainment. The pub is the only one in

the country to offer 24 draft beers and 450 international beers. There are nine different rooms and 500 seats, making it the largest pub in France. Leather booths make for a great late-night quiet drink.

 **FROMMER'S COOL FOR KIDS:
RESTAURANTS**

Meals at the grand restaurants of Paris are rarely suitable for young children. Nevertheless, many parents drag their children to these deluxe citadels, often to the annoyance of other diners. If you want to dine at a fancy restaurant, consider leaving the kids with a babysitter. However, if you prefer to dine with your children, then you may have to make some compromises. Perhaps you'll have to dine earlier than most Parisians. Some hotels have dining rooms, and this can be another good choice for family dining. They usually have children's menus, or at least one or two *plats du jour* cooked for children, such as spaghetti with meat sauce.

Most **cafés** throughout the day and early evening welcome children. At a café, children always seem to like the sandwiches (try a croque monsieur), the omelets, and most definitely their pommes frites (crispy french fries).

Les Drug Stores also welcome children, especially in the early evening, as do most tearooms, and you can tide the kids over with pastries and ice cream if dinner will be late. Try a picnic in the park. Also, there are lots of fast-food bars around the Eiffel Tower, where snacking and sightseeing go hand in hand.

La Samaritaine, 75, rue de Rivoli (tel. 45-08-33-33; Métro: Pont-Neuf), is a café that serves moderately priced food with a view of Paris.

If you'd like to take children to a steak house, try **Le Western** in the Hilton Hôtel (see "15th Arr.," above). They're accustomed to children there, and your kids may get a bang out of seeing the servers in western costumes.

Another good choice is **La Boutique a Sandwichs,** which is open throughout the day and welcomes early diners. See "8th Arr.," above.

Of course, if you're looking for fast-food eateries, such as **Pizza Hut** and **McDonald's,** you'll see these chains all over the city. Their prices may be a bit higher than you pay back home, but they're fast and convenient. Eating here is no way to teach your children how to appreciate French food, but the restaurants are always clean and sanitary.

If you take your child to one of the moderately priced or budget restaurants already mentioned, ask if the restaurant will serve a child's plate. If not, order a *plat du jour* or *plat garni*, which will be suitable for most children, particularly if a dessert is to follow.

For some of the best ice cream in Paris, take your child to **Bertillon,** 31, rue St-Louis-en-l'Ile, 4e (tel. 43-54-31-61; Métro: Pont-Marie), open Wednesday through Sunday from 10am to 8pm. This store sells some of the most delectable ice-cream flavors ever concocted. It was established in 1954 and has been famous ever since. Although it's open in winter and summer, in summer long lines form.

Most children like crêpes, and during a tour of the Latin Quarter with your child, consider **A La Bonne Crêpe,** 11, rue Grégoire-de-Tours, 6e (tel. 43-54-60-74; Métro: Odéon). Later at night, when Parisians take over, this typical Left Bank street might not be suitable for children, but during the day and early evening it's just fine. Both main-dish savory crêpes and dessert crêpes filled with luscious delights are served here. Crêpes cost 28–42 F ($5–$7.60) each. Instead of wine, your older child might prefer a glass of Breton cider, which the French children drink. One is enough—it has some alcohol in it. The crêperie is open Monday through Saturday from noon to 3pm and 7pm to midnight.

PICNIC FARE & WHERE TO EAT IT

Paris is full of shops that sell picnic ingredients; some can be found at most *charcuteries* (gourmet food shops) or *pâtisseries* or *boulangeries* (bakeries). Prices are a bit high, but that's just Paris.

My favorite picnic spot is the **Bois de Boulogne,** but, depending on which part of town you're in, you may find the Right Bank **Jardin des Tuileries** or the **Parc Monceau** equally enticing.

At the Bois de Boulogne, you can, if you have a child with you, tie in a visit here with a trip to the Jardin d'Acclimation (see "Cool For Kids," in Chapter 7).

Again, if you have children, you may want to take them to the **Bois de Vincennes** (Métro: Picpus), a big, popular patch of woodland with fine trees, two boating lakes, and a racecourse. This park, a favorite spot for family outings, adjoins the 14th-century Castle of Vincennes, open to visitors.

For the most elegant picnic makings in town, go to **Fauchon,** 26, place de la Madeleine, 8e (tel. 47-42-60-11; Métro: Madeleine), recommended in "Light Meals and Fast Food," above. Here you'll find a complete *charcuterie* and a famous pastry shop. It's the best-known food shop in town, said to offer 20,000 kinds of imported fruits, vegetables, and other exotic delicacies, snacks, salads, and canapés—all packed to take out.

Another gourmet supplier is **Chedeville Saint-Honoré,** 18, place du Marché Saint-Honoré, 1e (tel. 42-61-04-62; Métro: Pyramides), open Monday through Friday from 9am to 7pm and on Saturday from 9am to noon. For nearly a century, it has been preparing such homemade specialties as sausages, salami, pâtés, and various hams.

These are just two of thousands of shops throughout Paris. You can pick up a variety of pâtés or terrines, which can be consumed cold, as well as quiches and salads (but don't buy anything likely to go bad on a hot day). Many of the salads are made with a vinaigrette dressing, which preserves them better. And don't forget the condiments, such as olives and pickles. Food critic Patricia Wells has called the Parisian charcuterie a "little touch of heaven." She likes to go from shop to shop sampling this and that. That way, she claims, you can make a picnic lunch a "true Parisian feast."

Armed with some sauterne or champagne, or whatever it is you like to drink, you're ready to head for your picnic in the park.

PARIS ATTRACTIONS

I f it's your first visit to Paris, you are lucky. If it's your second, third, fourth, or your fiftieth you're even more fortunate. Like any good lover, Paris doesn't reveal all her charms and subtleties at once. The full impact of her beauty takes years to understand.

Paris is an old city, yet very much in the present, trying at times—almost hysterically—to be the style-setter of the world. Fads come and go with such rapidity that only New York and London could harbor so much fickleness. Somehow the old has learned to adapt to the new, and vice versa.

I'll spend a lot of time discussing monuments and art in this chapter, fashionable promenades and beautiful gardens. But even though I glorify monumental Paris, remember that its main attraction is and has always been the Parisians themselves. They're a unique breed, as even the most cursory visitor to the French capital finds out. The French from the provinces regard Parisians with interest, detachment, sometimes outright jealousy.

SIGHTSEEING STRATEGIES

If You Have 1 Day The most practical way to see Paris in a day is to take a guided tour, since you can't possibly master the city on your own in such a short period of time.

Start the day by ordering a café au lait or a café crème and croissants at a sidewalk café. The Cityrama tour, mentioned in "Organized Tours," below begins at 9:30am. A double-decker bus will take you around the city on a fast two-hour ride, past Notre-Dame and the Eiffel Tower. After the tour, have lunch and go to the Louvre for a guided tour of its most important artworks.

With what's left of the afternoon, stroll along the banks of the Seine, ending up at Notre-Dame as the sun sets over Paris. If you have an early dinner at a nearby bistro, you may still have the time and energy to attend the Lido or Folies Bergère (see "The Club and Music Scene" in Chapter 10).

If You Have 2 Days Start your second day by taking a Bateaux-Mouche cruise on the Seine (see "Organized Tours," below), with departures from Pont de l'Alma at place de l'Alma on the Right Bank (Métro: Alma-Marceau). Then go to the Eiffel Tower for lunch with a spectacular view (see my recommendation of Jules Verne in "Specialty Dining: Dining with a View" in Chapter 6).

Next, head for the Arc de Triomphe, a perfect place to begin a stroll down the Champs-Elysées, the main boulevard of Paris, until you reach the Egyptian obelisk at place de la Concorde. This grand promenade is one of the most famous long walks in the world.

If You Have 3 Days Spend your third morning exploring Sainte Chapelle and the Conciergerie. Have lunch, perhaps on the Ile St-Louis, and then take a walking tour of that island on the Seine. Afterward, I suggest spending two or three hours at the Musée d'Orsay.

If You Have 4 Days or More   On your fourth day, go on your own or take an organized tour to Versailles, 13 miles south of Paris. After viewing the palace and gardens, head back to the city for an evening stroll through the Latin Quarter, perhaps dining in a Left Bank bistro. With a good map, try walking along some of the livelier streets, such as rue de la Hachette and rue Monsieur-le-Prince.

On your fifth day, spend the morning roaming around Le Marais (see my walking tour in Chapter 8). By all means, pay a visit to the Picasso Museum and have lunch near the historic place des Vosges. Afterward, you might want to head toward Montmarte (again see the walking tour in Chapter 8 for a specific sightseeing route). Try to time your visit so you'll be at the Basilica of Sacré-Coeur at sunset.

ORGANIZED TOURS

BY BUS   Before plunging into more detailed sightseeing on your own, you might like to take the most popular get-acquainted tour in Paris. It's called **Cityrama**, 4, place des Pyramides, 1er, (tel. 42-60-30-14; métro: Tuilleries). On a double-decker bus with enough windows for the Palace of Versailles, you're taken on a nice and lazy two-hours ride through the city's streets. You don't actually go inside specific attractions—rather settle for a look at the outside of such places as Notre-Dame and the Eiffel Tower.

The language barrier is overcome as individual earphones are distributed with a canned commentary in ten different languages. In comfortable armchair seats, you sit back as Paris unfolds before you. Tours depart daily at 9:30am, 10:30am, 11:30am, 1:30pm, 2:30pm, and 3:30pm. The cost is 145 F ($26.10).

Another Cityrama offering, a tour of the nighttime illuminations, leaves daily in summer at 10pm, daily at 8:45pm in winter. The cost is 145 F ($26.10).

BY BOAT   A boat tour on Seine provides sweeping views of the riverbanks of Paris and some of the best views of the cathedral of Notre-Dame. Many of the boats have open sun decks, bars, and restaurants.

Bateaux-Mouche cruises (tel. 42-25-96-10 for information and reservation; métro: Alma-Marceau) on the Seine depart from the right bank of the Seine, adjacent to the Pont de l'Alma. Rides last about 75 minutes each. Tours depart every day of the week, at 30-minute intervals between 10am and 8:30pm, and at 15-minute intervals between 9 and 11pm. Lunch cruises depart at 1pm; dinner cruises at 8:30pm (jackets and ties are required for men on the dinner cruises).

Between 10am and 7:30pm fares are 30 F ($5.40) for adults and 15 F ($2.70) for children; after 8pm, 40 F ($7.20) for adults and 20 F ($3.60) for children. Luncheon cruises cost 300 F ($54) Monday through Saturday or 350 F ($63) on Sunday; and a dinner cruise costs 500 F ($90).

MUSEUM PASS

To save yourself both money and time spent waiting on ticket lines, purchase a Museum Pass for visits to 65 of the city's museums and monuments. A one-day pass costs 60 F ($10.80); a three-day pass, 120 F ($21.60); and a five-day pass, 170 F ($30.60).

Holders of the pass can head straight for the entrance—in fact the pass is known as a "queue-jumper."

The pass can be purchased at any of the attractions included; as well as at the main Métro and RER stations; and at the Paris Tourist Office, 127, av. des Champs Elysées, 8e (tel. 47-23-61-72; métro: Charles-de-Gaulle/Etoile), open daily from 9am to 8pm.

---

1. THE TOP ATTRACTIONS

MUSEE DU LOUVRE, rue de Rivoli, 1er. Tel. 40-20-53-17.

⭐ From far and wide they come—from North Dakota to Pakistan, from Nova Scotia to Japan—all bent on seeing the wonders of the legendary Louvre. People on one of those "Paris-in-a-day" tours try to break track records to get a glimpse of the two most famous ladies of the Louvre: the *Mona Lisa* and the armless *Venus de Milo*. (The scene in front of the *Mona Lisa* is best described as a circus. Viewers push and shove, and there seems minimal supervision from the staff. Flashbulbs, which are forbidden, pop all over the place. In all this fracas, you'll have anything else but a contemplative moment to view this world-famed attraction.) Those with an extra five minutes to spare go in pursuit of *Winged Victory*, that headless statue discovered at Samothrace and dating from about 200 B.C. You might as well appraise the considerable charms of these ageless favorites before making a big decision: which of the rest of the 300,000 works would you like to see?

The Louvre suffers from an embarrassment of riches. Hence, masterpieces are often ignored by the casual visitor—there is just too much of a good thing. It is the world's largest palace and the world's largest museum (some say greatest). As a palace, it leaves me cold, except for its old section, the Cour Carrée. As a museum, it's one of the great artistic heritages of the human race.

Marie Antoinette's head had rolled less than a month before the Revolutionary Committee decided that the king's collection of paintings and sculpture would be opened to the public. Between the Seine and the rue de Rivoli (Métro to Palais-Royal or Louvre, the latter the most elegant subway stop in the world), the Palace of the Louvre stretches for almost half a mile. In the days of Charles V it was a fortress, but François I, a patron of Leonardo da Vinci, had it torn down and rebuilt as a royal residence. At the lowest point in its history, in the 18th century, it was home for anybody who wanted to set up housekeeping. Laundry hung out the windows, corners were literally pig pens, and each family built a fire somewhere to cook a meal during the long Paris winter. Napoleon changed all that, chasing out the inhabitants and launching the restoration of the palace. In fact, the Louvre became the site of his wedding to Marie-Louise.

To enter the Louvre, you'll pass through a controversial 71-foot-high glass pyramid in the courtyard. Commissioned by Mitterrand and completed in 1990, it has received mixed reviews. Designed by I. M. Pei to allow sunlight to shine on an underground reception area, it shelters a complex of shops and restaurants. It also increases the gallery space of the Louvre by an astonishing 80% and provides underground garages for the tour buses that used to jam rue de Rivoli. Automatic ticket machines help relieve the long lines of yesteryear.

The collections are divided into six departments: Egyptian, Oriental, and Greek and Roman antiquities; sculpture; painting; and furniture and art objects. If you don't have to "do" Paris in a day, perhaps you can return to the Louvre for several visits, concentrating on different collections or schools of painting. Those with little time should go on one of the guided tours (in English), which last about 1¼ hours.

The Louvre's most important collections are in the wings devoted to painting and Greek and Roman sculpture. What to see after you've seen the big three (*Winged Victory, Venus de Milo, Mona Lisa*)? I'll give you a rough idea of some of the Louvre's masterpieces in the painting collection. After that, you're on your own—it would take a book to describe the Louvre in any detail (many have been written).

Da Vinci's much traveled *La Gioconda* was acquired by François I. Note the guard and the bullet-proof glass: it was stolen in the summer of 1911, found in Florence in the winter of 1913. Less well known (but to many even more enchanting) are Da Vinci's *Virgin and Child with St. Anne* and the *Virgin of the Rocks*.

One gallery displays 21 paintings by Rubens, done for Marie de Medici for her Luxembourg Palace in only two years. The Louvre stacks masterpiece upon masterpiece: Ingres's *The Turkish Bath*; David's portrait of Madame Récamier

? DID YOU KNOW . . . ?

- The Eiffel Tower outraged critics in its day, especially novelist Emile Zola, who denounced it as a "tower of Babel" and a "dishonor to Paris."
- Salvador Dalí did a portrait of Lenin dancing on piano keys, and you can see it displayed at the Pompidou Center.
- The most valuable painting in the world, Da Vinci's *Mona Lisa*, was estimated, for insurance purposes, at $100 million—too expensive for the French government to insure.
- In 1985 Bulgarian-born artist Christo wrapped the oldest bridge in Paris, the Pont-Neuf, in 440,000 square yards of polyamide fabric and 42,900 feet of rope.
- The Louvre sells five million postcards a year.
- Dame Nellie Melba, who appeared at the Paris Opéra, was the inspiration for Escoffier's acclaimed dessert peach Melba.
- George Washington was given the key to the Bastille (demolished by revolutionary mobs in 1789) as a gift from Lafayette.
- Underground Paris has 112 miles of tunnels through which the Métro runs.
- Paris has the greatest population density among highly industrialized cities in the world—nearly 54,000 people per square mile.
- Hitler ordered the burning of Paris, but the Nazi general in charge refused because he didn't want to go down in history "as the man who burned Paris."

lounging on her familiar sofa; the Botticelli frescoes from the Villa Lemmi; Raphael's *La Belle Jardinière;* Titian's *Open Air Concert;* a 1460 *Pietà* from Avignon; Dürer's self-portrait; Anthony Van Dyck's portrait of Charles I of England; Lucas Cranach's curious *Venus;* Fra Angelico's *Coronation of the Virgin;* Hans Memling's *Portrait of an Old Woman;* Jan Van Eyck's *Madonna with Chancellor Rolin;* Correggio's *The Mystic Marriage of St. Catherine;* Hans Holbein's (the Younger) *Portrait of Erasmus of Rotterdam;* Mantegna's *Calvary;* Ribera's *Clubfoot;* Rubens's portrait of Helena Fourment (his second wife) with her children; Vermeer's *Lacemaker;* Delacroix's bare-breasted *Liberty Leading the People;* the Titian portraits of Protestant-burning François I and his exquisite *Man with a Glove.* Usually no visit is complete without a look at some 'fluff': Boucher's *Diana Resting after Her Bath* and Fragonard's *Bathers.*

You ask, where did all these paintings come from? The kings of France, notably art patrons François I and Louis XIV, acquired many of them. Others have been willed to or purchased by the state. Many that Napoleon contributed were taken from reluctant donors (the church a heavy and unwilling giver). Much of Napoleon's plunder had to be returned, although France hasn't seen its way clear to giving back all the booty.

Of the Greek and Roman antiquities, the most notable collections, aside from the *Venus de Milo* and *Winged Victory,* are fragments of the frieze from the Parthenon. In Renaissance sculpture, two slaves by Michelangelo were originally intended for the tomb of Julius II but were sold into other bondage. Combine all that wealth of art with Sumerian and Babylonian treasures, Assyrian winged bulls and Persian friezes, bronze Egyptian queens and a world-renowned *Squatting Scribe,* Cellini's *Nymph of Fontainebleau,* and Marie Antoinette furniture—and you've got a busy three days . . . at least.

Admission: 33 F ($5.90) adults, free for children under 18.

Open: Thurs-Sun 9am-6pm, Mon and Wed 9am-9:45pm.

Tours: Mon and Wed-Sat at 10am, 11:30am, and 2-3:30pm for 30F ($5.40); purchase tickets at a window marked Acceuil des Groupes, beneath the Pyramid.

Metro: Palais-Royal–Musée-du-Louvre.

MUSÉE D'ORSAY, 1, rue de Bellechasse, 7e. Tel. 40-49-48-14.

In the middle of Paris, the defunct but handsome neo-classical rail station, the Gare d'Orsay, has been transformed into one of the greatest art museums in the world. Standing across the Seine from the Louvre and the Tuileries, it is a museum of the 19th century.

The Musée d'Orsay houses thousands of pieces of sculpture and painting spread across 80 different galleries. It also displays Belle Époque furniture, photographs, objets d'art, and architectural models, even a cinema. A detailed and wide-ranging

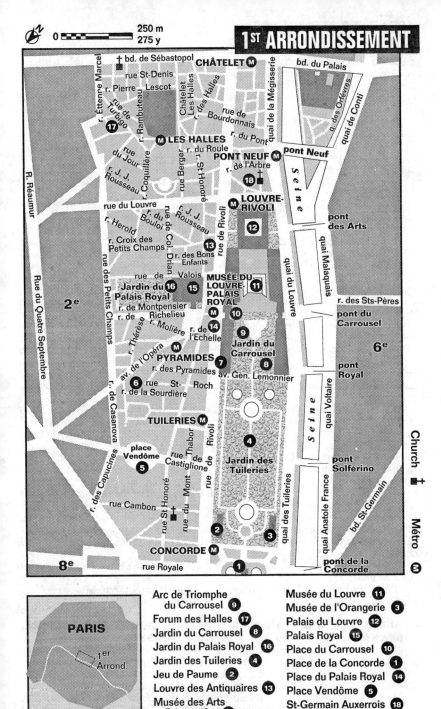

1ST ARRONDISSEMENT

0 — 250 m / 275 y

CHÂTELET
bd. de Sébastopol
rue St-Denis
r. Pierre Lescot
rue de Rambuteau
rue de Turbigo
r. Étienne Marcel
bd. du Palais
quai de la Mégisserie
av. des Orfèvres
quai de Conti

Châtelet Les Halles
rue des Halles
rue de Bourdonnais
r. du Pont

LES HALLES
r. du Roule
rue Berger
r. St-Honoré
rue du Jour
r. Coquillère
rue J. J. Rousseau

PONT NEUF
r. de l'Arbre
pont Neuf

rue du Louvre
r. J. J. Rousseau
rue de Rivoli

LOUVRE-RIVOLI

r. Herold
r. du Bouloi
r. de Col.-Driant
r. des Bons Enfants
r. Croix des Petits Champs
rue de Valois

pont des Arts
quai Malaquais

Jardin du Palais Royal
rue de Montpensier
r. de Richelieu
r. Thérèse
r. Molière
r. de l'Echelle
r. des Petits Champs

MUSÉE DU LOUVRE-PALAIS ROYAL

quai du Louvre
r. des Sts-Pères
pont du Carrousel

2e

PYRAMIDES
av. de l'Opéra
r. des Pyramides
rue St-Roch
r. de la Sourdière
r. de Casanova

Jardin du Carrousel
av. Gén. Lemonnier

6e

pont Royal

TUILERIES
rue de Rivoli
place Vendôme
rue de Castiglione
r. du Mont Thabor

Jardin des Tuileries
quai des Tuileries
quai Voltaire
quai Anatole France

pont Solférino
bd. St-Germain

rue Cambon
rue St-Honoré
r. du Mont Thabor

CONCORDE
rue Royale

pont de la Concorde

8e

Church
Métro

PARIS
1er Arrond.

Arc de Triomphe du Carrousel ⑨
Forum des Halles ⑰
Jardin du Carrousel ⑧
Jardin du Palais Royal ⑯
Jardin des Tuileries ④
Jeu de Paume ②
Louvre des Antiquaires ⑬
Musée des Arts Décoratifs ⑦

Musée du Louvre ⑪
Musée de l'Orangerie ③
Palais du Louvre ⑫
Palais Royal ⑮
Place du Carrousel ⑩
Place de la Concorde ①
Place du Palais Royal ⑭
Place Vendôme ⑤
St-Germain Auxerrois ⑱
St-Roch ⑥

panorama of international art is presented from the period between 1848 and 1914, from the birth of the Second French Republic to the dawn of World War I. In brief, it is a repository of art and civilization of the century just past. Conceived as a monument to the Industrial Revolution, the Orsay station, once called "the elephant," is covered by an arching glass roof, flooding the museum with light. The museum displays works ranging from the creations of academic and historic painters such as Ingres to romanticists such as Delacroix, to neo-Realists such as Courbet and Daumier. In a setting once used by Orson Welles to film a nightmarish atmosphere in *The Trial*, based on a Kafka work, are displayed the impressionists and post-impressionists, including Cézanne, Van Gogh, and the Fauves, along with Matisse, the cubists, expressionists, and the abstract painters. You get the sunny wheat fields by Millet, works from the Barbizon School, the misty landscapes of Corot, and brilliant-hued Gauguins.

But it is mainly the impressionists that keep the crowds lining up. Once the Louvre didn't want the works of these painters, although Americans appreciated them. If nothing else, the impressionists were independent, but unified in opposition to the dictatorial Académie des Beaux-Arts. For their subject matter they chose the world about them, and insisted on bathing their canvases in light, ignoring ecclesiastical or mythological scenes. They painted the Seine, Parisians strolling in the Tuileries, even railway stations such as the Gare St-Lazare (some critics considered Monet's choice of the latter unforgivable vulgarity). The impressionists were the first to paint the most characteristic feature of Parisian life: the sidewalk café, especially those in what was then the artists' quarter of Montmartre.

Perhaps the most famous painting displayed from this era is Manet's *The Picnic on the Grass*, which when it was first exhibited was decried as *au grande scandale des gens de bien*. Painted in 1863, it depicts a forest setting with a nude woman and two fully clothed men. Two years later his *Olympia* created another scandal, showing a woman lounging on her bed and wearing nothing but a flower in her hair and high-heeled shoes. Attending her is a black maid. Zola called Manet "a man among eunuchs."

One of Renoir's brightest, most joyous paintings is here—the *Moulin de la Galette*, painted in 1876. Of course there is always Degas with his racehorses and dancer series. His 1876 *Absinthe*—again, rejected when it was first shown—remains one of his most reproduced works. Paris-born Claude Monet was fascinated by the changing light effects on Rouen Cathedral, and in a series of five paintings he makes the old landmark live as never before.

One of the most celebrated works is by an American, James McNeill Whistler, represented by *Arrangement in Gray and Black: Portrait of the Painter's Mother*. It is said that this painting heralded the advent of modern art, although many critics denounced it at the time as "Whistler's Dead Mother" because of its funereal overtones. Today the painting has been hailed as a "veritable icon of our consciousness." As far as Whistler was concerned, he claimed he made "Mummy just as nice as possible."

Admission: 31 F ($5.60) adults, 16 F ($2.90) ages 18–24 and seniors, free for children under 18.

Open: Tues-Wed and Fri-Sun 10am-6pm, Thurs 10am-9:15pm. **Métro:** Solférino. **RER:** Musée-d'Orsay.

GEORGES POMPIDOU NATIONAL CENTER FOR ART AND CULTURE, place Georges-Pompidou, 4e. Tel. 42-77-12-33.

In 1969 Georges Pompidou, then president of France, decided to create a large cultural center to spotlight every form of 20th-century art. The center was finally opened in 1977 on the plateau Beaubourg, in the midst of a huge, car-free pedestrian district, east of boulevard de Sebastopol.

The structure, towering over a festive plaza, is the subject of much controversy. Parisians refer to the radical exoskeletal design as "the refinery." The Tinker Toy–like array of pipes and tubes surrounding the transparent shell are actually functional, serving as casings for the heating, air conditioning, electrical, and telephone systems for the center. The great worm-like tubes crawling at angles up the side of the building contain the escalators that transport visitors from one floor to the next. Inside, no interior walls block one's view. Each floor is one vast room, divided as necessary by movable partitions.

The unique structure has already proved a favorite attraction for Parisian and foreign visitors alike, drawing more viewers each year than Paris's former top sight, the Eiffel Tower. From the top of the center you can also enjoy one of the best views of the city. The center is made up of four separate attractions:

The **Musée National d'Art Moderne** (National Museum of Modern Art) offers a large collection of 20th-century art. The uniqueness of the Pompidou Center in cultural life today is shown vividly. The collections include French and American masterpieces. All the current trends of modern art are displayed on two floors (entrance on the fourth floor) in well-lit rooms of varying sizes. From the Fauves up to current abstract and expressionist works, the range is complete.

Featured are such artists as Max Ernst (a sculpture, *The Imbecile*), Kandinsky, Vuillard, Bonnard, Utrillo, Chagall, Dufy, Juan Gris, Léger, Pollock, as well as sketches by Le Corbusier and stained glass by Rouault. Modern sculpture includes works by Alexander Calder, Henry Moore, and Jacob Epstein. A gallery of contemporary artists (Galeries Contemporaines), on the ground floor, demonstrates the trends in artistic activity today. Special exhibitions and demonstrations are constantly being staged in the Grande Galerie to acquaint the public with the significant works of the 20th century. Guided tours are available.

The center also houses the **Public Information Library** where, for the first time in Paris's history, the public has free access to one million French and foreign books, periodicals, films, records, slides, and microfilms in nearly every area of knowledge.

The **Center for Industrial Design,** covering some 40,000 square feet of space, emphasizes the contributions made in the fields of architecture, visual communications, publishing, and community planning.

The **Institute for Research and Coordination of Acoustics/Music** brings together musicians and composers interested in furthering the cause of music, both contemporary and traditional. Concerts, workshops, and seminars are frequently open to the public.

In addition to its four main departments, the center also offers a children's workshop and library and a "cinémathèque," which tells the history of motion pictures.

Admission: One-day pass to all exhibits, 55 F ($9.90) adults, 50 F ($9) ages 18–24 and over 60; free for children under 18; free for everyone Sun 10am–2pm. Musée National d'Art Moderne, 27 F ($4.90) adults, 18 F ($3.20) ages 18–24 and over 60.

Open: Mon and Wed–Fri noon–10pm, Sat–Sun 10am–10pm. **Métro:** Rambuteau or Hôtel-de-Ville.

MUSEE PICASSO, Hôtel Salé 5, rue de Thorigny, 3e. Tel. 42-71-25-21.

When it opened at the beautifully restored Hôtel Salé (salt mansion), a state-owned property in Le Marais, the press hailed it as a "museum for Picasso's Picassos." And that's what it is. Almost overnight it became—and continues to be—one of the most popular attractions in Paris.

The greatest Picasso collection in the world, acquired by the state in payment of inheritance taxes totaling $50 million, consists of 203 paintings, 158 sculptures, 16 collages, 19 bas-reliefs, 88 ceramics, and more than 1,500 sketches and 1,600 engravings, along with 30 notebooks. These works are representative of the artist, spanning some 75 years of his life and changing styles.

The range of paintings includes a remarkable self-portrait in 1901 and goes on to embrace such masterpieces as *Le Baiser* ("the kiss") painted at Mougins in 1969. The museum also acquired another masterpiece he did a year later at the same place on the Riviera: it's called *Reclining Nude and the Man with a Guitar.* It's easy to stroll through the handsome museum seeking your own favorite work (mine is a delightfully wicked one, *Jeune Garcon à la Langouste,* "young man with a lobster," painted in Paris in 1941). The Paris museum owns several intriguing studies for *Les Demoiselles d'Avignon,* the painting that launched cubism. Many of the major masterpieces such as *The Crucifixion* and *Nude in a Red Armchair* should remain on permanent view. However, because the collection is so vast, temporary exhibitions, featuring such items as his studies of the Minotaur, will be held for the public at the rate of two a year. In addition to Picasso's own treasure trove of art, works by other masters from his private collection are displayed, including the contributions of such world-class artists as Cézanne, Rousseau, Braque, and André Derain, as well as Miró. Picasso was fascinated with African masks, and many of these are on view as well.

The collection opened here in 1979 (the artist died in 1973), but the mansion was constructed in 1656 by Aubert de Fontenay who collected the dreaded salt tax in Paris.

Admission: 28 F ($5) adults, 16 F ($2.90) ages 18–24 and over 60, free for children under 18.

Open: Wed 9:15am–10pm, Thurs–Mon 9:15am–5:15pm. **Métro:** St-Paul or Chemin-Vert.

MUSEE DE L'ORANGERIE DES TUILERIES, Jardin de Tuileries, 1er. Tel. 42-97-48-16.

This museum is a gem among art galleries. Often set aside for special exhibits, it has an outstanding collection of art and one celebrated display: Claude Monet's exquisite *Nymphéas,* executed between 1890 and 1921, a light-filtered tangle of lily pads and water, paneling the two oval, ground-floor rooms whose construction was supervised by the artist himself.

Creating his effects with hundreds and hundreds of minute strokes of his brush (one irate 19th-century critic called them "tongue lickings"), Monet achieved unity and harmony, as he did in his Rouen Cathedral series and his haystacks. Artists with lesser talent might have stirred up "soup." But Monet, of course, was a genius. See his lilies and evoke for yourself the mood and melancholy as he experienced it so many years ago. Monet continued to paint his water landscapes right up until his death in 1926, although he was greatly hampered by failing eyesight.

The renovated building also shelters the Walter-Guillaume collection, which includes more than 24 Renoirs, of which the most important is *Young Girl at a Piano.* Cézanne is represented by 14 works, notably *The Red Rock,* and Matisse by 11 paintings. Rousseau's nine works are highlighted by his *The Wedding,* and the dozen paintings by Picasso reach their brilliance in *The Female Bathers.* Other outstanding paintings are by Utrillo (10 works in all); Soutine (22), and Derain (28).

Admission: 26 F ($4.70) adults, free for children under 18.

Open: Wed–Mon 9:45am–5:15pm. **Métro:** Concorde.

ILE DE LA CITE

Medieval Paris, that architectural blending of grotesquerie and Gothic beauty, began on this island in the Seine. The venerated island ever since has been known as "the cradle" of the city. Actually, the river formed a protective moat around it. Sauval once observed: "The island of the City is shaped like a great ship, sunk in the mud, lengthwise in the stream, in about the middle of the Seine."

Few have written more movingly about 15th-century Paris than Victor Hugo, who invited the reader "to observe the fantastic display of lights against the darkness of that gloomy labyrinth of buildings; cast upon it a ray of moonlight, showing the city in glimmering vagueness, with its towers lifting their great heads from that foggy sea."

Medieval Paris was a city of legends and lovers, none more notable than Abélard, who was emasculated because of his love for Héloïse (afterward, he became a monk, she a nun), of blood-curdling tortures and brutalities. Explore as much of it as you can, but even if you're in a hurry, try to visit Notre-Dame, the Sainte Chapelle, and the Conciergerie.

NOTRE-DAME DE PARIS, 6, place du parvis de Notre-Dame, 4e. Tel. 43-26-07-39.

Notre-Dame is regarded as the venerable heart of Paris, even of France itself. For example, distances from Paris to all parts of France are calculated from its precincts.

PARIS

2e Arrondissement

Basilique Notre Dame
  des Victoires ❸
Bibliothèque Nationale ❻
Bourse des Valeurs ❷
Hôtel Colbert ❺
Musée Cognacq-Jay ❽
Notre Dame de
  Bonne Nouvelle ❶
Place de l'Opéra ❼
Place des Victoires ❹

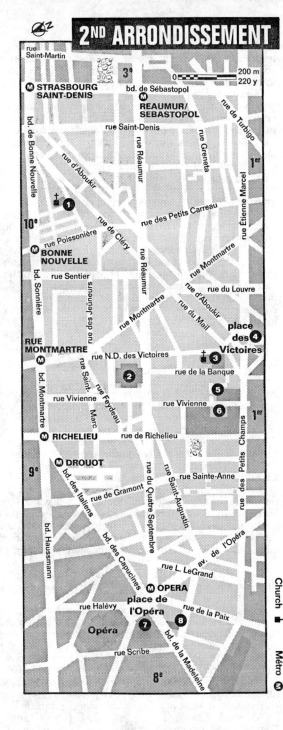

2ND ARRONDISSEMENT

Although many may disagree, Notre-Dame is, in my opinion, more interesting from the outside than in. Hence, you'll want to walk around the entire structure to appreciate this "vast symphony of stone" more fully. Better yet, cross over the bridge to the Left Bank and view it from the quay.

The history of Paris and that of Notre-Dame are inseparable. Many came here to pray before going off to lose their lives in the Crusades. Napoleon was crowned emperor here, taking the crown from Pius VII and placing it on his own head. Before that event, "Our Lady of Paris" had been sacked by revolutionaries, who destroyed the Galerie des Rois. But wars of religion, carelessness, vandalism, and "embellishments" had destroyed much that previously existed.

The cathedral was once scheduled for demolition, but, partly because of the Victor Hugo classic and the revival of interest in the Gothic, a movement mushroomed to restore the cathedral to its original glory. The task was completed under Viollet-le-Duc, an architectural genius.

The setting has always been memorable: on the banks of the Seine on the Île de la Cité. Founded in the 12th century by Maurice de Sully, bishop of Paris, Notre-Dame grew and grew. Over the years the cathedral has changed as Paris has—often falling victim to fads in decorative taste. Its flying buttresses were rebuilt in 1330.

Once the houses of old Paris crowded in on the structure, but Haussmann ordered them torn down to show off the edifice to its best advantage from the square known as Parvis. From that vantage point, you can view the trio of 13th-century sculptured portals. On the left, the portal of the Virgin depicts the signs of the Zodiac and the coronation of the Virgin. The association of the Virgin and the Cosmos is to be found in dozens of earlier and later medieval churches.

The restored central portal of the Last Judgment is divided into three levels: the first shows Vices and Virtues; the second, Christ and his Apostles; and above that, Christ in triumph after the Resurrection. The portal is a close illustration of the Gospel according to Matthew.

Finally, the portal of St. Anne is on the right, depicting such scenes as the Virgin enthroned with Child. It is the best preserved and probably the most perfect piece of sculpture in Notre-Dame. Over the central portal is a remarkable rose window, 31 feet in diameter, forming a showcase for a statue of the Virgin and Child.

Equally interesting (although often missed by the scurrying visitor) is the portal of the cloisters (around on the left), with its dour-faced 13th-century Virgin, a unique survivor of the many that originally adorned the façade. Unfortunately, the Child figure she is holding is decapitated. Finally, the portal of St. Stephen on the Seine side traces the martyrdom of that saint.

If possible, see the interior of Notre-Dame at sunset. Of the three giant medallions that warm the austere cathedral, the north rose window in the transept, dating from the mid-13th century, is best. The interior is in the typically Gothic style, with slender, graceful columns. The stone-carved choir screen from the early 14th century depicts such biblical scenes as the Last Supper. Near the altar stands the 14th-century Virgin and Child, highly venerated among the more faithful of Paris.

In the treasury, there is a display of vestments and gold objects, including crowns, behind glass. Exhibited are a cross presented to Haile Selassie, the former Emperor of Ethiopia, and a reliquary given by Napoleon. Notre-Dame is especially proud of its relic of the True Cross and the Crown of Thorns.

Finally, to visit those grimy gargoyles immortalized by Hugo you have to scale steps leading to the twin square towers, flat on top rising to a height of 225 feet. Once there, you can closely inspect those devils (some sticking out their tongues), hobgoblins, and birds of prey. You expect to see the imaginary character of Quasimodo in one of his celluloid hunchback interpretations (Charles Laughton, Anthony Quinn, or Lon Chaney, depending on which version you saw).

From October to May, history or theology lectures are given on Sunday at 4:45pm, followed by a free organ recital at 5:30pm and a mass at 6:30pm. During these hours, visitors are not encouraged to circulate in the cathedral.

Approached through a garden behind Notre-Dame is the **Memorial to the Deportation,** jutting out on the very tip of the Île de la Cité. Birds chirp nowadays, the Seine flows gently by—but the memories are far from pleasant. It is a memorial to

French martyrs of World War II, who were deported to camps like Auschwitz and Buchenwald. In blood-red are the words: "Forgive, but don't forget." It may be visited from 10am to noon and 2 to 7pm. Admission is free.

Admission: Cathedral, free; treasury, 15 F ($2.70) adults, 5 F (90¢) children under 18; gargoyles, 22 F ($3.90) in summer, 9 F ($1.60) in winter.

Open: Cathedral, daily 8am–7pm, except during Sun mass 10am–noon. Treasury, Mon–Sat 10am–6pm, Sun 2–6pm. Gargoyles, summer, daily 10am–4:30pm; off-season, daily 10am–3:30pm. **Métro:** Cité, Hôtel-de-Ville, or Maubert-Mutualité.

SAINTE CHAPELLE, 4, bd. du Palais, 1er. Tel. 43-54-30-09.

⭐ It is customary to call this tiny chapel a jewel box. That hardly suffices—nor does such a contemporary expression as a "light show." Go when the sun is shining, and you'll need no one else's words to describe the remarkable effects of natural light in Sainte Chapelle.

The church is approached through the Cour de la Sainte Chapelle of the Palais of Justice. If it weren't for the chapel's 247-foot spire, the law courts here would almost swallow it up.

Built in only five to seven years, beginning in 1246, the chapel has two levels. It was constructed to house relics of the True Cross, including the Crown of Thorns acquired by St. Louis (the Crusader king, Louis IX) from the Emperor of Constantinople. In those days, cathedrals throughout Europe were busy acquiring relics for their treasuries, regardless of authenticity. It was a seller's—perhaps a sucker's—market. Louis IX is said to have paid heavily for his precious relics, raising the money through unscrupulous means. He died of the plague on a Crusade and was canonized in 1297.

You enter through the lower chapel, supported by flying buttresses and ornamented with fleur-de-lis designs. The lower chapel was used by the servants of the palace, the upper chamber by the king and his courtiers. The latter is reached by ascending narrow spiral stairs.

Viewed on a bright day, the 15 stained-glass windows seem to glow with ruby red and Chartres blue. They vividly depict scenes from the Bible. The walls consist almost entirely of the glass, which had to be removed for safekeeping during the Revolution and again during both World Wars. In them are embodied the hopes, dreams, even the pretensions of the kings who ordered their construction.

Admission: 25 F ($4.50) adults, 6 F ($1) children under 18.

Open: Apr–Sept, daily 9:30am–6pm; off-season, daily 10am–4:30pm. **Métro:** Cité or St-Michel. **RER:** St-Michel.

LA CONCIERGERIE, 1, quai de l'Horloge, 4e. Tel. 43-54-30-06.

⭐ London has its Tower of London, Paris its Conciergerie. Although it had a long and regal history before the Revolution, it is visited today chiefly by those wishing to bask in the horrors of the Reign of Terror. The Conciergerie lives on as a symbol of infamy, recalling the days when carts pulled up daily to haul off the fresh supply of victims to the guillotine.

On the Seine, the Conciergerie is approached through its landmark twin towers, the Tour d'Argent and the Tour de César. The 14th-century vaulted Guard Room, which remains from the days when the Capets made the Palace of the Cité a royal residence, is the actual entrance to the chilling building. Also dating from the 14th century, and even more interesting, is the vast, dark, and foreboding Gothic Salle des Gens d'Armes (People at Arms), totally changed from the days when the king used it as a banqueting hall.

Architecture, however, plays a secondary role to the list of famous prisoners who spent their last miserable days on earth at the Conciergerie. Few in its history endured the tortures of Ravaillac, who assassinated Henry IV in 1610. He got the full treatment—pincers in the flesh, hot lead and boiling oil poured on him like bath water.

During the Revolution the Conciergerie became more than a symbol of terror to the nobility or the "enemies of the State." Meeting just a short walk from the prison, the Revolutionary Tribunal dispensed "justice" in a hurry. And the guillotine fell faster. If it's any consolation, these "freedom-loving" jurors did not believe in torturing their victims—only decapitating them.

In failing health and shocked beyond grief, Marie Antoinette was brought here to await her trial. Only a small screen (and sometimes not even that) protected her modesty from the glare of the guards stationed in her cell. The Affair of the Carnation failed in its attempt to abduct her and secure her freedom. In retrospect, one can perhaps feel sympathy for the broken and widowed queen. By accounts of that day, she was shy and stupid, although the evidence is that upon her death she attained the nobility of a true queen. Further, historians deny that she uttered the famous quotation attributed to her, "Let them eat cake," when told the peasants had no bread. It was shortly before noon on the morning of October 16, 1793, when her executioners came for her, grabbing her and cutting her hair, as was the custom for victims marked for the guillotine.

Today you can see lithographs and paintings depicting scenes from the Revolution, including a model of the dreaded guillotine. Also displayed is a facsimile of the final touching letter, or "testament," written by Marie Antoinette to Madame Elizabeth, sister of Louis XVI.

Later the Conciergerie housed yet more noted prisoners, including Madame Elizabeth; Madame du Barry, mistress of Louis XV; Mlle Roland ("O Liberty! Liberty! What crimes are committed in thy name!"); and Charlotte Corday, who killed Marat with a kitchen knife while he was taking a sulfur bath. In time the Revolution turned on its own leaders, such as Danton and Robespierre. Finally, even one of the most hated men in Paris, the public prosecutor Fouquier-Tinville, faced the same guillotine to which he'd sent so many others.

Admission: 31 F ($5.60) adults, 16 F ($2.90) ages 18–24 and over 60, free for children 17 and under.

Open: Apr–Sept, daily 9:30am–6:30pm; Oct–Mar, daily 10am–5pm. **Métro:** St-Michel, Cité, or Châtelet. **RER:** St-Michel.

PONT NEUF

After leaving the Conciergerie, turn left and stroll along the Seine past medievalesque towers till you reach the Pont Neuf or "New Bridge." The span isn't new, of course; actually, it's the oldest bridge in Paris, erected in 1604. In its day the bridge had two unique features: it was not flanked with houses and shops, and it was paved.

At the Hôtel Carnavalet, a museum in the Marais section (see below), is a painting, *Spectacle of Buffons,* showing what the bridge was like between 1665 and 1669. Duels were fought on the structure; great coaches belonging to the nobility crossed it; peddlers sold their wares; and as there were no public facilities, men defecated right on the bridge, as depicted in the painting. With all those crowds, it attracted entertainers, such as Tabarin, who sought a few coins from the gawkers. The Pont Neuf is decorated with corbels, a mélange of grotesquerie.

SQUARE DU VERT GALANT

Finally, continue on to the "prow" of the island, the Square du Vert Galant, pausing first to look at the equestrian statue of the beloved Henri IV, killed by an assassin. A true king of the people, Henry was (to judge from accounts) also regal in the boudoir. Hence the nickname "Vert Galant," or gay old spark. Gabrielle d'Estrées and Henriette d'Entragues were his best-known mistresses, but they had to share him with countless others—some of whom would casually catch his eye as he was riding along the streets of Paris.

In fond memory of the king, the little triangular park continues to attract lovers. If at first it appears to be a sunken garden, that's because it remains at its natural level; the rest of the Cité has been built up during the centuries.

THE GRAND PROMENADE

In 1891 that "Innocent Abroad" Mark Twain called the Champs-Élysées "the liveliest street in the world," designed for the favorite pastime of Parisians, promenading. It is rather too innocent to rank walking as a Parisian's number-one pastime, but surely it comes in second. Nowadays, tourists invariably take up that highly respectable custom of the 19th century. Visitors from Minnesota who normally would get into their automobiles to drive half a block to the drugstore are seen doing the sprint from Place Charles-de-Gaulle (Étoile) to Place de la Concorde. That walk is surely a grand promenade, and you won't know Paris till you've traversed it.

ARC DE TRIOMPHE, place Charles-de-Gaulle, 8e. Tel. 43-80-31-31.

At the western end of the Champs-Élysées, the Arc de Triomphe suggests one of those ancient Roman arches—only it's larger. Actually, it's the biggest triumphal arch in the world, about 163 feet high and 147 feet wide. To reach it, don't try to cross the square, the busiest traffic hub in Paris (death is certain!). Take the underground passage and live longer. With one dozen streets radiating from the "Star," the roundabout was called by one writer "vehicular roulette with more balls than numbers."

After the death of Charles de Gaulle, the French government—despite protests from anti-Gaullists—voted to change the name of the heretofore Place de l'Etoile to the Place Charles-de-Gaulle.

The arch has witnessed some of France's proudest moments—and some of its more shameful and humiliating defeats, notably those of 1871 and 1940. The memory of German troops marching under the arch that had come to symbolize France's glory and prestige is still painful to the French. And who could ever forget the 1940 newsreel of the Frenchman standing on the Champs-Élysées openly weeping as the haughty Nazi stormtroopers goose-stepped through Paris?

Commissioned by Napoleon in 1806 to commemorate his victories, the arch wasn't ready for the entrance of his new empress, Marie-Louise, in 1810. It served anyway; in fact, it wasn't completed until 1836, under the reign of Louis-Philippe. Four years later the remains of Napoleon—brought from his grave at St. Helena—passed under the arch on the journey to his tomb at the Invalides. Since that time it has become the focal point for state funerals. It is also the site of the permanent tomb of the unknown soldier.

The greatest state funeral was that of Victor Hugo in 1885; his coffin was placed under the center of the arch, and much of Paris turned out to pay tribute to the author. Another notable funeral was the one in 1929 of Ferdinand Foch, the supreme commander of the Allied forces in World War I. Perhaps the happiest moment occurred in 1944, when the Liberation of Paris parade passed through. That same year, Eisenhower paid a visit to the tomb of France's unknown soldier, a new tradition among leaders of state and important figures. An eternal flame is kept burning.

Of the sculpture on the monument, the best known is Rude's *Marseillaise,* also called *The Departure of the Volunteers. The Triumph of Napoleon in 1810,* by J. P. Cortot, and the *Resistance of 1814* and the *Peace of 1815,* both by Etex, also adorn the façade. The monument is engraved with the names of hundreds of generals (those underlined died in battle) who commanded French troops in Napoleonic victories.

You can take an elevator or climb the stairway to the top. Up there is an exhibition hall, with lithographs and photos depicting the arch throughout its history. From the observation deck, you have the finest view of the Champs-Élysées as well as such landmarks as the Louvre, the Eiffel Tower, and Sacré-Coeur.

Admission: 30 F ($5.40) adults, 16 F ($2.90) ages 18–24 and over 60, 5 F (90¢) children 7–17, free for children under 7.

Open: Apr-Sept, daily 10am–6pm; off-season, daily 10am–5pm. **Métro:** Charles-de-Gaulle (Etoile).

CHAMPS-ELYSEES

The greatest boulevard in Paris, perhaps in the world, has a two-faced character. Part is a drive through a chestnut-lined park, the other a commercial avenue of sidewalk cafés, automobile showrooms, airline offices, cinemas, lingerie stores, even hamburger joints. The dividing point between the park and the commercial sections is Rond-Point des Champs-Elysées. Close to that is a philatelist's delight, the best-known open-air stamp market in Europe, held Sunday and Thursday. To chronicle the people who have walked this broad avenue would be to tell the history of Paris through the last few centuries. Ever since the days of Thomas Jefferson and Benjamin Franklin, Americans have gravitated here. The Champs-Élysées has, of course, lost the fin-de-siècle elegance described by Proust in *The*

Remembrance of Things Past. For one thing, not all the kids playing in the park today are rich. Puppet shows, carousels, and other amusements entertain the present brood.

A slight detour from the Champs-Élysées takes you to—

PALAIS DE L'ELYSEE, rue du Faubourg St-Honoré, 8e.

The French "White House" is called the Palais de l'Élysée, and it occupies a block along fashionable Faubourg St-Honoré. It is now occupied by the president of France and cannot be visited by the public without an invitation.

Built in 1718 for the Count d'Evreux, the palace had many owners before it was purchased by the Republic in 1873. Once it was owned by Madame de Pompadour. When she "had the supreme delicacy to die discreetly at the age of 43," she bequeathed it to the king. The world première of the Voltaire play *The Chinese Orphan* was presented there. After her divorce from Napoleon, Josephine also lived there. Napoleon III also lived at l'Élysée when he was president, beginning in 1848. When he became emperor in 1852, he moved to the Tuileries. Such celebrated English visitors as Queen Victoria and Wellington have spent their nights there as well.

Included among the palace's works of art are tapestries madame at Beauvais in the 18th century, Raphael and Leonardo da Vinci paintings, and Louis XVI furnishings. A grand dining hall was built for Napoleon III, as well as an orangerie for the Duchess du Berry (now converted into a winter garden).

Métro: Miromesnil.

PLACE DE LA CONCORDE, 1er.

In the east, the Champs-Élysées begins at Place de la Concorde, an octagonal traffic hub ordered built in 1757 to honor Louis XV. The statue of the king was torn down in 1792 and the name of the square changed to Place de la Révolution. Floodlit at night, it is dominated nowadays by an Egyptian obelisk from Luxor, considered the oldest man-made object in Paris. It was carved circa 1200 B.C. and presented to France in 1829 by the Viceroy of Egypt.

In the Reign of Terror, the dreaded guillotine was erected on this spot, and claimed the lives of thousands—everybody from Louis XVI, who died bravely, to Madame du Barry, who went screaming and kicking all the way. Before the leering crowds, Marie Antoinette, Robespierre, Danton, Mlle Roland, and Charlotte Corday rolled away. (You can still lose your life on the Place de la Concorde; all you have to do is chance the traffic and cross over.)

For a spectacular sight, look down the Champs-Élysées—the view is framed by the Marly horses. On the opposite side, the gateway to the Tuileries is flanked by the winged horses of Coysevox. On each side of the obelisk are two fountains with bronze-tailed mermaids and bare-breasted sea nymphs. Gray-beige statues ring the square, honoring the cities of France. To symbolize the city's fall to Germany in 1871, the statue of Strasbourg was covered with a black drape that wasn't lifted until the end of World War I. Two of the palaces on the Place de la Concorde are today the Ministry of the Marine and the deluxe Crillon Hotel. They were designed in the 1760s by Ange-Jacques Gabriel.

Métro: Concorde.

JARDIN DES TUILERIES, place de la Concorde, 1er. Tel. 42-60-38-01.

Bordering the Place de la Concorde, the Tuileries are as much a part of the Paris scene as the Seine. These statue-studded gardens were designed by Le Nôtre, the gardener to Louis XIV, who planned the grounds of Versailles.

About 100 years before that, a palace was ordered built by Catherine de Medici. Connected to the Louvre, it was occupied by Louis XVI after he left Versailles. Napoléon I called it home. Twice attacked by the people of Paris, it was finally burnt to the ground in 1871 and never rebuilt. The gardens, however, remain. Like the orderly French mind, the trees are arranged according to designs. Even the paths are straight, as opposed to winding English gardens. To break the sense of order and formality are bubbling fountains.

The neoclassic statuary is often insipid and is occasionally desecrated by rebellious "art critics." Seemingly half of Paris is found in the Tuileries on a warm spring day, listening to the chirping birds and watching the daffodils and red tulips bloom.

Fountains bubble, and mothers roll their carriages over the grounds where 18th-century revolutionaries killed the king's Swiss guards.

At the end of your walking tour of the Tuileries—two miles from Place Charles-de-Gaulle (Etoile)—you'll be at the **Arc de Triomphe du Carrousel,** at the Cour du Carrousel. Pierced with three walkways and supported by marble columns, the monument honors the Grande Armée, celebrating Napoleon's victory at Austerlitz on December 5, 1805. The arch is surmounted by statuary, a chariot, and four bronze horses. "Paris needs more monuments," Napoleon once shouted. He got his wish.

Métro: Tuileries.

AROUND THE EIFFEL TOWER

Everyone visits the landmark that has become the symbol of Paris. For maximum enjoyment, however, don't just rush to it right at once. Approach it gradually. Take the Métro to Place du Trocadéro, dominated by a statue of Marshal Foch. Once you've surfaced from the underground, you'll be at the gateway to the—

PALAIS DE CHAILLOT

Replacing the 1878 Palais du Trocadéro, the new palace was built in 1937 for the International Exhibition. If you have time, try to visit at least two of the three important museums lodged in the building: one a maritime showcase, another a gallery of reproductions of many of the monuments of France, a third devoted to people. From the palace terrace (one writer called it "Mussolinian"), you have a panoramic view across the Seine to the Eiffel Tower. The **Jardins du Palais de Chaillot** in back sweep down to the Seine. They are noted for their fountain displays. From April to October the gardens are a babel of international tongues.

TOUR EIFFEL, Champ-de-Mars, 7e. Tel. 45-50-34-56.

⭐ Cross the Pont d'Iéna and you'll reach your goal, the incomparable Eiffel Tower at Champ-de-Mars, 7e (tel. 45-50-34-56). Except for perhaps the Leaning Tower of Pisa, it is the single most recognizable structure in the world. Weighing 7,000 tons but exerting about the same pressure on the ground as an average-size person sitting in a chair, the tower was never meant to be permanent. It was built for the Exhibition of 1889 by Gustáve Alexandre Eiffel, the French engineer whose fame rested mainly on his iron bridges. (Incidentally, one of the lesser-known aspects of his career is that he designed the framework for the Statue of Liberty.)

The tower, including its 55-foot television antenna, is 1,056 feet high. On a clear day you can see it from some 40 miles away. An open-framework construction, the tower ushered in the almost unlimited possibilities of steel construction, paving the way for the skyscrapers of the 20th century. Skeptics said it couldn't be built, and Eiffel actually wanted to make it soar higher than it did. For years it remained the tallest man-made structure on earth, until such skyscrapers as the Empire State Building usurped that record.

Artists and writers vehemently denounced it, although later generations sang its praise. People were fond of calling it names: "a giraffe," "the world's greatest lamppost," "the iron monster." Others suggested, "Let's keep art nouveau grounded." Nature lovers feared it would interfere with the flights of birds over Paris. The advent of wireless communication in the early 1890s preserved the tower from destruction.

You can visit the tower in three stages. Taking the elevator to the first landing, you have a view over the rooftops of Paris. A cinema museum can be visited, and restaurants and a bar are open year round. The second landing provides a panoramic look at the city. The third and final stage, gives the most spectacular view, allowing you to identify monuments and buildings that are visible. On the ground level, in the eastern and western pillars, you can visit the 1899 lift machinery when the tower is open.

Admission: First landing, 18 F ($3.20); second landing, 35 F ($6.30); third landing; 52 F ($9.30).

Open: Daily 9:30am–11pm. **Métro:** Trocadéro, Ecole-Militaire, or Bir-Hakeim.

CHAMP-DE-MARS AND ECOLE MILITAIRE, 7e.

With time remaining, explore the Champ-de-Mars, the gardens between the Eiffel Tower and the Military School. Traditionally, these gardens, laid out around 1770, were the World's Fair grounds of Paris, the scene of many a military parade.

Thanks in part to one of France's best-known mistresses, Madame de Pompadour, the École Militaire (Military School) was established; the plans were drawn up by A.-J. Gabriel. This classical school was founded in 1751 for about 500 young men who wanted a military career.

Napoleon entered in 1784, the year his father died of cancer. He graduated a year later as a lieutenant, aged 16. According to accounts, he wasn't popular with his classmates, many of whom openly made fun of him. One wrote, "All boots, no man." Pity those creatures when their names came up for promotions years later. Another French general, Charles de Gaulle, also studied at the school. Special permission is needed to go inside.

HOTEL DES INVALIDES [Napoléon's Tomb], place des Invalides, 7e. Tel. 45-55-37-70.

The glory of the French military lives on here, in the **Musée de l'Armée.** It was the Sun King who decided to build the "hotel" to house soldiers who'd been disabled. It wasn't entirely a benevolent gesture, since these veterans had been injured, crippled, or blinded while fighting his battles. Louvois was ordered in 1670 to launch this massive building program. When it was completed—and Louis was long dead—the corridors stretched for miles. Eventually the building was crowned by a gilded dome designed by Jules Hardouin-Mansart.

The Invalides is best approached by walking from the Right Bank across the turn-of-the-century Alexander III Bridge. Of this span, critic Ian Nairn wrote, "The whole thing is carried to the limit of mock pomposity, like Offenbach satirizing a romantic situation yet at the same time providing a beautifully tender melody for lovers." In the building's cobblestone forecourt is a display of massive cannons—a formidable welcome.

Before rushing on to Napoleon's tomb, you may want to take the time to visit the greatest army museum in the world. In 1794 a French inspector started collecting all these weapons, uniforms, and equipment.

With the continued accumulation of war material over the centuries, the museum has become a horrifying documentary of man's self-destruction. Viking swords, Burgundian bacinets, blunderbusses from the 14th century, Balkan khandjars, American Browning machine guns, war pitchforks, salamander-engraved Renaissance serpentines, "Haute Époque" armor, a 1528 Griffon, musketoons, grenadiers . . . if it could kill, it's enshrined in a place of honor here. As a sardonic touch, there's even the wooden leg of General Daumesnil. The museum was looted by the Germans in 1940.

Among the outstanding acquisitions are the suits of armor—especially in the new so-called Arsenal—worn by the kings and dignitaries of France, including Louis XIV. The best-known one—the "armor suit of the lion"—was made for François I. Henri II ordered his suit engraved with the monogram of his mistress, Diane de Poitiers, and (perhaps reluctantly) that of his wife, Catherine de Medici. The showcases of swords are reputedly among the finest in the world.

The mementos of World War I, including those of American and Canadian soldiers, are especially interesting. Included is the Armistice Bugle, which sounded the cease-fire on November 7, 1918, before the general cease-fire on November 11, 1918.

Much attention is focused on that Corsican general who became France's greatest soldier. A plaster death mask by Antommarchi is one of the most notable pieces on display. So, too, an oil by Delaroche, painted at the time of Napoleon's first banishment (April 1814), which depicted him as he probably looked, paunch and all. In the rooms relating to the First Empire are displayed the field bed of Napoleon with his tent. In the room devoted to the Restoration, the 100 Days, and Waterloo, you can see the reconstituted bedroom of Napoleon at the time of his death at St. Helena. On the more personal side, you can view Vizir, a horse he owned (stuffed), as well as a

IMPRESSIONS

The kid will come from Nebraska or Heidelberg, from Poland or Senegal, and Paris will be born again—new, brand new and unexpected, and the Arch of Triumph will rise again, and the Seine will flow for the first time, and there will be new areas, unknown and unexplored, called Montmartre and Montparnasse . . . and it will all be for the first time, a completely new city, built suddenly for you and you alone.
—Romain Gary

saddle used mainly for state ceremonies. The Turenne Salon contains other souvenirs of Napoleon, including the hat he wore at Eylau, his sword from his victory at Austerlitz, and his "Flag of Farewell" which he kissed before departing for Elba.

The Salle Orientale in the west wing shows arms for the Eastern world, including Asia and the Muslim countries of the Mideast, from the 16th to the 19th centuries. Turkish armor (see Bajazet's helmet) and weapons and Chinese and Japanese armor and swords are on display.

A walk across the Court of Honor delivers you to the **Church of the Dome,** designed by Hardouin-Mansart for Louis XIV. The great architect began work on the church in 1677, although he died before its completion. The dome is the second-tallest monument in Paris. In the Napoleon Chapel is the hearse used at the emperor's funeral on May 9, 1821.

To accommodate the **Tomb of Napoleon,** the architect Visconti had to redesign the high altar in 1842. First buried at St. Helena, Napoleon's remains were returned to Paris in 1840. Louis-Phillippe had demanded that of England. The triumphal funeral procession passed under the Arc de Triomphe, down the Champs-Élysées, en route to the Invalides. Snow swirled through the air.

The tomb is made of red Finnish porphyry, the base from green granite. Napoleon's remains were locked away inside six coffins. Surrounding the tomb are a dozen amazon-like figures representing his victories. Almost lampooning the small-ness of the man, everything is made large, big, awesome. You'd think a real giant was buried here, not a symbolic one. In his coronation robes, the statue of Napoleon stands 8½ feet high. The grave of Napoleon's son, "the King of Rome," lies at his feet.

Napoleon's tomb is surrounded by those of his brother, Joseph Bonaparte; the great Vauban; Foch, the Allied commander in World War I; Turenne; and La Tour d'Auvergne, the first grenadier of the Republic (actually, only his heart is entombed here).

Admission: 30 F ($5.40) adults, 20 F ($3.60) children 7–18 and those over 60, free for children under 7.

Open: Apr–Sept, daily 10am–6pm; Oct–Mar, daily 10am–5pm. **Closed:** Jan 1, May 1, Nov 1, and Dec 25. **Métro:** Latour-Maubourg, Varenne, or St-François-Xavier.

2. OTHER MAJOR ATTRACTIONS

MONTMARTRE

Soft-white three-story houses, slender, barren trees sticking up from the ground like giant toothpicks—that's how Utrillo, befogged by absinthe, saw Montmartre. On the other side of the canvas, Toulouse-Lautrec brush-stroked it as a district of cabarets, circus performers, and prostitutes. Today Montmartre remains truer to the dwarfish artist's conception than it does to that of Utrillo.

From the 1880s to the years preceding World War I Montmartre enjoyed its golden age as the world's best-known art colony. *La vie de bohème* reigned supreme. At one time the artistic battle in La Butte was the talk of the art world. There was, for one, the bold Matisse, and his band of followers known as "The Savage Beasts." Following World War I the pseudo-artists flocked to Montmartre in droves, with camera-snapping tourists hot on their heels. The real artists had long gone, perhaps to Montparnasse.

Before its discovery and subsequent chic, Montmartre was a sleepy farming community, with windmills dotting the landscape. The name has always been the subject of disagreement, some maintaining that it originated from the "mount of Mars," a Roman temple that crowned the hill, others asserting it means "mount of martyrs." The latter is a reference to the martyrdom of St. Denis, patron saint of Paris, who was beheaded on the mountain along with his fellow-saints Rusticus and Eleutherius.

See my walking tour in Chapter 8 for suggestions on how to see the sights of Montmartre.

BASILICA OF SACRE-COEUR, place St-Pierre, 18e. Tel. 42-51-17-02.

⭐ The crowning achievement of the butte is the Basilica of Sacré-Coeur. After the Eiffel Tower, it is the most characteristic landmark of the Parisian scene. Like the tower, it has always been—and still is—the subject of much controversy. One Parisian called it "a lunatic's confectionery dream." An offended Zola declared it to be "the basilica of the ridiculous." Sacré-Coeur has had warm supporters as well, including Max Jacob, the Jewish poet, and the artist Maurice Utrillo. Utrillo never tired of drawing and painting it, and he and Jacob came here regularly to pray.

In gleaming white, it towers over Paris—its five bulbous domes suggesting some Byzantine church of the 12th century, and its campanile inspired by Roman-Byzantine art. But it's not that old. After France's defeat by the Prussians in 1870, the basilica was planned as a votive offering to cure France's misfortunes. Rich and poor alike contributed money to build it. The National Assembly approved its construction in 1873. The church was not consecrated until 1919, but perpetual prayer of adoration has been made day and night since 1885.

On a clear day the vista from the dome can extend for 35 miles. You can also walk around the inner dome of the church, peering down like a pigeon (one is likely to be keeping you company).

Even if you have only 24 hours in Paris and can't explore most of the sights recommended in this chapter, try to make it to Sacré-Coeur at dusk. There, as you sit on the top steps, the church at your back, the Square Willette in front of you, nighttime Paris begins to come alive. First, a twinkle like a firefly; then all of the lights go on. One young American got carried away with it all: "Here, away from the whirling taxis, concierges, crazy elevators, and tipping problems, the sound of Paris permeates by osmosis."

Admission: Basilica, free; dome, 16 F ($2.90); crypt, 16 F ($2.90).

Open: Basilica, daily 7am–11pm. Dome and crypt, Apr–Sept, daily 9am–7pm; Oct–Mar, daily 9am–6pm. **Métro:** Abbesses or Anvers.

LE MARAIS

When Paris began to overflow the confines of Île de la Cité in the 13th century, the citizenry settled in Le Marais, the marsh that used to be flooded regularly by the high-rising Seine. By the 17th century the Marais had reached the pinnacle of fashion, becoming the center of aristocratic Paris. At that time, many of its great mansions—many restored or being restored—were built by the finest craftsmen in France.

See also my walking tour "Le Marais" in Chapter 8 "Strolling Around Paris."

In the 18th and 19th centuries, fashion deserted the Marais for the expanding Faubourg St-Germain and Faubourg St-Honoré. Industry eventually took over the quarter, and the once-elegant hotels were turned into tenements. There was talk of demolishing this seriously blighted sector, but in 1962 the alarmed Comité de Sauvegarde du Marais banded together and saved the historic district.

Today the 17th-century mansions are fashionable once again. The *Herald-Tribune* called it the latest refuge of the Paris artisan fleeing from the tourist-trampled St-Germain-des-Prés. The "marsh" sprawls across the 3rd and 4th Arrondissements, bounded by the Grands Boulevards, the rue du Temple, the Place des Vosges, and the Seine.

A good place to start your exploration of Le Marais is at—

PLACE DE LA BASTILLE

Here, on July 14, 1789, a mob of people attacked the Bastille and so began the French Revolution. Here? In all this traffic? Precisely, for nothing remains of the historic Bastille, built in 1369. It was completely torn down. A symbol of despotism, it once contained eight towers, rising 100 feet high. Many prisoners—some sentenced by Louis XIV for "witchcraft"—were kept within its walls, the best known being "The Man in the Iron Mask." And yet, when the fortress was stormed by the revolutionary mob, only seven prisoners were discovered. The Marquis de Sade had been transferred to the madhouse ten days earlier. The authorities had discussed razing it anyway. So in itself the attack meant nothing. What it symbolized, however, and what it started will never be forgotten. Bastille Day is celebrated with great festivity each July 14.

PLACE DES VOSGES, 4e.

It is the oldest square in Paris and was once the most fashionable. Right in the heart of Marais, it was called the Palais Royal in the days of Henri IV. The king planned to live here, but his assassin, Ravaillac, had other intentions for him. Henry II was killed while jousting on the square in 1559, in the shadow of the Hôtel des Tournelles. His widow, Catherine de Medici, had the place torn down.

Place des Vosges, once the major dueling ground of Europe, is considered one of the first planned squares in Europe. Its grand-siècle rosy-red brick houses are ornamented with white stone. The covered arcades allowed people to shop at all times, even in the rain—quite an innovation at the time. In the 18th century chestnut trees were added, sparking a controversy that continues to this day: critics say that the addition spoils the perspective.

Over the years such personages as Descartes, Pascal, Cardinal Richelieu, the courtesan Marion Delorme, Gautier, Daudet, and the most famous letterwriter of all time, Madame de Sévigné, lived there. Its best-known occupant was Victor Hugo (his home, now a museum, is the only house that can be visited without a private invitation). The great writer could be seen rushing under the arcades of the square to a rendezvous with his mistress. In the center of the square is a statue of Louis XIII on horseback.

Métro: St-Paul or Chemin-Vert.

HOTEL CARNAVALET, 23, rue de Sévigné, 3e. Tel. 42-72-21-13.

At the Hôtel Carnavalet, the history of Paris comes alive in intimately personal terms—right down to the chessmen Louis XVI used to distract his mind in the days before he went to the guillotine. A renowned Renaissance palace, it was built in 1544 by Pierre Lescot and Jean Goujon; later it was acquired by Madame de Carnavalet. The great François Mansart transformed it between the years 1655 and 1661.

But its best-known memories concern one of history's most famous letterwriters, Madame de Sévigné, who moved into the house in 1677, losing her dear friend La Rochefoucauld two years later. Fanatically devoted to her daughter (until she had to live with her), she poured out nearly every detail of her life in letters, virtually ignoring her son. A native of the Marais district, she died at her daughter's château in 1696. It wasn't until 1866 that the city of Paris acquired the mansion, eventually turning it into a museum.

Many salons depict events related to the Revolution: a bust of Marat, a portrait of Danton, and a replica of the Bastille (one painting shows its demolition). Another salon is devoted exclusively to the story of the captivity of the royal family at the Temple, including the bed in which Madame Elizabeth slept. The exercise book of the Dauphin is there—the pathetic legacy he left the world before his mysterious disappearance.

There is much to see: the Bouvier collection on the first floor, façades of old apothecary shops, extensive wrought-iron works, a bust of Napoleon by Charles-Louis Corbet, a Cazals portrait of Paul Verlaine that makes him look like Lenin, Jean

Beraud's parade of 19th-century opulence, and Baron François Gerard's painting of Madame Récamier—lounging, of course.

You end your tour in the immaculate courtyard in front of a statue of Louis XIV (which Coysevox originally did for l'Hôtel de Ville).

Admission: 30 F ($5.40) adults, 20 F ($3.60) ages 18–24 and over 60; free for children under 18.

Open: Tues–Sun 10am–5:40pm. **Métro:** St-Paul or Chemin-Vert.

MUSEE DE LA CHASSE ET DE LA NATURE, 60, rue des Archives, 3e. Tel. 42-72-86-43.

Nearby the Hôtel Carnavalet, the Hôtel Guénégaud—also built by François Mansart—has been restored and turned into the Musée de la Chasse et de la Nature by the Sommer Foundation. Photographs at the entrance depict the shocking state of the building's decay before its subsequent restoration.

Mounted heads are plentiful, ranging from the antelope to the elephant, from the bushbuck to the waterbuck, from the moose to the "bush pig." Rembrandt's sketch of a lion is here, along with a collection of wild-animal portraits by Desportes (1661–1743). The hunt tapestries are outstanding and often amusing—one a cannibalistic romp, another showing a helmeted man standing eye to eye with a bear he is stabbing to death. The rifles, some inlaid with pearls, others engraved with ivory, are exceptional, many dating from the 17th century. The museum also displays other historical weapons, along with a remarkable collection of paintings, including works by Rubens, Breughel, Oudry, Chardin, and Corot.

Admission: 25 F ($4.50).

Open: Wed–Mon 10am–12:30pm and 1:30–5:30pm. **Closed:** National holidays. **Métro:** Rambuteau or Hôtel-de-Ville.

NATIONAL ARCHIVES, 60, rue des Francs-Bourgeois, 3e. Tel. 40-27-62-18.

A short walk from the hunting museum deposits you at this Paris landmark steeped in Paris history.

On Napoleon's orders, the Palais Soubise was made the official records depository of France. But the building, designed by the much-underrated Delamair, is as fascinating as—or even more so than—the exhibits contained within. Apartments that once belonged to the Prince and Princess de Soubise have been turned into the Musée de l'Histoire de France.

You enter the colonnaded Court of Honor. Before going inside, walk around the corner to 58 rue des Archives to the medieval turreted gateway to the original Clisson mansion. (The Clisson mansion gave way to the residence of the dukes of Guise, who owned the property until it was purchased by the Soubise family. The Princess Soubise was once the mistress of Louis XIV, and apparently the Sun King was very generous, giving her the funds to remodel and redesign the palace.)

The archives contain documents that go back to Charlemagne and even earlier. The letter collection is highly valued, exhibiting the penmanship of Marie Antoinette (a farewell letter), Louis XVI (his will), Danton, Robespierre, Napoléon I, and Joan of Arc. The museum possesses the only known sketch made of the maid from Orléans while she was still alive. Even the jailer's keys to the old Bastille are found here.

For a much later Princess de Soubise, Germain Boffrand in 1735 designed a Salon Ovale, with *parfaites* (faultless) *expressions*. Adding to the lush décor, the gilt, and the crystal are paintings by Van Loo, Boucher, and Natoire.

Admission: 12 F ($2.10) adults, 8 F ($1.40) ages 18–24 and over 60, free for children under 18.

Open: Wed–Mon 1:45–5:45pm. **Métro:** St-Paul or Rambuteau.

THE LATIN QUARTER

This is the precinct of the University of Paris (often called the Sorbonne), lying on the Left Bank in the 5th Arrondissement—where students meet and fall in love over coffee and croissants. Rabelais called it the "Quartier Latin," because of the students and professors who spoke Latin in the classroom and on the streets. The sector teems with belly dancers, exotic restaurants (from Vietnamese to Balkan), sidewalk cafés, bookstalls, *caveaux,* and the *clochards* and *chiffonniers* (the bums and ragpickers).

A good starting point for your tour might be **Place St-Michel** (Métro: Pont St-Michel), where Balzac used to get water from the fountain when he was a youth. This center was the scene of much Resistance fighting in the summer of 1944. The quarter centers around **Boulevard St-Michel,** to the south (the students call it "Boul Mich").

From the "place," your back to the Seine, you can cut left down **rue de la Huchette,** the setting of Elliot Paul's *The Last Time I Saw Paris.* Paul first wandered into this typical street "on a soft summer evening, and entirely by chance," in 1923. Although much has changed since his time, some of the buildings are so old they often have to be propped up by timbers. Paul captured the spirit of the street more evocatively than anyone, writing of "the delivery wagons, makeshift vehicles propelled by pedaling boys, pushcarts of itinerant vendors, knife-grinders, umbrella menders, a herd of milk goats, and the neighborhood pedestrians." The local bordello has closed, however.

Branching off from Huchette is **rue du Chat Qui Pêche** (the "Street of the Cat Who Fishes"), said to be the shortest, narrowest street in the world, containing not one door and only one window. It is usually filled with garbage or lovers . . . or both.

MUSEE DE CLUNY, 6, place Paul-Painlevé, 5e. Tel. 43-25-62-00.

You stand in the cobblestone Court of Honor, admiring the flamboyant Gothic building with its clinging vines, turreted walls, gargoyles, and dormers with seashell motifs. Along with the Hôtel de Sens in Le Marais, the Hôtel de Cluny is all that remains of domestic medieval architecture in Paris. Originally the Cluny was the mansion—built over and beside the ruins of a Roman bath—of a rich 15th-century abbot. By 1515 it was the residence of Mary Tudor, teenage widow of Louis XII and daughter of Henry VII of England and Elizabeth of York.

Seized during the Revolution, the Cluny was rented in 1833 to Alexandre du Sommerard, who adorned it with his collection of medieval works of art. Upon his death in 1842, both the building and the collection were brought back by the government.

The present-day collection of arts and crafts of the Middle Ages is considered the finest in the world. Most people come primarily to see the **Unicorn Tapestries,** viewed by critics (and I heartily concur) as the most outstanding tapestries in the world. A beautiful princess and her handmaiden, beasts of prey, and just plain pets—all the romance of the age of chivalry lives on in these remarkable yet mysterious tapestries. They were discovered only a century ago in the Château de Boussac in Auvergne. Five seem to deal with the five senses (one, for example, depicts a unicorn looking into a mirror held up by a dour-faced maiden). The sixth shows a woman under an elaborate tent with jewels, her pet dog resting on an embroidered cushion beside her. The lovable unicorn and his friendly companion, a lion, hold back the flaps. The background in red and green forms a rich carpet of spring flowers, fruit-laden trees, birds, rabbits, donkeys, dogs, goats, lambs, and monkeys.

The other exhibitions are wide ranging, including several Flemish retables; a 14th-century Sienese (life-size) John the Baptist and other Italian sculptures; statues from Sainte Chapelle, dating from 1243–1248; 12th- and 13th-century crosses, studded with gems; golden chalices, manuscripts, ivory carvings, vestments, leather-work, jewelry, coins, a 13th-century Adam, and heads and fragments of statues from Notre-Dame de Paris recently discovered. In the fan-vaulted medieval chapel hang tapestries depicting scenes from the life of St. Stephen.

Downstairs are the ruins of the Roman baths, dating supposedly from around A.D. 200. You wander through a display of Gallic and Roman sculptures and an interesting marble bathtub engraved with lions. A votive pillar dates from the days of Tiberius.

Admission: 17 F ($3) Mon and Wed-Sat, 9 F ($1.50) Sun.
Open: Wed–Mon 9:45am–5:15pm. **Métro:** Cluny-Sorbonne.

THE SORBONNE, Boulevard St-Michel.

The University of Paris—everybody calls it the Sorbonne—is one of the most famous institutions in the world. Founded in the 13th century, it had become the most prestigious university in the West by the 14th century, drawing such professors as Thomas Aquinas. Reorganized by Napoleon in 1806, the Sorbonne is today the premier university of France.

At first glance from Place de la Sorbonne, it seems architecturally undistinguished. In truth, it was rather indiscriminately reconstructed at the turn of the century. Not so the **Church of the Sorbonne,** built in 1635 by Le Mercier, which contains the marble tomb of Cardinal Richelieu, a work by Girardon based on a design by Le Brun. At his feet, the statue *Science in Tears* is remarkable. **Métro:** St-Michel.

THE PANTHEON, place du Panthéon, 5e. Tel. 43-54-34-52.

Some of the most famous men in the history of France (Victor Hugo, for one) are buried here, at the Place du Panthéon, in austere grandeur, on the crest of the mount of St. Geneviève. In 1744 Louis XV made a vow that if he recovered from a mysterious illness, he would build a church to replace the decayed Abbey of St. Geneviève. He recovered. Madame de Pompadour's brother hired Soufflot for the job. He designed the church in 1764, in the form of a Greek cross, with a dome reminiscent of that of St. Paul's Cathedral in London. Soufflot died, and the work was carried out by his pupil, Rondelet, who completed the structure nine years after his master's death.

Came the Revolution and the church was converted into a "Temple of Fame"—ultimately a pantheon for the great men of France. The body of Mirabeau was buried here, although his remains were later removed. Likewise, Marat was only a temporary tenant. However, Voltaire's body was exhumed and placed here—and allowed to remain.

In the 19th century the building changed roles so many times—first a church, then a pantheon, then a church—that it was hard to keep its function straight. After Victor Hugo was buried here, it became a pantheon once more. Other notable men entombed within include Jean-Jacques Rousseau, Soufflot, Emile Zola, and Louis Braille.

The finest frescoes—the Puvis de Chavannes—are found at the end of the left wall before you enter the crypt. One illustrates St. Geneviève bringing supplies to relieve the victims of the famine. The very best fresco depicts her white-draped head looking out over moonlit medieval Paris, the city whose patroness she became.

Admission: 25 F ($4.50) adults, 14 F ($2.50) ages 18–24, free for children under 18.

Open: Daily 10am–5:45pm. **Métro:** St-Michel or Monge.

ILE ST-LOUIS, 4e.

As you walk across the little iron footbridge from the rear of Notre-Dame, you descend into a world of tree-shaded quays, aristocratic town houses and courtyards, restaurants, and antique shops.

The sister island of the Île de la Cité is primarily residential; its denizens fiercely guard their heritage, privileges, and special position. If you meet residents on the Riviera and ask them where they live, they don't answer just "Paris," they say perhaps "Île Saint-Louis," or more defiantly, "Île."

Saint-Louis was originally two "islets," one named "Island of the Heifers." It was popular as a dueling ground, prompting one foreigner to write home, "There isn't a Frenchman worth his salt who has not slain a man in a duel." The two islands were ordered joined by Louis XIII.

The number of famous people who have occupied these patrician mansions is now a legend. Plaques on the façades make it easier to identify them. Madame Curie, for example, lived at 36 Quai de Bethune, near Ponte de la Tournelle, from 1912 until her death in 1934.

The most exciting mansion (and there is almost universal agreement on that) is the **Hôtel de Lauzun,** built in 1657. It is surely one of the most elegant town houses of Paris. It is owned by the city, and permission to visit it requires bureaucratic red tape. At 17 Quai d'Anjou, it is named after the 17th-century rogue, the Duc de Lauzun, famous lover and on-again/off-again favorite of Louis XIV (he once hid under the Sun King's bed while the monarch made love to his mistress of the moment). At the hôtel, the French courtier was secretly married to "La Grande Mademoiselle" (the Duchess

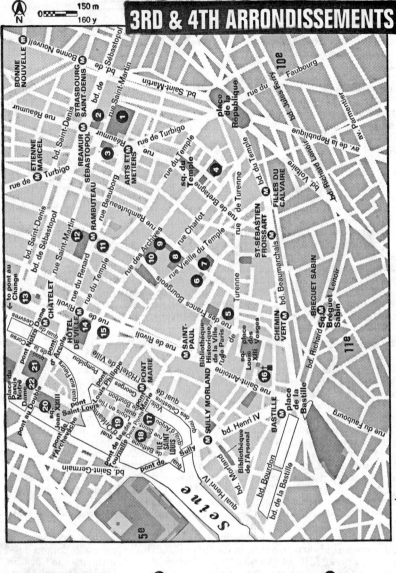

3RD & 4TH ARRONDISSEMENTS

0 ————— 150 m
0 ————— 160 y

N

PARIS
3ᵉ & 4ᵉ
Arrondissements

Archives Nationales ⑨
Carreau du Temple ④
Centre Georges
  Pompidou ⑫
Conservatoire National
  des Arts et Métiers ①
Hôtel Dieu de Cité ㉑
Hôtel de Rohan ⑧
Hôtel de Ville ⑭
Ile de la Cité ㉒
Ile Saint-Louis ⑰
Musée Carnavalet ⑤
Musée de l'Histoire
  de France ⑩
Musée Mickiewicz ⑲
Musée de la Musique
  Mécanique ⑪
Musée de la Serrure ⑥
Musée Picasso ⑦
Musée Victor Hugo ⑳
Notre Dame ⑯
Palais de la Jeunesse ②
Saint-Gervais et
  Saint-Protais ⑮
Saint-Louis-en-l'Ile ⑱
Saint-Nicholas-
  des-Champs ③
Tour Saint-Jacques ⑬

Church ✝   Métro Ⓜ

of Montpensier), much to the dislike of Louis XIV, who dealt with the matter by hustling him off to the Bastille.

That "Flower of Evil" Charles Baudelaire, French poet of the 19th century, lived at Lauzun with his "Black Venus," Jeanne Duval. At the same time that he was squandering the family fortune, Baudelaire was working on poems that celebrated the erotic. Although he had high hopes for them, they were dismissed by many as "obscene, vulgar, perverse, and decadent." (It was only in 1949 that the French court lifted the ban on all the works.) Baudelaire attracted such artists as Delacroix and Courbet to his apartment, which was often filled with the aroma of hashish. Occupying another apartment was the 19th-century novelist Théophile Gautier ("art for art's sake"), who is remembered today chiefly for his *Mademoiselle de Maupin*.

Voltaire lived at 2 Quai d'Anjou, in the **Hôtel Lambert**, with his mistress Emilie de Breteuil, the Marquise du Châteley, who had an "understanding" husband. The couple's quarrels at the Hôtel Lambert were known all over Europe (Emilie did not believe in confining her charms, once described as "nutmeggrater skin" and "bad teeth," to her husband or her lover). But not even Frederick, king of Prussia, could permanently break up her liaison with Voltaire.

The mansion was built by Louis Le Vau in 1645 for Nicolas Lambert de Thorigny, the president of the Chambre des Comptes. For a century the hôtel was the home of the royal family of Poland, the Czartoryskis, who entertained Chopin, among others.

Farther along, at no. 9, stands the house where Honoré Daumier, the painter, sculptor, and lithographer, lived between 1846 and 1863. From that house he satirized the petite bourgeoisie of his day. In hundreds upon hundreds of lithographs he attacked corruption in the French government. His caricature of Louis-Philippe netted him a six-month jail sentence.

Métro: Sully-Morland or Pont-Marie

PALAIS ROYAL, place du Palais-Royal on rue St-Honoré, 1er.

At the demolished Café Foy in the Palais Royal, Camille Desmoulins jumped up on a table and shouted for the mob "to fight to the death." The date was July 13, 1789. The French Revolution had begun. But the renown of the Palais Royal goes back much further. Facing the Louvre, the gardens were planted in 1634 for Cardinal Richelieu, who presented them to Louis XIII. As a child, the future Louis XIV played around the fountain, once nearly drowning. Children frolic here to this day.

In time the property became the residence of the dukes of Orléans. Philippe-Égalité, a cousin of Louis XVI, built his apartments on the grounds, and subsequently rented them to prostitutes. By the 20th century those same apartments were rented by such artists as Colette and Cocteau. Of the gardens Colette wrote, "It is as though I were living in the provinces under the shadow of the parish church! I go into the temple en passant." (A plaque at 9 rue Beaujolais marks the entrance to her apartment, which she inhabited until her death in 1954.)

New York–born American actor and playwright John Howard Payne wrote *Home, Sweet Home* while living in one of the apartments.

Let us turn the clock back again: Napoleon Bonaparte, then an 18-year-old lieutenant, met his first prostitute in the Palais Royal. Robespierre and Danton dined here. An actress, Mlle Montansier, "knew" many of them, including the Corsican. Charlotte Corday came this way, looking for a dagger with which to kill Marat. During the Directoire, when gambling dens flourished at the Palais Royal, foreigners reported seeing Frenchmen leaving the salons without their silk breeches—they had literally lost their trousers at the tables!

Today a sleepy provincial air remains. It's hard to imagine its former life. From the Place Colette, you enter the Court of Honor, colonnaded on three sides. The palace is the headquarters of the Councils of State these days, and the Court of Honor is a parking lot during the day. In the center of the Palais Royal is the Galerie d'Orléans, with two fountains and many a colonnade. You can stroll through the gardens or down the Galerie Montpensier, filled with little shops.

Métro: Louvre.

PLACE VENDOME

Always aristocratic, sometimes royal, Place Vendôme enjoyed its golden age in the heyday of the Second Empire. Dress designers—the great ones, such as Worth—introduced the crinoline there. Louis Napoléon lived here, wooing his future empress, Eugénie de Montijo, at his address at Hôtel du Rhin. In its halcyon days the waltzes of Strauss echoed across the plaza. But in time they were replaced by cannon fire.

Today the most prestigious tenant on the plaza is the Ritz. Banks and offices abound. Still, the Place Vendôme is considered one of the most harmonious squares in France, evoking the Paris of le grand siècle—that is, the age of Louis XIV.

The square is dominated today by a column crowned by Napoleon. The plaza was originally planned by Mansart to honor Louis XIV—so it's a good thing he died earlier. There was a statue of the Sun King here until the Revolution, when it was replaced briefly by "Liberty."

Then came Napoleon, who ordered that a sort of Trajan's Column be erected in honor of the victor at Austerlitz. That Napoleon himself won the battle was "incidental." The column was made of bronze melted from captured Russian and Austrian cannons.

After Napoleon's downfall the statue was replaced with one of Henri IV, everybody's favorite king and every woman's favorite man. Later Napoleon surmounted it once again, this time in uniform and without the pose of a Caesar.

The Communards of 1871, who detested royalty and the false promises of emperors, pulled down the statue. The artist Courbet is said to have led the raid. For his part in the drama, he was jailed and fined the cost of restoring the statue. He couldn't pay it, of course, and was forced into exile in Switzerland. Eventually, the statue of Napoleon, wrapped in a Roman toga, finally won out.

The plaza is one of the best known in Paris. It has attracted such tenants as Chopin, who lived at no. 12 until his death in 1849. Who was Vendôme, you ask? He was the son (delicate writers refer to him as "the natural son") of the roving Henri IV and his best-known mistress, Gabrielle d'Estrées.

Métro: Opéra.

LES HALLES DISTRICT

In the 19th century Zola called it "the underbelly of Paris." For eight centuries Les Halles was the major wholesale fruit, meat, and vegetable market of Paris. The smock-clad vendors, the carcasses of beef, the baskets of what many regarded as the most appetizing fresh vegetables in the world—all that belongs to the past. Today the action has moved to the steel-and-glass contemporary structure at Rungis, a suburb near Orly Airport. The original edifice, Baltard's old zinc-roofed Second Empire "umbrellas of iron," has been torn down.

Replacing these so-called umbrellas is **Le Forum des Halles,** which opened in 1979. This large complex, much of it underground, contains dozens of shops, plus several restaurants and movie theaters. Many of the shops aren't as good as one would wish, but others contain a wide display of merchandise that has made the complex popular with both residents and visitors alike.

For many tourists a night on the town is still capped by the traditional bowl of onion soup at Les Halles, usually at Au Pied de Cochon ("Pig's Foot") or at Au Chien Qui Fume ("Smoking Dog"), in the wee hours. One of the most classic scenes of Paris was night-owling tourists or elegantly dressed Parisians (many just released from Maxim's) standing at a bar drinking cognac with bloody butchers. Some writers have suggested that one Gérard de Nerval introduced the custom of frequenting Les Halles at such an unearthly hour. (De Nerval was a 19th-century poet whose life was considered "irregular." He hanged himself in 1855.)

A newspaper correspondent described the market scene today this way: "Les Halles is trying to stay alive as one of the few places in Paris where one can eat at any hour of the night."

Métro: Les Halles. **RER:** Châtelet/Les Halles.

There is still much to see in Les Halles district, beginning with the **Church of St-Eustache,** at 2, rue du Jour. This church, in the opinion of many, is rivaled only by Notre-Dame. In the old days cabbage vendors came there to pray for their produce.

Even before that it knew the famous and the infamous of its day—everybody from Madame de Pompadour (she was baptized here; so was Richelieu) to Molière, whose funeral was held here in 1673.

In the Gothic-Renaissance style, the church dates from the mid-16th century, although it wasn't completed until 1637. It has been known for its organ recitals ever since Liszt played here in 1866. Inside is the black-marble tomb of Jean Baptiste Colbert, the minister of state under Louis XIV. A marble statue of the statesman rests on top of his tomb, which is flanked by a Coysevox statue of *Abundance* (a horn of flowers) and a J. B. Tuby depiction of *Fidelity*. There is another entrance on rue Rambuteau.

Open: Daily 7:30am–7:30pm. **Métro:** Les Halles.

The district around the protective mother church of Les Halles has always had an unsavory reputation. Centuries ago a Parisian was saying how "ideal it was for assassinations." The best-known murder was that of Henri IV ("Vert Galant") in front of 11 rue de la Ferronnerie (the street of ironmongers). The assassin was Ravaillac, whose punishment I described above in the description of the Conciergerie.

Close at hand, rue des Lombards is worth seeking out. Once it was the banking center of Paris.

ST-GERMAIN-DES-PRES

In the époque de l'après-guerre, a long-haired girl in black slacks, black sweater, and black sandals drifted into St-Germain-des-Prés. Her name was Juliette Greco. She arrived in the heyday of the existentialists, when all the world seemed to revolve around Jean-Paul Sartre, Simone de Beauvoir, and Albert Camus. The Café de Flore, the Brasserie Lipp, and Deux-Magots were the stage settings for the newly arriving postwar bohemians who came there to "existentialize."

In time Sartre was eulogizing Miss Greco ("She has millions of poems in her throat"); her black outfit was adopted by girls from Paris to California; and eventually she earned the title of "la muse de St-Germain-des-Prés."

In the 1950s new names appeared: Françoise Sagan, Gore Vidal, James Baldwin. By the time the 1960s had arrived the tourists were as firmly entrenched at the Café de Flore and Deux-Magots. The old days are gone, but St-Germain-des-Prés remains an interesting quarter of nightclubs in "caves," publishing houses, bookshops, art galleries, Left Bank bistros, and coffeehouses—as well as two historic churches.

ST-GERMAIN-DES-PRES CHURCH, 3 place St-Germain-des-Prés, 6e. Tel. 43-25-41-71.

Outside it's an early-17th-century town house, a handsome one at that. But beneath that covering it's one of the oldest churches in Paris, going back to the 6th century when a Benedictine abbey was founded on the site by Childebert, son of Clovis, the "creator of France." Unfortunately, the marble columns in the triforium are all that remains from that period. At one time the abbey was a pantheon for Merovingian kings. Restoration of St. Symphorien Chapel, which is the site of the Merovingian tombs, at the entrance of the church, began in 1981. During that work, unknown Romanesque paintings were discovered on the triumphal arch of the chapel, making it one of the most interesting places of old Christian Paris.

Its Romanesque tower, topped by a 19th-century spire, is the most enduring landmark in the village of St-Germain-des-Prés. Its church bells, however, are hardly noticed by the patrons of Deux-Magots across the way.

The Normans were fond of destroying the abbey, and did so at least four times. The present building, the work of four centuries, has a Romanesque-style nave and a Gothic-style choir with fine capitals. Among the people interred at the church are Descartes and Jean-Casimir, the king of Poland who abdicated his throne.

When you leave St-Germain-des-Prés Church, just turn right in rue de l'Abbaye and have a look at the 17th-century Palais Abbatial, a pink palace.

Open: Daily 8am–7:30pm. **Métro:** St-Germain-des-Prés.

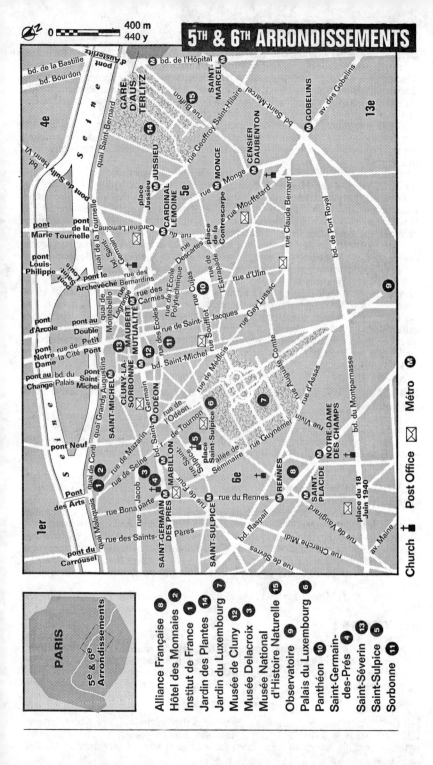

5TH & 6TH ARRONDISSEMENTS

400 m
440 y

Alliance Française 8
Hôtel des Monnaies 2
Institut de France 1
Jardin des Plantes 14
Jardin du Luxembourg 7
Musée de Cluny 12
Musée Delacroix 3
Musée National
d'Histoire Naturelle 15
Observatoire 9
Palais du Luxembourg 6
Panthéon 10
Saint-Germain-
des-Prés 4
Saint-Séverin 13
Saint-Sulpice 5
Sorbonne 11

Church †
Post Office ⌧
Métro Ⓜ

PARIS
5e & 6e
Arrondissements

CHURCH OF ST-SULPICE, rue St-Sulpice, 6e. Tel. 46-33-21-78.

Pause first on the 18th-century **Place St-Sulpice.** On the 1844 fountain by Visconti are sculpted likenesses of four 18th-century bishops: Fenelon, Massillon, Bossuet, and Flechier. Napoleon, then a general, was given a stag dinner there in 1799. He liked the banquet but not the square. When he was promoted he changed it. One of the two towers of the church was never completed.

Work originally began on the church in 1646; the façade, "bastardized classic," was completed in 1745. Many architects, including Le Vau, worked on the building. Some were summarily fired; others, such as the Florentine Servandoni, were discredited.

One of the most notable treasures inside the 360-foot-long church is Servandoni's rococo Chapel of the Madonna, with a marble statue of the Virgin by Pigalle. One critic wrote that you'd have to go to Versailles to find a peer of that chapel. The church contains one of the world's largest organs, with more than 6,500 pipes. The Sunday mass concerts—made known by Charles Widor—draw many visitors. Chalgrin designed the organ case in the 18th century.

One of the largest and most prestigious churches in Paris, St. Sulpice was sacked during the Revolution and converted into the Temple of Victory. Camille Desmoulins, the revolutionary who sparked the raiding of the Bastille, was married here.

But the real reason you come to St. Sulpice is to see the Delacroix frescoes in the Chapel of the Angels (first on your right as you enter). Seek out his muscular Jacob wrestling (or is he dancing?) with an effete angel. On the ceiling St. Michael is having his own troubles with the Devil, and yet another mural depicts Heliodorus being driven from the temple. Painted in the final years of his life, the frescoes were a high point in the career of the baffling, romantic Delacroix. If you are impressed by Delacroix, you can pay him a belated tribute by visiting the Delacroix museum previewed below.

Open: Daily 7:30am–7:30pm. **Métro:** St-Sulpice.

MUSEE EUGENE DELACROIX, 6, place de Fürstenberg, 6e. Tel. 43-54-04-87.

To art historians, Delacroix is something of an enigma. Even his parentage is a mystery. Many believed that Talleyrand had the privilege of fathering him. The Frank Anderson Trapp biography saw him "as an isolated and atypical individualist—one who respected traditional values, yet emerged as the embodiment of Romantic revolt."

By visiting his atelier, you will see one of the most charming squares on the Left Bank and also the romantic garden of the museum. You reach the studio through a large arch on a stone courtyard.

Delacroix died in this apartment on August 13, 1863. Lithographs, watercolors, oils, and reproductions fill the house where the artist sat up into the late hours writing his memorable and penetrating journals. In the Louvre is a portrait of Delacroix as a handsome, strong, mustachioed man. You'll also have to go to the Louvre to see some of the artist's best-known paintings, such as *Liberty Leading the People.*

Admission: 12 F ($2.10) adults, 7 F ($1.20) ages 18–25 and over 60, free for children under 18.

Open: Wed–Mon 9:15am–12:30pm and 2–5:15pm. **Métro:** St-Germain-des-Prés.

RUE VISCONTI

A short walk from the Delacroix museum is this street, obviously designed for pushcarts. At no. 17 is the maison where Balzac established his printing press in 1825. The venture ended in bankruptcy—which forced the author back to his writing desk. In the 17th century the French dramatist Jean-Baptiste Racine lived across the street. Such celebrated actresses as Champmeslé and Clairon were also in residence.

MONTPARNASSE

For the "lost generation," life centered around the literary cafés of Montparnasse. Hangouts such as Dôme, Coupole, Rotonde, and the Select became legendary. Artists, especially American expatriates, turned their backs on Montmartre, dismiss-

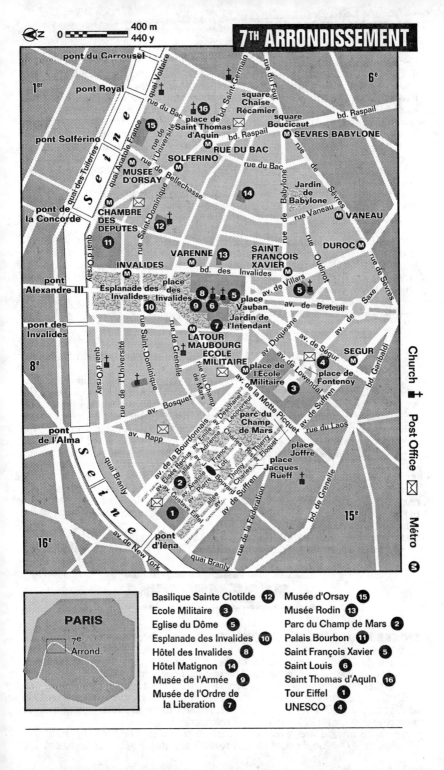

ing it as "too touristy." Picasso, Modigliani, and Man Ray came this way, and Hemingway was a popular figure. So was Fitzgerald when he was poor (when he was in the chips, you'd find him at the Ritz). William Faulkner, Archibald MacLeish, Isadora Duncan, Miró, James Joyce, Ford Madox Ford, even Trotsky—all were here. Except Gertrude Stein, who would not frequent the cafés. To see her, you would have to wait for an invitation to her salon at 27 rue de Fleurus. She bestowed her favor on Sherwood Anderson, Elliot Paul, and, for a time, Hemingway. However, Papa found that there wasn't "much future in men being friends with great women." John Malcolm Brinnin wrote in *The Third Rose:* "To have paid respects to Gertrude and to have sat with Alice [Alice B. Toklas] was to have been admitted into the charmed circle of those whose pretenses, at least, were interesting and fashionable."

When not receiving, Miss Stein was busy buying paintings—works by Cézanne, Renoir, Matisse, and Picasso. One writer said that her salon was engaged in an international conspiracy to promote modern art. At her Saturday-evening gatherings you might have met Braque.

The life of Montparnasse still centers around its cafés and exotic nightclubs, many of them only a shadow of what they used to be. Its heart is at the crossroads of the Boulevard Raspail and the Boulevard du Montparnasse, one of the settings of *The Sun Also Rises.* Hemingway wrote that "the Boulevard Raspail always made dull riding." Rodin's controversial statue of Balzac swathed in a large cape stands guard over the prostitutes who cluster around the pedestal. Balzac seems to be the only one in Montparnasse who doesn't feel the impact of time and change.

LA DEFENSE

LA GRANDE ARCHE DE LA DEFENSE, place du parvis de la Défense, 18e. Tel. 49-07-26-26.
Designed as the architectural centerpiece of the sprawling and futuristic satellite suburb of La Défense, this massive steel-and-masonry arch rises 35 stories from the pavement. Built with the blessing of President François Mitterand, and ringed with soaring office buildings and a circular avenue (*périphérique*), the design of which imitates the traffic circle surrounding the more famous Arc de Triomphe, the deliberately overscale archway is the latest major landmark to dot the Paris skyline. High enough to shelter the Cathedral of Notre-Dame below its heavily trussed canopy, the monument was designed as an extension of the panorama that interconnects the Louvre, the Arc du Carroussel, the Champs-Elysées, the Arc de Triomphe, avenue de la Grande-Armée, and place du Porte-Maillot into one magnificently engineered straight line. An elevator carries visitors to an observation platform, from which you can get an idea of the carefully conceived geometry of the surrounding street plan.
Admission: 30 F ($5.40) adults, 20 F ($3.60) children under 18.
Open: Mon–Fri 9am–5pm, Sat–Sun 10am–7pm. **RER:** La Défense.

3. MORE MUSEUMS

MUSÉE RODIN [HOTEL BIRON], 77, rue de Varenne, 7e. Tel. 47-05-01-34.
These days Rodin is acclaimed as the father of modern sculpture, but in a different era his work was labeled obscene. The world's artistic taste changed, and in due course the government of France purchased the gray-stone 18th-century luxury residence in Faubourg St-Germain. The mansion was the studio of Rodin from 1910 till his death in 1917. The rose gardens were restored to their 18th-century splendor, a perfect setting for Rodin's most memorable works.
In the courtyard are three world-famous creations: *The Gate of Hell, The Thinker,* and *The Burghers of Calais.* Rodin's first major public commission, *The*

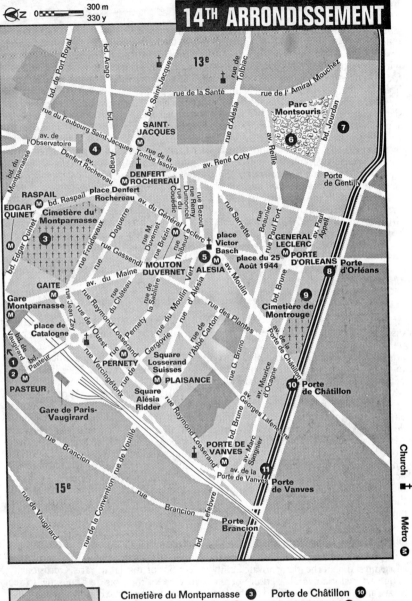

14TH ARRONDISSEMENT

0   300 m
    330 y

13e

rue de l' Amiral Mouchez

bd. de Port Royal

bd. Arago

rue de Tolbiac

rue de la Santé

Parc
Montsouris

rue du Faubourg Saint-Jacques

bd. Saint-Jacques

SAINT-
JACQUES

av. de
l'Observatoire

rue de la
Tombe Issoire

av. René Coty

av. Reille

bd. Jourdan

7

6

Porte
de Gentilly

Denfert Rochereau

av. Arago

av. Denfert Rochereau

DENFERT
ROCHEREAU

bd. du Montparnasse

RASPAIL

bd. Raspail

place Denfert
Rochereau

av. du Général Leclerc

rue Remy
Dumoncel

rue du
Couëdic

rue Bezout

rue Sarrette

rue
Beaunier

av. Paul
Appell

EDGAR
QUINET

bd. Edgar Quinet

Cimetière du
Montparnasse

3

rue Daguerre

rue Froidevaux

rue Gassendi

rue M.
Duverne

rue Brézin

rue
Thibaud

place
Victor
Basch

place du 25
Août 1944

GENERAL
LECLERC

PORTE
D'ORLEANS

PAUL FORT

8

Porte
d'Orléans

rue du Maine

MOUTON
DUVERNET

rue Vert

ALESIA

av. Moulin

5

GAITE

rue de
la Sablière

rue du Moulin

rue d'Alésia

rue des Plantes

Cimetière de
Montrouge

9

Gare
Montparnasse

av. du Maine

rue du Château

rue Raymond Losserand

rue de l'Ouest

Pernety

rue de
Gergovie

rue de
l'Abbé Carton

rue de

rue G. Bruno

bd. de Vaugirard

bd. Pasteur

place de
Catalogne

1

2

PASTEUR

rue Jean Zay

rue Vercingétorix

PERNETY

Square
Losserand
Suisses

PLAISANCE

Square
Alésia
Ridder

rue Raymond Losserand

av. de la
Porte de Chatillon

10

Porte
de Châtillon

Gare de Paris-
Vaugirard

rue Brancion

rue de Vouille

rue de la Convention

Brancion

PORTE DE
VANVES

av. Marc
Sangnier

av. de la
Porte de Vanves

11

Porte
de Vanves

15e

rue de Vaugirard

bd. Lefebvre

av. Maurice
d'Ocagne

bd. Brune

bd. Georges Lafenestre

Porte
Brancion

PARIS

14e
Arrondissement

Burghers commemorated the heroism of six burghers of Calais who, in 1347, offered themselves as hostages to Edward III in return for his ending the siege of their port. Perhaps the single best-known work, *The Thinker,* in Rodin's own words, "thinks with every muscle of his arms, back, and legs, with his clenched fist and gripping toes." Not yet completed at Rodin's death, *The Gate of Hell,* as he put it, is "where I lived for a whole year in Dante's Inferno."

Inside the building, the sculpture, plaster casts, reproductions, originals, and sketches reveal the freshness and vitality of that remarkable man. Many of his works appear to be emerging from marble into life. Everybody is attracted to *The Kiss* (of which one critic wrote, "the passion is timeless"). Upstairs are two different versions of the celebrated and condemned nude of Balzac, his bulky torso rising from a tree trunk (Albert E. Elsen commented on the "glorious bulging" stomach). Included are many versions of his *Monument to Balzac* (a large one stands in the garden), which was Rodin's last major work and which caused a furor when it was first exhibited.

Other significant sculpture includes Rodin's *Prodigal Son* (it literally soars), *The Crouching Woman* (called the "embodiment of despair"), and his *The Age of Bronze,* an 1876 study of a nude man, modeled by a Belgian soldier. (Rodin was accused—falsely—of making a cast from a living model.)

Admission: 22 F ($3.90) adults Mon–Sat, 11 F ($1.90) Sun; 11 F ($1.90) ages 18–24 and over 60; free for children under 18.

Open: Oct–Mar, Tues–Sun 10am–5pm; Apr–Sept, Tues–Sun 10am–6pm. **Métro:** Varenne.

A Digression: The Faubourg St-Germain

At the Hôtel Biron, you'll be on the threshold of what was the most elegant residential district of Paris in the 18th century, the **Faubourg St-Germain.** If you don't have to rush immediately to Napoleon's Tomb, try to explore some of that once-aristocratic district, lying roughly between the Invalides and St-Germain-des-Prés. At one time or another, some of the most celebrated names in France have lived there: Mme Récamier, Lafayette, Chateaubriand, Turgot, Queen Hortense, Mme de Montespan, André Gide, Ingres, Corot, Baudelaire, and Guillaume Apollinaire.

Deserted by fickle fashion, the former mansions are now occupied by foreign embassies or ministries such as the French Ministry of National Education. At 138 rue de Grenelle, Marshall Foch, the supreme Allied commander in World War I, died on March 20, 1929. On the same street, at 59 rue de Grenelle, Alfred de Musset lived from 1824 to 1839, before George Sand lured him away on an amorous adventure. The façade at the poet's residence is the most elegant on the street—note the *Fountain of the Four Seasons,* designed by Bouchardon in 1739. A woman, signifying the City of Paris, is seated on a throne of lions, dominating the figures of the Seine and the Marne at her feet. In niches to each side of her—favorite roosts of Parisian pigeons—are bas-reliefs depicting the four seasons. Autumn is illustrated with cherubs harvesting the grapes from the vineyards.

MARMOTTAN MUSEUM, 2, rue Louis-Boilly, 16e. Tel. 42-24-07-02.

A town-house mansion with all the trappings of the First Empire, the Marmottan Museum is one of the many private family collections on display in Paris. Occasionally a lone art historian would venture here on the edge of the Bois de Boulogne, to see what Paul Marmottan donated to the Académie des Beaux-Arts. Hardly anybody else did . . . until 1966, when Michel Monet, son of Claude Monet, died in a car crash, leaving a bequest of his father's art—valued at the time at $10 million—to the little museum. The Académie des Beaux-Arts suddenly found itself heir to more than 130 paintings, watercolors, pastels, and drawings—and a whole lot of Monet-lovers, who can, in one place, trace the evolution of the great man's work.

The gallery owns more than 30 pictures of his house at Giverny, and many of water lilies, his everlasting intrigue. The bequest included his *Willow,* painted in 1918, his *Houses of Parliament,* from 1905, even a portrait Renoir did of Monet when he was 32. The collection has been hailed "one of the great art treasures of the world," and that it is. Ironically, the museum had always owned Monet's *Impression,* from which the movement got its name.

Paul Marmottan's original collection includes fig-leafed nudes, First Empire antiques, assorted objets d'art, bucolic paintings, and crystal chandeliers. Many of the tapestries date from the Renaissance, and you can also see the extensive collection of miniatures donated by Daniel Waldenstein.

Admission: 35 F ($6.30) adults, free for children under 12.
Open: Tues–Sun 10am–5:30pm. **Métro:** La-Muette.

MUSEUM OF THE MONUMENTS OF FRANCE, Palais de Chaillot, place du Trocadéro, 16e. Tel. 47-27-35-74.

This museum houses moldings of the *grandes oeuvres* of French sculpture, including entire façades and portals, as well as reproductions of the most significant mural paintings up to the 16th century. Reproduced in detail are such landmarks in art as the southern façade of Chartres Cathedral (1220–1225) as well as the western one (1145–1150). The Romanesque and Gothic sculptures can be examined from an intimate perspective; in the original, much of the intricacy is lost or the sculpture too elevated to be appreciated.

Not only will you see some of the sculpture of such cathedrals as Notre-Dame and Reims, but also such sights as the 16th-century southern door of the transept of Beauvais Cathedral; that decorative masterpiece, the tomb of François II and of Marguerite de Foix at Nantes; the door to the chapter house of Bourges Cathedral; the 1560 north door of the transept in Rouen's Church of St. Maclou; and the 1535 Hôtel de Bernuy (school for boys) at Toulouse. Notable are the reproductions of the painted pillars at St-Savin-sur-Gartempe at Vienne.

Many of the Romanesque and Gothic mural paintings are reproduced right down to their faded glory (see, for example, the 14th-century dome of the Cathedral of Cahors, the town that was the ancient capital of Quercy). Perhaps the most ghoulish work is from La Brigue Chapel; the most humorous, the fork-tailed monsters devouring flesh from the château de Villeneuve-Lembron, Puy-de-Dôme (1515–1517).

Admission: 17 F ($3) adults, 7 F ($1.20) ages 18–25 and over 60, free for children under 18.
Open: Wed–Mon 9:30am–5pm. **Métro:** Trocadéro.

CITE DES SCIENCES ET DE L'INDUSTRIE, La Villette, 30, av. Corentin-Cariou, 19e. Tel. 40-05-80-00.

A city of science and industry has risen here. When its core was originally built in the 1960s, it was touted as the most modern slaughterhouse in the world. But when the site was abandoned as a failure in 1974, its echoing vastness and unlikely location on the northern edge of the city presented the French government with a problem. In 1986 the converted premises opened as the world's most expensive ($642 million) science complex designed to "modernize mentalities" as a first step in the process of modernizing society.

The place is so vast, with so many options, that a single visit gives only an idea of the scope of the Cité. What you'll see is something akin to a futuristic airplane hangar. Busts of Plato, Hippocrates, and a double-faced Janus gaze silently at a tube-filled space-aged riot of high-tech girders, glass, and lights—something akin to what a layman might think of the interior of an atomic generator.

The sheer dimensions of the place are awesome, a challenge to the arrangers of the constantly changing exhibits. Some of the exhibits are couched in an overlay of Gallic humor, including seismographic activity as presented in the comic-strip adventures of a jungle explorer. Among others is the silver-skinned Geodesic Dome (called the Géode) that shows the closest thing to a 3-D cinema in Europe on the inner surfaces of its curved walls. It is a 112-foot-high sphere with a 370-seat theater.

Explora, a permanent exhibit, is spread over the three upper levels of the building; its displays revolve around four themes: the universe, life, matter, and communication. The Cité also has a multimedia library and a planetarium. An "inventorium" is designed for children.

The Cité is set within La Villette park, the largest city park of Paris, with 136 acres of greenery—twice the size of the Tuileries. Here you'll find a belvedere, a video workshop for children, and information about exhibitions and events, along with a café and restaurant.

Admission: Cité Pass (entrance to all exhibits), 45 F ($8.10) adults, 35 F ($6.30) ages 7–25, free for children under 7; Géode, 50 F ($9) adults, 37 F ($6.60) children 17 and under.

Open: Tues 10am–6pm, Wed noon–9pm, Thurs–Fri 10am–6pm, Sat–Sun and holidays noon–8pm. Show times at Géode, Tues–Sun on the hour 10am–9pm. **Métro:** Line 7 to Porte de la Villette station.

MUSEE D'ART MODERNE DE LA VILLE DE PARIS, 11, av. du Président-Wilson, 8e. Tel. 47-23-61-27.

Right next door to the Palais de Tokyo, this interesting museum displays a permanent collection of paintings and sculpture owned by the city of Paris. In addition, the M.A.M. section of the city's modern art museum presents ever-changing temporary exhibitions on individual artists from all over the world or on international art trends. Bordering the Seine, the salons display works by such artists as Chagall, Matisse, Léger, Braque, Picasso, Dufy, Utrillo, Delaunay, Rouault, and Modigliani. See, in particular, Pierre Tal Coat's *Portrait of Gertrude Stein*. Picasso wasn't the only artist to tackle this difficult subject. Other sections in the museum are ARC, which shows work of young artists and new trends in contemporary art, and the Musée des Enfants, which has exhibitions and shows for children.

Admission: Permanent collection, 15 F ($2.70) adults, 8.50 F ($1.50) ages 18–25 and over 60; free for children under 18. Temporary exhibitions, 20–35 F ($3.60–$6.30) adults, 15–20 F ($2.70–$3.60) ages 18–25 and over 60; free for children under 18.

Open: Tues and Thurs–Sun 10am–5:30pm, Wed 10am–8:30pm. **Métro:** Iéna or Alma-Marceau.

MUSEE GUIMET, 6, place d'Iéna, 16e. Tel. 47-23-61-65.

Named after its founder and established originally at Lyon, the Guimet was transferred to Paris in 1889. It received in 1931 the collection of the Musée Indochinois du Trocadéro and, after World War II, the Asian collections of the Louvre. Today it is one of the world's richest museums of its genre.

The art ranges from Tibet to Japan to Afghanistan to Nepal to Java to India to China. There are even sculptures from Vietnam. The most interesting displays are on the ground floor, the exhibits encompassing Buddhas, heads of serpentine monsters, funereal figurines. See, for example, antiquities from the temple of Angkor Wat. The Jacques Bacot gallery is devoted to Tibetan art: fascinating scenes of the Grand Lamas entwined with serpents and demons.

On the first floor is the Indian section with the remarkable Mathura Serpent-King (2nd century A.D.), the Amaravati reliefs. René Grousset, a French art historian, was impressed with the "simple paganism, the innocent pleasure in the nude form." Of a harem group from that school (3rd century), he found its sensuality "refined," its freshness "agreeable." On the same floor is the Rousset collection.

On the top floor, the Michael Calmann collection is devoted to vases, statuettes in porcelain, ceramics, and pottery, including the Grandidier collection, that run the gamut of Chinese dynasties—going back six or seven centuries before the birth of Christ and forward to the Ts'ing Dynasty (1644–1911).

Admission: 26 F ($4.60) adults, 14 F ($2.50) ages 18–25 and over 60, free for children under 18.

Open: Wed–Mon 9:45am–6pm. **Métro:** Iéna or Alma-Marceau.

MUSEE CERNUSCHI, 7, av. Velásquez, 8e. Tel. 45-63-50-75.

Bordering the Parc Monceau, this small museum is devoted to the arts of China. It's another one of those mansions whose owners stuffed them with an art collection, then bequeathed them to the city of Paris. The address was quite an exclusive one when the town house was built in 1885.

Inside, there is, of course, a bust of Cernuschi—and that is as it should be, a

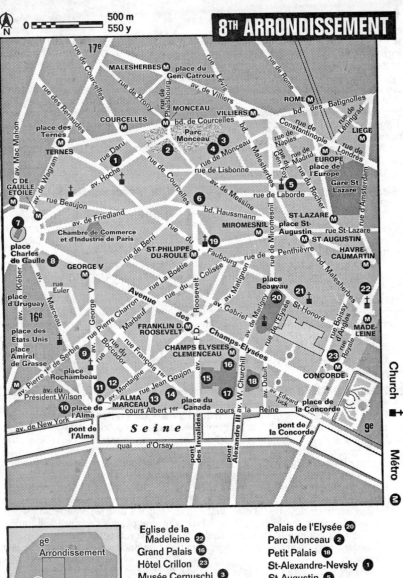

8TH ARRONDISSEMENT

500 m
550 y

8e Arrondissement

PARIS

Church ✝
Métro Ⓜ

American Cathedral in Paris ⑨
Arc de Triomphe ⑦
Crazy Horse Saloon ⑪

Eglise de la Madeleine ㉒
Grand Palais ⑯
Hôtel Crillon ㉓
Musée Cernuschi ③
Musée d'Art Moderne ⑩
Musée Jacquemart André ⑥
Musée Nissim de Camondo ④
Notre Dame de la Consolation ⑬
Office du Tourisme ⑧
Palais de la Découverte ⑮

Palais de l'Elysée ⑳
Parc Monceau ②
Petit Palais ⑱
St-Alexandre-Nevsky ①
St-Augustin ⑤
St-Jean-Baptiste ⑭
St. Michael's English Church ㉑
St-Philippe-du-Roule ⑲
Théâtres des Champs Elysées ⑫
Université Paris IV ⑰

self-perpetuating memorial to a man whose generosity and interest in the East was legend in his day. Now the collections include a fine assortment of Neolithic potteries, as well as bronzes from the 14th century B.C., the most famous perhaps the tiger-shape vase. The jades, ceramics, and funereal figures are exceptional, as are the pieces of Buddhist sculpture. Most admirable is a Bodhisattva originating from Yun-kang (6th century). Rounding out the exhibits are some ancient paintings, the best known of which is *Horses with Grooms,* attributed to Han Kan (8th century, T'ang Dynasty). The museum also houses a good collection of contemporary Chinese painting.

Admission: 12 F ($2.10) to the permanent collection, 20 F ($3.60) to temporary exhibitions.

Open: Tues–Sun 10am–5:40pm. **Métro:** Monceau or Villiers. **Bus:** 30 or 94.

MUSEE NISSIM DE CAMONDO, 63, rue de Monceau, 8e. Tel. 45-63-26-32.

This museum is a jewel box of elegance and refinement, evoking the days of Louis XVI and Marie Antoinette. The pre-World War I town house was donated to the Museum of Decorative Arts by Comte Moïse de Camondo (1860–1935) in memory of his son, Nissim, a French aviator killed in combat in World War I.

Entered through a courtyard, the museum is like the private home of an aristocrat of two centuries ago—richly furnished with needlepoint chairs, tapestries (many from Beauvais or Aubusson), antiques, paintings (the inevitable Guardi scenes of Venice), bas-reliefs, silver, Chinese vases, crystal chandeliers, Sèvres porcelain, and Savonnerie carpets. And, of course, a Houdon bust (in an upstairs bedroom). The Blue Salon, overlooking the Parc Monceau, is impressive. You can wander without a guide through the gilt and oyster-gray salons.

Admission: 18 F ($3.20) adults, 12 F ($2.10) children under 18 or seniors over 60.

Open: Wed–Sun 10am–noon and 2–5pm. **Closed:** Christmas and New Year's Day. **Métro:** Villiers.

MUSÉE DES ARTS DECORATIFS, Palais du Louvre, 107, rue de Rivoli, 1er. Tel. 42-60-32-14.

In the northwest wing of the Pavillon de Marsan of the Louvre, this museum offers a treasury of furnishings, fabrics, wallpaper, objets d'art, and other items that add up to displays of styles of living from the Middle Ages to the present day. Notable are the art deco boudoir, bath, and bedroom done in the 1920s for couturier Jeanne Lanvin by designer Rateau. This and other displays from 1900 to 1925 are on the first floor, together with collections of contemporary art and a 1900 room.

For many people the first floor holds the most interest, as it contains the prestigious collection of the works of Jean Dubuffet, which the artist donated to the museum. Decorative art from the Middle Ages to the Renaissance is on the second floor, while rich collections from the 17th, 18th, and 19th centuries occupy the third and fourth floors. The fifth floor contains specialized centers of the museum, such as wallpaper and drawings, and documentary centers detailing fashion, textiles, toys, crafts, and glass trends.

Admission: 23 F ($4.10) adults and students, free for children under 15.

Open: Wed–Sat 12:30–6pm, Sun 11am–6pm. **Métro:** Palais-Royal or Tuileries.

PETIT PALAIS, Petit Palais, av. Winston-Churchill, 8e. Tel. 42-65-12-73.

Built by architect Charles Girault, the small palace faces the Grand Palais (housing special exhibitions)—both erected for the 1900 Exhibition.

The Petit Palais contains works of art belonging to the city of Paris. Most prominent are the Dutuit and Tuck collections. In the Dutuit collection are Egyptian, Greek, and Roman bronzes, rare ivory statues (the most prominent of which is of a Roman actor), and a series of ancient Greek porcelains. From the Middle Ages are enamels, sculpture, and hand-lettered and -painted manuscripts. A good collection of 17th-century Dutch and Flemish paintings are also on view, with representative artists including Breughel the Younger (*Wedding Pageant*), Rubens, Hobbema, Ruysdaël, and others.

The museum's other major collection was donated by Edward Tuck in 1930. It's composed mainly of decorative artwork of the 18th century, including tapestries, furniture (much gilt), wood-paneled salons, and porcelains, which give a good overview of the aesthetic sense of France at the time of the fall of the ancien régime.

A number of rooms are dedicated to 19th-century French painting, including a few works by major impressionists. In the collection are canvases by Courbet, Daumier, Corot, Delacroix, Manet, Sisley, Mary Cassatt (*Le Bain*), Maurice Denis, Odilon Redon, a series of portraits (one of Sarah Bernhardt by Clairin), and art by Edouard Vuillard and Pierre Bonnard. The 19th century, as you will have seen by now, is the best represented at the museum, with stress on the "academic school," especially the enormous compositions of Gustave Doré. Other important artists come from the symbolist school, including *Soir Antique* by Osbert. Notable paintings displayed include *The Death of Seneca* by David, the *Portrait of Lalande* by Fragonard, and the *Young Shepherd Holding a Flower* by Greuze. Sculptures are by Rodin, Bourdelle, and Maillol, and creations of what is currently the craze in antique stores can be seen as well—glassworks by Galle and Lalique. There is an impressive collection of sculpture by Carpeaux as well.

Admission: 15 F ($2.70); special exhibitions, 30–40 F ($5.40–$7.20); free Sun.
Open: Tues–Sat 10am–5:40pm. **Métro:** Champs-Elysées.

MUSEE JACQUEMART-ANDRE, 158, bd. Haussmann, 8e. Tel. 45-62-39-94.

This late-19th-century town house was built by Edouard André, who later married Nélie Jacquemart, an artist. Together they formed a collection of rare French 18th-century decorative art and Italian Renaissance works. Mlle André, who died shortly before World War I, willed the building and its contents to the Institut de France. It is perhaps the best of the little decorative art museums of Paris.

You enter through an arcade leading into an enclosed courtyard. Two white lions guard the doorway. Inside are Gobelin tapestries, Houdon busts, Savonnerie carpets—and a rich art collection, including Rembrandt's *The Pilgrim of Emmaüs*. Represented by paintings are Van Dyck, Tiepolo, Rubens, Watteau, Fragonard, Boucher, Carpaccio, and Mantegna (*Virgin and Child*). Donatello torchères, statuary (including a wingless victory), Slodtz busts, della Robbia terracottas (Ganymede with the eagle), and antiques round out the collection. The salons drip with gilt, and the winding stairway to the top floor is elegant.

Admission: 15 F ($2.70).
Open: Wed–Sun 1–5:30pm. **Closed:** Aug. **Métro:** Miromesnil or St-Philippe-du-Roule.

MANUFACTURE NATIONALE DE SEVRES, place de la Manufacture, Sèvres, 7e.

Madame de Pompadour loved Sèvres porcelain. She urged Louis XV to order more and more of it, thus ensuring its position among the fashionable people of the 18th century. Two centuries later, it is still fashionable.

The Sèvres factory, next door to a museum, has been owned by the state of France for more than two centuries. It was founded originally in Vincennes, and moved to Sèvres, a riverside suburb of Paris, in 1756. The factory may be visited on Thursday, except holidays and in July and August. The visits are free. The factory's commercial service sells porcelains to the public daily except Sunday and holidays.

Next door, the **Musée National de Ceramique de Sèvres** (tel. 45-34-99-05) shelters one of the finest collections of faïence and porcelain in the world. Some of it belonged to Madame du Barry, Pompadour's hand-picked successor. You can see the Sèvres ware as it looked from the day it was created and as it looks straight from the factory today. On view, for example, is the "Pompadour rose" (which the English insisted on calling the "rose du Barry"), a style much in vogue in the 1750s and 1760s. The painter Boucher made some of the designs used by the factory, as did the sculptor Pajou (he did the bas-reliefs for the Opéra at Versailles). The factory pioneered what became known in porcelain as the Louis Seize style—it's all here, plus lots more, including works from Meissen (archrival of Sèvres).

Admission: 16 F ($2.80) adults, 8 F ($1.40) seniors and ages 19–25, free for children under 19.

Open: Wed–Mon 10am–noon and 1:30–5:15pm. **Métro:** Pont-de-Sèvres; then walk across the Seine to the Left Bank.

MUSEE ZADKINE, 100 bis, rue d'Assas, 6e. Tel. 43-26-91-90.

This museum near the Luxembourg Gardens and Boulevard St-Michel, is one of the newest of the museums of Paris. Once it was the private residence of Ossip Zadkine, the sculptor. Now the collection of this famous artist has been turned over to the city of Paris for public viewing. Included are some 300 pieces of sculpture, displayed both within the museum and in the garden, which gives a rural charm to the heart of the city. In addition, some drawings and tapestries are also exhibited.

Admission: 12 F ($2.10).

Open: Tues–Sun 10am–5:30pm. **Métro:** Luxembourg or Vavin.

LES GOBELINS, 42, av. des Gobelins, 13e. Tel. 43-37-12-60.

The founding father of the dynasty, Jehan Gobelin, came from a family of dyers and clothmakers. In the 15th century he discovered a scarlet dye that was to make him famous. By 1601 Henry IV had become interested, bringing up 200 weavers from Flanders whose full-time occupation was to make tapestries (many now scattered across the museums and residences, both public and private, of Europe). Oddly enough, until then the Gobelin family had not made any tapestries, although the name would become synonymous with that art form.

Colbert, the minister of Louis XIV, purchased the works, and under royal patronage the craftsmen set about executing designs by Le Brun. Closed during the Revolution, the industry was reactivated by Napoleon.

The factory is still going strong and you can visit the studios of the craftspeople—called *ateliers*. Some of the ancient high-warp looms are still in use. The craftspeople turn out modern tapestries inspired by such artists as Picasso, Léger, Matisse, and Miró.

For information, contact Caisse Nationale des Monuments Historiques, 62, rue St-Antoine, 4e (tel. 44-61-21-69).

Admission: 26 F ($4.70) adults, free for children under 18.

Open: Guided tours Wed–Thurs at 2 and 2:45pm. **Métro:** Gobelins.

4. MORE CHURCHES

VAL-DE-GRACE, 1, place Alphonse-Laveran, 5e. Tel. 40-51-47-02.

According to an old proverb, to understand the French you must like Camembert cheese, the Pont Neuf, and the dome of Val-de-Grâce.

After 23 years of a barren marriage to Louis XIII, Anne of Austria gave birth to a boy who would one day be known as the Sun King. In those days, if monarchs wanted to express gratitude, they built a church or monastery. On April 1, 1645, seven years after his birth, the future Louis XIV laid the first stone of the church. At that time, Mansart was the architect. To him we owe the façade in the Jesuit style. Le Duc, however, designed the dome, and the painter Mignard decorated it with frescoes. Other architects included Le Mercier and Le Muet.

The origins of the church go back even further, to 1050, when a Benedictine monastery was founded on the grounds. In 1619 Marguerite Veni d'Arbouze was appointed abbess by Louis XIII. She petitioned Anne of Austria for a new monastery, as the original one was decaying. Then came Louis XIV's church, which in 1793 was turned into a military hospital and in 1850 an army school.

Admission: Free.

Open: Mon–Sat 9am–noon and 2–5pm. Touring prohibited during services. **Métro:** Port-Royal. To reach it, walk up rue Val-de-Grâce from Boulevard St-Michel. **Bus:** 38.

ST-ETIENNE-DU-MONT, place Ste-Geneviève, 5e. Tel. 43-54-11-79.

Once there was an abbey on this site, founded by Clovis and later dedicated to Ste. Geneviève, the patroness of Paris. Such was the fame of this popular saint that the abbey proved too small to accommodate the pilgrimage crowds. Now part of the Lycée Henri IV, the **Tower of Clovis** is all that remains from the ancient abbey (you can see the Tower from rue Clovis).

Today the task of keeping alive the cult of Ste. Geneviéve has fallen on the Church of St-Etienne-du-Mont, on Place Ste-Geneviève, practically adjoining the Panthéon. The interior is in the Gothic style, unusual for a 16th-century church. Construction on the present building began in 1492 and lasted until 1626.

Besides the patroness of Paris, such men as Pascal and Racine were entombed in the church. Incidentally, the tomb of the saint was destroyed during the Revolution. However, the stone on which her coffin rested was discovered later, and the relics were gathered for a place of honor at St. Étienne.

The church possesses a remarkable rood screen, built in the first part of the 16th century. Across the nave, it is unique in Paris—uncharitably called spurious by some, although others have hailed it as a masterpiece. Another treasure is a wood-carved pulpit, held up by a semi-nude Samson who clutches a bone in one hand, having slain the lion at his feet. The fourth chapel on the right (when entering) contains most impressive stained glass, from the 16th century.

Open: Daily 7:30am–noon and 2:30–7pm. **Closed:** Mon July–Aug. **Métro:** Cardinal-Lemoine.

ST-GERMAIN L'AUXERROIS, 2, place du Louvre, 1er. Tel. 42-60-13-96.

Once it was the church for the Palace of the Louvre, drawing an assortment of courtesans, men of art and of law, artisans from the quartier, even royalty. Sharing the Place du Louvre with Perrault's colonnade, the church contains only the foundation stones of its original belfry built in the 11th century. It was greatly enlarged in the 14th century by the addition of side aisles. The little primitive chapel that had stood on the spot eventually gave way to a great and beautiful church, with 260 feet of stained glass, including some rose windows from the Renaissance.

The saddest moment in its history was on August 24, 1572. The unintentional ringing of its bells signaled the St. Bartholomew Massacre, in which the Protestants suffered a blood bath. The churchwardens' pews are outstanding, with intricate carving, based on designs by Le Brun in the 17th century. Behind the pew is a 15th-century triptych and Flemish retable (so badly lit you can hardly appreciate it). The organ was originally ordered by Louis XVI for the Sainte Chapelle. In that architectural mélange, many famous men were entombed, including the sculptor Coysevox and Le Vau, the architect. Around the chancel is an intricate 18th-century grille.

Open: Daily 8am–7:30pm. **Métro:** Musée-du-Louvre.

CHURCH OF ST-SEVERIN, rue des Prêtres, 5e. Tel. 43-25-96-63.

This flamboyant Gothic building, just a short walk from the Seine, hardly recaptures the lifestyle of its namesake, the ascetic recluse of the 6th century. An act of Henri I in the 11th century gave the church to Paris, and by the end of the 15th century it was imitating some of the architectural features of Notre-Dame across the river. In the 17th century Mlle de Montpensier (La Grande Mademoiselle) was one of its parishioners and certainly its heaviest financial contributor.

Before entering, walk around the church to see its gargoyles, birds of prey, and reptilian monsters projecting from the top. To the right, facing the church, is the "garden of ossuaries" of the 15th century. The entrance on rue des Prêtres leads to the wide interior. Inside, the stained glass is its most obvious adornment—in cobalt, burgundy, amber, magenta, white-gold, royal-blue, indigo, oyster-pink, ruby-red. It is interesting to contrast the modern stained glass by Jean Bazaine in 1970 with the panels from the 14th and 15th centuries.

The present church was built from 1210 to 1230, then reconstructed in 1458. The tower was completed in 1487, the chapels between 1498 and 1520. Hardouin-Mansart designed the Chapel of the Communion in 1673 when he was 27 years old.

Admission: Free.
Open: Daily 8am–7pm. **Metro:** St-Michel or Maubert-Mutualité.

5. GARDENS & PARKS

We've already walked through the Jardin des Tuileries (in "The Top Attractions: The Grand Promenade"). In this section we explore some other oases, beginning with the—

JARDIN DU LUXEMBOURG, 6e. Tel. 43-29-12-78.

Hemingway told a friend that the Luxembourg Gardens "kept us from starvation." He related that in his poverty-stricken days in Paris, he wheeled a baby carriage (the vehicle was considered luxurious) and child through the gardens because it was known "for the classiness of its pigeons." When the gendarme went across the street for a glass of wine, the writer would eye his victim, preferably a plump one, then lure him with corn . . . "snatch him, wring his neck," then flip him under Bumby's blanket. "We got a little tired of pigeon that year," he confessed, "but they filled many a void."

Before it became a feeding ground for struggling Montparnasse artists of the 1920s, Luxembourg knew greater days. But it's always been associated with artists, although students from the Sorbonne and children predominate nowadays. Watteau came this way, as did Verlaine. Balzac, however, didn't like the gardens at all. In 1905 Gertrude Stein would cross the gardens to catch the Batignolles-Clichy-Odéon omnibus pulled by three gray mares across Paris, to meet Picasso in his studio at Montmartre, where she sat while he painted her portrait.

The gardens are the best on the Left Bank (some say in all of Paris). Marie de Medici, the much-neglected wife and later widow of the roving Henri IV, ordered a palace built on the site in 1612. She planned to live there with her "witch" friend, Leonora Galigaï. A Florentine by birth, the regent wanted to create another Pitti Palace, or so she ordered the architect, Salomon de Brossee. She wasn't entirely successful, although the overall effect is most often described as Italianate.

The queen didn't get to enjoy the palace for very long after it was finished. She was forced into exile by her son, Louis XIII, after it was discovered that she was plotting to overthrow him. Reportedly, she died in Germany in poverty, quite a comedown from that luxury she had once known in the Luxembourg. Incidentally, the 21 paintings she commissioned from Rubens that glorified her life were intended for her palace, although they are now in the Louvre. The palace can't be visited without special permission in advance.

But you don't come to the Luxembourg to visit the palace, not really. The gardens are the attraction. For the most part, they are in the classic French tradition: well groomed and formally laid out, the trees planted in designs. A large water basin in the center is encircled with urns and statuary on pedestals—one honoring Ste. Geneviéve, the patroness of Paris, depicted with pigtails reaching to her thighs. Another memorial is dedicated to Stendhal.

Crowds throng through the park on May Day, when Parisians carry their traditional lilies of the valley. Birds sing, and all of Paris (those who didn't go to the country) celebrates the rebirth of spring.

Admission: Park, free; palace, special permission required in advance.
Métro: Odéon. **RER:** Luxembourg.

BOIS DE BOULOGNE, Porte Dauphine, 16e. Tel. 40-67-97-02.

One of the greatest and most spectacular parks in Europe, the Bois is often called the main lung of Paris. Horse-drawn carriages traverse it, but you can also take your car through. Many of its hidden pathways, however, must be discovered by walking. If you had a week to spare, you could spend it all in the Bois de Boulogne and still not see everything.

Porte Dauphine is the main entrance, although you can take the Métro to Porte Maillot as well. West of Paris, the park was once a forest kept for royal hunts. In the late 19th century it was in vogue. Carriages containing elegantly attired and coiffured Parisian damsels with their foppish escorts rumbled along the Avenue Foch.

Nowadays, it's more likely to attract picnickers from the middle class. (And at night, hookers and muggers are prominent, so be duly warned.)

When Emperor Napoleon III gave the grounds to the city of Paris in 1852, they were developed by Baron Haussmann. Separating Lac Inférieur from Lac Supérieur is the Carrefour des Cascades (you can stroll under its waterfall). The Lower Lake contains two islands connected by a footbridge. From the east bank, you can take a boat to these idyllically situated grounds, perhaps stopping off at the café-restaurant on one of them.

Restaurants in the Bois are numerous, elegant, and expensive. The Pre-Catelan contains a deluxe restaurant of the same name and a Shakespearean theater in a garden said to have been planted with trees mentioned in the bard's plays.

The **Jardin d'Acclimation** at the northern edge of the Bois de Boulogne is for children, with a small zoo, an amusement park, and a narrow-gauge railway. (See "Cool for Kids," below for more details.)

Two **racetracks,** Longchamp and the Auteuil, are in the park. The annual Grand Prix is run in June at Longchamp (the site of a medieval abbey). The most fashionable people of Paris turn out, the women gowned in their finest haute couture. Directly to the north of Longchamp is Grand Cascade, the artificial waterfall of the Bois de Boulogne.

In the 60-acre Bagatelle Park, the Comte d'Artois (later Charles X) brother-in-law of Marie Antoinette, made a bet with her—he could erect a small palace in less than three months—and won. If you're in Paris in late April, go to the **Bagatelle** to look at the tulips, if for no other reason. In late May one of the finest and best-known rose collections in all of Europe is in full bloom.

Note: Beware of muggers and prostitutes at night.

Métro: Les-Sablons, Porte-Maillot, or Porte Dauphine.

PARC MONCEAU, 8e. Tel. 42-27-39-56.

One widely known American writer once said that all babies in the Parc Monceau were respectable. Having never known one who wasn't, I can only agree with the pundit. At any rate, babies like Parc Monceau. Or at least their mothers and/or nurses are fond of wheeling their carriages through it. Much of the park is ringed with 18th- and 19th-century mansions, some of them evoking Proust's *Remembrance of Things Past.*

The park was opened to the public in the days of Napoleon III's Second Empire. It was built in 1778 by the Duke of Orléans, or Philippe-Égalité, as he became known. Carmontelle designed the park for the duke, who was considered at the time the richest man in France. "Philip Equality" was noted for his debauchery and his pursuit of pleasure. No ordinary park would do.

Monceau was laid out with an Egyptian-style obelisk, a dungeon of the Middle Ages, a thatched alpine farmhouse, a Chinese pagoda, a Roman temple, an enchanted grotto, various chinoiseries, and of course a waterfall. These fairytale touches have largely disappeared except for a pyramid and an oval *naumachie* fringed by a colonnade. Many of the former fantasies have been replaced with solid statuary and monuments, one honoring Chopin. In spring, the red tulips and magnolias are worth the air ticket to Paris.

Métro: Monceau or Villiers.

6. COOL FOR KIDS

Boasting playgrounds with tiny merry-go-rounds and gondola-style swings, the large parks of Paris are always a treat for kids.

If you're staying on the Right Bank, take the children for a stroll through the Tuileries (see "The Top Attractions," above in this chapter), where there are donkey rides, ice-cream stands, and a marionette show; at the circular pond, you can rent a toy sailboat. On the Left Bank, similar delights exist in the Jardin du Luxembourg (see

"Gardens and Parks" above in this chapter). After a visit to the Eiffel tower, you can take the kids for a donkey ride in the nearby gardens of the Champ-de-Mars (see "The Top Attractions", above in this chapter).

A great Paris tradition, puppet shows are worth seeing for their enthusiastic, colorful productions—they're a genuine French child's experience.

At the Jardin du Luxembourg, you'll see puppet productions with sinister plots set in Gothic castles and Oriental palaces; some young critics say the best puppet shows are held in the Champ-de-Mars (performance times at the Luxembourg Gardens and Champs-de-Mars vary). In the Tuileries there are shows on Wednesday, Saturday, and Sunday at 3:15pm all summer long.

On Sunday afternoons, French families head up to the Butte Montmarte to bask in the fiesta atmosphere. You can join in the fun: Take the Métro to Anvers and walk to the Funiculaire de Montmarte (the silver cable car that carries you up to Sacré-Coeur). Once up top, follow the crowds to place du Tertre, where a band will usually be blasting off-key and where you can have the kids' picture sketched by local artists. You can take in the views of Paris from the various vantage points and treat the kids to ice cream in an outdoor café.

A ZOO

PARC ZOOLOGIQUE DE PARIS, Bois de Vincennes, 53, av. de Saint-Maurice, 12e. Tel. 43-43-84-95.
There is a modest zoo in the Jardin des Plantes, near the natural history museum. But without a doubt, the best zoo Paris has to offer is in the Bois de Vincennes—it's on the outskirts but quickly reached by subway. This modern zoo displays its animals in settings similar to their natural habitats. The lion has an entire veldt to itself, and you can view each other comfortably across a deep protective moat. On a concrete mountain reminiscent of Disneyland's Matterhorn, lovely Barbary sheep leap from ledge to ledge or pose gracefully for hours watching the penguins in their pools at the mountain's foot. The animals seem happy here and are consequently playful. Keep well back from the bear pools.

Admission: 35 F ($6.30) adults, 20 F ($3.60) students and those over 60, 7 F ($1.20) children under 18.
Open: Mon–Sat 9am–5:30pm, Sun 9am–6pm. **Métro:** Porte-Dorée.

AN AMUSEMENT PARK

JARDIN D'ACCLIMATION, Bois de Boulogne, 16e. Tel. 40-67-90-82.
The definitive children's park in Paris is the Jardin d'Acclimation, a 25-acre amusement park on the northern edge of the Bois de Boulogne. The visit starts with a ride from Porte Maillot to the jardin entrance, through a stretch of wooded park, on a jaunty green-and-yellow narrow-gauge train. Inside the gate is an easy-to-follow layout map. The park is circular—follow the road in either direction and it will take you all the way around and bring you back to the train at the end. En route you will discover a house of funny mirrors, an archery range, a miniature-golf course, zoo animals, an American-style bowling alley, a puppet theater (performances only on Thursday, Saturday, Sunday, and holidays), a playground, a hurdle-racing course, and a whole conglomeration of junion-scale rides, shooting galleries, and waffle stalls.

You can trot the kids off on a pony or join them in a boat on a lagoon. Also fun to watch is "La Prévention Routière," a miniature roadway operated by the Paris police. The youngsters drive through in small cars equipped to start and stop and are required by two genuine Parisian gendarmes to obey all street signs and light changes.

Admission: 9F ($1.60) adults, 4 F (70¢) children.
Open: Mon–Sat 10am–6:30pm, Sun 10am–7:30pm. **Métro:** Les-Sablons.

MUSEUMS

Set within the city's largest park and having special areas dedicated to children, the **Cité des Sciences et de l'Industrie** is one of the best museums for kids in Paris; for a full description, see "More Museums," above in this chapter.

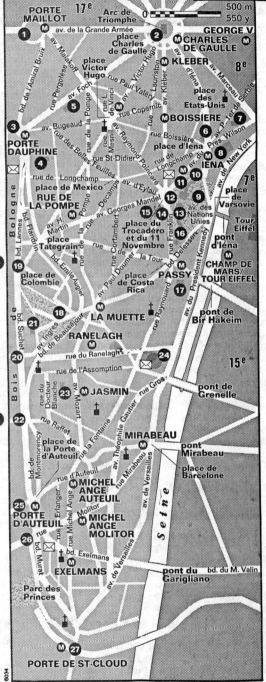

PARIS

16e Arrondissement

Church ✝

Post Office ⊠

Métro Ⓜ

MUSÉE DE LA MARINE (Marine Museum), Palais de Chaillot, 16e. Tel. 45-53-31-70.

A lot of what is here is pomp: gilded galleys and busts of stiff-necked admirals. There's a great number of old ship models, including, for instance, the big galley *La Réale*, the *Royal-Louis*, the rich ivory model *Ville de Dieppe*, the gorgeous *Valmy*. A barge constructed in 1811 for Napoleon I was used to carry another Napoleon (the Third) and his empress, Eugenie, on their first visit to the port of Brest in about 1858. The imperial crown is held up by winged cherubs.

There are many documents and artifacts concerning merchant fishing and pleasure fleets, oceanography, hydrography, with films illustrating the subjects. Thematic exhibits explain, for instance, ancient wooden shipbuilding, development of scientific instruments, merchant navy, fishing, steam, and sea traditions, and show some souvenirs of explorer Laperouse's wreck in Vanikoro Island in 1788. Important paintings include Joseph Vernet's *The Ports of France* during the 18th century.

Admission: 28 F ($5) adults, 14 F ($2.50) children 5–12 and seniors over 60, free for children under 5.

Open: Wed–Mon 10am–6pm. **Métro:** Trocadéro.

MUSÉE DE L'HOMME, Palais de Chaillot, 16e. Tel. 45-53-70-60.

This museum, which deserves to be better known, is devoted to the history of people and their way of life.

A case contains the most important exhibit, the Cro-Magnon "Menton man," discovered in 1872 in the Grimaldi grottoes on the French Riviera. Among the replicas are South African and Sahara cave paintings. One long gallery depicts African cultures, with some of the best-known pieces of African art. Then follow Ethiopia, with a beautiful and rare set of church paintings, North Africa, the Middle East, and Europe, with a series of traditional garb displayed. The upstairs galleries are filled with representative artifacts from the Arctic, Asia, Oceania, and the Americas. The North American section contains some of the oldest Plains Indian pieces in existence. Of particular note are the chaman costumes from Siberia, the renewed exhibits dealing with Laos and Cambodia, a complete set of door carvings from New Caledonia, some of the best-known carvings from Polynesia, and pre-Columbian art from South and Central America.

One room is turned over to temporary exhibitions, dealing with prehistoric or ethnographical themes. A library sells scientific books dealing with the history of man and his cultures. On the third floor, a Photographic Documentation Department (Photothèque) is also open to the public.

Admission: 25 F ($4.50) adults, 15 F ($2.70) children 7–18, free for children under 7.

Open: Daily 9:45am–5:15pm. **Métro:** Trocadéro.

MUSÉE GRÉVIN, 10, bd. Montmarte, 9e. Tel. 47-70-85-06.

The desire to compare this museum in Montmartre to Madame Tussaud's of London is almost irresistible. Grévin is the number-one waxworks of Paris. It isn't all blood and gore, and doesn't shock some as Tussaud's might. Presenting a panorama of French history from Charlemagne to the mistress-collecting Napoleon III, it shows memorable moments in a series of tableaux.

Depicted are the consecration of Charles VII in 1429 in the Cathedral of Reims (Joan of Arc, dressed in armor and carrying her standard, stands behind the king); Marguerite de Valois, first wife of Henri IV, meeting on a secret stairway with La Molle, who was soon to be decapitated; Catherine de Medici with the Florentine alchemist Ruggieri; Louis XV and Mozart at the home of the Marquise de Pompadour; and Napoleon on a rock at St. Helena, reviewing his victories and defeats.

There are also displays of contemporary sports and political figures, as well as 50 of the world's best loved film stars.

Two shows are staged frequently throughout the day. The first, called the "Palais des Mirages," starts off as a sort of Temple of Brahma, and through magically distorting mirrors, changes into an enchanted forest, then a fête at the Alhambra at Granada. A magician is the star of the second show, "Le Cabinet Fantastique"; he entertains children of all ages.

Admission: 48 F ($8.60) adults, 34 F ($6.10) children under 14.

Open: June–Sept, daily 10am–7pm; Oct–May, daily 1–7pm (ticket office closes at 6pm). **Métro:** Montmartre or Richelieu-Drouot.

MUSEE NATIONAL D'HISTOIRE NATURELLE (Museum of Natural History), 57, rue Cuvier, 5e. Tel. 40-69-30-30.

Founded in 1635 as a scientific research center, this Museum of Natural History, in the Jardin des Plantes, today has a wide range of exhibits—including galleries of paleontology, anatomy, mineralogy, and botany, with massive skeletons of dinosaurs and mastodons, among many other collections.

Within the museum's grounds are tropical hothouses containing thousands of species of unusual plant life and a menagerie with small animal life in simulated natural habitats.

Admission: 18 F ($3.20) adults, 12.50 F ($2.25) children under 18.

Open: Wed–Mon 10am–5pm. **Métro:** Jussieu or Austerlitz.

PALAIS DE LA DECOUVERTE (Palais of Discovery), Grand Palais, av. F-D-Roosevelt, 8e. Tel. 43-59-18-21.

Although everything here is in French, if your kids are interested in science take them to the Palais of Discovery anyway. With live experiments to watch, daily science films, special temporary exhibits, machines to test your muscular reactions—this is a real funhouse. White-coated technicians give more than 50 lectures a day on physics, chemistry, and biology.

Admission: 20 F ($3.60) adults, 10 F ($1.80) children under 18 and those over 60. Planetarium show, 13 F ($2.30) per person extra.

Open: Palais, Tues–Sat 9:30am–6pm; Sun 10am–7pm. Planetarium shows, Tues–Fri at 11am, 2pm, 3:15pm, 4:30pm; Sat–Sun at 11:30am, 2pm, 3:15pm, 4:30pm, and 5:45pm. **Métro:** F-D Roosevelt or Champs-Elysées–Clemenceau.

7. SPECIAL-INTEREST SIGHTSEEING

FOR THE LITERARY ENTHUSIAST

MAISON DE VICTOR HUGO, 6, place des Vosges, 4e. Tel. 42-72-16-65.

Appraisals of Hugo have been varied. Some have called him a genius. Cocteau said he was a madman, and an American composer discovered that in the folly of his dotage he carved furniture—with his teeth! From 1832 to 1848 the novelist and poet lived on the second floor at 6 Place des Vosges, in the old Hôtel Rohan Guéménée, built in 1610 on what was then the Place Royale. His maison is owned by the city of Paris, which has taken over two additional floors.

A leading figure in the French Romantic movement, Hugo is known for such novels as *The Hunchback of Notre Dame* and *Les Misérables*. The museum owns some of Hugo's furniture as well as pieces that once belonged to Juliette Drouet, the mistress with whom he lived in exile on Guernsey, one of the Channel Islands.

Worth the visit are Hugo's drawings, more than 450, illustrating scenes from his own works. See, in particular, his *Le Serpent*. Mementos of the great writer abound: samples of his handwriting, his inkwell, first editions of his works, and the death mask in his bedroom. A painting of his funeral procession at the Arc de Triomphe in 1885 is on display. Portraits and souvenirs of Hugo's family are also plentiful. Of the furnishings, especially interesting is a chinoiserie salon. The collection even contains Daumier caricatures and a bust of Hugo by David d'Angers, which—when compared to Rodin's—looks saccharine.

Admission: 12 F ($2.10) adults, 6.50 F ($1.10) children under 19.

Open: Wed–Sun 10am–5:40pm. **Closed:** Holidays. **Métro:** St-Paul, Bastille, or Chemin-Vert.

MAISON DE BALZAC, 47, rue Raynouard, 16e. Tel. 42-24-56-38.
In the residential district of Passy, near the Bois de Boulogne, sits a modest house. Here the great Balzac lived for seven years beginning in 1840. Fleeing there after his possessions and furnishings were seized, Balzac cloaked himself in secrecy (you had to know a password to be ushered into his presence). Should a creditor knock on the Raynouard door, Balzac could always escape through the rue Berton exit.

The museum's most notable memento is the Limoges coffee pot (the novelist's initials are in mulberry pink) that his "screech-owl" kept hot throughout the night as he wrote *La Comédie Humaine* to stall his creditors. Also enshrined here are Balzac's writing desk and chair. It also contains a library of special interest to scholars.

The little house is filled with reproductions of caricatures of Balzac. (A French biographer once wrote: "With his bulky baboon silhouette, his blue suit with gold

---

IN THEIR FOOTSTEPS

Victor Hugo (1802–85) The leading author of the French Romantic movement, Victor Hugo wrote novels, plays, and lyric poems. His most famous works were *Les Misérables* (1862) and *The Hunchback of Notre Dame* (1831). A highly controversial figure, Hugo was a hero to the liberals of his era, but a demon to the conservatives and imperialists. For several years he lived in exile on the Channel island of Guernsey, writing scathing denunciations of the Napoleonic dynasty, including one pamphlet entitled *Napoléon le Petit.*
- **Birthplace:** Besançon, at the Mission Barrette on place St-Quentin, on February 26, 1802. Son of a French captain sent there to command a battalion.
- **Residences:** Most famous was 6, place des Vosges in Paris, the old Hôtel Rohan-Guéménée, built in 1610 and now a museum. He also lived at 21, rue de Clichy sometime after 1870; he died at what is now 124, av. Victor-Hugo. A statue of the novelist at place Victor-Hugo honors him.
- **Favorite Haunts:** Le Procope, 13, rue de l'Ancienne-Comédie, in Paris, the oldest café in Paris (and still going); Théâtre l'Odéon (now Théâtre de France), where his controversial play *Hernani* opened in 1830.
- **Resting Place:** The Panthéon. When he died on May 22, 1885, his body lay in state for 24 hours beneath the Arc de Triomphe in Paris. Thousands of mourners followed the unadorned hearse to the Left Bank.

Colette (1873–1954) The creator of *Gigi*, *Chéri*, and *Claudine in Paris*, celebrated as much for her controversial personality as for her writings.
- **Birthplace:** St. Sauveur-en-Puisaye in Burgundy (the "Montigny" of her early Claudine novels), on January 28, 1873.
- **Residences:** At 20 she married Belle Epoque newspaper publisher Henri Gauthier-Villars and settled in Left Bank Paris at 18, rue Jacob, where she wrote and did "miming" in music halls. By 1920, with the publication of *Chéri*, she had become famous. During her second marriage, to Henri de Jouvenel, she lived at the Château de Castel-Novel in the Dordogne (now a hotel). Her final address was 9, rue de Beaujolais at the Palais Royal in Paris.
- **Favorite Haunts:** Grand Véfour, the deluxe restaurant at the Palais Royal in Paris; the Moulin Rouge, where in 1907 she was involved in *Le Scandale du Moulin-Rouge*, in which her kiss to the marquise de Belboeuf brought out the police who closed the performance.
- **Resting Place:** The archbishop of Paris refused her burial service at the Eglise Saint-Roche, and she was interred at Père-Lachaise cemetery—marked by a tombstone of black and rose-colored granite, following a state funeral at the Palais Royal.

buttons, his famous cane like a golden crowbar, and his abundant, disheveled hair, Balzac was a sight for caricature.")

The house is built on the slope of a hill, with a small courtyard and garden.

Admission: 12 F ($2.10) adults, 6.50 F ($1.10) children 18 and under, free for seniors over 60.

Open: Tues–Sun 10am–5:40pm. **Métro:** Passy or La-Muette.

FOR THE UNDERGROUND ENTHUSIAST

CATACOMBS, 1, place Denfert-Rochereau, 14e. Tel. 43-22-47-63.

Every year an estimated 50,000 tourists explore some 1,000 yards of tunnel in these dank Catacombs to look at some six million skeletons ghoulishly arranged in artistic skull-and-crossbones fashion. It has been called the empire of the dead. First opened to the public in 1810, the Catacombs are now illuminated with overhead electric lights over their entire length.

In the Middle Ages the Catacombs were originally quarries, but in 1785 city officials decided to use them as a burial ground. So the bones of several million persons were moved here from their previous resting places, the overcrowded cemeteries being considered health menaces. In 1830 the prefect of Paris closed the Catacombs to the viewing public, considering them obscene and indecent. He maintained that he could not understand the morbid curiosity of civilized people who wanted to gaze upon the bones of the dead. Later, in World War II, the Catacombs were the headquarters of the French Underground.

Admission: 15 F ($2.70) adults, 10 F ($1.80) children under 18.

Open: Tues–Fri 2–4pm, Sat–Sun 9–11am and 2–4pm. **Métro:** Denfert-Rochereau.

THE SEWERS OF PARIS (Les Egouts de Paris), pont de l'Alma 7e. Tel. 47-05-10-29.

Some say Baron Haussmann will be remembered mainly for the vast, complicated network of Paris sewers he erected. The *égouts* of the city, as well as telephone and telegraph pneumatic tubes, are constructed around a quartet of principal tunnels, one 18 feet wide and 15 feet high. It's like an underground city, with the street names clearly labeled. Further, each branch pipe bears the number of the building to which it is connected. These underground passages are truly mammoth, containing pipes bringing in drinking water and compressed air as well as telephone and telegraph lines.

That these sewers have remained such a popular attraction is something of a curiosity. They were made famous by Victor Hugo's *Les Misérables*. "All dripping with slime, his soul filled with a strange light," Jean Valjean in his desperate flight through the sewers of Paris is considered one of the heroes of narrative drama.

Tours begin at Pont de l'Alma on the Left Bank. A stairway there leads into the bowels of the city. However, you often have to wait in line as much as half an hour. Visiting times might change when there is bad weather, as a storm can make the sewers dangerous. The tour consists of seeing a movie on sewer history, visiting a small museum, and then a short trip through the maze.

Warning: This is not the atmosphere of *Les Misérables* with Jean Valjean, because the sewers are perilous without light, odoriferous, and deep. But the visit at the Pont de l'Alma is interesting and draws many tourists.

Admission: 22 F ($3.90) adults, 17 F ($3) ages 18–24 and over 60.

Open: Sat–Wed 11am–5pm. **Closed:** Three weeks in Jan for maintenance. **Métro:** Alma-Marceau. **RER:** Pont de l'Alma.

"THE GRANDEST ADDRESS IN PARIS"

CEMETIERE DU PERE-LACHAISE, 16 rue de Repos, 20e. Tel. 43-70-70-33.

When it comes to name-dropping, this cemetery knows no peer; it's been called the "grandest address in Paris." Everybody from Madame Bernhardt to Oscar Wilde (his tomb by Epstein) was buried here. So were Balzac, Delacroix, and Bizet. The body of Colette was taken here in 1954, and in time the little sparrow, Piaf, would follow. The lover of George Sand, Alfred de Musset, the poet, was buried under a weeping willow. Napoleon's marshals, Ney and Masséna, were entombed here, as were Chopin and Molière. Marcel Proust's black tombstone rarely lacks a tiny bunch of violets. Colette's black granite slab always sports flowers, and legend has it that the cats replenish the red roses.

Some tombs are sentimental favorites, the tomb of Jim Morrison, American rock star who died in 1971, reportedly drawing the most visitors. The great dancer Isadora Duncan is reduced to a "pigeon hole" in the Columbarium where bodies have been cremated and then "filed." If you search hard enough, you can find the tombs of that star-crossed pair, Abélard and Héloïse, the ill-fated lovers of the 12th century. At Père-Lachaise they have found peace at last. Lovers of a different kind can also be found here. One stone is marked Alice B. Toklas on one side, Gertrude Stein on another.

Spreading over more than 40 acres, Père-Lachaise was acquired by the city of Paris in 1804. Nineteenth-century French sculpture abounds, each family trying to outdo the other in ornamentation and cherubic ostentation. Some French Socialists still pay tribute at the Mur des Fédérés, the anonymous grave site of the Communards who were executed on May 28, 1871. Frenchmen who died in the Resistance or in Nazi concentration camps are also honored by the monument.

A guide at the entrance may give you a map outlining some of the well-known grave sites.

Open: Mar 15–Nov 5, Mon–Fri 7:30am–6pm, Sat 8:30am–6pm, Sun 9am–6pm; Nov 6–Mar 14, Mon–Fri 8am–5:30pm, Sat 8:30am–5:30pm, Sun 9am–5:30pm. **Métro:** Père-Lachaise.

FOR VISITING AMERICANS

HARRY'S NEW YORK BAR, 5, rue Daunou, 2e. Tel. 42-61-71-14.

F. Scott Fitzgerald and Ernest Hemingway drank a lot here, Gloria Swanson talked about her affair with Joseph Kennedy, and even Gertrude Stein showed up. And the place is still going strong. See also "Specialty Bars and Clubs" in Chapter 10.

Métro: Opéra or Pyramides.

LA ROTONDE, 105, bd. Montparnasse, 6e. Tel. 43-26-68-84.

Americans tended to drink on the Right Bank, notably in the Ritz Bar, when they had money. When they didn't, they headed for one of the cafés of Montparnasse, which, according to Hemingway, usually meant La Rotonde.

Métro: Raspail.

DEUX MAGOTS, 170, bd. St-Germain, 6e. Tel. 45-48-55-25.

This long-established watering hole of St-Germain-des-Prés is where Jake Barnes meets Lady Brett in Hemingway's *The Sun Also Rises*.

Métro: St-Germain-des-Prés.

SHAKESPEARE AND COMPANY, 37, rue de la Bûcherie, 5e.

The most famous bookstore on the Left Bank was Shakespeare and Company, on rue de l'Odéon, home to the legendary Sylvia Beach, the "mother confessor to the Lost Generation." Hemingway, Fitzgerald, and Gertrude Stein were all frequent patrons. In recent decades, visitors would be likely to find Anaïs Nin, the diarist noted for her descriptions of struggling American artists in 1930s Paris, in the store. At one point she helped her companion, Henry Miller, publish *Tropic of Cancer,* a book so notorious in its day that returning Americans trying to slip a copy through Customs often had it confiscated as pornography. When times were hard, Ms. Nin herself wrote pornography at a dollar a page.

Today the shop is located on rue de la Bûcherie, where expatriates still come to swap books and the latest literary gossip.

Open: Daily 11am–midnight. **Métro:** St-Michel.

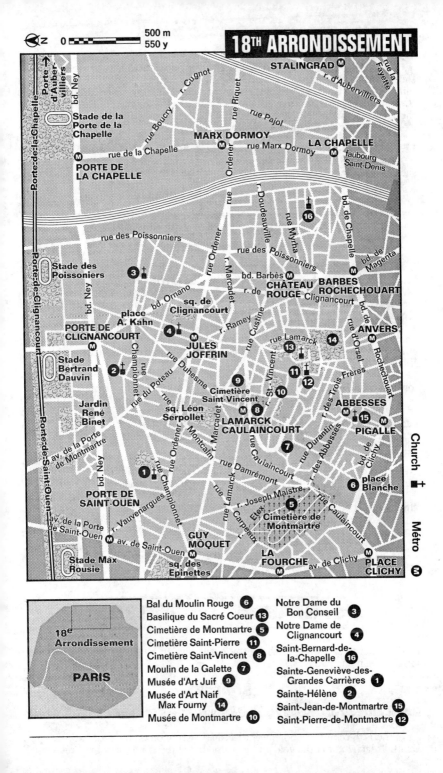

18TH ARRONDISSEMENT

0   500 m
550 y

STALINGRAD

Stade de la
Porte de la
Chapelle

MARX DORMOY

LA CHAPELLE

faubourg
Saint-Denis

PORTE DE
LA CHAPELLE

rue de la Chapelle

r. Cugnot

rue Riquet

rue Pajol

rue Marx Dormoy

rue de la Chapelle

bd. Ney

rue Boucy

Porte
d'Auber-
villiers

rue la
Fayette

r. d'Aubervilliers

bd. de Chapelle

bd. de
Magenta

Porte-de-la-Chapelle

Porte-de-Clignancourt

Porte-de-Saint-Ouen

rue des Poissonniers

Stade des
Poissoniers

rue des Poissonniers

bd. Barbès

CHÂTEAU
ROUGE

BARBES
ROCHECHOUART

Clignancourt

ANVERS

bd. Ney

bd. Ornano

place
A. Kahn

sq. de
Clignancourt

r. de Clignancourt

r. Marcadet

r. Ramey

rue Custine

rue Lamarck

r. des Trois Frères

bd. de Rochechouart

r. d'Orsel

PORTE DE
CLIGNANCOURT

Stade
Bertrand
Dauvin

JULES
JOFFRIN

rue Duhesme

rue Championnet

rue du Poteau

ABBESSES

PIGALLE

Jardin
René
Binet

Cimetière
Saint-Vincent

sq. Léon
Serpollet

LAMARCK
CAULAINCOURT

St-Vincent

Montcalm

r. des Abbesses

bd. de Clichy

rue Ordener

rue Marcadet

rue Caulaincourt

r. Durantin

PORTE DE
SAINT-OUEN

rue Championnet

rue Damrémont

rue Lamarck

place
Blanche

av. de la Porte
de Montmartre

r. Vauvenargues

rue Carpeaux

Etex.

r. Joseph Maistre

Cimetière de
Montmartre

rue Caulaincourt

av. de la Porte
de Saint-Ouen

Stade Max
Rousie

GUY
MOQUET

sq. des
Epinettes

av. de Saint-Ouen

LA
FOURCHE

av. de Clichy

PLACE
CLICHY

Church

Métro

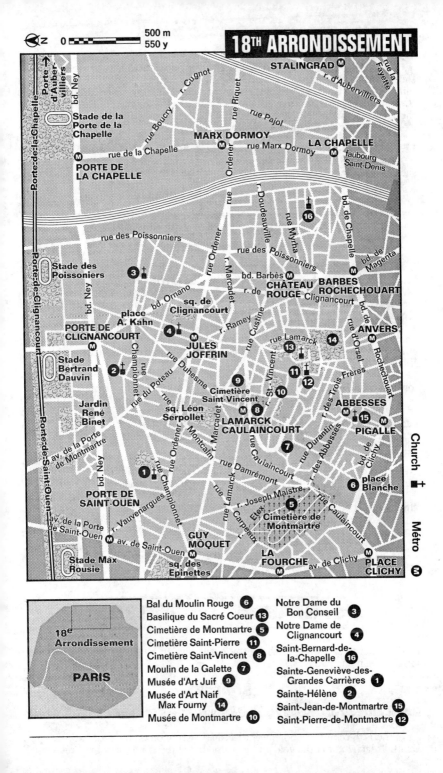

18e
Arrondissement

PARIS

Bal du Moulin Rouge **6**
Basilique du Sacré Coeur **13**
Cimetière de Montmartre **5**
Cimetière Saint-Pierre **11**
Cimetière Saint-Vincent **8**
Moulin de la Galette **7**
Musée d'Art Juif **9**
Musée d'Art Naif
  Max Fourny **14**
Musée de Montmartre **10**

Notre Dame du
  Bon Conseil **3**
Notre Dame de
  Clignancourt **4**
Saint-Bernard-de-
  la-Chapelle **16**
Sainte-Geneviève-des-
  Grandes Carrières **1**
Sainte-Hélène **2**
Saint-Jean-de-Montmartre **15**
Saint-Pierre-de-Montmartre **12**

2 RUE DE L'UNIVERSITE, 7e.

When Benjamin Franklin arrived in Paris in December 1776, he stayed here. In short time, he moved to 52, rue Jacob, 6e (Métro: St-Germain-des-Prés), and later, as minister to the Court at Versailles, he moved into the Hôtel de Valentinois, 62, rue Raynouard, 16e (Métro: Passy), about half a mile from the center of Paris. Beloved by the French, Franklin left Passy on July 11, 1785, at the age of 79.

Métro: Rue-du-Bac or St-Germain.

LE PROCOPE, 13, rue l'Ancienne-Comédie, 6e. Tel. 43-26-99-20.

Dating from 1686, this is the oldest café in Paris and the restaurant of choice for such historical figures as Franklin and Jefferson (see "5th and 6th Arr." in Chapter 6).

Métro: Odéon.

8. SPECIAL & FREE EVENTS

It won't cost you a franc to explore the streets of Paris. Walk along the quays of the Seine, browse through the shops and stalls; each street opens onto a new vista.

If you're an early riser, a walk through Paris at dawn can be memorable; you'll see the city come to life. Shopfronts are washed clean for the new day, cafés open, and vegetable vendors arrange their produce.

The spacious forecourt of the Centre Georges Pompidou, place Georges-Pompidou, is a free "entertainment center" featuring mimes, fire-eaters, would-be circus performers, and sometimes first-rate musicians. Métro: Rambuteau or Hôtel de Ville.

In the corridors of the Métro, classical music students (often from the Conservatoire National) perform; a hat (or violin case) is passed for donations.

If you're in Paris during one of the major festivals, you can join in the fun on the streets for free. On Summer Solstice (June 21), clowns, fire-eaters, and other performers roam the streets. On Bastille Day (July 14), the French traditionally drink wine and dance in the streets—fireworks are displayed, free concerts are given, and a parade of tanks heads down the Champs-Elysées.

Many cultural events (such as concerts, films, and lectures) in Paris are free; these events are often sponsored by foreign nations, such as Great Britain. Inquire at the Centre Culturel Britannique, 9-11, rue de Constantine, 7e (tel. 49-55-73-00).

For wonderful free organ concerts in some of the city's old churches on Sunday afternoons, check *Pariscope,* the guide to entertainment events.

Free concerts featuring jazz, classical, and contemporary music from the Netherlands are held at the Institut Neerlandais, 121, rue de Lille, 7e (tel. 47-05-85-99; Métro: Assemblée-Nationale).

At the American Church, 65, quai d'Orsay, 7e (tel. 47-05-07-99; Métro: Invalides), free chamber-music concerts are presented.

9. NEARBY ATTRACTIONS

In the suburbs of Paris—reachable by either bus or Métro are more sightseeing targets, beginning with:

ST-DENIS

BASILIQUE ST-DENIS, 22 bis, rue Gabriel-Peri, St-Denis, 8e. Tel. 42-43-05-10.

In the 12th century Abbot Suger placed an inscription on the bronze doors of St. Denis: "Marvel not at the gold and expense, but at the craftsmanship of the work."

FROMMER'S FAVORITE PARIS EXPERIENCES

A Stroll Along the Faubourg St-Honoré In the 1700s it was home to the wealthiest of Parisians, but today it's home to the stores that cater to the wealthy. Even if you don't purchase anything, it's great window-shopping with all the big names: Hermès, Larouche, Courrèges, Cardin, St. Laurent, Lagerfeld.

A Languid Afternoon of Café Sitting The Parisian café is an integral part of life. Even if it means skipping a museum, spend some time at a café. Whether you have one small coffee or the most expensive cognac in the house, nobody will hurry you.

Afternoon Tea at Muscade Drinking tea in London has its charm, but the Parisian *salon de thé* is unique. Skip those cucumber-and-watercress sandwiches and get down to the business of rich, luscious desserts, like golden pains au chocolate. Muscade, 36, rue de Monpensier, 1er (tel. 42-97-51-36; Métro: Louvre), is open daily from 3:30 to 7pm. From May to September, you can sit on the garden terrace, enjoying a view of the rose garden of the Palais-Royal, as you savor a lush ruby-red strawberry tart.

A Night at the Ballet Renoir may have hated the building, but a night at the Opéra is still one of the highlights of any trip to Paris. The Opéra, at place de l'Opéra, is now the major center for ballet in Paris (the Opéra at the Bastille is for opera), and an evening here takes you back to the Second Empire world of marble and gilt and grand staircases, all sheltered under a controversial ceiling by Chagall. Dress with pomp and circumstance.

A Day at the Races Paris has eight racing tracks, some within the boundaries of the city. The most famous (and the classiest) is Longchamp, in the Bois de Boulogne, 16e. The site of the Prix de l'Arc de Triomphe and Grand Prix, Longchamp is considered the longest racetrack on earth. If it's a major social event, you'll have to dress up, of course. Take the Métro to Porte d'Auteuil, then a special bus from there to the track. *Paris-Turf,* the racing paper, has details about racing times.

The first Gothic building in France that can be dated precisely, St. Denis was the "spiritual defender of the State" during the reign of Louis VI ("The Fat"). The massive façade, with its crenelated parapet on the top similar to the fortifications of a castle, has a rose window. The stained-glass windows, in stunning colors—mauve, purple, blue, and rose—were restored in the 19th century. In the Middle Ages it was believed that Suger had ground up sapphires, emeralds, and rubies to create the rich colors.

St. Denis, the first bishop of Paris, became the patron saint of the French monarchy. Royal burials began here in the 6th century and continued until the Revolution. In all, it was the burial place of five royal dynasties. The church has had a long and colorful history. In 1429 Joan of Arc delivered up her arms here, and three centuries later Napoleon married Marie Louise. This is also considered "the birthplace of the Crusades." The sculptures designed for tombs—some two stories high—span the country's artistic development from the Middle Ages to the Renaissance. You are conducted through the crypt on a guided tour (in French only). François I was entombed at St. Denis. His funeral statue is nude, although he demurely covers himself with his hand. Other kings and queens here include Louis XII and Anne of Brittany, as well as Henri II and Catherine de Medici. However, the Revolutionaries stormed through, smashing many marble faces and dumping royal remains in a lime-filled ditch in the garden. Royal remains were reburied under the main altar during the 19th century.

Admission: 24 F ($4.30) adults, 13 F ($2.30) for those under 25 and over 60.

Open: Apr–Sept, daily 10am–7pm; Oct–Mar, daily 10am–5pm. **Métro:** St-Denis.

ECOUEN

This next sight can easily be tied in with a visit to St-Denis.

MUSEE NATIONAL DE LA RENAISSANCE, Chateau d'Ecouen, Ecouen. Tel. 39-90-04-04.

At a charmingly situated place right outside Paris, heading north on the route to Chantilly, Valéry Giscard d'Estaing, the former French president, inaugurated this museum devoted to works of the Renaissance. Called Le Château d'Ecouen, the castle in the hamlet of Ecouen was constructed between 1538 and 1555 for the high constable, Anne de Montmorency. In 1806 Napoleon assigned the building as a school for daughters of La Légion d'Honneur. On a promontory in a park-like setting, the château contains an exceptional collection of works from the Renaissance—tapestries, paintings, and objects of art—which betray a heavy Italian influence. See especially the best-known tapestry, *David and Bathsheba*, 245 feet long.

Admission: 20 F ($3.60) Mon–Sat, 13 F ($2.30) Sun.

Open: Wed–Mon 9:45am–12:30pm and 2–5:15pm. **Métro:** St-Denis/Porte-de-Paris; then bus no. 268C to Ezanville, which stops near the museum.

VINCENNES

A suburb of parks, Vincennes is about five miles east of Notre-Dame and is visited mainly for the Château de Vincennes. (See also Parc Zoologique in the Bois de Vincennes, previewed above in this chapter in "Cool for Kids.")

CHATEAU DE VINCENNES, av. de Paris, 12e.

It's been called the Versailles of the Middle Ages, and it's had a checkered career. Encircled by the once-great forest, the Bois de Vincennes, the château, like Versailles, was originally a hunting lodge. At the south of the town of Vincennes, the castle was founded by Louis VII ("The Young") in 1164, but it has subsequently been rebuilt many times. What you see today is merely a shell of its former self.

St. Louis (Louis IX) was fond of the castle; it is said that he administered justice while sitting under his favorite oak tree in the forest. Inspired by the Sainte Chapelle in Paris, Charles V ordered a chapel built in 1379. That "citizen of the world," Mazarin, and the mother of Louis XIV directed the completion of two pavilions.

Louis XIV, however, wasn't especially fond of Vincennes, because he had another home in mind. In time the château was to become a porcelain factory, an arsenal under Napoleon, and a supply depot for the Nazis. Now it is being restored by the government. Its most memorable role was that of a prison or dungeon, the most famous prisoner being Mirabeau, the French revolutionary and statesman.

Admission: 26 F ($4.60) for guided tour.

Open: May–Sept, daily 10am–7pm; Oct–Apr, daily 10am–5pm. **Métro:** Château-de-Vincennes. **RER:** Vincennes.

ST-GERMAIN-EN-LAYE

Gourmet cooks know that béarnaise sauce was invented here, although the town has other distinctions. Only 13 miles northwest of Paris, St-Germain-en-Laye traditionally drew Parisians wishing to escape the summer heat.

CHATEAU VIEUX. Tel. 34-51-53-65.

Louis XIV lived here, but he was to desert it for Versailles. Still, St-Germain-en-Laye has been the seat of the royal court. The Métro line from Paris will take you directly to the entrance to the Château Vieux, standing in the heart of town and dating from the 12th century. Built by François I, the castle is made of brick and stone. Once James II stayed here, enjoying French hospitality while hoping to regain the throne of England. However, this Stuart king died here. Napoléon III ordered that the château—built on a hill on the left bank of the Seine—be turned into a museum, tracing the history of France from the cave dwellers until the Carolingian era. And so it is today: the **French Museum of National Antiquities,** with displays of tools, stones, even arms and jewelry used or worn by the early settlers of Gaul.

Chapelle, the oldest section of the Château Vieux, is of special interest. It was built by St. Louis in the 1230s. At the end of the tour of the château, stroll through Le Nôtre's **gardens.**

Admission: 20F ($3.60).

Open: Château, Wed–Mon 9am–5:15pm; gardens, daily 7am–9:30pm. **Métro:** A-1 to St-Germain-en-Laye.

LE MUSEE DE DEPARTEMENTAL DE PRIEURE, 2 bis, rue Maurice-Denis. Tel. 39-73-77-87.

This museum, installed in the oldest building in St-Germain-en-Laye, was built in 1678 by the marquise de Montespan, a paramour of Louis XIV. From World War I to World War II it was inhabited by Maurice Denis, a painter who lived here until his death in 1943. Here he befriended a group of artists, known as "Nabis," including Paul Serusier. Nabis masters such as Bonnard and Vuillard are represented in the exhibition, along with members of the Pont-Aven group, including Gauguin and Emile Bernard. Works by other artists, including Toulouse-Lautrec, are also exhibited. You can visit a chapel decorated by Denis, as well as his atelier.

Admission: 20 F ($3.60) adults, free for children under 12.

Open: Wed–Fri 10am–5:30pm, Sat–Sun 10am–6:30pm. **Métro:** A-1 to St-Germain-en-Laye.

Where to Stay and Dine

PAVILLON HENRI IV, 21, rue Thiers, 78100 St-Germain-en-Laye. Tel. 39-10-15-15. Fax 39-73-93-73. 39 rms (all with bath). TV TEL **Métro:** RER Line 1 to St-Germain-en-Laye, then a five-minute walk.

$ Rates: 500–750 F ($90–$135) single; 1,000–1,300 F ($180–$234) double. Breakfast 50 F ($9) extra. AE, DC, MC, V.

In the 1500s, Henri IV, possibly the most promiscuous king in French history, built the Château Neuf on this terrace as a hideaway for his illegitimate children. The castle was later bequeathed to the comte d'Artois, the brother of Louis XVI, who planned to demolish it until the Revolution aborted his plans.

The château was partly rebuilt in 1836, and today the remains comprise the illustrious Pavillon Henri IV hotel, where Dumas wrote *The Three Musketeers.* Standing at the edge of the belvedere gardens, which were originally laid out during the Renaissance, it is still elegantly old-fashioned. A corner room has been set aside as a museum, in remembrance of where the Sun King romped with Madame de Montespan. A chapel in one of the wings is famous for its painted ceilings.

The fortunate visitors who get to spend a night here will find handsomely furnished bedrooms and a good restaurant. You can always order the classic dishes here—carré d'agneau rôti, rognon de veau (veal kidney) dijonnaise, and, of course, pommes soufflés, which were invented here, along with sauce béarnaise, which is just the thing to top your chateaubriand. Most à la carte lunches or dinners average around 400 F ($72) without wine; a fixed-price lunch is offered for 240 F ($43.20) Monday through Friday.

CHAPTER 8

STROLLING AROUND PARIS

1. MONTMARTRE
2. LE MARAIS
3. THE QUAYS OF THE SEINE
4. THE LITERARY LEFT BANK

The only way to discover Paris is on foot, using your own shoe leather. And it won't cost you a franc to explore the streets of the City of Light. Walk along the quays of the Seine, browse through the shops and stalls; each street opens onto a new vista.

If you're an early riser, a walk through Paris at dawn can be memorable; you'll see the city come to life. Shopfronts are washed clean for the new day, cafes open, and vegetable vendors arrange their produce.

Try to spend one day walking the grand promenade of the Champs Elysees, which will take you from the Arc de Triomphe to the Tuileries (follow the outline in "The Grand Promenade" in "The Top Attractions" in Chapter 7).

This chapter is organized into a series of walking tours of the some of the major attractions and districts of Paris.

Unless you are in Paris for several weeks, it's virtually impossible to visit all its major attractions. Most people are lucky to see merely the highlights. Your busy itinerary may not allow you to take all of the strolls in this chapter, but try to fit in as many as possible.

A day spent exploring the history-rich attractions of Le Marais will include the place de la Bastille, place des Vosges, and the National Archives (see "Le Marais," the second walking tour of this chapter).

A day spent walking along the banks and quays of the Seine is for many visitors their most memorable walk in Paris. Notre-Dame and Ile de la Cite are best viewed from the bank of the river (see "The Quays of the Seine," the third walking tour of this chapter).

WALKING TOUR — MONTMARTRE

Start: Place Pigalle.
Finish: Place Pigalle.
Time: 5 hours, more if you break for lunch; it's a three-mile trek.
Best Time: Any day that it isn't raining. Set out in the morning, 10am at the latest.
Worst Time: At dusk, when the pickpockets begin another night's work.

The traditional way to explore Montmartre is on foot. It's the highest point in the city, and visitors who find it too much of a climb will want to take the miniature train along the steep streets (45 minutes). **Le Petit Train de Montmartre** passes all the major landmarks, taking 72 passengers who can listen to the English commentary. Board at either place du Tertre (the Church of St-Pierre) or place Blanche (near the Moulin Rouge). Trains run March to October, daily from 10am to 7pm. For information, contact Promotrain, 38, bd. Flandrin, 16e (tel. 45-04-87-47).

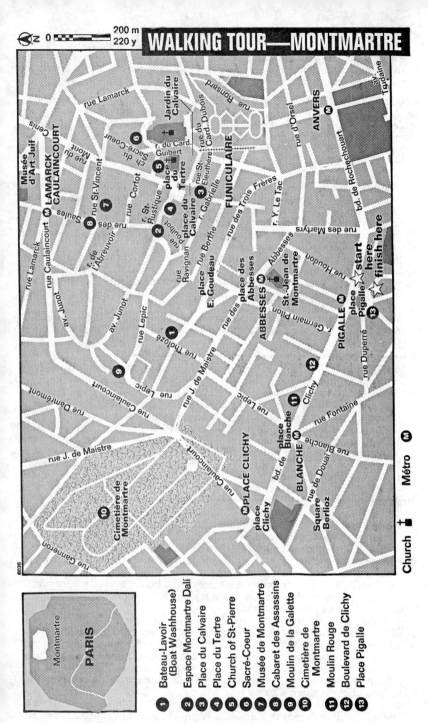

WALKING TOUR—MONTMARTRE

N 0 200 m
        220 y

start here
finish here

Church ✝ Métro Ⓜ

PARIS
Montmartre

① Bateau-Lavoir (Boat Washhouse)
② Espace Montmartre Dalí
③ Place du Calvaire
④ Place du Tertre
⑤ Church of St-Pierre
⑥ Sacré-Coeur
⑦ Musée de Montmartre
⑧ Cabaret des Assassins
⑨ Moulin de la Galette
⑩ Cimetière de Montmartre
⑪ Moulin Rouge
⑫ Boulevard de Clichy
⑬ Place Pigalle

The simplest way to reach Montmartre is to take the Métro to Anvers, then walk up rue Steinkerque toward the funicular. Funiculars run to the precincts of Sacré-Coeur every day from 6am to 11pm.

FROM PLACE PIGALLE TO MONT CENIS   Those who prefer to walk can take the Métro to Place-Pigalle. Turn right after leaving the station, proceed down boulevard de Clichy, turn left at the Cirque Medrano, and begin the climb up rue des Martyrs. Upon reaching rue des Abbesses, turn left onto rue Ravignan, then right, and eventually you'll come to place Emile-Goudeau, a tree-studded square in the middle of rue Ravignan. At no. 13, across from the Timhotel, stood:

1. Bateau-Lavoir (Boat Washhouse), called the cradle of cubism. Fire gutted it in 1970, but it has been reconstructed by the city of Paris. Picasso once lived here and, in the winter of 1905–06, painted one of the world's most famous portraits, *The Third Rose* (Gertrude Stein). Other residents have included Kees van Dongen and Juan Gris. Modigliani had his studio nearby, as did Henri Rousseau and Braque.

Rue Ravignan ends at place Jean-Baptiste-Clement. Go to the end of the street and cross it onto rue Norvins (which will be on your right). This intersection, one of the most famous street scenes of Montmartre (and painted by Utrillo) is the meeting point of rues Norvins, St-Rustique, and des Saules. Turn right and head down rue Poulbot. At no. 11, you'll come to the:

2. Espace Montmartre Dalí   This phantasmagorical world of Dalí features 300 original works by the artist, including his famous 1956 lithograph of *Don Quixote.*

REFUELING STOPS   Chances are, you'll be in Montmartre for lunch. Many restaurants, especially those around place du Tertre, are unabashed tourist traps. You'll be asked eight times if you want your portrait sketched in charcoal. However, **La Maison-Rose,** 2, rue de'Abreuvoir, 18e (see Chapter 6 for a complete description), is a good bargain. This was once the atelier of Utrillo, and the famous French singer Charles Aznavour used to sing here. The little pink house is about 300 yards from place du Tertre. But if you want better food, then leave the place du Tertre area and take a 12-minute walk down the Butte to **Le Maquis,** 69, rue Caulaincourt, 18e (see Chapter 6 for details), open Tuesday through Saturday. The food is surprisingly reasonable, and in sunny weather you can try for a seat on the tiny terrace.

Poulbot crosses the tiny:

3. Place du Calvaire, which offers a panoramic view of Paris. On this square (a plaque marks the house) lived artist, painter, and lithographer Maurice Neumont (1868–1930). From here, follow the sounds of an oompah band to:

4. Place du Tertre, the old town square of Montmartre. Its cafés are overflowing, its art galleries (indoors and out) always overcrowded. Some of the artists still wear berets, and the cafés bear such names as La Bohème—you get the point. Everything is so loaded with local color—applied as heavily as on a Seurat canvas—it gets a little redundant.

Right off the square fronting rue du Mont-Cenis is the:

5. Church of St-Pierre. Originally a Benedictine abbey, it has played many roles—Temple of Reason during the Revolution, a food depot, a clothing store, even a munitions factory. Nowadays it's back to being a church. In 1147 the present church was consecrated; it's one of the oldest in Paris. Two of the columns in the choir stall are the remains of a Roman temple. Note among the sculptured works a nun with the head of a pig, a symbol of sensual vice. At the entrance of the church are the three bronze doors sculpted by Gismondi in 1980. The middle door depicts the life of St. Peter. The left door is dedicated to St. Denis, patron saint of Paris, and the right door to the Holy Virgin.

After visiting St. Peter's, veer left around the huge reservoir of Montmartre and go through the Jardin du Calvaire until you arrive at the terrace of:

6. **Sacré-Coeur,** overlooking Square Willette. After a visit to Sacré-Coeur, walk between the basilica and the Cemetery of St-Pierre, turning left (west) and heading along rue Chevalier-de-la-Barre, taking a right turn onto rue du Mont-Cenis.

FROM MONT-CENIS TO PLACE PIGALLE Continue on this street until you reach rue Corot, at which point turn left. At no. 12 is the:

7. **Musée de Montmartre** (tel. 46-06-61-11), with a wide collection of mementos of *Vieux Montmartre*. This famous 17th-century house was formerly occupied by Utrillo, Dufy, van Gogh, and Renoir. Suzanne Valadon and her son, Utrillo, also lived here. Open Tuesday through Sunday from 11am to 6pm; admission is 20 F ($3.60).

From the museum, turn right heading up rue des Saules past a winery, a reminder of the days when Montmartre was a farming village on the outskirts of Paris. A grape-harvesting festival is held here every October.

The intersection of rue des Saules and rue St-Vincent is one of the most visited and photographed corners of the Butte. Here, on one corner, sits the famous old:

8. **Cabaret des Assassins,** long ago renamed Lapin Agile (see Chapter 10, "Paris Evening Entertainment," for details).

Continue along rue St-Vincent, passing the Cimetière St-Vincent on your right. Utrillo is just one of the many famous artists buried here. Take a left turn onto rue Girardon and climb the stairs. In a minute or two, you'll spot on your right two of the windmills (*moulins*) that used to dot the Butte. One of these:

9. **Moulin de la Galette** (entrance at 1, av. Junot), was immortalized by Renoir.

Turn right onto rue Lepic and walk past no. 54. In 1886 van Gogh lived here with Guillaumin. Take a right turn onto rue Joseph-de-Maistre, then left again on rue Caulaincourt until you reach the:

10. **Cimetière de Montmartre,** second in fame only to Père-Lachaise, and the resting place of many famous personages. The burial ground (Métro: Clichy) lies west of the "Butte," north of boulevard de Clichy. Opened in 1795, the cemetery shelters such composers as Berlioz (d. 1869) and Offenbach (d. 1880), Heinrich Heine, Stendhal, the Goncourt brothers, and poets Alfred de Vigny and Théophile Gautier. I like to pay my respects at the tomb of Alphonsine Plessis, the heroine of *La dame aux camélias,* and Madame Récamier, who taught the world how to lounge.

From the cemetery, take avenue Rachel, turn left onto boulevard de Clichy, and go to place Blanche, where an even better-known windmill than the one in Renoir's painting stands, the:

11. **Moulin Rouge,** one of the most talked-about nightclubs in the world. It was immortalized by Toulouse-Lautrec.

From place Blanche, you can begin a descent down:

12. **Boulevard de Clichy,** fighting off the pornographers and hustlers trying to lure you into tawdry sex joints. With some rare exceptions—notably the citadels of the *chansonniers*—boulevard de Clichy is one gigantic tourist trap. Still, as Times Square is to New York, boulevard de Clichy is to Paris: Everyone who comes to Paris invariably winds up here. The boulevard strips and peels its way down to:

13. **Place Pigalle,** center of nudity in Paris. The square is named after a French sculptor, Pigalle, whose closest association with nudity was a depiction of Voltaire in the buff. Place Pigalle, of course, was the notorious "Pig Alley" of World War II. Toulouse-Lautrec had his studio right off Pigalle at 5, av. Frochot. In those days when she was lonely and hungry, Edith Piaf (the "little sparrow") sang in the alleyways of Pigalle, hoping to earn a few francs.

WALKING TOUR — LE MARAIS

Start: Place de la Bastille.
Finish: Place de la Bastille.
Time: 5 hours without any major stops; the distance is 2½ miles.
Best Time: Monday through Friday when more buildings are open. (If interiors are closed, often you can walk into courtyards.)
Worst Time: Weekends, because of closings.

FROM PLACE DE LA BASTILLE TO VIEILLE-DU-TEMPLE A good place to begin your tour of Le Marais is:

1. **Place de la Bastille.** (For details about the major attractions, see Chapter 7.) Today, the once-depressed area around the former Bastille is gaining a new reputation, particularly since the Bastille Opéra opened, attracting *le tout Paris*. It was at place de la Bastille on July 14, 1789, that a Paris mob attacked the old prison, launching the French Revolution. It's hard to imagine it today, since the Bastille, built in 1369, was completely razed. A symbol of despotism, it once contained eight towers rising 100 feet high. Many prisoners—some sentenced by Louis XIV for "witchcraft"—were kept within its walls, the best known being "The Man in the Iron Mask." And yet, when the fortress was stormed by the revolutionary mob, only seven prisoners were discovered. So in one sense the attack meant nothing. What is symbolized, however, and what it started, will never be forgotten. Bastille Day is celebrated with great festivity each July 14.

   It was probably easier to storm the Bastille than it is to slip by the speeding cars to the center of the square to see the:
2. **Colonne de Juillet (July Column),** which does not commemorate the Revolution. Instead, it honors the victims of the July Revolution of 1830, which put Louis-Philippe on the throne. The tower is crowned by a winged nude, the God of Liberty, a star emerging from his head.

   From place de la Bastille, walk up rue St-Antoine and turn right onto rue des Tournelles, noting the:
3. **Statue of Beaumarchais** (1895), honoring the 18th-century dramatist (*The Barber of Seville* and *The Marriage of Figaro*). Cut left again, onto the colorful and typical rue Pas-de-la-Mule (Footsteps of the Mule), and you'll soon realize by the posters and graffiti that you're in a hotbed of left-wing French politics. Then, suddenly, you enter the enchanted:
4. **Place des Vosges,** completed in 1612. You'll want to walk around the entire square. If you take an immediate left, you will find, at the far end of the square, the:
5. **Maison de Victor Hugo,** now a museum that can be visited by the public. Hugo lived here in 1832–48. You can see his sketch for *The Hunchback of Notre Dame.*

REFUELING STOP If you're ready for some nourishment, try **Ma Bourgogne,** 19, place des Vosges, 4e (for details, see Chapter 10, "Paris Evening Entertainment"). Here you can sit and appreciate the view of this historic square dating from 1407.

From the northwest corner of the square, turn left onto rue des Francs-Bourgeois. At the intersection with rue de Sévigné, take a right turn. At no. 23 is the:
6. **Hôtel Carnavalet,** a 16th-century mansion that is now a museum devoted to the history of Paris and the French Revolution. Here you can see a model of the Bastille as it looked before it was torn down.

   Continue to the end of rue de Sévigné, noting no. 29 (now part of the Carnavalet Museum). This is the:

7. Hôtel Le-Peletier-de-St-Fargeau, bearing the name of its former occupant, who was considered responsible for the death sentence of Louis XVI. At the end of the street, you reach rue du Parc-Royal. Take a left onto this lovely street lined with 17th-century mansions. The street leads to place de Thorigny, where the:

8. Musée Picasso is at no. 5 in the Hôtel Salé, originally built by a salt-tax collector. You can visit the museum either now or later in the tour.

Retrace your steps toward place de Thorigny, cutting right onto rue de la Perle. Continue along this street until you reach the crossroads with rue Vieille-du-Temple. Turn left. At 87, rue Vieille-du-Temple, Delamair's:

9. Hôtel de Rohan was once occupied by the cardinal of the "diamond necklace scandal," which implicated Marie Antoinette. He was the fourth Cardinal Rohan. The first, the original occupant of the hotel, was reputed to be the son of Louis XIV. The interior is open to the public only when exhibitions are on. The main attraction is the amusing 18th-century Salon des Singes (Monkey Room). In the courtyard (open Monday through Friday from 9am to 6pm), you can see a stunning bas-relief depicting a nude Apollo and four horses against a background exploding with sunbursts.

Also on rue Vieille-du-Temple, at no. 47, is the:

10. Hôtel des Ambassadeurs de Hollande, where Beaumarchais wrote *The Marriage of Figaro*. It is one of the most splendid mansions in Le Marais—and was never actually occupied by the Dutch embassy. It's not open to the public.

FROM RUE DES ROSIERS TO PLACE DE LA BASTILLE Continue along rue Vieille-du-Temple until you reach:

11. Rue des Rosiers (Street of the Rosebushes), and turn left. It's one of the most colorful and typical streets remaining from the old Jewish quarter. The Star of David shines here, Hebrew letters flash (in neon, no less), couscous is sold from the shops run by Moroccan or Algerian Jews, bearded old men sit in doorways, restaurants serve strictly kosher meats, and signs appeal for Jewish liberation. Whatever you're in the market for—good sausage stuffed in a goose neck, roots of black horseradish, pickled lemons—you'll find it here.

REFUELING STOP Stop for lunch at **Chez Jo Goldenberg,** 4, rue des Rosiers, 4e (see Chapter 6, "Paris Dining," for details). This restaurant was founded by the doyen of Jewish restaurateurs in Paris, Albert Goldenberg. All the dishes that its habitués have come to know and love, everything from stuffed carp to pastrami, are still sold here and made according to the old recipes.

At the intersection of rue des Rosiers and rue Pavée, turn right and walk until you reach the St-Paul Métro stop. At that point, make a right turn along rue François-Miron. Although the facade at the 17th-century:

12. Hôtel de Beauvais, 68, rue François-Miron, was badly damaged in the French Revolution, it remains one of the most charming in Paris. A plaque commemorates the fact that Mozart inhabited the maison in 1763. When he was only 7 years old he played at the court of Versailles. Louis XIV presented the mansion to Catherine Belier, wife of Pierre de Beauvais, who reportedly had the honor of introducing Louis, then 16, to the facts of life. To visit inside, apply to the Association du Paris Historique, on the ground floor of the building, any afternoon.

Continue your walk along rue François-Miron until you come to a crossroads. At that point, take a sharp left along rue de Jouy. Continue along the street, cross rue Fourcy, and head down rue du Figuier. The:

13. Hôtel de Sens, a Paris landmark at 1, rue de Figuier, 4e (tel. 42-78-14-60), was built between the 1470s and 1519 for the archbishops of Sens. Along with the Cluny on the Left Bank, it is the only domestic architecture remaining from the 15th century. Long after the archbishops had departed in 1605, it was occupied

PARIS

Le Marais

1 Place de la Bastille
2 Colonne de Juillet
   (July Column)
3 Statue of Beaumarchais
4 Place des Vosges
5 Maison de Victor Hugo
6 Hôtel Carnavalet
7 Hôtel Le-Peletier-
   Saint-Fargeau
8 Musée Picasso
9 Hôtel de Rohan
10 Hôtel des Ambassadeurs
   de Hollande
11 rue des Rosiers
12 Hôtel de Beauvais
13 Hôtel de Sens
14 Hôtel de Béthune-Sully

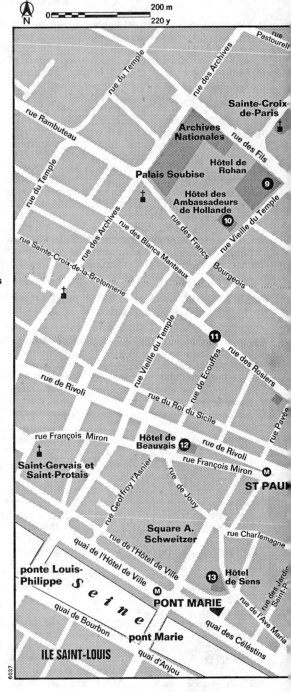

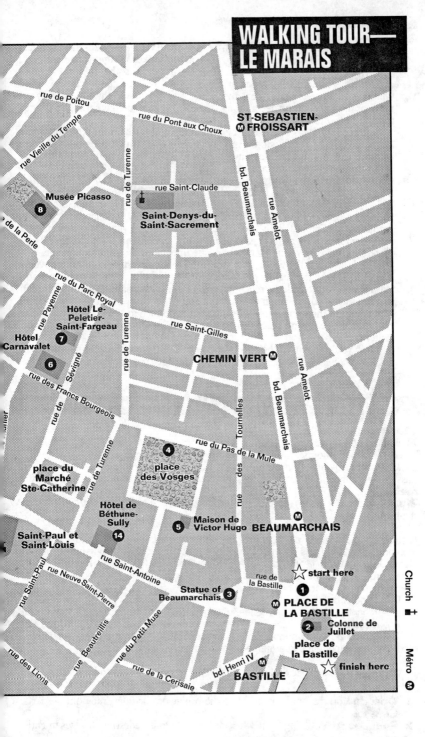

WALKING TOUR—
LE MARAIS

rue de Poitou

rue du Pont aux Choux

ST-SEBASTIEN-
Ⓜ FROISSART

rue Vieille du Temple

rue de Turenne

rue Saint-Claude

bd. Beaumarchais

rue Amelot

Musée Picasso

8

✝

de la Perle

Saint-Denys-du-
Saint-Sacrement

rue du Parc Royal

Hôtel Le-
Peletier-
Saint-Fargeau

7

rue Payenne

rue de Turenne

rue Saint-Gilles

Hôtel
Carnavalet

6

rue de Sévigné

CHEMIN VERT Ⓜ

rue Amelot

rue des Francs Bourgeois

rue de

bd. Beaumarchais

rue du Pas de la Mule

4

place
des Vosges

rue des Tournelles

place du
Marché
Ste-Catherine

rue de Turenne

Hôtel de
Béthune-
Sully

14

Maison de
Victor Hugo

5

rue des

BEAUMARCHAIS Ⓜ

Saint-Paul et
Saint-Louis

rue Saint-Antoine

rue Saint-Paul

rue Neuve Saint-Pierre

Statue of
Beaumarchais

3

rue de
la Bastille

☆ start here

1

Ⓜ PLACE DE
LA BASTILLE

Church ✝

rue Beautreillis

rue du Petit Muse

2

Colonne de
Juillet

place de
la Bastille

Métro Ⓜ

rue des Lions

rue de la Cerisaie

bd. Henri IV Ⓜ

BASTILLE

☆ finish here

by the scandalous Queen Margot, wife of Henri IV. Her new lover—"younger and more virile"—slew the discarded one as she looked on in great amusement. The restoration of the Hôtel de Sens, as usual, was the subject of great controversy; nonetheless, today it houses the Bibliothèque Forney. Leaded windows and turrets characterize the facade; you can go into the courtyard to see more of the ornate stone decoration—the gate is open Tuesday through Saturday from 1:30 to 8pm.

Retrace your steps to rue Fourcy, turn right, and walk up the street until you reach the St-Paul Métro stop again. Turn right onto rue St-Antoine, the street where Henri II was fatally wounded in a jousting tournament in 1559. Walk along this street until you reach the:

14. Hôtel de Bethune-Sully, 62, rue St-Antoine, 4e (tel. 42-74-22-22). Work began on this mansion in 1625, on the order of Jean Androuet de Cerceau. In 1634 it was acquired by the duc de Sully, who had been Henri IV's minister of finance before the king was assassinated in 1610. After a straitlaced life as "the accountant of France," Sully broke loose in his declining years, adorning himself with diamonds and garish rings—and a young bride, who is said to have had a preference for very young men, whom she openly invited into their home.

The Hôtel de Sully was acquired by the French government just after World War II. It is now the seat of the National Office of Historical Monuments and Sites. Recently restored, the relief-studded facade is especially appealing. You can visit the interior of the hotel with a guide, on either Saturday or Sunday at 3pm, depending on the program. There is daily admittance to the courtyard and the garden that opens onto place des Vosges. In the building there's an information center and a bookshop.

Now you've come to the end of the tour. Continue walking along the street until you come to place de la Bastille and the Métro stop.

WALKING TOUR —— THE QUAYS OF THE SEINE

Start: The Louvre.
Finish: The Louvre.
Time: At least 3 hours, not including stops; it's a three-mile walk.
Best Time: Any time of the day or night. You'll see more during the day, but you'll miss the nighttime illuminations. Consider doing part of this tour during the day, the rest at night.
Worst Time: A sunny Saturday afternoon, when it's the most crowded with strollers.

A stroll along the banks and quays of the noble Seine is for many visitors the most memorable walk in Paris. Some of the city's most important monuments—such as Notre-Dame on the Ile de la Cité—are best viewed from the riverbank. Many attractions, such as the mighty facade of the Louvre, take on even more interest at night when they're floodlit.

The Seine is called the loveliest avenue in Paris. You'll walk past flower vendors, seed merchants, pet shops, and sellers of caged birds, and perhaps you'll stop at one of the *bouquinistes*, or booksellers, who line the parapets. If you should fall in love with the Seine, you can always moor your houseboat here, as did the writer Anaïs Nin, recording her experience in a memorable short story, "Houseboat."

With your back to place du Louvre, facing the Seine, turn right and walk along the:

1. Quai du Louvre until you come to the bridge on the quay, the pont des Arts. Cross the:
2. Pont des Arts, dating from 1803, one of only four pedestrian bridges in Paris.

The first iron bridge in the city, it gives you a spectacular view of the Louvre and Sainte Chapelle, and, in the distance, the spires of Notre-Dame. You emerge onto the:

3. **Quai de Conti,** on the Left Bank. Bypassing the Institut de France, head along the river. Pause for a look at the:

4. **Pont Neuf,** on your left, which is the most famous and the oldest bridge in Paris, recalling the Middle Ages. In those days you came to the bridge to have a tooth pulled. The Pont Neuf, begun in 1578, has never been enlarged in four centuries. From it, you can see the little Square du Vert Galant, jutting out like the prow of a ship from Ile de la Cité. You'll pass the Palais de Justice (the law courts) and Sainte Chapelle on Cité. Here scientist Pierre Curie, husband of the famous Marie, was killed by a horse-drawn carriage in 1906.

REFUELING STOP Drop in at **Taverne Henri IV,** 13, place du Pont-Neuf, 1er (tel. 43-54-27-90), a 17th-century building opposite the statue of the "Vert Galant" at the Pont Neuf. This is one of the most famous wine bars of Paris (see Chapter 10 for a complete description).

Continuing along the river, you'll come to the:

5. **Quai des Grands-Augustins,** constructed by Philip the Fair in 1313. It's named after an Augustine monastery that stood there. Rue des Grands-Augustins juts off to your right. Picasso had his studio at no. 7, and there he painted *Guernica.*

Continuing along the river, you reach the:

6. **Pont St-Michel,** with its fountain by Davioud. The scene of some of the bitterest fighting in 1944 against the Nazis, it again became a scene of turmoil during the student riots in the May Revolution of the late 1960s.

At this point, the promenade becomes the:

7. **Quai St-Michel.** Lined with booksellers' stalls, it is intersected by two of the most charming old and narrow streets of Paris, rue du Chat-qui-Pêche and rue Xavier-Privas. Stroll along either or both of them.

REFUELING STOP Head for **Café le Départ,** 1, place St-Michel, 5e (tel. 43-54-24-55), an art nouveau café long popular with students. It's open 24 hours a day. (See Chapter 6 for details.)

Quai St-Michel leads to the:

8. **Quai de Montebello.** Pause here at the intersection with Square René-Viviani for a remarkable view—Notre-Dame on one side, the Left Bank church of St-Julien-le-Pauvre on the other.

Still strolling, you reach the:

9. **Quai de la Tournelle,** the setting for one of the world's most famous restaurants, Tour d'Argent. At the:

10. **Pont de la Tournelle,** you will be at one of the newest bridges of Paris, dating from 1928. From the bridge there's a magnificent panoramic view of Notre-Dame.

At the end of the quay, turn left onto the:

11. **Pont de Sully,** which cuts across Ile St-Louis and takes you back to the Right Bank. The bridge, dating from 1876, also offers a splendid view of Notre-Dame and of Ile St-Louis itself. You arrive at:

12. **Square Henri-Galli,** containing, in part, stones from the Bastille destroyed by the revolutionary mob. Keeping right, you emerge onto the:

13. **Quai des Célestins,** enjoying yet another view of Ile St-Louis as you walk along. Pause to take in the Pont Marie, which connects the Right Bank with Ile St-Louis. You are now on the:

14. **Quai de l'Hôtel-de-Ville.** On your right you'll pass the Hôtel de Ville (city hall). Passing it, you'll arrive at the:

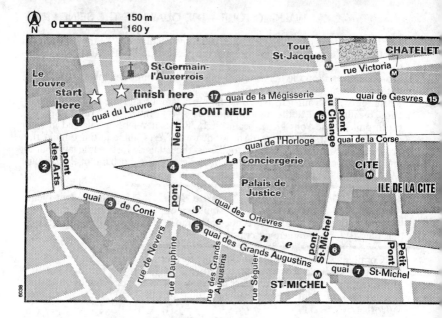

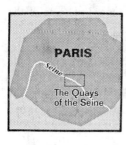

PARIS

The Quays of the Seine

① Quai du Louvre	**⑨** Quai de la Tournelle
② Pont des Arts	**⑩** Pont de la Tournelle
③ Quai de Conti	**⑪** Pont de Sully
④ Pont Neuf	**⑫** Square Henri Galli
⑤ Quai des Grands-	**⑬** Quai des Célestins
Augustins	**⑭** Quai de l'Hôtel de Ville
⑥ Pont St-Michel	**⑮** Quai des Gesvres
⑦ Quai St-Michel	**⑯** Pont au Change
⑧ Quai de Montebello	**⑰** Quai de la Mégisserie

15. Quai de Gesvres and its Pont Notre-Dame, dating from 1913. The next bridge along the river is the:

16. Pont au Change (Money-changer's Bridge). It leads to place du Châtelet, with an 1808 fountain commemorating the victories of Napoléon. The riverbank walk now becomes the:

17. Quai de la Mégisserie, once, long ago, the site of the public slaughterhouse of Paris. Seed merchants and pet shops line this quay, from which you can enjoy a good view of the Conciergerie and the Law Courts.

    Now you're back at the Pont Neuf, that famous landmark bridge again. If you continue along, you'll return to the Louvre where you began.

Hôtel de Ville

† St-Gervais and St-Protais

Ⓜ PONT MARIE

S e i n e

⑭ quai de l'Hôtel de Ville

pont Louis-Philippe

quai des ⑬ Célestins

rue St-Paul

pont Marie

quai aux Fleurs

quai de Bourbon   quai d'Anjou

⑫

ILE SAINT-LOUIS

pont St-Louis

St-Louis-en-l'Ile †

† Cathédrale Notre Dame

quai d'Orléans   quai de Béthune

pont de Sully

pont de l'Archevêché

quai de la Tournelle

⑩

⑪

Métro Ⓜ Church

quai de ⑧ Montebello   quai de la ⑨ Tournelle

bd St-Germain

quai St-Bernard

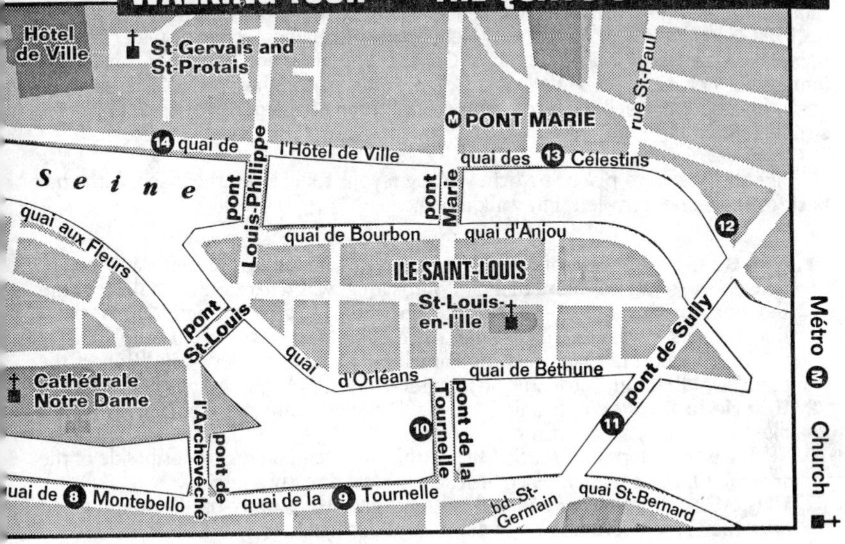

WALKING TOUR — THE LITERARY LEFT BANK

Start: Place St-Michel.
Finish: Rue de Seine.
Time: 3 hours, not counting stops.
Best Time: Any pleasant, sunny day. Try to begin at 9am and end by 4pm.
Worst Time: Morning or late-afternoon rush hour.

Paris is filled with streets, former homes or studios, monuments, and cafés where famous writers and artists lived, worked, and played. Many of these were Americans, such as Gertrude Stein and Ernest Hemingway, to name a couple. Other famous names include Henry Miller (*Tropic of Cancer*) and his friend and lover, Anaïs Nin, famous for her controversial *Diaries*. Some of the places they patronized, although vastly changed, are still there to greet visitors. Many have gone, of course, but the streets remain.

Take the Métro to place St-Michel to begin your tour. From the place, with your back to the Seine, turn left and walk along:

1. **Rue de la Huchette,** one of the most typical and famous of Left Bank streets. This short street, not more than 300 yards long, was where Elliot Paul lived, and the story of this street—its shopkeepers, radicals, growing children, workers, hotelkeepers—was described in the memorable *The Last Time I Saw Paris*.
    After exploring that street, perhaps looking for a modern-day "Robert the pimp" or "l'Hibou," cross rue St-Julien-le-Pauvre and Square René-Viviani onto:
2. **Rue de la Bûcherie,** heading for no. 27, Shakespeare and Company, which is filled with many wonderful old books.
    Trace your steps to place St-Michel (this time walk on the opposite side of the streets). Once you reach place St-Michel, head directly south to:
3. **Place St-André-des-Arts** and a street that begins here, rue Danton, named after the French revolutionary who was guillotined.

REFUELING STOP   If you want a short rest, go to **Café le Départ,** 1, place St-Michel, 5e (tel. 43-54-24-55), which has views of both the spire of Sainte Chapelle and the dragon statue of place St-Michel (see Chapter 6 for details). Have a coffee and pause to remember.

That memory might be of the Beat Generation. Jack Kerouac described the Café Gentilhomme here in his *Satori in Paris*. The once-favorite hotel of Allen Ginsberg stands just around the corner. Members of the Beat Generation, or those in search of them, still come to Hôtel du Vieux Paris, 9, rue Gît-le-Coeur, 6e (tel. 43-54-41-66) (see Chapter 5 for complete information). William Burroughs came this way—"a magical interlude"—and Peter Orlovsky occupied Room 25.
    Back at place St-André-des-Arts, walk along rue Danton, turn right onto rue Suger, one of the fine old Left Bank streets. At no. 11, J. K. Huysmans was born in 1848. This French novelist is best known for his morbid psychological studies such as *A Rebours* (Against the Grain). At the end of the street, turn left onto rue de l'Eperon, which leads to boulevard St-Germain and:
4. **Carrefour de l'Odéon.** Danton ("we need audacity") lived here. Today, a pigeon-decorated statue stands where his house once did. From here, turn left onto:
5. **Rue Monsieur-le-Prince.** Practically everybody used to live on this street, including French philosopher Pascal, at no. 54. The street has been called a "Yankee alleyway." The street's roster of figures includes Richard Wright (no. 14), James McNeill Whistler (no. 22), Henry Wadsworth Longfellow (no. 49), and Oliver Wendell Holmes (no. 55).

REFUELING STOP   At 62, rue Monsieur-le-Prince, 6e, **Slice** (tel. 43-54-21-67) is said to have the best pizza in town, and I'm talking Big Apple–style pizza here. Finish with a rich chocolate-banana cake. Open daily from 11am to 11pm.

At the intersection with rue Racine, cut right into:
6. **Place de l'Odéon,** with its landmark Théater de l'Odéon, where the premier of *The Marriage of Figaro* in 1794 landed Beaumarchais in jail. During the postwar era, this theater hosted the avant-garde, presenting plays by Ionesco, Edward Albee, and Beckett.

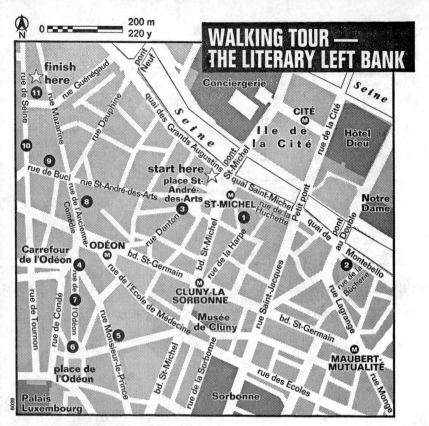

**WALKING TOUR —
THE LITERARY LEFT BANK**

① Rue de la Huchette
② Rue de la Bûcherie
③ Place St-André-
   des-Arts
④ Carrefour de l'Odéon
⑤ Rue Monsieur-le-Prince
⑥ Place de l'Odéon
⑦ Rue de l'Odéon
⑧ Rue de l'Ancienne
   Comédie
⑨ Rue de Buci
⑩ Rue de Seine
⑪ Librairie Fischbacher

REFUELING STOP   For lunch, try **La Méditerranée**, 2, place de l'Odéon, 6e (tel. 43-26-46-75), still going strong after all these years. Known for its seafood specialties, such as bouillabaisse, it was once the haunt of Jean Cocteau, who often showed up with Marlene Dietrich. It serves lunch daily from 12:15 to 2:45pm, costing 155 F ($27.90) for a fixed-price menu, and dinner daily from 7:15 to 10:45pm, costing 255 F ($45.90) for a fixed-price menu.

Place de l'Odéon is the site of the Institut Benjamin-Franklin, an American cultural institute on the square. The same location was once occupied by Café Voltaire, a celebrated gathering point for the *philosophes* and much frequented in the 1920s by American expatriates. From the square, take:
7. Rue de l'Odéon north. The original Shakespeare and Company stood at no. 12. Here Sylvia Beach entertained such writers as MacLeish, Pound, Fitzgerald, and Hemingway. She also helped publish Joyce's *Ulysses*.

Cross carrefour de l'Odéon again onto:

8. **Rue de l'Ancienne-Comédie,** the setting of the café Le Procope at no. 13 (see Chapter 6 for details). A literary haunt since 1686, it was patronized by Balzac, Hugo, Racine, and Molière. At the intersection, turn onto:

9. **Rue de Buci,** site of the Buci Market, one of the most charming in Paris. It's open Tuesday through Saturday from 9am to 1pm and 4 to 7pm, and on Sunday from 9am to 1pm. Turn right onto:

10. **Rue de Seine.** The house at no. 21 was once occupied by George Sand. The art gallery and craft center now there was founded by Isadora Duncan. Jean-Paul Sartre lived at Louisiane, 60, rue de Seine, 6e (tel. 42-29-59-30), one among many other famous names.

REFUELING STOP   Try **La Palette,** 43, rue de Seine, 6e (tel. 43-26-68-15), for an experience of what used to be called "a bohemian café." You may remember it from the James Ivory film *Quartet*, starring Maggie Smith and Alan Bates. You can enjoy fresh salads and slices of country ham, while checking out the artists' palettes hanging on the wall. A café au lait costs 18 F ($3.20). Open daily from 8am to 2am; closed in August.

Finally, you might want to end this literary tour appropriately enough at:

11. **Librairie Fischbacher,** 33, rue de Seine, 6e (tel. 43-26-84-87), a bookshop that sells many English titles and carries a superb array of fine art editions. Open Monday through Friday from 9am to 7pm and on Saturday from 10am to 7pm.

CHAPTER 9

PARIS SAVVY SHOPPING

1. **THE SHOPPING SCENE**
2. **SHOPPING A TO Z**
- **FROMMER'S SMART TRAVELER: SHOPPING**

Like visiting the Louvre, shopping is an integral part of the Parisian experience. Paris presents a formidable array of choices: from classic Chanel suits, crystal, and perfume to discounted designer clothes, bonbons, and hand-painted toys. The shopping and browsing opportunities are endless.

1. THE SHOPPING SCENE

SHOPPING AREAS

Although Paris may seem like an intimidating place to shop, it can easily be broken down into accessible shopping districts with some advance planning.

The **1st and 2nd arrondissements,** where you'll find the famous rue de Rivoli, are filled with shops. Rue St-Honoré, parallel to rue de Rivoli, is also renowned for its many stores, which become less elegant as you head toward the Louvre and more upscale as you approach the 8th arrondissement. The 1st is the site of one of the best family department stores in Paris, Samaritaine, and Forum des Halles, the city's biggest shopping mall (see below). A stroll along avenue de l'Opéra will bring you to the chic boutiques on place de l'Opéra. The great jewelry stores are clustered on the prestigious place Vendôme.

From the chic avenue Montaigne to rue du Faubourg St-Honoré, the **8th arrondissement** is where the international elite goes to buy haute couture. The 8th also includes the Champs-Elysées, although its former elegance has long since been replaced by rampant commercialism.

Most of the *grands magasins,* or department stores, including Galeries Lafayette and Au Printemps, are found in the **9th arrondissement** (see below). The nearby boulevards Haussmann, des Italiens, and des Capucines are also good for browsing. If you're looking for crystal and china, however, your best bet is rue de Paradis in the **10th arrondissement.**

Rue de Passy is lined with stores catering to the wealthy residents of the **16th arrondissement.**

I recommend the Marais, in the **3rd and 4th arrondissements,** if you're interested in antiques. Place des Vosges, of Victor Hugo fame, is the place for old engravings and curios. From there you can head to rue des Francs-Bourgeois, where, as you progress toward the Centre Georges-Pompidou, the neighborhood is packed with old galleries, boutiques, and antique shops.

On the Left Bank, the **5th and 6th arrondissements** contain charming specialty shops, boutiques, and bookstores. Boulevard St-Germain is the main shopping venue, while boulevard St-Michel is filled mostly with souvenir and fast-food shops. Shopping is usually better in the 6th, with its stylish fashions and expensive antiques.

Venturing onto rue du Bac in the **7th arrondissement,** you will come upon a neighborhood of art galleries and pricey fashion boutiques.

SHIPPING IT HOME

There are restrictions on what merchandise can be shipped. Customs regulations change, so when in doubt it's best to check before you buy so that your purchase doesn't show up on a "prohibited" list.

If you buy something at a Parisian department store or an upscale boutique, ask the clerk about reliable shippers. Most major hotel desks in Paris also maintain up-to-date lists of shipping companies. Many shoppers even talk to their local shipping companies before they go. Remember, however, that there is always some degree of risk involved in shipping goods.

Check with the shipper in Paris to make sure you understand the arrangement that you've made, and ask about insurance. Don't forget to ask about duties and clearance fees in your home country, what kind of packing will be used, and whether there will be any warehouse penalties if you can't pick up the item right away.

TAX REFUND

Tourists staying in France for less than six months are entitled to a refund on the Value-Added Tax (VAT) on certain purchases made within the country, but only under carefully defined conditions. These refunds usually average around 13%–15.7%, and are allowed only on purchases of more than 2,000 F ($360) made in a single store, and apply only to citizens of countries that are not members of the EC. The refund, however, is not automatic (some forms and paperwork need to be completed at the time of purchase), and food, wine, and tobacco don't count. Procedures for receiving the refund are slightly different for merchandise you carry with you outside of France than it is for merchandise you arrange to have shipped, although any reputable merchant will have the necessary forms and paperwork in inventory.

You must take several steps to receive your refund. First, show the clerk your passport to prove your eligibility. You'll then be given an export sales document in triplicate (two pink sheets and a green one), which you must sign, as well as an envelope addressed to the store. Arrive at your departure point as early as possible to avoid lines at the *détaxe* (refund) booth at French Customs. If you're traveling by train, go to the *détaxe* area in the station before boarding—you can't get your refund documents processed on the train. The refund booths are outside the passport checkpoints, so you must handle your refund before you proceed with the passport check.

Only the person who signed the documents at the store can present them for refund. Give the three sheets to the Customs official, who will countersign and hand you back the green copy. (Save it in case any problems arise.) Give the official the stamped envelope addressed to the store. One of the processed pink copies will be mailed to the store for you. Your reimbursement will either be mailed by check (in convertible French francs) or credited to your credit-card account. In some cases you may get your refund immediately, paid at an airport bank window. If you don't receive your tax refund in four months, write to the store, giving the date of purchase and the location where the forms were given to Customs officials. Include a photocopy of your (green) refund sheet.

BEST BUYS

Perfumes and cosmetics, including such famous brands as Guerlain, Chanel, Schiaparelli, and Jean Patou, are almost always cheaper in Paris than in the U.S.

Paris is also a good place to buy Lalique and Baccarat **crystal.** They're expensive, but they're still priced below the international market value.

Of course, many visitors come to Paris just to shop for **fashions.** From Chanel to Yves Saint-Laurent, from Nina Ricci to Sonia Rykiel, the city overflows with fashion boutiques, ranging from haute couture to the truly outlandish. Fashion accessories, such as those designed by Louis Vuitton and Céline, are among the finest in the world.

Lingerie is another great French export. All the top lingerie designers are represented in boutiques as well as in the major department stores, Galeries Lafayette and Au Printemps.

AIRPORT TAX-FREE BOUTIQUES

You're better off buying certain products in the airport. In the duty-free shops at Orly and Charles de Gaulle airports, you'll get a minimum discount of 20% on all items, and up to 50% on liquor, cigarettes, and watches. Among the items on sale are crystal, cutlery, chocolates, luggage, wines and whiskeys, pipes and lighters, lingerie, silk scarves, perfume, knitwear, jewelry, cameras and equipment, cheeses, and antiques.

The drawbacks of airport shopping are that the selections are limited, and of course, you must carry your purchase with you onto the plane.

2. SHOPPING A TO Z

In alphabetical order, here's a quick preview of specialty shopping in Paris, along with the markets and the major department stores. Most stores are open Monday through Saturday from 9 or 9:30am (sometimes 10am) to 6 or 7pm, without a break for lunch. Some of the smaller stores break for lunch for one to three hours, beginning at 1pm.

ANTIQUES

LA COUR AUX ANTIQUAIRES, 54, rue du Faubourg St-Honoré, 8e. Tel. 42-66-58-77.
This elegant Right Bank arcade contains 18 independent shops offering a variety of antiques, paintings, and objets d'art (usually from the 16th to the 20th century). The complex is located near the president's residence at the Elysée Palace. Métro: Concorde or Madeleine.

LE LOUVRE DES ANTIQUAIRES, 2, place du Palais-Royal, 1er. Tel. 42-97-27-00.
Le Louvre des Antiquaires is the largest antiques center in Europe, stocking

 FROMMER'S SMART TRAVELER: SHOPPING

VALUE-CONSCIOUS TRAVELERS SHOULD
CONSIDER THE FOLLOWING:

1. Shop at discount stores (I recommend several) featuring merchandise that didn't sell at some of the better-known fashion houses. Discounts range from 20% to 50%.
2. Read the section on tax refunds or *détaxe*, as the French call it (see above). It's complicated, and there's a lot of red tape involved, but refunds save you substantial money.
3. Haggle in the open-air flea markets of Paris. Depending on how much the owner wants to sell, you can secure some good buys by strong, steady, and firm bargaining.
4. Sometimes if you pay cash instead of using a credit card, the shopkeeper will lower the price.
5. Don't assume that because a certain product is made in France that it's cheaper. Check prices at home before leaving so that you'll know what's a good buy.

everything from Russian icons to 19th-century furniture to art deco pieces. Located across from a giant parking lot beside the Louvre, it houses 250 dealers in its 2½ acres of well-lit modern salons. Customers go down an enormous flight of stairs, past a café and a reception area, before reaching the art dealers' inner sanctum. This former department store was built in 1852 according to Napoléon's plans for rue de Rivoli. Métro: Louvre.

THE VILLAGE SUISSE, 78, av. de Suffren, 15e, and 54, av. de la Motte-Picquet, 15e.
This is a vast Left Bank complex of 200 antiques shops and boutiques. Parisian interior decorators frequent the gallery for their wealthy clients, looking for oil paintings, silver, copper, pewter, or antique furniture from all major periods and styles. Bargain hunters should look elsewhere. Métro: La Motte-Picquet.

ART

CARNAVALETTE, 2, rue des Francs-Bourgeois, 3e. Tel. 42-72-91-92.
Carnavalette is just off place des Vosges in the Marais. It sells unusual, one-of-a-kind engravings, plus a large collection of satirical 19th-century magazines and newspapers. Métro: St-Paul.

GALERIE DOCUMENTS, 53, rue de Seine, 6e. Tel. 43-54-50-68.
Galerie Documents contains one of the most original collections of old posters (1870–1930) in Paris. Many are inexpensive, although you could easily pay 1,200 F ($216) for an original. The store will mail your poster home. Métro: Odéon.

GALERIE 27, 27, rue de Seine, 6e. Tel. 43-54-78-54.
Galerie 27 sells lithographs by some of the most famous artists of the early 20th century, including Picasso. The inventory ranges from art posters selling for 50 F ($9) each to original paintings by Chagall, Miró, Picasso, and Léger. Métro: St-Germain-des-Prés.

MAEGHT EDITEUR & ADRIEN MAEGHT GALLERY, 42, rue du Bac, 7e. Tel. 45-48-31-01.
This gallery has an interesting collection of posters and pictorial books by important artists, such as Matisse. Exhibits include modern sculpture and engravings by established and unknown artists. Métro: Rue-du-Bac.

SCHMOCK BROC, 15, rue Racine, 6e. Tel. 46-33-79-98.
Located on the Left Bank near the Odéon, Schmock Broc is a specialty shop run by one of the city's leading collectors of jewelry from the '40s and '50s, paintings, and drawings. Explore the collection of jewelry, art, and other items discovered during the owner's frequent shopping expeditions. Métro: Odéon.

BOOKS

THE ABBEY BOOKSHOP, 29, rue de la Parcheminerie, 5e. Tel. 46-33-16-24.
An offshoot of the Abbey Bookshop of Toronto, this Left Bank shop specializes in works of Canadian writers. Browse through new and used books while sipping complimentary tea or coffee. The shop also specializes in high-quality hardcovers dealing with history, politics, literature, and philosophy. Métro: St-Michel.

BRENTANO'S, 37, av. de l'Opéra, 2e. Tel. 42-61-52-50.
Brentano's is one of the leading English-language bookstores in Paris, offering guides, maps, novels, and nonfiction. Métro: Opéra.

W. H. SMITH AND SON, 248, rue de Rivoli, 1er. Tel. 42-60-37-97.
Right across from the Tuileries Gardens, W. H. Smith and Son is the best English bookstore in Paris. Books, magazines, and newspapers published in the English-speaking world are widely available. The *New York Times* is available every Monday. The store stocks many American magazines, as well as a fine selections of maps, reference books, language books, and children's books. Métro: Concorde.

CHINA & CRYSTAL

BACCARAT, 30 bis, rue de Paradis, 10e. Tel. 47-70-64-30.
Purveyor to kings and presidents since 1764, Baccarat produces world-renowned full-lead crystal for an international clientele. Paying and nonpaying customers alike are welcome to look at the company's historical models in the Baccarat museum. Métro: Château-d'Eau, Poissonière, or Gare de l'Est.

LALIQUE, 11, rue Royale, 8e. Tel. 42-65-33-70.
Lalique is run by Marie-Claude Lalique, the granddaughter of its original founder, Réné Lalique, a silversmith who launched the shop during the Belle Epoque. Known around the world for its glass sculpture and decorative lead crystal, the shop sells a wide range of merchandise at slightly lower prices than those found abroad. Métro: Concorde.

LIMOGES-UNIC, 12 and 58, rue de Paradis, 10e. Tel. 47-70-54-49.
Limoges-Unic sells a wide stock of Limoges china—such as Ceralane, Haviland, and Bernardaud—as well as Baccarat, Villeroy & Boch, Hermès, Dior, Lanvin, Lalique, Daum, St. Louis, and Sèvres crystal. Customers will also find Christofle & Ercuis silverware and countless other items. Métro: Gare de l'Est or Poissonnière.

CHOCOLATES

DALLOYAU, 99–101, rue du Faubourg St-Honoré, 8e. Tel. 43-59-18-10.
When Dalloyau was established in 1802, the newly rich bourgeoisie rushed to its doorstep to sample its chocolates, pastries, petits-fours, and cakes. Today this store, located near some of the most fashionable boutiques in Europe, will ship its elegantly packaged confections anywhere in the world. Métro: Champs-Elysées–Clemenceau.

LA MAISON DU CHOCOLAT, 225, rue du Faubourg St-Honoré, 8e. Tel. 42-27-39-44.
One of the best places in Paris to buy chocolates, the subtle decor contains racks and racks of chocolates, priced individually or by the kilo. Each is made from a blend of as many as six different kinds of South American chocolate, flavored with just about everything imaginable. All the merchandise, including the chocolate pastries, is made in the store's supermodern cellar facilities. Closed: Aug. Métro: Ternes.

CRAFTS

BOUTIQUE DU MUSEE DES ARTS DECORATIFS, Palais du Louvre, 107, rue de Rivoli, 1er. Tel. 42-61-04-02.
This boutique, connected with the Musée des Arts Décoratifs, offers attractive household goods, some museum replicas. Craftspeople have copied museum pieces in faïence and molded crystal, jewelry and porcelain boxes, even scarves. Also there is a selection of the work of young French artists in ceramic, jewelry, and glass. Métro: Palais Royal or Tuileries.

LE PRINTEMPS, 64, bd. Haussmann, 9e. Tel. 42-82-50-00.
In addition to its other merchandise, Le Printemps offers one of the largest selections of handcrafts in Paris. Métro: Havre-Caumartin.

TROUSSELIER, 73, bd. Haussmann, 8e. Tel. 42-66-97-95.
The century-old Trousselier is one of the few places still dedicated to crafting artificial flowers. At first glance it seems to be an ordinary flower shop, but a second look or touch will reveal silk flowers that have been hand-painted by artisans who work in the back of the store. The exquisite flowers are expensive but worth the price. Métro: Havre-Caumartin.

DEPARTMENT STORES

GALERIES LAFAYETTE, 40, bd. Haussman, 9e. Tel. 42-82-34-56.
A landmark in the Parisian fashion world and a beautiful example of the city's Belle Epoque architecture, Galeries Lafayette is one of the world's leading department

stores. A special entrance marked WELCOME directs you to English-speaking hostesses available to assist you. The Galeries Lafayette includes the Galfa Club men's store, Lafayette Sports, and the main store, featuring the latest in international fashion designs, unusual gifts, perfumes, and quality housewares. Finish your shopping day with an exceptional view of Paris on the Galeries Lafayette rooftop terrace. Métro: Chausée-d'Antin or Opéra.

LE PRINTEMPS, 64, bd. Haussmann, 9e. Tel. 42-82-50-00.

Le Printemps is the city's largest department store, consisting of three stores connected by bridges on the second and third floors. Brummell offers men's clothing, while Printemps de la Mode sells clothes for women, juniors, and children. Printemps de la Maison is mainly for records, books, furniture, and housewares. The ground floor has one of the largest perfumeries in Paris, as well as cosmetics, gifts, and handcrafts. Interpreters stationed at the Welcome Service on the ground floor will help you claim your discounts and guide you to departments. International customers are also invited to the store's fashion shows, held under the historic 1923 glass dome every Tuesday throughout the year and every Tuesday and Friday at 10am March through October. Métro: Havre-Caumartin. RER: Auber.

SAMARITAINE, 19, rue de la Monnaie, 1er. Tel. 40-41-20-20.

Samaritaine is a much less expensive, family-oriented department store. It is one of the *grands magasins* (department stores) of Paris, with some good buys in clothing, and a little bit of everything. A restaurant on the premises serves meals Monday through Saturday from 11:30am to 3pm. Métro: Pont-Neuf.

DISCOUNT STORES

Discount houses tend to be crowded, and customers often feel rushed. At each of the following stores, however, at least one of the employees speaks English.

ANNA LOWE, 35, av. Matignon, 8e. Tel. 43-59-96-61.

Anna Lowe is the premier boutique in Paris for high-quality clothing at discount prices. The boutique is only half a block from rue du Faubourg St-Honoré, where haute couture is much more expensive. All items sold by former model Anna Lowe have the designer's label still attached, including Chanel, Valentino, Givenchy, Ungaro, La Croix, and Guy Laroche. Prices are often half the usual prices of the garments. The merchandise from last season's collection of famous designs does not contain factory rejects or seconds, although some of the clothes are models' samples. Alterations are done for a normal price, often within two or three days. Métro: Miromesnil.

MENDES [ST-LAURENT], 65, rue Montmartre, 2e. Tel. 42-36-83-32.

Many fashion-conscious and budget-conscious Parisian women come to Mendes, on the edge of the garment district, to buy St-Laurent sportswear. Sometimes discounts on "last season's" clothing average as much as 50%. There are no dressing rooms, no alterations, and no exchanges or refunds. Clothes from the winter collection are available at reduced prices after mid-January, and similarly, clothes from the summer collection become available after mid-July. None of the clothing has been worn. Métro: Les Halles.

FASHION FOR CHILDREN

BONPOINT, 15, rue Royale, 8e. Tel. 47-42-52-63.

Located near Maxim's, Bonpoint is part of a well-known haute couture chain for children. Clothing is well tailored—and very expensive. The shop sells clothes for boys and girls ages 1 day to 16 years. Its strongest inventories are in formal dresses, confirmation dresses, and the long and elegant baptism robes, embroidered in France and edged in lace. Métro: Concorde.

FASHION FOR WOMEN

BOUTIQUE ALAIA, 7, rue de Moussy, 4e. Tel. 42-72-19-19.

Enormously popular with stylish, young-at-heart French women, who often swear by its merchandise, this is one of Paris's up-and-coming new designers whose prices have not yet reached the stratospheric level of the city's better-known couturiers. Based on the designs of a talented French-speaking Tunisian (Azzedine Alaïa), the store is definitely worth a look. Métro: Hôtel-de-Ville.

CELINE, 24, rue François-1er, 8e. Tel. 47-20-22-83.
Céline is one of the best choices for ultraconservative, well-made clothes that are said to last forever. There's also a selection of elegant shoes and handbags. Métro: F-D-Roosevelt.

CHANEL, 31, rue Cambon, 1er. Tel. 42-86-28-00.
Located across from the Ritz, Chanel is a haute couture landmark. Prices, of course, are astronomical. The shop also sells accessories, perfumes, cosmetic lines, and watches. Métro: Concorde or Tuileries.

CHANEL, 42, av. Montaigne, 8e. Tel. 47-23-74-12.
This Chanel boutique offers reasonably priced, but still very expensive, ready-to-wear clothes. Here customers will find the classic designs and accessories that never go out of style. Métro: F-D-Roosevelt.

CHRISTIAN DIOR, 28-32, av. Montaigne, 8e. Tel. 40-73-54-44.
Christian Dior offers a wide selection of women's and men's sportswear and accessories. There are separate salons for shoes and leather goods, furs, children's clothing, jewelry, and other items. Métro: F-D-Roosevelt.

HERMES, 24, rue du Faubourg St-Honoré, 8e. Tel. 44-17-47-17.
The legendary Hermès shop is noted for its silk scarves printed with antique motifs. Ties, fragrances, clothing, and other items also are available. Hermès leather goods, such as reindeer hide, kid, and doeskin gloves, are known worldwide. Handbags are crafted on the premises. Métro: Concorde.

JOSEPHINE FISSE, 5, rue Clement-Marot, 8e. Tel. 47-23-45-27.
Situated near avenue Montaigne, Josephine Fisse is a superchic, high-tech boutique that carries the latest styles of Sonia Rykiel. Métro: F-D-Roosevelt.

LANVIN, 22, rue du Faubourg St-Honoré, 8e. Tel. 47-63-80-21.
Lanvin specializes in women's fashions and accessories. On the second floor, haute couture dresses are presented in the salon. On the first floor, customers will find chic and contemporary *prêt-à-porter* (ready-to-wear) dresses and ensembles. Métro: Concorde.

AUX MUSES D'EUROPE, 64, rue de Seine, 6e. Tel. 43-26-89-63.
Aux Muses d'Europe sells beautiful antique lace dresses, as well as vintage clothing (1900–50) and accessories. With items collected from all over France by the mother-daughter team of Marguerite and Katia Belleville, the shop frequently outfits actresses in period costumes. Linens, accessories, costume jewelry, bags, gloves (1940–50), and lace-trimmed baby dresses also are available. Métro: Odéon or St-Germain-des-Prés.

SARA SHELBURNE, 10, rue du Cygne, 1er. Tel. 42-33-74-40.
Sara Shelburne, a law student turned designer, has created a luxurious ready-to-wear boutique for women, with dresses, separates, gowns, coats, knits, and sexy evening wear. Shelburne designs and makes most of her fabrics; machine-washable combed-wool knits, Egyptian cotton, dyed-to-match silks, velvets, and lace. She'll make garments to your measurements for the same price as ready-to-wear within two days. In addition to her world-renowned wedding dress department, Sara Shelburne has added a collection of handmade shoes coordinated with the colors of her clothes, in suede, leather, or the same silk as a dress. Métro: Les Halles or Etienne-Marcel.

FASHION FOR MEN

ALAIN FIGARET, 21, rue de la Paix, 2e. Tel. 42-65-04-99.
Alain Figaret has one of Paris's best selections of men's shirts. Although there is a

broad range of fabrics, each shirt has the same classic appeal. The store prides itself on selling cotton (never silk) shirts and all-silk (never synthetic) neckties. They also sell men's underwear and elegant pajamas. Métro: Opéra.

CERRUTI, 1881, 27, rue Royale, 8e. Tel. 42-65-66-72.
Cerruti, just down the street from Maxim's, is my favorite store for men's designer clothing. The clothes are beautiful but expensive. The store is named after a Milanese couturier who established the first branch, as the name implies, in 1881. It specializes in well-styled and lightweight men's clothing, closely fitted in the Italian style to men of medium builds. Much of the apparel is designed for warm-weather climates. Métro: Concorde.

LANVIN, 15, rue du Faubourg St-Honoré, 8e. Tel. 42-65-14-40.
This shop, one of the most elegant in Paris, is just one of many Lanvin boutiques throughout the city. Specializing in "the latest" conservative but stylish fashion, Lanvin also sells a handsome collection of shirts and ties (and will custom-make shirts and suits). Métro: Concorde.

PIERRE CARDIN BOUTIQUE HOMMES, 59, rue du Faubourg St-Honoré, 8e. Tel. 42-66-92-25.
Pierre Cardin carries a large assortment of sophisticated men's clothing and some of the finest accessories available, including an unusual selection of men's shoes. As you'd expect, everything is expensive. Métro: Champs-Elysées–Clemenceau.

FOOD

FAUCHON, place de la Madeleine, 8e. Tel. 47-42-60-11.
A vast shop filled with gastronomic goodies, Fauchon is one of the most popular city sights. The window display, often including plump chickens or lamb filled with fresh vegetables, entices passersby on place de la Madeleine. Once you're inside, English-speaking clerks help you choose from the wide selection. The fruit-and-vegetable department offers such items as rare mushrooms and *fraises des bois* (wild strawberries). The confectionery store features different types of pastry and especially good candies. Also on the premises is a self-service stand-up bar, a cocktail department, a gifts department, a selection of porcelain and table settings, and an impressive collection of wines. Métro: Madeleine.

GLASSWARE

AMON GALLERY [Galerie d'Amon], 28, rue St-Sulpice, 6e. Tel. 43-26-96-60.
Just off the Jardin du Luxembourg, near the Church of St-Sulpice, Amon Gallery has a permanent exhibition of glasswork, with a wide range of items from France and abroad. Madeleine and Jean-Pierre Maffre display items in blown glass, blown engraved glass, scent bottles for collectors, and paperweights created by the best "glass artists" in the field. Métro: Odéon.

HATS

E. MOTSCH, 42, av. George-V, 8e. Tel. 47-23-79-22.
Located just off the Champs-Elysées, E. Motsch has been, since 1887, one of the most distinguished outlets for classic handmade hats for both men and women. The staff offers almost every type of headgear, from berets to Scottish tam-o'-shanters. The women's section contains some of the most stylish, albeit conservative, hats in Paris. Métro: George-V.

HOME FURNISHINGS & ACCESSORIES

ELINAS L. R., 2, rue Duphot, 8e. Tel. 42-86-02-40.
At this small emporium/showroom, a former student of art history, Marie-Christine de la Rochefoucauld, has created unique items, including custom-made screens, tabletop accessories, and even her own signature chairs. She also designs

tables in unusual woods, including lemon wood, shagreen, and ebony. These tables are most often painted in abstract themes. Métro: Madeleine.

NUIT BLANCHE, 55, rue Boissière, 16e. Tel. 47-04-42-43.
An elegantly chic Parisian woman, Sabine Marchal, has opened this boutique devoted to the comforts of the bedroom. That means an array of exquisite sheets and pillowcases, many with hand-embroidered work. Sheet sizes are made to fit American beds. Métro: Boissière.

JEWELRY

VAN CLEEF & ARPELS, 22, place Vendôme, 1er. Tel. 42-61-58-58.
Established around the turn of the century, Van Cleef & Arpels is world renowned. This exclusive shop, one of many branches found throughout the world, is known for its special settings, and carries a range of deluxe watches as well. Métro: Opéra or Tuileries.

LEATHER GOODS

GUCCI, 2, rue du Faubourg St-Honoré, 8e. Tel. 42-96-83-27.
This Gucci store is one of the world's largest showcases for the Milan-based designer, with his trademark red-and-green-trimmed leather goods. Gucci makes some of the world's most outstanding shoes and handbags, as well as other accessories, including wallets, handbags, gloves, and clothing items. This branch also has an excellent selection of scarves, two-piece ensembles, and sweaters. Métro: Concorde.

LINGERIE & BATHING SUITS

CADOLLE, 14, rue Cambon, 1er. Tel. 42-60-94-94.
The store's original owner, Herminie Cadolle, invented the brassiere in 1889. Today the store is managed by Herminie's descendants, Alice and Poupie Cadolle, who offer made-to-order and ready-to-wear lingerie. Custom-made whalebone corsets are still available, and the nightgowns range from the demure to the scandalous. There is also a collection of bathing suits, as well as the famous perfume, Le No. 9. Métro: Concorde or Madeleine.

MALLS

FORUM DES HALLES, 1-7, rue Pierre-Lescot, 1er. Tel. 42-96-68-74.
Once the great old vegetable markets, Les Halles is now a vast crater in the middle of Paris, selling, among other things, clothing, accessories, food, and gifts. Métro: Etienne-Marcel.

MONTPARNASSE SHOPPING CENTRE, between rue de l'Arrivée and rue du Départ, 14e.
Boutiques in this shopping center offer men's and women's fashions, jewelry, perfume, cosmetics, gifts, shoes, art, wool, records, glasses, and children's wear. Shoppers will also find a branch of Galeries Lafayette, restaurants, a travel agent, and even a swimming pool inside. Métro: Montparnasse-Bienvenue.

PALAIS DES CONGRES DE PARIS BOUTIQUES, 2, place de la Porte-Maillot, 17e. Tel. 40-68-26-24.
Palais des Congrès de Paris Boutiques, located inside the convention building, offers art, fine food, fashion, jewelry, toys, books, records, and children's wear. You'll also find a Japanese department store and hairdressers. Métro: Porte-Maillot.

MARKETS

MARCHE AUX PUCES, av. de la Porte de Clignancourt.
Marché aux Puces has an enormous mixture of vintage bargains and old junk, some of which was stolen only the night before. It's estimated that the complex has 2,500–3,000 open stalls spread over half a mile.

Monday is traditionally the day for bargain hunters, and negotiating is a must. Finds are rare, however, because the best buys have been skimmed by dealers.

Once you arrive at Porte de Clignancourt, turn left and cross boulevard Ney, then walk north on avenue de la Porte de Clignancourt. You'll pass stalls offering cheap clothing, but continue walking until you see the entrances to the first maze of flea-market stalls on the left. Open Saturday through Monday from 9am to 6pm. Métro: Porte-de-Clignancourt. Bus: 56.

MARCHE AUX FLEURS AND MARCHE AUX OISEAUX, place Louis-Lépine, Ile de la Cité, 4e.

The Flower Market, on the Ile de la Cité in the 4th arrondissement, behind the Tribunal de Commerce, has always provided inspiration for artists and a breath of fresh air for tourists. The stalls burst with color, displaying flowers, usually from the French Riviera—at least those that have escaped the perfume factories, of course.

The Marché aux Oiseaux (Bird Market) is also located at place Louis-Lépine. Even if you're not in the market for a rare bird, you'll want to have a look. The stalls run along the Seine, from the Louvre to the Hôtel de Ville. The Flower Market is open daily from 8am to 4pm; the Bird Market, on Sunday from 9am to 7pm. Métro: Cité.

PERFUMES

FREDDY OF PARIS, 10, rue Auber, 9e. Tel. 47-42-63-41.

Located near the American Express office and the Opéra, Freddy of Paris offers discounts of up to 40% on all name-brand perfumes, creams, novelties, gifts, top-fashion handbags, scarves, ties, and costume jewelry. Métro: Auber or Opéra.

MICHEL SWISS, 16, rue de la Paix, 2e. Tel. 42-61-61-11.

On the surface, Michel Swiss looks like many of the ultrachic boutiques near place Vendôme. But once you're inside (there's no storefront window), you'll see the major brands of luxury perfumes, makeup, leather bags, pens, neckties, fashion accessories, and giftware, all discounted by 25%, plus an additional tax discount for non-EC residents amounting to 15.7%. It's a good idea to avoid the crowds who pile in here at lunchtime. Métro: Opéra.

PARFUMERIE FRAGONARD, 9, rue Scribe, 9e. Tel. 47-42-93-40.

In a Napoléon III town house, near the Paris Opéra, this perfume house contains a more edited version of the museum of perfume in Grasse (established in 1782 on the French Riviera). This Parisian shop is an outlet for the scent factories in Eze and Grasse. The aluminum containers in which it sells its scents are said to keep the perfume fresh for up to 10 years. Métro: Opéra. RER: Auber.

SOUVENIRS & GIFTS

EIFFEL SHOPPING, 9 av. de Suffren, 7e. Tel. 45-66-55-30.

Eiffel Shopping offers a free glass of cognac while you browse through the designer collection (Céline, St-Laurent, Lanvin, Cartier, and Chanel, to name just a few) of handbags, ties, scarves, watches, sunglasses, jewelry, perfumes, Lalique crystal, and much more. This tax-free shopping center, only a block from the Eiffel Tower, offers top-quality merchandise at discount prices, and all the salespeople are bilingual. Métro: Bir-Hakeim.

STATIONERY

CASSEGRAIN, 422, rue St-Honoré, 8e. Tel. 42-60-20-08.

Cassegrain, which has another store at 81, rue des Sts-Pères, 6e. (tel. 42-22-04-76; Métro: Sèvres), opened right after World War I and is considered the premier stationery shop in the city. The store offers beautifully engraved traditional stationery, as well as buiness cards and gift items. Métro: Concorde.

TABLEWARE & BED LINEN

AU BAIN MARIE, 10, rue Boissy-d'Anglas, 8e. Tel. 42-66-59-74.

Located between Hermès at Faubourg St-Honoré and the Hôtel de Crillon, this is one of the best choices in town for new, antique, and embroidered table and bedroom linen. The store also sells virtually everything for a dining table, including antique and modern tableware and about 5,000 English and French books on food and wine. A mail-order catalog is available. Métro: Concorde.

TOYS

AU NAIN BLEU, 406, rue St-Honoré, 8e. Tel. 42-60-39-01.

In business since 1836, "The Blue Dwarf" is filled with toy soldiers, stuffed animals, games, model airplanes, technical toys, model cars, and puppets. France's oldest toy shop has attracted such customers as Sarah Bernhardt and Marcel Proust. The shop is also known for its repair service, its craftspeople specializing in mending "golden toy oldies." Métro: Concorde.

LE MONDE EN MARCHE, 34, rue Dauphine, 6e. Tel. 43-26-66-53.

Le Monde en Marché has a large assortment of reasonably priced, creative toys, including music boxes and tin animals. It's been at the address since 1965. Métro: Odéon.

RIGODON, 13, rue Racine, 6e. Tel. 43-29-98-66.

This might be one of the most famous stores of its kind in Europe. It contains one of the most varied puppet and marionette collections anywhere hanging from its ceiling. They come in all characters, sizes, and prices, and include angels, witches on broomsticks, bat women with feathered wings, and delicately elegant re-creations of porcelain dolls in 18th-century costumes. About half the inventory is fabricated by French subcontractors near Paris; others come from Italy and Southeast Asia. In recent years, many of the products here have been used as props by the California film industry. Métro: Odéon.

CHAPTER 10

PARIS EVENING ENTERTAINMENT

Parisians tend to do everything later than their Anglo-American counterparts. Once the workday is over, people head straight to the café, where they meet up with friends, and from there they go to the restaurant or bar and finally to the nightclub.

1. THE CAFES OF PARIS

To a Parisian a café is a combination club, tavern, and snack bar. You can read your newspaper, meet a friend, do your homework, or write your memoirs in a café. You can nibble at a hard-boiled egg or drink yourself into oblivion. Often people meet at cafés to relax and talk before going to a show.

Cafés aren't restaurants, although the larger ones may serve complete and excellent meals. They aren't bars either, although they do offer a variety of alcoholic drinks. And they aren't coffee shops in the American sense, because you can order a bottle of champagne just as readily as an iced chocolate.

Contrary to general belief, the coffeehouse is not a French invention. It began in 17th-century Vienna and flourished in London long before taking root in France. Parisians transformed it into the symbol of their inimitable brand of *joie de vivre*. Cafés are plentiful—a single block in one of the centrally located arrondissements may sport three or four.

A few of my nightlife choices are classic Paris cafés, whose texture changes radically over the course of a day. Considered the living rooms and unofficial salons of many neighborhood residents, these cafés thrive during the workday, when their premises burgeon with clients and activities. They adopt a different, less hurried, aura at night, when wine and brandy replace café au lait as the drink of choice, and the dark shadows and bright lights of nocturnal Paris give life a different perspective.

BRASSERIE LIPP, 151, bd. St-Germain, 6e. Tel. 45-48-53-91.
The Lipp has been called the "rendezvous for le tout Paris." Picasso and Charles de Gaulle patronized this St-Germain-des-Prés landmark, as did Max Ernst, Sartre, André Gide, Man Ray, Simone de Beauvoir, James Joyce, and James Baldwin. After the 1944 Liberation, Hemingway was, according to the former owner, Roger Cazes, the first to return to the café. Today you might see Catherine Deneuve sitting on a mole-skin banquette, her face reflected in the "hall of mirrors." An Alsatian named Lipp opened the café after the Franco-Prussian War of 1870–71. He preferred not to live in Germany, he said, but could not do without Alsatian beer, which is still served today.

The restaurant has an upstairs dining room, but it's more fashionable to sit in the back room. During the rush hours it's very difficult to get a seat unless you're a regular. For breakfast, order the traditional black coffee and croissants. At lunch or dinner, the house specialty is pork and choucroute (sauerkraut)—some say it's the best sauerkraut in Paris. There are usually three or four plats du jour offered. Meals cost 200–250 F ($36–$45). The waiters in their black jackets and white aprons are reminiscent of fin-de-siècle Paris. May it live forever! Open daily from 9am to 2am—it's fashionable to arrive late. Métro: St-Germain-des-Prés.

CAFE DE CLUNY, 20, bd. St-Michel, or 102, bd. St-Germain, 5e. Tel. 43-26-68-24.

Placed strategically at the intersection of these two famous avenues, the Café de Cluny overlooks the hub of the Left Bank and the Musée de Cluny. It's a popular meeting place for residents and tourists. In addition to the traditional drinks, meals are served. For example, a plate of entrecôte with french-fried potatoes costs 55 F ($9.90). Beer is 22 F ($4); coffee, 12 F ($2.20). Open daily from 7am to 2am. Métro: St-Michel.

CAFE DE FLORE, 172, bd. St-Germain, 6e. Tel. 45-48-55-26.

Sartre, the granddaddy of existentialism, often came here during the war and was a key figure in the Resistance. Wearing a leather jacket and beret, he sat at his table and wrote his trilogy, *Les Chemins de la Liberté* (The Roads to Freedom). In *A Memoir in the Form of a Novel (Two Sisters)*, Gore Vidal introduces his two main characters with "I first saw them at the Café de Flore in the summer of 1948. They were seated side by side at the center of the first row of sidewalk tables, quite outshining Sartre and de Beauvoir, who were holding court nearby." Camus, Picasso, and Apollinaire also frequented the Flore. The café is still going strong, although the famous folks have moved on. Espresso costs 21 F ($3.80) and a glass of beer goes for 40 F ($7.20). Open daily from 7am to 1:30am (closed July). Métro: St-Germain-des-Prés.

CAFE DE LA PAIX, place de l'Opéra, 9e. Tel. 40-07-30-12.

This has been a popular American enclave since the Yankee troops marched down the street in their victory parade after World War I. After picking up your mail at the nearby American Express, read it at your leisure at a sidewalk table under the green canopy. There's also a stunning view of the Opéra. Famous visitors have included Emile Zola, Oscar Wilde, Edward VII, de Maupassant, Chevalier, Caruso, and Chagall. No one can remember Charles de Gaulle dining here, but a messenger arrived and ordered a "tinned" ham for the general's first supper when he returned to Paris in 1944 at the Liberation. Whiskey costs 46–57 F ($8.30–$10.30), a soda is 26 F ($4.70), and café espresso, 19 F ($3.40). Open daily from 10am to 1:30am. Métro: Opéra.

LA COUPOLE, 102, bd. Montparnasse, 14e. Tel. 43-20-14-20.

This Montparnasse café is so well known that some tourists stop here with suitcases in tow for a beer or coffee before beginning the search for a hotel. The café is big, bold, and brassy, with pillars decorated by artists between the two world wars. The clientele ranges from artists' models to young men dressed like Rasputin. In 1928 Fraux and Lafon—two waiters at the Café du Dôme—opened La Coupole. At first the new café was unwelcome; now it's a landmark. Many of the Dôme's faithful customers were lured here, including Kiki, the prostitute who wrote a memoir with a forward by Hemingway.

Order a coffee or cognac VSOP at one of the sidewalk tables. The dining room looks like a railway station but serves surprisingly good food. Try the sole meunière, curry d'agneau (lamb), or cassoulet. The fresh oysters and shellfish are especially popular. A buffet breakfast is served from 7:30 to 10:30am Monday through Friday only for 78 F ($14). Coffee costs 20 F ($3.60), and a complete meal begins at 275 F ($49.50) Open daily from 7:30am to 2am. Métro: Vavin.

DEUX MAGOTS, 170, bd. St-Germain, 6e. Tel. 45-48-55-25.

This legendary café and brasserie is still the hangout for the sophisticated residents of St-Germain-des-Prés and a tourist favorite in summer. Tourists virtually monopolize the limited number of sidewalk tables. Waiters rush about, seemingly oblivious to your needs. Off-season, it's not a lonesome café, as the regulars quickly learn who's who.

The Deux Magots was once a gathering place of the intellectual elite, including Sartre, Simone de Beauvoir, and Jean Giraudoux. Inside are two large Oriental statues that give the café its name. The crystal chandeliers are too brightly lit, but the regulars seem used to the glare. After all, some of them even read newspapers there. An espresso is 19 F ($3.40); beer goes for 24–38 F ($4.30–$6.80). Open daily from 7:30am to 1:30am. Métro: St-Germain-des-Prés.

LE DOME, 108, bd. du Montparnasse, 14e. Tel. 43-35-25-81.

Many Parisians regretted when Le Dôme's dowdy but authentic original decor was ripped out and replaced with a glossy art nouveau reproduction. Today, although the style of the old café is just a memory, it's the most self-consciously glamorous of the *brasseries de luxe* of the Montparnasse neighborhood, and perhaps the most expensive. Many tourists today stop for a cup of coffee or for a sampling of the fresh oysters that are displayed in refrigerated cases. Menu specialties include pot-au-feu of seafood, turbot with hollandaise sauce, filet of sea wolf with morels and fresh asparagus, and beefsteaks. Coffee costs 12 F ($2.20) and complete meals run 350–450 F ($63–$81). Open Tuesday through Sunday from 8:30 to 12:45am. Meals are served Tuesday through Sunday from noon to 3pm and 7pm to 12:45am. During August, both the café and restaurant are also closed on Sunday. Métro: Vavin.

FOUQUET'S, 99, av. des Champs-Elysées, 8e. Tel. 47-23-70-60.

Founded at the turn of the century, Fouquet's is the premier sidewalk café on the Champs-Elysées. It has attracted many famous celebrities, including Chaplin, Chevalier, Dietrich, Mistinguett, and even Churchill and Roosevelt. Outside tables are separated from the sidewalk by a barricade of potted flowers. Inside is an elegant grill room with leather banquettes and rattan furniture, as well as private banquet rooms and a restaurant on the upper level. In the café and grill room, main courses run 125–160 F ($22.50–$28.80) and the fixed-priced menu is 240 F ($43.20); sandwiches go for 65 F ($11.70) and a glass of wine is 42 F ($7.60).

The café and grill room are open daily from 8am to midnight; the restaurant and banquet rooms, Monday through Friday from 8am to midnight (the restaurant and banquet rooms are closed mid-July to late August). Métro: George-V.

LE MANDARIN, 148, bd. St-Germain, 6e. Tel. 46-33-98-35.

This elegantly decorated corner café is always packed with a young Left Bank crowd and visitors to St-Germain-des-Prés. Fine wines and coffee are served at the brass bar. Bentwood chairs are scattered over several raised platforms and spill out onto the sidewalk in warm weather. The decor includes lace-covered hanging lamps, brass trim, and lots of exposed wood. The specialties are punch and onion soup auvergnat. Crêpes run 22–38 F ($4–$6.80) and coffee costs 14–17 F ($2.50–$3.10); the higher prices are in effect after 10pm. Open Sunday through Thursday from 8am to 2am, on Friday to 3am, and on Saturday to 4am. Métro: Odéon or Mabillon.

LA ROTONDE, 105, bd. du Montparnasse, 6e. Tel. 43-26-68-84.

Once patronized by Hemingway, the original Rotonde faded into history. Lavishly upgraded, this reincarnation, which is both a restaurant and a café, has art deco paneling and shares the original hallowed site with a movie theater. A complete meal costs 225 F ($40.50); a glass of wine, 20 F ($3.60); prices are lower if you stand at the bar. Open Sunday through Thursday from 7:30am to 2am and on Friday and Saturday from 7:30am to 3am. Métro: Vavin.

LE SELECT, 99, bd. du Montparnasse, 6e. Tel. 42-22-65-27.

In *The Sun Also Rises*, Hemingway's hero walked past the "sad tables" of the Rotonde to the Select. Physically, not much has changed here since Jean Cocteau was a patron. The literary café basks in its former glory and continues to flourish, impervious to fads. It's based on the eternal truth that everyone needs a drink and drinking companions. There are 40 different whiskeys and 20 different cocktails from which to choose. Coffee costs 10–14 F ($1.80–$2.50); cocktails, 50–55 F ($9–$9.90).

Open Sunday through Thursday from 8am to 2:30am and on Friday and Saturday from 8am to 3:30am. Métro: Vavin.

2. THE ENTERTAINMENT SCENE

Announcements of shows, concerts, and even the opera programs are plastered on kiosks all over town. Listings of what's playing can be found in **Pariscope,** a weekly entertainment guide, or the English-language **Paris Passion.** Performances start later in Paris than in London or New York—anywhere from 8 to 9pm—and Parisians tend to dine after the theater. You don't have to follow suit; you may not want to, in fact, as many of the less expensive restaurants close as early as 9pm.

There are many ticket agencies in Paris, but most are found near the Right Bank hotels. Avoid them if possible. The cheapest tickets can be purchased at the theater box office. Remember to tip the usher who shows you to your seat in a theater or movie house 3 F (50¢).

DISCOUNTS

Several agencies sell tickets for cultural events and plays at discounts of up to 50%. One outlet for discount tickets is the **Kiosque Théâtre** at 15, place de la Madeleine, 8e (no phone; Métro: Madeleine), offering leftover tickets for about half price on the day of the performance. Tickets for evening performances are sold Tuesday through Friday from 12:30 to 8pm and on Saturday from 2 to 8pm. If you'd like to attend a matinée, buy your ticket on Saturday from 12:30 to 2pm or on Sunday from 12:30 to 4pm.

For discounts of 20%–40% on tickets for festivals, concerts, and theater performances, try two locations of the **FNAC** department store chain: 136, rue de Rennes, 6e (tel. 44-09-18-00; Métro: Montparnasse-Bienvenue); or in the Forum des Halles, 1-7, rue Pierre-Lescot, 1er (tel. 42-61-81-18; Métro: Châtelet–Les-Halles). To receive these discounts, you must first purchase a *carte alpha* for 80 F ($14.40), which is good for one year. These agencies are usually open Tuesday through Saturday from 10am to 7pm.

THE MAJOR CONCERT & PERFORMANCE HALLS

Comédie Française, 2, rue de Richelieu, 1er (tel. 40-15-00-15). French and contemporary theater. Métro: Palais Royal.

L'Opéra Paris Garnier, 8, rue Scribe, 9e (tel. 47-42-53-71). Ballet and musical performances. Métro: Opéra.

L'Opéra Paris Bastille, place de la Bastille, 4e (tel. 40-01-16-16). Traditional opera and symphony performances. Métro: Bastille.

Opéra-Comique, 5, rue Favart, 2e (tel. 42-96-12-20). Light-opera productions. Métro: Richelieu-Drouot.

Radio France Auditorium, 116, av. du Président-Kennedy, 16e (tel. 42-30-15-16). Among the best orchestra concerts in Paris. Métro: Passy.

Salle Pleyel, 5, rue du Faubourg St-Honoré, 8e (tel. 45-61-06-30). Home of the Orchestre de Paris. Métro: Ternes.

Théâtre des Champs-Elysées, 15, av. Montaigne, 8e (tel. 49-52-50-00). Operas, concerts, and ballets. Métro: Alma-Marceau.

Théâtre Musical de Paris, 1, place du Châtelet, 1er (tel. 40-28-28-40). Opera and ballet. Métro: Châtelet.

Théâtre National de Chaillot, place du Trocadéro, 16e (tel. 47-27-81-15). One of the largest concert halls in Paris. Métro: Trocadéro.

3. THE PERFORMING ARTS

THEATER

COMEDIE FRANÇAISE, 2, rue de Richelieu, 1er. Tel. 40-15-00-15.
Language is the only limitation to enjoying French theater. Those of you with modest French can still delight in a lively, sparkling production of Molière at this national theater, established to keep the classics alive and promote the most important contemporary authors. Nowhere else will you see the works of Molière and Racine so beautifully staged. In 1993, a much-neglected wing of the building was renovated and launched as Le Théâtre du Vieux Colombier and opened with fanfare to an appreciative French audience. Dedicated to the presentation of contemporary French-language plays, it charges a constant 130 F ($23.40) for tickets. A "jewel-box" containing only 420 seats, its repertoire is both contemporary and experimental.

Both theaters are closed on Monday. Otherwise, performances begin at 8:30pm with three thumps of a baton—a ritual imposed since the days of Louis XIV. Closed August 1 to September 15. The only matinees are on Sunday at 3pm. Métro: Palais Royal.

Admission: Tickets, 45–165 F ($8.10–$29.70).

OPERA

OPERA-COMIQUE, 5, rue Favart, 2e. Tel. 42-96-12-20.
For light-opera productions, try the Opéra-Comique. If possible, make arrangements two weeks before the performance. The box office is open Monday through Saturday from 11am to 7pm; closed July and August. Call 42-86-88-83 for reservations. Métro: Richelieu-Drouot.

Admission: Tickets, 40–600 F ($7.20–$108).

L'OPERA DE PARIS BASTILLE, place de la Bastille, 4e. Tel. 40-01-17-89.
The controversial building was designed by Canadian architect Carlos Ott, with curtains created by Issey Miyake, the Japanese fashion designer. The giant showplace was inaugurated in July 1989, and on March 17, 1990, the curtain rose on Hector Berlioz's opera *Les Troyens*. Since its much-publicized opening, the opera house has presented masterworks such as Mozart's *Marriage of Figaro* and Tchaikovsky's *Queen of Spades*. The main hall is the largest of any opera house in France, with 2,700 seats. The building also contains two additional concert halls, including an intimate room, usually used for the presentation of chamber music, with only 250 seats. Both traditional opera performances and symphony concerts are presented here.

Several concerts are presented free, in honor of certain French holidays. Write ahead for tickets to the Opéra de Paris Bastille, 120, rue de Lyon, 75012 Paris. Closed in August. Métro: Bastille.

Admission: Tickets, 40–520 F ($7.20–$93.60).

THEATRE MUSICAL DE PARIS, 1, place du Châtelet, 1er. Tel. 40-28-28-40.
The Théâtre Musical de Paris, whose prices are usually lower than those of other Paris theaters, sits behind a dignified neoclassical facade near Paris's City Hall. Built in 1862 on the site of an ancient Roman stadium, it is largely subsidized by the city government of Paris and is known for its good acoustics. Closed in July and August. Métro: Châtelet.

Admission: Tickets, opera, 70–495 F ($12.60–$89.10); concerts, 70–300 F ($12.60–$54); ballet, 70–200 F ($12.60–$36).

CLASSICAL MUSIC

There are numerous concerts throughout the year, with daily listings taking up full columns in the newspaper. Organ recitals are featured in the churches (the largest organ is in St-Sulpice); and jazz is played at the modern-art museum.

RADIO FRANCE AUDITORIUM, 116, av. du Président-Kennedy, 16e. Tel. 42-30-15-16.

One of the largest, and probably the most famous, orchestral halls in France is this mammoth auditorium, whose fine acoustics were carefully planned during its construction in 1963. The building is home to both the Orchestra National de France and the Orchestre Philharmonique. Métro: Passy.

Admission: Tickets, 80–120 F ($14.40–$21.60).

SALLE PLEYEL, 5, rue du Faubourg St-Honoré, 8e. Tel. 45-61-06-30.

A few blocks northeast of the Arc de Triomphe, the Salle Pleyel is host to the Orchestre de Paris, whose season runs from September to Easter. Tickets are sold daily from 11am to 6pm on the day of concerts. Métro: Ternes.

Admission: Tickets, 80–250 F ($14.40–$45).

THEATRE DES CHAMPS-ELYSEES, 15, av. Montaigne, 8e. Tel. 49-52-50-00.

Operas, concerts, and ballets are performed here by national and international companies. The box office is open Monday through Saturday from 11am to 7pm. Métro: Alma-Marceau.

Admission: Tickets, 60–450 F ($10.80–$81).

THEATRE NATIONAL DE CHAILLOT, place du Trocadéro, 16e. Tel. 47-27-81-15.

One of the largest concert halls in Paris, this theater is part of the complex of buildings preceding the upward thrust of the Eiffel Tower. Programs are announced on big showboards out front. Métro: Trocadéro.

Admission: Tickets, 40–400 F ($7.20–$72).

BALLET

L'OPERA PARIS GARNIER, 8, rue Scribe, 9e. Tel. 40-01-17-89.

L'Opéra is the premier stage for ballet and musical productions. Since the competition from the Opéra at the Bastille, the original opera has made great efforts to present more up-to-date works, including choreography by Jerome Robbins, Twyla Tharp, Agnes de Mille, and Georges Balanchine. This architectural wonder was designed as a contest entry by a young architect in the heyday of Napoléon III's Second Empire. The facade is adorned with marble and sculpture, including *The Dance* by Carpeaux. The great musical performers of the world, including Sarah Bernhardt, have appeared here. Métro: Opéra.

Admission: Tickets, 30–600 F ($5.40–$108).

MUSIC HALLS

A slick combination of song, dance, juggling, and acrobatics adds up to a top entertainment value for the visitor. The best music halls offer packed programs of professional talent and international stars.

OLYMPIA, 28, bd. des Capucines, 9e. Tel. 47-42-82-45.

Charles Aznavour and other big names make frequent appearances in this cavernous hall. Yves Montand appeared once—and the performance was sold out four months in advance. A typical lineup might include an English rock group singing its latest hit, a showy group of Italian acrobats, a well-known French singer, a talented dance troupe, an American juggler/comedy team (doing much of their work in English), plus the featured star. A witty emcee and an on-stage band provide a smooth transition between acts. Performances usually begin Tuesday through Sunday between 8 and 8:30pm; Saturday matinees are at either 2:30 or 5pm. Very few performances are presented in July and August. Métro: Opéra.

Admission: Tickets, 60–480 F ($10.80–$86.40).

FOLK SONGS & CHANSONNIERS

The *chansonniers* (literally "song writers") provide a bombastic musical satire of the day's events. This combination of parody and burlesque is a time-honored Gallic amusement and a Parisian institution. The wit and ridicule these performers shower upon prostitutes and presidents alike make for an extravagant revue. Songs are often created on the spot, depending for their inspiration on "the disaster of the day." The best theaters of the chansonniers are on the tawdry boulevard de Clichy.

AU LAPIN AGILE, 22, rue des Saules, 18e. Tel. 46-06-85-87.

Picasso and Utrillo once patronized this little cottage near the top of Montmartre, formerly known as the Café des Assassins. It has been painted by artists, known and unknown, including Utrillo. For many decades it has been the heartbeat of French folk music, featuring folk songs, sing-alongs, and poetry readings. You'll sit at carved wooden tables in a low, dimly lit room with walls covered with bohemian memorabilia.

Songs include old French folk tunes, love ballads, army songs, sea chanteys, and music-hall ditties. You're encouraged to sing along, even if it's only the "oui, oui, oui—non, non, non" refrain of "Les Chevaliers de la Table Ronde." You can always hum along with "Larilette" and "Madelon." The best sing-alongs are on weeknights after tourist season ends. Drinks cost 25 F ($4.50). Open Tuesday through Sunday from 9:15pm to 2am. Métro: Lamarck.

Admission: 110 F ($19.80), including the first drink.

AU CAVEAU DE LA BOLEE, 25, rue de l'Hirondelle, 6e. Tel. 43-54-62-20.

This cellar, built in 1317 as part of the historic Abbey of St-André, has been both a prison and a literary club. Paul Verlaine and Oscar Wilde drank absinthe here. There are 70 seats in niches, below a vaulted ceiling. Balladeers, poets, and storytellers perform, and the audience is encouraged to join in. It's especially popular with Left Bank students who know the "dirty old French songs." You won't understand the jokes and references made in the show unless your knowledge of French is extremely good. A fixed-price dinner costing 230 F ($41.40) is served Monday through Saturday at 9pm, followed by a cabaret show at 10:30pm. On Sunday a jazz show begins at 10:30pm. Drinks begin at 30 F ($5.40). This caveau is on a tiny street off the western edge of place St-Michel, beneath one of the square's grandiose buildings. Métro: St-Michel.

Admission: Free with fixed-price dinner, 100 F ($18) without dinner.

CAVEAU DES OUBLIETTES, 11, rue St-Julien-le-Pauvre, 5e. Tel. 43-54-94-97.

One of the most popular tourist attractions, this caveau presents French *chansons* (sentimental or bawdy love songs) dating from the 11th to the 20th century. Performers wear costumes from different eras. After the show, a guide will take you through the museum, where a chastity belt, arms and armor, and thumbscrews are on display. In the Latin Quarter, across from Notre-Dame, this caveau was opened by Marcel François in 1920, beneath the church's subterranean vaults that many centuries ago were connected to the fortress prison of the Petit Châtelet. It's best to reserve a table. Open Monday through Thursday from 9pm to 1am and on Friday and Saturday from 9pm to 2am. Métro: St-Michel.

Admission: 140 F ($25.20), including the first drink.

THEATRE DES DEUX ANES, 100, bd. de Clichy, 18e. Tel. 46-06-10-26.
If you speak colloquial French, you'll enjoy this revue of song and satire that has thrived in more or less the same format since the 1920s. Despite a much-needed renovation in 1992, the theater reminds many Parisians of a comic-operetta house which might have thrived in Marseilles during the 1930s. It lies a short distance from the much more famous Moulin Rouge. Performances are Tuesday through Sunday at 9pm; the box office is open Tuesday through Sunday from 11am to 7pm. Métro: Blanche.
Admission: Tickets, 180 F ($32.40).

4. THE CLUB & MUSIC SCENE

Paris today is still a mecca for night owls, even though some of the once-unique attractions now glut the market. The fame of Parisian nights was established in those distant days of innocence when Anglo-Americans still gasped at the sight of a bare bosom in a chorus line. The fact is that contemporary Paris has less nudity than London, less vice than Hamburg, and less drunkenness than San Francisco.

Nevertheless, both the quantity and the variety of Paris nightlife still beat those of any metropolis on earth. Nowhere else will you find such a huge and mixed array of clubs, bars, discos, cabarets, jazz dives, music halls, and honky-tonks.

NIGHTCLUBS/CABARET

CABARET LIDO NORMANDIE, 116 bis, av. des Champs-Elysées, 8e. Tel. 40-76-56-10.
Sitting in the panoramic Lido Cabaret, the audience is overwhelmed with glamour and talent. The permanent attractions are the Bluebell Girls, a fabulous precision ensemble of long-legged, beautiful international women. The show, which is visible from any seat in the theater, is subject to change. Dinner is served at 8:30pm, and the revue begins at 10pm and 12:15am daily. Métro: George-V.
Admission: 640–810 F ($115.20–$145.80) including dinner, 465 F ($83.70) without dinner including a half bottle of wine.

CRAZY HORSE SALOON, 12, av. George-V, 8e. Tel. 47-23-32-32.
Arthur Sainer wrote a review of the Sam Shepard play *Shaved Splits* that would have been appropriate as a description of the show at the Crazy Horse Saloon: "frantic, wondrous, surly, delicious . . . blatant, elegiac, fatiguing, corrupting, virginal . . . stupefying, messy, giggly, two-dimensional, corrosive, counter-erotic . . . rhetorical, convulsive, metallic . . . convivial, gyrational, overheated, pop-eyed, flat-eyed, wide-eyed." That should tell you that Alain Bernardin's stripteasery is no ordinary cabaret. It's a French parody of a Far West saloon, which became the first emporium in France where the strippers tossed their G-strings to the winds, throwing up their hands for the big "revelation."
The management invites you to "Be cool! Do it yourself! We dig English like Crazy!" and indeed, the place is always packed with out-of-towners. Between acts there are vaudeville skits. The first drink (admission) price includes the cover charge and two drinks. After that, you pay an additional charge for each drink. The first drink charge depends on whether you sit in the orchestra (most expensive), the mezzanine (middle range), or the wings (least expensive). On Friday and Saturday, shows are at 8 and 10:30pm and 12:50am; Sunday through Thursday, at 8:45 and 11:15pm. Reservations are important. Métro: George-V.
Admission: 290–530 F ($52.20–$95.40), including the cover charge and two drinks; third drink from 55 F ($9.90).

FOLIES BERGERE, 32, rue Richer, 9e. Tel. 42-46-77-11.
The Folies Bergère is a Parisian institution. Since 1886 foreigners have been flocking to this cabaret for the performances, the excitement, and of course, the scantily clad dancers. The risqué spectacle is probably as famous for its

elaborate costumes as it is for nudity. From the towering plumes to the bushy tails, there can be literally thousands of costumes worn in each show.

Josephine Baker, the black American singer who used to throw bananas into the audience, became "the toast of Paris" at the Folies Bergère. According to legend, the first G.I. to reach Paris at the Liberation in 1944 asked for directions to the club. Today Parisians tend to be indifferent toward the show, but it's still packed in July.

The seats range from the *galerie* (usually the least expensive) to a loge in the orchestra or balcony. A scale model at the box office shows locations of the various seats. The box office is open daily from 10am to 10pm; the revue is presented Tuesday through Sunday at 9:30pm. Closed in January. Métro: Rue-Montmartre or Cadet.

Admission: 129–379 F ($23.20–$68.20) show only, 640–712 F ($115.20–$128.10) dinner and show.

MILLIARDAIRE, 68, rue Pierre-Charron, 8e. Tel. 42-25-25-17.

The stylishly elegant Milliardaire is just off the Champs-Elysées, reached through a backyard that's not nearly as plush as the interior. Many beautiful women appear in the show, their stylish nudity interspersed with international humor and comedy acts. Two different shows are staged nightly Monday through Saturday, at 10pm and midnight. The place maintains a popular and discreet piano bar open every night after the last show from 1:30am until dawn. Métro: F-D-Roosevelt.

Admission: 340 F ($61.20) show and two drinks, 390 F ($70.20) show and a half bottle of champagne.

MOULIN ROUGE, place Blanche, 18e. Tel. 46-06-00-19.

The Moulin Rouge was immortalized in the paintings of Toulouse-Lautrec. Later on, Colette created a scandal at the club by offering an on-stage kiss to Madame de Morny. Today the shows still have shock value. The revue itself is stunning, with elaborate feather costuming and the best cancan in France. There was the time that a nude couple jumped into a tank for some underwater recreation; or you may be treated to a ballet, with a slightly bawdy twist, of course. All in all, however, it's not that different from the Lido. Try to get a table, as the view is much better on the main floor than from the bar. Reservations are essential, but it's possible to sit at a bar stool and see the show. The bar is open 15 minutes before the beginning of each show; stools are not reserved. Drinks at the bar cost 200 F ($36), with no minimum. Dinner, served nightly between 8 and 10pm, is completed before the spectacle begins. Spectacles are nightly at 10pm and again at midnight. Métro: Place Blanche.

Admission: 670 F ($120.60) including dinner, 465 F ($83.70) without dinner including a half bottle of champagne.

LE PARADIS LATIN, 28 rue Cardinal-Lemoine, 5e. Tel. 43-25-28-28.

Built by Gustave Eiffel with the same metallic skeleton as his famous tower, Le Paradis Latin represents the architect's only venture into theater design. The theater itself is credited with introducing vaudeville and musical theater to Paris. In 1903 the building functioned as a warehouse. In the 1970s, however, it was transformed into one of the most successful cabarets in Paris. The master of ceremonies speaks in French and English. Performances are given Wednesday through Monday. Dinner is at 8pm, and the revue is presented from 10pm to midnight. Métro: Jussieu or Cardinal-Lemoine.

Admission: 670 F ($120.60) including dinner, 465 F ($83.70) including only champagne.

VILLA D'ESTE, 4, rue Arsene-Houssaye, 8e. Tel. 42-56-14-65.

In days of yore this club has booked such top talent as Amalia Rodrigues, the leading fadista of Portugal, or the French chanteuse, Juliette Greco. Today, you're more likely to hear the French singer François de Guelte. Its owners book top talent from Europe and America. A short stroll from the Champs-Elysées, the Villa d'Este has been around for a long time, and the quality of its offerings remains high. The place is a diner-dansant club more than pure cabaret. The doors open at 8pm, with an orchestra playing from 9pm. A comedy/cabaret/magic act lasts until around midnight, with dancing until 2am. The place is closed in August. Reservations are necessary. The fixed-price menus include wine that grows increasingly better as the price rises. These menus cost 200–720 F ($36–$129.60). It's also possible to attend and order only a drink. Every Sunday afternoon a tea dance with a live orchestra is presented from 3 to 7pm. Métro: Charles-de-Gaulle (Etoile).

Admission: One-drink minimum, 150 F ($27) each; tea dance, 90 F ($16.20), including first drink.

JAZZ CLUBS

Paris is the jazz center of Europe. From the caveaux of the Left Bank to the clubs on the Right, you'll hear Dixieland or Chicago rhythms. Many of the clubs recommended below combine jazz and rock.

LE BILBOQUET, 13, rue St-Benoit, 6e. Tel. 45-48-81-84.

This restaurant, jazz club, and piano bar offers some of the best music in Paris. In the heart of St-Germain-des-Prés, the site was famous during the heyday of existentialism. The film *Paris Blues* was shot here. Jazz is played on the upper level in Le Bilboquet restaurant. The wood-paneled room has a copper ceiling, a sunken bar with brass trim, and a Victorian candelabra. Tables are on a raised tier and elevated balcony. The menu is limited but classic French, specializing in carré d'agneau, fish, and beef. Appetizers include smoked salmon and terrines. Open nightly from 8pm to 2:45am. Live music is presented from 10:45pm to 2:45am.

Under separate management is the disco, Club St-Germain, downstairs, open Tuesday through Saturday from 11:30pm to dawn. Entrance is free, but drinks cost 60–90 F ($10.80–$16.20). Clients can walk from one club to the other, but they have to buy a new drink each time they change venues. Dinner at Le Bilboquet costs 250–300 F ($45–$54).

Admission: 120 F ($21.60), including first drink.

CAVEAU DE LA HUCHETTE, 5, rue de la Huchette, 5e. Tel. 43-26-65-05.

This celebrated jazz cave draws a young crowd, mostly students, who dance to the music of well-known jazz combos. This caveau is reached by a winding staircase. In pre-jazz days, it was frequented by Robespierre and Marat. Drinks begin at 18 F ($3.20). Open Sunday through Friday from 9:30pm to 3am, and on Saturday and holidays from 9:30pm to 4am. Métro: St-Michel.

Admission: 55 F ($9.90) Sun–Thurs, 65 F ($11.70) Fri, 70 F ($12.60) Sat; women students, 50 F ($9).

JAZZ CLUB LIONEL HAMPTON, in the Hôtel Méridien, 81, bd. Gouvion-Saint-Cyr, 17e. Tel. 40-68-30-42.

Some of the world's jazz greats, including namesake Lionel Hampton, have performed in the Hôtel Méridien's central courtyard. The hotel is near the Champs-Elysées and the Arc de Triomphe. It's open daily from 10pm to 2am. Métro: Porte-Maillot.

Admission: 130 F ($23.40), including the first drink.

NEW MORNING, 7-9, rue des Petites-Ecuries, 10e. Tel. 45-23-51-41.

Jazz maniacs come here to drink, talk, and dance. The high-ceilinged loft, formerly a newspaper office, was turned into a nightclub in 1981. The name comes from Bob Dylan's 1969 album. Many styles of music are played and performed, except disco. The place is especially popular with jazz groups from South and Central Africa. It's usually open Monday through Saturday from 9:30pm to 2am, although times and days can vary. Call ahead for the program and hours before you go. Shows usually begin at 8:30pm or 9:30pm. The club used to be the favorite Parisian venue for two jazz greats, Stan Getz and Dizzy Gillespie, both of whom died in 1992. No food is served. Métro: Château-d'Eau.

Admission: 100–150 F ($18–$27).

SLOW CLUB, 130, rue de Rivoli, 1er. Tel. 42-33-84-30.

One of the most famous jazz cellars in Europe, the Slow Club features the well-known French jazz band of Claude Luter, who played 10 years with the late Sidney Bechet. Drinks cost 18 F ($3.20) and up. Open Tuesday through Thursday from 10pm to 3am, and on Friday, Saturday, and holidays from 10pm to 4am. Métro: Châtelet.

Admission: 50 F ($9) Tues–Thurs, 70 F ($12.60) Fri–Sat and holidays.

TROIS MAILLETZ, 56, rue Galande, 5e. Tel. 43-54-42-94.

This medieval cellar once housed the masons who built Notre-Dame, many of whom carved their initials into the walls. Today it attracts jazz aficionados from all over the world. It's one of the few places in the district where students don't predominate. Musical celebrities appearing here have included Memphis Slim, Bill Coleman, and Nina Simone. It's open nightly from 10:30pm to "whenever"; the piano bar, daily from 5pm to 5am. Traditional French meals, such as salmon tartare and grills, are served in a restaurant adjacent to the piano bar during its entire opening time. Meals begin at 220 F ($39.60) each. Reservations are recommended on weekends. The restaurant and piano bar are on the main level, and the jazz is in the cellar. Drinks run 50–85 F ($9–$15.30). Métro: Maubert-Mutualité.

Admission: Cellar, 60–70 F ($10.80–$12.60); restaurant and piano bar, free.

DANCE CLUBS/DISCOS

Paris is supposedly the cradle of discothèques, but the definition of disco is less clear than it was when the trend started in the '60s. Originally discos were small, intimate dives where people danced to discs—hence the term. Today, however, discos can be anything from playground-size ballrooms with full orchestras to tiny bars with taped tunes where they don't let you dance at all.

The nightspots listed below are a few of the hundreds of places where people go chiefly to dance—distinct from others where the main attraction is the music.

The area opposite and around the Church of St-Germain-des-Prés is full of dance dives. They come and go so quickly that many could be hardware stores by the time you get there—but new ones will no doubt spring up to take their place.

LE PALACE, 8, rue du Faubourg-Montmartre, 9e. Tel. 42-46-10-87.

One of the leading nightclubs of Paris, La Palace re-creates 1940s Hollywood glamour. It's designed in the spirit and allure of a Roman or Greek amphitheater, with four different bars scattered over three different levels. Music is recorded, and there's plenty of room to dance. In 1992, it was acquired by Régine, empress of the Paris night, who plans to retain its youthful ambience. Management does not allow sneakers or jeans with holes pierced in indiscreet places. Open from 11pm to dawn nightly. Métro: Montmartre.

Admission: 100 F ($18) Wed and Fri–Sat, 80 F ($14.40) Sun–Tues and Thurs, including first drink.

LA BALAJO, 9, rue de Lappe, 11e. Tel. 47-00-07-87.

This club is practically a national shrine to the famous French chanteuse Edith Piaf, known as the "little sparrow," who used to perform here frequently. The place is still popular, drawing the young and the young at heart, but the music is recorded now. It's a good place to go after a performance at l'Opéra Paris Bastille. Open Thursday through Sunday from 11:30pm to 5am. Métro: Bastille.

Admission: 100 F ($18), including the first drink.

CLUB ZED, 2, rue des Anglais, 5e. Tel. 43-54-3-78.

This popular nightspot in what was originally a bakery may surprise you with its mix of musical offerings; samba music from Rio, rock, 1960s pop tunes, or jazz. Open on Wednesday and Thursday from 10:30pm to 3:30am and on Friday and Saturday from 10:30pm to 4:30am (closed in August). Métro: Maubert-Mutualité.

Admission: 50–100 F ($9–$18), including the first drink.

LA COUPOLE, 102, bd. Montparnasse, 14e. Tel. 43-20-14-21.

Below this landmark café is a basement ballroom. La Coupole is a former mecca of bohemia in Montparnasse. Today it remains a popular place to waltz and tango to orchestra music. (To prepare yourself, see *Last Tango in Paris*.) The upstairs café is previewed separately. The musical style is "disco retro" (the best disco tunes of the 1960s, '70s, and '80s). Open on Saturday and Sunday afternoons from 3 to 7pm, on

Friday and Saturday nights from 9:30pm to 4am, and on Sunday from 9:30pm to 3am. Métro: Vavin.

Admission: Café, free; ballroom, Sat matinee 60 F ($10.80), Sunday matinée 80 F ($14.40), Fri–Sat nights 90 F ($16.20).

L'ESCALE, 15, rue Monsieur-le-Prince, 6e. Tel. 43-54-63-47.

The oldest salsa and Latin music nightclub in Paris, L'Escale is located in a charming 17th-century building in St-Germain-des-Prés. The atmosphere and artistry makes the expense worthwhile. The bar is intimate and dimly lit, with a Mexican mural barely visible on the wall. Musicians play Latin American songs—not the diluted stuff you usually hear, but rather the really melancholy and wild gaucho airs. The club also has a "cave" where you can dance to a Latin combo. Open daily from 11pm to 4am. Métro: Odéon.

Admission: 80 F ($14.40), including the first drink.

NEW RIVERSIDE CLUB, 7 rue Grégoire-de-Tours, 6e. Tel. 43-54-46-33.

There's usually a line at the door to this typical Left Bank cellar disco with an interesting international crowd. Some dance *comme des foux* (like lunatics) to the rock music. Drinks run 40–60 F ($7.20–$10.80). Open daily from 11pm to either 6 or 7am. Métro: St-Michel or Odéon.

Admission (including first drink): 75 F ($13.50) Sun–Thurs, 90 F ($16.20) Fri–Sat.

5. THE BAR SCENE

WINE BARS

Many Parisians now prefer the wine bar to the traditional café or bistro. The food is often better and the ambience more inviting. Wine bars come in a wide range of styles, from old to modern.

WILLI'S WINE BAR, 13, rue des Petits-Champs, 1er. Tel. 42-61-05-09.

Journalists and stockbrokers patronize this increasingly popular wine bar in the center of the financial district, close to the Bourse. It's run by two Englishmen, Mark Williamson and Timothy P. Johnson. About 250 different kinds of wine are offered, including a dozen "wine specials," which you can taste by the glass. Lunch is the busiest time of the day—on quiet evenings, you can better enjoy the warm ambience and 16th-century beams. Daily specials, written on a blackboard, are likely to include brochette of lamb flavored with cumin or lyonnaise sausage in a truffled vinaigrette with pistachios, and a spectacular dessert, the chocolate terrine. The Fixed-price menu costs 148 F ($26.60); wine by the glass begins at 18 F ($3.20). Open Monday through Saturday from noon to 2:30pm and 7 to 11pm. Métro: Bourse, Louvre, or Palais-Royal.

AU SAUVIGNON, 80, rue des Sts-Pères, 7e. Tel. 45-48-49-02.

This tiny wine bar, with tables overflowing onto a covered terrace, is the best known in Paris. The owner is from Auvergne, and when he's not polishing his zinc countertop or preparing a plate of charcuterie for a client, he will sell you beaujolais. Wines range from the cheapest beaujolais to the most expensive Puligny Montrachet. A glass of wine runs 17–27 F ($3.10–$4.90) at the bar, 2 F (40¢) extra at a table. To go with your wine, choose a specialty from Auvergne, including goat cheese and terrines. The fresh Poilane bread is ideal with the Auvergne ham, the pâté, or the goat cheese. The place is decorated with old ceramic tiles and frescoes done by Left Bank artists. Open Monday through Saturday from 8:30am to 10:30pm (closed holidays and August). Métro: Sèvres-Babylone.

MA BOURGOGNE, 19, place des Vosges, 4e. Tel. 42-78-44-64.

The arcades here are reminiscent of Italy. There are rattan sidewalk tables and a cozy room with a beamed ceiling. Monsieur Aimé, the owner, selects the wines himself from wine growers, and his wife offers a wide choice of country dishes—I recommend her famous tartar steak. Coffee costs 12 F ($2.20) at a table or 5 F (90¢) at the bar, and a glass of beaujolais is 18 F ($3.20). A fixed-price meal costs 180 F ($32.40) (Saturday and Sunday only); an à la carte meal, 200 F ($36). The brasserie is most exciting during festivals in the Marais district. Open daily from 8am to 1am (closed in February). Métro: St-Paul or Bastille.

LA TARTINE, 24, rue de Rivoli, 4e. Tel. 42-72-76-85.

Mirrors, brass detail, and frosted-globe chandeliers make La Tartine look like a movie set of Old Paris. Infamous former patrons include Tito, Trotsky, and Lenin. At least 60 wines are offered at reasonable prices, including seven kinds of beaujolais and a large selection of bordeaux, all served by the glass. I recommend the light wine Sancerre and goat cheese from the Loire Valley. Sandwiches cost 14 F ($2.50), and a platter of charcuterie is 40 F ($7.20). A glass of wine, depending on vintage, goes for 8.50–14 F ($1.50–$2.50). Open Thursday through Monday from 8am to 10pm and on Wednesday from noon to 10pm (closed three weeks in August—dates vary). Métro: St-Paul.

BARS & PUBS

These "imported" establishments try to imitate American cocktail bars or masquerade as British pubs—most strike an alien chord. But that doesn't prevent fashionable Parisians from bar-hopping (not to be confused with café-sitting). The best bars are the famous ones in the deluxe hotels. Bars generally charge more than cafés for drinks. If you prefer the local culture, stick to the cafés, listed separately.

GEORGE V BAR, 31, av. George-V, 8e. Tel. 47-23-54-00.

The decor is elegant and symmetrical, with black accents over beige, maroon marble, and a massive crystal lighting fixture illuminating this stagelike setting. For more privacy, try the nearby salon, with couches and Regency antiques. Drinks are 90 F ($16.20). Open daily from 11am to 1:30am. Métro: George-V.

LE BAR, 10, rue de l'Odéon, 6e. Tel. 43-26-66-83.

Each evening, university students crowd this popular Left Bank hangout right off place de l'Odéon, contained on two floors. The walls are decorated with posters, and a jukebox keeps the place jumping. Many people speak English, but French is still helpful. Drinks begin at 20 F ($3.60). Open daily from 5:30am to 2am. Métro: Odéon.

BAR ANGLAIS, in the Hôtel Plaza Athenée, 25, av. Montaigne, 8e. Tel. 47-23-78-33.

This elegant bar, on the lower level, has classical Anglo-Saxon decor. The service is French, and the drinks, priced at 90 F ($16.20), are international. Open daily from 10am to 1am. Métro: Alma-Marceau.

BAR DES THEATRES, 6, av. Montaigne, 8e. Tel. 47-23-34-63.

Famous throughout Paris, the Bar des Théâtres is crowded with theatergoers before and after shows. It's across from the Théâtre des Champs-Elysées, on the "most expensive street in the world." The chic clientele seems to enjoy the cramped tables in the paneled dining room in back. Coffee at bar costs 5.50 F ($1); full meal goes for 100–300 F ($18–$54). Open daily from 6am to 2am. Métro: F-D-Roosevelt.

HOTEL DE CRILLON, 10, place de la Concorde, 8e. Tel. 44-71-15-00.

The bar is just as famous as the luxury hotel where it's located. In the past it attracted many of the Lost Generation, including Hemingway and F. Scott and Zelda Fitzgerald. Hemingway's fictional heroine, Brett Ashley, broke her promise to rendezvous here with Jake Barnes in *The Sun Also Rises*. More recent guests have included Madonna, Tom Cruise, Debra Winger, and upper-level staff of the American Embassy. Classified as a historic monument, the hotel was recently refurbished by fashion designer Sonia Rykiel. Wood paneling has been added. Drinks run 90 F ($16.20). Open daily from 11:30am to midnight. Métro: Concorde.

HOTEL BRISTOL BAR, 112, rue du Faubourg St-Honoré, 8e. Tel. 42-66-91-45.

The bar overlooks the hotel's central courtyard, with wicker chairs set out among pink marble columns and thick Oriental rugs. The spacious Regency-style bar is tended by Michel Le Regent, famous for his prize-winning specialties, like the "crazy horse cocktail" (strawberries, bananas, scotch, and champagne), the nanny's cocktail (lemon and pineapple juice, blue curaçao, banana liqueur, and vodka), and the Pluton (orange juice, pineapple juice, Pernod, vodka, and strawberries). Drinks are 90 F ($16.20). Open daily from 11am to midnight, with piano music from 7:30pm to midnight. Métro: Miromesnil.

6. SPECIALTY BARS & CLUBS

GAY PARIS

Gay life is mostly centered around Les Halles and Le Marais, with the greatest concentration of gay clubs, restaurants, bars, and shops located between the Hôtel-de-Ville and Rambuteau Métro stops. Gay discos come and go so fast that even a magazine devoted somewhat to their pursuit, **Gay Pied,** has a hard time keeping up. That magazine is sold at many news kiosks, as is **Lesbia,** a monthly national lesbian magazine.

LE BAR CENTRAL, 33, rue Vielle-du-Temple, 4e. Tel. 48-87-99-33.
Le Bar Central, with no cover charge, is one of the leading bars for men in the Hôtel-de-Ville area. In fact, it's probably the most famous gay men's bar in Paris today. Beer costs 15 F ($2.70) per glass. Open daily from 4pm to 2am. The club has established a small hotel upstairs, with a few facilities and only seven bedrooms. Singles are 400 F ($72) daily and doubles are 490 F ($88.20), excluding breakfast. Both the bar and its little hotel are in a 300-year-old building in the heart of the Marais. The hotel caters especially to gay men, less frequently to lesbians. Métro: Hôtel-de-Ville.

LA CHAMPMESLE, 4, rue Chabanais, 2e. Tel. 42-96-85-20.
With dim lighting, background music, and comfortable banquettes, La Champmesle offers a cozy and discreet meeting place for women, although men are welcome. It is, in fact, a leading women's bar of Paris. The club is in a 300-year-old building, decorated with exposed stone and heavy ceiling beams, with "retro"-style furnishings evocative of the 1950s. Every Thursday night one of the premier lesbian events of Paris is a cabaret held here beginning at 10pm. The entrance and drinks prices are the same on Thursday as any other time. Drinks run 25–80 F ($4.50–$14.40). Josy is the charming entrepreneur who established this place some 14 years ago. Open daily from 6pm to 2am. Métro: Opéra.

CLUB 18, 18, rue de Beaujolais, 1er. Tel. 42-97-52-13.
At press time, this was the leading gay bar and disco in Paris, filled mostly with men, but accommodating to women and sympathetic heterosexuals as well. Adapted from the premises of a coyly provocative bar once well known as "Whiskey-à-Go-Go," it contains a crowded bar on the street level and an animated disco in the basement. Drinks cost 50 F ($9) each. Open Tuesday through Sunday from 11pm to dawn. Métro: Bourse.
   Admission: 50 F ($9).

MADAME ARTHUR, 75 bis, rue des Martyrs, 18e. Tel. 42-64-48-27.
Madame Arthur is one of the leading female-impersonator cabarets of Europe. This place Pigalle showplace, drawing both straights and gays, is directed by Madame Arthur, who is no lady. The joke is, this place has been around so long it welcomed the invading armies of Julius Caesar—and it's still going strong. The two-hour show begins nightly between 10:45 and 11pm. You can visit just to drink, at 95 F ($17.10) each, or you can dine from a choice of fixed-price menus, the most expensive of which includes caviar; fixed-price menus cost 280–695 F ($50.40–$125.10). Reservations are a good idea. Métro: Abbesses.
   Admission: 165 F ($29.70), including the first drink.

LE NEW MONOCLE, 60, bd. Edgar-Quinet, 14e. Tel. 43-20-81-12.

Located in the center of Montparnasse, Le New Monocle has been a traditional lesbian hangout since the days of Gertrude and Alice. It is a *disco féminin,* but does admit gay male couples. All drink prices are the same—100 F ($18) for the first drink, 50 F ($9) for subsequent drinks—and there's no cover charge. Inside is a bar, plus a dance floor ringed with seats and banquettes, and comfortably battered 1950s-inspired accessories. Live entertainment is interspersed with disco music. Open Monday through Saturday from 11pm to dawn; closed in August. Métro: Edgar-Quinet.

LE PIANO ZINC, 49, rue des Blancs-Manteaux, 4e. Tel. 42-74-32-42.

This ever-popular place with no cover charge is unusual. Founded by a German-born francophile named Jürgen about 10 years ago, it's both a piano bar and a cabaret, filled with singing patrons who belt out old French *chansons* with humor and gusto. It defines itself as a gay bar, "but you can happily bring your grandmère, as some of our clients do," management assures us. The place is on three different floors of a building, with the cabaret presented in the basement nightly at 10pm for no charge. Drinks go for 42 F ($7.60); beer, 19 F ($3.40). It's open daily from 6pm to 2am. Métro: Rambuteau.

LITERARY HAUNTS

LA CLOSERIE DES LILAS, 171, bd. du Montparnasse, 6e. Tel. 43-26-70-50.

Hemingway, Picasso, Gershwin, and Modigliani all loved the Closerie, and it has once again become one of the hottest bars in Paris. Look for the brass name plate of your favorite Lost Generation artist along the banquettes or at the well-oiled bar. Scotch and soda costs 75 F ($13.50); beer, 30 F ($5.40). Open daily from 11am to 2am. Métro: Port-Royal.

HARRY'S NEW YORK BAR, 5, rue Daunou, 2e. Tel. 42-61-71-14.

⭐ Harry's, the best-known bar in Europe and the most popular American watering hole in Paris, has spawned a host of imitators. Famous patrons have included Fitzgerald, Faulkner, Steinbeck, Elliot Paul (*The Last Time I Saw Paris*), Stein, Ford Madox Ford, and Ring Lardner. It was also an oasis for American journalists in Paris and the birthplace of the Bloody Mary. Primo Carnera hung up his gloves at Harry's in 1929, after losing the world's heavyweight championship; they're still there, dangling from a wooden monkey. In 1932 J. H. Cochrane set the world's drinking-speed record here, downing 4.4 pints in 11 seconds.

A Scotsman named Harry opened the bar on Thanksgiving Day 1911 and ran the place until he died in 1958. Today the bar is managed by his son, Duncan C. Mac Elhone, a Georgetown University graduate. The IBF (International Bar Flies Association) meets here regularly. A variety of whiskeys is sold, including a 1965 MacAllan single-malt scotch for just 128 F ($23). A dry martini costs 48 F ($8.60); whiskey runs 50–185 F ($9–$33.30). Open daily from 10:30am to 4:30am; there's piano music from 10pm to 2am. Métro: Opéra or Pyramides.

ROSEBUD, 11 bis, rue Delambre, 14e. Tel. 43-35-38-54.

This place—whose name is reminiscent of Orsen Welles's classic, *Citizen Kane,* and Otto Preminger's flop, *Rosebud*—is a combination coffeehouse, bar, and social center. It's not unusual to see some of the patrons dressed 1920s style, with headbands and cloches. The walls are lined with wine bottles, the tables are crowded, and the shades are drawn. Meals cost 150 F ($27); drinks run 53–58 F ($9.50–$10.40), and beer is 29 F ($5.20). Open daily from 7pm to 2am; closed August. Métro: Vavin.

HISTORIC TAVERNS

AU FRANC PINOT, 1, quai de Bourbon, 4e. Tel. 43-29-46-98.

This is the oldest wine bistro in Paris, dating from the early 17th century. It's built on a double tier of vaulted cellars at the foot of Pont Marie. The owners renovated the tavern in 1980, adding an inventory of two dozen wines, sold by the glass. Try a glass of the red Sancerre, beaujolais, or riesling. The wooden bar is crowned by a large metal rooster and tables with bentwood chairs are lit by stained-glass windows. Descend into one of the deepest cellars of Paris, where you'll find an intimate restaurant. Specialties include lamb with crayfish in a tarragon-cream sauce, terrine of foie gras with fresh duckling from Landes, and a small selection of other classic French dishes. A fixed-price meal costs 200 F ($36); a glass of wine runs 15–40 F ($2.70–$7.20). Open Tuesday through Saturday from 6:30pm to midnight. Métro: Pont-Marie.

TAVERNE HENRY IV, 13, place du Pont-Neuf, 1er. Tel. 43-54-27-90.
   In a dramatic location for an apéritif, this tavern is housed in a 17th-century building opposite the statue of the "Vert Galant" at Pont Neuf. It's best at sunset. Your host, Monsieur Cointepas, bottles his own wines, including beaujolais and the earthier Chinon. A glass of wine is 20–25 F ($3.60–$4.50); drinks are cheaper at the bar. Snacks costing 20–25 F ($3.60–$4.50), include wild boar pâté. Ten farmer's-style lunches also are offered, for 55 F ($9.90). Open Monday through Saturday from 11:30am to 9:30pm (closed in August). Métro: Pont-Neuf.

7. MOVIES

Paris has had a love affair with film for years. You can find English-language films listed in *Pariscope* and in the papers. The letters "V.O." stand for *Version Originale,* indicating that the soundtrack is in the original language and the film is subtitled, not dubbed, in French. Movies run daily from 2pm to midnight with several breaks. You often have to stand in line at the theater even in the middle of the week. Many of the major first-run theaters are along the Champs-Elysées.
   Cinémathèque Française, 7, av. Albert-de-Mun, 16e (tel. 47-04-24-24; Métro: Trocadéro), is a government-supported theater that's a favorite of Parisian film aficionados. Foreign films are often shown here in their original language, with French subtitles. Up to five films are shown Tuesday through Sunday at two theaters: Palais de Chaillot, 7, av. Albert-de-Mun, 16e (Métro Trocadéro); and Palais de Tokyo, avenue du Président-Wilson, 16e (Métro: Iéna). Admission is 22 F ($4); call the number above for schedules of both theaters. Cinémathèque Française is also a museum, showing the history of movies, with a model of stage settings, posters, and old costumes, and objects of film history. Charging an admission of 22 F ($4), it can be visited only on a conducted tour daily at 10am, 11am, 2pm, 3pm, and 4pm. Entrance is at the Musée du Cinéma, 1, place du Trocadéro, 16e (Métro: Trocadéro).
   The largest cinema in Paris (a virtual attraction itself) is **Le Grand Rex,** 1, bd. Poissonnière, 2e (tel. 42-36-83-93), seating 2,800. First-run films, in their original language, are featured. It contains seven theaters. Seats range from 34 to 45 F ($6.10 to $8.10). Métro: Bonne-Nouvelle.

CHAPTER 11

THE ILE DE FRANCE

First, Versailles, then Fontainebleau and the Cathedral of Chartres. Those are the places known to international visitors, and those are the meccas that draw the tour buses. Indeed, they are the principal stars in the galaxy of the Île de France— and rightly so. They need no selling from me, but the lesser-known spots in this green belt surrounding Paris do.

Everything recommended in the chapter that follows lies within a one-day trip from Paris. You can, for example, wander through the archeological garden of medieval Senlis in the morning, thrill to the Château of Chantilly in the afternoon, and enjoy the showgirls at the Moulin Rouge in Paris that evening.

Much of the "Island of France" is known to us through the paintings of such artists as Corot, Renoir, Sisley, Degas, Monet, and Cézanne. This ancient land through which Caesar's armies marched is often called the heart of France. Seemingly, it is the dream of every Parisian to have a little rustic cottage or farmhouse in this province. Romanesque ruins, Gothic cathedrals, castles left over from the age of feudalism, châteaux evoking the splendor of the 18th century, great forests such as Fontainebleau or Chantilly, sleepy villages, even an African game reserve— you'll find all of these and more. Besides the attractions, small regional restaurants will introduce you to the provincial cooking of France.

SEEING THE ILE DE FRANCE

Most towns in the Ile de France can be reached by rail, but a car is essential if you want to visit Fontainebleau in the morning, drive through the forest in the afternoon, and end the day with dinner in Barbizon.

1. VERSAILLES

13 miles SW of Paris, 44 miles NE of Chartres

GETTING THERE **By Train** Take the RER line (C5), which leaves every 15 minutes from Paris, to Versailles–Rive Gauche. Turn right when you exit. Eurailpass holders travel free.

By Métro Get off at Pont de Sèvres and transfer to bus no. 171. The trip takes 15 minutes. To get there from Paris, it's cheaper to pay with three Métro tickets from a *carnet* packet. You'll be let off near the gates of the palace.

WHAT'S SPECIAL ABOUT THE ILE DE FRANCE

Great Towns/Villages
- ☐ Barbizon, famed for its 19th-century school of painting.
- ☐ Illiers-Combray, torn from the pages of Marcel Proust's *Remembrance of Things Past.*

Ancient Monuments
- ☐ The Cathedral of Chartres, a gem of medieval stone carving; its stained glass also gave the world "Chartres blue."
- ☐ Malmaison, the home of Martinique-born Josephine, wife of Napoléon Bonaparte.

Gardens
- ☐ Giverny, where Claude Monet lived for 43 years and the gardens in which he "invented light."

Castles and Palaces
- ☐ Château de Versailles, where French art reached its zenith in the 17th and 18th centuries.

- ☐ Palace of Fontainebleau, where Napoléon bid farewell to France.

Architectural Highlights
- ☐ The 236-foot-long Hall of Mirrors at Versailles, where the treaty ending World War I was signed.
- ☐ Vaux-le-Vicomte, a château north of the Forest of Fontainebleau, built in 1656 by the finance minister to Louis XIV—a monument to *le grand siècle.*

Events/Festivals
- ☐ Versailles Spectacle, evening fireworks and illuminated fountains throughout the summer.
- ☐ Versailles Grandes Eaux Musicales, a display of fountains in the park on summer Sundays, with classical music.

By Car   Take Rte. N10. Park on place d'Armes in front of the palace.

ESSENTIALS   Orientation   The town is dominated by the palace. Three main avenues radiate from place d'Armes in front of the palace.

Information   The tourist office is at 7, rue des Réservoirs (tel. 39-50-36-22).

Back in *le grand siècle,* all you needed was a sword, a hat, and a bribe for the guard at the gate. Providing you didn't look as if you had smallpox, you'd be admitted to the inner precincts of the palace, there to stroll through glittering salon after dazzling chamber—watching the Sun King at his banqueting table, or else doing something more personal. Louis XIV was indeed the State, and was accorded about as much privacy as an institution.

THE PALACE OF VERSAILLES

In 50 years Versailles went from the simple hunting lodge of Louis XIII to a lavish palace, a monument to the age of absolutism. What you see today has been called the greatest living museum of a vanished life on the face of our planet. Conceived in 1661, the construction involved anywhere from 32,000 to 45,000 workmen, some of whom had to drain marshes—often at the cost of their lives—and move forests.

Enraged with jealousy that his finance minister, Fouquet, could live better at Vaux-le-Vicomte than he did at Fontainebleau, Louis XIV set out to create a palace that would be the awe of Europe. He entrusted Louis Le Vau with the architecture, although Hardouin-Mansart was to play a great role later on. Le Brun decorated the interior. Together these men created grandeur and elegance that were to be copied, but never duplicated, all over Europe. Versailles became a symbol of pomp, ceremony, and opulence.

To keep an eye on them (and with good reason), Louis XIV summoned the nobles of France to live at his court. There he amused them with constant entertainment and lavish banquets. To some he awarded such tasks as holding his ermine-lined robe. While the French aristocrats played away their lives, often in silly intrigues, the peasants back on the estates were sowing more than grain. They were planting the seeds of the Revolution.

When the Sun King shone no more in 1715, he was succeeded by his great-grandson, Louis XV, who continued the outrageous pomp, although he is said to have predicted the outcome: *"Apres moi, le déluge"* ("After me, the deluge"). His wife, Marie Leczinska, was shocked at the morality, or lack of it, at Versailles. When her husband tired of her, she lived as a nun, while the king's attention wandered to Madame de Pompadour, who was accused of running up a debt for her country far beyond that of a full-scale war. On her death, Madame du Barry replaced her.

Louis XVI, however, found his grandfather's behavior scandalous—in fact, he ordered that the "stairway of indiscretion" be removed. This rather dull, weak king and his queen, Marie Antoinette, were at Versailles when they were notified, on October 6, 1789, that mobs were marching on the palace. As predicted, *le déluge* had arrived.

Napoleon stayed at Versailles, but he never seemed overly fond of it. Perhaps the image of the Sun King burned too strongly in his mind. The Citizen King, Louis-Philippe, who reigned from 1830 to 1848, prevented the destruction of Versailles by converting it into a museum dedicated to the glory of France. To do that, he had to surrender some of his own not-so-hard-earned currency. John D. Rockefeller contributed heavily toward the restoration of Versailles, and work continues to this day.

The six magnificent **Grands Appartements** are in the Louis Quatorze style, taking their names from the allegorical ceiling paintings. The best known is the Salon of Hercules, painted by François Le Moyne, using Pompadour red and depicting the club-carrying strongman riding in a chariot. Beginning in 1733 the artist worked on that ceiling for three years, completing it in time for his suicide. Louis XV was delighted (by the painting, not the suicide). In one of these apartments, the Salon of Mercury, Louis XIV died in 1715 after one of the longest reigns in history, lasting 72 years.

Visitors pass through the Salon of War, viewing a bas-relief by Coysevox depicting

---

IN THEIR FOOTSTEPS

Madame de Pompadour (1721–64) As a little girl, Jeanne Antoinette Poisson La Normant d'Etoiles was told by a fortuneteller that she would "reign over the heart of a king." Married at age 21 to the marquis de Pompadour, she pledged eternal fidelity "unless the king should call." Four years later he did, after meeting her at a masked ball at Versailles, where he was disguised as a clipped yew tree.

• **Birthplace:** Paris, on December 29, 1721. She was baptized in the Church of St-Eustache.

• **Residences:** Her most famous address was the Château de Versailles; her Paris address was the Palais de l'Elysée, now the official residence of the president of the French Republic.

• **Resting Place:** When she was unseated as the king's mistress, she helped select her replacement: Madame du Barry (1743–93). On April 15, 1764, Madame de Pompadour—so the saying went—"had the supreme delicacy to die discreetly at the age of 43." Upon learning of her death at her own church, St-Eustache in Paris, a priest remarked uncharitably, "France's greatest burden has been removed."

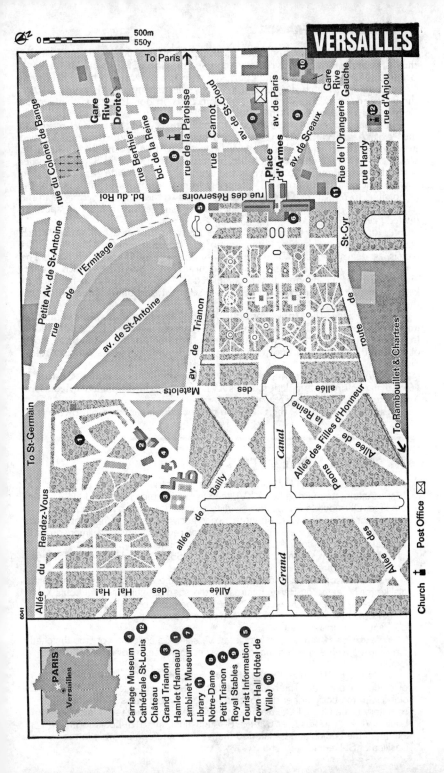

VERSAILLES

0 | 500m
550y

To Paris ↑

Gare Rive Droite

Gare Rive Gauche

To Paris ↑

Place d'Armes

To St-Germain

To Rambouillet & Chartres

Streets and places labelled on map:

rue du Colonel de Bange
rue Berthier
bd. de la Reine
rue de la Paroisse
rue Carnot
av. de St-Cloud
av. de Paris
av. de Sceaux
rue de l'Orangerie
rue d'Anjou
rue Hardy
Place d'Armes
rue des Réservoirs
bd. du Roi
Petite Av. de St-Antoine
rue de l'Ermitage
av. de St-Antoine
av. de Trianon
allée des Matelots
St-Cyr
route de
Canal
Grand
Allée de la Reine
Allée des Filles d'Honneur
Allée des Paons
Bailly
allée de
Allée du Rendez-Vous
Allée des Hal Hal

PARIS
Versailles

Carriage Museum 4
Cathédrale St-Louis 12
Château 6
Grand Trianon 3
Hamlet (Hameau) 1
Lambinet Museum 7
Library 11
Notre-Dame 8
Petit Trianon 2
Royal Stables 9
Tourist Information 5
Town Hall (Hôtel de Ville) 10

Church ✝   Post Office ⊠

6041

a triumphant Sun King on horseback trampling on his enemies (or victims). Finally, they arrive at the most famous room at Versailles: the **Hall of Mirrors,** 236 feet long. Begun by Mansart in 1678 in the Louis XIV style, it was decorated by Le Brun with 17 large windows matched with corresponding reflecting mirrors. On June 28, 1919, the treaty ending World War I was signed in this corridor. Ironically, the German Empire was also proclaimed there in 1871.

The royal apartments were for show, but Louis XV and Louis XVI retired to the **Petits Appartements** to escape the demands of court etiquette. Louis XV died in his bedchamber in 1774, the victim of smallpox. In a second-floor apartment, which can be visited only with a guide, he stashed away Mme du Barry and earlier Mme de Pompadour. Also shown is the apartment of Mme de Maintenon, who was first the mistress of Louis XIV, later his wife. Attempts have been made, as far as possible, to return the **Queen's Apartments** to their original setting as in the days of Marie Antoinette, when she played her harpsichord in front of specially invited guests.

Her king, Louis XVI, had an impressive **Library,** designed by Gabriel, which was sumptuous enough; but, library or no, the monarch remained dimwitted. Its panels are delicately carved, and the room has been restored and refurnished. The Clock Room contains Passement's astronomical clock, encased in gilded bronze. Twenty years in the making, it was completed in 1753. The clock is supposed to keep time until the year 9999. At the age of seven Mozart played in this room for the court.

Gabriel designed the **Opéra** for Louis XV in 1748, although it wasn't completed until 1770. The bas-reliefs are by Pajou, and bearskin rugs once covered the floor. In its heyday it took 3,000 powerful candles to light the place. The final restoration of the theater was carried out in 1957, replacing Louis-Philippe's attempt at refurbishing.

With gold and white harmony, Hardouin-Mansart built the **Royal Chapel** in 1699, dying before its completion. Louis XVI, when still the dauphin, married Marie Antoinette there. Both were teenagers.

Spread across 250 acres, the **Gardens of Versailles** were laid out by the great

---

IN THEIR FOOTSTEPS

Marie Antoinette (1755–93) Princess of Austria and Queen of France. Marie Antoinette married Louis XVI, thereby uniting the French and the Austrian empires. Oblivious to the politics swirling around her, she understood too late the violent forces that were about to sweep her world away. When her calls for assistance to Austria went unheeded, she was reviled, humiliated, imprisoned, separated from her children, and eventually guillotined.

• **Birthplace:** Vienna, on November 2, 1755; ninth child of Maria Theresa and Emperor Francis I.

• **Residences:** The Château de Versailles, where she developed an intense dislike for Madame du Barry, mistress of the aged but still-powerful Louis XV. She became queen on May 10, 1774, upon the death of Louis XV. Neglected by her cold and apathetic husband, she turned to a young and dissolute circle of dilettantes for amusement.

• **Favorite Haunts:** The Hamlet at Versailles, a collection of little thatched farmhouses where she pretended to be a shepherdess, tending to perfumed lambs.

• **Resting Place:** St-Denis. She was guillotined on October 16, 1793, at place de la Concorde. The body of the beheaded Marie Antoinette was thrown, along with the body of her decapitated husband, into a mass grave in the cemetery of La Chapelle Expiatoire at an address renamed years later Square Louis XVI, 29, rue Pasquier (Métro: St-Augustins). In 1818, Louis XVIII exhumed the bodies and transferred them to the *nécropole royale* in the Basilica of St-Denis near Paris.

landscape artist André le Nôtre. At the peak of their glory, 1,400 fountains spewed forth. *The Buffet* is an exceptional one, having been designed by Mansart. One fountain depicts Apollo in his chariot pulled by four horses, surrounded by tritons emerging from the water to light the world.

Le Nôtre created a Garden of Eden in the Île de France, using ornamental lakes and canals, geometrically designed flower beds, and avenues bordered with statuary. On the mile-long "Grand Canal" Louis XV—imagining he was in Venice—used to take gondola rides with his "favorite," whoever that was.

A long walk across the park will take you to the **Grand Trianon,** in pink-and-white marble, designed by Hardouin-Mansart for Louis XIV in 1687. Traditionally, it's been a place where France has lodged important guests, although De Gaulle wanted to turn it into a weekend retreat for himself. Nixon slept there in the room where Madame de Pompadour died. Queen Victoria did not, failing to show up for an expected visit. Madame de Maintenon—once called "a devil in the guise of a woman"—also slept there, as did Napoléon I. The original furnishings are gone, of course, with mostly Empire pieces there today.

Gabriel, the designer of the Place de la Concorde in Paris, built the **Petit Trianon** in 1768 for Louis XV. Actually, its construction was inspired by Madame de Pompadour, who died before it was readied. So Louis used it for his trysts with Madame du Barry. In time, Marie Antoinette adopted it as her favorite residence. There she could escape the rigid life at the main palace. Many of the current furnishings, including a few in her rather modest bedroom, belonged to the ill-fated queen. Napoleon I once presented it to his sister, Pauline Borghese, but the emperor ungallantly took it back and gave it instead to his new bride, Marie-Louise.

Behind the Petit Trianon is the **Hamlet,** that collection of little thatched farmhouses—complete with a water mill—where Marie Antoinette could pretend she was a shepherdess, tending to her perfumed lambs. Lost in a bucolic world, she was there on the morning the news came from Paris that the Revolution was launched. Nearby is the Temple of Love, built in 1775 by Richard Mique, the queen's favorite architect. In the center of its Corinthian colonnade is a reproduction of Bouchardon's Cupid shaping a bow from the club of Hercules.

Between the Grand and the Petit Trianons is the entrance to the **Carriage Museum,** housing coaches from the 18th and 19th centuries—among them one used at the coronation of Charles X, another used at the wedding of Napoleon I to Marie-Louise. One sleigh rests on tortoise runners. (Your ticket to the Petit Trianon will also admit you to see these *voitures.*)

The Grands Appartements, the Royal Chapel, and the Hall of Mirrors can be visited without a guide Tuesday through Sunday between 9:45am and 5pm; the charge is 40 F ($7.20) for adults and 26 F ($4.70) for those under 26. Other sections of the château may be visited only at specific hours or on special days. Some of the sections are closed temporarily as they undergo restoration. The palace is closed on Monday and holidays.

The Grand Trianon is open Tuesday through Sunday from 9:45am to noon and 2 to 5pm; admission is 20 F ($3.60). The Petit Trianon is open Tuesday through Sunday from 2 to 5pm; admission is 12 F ($2.20).

A reduced rate is offered for all visitors on Sunday, and Tuesday through Saturday for those 18–25 and over 60. In these cases, a general ticket for the château costs only 26 F ($4.70). The charge is 13 F ($2.30) for the Grand Trianon and 8 F ($1.40) for the Petit Trianon. For more information, call 30-84-74-00.

VERSAILLES EVENTS

The tourist office in Versailles offers a program of **evening fireworks and illuminated fountains** on several occasions throughout the summer. These spectacles are announced a full season in advance. Dates usually fall on Saturday night, although schedules change from year to year. Spectators sit on bleachers clustered at the boulevard de la Reine entrance to the Basin of Neptune. The most desirable frontal-view seats cost 180 F ($32.40), seats with a side view go for 80 F ($14.40), and standing room on the promenoir costs 50 F ($9) for adults, free for children under 10. Gates admitting you to Grand Fête de Nuit de Versailles open 1½ hours before show time.

Tickets can be purchased in advance at the tourist office in Versailles, 7, rue des Réservoirs (tel. 39-50-36-22). You can also purchase tickets in Paris at Agence Perrossier, 6, place de la Madeleine, 8e (tel. 42-60-58-31), and Agence des Théâtres, 78, av. des Champs-Elysées, 8e (tel. 43-59-24-60). If you've just arrived in Versailles from Paris, you can take a chance and purchase tickets an hour before show time on boulevard de la Reine. The show lasts 1½ hours.

May through September, a less elaborate spectacle is staged each Sunday. Called **Grandes Eaux Musicales,** it is a display of fountains in the park, accompanied by classical music.

WHERE TO STAY

Consider staying over in the Versailles area; it's usually impossible to see all of the palace in one day.

Expensive

TRIANON-PALACE, 1, bd. de la Reine, 78000 Versailles. Tel. 30-84-38-00, or toll free 800/772-30-41 in the U.S. Fax 39-49-00-77. 69 rms (all with bath or shower), 25 suites. MINIBAR TV TEL
$ Rates: 990–2,050 F ($178.20–$369) single; 1,370–2,300 F ($246.60–$414) double; from 3,500 F ($630) suite. Breakfast 100 F ($18) extra. AE, DC, MC, V. **Parking:** Free.

In 1919 this hotel was the headquarters of the Versailles Peace Conference where Woodrow Wilson, Lloyd George, Georges Clemenceau, and national leaders from Italy and Belgium gathered. A stay here is almost like living at the Grand Trianon. A classically designed palace with stately charm, it is set in its own five-acre garden bordering those of the Trianons of the Château de Versailles. Guests stay either in the palace or in a new building, the Trianon Hôtel, separated from the palace by a garden. Today the Trianon-Palace graciously serves many visitors who make it their base for exploring Paris. It's only 25 minutes by car from the Champs-Elysées.

Though many of the dignified bedrooms are old-fashioned, others are modern. The rooms are decorated traditionally with subdued colors, antiques, and many fine reproductions.

Dining/Entertainment: Breakfast is served in the sumptuous Salle Clemenceau where the Treaty of Versailles was negotiated. On the 18th-century-style glass veranda, overlooking the park, chef Gérard Vié, the finest in Versailles, has moved his world-class restaurant, Les Trois Marches (see "Where to Dine," below). Guests can dine less expensively by ordering a *menu du jour* at 165 F ($29.70) in the Brasserie La Fontaine. After 5pm daily, you can relax and listen to good music in the Marie-Antoinette Piano Bar.

Services: 24-hour room service, babysitting, laundry.

Facilities: Sports and health center, spa, indoor swimming pool, tennis courts.

Moderate

NOVOTEL VERSAILLES LE CHESNAY, 4, bd. St-Antoine, 78150 le Chesnay. Tel. 39-54-96-96. Fax 39-54-94-40. 105 rms (all with bath). A/C MINIBAR TV TEL
$ Rates: Mon–Thurs, 520 F ($93.60) single; 550 F ($99) double. Fri–Sat, 490–495 F ($88.20–$89.10) single or double. Breakfast 52 F ($9.40) extra. Children under 16 free in parents' room. AE, DC, MC, V. **Parking:** 30 F ($5.40) indoor, free outdoor.

A 15-minute walk from one of the side wings of the Château de Versailles, this hotel, built in 1988, has a modern facade with columns and big windows. The practical, identical bedrooms have radios, and four of them are equipped for the disabled. The restaurant and grill are open daily from 6am to midnight.

Inexpensive

BELLEVUE HOTEL, 12, av. de Sceaux, 78000 Versailles. Tel. 39-50-13-41. Fax 39-02-05-67. 24 rms (all with bath or shower). MINIBAR TV TEL
$ Rates: 350 F ($63) single; 450 F ($81) double. Breakfast 40 F ($7.20) extra. AE, DC, MC, V. **Parking:** 12 F ($2.20).

On one of the city's grandest tree-lined avenues, this hotel is only a three-minute walk from the entrance to the château. Built in 1850, the hotel was last renovated in 1990. The lobby is simple and modern, and the bedrooms are styled in either a Louis XV or Louis XVI fashion.

HOTEL LA RESIDENCE DU BERRY, 14, rue Anjou, 78000 Versailles. Tel. 39-49-07-07. 38 rms (all with bath or shower). TV TEL
$ Rates: 390–430 F ($70.20–$77.40) single or double. Breakfast 40 F ($7.20) extra. AE, DC, MC, V. **Parking:** Free.

Entirely renovated in 1987, this is one of the only small, three-star hotels in Versailles. Each of its bedrooms is equipped with a hairdryer and radio. Breakfast is the only meal served. The hotel is located in the heart of the St. Louis district, five minutes from the château and the Palais des Congrès. From one of three nearby terminals, you can easily get back to Paris.

HOTEL RICHAUD, 16, rue Richaud, 78000 Versailles. Tel. 39-50-10-42. Fax 39-53-43-36. 39 rms (all with bath or shower). TV TEL
$ Rates: 250–350 F ($45–$63) single; 280–350 F ($50.40–$63) double. Breakfast 25 F ($4.50) extra. DC, MC, V. **Parking:** Free.

Located on a small street opposite the Versailles Hospital, this hotel was built in the 19th century and renovated most recently in 1992. It has been completely redecorated, with modernized rooms and plumbing; the decor is classic, and the furniture is comfortable.

WHERE TO DINE

Expensive

LE RESCATORE, 27, av. St-Cloud. Tel. 39-50-23-60.
Cuisine: FRENCH. **Reservations:** Required.
$ Prices: Appetizers 75–150 F ($13.50–$27); main dishes 125–220 F ($22.50–$39.60); fixed-price meal 255 F ($45.90) at lunch, 375 F ($67.50) at dinner. AE, MC, V.
Open: Lunch Mon–Fri 12:30–2pm; dinner Mon–Sat 7:30–10pm.

This seafood restaurant in the center of town has a classic and conservative decor. The high-ceilinged dining room has tall French doors leading to wrought-iron balconies, which overlook the busy avenue below. Chef Jacques Bagot's specialties include cassoulet of fish, turbot sweetened with mild garlic, and pot-au-feu of seafood. Occasionally he offers a selection of grilled exotic fish.

RESTAURANT LES TROIS MARCHES, in the Hôtel Trianon-Palace, 1 bd. de la Reine. Tel. 39-50-13-21.
Cuisine: BOURGEOISE. **Reservations:** Required.
$ Prices: Appetizers 120–250 F ($21.60–$45); main dishes 175–300 F ($31.50–$54); fixed-price meals 260–750 F ($46.80–$135) at lunch, 395–750 F ($71.10–$135) at dinner. AE, DC, MC, V.
Open: Lunch Tues–Sat noon–2pm; dinner Tues–Sat 7–10pm.

This restaurant is the most elegant and renowned in Versailles, frequently attracting a curious and devoted clientele from Paris and beyond. Its chef, Gérard Vié, after many much-publicized digressions into *cuisine moderne,* is today one of the best known in the region for the inventiveness of his *cuisine bourgeoise*. In a soaring greenhouse-inspired dining room remarkable for both its generous expanses of glass and its intimate size (only 55 seats), his restaurant enjoys a view over the shepherdess's meadow of the Parc de Versailles. In summer, a terrace in front is adorned with a canopy and additional tables, as well as formal flower and vegetable beds whose Renaissance-style patterns were personally designed by Gérard Vié himself.

Menu specialties change with the seasons, but are likely to include an appetizer of baked potato suffused with lard and stuffed with caviar, a warm flan of foie gras and oysters, raw marinated lobsters served with sea salt, shoulder of lamb baked in a zucchini crust, guinea fowl braised with cabbage, canard (duck) de Challons with cider vinegar and honey, and a fondant de boeuf à la royale with chambertin (a red burgundy wine) and foie gras. One of the most frequently ordered desserts is roasted peaches with Cassis sauce and Szechuan pepper ice cream.

Moderate

LE POTAGER DU ROY, 1, rue du Maréchal-Joffre. Tel. 39-50-35-34.
Cuisine: FRENCH. **Reservations:** Required.
$ Prices: Appetizers 70–165 F ($12.60–$29.70); main dishes 155–175 F ($27.90–$31.50); fixed-price meal 120–169 F ($21.60–$30.40). V.
Open: Lunch Tues–Sat noon–2pm; dinner Tues–Sat 7:30–10pm.

Philippe LeTourneur used to work for another Versailles chef, Gérard Vié (see above), before setting up his own attractive restaurant. Located in the commercial St. Louis part of town, the restaurant has a modern, warm decor. Begin with a lamb terrine with raisins and pistachio nuts, then follow with calf's head in a ravigote sauce, steamed filet of sole with summer vegetables, or roast stuffed duckling.

LE QUAI NO 1, 1, av. de St-Cloud. Tel. 39-50-42-26.
Cuisine: FRENCH. **Reservations:** Required.
$ Prices: Appetizers 45–100 F ($8.10–$18); main dishes 65–170 F ($11.70–$30.60); fixed-price meals 115–160 F ($20.70–$28.80) V.
Open: Lunch Tues–Sun 12:30–2pm; dinner Tues–Sat 7:30–11pm.

This agreeable restaurant, occupying two floors, is decorated with light-grained paneling. The fast-rising chef, Philippe Roche, offers well-planned menus that specialize in seafood. The prices are reasonable, and the fixed-price meals make this restaurant one of the bargains of Versailles. Typical dishes include fresh oysters, a flan made with lobster, and a sauerkraut of fish.

Inexpensive

LA FLOTTILLE, in the Parc du Château. Tel. 39-51-41-58.
Cuisine: FRENCH. **Reservations:** Recommended.
$ Prices: Restaurant, appetizers 35–55 F ($6.30–$9.90); main dishes 88–110 F ($15.80–$19.80); fixed-price meals 130 F ($23.40). Brasserie, snacks 25–60 F ($4.50–$10.80). MC, V.
Open: Brasserie, daily 8:30am–7pm for coffee, ice cream, and snacks; restaurant, lunch daily noon–3:30pm.

This establishment was originally built around 1896 as a bar for the laborers who maintained the gardens surrounding the château. Today, the only restaurant inside the park, it occupies an enviable position at the head of the Grand Canal, with a sweeping view over some of the most famous landscaping in Europe. There are outside tables for having lunch in clement weather, and a charmingly old-fashioned, pavilion-inspired dining room maintained by a pair of English-speaking French partners.

Throughout the day, a brasserie-style snack bar serves hot dogs, omelets, crêpes, salads, and ice cream. Most lunchtime diners, however, prefer the dining room, where menu specialties include une assiette La Flottille composed of several kinds of raw marinated fish served with olive oil and anise, roast rack of lamb with herbs, filets of beef, fried salmon with saffron sauce, and filet of sole with baby vegetables.

2. FONTAINEBLEAU

37 miles S of Paris, 46 miles NE of Orléans

GETTING THERE   By Train and Bus   Trains to Fontainebleau depart from the Gare de Lyon in Paris and take 35 minutes to an hour. Fontainebleau station is just outside the town in Avon, a suburb of Paris; a local bus makes the two-mile trip to the château every 10 to 15 minutes from Monday to Saturday (every 30 minutes on Sunday).

ESSENTIALS   Orientation   Dominated by its château, the town is surrounded by the thickly wooded Forêt de Fontainebleau. The main squares are place du Général-de-Gaulle and place d'Armes.

Information   The Office de Tourisme is at 31, place Napoléon-Bonaparte (tel. 64-22-25-68).

Napoleon called the Palace of Fontainebleau the house of the centuries. Much of French history has taken place within its walls, perhaps no moment more memorable than when Napoleon I stood on the horseshoe-shaped stairway and bade a loving farewell to his army before his departure to Elba and exile. That scene has been the subject of seemingly countless paintings, including Vernet's *Les Adieux* of the emperor.

THE PALACE OF FONTAINEBLEAU

Napoleon's affection for Fontainebleau (perhaps Versailles carried too many memories of Louis XIV) was understandable. He was following the pattern of a grand parade of French kings in the pre-Versailles days who used Fontainebleau as a resort, hunting in its magnificent forest. Under François I the hunting lodge became a royal palace, much in the Italian Renaissance style that the king so admired and wanted to imitate. The style got botched up, but many artists, including Benvenuto Cellini, came from Italy to work for the French monarch.

Under the patronage of François I, the School of Fontainebleau—led by the painters Rosso Fiorentino and Primaticcio—grew in prestige. These two artists adorned one of the most outstanding rooms at Fontainebleau: the **Gallery of François I,** 210 feet long. (The restorers under Louis-Philippe did not completely succeed in ruining it.) Surrounded by pomp, François I walked the length of his gallery while artisans tried to tempt him with their wares, job seekers asked favors, and heavily scented courtesans tried to lure him away from the Duchess d'Etampes. The stucco-framed panels depict such scenes as Jupiter (portrayed as a bull) carrying off Europa, the *Nymph of Fontainebleau* (with a lecherous dog appearing through the reeds), and the monarch holding a pomegranate, a symbol of unity. However, the frames compete with the pictures. Everywhere is the salamander, symbol of the Chevalier King.

If it is true that François I built Fontainebleau for his mistress, then Henri II, his successor, left a fitting memorial to the woman he loved, Diane de Poitiers. Sometimes called the Gallery of Henri II, the **Ballroom** is in the mannerist style, the second splendid interior of the château. The monograms H & D are interlaced in the decoration. The king didn't believe in keeping his affection for his mistress a secret. At one end of the room is a monumental fireplace supported by two bronze satyrs, made in 1966 (the original ones were melted down in the Revolution). At the opposite side is the salon of the musicians, with sculptured garlands. The ceiling contains octagonal coffering adorned with rosettes. Above the wainscoting is a series of frescoes, painted between 1550 and 1558, depicting such mythological subjects as *The Feast of Bacchus.*

An architectural curiosity is the **Louis XV Staircase,** richly and elegantly adorned. Originally, the ceiling was decorated by Primaticcio for the bedroom of the Duchesse d'Etampes. When an architect was designing the stairway, he simply ripped out her floor and used the bedroom ceiling to cover the stairway. Of the Italian frescoes that were preserved, one depicts the Queen of the Amazons climbing into Alexander's bed.

When Louis XIV ascended to the throne, Fontainebleau was virtually neglected because of his preoccupation with Versailles. However, he wasn't opposed to using the palace for house guests—specifically such unwanted ones as Queen Christina, who had abdicated the throne of Sweden. Apparently thinking she still had "divine right," she ordered one of the most brutal royal murders on record—that of her lover, Monaldeschi, who had ceased to please her.

Although in the main neglected by Louis XIV and his heirs, Fontainebleau found renewed glory—and shame—under Napoleon I. You can wander around much of the palace on your own, but most of the **Napoleonic Rooms** are accessible by guided tour only. Impressive are his throne room and his bedroom (look for his symbol, a bee). You can also see where the emperor signed his abdication (the document exhibited is a copy). The furnishings in the Empress Josephine's apartments and the grand apartments of Napoleon evoke the imperial heyday.

Minor apartments include those once occupied by Mme de Maintenon, the much-neglected wife of Louis XIV. Another was occupied by Pope Pius VII, who was kept a virtual prisoner by Napoleon; still another by Marie Antoinette. A bed she ordered didn't arrive on time, although the Empress Eugénie, wife of Napoléon III, later slept in it.

The apartments (tel. 64-22-27-40) are open Wednesday through Monday from 9:30am to 12:30pm and 2 to 5pm. Entrance to the Grands Appartements is 26 F ($4.70); to the Petits Appartements, 14 F ($2.50).

After your long trek through the palace, visit the **gardens** and, especially, the carp pond; the gardens, however, are only a prelude to the Forest of Fontainebleau.

WHERE TO STAY

Expensive

HOTEL DE L'AIGLE-NOIR [The Black Eagle], 27, place Napoléon-Bonaparte, 77300 Fontainebleau. Tel. 64-22-32-65. Fax 64-22-17-33. 57 rms (all with bath), 6 suites. A/C MINIBAR TV TEL

$ Rates: 950 F ($171) single or double; from 1,200 F ($216) suite. Breakfast 80 F ($14.40) extra. AE, DC, MC, V. **Parking:** 50 F ($9).

Directly opposite the château, this hotel has its own dignity and glamour. Once the private home of the Cardinal de Retz, it was built with a formal entrance to its courtyard, through the high iron grill and pillars crowned by the namesake black eagles. The private mansion was converted into a hotel in 1720 and has recently been completely remodeled, making it the finest lodgings in Fontainebleau. The rooms are tastefully decorated with antiques and big double windows and also have radios. There is also a fabulous Napoléon III–style piano bar.

Facilities: Indoor swimming pool, gymnasium, sauna, underground parking garage.

NAPOLEON, 9, rue Grande, 77300 Fontainebleau. Tel. 64-22-20-39. Fax 64-22-20-87. 57 rms (all with bath or shower), 1 suite. MINIBAR TV TEL

$ Rates: 600–650 F ($108–$117) single; 650–700 F ($117–$126) double; 990 F ($178.20) suite. Breakfast 60 F ($10.80) extra. AE, DC, MC, V. **Parking:** 50 F ($9).

This classically designed, formal hotel is a short walk from the château. A coaching inn a century ago, it has turned its carriage yard into a pleasant courtyard with lots of flowers and shrubbery. The lobby area has lots of Oriental rugs, big arched windows looking out over the street, and a garden tea room. An inviting bar off the reception area has an ornate oval ceiling, Louis-Philippe chairs, and a neoclassical fireplace. The bedrooms are filled with blond reproductions of antiques with eye-catching padded and flowered headboards. All rooms are well furnished and comfortable.

Dining/Entertainment: Since the Napoléon is so close to the château, many

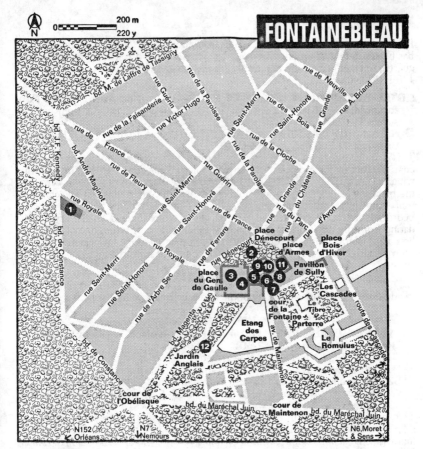

FONTAINEBLEAU

Cour du Cheval-Blanc ❸
Cour du Offices ⓫
Cour Ovale ❻
Galerie de Diane ❿
Jardin Anglais ⓬
Jardin Diane ❷

Louis XV Staircase ❹
Musée Bibliothèque ❶
Napoléon's Apartment ❺
Porte du Baptistère ❽
Salle de Bal ❼
Throne Room ❾

visitors may want to patronize its first-class restaurant, La Table des Maréchaux—the food is among the finest served in Fountainbleau. Fixed-price meals cost 130 F ($23.40), and à la carte dinners average 250 F ($45).

Moderate

HOTEL DE LONDRES, 1, place du Général-de-Gaulle, 77300 Fontaine-bleau. Tel. 64-22-20-21. Fax 60-72-39-16. 22 rms (all with bath). TV TEL
$ Rates: 230–500 F ($41.40–$90) single or double. Breakfast 45 F ($8.10) extra. AE, DC, MC, V.

Attractive and modestly priced, this hotel is conveniently located across from the

Palace of Fontainebleau. The hotel dates from the days of the Second Empire, but it has been substantially modernized over the years. Rooms are suitable for one or two guests. You can order food and drinks on the terrace; the fixed-price meals begin at 130 F ($23.40).

HOTEL-RESTAURANT LEGRIS ET PARC, 36, rue du Parc, 77300 Fontainebleau. Tel. 64-22-24-24. Fax 64-22-24-24. 25 rms (all with bath), 6 suites. TV TEL

$ Rates: 270 F ($48.60) single; 440 F ($79.20) double; from 510 F ($91.80) suite. Breakfast 42 F ($7.60) extra. MC, V.

This is my favorite hotel in its price range, located on a country lane just steps from the château. Part of the facade is art nouveau, unusual for Fontainebleau, and another wing is much older. The classical lobby contains elegant reproduction furniture, marble floors, a few antiques, and gold-and-blue fabric-covered walls. The charming staff—mostly members of the Legris family—speak English. Some of the cozy bedrooms are freshly painted and papered, with a scattering of 17th-century timbers dating from the original construction of the house. Racine wrote one of his works here and, later, Louis XV bought the establishment to lodge his personal corps of bodyguards. There's a restaurant across the courtyard from the lobby.

WHERE TO DINE

In addition to the following, a few of the hotels listed above have superb restaurants.

Expensive

LE BEAUHARNAIS, in the Hôtel de l'Aigle-Noir, 27, place Napoléon-Bonaparte. Tel. 64-22-32-65.

Cuisine: FRENCH. **Reservations:** Required.

$ Prices: Appetizers 80–140 F ($14.40–$25.20); main dishes 95–145 F ($17.10–$26.10); fixed-price meals 180–290 F ($32.40–$52.20). AE, DC, MC, V.

Open: Lunch daily noon–2pm; dinner daily 7:30–9:30pm. **Closed:** July 15–Aug 13 and Dec 23–30.

This is the most beautiful restaurant in town, occupying a former courtyard; the refined interior is decorated with Empire furniture and potted palms. Try the salmon mariné, with cucumbers and caviar-filled blinis, or the chef's special version of zander. His Rouen duckling is superb, as is a special chocolate concoction for dessert, which he serves with pistachio-cream sauce.

LE FRANÇOIS 1ER, 3, rue Royale. Tel. 64-22-24-68.

Cuisine: FRENCH. **Reservations:** Required.

$ Prices: Appetizers 95–142 F ($17.10–$25.60); main dishes 130–195 F ($23.40–$35.10); fixed-price meals 150–250 F ($27–$45). AE, DC, MC, V.

Open: Lunch Wed–Mon 12:30–2pm; dinner Wed–Mon 7:30–9:30pm.

The premier dining choice for Fontainebleau has Louis XIII decor, which means lots of rich woods and beams. Try to sit on the terrace overlooking the château and the cour des Adieux. The cuisine is consistently good; in game season, the menu includes hare, roebuck, duck's liver, and partridge. Jean-Pierre Lenormand, the owner and chef, also specializes in foie gras of duckling with an aspic of sauterne wine, lobster salad, and filet of beef with marrow and a wine from the Loire.

Inexpensive

LE DAUPHIN, 24-26, Grande-Rue. Tel. 64-22-27-04.

Cuisine: FRENCH. **Reservations:** Recommended.

$ Prices: Appetizers 22–72 F ($4–$13); main dishes 50–94 F ($9–$16.90); fixed-price meal 80 F ($14.40) Mon–Sat, 150 F ($27) Sun. MC, V.

Open: Lunch Thurs–Tues noon–2pm; dinner Thurs–Mon 7–9:30pm. **Closed:** Feb and one week in Sept.

This country tavern offers one of the best and most reasonable fixed-price meals in town. Near the tourist office, it's a short walk from the château. Specialties include endive in roquefort dressing, steak au poivre flambé in cognac, and confit de canard (duck) from Landes with flap mushrooms. Dessert might be either a tarte tatin or a pear sorbet.

3. VAUX-LE-VICOMTE

29 miles SE of Paris, 12 miles NE of Fontainebleau

GETTING THERE By Train and Bus It's a 45-minute train ride from Gare de Lyon in Paris to Melun, then a direct bus ride.

The ✪ **Château Vaux-Le-Vicomte** (mailing address 77950 Maincy) (tel. 60-66-97-09), was built in 1656 by Nicolas Fouquet, Louis XIV's ill-fated minister of finance. To save the reputation of his godfather, Cardinal Mazarin, who had amassed a fabulous fortune while he was prime minister, Louis XIV (inspired by Colbert) decided to lay the responsibility for mismanaging the French Treasury on Fouquet and have him arrested and tried; but first Louis hired the same artists and architects who had built the Château Vaux-le-Vicomte to begin the grand task of building Versailles. Visitors will see the striking similarities between the two monuments to *le grand siècle*.

The view of the château from the main gate will give you a sense of the splendor of 17th-century France. On the south side, a majestic staircase sweeps toward the formal gardens, designed by Le Nôtre. Lined by a border of trees and statues, the gardens are dominated by a copy of the Farnese *Hercules*. The grand canal, flanked by cascading waterfalls, divides the lush greenery.

The interior of the château, now a private residence, is completely furnished and decorated with 17th-century pieces. The great entrance hall leads to 12 state rooms, including the oval rotunda. Many of the rooms are hung with Gobelin tapestries and decorated with painted ceiling and wall panels by Le Brun with sculpture by Girardon. A tour of the interior also includes Fouquet's personal suite, the huge basement with its wine cellar, the servants' dining room, and the copper-filled kitchen.

A **Carriage Museum,** housed in the stables of the castle, was opened in 1979. The carriages are of three different types—country, town, and sports and hunting. Some 25 perfectly restored 18th- and 19th-century carriages are on exhibit, with mannequin horses and people.

From May to October, candlelight evenings are held every Saturday, when the château can be visited by the light of more than a thousand candles from 8:30 to 11pm. On those evenings, the Ecureuil cafeteria and the Carriage Museum stay open until midnight. On the second and last Saturday of each month the fountains of the 13 main pools bubble from 3 to 6pm.

Admission to the garden and carriage museum is 27 F ($4.90); a full visit, including the Carriage Museum, château, and gardens, costs 48 F ($8.60). The château is open from February 13 through March, daily from 11am to 6pm; April through October, daily from 10am to 6pm; November 1–14, daily from 11am to 5pm; and December 22 to January 4, daily from 11am to 5pm.

WHERE TO DINE

RESTAURANT L'ECUREUIL, Château Vaux-le-Vicomte. Tel. 60-66-97-09.
    Cuisine: FRENCH. **Reservations:** Not required.
$ Prices: Appetizers 18–34 F ($3.20–$6.10); main dishes 60–75 F ($10.80–$13.50). No credit cards.
    Open: Sun–Fri 11:30am–6pm, Sat 11:30am–11pm (Fri in July–Aug 11:30am–11pm).

The only restaurant in the village is this self-service eatery which lies near the château's entrance, within what was originally built as the stables. Amid a surprisingly elegant Louis XIV decor, you can order such upscale cafeteria food as suprême of chicken in a white wine sauce, steaks in red wine sauce with gratinéed potatoes, and filet of sole with butter-and-parsley sauce. For more formal meals, virtually everyone in town heads to the nearby town of Melun.

4. BARBIZON

35 miles SE of Paris, 6 miles NW from Fontainebleau

GETTING THERE   By Train and Bus   You can take the train from Paris to Fontainebleau (see above) and then continue on to Barbizon via a connecting bus. Several buses run between Fontainebleau and Barbizon daily.

ESSENTIALS   Information   The Office de Tourisme is at 41, Grande-Rue (tel. 60-66-41-87).

In the 19th century the Barbizon School of painting gained world renown. On the edge of the Forest of Fontainebleau, the village was a refuge for such artists as Théodore Rousseau, J. F. Millet, and Corot, many of whom could not find acceptance in the more conservative salons of Paris. In Barbizon they turned to nature for inspiration and painted more realistic pastoral scenes—as they saw them—without nude nymphs and dancing fauns. These artists attracted a school of lesser painters, including Charles Daubigny and Diaz. Charles Jacques, Decamps, Paul Huet, Ziem, Troyon, and many others would follow.

Today, Barbizon's chic attracts some of the most fashionable Parisians with its celebrated inns, such as Bas-Bréau, that flank the main street. Some dismiss the village as affected and complain about its outrageous prices, but others just enjoy Barbizon's sunshine and clean air.

WHAT TO SEE & DO

Along the Grande-Rue you can visit the **ateliers** of some of the noted painters, such as Millet. Inside his studio (now an art gallery, with free admission—open Wednesday through Monday until 6pm) is an etching of *The Man with the Hoe,* as well as some of his original furnishings. Born of a peasant family in Normandy, Millet used to take his sketch pad into the fields during the day and then return to his studio in the late afternoon to add the finishing touches. You can also visit the vine-covered second-floor atelier of Rousseau on the same street, next door to a little chapel.

L'Auberge du Père-Gannes, 92, Grande-Rue (tel. 60-66-46-73), an ancient inn, has been turned into a gallery open to the public. In its heyday, Millet, Charles Jacques, Corot, Rousseau, Rosa Bonheur, even Delacroix and Ingres used to drop in. Writers were welcome here, too: Verlaine, Robert Louis Stevenson, and George Sand with her effete lover, poet Alfred de Musset, used to frequent this inn. It's open Easter to October, Wednesday through Monday from 10am to 5:30pm; and November through Easter, only on Wednesday, Friday, and Sunday from 10am to 5:30pm.

WHERE TO STAY

Expensive

HOTELLERIE DU BAS-BREAU, 22, Grande-Rue, 77630 Barbizon. Tel. 60-66-40-05. Fax 60-69-22-89. 12 rms (all with bath), 8 suites. TV TEL
$ Rates: 1,300–1,500 F ($234–$270) double; from 1,800 F ($324) suite. Breakfast 90 F ($16.20) extra. AE, DC, MC, V. **Parking:** Free. **Closed:** Early Jan to mid-Feb.

This is one of the great old inns of France. In the 1830s, when it was known as Monsieur Siron's auberge, many famous artists stayed here, and Robert Louis Stevenson wrote his *Forest Notes* in one of the bedrooms. When Napoléon III

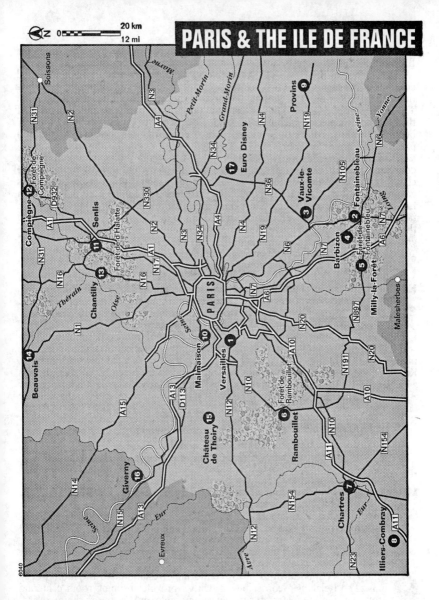

PARIS & THE ILE DE FRANCE

20 km
0
12 mi

N

Soissons

Forêt de Compiègne

Compiègne 12

Senlis 11

Forêt d'Halatte

Chantilly 13

Thérain

Oise

Beauvais 14

Giverny 16

Château de Thoiry 15

Malmaison 10

Versailles 1

PARIS

Forêt de Rambouillet

Rambouillet 6

Chartres 7

Illiers-Combray 8

Evreux

Euro Disney 17

Vaux-le-Vicomte 3

Provins 9

Fontainebleau 2

Forêt de Fontainebleu

Barbizon 4

Milly-la-Forêt 5

Malesherbes

Seine

Marne

Petit-Morin

Grand-Morin

Yonne

Eure

Aure

Sèvre

and his empress stayed for a day in 1868 to purchase some paintings from the Barbizon School, the inn became known as the Hôtel de l'Exposition.

At the edge of the Forest of Fontainebleau, the hotel is set amid shade trees and courtyards. It's furnished in rich, lustrous provincial antiques and fantastic reproductions. In the colder months, guests gather around the brick fireplace in the living room. The bedrooms of this Relais & Châteaux are furnished in part with antiques, many of them collector's pieces. Each room is a double or suite. Many clients prefer the rear building's rooms, which open directly onto semiprivate terraces with chairs and parasols and flower boxes.

Dining/Entertainment: Whether in an old-world dining room or in the courtyard, you can enjoy such specialties as filet de charolais en feuilleté and soufflé chaud aux framboises (raspberries). In summer, guests enjoy good-tasting fish dishes flavored with herbs from the hotel's own garden. Try Saint-Pierre à l'oseille, a full-flavored white fish (John Dory in English), firm in texture, served with a tangy-tasting sorrel sauce. During the brisk autumn months you'll find wild game on the menu, none finer than the well-known specialty of the house: pâté chaud de grouse (a gamey Scottish grouse pâté that has been wrapped in a pastry puff and coated with a consommé-clear brown sauce). Meals begin at 450 F ($81).

Moderate

HOSTELLERIE LES PLEIADES, 21, Grande-Rue, 77630 Barbizon. Tel. 60-66-40-25. Fax 60-66-41-68. 23 rms (all with bath or shower), 1 suite. TV TEL
$ Rates: 320–550 F ($57.60–$99) single or double; from 540 F ($97.20) suite. Breakfast 50 F ($9) extra. AE, DC, MC, V. **Parking:** Free.

Les Pléiades combines decoration of the olden days with modern comforts. It's the seat of a monthly conference to which important politicians, artists, and writers are invited. The establishment is run and directed by the town's local historian, Roger S. Karampournis, and his wife, Yolande. Before he bought the place 12 years ago, he was a dishwasher near the fish piers in Boston and later managed several PX operations for American soldiers in Europe. Today he's one of the best-known chefs in the gourmet circle of Barbizon. His cuisine has flair and style. Meals cost 150–280 F ($27–$50.40). Reservations are recommended.

WHERE TO DINE

In addition to the following, a few of the hotels listed above have some of the finest restaurants in town.

LE RELAIS, 2, av. Charles-de-Gaulle, 77630 Barbizon. Tel. 60-66-40-28.
Cuisine: FRENCH. **Reservations:** Recommended.
$ Prices: Appetizers 35–45 F ($6.30–$8.10); main dishes 85–110 F ($15.30–$19.80); fixed-price meal 130 F ($23.40) Mon–Tues and Thurs–Fri, 165 F ($29.70) Sat–Sun. V.
Open: Lunch Thurs–Tues noon–2:15pm; dinner Wed–Mon 7:30–9:30pm.
Closed: Last two weeks of Aug.

Many prefer this down-to-earth, comfortable restaurant to the more pricey inns. The Relais is a corner tavern, with a provincial dining room centering around a small fireplace. In sunny weather, tables are set out in the rear yard, with a trellis, an arbor, and trees. Typical dishes include quenelle de brochet, roast quail with prunes, and grilled beef.

5. MILLY-LA-FORET

38 miles S of Paris, 12 miles W from Fontainebleau

Jean Cocteau believed that religion and artistic freedom did not necessarily conflict. As if to prove his point, he decorated the interior of the little stone 12th-century **Chapel of St-Blaise** (tel. 64-98-96-68) right outside this little village. Painted in the closing years of his life (he died in 1963), the chapel formed his own memorial and his tomb was placed here. The man who influenced the pre–World War II decades in France with his daring unconventionality made for himself a peaceful resting place.

Inside, the frescoes are secular. One depicts a wide-eyed whiskered cat looking haplessly at a giant flower; another shows a Christlike figure wearing a crown of thorns.

In his day Cocteau was considered immoral because of his homosexuality, but by 1955, following his election to the Académie Française, his reputation was assured. He wrote candidly in his *White Paper* about his homosexuality and pointed out that he did not want mere toleration. The poet, who was considered avant-garde in the 1920s, got his wish.

6. RAMBOUILLET

34 miles SW of Paris, 26 miles NE of Chartres

GETTING THERE **By Train** Take the SCNF train from Paris's Gare Montparnasse.

ESSENTIALS **Orientation** The center of the town, which is dominated by its 18th-century château, is place de la Gare.

Information The Office de Tourisme is in the Hôtel de Ville, place de la Libération (tel. 34-83-21-21).

Pompidou used to visit the **Château de Rambouillet** (tel. 30-88-84-84), as did Louis XVI and Charles de Gaulle. Dating from 1375, the château is surrounded by a park and one of the most famous forests in France. Once it was occupied by the marquise de Rambouillet, before it became a royal residence; supposedly she taught the haut monde of Paris how to talk and she brought a string of poets, painters, and cultured ladies and gentlemen to her home.

François I, the Chevalier King, died of a fever at Rambouillet in 1547 at the age of 52. When the château was later occupied by the comte de Toulouse, Rambouillet was often visited by Louis XV, who was amused by the comte's witty and high-spirited wife. Louis XVI acquired the château; his wife, Marie-Antoinette, was bored with the whole place and called it "the toad." In his surprisingly modest boudoir are four panels representing the continents.

Marie-Louise came here in 1814, after leaving Napoléon. She was on her way to Vienna with "the king of Rome." A sad Napoléon slept here shortly before leaving on the long voyage into exile at St. Helena.

In 1830 Charles X, Louis XVI's brother, abdicated after the July Revolution. After that, Rambouillet became privately owned. At one time it was a fashionable restaurant, attracting Parisians, who could also go for rides in gondolas. Napoléon III, however, returned it to the Crown. In 1897 it was designated as a residence for the presidents of the Republic. Superb woodwork is used throughout, and the walls are adorned with tapestries, many dating from the era of Louis XV.

The château is open April through September, daily from 10am to noon and 2 to 6pm; off-season, daily from 10am to noon and 2 to 5pm. Admission is 25 F ($4.50) Monday through Saturday and 12 F ($2.20) on Sunday and holidays.

WHERE TO STAY

CLIMAT DE FRANCE, Lieu-dit "La Louvière," 78120 Rambouillet. Tel. 34-85-62-62. Fax 30-59-23-57. 67 rms (all with bath). TV TEL

$ Rates: 229–275 F ($41.20–$49.50) single or double. Extra bed 50 F ($9). Breakfast 39 F ($7) extra. AE, DC, MC, V. **Parking:** Free.

This may be the most reliable overnight stop you'll find; the bedrooms are comfortable and basic. The hotel, located near the natural park of the Vallée de Chevreuse, is run by a chain well known for its modern prices. There is also a good restaurant, La Soupière. The hotel has a heated outdoor swimming pool and tennis courts. To reach it from Rambouillet, take the N10 in the direction of Chevreuse.

WHERE TO DINE

LA POSTE, 101, av. du Général-de-Gaulle. Tel. 34-83-03-01.
   Cuisine: FRENCH. **Reservations:** Required Sun.
$ **Prices:** Appetizers 60–108 F ($10.80–$19.40); main dishes 150–250 F ($27–$45); fixed-price menu 118–186 F ($21.20–$33.50). AE, MC, V.
   Open: Lunch Tues–Sun noon–2:30pm; dinner Tues–Sat 7–10pm.

After visiting the château, have lunch at La Poste, where some of the best food in town is served. It lies on the main street of town, across from the police station, 300 yards from the château. It was originally built in the early 19th century as a relay station for the postal services. The restaurant is full of rustic and provincial charm. Specialties include fricassée of chicken and lobster and also a terrine de foie gras maison. Another most interesting specialty is tournedos de la mer, a "steak" made from fresh salmon, smoked salmon, and monkfish.

VILLA MARINETTE, 20, av. du Général-de-Gaulle, 78120 Gazeran. Tel. 34-83-19-01.
   Cuisine: FRENCH. **Reservations:** Required.
$ **Prices:** Fixed-price meals 100–140 F ($18–$25.20). MC, V.
   Open: Lunch Thurs–Tues 12:30–2pm; dinner Thurs–Mon 7:30–9pm. **Closed:** Aug 20–Sept 12.

Located in the hamlet of Gazeran, west of Rambouillet, this is a great choice. The restaurant is in an old-fashioned house, with its own garden where tables are set for outside dining. It's owned by Alsatians, who prepare their own regional recipes, as well as specialties from all over France. They cook hearty and filling dishes with fresh ingredients. Try their chicken with riesling (if it's available) or duck sausage. Only fixed-price meals are offered, but the choice is wide. The little inn also rents six comfortably furnished bedrooms, three with private bath. Rates range from 140 F ($25.20) in a single without bath to 200 F ($36) in a double with bath.

---

7. CHARTRES

60 miles SW of Paris, 47 miles NW of Orléans

GETTING THERE   By Train   From Paris's Gare Montparnasse, trains run directly to Chartres, taking less than an hour and passing through the sea of wheatfields that characterize Beauce, the granary of France.

By Car   The town of Chartres, 60 miles southwest of Paris, can be reached by autoroute.

ESSENTIALS   Orientation   Place de la Cathédrale with the massive bulk of Our Lady of Chartres, and its two dissimilar towers, is the center of town.

Information   The Office de Tourisme is on place de la Cathédrale (tel. 37-21-50-00).

Many observers have felt that the building aspirations of medieval man in France reached their highest expression in the Cathedral of Chartres, or in French, Cathedrale de Notre-Dame-de Chartres, 11, rue des Lisses (tel. 37-21-32-33). Down through the centuries it has been known as the "Stone Testament of the Middle

Ages." Go there to see its architecture, its sculpture, and—perhaps most important—its stained glass, which gave the world a new and unique color, Chartres blue.

CATHEDRALE DE NOTRE-DAME-DE-CHARTRES

Before entering the cathedral, stand in awe in front of the royal portal. Reportedly, Rodin sat for hours on the edge of the sidewalk, drinking in the Romanesque sculpture. His opinion: Chartres is the French Acropolis. When a shower descended, a friendly soul offered him an umbrella—which he declined, so transfixed was he by the magic of his precursors.

First, how did it begin? The origins are uncertain; some have suggested that the cathedral grew up over an ancient Druid site, which had later become a Roman temple. As early as the 4th century it was a Christian basilica. A fire in 1194 destroyed most of what had then become a Romanesque cathedral, but it spared the western façade and the crypt. The cathedral that you see today dates principally from the 13th century, when it was built with the combined efforts and contributions of kings, princes, churchmen, and pilgrims from all over Europe.

One of the greatest of the world's High Gothic cathedrals, it was the first to use flying buttresses. In size, it ranks third in the world, bowing only to St. Peter's in Rome and the Cathedral of Canterbury in Kent, England.

The **Old Tower** (Clocher Vieux) with its 350-foot-high steeple dates from the 12th century. The so-called **New Tower** (Clocher Neuf) is from 1134, although the elaborate ornamental tower was added in 1506 by Jehan de Beauce, following one of the many fires that have swept over the cathedral.

French sculpture in the 12th century broke into full bloom when the western façade or **Royal Portal** was added. A landmark in Romanesque art, the sculptured bodies are elongated, often formalized beyond reality, in their long, flowing robes. But the faces are amazingly (for the time) lifelike, occasionally betraying *Mona Lisa* smiles. In the central tympanum, Christ is shown at the Second Coming, while his descent is depicted on the right, his ascent on the left. Before entering, you should walk around to both the north and south portals, each dating from the 13th century. The bays depict such biblical scenes as the expulsion of Adam and Eve from the Garden of Eden.

Inside is a celebrated **choir screen;** work on it began in the 16th century and lasted until 1714. The niches, 40 in all, contain statues illustrating scenes from the life of the Madonna and Christ—everything from the massacre of the innocents to the coronation of the Virgin.

But few of the rushed visitors ever notice the screen: they're too transfixed by the light from the **stained glass.** Covering an expanse of more than 3,000 square yards, the glass is without peer in the world and is truly mystical. It was spared in both World Wars because of a decision to remove it painstakingly piece by piece.

See the windows in the morning, at noonday, at sunset—whenever and as often as you can. Like a kaleidoscope, they are never the same. Most of the stained glass dates from the 12th and 13th centuries.

It is difficult to single out one panel or window of special merit; however, an exceptional one is the 12th-century *Vierge de la Belle Verrière* ("Our Lady of the Beautiful Window") on the south side. Of course, there are three fiery rose windows, but you couldn't miss those even if you tried.

The nave—the widest in France—still contains its ancient maze. The wooden *Virgin of the Pillar,* to the left of the choir, dates from the 14th century. The crypt was built over a period of two centuries, beginning in the 9th. Enshrined within is *Our Lady of the Crypt,* a 1976 Madonna that replaces one destroyed during the French Revolution.

You can visit the crypt daily at 11am and at 2, 3:15, and 4:30pm for 10 F ($1.80). Apply at La Crypte, 18, Cloître Notre-Dame (the south portal). Try to get a tour conducted by Malcolm Miller, an Englishman who has spent some three decades studying the cathedral and giving the tours in English. His rare blend of solid scholarship, with, enthusiasm, and humor will help your understanding and appreciation of the cathedral. He discusses and provides insight into the history, stained glass, and sculpture of the cathedral. He usually conducts tours at noon and 2:45pm Monday through Saturday. The cathedral is open daily from 7am to 7pm.

After your visit, stroll through the **episcopal gardens** and enjoy yet another view of this remarkable French cathedral.

THE OLD TOWN

If time remains, you may want to explore the medieval cobbled streets of the Vieux Quartiers (Old Town). At the foot of the cathedral, the lanes contain gabled medieval houses. Humped bridges span the Eure River. From the Bouju Bridge, you can see the lofty spires in the background. Try to find rue Chantault, which has houses with colorful facades. One dwelling is eight centuries old.

One of the highlights of your visit might be the **Musée des Beaux-Arts de Chartres,** 29, Cloître Notre-Dame (tel. 37-36-41-39), which is open April to October, Wednesday through Monday from 10am to 6pm; off-season, Wednesday through Monday from 10am to noon and 2 to 5pm. Next door to the cathedral, this museum of fine arts charges no admission. Installed in a former episcopal palace, the museum building at times competes with its exhibitions. One part dates from the 15th century and is set around an inner courtyard. The permanent collection of paintings covers mainly the 16th through the 19th century, offering the works of such old masters as Zurbarán, Watteau, and Brosamer. See David Ténier's *Le Concert.* There are also rare modern works, such as a Bernard Rancillac *Portrait of Giacometti,* an acrylic on canvas (1966).

WHERE TO STAY
Moderate

LE GRAND MONARQUE BEST WESTERN, 22, place des Epars, 28005 Chartres. Tel. 37-21-00-72, or toll free 800/528-1234 in the U.S. Fax 37-36-34-18. 49 rms (all with bath or shower), 5 suites. MINIBAR TV TEL
$ Rates (including continental breakfast): 456–577 F ($82.10–$103.90) single; 605–705 F ($108.90–$126.90) double; from 1,016 F ($182.90) suite. AE, DC, MC, V. **Parking:** 30 F ($5.40).
The leading hotel of Chartres, the Grand Monarque is housed in a classic building enclosing a courtyard. Recent renovations have improved this hotel, which still attracts a handsome clientele who enjoy its old-world charm—such as art nouveau stained glass and Louis XV chairs in the dining room. The bedrooms, quiet and comfortable, are decorated with reproductions of antiques; most have sitting areas. The hotel also has a notable restaurant, where meals begin at 200 F ($36).

HOTEL MERCURE, 6-8, av. Jehan-de-Beauce, 28000 Chartres. Tel. 37-21-78-00. Fax 37-36-23-01. 48 rms (all with bath). TV TEL
$ Rates: 450–510 F ($81–$91.80) single or double. Third person 65 F ($11.70) per day extra; breakfast 48 F ($8.60) extra. AE, DC, MC, V. **Parking:** Free.
Though this 1982 hotel is one in a chain, it has many traditional touches, and the bedrooms are warm and inviting, with reproductions of Louis XV and Louis XVI furniture. Most of the accommodations face a garden, and many windows open out to a splendid view of the cathedral. In chilly weather, guests gather around the log fire. Only breakfast is served, but there are numerous restaurants nearby. It's located right in the center of town.

Inexpensive

HOTEL DE LA POSTE, 3, rue du Général-Koenig, 28003 Chartres. Tel. 37-21-04-27. Fax 37-36-42-17. 60 rms (all with bath). TV TEL
$ Rates: 240–270 F ($43.20–$48.60) single; 260–280 F ($46.80–$50.40) double. Breakfast 36.50 F ($6.60) extra. AE, DC, MC, V. **Parking:** 32 F ($5.80).
A Logis de France, this hotel offers one of the best values in Chartres. It's located in the center of town, across from the main post office. The rooms are soundproofed and comfortably furnished and have wall-to-wall carpeting. A

fixed-price dinner in the restaurant costs 74 F ($13.30), 92 F ($16.60), and 160 F ($28.80). There's an in-house garage.

WHERE TO DINE

LE BUISSON ARDENT, 10, rue au Lait. Tel. 37-34-04-66.
Cuisine: FRENCH. **Reservations:** Recommended.
$ Prices: Appetizers 45–65 F ($8.10–$11.70); main dishes 95–150 F ($17.10–$27); fixed-price menus 100 F ($18) and 250 F ($45). AE, DC, MC, V.
Open: Lunch Thurs–Tues 12:30–2pm; dinner Thurs–Sat and Mon 7:30–9:30pm.
Contained in an especially charming and beautiful house in the most historic section of the town, this establishment offers seating both on the street level and upstairs. From the upstairs windows, the traditionally decorated establishment has a view of the cathedral. Specialties include salmon baked in its own skin and served with a warm vinaigrette sauce, fresh codfish with coriander and parsley flan, and a fricassée of lamb sweetbreads perfumed with an essence of morels. The 100-F ($18) fixed-price menu is offered only Monday through Friday.

LA VIEILLE MAISON, 5, rue au Lait. Tel. 37-34-10-07.
Cuisine: FRENCH. **Reservations:** Recommended.
$ Prices: Appetizers 98–150 F ($17.60–$27); main dishes 110–200 F ($19.80–$36); fixed-price menus 155 F ($27.90), 220 F ($39.60), and 340 F ($61.20). AE, DC, MC, V.
Open: Lunch Tues–Sun noon–2pm; dinner Tues–Sat 7–9:15pm.
There are only a few tables here set amid the antique decor in a house dating from the Middle Ages. The restaurant lies at the foot of the cathedral and is maintained by its chef, Bruno Letartre. The short menu is created from the best ingredients; the service is impeccable. Fresh fish is a specialty—in fact, the 220-F ($39.60) menu cited above consists entirely of fresh fish. Monsieur Letartre showcases his culinary skill in a 340-F ($61.20) *menu dégustation.*

NEARBY ACCOMMODATIONS & DINING

LE MANOIR DU PALOMINO, 28300 St-Prest. Tel. 37-22-27-27. Fax 37-22-24-92. 20 rms (all with bath). MINIBAR TV TEL
$ Rates: 270–550 F ($48.60–$99) single or double. Breakfast 40 F ($7.20) extra. MC, V. **Parking:** Free. **Closed:** Dec 24–Feb 24.
This hotel, located five miles from Chartres, has the most desirable accommodations in the area. An old private dwelling with lots of architectural character, it was completely renovated and restored in 1986 and offers elegant rooms. The manor house is set in a 36-acre park that has a golf course and is bisected by the river l'Eure. This tile-roofed, rustic building has been enlarged over the years and is covered with ivy and graced with gables and chimneys.
   The decor in the dining room was inspired by the decor of the Napoleonic empire. Excellent meals are served at reasonable prices: Dinner costs 135–250 F ($24.30–$45). The restaurant is open for lunch Tuesday through Sunday from noon to 2:30pm and for dinner Tuesday through Saturday from 7:30 to 9:30pm. From Chartres, take the road to Maintenon following the Vallée de l'Eure.

---

8. ILLIERS-COMBRAY

54 miles SW of Paris, 15 miles SW of Chartres

GETTING THERE By Train The town is a 45-minute ride from Chartres. You'll arrive at the station at place de la Gare.

Once upon a time this small town was called simply Illiers. Then tourists started to come and signs were posted: ILLIERS, LE COMBRAY DE MARCEL PROUST. Illiers was and is a real town, but Marcel Proust in his imagination made it world famous as

Combray in *A la recherche du temps perdu (Remembrance of Things Past)*. Today, as a result, Illiers is known as "Illiers-Combray."

It was the taste of a madeleine that launched Proust on his immortal recollection. To this day hundreds of his readers from all over the world flock to the pastry shops in Illiers to eat a madeleine dipped in limeflower tea. Following the Proustian labyrinth, you can explore the gardens, streets, and houses that he wrote about so richly and had frequently visited until he was 13 years old. The town is epitomized by its Church of St-Jacques, where Proust as a boy placed hawthorn on the altar.

Some members of the Proust family have lived at Illiers for centuries. Proust's grandfather, François, was born here on rue de Cheval-Blanc. At 11, place du Marché, just opposite the church, he ran a small candle shop. His daughter, Elisabeth, married Jules Amiot, who ran another shop, at 14, place du Marché. Down from Paris, young Marcel would visit his aunt at 4, rue du St-Esprit, which has now been renamed rue du Docteur-Proust, honoring Marcel's grandfather.

The **Maison de Tante Léonie,** 4, rue du Docteur-Proust (tel. 37-24-30-97), is now a museum, charging a 12-F ($2.20) entrance fee. In the novel this was the house of "Aunt Léonie." Filled with antimacassars, it's typical of the solid bourgeois comfort of its day. Upstairs you can visit the bedroom where the young Marcel slept; today it contains souvenirs of key episodes in the novel. You can also see the room where his aunt spent many years, before dying of an illness. The house can be visited Wednesday through Monday at 3 and 4pm.

In the center of town, a sign will guide you to further sights that are related to the great writer.

---

9. PROVINS

50 miles SE of Paris, 30 miles E of Melun

GETTING THERE By Train   Take the SNCF train from Paris.

ESSENTIALS Orientation   The town is divided into the Upper Town, which is the historic district, with 12th- and 13th-century ramparts, and the newer Lower Town.

Information   The Office de Tourisme is at Tour César (tel. 64-00-05-31).

Feudal Provins, the "city of roses," is one of the most interesting tourist destinations in the Ile de France. Historic, romantic, and beautiful, Provins soared to the pinnacle of its power and prosperity in the Middle Ages, then fell to ruin in the Hundred Years' War. Given its proximity to Paris, it's surprising that Provins remains so relatively little known by foreigners.

Once it was the third town of France, after Paris and Rouen, and its Fair of Champagne rivaled those of Troyes. The city is also known for its "Damask Rose," brought back from the Crusades by Thibault IV. The Duke of Lancaster, through marriage, became the comte de Provins, including the rose in his coat-of-arms. A century and a half later, the red rose of Lancaster confronted the white rose of York in the "War of the Roses."

WHAT TO SEE & DO

With its towers and bastions, Provins was surrounded by ramparts in the 13th century that protected it from the vast plains of Brie. From the Porte St-Jean, you can tour the well-preserved **ramparts.**

The Upper Town (*ville-haute*) is perched on a promontory, and the Lower Town (*ville-basse*) is crossed by two rivers, the Durteint and the Voulzie, the latter an affluent of the Seine.

In the Upper Town, the **Tour César** (Caesar's Tower; tel. 64-00-05-31), erected on the site of a Roman fort, can be visited for a 10-F ($1.80) admission charge daily from 10am to noon and 2 to 6pm; it closes at 5pm in winter. The tower holds the bell to the adjoining **Church of St-Quiriace,** built in the 12th and 13th centuries. The church contains a majestic, primitive Gothic choir and a modern dome. Joan of Arc stopped here on her way to Orléans. A short walk away along rue de Jouy is **Grange-aux-Dimes,** which contains three 12th-century rooms, one above the other. It's open daily from Easter through October, from 10am to noon and 2:30 to 5pm, charging 6 F ($1.10) for admission.

In the Lower Town, the major attraction is the **Hôtel-Dieu,** which was formerly the palace of the comtesses de Champagne. Visitors can explore its underground passages with graffiti.

WHERE TO STAY

HOTELLERIE AUX VIEUX REMPARTS, 3, rue Couverte, 77160 Provins. Tel. 64-08-94-00. Fax 60-67-77-22. 25 rms (all with bath or shower). MINIBAR TV TEL
$ Rates: 330–420 F ($59.40–$75.60) single; 390–540 F ($70.20–$97.20) double. Breakfast 50 F ($9) extra. AE, DC, MC, V. **Parking:** Free.
The finest accommodations in the heart of this medieval district combine traditional charm with modern amenities. It also has a quiet garden. The hotel offers first-rate comfort and a good restaurant, featuring many regional and national dishes. Meals begin at 180 F ($32.40). Private parking is available.

WHERE TO DINE

LE MEDIEVAL, 6, place Honoré-de-Balzac. Tel. 64-00-01-19.
Cuisine: FRENCH. **Reservations:** Recommended.
$ Prices: Appetizers 55–135 F ($9.90–$24.30); main dishes 90–140 F ($16.20–$25.20); fixed-price menus 135–178 F ($24.30–$32). AE, MC, V.
Open: Lunch Tues–Sun 12:30–2pm; dinner Tues–Sat 7:30–9pm.
Opposite the Palace of Justice (the city courtrooms) in the town center is one of the leading culinary delights in this "city of roses." The cuisine is classical with many innovative touches; try filets of sole in orange butter or filet of lamb accompanied with a preparation of lamb kidneys. The menu is always determined by what's fresh at the marketplace, and the service is impeccable.

10. MALMAISON

10 miles W of Paris, 3 miles NW of St-Cloud

GETTING THERE   By Métro   Take the Métro A-1 line from place Charles-de-Gaulle to La Défense. Transfer to bus no. 158A for the six-mile run to the country house—the bus stop is Rueil, le Château.

The **Musée National du Château de Malmaison,** avenue du Château, 92500 Rueil, Malmaison (tel. 47-49-20-07), is an old house with a lot of history. In the 9th century Norman invaders landed here and devastated the countryside—hence the name Malmaison, or "bad house." The château—really a country residence far removed from the grandeur of the Tuileries or Compiègne (other Napoleonic residences)—was built in the 17th century, beginning in 1622. It was purchased in 1799 by Joséphine, Napoléon's wife, who had it restored and fashionably decorated. She subsequently enlarged the estate (but not the château). Popular references to Malmaison as a leper's sanitorium are unfounded. Today it is filled with mementos and Empire furnishings.

The veranda and the council room are obviously inspired by Napoléon's tent from his military campaigns. His study and desk are exhibited in his library. Marie-Louise, his second wife, took Napoléon's books with her when she left France; however, these books were purchased by an English couple who presented them to the museum at Malmaison. Most of the furnishings are the originals; some came from the Tuileries and St-Cloud. Napoléon always attached a sentimental importance to Malmaison, and he spent a week here before his departure for St. Helena.

Many of the portraits and sculpture immortalize a Napoleonic deity: see, for example, David's equestrian portrait of the emperor and also a flattering portrait of Joséphine by Gérard.

In 1809, following her divorce because of childlessness, Joséphine retired here, and she was passionately devoted to her roses until her death in 1814 at the age of 51. The roses in the garden today are a fitting memorial to Napoléon's "sweet and incomparable love of my life." A towering tree on the premises is said to have been planted by the wife of the First Consul after one of his victories. The bed in which Joséphine died is exhibited, as is her toilet kit—including her toothbrush.

Admission on Monday and Wednesday through Saturday is 26 F ($4.70); on Sunday, 17 F ($3.10). Children under 18 are admitted free. The museum is open in summer Wednesday through Monday from 10am to noon and 1:30 to 5pm; in winter it closes at 4:30pm.

11. SENLIS

32 miles S of Paris, 62 miles S of Amiens

GETTING THERE By Train and Bus In Paris, take a train from Gare du Nord to Chantilly, where it's a one-hour bus ride to Senlis.

ESSENTIALS Information The Office de Tourisme is on place Parvis-Notre-Dame (tel. 44-53-06-40).

Today Senlis is a quiet, ancient Roman township surrounded by forests. Barbarians no longer threaten its walls as they did in the 3rd century; royalty is gone, too—all those kings of France from Clovis to Louis XIV who either passed through or took up temporary residence here.

A visit to this northern French town can be tied in with a trek to nearby Chantilly. Today the core of Vieux Senlis is an archeological garden, which attracts visitors from all over the world.

WHAT TO SEE & DO

The **Cathedral of Notre-Dame** on place Notre-Dame in the town center, has a graceful and elegant 13th-century spire, which towers 256 feet and dominates the countryside for miles around. The severe western facade contrasts with the flamboyant Gothic southern portal. A fire swept over the building in 1504 and much rebuilding followed—so the original effect is lost. A 19th-century decorative overlay was applied to the original Gothic structure, which was begun in 1153 to honor Notre-Dame. Before entering the cathedral, walk around to the western porch to see the sculptures. Depicted in stone is an unusual calendar of the seasons, along with scenes showing the ascension of the Virgin and the entombment. The builders of the main portal imitated the work at Chartres. Inside, the light, airy feeling of Gothic echoes the words of a critic who said it was "designed so that man might realize that he was related to the infinite and the eternal." In the forecourt are memorials to Joan of Arc and Marshal Foch.

The **Château Royal and Parc** are a short walk from the cathedral. Built on the ruins of a Roman palace, the castle followed the outline of the Gallo-Roman walls, some of the most important in France owing to their state of preservation. Once inhabited by such monarchs as Henri II and Catherine de Medici, the château—now in ruins—encloses a complex of buildings. Of the 28 towers originally constructed against the Gallo-Roman walls, only 16 remain. One ruin houses the King's Chamber, the boudoir of French monarchs since the time of Clovis. Within the complex is the Priory of St. Mauritius, which not only honors a saint but also was founded by one, the French king, Louis IX.

The **Musée de la Vénerie** (Hunting), in the Château Royal, is in the middle of the Royal Castle's garden. This museum, housed in an 18th-century prior's building, is unique in Europe. It presents works of art relating to the story of hunting from the 15th century to the present day. Paintings, drawings, engravings, collections of old hunting suits, arms, horns, and trophies are exhibited. The Hunting Museum and the Royal Castle garden are open Thursday through Monday from 10am to noon and 2 to 6pm and on Wednesday from 2 to 6pm. Guided visits cost 6 F ($1.10) for the garden and 12 F ($2.20) for both the museum and the garden. For information, call 44-53-00-80.

WHERE TO STAY

HOSTELLERIE DE LA PORTE BELLON, 51, rue Bellon, 60300 Senlis. Tel. 44-53-03-05. Fax 44-53-29-94. 19 rms (all with bath), 1 suite. TV TEL

$ Rates: 210 F ($37.80) single; 400 F ($72) double; 500 F ($90) suite. Breakfast 33 F ($5.90) extra. MC, V. **Parking:** Free.

My choice in Senlis is this combined hotel and restaurant, on a quiet cobblestone street with an adjacent parking lot, about a block from the junction of the main road from Paris to Lille with rue de Meaux. It lies opposite the bus station and a 10-minute walk from the cathedral. The 300-year-old building was a former abbey and is designed with three floors of big windows, shutters, and flower boxes filled with blue and violet pansies. The ground floor contains a bar area surrounded by provincial French paneling, a bubbling fish tank, and a collection of old pewter.

The adjacent restaurant is accented with flowered wallpaper, charmingly rustic accessories, and massive fireplace. Fixed-price meals run 105–189 F ($18.90–$34).

WHERE TO DINE

In addition to the Hostellerie de la Porte Bellon (above), I recommend the following:

LES GOURMANDINS, 3, place de la Halle. Tel. 44-60-94-01.
Cuisine: FRENCH. **Reservations:** Required on weekends.
$ Prices: Fixed-price meals 210–310 F ($37.80–$55.80); fixed-price lunch (Mon and Wed–Fri only) 120 F ($21.60). MC, V.
Open: Lunch Wed–Mon noon–2pm; dinner Wed–Sun 7–10pm.

Set in a 16th-century building about a five-minute walk south of the town's famous cathedral, this is one of the best and most reliable restaurants in Senlis. Amid a conservatively modern decor of pinks and yellows, you can appreciate the modernized French cuisine and delectable seafood of Sylvain Knecht, who is ably assisted in the dining room by his wife, Marie-Christine. Menu specialties include a chartreuse of scallops with lobster in a champagne sauce, a grande assiette of several varieties of fresh fish, served with a fumet de poisson and saffron; a charlotte of lamb in the style of Nice; and desserts which lean heavily toward ample use of chocolate in differing degrees of sweetness. (Mr. Knecht's grande assiette au chocolat contains chocolate-based ingredients from around the world.)

12. COMPIEGNE

50 miles N of Paris, 50 miles S of Amiens

GETTING THERE By Train There are frequent connections from Gare du Nord in Paris. The ride takes 50 minutes. The station is across the river from the town center.

By Car Take the northern Paris–Lille motorway (E3) for 50 miles.

ESSENTIALS Information The Office de Tourisme is on place Hôtel-de-Ville (tel. 44-40-01-00).

A visit to this Oise River valley town is usually tied in with an excursion to Senlis.
The most famous dance step of all time was photographed in a forest about four miles from town: Hitler's "jig of joy" on June 22, 1940, which heralded the ultimate humiliation of France and shocked the world. At the peak of his power, Hitler forced the vanquished French to capitulate in the same railway coach where German plenipotentiaries signed the Armistice on November 11, 1918. The coach was transported to Berlin, where it was exhibited. The **Wagon du Maréchal Foch,** Forêt de Compiegne (tel. 44-40-09-27), can be visited daily from 9am to 12:30pm and 2 to 6:30pm. Three-dimensional slides are projected on a screen showing scenes from "The Great War." Admission is 10 F ($1.80) for adults, 5 F (90¢) for children 7–14. The **Glade,** as it is known, is on the Soissons Road.

But you don't go to Compiègne—which the French call *la ville de l'armistice*—just for war memories. In the town's heyday, before it was occupied by the Germans in 1870, World War I, and again in 1940, royalty and the two Bonaparte emperors flocked here.

WHAT TO SEE & DO

Life at Compiegne centered around what is now the **Musée National du Château de Compiègne,** place du Palais (tel. 44-40-02-02). But it wasn't always a place of pagentry. Louis XIV once said: "In Versailles, I live in the style befitting a monarch. In Fontainebleau, more like a prince. At Compiègne, like a peasant." But the Sun King returned again and again. (Some historians doubt this remark, incidentally.) His successor, Louis XV, started rebuilding the château, based on plans drawn up by Gabriel. The king died before work was completed, but Louis XVI and Marie Antoinette continued to expand it. The palace always had special memories for the couple, who were both teenagers when they first met here on a spring day in 1770. An up-and-coming dauphin, the future king was so embarrassed by the encounter that, it is said, he never once dared look into her face—rather, he just gazed at her feet.

Marie-Louise arrived at Compiègne to marry Napoléon I, and in a dining room that you can visit on a guided tour, she had her first meal with the mighty ruler. Accounts maintain that she was paralyzed with fear of this older man (Napoléon was in his 40s at the time). After dinner, he seduced her, and in so doing is said to have only increased her fears.

It wasn't until the Second Empire that Compiègne reached its pinnacle of social success. Under Napoléon III and his empress, Eugénie, the autumnal hunting season was the occasion for gala balls and parties, some, according to accounts, lasting 10 days without a break. It was the "golden age": Women arrived in crinolines and danced to the waltzes of Strauss, Offenbach's operas echoed through the chambers and salons, and Eugénie, who fancied herself an actress, performed in the palace theater for her guests.

On the guided tour you'll see the gold-and-scarlet Empire Room, where Napoléon I spent many a troubled night. His library, known for its "secret door," is also on the tour. In the Queen's Chamber, the "horn of plenty" bed was used by Marie-Louise. The furniture is by Jacob, and the saccharine nude on the ceiling by Girodet. Dubois decorated the charming Salon of Flowers, and the largest room, the Ball Gallery, was adorned by Girodet.

In the park, Napoléon I ordered the gardeners to create a green bower to remind his new queen, Marie-Louise, of the one at Schönbrunn in Austria.

One wing of the palace houses the **National Automobile and Touristic Museum,** which exhibits about 150 vehicles: everything from *Ben Hur* chariots to bicycles to a Citroën "chain-track" vehicle. Also try to see the **Musée du Second-Empire,** which has a collection of paintings, sculpture, and furniture from that period, including works by Carpeaux; and the **Musée de l'Impératrice** has souvenirs from the imperial family.

The château is open Wednesday through Monday from 9:30am to noon and 1:30 to 5pm. Admission is 25 F ($4.50). You can also visit the other museums in the château with this ticket.

The *picantins* strike the hours at the **Hôtel de Ville,** erected in the early 16th century with a landmark belfry. Nearby is a **Museum of Historical Figurines,** place de l'Hôtel-de-Ville (tel. 44-40-26-00), a unique collection of about 100,000 tin soldiers, from a Louis XIV trumpeter to a soldier from World War II. The Battle of Waterloo is depicted. This museum can be visited Tuesday through Sunday from 9am to noon and 2 to 6pm; it closes earlier off-season. Admission is 11 F ($2).

The **statue of Joan of Arc,** who was taken prisoner at Compiègne by the Burgundians on May 23, 1430, before she was turned over to the English, stands at the town square.

WHERE TO STAY

The restaurant listed under "Where to Dine," below, also rents guest rooms.

HOSTELLERIE DU ROYAL-LIEU, 9, rue de Senlis, 60200 Compiègne. Tel. 44-20-10-24. Fax 44-86-82-27. 20 rms (all with bath), 3 suites. TV TEL

$ Rates: 395 F ($71.10) single or double; from 520 F ($93.60) suite. Breakfast 39 F ($7) extra. AE, DC, MC, V. **Parking:** Free.

This hotel, about a mile and a quarter from town, offers pleasant accommodations and a good restaurant. Monsieur and Madame Bonechi have carefully decorated the rooms in this rambling two-story annex, each in a different style. The accommodations have names such as Madame Pompadour, Madame Butterfly, and La Goulue; less fancifully named units include rooms done in a representative scattering of different "Louis" periods or Empire style. Both the rooms and the terrace of the restaurant look out over an immaculate garden centered around an enormous cauldron once used for making gruyère cheese and now serving as a flower pot.

Meals in the elegantly rustic dining room might include a four-fish stew with red butter, a scallops dish with endive, filet of beef with morels in cream sauce or with foie gras, and an award-winning cassolette of snails with anise. Dessert soufflés are available if you order them 30 minutes in advance. Meals cost 200–340 F ($36–$61.20). The dining room is open daily from noon to 2pm and 8 to 9:30pm.

WHERE TO DINE

ROTISSERIE DU CHAT QUI TOURNE, in the Hôtel de France, 17, rue Eugène-Floquet, 60200 Compiegne. Tel. 44-40-02-74. Fax 44-40-48-37. **Cuisine:** FRENCH. **Reservations:** Recommended.

$ Prices: Appetizers 55–145 F ($9.90–$26.10); main dishes 85–145 F ($15.30–$26.10); fixed-price menus 98 F ($17.60), 145 F ($26.10), and 205 F ($36.90). MC, V.

Open: Lunch daily noon–2pm; dinner daily 7:15–9pm.

The name, "Inn of the Cat That Turns the Spit," dates from 1665. The bar and a traditional country inn–style dining room are downstairs. Madame Robert, the proprietor, believes in judicious cooking and careful seasoning, and she prices her table d'hôte menus to appeal to a wide range of budgets. The *menu gastronomique* is likely to include terrine de canard (duck), then trout meunière, followed by poulet rôti (roast chicken) à la broche, and finally dessert.

Madame Robert also rents some clean and comfortable bedrooms. Singles run 120–285 F ($21.60–$51.30), and doubles are 155–332 F ($27.90–$59.80), plus another 38 F ($6.80) for breakfast.

---

13. CHANTILLY

26 miles N of Paris, 31 miles SE of Beauvais

GETTING THERE   By Train   Trains depart frequently for Chantilly from Gare du Nord in Paris; the ride takes about an hour.

ESSENTIALS Orientation The main attraction, the château, is in a park on the edge of the forest, reached via rue de Connétable.

Information The Office de Tourisme is at 23, av. du Maréchal-Joffre (tel. 44-57-08-59).

_____

This is a resort town for Parisians who want a quick weekend getaway. Known for its frothy whipped cream and its black lace, it also draws visitors for its racetrack and its château. The first two Sundays in June are the highlight of the turf season, bringing out a very fashionable crowd.

WHAT TO SEE & DO

Once the seat of the Condé, **Château de Chantilly** and **Musée Condé** are situated on an artificial carp-stocked lake. You approach along the same forested drive that Louis XIV, along with hundreds of guests, rode for a banquet prepared by Vatel, one of the best-known French chefs. One day, when the fish didn't arrive on time, Vatel committed suicide. The château is French Renaissance, with gables and domed towers, but a part of it was rebuilt in the 19th century. It is skirted by a romantic, mysterious forest once filled with stag and boar.

In 1886 the owner of the château, the duc d'Aumale, bequeathed the park and palace to the Institute of France, along with his fabulous art collection and library. Aside from the sumptuous furnishings, the château is a museum, housing works by such artists as Memling, van Dyck, Botticelli, Poussin, Watteau, Ingres, Delacroix, Corot, Rubens, and Vernet. See especially Raphael's *Madonna of Lorette, Virgin of the House d'Orléans,* and his *Three Graces* (sometimes called the *Three Ages of Woman*). The foremost French painter of the 15th century, Jean Fouquet, did a series here of about 40 miniatures, and the museum is also rich in Clouet portraits, such as one of Marguerite de France as an *enfant.* A copy of the rose diamond that received worldwide attention when it was stolen in 1926 is on display in the jewel collection. Also see one of the most celebrated Condé library acquisitions, *Les très riches heures du duc de Berri,* an illuminated manuscript from the 15th century illustrating the months of the year.

The petit château was built about 1560 by Jean Bullant for one of the members of the Montmorency family. The stables (see below), a hallmark of French 18th-century architecture, were built to house 240 horses with adjacent kennels for 500 hounds. If you have time, take a walk in the garden laid out by Le Nôtre. A hamlet of rustic cottages and the House of Sylvie, a graceful building constructed in 1604 and rebuilt by Maria-Felice Orsini, are in the park.

The château (tel. 44-57-08-00) charges 35 F ($6.30) admission for adults or 9 F ($1.60) for those under 12. It's open October to March, Wednesday through Monday from 10am to 6pm; off-season, Wednesday through Monday from 10:30am to 12:45pm and 2 to 5pm.

The **Musée Vivant du Cheval,** rue du Connétable (tel. 44-57-40-40), occupies the restored Grandes Ecuries, the stables built between 1719 and 1735 for Louis-Henri, duc de Bourbon and prince de Condé, who occupied the château and estate. Besides being fond of horses, he believed in reincarnation and expected to come back as a horse in his next life; therefore he built the stables fit for a king.

The stables and an adjoining kennel structure for 500 hounds fell into ruins over a couple of centuries, but they have now been restored as a museum of the living horse, with thoroughbreds housed alongside old breeds of draft horses, Arabs and Hispano-Arabs, and farm horses. Yves Bienaimé, a certified riding instructor who undertook the restoration and establishment of the museum, has exhibitions tracing the history of the horse's association with humans, as well as displays of saddles, a blacksmith shop, equipment for care of the animals, and horse-race memorabilia. The museum is open April through October, Wednesday through Monday from 10:30am to 5:30pm; the rest of the year it's open from 2 to 5:30pm. Entrance is 45 F ($8.10) for adults, 35 F ($6.30) for children. There are three equestrian displays April through October, daily at 11:30am, 3:30pm, and 5:15pm; during the rest of the year, there's one display, at 3:30pm. These last about half an hour, and they explain how the horse is ridden and trained.

WHERE TO STAY

HOTEL CAMPANILE, route de Creil, R.N. 16, 60600 Chantilly. Tel. 44-57-39-24. Fax 44-58-10-05. 50 rms (all with bath). TV TEL
$ Rates: 268 F ($48.20) single or double. Breakfast 29 F ($5.20) extra. MC, V.
Parking: Free.
Less than a mile north of Chantilly, this 1980s hotel is tranquil and well run. The well-furnished bedrooms have radios. The hotel operates a good and reasonably priced restaurant, which features meals for 90 F ($16.20) and up.

WHERE TO DINE

LE RELAIS CONDE, 42, av. du Maréchal-Joffre. Tel. 44-57-05-75.
Cuisine: FRENCH. **Reservations:** Recommended.
$ Prices: Appetizers 80–150 F ($14.40–$27); main dishes 102–138 F ($18.40–$24.80); fixed-price menus 180–280 F ($32.40–$50.40) Tues–Fri. AE, DC, V.
Open: Lunch Wed–Mon noon–2:30pm; dinner Wed–Sun 7–10pm.
This is a popular restaurant both for fans of the nearby racetrack and for tourists coming only to visit the château. Once a chapel, this building was expanded to serve the gourmet demands of today's horse-loving clients—many of whom inhabit lovely villas in the surrounding countryside. The owner has provided an elegant setting for his traditional recipes, including such appetizers as duckling foie gras, a cassolette of snails in the Burgundy style, or a lobster terraine. Main dishes include shellfish-stuffed ravioli flavored with herb butter, lamb cutlets, and veal kidneys. For dessert, try the black chocolate mousse. The wine list includes vintages from throughout France, and the service is attentive. There's also a garden for outdoor dining.

LE TIPPERARY, 6, av. du Maréchal-Joffre. Tel. 44-57-00-48.
Cuisine: FRENCH. **Reservations:** Recommended.
$ Prices: Appetizers 50–120 F ($9–$21.60); main dishes 90–140 F ($16.20–$25.20); fixed-price menus 155–250 F ($27.90–$45). AE, DC, MC, V.
Open: Lunch daily noon–2:30pm; dinner daily 7–10pm.
This a favorite in town, and the owners will welcome you to their traditional establishment on the main floor of a 19th-century town house. There are also café tables outdoors, where you can enjoy an apéritif. To begin your meal, try the chef's specialty, ravioli stuffed with snails and shrimp. Other dishes likely to be featured include scallops in the style of Provence, a fricassée of sweetbreads flavored with port, Barbary duckling in a sauce flavored with the herbs of Provence, and a salad of crayfish tails.

NEARBY ACCOMMODATIONS & DINING

If you'd like to stay within driving distance of Chantilly but would like better accommodations, more atmosphere, and delicious food, I recommend the following:

CHATEAU DE CHAUMONTEL, 21, rue André-Vassord-Chaumontel. Tel. 34-71-00-30. Fax 34-71-26-97. 18 rms (all with bath), 2 suites. TV TEL
$ Rates (including half board): 690 F ($124.20) single; 900 F ($162) double; 1,120 F ($201.60) suite. AE, MC, V. **Parking:** Free.
Northeast of Luzarches, about four miles south of Chantilly, is this hotel and restaurant dating from the latter part of the 16th century. It has had many aristocratic owners and was once the hunting lodge of the prince de Condé, who lived at Chantilly. By 1956 it was turned into a hotel, with well-furnished rooms. The rustic dining room has excellent food, offering such specialties as roast lamb and poached turbot. Fixed-price meals cost 159 F ($28.60), running all the way up to 380 F ($68.40) for a gourmet repast.

14. BEAUVAIS

46 miles NW of Paris, 50 miles E of Rouen

GETTING THERE By Train More than a dozen trains daily make the 90-minute trip from Gare du Nord in Paris.

ESSENTIALS Information The Office de Tourisme is at 1, rue Beauregard (tel. 44-45-08-18).

Because Beauvais, where Victor Hugo spent "mellow hours," is at the crossroads of Paris, Rouen, Reims, and Amiens, it has been ravaged by war involving the Normans, the English, the Burgundians, and the Germans. The last attack was by the Nazis in June 1940; although the town was destroyed, Beauvais has been rebuilt according to the original plan.

WHAT TO SEE & DO

Before the war Beauvais was known for its tapestries, the manufacture of which was started by Colbert in 1664. The looms and the artists are now at Gobelins in Paris. However, to honor the old tradition, a National Tapestry Gallery was opened next to the cathedral. The **Galerie Nationale de la Tapisserie et d'Art Textile,** 1, rue St-Pierre (tel. 44-05-14-28), is open Tuesday through Sunday from 9:30 to 11:30am and 2 to 6pm; it closes at 5pm in winter. Admission is 20 F ($3.60). A workshop with four low-warp looms is tended by weavers here, and exhibitions are regularly staged. The study of all the trends of tapestry making, both ancient and modern, is pursued. And most important, the gallery allows Beauvais to retain its link with its long-standing tradition.

The **Cathédrale de St-Pierre,** place St-Pierre (tel. 44-48-11-60), was spared the 1940 bombardment. In the words of Viollet-le-Duc, this cathedral was "the Parthenon of France." Still uncompleted, this masterpiece of Gothic architecture dates from 1225–72, when it incorporated part of a Carolingian church. It is said to have the highest Gothic choir in the world, 158 feet under the vault. In fact, the pillars were so tall that the vaulting fell in 1284. After this inauspicious beginning, a stone bell tower was erected that soared more than 500 feet high—the tallest in the world at that time. However, it collapsed in 1573, just four years after it was built.

The Beauvais cathedral suffered so many wars and structural collapses that only the transept choir, a single bay of the nave, plus seven apse chapels, were ever completed. It has been said that the nave of Amiens, the portal at Reims, the towers of Chartres, and the choir at Beauvais would make the greatest cathedral in the world.

Some of the stained glass is from the 13th century and some from the 16th-century school of Angrand-le-Prince. On the north portal is a remarkable carving, *The Man in the Wheelbarrow*. The cloisters are from the 14th century.

The curiosity of the cathedral is an astronomical clock, built from 1865 to 1868 by August Vérité and said to be the largest in the world. It was based on another celebrated clock, the one at Strasbourg. At certain times of the day it presents a scene from the Last Judgment. The cathedral is open daily from 9am to noon and 2 to 5:30pm. Admission is free; however, to view the astronomical clock costs 20 F ($3.60) for adults and 5 F (90¢) for children. The clock is on view only from May through November: daily from 10:40am to 2:40pm and Monday through Saturday from 3:30 to 4:40pm.

Try to visit the **Church of St-Etienne,** south of place de la Hachette, which represents a harmonious marriage of Romanesque (nave) and Gothic (choir). The 1940 bombs badly damaged the choir, although it has subsequently been repaired. Of the 16th-century stained glass, the most outstanding is the *Tree of Jéssé* by Angrand-le-Prince. Goering wanted to own the 16th-century bearded statue of St. Wilgeforte in the nave. On the facade is a *roue de la fortune* (wheel of fortune) in the rose window of the north transept. The church is open only for masses on Sunday at 11am and 5pm and Monday through Saturday at 7pm.

WHERE TO STAY

CHENAL HOTEL, 63, bd. du Général-de-Gaulle, 60000 Beauvais. Tel. 44-45-03-55. Fax 44-45-07-81. 29 rms (all with bath). TV TEL
$ Rates: 320 F ($57.60) single; 365 F ($65.70) double. Breakfast 37 F ($6.70) extra. AE, DC, MC, V. **Parking:** 30 F ($5.40).

Near the rail station, this is the most modern hotel in town and has efficient, individualized bedrooms. The in-house video offers two programs every night on the TV in each bedroom. There's a bar on the premises, but no restaurant.

WHERE TO DINE

A LA COTELETTE, 8, rue des Jacobins. Tel. 44-45-04-42.
Cuisine: FRENCH. **Reservations:** Recommended.
$ Prices: Appetizers 60–130 F ($10.80–$23.40); main dishes 75–160 F ($13.50–$28.80); fixed-price menu 185 F ($33.30). AE, MC, V.
Open: Lunch Mon–Sat noon–2pm; dinner Mon–Sat 7–10pm.

Denis Sérouart has lightened the decor of soft pastels, plants, paneling, and equestrian lithographs. Fresh oysters are always a good choice here, as is the chef's selection of homemade goose and duck foie gras. You might enjoy a savory kettle of fish from Dieppe or leg of hare with homemade noodles. For dessert, try the regional specialty, pavé de Beauvais with Grand Marnier—a cake in the shape of a paving stone.

LA CREMAILLERE, 1, rue Gui-Patin. Tel. 44-45-03-13.
Cuisine: FRENCH. **Reservations:** Recommended.
$ Prices: Appetizers 49–135 F ($8.80–$24.30); main dishes 69–148 F ($12.40–$26.60); fixed-price menus 105–170 F ($18.90–$30.60). MC, V.
Open: Lunch Thurs–Mon noon–2:30pm; dinner Thurs–Mon 7–10pm.

⑤ This family-run restaurant, in a charming, rustic-style house, offers excellent regional specialties. Daniel Leménager, the talented chef de cuisine, maintains a consistent quality in the *bonne tradition familiale*. He is assisted by his mother, Renée-Marie. A superb specialty is the chef's trout with peppercorns served in a sorrel sauce. Or try his tripe cooked in Norman cider or the rack of lamb.

15. CHATEAU DE THOIRY

25 miles W of Paris

GETTING THERE   By Car   Take the Autoroute de l'Ouest (A13) toward Dreux, exiting at Bois-d'Arcy. Then take the N12, following the signs on the D11 to Thoiry.

The **Château et Parc Zoologique de Thoiry,** 78770 Yvelines (tel. 34-87-52-25), is a major tourist attraction that in one year drew more visitors than either the Louvre or Versailles. The 16th-century château, owned by the Count de La Panouse family (now run by son Paul and his wife, Annabelle), displays two unpublished Chopin waltzes, antique furniture, more than 343 handwritten letters of French or European kings, as well as the original financial records of France from 1745 to 1750. But these are not the things that lure tourists.

They come to the grounds, which have been turned into a game reserve of elephants, giraffes, zebras, monkeys, rhinoceroses, alligators, lions, tigers, kangaroos, bears, and wolves—more than 1,000 animals and birds roam at liberty. The reserve and park cover 300 acres, although the estate is on 1,200 acres.

In the French gardens you can see llamas, Asian deer and sheep, and many types of birds, including flamingos and cranes. In the tiger park a promenade has been designed above the tigers. In addition, the *caveau* of the château is a vivarium. Paul and Annabelle are also restoring the 17th-, 18th-, and 19th-century gardens as well as creating new ones.

To see the animal farm, you take a minibus from the parking lot of the château, or drive your own car, providing it isn't a convertible—an uncovered car may be dangerous. Anticipating troubles, the owners carry thousands upon thousands of francs' worth of insurance. However, all that's likely to happen to you is that an elephant might stick his trunk in your window if you leave it open.

The park is most crowded on weekends, but if you want to avoid the crush at these times, visit on Saturday or Sunday morning. The château grounds are open daily all year from 10am to 6pm. To visit the château costs 25 F ($4.50) for adults, 20 F ($3.60) for children. To visit the nature reserve and the botanical gardens is 95 F ($17.10) for adults, 76 F ($13.70) for children. A comprehensive ticket, including the château, nature reserve, gardens, and zoo, sells for 120 F ($21.60) for adults or 96 F ($17.30) for children.

WHERE TO STAY & DINE

HOTEL DE L'ETOILE, 78770 Thoiry. Tel. 34-87-40-21. Fax 34-87-49-57. 12 rms (all with bath). TEL

$ Rates: 200 F ($36) single; 310 F ($55.80) double. Breakfast 40 F ($7.20) extra. AE, DC, MC, V. **Parking:** 30 F ($5.40).

This rustic three-story inn has a stone-and-timber garden sitting room for guests. Rooms are comfortably furnished and maintained. There is a dolphin fountain decorating one of the walls, and a pleasant restaurant with masonry trim. Meals consist of homemade French dishes; expect to pay 100–260 F ($18–$46.80) for a fixed-price meal.

---

16. GIVERNY

50 miles NW of Paris

GETTING THERE   By Train   Take the Paris–Rouen line (Paris–St-Lazare) to Vernon station. A taxi can take you the three miles to Giverny.

By Bus   Bus tours are operated from Paris by American Express and Cityrama.

By Car   Take the Autoroute de l'Ouest (Port de St-Cloud) toward Rouen. Leave the autoroute at Bonnières, then cross the Seine on the Bonnières Bridge. From there, a direct road with signs will bring you to Giverny. Expect about an hour of driving, and try to avoid weekends.

Another way to get to Giverny is to leave the highway at the Bonnières exit and go in the direction of Vernon. Once in Vernon, cross the bridge over the Seine. On the other side, follow the signs directing you to Giverny or to Gasny (Giverny is before Gasny). This is easier than going through Bonnières, where there aren't many signs.

On the border between Normandy and the Ile de France, the ✪ **Claude Monet Foundation,** rue Claude-Monet (tel. 32-51-28-21), is the house where Claude Monet lived for 43 years. The restored house and its gardens are open to the public. Born in 1840, the French impressionist painter was a brilliant innovator, excelling in presenting the effects of light at different times of the day. In fact, some critics claim that he "invented light." His series of paintings of the Rouen Cathedral and of the water lilies, which one critic called "vertical interpretations of horizontal lines," are just a few of his masterpieces.

Leaving Poissy, Monet came to Giverny in 1883. While taking a small railway linking Vetheuil to Vernon, he discovered the village at a point where the Epte stream joined the nearby Seine. Many of his friends used to visit him at his home, which he called *Le Pressoir,* including Clemenceau, Cézanne, Rodin, Renoir, Degas, and Sisley. When Monet died in 1926, his son, Michel, inherited the house but left it abandoned until it decayed in ruins. The gardens became almost a jungle, inhabited by river rats. In 1966 Michel Monet died and the house was left to the Beaux Arts Academy. It wasn't until 1977 that Gerald van der Kemp, who restored Versailles, decided to work on Giverny. A large part of it was restored with gifts from American benefactors, especially the late Mrs. Lila Acheson Wallace, former head of *Reader's Digest,* who contributed $1 million.

Guests can stroll through the garden and view the thousands of flowers, including the nymphéas. The Japanese bridge, hung with wisteria, leads to a dreamy setting of weeping willows and rhododendrons. Monet's studio barge was installed on the pond.

The foundation is open April through October, Tuesday through Sunday from 10am to 6pm, charging an admission of 35 F ($6.30). You can visit just the gardens for 25 F ($4.50).

WHERE TO DINE

AUBERGE DU VIEUX MOULIN, 21, rue de la Falaise. Tel. 32-51-46-15.
  Cuisine: FRENCH. **Reservations:** Not required.
$ Prices: Appetizers 45–60 F ($8.10–$10.80); main dishes 60–100 F ($10.80–$18); fixed-price menus 130–190 F ($23.40–$34.20). MC, V.
  Open: Lunch Tues–Sun noon–3pm; dinner Tues–Sun 7:30–10pm. **Closed:** Two weeks in late Jan and early Feb (dates vary).

This is a convenient luncheon stop for visitors exploring the Monet house. The Boudeau family maintains a series of cozy dining rooms filled with original paintings by the impressionists. Since you can walk here from the museum in about five minutes, leave your car in the museum lot. Specialties include such appetizers as a seafood terrine with baby vegetables. Main dishes include escalope of salmon with a sorrel sauce and auiguillettes of duckling served with peaches. The hundred-year-old stone building is ringed with lawns and has a pair of flowering terraces. It was originally built as a mill until the construction of a highway destroyed its original function.

17. EURO DISNEY RESORT

20 miles E of Paris

GETTING THERE By Train The resort is linked to the RER commuter express rail network (Line A), which maintains a stop within walking distance of the theme park. Board the RER at such inner-city Paris stops as Charles-de-Gaulle-Étoile, Châtelet–les-Halles, or Nation. Get off at Line A's last stop, Marne-la-Vallée/Chessy, a 45-minute ride from central Paris. The round-trip fare from central Paris is 85 F ($15.30). Trains run every 10 to 20 minutes, depending on the time of day.

By Bus Each of the hotels in the resort is connected by shuttlebus to and from both Orly airport and Roissy–Charles de Gaulle. Buses depart from both airports at intervals of between 30 and 45 minutes, depending on the time of day and day of the year. One-way transport to the park from either of the airports costs 75 F ($13.50) per person.

By Car Take the A-4 highway east from Paris, getting off at Exit 14 where it's marked PARC EURO DISNEYLAND. Guest parking at any of the thousands of parking spaces costs between 30 F to 50 F ($5.40–$6), depending on the size of the vehicle. An interconnected series of moving sidewalks speeds up pedestrian transit from the parking areas to the entrance of the theme park. Parking for guests of any of the hotels within the resort is free.

ESSENTIALS Information All the hotels recommended below offer general information about the theme park, but for specific theme park information in all languages, contact the **Euro Disney Guest Relations** office, located in City Hall on Main Street, U.S.A. (tel. 64-74-30-00).

Fast Facts Coin-operated lockers can be rented for 10 F ($1.80) per use, and larger bags can also be stored for 15 F ($2.70) per day. Children's strollers and wheelchairs can be rented for 30 F ($5.40) per day, with a 20 F ($3.60) deposit.

Babysitting is available within accommodations at any of the resort's hotels if 24-hour notice is given in advance.

After evoking some of the most enthusiastic and most controversial reactions in recent French history, in 1992 the Euro Disney Resort opened its doors to one of the most lavish theme parks in the world. Set on a 5,000-acre site (about one-fifth the size of Paris) in the Paris suburb of Marne-la-Vallée, the park incorporates the most successful elements of its Disney predecessors—but with a European flair.

WHAT TO SEE & DO

The resort is conceived as a total vacation destination, clustering into one enormous unit the Euro Disneyland Park with its five different "lands" of entertainment, six massive and well-designed hotels, a campground, an entertainment center (Festival Disney), a 27-hole golf course, and dozens of restaurants, shows, and shops.

Visitors from virtually every country in Europe stroll amid an abundance of flowerbeds, trees, reflecting ponds, fountains, and a large artificial lake flanked with hotels (see below). An army of smiling employees and Disney characters—many of whom are multilingual, including Buffalo Bill, Mickey and Minnie Mouse, and French-born Caribbean pirate Jean Laffitte—are on hand to greet and delight the thousands of children in attendance.

Of the attractions, **Main Street, U.S.A.,** is replete with horsedrawn carriages and street-corner barbershop quartets. From there, steam-powered railway cars embark from the "Main Street Station" for a trip through a Grand Canyon Diorama to **Frontierland,** with its paddlewheel steamers reminiscent of the Mississippi Valley of Mark Twain's era. Other attractions include "The Critter Corral at the Cotton-wood Creek Ranch" petting zoo, and "The Lucky Nugget Saloon," whose inspiration comes straight from the gold-rush era. There, visitors find a can-can show whose dance steps and costumes, ironically, originated from the cabarets of turn-of-the century Paris.

The park's steam trains chug past **Adventureland**—with its swashbuckling pirates of the 18th century, the treehouse of the Swiss Family Robinson, and reenacted legends from the *Arabian Nights*—to **Fantasyland.** There lies the symbol of the theme park, the Sleeping Beauty Castle ("Le Château de la Belle au Bois Dormant"), the soaring pinnacles and turrets of which are an idealized (and spectacular) interpretation of the châteaux of France. Parading within its shadow are time-tested but Europeanized versions of Blanche Neige et les Sept Nains (Snow White and the Seven Dwarfs), the Flight of Peter Pan, Dumbo the Flying Elephant, Alice (in Wonderland's) Curious Labyrinth, the Mad Hatter's Tea Cups, and Sir Lancelot's Magic Carrousel.

Visions of the future are exhibited at **Discoveryland,** whose tributes to human invention and imagination are drawn from the works of Leonardo da Vinci, Jules Verne, H. G. Wells, the modern masters of science fiction, and the *Star Wars* series.

In addition to the theme park, Disney maintains an entertainment center, **Festival Disney**—the layout of which might remind visitors of a mall in California. Illuminated inside by a spectacular gridwork of lights suspended 60 feet above the ground, the complex contains dance clubs, shops, restaurants (one of which offers a dinner spectacle, "Buffalo Bill's Wild West Show"), bars for adults trying to escape from their children for a while, a French Government Tourist Office, a post office, and a marina.

Admission: Admission to the park for one day costs between 175 F and 250 F ($31.50–$45) for adults, and from 125 F to 175 F ($22.50–$31.50) for children under 12. Children 2 years and younger enter for free. Admission to the park for 2 days ranges from 335 F to 475 F ($60.30–$85.50) for adults, and from 240 F to 335 F ($43.20–$60.30) for children. Admission costs vary with the season, with peak season scheduled from mid-June to mid-September, and during Christmas and Easter weeks. Entrance to Festival Disney, the resort's consortium of shops, dance clubs, and restaurants, is free, although there's usually a cover charge to enter the dance clubs.

Open: June 12–Sept 12, daily 9am–11pm. Sept 13–June 11, Mon–Fri 9am–7pm; Sat–Sun 9am–11pm. Opening and closing hours, however, vary with the weather and the season. It's usually a good idea to phone the Information Office (see above).

Tours: Guided tours can be arranged for 45 F ($8.10) for adults and 35 F ($6.30) for children ages 3 to 11. Lasting 3½ hours and incorporating 20 or more people, the tours offer an opportunity for a complete visit. Note that whether or not, you participate in a guided tour, you will still be required to wait in line.

WHERE TO STAY

The resort contains six hotels, each of which evokes a different theme and shares a common reservations service. For more information in North America, call 407/W-DISNEY (934-7639). For information or reservations in France, contact the Central Reservations Office, Euro Disney S.C.A., B.P. 105, F-77777 Marne-la-Vallée Cedex 4 (tel. 49-41-49-10).

Expensive

DISNEYLAND HOTEL, Euro Disney Resort, B.P. 105, F-77777 Marne-la-Vallée Cedex 4. Tel. 60-45-65-00. Fax 60-45-65-33. 479 rms, 21 suites (all with bath). A/C MINIBAR TV TEL

$ Rates: 1,400–1,950 F ($252–$351) for 1 to 4 people; suites 2,900–12,500 F ($522–$2,250). Continental breakfast 75 F ($13.50) adults, 35 F ($6.30) children. AE, DC, MC, V.

Considered the flagship hotel of the resort and positioned at the entrance to the park, this establishment resembles a massive Victorian resort hotel, with red-tile turrets and jutting balconies, which some observers liken to the town hall of a major European city. Bedrooms are plushly and conservatively furnished, and contain private safes. On the "Castle Club" floor, free newspapers, all-day beverages, and access to a well-equipped private lounge are provided.

Dining/Entertainment: Three restaurants (the California Grill is recommended separately; see "Where to Dine," below) and two bars.

Facilities: Health club with indoor/outdoor pool, whirlpool, sauna, private dining and banqueting rooms.

Services: Room service, laundry, babysitting.

HOTEL NEW YORK, Euro Disney Resort, B.P. 105, F-77777 Marne-la-Vallée Cedex 4. Tel. 60-45-73-00. Fax 60-45-73-33. 537 rms, 36 suites (all with bath). A/C MINIBAR TV TEL

$ Rates: 1,090–1,480 F ($196.20–$266.40) for 1 to 4 people; from 2,100 F ($378) suite. Continental breakfast 75 F ($13.50) for adults, 35 F ($6.30) for children. AE, DC, MC, V.

Inspired by the Big Apple at its best, this hotel was designed around a nine-story central "skyscraper" flanked by the Gramercy Park Wing and the Brownstones Wing. (The exteriors of both of these wings evoke the row houses of their respective Manhattan neighborhoods.) Set at the edge of Lake Disney, the hotel incorporates an ornamental pool that in winter is transformed into a look-alike version of the skating rink at Rockefeller Center. Bedrooms are comfortably appointed with art deco accessories and New York–inspired memorabilia.

Dining/Entertainment: The hotel has a diner, a cocktail and wine bar, and a jazz club.

Services: Room service, laundry, babysitting.

Facilities: Indoor/outdoor pool, two outdoor tennis courts, health club.

Moderate

NEWPORT BAY CLUB, Euro Disney Resort, B.P. 105, F-77777 Marne-la-Vallée Cedex 4. Tel. 60-45-55-00. Fax 60-45-55-33. 1,083 rms, 15 suites (all with bath). A/C MINIBAR TV TEL

$ Rates: 650–990 F ($117–$178.20) for 1 to 4 people; from 1,700 F ($306) suite. Continental breakfast 55 F ($9.90) adults; 35 F ($6.30) children. AE, DC, MC, V.

This hotel is designed with a central cupola, jutting balconies, and a fresh color scheme of blue and cream, inspired by a harborfront New England hotel. The hotel is ringed with verdant lawns and a large front porch with comfortable rocking chairs. Each of the nautically decorated bedrooms contains closed-circuit TV movies. The upscale Yacht Club and the less formal Cape Cod restaurants are the dining choices. Facilities include a lakeside promenade, a croquet lawn, a glassed-in pool pavilion, an outdoor pool, and a health club with sun beds and a sauna.

SEQUOIA LODGE, Euro Disney Resort, B.P. 105, F-77777 Marne-la-Vallée Cedex 4. Tel. 60-45-51-00. Fax 60-45-51-33. 997 rms, 14 suites (all with bath). A/C MINIBAR TV TEL
$ Rates: 590–950 F ($106.20–$171) for 1 to 4 persons. Continental breakfast 55 F ($9.90) adults, 35 F ($6.30) children. AE, DC, MC, V.
Built of gray stone and roughly textured planking, and capped with a gently sloping green copper roof, this hotel evokes a rough-hewn but comfortable lodge in a remote section of the Rocky Mountains. Located at the edge of the resort's lake, the hotel consists of a large central building with five additional chalets (each containing 100 bedrooms) nearby. Rooms are comfortably rustic—a departure from the glossiness of other sections of the resort. By the light of an open fireplace, the Hunter's Grill serves juicy portions of spit-roasted meats carved directly onto your plate. Less formal is the Beaver Creek Tavern. Facilities include an indoor pool and health club.

Inexpensive

HOTEL CHEYENNE AND HOTEL SANTA FE, Euro Disney Resort, B.P. 105, F-77777 Marne-la-Vallée Cedex 4. Tel. 60-45-62-00 (Cheyenne) or 60-45-78-00 (Santa Fé). Fax 60-45-62-33 (Cheyenne) or 60-45-78-33 (Santa Fé). 2,000 rms (all with bath). TV TEL
$ Rates: Hotel Cheyenne, 475–790 F ($85.50–$142.20) for 1 to 4 people, Hotel Santa Fé, 375–590 F ($67.50–$106.20) for 1 to 4 people. Continental breakfast 55 F ($9.90) adults, 35 F ($6.30) children. AE, DC, MC, V.
Set adjacent to one another, these qualify as the two most cost-conscious hotels at the resort. Both rise from a spot near a recreation of Texas' Rio Grande and evoke different aspects of the Old West. The Cheyenne houses visitors within 14 two-story buildings scattered along "Desperado Street." Each building is a re-creation of a clapboard-sided outpost from the gold-rush era. Its companion hotel, the Santa Fé, sports a desert theme, and houses four different "nature trails" winding among 42 adobe-style pueblos. Towering above the Santa Fé is a giant drive-in movie screen painted with a likeness of Clint Eastwood. Nearby, an artificial volcano erupts regularly.

Tex-Mex specialties are offered at La Cantina (Hotel Santa Fé), while barbecue and smokehouse specialties are served at the Chuck Wagon Café (Hotel Cheyenne). Two-fisted drinks are the order of the day at the Cheyenne's Red Garter Saloon and at the Santa Fé's Apache Bar. Children's play areas include a log fort, a corral, a teepee village, a covered wagon, the Totem Pole playground, and the Pow Wow video arcade.

WHERE TO DINE

Within the resort, there are at least 45 different restaurants and snack bars, each trying hard to please millions of European and North American palates. Here follow a few recommendations:

THE CALIFORNIA GRILL, in the Disneyland Hotel. Tel. 60-45-65-00.
Cuisine: CALIFORNIAN. **Reservations:** Required.
$ Prices: Appetizers 55–95 F ($9.90–$17.10); main dishes 160–265 F ($28.80–$47.70). Children's menus from 85 F ($15.30). AE, DC, MC, V.
Open: Dinner only, daily 6pm–midnight.
Dedicated to the new and lighter recipes that have placed the Golden State on the world's culinary map, this airy and elegant restaurant features specialties from a California harvest, many of them cooked on mesquite grills or in wood-burning ovens. Specialties include maple-glazed salmon roasted on a wooden plank with a mushroom and beet ragoût; field lettuces with sundried tomatoes, farmers bread croûtons, and lemon-chive dressing; seared and spiced tuna filet served rare with a

beansprout salad and soy vinaigrette; pan-roasted sea bass with red pepper and fennel julienne, warm cilantro, and a tomato-lime vinaigrette; and such desserts as a warm feuilleté of mango with caramel sauce. A children's menu (which might include Goofy's fried chicken, the Mad Hatter's minute steak, Dumbo's desserts) is also available. The wine cellar is heavily stocked with California vintages. An appropriate apéritif might be an American version of French kir, made with loganberry juice and sparkling wine. Jackets are required for men.

KEY WEST SEAFOOD, in Le Festival Disney Building. Tel. 49-32-40-15.

Cuisine: SEAFOOD. **Reservations:** Required.

$ Prices: Appetizers 20–55 F ($3.60–$9.90); main dishes 75–250 F ($13.50–$45). Children's menus 65 F ($11.70). AE, DC, MC, V.

Open: Lunch daily 11:30am–3:30pm, dinner daily 6pm–midnight.

Evocative of a seafood restaurant in the Florida Keys, this restaurant regales European diners with exposed timbers, a raffish hint of salt spray, and one of the most amply stocked oyster bars anywhere. Drinks include a spice-laden Bloody Mary or a margarita made with a mixture of tequilas. Your meal might consist of a sand digger's bucket brimming with steamed mussels, crabs served either steamed or fried with garlic, Islamorada clam chowder, garlic crabs, heaping platters of shrimp, oysters, and clams, and dessert pies made either from Key limes or southern pecans.

THE YACHT CLUB, in the Hotel Newport Bay Club. Tel. 64-74-30-00.

Cuisine: AMERICAN. **Reservations:** Required.

$ Prices: Appetizers salad included in price of main course. Main dishes 160–250 F ($28.80–$45). Children's menu 55 F ($9.90). AE, DC, MC, V.

Open: Dinner only, daily 5pm–midnight.

Decorated like the dining room of a rustically elegant yacht club on the New England coast, this restaurant serves simple but wholesome preparations of shrimp, steak, and lobster in copious portions. Specific dishes include spicy sautéed shrimp with tomatoes and mushrooms, grilled fresh Maine lobster with an optional crabmeat stuffing, and several combinations of surf & turf. Several fresh vegetables of the day round out a meal here nicely.

EVENING ENTERTAINMENT

Although you might find it hard to escape the presence of children and the props which were designed to entertain them, Euro Disney offers hideaways for adults as well. Here is a selection of the most visible.

HURRICANES BEACH CAFÉ, in the Festival Disney Building. Tel. 60-45-70-00.

Skilled at entertaining adults as well as children, Disney offers at this beach café electronic music, a dance floor disguised as a tropical beach, and an amply stocked bar for adults who want to get away from their offspring for a while. At regular intervals, artificial hurricanes add to the shake, rattle, and roll. Admission is free before 9pm and for children under 12. After 9pm, admission is 50 F ($9) for hotel guests; 75 F ($13.50) for non-residents, including your first drink. Open daily from 1pm to 1am.

ROCK 'N ROLL AMERICA, in the Festival Disney Building. Tel. 60-45-70-00.

Its theme includes the best American music of the '50s and '60s, hamburgers, milkshakes, and occasional presentations of live rock and roll bands. It manages to incorporate rock and roll breakfasts, complete with videos of Roger Rabbit, with late night disco action for adults.

After 9pm, admission is 50 F ($9) for hotel guests; 75 F ($13.50) for non-residents, including your first drink. It's open daily from 7am to 1am.

MANHATTAN JAZZ CLUB, in the Hotel New York. Tel. 60-45-73-00.

Its ambience re-creates the city skyline of Manhattan and the sounds of the Jazz Age. Within a black and white art deco setting, you can drink cocktails ranging from a Bellini to a highly potent Long Island iced tea, or dine on platters of Cajun specialties priced at from 135–170 F ($24.30–$30.60) each. Music is hosted by a resident master of ceremonies, and includes a revolving assortment of jazz musicians from France and abroad. The setting attracts residents of Paris who come out for the music and the evocation of New York at its best.

Admission is free for dinner guests and people under 16; all others 75 F ($13.50), which includes one free drink. It's open nightly from 7pm to very late. Music begins at 9pm.

CHAPTER 12

THE LOIRE VALLEY

The Val de Loire is called "The Garden of France." Bordered by vineyards, the winding Loire Valley cuts through the soft contours of the land of castles deep in the heart of France. Along the way are *levées* (dikes), some dating from centuries ago, built to hold back the lazy Loire should it become the turbulent Loire.

Many Crusaders returning to their medieval dungeon-like quarters brought with them the news of the elegance and opulence of the East. Soon enough, they began to rethink their surroundings. Later, word came across the Alps from neighboring Italy of a great artistic flowering, of artists such as Leonardo da Vinci and Michelangelo. And so, in the days of the French Renaissance, when the kings of France built châteaux throughout this valley, the emphasis was on sumptuousness. An era of pomp and circumstance was to reign here until Henri IV moved the court to Paris, marking the decline of the Loire.

The Valley of the Loire has played a major part in the national consciousness. Joan of Arc, the maid of Orléans, came this way looking for her dauphin, finding him at Chinon. Carried around from castle to castle were mistresses, the list now legendary, ranging from Agnès Sorel (the mistress of Charles VII) to Diane du Poitiers (the mistress of Henri II). In his heyday, the Chevalier King brought Leonardo da Vinci from Florence, installing him at Amboise. Catherine de Medici and her "flying squadron" of beauties, Henry III and his handsome minions—the people and the events make a rich tapestry. The Loire has a tale to tell, as even the most cursory visitor to its châteaux discovers. Its sights and curiosities are multifarious, ranging from Renaissance, medieval, and classical châteaux to residences where Balzac wrote or Rabelais lived, to Romanesque and Gothic churches, to Roman ramparts, to such art treasures as the Apocalypse Tapestries. There's even the castle that inspired the fairytale "Sleeping Beauty."

SEEING THE LOIRE VALLEY

GETTING THERE The nearest international airport for the Centre–Loire Valley is in Paris (Charles de Gaulle or Orly). From there, motorways A6, A10, and A11 lead easily to the main towns of the region.

WHAT'S SPECIAL ABOUT THE LOIRE VALLEY

Great Towns/Villages
- ☐ Chinon, birthplace of Rabelais, is the oldest fortress-château in the Loire Valley; Joan of Arc changed the course of history here.
- ☐ Loches, the cité médiévale of the Loire Valley, former home of legendary beauty Agnès Sorel.

Ancient Monuments
- ☐ Fontevraud-l'Abbaye, the burial abbey for the Plantagenet kings of England.

Gardens
- ☐ The spectacular Renaissance gardens at Villandry, laid out in three cloisters with a water garden.

Châteaux
- ☐ Chambord, the largest of the Loire Valley châteaux, and Renaissance King François I's favorite residence; its grandeur represents the pinnacle of 16th-century French power.

- ☐ Château d'Amboise, associated with Charles VII and François I; Leonardo da Vinci died here.
- ☐ Château de Blois, seat of the comtes de Blois in the 13th century, and later briefly the capital of France.
- ☐ Chaumont-sur-Loire, a medieval fortress, to which Diane de Poitiers was banished after the death of her lover, King Henri II.
- ☐ Chenonceaux, an architectural masterpiece of the Renaissance.

Architectural Highlights
- ☐ Château d'Azay-le-Rideau, whose beauty and expense was said to have destroyed its original owners.

Events/Festivals
- ☐ Son-et-lumière (sound-and-light) shows each summer bring to life the royal past of the Loire Valley.

Main-line trains take travelers to Orléans, Blois, and Tours.

The best way to see the Loire is in your own car, free from tour buses and guides herding you in and out of castles. Attempts to explore the valley in two to three days are doomed. If your schedule can accommodate it, allow at least a week. If you wish, you can stay in one of the big towns, such as Tours, with their wide range of accommodations. But you may prefer to seek out a central yet seemingly isolated village with an old inn where the pace is less frenetic, the food worthy of the finest tables in the Loire, and the price the kind you don't mind paying.

Autumn or spring is ideal, although most of the intriguing son-et-lumière (sound-and-light) programs take place in summer when the châteaux are floodlit. First performed on the banks of the Loire, these pageants have become one of the main attractions of France.

A SUGGESTED ROUTE If you're pressed for time, concentrate on the eastern Loire Valley. On your first day, arrive in Tours, the capital; while based in Tours or nearby Amboise, visit Azay-le-Rideau and Chinon. On your second day, take in the attractions of Amboise and Chenonceaux. On your third day, explore Chaumont and drive to Blois for an overnight stay. On your fourth day, go to Orléans, with a stopover in Chambord.

---

1. CHATEAUDUN

64 miles SW of Paris, 27 miles SW of Chartres

GETTING THERE **By Bus** Buses run frequently from Chartres.

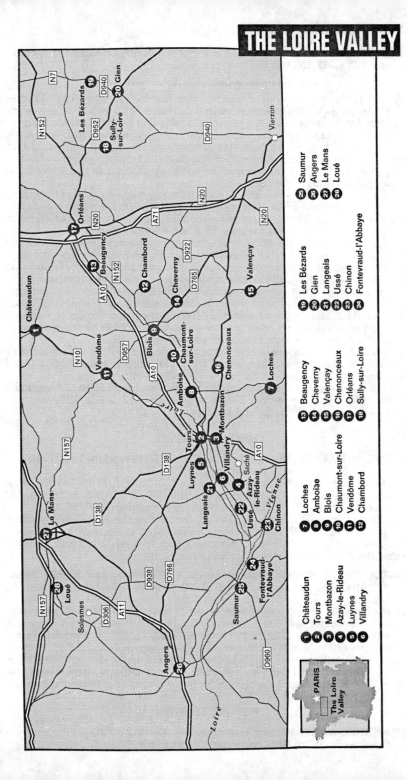

THE LOIRE VALLEY

1 Châteaudun
2 Tours
3 Montbazon
4 Azay-le-Rideau
5 Luynes
6 Villandry
7 Loches
8 Amboise
9 Blois
10 Chaumont-sur-Loire
11 Vendôme
12 Chambord
13 Beaugency
14 Cheverny
15 Valençay
16 Chenonceaux
17 Orléans
18 Sully-sur-Loire
19 Les Bézards
20 Gien
21 Langeais
22 Ussé
23 Chinon
24 Fontevraud-l'Abbaye
25 Saumur
26 Angers
27 Le Mans
28 Loué

PARIS
The Loire Valley

ESSENTIALS Information The Office de Tourisme is located at 1, rue de Luynes (tel. 37-45-22-46).

South of the cathedral city of Chartres, your first château in the Loire Valley—**Château de Châteaudun,** place Jean de Dunois (tel. 37-45-22-70)—emerges. Austere, foreboding, it rises on a stonebound table over a tributary of the Loire.

Looking like an impregnable fortress, it isn't the most "warm-hearted" gateway to the château country, but it's imposing and interesting. Originally it was erected as an important fortress to protect the surrounding countryside from its jealous and restless neighbors. In 911 the Normans went on a rampage in this area and succeeded in burning much of the castle.

The comrade in arms of Joan of Arc, Jean Dunois, called the Bastard of Orléans, rebuilt the chapel and the façade in the 15th century. The donjon, a huge round tower 150 feet high, had been reconstructed in the 12th century. The façade on the right, elaborately ornamented, was the result of a 16th-century restoration.

Although begun in the Middle Ages, the château is a mixture of medieval and Renaissance architecture. The roof is pierced with towering chimneys and large dormers. After a great fire swept over Châteaudun in the 18th century, Hardouin, an architect of Louis XV's, directed what was almost an entire reconstruction of the town, indiscreetly turning over the castle to the homeless, who stripped it of its finery. By 1935 the government had acquired the fortress and a major restoration program was launched. Even today it's not richly furnished, but a collection of tapestries depicting such scenes as the worship of the golden calf now cover the walls. The most admirable architectural features are the two carved staircases.

Inside the Saint-Chapelle, a keep dating from the Middle Ages, is a collection of more than a dozen 15th-century robed statues, including a woman with a sword standing on a man's head.

The château is open daily: April through September, from 9:30 to 11:45am and 2 to 6pm; October through March, from 10 to 11:45am and 2 to 4pm. Admission is 24 F ($4.30), half price on Sunday and holidays.

WHERE TO STAY

HOTEL DE BEAUCE, 50, rue Jallans, 28200 Châteaudun. Tel. 37-45-14-75. Fax 37-45-87-53. 24 rms (18 with bath). TV TEL
$ Rates: 145 F ($26.10) single without bath, 210–230 F ($37.80–$41.40) single with bath; 160 F ($28.80) double without bath, 250–270 F ($45–$48.60) double with bath. Breakfast 30 F ($5.40) extra. MC, V. **Parking:** 26 F ($4.70).
Built in the late 1960s, this hotel is clean, modern, and simple, and although it lacks a restaurant, it has a small cocktail lounge for the use of guests only. It lies about a two-minute walk from the heart of town, on a quiet residential street with very little noise. Rooms are furnished in an uncomplicated style.

HOTEL SAINT-MICHEL, 28, place du 18-Octobre, and 5, rue Péan, 28200 Châteaudun. Tel. 37-45-15-70. 19 rms (14 with bath or shower). TV TEL
$ Rates: 170 F ($30.60) single without bath or shower, 230 F ($41.40) single with bath or shower; 190 F ($34.20) double without bath or shower, 300 F ($54) double with bath or shower. Breakfast 27 F ($4.90) extra. AE, MC, V. **Parking:** Free.
Monsieur and Madame Halbout own this hotel conveniently located on the main square of town. Rooms are simply furnished, with hot-and-cold-water basins. Nine rooms have minibars. There's no restaurant, although the hotel offers a sauna and solarium. Breakfast is served in the lounge, in your room, or in the winter garden.

WHERE TO DINE

LE MICHEL-ANGE, 33, rue Fouleries. Tel. 37-45-23-72.
Cuisine: FRENCH. **Reservations:** Recommended.

$ Prices: Appetizers 55–95 F ($9.90–$17.10); main dishes 115–170 F ($20.70–$30.60); fixed-price meals 110–140 F ($19.80–$25.20). DC, V.
Open: Lunch Tues–Sun 12:30–2pm; dinner Tues–Sun 7:15–9:30pm.

Some of the best food in Châteaudun is served in this rough-hewn "troglodytic" *caveau*, with a flower garden that borders the Loire. The service is helpful and efficient. The menu includes terrine fondante of duckling with a confiture of onions, salmon in papillote with scallops, and chateaubriand with foie-gras butter. The cave makes a fine air-conditioned luncheon stop if you're en route from Paris to the Loire Valley.

---

2. TOURS

144 miles SW of Paris, 70 miles SW of Orléans

GETTING THERE By Train Tours is a 2½-hour ride from Paris's Gare d'Austerlitz.

ESSENTIALS Orientation The heart of town is place Jean-Jaurès. Rue Nationale is the principal street (the Loire's Valley's "Champs-Elysées"), running north to the Loire River. Head along rue du Commerce and rue du Grand-Marché to reach *la vieille ville* (the old town).

Information The Office de Tourisme is located on boulevard Heurteloup (tel. 47-05-58-08).

Although without a major château, the industrial and residential city of Tours is the traditional center for exploring the Loire Valley. At the junction of the Loire and Cher Rivers, it was one of the great pilgrimage sites of Europe in the Middle Ages. The devout en route to Santiago de Compostela in northwest Spain stopped off at Tours to pay homage at the tomb of St. Martin, the Apostle of Gaul, who had been bishop of Tours in the 4th century. One of the most significant conflicts in world history, the Battle of Tours in 732, checked the Arab advance into Gaul.

The townspeople are fond of pointing out that Tours, not Paris, is the logical site for the capital of France. It virtually *was* the capital in June of 1940, when Churchill flew there to meet with Paul Reynaud.

WHAT TO SEE & DO

CATHEDRALE DE ST-GATIEN, 5, place de la Cathédrale. Tel. 47-05-05-54.

This cathedral, the chief attraction of Tours, honors an evangelist of the 3rd century. Its façade is in the flamboyant Gothic style, flanked by two towers the bases of which date from the 12th century, although the lanterns are Renaissance. This medley of styles has a certain charm which Balzac called "a scent of heaven." The choir was built in the 13th century, and each century up to and including the 16th produced new additions. Sheltered inside is the handsome 16th-century tomb of the children of Charles VIII. Some of the stained-glass windows, the building's glory, date from the 13th century and are said to be among the finest in France.

Admission: 30 F ($5.40) adults, 15 F ($2.70) children 13–18, free for children under 13.

Open: Wed–Mon 9am–12:45pm and 2–6pm.

MUSEE DE L'HISTORIAL DE TOURAINE, Château Royal, quai d'Orléans. Tel. 47-61-02-95.

A perfect introduction to the Loire Valley, this museum features 30 scenes and 165 wax figures tracing 1,000 years of Touraine history.

Admission: 29 F ($5.20) adults, 19 F ($3.40) children under 16.

Open: June–Sept, daily 9am–6:30pm; Oct–Nov and Apr–May, daily 9am–noon and 2–6:30pm; Dec–Mar, daily 2–5:30pm.

WHERE TO STAY

Moderate

HOTEL ALLIANCE, 292, av. de Grammont, 37000 Tours. Tel. 47-28-00-80. Fax 47-27-77-61. 110 rms (all with bath), 6 suites. A/C MINIBAR TV TEL **Bus:** 1, 4, or 5.
$ Rates: 420 F ($75.60) single; 495 F ($89.10) double; from 800 F ($144) suite. Breakfast 60 F ($10.80) extra. AE, DC, MC, V. **Parking:** Free.

This is the largest and probably the most visible modern hotel in Tours. Built in the 1970s on the banks of the Cher, it lies about a mile south of the town center, on one of the city's main commercial boulevards. Despite its relative youth, the hotel is decorated in the *grand siècle* style of an 18th-century Loire Valley house, and contains a formal reception area with crystal chandeliers and boxwood planters. The bright-colored rooms are soundproof and furnished with a blend of modern pieces and antique reproductions. There's plenty of open space, a French garden, and a swimming pool. Breakfast and drinks are served in a sitting area. The hotel has a distinguished restaurant with a terrace; full meals cost 225–250 F ($40.50–$45), and the fixed-price menu is 150 F ($27).

HOTEL DE L'UNIVERS, 5, bd. Heurteloup, 37000 Tours. Tel. 47-05-37-12. Fax 47-61-51-80. 90 rms (all with bath). TV TEL
$ Rates: 350 F ($63) single; 750 F ($135) double. Breakfast 60 F ($10.80) extra. AE, DC, MC, V. **Parking:** 40 F ($7.20).

Highly rated, this hotel on the main artery of Tours is the oldest place in town and has hosted Thomas Edison, Rudyard Kipling, Ernest Hemingway, John D. Rockefeller, and former kings of Spain, Portugal, and Romania. The public rooms are carpeted and have been entirely renovated. The hotel's main dining room, La Touraine (open Sunday through Friday), serves excellent Loire dishes. The fixed-price menu costs 180 F ($32.40).

LE ROYAL, 65, av. de Grammont, 37000 Tours. Tel. 47-64-71-78. Fax 47-05-84-62. 50 rms (all with bath). TV TEL **Bus:** 1, 4, or 5.
$ Rates: 322 F ($58) single; 382 F ($68.80) double. Breakfast 38 F ($6.80) extra. AE, DC, MC, V. **Parking:** 25 F ($4.50).

Here you can enjoy modern conveniences without sacrificing tradition. Lounges and rooms are imaginatively furnished in the styles of Louis XV and Louis XVI. There's no restaurant here, but a country tavern offers drinks. Underground parking is available.

TOURS SUD NOVOTEL, Zac de la Vrillonnerie, 37170 Chambray-les-Tours. Tel. 47-27-41-38. Fax 47-27-60-03. 127 rms (all with bath). A/C TV TEL **Bus:** 6.
$ Rates: 420 F ($75.60) single; 460 F ($82.80) double. Breakfast 48 F ($8.60) extra. Children under 16 stay free in parents' room. AE, DC, MC, V. **Parking:** Free.

Set on special grounds amid a labyrinth of access roads and warehouses, this comfortable hotel, built in the late 1970s, was designed to offset the dozens of trees arranged on flat lawns around it. With comfortable and simply designed rooms, it's the preferred stopover of thousands of business travelers. All rooms are exactly alike, each with both a double and a single bed and a radio. For recreation, the Novotel offers a swimming pool and a children's play area. Facilities include a grill restaurant, open daily from 6am to midnight. The hotel is located three miles south of the town center, in Chambray, close to the Paris–Bordeaux motorway.

Inexpensive

LE CENTRAL, 21, rue Berthelot, 37000 Tours. Tel. 47-05-46-44. Fax 47-66-10-26. 41 rms (37 with bath, 2 with shower, 2 with wash basin and bidet). TEL **Bus:** 1, 4, or 5.
$ Rates: 180 F ($32.40) single or double with wash basin and bidet, 290 F ($52.20) single or double with shower, 340 F ($61.20) single or double with bath. Breakfast 30 F ($5.40) extra. AE, DC, MC, V. **Parking:** 35 F ($6.30).

Off the main boulevard, this old-fashioned hotel is within walking distance of the river and cathedral. It's set back from the street and surrounded by gardens, lawns, and trees. The Tremouilles family offers comfortable rooms at reasonable rates, and there are two French salons with reproductions of 18th- and 19th-century pieces. Thirty-two of the rooms have TVs and minibars. A garage is available.

HOTEL DU THEATRE, 57, rue de la Scellerie, 37000 Tours. Tel. 47-05-31-29. Fax 47-61-12-72. 32 rms (all with bath or shower). TV TEL **Bus:** 1, 4, or 5.
$ Rates: 100–225 F ($18–$40.50) single; 150–260 F ($27–$46.80) double. Breakfast 27 F ($4.90) extra. AE, DC, MC, V.

Named after the Grand Théâtre, which it faces, this small hotel is often patronized by actors appearing at the theater. The old building has been restored and is personal and homelike; the central location and price are also enticing. Breakfast is the only meal served, but there are several restaurants nearby.

HOTEL GAMBETTA, 7, rue Gambetta, 37000 Tours. Tel. 47-05-08-35. Fax 47-05-58-59. 39 rms (35 with bath or shower). TV TEL **Bus:** 1, 4, or 5.
$ Rates: 175 F ($31.50) single without bath or shower, 200–275 F ($36–$49.50) single with bath or shower; 195 F ($35.10) double without bath or shower, 270–295 F ($48.60–$53.10) double with bath or shower. Breakfast 35 F ($6.30) extra. AE, MC, V. **Parking:** 28 F ($5).

In the town center, this pleasant hotel offers spacious, conservatively decorated rooms. The quietest units are those clustered around an interior courtyard. The hotel has a bar with Greek-style columns.

WHERE TO DINE

Expensive

JARDIN DU CASTEL, 16, rue Groison, 37000 Tours. Tel. 47-41-94-40. Fax 47-51-50-28.
Cuisine: FRENCH. **Reservations:** Required. **Bus:** 1, 4, or 5.
$ Prices: Appetizers 45–135 F ($8.10–$24.30); main dishes 100–175 F ($18–$31.50); fixed-price menus 220 F ($39.60), 280 F ($50.40), and 400 F ($72). AE, DC, MC, V.
Open: Apr–Oct, lunch Wed–Sun noon–2:30pm; dinner Wed–Sun 7:30–11pm. Nov–Dec and Feb–Mar, lunch Tues–Sat noon–2:30pm; dinner daily 7:30–11pm. **Closed:** Jan.

Set at the edge of the Loire, this elegant 19th-century villa was originally built as the second home of the président des Comptes (director of the French Treasury) under Louis-Philippe. In 1987, it was acquired by Jean André and Guy Tricon and transformed into an elegant restaurant. A garden, enclosed by a stone wall, contains three enormous trees, one of them a tulip tree, whose shade protects diners on the flower-bordered terrace. Inside, opulently carved marble fireplaces add to the Directoire elegance.

The modern cuisine includes such specialties as oyster soup, zucchini spaghetti with a chive-flavored cream sauce and tomato purée, and a croustillant de brochet (a saltwater fish) flavored with vinegar.

In the early 1990s, the partners opened the **Hôtel de Groison** by adding 10 comfortably furnished bedrooms, each with TV, telephone, and minibar, priced at 520–920 F ($93.60–$165.60) per room, single or double occupancy. A sumptuous breakfast costs an additional 85 F ($15.30) per person extra. Parking is free on the narrow street outside, and around 60 F ($10.80) in a nearby garage.

JEAN BARDET, 57, rue Groison, 37000 Tours. Tel. 47-41-41-11. Fax 47-51-68-72.

    Cuisine: FRENCH. **Reservations:** Required. **Bus:** 1, 2, 7, or 9.

$ Prices: Appetizers 180–280 F ($32.40–$50.40); main dishes 200–500 F ($36–$90); fixed-price menus 610 F ($109.80), 700 F ($126), and 850 F ($153). AE, DC, MC, V.

    Open: Lunch Tues–Sun noon–2pm; dinner Tues–Sat 7:30–9:30pm. **Closed:** Feb 23–Mar 10.

    ★ Chef Bardet is known as "the prince of the chefs of Tours," and his cuisine has been described as "sensitive and sensual." The restaurant is a three-minute drive from the Loire on a hillside at the end of a one-way street. The early 19th-century villa and six-acre garden, which contains century-old sequoias and rare shrubs, are enclosed by a high wall. Apéritifs are served in a conservatory with bay windows, and the dining rooms are in several additions with Doric stone columns. The highly praised cuisine is the most expensive in town; the menu includes ragoût of oysters on a light-textured mousse of watercress and muscadet, Périgord truffles in puff pastry, and roast duck gizzards with lobster and essence of Graves wine. For dessert, try the bitter coffee sorbet or one of the many pastries.

If you also need a place to stay, Bardet and his wife, Sophie, rent 16 plush rooms—several containing Jacuzzis and working fireplaces. The decor is done in English themes with vibrant colors. Rooms cost 700–1,900 F ($126–$342) single or double.

LA ROCHE LE ROY, 55, route St-Avertin. Tel. 47-27-22-00.

    Cuisine: FRENCH. **Reservations:** Recommended.

$ Prices: Appetizers 70–130 F ($12.60–$23.40); main dishes 90–140 F ($16.20–$25.20); fixed-price meals 150–295 F ($27–$53.10). AE, MC, DC, V.

    Open: Lunch Mon–Fri 12:15–1:45pm; dinner Mon–Sat 7:15–10pm. **Closed:** First three weeks in Aug.

One of Tours's hottest chefs, Alain Couturier, blends new and old culinary techniques. The restaurant is in a 15th-century manor house with elegant but simple decor; the emphasis here is on the food. Try his warm salad of pigeon and grapes, followed by bass prepared with wine from the Loire or a rack of hare with rosemary-flavored honey. The rockfish with foie gras and a sweet-and-sour sauce is delectable. For dessert, there's a mélange of seasonal fruits served with a sabayon made with Vouvray valley wine.

Moderate

ROTISSERIE TOURANGELLE, 23, rue du Commerce. Tel. 47-05-71-21.

    Cuisine: FRENCH. **Reservations:** Required. **Bus:** 1, 4, or 5.

$ Prices: Appetizers 90–135 F ($16.20–$24.30); main dishes 110–135 F ($19.80–$24.30); fixed-price menus 95 F ($17.10), 135 F ($24.30), and 175 F ($31.50). AE, DC, MC, V.

    Open: Lunch Tues–Sun 12:15–1:45pm; dinner Tues–Sat 7:30–9:45pm. **Closed:** Feb.

Located in the modern commercial district, this pleasant restaurant is one of the best in Tours. Specialties, prepared with regional ingredients and local wines, include pike perch with sabayon and aiguillettes de filet de canard (duckling), followed by a strawberry parfait with a coulis of raspberries. You can dine on the terrace in summer.

LES TUFFEAUX, 19, rue Lavoisier. Tel. 47-47-19-89.

    Cuisine: FRENCH. **Reservations:** Required. **Bus:** 1, 4, or 5.

$ Prices: Appetizers 70–89 F ($12.60–$16); main dishes 90–110 F ($16.20–$19.80); fixed-price menus 110 F ($19.80), 150 F ($27), and 200 F ($36). MC, V.
Open: Lunch Tues–Sat noon–1:45pm; dinner Mon–Sat 7–10pm.

This 18th-century house in the old town holds one of the best restaurants in Tours. The restaurant has exposed beams and several walls constructed with the same type of beige-colored stone—called *le tuffeaux*—used to build many of the châteaux in the Loire Valley. A meal might consist of a soup of langoustines flavored with thyme, suprême of pike perch, filet of sole with asparagus, roast pigeon with pink grapefruit, salmon with fennel, and sumptuous desserts. The least expensive way to dine here is to order a fixed-price menu, although the 110-F ($19.80) menu is not available on Saturday night.

Inexpensive

LE RELAIS BURE, 1, place de la Résistance. Tel. 47-05-67-74.
   Cuisine: FRENCH. **Reservations:** Not required. **Bus:** 1, 4, or 5.
$ Prices: Appetizers: 27–100 F ($4.90–$18); main dishes 70–460 F ($12.60–$82.80). DC, MC, V.
   Open: Lunch daily noon–3pm; dinner daily 7pm–midnight.

Set within a five-minute walk east of the town's historic center, at the edge of a modern square whose center is used as a parking lot, this brasserie specializes in shellfish, regional recipes, and turn-of-the-century nostalgia. In addition to a busy bar area and a warm-weather front terrace, inside tables are scattered amid the street level and a raised mezzanine, each warmly decorated with lots of exposed wood. Most main courses here are reasonably priced at 70–100 F ($12.60–$18), with the exception of shellfish, whose rarity will usually bring the price of a main course here much higher. Menu items include six well-flavored versions of sauerkraut, a wide choice of grilled meats (including a peppery steak au poivre), foie gras and smoked salmon (both prepared in-house), and a tempting array of ultra-fresh desserts prepared by a resident pastry chef.

NEARBY ACCOMMODATIONS & DINING

CHATEAU DE BEAULIEU, 37300 Joué-les-Tours. Tel. 47-53-20-26. Fax 47-53-84-20. 19 rms (all with bath). TV TEL **Directions:** Take the D86 from Tours, then the D207 for Beaulieu, 4½ miles southwest of Tours. **Bus:** 3.
$ Rates: 370–670 F ($66.60–$120.60) single or double. Breakfast 48 F ($8.60) extra. AE, DC, MC, V. **Parking:** Free.

At this secluded 18th-century country estate, which contains a restaurant and a three-star hotel, you can experience the lifestyle of another era. The gravel driveway encircles a bronze fountain with cherubs and urns of flowers. Beyond the formal entrance, a double curving stairway takes you to the reception hall. The rooms are furnished with mahogany and chestnut pieces, paneled recessed windows, fireplaces, and good plumbing.

   Jean-Pierre Lozay, the owner, is also an excellent chef, so at least try to visit for a meal. In the beam-ceilinged dining room, classic French windows open onto views of the gardens, complete with two public swimming pools (open from July to September) and four tennis courts. Fixed-price meals run 195–420 F ($35.10–$75.60); à la carte meals are available. The hotel has a terrace overlooking the garden. Call the château in advance to reserve a room or a table in the dining room.

---

3. MONTBAZON

154 miles SW of Paris, 7 miles SE of Tours

GETTING THERE   By Car   From Tours, motorists can head south along N10 for 7 miles.

ESSENTIALS Information The Pavillon du Tourisme, avenue de la Gare (tel. 47-26-97-87), is open from June 15 through September.

The Indre River winds its way below. Cows graze in the fields. All is quiet now. Once, however, the sound of battle was heard between the forces of the warring counts of Anjou and Blois. In time Henri III made Montbazon a grand duchy, but the Revolution ended that bit of pomposity.

The ruins of a 10th-century **keep**—built by Foulques Nerra, known as the Black Falcon—can be explored from 9am to noon and 2:30 to 7pm March to October.

Nearby you can visit **Montlouis-sur-Loire,** where the castle of **La Bourdaisière** has been rebuilt since its destruction. Only the stables are authentically 17th century. Lilian Whitteker, the American painter born in Cincinnati, Ohio, in 1881 and known for her paintings of flowers, retired there. The Franco-American Foundation displays a permanent exhibit of paintings on the grounds.

WHERE TO STAY & DINE

LE CHATEAU D'ARTIGNY, route d'Azay-le-Rideau, 37250 Montbazon. Tel. 47-26-24-24. Fax 47-65-92-79. 51 rms (all with bath), 2 suites. TV TEL
Directions: Take the D17 one mile southeast of Montbazon.
$ Rates: 820 F ($147.60) single; 945–1,575 F ($170.10–$283.50) double; from 3,150 F ($567) suite. Breakfast 85 F ($15.30) extra; half board 905–1,220 F ($162.90–$219.60) per person extra. MC, V. **Parking:** Free. **Closed:** Dec 1–Jan 11.

This château was built for the perfume king François Coty, who lavishly lived and entertained here. Today the mansion is a deluxe hotel for guests who want to spend their holiday in the country in grandeur and in total comfort. Luxury is certainly a tradition here. For example, what is now the wine cellar was once a private cold storage for Madame Coty's furs, and the former pantry room is lined with pink marble. In the rotunda ballroom an artist did a ceiling painting of the red-caped tycoon and his wife in white surrounded by their family. The proprietor, Alain Rabier, will tell you about an unfinished chapel, a pavilion half the size of the one at Versailles, and why the kitchen was installed upstairs (Monsieur Coty didn't want the cooking odors, which ascend, to interfere with his enjoyment of flowers). Famous visitors have included Henry Ford II and Elizabeth Taylor.

Weekend soirées are popular here, as are musical evenings, sometimes featuring a violinist. The drawing room and corridors are classically furnished, with fine antiques, gilt torchères, Louis XV–style chairs, and bronze statuary. In typical château style, there are acres of private parkland, as well as a large formal garden at the front entrance with a round reflecting pool. Set among the trees is a flagstone-edged swimming pool. Rooms are furnished in various periods, with a generous use of antiques (especially Louis XVI and Directoire).

Another reason to stay here is the superb cuisine served in the gilt-and-paneled dining room. There's a wide selection of wines, including Chinon and Montlouis. Fixed-price menus cost 285 F ($51.30), 370 F ($66.60), and 440 F ($79.20).

DOMAINE DE LA TORTINIERE, Les Gués de Veigné, 37250 Montbazon. Tel. 47-26-00-19. Fax 47-65-95-70. 21 rms (all with bath), 7 suites. TV TEL
Directions: Take the N10 one mile north of Montbazon, then the D287 toward Ballan-Mire.
$ Rates: 545 F ($98.10) single; 665–830 F ($119.70–$149.40) double; from 1,100 F ($198) suite. Breakfast 60 F ($10.80) extra. MC, V. **Closed:** Dec 20–Feb 28.

This picture-postcard château, just one mile off the N10 between Tours and Montbazon, is perched high on a hillside overlooking the Vallée de l'Indre. It was built in the Belle Epoque style in 1861, with high peaked towers, baroque gables and windows, and curving exterior staircases leading from the rolling lawns to the ivy-covered terraces. The interior furnishings are modest compared with the architecture. Some of the rooms are in an ivy-covered, petite Renaissance pavilion in the garden, amid cedar trees.

If you can't stay at the château, consider visiting for a meal. The fixed-price lunch costs 220 F ($39.60); a fixed-price dinner, 290 F ($52.20) and 370 F ($66.60). The restaurant is open daily.

4. AZAY-LE-RIDEAU

162 miles SW of Paris, 13 miles SW of Tours

GETTING THERE By Train or Bus There is train and bus service from Tours.

ESSENTIALS Information The Syndicat d'Initiative (tourist office), at place de l'Europe (tel. 47-45-44-40), is open from March 15 through September.

Its machicolated towers and blue-slate roof pierced with dormers shimmer in the moat, creating a reflection like one in a Monet painting. Then a white swan glides by, rippling the waters. The defensive medieval look is all for show. The Chateau d'Azay-le-Rideau, 37190 Azay-le-Rideau (tel. 47-45-42-04) was created as a private residence during the Renaissance. A site was selected at an idyllic spot on the banks of the Indre River, about 13 miles southwest of Tours. A previous château that stood there was in ruins. (In fact, the whole village was known as Azay-le-Brûlé or Azay the Burnt. Passing through with his court in 1418, the dauphin, later Charles VII, was insulted by the Burgundians. A whole garrison was killed for this "outrage," the village and its fortress razed.)

Gilles Berthelot, the finance minister of François I, built the château beginning in 1518. Actually, his big-spending wife, Philippa, supervised its construction. Both of them should have known better. So elegant and harmonious, so imposing was the creation that the Chevalier King grew immensely jealous. In time Berthelot fled, the château reverting to the king. François I didn't live there, however, but started the custom of granting it to "friends of the Crown." After a brief residency by Prince Frederick of Prussia in 1870, the château became the property of the state in 1905.

Before entering you can circle the mansion, enjoying its near-perfect proportions. Many critics consider it the crowning achievement of the French Renaissance in Touraine. Architecturally, its most fancifully ornate feature is a great bay enclosing a grand stairway with a straight flight of steps. The Renaissance interior is a virtual museum.

The largest room at Azay, the Banqueting Hall, is adorned with four 16th-century Flemish tapestries representing scenes from the life of Solomon (it took a craftsperson one year to weave just four square feet). In the kitchen is a collection of utensils. The corner carvings are most unusual: one, for example, shows a dog biting its own ear. In the second room is a trio of 16th-century Flemish tapestries. The fireplace is only a plaster molding of a chimneypiece made by Rodin for the Château of Montal. The fireplace masterpiece, however, is in a ground-floor bedroom containing a 16th-century four-poster. Over the stone fireplace hovers a salamander, the symbol of François I.

From the second-floor Royal Chamber, look out at the gardens—the scenery described by Balzac in *The Lily of the Valley*. He also called the château a "cut diamond mounted on pilings masked with flowers." This bedroom, also known as the Green Room, is believed to have sheltered both Louis XIII and Louis XIV. The adjoining Red Chamber—so named because of its damask—contains a portrait gallery, including a *Lady in Red* (erroneously attributed to Titian) and a scene showing Gabrielle d'Estrées (the favorite of Henri IV) in her bath.

The château is open July through August, daily from 9am to 7pm; and April through June and September, daily from 9:30am to 6pm. Adults pay 26 F ($4.70); ages 18–25, 17 F ($3.10); children 7–17, 6 F ($1.10). From the beginning of June until around the last of September, a son-et-lumière program is staged; admission is 45 F ($8.10) for adults, 35 F ($6.30) for children.

WHERE TO DINE

L'AIGLE D'OR, 10, av. Adélaïde-Riché. Tel. 47-45-24-58.
   Cuisine: FRENCH. **Reservations:** Recommended.
$ Prices: Appetizers 53–95 F ($9.50–$17.10); main dishes 80–230 F ($14.40–$41.40); fixed-price menus 135 F ($24.30), 190 F ($34.20), and 265 F ($47.70). V.
   Open: Lunch Thurs–Tues 12:30–2pm; dinner Mon–Tues and Thurs–Sat 7:30–9:30pm. **Closed:** Jan 15–Feb 15 and Dec 10–20.

One of the best places to dine in town, this restaurant has been newly decorated in pastel shades. The food is excellent, including such dishes as stingray with artichokes and minced lamb with a zucchini flan. A specialty is rabbit with Vouvray wine. The service is professional, and the welcome is charming.

AN EASY EXCURSION TO SACHE

Just 4½ miles from Azay-le-Rideau, you can visit the hometown of Honoré de Balzac, where he wrote *The Lily of the Valley*. The **Château de Saché** (tel. 47-26-86-50) houses a Balzac museum, with his bedroom preserved as it was when he lived there. It's open July and August, daily from 9:30am to 6:30pm; in September and March 15 to June 30, daily from 9am to noon and 2 to 6pm; and October to March 14, Thursday through Tuesday from 9am to noon and 2 to 5pm (closed: December and January). Admission is 18 F ($3.20). Alexander Calder, who died in 1976 and is known for his stabiles and mobiles, also lived at Saché.

---

5. LUYNES

155 miles SW of Paris, 6½ miles W of Tours

GETTING THERE   By Car   From Tours, head west along N152 for about 6½ miles; the turnoff to Luynes is signposted.

ESSENTIALS   Information   The Syndicat d'Initiative (tourist office) is at la Mairie (tel. 47-55-50-31).

A stark 15th-century castle rises on the banks of the Loire on an ancient Gallo-Roman site. Underneath the mountain the local vineyard owners use the caves as storage warehouses. The château was originally built by the Maillé family, but its name was changed when it was acquired by Charles d'Albert de Luynes, whom the king made a duke in 1619. His descendants still own the château today and have not opened it to the public.

WHERE TO STAY & DINE

DOMAINE DE BEAUVOIS, route de Cleré, 37230 Luynes. Tel. 47-55-50-11. Fax 47-55-59-62. 40 rms (all with bath), 2 suites. MINIBAR TV TEL
$ Rates: 700–1,360 F ($126–$244.80) single or double; from 1,460 F ($262.80) suite. Breakfast 80 F ($14.40) extra. AE, DC, MC, V. **Parking:** Free. **Closed:** Mid-Jan to mid-Mar.

This is classic château architecture, with a central tower, a formal entrance, and a terraced reflecting pool. Dating from the 15th century, the hotel overlooks the Loire and is surrounded by 300 acres of parkland, including a large pond for fishing and canoeing. From the tower you can survey the "domaine," which includes bridle paths, tennis courts, and a pool. The drawing room contains a marble fireplace, an iron chandelier with colored glass, and three tall windows opening onto the pool. The bedrooms are individually decorated with coordinated fabric on the walls, draperies, and upholstery. Furniture is a mix of reproductions and antiques. Suites and accommodations in the villa annex, La Closerie, are at the upper end of the prices given above. Room 12 is on a grand-opera scale, with a 10-foot fireplace and an armoire.

There are several theme dining rooms: an opulent Louis XV room, a rustic Louis XIII room, and the more rustic 15th-century tower room with a stone fireplace. One wing contains a large dining room, which can cater up to 100 people.

The château is about 6½ miles from Tours, one mile north of Luynes, off the D49.

---

6. VILLANDRY

157 miles SW of Paris, 20 miles NE of Chinon, 11 miles W of Tours, 5 miles E of Azay-le-Rideau

GETTING THERE   Unfortunately, Villandry doesn't have bus service from Tours. Rent a bike and ride along the Cher or go by car.

The 16th-century-style gardens of the medieval and Renaissance   **۞ Château de Villandry,** 37510 Joué-les-Tours (tel. 47-50-02-09), are celebrated throughout the Touraine. Forming a trio of superimposed "cloisters," with a water garden on the highest level, they were planned by Dr. Carvallo, founder of La Demeure Historique. The grounds contain 10½ miles of boxwood sculpture, which the gardeners must cut to style in only two weeks in September. Every square of the gardens seems like a mosaic. The borders represent the many faces of love: tender, tragic (with daggers), or crazy, the last evoked by a labyrinth in the middle that doesn't get you anywhere. Pink tulips and dahlias suggest sweet love; red, tragic; and yellow, unfaithful. Crazy love is symbolized by all colors. The vine arbors, citrus hedges, shady walks—all this keeps six men busy full time. One garden contains all the common French vegetables except the potato, which wasn't known in France in the 16th century (even as late as 1771 the potato was considered "unfit for human consumption," until its virtues were extolled by Parmentier).

Originally a feudal castle stood at Villandry, but in 1536 Jean Lebreton, the chancellor of François I, built the present château, whose buildings form a U and are surrounded by a two-sided moat. Near the gardens is a terrace from which you can see the small village and the 12th-century church of Villandry.

Admission to the gardens with a tour of the château is 37 F ($6.70). To visit the gardens separately without a guide, admission is 24 F ($4.30). The château is open from mid-March to mid-November, and guided tours are conducted daily from 9am to 6:30pm (until 5:30pm off-season). The gardens are open from 9am to sunset.

WHERE TO STAY & DINE

LE CHEVAL ROUGE, Villandry, 37510 Joué-les-Tours. Tel. 47-50-02-07. Fax 47-50-08-77.

Cuisine: FRENCH. **Reservations:** Recommended.

$ Prices: Appetizers 60–250 F ($10.80–$45); main dishes 80–250 F ($14.40–$45); fixed-price meals 80–240 F ($14.40–$43.20). MC, V.

Open: Lunch daily noon–2pm; dinner daily 7:30–9pm. **Closed:** Jan 10–Mar 10; and Sun night and Mon during Mar–Apr and Sept–Oct.

The best food in town is served with polite dignity at this restaurant, run by the Rody family. This structure was built in 1953 from native beige stones used in the château nearby. Many of the famous gardens of the château are visible from the windows of the dining room, and the Cher flows within 100 yards of the hotel. Specialties include fresh grilled salmon, farm-bred pigeon with garlic, and filet of pork with plums.

This inn also rents 20 comfortably and well-equipped rooms, 18 with private bath. A single rents for 295 F ($53.10), a double is 305 F ($54.90), and a triple costs 400 F ($72), plus another 35 F ($6.30) for breakfast.

7. LOCHES

160 miles SW of Paris, 25 miles SE of Tours

GETTING THERE   By Bus   Two buses a day leave from Tours, and the trip takes one hour.

ESSENTIALS   Information   The Office de Tourisme is near the bus station on place Wermelskirchen (tel. 47-59-07-98).

Forever linked to the memory of that legendary beauty Agnès Sorel, Loches is the *cité médiévale* of the château country. In the hills on the banks of the Indre River, it is called the city of kings. Known as the acropolis of the Loire, the château and its satellite buildings form a complex called the **Cité Royale.** The House of Anjou, from which the Plantagenets descended, owned the castle from 886 to 1205. The kings of France occupied it from the mid-13th century until the days of Charles IX, the son of Catherine de Medici, who was king from 1560.

WHAT TO SEE & DO

The **Château de Loches,** 5, place Charles-VII (tel. 47-59-01-32), is remembered for *la belle des belles* (the beauty of beauties), Agnès Sorel. Inside the castle is her tomb—two angels guard her velvet cushion and her feet rest on two rams. In 1777 her tomb was opened; inside the coffin was a set of dentures and some locks of hair—all that remained from the one who was considered the most dazzling beauty of the 15th century. Maid of honor to Isabelle de Lorraine, she was singled out by the dauphin (Charles VII) to be his mistress. She had great influence with the king until her mysterious death. The future king, Louis XI, wasn't captivated by Mademoiselle Sorel; he once slapped her in the face and chased her at sword point. After her death, Fouquet painted her as the Virgin (Antwerp owns the masterpiece).

The château also contains the oratory of Anne of Brittany, decorated with sculptured ermine tails. One of its most outstanding treasures is a triptych of *The Passion* from the Fouquet School, dating from 1485.

Admission is 26 F ($4.70) for adults, 16 F ($2.90) for children, and includes the donjon described below. During the summer the château is open daily from 9am to noon and 2 to 6pm; October to mid-March it's open Thursday through Tuesday and closes at 5pm. The château is closed in December and January.

The ancient **keep** (donjon), reached along Mail du Donjon, of the comtes d'Anjou can also be visited during the same hours as the château. The Round Tower of Louis XI contains rooms formerly used for torture; a favorite method was to suspend the victim in an iron cage. Cardinal Balue was held that way for more than 10 years. In the 15th century the duke of Milan, Ludovico Sforza (Ludvico il Moro), was imprisoned in the Martelet, and he painted frescoes on the walls to pass the time; he died at Loches in 1508.

Nearby, the **Collegiate Church of St-Ours,** 1, rue Thomas Pactius (tel. 47-59-02-36), spans the 10th to the 15th centuries and is an interesting example of Romanesque architecture. The portal is richly decorated with sculptured figures, unfortunately damaged by time and renovations but still attractive. Monumental stone pyramids (*dubes*) surmount the nave. The west door is exceptionally carved. The church is open daily from 8am to 7pm.

Finally, you may want to walk the **ramparts** and enjoy the view of the town, including a 15th-century gate and Renaissance inns.

WHERE TO STAY

GEORGE SAND, 39, rue Quintefol, 37600 Loches. Tel. 47-59-39-74. Fax 47-91-55-75. 20 rms (all with bath). TV TEL **Bus:** 10.

$ **Rates:** 260–400 F ($46.80–$72) single or double. Breakfast 30 F ($5.40) extra. MC, V. **Closed:** Nov 27–Dec 27.

Loaded with rustic objects, this tastefully redecorated inn dates from the 17th century and is conveniently located just a few steps from the base of the château. The inn, owned by Monsieur and Madame Fortin, was completely renovated in 1982. Several of the bedrooms look out over a tributary of the Indre River; the quieter ones are at the rear.

This Logis de France hotel has a restaurant with a view of the Indre. A la carte dishes feature the cuisine of Touraine, including a fondue of goat with confit of leeks, filet of pike perch (a river fish) in white butter, and breast of duck George Sand. Fixed-price menus cost 80–190 F ($14.40–$34.20).

GRAND HOTEL DE FRANCE, 6, rue Picois, 37600 Loches. Tel. 47-59-00-32. 20 rms (all with bath or shower). TV TEL **Bus:** 10.

$ **Rates:** 130–320 F ($23.40–$57.60) single or double. Breakfast 30 F ($5.40) extra. DC, MC, V. **Closed:** Jan 5–Feb 15.

Charmingly French, this hotel has an inner courtyard, which many bedrooms overlook. The rates are low for the area, and English is spoken. There's a petite dining room with paneling and crystal, and you can also dine under parasols in the courtyard. Three fixed-price meals are offered, for 80 F ($14.40), 110 F ($19.80), and 150 F ($27). The restaurant is closed Sunday for dinner, all day Monday, and from September to the end of June.

LUCCOTEL, rue de Lézards, 37600 Loches. Tel. 47-91-50-50. Fax 47-94-01-18. 42 rms (all with bath). TV TEL **Bus:** 10.

$ **Rates:** 230–320 F ($41.40–$57.60) single or double. Breakfast 35 F ($6.30) extra. MC, V. **Parking:** Free.

This quiet, comfortable hotel on a hill overlooks Loches and the château and is surrounded by a 2½-acre park. Two of the units are suitable for the disabled. The hotel has a heated indoor swimming pool, a Jacuzzi, and a sauna, as well as an excellent restaurant, Le Colvert. Fixed-price menus and à la carte meals go for 90–190 F ($16.20–$34.20).

8. AMBOISE

136 miles SW of Paris, 22 miles E of Tours

GETTING THERE   By Bus   In summer, regular bus service connects Amboise with Tours, Blois, and Chenonceaux.

By Train   A train from Tours will deposit you at Gare SNCF. The train station is across the river.

ESSENTIALS   Information   The Office de Tourisme is on quai Général-de-Gaulle (tel. 47-57-01-37).

On the banks of the Loire, Amboise is in the center of vineyards known as Touraine-Amboise. Leonardo da Vinci, the quintessential Renaissance man, spent his last years in this ancient city.

WHAT TO SEE & DO

Dominating the town is the ✪ **Château of Amboise** (tel. 47-57-00-98), the first in France to reflect the impact of the Italian Renaissance.

A combination of both Gothic and Renaissance, this 15th-century château is mainly associated with Charles VIII, who built it on a rocky spur separating the valleys of the Loire and the Amasse. The only son of Louis XI of France and Charlotte of Savoy, the future Charles VIII was born at Amboise on June 30, 1470. At the age of

25, he returned to France after his Italian campaign. With him he brought artists, designers, and architects from "that land of enchantment." In a sense, he was bringing the Italian Renaissance to France. His workers built the *logis du roi,* the apartments of the king, its façade pierced by large double-mullioned windows and crowned by towering dormers and sculptured canopies. Charles VIII died at Amboise on April 8, 1498, after an accident: he banged his head against the lintel of a very low door. The blow didn't kill him until after he'd witnessed a fête planned that day for his entertainment. At the end of the terrace, near the room of his queen, Anne of Brittany, is the doorway where it is said the mishap took place.

Later Louise of Savoy and her children lived at Amboise. One of her offspring in 1515 became King François I; the other was Margaret of Navarre. François continued to live at Amboise, making additions to the castle. The château enjoyed its golden hours under the Chevalier King, as he sponsored a number of brilliant festivals, including some that featured contests between wild animals. The most memorable event was the arrival of Charles V in 1539. Preceded by torchbearers, the emperor grandly began to climb up one of the ramps, but a torch ignited a banner in the fabric-draped tower and he was nearly burned alive.

The skyline of Amboise is characterized by two squat towers, the Hurtault and the Minimes, which contain ramps of huge dimensions so that cavaliers on horseback or nobles in horse-drawn chariots could ascend them.

The name Amboise became linked in 1560 with a series of some of the most savage executions in France—executions that followed the Amboise Conspiracy, a Huguenot plot led by a La Renaudie. Its aim was to remove François II from the influence of the House of Guise. Decapitations and mass hangings followed, much to the after-dinner amusement of the young François II and his queen, Mary Stuart (later Mary Queen of Scots). During the 19th century much of Amboise was destroyed, and it was only partially restored later.

You visit first the flamboyant Gothic Chapel of St. Hubert, built on the ramparts in the late 15th century and distinguished by its lace-like tracery. It allegedly contains the remains of da Vinci. Actually the great artist was buried in the castle's Collegiate Church, which was destroyed between 1806 and 1810. During the Second Empire excavations were undertaken on the site of the church, and bones discovered were "identified" as those of Leonardo.

Today the walls of the château are hung with tapestries, the rooms furnished in the style of the époque. From the terraces are panoramic views of the town and of the Loire Valley.

The château may be visited daily from 9am to noon and 2 to 6:30pm. In winter it's open until sunset, and in July and August it's open all day without interruption. Admission is 28 F ($5) for adults and 18 F ($3.20) for children.

Finally, you might visit **Clos-Lucé,** 2, rue de Clos-Lucé (tel. 47-57-62-88), a 15th-century manor house of brick and stone. In what had been an oratory for Anne of Brittany, François I installed "the great master in all forms of art and science," Leonardo da Vinci. Loved and venerated by the Chevalier King, da Vinci lived there for three years, dying at the manor in 1519. (Incidentally, those death-bed paintings depicting Leonardo in the arms of François I are probably symbolic; the king was supposedly out of town when the artist died.) From the window of his bedroom Leonardo liked to look out at the château where François lived. Whenever he was restless, the king would visit Leonardo via an underground tunnel, discovered in modern times by the Beaux-Arts. Nine days before his death, the artist made a will leaving untold riches of books, drawings, and instruments to his "beloved pupil and faithful companion" Francescoda Metzi. You can visit what is believed to have been the kitchen—the domain of the faithful servant Mathurine, mentioned by da Vinci in his will, to whom he left his cloak of "good black cloth, trimmed with leather."

Inside, the rooms are well furnished, some containing reproductions from the period of the artist. The lower level is reserved for da Vinci's designs, models, and inventions, including his plans for a turbine engine, an airplane, and a parachute.

There's also a video on da Vinci's life, an exhibition room for children, and a bookshop.

Clos-Lucé is open June through September, daily from 9am to 7pm; the rest of the year, daily from 9am to noon and 2 to 7pm. The museum is closed for Christmas and in January. Admission is 30 F ($5.40) for adults and 22 F ($4) for children.

Clos-Lucé has a tearoom and a pancake shop open daily from noon to 7pm.

WHERE TO STAY

Expensive

LE CHOISEUL, 36, quai Charles-Guinot, 37400 Amboise. Tel. 47-30-45-45. Fax 47-30-46-10. 32 rms (all with bath). 4 suites. MINIBAR TV TEL

$ Rates: 500–900 F ($90–$162) single or double; 980–1,300 F ($176.40–$234) suite. Breakfast 75 F ($13.50) extra. MC, V. **Parking:** Free. **Closed:** Nov 27–Jan 15.

The rooms in this 18th-century hotel, 15 of which are air-conditioned, are luxurious. On the grounds is a garden with aromatic, flowering terraces. This hotel is set in the valley between a hillside and the Loire River, close by the Château d'Amboise.

Dining/Entertainment: The formal dining room has a view of the Loire and welcomes nonresidents who phone in advance. It's open daily from noon to 2pm and 7 to 9:30pm; fixed-price menus are 200 F ($36), 280 F ($50.40), and 380 F ($68.40).

Facilities: Outdoor swimming pool, tennis.

HOSTELLERIE DU CHATEAU-DE-PRAY, route de Charge (D751), 37400 Amboise. Tel. 47-57-23-67. 19 rms (all with bath). TEL

$ Rates: 550–650 F ($99–$117) single or double; from 800 F ($144) suite. Breakfast 45 F ($8.10) extra; half board 195 F ($35.10) extra. AE, MC, V. **Parking:** Free. **Closed:** Jan–Feb 10.

Set in a forested park about a mile east of the center of Amboise, this château was originally conceived as a fortress by Geoffroy de Pray in 1244. Although it had served for many years as a hotel, in 1991 it was acquired by an aggressive new management, who poured millions of francs into a complete restoration. Today, from its position above parterres surveying the Loire, it resembles some of the tower-flanked castles on the Rhine. Inside, you'll find antlers, hunting trophies, venerable antiques, and a paneled drawing room with a fireplace and a collection of antique oil paintings. Bedrooms are stylishly conservative and very comfortable.

Dining/Entertainment: Open to nonresidents, the restaurant offers fixed-price menus ranging from 195 to 250 F ($35.10 to $45), and a cost-conscious lunch priced at 150 F ($27). During warm weather, tables are placed outside on a terrace overlooking formal gardens. A typical dinner might include grilled salmon with beurre blanc, lobster cannelloni, and roast rabbit with wine sauce.

Moderate

BELLE-VUE, 12, quai Charles-Guinot, 37400 Amboise. Tel. 47-57-02-26. 34 rms (all with bath or shower). TEL

$ Rates: 220 F ($39.60) single; 320 F ($57.60) double. Breakfast 30 F ($5.40) extra. MC, V. **Parking:** Free. **Closed:** Nov 15–Mar 15.

This efficient inn lies at the bridge crossing the Loire. It has rows of French doors and outside tables on two levels shaded by umbrellas in summer. The interior lounges are functionally furnished and well maintained. Rooms are modernized and comfortable, providing you avoid the attic rooms, reached after traversing narrow halls. Only breakfast is served.

LION D'OR, 17, quai Charles-Guinot, 37400 Amboise. Tel. 47-57-00-23. 23 rms (19 with bath or shower, all with toilet and basin). TEL

$ Rates: 192 F ($34.60) single or double without bath; 286–306 F ($51.50–$55.10) single or double with bath or shower. Breakfast 35 F ($6.30) extra. MC, V. **Parking:** 35 F ($6.30). **Closed:** Nov to mid Mar.

"The Golden Lion" (its English name) is comprised of an 18th-century and a 19th-century wing which were joined together to form a coherent whole. The inn sits in the historic heart of Amboise, near the foundation of the château. Steep slate roofs and wide windows characterize the architecture, and many rooms open onto a view of the Loire. Bedrooms are comfortably but simply furnished. Nonresidents must call ahead to reserve a table in the high-ceilinged dining room; full meals cost 143–249 F ($25.70–$44.80). A typical meal includes dentelle de saumon à la ciboulette, épaule d'agneau (lamb) farcie with salad, cheese, and, for dessert, fleur de sorbet au coulis de framboise (raspberries). Specialties include foie gras de canard (duck), scallops with endive, medallions of veal and mushrooms, and sabayon of peaches with champagne.

NOVOTEL, 17, rue des Sablonnières, 37400 Amboise. Tel. 47-57-42-07.
   Fax 47-30-40-76. 121 rms (all with bath). TV TEL **Directions:** Exit from the A10 autoroute at Amboise, follow the signs for Chenonceaux, then follow the blue signs for Novotel.
$ Rates: 400–440 F ($72–$79.20) single; 520–560 F ($93.60–$100.80) double. Breakfast 50 F ($9) extra. AE, DC, MC, V. **Parking:** Free.

Built about half a mile west of the town's château in the early 1980s, this member of the nationwide hotel chain was completely renovated in 1991. Today, it adheres to a time-tested and very successful architectural formula which includes clean and contemporary bedrooms in monochromatic colors, and sofas that can be converted into extra beds upon demand. About half the bedrooms offer sweeping views of the château and minibars, and are priced at the upper end of the above-mentioned price scale. On the premises is a modern and unpretentious restaurant offering platters and fixed-price menus for around 135 F ($24.30) each, two tennis courts, a swimming pool, and a protected parking lot that is locked after dark.

WHERE TO DINE

In addition to the following, see "Where to Stay," above, for the hotel restaurants.

LE MANOIR ST-THOMAS, place Richelieu. Tel. 47-57-22-52.
   Cuisine: FRENCH. **Reservations:** Required.
$ Prices: Appetizers 85–90 F ($15.30–$16.20); main dishes 110–140 F ($19.80–$25.20); fixed-price menu 195 F ($35.10) for four courses, 300 F ($54) for seven courses. AE, DC, MC, V.
   Open: Lunch Tues–Sun 12:15–2:30pm; dinner Tues–Sat 7:15–9:30pm.
   Closed: Jan 15–Mar 15.

The best food in town is served at this Renaissance house, which lies in the shadow of the Château d'Amboise. The owner and chef is François Le Coz. The restaurant is in a pleasant garden within the stone-and-brick wall of a Renaissance house whose foundations are from the 15th century. The elegant dining room is richly decorated with a polychrome ceiling and a massive stone fireplace. Specialties include filet of lamb with port, a confit of duck liver with Vouvray sauce, and filet of red mullet with a cream of sweet-pepper sauce.

9. BLOIS

112 miles SW of Paris, 37 miles NE of Tours

GETTING THERE By Train Blois is a one-hour train ride from Tours, a 40-minute ride from Amboise.

ESSENTIALS Orientation Usually visited in conjunction with nearby Chambord, Blois lies 35 miles from Orléans. On the right bank of Loire, Blois is the center of the château district. (In 1429 Joan of Arc launched her expeditionary forces from here to oust the English from Orléans.)

Information The Office de Tourisme is located at Pavillon Anne-de-Bretagne, 3 av. Jean-Laigret (tel. 54-74-06-49).

A wound in battle had earned him the name "Balafré" (Scarface), but he was quite a ladies' man nonetheless. In fact, on that cold misty morning of December 23, 1588, the Duke of Guise had just left a warm bed and the arms of one of Catherine de Medici's lovely "flying squadron" girls. His archrival, Henri III, had summoned him.

As he made his way to the king's chambers, perhaps he was dreaming of the day when the effeminate little monarch would be overthrown and he, the champion of the Catholics, would become ruler of France.

The king's minions were about. Nothing unusual—Henri was always surrounded with attractive young men these days. Then it happened. The guards moved menacingly toward him with daggers. Wounded, the duke was still strong enough to knock a few down. He made his way toward the door, where more guards awaited him. Staggering back, he fell to the floor in a pool of his own blood. Only then did Henri emerge from behind the curtains. "My God," he is reputed to have exclaimed, "he's taller dead than alive!" The body couldn't be shown: the duke was too popular. Quartered, it was burned in a fireplace in the château. Then Henri's mother, Catherine de Medici, had to be told the "good news."

SEEING THE CHATEAU DE BLOIS

The murder of the Duke of Guise—one of the most famous assassinations in French history—is only one of the memories of the **☼ Château de Blois** (tel. 54-78-06-62), which was begun in the 13th century by the counts of Blois. Charles d'Orléans (son of Louis d'Orléans, assassinated by the Burgundians in 1407), the "poet prince," lived at Blois after his release from 25 years of English captivity. He had married Mary of Cleves and had brought a "court of letters" to Blois. In his 70s, Charles became the father of the future Louis XII, who was to marry Anne of Brittany. Blois was launched in its new role as a royal château. In time it was to be called the second capital of France, and Blois the city of kings. However, Blois became a palace of banishment. Louis XIII for a time got rid of his interfering mother, Marie de Medici, by sending her there; but this plump matron escaped by sliding into the moat on a coat down a mound of dirt left by the builders. Then in 1626 the king sent his conspiring brother, Gaston d'Orléans, there. He stayed.

If you stand in the courtyard of the great château, you'll find it's like an illustrated storybook of French architecture. The Hall of the Estates-General is a beautiful work from the 13th century; the so-called gallery of Charles d'Orléans was actually built by Louis XII in 1498–1501, as was the Louis XII wing. The François I wing is a masterpiece of the French Renaissance; the Gaston d'Orléans wing was built by François Mansart between 1635 and 1637. Of them all, the most remarkable is the François I wing, containing a spiral staircase, with elaborately ornamented balustrades and the king's symbol, the salamander. In the Louis XII wing, seek out paintings by Antoine Caron, court painter to Henri III, depicting the persecution of Thomas More.

Restoration of the interior is continuing, but the royal emblems were destroyed during the Revolution. Note the paneling behind which many people placed secrets, perhaps Catherine de Medici her poisons. The room where the Estates-General met in 1588 is the oldest part of the château, nowadays containing tapestries from the 17th century, some based on cartoons by Rubens, others in the Renaissance style illustrating scenes from the life of Marc Antony.

The château is open daily: March 15 through October, from 9am to 6pm; November through March 14, from 9am to noon and 2 to 5pm. Admission to the château and museum is 30 F ($5.40) for adults, 15 F ($2.70) for ages 7–25. A son-et-lumière program is presented in summer for an additional 60 F ($10.80).

WHERE TO STAY

L'HORSET BLOIS, 26, av. Maunoury, 41000 Blois. Tel. 54-74-19-00. Fax 54-74-57-97. 78 rms (all with bath or shower). MINIBAR TV TEL **Bus:** 1.

$ Rates: 435 F ($78.30) single; 490 F ($88.20) double. Children under 12 stay free in parents' room. American buffet breakfast 55 F ($9.90) extra. AE, DC, MC, V.
Parking: Free.

Opened in 1988, this leading hotel has all the modern amenities as well as a respect for traditional French charm. A three-star hotel, it's a member of a small but widely respected French-based hotel chain. Rooms are furnished with contemporary flair. There is a good restaurant, where meals go for 115–168 F ($20.70–$30.20). Children's meals are available.

IMPRESSIONS

The murders, or political executions perpetrated in this castle, though not uninteresting, were inflicted on, and by men that command neither our love nor our veneration. The character of the period, and of the men that figured in it, were alike disgusting. Bigotry and ambition, equally dark, insidious and bloody, allow no feelings of regret. The parties could hardly be better employed than in cutting each others' throats.
—Arthur Young, 1792

MERCURE, 28, quai St-Jean, 41000 Blois. Tel. 54-56-66-66. Fax 54-56-67-00. 96 rms (all with bath). MINIBAR TV TEL **Bus:** Take the quayside bus marked PISCINE.
$ Rates: 430–600 F ($77.40–$108) single; 495–600 F ($89.10–$108) double. Breakfast 50 F ($9). AE, DC, MC, V. **Parking:** 35 F ($6.30).
This is the newest and one of the best-located hotels in Blois. Opened in May 1993, it sits beside the quays of the Loire, a five-minute walk from the château. Built in a three-story design of reinforced concrete and big windows, it contains larger-than-expected bedrooms filled with contemporary furniture and color schemes of blue, gray, or bordeaux. A greenhouse-style lobby leads into a pleasant restaurant where meals are served every day from noon to 2:30pm and 7 to 10:30pm.

NOVOTEL BLOIS, 1, rue de l'Almandin, à la Chaussée-Saint-Victor, 41260 Blois. Tel. 54-78-33-57. Fax 54-74-25-13. 116 rms (all with bath). MINIBAR TV TEL **Directions:** From the center, follow the signs toward Orléans on the RN-152.
$ Prices: 390 F ($70.20) single; 450 F ($81) double. Breakfast 48 F ($8.60). Children under 16 stay free in parents' room. AE, DC, MC, V. **Parking:** Free.
Built in 1976, and renovated at least once since then, this functional and comfortable member of a nationwide chain lies within a residential neighborhood about 2½ miles northeast of the town center. Bedrooms are monochromatic and contemporary, and contain large writing desks and sofas that can easily be converted into additional beds. A modern, big-windowed restaurant is open continuously from 6am to midnight, and serves fixed-price meals for around 120 F ($21.60) each.

ST-JACQUES, place de la Gare, 41000 Blois. Tel. 54-78-04-15. 33 rms (all with shower). TEL **Bus:** 149.
$ Rates: 130 F ($23.40) single; 190–250 F ($34.20–$45) double. Breakfast 23 F ($4.10) extra. MC, V.
Open all year, this little hotel across from the railway station offers comfortable rooms, 10 of which contain TVs. A continental breakfast is the only meal served.

WHERE TO DINE

LE MEDICIS, 2 allée François-1er, 41000 Blois. Tel. 54-43-94-04.
Cuisine: FRENCH. **Reservations:** Required. **Bus:** 149.
$ Prices: Appetizers 95–125 F ($17.10–$22.50); main dishes 110–185 F ($19.80–$33.30); fixed-price menus 98 F ($17.60), 140 F ($25.20), 198 F ($35.60), and 298 F ($53.60). AE, DC, MC, V.
Open: Lunch daily 12:30–2pm; dinner daily 7–10pm. **Closed:** Jan.
Christian and Annick Garanger maintain what may be the most sophisticated inn in Blois—ideal for a gourmet meal or an overnight stopover. Fresh fish is the chef's specialty. The menu is subject to change, but typical dishes include asparagus in a mousseline sauce, scampi ravioli with a saffron sauce, suprême of perch with morels, boned pigeon (served pink) with foie gras sauce, and thinly sliced duck breast with a

Touraine Cassis sauce. Chocolate in many manifestations appears as the dessert specialty.

In addition, the Garangers also rent 12 elegant and traditionally furnished bedrooms, each with private bath. Charges are 380 F ($68) daily for a single or double, or 700 F ($126) for a suite; breakfast costs an extra 38 F ($6.80).

RENDEZVOUS DES PECHEURS, 27, rue du Foix. Tel. 54-74-67-48.
  Cuisine: FRENCH. **Reservations:** Not required. **Bus:** 149.
$ Prices: Appetizers 45–90 F ($8.10–$16.20); main dishes 110–195 F ($19.80–$35.10); fixed-price meal 130 F ($23.40). MC, V.
  Open: Lunch Tues–Sat 12:30–2pm; dinner Mon–Sat 7:30–9:30pm.

The name of the restaurant means "meeting point of the fishermen." The restaurant lies in an old building in the historic heart of town, near the château, beside the quays of the Loire. The chef, who runs the restaurant, makes sure that the fish is always fresh and well prepared, with the natural flavors intact. Only fish, not shellfish of any kind, is served. The menu changes daily according to the availability of fish in the markets; sea urchins raw from the shell is a favorite dish. Other specialties include a filet of Loire valley sandre (zander) in wine and butter sauce, and crayfish-stuffed cabbage. You can also order main dishes other than fish—for example, sautéed foie gras with warm potatoes.

10. CHAUMONT-SUR-LOIRE

124 miles SW of Paris, 25 miles E of Tours

GETTING THERE   By Train   About eight trains a day leave from Blois, the ride taking 12 minutes. Eight trains a day also make the 30-minute journey from Tours.

ESSENTIALS   Orientation   The train station lies about a mile north of the château, a pleasant walk.

Information   The Office de Tourisme is on rue du Maréchal-Leclerc (tel. 54-20-91-73).

O n that long-ago morning when Diane de Poitiers crossed the drawbridge, the ✪ **Château of Chaumont** (tel. 54-20-98-03) looked grim. Its battlements, its pepper-pot turrets crowning the towers—the whole effect resembled a prison. Henri II, her lover, had died. The king had given her Chenonceaux, which she loved, but Catherine de Medici in her widow's weeds had banished her from her favorite château and shipped her off to Chaumont. Inside, portraits reveal the king's mistress to have truly lived up to her reputation as forever beautiful. Another portrait—that of Catherine de Medici, wife of Henri II, looking like a devout nun—invites unfavorable comparison.

Chaumont (Burning Mount) was built during the reign of Louis XII by Charles d'Amboise. Looking down at the Loire, it is approached by a long walk up from the village through a tree-studded park. The original fortress had been dismantled by Louis XI. In 1560 it was acquired by Catherine de Medici. At one time Madame de Staël, banished from Paris by Napoleon, resided there. Chaumont was privately owned and inhabited until it was acquired by the state in 1938.

Architecturally, the castle spans the intermediate period between the Middle Ages and the Renaissance. Inside, the prize exhibit is a rare collection of medallions by Nini, an Italian artist. A guest of the château for a while, he made medallion portraits of kings, queens, nobles—even Benjamin Franklin, who once visited Chaumont.

In the bedroom occupied by Catherine de Medici there is a rare portrait of Catherine, painted when she was young, wearing many jewels, including a ruby later owned by Mary Queen of Scots. Catherine was superstitious, always keeping her astrologer, Cosimo Ruggieri, at her beck and call. She had him housed in one of the tower bedrooms (a portrait of him remains). It is reported that he foretold the disasters awaiting her sons, including Henri III. In the astrologer's bedroom is a most unusual tapestry depicting Medusa with a flying horse escaping from her head.

The château is open daily: in July and August, 9:15am to 5:30pm; April to June and in September, 9:15 to 11:30am and 1:45 to 5:30pm; and October to March, 9:15 to 11:30am and 1:45 to 3:50pm. Admission is 24 F ($4.30) for adults and 14 F ($2.50) for children.

WHERE TO STAY & DINE

HOTEL LE CHATEAU, 2, rue du MI-de-Lattre-de-Tassigny, 41150 Chaumont-sur-Loire. Tel. 54-20-98-04. Fax 54-20-97-98. 13 rms (all with bath or shower), 2 suites. TEL

$ Rates: 390–470 F ($70.20–$84.60) single or double; 550 F ($99) suite. Breakfast 40 F ($7.20) extra. V. **Parking:** Free.

This fine early 20th-century house has the kind of exposed timbers and black-and-white facade you'd have expected to find in Normandy. Set a 10-minute walk downhill from the famous château, in a village containing no more than 900 people, it has a small garden and a swimming pool. The hotel has a kindly staff, comfortably furnished bedrooms, and the best and most reasonably priced restaurant in the village. Regional specialties are served, with fixed-price meals priced at 85–235 F ($15.30–$42.30).

11. VENDÔME

106 miles SW of Paris, 20 miles NE of Blois

GETTING THERE **By Bus** Daily buses run to Vendôme from Blois.

ESSENTIALS **Information** The Office de Tourisme, 47, rue Poterie (tel. 54-77-05-07), will guide you with a map. It lies at the base of the ramp running to the château from the Loir River.

The clock towers, slate gables, and 14th- and 16th-century facades in Vendôme are reflected in the still waters of the Loir River, which winds around the foot of a hill crowned by the ruins of a feudal castle. (The Loir flows into the more familiar Loire River at Angers.) The setting of several Balzac novels, the town was partly built on islands in the Loir and is quilted with flower gardens; it dates from Gallo-Roman times.

WHAT TO SEE & DO

Vendôme's castle was rebuilt in the 11th century by Geoffroy Martel, one of the comtes de Vendôme, who founded the Abbey of the Trinity. During the Hundred Years' War, the castle became a British possession. Badly damaged, it was restored in the 17th century by César de Vendôme, son of Henri IV. The **Musée du Château** lying off Faubourg St-Bienheuré (tel. 54-77-26-13), which contains the château's artifacts and memorabilia, is open Wednesday through Monday from 9am to noon and 2 to 6pm; admission is 12 F ($2.20). In addition to exploring the castle's ruins, wander through the castle gardens.

The **Abbey of the Trinity,** off rue de la République, is considered by many the best example of flamboyant Gothic architecture in France. Its *misérecords* (under-the-seat wood carvings in the choir) are said to be the finest in the country. Sold as a national property in 1791, the abbey was used, in various parts, as a prison and as government offices. From the days of Napoléon I until the Nazi invasion of 1940, the abbey was a military headquarters. Today some of the buildings house offices. The abbey's **Musée du Cloître** (tel. 54-77-26-13) contains interesting relics and is open Wednesday through Monday from 10am to noon and 2 to 6pm; admission is 13 F ($2.30) for adults; free for children under 16.

WHERE TO STAY

GRAND HOTEL SAINT-GEORGES, 14, rue Poterie, 41100 Vendôme. Tel. 54-77-25-42. Fax 54-80-66-03. 35 rms (27 with bath, 8 with sink). TV TEL
$ Rates: 230 F ($41.40) single; 280 F ($50.40) double. Breakfast 30 F ($5.40) extra. AE, MC, V. **Parking:** Free.

In a corner building near St-Georges Gate, this hotel is a *relais gastronomique,* which means it's a good choice for both food and lodging. It was built in 1950 as a replacement for a building demolished in World War II. The traditional rooms have many homelike touches, and in the elegant restaurant, you can enjoy fixed-price meals, costing 85 F ($15.30), 140 F ($25.20), and 195 F ($35.10).

HOTEL VENDOME, 15, faubourg Chartrain, 41100 Vendôme. Tel. 54-77-02-88. Fax 54-73-90-71. 35 rms (all with bath or shower). TV TEL
$ Rates: 200–370 F ($36–$66.60) single; 250–435 F ($45–$78.30) double. Breakfast 50 F ($9) extra. MC, V. **Parking:** 40 F ($7.20).
The leading hotel in town, run by J. M. Leroy, this is a much altered, much changed medieval building which was last renovated in 1989. It lies a five-minute walk from the château in the historic center's pedestrian zone. Rooms are decorated in a traditional French style. The restaurant serves good food, and the wine list is one of the most extensive in the area; meals begin at 110 F ($19.80).

WHERE TO DINE

In addition to the following, see "Where to Stay," above, for the hotel restaurants.

PETIT BILBOQUET, route de Tours. Tel. 54-77-16-60.
Cuisine: FRENCH. **Reservations:** Required.
$ Prices: Appetizers 50–100 F ($9–$18); main dishes 75–110 F ($13.50–$19.80); fixed-price meals 110–167 F ($19.80–$30.10). MC, V.
Open: Lunch Tues–Sun 12:30–2pm; dinner Tues–Sat 8–9:30pm. **Closed:** Part of Aug.
The finest continental and regional cuisine in town is served at this restaurant, located at the southern edge of town. The restaurant is installed in what was originally built as an officers' mess for a French cavalry regiment stationed in Vendôme during the 19th century. Jerry H. Simpson, Jr., of Charlotte, N.C., discovered the Petit Bilboquet for me and called it "the very best restaurant—for the money—in France." Freshly ironed linen and fine china, crystal, and silver make dining here an elegant experience. Diners can eat in the garden during fair weather. The service is attentive but unobtrusive, and the selection of wines is adequate. Try such dishes as warm asparagus in a truffle sauce, crayfish with baby vegetables, sautéed foie gras, or turbot with a Basque-style piperade.

12. CHAMBORD

118 miles SW of Paris, 11 miles E of Blois

GETTING THERE   By Car or Bicycle   It's best to travel to Chambord by car. Otherwise, you could rent a bicycle in Blois and cycle the eleven miles to Chambord, or take one of the many organized tours to Chambord leaving from Blois in summer.

ESSENTIALS   Information   The Office de Tourisme is on place St-Michel (tel. 54-20-34-86).

When François I, the Chevalier King, used to say, "Come on up to my place," he meant the **Château de Chambord,** 41250 Bracieux (tel. 54-20-32-20), not Fontainebleau or Blois. Construction workers, some 2,000 strong, began to piece together "the pile" in 1519. What emerged after 20 years was the pinnacle of the French Renaissance, the largest château in the Loire Valley. It was ready for the visit of Charles V of Germany, who was welcomed by nymphets in transparent veils gently tossing wildflowers—fresh from the encircling forest of Sologne—in the emperor's path.

In the years that ensued, French monarchs—Henri II and Catherine de Medici, Louis XIII, Henri II—came and went from Chambord, but not one of them developed the affection for it held by François I. The brother of Louis XIII, Gaston d'Orléans, restored the château in part. His daughter, "La Grande Mademoiselle" (Mlle de Montpensier), related in her writings that she used to force her father to run up and down Chambord's famous double spiral staircase after her. Because of its curious structure, he never caught her.

Louis XIV made nine visits there. Molière's *Monsieur de Pourceaugnac* was performed at Chambord for the Sun King. According to a much-repeated theatrical legend, the playwright saved the play by leaping into the orchestra pit, eliciting a hearty roar from the up-to-then stony-faced king. Molière also previewed *Le Bourgeois Gentilhomme* there.

Driven from the throne of Poland, Stanislas Leczinski, the father-in-law of Louis XV, took up residence in 1725, spending eight years at Chambord. Perhaps its most colorful resident, however, was Maurice Saxe, the marshal of France in 1743 and an illegitimate son of Augustus II of Saxony. To Chambord he imported cavalrymen from the West Indies. Ruling with an iron fist (even invoking the death penalty), he apparently applied the standard of brutality to his mistress, Madame Favart. Falling into decay, the château became—at the lowest point in its history—a munitions factory. The state acquired Chambord in 1932.

The château is set in a park of more than 13,000 acres, enclosed within a wall stretching some 20 miles. Looking out one of the windows from one of the 440 rooms, François I is said to have carved on a pane, with a diamond ring, these words: "A woman is a creature of change; to trust her is to play the fool." On seeing the estate, Chateaubriand said Chambord was like "a lady whose hair has been blown by the wind." Its façade is characterized by four monumental towers. The keep contains a spectacular terrace, which the ladies of the court used to stand on to watch the return of their men from the hunt. From that platform you can inspect the dormer windows and the richly decorated chimneys, some characterized by winged horses.

The three-story keep also encloses the already-mentioned corkscrew staircase—superimposed so that one person may descend at one end and another ascend at the other without ever meeting. The apartments of Louis XIV, including his redecorated bedchamber, are also in the keep. A trio of rooms was restored by the government, but not with the original furnishings, of course.

The château is open in July and August, daily from 9:30am to 6:45pm; September through June, daily from 9:30 to 11:45am and 2 to 4:45pm. Admission is 31 F ($5.60) for adults or 17 F ($3.05) for children.

WHERE TO STAY & DINE

HOTEL DU GRAND-ST-MICHEL, 103, place St-Michel, Chambord, 41250 Bracieux. Tel. 54-20-31-31. 39 rms (27 with bath or shower). TEL
$ Rates: 180 F ($32.40) single without bath; 290–420 F ($52.20–$75.60) double with bath. Breakfast 36 F ($6.50) extra. MC, V. **Parking:** Free. **Closed:** Mid-Nov to mid-Dec.

Directly across from Chambord, this country inn has front bedrooms that overlook the château, which is especially handsome when illuminated in the evening. Rooms are plain and comfortable, and the decor is provincial. Good food is offered daily in the restaurant—try the regional dishes. In summer, meals are served on the terrace under an awning; for a table in front of the château, make a reservation.

The fixed-price menus begin at 125 F ($22.50); à la carte meals begin at 190 F ($34.20).

13. BEAUGENCY

93 miles SW of Paris, 53 miles NE of Tours

GETTING THERE By Train   There is train service to Beaugency from Orléans and Blois.

By Bus   From Orleans there are about ten buses a day making the trip to Beaugency.

ESSENTIALS Information   The Office de Tourisme is located at 3, place du Dr.-Hyvernaud (tel. 38-44-54-42).

The heart of this ancient Loire Valley town is an archeological garden called the **City of the Lords,** named after the counts who enjoyed great power in the Middle Ages. A major event in the history of medieval Europe took place there: the marriage of Eleanor of Aquitaine and Louis VII was dissolved in 1152. These two monarchs had fallen into a bitter dispute during the Second Crusade, and attempts at a reconciliation had failed. The tempestuous Eleanor sought a divorce on the grounds of consanguinity—that is, they were cousins in the fourth degree, and such relatives were forbidden to marry according to the rules of the day. This remarkable woman later became queen consort of Henry II of England, bringing southwestern France as her dowry. She was also, of course, the mother of Richard the Lion-Hearted. At a much later date, in 1429, Joan of Arc rid Beaugency of the English.

On the right bank of the Loire, the town boasts a bridge dating from the 14th century. It's unusual in that each of its 26 arches is in a different style.

The 15th-century **Château Dunois,** 2 place Dunois (tel. 38-44-55-23), floodlit at night, contains a folklore museum of the Orléans district. Exhibits are of archeological artifacts discovered in the district, the collection embracing antique toys, hairpieces, furniture, antique costumes, paintings, and pieces of sculpture. The museum is open Wednesday through Monday from 10am to noon and 2 to 5pm; it closes at 6:30pm in summer. Admission is 18 F ($3.20) for adults and 14 F ($2.50) for children 6–17.

Near the château is **St. George's Vault,** a gate of the former castle of the Lords of Beaugency, which opened from the fortress onto the Rû Valley and the lower part of town.

The **Church of Notre-Dame** would have been a good example of Romanesque art of the 12th century if the Gothic hadn't intruded. Originally it was attached to a Benedictine abbey. Nearby is **St. Firmin's Tower,** all that remains of an old church that once stood on the Place St-Firmin. A trio of bells is sheltered in this tower, whose spire rises to a height of 180 feet. From the structure a magnificent view of the river valley unfolds before you.

In the archeological garden, the **Hôtel-Dieu** (the old hospital) is one of the oldest buildings in Beaugency, having been erected in the 11th century, its roofing edge in the Romanesque style. **St. Étienne's Church,** built in the 11th century, is one of the oldest churches of France, and **Caesar's Tower** is a good example of 11th-century military art.

WHERE TO STAY

L'ABBAYE DE BEAUGENCY, 2, quai de l'Abbaye, 45190 Beaugency. Tel. 38-44-67-35. 18 rms (all with bath or shower). TV TEL
$ Rates: 460 F ($82.80) single; 540 F ($97.20) double. Breakfast 42 F ($7.60) extra. AE, DC, MC, V. **Parking:** Free.
This ancient building from the 11th century offers rooms with stunning views of the

Loire and the old bridge. It was transformed into a hotel in the 1930s. The large, sunny bedrooms were recently renovated, and the bathrooms are spacious and modern. The restaurant is known for classic dishes such as coq au vin, and in season, game is a specialty. Fixed-price menus begin at 185 F ($33.30).

LA SOLOGNE, 6, place St-Firmin, 45190 Beaugency. Tel. 38-44-50-27.
Fax 38-44-90-19. 16 rms (10 with bath or shower). TV TEL
$ Rates: 170 F ($30.60) single without bath; 300 F ($54) double with bath. Breakfast 40 F ($7.20) extra. MC, V. **Closed:** Dec 20–Feb 1.

This small, family-run hotel is in a distinguished neighborhood in the heart of the old city. Rooms are well maintained but slightly old-fashioned, and each one has a personal touch. The hotel doesn't have a restaurant, but breakfast is served. There is a winter garden with a reading lounge.

LA TONNELLERIE, 12, rue des Eaux-Bleues, Tavers, 45190 Beaugency. Tel. 38-44-68-15. Fax 38-44-10-01. 20 rms (all with bath or shower), 5 suites. TEL **Directions:** Take the N152 about two miles from Beaugency.
$ Rates: 740–890 F ($133.20–$160.20) single or double; from 880 F ($158.40) suite. Breakfast 55 F ($9.90) extra; half board for two people 1,495–1,945 F ($269.10–$350.10) daily. MC, V. **Parking:** Free.

This pleasant old house has comfortable rooms, an outdoor pool, and a garden view. The Aulagnon family runs the place. In the restaurant, lunch, served Monday through Saturday, costs 116 F ($20.90); a *menu dégustation* goes for 316 F ($56.90).

WHERE TO DINE

In addition to the following, see "Where to Stay," above, for some hotel restaurants.

HOSTELLERIE DE L'ECU DE BRETAGNE, place du Martroi, 45190 Beaugency. Tel. 38-44-68-07.
Cuisine: FRENCH. **Reservations:** Recommended.
$ Prices: Fixed-price menus 150 F ($27), 180 F ($32.40), and 220 F ($39.60). AE, DC, MC, V.
Open: Apr–Sept, lunch daily noon–2pm; dinner daily 7:30–10pm. Oct–Mar, lunch Tues–Sun noon–2pm; dinner Tues–Sat 7:30–10pm. **Closed:** Feb and first week of Mar.

This old restaurant is located on a quiet square in an old coaching inn owned by Madame Renucci. Enjoy a drink at the outside café or in the country tavern, which has provincial tables and Breton-style carved paneling. The menu is divided into classic and regional dishes; try the Loire zander (a white fish) or filet of beef à la Beaugency. Local goat cheese is a favorite, as is a nut-studded soufflé for dessert. The homemade fruit tarts are also very good. The inn also rents 26 simply furnished rooms—a double without bath costs 300 F ($54), and a double with bath begins at 460 F ($82.80), plus 45 F ($8.10) for breakfast.

14. CHEVERNY

119 miles SW of Paris, 8 miles SE of Blois

GETTING THERE The town of Cheverny is best reached by car or on an organized bus tour from nearby Blois.

The *haut monde* still comes to the Sologne area for the hunt. It's as if the 17th century never ended. It did, of course, and 20th-century realities such as taxes are *formidable*—hence the **Château de Cheverny** (tel. 54-79-96-29) must open some of its rooms for inspection by paying guests. At least that keeps the tax collector at bay and the hounds fed in winter.

Unlike most of the Loire châteaux, Cheverny is inhabited, actually lived in by the descendants of the original owner, the vicomte de Sigalas. Lineage is traced back to

Henri Hurault, the son of the chancellor of Henri III and Henri IV, who built the first château in 1634.

This particular ancestor married an 11-year-old girl, Françoise Chabot. When that lady grew up, she developed a passion for page boys that lasted until her husband interrupted her nocturnal activities. After killing her frightened lover, he offered his spouse two choices: she could either swallow poison or else have his sword plunged into her heart. She elected to swallow from the bitter cup. Perhaps to erase the memory, he had the old castle torn down and a new one—the present château—built for his second wife. It attracted many fashionable visitors over the centuries, among them the "Grande Mademoiselle," who compared its beauty to "the Alcine Island or the Apolidor Palace." In a sense the château is "pure"—that is, it was constructed in a short period of time and has remained substantially as it was intended. Designed in the classic Louis XIII style, it contains square pavilions flanking the central pile.

Inside, the antique furnishings, tapestries, rich decorations, and objects of art warm things up considerably. A 17th-century French artist, Jean Mosnier, decorated the fireplace with motifs from the legend of Adonis. In the Guards' Room is a collection of medieval armor resting under a painted ceiling. Also displayed is a Gobelins tapestry depicting *The Abduction of Helen of Troy.* In the king's bedchamber, another Gobelins tapestry traces the *Trials of Ulysses,* such as his landing on the island of Circe. Most impressive, however, is a stone stairway of carved fruit and flowers.

Bypassing a kennel of hounds, you reach the **Salle de Trophées,** a hunting museum with an outstanding collection of antlers—more than 2,000 of them. You needn't spend much time there unless you dig weird headgear. The tree-shaded park of streams and ponds—although offering only a hint of its former glory—is impressive enough.

The château is open June through mid-September, daily from 9:15am to 6:45pm; and October through May, daily from 9:30am to noon and 2:15 to 5 or 6pm. Admission is 29 F ($5.20) for adults, 19 F ($3.40) for children 7 to 14.

WHERE TO DINE

SAINT-HUBERT, rue Nationale, 41700 Cour-Cheverny. Tel. 54-79-96-60.

Cuisine: FRENCH. **Reservations:** Not required.
$ **Prices:** Fixed-price meals 100 F ($18). MC, V.
Open: Lunch Thurs–Tues 12:15–1:15pm; dinner Thurs–Tues 7:30–8:45pm. **Closed:** Dec 20–Feb 1.

Located about 800 yards from the château, this roadside inn was built in the old provincial style. The chef de cuisine, Jean-Claude Pillaut, is the secret of Saint-Hubert's success. The least expensive menu might include a terrine of quail in gelatin, pike perch with beurre blanc, a selection of cheese, and a homemade fruit tart. The most expensive menu is likely to offer lobster or fresh spring asparagus. Game is featured here in season.

Most visitors pass through Cour-Cheverny on a day trip, but it's also possible to spend the night. Saint-Hubert offers 20 bedrooms with baths, charging from 280 F ($50.40) daily for a single and 320 F ($57.60) for a double, plus another 35 F ($6.30) for breakfast.

LES TROIS MARCHANDS, place de l'Eglise, 41700 Cour-Cheverny. Tel. 54-79-96-44. Fax 54-79-25-60.

Cuisine: FRENCH. **Reservations:** Not required.
$ **Prices:** Appetizers 55–110 F ($9.90–$19.80); main dishes 80–120 F ($14.40–$21.60); fixed-price meals 100 F ($18) and 295 F ($53.10). AE, DC, MC, V.
Open: Lunch daily noon–2pm; dinner daily 7:30–8:45pm. **Closed:** Mon Oct–June.

This much-renovated coaching inn, whose name translates as "The Three Merchants," has been handed down for many generations from father to son. Adjacent to the village church, and flanked with enormous linden trees, it dates from 1665. Today,

Jean-Jacques Bricault owns the three-story building which sports awnings, a mansard roof, a glassed-in courtyard, and sidewalk tables with bright-colored umbrellas, where diners can enjoy fine regional cuisine. In the large tavern-style dining room, amid beamed ceilings and provincial furnishings, the menu at 295 F ($53.10) might include a ballotine de canard (duckling) with pistachio nuts, followed by fresh salmon, then quail flambé, plus fresh string beans, a garden salad, a selection from the cheese board, and a homemade lapereau (young rabbit) sautéed in a red wine and stock. Cour-Cheverny is a very good house white wine.

The inn also rents 38 guest rooms. Furnishings are traditional, with padded headboards and provincial chests. All rooms have TVs and telephones. A single without bath costs 170 F ($30.60), rising to 240 F ($43.20) in a single with bath. A double without bath also costs 170 F ($30.60), going up to 240–310 F ($43.20–$55.80) with bath. Breakfast is another 38 F ($6.80) per person.

---

15. VALENÇAY

145 miles SW of Paris, 35 miles S of Blois

GETTING THERE By Train There are frequent SNCF rail connections from Blois.

ESSENTIALS Orientation The village is completely dominated by its château, which is surrounded by a park.

Information The Office de Tourisme is located at the Hôtel de Ville (tel. 54-00-14-33).

One of the handsomest Renaissance buildings in the château country, the **Château de Valençay** (tel. 54-00-10-66) was acquired in 1803 by Talleyrand on the orders of Napoleon, who wanted his shrewd minister of foreign affairs to receive dignitaries in great style. During its occupancy by Talleyrand, some of the most important personages in Europe passed under the portal of Valençay. Not all those guests, notably Ferdinand VII of Spain, wanted to visit the château. Driven from his homeland in 1808, the king was housed at Valençay for six years, on orders of Napoleon, as "the guest of Talleyrand."

In 1838 Talleyrand was buried at Valençay, the château passing to his nephew, Louis de Talleyrand-Périgord. Before the Talleyrand ownership, Valençay was built in 1550 by the d'Estampes family on the site of an old feudal castle of the lords of Châlons. The dungeon and the great west tower are of this period, as is the main body of the building; but other wings were added in the 17th and 18th centuries. The effect is grandiose, almost too much so, with domes, chimneys, and turrets.

The interior furnishings are especially rewarding, as the apartments are sumptuously furnished, mostly in the Empire style but with Louis XV and Louis XVI trappings as well. In the main drawing room is a star-footed table, said to have been the one on which the Final Agreement of the Congress of Vienna was signed in June 1815 (Talleyrand represented France).

Ten private apartments are open to the public. Visits to Valençay usually are the longest of any château in the Loire, lasting 45 minutes. The Museum of Talleyrand that used to stand on the premises is now closed, but some of the collection is displayed in the new rooms of the castle. In the park is a museum of some 60 antique cars (circa 1890–1950). After your visit to the main buildings, you can walk through the garden and deer park. On the grounds are many exotic birds, including flamingos.

Admission to the castle, car museum, and park is 30 F ($5.40) for adults, 23 F ($4.10) for seniors age 60 or over, and 18 F ($3.20) for children under 18. It's all open mid-March through mid-November, daily from 9am to noon and 2 to 7pm;

mid-November through mid-March, only on Saturday and Sunday from 9am to noon and 1:30 to 4:30pm.

WHERE TO STAY & DINE

HOTEL D'ESPAGNE, 9, rue du Château, 36600 Valençay. Tel. 54-00-00-02. Fax 54-00-12-63. 8 rms (all with bath), 6 suites. TV TEL
$ Rates: 450–650 F ($81–$117) single or double; from 1,000 F ($180) suite. Breakfast 75 F ($13.50) extra. AE, DC, MC, V. **Parking:** 25 F ($4.50). **Closed:** Jan–Feb.

This former coaching inn has a wide-arched entrance leading to a U-shaped building and a flagstone courtyard with trimmed boxwood shrubbery and tubs of flowers. Monsieur and Madame Fourré and their family provide an old-world ambience combined with comforts and a first-class kitchen; the family has maintained a smooth operation since 1875. The bedrooms have their own names and individuality—your room might have authentic decor from one of the Empire, Louis XV, or Louis XVI periods. The hotel has a cluster of adjoining buildings.

Lunch is served in the dining room or gardens Tuesday through Sunday. The chef's specialties include noisettes of lamb in tarragon, sweetbreads with morels, and a special dessert, délicieuse au chocolat. Fixed-price menus range from 180 F ($32.40), with a spectacular à la carte meal, including wine, costing 380 F ($68.40) and up. The restaurant is open daily from June through September; off-season, it's closed on Monday.

16. CHENONCEAUX

139 miles SW of Paris, 21 miles E of Tours

GETTING THERE By Train There are four daily trains from Tours to Chenonceaux (trip time: 45 minutes). The train deposits you a mile from the château.

ESSENTIALS Information The Syndicat d'Initiative (tourist office) is located at 13 bis, rue du Château (tel. 47-23-94-45), open Easter to September.

The chef d'oeuvre of the Renaissance, the **Château de Chenonceaux** (tel. 47-23-90-07) has essentially orbited around the series of famous *dames de Chenonceaux* who have occupied it. Originally the château was owned by the Marqués family, but its members were extravagant beyond their means. Deviously, Thomas Bohier, the comptroller-general of finances in Normandy, began buying up land around the château. Finally, the Marqués family was forced to sell to Bohier, who tore down Chenonceaux, preserving only the keep, and building the rest in the emerging Renaissance style. In that undertaking, he was ably assisted by Catherine Briçonnet, the daughter of a wealthy family from Tours. After her husband died in 1524, Catherine lived for only two more years; at her death François I seized the château.

In 1547 Henri II gave Chenonceaux to his mistress, Diane de Poitiers, who was 20 years his senior. For a time this remarkable woman was virtually the queen of France, in spite of Henri's wife, Catherine de Medici. Apparently Henri's love for Diane continued unabated, even though she was in her 60s when the king died in a jousting tournament in 1559. Critics of Diane de Poitiers accused her of using magic not only to preserve her celebrated beauty but to keep Henri's attentions from waning.

Upon Henri's death, his jealous wife became regent of France. She immediately forced Diane de Poitiers to return the jewelry Henry had given her and to abandon her beloved Chenonceaux in exchange for Chaumont, which she did not want. Catherine added her own touches to the château, building a two-story gallery across the bridge—obviously inspired by her native Florence. The long gallery running along the Cher River contains a black-and-white diamond floor.

It was at Chenonceaux that Catherine received a pair of teenage honeymooners: her son, François II, and his bride, Mary Stuart. Another son, Henri III, sponsored an infamous fête at Chenonceaux. As described by the historian Philippe Erlanger: "Under the trees of this admirable park the King presided over the banquet, dressed as a woman. He wore a gown of pink damask, embroidered with pearls. Emerald, pearl, and diamond pendants distended the lobes of his ears, and diamonds shone in his hair which, like his beard, was dyed with violet powder." After Henri III was assassinated (by Jacques Clément), Chenonceaux was occupied by his widow, Louise de Lorraine. Even though the king had preferred his "curly-haired minions" to her she nevertheless mourned his death for the rest of her life, earning the name *La Reine Blanche* ("White Queen").

In the 18th century Madame Dupin, the grandmother of George Sand, acquired the château. A lady of the aristocracy, she was the wife of the "farmer-general" of France. She is said to have brought the "talents of the époque" to her château, employing Rousseau as a tutor for her sons. However, when the author of *The Social Contract* declared his undying love for her, she asked him not to return. Rousseau is said to have fallen violently ill, "sick with humiliation."

In the 19th century Madame Pelouse took over the château and began the difficult task of restoring it to its original splendor. That duty is still being admirably carried out by the present owners, the chocolate-making Menier family.

Many of the walls today are covered with Gobelins tapestries, including one depicting a woman pouring water over the back of an angry dragon, another of a three-headed dog and a seven-headed monster. The chapel contains a delicate marble Virgin and Child, plus portraits of Catherine de Medici in her traditional black and white. There's even a portrait of the stern Catherine in the former bedroom of her rival, Diane de Poitiers. But in the Renaissance bedchamber of François I, the most interesting portrait is that of Diane de Poitiers as the huntress Diana, complete with a sling of arrows on her back. *The Three Graces* are by Van Loo.

The château is open daily: mid-March through mid-September, from 9am to 7pm; mid-September through October, from 9am to 6pm; in November, from 9am to 5pm; in December and January, from 9am to noon and 2 to 4pm; and February to mid-March, from 9am to noon and 2 to 5pm. Admission is 35 F ($6.30) for adults, 25 F ($4.50) for children 7–15.

The history of Chenonceaux is related in 15 tableaux in the wax museum, which charges an additional 8 F ($1.40). Diane de Poitiers, who, among other accomplishments, introduced the artichoke to France, is depicted in three of the tableaux. Another portrays Catherine de Medici tossing out her husband's mistress.

A **son-et-lumière** spectacle, called *In the Old Days of the Dames of Chenonceaux,* is staged in summer; admission is 33 F ($5.90).

WHERE TO STAY

HOTEL DU BON-LABOUREUR ET DU CHATEAU, Chenonceaux, 37150

Bléré. Tel. 47-23-90-02. Fax 47-23-82-01. 40 rms (all with bath), 1 suite. TEL
$ Rates: 280–500 F ($50.40–$90) single; 320–600 F ($57.60–$108) double; from 1,000 F ($180) suite. Breakfast 45 F ($8.10) extra. AE, DC, MC, V. **Parking:** Free. **Closed:** Mid-Dec to Mar.

This country inn, which has an ivy-covered facade and tall chimneys, is within sight of the Loire and walking distance of the château; it's located on the village's main road. The rear garden has a little guesthouse, plus formally planted roses. The owner and chef de cuisine is Louis-Claude Jeudi. Founded in 1880, the hotel still maintains the flavor of that era, but modern bathrooms have been added to the bedrooms, 10 of which contain TVs. If fair weather permits, request a table in the courtyard, under a maple tree. Inside, the beamed dining room has a tall grandfather clock, high-back ladder chairs, and an open cupboard with pewter bottles and regional ceramics. The fixed-price menus in this French gastronomic restaurant, Le Bon Laboureur, run 180–320 F ($32.40–$57.60). Guests can also order grill specialties in a second restaurant, Les Gourmandises de Touraine, where meals are less expensive, beginning at 100 F ($18). Other amenities include an English bar and outdoor heated swimming pool.

HOTEL OTTONI, Chenonceaux, 37150 Blois. Tel. 47-23-90-09. Fax 47-23-91-59. 15 rms (all with bath). TV TEL

$ Rates: 320 F ($57.60) single; 480 F ($86.40) double. Breakfast 38 F ($6.80) extra; half board 275–390 F ($49.50–$70.20) per person. AE, DC. **Parking:** Free. **Closed:** Dec–Jan, and Wed Jan–Apr.

This is a traditional French inn, enjoying a leafy setting with a rear garden, a short walk from the château. Bedrooms are furnished in a classic boudoir style and offer much comfort at a good price. Under a beamed ceiling, some of the finest meals in town are served in the restaurant with its steakhouse. Good regional specialties are featured, and meals can also be served outside on a terrace in the garden. Complete diners cost 100–300 F ($18–$54). The restaurant is closed from mid-November to mid-February and on Wednesday from February through April.

WHERE TO DINE

In addition to the restaurant in the inn mentioned above, I recommend the following:

AU GATEAU BRETON, 16, rue Bretonneau. Tel. 47-23-90-14.
Cuisine: FRENCH. **Reservations:** Required July–Aug.
$ Prices: Fixed-price menus 60 F ($10.80), 75 F ($13.50), 85 F ($15.30), and 100 F ($18). MC, V.
Open: Lunch Wed–Mon 11:30am–2pm; dinner Wed–Mon 7–9:30pm. **Closed:** Mid-Nov to mid-Dec.

The sun-terrace dining area in back of this little Breton-type inn, which is a short walk from the château, is a refreshing place for dinner or tea. Gravel paths run between little beds of pink geraniums and lilacs, and the red tables have bright canopies and umbrellas. Chef Herembert provides home-cooking and a cherry liqueur—a specialty of the region. In cool months meals are served in the rustic dining rooms. Specialties include small chitterling sausages of Tours, chicken with Armagnac sauce, and crêpes flambéed in Grand Marnier. Tasty pastries are sold in the front room.

17. ORLEANS

74 miles SW of Paris, 45 miles SE of Chartres

GETTING THERE **By Train** From Paris (Gare d'Austerlitz), about two dozen trains leave daily for Orléans (trip time: one hour).

ESSENTIALS **Orientation** The main square is place du Martroi. The transportation depots and the tourist office are located on the north side of the old town.

Information The Office de Tourisme is located at place Albertler (tel. 38-53-05-95).

Orléans suffered heavy damage in World War II, so those visiting who hope to see how it looked when the Maid of Orléans was there are likely to be disappointed. However, the reconstruction of Orléans has been judiciously planned, and there are many rewarding targets for visitors.

WHAT TO SEE & DO

Orléans is the chief town of Loiret, on the Loire, about 80 miles from Paris. Joan of Arc relieved the city in 1429 from the attacks of the Burgundians and the English. That deliverance is celebrated every year on May 8, the anniversary of her victory. An equestrian statue of Joan of Arc stands in the **Place du Martroi,** which was created by Foyatier in 1855.

From that square you can drive down rue Royal—rebuilt in the 18th-century style—across the **Pont George-V,** erected in 1760. After crossing the bridge you'll have a good view of the town. A simple cross marks the site of the Fort des Tourelles, which Joan of Arc and her men captured.

Back in the heart of town, you can go to the **Cathedral Ste-Croix,** place Ste-Croix (tel. 38-66-64-17), begun in 1287 in the High Gothic period, although burned by the Huguenots in 1568. The first stone on the present building was laid by Henri IV in 1601, and work continued on the cathedral until 1829. Inside, the church of the Holy Cross contains an excellent organ from the 17th century, and some magnificent woodwork from the early 18th century in its chancel, the masterpiece of Jules Hardouin-Mansart and other artists of Louis XIV. You'll need a guide to tour the chancel and the crypt, and to see the treasury with its Byzantine enamels, its goldwork from the 15th and 16th centuries, and its Limoges enamels. There is no admission fee, but you should tip the guide. It's open daily 8:15am to noon and 1 to 6pm. Take bus J or G.

To the northwest of the cathedral is the **Groslot Hôtel,** place de l'Etape (tel. 38-42-22-30). This Renaissance mansion was built from 1550, under Henri II, and embellished in the 19th century. François II lived in it during the fall of 1560 and died here on December 5. He was the first husband of Mary Queen of Scots. Other kings came here. On a lighter note, it was here that Charles IX met his lovely Marie Touchet. The statue of Joan of Arc praying (at the foot of the flight of steps) was the work of a daughter of King Louis-Philippe. She was Princess Marie of Orléans. In the garden you can see the remains of the 15th-century chapel of St. Jacques. The Groslot Hôtel was the town hall from 1790 to 1982. Admission is free, and hours are daily from 10am to noon and 2 to 5pm. In front of the Groslot Hôtel is the new municipal center.

Another church of much interest, lying near the Loire, is the **Church of St-Aignan,** place St-Aignan (no phone). Consecrated in 1509, the choir and transept remain, but the nave was burned by the Protestants. In a gilded, carved wooden shrine lie the remains of the church's patron saint. The crypt, completed in 1029, is intriguing, containing some decorated capitals. This surely must be one of the earliest vaulted hall-crypts in France. It's open daily from 8am to noon and 2:15 to dusk. Take bus J or G.

The **Musée des Beaux-Arts,** 1, rue Ferdinand-Rabier (tel. 38-53-39-22), is mainly a picture gallery of French works from the 16th to the 20th centuries. Some of the works once hung in Richelieu's château. Other pieces of art include busts by Pigalle, *St. Sebastian with Lantern* by Georges de La Tour, and a fine array of portraits, including one of Mme de Pompadour, of whom, when she first crossed the Pont George-V, the people of the town remarked: "Our bridge has just borne France's heaviest weight." See also works by Corrège, Le Nain, Philippe de Champaigne, La Hire, Boucher, Watteau, Courbet, and Gauguin, as well as a salon of pastels by Perronneau. Several foreign works are also displayed, including a lovely Velásquez. The museum is open Wednesday through Monday from 10am to noon and 2 to 6pm. Admission is 14 F ($2.50).

WHERE TO STAY

HOTEL MERCURE ORLEANS, 44-46, quai Barentin, 45000 Orléans. Tel. 38-62-17-39. Fax 38-53-95-34. 109 rms (all with bath). A/C MINIBAR TV TEL **Bus:** J or G.
$ Rates: 450–550 F ($81–$99) single or double. Breakfast 55 F ($9.90) extra. AE, DC, MC, V. **Parking:** 30 F ($5.40).
Located along the river at Pont Joffre, in the center of town, this modern band-box structure is within walking distance of place du Martroi and its statue of Joan of Arc. The restaurant and bar, Le Gourmandin, serves regional specialties. A table d'hôte menu with wine costs 160 F ($28.80). The hotel also has a big, heated swimming pool.

NOVOTEL ORLEANS LA COURCE, 2, rue Honoré-de-Balzac, 45100 Orléans. Tel. 38-63-04-28. Fax 38-69-24-04. 119 rms (all with bath or

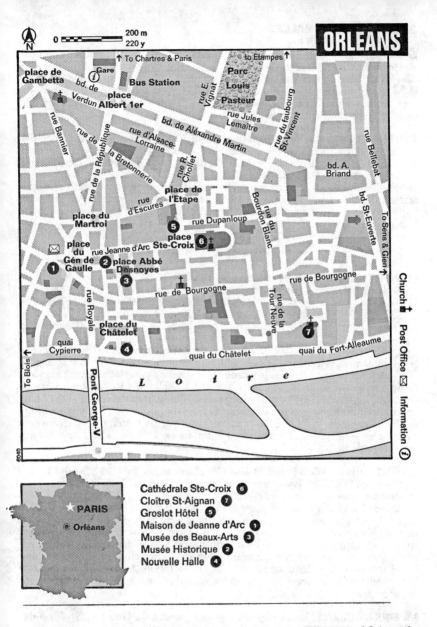

ORLEANS

0 ___ 200 m
___ 220 y

To Chartres & Paris ↑   to Etampes ↑

place de Gambetta

Gare (i)

bd. de Verdun

Bus Station

place Albert 1er

Parc Louis Pasteur

rue E. Vignat

rue Jules Lemaître

rue du faubourg St-Vincent

rue Bellebat

place du Martroi

rue d'Alsace-Lorraine

bd. de Alexandre Martin

rue de la République

rue de la Bretonnerie

rue R. Chollet

bd. A. Briand

bd. St-Euverte

To Sens & Gien →

rue d'Escures

place de l'Etape

place du Martroi

5

rue Dupanloup

rue du Bourdon Blanc

place du Gén de Gaulle

1

rue Jeanne d'Arc

place Ste-Croix **6**

2 place Abbé Desnoyes

3

rue de Bourgogne

rue de Bourgogne

rue Royale

rue de la Tour Neuve

7

place du Châtelet

4

quai Cypierre

quai du Châtelet

quai du Fort-Alleaume

To Blois

Pont George-V

L o i r e

Church ✝   Post Office ⊠   Information (*i*)

★ PARIS

⦿ Orléans

Cathédrale Ste-Croix **6**
Cloître St-Aignan **7**
Groslot Hôtel **5**
Maison de Jeanne d'Arc **1**
Musée des Beaux-Arts **3**
Musée Historique **2**
Nouvelle Halle **4**

---

shower). A/C MINIBAR TV TEL **Directions:** Follow the N20 south of Orléans for seven miles.

$ Rates: 430 F ($77.40) single; 475 F ($85.50) double. Breakfast 48 F ($8.60) extra. AE, DC, MC, V. **Parking:** Free.

This 1980s hotel, in a beautiful park, offers such diversions as *pétanque* (French bowling), golfing practice, swimming, and tennis. Rooms are comfortable and tastefully decorated. The hotel's grill, open until midnight, offers a fixed-price meal for only 85 F ($15.30).

ST-MARTIN, 52, bd. Alexandre-Martin, 45000 Orléans. Tel. 38-62-47-47. Fax 38-83-13-28. 22 rms (12 with bath or shower). TEL **Bus:** J or G.

$ Rates: 125 F ($22.50) single without bath; 266 F ($47.90) double with bath. Breakfast 22 F ($4) extra. MC, V.

This hotel—near the cathedral, the sights, and the shops of Orléans—has clean, simple rooms. Although the St-Martin is on a broad boulevard, the rooms are fairly quiet—nine contain TVs. There's no restaurant, but you'll be close to some excellent ones (see below).

TERMINUS, 40, rue de la République, 45000 Orléans. Tel. 38-53-24-64.
Fax 38-53-24-18. 50 rms (all with bath or shower). TV TEL **Bus:** A, B, E, F, or H.
$ Rates: 310 F ($55.80) single; 350 F ($63) double. Breakfast 35 F ($6.30) extra. AE, DC, MC, V. **Parking:** 40 F ($7.20).

Despite its unromantic name, this hotel is comfortable and reasonably priced, located across from the railway station. A century old, it was last renovated in 1990. Rooms are immaculate and soundproof, and the service is attentive. There's no restaurant, but breakfast is served.

WHERE TO DINE

LES ANTIQUAIRES, 2-4, rue au Lin. Tel. 38-53-52-35.
Cuisine: FRENCH. **Reservations:** Required. **Bus:** J or G.
$ Prices: Appetizers 60–120 F ($10.80–$21.60); main dishes 65–180 F ($11.70–$32.40); fixed-price meals 120–190 F ($21.60–$34.20). AE, DC, MC, V.
Open: Lunch Tues–Sat noon–2pm; dinner Tues–Sat 7:30–10pm. **Closed:** Aug 1–24.

This rustically elegant mansion on a small street near the river was originally built before the Renaissance, and still retains its two-story format and its original ceiling beams. A large and accommodating fireplace warms a cozy and rustic interior. Most of the emphasis here is on a solid and well-grounded French cuisine, using seasonal ingredients which usually derive from the region of the Loire. Specialties include seasonal game dishes, fish from the nearby river (including a friture des petits poissons) and Loire Valley salmon with parsley butter, filet of sole with a fricassée of asparagus, and terrine of rabbit in its own gelatin. The dining room is air-conditioned.

LA CREMAILLERE, 34, rue N-D-de-Recouvrance. Tel. 38-53-49-17.
Cuisine: FRENCH. **Reservations:** Required. **Bus:** FB from the station.
$ Prices: Fixed-price menus 98–200 F ($17.60–$36). AE, DC, MC, V.
Open: Lunch daily noon–1:30pm; dinner Mon–Sat 7–9:30pm.

In 1992, the premises of this older restaurant were radically modernized into a tasteful, ultra-contemporary new design, and the kitchens were infused with a new culinary style directed by Claude Louboutin. Today, a wide choice exists within each of the fixed-price menus listed above, any of which might include such dishes as Loire Valley salmon and zander in several kinds of sauces, ravioli of crayfish, and such Loire Valley game dishes as filet of roebuck with a sweet-herb sauce or saddle of rabbit with red wine sauce.

LA GRANGE, 205, faubourg Bourgogne, route de Nevers, St-Jean-de-Braye. Tel. 38-86-43-36.
Cuisine: FRENCH. **Reservations:** Recommended. **Directions:** Take the N152 two miles east of Orléans.
$ Prices: Appetizers 70–100 F ($12.60–$18); main dishes 80–120 F ($14.40–$21.60); fixed-price meals 100–140 F ($18–$25.20). V.
Open: Lunch Tues–Sat noon–2pm; dinner Tues–Sat 7:45–9pm. **Closed:** Mar 1–10 and Aug.

The building containing this charmingly rustic enclave was originally built in 1875 as a barn for horses, cows, and the storage of wheat. It lies midway between Orléans and the satellite city of St-Jean-de-Bray. Today, Robert DuPuy prepares delicious meals which might include a mousse of turbot with watercress; a mousseline of zander with carrots and grapefruit; boneless slices of duck with red pepper, sweetbreads, and hurtleberries; and veal kidneys in a mustard sauce.

LA POUTRIERE, 8-10, rue de la Brêche. Tel. 38-66-02-30.
  Cuisine: FRENCH. **Reservations:** Required.
$ **Prices:** Appetizers 80–90 F ($14.40–$16.20); main dishes 130–150 F ($23.40–$27); fixed-price menus 150–350 F ($27–$63). AE, DC, MC, V.
  Open: Lunch Tues–Sun noon–2pm; dinner Tues–Sat 7:30–10pm. **Closed:** Dec 20–Jan 5.

Set on the relatively underpopulated left bank of the Loire, this restaurant occupies the premises of a farmhouse whose foundations were originally built in the early 1600s. Beneath heavy ceiling beams, you can enjoy specialties from the kitchens of Simon Lebras, which include a gâteau of lobster with a coulis of chervil, veal kidneys with sauterne sauce, and a wide array of Loire Valley fish and game dishes.

18. SULLY-SUR-LOIRE

96 miles S of Paris, 30 miles SW of Orléans

GETTING THERE   By Bus   From Orléans, five to seven buses per day run to Sully, taking 1 hour.

By Car   Motorists from Orléans head southwest along Route 952 until they reach the junction with Route 948, at which point they head south.

ESSENTIALS   Information   The Office de Tourisme is on place du Général-de-Gaulle (tel. 38-36-23-70).

Southeast of Orléans stands the beautiful **Château de Sully,** av. de Bethune (tel. 38-36-36-86), where Joan of Arc persuaded Charles VII to go to Reims and proclaim himself king of France. A minister of Henri IV bought the Castle of Sully in 1602 and became the first Duke of Sully in 1606. The castle was mostly destroyed in World War II, but it has been restored. It was originally constructed in the 14th century, although enlarged after 1602. Exiled from Paris, Voltaire spent two years in Sully. A theater was built for the writer in which his plays could be performed.

Several apartments in the 14th-century wing of the castle are open to the public. Sully's remains were placed in the oratory. On the second floor an apartment was covered with timberwork, which is considered the finest such work from medieval days. It is so well preserved it is hard to believe that it's actually 600 years old. In the Renaissance pavilion you can see the minister's study and his bedroom. Both rest under painted ceilings.

The château is open May 1 to June 15 and September 16 to October, daily from 10am to noon and 2 to 6pm; June 16 to September 15, daily from 10am to 6pm. In the off-season, in March, April, and November, it's open daily from 10am to noon and 2 to 5pm. The château is closed at other times. Admission is 12 F ($2.20).

WHERE TO STAY & DINE

HOSTELLERIE DU GRAND-SULLY, 10, bd. Champ-de-Foire, 45600
  Sully-sur-Loire. Tel. 38-36-27-56. Fax 38-36-44-54.
  Cuisine: FRENCH. **Reservations:** Required.
$ **Prices:** Fixed-price menus 150–280 F ($27–$50.40). AE, DC, MC, V. **Parking:** Free.
  Open: Lunch daily noon–3pm; dinner Mon–Sat 5:30–9:30pm.

Part of this inn was built by the finance minister to Henri IV in the 17th century about 150 yards from the base of the château. This inn, better known as a restaurant than as a hotel, is in fact the finest dining establishment in town. The bar is pleasant, and a garden is on the premises.

This is also a good place to spend the night, especially if you're en route to

Burgundy and the French Alps. The 10 rooms are modestly furnished, with TVs, minibars, and telephones. A single or double costs 200–250 F ($36–$45), plus 38 F ($6.80) for breakfast.

19. LES BEZARDS

This village, at the edge of the Forest of Orléans, is the far eastern extremity of the Loire Valley. It lies on the main route (N7) between Paris and Nevers (it's 85 miles south of Paris and 43 miles southeast of Orleans). Les Bezards is a popular stopping-off point with Parisians, who stay at the following recommendation, exploring the lovely towns of Gien and Briare farther along the Loire.

WHERE TO STAY & DINE

AUBERGE DES TEMPLIERS, N7 at Boismorand, Les Bézards, 45290 Nogent-sur-Vernisson. Tel. 38-31-80-01. Fax 38-31-84-51. 30 rms (all with bath), 8 suites. TV TEL

$ Rates: 600 F ($108) single; 1,400 F ($252) double; from 1,600 F ($288) suite. Breakfast 90 F ($16.20) extra. AE, DC, MC, V. **Parking:** Free. **Closed:** Feb.

This haven of luxury, comfort, and recreation is disguised on the outside as a rustic inn. The ancient Relais & Châteaux was built on the site of an older hospice belonging to the Knights Templars and was once a stagecoach stop. Accommodations are available in the annex, the thatch-roofed La Chaumière, and the little manor house. The most modern accommodations are in a pavilion by the pool. Ask for the tiny tower room if you prefer a snug nest; it's completely round, with old beams. The rooms are furnished with reproductions of antiques. Even the bathrooms are well decorated, with beautiful tiles and wallpaper. Be sure to take a stroll through the flower gardens.

Dining/Entertainment: The bar has a fireplace, beamed ceilings, and brass chandeliers. Dining is by candlelight. Chef de cuisine Monsieur Dépée specializes in wild-game dishes during autumn hunting season, including woodcock, pheasant, and young rabbit. Other dishes include white mousse of liver, veal liver cooked in cider vinegar, sole à l'orange, and young guinea hen with lime. For dessert, the soufflé glacé with a whisky-and-honey sauce is sinful. Meals are served in the garden in fair weather. Fixed-price menus cost 400–620 F ($72–$111.60), and à la carte meals average 600 F ($108). Fine regional wines, such as sancerre, and more expensive wines are stocked here.

Facilities: Heated swimming pool, tennis courts.

20. GIEN

96 miles S of Paris, 40 miles SE of Orléans

GETTING THERE By Train There are frequent SNCF rail connections to the town of Gien from Orléans.

ESSENTIALS Information The Office de Tourisme is located at rue Anne-de-Beaujeu (tel. 38-67-25-28); the office is open from March to November.

A town of flowers, known for its porcelain, Gien was heavily bombed in the early months of World War II. But the reconstruction has been skillful, the town planners showing a healthy respect for traditional architectural styles. The town is in red brick that contrasts with the geometric designs and edgings in black brick.

Stroll along the Loire River promenade with its shade trees, and cross the humpback bridge dating from the 15th century for a good view. If you're planning to stay over, avoid the weekends, especially in autumn. French hunters after wild game in the surrounding area (woodcock, pheasant, rabbit) seem to book up all the rooms.

WHAT TO SEE & DO

Founded in 1821, the faïence factory, **Faïencerie de Gien** (tel. 38-67-00-05), is at place de la Victoire in the western part of Gien, covering about ten acres. Visits to the factory (Monday through Friday only) must be arranged in advance, so call for an appointment. There is no bus service to the factory, so you'll need a car.

A museum of faïence on the grounds is open daily from 9am to noon and 2 to 6pm, charging 12 F ($2.20) admission. Also here is a "second-choice" shop, where slightly flawed faïence is for sale at discounted prices. The shop is open Monday through Saturday from 9am to noon and 2 to 6pm.

The **Château de Gien**, place du Château, rebuilt in 1484, once belonged to Anne de Beaujeu, the Comtesse of Gien, eldest daughter of Louis XI. The most interesting section of the restored castle is the Great Hall, with its paintings by Desportes.

In the castle is an **International Hunting Museum** (tel. 38-67-69-69), which includes a collection of weapons, pictures, and prints, all devoted to *la chaise* down through the ages. The castle/museum is open daily from Easter through the end of October from 9:30am to 6:30pm; off-season it closes at 5:30pm. Admission is 23 F ($4.10) for adults, 15 F ($2.70) for children.

The **Church of St. Joan of Arc** stands nearby on the place du Château, but it is modern, the design pleasing and harmonious. Only the tower dates from the 15th century, the time of Anne de Beaujeu. After its destruction in 1940, the church was rebuilt in the postwar years in red brick with black geometric designs. Inside the baptistery, the baked-earth capitals, the ceramic statues, and the stained-glass windows should be observed, as well as the uncommon "Way of the Cross" made in the local earthenware works.

WHERE TO STAY & DINE

If you're planning to stay overnight, avoid the weekends, especially in autumn— French hunters tend to book all the rooms.

HOTEL BEAU-SITE/RESTAURANT LA POULARDE, 13, quai de Nice, 45500 Gien. Tel. 38-67-36-05. Fax 38-38-18-68. 10 rms (all with bath). TV TEL
$ Rates: 230 F ($41.40) single; 270 F ($48.60) double. Breakfast 40 F ($7.20) extra. AE, DC, MC, V. **Parking:** Free. **Closed:** Jan 1–15.
This hotel and restaurant was built right after World War II, and sits at the edge of the Loire, near the center of Gien. The rooms here are simply furnished, with private bathrooms. In the restaurant, generous, well-prepared, family-style meals based on old regional recipes are politely served. Specialties include brochette of Loire Valley fish, several trout dishes, and duck with peaches. Fixed-price menus cost 80 F ($14.40) (Monday through Friday only), 128 F ($23), and 285 F ($51.30). The restaurant is closed Sunday night during most of the year, but in July and August remains open for both lunch and dinner every day.

HOTEL DU RIVAGE, 1, quai de Nice, 45500 Gien. Tel. 38-37-79-00. Fax 38-38-10-21. 22 rms (all with bath), 3 suites. TV TEL
$ Rates: 355–495 F ($63.90–$89.10) double; 695 F ($125.10) suite. Breakfast 42 F ($7.60) extra. AE, DC, MC, V. **Parking:** Free. **Closed:** Mid-Feb to mid-Mar.
Christian Gaillard heartily welcomes hunters on the weekend to his hotel near the river promenade. Rooms are pleasantly decorated and comfortable. The food is exceptional: Specialties include parfait of Loire pike perch, duckling with morels, a feuilleté of snails with sancerre, salmon filet in season, and a fricassée of lamb sweetbreads with cider vinegar and honey. The hotel also offers a convivial bar. Fixed-price menus cost 155 F ($27.90), 220 F ($39.60), and 320 F ($57.60); à la

carte meals average 320 F ($57.60). The 155-F ($27.90) menu is not served Saturday at dinner or Sunday at lunch.

---

21. LANGEAIS

161 miles SW of Paris, 16 miles W of Tours

GETTING THERE By Train There are frequent SNCF rail connections from Tours, and several trains a day stop in Langeais en route to Saumur.

ESSENTIALS Orientation The château is just a short walk from the rail station (follow the signs).

Information The Bureau du Tourisme is located at 15, place de Brosse (tel. 47-96-58-22).

The formidable gray pile, the **Château de Langeais**, 37130 Langeais (tel. 47-96-72-60), a true fortress of the Middle Ages, dominates the town. It is one of the few châteaux actually located on the Loire. The façade is forbidding, but once you cross the drawbridge and go inside, the apartments are so richly decorated that the severe effect is softened or forgotten. The castle dates back to the 9th century, when the dreaded Black Falcon erected what was considered the first dungeon in Europe, the ruins of which remain to this day. The present structure was built in 1465 in the reign of Louis XI. That the interior is so well preserved and furnished is because of Jacques Siegfried, who not only restored it over a period of 20 years but bequeathed it to the Institut de France in 1904.

"She arrived at Langeais carried in a litter decked with gold cloth, dressed in a gown of black trimmed with sable. Her wedding gown of gold cloth was ornamented with 160 sables." The date was December 6, 1491. The marriage of Anne of Brittany to Charles VIII was to be the golden hour of Langeais. Their symbols—scallops, fleurs-de-lis, and ermine—set the motif for the Guard Room. In the Wedding Chamber, where the marriage took place, the walls are decorated with a series of seven tapestries known as the *Valiant Knights*.

At the entrance to Langeais, a large tapestry illustrating the life of Nebuchadnezzar shows him covered with hair and stricken with madness. In a bedchamber known sardonically as "The Crucifixion," the 15th-century black-oak four-poster is reputed to be one of the earliest known. The room takes its odd name from a tapestry of the Virgin and St. John standing on a flower-bedecked ground. In the Monsieur's Room a rare Flemish tapestry depicts such motifs as Virginia snake-root leaves and pheasants on railings, surrounded by a border of fruit. The Chapel Hall was built by joining two stories under a ceiling of Gothic arches. In the Luini Room is a large fresco by that artist, dating from 1522, removed from a chapel on Lake Maggiore, Italy. It represents St. Francis of Assisi and St. Elizabeth of Hungary with Mary and Joseph. The Byzantine Virgin in the drawing room is considered an early work of Cimabue, the Forentine artist. The best for last: the *Tapestry of the Thousand Flowers* in the Drawing Room is like an ageless celebration of spring, a joyous riot of growth, a symbol of life's renewal.

The château is open mid-March to November 1, daily from 9am to 6:30pm; off-season, Tuesday through Sunday from 9am to noon and 4 to 5pm. It's closed November 2 and March 14. Admission is 30 F ($5.40) for adults and 17 F ($3.10) for children.

WHERE TO STAY & DINE

LA DUCHESSE ANNE, 10, rue de Tours, 37130 Langeais. Tel. 47-96-82-03. Fax 47-96-68-60. 23 rms (9 with bath or shower). TEL
$ Rates: 220 F ($39.60) single or double without bath, 270–295 F ($48.60–$53.10) single or double with bath. Breakfast 32 F ($5.80) extra. V. **Parking:** Free.

Set on the eastern outskirts of town, this hotel originally served as a coaching inn during the 18th century. Today, its white-painted facade still has its covered carriage passageway, which leads to an inner courtyard. Rooms are simply furnished but comfortable. Garden tables are set out for dining, and there's a holding tank for the fresh trout that is one of the specialties of the restaurant. Other dishes include Loire Valley pike with beurre blanc and vegetables, and quail gourmande studded with small crayfish. Fixed-price menus cost 86–195 F ($15.50–$35.10); à la carte meals average around 250 F ($45) each. About a dozen of the rooms contain TVs.

HOSTEN ET RESTAURANT LANGEAIS, 2, rue Gambetta, 37130
Langeais. Tel. 47-96-82-12. Fax 47-96-56-72. 11 rms (all with bath), 1 suite.
$ Rates: 290–550 F ($52.20–$99) single or double; 580 F ($104.40) suite.
Breakfast 48 F ($8.60) extra. AE, DC, MC, V. **Parking:** Free. **Closed:** Jan
10–Feb 10 and June 20–July 12.

This country inn has an informal atmosphere and excellent food and service. The restaurant is expensive, but the hotel is budget to medium-priced. The Hosten family bought this 75-year-old hotel in 1948; Madame Hosten takes care of the guest accommodations, and her husband, Jean-Jacques, is the chef (he was trained at the Savoy in London and at the Ledoyen on the Champs-Elysées in Paris). Rooms—all doubles—are well furnished and comfortable.

The restaurant has received many honors over the years. In addition to the dining room, tables are set up in the open courtyard under umbrellas and flowering trees. The *menu de prestige* includes blanquette de soles et turbots, escalope de saumon à l'oseille (sorrel), terrine chaude de brochets with a sauce Nantua, and homard (lobster) Cardinal. Desserts are likely to include the classic soufflé au Grand-Marnier and charlotte au coulis de framboises (raspberries). A meal costs 300–350 F ($54–$63). The restaurant is open for lunch Wednesday through Monday and for dinner Wednesday through Sunday.

---

22. USSE

183 miles SW of Paris, 9 miles NE of Chinon

GETTING THERE It's best visited by car or on an organized bus tour from Tours.

ESSENTIALS Information The château (clearly seen from below) stands on a hill looking down on the Indre River. To the south of Ussé, the forest of Chinon contains more than 31 miles of trees, including picnic areas.

At the edge of the hauntingly dark forest of Chinon, the **Château d'Ussé** was the inspiration behind Perrault's legend of "The Sleeping Beauty" (called in French "Belle au Bois Dormant"). On a hill overlooking the Indre River, it is a virtual forest of steeples, turrets, towers, chimneys, and dormers. Originally conceived as a medieval fortress, it was erected at the dawn of the Renaissance. Two powerful families—Bueil and d'Espinay—lived in the château in the 15th and 16th centuries.

Vauban, the military engineer who in the 17th century designed systems of fortifications for French cities, was a frequent visitor when Ussé was owned by his son-in-law, the Marquis de Valentinay. At one point in its history Mlle d'Ussé ordered royal apartments built for an anticipated visit of Louis XIV that never materialized. In time the château was owned by the Duke of Duras and later by Mme de la Rochejacquelin before coming into its present ownership by the Marquis de Blacas. The terraces, laden with orange trees, were laid out in the 18th century. When the need for a "fortified" château had long since passed, the north wing was demolished, opening up a greater view, as the occupants wished to enjoy the sun and the landscape.

The marquis has opened a large number of rooms to the public. The guided tour begins in the Renaissance chapel, with its sculptured portal and handsomely designed stalls. Then you are escorted through the royal apartments, furnished with tapestries and antiques, including a four-poster in red damask. One gallery displays an extensive collection of swords and rifles.

The château is open daily March 15 to July 15, 9am to noon and 2 to 6pm; July 16 through August, daily 9am to 6:30pm; September, daily 9am to noon and 2 to 7pm; closed rest of year. Admission is 52 F ($9.40) for adults, 19 F ($3.40) for children.

---

23. CHINON

176 miles SW of Paris, 30 miles SW of Tours, 19 miles from Langeais

GETTING THERE   By Train   There are two trains daily from Tours (trip time: 1 hour).

ESSENTIALS   Orientation   The town center is place de l'Hôtel-de-Ville.

Information   The Office de Tourisme is located at 12, rue Voltaire (tel. 47-93-17-85).

Remember when Ingrid Bergman as Joan of Arc sought out the dauphin even though he tried to conceal himself among his courtiers? The action in real life took place at Chinon, one of the oldest fortress-châteaux in France. Charles VII, mockingly known as the King of Bourges, centered his government at Chinon from 1429 to 1450. In 1429, with the English besieging Orléans, the maid of Orléans, that "messenger from God," prevailed upon the weak dauphin to give her an army. The rest is history.

The seat of French power stayed at Chinon until the Hundred Years' War ended. It was here that Louis XII in 1498 received Cesare Borgia, the son of the notorious Pope Alexander VI, when he brought permission from Rome to dissolve Louis's marriage to his "deformed" wife. Later he married Anne of Brittany.

WHAT TO SEE & DO

On the banks of the Vienne, in the heart of Rabelais country, Chinon retains a medieval atmosphere with its grim feudal ruins. Nineteen miles from Langeais, it consists of winding streets and turreted houses, many built in the 15th and 16th centuries in the heyday of the court. For the best view, drive across the river, turning right onto the Quai Danton. From that vantage point you'll have the best perspective of the town, seeing the castle in relation to the village and the river. The gables and towers make Chinon look like a toy village.

The most typical street is **rue Voltaire,** lined with 15th- and 16th-century town houses. At no. 44, Richard the Lion-Hearted died on April 6, 1199, after suffering a mortal wound while besieging Chalus in Limousin. In the heart of town, the **Grand Carroi** was the crossroads of the Middle Ages.

The most famous son of Chinon, Rabelais, the great Renaissance writer, walked these streets. He was born at La Devinière, on the D17 near the N751, now the **Musée Rabelais.** It's open mid-March through September, daily from 9am to noon and 2 to 6pm; off-season it closes at 5pm and on Wednesday. The château is also closed in December and January. Admission is 15 F ($2.70). Rabelais used his native scenery as background in many of his stories.

The **Château de Chinon** (tel. 47-93-13-45) is three separate strongholds, badly ruined. Some of the grim walls remain, although many of the buildings—including the Great Hall where Joan of Arc sought out the dauphin—have been torn down. Some of the most destructive owners were the heirs of Cardinal Richelieu. Now gone, the **Château de St-Georges** was built by Henry II of England, who died there in 1189. The **Château de Mileu** dates from the 11th to the 15th centuries, containing the keep and the clock tower, where a **Museum of Joan of Arc** has been installed. Separated from the latter by a moat, the **Château du Coudray** contains the Tour du Coudray, where Joan of Arc stayed during her time at Chinon. In the 14th century the Knights Templar were imprisoned there (they are responsible for the graffiti on the walls) before meeting their violent deaths.

The Château de Chinon is open in July and August, daily from 9am to 7pm; in September, May, and June, daily from 9am to 6pm; in October and November and February to March 14, daily from 9am to noon and 2 to 6pm; closed December and January. Admission is 21 F ($3.80) for adults and 17 F ($3.10) for children.

WHERE TO STAY

CHRIS' HOTEL, 12, place Jeanne-d'Arc, 37500 Chinon. Tel. 47-93-36-92. Fax 47-98-48-92. 40 rms (all with bath), 2 suites. TV TEL

$ Rates: 240 F ($43.20) single; 350–400 F ($63–$72) double; from 800 F ($144) suite. Breakfast 40 F ($7.20) extra. AE, DC, MC, V. **Parking:** 15 F ($2.70).

The tranquil setting of this well-run hotel is a 19th-century building near the historic district of town. Many of the bedrooms have views of the castle and the river. The rooms are comfortable, and most are furnished in a Louis XV style; all have modern amenities. Breakfast is the only meal served.

HOSTELLERIE GARGANTUA, 73, rue Voltaire, 37500 Chinon. Tel. 47-93-04-71. 7 rms (6 with bath). TEL

$ Rates: 480 F ($86.40) single or double without bath, 550–600 F ($99–$108) single or double with bath. Half board 200 F ($36) per person extra. MC, V. **Parking:** 20 F ($3.60). **Closed:** Mid-Nov to Feb 1.

Named after Rabelais's amiable giant, this 15th-century town mansion is in a row of ancient buildings near the river. It stands almost opposite the house where Richard the Lion-Hearted died. The Gargantua features a terrace with a view of the château, and some rooms have four-poster beds. Try to visit, at least for a meal; food is formally served in a stylish medieval hall. Don't miss the fluffy omelet Gargamelle; one of the ingredients is a creamy fondue sauce. Fixed-price menus cost 100–150 F ($18–$27).

HOTEL DIDEROT, 4, rue Buffon, 37500 Chinon. Tel. 47-93-18-87. Fax 47-93-37-10. 25 rms (all with bath or shower). TEL

$ Rates: 220–250 F ($39.60–$45) single; 350–400 F ($63–$72) double. Breakfast 35 F ($6.30) extra. AE, DC, MC, V. **Parking:** Free. **Closed:** Dec 20–Jan 10.

This 18th-century manor house, a short walk from place Jeanne-d'Arc, was converted into a hotel after World War II. A small annex in the courtyard is built in the same style as the main building. Theodore Kazamias and his wife, who used to be a doctor, bought and renovated the place in the 1970s. Rooms are furnished with antiques. In the breakfast room (breakfast is the only meal served), the fireplace dates from the 1400s. Try some of the homemade jam with your morning croissant.

HOTEL LE CHINON, Digue St-Jacques, 37500 Chinon. Tel. 47-98-46-46. Fax 47-98-35-44. 54 rms (all with bath or shower). MINIBAR TV TEL

$ Rates: 340 F ($61.20) single; 380 F ($68.40) double. Breakfast 40 F ($7.20) extra. AE, DC, MC, V. **Parking:** Free.

Modern and streamlined, this hotel, built in 1988, contains comfortable, carpeted rooms with functional furniture. French casement windows open onto a balcony or terrace. Some rooms offer views of the nearby Château de Chinon, which rises from a rocky outcrop on the opposite bank of the River Vienne. The hotel's dining room serves meals daily, costing 70–100 F ($12.60–$18) each. Children's menus are available for around 40 F ($7.20) each.

WHERE TO DINE

In addition to the following, see "Where to Stay," above, for hotel restaurants.

AU PLAISIR GOURMAND, 2, rue Parmentier. Tel. 47-93-20-48.
 Cuisine: FRENCH. **Reservations:** Required.

$ Prices: Appetizers 65–95 F ($11.70–$17.10); main dishes 95–120 F ($17.10–$21.60); fixed-price menus 175–240 F ($31.50–$43.20). MC, V.

 Open: Lunch Tues–Sun noon–2pm; dinner Tues–Sat 7:30–9:30pm. **Closed:** Feb.

This is the premier restaurant in the area, and it is owned by Jean-Claude Rigollet, who used to direct the chefs at Les Templiers in Bézards. His restaurant offers an intimate dining room with a limited number of tables in a charming 18th-century building that was once a convent. Menu items change frequently. The selection might include a salad of warm turnips with foie gras, warm oysters with leeks, steamed chicken with truffles, and fricassée of monkfish with lobster butter.

NEARBY ACCOMMODATIONS & DINING

CHATEAU DE MARCAY, Marcay, 37500 Chinon. Tel. 47-93-03-47. Fax 47-93-45-33. 38 rms (all with bath), 3 suites. TV TEL **Directions:** Take the D116 4½ southwest of Chinon.

$ Rates: 520–1,575 F ($93.60–$283.50) single or double; from 1,650 F ($297) suite. Extra bed 150 F ($27). Half board 680–1,180 F ($122.40–$212.40) per person. AE, DC, MC, V. **Parking:** Free.

⭐ This Relais & Châteaux with pepperpot roofs was once a 15th-century fortress, and it remained untouched by the region's civil wars. It is sumptuously decorated, and the rooms are well furnished. A top-notch chef maintains high standards in the restaurant; specialties change with the seasons. There is a panoramic view from the garden terrace and dining room, where the accessories are elegantly rustic. A la carte meals start at 350 F ($63); fixed-price menus run 230–385 F ($41.40–$69.30).

MANOIR DE LA GIRAUDIERE, Beaumont-en-Veron, 37420 Avoine. Tel. 47-58-40-36. Fax 47-58-46-06. 20 rms (all with bath or shower), 5 suites. TV TEL **Directions:** Head three miles west of Chinon along the D749 in the direction of Bourgueil.

$ Rates: 200–350 F ($36–$63) single or double; 420 F ($75.60) suite. Breakfast 32 F ($5.80) extra. AE, DC, MC, V. **Parking:** Free.

In a six-acre park, three miles from Chinon, this 17th-century family-run manor offers classic decor and modern comforts. A good restaurant is on the premises. The restaurant—not the hotel—closes in January; otherwise, the restaurant is open daily except Tuesday and Wednesday at lunch. A daily fixed-price menu is featured for 105 F ($18.90), and seasonal à la carte meals range from 150 to 250 F ($27 to $45). Typical local products and Loire wines are featured, including fresh asparagus in the spring, pike perch, duck stew, goat's cheese, and, for dessert, a pear charlotte drippy with strawberry sauce.

24. FONTEVRAUD-L'ABBAYE

189 miles SW of Paris, 10 miles SE of Saumur

GETTING THERE   By Bus   Three buses leave daily from Saumur, taking 30 minutes.

By Car   If you're driving, take the N147 about 2½ miles from the village of Montsoreau.

ESSENTIALS   Information   The Office de Tourisme is located at Chapelle Sainte-Catherine (tel. 41-51-79-45). It's open June through September.

You're likely to trip over a British colonel muttering, "These tombs should be in Westminster Abbey where they belong!" For in the **Abbaye Royale de Fontevraud** (tel. 41-51-71-41), the Plantagenet dynasty of the kings of England are buried. Why there? These monarchs, whose male line vanished in 1499, were also the counts of Anjou, and they left instructions that they be buried on their native soil.

Contained within the 12th-century Romanesque church—with its four Byzantine domes—are the remains of the two English kings or princes, including Henry II of England, the first Plantagenet king (the one who fought with Thomas Becket) and his wife, Eleanor of Aquitaine, the single most famous woman of the Middle Ages (at one time she was married to Louis VII of France). Her crusading son, Richard the Lion-Hearted, was also entombed here. The Plantagenet line ended with the death of Richard III at the Battle of Bosworth in 1485. The last occasion when the matter of returning the tombs of the Plantagenet kings to England was raised was on the eve of the 1867 Universal Exhibition. In a spirit of goodwill, Napoleon III offered the reclining statues to Queen Victoria. This led to a strong protest on the part of Angevin archeologists. The emperor had to write to the queen, begging her to free him from such a rash promise. To save Napoleon from embarrassment, the queen recognized that, after all, it would be contrary to the wishes of the two kings who, as they were dying, expressly requested that their remains be buried in the abbey church of Fontevraud. The tombs fared badly in the Revolution, as mobs invaded the church, desecrating the sarcophagi and scattering their contents on the floor.

More interesting than the tombs, however, is the octagonal Tour d'Evraud, the last remaining Romanesque kitchen in France. Surrounding the tower is a group of apses crowned by conically roofed turrets. A pyramid tops the conglomeration, capped by an open-air lantern tower pierced with lancets.

The abbey was founded in 1099 by Robert d'Arbrissel, who had spent much of his life as a recluse, although he enjoyed a reputation at one time as a sort of Billy Sunday of the Middle Ages. His abbey was like a public-welfare commune, very liberal in its admission policies. One part, for example, was filled with aristocratic ladies, many of them banished from court, including discarded mistresses of kings. The four youngest daughters of Louis XV were educated there as well. Aside from the nuns and monks, there were lepers, and a hospital for the lame and sick who arrived almost daily at the abbey's doorstep. The foundation was controlled by powerful "abbesses" appointed by the king. Under Napoleon I the abbey was converted into a prison and remained so for 160 years. Now the prisoners are gone and the abbey is being restored—actually rebuilt in parts—at great expense to the French government.

In the chapterhouse are some interesting 16th-century frescoes. A cloister dates from the same period, although one section goes back to the 12th century. The refectory is also from the 1500s.

The abbey can be visited daily, but hours are seasonal: September 16 to October 31, 9:30am to 12:30pm and 2 to 6pm; November to March 26, 9:30am to 12:30pm and 2 to 5pm; March 27 to May 31, 9:30am to 12:30pm and 2 to 6:30pm; June 1 to September 15, 9am to 7pm. Admission is 25 F ($4.50) for adults, 14 F ($2.50) for ages 18–24 and those 65 or over.

WHERE TO STAY

HOTELLERIE DU PRIEURE ST-LAZARE, 49590 Fontevraud-l'Abbaye. Tel. 41-51-73-16. Fax 41-51-75-50. 50 rms (all with bath). MINIBAR TV TEL
$ Rates: 335 F ($60.30) single; 400 F ($72) double; 480 F ($86.40) triple. Breakfast 48 F ($8.60) extra. AE, MC, V. **Parking:** Free.

Despite its deliberate simplicity, this is probably one of the most unusual hotels in Europe. Set upon 11th-century foundations, amid walls which were added to the abbey during the 18th century, the hotel is contained within what functioned long ago as cells for penitent monks. As part of the continuing restoration of the world-famous abbey, one of its four-story wings was transformed into a conference center during the 1970s. In 1990, those facilities were turned over to a private management company, which today maintains them as a hotel.

Bedrooms are clean, well maintained, and monastically simple, with white walls and appropriately spartan modern furniture. (An elevator adds a convenience not known to the medieval monks who lived here previously.) On the premises is a big-windowed, stone-sided restaurant, Le Cloître, built as a panoramic enclosure of the 11th-century medieval cloister. Fixed-price menus cost 86–216 F ($15.50–$38.90) and are served every day at lunch and dinner. An additional dining room, for groups and conferences, is in the monastery's famous rectory, beneath a vaulted ceiling, near a monumental and very historic fireplace. Despite the lack of plushness, most guests at this establishment appreciate the abbey's calm and its well-established incentives to meditation.

WHERE TO DINE

LA LICORNE, allée Ste-Catherine. Tel. 41-51-72-49.
Cuisine: FRENCH. **Reservations:** Required.
$ Prices: Appetizers 50–125 F ($9–$22.50); main dishes 80–160 F ($14.40–$28.80); fixed-price menus 110 F ($19.80) (weekdays only) and 185–250 F ($33.30–$45). AE, MC, V.
Open: June to mid-Sept, lunch daily noon–1:30pm; dinner daily 7–9pm. Mid-Sept to May, lunch Tues–Sun noon–1:30pm; dinner Tues–Sat 7–9pm.

Some sightseers consider a visit to the nearby abbey and a meal at this restaurant to be the perfect combination of medieval history and sensuality. Containing only 30 seats, the restaurant lies along a sycamore-lined pedestrian walkway which stretches between the abbey and a nearby parish church. It was built in the 1700s as a *maison bourgeoise,* and its neoclassical pilasters and proportions are considered significantly beautiful in their own right.

During warm weather, tables are set up in a flowered garden overlooking the walkway; otherwise, in the contemporary dining room. Menu items are prepared by one of the region's best-trained chefs, Michel Lecomte, and might include a couscous of lobster with lima beans, crayfish-stuffed ravioli with morel sauce, filet of salmon with vanilla sauce, sea scallops with orange zest, zander with oysters and ginger, and such luscious desserts as a warm chocolate tart with pears and lemon-butter sauce.

25. SAUMUR

186 miles SW of Paris, 33 miles SE of Angers

GETTING THERE   By Train   Trains run frequently between Tours and Nantes, with stopovers at Saumur.

ESSENTIALS   Orientation   The train station is on the north side of town. Most major points of interest, including the château (see below), are on the south bank. From the station, take bus A into town.

Information   For information, contact the Office de Tourisme on place de la Bilange (tel. 41-51-03-06).

At a point where the Loire separates to encircle an island, Saumur is set in a region of vineyards. (Do sample some of the local produce, like the Saumur mousseux.) Founded in 1768, its Cavalry School, as well as its riding club, the Black Cadre, are world renowned. Its horsemen are considered among the finest in Europe (to see a rider carry out a *curvet* is to thrill at the training of both man and beast). The townspeople have even installed a **Musée du Cheval**—that is, a museum devoted to the history of the horse down through the ages, complete with stirrups, antique saddles, spurs, and whatever.

The museum is housed in the **Château de Saumur** (tel. 41-51-30-46), towering over the town from a promontory overlooking the Loire. The Poet Prince, René of Anjou, called it "the castle of love." In the famous *Book of Hours* of the duc de Berry at Chantilly, a 15th-century painting shows Saumur as a fairytale castle of bell turrets and gilded weathercocks. But these adornments are largely gone, leaving a rather stark and foreboding fortress.

Under Napoleon the castle became a prison, eventually degenerating into a barracks and munitions depot. The town of Saumur acquired it in 1908 and began the herculean task of restoration. Now an interesting regional museum, the **Musée des Arts Decoratifs,** devoted to decorative arts, has been installed. The galleries grew out of the collection begun by Count Charles Lair. The museum is noted mainly for its ceramics, dating from the 16th through the 18th centuries. A series of 13th-century enamel crucifixes from Limoges is remarkable, and also displayed are illustrated 15th-century manuscripts, polychrome sculpture (some from the 14th century), tapestries, and antique furnishings.

The château is open daily: June 15 to September 15, 9am to 7pm (in July and August, also on Wednesday and Saturday night from 7 to 10pm); April to June 14 and September 16–30, 9am to noon and 2 to 6pm; October through March, 10am to noon and 2 to 5pm. Admission is 32 F ($5.80) for adults, 15 F ($2.70) for children. Take bus C.

WHERE TO STAY

HOTEL ANNE-D'ANJOU, 32, quai Mayoud, 49400 Saumur. Tel. 41-67-30-30. Fax 41-67-51-00. 50 rms (all with bath). TV TEL **Bus:** A.
$ Rates: 390 F ($70.20) single; 495 F ($89.10) double. Breakfast 45 F ($8.10) extra. AE, DC, MC, V.

This antique building was originally built in the 18th century as a family home. The magnificent stairwell below a trompe-l'oeil ceiling is classified as a historic monument. Rooms in the back overlook the château, while the main facade faces the Loire. This became a hotel in 1984, when it was completely renovated. Five of the accommodations still have their original decor, ranging from Louis XVI to Empire. Former famous guests include Jean Marais (the French actor), Ginger Rogers, and the Prince of Monaco. The hotel also operates one of the most prestigious restaurants in Saumur, Les Menestrels (see "Where to Dine," below).

LE ROI RENE, 94, av. du Général-de-Gaulle, 49400 Saumur. Tel. 41-67-45-30. Fax 41-67-74-59. 38 rms (all with bath or shower). TV TEL **Bus:** A.
$ Rates: 250–310 F ($45–$55.80) single or double. Breakfast 30 F ($5.40) extra. AE, MC, V. **Parking:** 25 F ($4.50).

This traditional favorite is on a quiet square overlooking the Loire. Many comforts have been added recently. Rooms are well furnished and have double-pane windows. The inn also serves good food daily.

WHERE TO DINE

DELICES DU CHATEAU, Les Feuquières, Château de Saumur. Tel. 41-67-65-60.
Cuisine: FRENCH. **Reservations:** Required. **Bus:** 6.
$ Prices: Appetizers 70–110 F ($12.60–$19.80); main dishes 100–140 F ($18–$25.20); fixed-price menus 170–270 F ($30.60–$48.60). AE, DC, MC, V.
Open: Oct–Apr, lunch Tues–Sun 12:30–2pm; dinner Tues–Sat 7–10:30pm. May–Sept, lunch daily 12:30–2pm; dinner daily 1:30–10:30pm. **Closed:** Dec.

This well-maintained and elegant restaurant, in a restored 12th-century house on the château grounds, contains a large fireplace and antique furniture; there are great views of the city and the Loire below from the restaurant's flowery terrace. Pierre Millon is the outstanding chef de cuisine—the food is classic but personalized. Try the filet of beef sautéed with duck liver and an essence of truffles, shrimp with red currants and cucumbers, or the bavarois of lobster. A newer specialty is Loire Valley zander encased in a shell of puréed potatoes and served with a coulis of a local wine (Saumur Champigny). The cheaper of the fixed-price menus is one of the dining bargains in Saumur.

L'ESCARGOT, 30, rue du Maréchal-Leclerc. Tel. 41-51-20-88.
Cuisine: FRENCH. **Reservations:** Required. **Bus:** A.
$ Prices: Appetizers 25–57 F ($4.50–$10.30); main dishes 57–90 F ($10.30–$16.20); fixed-price menus 78–125 F ($14–$22.50). AE, MC, V.
Open: Lunch Thurs–Tues noon–2:30pm; dinner Thurs–Tues 7–10pm. **Closed:** Jan.

This typical French bistro, named "The Snail," contains two dining rooms with a mellow atmosphere. Fixed-price menus include hors d'oeuvres, a fish and a meat course, plus dessert. Service and drinks are extra. Specialties include a cassolette of snails with garlic butter, filet of zander with the famous beurre blanc ("white butter") of the Loire, and a Loire salmon soufflé "in the style of the chef."

RESTAURANT LE GAMBETTA, 12, rue Gambetta. Tel. 41-67-66-66.

Cuisine: FRENCH. **Reservations:** Recommended. **Bus:** A
$ **Prices:** Appetizers 45–110 F ($8.10–$19.80); main dishes 75–110 F ($13.50–$19.80); fixed-price menus 96–192 F ($17.30–$34.60). AE, DC, MC, V.
Open: Lunch daily noon–2pm; dinner daily 7–10pm.

Set on a quiet side street near the cavalry school, a five-minute walk from the town center, this late 19th-century town house has a pleasant garden in back for fair-weather dining, and an elegantly appointed dining room. You'll be welcomed by the English-speaking Floriane Thibault, whose husband, Jean, prepares a sophisticated cuisine in back. Menu choices change with the season, but are likely to include such dishes as an escalope of foie gras with cherries and honey sauce, filet of potted zander with a coulis of seasonal greens and parsley, breast of duckling with a confit of ginger, and seasoned pig's foot stuffed with sweetbreads and morels. The wines of Saumur make everything taste even better.

RESTAURANT LES MENESTRELS, 11-13, rue Raspail. Tel. 41-67-71-10.
Cuisine: FRENCH. **Reservations:** Required. **Bus:** C.
$ **Prices:** Appetizers 86–150 F ($15.50–$27); main dishes 90–150 F ($16.20–$27); fixed-price menus 160 F ($28.80) (Mon–Wed only), 210 F ($37.80), 270 F ($48.60), and 340 F ($61.20). AE, DC, MC, V.
Open: Lunch Tues–Sat 12:30–2pm; dinner Tues–Sat 7:30–9:30pm.

The Hôtel Anne-d'Anjou (see "Where to Stay," above) operates one of the leading restaurants in the city. The entrance is between the château and the hotel. The decor includes heavy timbers, chiseled stone, plaster walls, and some architectural features unchanged from the 1500s. The restaurant has a nice view of the château and its own garden. When the upper floors are full, more seating is available in a vaulted cellar. Menus are based on the supply of fresh local and regional produce. Try the pot-au-feu of lobster or Loire salmon with sorrel.

NEARBY ATTRACTIONS

The **Château de Montsoreau,** 49730 Montsoreau (tel. 41-50-70-25), is six miles east of Saumur on the N751. It contains the Musée des Goums, devoted to Moroccan troops who fought with the Allies in World War II. Immortalized by Dumas in *La Dame de Montsoreau,* the château itself is worthy of a visit. It was constructed in the 15th century in the Gothic style by a courtier of Charles VII. A Renaissance stairway was added in the 16th century. The château is open Wednesday through Monday from 10am to noon and 2 to 6pm. Admission is 22 F ($4).

NEARBY ACCOMMODATIONS

HOSTELLERIE DU PRIEURE, Chênehutte-les-Tuffeaux, 49350 Gennes.
Tel. 41-67-90-14. Fax 41-67-92-24. 35 rms (all with bath), 2 suites. MINIBAR TV TEL **Directions:** Take the D751 four miles west of Saumur.
$ **Rates:** 500–1,000 F ($90–$180) single; 500–1,360 F ($90–$244.80) double; 1,350–1,750 F ($243–$315) suite. Breakfast 75 F ($13.50) extra. AE, MC, V.
Parking: Free. **Closed:** Jan–Feb.

Dating from the 12th century, this ancient *prieuré* (priory) in the château district has a steep roof, dormer windows, and a large peaked tower. Designed for meditation, it's located in a 60-acre park on a plateau. The Relais & Châteaux's facilities include a miniature-golf course and a heated swimming pool. While not rated as a luxury establishment, the Hostellerie does offer comfortable and gracious accommodations. Two of the most beautiful of the newly added bedrooms are in a 10th-century chapel, one of the outbuildings. The least expensive rooms are in a simple outlying pavilion, not in the château itself. The Grand Salon has an ornately carved stone fireplace, crystal chandeliers, oak furniture, and a bar with a fleur-de-lis motif. Each room is different, but all are traditional. Monsieur Doumerc is the director.

The dining room has one of the finest views of the Loire, a span of 40 miles; it's truly beautiful at sunset. The rognons de veau sautés à la moutarde (sautéed veal kidneys in a mustard sauce) is heavenly. Fixed-price meals cost 250–400 F ($45–$72).

26. ANGERS

179 miles SW of Paris, 55 miles E of Nantes

GETTING THERE By Train Trains from Tours take one hour; connections from Saumur take only 30 minutes. From Paris's Gare Montparnasse, it's about a 1½-hour trip.

ESSENTIALS Orientation The train station at place de la Gare is within a convenient walk of the château. To the east of the château is the monumental center.

Information The Office de Tourisme is at place Kennedy (tel. 41-88-69-93).

Once the capital of Anjou, Angers straddles the Maine River. Although it suffered extensive damage in World War II, it has been considerably restored. Somehow it blends the charm of the provinces with the suggestion of the sophisticated life. It is often used by visitors as a base for exploring the châteaux district in the west.

WHAT TO SEE & DO

The moated **Château d'Angers** (tel. 41-87-43-47), was once the home of the counts of Anjou, its origin going back to the 9th century. The notorious "Black Fulk" lived there, and in time the Plantagenets, who became the kings of England. (One of their descendants, Geoffrey the Handsome, married Matilda, the granddaughter of William the Conqueror. Their son, Henry Plantagenet, later Henry II of England, married the legendary Eleanor of Aquitaine after she was divorced by the king of France.)

After the castle was destroyed, it was reconstructed by St. Louis. From 1230 to 1238 the outer walls and 17 massive towers were built—a formidable fortress well prepared to withstand almost any invader. The château was especially favored by the Good King René, in whose reign a brilliant court life flourished until he was forced to surrender Anjou to Louis XI. Louis XIV, in time, turned the château into a prison, dispatching his former finance minister, Fouquet, to a cell there. In the 19th century the castle was again a prison, and in World War II it was used by the Germans as a munitions depot. Allied planes bombed it in 1944.

The castle should be visited if for no other reason than to see the **Apocalypse Tapestries,** considered one of the great masterpieces of art to come down from the Middle Ages. This series of tapestries wasn't always so highly regarded, serving once as a canopy for orange trees to protect the fruit from unfavorable weather conditions and at another time to cover the damaged walls of a church. Based on cartoons by Hennequin of Bruges, they were made by Poisson beginning in 1375. Louis I of Anjou had ordered them for the walls of his castle. In the 19th century they were purchased for only a nominal sum.

Seventy-seven pieces of them stretch a distance of 335 feet, the series illustrating the book of Saint John. One scene is called *La Grande Prostituée.* Another shows Babylon invaded by demons; yet another depicts men in combat with a seven-headed dragon or a peace scene with two multiheaded monsters holding up a fleur-de-lis staff. In still another, warriors are riding on the backs of lions.

After seeing the tapestries, you can go on a tour of the fortress, including the courtyard of the nobles, the prison cells, the ramparts, the windmill tower, a 15th-century chapel, and the restored royal apartments.

The château is open June 1 through September 15, daily from 9am to 7pm; off-season, daily from 9:30am to 12:30pm and 2 to 6pm. Admission is 31 F ($5.60) for adults, 20 F ($3.60) for seniors age 60 or over, 6 F ($1.10) for children 7–17.

The **Cathédrale de St-Maurice,** place Freppel (tel. 41-87-58-45) is from the 12th and 13th centuries, the previous church that stood on this site having been destroyed in a fire. The main tower, however, is from the 16th century, and the statues on the portal represent everybody from the Queen of Sheba to David at the harp. On the tympanum is depicted *Christ Enthroned;* the symbols, such as the lion for St.

Mark, represent the Evangelists. Inside, the stained-glass windows from the 12th through the 16th centuries have made the cathedral known throughout Europe. The oldest one illustrates the martyrdom of St. Vincent (the most unusual window is from a later period: ex-St. Christopher with the head of a dog). Once all the Apocalypse Tapestries were exhibited here; now only a few remain. It is said that Henri Gervais, who designed the imposing central altar, did so from his death bed. The 12th-century nave is a landmark in cathedral architecture, a clear, simple, coherent plan that is a work of harmonious beauty and refinement. It is covered with Angevin vaulting. It's open daily from 8am to 5pm.

WHERE TO STAY

HOTEL CONCORDE, 18, bd. Foch, 49100 Angers. Tel. 41-87-37-20. Fax 41-87-49-54. 69 rms (all with bath or shower). MINIBAR TV TEL
$ Rates: 540 F ($97.20) single; 620 F ($111.60) double. Breakfast 55 F ($9.90) extra. AE, DC, MC, V. **Parking:** 40 F ($7.20).
Set in the commercial heart of town behind a concrete facade, this modern, four-story hotel was built in 1972 and renovated several times since then. The reception area has a high ceiling and much exposed stone. Rooms have modern comforts and radios. The in-house brasserie, Le Grand Cercle, serves food either inside or on a terrace opening onto the boulevard. Fixed price menus run 90–140 F ($16.20–$25.20).

HOTEL D'ANJOU, 1, bd. Foch, 49100 Angers. Tel. 41-88-24-82. Fax 41-87-22-21. 53 rms (all with bath). MINIBAR TV TEL
$ Rates: 350–550 F ($63–$99) single or double. Breakfast 50 F ($9) extra. AE, DC, MC, V. **Parking:** 40 F ($7.20).
The prices are reasonable at this four-story hotel located on the main boulevard, next to a large park. The rooms are clean and comfortably furnished with traditional pieces, and guests are politely welcomed and cared for. The hotel restaurant, La Salamandre, is one of the better ones in town, offering regional specialties and fresh-tasting fish dishes. Try the sole in tomato sauce and filets of duck with spring turnips. Fixed-price meals cost 115 F ($20.70) (lunch only), 144 F ($25.90), and 210 F ($37.80); à la carte meals average 300 F ($54). The restaurant is closed Sunday night.

HOTEL DE FRANCE, 8, place de la Gare, 49100 Angers. Tel. 41-88-49-42. Fax 41-86-76-70. 57 rms (all with bath). MINIBAR TV TEL
$ Rates: 330 F ($59.40) single; 600 F ($108) double. Breakfast 50 F ($9) extra. AE, DC, MC, V. **Parking:** Free.
One of the most respected hotels in town, this well-run 19th-century hotel is located near the rail station. It has been run by the Bouyer family since 1893. The restaurant, Les Plantagenets, serves fixed-price meals beginning at 95 F ($17.10).

HOTEL SAINT-JULIEN, 9, place du Ralliement, 49100 Angers. Tel. 41-88-41-62. Fax 41-20-95-19. 34 rms (all with bath or shower). TV TEL
$ Rates: 160–270 F ($28.80–$48.60) single; 260–300 F ($46.80–$54) double. Breakfast 28 F ($5) extra. MC, V. **Parking:** Free.
Located across from Angers's main theater and midway between the convention center and the château, the Saint-Julien is a family-run hotel with a good reputation and a polite staff. Reservations are important, as it's often fully booked. Rooms are comfortably and traditionally furnished. Seventeen units contain minibars. Although the hotel doesn't include a restaurant, it shares the building with one.

WHERE TO DINE

In addition to the following, see "Where to Stay," above, for hotel restaurants.

LE LOGIS, 9, place du Ralliement. Tel. 41-87-44-15.
Cuisine: SEAFOOD. **Reservations:** Recommended.
$ Prices: Appetizers 80–100 F ($14.40–$18); main dishes 100–130 F ($18–$23.40); fixed-price menus 115–180 F ($20.70–$32.40). AE, DC, MC, V.
Open: Lunch Mon–Sat noon–2pm; dinner Tues–Sat 7:30–9:30pm.
Set one floor above street level in a building which rises opposite the Municipal

Theater, this heart-of-town restaurant specializes in seafood, as well as a very limited array of meat dishes. André Guinet, assisted by a cooperative staff, prepares such dishes as crabmeat-stuffed mushrooms, homemade pâté of fish, escalopes of turbot with periwinkles and a saffron sauce, grilled filet of skate with rosemary-butter sauce, and filet of Loire Valley zander with white wine sauce. The decor is vaguely Louis XIII and mingles an eclectic mixture of antique and reproduction furniture.

LE TOUSSAINT, 7, place du Président-Kennedy. Tel. 41-87-46-20.
   Cuisine: FRENCH. **Reservations:** Recommended.
$ Prices: Appetizers 70–120 F ($12.60–$21.60); main dishes 65–155 F ($11.70–$27.90); fixed-price menus 115 F ($20.70), 180 F ($32.40), and 300 F ($54). AE, MC, V.
   Open: Lunch Tues–Sun noon–2pm; dinner Tues–Sat 7:45–9:30pm.

This leading restaurant, located on the same street as the cathedral, serves the imaginative cuisine of the well-known chef Michel Bignon. The second-floor dining room offers a sweeping view of the château. Recipes are well researched and use only the freshest ingredients. Specialties include foie gras with Layon wine, farm-bred pigeon stuffed with foie gras, a matelotte of Loire eels with a local red wine sauce, and an array of fresh fish and shellfish. The dessert specialty is a soufflé glacé with Cointreau.

NEARBY ACCOMMODATIONS & DINING

CHATEAU DE LA JAILLIERE, 44370 La Chapelle St-Sauveur, at Varades. Tel. 40-98-62-54. 4 rms (all with bath), 1 suite. **Directions:** Take the D6 22 miles west of Angers; the D6 intersects with the N23 between Angers and Nantes.
$ Rates (including continental breakfast): 660–840 F ($118.80–$151.20) double; 4,800 F ($864) suite for six weekly. **Parking:** Free. **Closed:** Oct 15–May 15.

Heavily embellished, this 19th-century château has dozens of marble fireplaces, tapestries, and period furniture. It's owned by the comtesse d'Anthenaise, who offers insights into the region's history. There are flowering gardens, expansive lawns, a private tennis court, and a swimming pool. Rooms are beautifully furnished with antiques, and all are doubles. Well-prepared dinners begin at 200 F ($36).

NORMANDY

Ten centuries have gone by since the Vikings invaded the province of Normandy. The early Scandinavians might have come to ravish the land, but they stayed to cultivate it, bringing their cattle and their women. Of course, they didn't entirely revert from warriors to butter-and-egg men. Rather, they set out on conquests that were to give them England and even Sicily. The Normans produced great soldiers, none more famous than William the Conqueror, who defeated the forces of King Harold at Battle Abbey in 1066. The English and the French continued to do battle on and off for 700 years—a national rivalry that climaxed at the 1815 Battle of Waterloo.

Much of Normandy was later ravaged in the 1944 invasion that began on a June morning when parachutists and airborne troops dropped from the sky at Sainte-Mère-Eglise and Bénouville-sur-Orne. The largest armada ever assembled was about to begin one of the most momentous sagas in world history, the reconquest of continental Europe from the Nazis. Today, many come to Normandy just to see the D-Day beachheads.

Some of the province evokes a Millet landscape. Cattle graze sleepily in the fields turned a verdant green by the heavy Atlantic rainfall. Wood-framed houses exist side by side with postwar modern buildings that rose out of the ashes of World War II. Miraculously spared from the bombardments heaped on Normandy in the battle are stained-glass windows, sculptured woodwork, and Gothic architecture. Many great buildings, regrettably, were leveled to the ground.

The wide beaches attract those seeking a family holiday, although in August the sands of Deauville draw the most chic Europeans and North Americans. Not far from the banks of the Seine you come upon a tiny hamlet where Monet painted his water lilies. Transatlantic liners pull into Le Havre, the fishermen's nets are set off by a background of cliffs, and yachts clog the harbor. Normandy, like Brittany, seems to look toward the sea. Or so you think until you venture into its heartland and glimpse lush pastures and fragrant apple orchards.

SEEING NORMANDY

Many visitors arrive from England. There are many sea connections, including from Portsmouth to Le Havre, Caen, or Cherbourg, or from Newhaven to Dieppe.

GETTING THERE There is air service from London to Caen, Cherbourg, Deauville, Le Havre, and Rouen.

There are direct rail connections from both Gare St-Lazare and Gare Montparnasse in Paris to all the main cities in Normandy.

If you want to "do" Normandy by bus, contact Bus Verts, 11, rue des Chanoines, 14000 Caen (tel. 31-44-77-44), for information.

A modern freeway links Paris to Rouen and Caen.

WHAT'S SPECIAL ABOUT NORMANDY

Beaches

☐ Corniche Normande, a nine-mile coastline of Normandy's grandest beach resorts: Deauville, Trouville, and Honfleur, with sandy beaches, gambling, the works.

☐ D-Day beaches, where Allied troops landed on June 6, 1944—all the legendary names are here: Omaha, Utah, and Juno.

☐ Côte Fleurie, a 12-mile stretch of sandy beach from Deauville–Trouville to Cabourg of Marcel Proust fame.

☐ Dieppe, the oldest French seaside resort; it's the beach closest to Paris.

Great Towns/Villages

☐ Bayeux, for a glimpse of Queen Mathilda's tapestry.

☐ Rouen, capital of Upper Normandy, forever associated with Joan of Arc's burning at the stake.

Ancient Monuments

☐ Mont St-Michel, "wonder of the Western world," the great abbey and No. 1 attraction of Normandy.

☐ Cathédrale de Rouen, a stunning example of French Gothic architecture.

☐ Cathédrale de Bayeux, called "the Reims of Normandy."

Architectural Highlights

☐ Abbaye aux Hommes (in Caen), built in Norman Romanesque style, site of William the Conqueror's tomb.

☐ Jumièges, on the lower Seine, "one of the greatest ruins in France."

Events/Festivals

☐ Grande Fête Normande (Festival of Normandy), Etretat (Ascension weekend).

☐ Fête de Jeanne d'Arc (Joan of Arc Festival), Rouen (Sunday nearest May 30).

A SUGGESTED ROUTE   Here's Normandy in a nutshell: On your first day, head for Rouen and spend the day exploring its old town and Rouen Cathedral. On your second day, go to Caen, William the Conqueror's seat of government. Stay overnight in Caen or in Bayeux, where you can see its cathedral and the Bayeux tapestry. On your third day (based in either Caen or Bayeux), explore the D-Day beaches. On your fourth day, continue west toward Mont-St-Michel, an ancient abbey and one of the premier attractions of Europe.

1. ROUEN

84 miles NW of Paris, 55 E of Le Havre

GETTING THERE   By Train   From Paris (Gare St-Lazare), trains leave for Rouen about once every hour; the ride takes an hour and 10 minutes.

ESSENTIALS   Orientation   The Seine River, as in Paris, splits Rouen into a Rive Gauche (Left Bank) and Rive Droite (Right Bank). The old city is on the right bank.

Information   The Office de Tourisme is located at 25, place de la Cathédrale (tel. 35-71-41-77).

"We've got one of the greatest cathedrals in Europe, many attractions," the woman at the Tourist Office laments, "but always, always, they want to know where *she* was burned alive." *She* is Joan of Arc, and she died "on the Place du Vieux-Marché," answers the woman automatically.

The capital of Normandy, Rouen is the second most important tourist center in the north of France. It is also a hub of industry and commerce, the third-largest port in France. Victor Hugo called it "the city of a hundred spires." Half of it was destroyed in World War II, mostly by Allied bombers, and many Rouennais were killed. In the reconstruction of the old quarters some of the almost forgotten crafts of the Middle Ages were revived.

On the Seine, 84 miles northwest of Paris, the city of Rouen is a good center for exploring much of Normandy. It is rich in historical associations: William the Conqueror died here in 1087, Joan of Arc in 1431.

WHAT TO SEE & DO

This city has its share of formidable attractions beginning with Rouen Cathedral, in French called ✪ **Cathédrale Notre-Dame,** place de la Cathédrale. Most of the world knows Rouen's cathedral, immortalized by Monet in an impressionistic series of paintings depicting the three-portal main front with its galaxy of statues.

The present cathedral, a symphony of lace-like stonework, was reconstructed in part after the bombings of World War II. Consecrated in 1063, it was rebuilt after the "great fire" of 1200, the work lasting for centuries. Two soaring towers distinguish it; one, the **Tour de Beurre** (Tower of Butter), was financed by the faithful willing to pay good money in exchange for the privilege of eating butter at Lent. The tower is a masterpiece of the flamboyant Gothic style. Containing a carillon of 56 bells, a three-story lantern tower—built in 1877 and utilizing 740 tons of iron and bronze—rises to a height of almost 500 feet.

Especially interesting in the interior, the **Chapelle de la Vierge** is adorned with the Renaissance tombs of the cardinals d'Amboise as well as Jean de Brézé. Also entombed inside was the "lion" heart of Richard the Lion-Hearted, a token of his affection for the people of Rouen.

The cathedral is open daily but closed Monday through Saturday from noon to 2pm and on Sunday from 1 to 3pm. No admission is charged.

Behind the cathedral, the **Archbishop's Palace** was bombed during the war. Now it stands naked against the sky. The broken arches and rosette windows witnessed the trial of Joan of Arc in 1431. At this same spot her rehabilitation was proclaimed in 1456.

To and Through the Place du Vieux-Marché

A lane running between the cathedral and Place du Vieux-Marché is called **rue du Gros-Horloge** (Street of the Great Clock). Now a traffic-free pedestrian mall, it is named for an ornate gilt Renaissance clock mounted on an arch, Rouen's most popular monument. The arch bridges the street and is connected to a Louis XV sculpted fountain with a bevy of cherubs and a belltower. At night the bells still toll a curfew. Visitors who purchase a ticket at the Beaux-Arts (see below) are entitled to visit the belfry to see the iron clockworks and the bells. It's open Easter through mid-September, daily on Wednesday from 2 to 6pm and Thursday through Monday from 10am to noon and 2 to 6pm.

Of course you'll want to visit **Place du Vieux-Marché** (Old Marketplace), marking "the final abode" of Joan of Arc. Tied to a stake, she was burned alive on a pyre set by the English on May 30, 1431. Kissing a cross while she was being chained, she is reported to have called out "Jesus!" as the fire was set. Afterward her ashes were gathered up and tossed into the Seine.

In the center of a monumental complex in the square is a modern church displaying stained-glass windows from St. Vincent. Beside it a bronze cross marks the position of St. Joan's stake.

Nearby at 15 Place de la Pucelle (Square of the Maid), stands the **Hôtel de Bourgtheroulde** (tel. 35-08-64-00), which is Gothic inspired, although it shows traces of the beginning of the Renaissance. It dates from the 16th century and was

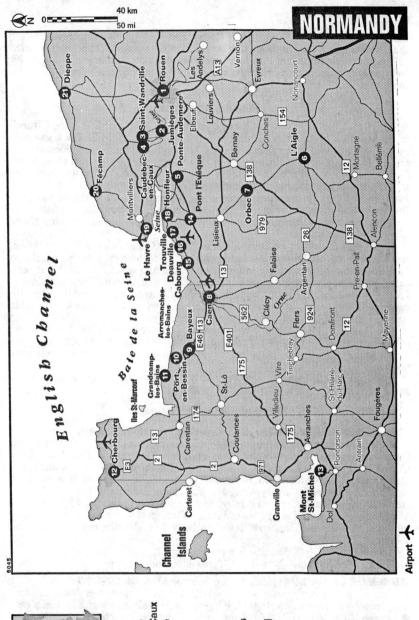

NORMANDY

0 — 40 km
0 — 50 mi

N

English Channel

Baie de la Seine

Dieppe **21**

Fécamp **20**

Le Havre **19** ✈
Montivilliers

Saint-Wandrille
Rouen **1**
Les Andelys
Vernon
A13
Louviers
Evreux
Nonancourt

4 3 Caudebec-en-Caux
2 Jumièges
Elbeuf
Seine
5 Pont-Audemere
Bernay
Conches
L'Aigle **6**
154

Honfleur **18**
Pont l'Evêque **14**
Orbec **7**
138
Mortagne
Bellême
12

Trouville **17** ✈
Deauville **16**
Cabourg **15**
Lisieux
979
Alençon
138

Falaise
26
Argentan
Pre-en-Pail
Mayenne

Arromanches-les-Bains
13
Ciécy
Orme
562
Flers
924
Domfront
12

Iles St-Marcouf
Grandcamp-les-Bains
Port-en-Bessin **11**
Bayeux **9**
10 E46 13
Caen **8**
E401
St-Lô
175
Villedieu
Vire
Tinchebray
St-Hilaire-du-Harc
Fougères

Cherbourg **12**
E3
2
174
Carentan
Coutances
Avranches
Pontorson
Antrain

Carteret
2
175
Granville
971
Mont St-Michel **13**
Dol

Channel Islands

Airport ✈

8045

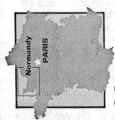

Normandy
PARIS

1 Rouen
2 Jumièges
3 Saint-Wandrille
4 Caudebec-en-Caux
5 Pont-Audemere
6 L'Aigle
7 Orbec
8 Caen
9 Bayeux
10 Port-en-Bessin
11 D-Day Beaches
12 Cherbourg
13 Mont St-Michel
14 Pont l'Evêque
15 Cabourg
16 Deauville
17 Trouville
18 Honfleur
19 Le Havre
20 Fécamp
21 Dieppe

built by William the Red (Guillaume le Roux). The inside yard is exceptional. Once in the courtyard, look back at the Gothic building with its octagonal stair tower. The left gallery is entirely Renaissance. A bank uses the hôtel now, and access is free during working hours. On Saturday and Sunday you can visit by ringing a bell and asking for the porter.

More Churches

Besides the cathedral, two other Rouen churches seek attention. One is the **Church of St-Maclou,** behind the cathedral, at 3, rue Dutuit (tel. 35-71-71-72). It was built in the florid Gothic style, with a step-gabled porch and handsome cloisters. It is known for the remarkable panels on its doors, dating from the 16th century; my favorite (to the left) is the "Portal of the Fonts." The church was originally constructed in 1200, rebuilt in 1432, and finally consecrated in 1521, although its lantern tower is from the 19th century. It sits on a square of old Norman crooked-timbered buildings. Inside, pictures dating from June 4, 1944, document St-Maclou's destruction.

The Church of St-Maclou is open daily from 10am to noon and 2 to 6pm; closed May 1 and July 14.

If you walk from rue de la République to Place du Général-de-Gaulle, you'll be at the **Church of St-Ouen,** the outgrowth of a 7th-century Benedictine abbey. Flanked by four turrets, its 375-foot octagonal lantern tower, in the Gothic style, is called "the ducal crown of Normandy." One of the best-known Gothic buildings in France, the present church represents the work of five centuries. Its nave is of the 15th century, its choir from the 14th (but with 18th-century railings), and its remarkable stained glass from the 14th through the 16th centuries.

On May 23, 1431, Joan of Arc was taken to the cemetery of St. Ouen, where officials sentenced her to be burnt at the stake unless she recanted. An abjuration was signed by her, thus condemning her to life imprisonment; that sentence was later revoked.

The Church of St-Ouen is open Wednesday through Monday from 10am to noon and 2 to 5pm; closed from November 1 to March 15.

The Museums of Rouen

MUSEE DES BEAUX-ARTS, place Verdel. Tel. 35-71-28-40.
This is one of the most important provincial museums in France, with portraits by David, plus works by Delacroix and Ingres (don't miss his *La Belle Zélie*). A retable by Gérard David, called *La Vierge et les Saints (The Virgin and the Saints),* is a masterpiece. One whole salon is devoted to Géricault, including a portrait of Delacroix. Other works are by Veronese, Velásquez, Caravaggio, Rubens, Poussin, Fragonard, Ingres, and Corot. There is a large collection of paintings by Sisley and Monet, including a version of Monet's *Rouen Cathedral*—one of his most famous studies. There are also important paintings by Dufy and sculptures by Duchamp-Villon.

Admission: 11 F ($2) adults, free for children.
Open: Wed 2–6pm, Thurs–Mon 10am–noon and 2–6pm.

MUSEE DE LA CERAMIQUE, 1, rue Faucon. Tel. 36-07-31-74.
One of the greatest treasures in this 17th-century house is the Rouen faïence, which pioneered a special red in 1670. The exhibits provide a showcase for the talents of Masseot Abaquesne (1500–64), considered the premier French artist in faïence. In time, his position was usurped by Louis Poterat (1673–96). As well, an exceptional showcase is devoted to chinoiseries dating from 1699 to 1745.

Admission: 11 F ($2) adults, free for children.
Open: Wed 2–6pm, Thurs–Mon 10am–noon and 2–6pm.

LE SECQ DES TOURNELLES, rue Jacques-Villon. Tel. 35-08-81-81.
The Wrought Ironworks Museum is housed in the 15th-century Church of St-Laurent. Its collection ranges from what the press once called "forthright masculine forging to lacy feminine filigree, from Roman keys to the needlepoint balustrade that graced Mme de Pompadour's country mansion." An aristocrat in

ROUEN

0 ⌐ 150 m
N ⌐ 165 y

↑ rue Thiers   ↑ To Gare Rive-Droite   ④ To Musée d' Antiquités

rue Gauchoise   rue des Bon-Enfants   rue Thiers   ⑤   ⑥

↑ To Musée Flaubert

rue Guil.-le-Conquérant   rue Ganterie   rue Beauvoisine   rue Louis Ricard

place du Vieux-Marché   rue Rollon   rue Socrate   rue de l'Hôpital   place du Général-de-Gaulle

①   rue St-Lô   LE VIEUX   rue de Chaine   ⑧

②   rue aux Juifs   ROUEN

③   rue du Gros-Horloge   rue des Carmes   rue St-Nicholas   rue d'Amiens

rue du Gén. Giraud   rue aux Ours   rue Jeanne d'Arc   Champmeslé   rue St-Romain   rue de Damiette   ⑨ rue Martainville

Bus Station   ⓘ place de la Cathédrale   ⑩

quai du Havre   rue du Change   rue du Gén. Leclerc   rue de la République

Seine   ↓ To Gare Rive Gauche & Airport   ✝ ⑦

Church ■✝

Post Office ✉

Information ⓘ

↗ To Gard du Nord

Aître St-Maclou ⑨
Cathédrale Notre-Dame ⑦
Eglise St-Maclou ⑩
Eglise St-Ouen ⑧
Hôtel de Bourgtheroulde ②

Musée des Beaux-Arts ⑤
Musée de la Céramique ④
Musée Jeanne-d'Arc ①
Musée le Secq des Tournelles ⑥
Tour du Gros-Horloge ③

● Rouen
★ PARIS

Paris, Le Secq des Tournelles began the collection in 1870. So passionately was he devoted to it that his wife divorced him, charging alienation of affection. Donated to the city of Rouen, the collection now has as many as 14,000 pieces, including kitchen utensils, jewelry, scissors, and a gate.

Admission: 11 F ($2) adults, free for children.
Open: Wed 2–6pm, Thurs–Mon 10am–noon and 2–6pm.

MUSEE FLAUBERT ET D'HISTOIRE DE LA MEDECINE, Hôtel-Dieu, 51, rue de Lecat. Tel. 35-15-59-95.

Gustave Flaubert, author of *Madame Bovary,* was born here, in the director's quarters of Rouen's public hospital (his father was the director). Flaubert spent the first 25 years of his life in the city, and the bedroom where he was born in 1821 is still intact. In addition, family furniture and medical paraphernalia are displayed. Only a glass door separated the Flaubert family from the ward filled with moaning patients. Contiguous to the family's billiard room was the dissection ward, where Flaubert would go to peek at the corpses.

Admission: Free.
Open: Tues–Sat 10am–noon and 2–6pm. **Closed:** Holidays.

FLAUBERT PAVILION, Croisset. Tel. 35-36-43-91.

Flaubert fans may want to visit the author's family home in this industrial suburb of Rouen. Flaubert wrote *Madame Bovary* and *Salammbô* here.

Admission: 6 F ($1.10), free Sun and holidays.
Open: Wed 2–6pm, Thurs–Mon 10am–noon and 2–6pm.

MUSEE JEANNE-D'ARC, 33, place du Vieux-Marché. Tel. 35-88-02-70.

The life and tragic martyrdom of Joan of Arc, France's national heroine, are traced at this museum, located on the old market square where Joan was burned to death in 1431. In a vaulted cellar are waxworks depicting the main stages of her life from Domrémy, where she was born, to the stake, where she died.

Admission: 22 F ($4) adults, 12 F ($2.20) children.

Open: May–Oct, daily 9:30am–6:30pm; Nov–Apr, Tues–Sun 10am–noon and 2–6pm.

WHERE TO STAY

Finding a room in Rouen can be a bit tricky if you don't have a reservation: In summer, tourists fill the limited accommodations; during the rest of the year, business travelers often book the hotels.

Expensive

MERCURE CENTRE, rue Croix-de-Fer, 76000 Rouen. Tel. 35-52-69-52.
Fax 35-89-41-46. 121 rms (all with bath), 4 suites. A/C MINIBAR TV TEL **Bus:** 1, 3, 5, 7, or 10.

$ Rates: Sun–Thurs, 510 F ($91.80) single or double; Fri–Sat, 430 F ($77.40) single or double. Suites from 1,100 F ($198). Breakfast 55 F ($9.90) extra. AE, DC, MC, V. **Parking:** 40 F ($7.20).

Modern, unpretentious, and well located in the heart of Rouen, this is a good choice for value and modern comfort. Originally built in a four-floor design in 1976, it was bought by the nationwide Mercure chain in 1992. The location is unbeatable—right at the cathedral of Rouen and rue du Gros-Horloge. Rooms, efficiently furnished in a contemporary functional design, are clean and well maintained. There's a bar on the premises, but breakfast is the only meal served.

Moderate

HOTEL DE DIEPPE, place Bernard-Tissot, 76000 Rouen. Tel. 35-71-96-00, or toll free 800/528-1234 in the U.S. and Canada. 42 rms (all with bath). TV TEL **Bus:** 1, 3, 5, 7, or 10.

IN THEIR FOOTSTEPS

Gustave Flaubert (1821–80) Not as prodigious as Balzac, Flaubert wrote with infinitely more care, searching obsessively for *le mot juste* and laboring over the construction, balance, emotional precision, temporal specificity, and sonority of each sentence. He is best known for his immortal heroine, Madame Bovary, a woman trapped in a boring marriage within a stifling provincial society. When asked, at the end of his life, the name of the woman upon whom he modeled Emma Bovary, he responded, *"Madame Bovary, c'est moi!"* (I myself am Madame Bovary!).

• **Birthplace:** Rouen, Normandy, on December 12, 1821, at Hôtel-Dieu, 51, rue de Lecat, where a museum today commemorates his achievements. He was the son of a surgeon and clinical professor, and doctor's daughter.

• **Residences:** In Paris, he lived at 42, bd. du Temple. After 1846 he spent most of his life in Normandy, at Croisset, but only the 18th-century pavilion in which he used to write remains. His library has been preserved in the Mairie at Canteleu-Croisset.

• **Favorite Haunts:** The Breton town of Brest, where he described the bordello district and prison in *Par les champs et par les greves* (1886). In the Massif Central, he was entertained by George Sand at the 18th-century mansion le Château de Nohant. The village of Ry (Eure) was the Yonville-l'Abbaye of *Madame Bovary*, and the Hôtel de Rouen is still there.

• **Resting Place:** Croisset, Normandy. The novelist died suddenly on May 8, 1880, of a stroke, leaving on his table an unfinished page of manuscript. He is buried in the cemetery at Croisset.

$ Rates: 415–485 F ($74.70–$87.30) single; 475–585 F ($85.50–$105.30) double. Breakfast 40 F ($7.20) extra. AE, DC, MC, V. **Parking:** Free.

This hotel has been run by the Gueret family since 1880, and each generation has modernized the premises somewhat. However, this still remains a traditional French inn, located across from the train station. The rooms are decorated in either period or contemporary styling. In the adjoining rôtisserie, Le Quatre Saisons, you can select a fixed-price menu for 135 F ($24.30) or order such à la carte specialties as duckling à la presse and sole poached in red wine.

HOTEL DU GROS-HORLOGE, 91, rue du Gros-Horloge, 76000 Rouen. **Tel. 35-70-41-41.** Fax 35-88-44-45. 62 rms (all with bath). TV TEL **Bus:** 1, 3, 5, 7, or 10.

$ Rates: 265–295 F ($47.70–$53.10) single; 300–340 F ($54–$61.20) double. Breakfast 35 F ($6.30) extra. MC, V. **Parking:** 20 F ($3.60).

I'd rank this hotel no. 5 in Rouen, but it's not nearly as expensive as the frontrunners. The four-story, two-star hotel, with rustic and traditionally furnished rooms, is located in the center of the town's commercial district. Breakfast is the only meal served.

Inexpensive

HOTEL DE LA CATHEDRALE, 12, rue St-Romain, 76000 Rouen. Tel. **35-71-57-95.** 24 rms (all with bath or shower). TV TEL **Bus:** 1, 3, 5, 7, or 10.

$ Rates: 225–310 F ($40.50–$55.80) single; 275–365 F ($49.50–$65.70) double. Breakfast 32 F ($5.80) extra. MC, V. **Parking:** 30 F ($5.40).

Staying here is like staying in a private home. The bedrooms are clean and simply furnished. The location is choice—behind the cathedral and opposite the Archbishop's Palace, where Joan of Arc was tried. The hotel's street has been restored and now has the original black-and-white timbered facades.

HOTEL DE QUEBEC, 18–24, rue de Québec, 76000 Rouen. Tel. 35-70- **09-38.** 38 rms (30 with bath). TV TEL **Bus:** 1, 3, 5, 7, or 10.

$ Rates: 160 F ($28.80) single without bath; 285–300 F ($51.30–$54) double with bath. AE, MC, V. **Parking:** Free.

This modern, brick corner hotel is well run and is a block from the Seine, within walking distance of the cathedral and some of the city's best restaurants. The bedrooms are small but serviceable, and many open onto a rear courtyard where parking is available.

HOTEL LE CARDINAL, 1, place de la Cathédrale, 76000 Rouen. Tel. **35-70-24-42.** Fax 35-89-75-14. 22 rms (all with bath). TV TEL **Bus:** 1, 3, 5, 7, or 10.

$ Rates: 230–330 F ($41.40–$59.40) single; 255–355 F ($45.90–$63.90) double. Breakfast 34 F ($6.10) extra. MC, V. **Parking:** 28 F ($5).

Madame Picard rents rooms in the best location in the city for those who want a view of the cathedral—as Monet did. Reconstructed after World War II damage, the Cardinal is modest in its appointments, but it's clean and well run.

HOTEL LE VIKING, 21, quai du Havre, 76000 Rouen. Tel. 35-70-34-95. Fax 35-89-91-12. 38 rms (all with bath or shower). TV TEL **Bus:** 1, 3, 5, 7, or 10.

$ Rates: 195–300 F ($35.10–$54) single; 255–320 F ($45.90–$57.60) double. Breakfast 32 F ($5.80) extra. MC, V. **Parking:** 45 F ($8.10).

Located on the riverbank overlooking the Seine, this hotel has charming views from its front rooms, although the noise of traffic can be bad at times. In July and August you should reserve at least two weeks in advance. Breakfast is the only meal served.

LA VIEILLE-TOUR, place de la Haute-Vieille-Tour, 76000 Rouen. Tel. **35-70-03-27.** 23 rms (16 with bath or shower). TV TEL **Bus:** 1, 3, 5, 7, or 10.

$ Rates: 160 F ($28.80) single or double without bath; 215 F–260 F ($38.70–$46.80) single with bath or shower; 250 F–290 F ($45–$52.20) double with bath or shower. Breakfast 25 F ($4.50) extra. AE, DC, MC, V. **Parking:** 30 F ($5.40).

This small, modern hotel is a block from the Seine, within walking distance of the cathedral. In fact, you'll often hear the chimes from your bedroom window. The lobby is tiny, the breakfast lounge small. But many of the bedrooms are spacious, some with two double beds. Furnishings are contemporary. The most desirable accommodations face the square. Breakfast consists of coffee and croissants with jam and Normandy butter.

WHERE TO DINE
Expensive

LE BEFFROY, 15, rue Beffroy. Tel. 35-71-55-27.
　Cuisine: FRENCH. **Reservations:** Required. **Bus:** 1, 3, 5, 7, or 10.
$ Prices: Appetizers 105–155 F ($18.90–$27.90); main dishes 125–230 F ($22.50–$41.40); fixed-price meals 155 F ($27.90) at lunch, 180–275 F ($32.40–$49.50) at dinner. AE, MC, V.
　Open: Lunch Tues–Sat noon–2pm; dinner Tues–Sat 7:30–9:15pm.
Run by Mr. and Mrs. Engel and their daughter, Carole, this restaurant's cuisine depends on the market availability of ingredients. Well-prepared specialties include versions of cassolette of snails with burgundy, aiguillettes of duckling rouennais, poached oysters with scallops, and fish salad. The wine list is thoughtfully chosen. The setting itself—an old Norman-style house with time-blackened timbers and a stone fireplace—is part of the allure.

LA COURONNE, 31, place du Vieux-Marché. Tel. 35-71-40-90.
　Cuisine: FRENCH. **Reservations:** Required. **Bus:** 2, 5, 6, 10, or 12.
$ Prices: Appetizers 95–150 F ($17.10–$27); main dishes 105–180 F ($18.90–$32.40); fixed-price menus 150 F ($27), 195 F ($35.10), and 270 F ($48.60); fixed-price lunch (main course and dessert) 130 F ($23.40). AE, DC, MC, V.
　Open: Lunch daily noon–2:30pm; dinner daily 7:30–10:30pm.
Not only is this the oldest restaurant in Rouen, dating from 1345, but also it claims to be the oldest inn in France. Housed in a half-timbered building that looks like a setting for *Hansel and Gretel*, it stands directly on the square where Joan of Arc was burned at the stake. During World War II, a 500-pound bomb exploded in its rear courtyard, but, amazingly, its wooden pegs held La Couronne together.

IN THEIR FOOTSTEPS

Joan of Arc (1412?–31) Jeanne d'Arc was a religious and military leader of France. Her success is so unusual, so against the grain of the sexual, military, and religious standards of the 15th century, that her most devoted admirers cite divine intervention as its cause. She persuaded the weak and indecisive dauphin to place her at the head of his armies, and she defeated the English and began to drive them out of Aquitaine and Calais.
　• **Birthplace:** Domrémy in Lorraine, January 6, 1412 [?], to a lowly family. When she was 16, she heard "voices," which she claimed came from a congregation of saints, telling her to rid France of the English and place Dauphin Charles VII on the throne.
　• **Favorite Haunts:** Many sites are associated with her, including Chinon in the Loire Valley, where she first appeared before the dauphin; Orléans, which she entered in triumph with the French army; and Reims, where she had the dauphin crowned King of France.
　• **Resting Place:** Captured by the English, tortured, starved, and forced to recant her story of her "visions" and "voices," she later revoked her recantation and was burned at the stake on May 30, 1431, at place du Vieux-Marché in Rouen. She was beatified in Rome in 1909 and canonized in 1920.

The dining rooms, on several floors, are reached by wooden stairs leading around the fireplaces. La Couronne has won fame for its caneton (duckling) rouennais, and the seafood couldn't be fresher. Other specialties are fresh filet of sole cardinal (with lobster and lobster sauce), sautéed veal kidneys flambéed with cognac, and soufflé normand with Calvados.

GILL, 9, quai de la Bourse. Tel. 35-71-16-14.
   Cuisine: FRENCH. **Reservations:** Recommended. **Bus:** 1, 3, 5, 7, or 10.
$ **Prices:** Appetizers 80–150 F ($14.40–$27); main dishes 128–150 F ($23–$27); fixed-price meals 185–350 F ($33.30–$63). AE, DC, MC, V.
   Open: Lunch Tues–Sat noon–2:15pm; dinner Tues–Sat 7–9:45pm. **Closed:** Winter Sun lunch.

⭐ One of the city's most talked-about upper-bracket restaurants is in a building reerected after the bombings of World War II, beside the roaring traffic of the quais of the Seine. Inside, a calm and uncluttered modern decor of off-white walls and hi-tech accessories is an appropriate foil for the sophisticated cuisine of Gilles Tournadre. Known for their subtlety, the dishes change with the season, but might include a ravioli of crayfish or chutney-roasted crayfish with red peppers, turbot roasted with a fondue of endive, sliced duck liver with leeks, a mixed platter of assorted fish, and a North Atlantic lobster stew. Dessert might include a millefeuille nature, one of France's most prevalent many-layered pastries, but which in the hands of Mr. Tournadre becomes an elegant art form.

Moderate

AU BOIS CHENU, 23, place Pucelle-d'Orléans. Tel. 35-71-19-54.
   Cuisine: FRENCH. **Reservations:** Not required. **Bus:** 1, 3, 5, 7, or 10.
$ **Prices:** Fixed-price menus 98–150 F ($17.60–$27). AE, DC, MC, V.
   Open: Lunch Thurs–Mon noon–2:15pm; dinner Thurs–Mon 7–10pm. **Closed:** Sept 1–15.
This well-managed restaurant, not far from rue du Gros-Horloge, near the market, raised many local eyebrows and received much praise within the city for a tasteful but sweeping interior renovation which was completed in 1992. Today, amid yellow- and blue-lacquered walls, and solid mahogany chairs, you can enjoy specialties that include salmon in a beurre-blanc sauce, white brill flavored with mustard, roasted veal kidneys, and, in season, roast pheasant flavored with Calvados. For dessert, you'll be tempted by a plate of Normandy cheese or a tart made with the fruit of the season, perhaps strawberries. Only fixed-price menus are offered.

MAISON DUFOUR, 67, rue St-Nicholas. Tel. 35-71-90-62.
   Cuisine: FRENCH. **Reservations:** Required. **Bus:** 1, 3, 5, 7, or 10.
$ **Prices:** Appetizers 40–120 F ($7.20–$21.60); main dishes 50–180 F ($9–$32.40); fixed-price menus 160–240 F ($28.80–$43.20). AE, V.
   Open: Lunch Tues–Sun noon–2pm; dinner Tues–Sat 7–9:30pm. **Closed:** Aug 2–23.
One of the best-preserved 17th-century inns of Normandy, this five-story corner building was built in the Norman style. Inside, there are several dining rooms with a colorful atmosphere: copper pans and pots, spices, wood carvings, and engravings.
   The dishes, prepared and served under the eagle eye of the Dufour family, are so outstanding that it's difficult to single out specialties. Many are based on classic recipes; others are from the *cuisine moderne* repertoire. A kettle of black mussels in a creamy sauce is a reliable opener. You might also enjoy chicken from the Auge Valley, brains in a black-butter sauce, or lamb in a garlic-cream sauce.

Inexpensive

BRASSERIE DE LA GRANDE POSTE, 43, rue Jeanne-d'Arc. Tel. 35-70-08-70.
   Cuisine: FRENCH. **Reservations:** Not required. **Bus:** 1, 3, 5, 7, or 10.
$ **Prices:** Appetizers 15–30 F ($2.70–$5.40); main dishes 30–70 F ($5.40–$12.60); fixed-price meals 58 F ($10.40) (available only weekdays at lunchtime) and 85 F ($15.30). MC, V.

Open: Daily 11:15am–11:30pm.

Popular, crowded, and with an enviable turn-of-the-century decor that has changed very little since the place was established in the 1880s, this restaurant is one of the most reliable and time-tested brasseries in Rouen. Rising from a medieval street across from the Palais de Justice, it offers a tiny front terrace (suitable really only for drinks) and a large interior staffed by a corps of veteran waiters. Menu items include the full roster of brasserie-style dishes, such as hard-boiled eggs with mayonnaise, grilled meats (included steak au poivre), filets of sole meunière, and entrecôte with french fries. An unpretentious wine list is reasonably priced.

PASCALINE, 5, rue de la Poterne. Tel. 35-89-67-44.
   Cuisine: FRENCH. **Reservations:** Recommended. **Bus:** 1, 3, 5, 7, or 10.
$ **Prices:** Appetizers 28.50–40 F ($5.10–$7.20); main dishes 48–75 F ($8.60–$13.50); fixed-price menus 95–120 F ($17.10–$21.60). V.
   Open: Lunch daily noon–2:30pm; dinner daily 7:30–11:30pm.

The cheapest fixed-price menu here seems to be the best bargain in town. This informal bistro has a turn-of-the-century decor and is often filled with those who make this a regular rendezvous. The à la carte menu offers fresh seafood, tenderloin steaks, and sauerkraut Alsatian style. Desserts are an ice-cream-lover's delight.

NEARBY ACCOMMODATIONS & DINING

Motorists who prefer not to cope with the streets of Rouen might want to stay at the following hotel:

NOVOTEL ROUEN-SUD, Le Madrillet, 76800 Saint-Etienne-du-Rouvray.
   Tel. 35-66-58-50. Fax 35-66-15-56. 134 rms (all with bath). A/C MINIBAR TV TEL
$ **Rates:** 440 F ($79.20) single; 490 F ($88.20) double. Breakfast 50 F ($9) extra. Children under 16 stay free in parents' room. AE, DC, MC, V. **Parking:** Free.
Located about four miles south along the N138, facing the Parc des Expositions, is this hotel, designed for ease of accessibility and businesslike convenience. There are two tennis courts, an outdoor pool, a bar that serves exotic drinks, and a modern grill that's open from 6am to midnight. You wheel your own luggage to one of the comfortable bedrooms—each with one single bed, one double bed, and a desk.

2. JUMIEGES

102 miles NW of Paris, 17 miles W of Rouen

GETTING THERE A bus goes to Jumièges once a day from Rouen, but there's no train service.

ESSENTIALS The abbey lies 2½ miles off the D982.

Called one of the most beautiful ruins in France, the **Abbaye de Jumièges,** Le Bourg, 76480 Duclair (tel. 35-37-24-02), was founded by St. Philbert in the 7th century and rebuilt in the 10th century by Duke Guillaume ("Long Sword"). The abbey church was consecrated in 1067 by the archbishop of Rouen in the presence of William the Conqueror.

One of the architectural wonders of Normandy, the abbey was seized by the state during the French Revolution. It was later sold to a wood merchant and subsequently vandalized. Salvaged finally in the mid-1800s, it has been turned over to the state. The 100-foot-high nave is complete, and the porch is surrounded by two towers 150 feet high.

From April through the end of September, it's open daily from 9am to 6:30pm; off-season, daily from 10am to noon and 2 to 4pm. Admission is 24 F ($4.30) for adults, 5 F (90¢) for children under 18.

3. SAINT-WANDRILLE

108 miles NW of Paris; 33 miles NW of Rouen

GETTING THERE By Bus There's daily bus service from Rouen.

By Car Drive 6½ miles from Jumièges, along the D982.

The **Abbey of Saint-Wandrille**, 76490 Saint-Wandrille (tel. 35-96-23-11), was founded in 649 by Wandrille, an official of the court of King Dagobert. Wandrille was called an "athlete of God" because of his great spiritual training and influence. Over the centuries the buildings have suffered from fire, thunder, and lightning, as well as attacks by Vikings, and nothing remains of the original 7th-century monastery. Monks have lived in the abbey since 649 (except for 100 years or so because of French political troubles).

A huge blue gate from the 18th century frames the entrance to the monastery. Inside the great courtyard you can see a building that houses a factory in which household products, such as wax and polish, are manufactured to help the community make a living. The microfilm workroom and several workshops are next to the factory.

The cloisters are from the 14th to the 16th century. In the north gallery is a beautiful and unique lavabo (wash basin) from about 1500. A 14th-century barn, originally located 30 miles from the abbey, was transplanted in 1967–69 as the abbey church.

A guided tour is given Monday through Saturday at 3 and at 4pm (on Sunday and holidays also at 11:30am). Admission is 20 F ($3.60) for adults, free for children. Products made by the monks are on sale.

WHERE TO DINE

AUBERGE DEUX-COURONNES, 76490 Saint-Wandrille-Rancon. Tel. 35-96-11-44.
  Cuisine: FRENCH. **Reservations:** Required.
$ **Prices:** Appetizers 30–95 F ($5.40–$17.10); main dishes 35–180 F ($6.30–$32.40); fixed-price menus 120–145 F ($21.60–$26.10). AE, MC, V.
  Open: Lunch Tues–Sun noon–2pm; dinner Tues–Sat 7–9pm. **Closed:** Last two weeks of Sept.

This 17th-century Norman inn is a good choice for lunch or dinner. It has all the ceiling beams and rich patina you'd expect from such a mellow old place, along with a fireplace. A leg of lamb or a sirloin steak can be grilled to your taste by the chef himself. This gem of a restaurant is beautifully run, and chef Jacques Grangier and his son, François, prepare all their Norman specialties well, a cuisine using butter, cream, cheese, and cider. There are other standard French dishes as well. I recommend escalope of veal Vallé d'Auge with a cream sauce, roast guinea fowl with apples, and, for dessert, crêpes normandes flambéed with Calvados at your table. In addition to good food, the service is efficient.

4. CAUDEBEC-EN-CAUX

103 miles NW of Paris; 22 miles NW of Rouen

GETTING THERE By Bus Take the 191/192 bus line from Rouen.

Set in an amphitheater on the banks of the Seine, this charming town was nearly destroyed in World War II. At the end of the Ste-Gertrude Valley, it is the scene of the "Mascaret," which is a tidal wave occurring in the estuary of the Seine at the time of the fall and spring equinoxes.

WHAT TO SEE & DO

Its Gothic **Church of Notre-Dame,** which dates from the early 15th century, was saved from the 1940 fires. Henri IV considered it the handsomest chapel in his kingdom. Restoration work in the 16th century was carried out by Guillaume Le Tellier. On the west side is a trio of flamboyant doorways, topped by a rose window.

Although damaged in the war, the **Maison des Templiers,** rue de la Boucherie (tel. 35-56-96-06), has been restored and proves to be an outstanding example of secular architecture from the 13th century. Paintings and carvings can be seen on the ground floor. The interesting carvings on the first floor, from the time of the Templars, show monks' faces and animals. The attraction is open June through September, daily from 3 to 7pm; in April and May, only on Saturday and Sunday from 3 to 7pm. Admission is 15 F ($2.70).

WHERE TO STAY & DINE

Le Normandie, listed under "Where to Dine," below, also rents guest rooms.

MANOIR DE RETIVAL, 2, rue St-Clair, 76490 Caudebec-en-Caux. Tel. 35-96-11-22. Fax 35-96-29-22. 2 rms (both with bath). TV TEL
$ Rates: 600 F ($108) single or double. Breakfast 50 F ($9) extra. MC, V. **Closed:** Mon night.

Originally built late in the 18th century, and enlarged about 30 years later, this building originally functioned as a hunting lodge. Its site on a bluff overlooking the village of Caudebec-en-Caux was selected for its sweeping view up and down the valley of the Seine. Today, it functions as the finest restaurant in the neighborhood, attracting a clientele from as far away as Paris. On the premises are two exceptionally beautiful bedrooms, one furnished in the style of Louis XVI, the other in the Directoire style—but they are rented only to clients who opt to dine at the in-house restaurant.

Fixed-price menus cost 280–420 F ($50.40–$75.60); à la carte items cost 95–200 F ($17.10–$36) for appetizers and 120–200 F ($21.60–$36) for main courses. Menu items change with the season, but might include a risotto of lobster, bar croustillant avec crème fleurette à l'huile de Tandoori (a sophisticated preparation of a local whitefish), and a traditional Norman dish, Rouennais-style pigeon, served with a sauce bound together with blood, foie gras, and shallots. The restaurant is closed all day Monday and Tuesday at noon, and the hotel section is closed on Monday night.

WHERE TO DINE

LE NORMANDIE, 19, quai Guilbaud, 76490 Caudebec-en-Caux. Tel. 35-96-25-11. Fax 35-96-68-15.
Cuisine: FRENCH. **Reservations:** Recommended.
$ Prices: Fixed-price meals 60–169 F ($10.80–$30.40). AE, DC, MC, V.
Open: Lunch daily noon–2:30pm; dinner Mon–Sat 7–9:30pm. **Closed:** Feb.

At Le Normandie, owner Edith Gremond offers well-prepared cuisine in a setting overlooking the Seine. The chef presents such dishes as grilled fresh sardines, eggplant fritters, fried sand eels, and Norman chicken. Meals are reasonably priced considering the quality and the generous portions. The higher-priced meals may be more food than you'll be able to eat.

In addition, the owner of this *restaurant avec chambres* has enlarged the room capacity to 16, each with private bath or shower, TV, and telephone. The accommodations are adequate in comfort and cost from 196 F ($35.20) for a single and from 330 F ($59.40) for a double.

5. PONT-AUDEMER

105 miles NW of Paris, 30 miles SE of Le Havre, 23 miles NE of Lisieux

GETTING THERE By Bus There are SNCF bus connections from Le Havre.

ESSENTIALS Orientation The town lies among canal branches of the River Risle.

Information The Syndicat d'Initiative (tourist office) is on place Maubert (tel. 32-41-08-21).

The most historic streets are rue de la Licorne and rue de la République, off which lie a number of half-timbered buildings.

William the Conqueror's father used to storm through this historic town of markets and tanners, which today is a convenient stopover between Deauville and Rouen. A number of old houses still stand on **rue de la Licorne** (the Street of the Unicorn). A few visitors pass through to see the **Church of St-Ouen**, which dates from the 11th century and has a 1450 facade and Renaissance stained-glass windows. But the real reason foreigners head this way is to stay at a remarkable old Norman inn, called the Auberge du Vieux-Puits.

WHERE TO STAY

AUBERGE DU VIEUX-PUITS, 6, rue Notre-Dame-du-Pré, 27500 Pont-Audemer. Tel. 32-41-01-48. 12 rms (7 with bath or shower). TV TEL

$ Rates: 240–360 F ($43.20–$64.80) single with bath; 250–290 F ($45–$52.20) double without bath, 390 F ($70.20) double with bath. Breakfast 38 F ($6.80) extra. MC, V. **Parking:** Free. **Closed:** Dec 21–Jan 28.

"The Inn of the Old Well" is a 17th-century Norman inn decorated with beamed ceilings, half-timbered walls, country chairs, and wooden tables. The L-shaped building partially encloses an old garden. Copper and brass pots and pans hang from the beams, and a pewter collection is above the fireplace. The inn is owned by M and Mme Jacques Foltz. Bedrooms in the 17th-century part of the house are small but charmingly decorated. Other bedrooms, with more modern facilities, are larger and more comfortable and housed in a modern wing. They offer fixed-price meals for 175 F ($31.50) and 280 F ($50.40), including grilled andouillette of the sea with beurre blanc, roast pigeon, and roast lamb kidneys, topped by a Benedictine-flavored orange soufflé. Many diners, however, prefer to finish their meal with the three classic cheeses of Normandy: Camembert, Livarot, and Pont-l'Evêque. The local cider is also a treat. The restaurant is also closed Monday night and Tuesday.

LA RICARDIERE, B.P. 501, Tourville, 27500 Pont-Audemer. Tel. 32-41-09-14. 4 rms (all with bath).

$ Rates (including continental breakfast): 295–345 F ($53.10–$62.10) double. No credit cards. **Parking:** Free.

This inn offers one of the most charming accommodations in the area—an 18th-century house with four spacious double bedrooms to rent. The house lies off the D139 on the outskirts of town. In a secluded setting in the Norman countryside, this is a mother-daughter operation. The house is warmly furnished and decorated; the daughter's background as an artist is apparent. The mother once wrote a guidebook on the history of the area. Since this is a private home, you must telephone for a reservation in advance—never just arrive on the doorstep. Also, when your reservation is made, detailed directions about the route will be given to you.

6. L'AIGLE

86 miles W of Paris, 34 miles SE of Lisieux

GETTING THERE By Train   There are SNCF rail connections from Rouen.

ESSENTIALS Information   The Office de Tourisme is on place Fulbert-de-Beina (tel. 33-24-12-40).

A good base for touring the upper valley of the Risle, L'Aigle is the setting for **St. Martin's Church,** which has a 15th-century square tower and another smaller tower dating from the 12th century. In addition, it also has an interesting waxworks museum: the **Musée Juin 44: Bataille de Normandie,** 44, place Fulbert-de-Beina (tel. 33-24-19-44), which has a re-creation of some of the major personalities of the Battle of Normandy, including Churchill and Charles de Gaulle. Their voices, recorded at the time, can also be heard. The museum is open Easter to November 11, Tuesday through Sunday from 10am to noon and 2 to 6pm. Admission is 12 F ($2.10) for adults, 6.50 F ($1.10) for children.

L'Aigle is a metal-working center—a tradition dating from ancient times. Frankly, the town isn't a major sightseeing attraction. My main reason for recommending it is the Hôtel du Dauphin.

WHERE TO STAY

HOTEL DU DAUPHIN, place de la Halle, 61300 L'Aigle. Tel. 33-24-43-12. Fax 33-34-09-28. 30 rms (all with bath). MINIBAR TV TEL
$ Rates: 337–398 F ($60.60–$71.60) single; 398–490 F ($71.60–$88.20) double. Breakfast 38 F ($6.80) extra. AE, DC, MC, V. **Parking:** Free.

This place was originally constructed in the 1500s as an inn, and today its three-story premises sit beside one of the main squares of L'Aigle in the town center. The hotel has to have one of the most charmingly decorated interiors of any hostelry in Normandy. In grand provincial comfort, Michel Bernard will welcome you to one of his color-coordinated rooms. Tea and pastry are a delight in the salon known as Coin du Feu, which has a fireplace. The food at the Dauphin is among the most outstanding in the area; specialties include sole normande, langouste (lobster) flavored with port wine, caneton (duckling) à la bigarade, and homemade ice creams and fruit tarts. If you order à la carte, you're likely to pay 330 F ($59.40); a fixed-price menu begins at 123 F ($22.10). The hotel is open all year.

7. ORBEC

104 miles NW of Paris, 12½ miles S of Lisieux, 22 miles NW of L'Aigle, 43 miles SE of Caen

GETTING THERE By Car   From Lisieux, motorists can head 12½ miles south on D519.

ESSENTIALS Orientation   Orbec's main artery is rue Grande.

Information   The Syndicat d'Initiative (tourist office), rue Guillonière (tel. 31-32-87-15), is open mid-April to September.

In a peaceful valley of the Pays d'Auge, near the source of the Orbiquet River, Orbec is a Norman town that has preserved its character. Although the town has an interesting **Church of Notre-Dame,** from the 15th and 16th centuries, the real reason people come here is to sample the food at Au Caneton (previewed below).

WHERE TO DINE

AU CANETON, 32, rue Grande. Tel. 31-32-73-32.
   Cuisine: FRENCH. **Reservations:** Required.
$ **Prices:** Appetizers 70–120 F ($12.60–$21.60); main dishes 95–160 F ($17.10–$28.80); fixed-price menus 130 F ($23.40), 195 F ($35.10), and 280 F ($50.40). AE, MC, V.
   Open: Lunch Wed–Mon noon–2pm; dinner Wed–Sun 7:45–9pm. **Closed:** Feb.

In this rustic 17th-century Norman house located along the main business route, a five-minute walk from the village church, you can dine in small dark rooms by lamplight reflecting the illuminated chimneypiece. The owners, Chantal and Didier Tricot, know the value of classic seasoning and prepare excellent sauces. The food draws visitors all the way from Paris. Specialties include duckling with either lemon or apples, lobster with nettles, roasted sauvageon (a hybrid cross between two types of European ducks), scallops in puff pastry with a julienne of baby vegetables, a gigot of roebuck, and, for dessert, a soufflé au Calvados. Of course, this is Calvados country, so one of those mellow mulled drinks with your meal would be in keeping with an age-old tradition.

---

8. CAEN

148 miles NW of Paris, 74 miles SE of Cherbourg

GETTING THERE   By Train   It's a two-hour train ride from Paris's Gare St-Lazare. The train station is not in the center, but there's bus service to the town center.

ESSENTIALS   Information   The Office de Tourisme is located at place St-Pierre (tel. 31-86-27-65).

On the banks of the Orne, the port city of Caen suffered great damage in the Allied invasion of Normandy in 1944. Nearly three-quarters of the city's buildings, some 10,000 in all, were destroyed, although the twin abbeys founded by William the Conqueror and his "good wife, Mathilda," were spared. The city today is essentially modern and has many broad avenues and new apartment buildings.

William the Conqueror made Caen his seat of government. The son of Robert the Devil and a tanner's daughter, young William had been known as "The Bastard" in the days before he conquered England. He proposed marriage to his cousin Mathilda, the daughter of Baldwin V of Flanders. She is said to have told her ladies-in-waiting that she'd "rather take the veil than marry a bastard." However, William galloped on horseback to Flanders and grabbed Mathilda by the hair, and she changed her mind. The Papal Council at Reims had prohibited the alliance because of their close kinship, but in 1059 Pope Nicholas II granted them dispensation. To show their penance, William and Mathilda founded the Abbaye aux Hommes and the Abbaye aux Dames at Caen.

WHAT TO SEE & DO

The **Abbaye aux Hommes,** Esplanade Jean-Marie-Louvel (tel. 31-30-42-01), is adjacent to the **Eglise St-Etienne** and is entered on place Monseigneur-des-Hameaux. During the height of the Allied invasion of 1944, denizens of Caen flocked to St-Etienne for protection from the bombardment.

The church is characterized by twin Romanesque towers from the 11th century, which rise to 276 feet. Its 15th-century spires helped earn for Caen the appellation of "a city of spires." A simple marble slab inside the high altar commemorates the site of William's tomb. The Huguenots destroyed the tomb in the uprising of 1562, save for a hipbone that was recovered. However, during the French Revolution the last bit of William the Conqueror's dust was scattered to the wind.

You can take a conducted tour of the abbey, open daily from 9am to noon and 2 to

5pm. Tours of the abbey cost 10 F ($1.80). Inside, the hand-carved wooden doors and the elaborately sculpted wrought-iron staircase are exceptional. From the cloisters, you get a good view of the two towers of St-Etienne. Part of the former abbey houses municipal offices.

On the opposite side of town, the **Abbaye aux Dames,** place de la Reine-Mathilde (tel. 31-06-98-98), was founded by Mathilda, and it embraces the **Eglise de la Trinité,** which, like St-Etienne, is flanked by two Romanesque square towers. Destroyed during the Hundred Years' War, its spires were never rebuilt. In the 12th-century choir rests the tomb of Queen Mathilda; also notice the ribbed vaulting. To see the choir, the transept, and the crypt, take a guided tour, offered daily between 9am and noon or 2 and 7pm (6pm in winter). Entrance is free.

If time remains, you may want to visit the **château,** near the Relais des Gourmets, where you may enjoy a walk in the castle gardens, from which you can look out over Caen. The citadel is from the 14th and 15th centuries; it was badly damaged in the war. The approach ramp is from the front of the Church of St-Pierre. The château is open May through September, daily from 6am to 9:30pm; off-season, daily from 6am to 7:30pm. Entrance is free.

WHERE TO STAY

The city has no expensive lodgings, only moderately priced and budget. Le Dauphin, listed under "Where to Dine," below, also rents guest rooms.

Moderate

HOTEL LE MODERNE, 116, bd. du Maréchal-Leclerc, 14000 Caen. Tel. 31-86-04-23. Fax 31-85-37-93. 40 rms (all with bath). MINIBAR TV TEL **Bus:** 1, 3, 4, 10, or 11.

$ **Rates:** 310–425 F ($55.80–$76.50) single; 425–460 F ($76.50–$82.80) double. Breakfast 45 F ($8.10) extra. AE, DC, MC, V. **Parking:** 35 F ($6.30).

Built after World War II, this hotel was renovated in 1990. Located in a pedestrian zone of the inner city, across the street from the Chambre de Commerce, it offers quiet and dependable lodgings. Most accommodations are decorated in a classical, traditional style, and a sauna was added on the fifth floor. The breakfast room has a good view of the town. Breakfast is the only meal served, but the staff will direct you to several good restaurants nearby.

HOTEL MALHERBE, place du Maréchal-Foch, 14000 Caen. Tel. 31-27-57-57. Fax 31-27-57-58. 92 rms (all with bath or shower). TV TEL **Bus:** 1, 3, 4, 10, or 11.

$ **Rates:** 390–510 F ($70.20–$91.80) single; 440–560 F ($79.20–$100.80) double. Breakfast 50 F ($9) extra. AE, DC, MC, V. **Parking:** Free.

Built sometime after World War II in the commercial heart of town, opposite an angel-capped monument dedicated to a French military hero, this hotel was radically modernized and enlarged in 1991. Today, it offers a cozy and traditionally furnished bar much favored by Americans visiting the D-Day beaches, and an efficient modern restaurant, Le Rabelais. Fixed-price menus inside cost 110–160 F ($19.80–$28.80) each. Bedrooms are comfortable, predictably modern, and well maintained.

LES RELAIS DES GOURMETS, 15, rue de Geôle, 14300 Caen. Tel. 31-86-06-01. Fax 31-39-06-00. 28 rms (all with bath), 7 suites. TV TEL **Bus:** 1, 3, 4, 10, or 11.

$ **Rates:** 505 F ($90.90) single or double; from 735 F ($132.30) suite. Breakfast 42 F ($7.50) extra. AE, DC, MC, V.

At the foot of the Château de Guillaume-le-Conquérant is this charming four-star hotel. Many antiques, including a 13th-century closet, and reproductions adorn the lounges and reception area. The personalized bedrooms are generally spacious, many with views of the garden or the château; most contain minibars. Proprietor and chef Jean Legras-Daragon has been awarded many culinary honors. You can dine on the hotel's little terraced garden, where excellent seafood—including lobster, oysters, and the fish of the Channel—is served. Meals cost 145–240 F ($26.10–$43.20) at both restaurants. There is also a high-quality restaurant next door, L'Ecaille, 13, rue de Geôle (tel. 31-86-49-10), facing the castle of William the Conqueror.

Inexpensive

BRISTOL, 31, rue du 11-Novembre, 14000 Caen. Tel. 31-84-59-76. Fax 31-52-29-28. 25 rms (20 with bath or shower). TV TEL **Bus:** 1, 3, 4, 10, or 11.

$ Rates: 150 F ($27) single or double without bath; 195 F ($35.10) single with bath or shower; 200–250 F ($36–$45) double with bath or shower. Breakfast 25 F ($4.50) extra. MC, V. **Parking:** Free.

Built in 1954 and renovated in 1992, this hotel is on a block of modern apartments and shops, not far from the park. Consider the Bristol more as a stopover hotel than a charming inn. A continental breakfast is the only meal served.

HOTEL DES QUATRANS, 17, rue Gémare, 14300 Caen. Tel. 31-86-25-57. Fax 31-85-27-80. 32 rms (all with bath). TEL **Bus:** 1, 3, 4, 10, or 11.

$ Rates: 155 F ($27.90) single; 260 F ($46.80) double. Breakfast 30 F ($5.40) extra. MC, V.

This agreeable hostelry, suitable for an overnight stay, is one of the best bargains in Caen. Rooms are simply furnished and offer basic amenities. Breakfast is the only meal served.

WHERE TO DINE

Caen is famous for its tripe à la mode de Caen. Even if you don't normally like tripe, you might want to give it a try here. Caen shares nearly all the culinary specialties of Normandy. The traditional Caen chefs rely heavily on the use of cream, and everything, of course, tastes better with the celebrated cheeses of the region, along with that spirited cider, Calvados.

LE BOURRIDE, 15-17, rue du Vaugueux. Tel. 31-93-50-76.
   Cuisine: FRENCH. **Reservations:** Required. **Bus:** 1, 3, 4, 10, or 11.
$ Prices: Appetizers 108–193 F ($19.40–$34.70); main dishes 113–195 F ($20.30–$35.10); fixed-price meals 290–420 F ($52.20–$75.60). AE, DC, MC, V.
   Open: Lunch Tues–Sat 12:30–2pm; dinner Tues–Sat 7:15–10pm. **Closed:** Jan 3–24 and Aug 16–Sept 3.

La Bourride offers the best food in Caen. As the restaurant's name implies, there is indeed a bourride served here, concocted from five kinds of fish, delicately seasoned and cooked under the expert eye of Michel Bruneau. The restaurant is in a beautiful old house near the château, in the center of the oldest part of Caen. The dining room has thick stone walls and a magnificent Renaissance fireplace. The service, directed by Françoise Bruneau, includes tactful advice on an array of prominent wines to accompany any of the specialties, such as fresh foie gras of Norman duckling, a papillote of salmon, or roast lamb with a confit of onions. Desserts, which depend on the fruits in season, are excellent, or try the Calvados sorbet.

LE DAUPHIN, 29, rue Gémare, 14300 Caen. Tel. 31-86-22-26. Fax 31-86-35-14.
   Cuisine: FRENCH. **Reservations:** Required. **Bus:** 1, 3, 4, 10, or 11.
$ Prices: Appetizers 60–105 F ($10.80–$18.90); main dishes 75–120 F ($13.50–$21.60); fixed-price menus 95–290 F ($17.10–$52.20). AE, DC, MC, V.
   Open: Lunch Sun–Fri noon–2:30pm; dinner Sun–Fri 7–9:30pm. **Closed:** July 24–Aug 10.

Not only is this one of the outstanding restaurants of Caen, but also it offers good accommodations. The chef de cuisine is Robert Chabredier. The cuisine consists of fresh ingredients and is imaginative, and there are many interesting dishes and specialties, including a ragoût of small lobster with fresh pasta, sweetbreads forester style, and warm oysters in red butter. His dessert specialty is apple charlotte.

All 22 bedrooms, with private baths and showers, are well furnished and maintained. A single with shower costs 310–360 F ($55.80–$64.80), and doubles with private bath cost 340–390 F ($61.20–$70.20), plus 45 F ($8.10) for breakfast. Parking is available.

LES ECHEVINS, 35, route de Trouville. Tel. 31-84-10-17.
   Cuisine: FRENCH. **Reservations:** Not required.
$ Prices: Appetizers 85–145 F ($15.30–$26.10); main dishes 92–255 F ($16.50–$45.90); fixed-price menus 155 F ($27.90), 210 F ($37.80), and 320 F ($57.60). MC, V.
   Open: Lunch Mon–Sat noon–2:30pm; dinner Mon–Sat 7:30–9:30pm. **Closed:** Aug.

In a house built in 1882, this restaurant is about two miles from the center of town on the Deauville–Cabourg road, near the motorway from Paris. The restaurant has two dining rooms and a lounge bar, plus a large garden and ample parking. Patrick Regnier, the owner and chef, prepares the kind of dishes he once cooked with flair at an exclusive Paris restaurant before establishing his own domain in Caen. Menu specialties reveal a rich collection from his repertoire, augmented by perfectly blended sauces, including veal cutlet stuffed with morels, scallops with whisky, turbot with two kinds of exotic mushrooms, and deboned pigeon stuffed with foie gras. Regional dishes include Caen-style tripe and marmite dieppoise, followed by a Calvados soufflé for dessert.

NEARBY ACCOMMODATIONS

Le Manoir d'Hastings, listed under "Nearby Dining," below, also rents guest rooms.

NOVOTEL, av. de la Côte-de-Nacre, 14000 Caen. Tel. 31-93-05-88. Fax 31-44-07-28. 126 rms (all with bath). MINIBAR TV TEL **Directions:** Take the Caen Université exit from the Caen Périphérique in the north of Caen.
$ Rates: 430 F ($77.40) single; 480 F ($86.40) double. Children under 16 stay free in parents' room. Breakfast 50 F ($9) extra. AE, DC, MC, V. **Parking:** Free.
These superior accommodations are located about a mile and a half north of the city center. Built in 1976, the hotel is part of a nationwide chain with high standards. Each of the well-furnished and well-maintained rooms contains both a single and a double bed, making them ideal for families. A swimming pool is on the landscaped grounds, and the grill serves both French and international dishes, including the regional tripe à la mode de Caen.

RELAIS CHATEAU D'AUDRIEU, 14250 Audrieu. Tel. 31-80-21-52. Fax 31-80-24-73. 21 rms (all with bath), 9 suites. TV TEL **Directions:** From Caen, take the N13 for 11 miles, then the D158 for 2 miles.
$ Rates: 585–1,200 F ($105.30–$216) single or double; 1,565–1,880 F ($281.70–$338.40) suite. Breakfast 80 F ($14.40) extra. MC, V. **Parking:** Free.
This château set in a 50-acre park offers the most luxurious accommodations at Audrieu. Gérard and Irène Livry-Level have decorated many of their lovely, well-appointed rooms with antiques and calla lilies. Guests enjoy the heated outdoor swimming pool, as well as the spectacular setting.
   The chef in the superb restaurant offers excellent specialties, including a bouillon of duckling with cider and poached foie gras, roasted crayfish in a cream sauce, and veal brains with an onion confit. Some of the produce, such as raspberries in summer, come from their own garden. A la carte dinners average 350 F ($63).

NEARBY DINING

Both the hotels listed under "Nearby Accommodations," above, also have fine restaurants.

LE MANOIR D'HASTINGS, 14970 Bénouville. Tel. 31-44-62-34. Fax 31-44-76-18.
   Cuisine: FRENCH. **Reservations:** Required. **Directions:** From Caen, follow the signs for Ouistreham, then go 6½ miles after turning off for Bénouville; The manor is next to the village church.

$ Prices: Appetizers 30–60 F ($5.40–$10.80); main dishes 88–170 F ($15.80–$30.60); fixed-price meals 120 F ($21.60), 160 F ($28.80), 280 F ($50.40), and 360 F ($64.80). AE, DC, MC, V.
Open: Lunch daily 12:30–2pm; dinner daily 7–9:30pm. **Closed:** Sun night and Mon Oct–Apr.

✪ This establishment is housed in a converted priory from the 17th century and has an enclosed Norman garden. Its owners, José and Carole Aparicio, serve *cuisine moderne.* If you're tired of cream and Calvados with everything, then head here for a refreshing lighter meal. The chef has developed his own style, as reflected by a wide variety of dishes, including lobster cooked in cider or a delicately flavored sea bass. For dessert, I suggest a tart normand flambé with Calvados. Of the fixed-price menus, the most expensive is a *menu gourmand* with seven *petits plats dégustation,* based on the best available at the market.

The manor also offers 11 handsomely furnished bedrooms facing a garden, each with a separate bathroom. A single costs 440 F ($79.20) and a double goes for 500 F ($90), plus another 50 F ($9) for breakfast.

---

9. BAYEUX

166 miles NW of Paris, 16 miles NW of Caen

GETTING THERE   By Train   Trains from Paris to Cherbourg stop in Bayeux.

ESSENTIALS Orientation   The major commercial boulevard is rue St-Martin. A traffic-free zone begins at rue St-Jean.

Information   The Office de Tourisme is located at 1, rue des Cuisiniers (tel. 31-92-16-26).

The dukes of Normandy sent their sons to this Viking settlement to learn the Norse language. Bayeux has changed a lot since then, but miraculously it was spared from bombardment in the 1944 Allied invasion of Normandy. The first town liberated in France, Bayeux gave de Gaulle an enthusiastic welcome when he arrived there on June 14. Today the sleepy town, 17 miles northwest of Caen, is filled with Norman timbered houses, stone mansions, and cobbled streets.

WHAT TO SEE & DO

CATHEDRAL OF BAYEUX, 5, rue Maitrise. Tel. 31-92-01-85.
Called "the Reims of Normandy," the cathedral was consecrated in 1077 by William the Conqueror's brother, Odo. The ruler's son, Beauclerc, partially destroyed it in 1105. Left over from an earlier church, its Romanesque towers rise on the western side, although the central tower is from the 15th century, with an even later topping. Inside, the nave is a fine example of the Norman Romanesque style. Rich in sculptural decorations, the 13th-century choir contains handsome Renaissance stalls. To see the crypt and the 13th-century chapter house, apply to the sexton. Incidentally, the crypt was built in the 11th century and was then sealed; its existence remained unknown until it was discovered in 1412.
   Admission: Free.
   Open: July–Aug, daily 8am–7pm; Sept–June, daily 8am–noon and 2–7pm.

MUSÉE DE LA TAPISSERIE DE BAYEUX, Centre Guillaume-le-Conquérant, rue de Nesmond. Tel. 31-92-05-48.
✪ This museum displays the Bayeux tapestry—the most famous tapestry in the world. Actually, it isn't even a tapestry; it's an embroidery on a band of linen, 231 feet long and 20 inches wide, depicting some 58 scenes in eight colors. Contrary to legend, it wasn't made by Mathilda, the wife of William the Conqueror. It was probably commissioned in Kent and made by unknown Saxon embroiderers

between 1066 and 1077. The first recorded mention of the embroidery was in 1476, when it was explained that the tapestry was used to decorate the nave of the Cathedral of Bayeux.

Housed in a glass case, the embroidery tells the story of the conquest of England by William the Conqueror, including such scenes as the coronation of Harold as the Saxon king of England, Harold returning from his journey to Normandy, "the personage of Aelfgyve," the surrender of Dinan, Harold being told of the apparition of a comet (the portent of misfortune), William the Conqueror in war dress, and the death of Harold. Decorative borders include scenes from Aesop's Fables. Men, horses, ships, and weapons—the panorama of history—sweeps by as you view this masterpiece.

Admission: 25 F ($4.50) adults, 12 F ($2.10) children 10 and under.

Open: Mid-May to mid-Sept, daily 9am–7pm; mid-Mar to mid-May and mid-Sept to mid-Oct, daily 9am–12:30pm and 2–6:30pm; mid-Oct to mid-Mar, daily 9:30am–12:30pm and 2–6pm.

MUSEE MEMORIAL DE LA BATAILLE DE NORMANDIE, bd. Fabian-Ware. Tel. 31-92-93-41.

This museum, located across from the cemetery of Brittany, deals exclusively with the military and human history of the battle for Normandy. Inside are about 440 feet of window and film displays, plus a diorama. Wax dummies of soldiers in their uniforms, along with the tanks and guns used to win the battle, are exhibited. The museum has been enlarged to contain exhibitions dealing only with military developments of the Battle of Normandy (Operation Overlord, June 6–August 22, 1944).

Admission: 20 F ($3.60) adults, 10 F ($1.80) children.

Open: July–Aug, daily 9am–7pm; Sept–June, daily 10am–12:30pm and 2–6pm.

WHERE TO STAY & DINE
Moderate

LE LION D'OR, 71, rue St-Jean, 14400 Bayeux. Tel. 31-92-06-90. Fax 31-22-15-64. 28 rms (all with bath or shower), 2 suites. TV TEL **Bus:** 3.

$ Rates: 400–430 F ($72–$77.40) single; 400–450 F ($72–$81) double; 850 F ($153) suite. Breakfast 50 F ($9) extra. AE, DC, MC, V. **Parking:** Free. **Closed:** Dec 20–Jan 20.

Like an old French coaching inn, Le Lion d'Or has a large open courtyard and a mansard roof. Lush flower boxes decorate the facade. You can sleep or dine well here. One meal is required of overnight guests. The renovated hotel has that old-world-inn atmosphere and is pleasant and comfortable. The personalized rooms are set back from the street.

The beamed dining room has elegant, cloth-covered walls decorated with reproductions of the Bayeux tapestry. The restaurant has a view of a courtyard filled with baskets of geraniums. The cuisine here is famous: Try the meatloaf, a specialty of the house; fresh poached trout with shallot butter; chicken à la Vallée d'Auge flambé (cooked in cider with cream and mushrooms); Normandy cheese; and, to top it off, a meringue cake called Saint-Eve, a specialty of Bayeux. There are lots of excellent wines, plus an attractive bar with a fireplace. Meals cost 110–320 F ($19.80–$57.60).

LUXEMBOURG, 25, rue Bouchers, 14400 Bayeux. Tel. 31-92-00-04, or toll free 800/528-1234 in the U.S. and Canada. Fax 31-92-54-26. 22 rms (all with bath), 3 suites. MINIBAR TV TEL **Bus:** 3.

$ Rates: 350 F ($63) single; 420–470 F ($75.60–$84.60) double; from 1,200 F ($216) suite. Half board 370–550 F ($66.60–$99) per person daily. Breakfast 50 F ($9) extra. AE, DC, MC, V. **Parking:** Free.

This is the finest hotel in the area. Part of its original core was constructed about a hundred years ago as a post office. The completely restored interior has terrazzo floors and a decor combining both neoclassical and art deco periods. There's a richly decorated bar, an elegant restaurant, plus a basement disco that's open until 4am. The restaurant is filled with Louis XIII chairs, rich velvet upholstery, a coffered ceiling, and embroidered napery. Try the fricassée of lobster, followed by a Norman-style apple tart. Meals cost 99–396 F ($17.80–$71.20).

NOVOTEL BAYEUX, 117, rue St-Patrice, 14400 Bayeux. Tel. 31-92-16-11. Fax 31-21-88-76. 78 rms (all with bath). A/C MINIBAR TV TEL **Bus:** 3.

$ **Rates:** 430 F ($77.40) single; 500 F ($90) double. Breakfast 50 F ($9) extra. AE, DC, MC, V. **Parking:** Free.

This modern hotel is set in a park with a pleasant swimming pool. The bedrooms are functionally furnished, and you may dine in the main restaurant or, in fair weather, on the terrace. The average meal costs 160 F ($28.80) per person.

Inexpensive

CHURCHILL HOTEL, 14-16, rue St-Jean, 14404 Bayeux. Tel. 31-21-31-80. Fax 31-21-41-66. 32 rms (all with bath), 1 suite. TV TEL **Bus:** 3.

$ **Rates:** 280 F ($50.40) single; 320–420 F ($57.60–$75.60) double; 480–620 F ($86.40–$111.60) suite. Breakfast 38 F ($6.80) extra. AE, DC, MC, V. **Parking:** Free.

Located in the center of old Bayeux, near Queen Mathilda's tapestry, this three-star hotel was built in 1986. On a pedestrian street, it is traditional in style but has all the modern amenities. Monsieur and Madame Selmi welcome you to one of their individually decorated bedrooms, each with a private bath or shower. The hotel also has an excellent restaurant, which offers quality family and regional cooking using local produce. A parking lot adjoins the hotel.

HOTEL D'ARGOUGES, 21, rue St-Patrice, 14402 Bayeux. Tel. 31-92-88-86. Fax 31-92-69-16. 25 rms (all with bath or shower). MINIBAR TEL **Bus:** 3.

$ **Rates:** 280–300 F ($50.40–$54) single; 260–380 F ($46.80–$68.40) double. Breakfast 35 F ($6.30) extra. AE, DC, MC, V. **Parking:** Free.

Monsieur and Madame Auregan have handsomely restored this 18th-century hotel into some of the finest accommodations in Bayeux. In fair weather, guests enjoy sipping drinks in the garden. The rooms also have radios, and a garage is available. Eighteen rooms contain TVs. Breakfast is the only meal served.

Budget

FAMILY HOME, 39, rue du Général-de-Dais, 14400 Bayeux. Tel. 31-92-15-22. Fax 31-92-55-72. 13 rms (all with bath). **Bus:** 3.

$ **Rates** (including continental breakfast): 160 F ($28.80) single; 200 F ($36) double. AE, MC, V.

This 16th- and 17th-century presbytery, now a private house, is located in the center of Bayeux, near the cathedral and museums on a quiet street leading to the main street, rue St-Malo. It consists of a compound of four interconnected buildings. In winter, there's usually a fire blazing in the lounge fireplace. The bedrooms are simply furnished, and you can cook your own meals in the kitchen. Madame Lefèvre also serves copious and varied meals to her guests for 65 F ($11.70), which includes wine and service charge. These are served at a long communal table. The wine served is a smooth Anjou produced by Madame Lefèvre's family at their own vineyards.

---

10. PORT-EN-BESSIN

171 miles NW of Paris, 5½ miles NW of Bayeux

GETTING THERE By Bus Take bus Vert no. 70 from Bayeux.

ESSENTIALS Port-en-Bessin does not have a tourist office. The nearest information center is at Bayeux (see above).

If you want to get away from the popular tourist centers, consider visiting the Port, as it's called locally. In the Calvados section, Port-en-Bessin opens onto a harbor enclosed by two half-moon jetties. Try to arrive early in the morning, except Sunday, to see the fish auction.

WHERE TO STAY & DINE

LE CHENEVIERE, 14520 Port-en-Bessin–Huppain. Tel. 31-21-47-96. Fax 31-21-47-98. 15 rms (all with bath or shower). MINIBAR TV TEL
$ Rates: 700–900 F ($126–$162) single; 800–1,000 F ($144–$180) double. Breakfast 55 F ($9.90) extra. AE, DC, MC, V. **Parking:** Free. **Closed:** Dec 21–Feb.

If elegance is what you're after, stay at Le Chenevière, located less than a mile from the port. Many English visitors often come here just for the weekend; in fact, this 19th-century Norman château evokes an English manor house (albeit with a Norman roof). The hotel, opened in 1988 after a massive restoration, is set in a park and is adjacent to the 27-hole Omaha Beach Golf Course. Because Le Chenevière lies between Bayeux and Omaha Beach (which earned its fame in the Normandy invasion of 1944), it's a convenient base for touring. The bedrooms are individually decorated in a floral motif and have all the amenities.

The hotel also offers superb cuisine, with many regional dishes. Fixed-price meals begin at 125 F ($22.50) at lunch, and they're 195 F ($35.10) and 295 F ($53.10) at dinner.

HOTEL DE LA MARINE, quai Letourneur, 14520 Port-en-Bessin. Tel. 31-21-70-08. Fax 31-21-90-36. 16 rms (all with bath or shower). TEL
$ Rates: 350 F ($63) single or double. Breakfast 38 F ($6.80) extra. DC, MC, V. **Parking:** Free.

Consider stopping overnight or for a meal at this hotel located right next to the harbor. It was rebuilt in 1952 after the bombings of World War II, then renovated in 1992. The pleasant interior has carpeting and rustic furniture, and the bedrooms are comfortable. The air-conditioned dining room on the second floor has a view of the sea. A fixed-price meal, costing 105–255 F ($18.90–$45.90), often includes filet of sole flavored with cider, John Dory in an orange-cream sauce, and medallions of veal in a Normandy sauce. The service is good.

11. D-DAY BEACHES

Arromanches-les-Bains, 169 miles NW of Paris, 6½ miles NW of Bayeux; Grandcamp-Maisy (near Omaha Beach), 186 miles NW of Paris, 35 miles NW of Caen.

GETTING THERE By Bus Out of Bayeux bus service is a bit uneven and sometimes involves long delays. Bus Verts head for Port-en-Bessin and points west along the coast, and no. 74 offers service to Arromanches and other targets in the east.

By Car It's best to explore the coast by car and to not have to depend on public transportation.

ESSENTIALS Information The Office de Tourisme is located at 4, rue du Maréchal-Joffre, Arromanches-les-Bains (tel. 31-21-47-56). It's open April through September.

From June 6 to the breakthrough on July 18, "the longest day" was very long indeed.
The greatest armada the world had ever known—men, warships, landing craft, tugboats, Jeeps, whatever—had assembled along the southern coast of England in the spring of 1944.

On June 5, at 9:15 p.m., the BBC announced to the French Resistance that the invasion was imminent, signaling the underground to start dynamiting the railways. Before midnight, Allied planes were bombing the Norman coast fortifications. By

1:30 on the morning of June 6, members of the 101st Airborne were parachuting to the ground on German-occupied French soil. At 6:30 a.m. the Americans were landing on the beaches code-named Utah and Omaha. One hour later the British and Canadian forces were making beachheads at Juno, Gold, and Sword.

The Nazis had mocked Churchill's promise in 1943 to liberate France "before the fall of the autumn leaves." When the invasion did come, it was swift, sudden, and a surprise to the formidable "Atlantic wall." Today veterans from Canada, the United States, and Britain walk with their families across the beaches where "Czech hedgehogs," "Belgian grills," pillboxes, and "Rommel asparagus" once stood.

SEEING THE D-DAY BEACHES

The exploration of the D-Day Beaches begins at the modest little seaside resort of **Arromanches-les-Bains,** 6½ miles from Bayeux. In June of 1944 it was a little fishing port, until it was taken by the 50th British Division. Towed across the English Channel, a mammoth prefabricated port known as "Winston" was installed to supply the Allied forces. "Victory could not have been achieved without it," said Eisenhower. The wreckage of that artificial harbor—also known as "Mulberry"—lies right off the beach, *la plage du débarquement.* The **Musée du Débarquement** (tel. 31-22-34-31) has been installed, featuring relief maps, working models, a cinema, and photographs showing such scenes as the opening "Pontoons." A diorama of the landing, with an English commentary, is featured, including showing of the British film *Port Wilson.*

Admission to the Musée du Debarquement is 25 F ($4.50). From mid-April through the end of May, the museum is open daily from 9am to noon and 2 to 6:30pm; from the end of May through the end of August, daily from 9am to 6:30pm; September 1–15, daily from 9am to noon and 2 to 6:30pm; and from September 16 through mid-April, daily from 9am to noon and 2 to 6pm.

Moving along the coast, you arrive at **Omaha Beach,** where the wreckage of war can still be seen. "Hanging on by their toenails," the men of the 1st and 29th American Divisions occupied the beach that June day. The code-name Omaha became famous throughout the world, although the French up to then had called the beaches St-Laurent, Vierville-sur-Mer, and Colleville. A monument commemorates the heroism of the invaders.

Covering some 173 acres at Omaha Beach, the **Normandy American Cemetery** (tel. 31-22-40-62) is filled with crosses and stars of David in Lasa marble. The remains of 9,386 American military dead were buried there on territory now owned by the United States, a gift from the French nation. The cemetery is open daily from 9am to 5pm.

Farther along the coast, the jagged lime cliffs of the **Pointe du Hoc** come into view. A cross honors a group of American Rangers led by Lt.-Col. James Rudder who scaled the cliff using hooks to get at the pillboxes. The scars of war are more visible here than at any other point along the beach.

Much farther along the Cotentin Peninsula is **Utah Beach,** where the 4th U.S. Infantry Division landed at 6:30 a.m. The landing force was nearly two miles south of their intended destination, but, fortunately, Nazi defenses were weak at this point. By midday the infantry had completely cleared the beach. A U.S. monument commemorates their heroism.

Nearby you can visit **Sainte-Mère-Église,** which not too many people had heard of until the night of June 5 and 6 when parachutists were dropped over the town. They were from the 82nd U.S. Airborne Division, under the command of Gen. Matthew B. Ridgeway. Members of the 101st U.S. Airborne Division, commanded by Gen. M. B. Taylor, were also involved. Thus little Sainte-Mère-Église became the first town in France to be liberated in the long war against Germany.

In the town is the **Musée des Troupes Aéroportées** (Airborne Museum), Place du 6 Juin, at which you can see many relics, including the C-47 that transported the U.S. paratroopers who landed in this district the night of June 5 and 6, 1944, as well as a U.S. CG4-A glider.

The museum is open February to June and September 16 through November 15, from 10am to noon and 2 to 6pm; from July 1 through September 15, from 9am to 7pm. Admission is 15 F ($2.70) for adults and 6 F ($1) for children.

Also in Sainte-Mère-Église is the **Kilometer "0"** on the **Liberty Highway,** marking the first of the milestones the American armies reached on their way to Metz and Bastogne.

WHERE TO DINE

At Grandcamp-Maisy, near Omaha Beach, you'll find a little fishing village in danger of silting up. In summer, French families turn it into a modest seaside resort.

The Hôtel Duguesclin also rents guest rooms.

HOTEL DUGUESCLIN, 4, quai Crampon, 14450 Grandcamp-Maisy. Tel. 31-22-64-22. Fax 31-22-34-79.
  Cuisine: FRENCH. **Reservations:** Recommended.
$ Prices: Appetizers 30–65 F ($5.40–$11.70); main dishes 75–110 F ($13.50–$19.80); fixed-price meals 50–250 F ($9–$45). MC, V.
  Open: Lunch daily noon–2pm; dinner daily 7–9pm. **Closed:** Jan 15–Feb 6.

I recommend this typical Norman inn as a luncheon stopover or even as an overnight stay. The fish soup is excellent, and I also recommend the Norman sole if it's available. Everything tastes better with the country bread and Norman butter.

The hotel rents 31 simply but comfortably furnished rooms—25 have baths or showers, and all have TVs. A single without bath rents for 150 F ($27), rising to 250 F ($45) with bath. A double without bath is also priced at 150 F ($27), going up to 260 F ($46.80) with bath, plus 25 F ($4.50) per person for breakfast.

LE MAREE, 5, quai Chéron. Tel. 31-22-60-55.
  Cuisine: FRENCH. **Reservations:** Required.
$ Prices: Appetizers 40–140 F ($7.20–$25.20); main dishes 100–183 F ($18–$32.90); fixed-price meals 99–220 F ($17.80–$39.60). MC, V.
  Open: Apr–Oct, lunch daily 12:30–2:30pm; dinner daily 7–9:30pm. Nov–Mar, lunch Thurs–Tues 12:30–2:30pm; dinner Thurs–Mon 7–9:30pm.

Located directly at the port, this small restaurant in a 1920s building is perfect for seafood devotees. The fish, always fresh and savory, is often bought from the boats that gathered the sea harvest. First try the fresh oysters; then I recommend the medley of monkfish, morels, and sweetbreads cooked in the same dish. Meals are served in the rustic dining room or on the outdoor terrace.

12. CHERBOURG

223 miles NW of Paris, 74 miles NW of Caen

GETTING THERE   By Train   Trains leave hourly from Caen; the trip takes 1½ hours. The rail station is a 12-minute walk from the ferry dock.

ESSENTIALS   Information   The Office de Tourisme is at 2, quai Alexandre-III (tel. 33-93-52-02).

At the tip of the Cotentin Peninsula, Cherbourg was the chief supply port for the Allied landings in the invasion of Normandy in 1944. On the English Channel, at the mouth of the Divette River, Cherbourg is the third great naval base of France. Its naval port was begun on orders of Napoléon Bonaparte, and it contains extensive drydocks and shipbuilding yards. Because of its location, 60 miles south of England's Isle of Wight, it was connected by the "Pluto" pipeline under the ocean, which transported fuel from the Isle of Wight to Cherbourg. Today you can take a motorboat trip through the great artificial port.

WHAT TO SEE & DO

EGLISE DE LA TRINITE, place Napoléon. Tel. 33-53-10-63.

This church, on the south side of place Napoléon, was built from 1423 to 1504 and is a fine example of the flamboyant style. It is one of the few historic buildings still left in Cherbourg.

Admission: Free.
Open: Daily 8am–5pm.

MUSÉE DE LA LIBÉRATION, Fort du Roule. Tel. 33-20-14-12.

The history of the battle of Cherbourg—in fact, the story of the Allied landings at Normandy—unfolds at this museum, which is reached by a winding road. At the top you'll have a good view of the town and the port. Photographs show the Germans surrendering, and an armory room displays artillery and equipment. One of the most interesting sections is devoted to modern propaganda, including the underground press and a moving Paul Colin poster, *Wounded France Awakes to Liberty*. The French contribution to the Allied victory is also well represented.

Admission: 10 F ($1.80).
Open: Apr–Sept, daily 9am–noon and 2–6pm; Oct–Mar, Wed–Mon 9:30am–noon and 2–5:30pm.

MUSÉE THOMAS-HENRY, rue Vastel. Tel. 33-44-40-22.

Housed in the Hôtel de Ville de Cherbourg (town hall), this museum has a collection of European paintings, including some Spanish and German ones. A statue of a local painter, Jean-François Millet, stands in the public garden, and inside the museum you can see examples of his work. Look for a panel by Fra Angelico Lippi. Other works are by Poussin, Vernet, and David.

Admission: 10 F ($1.80).
Open: May–Oct, Wed–Mon 10am–noon and 2–6pm; Nov–Apr, daily 10am–noon and 2–5pm.

WHERE TO STAY

LE LOUVRE, 2, rue Henri-Dunant, 50100 Cherbourg. Tel. 33-53-02-28.

Fax 33-53-43-88. 42 rms (35 with bath). TV TEL
$ Rates: 240 F ($43.20) single without bath, 280–300 F ($50.40–$54) single with bath; 260–290 F ($46.80–$52.20) double without bath, 300–320 F ($54–$57.60) double with bath. Breakfast 30 F ($5.40) extra. AE, MC, V. **Parking:** 25 F ($4.50).

One of the finest bargain accommodations in Cherbourg is this one, located in the center of town. Though it doesn't have a restaurant and the furnishings are modest, the rooms are comfortable and well maintained. The owners extend a warm welcome.

MERCURE CHERBOURG, Gare Maritime, 50100 Cherbourg. Tel. 33-44-01-11. Fax 33-44-51-00. 84 rms (all with bath or shower). MINIBAR TV TEL **Bus:** 1.

$ Rates: 265–605 F ($47.70–$108.90) single; 380–625 F ($68.40–$112.50) double. Breakfast 50 F ($9) extra. AE, DC, MC, V. **Parking:** Free.

Located on a seabank, this is the best place to stay in the port. It faces the Port de Plaisance, as well as the Gare Maritime. Your room may have a view of a fishing fleet, most of which is from Britain. The Clipper restaurant faces the sea and features good food, especially seafood. The bar, La Timonerie, also opens onto the sea and is a scenic place to stop for a drink.

WHERE TO DINE

Also see the Mercure Cherbourg, listed under "Where to Stay," above.

CAFÉ DU THÉÂTRE, place du Général-de-Gaulle. Tel. 33-43-01-49.

Cuisine: FRENCH. **Reservations:** Not required. **Bus:** 1.
$ Prices: Appetizers 12–65 F ($2.10–$11.70); main dishes 55–82.50 F ($9.90–$14.80); fixed-price menu 69.50 F ($12.50). MC, V.
Open: Lunch daily noon–3pm; dinner Mon–Sat 6–11pm.

⑤ This is the most visible restaurant in a complex of theaters, concert halls, and art facilities—all contained within the premises of the Théâtre National de Cherbourg. Very much like a posh Parisian brasserie, it's the preferred café and restaurant of the region's artists and performers. The large restaurant has a soaring ceiling, and its fixed-price menu is the bargain of the town. The main specialty is choucroute (sauerkraut) garni with pork products; other dishes include terrine of fish, fresh shellfish, filet of duckling, lamb cutlets, and grilled steaks.

LE SAINT-JOURS, 59, rue au Blé. Tel. 33-53-67-64.
Cuisine: FRENCH. **Reservations:** Recommended.
$ Prices: Appetizers 30–130 F ($5.40–$23.40); main dishes 85–210 F ($15.30–$37.80); fixed-price meals 130 F ($23.40), 190 F ($34.20), 210 F ($37.80), and 280 F ($50.40). AE, MC, V.
Open: Lunch Mon–Fri noon–2pm; dinner Mon–Sat 7:30–10pm. **Closed:** June 30–Sept 5 and Dec 22–28.

This leading restaurant of town is set on the ground floor in a 19th-century house. It lies in the center of the oldest section of town and is one of the rare Cherbourg buildings to escape the bombings. The restaurant is distinguished for its fixed-price menus, including a *menu de l'océan,* featuring fish in every dish—even the lasagne is baked with salmon in a basil-flavored cream sauce. Other dishes include a cassoulet au confit de canard (duckling), lobster with rice pilaf, and roast pigeon en cocotte.

---

13. MONT ST-MICHEL

201 miles W of Paris, 80 miles SW of Caen, 47 miles E of Dinan, 30 miles E of St-Malo

GETTING THERE   By Train and Bus or Taxi   Mont St-Michel can be reached by train from Paris (Gare Montparnasse); take the train to Dol then transfer to Pontorson, which is the closest rail station to the "Mont." From Pontorson, there is bus service to Mont St-Michel, six miles away. Bus schedules are somewhat erratic, so you may have to take a taxi.

ESSENTIALS   Orientation   To reach the abbey, you have to climb the steep Grande Rue. Along the way, you may have to fight off souvenir peddlers and Normans hawking their omelet specialties.

Information   The Office de Tourisme is in the Corps de Garde des Bourgeois (in English, the Old Guard Room of the Bourgeois, tel. 33-60-14-30), located at the left of the town gates. The office is open from February to November, and they can provide you with free tables of the annual tides.

Tides   Mont St-Michel is noted for its tides, considered the highest on the continent of Europe, measuring at certain times of the year a 50-foot difference between high and low tide. Unsuspecting tourists wandering across the sands—notorious for quicksands—can be trapped as the sea rushes toward the Mont at a speed comparable to that of a galloping horse. Every day there are two high tides, varying from 20 to 50 minutes. About twice a month the granite hilltop is completely surrounded by water, but the causeway leading to it is never submerged.

Parking   It's free to park your car on the causeway-bridge, but spaces are tight as you approach the Mont, itself. There are also some small free lots near the end of the causeway. The largest of the public parking lots, however, charges 15 F ($2.70) per day—note that this lot becomes flooded at high tide and cars make a scramble to get off the lot before the waters arrive; there's ample time warning for drivers.

Considered one of the greatest sightseeing attractions in Europe, Mont St-Michel is surrounded by massive walls measuring more than half a mile in circumference. Connected to the shore by a causeway, it crowns a rocky islet at the border between Normandy and Brittany. The rock is 260 feet high.

SEEING THE ABBEY

It's a steep climb up Grande Rue, lined with 15th- and 16th-century houses, to reach the abbey (tel. 33-60-14-14). Those who make it to the top can begin their exploration of the "Marvel of the West."

In the 8th century an oratory was founded on the spot by St. Aubert, the bishop of Avranches. It was replaced by a Benedictine monastery, founded in 966 by Richard I, Duke of Normandy. That met with destruction by fire in 1203. Large parts of the abbey were financed by Philip Augustus in the 13th century.

Ramparts encircle the church and its ensemble of buildings, a part of which includes the "Merveille" (Marvel), one of the most important Gothic masterpieces in Europe. One of these, the Salle des Chevaliers, is most graceful. Begun in the 11th century, the abbey church consists of a Romanesque nave and transept, plus a choir in the flamboyant Gothic style. The rectangular refectory is from 1212, the cloisters with their columns of pink granite from 1225.

Hours: The abbey is open daily (with mass daily at 12:15pm): May 15 to September 15, from 9:30am to 6pm; February 16 to May 14 and September 16 to November 10, 9:30 to 11:45am and 1:45 to 5pm; November 11 to February 15, 9:30 to 11:45am and 1:45 to 4:15pm.

Tours: Guided tours, leaving every 15 minutes are 45 minutes long. Tours in English are conducted daily at 10am, 11am, noon, and 1:30, 2:30, 3:30, 4:30, and 5:30pm—no tours in English are conducted on Friday. After the tour, you can enter the abbey gardens.

The **Logis Tiphaine** (tel. 33-60-23-34) can also be visited; it was the home of Tiphaine de Raguenel, spouse of Bertrand Duguesclin, constable of France in the 16th century. It's open daily from 9am to 6:30pm; admission is 20 F ($3.60) for adults, 15 F ($2.70) for students, and 10 F ($1.80) for children under 12.

WHERE TO STAY

Plan to spend at least a night here at one of the town's typically French inns. La Mère Poulard, listed under "Where to Dine," below, also rents rooms.

HOTEL DU MOUTON-BLANC, Grande Rue, 50116 Mont St-Michel. Tel. 33-60-14-08. Fax 33-60-05-62. 26 rms (all with bath or shower). TEL

$ Rates: 350–480 F ($63–$86.40) single or double. Breakfast 45 F ($8.10) extra. MC, V.

This inn lies midway up the village slope, halfway between the sea and the famous basilica. Sections of it date from the 14th century; other sections were added in the 1950s. The lower floors of this village house complex have been converted into a restaurant; the simply furnished double bedrooms available for guests are upstairs. Four contain TVs.

Tables are set in a Norman-style dining room and also outside on a terrace that overlooks the sea. As with most of the restaurants in Mont St-Michel, omelets are offered, along with fruits de mer (seafood). Two of the local specialties are mussels in cream sauce and several different preparations of lobster. Fixed-price menus are featured, at 82 F ($14.70) and 240 F ($43.20).

LES TERRASSES POULARD, Grande Rue, 50116 Mont St-Michel. Tel. 33-60-14-09. Fax 33-60-37-31. 29 rms (all with bath or shower). MINIBAR TV TEL

$ Rates: 300–950 F ($54–$171) single or double. Breakfast 60 F ($10.80) extra. AE, DC, MC, V.

This inn was formed when two village houses—one medieval, the other built in the 1800s—were united into a coherent whole. Today, the establishment is considered one of the best in town, with an English-speaking staff and an enviable position across from a parish church founded in the 11th century. Prices depend on the views, which encompass either the dense pedestrian traffic of the Mont's main street, a pleasant garden, or the medieval ramparts. The largest and most expensive rooms contain fireplaces.

There's a restaurant on the premises with a sweeping view over the bay; inside it serves seafood and regional specialties. Fixed-price meals, available every day at lunch and dinner, cost 69–150 F ($12.40–$27) each.

WHERE TO DINE

In addition to the following, the Hôtel du Mouton-Blanc, listed above, has a superb restaurant.

LA MERE POULARD, Grande Rue, 50116 Mont St-Michel. Tel. 33-60-14-01.
Cuisine: FRENCH. **Reservations:** Recommended.
$ **Prices:** Appetizers 65–110 F ($11.70–$19.80); main dishes 75–190 F ($13.50–$34.20); fixed-price menus 150–400 F ($27–$72). AE, DC, MC, V.
Open: Lunch daily noon–2pm; dinner daily 7–9pm.

This French country inn is really a shrine to those who revere the omelet that Annette Poulard created in 1888 when the hotel was founded. Her omelet "secret" has been passed on to the operators of the inn today. The beaten eggs are cooked over an oak hearth fire in a long-handled copper skillet. Baskets holding hundreds of fresh eggs are stacked on a counter. The foamy, frothy mixture of beaten eggs really creates more of an open-fire soufflé than an omelet. Other specialties include lamb raised on the saltwater marshes near the foundations of the abbey and an array of fish, including lobster.

The inn also rents 27 renovated, typically Norman guest rooms, each with private bath. A single or double ranges from a low of 250 F ($45) to a high of 950 F ($171). A suite rents for 1,600 F ($288). Breakfast is another 60 F ($10.80) per person extra.

NEARBY ACCOMMODATIONS & DINING

LA VERTE CAMPAGNE, Hameau Chevalier par Trelly, 50660 Quettreville. Tel. 33-47-65-33. 7 rms (4 with bath). TEL **Directions:** Take the D7 north from Avranches to Lengronne and follow the signs 2½ miles north from Trelly.
$ **Rates:** 200 F ($36) single or double without bath, 350 F ($63) single or double with bath. MC, V. **Parking:** Free. **Closed:** Two weeks in Nov and two weeks in Feb.

When you've had enough of the casinos of Deauville and the tides of Mont St-Michel, head for this rustic Norman farmhouse, located about 30 miles north of Mont St-Michel. A small road winds through groves and orchards and brings you to a white wooden barrier with a 1717 stone farmhouse just beyond. You will be welcomed by Madame Bernou and her cats. The farmhouse has been entirely renovated and sumptuously decorated with antiques and lots of brass. The bar is cozy. The atmosphere is comfortable, yet formal. If you're spending the night, ask for the "splurge" double bedroom that has red carpeting, curtains, bedcover, and vanity—all in harmony with the pink "Vichy" pattern.

In the restaurant, fixed-price menus cost 140 F ($25.20) and 210 F ($37.80); à la carte meals begin at 225 F ($40.50). Specialties include chicken and lamb raised on the property, along with magrêt of duckling with walnut-butter sauce or monkfish flavored with saffron. Hours are 12:30 to 2:30pm and 7:30 to 9:30pm; no meals are served Sunday night or Monday in winter. Nonresidents are welcome, but they should always phone in advance for a table.

14. PONT L'EVEQUE

121 miles NW of Paris, 11 miles N of Lisieux

GETTING THERE   By Car   From Lisieux, motorists can head north for 11 miles on D579.

ESSENTIALS Orientation Two old streets are the main points of interest, rue St-Michel and rue de Vaucelles.

Information Contact the Office de Tourisme, à la Mairie (tel. 31-64-12-77), for information.

Famous for its cheese since the 13th century, Pont l'Evêque was severely damaged during the liberation of Normandy from the Nazis in 1944. Many discerning French people use it as a special retreat for food and lodging, since they don't like paying the more rarified tariffs at nearby Trouville or Deauville.

WHERE TO STAY

LE LION D'OR, 8, place du Calvaire, 14130 Pont l'Evêque. Tel. 31-65-01-55. Fax 31-65-05-64. 25 rms (15 with bath or shower). TV TEL
$ Rates: 220 F ($39.60) single or double without bath, 300–320 F ($54–$57.60) single or double with bath. Breakfast 33 F ($5.90) extra. AE, DC, MC, V. **Parking:** Free.

An attractive and charming hotel, Le Lion d'Or is usually heavily booked for *le weekend*. It was originally built in the late 19th century, and last renovated in 1984. The rooms are modestly furnished, well kept, and comfortable. The hotel, located near the train station, is open all year. It also serves good food: A fixed-price meal costs 110–175 F ($19.80–$31.50), and à la carte dinners average 200 F ($36). The classic Norman food, including filets of sole normande and a blanquette of scallops, is served daily from noon to 2:30pm and 7 to 10pm.

WHERE TO DINE

AUBERGE DE LA TOUQUES, place de l'Eglise. Tel. 31-64-01-69.
Cuisine: FRENCH. **Reservations:** Required.
$ Prices: Appetizers 35–96 F ($6.30–$17.20); main dishes 65–130 F ($11.70–$23.40). AE, MC, V.
Open: Lunch Thurs–Tues noon–2pm; dinner Thurs–Tues 7–9:30pm. **Closed:** Jan 3–27 and Dec 6–22.

This restaurant offers the chance to dine Norman style on the specialties of chef de cuisine Dominique Froger. The large dining room in this 15th- or 16th-century building is warmed by two fireplaces. Main dishes include pepper steak, lobster flan, mousseline of scallops, and several well-prepared meat dishes.

---

15. CABOURG

139 miles NW of Paris, 15 miles NE of Caen

GETTING THERE By Train and Bus From Caen, you can catch a bus to Cabourg or a train connection that will take you to Dives, across the river.

ESSENTIALS Orientation The heart of the resort is laid out symmetrically, like a giant fan. Promenade Marcel-Proust borders the water.

Information The Office de Tourisme is located in the Jardins du Casino (tel. 31-91-01-09).

Literary fans will know this small resort as "Balbec" from *Remembrance of Things Past* by Marcel Proust, who used to spend his summers here. The French writer vividly evoked this "Second Empire" resort as it existed in the Belle Epoque. Proust found lodgings at the Grand Hotel (see below).

It's still fashionable to stroll along boulevard des Anglais, which runs along the sandy beach. The town is preferred by many who shun the atmosphere of Deauville and Trouville—two much larger and better-known resorts.

If you're interested in history, see **Dives-sur-Mer,** a hamlet that was once far more important than it is today. In 1066, William the Conqueror set out from this large port to capture England. Visit the former pilgrimage church of Notre-Dame de Dives, which dates from the 14th century, although its transept is from the 11th century. Also visit Les Halles, the covered market of Dives-sur-Mer, which was originally built in the 15th century.

However, for the atmosphere of a sea resort, you'll want to return to the Côte Fleurie and Cabourg, which boasts a **casino** on the beach.

WHERE TO STAY

HOTEL DE PARIS, 39, av. de la Mer, 14390 Cabourg. Tel. 31-91-31-34.
24 rms (all with bath or shower).
$ Rates: 195–350 F ($35.10–$63) single or double. Breakfast 30 F ($5.40) extra. V. **Parking:** 15 F ($2.70).

Built at the end of the 19th century, this hotel is on a quiet residential street in the center of town. Of its five gables, the central one is capped with an iron griffin, which looks over the street. This family-run hotel rents simply but comfortably furnished bedrooms. Breakfast is the only meal served.

PULLMAN GRAND HOTEL, promenade Marcel-Proust, 14390 Cabourg. Tel. 31-91-01-79, or toll free 800/223-9862 in the U.S. Fax 31-24-03-20. 68 rms (all with bath), 1 suite. TV TEL
$ Rates: 800 F ($144) single; 1,300 F ($234) double; from 2,500 F ($450) suite. Breakfast 70 F ($12.60) extra. AE, DC, MC, V. **Parking:** Free.

This fine hotel is still a reminder of the opulent days of the late 19th century, when its most famous guest was Marcel Proust. A bedroom called Marcel Proust Memory, which was restored from Proust's description in his books, can be reserved by hotel guests. The hotel is located on the edge of the water and has terraces for outdoor dining in the restaurant Le Balbec (see my recommendation below, under "Where to Dine"), and dozens of balconies set between the oversize rooms and the open sea. Many Parisians come here just for the weekend.

WHERE TO DINE

RESTAURANT LE BALBEC, in the Pullman Grand Hôtel, promenade Marcel-Proust. Tel. 31-91-01-79.
Cuisine: FRENCH. **Reservations:** Recommended.
$ Prices: Appetizers 35–145 F ($6.30–$26.10); main dishes 120–195 F ($21.60–$35.10); fixed-price meals 180–320 F ($32.40–$57.60). AE, DC, MC, V.
Open: Lunch daily 12:30–2:30pm; dinner daily 7:30–10pm.

This restaurant draws a loyal crowd of regular customers from the area. The premier dining choice in town, it's located in the town's best hotel (see my recommendation in "Where to Stay," above). The international cuisine includes many classic French dishes and is served in a sumptuous turn-of-the-century setting. Polite, efficient, formal service is a hallmark of the hotel.

NEARBY ACCOMMODATIONS

LE MOULIN DU PRE, route de Gonneville-en-Auge, 14860 Ranville. Tel. 31-78-83-68. Fax 31-78-21-05. 10 rms (5 with bath).
$ Rates: 220–235 F ($39.60–$42.30) single or double without bath, 250–310 F ($45–$55.80) single or double with bath. Breakfast 39 F ($7) extra. AE, DC, MC, V. **Parking:** Free.

Located 4½ miles east of the center of Cabourg, this hotel is the personal statement of the Hamchin and Holtz families. The daughter of the Hamchins married a poet named Holtz and remained to operate the establishment. Set inside a 19th-century millhouse, the hotel's bedrooms are all decorated in shades of pink or blue, and have windows with views of the verdant countryside.

Meals are prepared by the inventive Jocelyn Holtz and feature such specialties as terrine of suckling pig en gelée, turbot flan with sage, vegetable terrine with foie gras, and an aromatic array of grilled meats. A la carte meals cost 200–260 F ($36–$46.80), with a fixed-price menu going for 245 F ($44.10). The restaurant is closed Sunday night and Monday (except in July and August). It also closes for two weeks in March and in October.

NEARBY DINING

GUILLAUME LE CONQUERANT, 2, rue Hastings, Dives-sur-Mer. Tel. 31-91-07-26.
   Cuisine: FRENCH. **Reservations:** Recommended.
$ **Prices:** Fixed-price meals 105–320 F ($18.90–$57.60). AE, MC, V.
   Open: May–Sept, lunch daily noon–2:30pm; dinner daily 7:30–9:30pm. Oct–Nov 21 and Dec 22–Apr, lunch Tues–Sun noon–2:30pm; dinner Tues–Sat 7:30–9:30pm. **Closed:** Nov 22–Dec 21.

Located on the outskirts of Cabourg at Dives-sur-Mer, this is one of the most famous restaurants of Normandy. This ancient postal relay dates from the 16th century, and over the years it has hosted some of the greatest names in France, including Madame de Sévigné. Dumas stopped here, as have various crowned heads of Europe. Patrons enter a well-preserved Norman courtyard before going into the elegant yet rustic dining rooms. Specialties include turbot suprême braised with shallots, fresh lobster, and foie gras with a fondue of morels.

16. DEAUVILLE

128 miles NW of Paris, 29 miles NE of Caen

GETTING THERE   By Train   There are daily rail connections from Paris, leaving from Gare St-Lazare. The SNCF rail depot is between Trouville and Deauville, south of the town.

By Bus   Bus Verts du Calvados serves the lower Normandy coast from Caen to Le Havre.

ESSENTIALS   Orientation   Avenue de la République is the main road through the resort, and promenade des Planches is the fashionable place to be seen.

Information   The Office de Tourisme is on place Mairie (tel. 31-88-21-43).

SPECIAL EVENTS   Every year since 1975, for a week in early September, the Deauville Film Festival is held, honoring movies made in the United States only. Screen actors, producers, directors, and writers flock here and briefly eclipse the high-rollers at the casinos and the horse-race and polo crowd. The film festival has drawn a wide range of stars, many from the golden age of Hollywood, including Kirk Douglas, Gene Kelly, Lana Turner, Gregory Peck, Rock Hudson, Gloria Swanson, and Elizabeth Taylor. No prizes are awarded to the films shown; oddly, a prize for literature is the only award given.

Deauville has always been associated with the rich and famous. In 1913 Coco Chanel began her career here by opening a boutique that sold tiny hats. The fashion at the time was huge fruit and flower hats, and Coco asked, "How can the mind breathe under those things?" Today, visitors still put on their best for the evening activities, including concerts, ballets, and the nightclub casino where some of the biggest names in Europe perform.

Parasols dot the beach and jetsetters abound—especially in August. Many bathers strut the boardwalk just to see and be seen and drop in occasionally for an apéritif at Le Bar du Soleil. One French countess confided that she diets for three months straight before sunning at Deauville. Visit the aptly named **Plage Fleurie;** it's covered with bright flowers.

The resort of Trouville, built in the days of Louis-Philippe, was once the most fashionable place to go—until 1859, that is, when the duc de Morny (Napoléon III's half brother) founded Deauville, which quickly replaced Trouville. With its golf courses, casinos, deluxe hotels, two race tracks (La Touques and Clairefontaine), regattas, yachting harbor, polo grounds, and tennis court, Deauville is a formidable contender for the business of the smart crowd.

WHAT TO SEE & DO

Launched in the 1920s, the **Casino de Deauville,** rue Edmond-Blanc (tel. 31-98-66-66), is open all year. It's in the heart of the nighttime complex of Deauville, which includes the super-expensive Le Régine's nightclub. There is a theater, as well as the superb La Rotonde restaurant, where fixed-price meals cost 180–320 F ($32.40–$57.60). Other dining facilities include Le Banco, La Brasserie de la Boule, and La Dolce Vita. The casino is open July to September 15, Monday through Friday from 11am to 3am and on Saturday and Sunday from 11am to 3:30am; off-season, daily from 3pm to 3am. Admission is 60 F ($10.80).

If you don't want to go swimming at the beach, you can visit the $2-million Olympic-size pool, **La Piscine.**

WHERE TO STAY

Expensive

HOTEL DU GOLF, at New-Golf, 14800 Deauville. Tel. 31-88-19-01. Fax 31-88-75-99. 165 rms (all with bath), 10 suites. MINIBAR TV TEL **Directions:** From Deauville, take the D278 for 1½ miles.
$ **Rates:** 600–1,350 F ($108–$243) single or double; 2,200–3,000 F ($396–$540) suite. Breakfast 90 F ($16.20) extra. AE, DC, MC, V. **Parking:** Free. **Closed:** Nov 16–Mar 12.

Sports fans—especially golfers—will enjoy staying at this colossal Norman hotel, which has an adjoining golf course and is near the race track and stadium. The bedrooms are well appointed. Meals are served in the dining room, where big windows overlook the country setting. Guests gather in the refurbished lounge, relaxing in armchairs and exchanging golf scores.

NORMANDY, 38, rue Jean-Mermoz, 14800 Deauville. Tel. 31-98-66-22. Fax 31-98-66-23. 276 rms (all with bath), 25 suites. MINIBAR TV TEL
$ **Rates:** 780–2,000 F ($140.40–$360) single or double; from 1,275 F ($229.50) suite. Breakfast 90 F ($16.20) extra. AE, DC, MC, V. **Parking:** Free.

This is the best hotel in Deauville. It's a block-long structure built to resemble a Norman village, with turrets, gables, and tiny windows in sloping roofs. Opposite the casino, this year-round hotel opens onto a park of trimmed shrubs, beds of red geraniums, and lawns. The interior is as warm and comfortable as a vast rambling country house. Activity centers around the main rotunda, which is encircled by a colonnade of marble pillars, and the dark-paneled lounge. Bedrooms are furnished with antiques or reasonably good reproductions. The price of a room is determined by its view and size, and the best ocean-view doubles cost more than the smaller suites. A complete lunch or dinner costs from 250 F ($45). Lunches in summer are served in the main restaurant or outdoors under umbrellas. Facilities include tennis courts.

LE ROYAL, bd. Eugène-Cornuché, 14800 Deauville. Tel. 31-98-66-33. Fax 31-98-66-34. 298 rms (all with bath), 16 suites. A/C MINIBAR TV TEL
$ **Rates:** 1,500–2,000 F ($270–$360) single or double; from 2,800 F ($504) suite. Breakfast 90 F ($16.20) extra. AE, DC, MC, V. **Parking:** Free. **Closed:** Nov–Mar.

This impressive hotel, built in 1913, adjoins the casino and fronts a blockwide park between the hotel and the water. High-trimmed yew hedges are arranged to make various terrace levels for lawns and flower beds. The Royal is like a great regal palace; it provides grandiose living for big spenders. The price of the rooms, some of which are mammoth in size, varies according to the view and whether you have a shower or a bathtub. The bedrooms are decorated with period furniture and loomed carpets, and some have spacious sitting rooms fronting the ocean. This is an ideal place to spend a holiday *à la française.*

In fair weather, lunch is provided on the terrace or lawn. There's also a grill where quick meals are served. Guests can dine more formally in either L'Etrier or Le Royal. In either dining room, each elegantly decorated, meals begin at 160 F ($28.80). Facilities include a heated swimming pool, sauna, and two recreation rooms, one for children.

Moderate

LE CONTINENTAL, 1, rue Désiré-le-Hoc, 14800 Deauville. Tel. 31-88-21-06. Fax 31-98-93-67. 42 rms (all with bath), 6 suites. TV TEL
$ Rates: 360–390 F ($64.80–$70.20) single or double; from 500 F ($90) suite. Breakfast 32 F ($5.70) extra. AE, DC, MC, V. **Closed:** Nov 15–Dec 3.

This simple and clean hotel is good for an overnight stop. Bedrooms are comfortably furnished and well kept. Breakfast is the only meal served here, but the hotel has a bar. The owner is usually on hand to assist you.

HELIOS HOTEL, 10, rue Fossorier, 14800 Deauville. Tel. 31-88-28-26. Fax 31-88-53-87. 44 rms (all with bath or shower). TV TEL
$ Rates: 480 F ($86.40) single or double. Breakfast 45 F ($8.10) extra. AE, DC, MC, V.

This is located midway between the monumental center of the resort and the beach, behind a flowering courtyard with a swimming pool. Each of its comfortable bedrooms has all the modern conveniences. Breakfast is the only meal served at this year-round hotel.

HOTEL IBIS, 9, quai de la Marine, 14800 Deauville. Tel. 31-98-38-90. Fax 91-98-38-36. 95 rms (all with bath), 11 suites. TV TEL
$ Rates: 280–380 F ($50.40–$68.40) single; 310–450 F ($55.80–$81) double; from 600 F ($108) suite. Breakfast 38 F ($6.80) extra. MC, V. **Parking:** 38 F ($6.80).

Part of a nationwide chain, the Hôtel Ibis is scenically located and offers some of the best values of any hotel in Deauville. The modern building, built in 1985, overlooks the yacht harbor; the bedrooms are comfortably furnished. The hotel restaurant offers a traditional French menu, with meals starting at 95 F ($17.10).

MARIE-ANNE, 142, av. de la République, 14800 Deauville. Tel. 31-88-35-32. Fax 31-88-35-32. 24 rms (all with bath). TEL
$ Rates: 380 F ($68.40) single; 515 F ($92.70) double. Breakfast 36 F ($6.40) extra. AE, DC, MC, V. **Closed:** Nov 15–Dec 3.

This ornate building is in the middle of a charming private garden. There's no restaurant on the premises, but breakfast is available. All the bedrooms have radios, 17 contain TVs, and 10 contain minibars.

PULLMAN ALTEA, bd. Corniche, 14800 Deauville. Tel. 31-88-62-62. Fax 31-88-54-93. 65 rms (all with bath). MINIBAR TV TEL
$ Rates: 360–670 F ($64.80–$120.60) single; 400–730 F ($72–$131.40) double. Breakfast 52 F ($9.30) extra. AE, DC, MC, V.

Romantically situated on a promontory jutting out into the sea, the Pullman Altea is more vacation complex than hotel. The 1986 structure is filled with wooden balconies and prominent gables and has a view of the harbor. The well-furnished bedrooms are rented all year.

WHERE TO DINE

Expensive

AUGUSTO, 27, rue Désiré-le-Hoc. Tel. 31-88-34-49.
Cuisine: FRENCH. **Reservations:** Required.
$ Prices: Appetizers 40–150 F ($7.20–$27); main dishes 89–165 F ($16–$29.70); fixed-price menus 125–340 F ($22.50–$61.20). AE, DC, MC, V.
Open: Lunch daily noon–2:30pm; dinner daily 7pm–midnight.

This intimate bistro is run by Jean-Claud Lebreton, who maintains high standards for cuisine and service. The restaurant has four dining rooms, one with silk-covered walls and another with a nautical decor. Upstairs are garden-style and Norman rooms. The specialty here is lobster from Brittany, the latest creation a lobster civet in burgundy. The price of lobster depends on market quotations. Other dishes include thin slices of raw salmon with dill and green pepper, spiny lobster medallions served with sherry, hot oysters with shredded vegetables, and stuffed sole with champagne sauce. For dessert, I recommend the gratin of fresh and exotic fruit with a tangerine sabayon.

LE CIRO'S, promenade des Planches. Tel. 31-88-18-10.
   Cuisine: FRENCH. **Reservations:** Not required.
$ Prices: Appetizers 62–195 F ($11.10–$35.10); main dishes 115–390 F ($20.70–$70.20); fixed-price meals 175–350 F ($31.50–$63). AE, DC, MC, V.
   Open: Lunch daily noon–2:30pm; dinner daily 7:15–10:30pm.

Should you arrive on your yacht, this is a convenient luncheon stop. You couldn't get much closer to the water or be more chic. Ciro's provides the best seafood in Deauville—it's expensive but worth it. Tables are placed on two levels; both have glass walls that allow a fine view of the sea.

As you enter, you can make your lobster selection from a tank. The kitchen always stocks a wide range of delectable French oysters and mussels. If you want a little bit of everything, ask for the plateau de fruits de mer, which contains not only lobster but also the various oysters and clams. The most expensive item on the menu is grilled lobster, but there are many other interesting fish dishes, including barbue (brill) cooked in Norman cider. For an elaborate appetizer, I recommend a foie gras of duckling or a lobster salad with truffles. Classic French dishes, such as a grilled filet of beef with a béarnaise sauce and grilled lamb cutlets, also are offered. Everything is prepared well, and the least expensive way to dine here is to order one of the fixed-price meals.

LE SPINNAKER, 52, rue Mirabeau. Tel. 31-88-24-40.
   Cuisine: FRENCH/NORMAN. **Reservations:** Recommended.
$ Prices: Appetizers 80–150F ($14.40–$27); main dishes 130–210 F ($23.40–$37.80); fixed-price meals 130–320 F ($23.40–$57.60). AE, MC, V.
   Open: Lunch Thurs–Tues 12:30–2:30; dinner Thurs–Tues 7:30–9:30pm.
   Closed: Jan, and Thurs Oct–Mar.

Set in the heart of town in a Norman-style half-timbered building, this is one of the best-recommended and most charming restaurants in town. Directed by the owner/chef Pascal Angenard, it features Norman and regional cuisine, and has a semi-antique decor filled with English chintz and white napery to accompany it. Menu specialties are ultra-fresh and richly satisfying. They include a terrine of foie gras with four spices, roasted lobster with cider vinegar and cream-enriched potatoes, slow-cooked flank of baby veal, prepared with onions and gratin of macaroni, and a succulent thin-baked tart with hot apples. A fine array of wines can accompany your meal.

Moderate

BRASSERIE-CREPERIE DEAUVILLE-TROUVILLE, 90, rue Eugène-Colas. Tel. 31-88-81-72.
   Cuisine: FRENCH. **Reservations:** Not required.
$ Prices: Appetizers 25–40 F ($4.50–$7.20); main dishes 50–80 F ($9–$14.40); crêpes 28–50 F ($5–$9); sandwiches from 20 F ($3.60); fixed-price menus 79 F ($14.20), 85 F ($15.30), and 98 F ($17.60). V.
   Open: Lunch daily noon–3pm; dinner daily 6–11pm. **Closed:** Tues–Wed in June and two weeks in Oct.

This popular brasserie serves one of the most reasonably priced menus in town. Try the tasty cut of beef, onglet, served with shallots, or one of the plats du jour. You can make selections from the shellfish and fish menus or, for something simpler, order a crêpe. The brasserie also serves great ice cream. At the self-service cafeteria downstairs, you can order sandwiches and salads. One floor above street level is the more formal brasserie with waiter service. Also on the premises is Pub 90, an English-style pub open daily from 9pm to 4am, charging from 15 F ($2.70) for a beer.

CHEZ MIOCQUE (Bar Cintra), 81, rue Eugène-Colas. Tel. 31-88-09-52.
  Cuisine: FRENCH. **Reservations:** Recommended.
$ Prices: Appetizers 55–120 F ($9.90–$21.60); main dishes 120–200 F ($21.60–$36). No credit cards.
  Open: Lunch Thurs–Mon noon–3pm; dinner Thurs–Mon 7pm–midnight.
  Closed: Jan–Feb.

This brasserie-café does a bustling business at its sidewalk café tables. Located right in the center of Deauville, Chez Miocque is near the casino, the luxurious Normandy Hôtel, and the fashionable boutiques. The owner, known simply as Jack, is an American from New York City, who will welcome you for lunch, dinner, or just drinks. I recommend his fish of the day, his pepper steak, and his sole meunière, followed by a tarte Tatin.

17. TROUVILLE

128 miles NW of Paris, 27 miles NE of Caen

GETTING THERE By Train There are rail connections from Gare Saint-Lazare in Paris to Trouville.

By Bus Bus Verts du Calvados serves the coast from Caen to Le Havre. Bus Inter Normandie serves the region from Caen to Rouen.

ESSENTIALS Orientation Boulevard Hautpoul is the main road through the resort, and promenade des Planches stretches across the waterfront.

Information The Syndicat d'Initiative (tourist office) is located at 32, quai Fernand-Moureaux (tel. 31-88-36-19).

This resort launched the Côte Fleurie—the "Flower Coast"—at the start of the Second Empire. As the first major seaside resort in France, it was developed during the days of Louis-Philippe, the "Citizen King," and has long been fashionable. It lies just across the Touques River from its more sophisticated (and more expensive) rival, Deauville.

Admittedly, Trouville is old, but like a charming countess it wears its years with a hautiness, covering a wrinkle with a mere blush. Time was when Trouville was the formal resort; nowadays it gives Deauville that privilege, as it is noisier and more fun for some.

When the sea bathers have left Trouville's splendid sands to return to Paris or wherever, Trouville lives. Its hardcore resident population of fisherfolk see to that.

On the seafront Promenade des Planches is a large swimming pool, called the Piscine Olympique, and an impressive casino, which, nevertheless, isn't as grand as the one at Deauville.

WHERE TO STAY

CARMEN, 24, rue Carnot, 14360 Trouville. Tel. 31-88-35-43. Fax 31-88-08-03. 15 rms (12 with bath). MINIBAR TV TEL
$ Rates: 180 F ($32.40) single without bath; 340 F ($61.20) single or double with bath. Breakfast 32 F ($5.70) extra. AE, DC, MC, V.

This small hotel is run by the Bude family. Some rooms overlook a courtyard filled with flowers. There is a simple dining room in the hotel, where guests can order meals ranging from 100 to 200 F ($18 to $36). The restaurant is closed on Tuesday and during most of January.

HOTEL ST. JAMES, 16, rue de la Plage, 14360 Trouville. Tel. 31-88-05-23. 14 rms (all with bath).

$ Rates: 455 F ($81.90) single; 525 F ($94.50) double. Breakfast 150 F ($27) extra. MC, V. **Parking:** Free.

Built in 1834 as a private mansion, this is the most interesting place to stay at the resort. It was turned into a hotel in 1957 by Madame Christiane Masselin. The social center of the hotel is a Louis XIII salon, and each of the rooms is charmingly decorated. The hotel also serves good food, such as mussels in cream sauce, salmon trout, and rabbit in cocotte with morels; meals cost 160–200 F ($28.80–$36).

MAISON NORMANDE, 4, place Maréchal-de-Lattre-Tassigny, 14360 Trouville. Tel. 31-88-12-25. 20 rms (all with bath or shower). TEL
$ Rates: 280–440 F ($50.40–$79.20) single or double. Breakfast 35 F ($6.30) extra. MC, V. **Closed:** Oct–Feb.

This little hotel is a good bargain on the main street of the resort, only a few blocks from the beach. The facade is a product of the 19th century. Inside, the lounges are cozy with rustic touches, including heavy beams and a fireplace. Bedrooms are simply but comfortably furnished. Breakfast is the only meal served.

LES SABLETTES, 15, rue Paul-Besson, 14360 Trouville. Tel. 31-88-10-66. 18 rms (14 with bath or shower). TEL
$ Rates: 180 F ($32.40) single or double without bath, 320 F ($57.60) single or double with bath. Breakfast 26 F ($4.60) extra. MC, V. **Closed:** Dec–Jan.

This small, unpretentious five-story hotel is on a quiet residential street, one block from the port, near the casino. It has a 19th-century facade, and the bedrooms are comfortable. Breakfast is the only meal served.

WHERE TO DINE

LA PETITE AUBERGE, 7, rue Carnot. Tel. 31-88-11-07.
Cuisine: FRENCH. **Reservations:** Recommended.
$ Prices: Appetizers 53–110 F ($9.50–$19.80); main dishes 98–145 F ($17.60–$26.10); fixed-price meals 99 F ($17.80), 159 F ($28.60), and 219 F ($39.40). MC, V.
Open: Summer, lunch daily noon–2pm; dinner daily 7:15–9:30pm. Off-season, lunch Thurs–Mon noon–2pm; dinner Thurs–Mon 7:15–9:30pm.

If you want something inexpensive without sacrificing quality, try this Norman bistro with crowded tables—it's just a block from the casino. I recently enjoyed an excellent meal for 99 F ($17.80). Try the soupe de poissons (fish soup), one of the finest along the "Flower Coast," or a seafood pot-au-feu. You can also order grilled beef and roast lamb.

LES VAPEURS, 160, bd. Fernand-Moureaux. Tel. 31-88-15-24.
Cuisine: FRENCH. **Reservations:** Recommended.
$ Prices: Appetizers 38–110 F ($6.80–$19.80); main dishes 85–135 F ($15.30–$24.30). AE, V.
Open: Daily 12:30pm–1am. **Closed:** Tues night and Wed in winter; Jan 6–Feb 8.

This art deco brasserie, one of the most popular spots on the Norman coast, is heavily frequented by Parisians on the weekends. Located across from the fish market at the port, this has been called the Brasserie Lipp of Normandy. The windows face the port, and in warm weather you can dine at sidewalk tables. Seafood is the specialty, and a wide range of fresh shrimp, mussels laced with cream, crinkle-shelled oysters, and fish is offered. Sauerkraut is also popular here.

18. HONFLEUR

125 miles NW of Paris, 39 miles NE of Caen

GETTING THERE By Bus Bus Verts du Calvados serves the coast from Caen to Le Havre.

ESSENTIALS Orientation Vieux Bassin (or the "old harbor") is the heart of the resort, and it's protected from the sea. Coming in from Pont l'Evêque to the south, the D579 leads to the major boulevard, rue de la République. Follow it until the end and you're in the town center.

Information The Office de Tourisme is at place Arthur-Boudin (tel. 31-89-23-30).

At the mouth of the Seine, opposite Le Havre, Honfleur is one of Normandy's most charming fishing ports. It is actually 500 years older than Le Havre—it dates from the 11th century. Early in the 17th century colonists set out for Québec. The township has long been favored by artists, including Daubigny and Corot. Monet also found inspiration here, and Baudelaire wrote *Invitation au Voyage* at Honfleur.

From place de la Porte-de-Rouen you can begin your tour of the town, which should take about an hour. Stroll along the **Vieux Bassin,** the old harbor, which has fishing boats and tall, slate-roofed, narrow houses. The former governor's house, **Lieutenance,** on the north side of the basin, dates from the 16th century. Nearby is the **Church of Ste-Catherine,** built entirely of timber in the 15th century by shipbuilders. The belfry stands on the other side of the street and is also built of wood.

The **Musée Eugène-Boudin,** place Erik-Satie (tel. 31-89-54-00), has a good collection of the painters who flocked to this port. The largest collection is of the pastels and paintings of Eugène Boudin, of course. It's open March 15 to September 30, Wednesday through Monday from 10am to noon and 2 to 6pm; October to March 14, it's open Monday and Wednesday through Friday from 2:30 to 5pm, and on Saturday and Sunday from 10am to noon and 2:30 to 5pm. Admission is 18 F ($3.20).

WHERE TO STAY

In addition to these hotels, Le Cheval Blanc Hôtel, listed under "Where to Dine," below, also has rooms for rent.

LA FERME ST-SIMEON, route Adolphe-Marais, 14600 Honfleur. Tel. 31-89-23-61. Fax 31-89-48-48. 38 rms (all with bath), 4 suites. MINIBAR TV TEL

$ Rates: 750 F ($135) single; 1,390–2,850 F ($250.20–$513) double; from 3,350 F ($603) suite. Breakfast 95 F ($17.10) extra. MC, V. **Parking:** Free.

An old cider press is a focal point in front of this 17th-century Norman wood-and-slate house. From the back patio you can see Le Havre and the English Channel. The light and shimmering water drew artists to this hilltop inn, which is said to be the place where impressionism was born at the end of the 19th century. Boudin dazzled Monet here, and here Courbet met Baudelaire.

Today the atmosphere is tranquil thanks to the hospitality of owner Roland Boelen. Much of the hotel is lined with terra-cotta floors, carved wood, and copper and faïence touches. The bedrooms are decorated in an 18th-century style.

Food is served either in the restaurant or on the terrace, which has a view of the Seine estuary and Le Havre. The classic yet simple cuisine is superb: Try the chausson of lobster, a fricassée of rice and kidneys, or the sole normande. Meals are 420–550 F ($75.60–$99). There is also a bar, used for drinks and breakfast.

Facilities include tennis courts, a heated indoor swimming pool with a sauna, plus a solarium, massage service, fitness center, and whirlpool baths.

HOSTELLERIE LECHAT, 3, place Ste-Catherine, 14600 Honfleur. Tel. 31-89-23-85. Fax 31-89-28-61. 22 rms (all with bath), 1 suite. TV TEL **Bus:** 20 or 50.

$ Rates: 350–450 F ($63–$81) single or double; 600 F ($108) suite. Breakfast 40 F ($7.20) extra. AE, DC, MC, V. **Parking:** Free. **Closed:** Jan.

This hotel is run to perfection under the close supervision of owner Jean-Luc Blais. The comfortably furnished rooms, although modest, are fine for an overnight stopover at the center of the port. The rustic restaurant in the hotel offers an array of seafood, including sole, salmon, and turbot, along with shellfish, such as lobster (very expensive) and oysters. The chef also does some superb terrines. A fixed-price meal costs 135 F ($24.30). The restaurant is closed on Wednesday and for lunch on Thursday.

WHERE TO DINE

The hotels listed under "Where to Stay," above, also have superb restaurants.

LE CHEVAL BLANC HOTEL, 2, quai Passagers, 14600 Honfleur. Tel. 31-81-65-00. Fax 31-89-52-80.
   Cuisine: FRENCH. **Reservations:** Required. **Bus:** 20 or 50.
$ **Prices:** Appetizers 98–145 F ($17.60–$26.10); main dishes 110–185 F ($19.80–$33.30); fixed-price meals 148 F ($26.60), 215 F ($38.70), and 380 F ($68.40). AE, MC, V.
   Open: Lunch daily noon–2pm; dinner Wed–Mon 7–9:30pm. **Closed:** Jan.
A portside villa dating from the 1400s, this is one of Honfleur's most desirable privately owned buildings. The restaurant is perhaps the prime reason for an overnight stay. While dining, you'll enjoy a view of one of the most charming ports in the north of France. Menu specialties, prepared by owner and chef Gérard Bonnefor, feature creative sauces and garnishes and include salmon marinated with herbs and scampi with cider vinegar.
   This establishment also rents 33 bedrooms—all have telephones, TVs, a view of the port, and private baths. A single costs 350 F ($63) and a double runs 580 F ($104.40), continental breakfast included.

RESTAURANT L'ABSINTHE, 10, quai de la Quarantaine. Tel. 31-89-39-00.
   Cuisine: FRENCH. **Reservations:** Required. **Bus:** 20 or 50.
$ **Prices:** Appetizers 83–135 F ($14.90–$24.30); main dishes 125–200 F ($22.50–$36); fixed-price meals 149 F ($26.80), 220 F ($39.60), and 350 F ($63). AE, DC, MC, V.
   Open: Lunch daily 12:15–2:15pm; dinner daily 7:15–9:15pm. **Closed:** Mon night and Tues off-season; mid-Nov to mid-Dec.
This 17th-century tavern is known by practically everyone in town for its beautiful decor, extravagant portions, and well-prepared and savory cuisine. Chef Antoine Ceffrey, who apprenticed for many years at Troisgros, will probably make an appearance in the dining room before the end of your meal. A dinner might consist of veal kidneys with Calvados, rack of lamb with thyme, well-garnished shellfish, monkfish with ginger, and attractive desserts, such as an assortment of fresh fruit with essence of raspberries.

---

19. LE HAVRE

126 miles NW of Paris, 67 miles NE of Caen

GETTING THERE   By Train   Rail connections from Rouen take 45 minutes, and those from Paris take two hours.

ESSENTIALS   Orientation   Two major boulevards, boulevard de Strasbourg and rue de Paris, come together at place de l'Hôtel-de-Ville. From there, avenue Foch leads to the water.

Information   The Office de Tourisme is on place de l'Hôtel-de-Ville (tel. 35-21-22-88).

France's major Atlantic port, at the mouth of the Seine, Le Havre lay in ruins in 1945, the worst-damaged port at the end of World War II, and the competition was stiff for that distinction. The city had been the target of more than 170 bombings. But the recovery of Le Havre was amazing, and now the largest container ships and oil tankers afloat can dock there easily. You can reach Trouville and Deauville by boat during the summer or you can go across one of Europe's longest suspension bridges, which celebrated its first anniversary in 1960.

WHAT TO SEE & DO

A modern city, with tall blocks of apartment houses and large, pleasant squares, Le Havre, unlike some French towns, has radically changed since it was created in the 16th century by François I. There's a lot to see in Le Havre and its surrounding areas, and in summer it's possible to tour the port by boat. For information about all of the available **boat tours,** contact the tourist office (see "Essentials," above).

If you drive out to **Le Heve Lighthouse,** you'll have a good view of the port, the "Flower Coast," and an estuary of the Seine. In summer, lighthouse tours begin daily at 10am; the guide expects a tip.

The **Eglise St-Joseph,** boulevard François, which has a bell tower nearly 350 feet high, is the tallest building made of reinforced concrete in the country. The vast interior is awesome: It has square pillars supporting a lantern tower, and light pours in through colored glass. From the top of the tower, visitors can enjoy a vista of Le Havre. The church is open daily from 9am to noon and 2 to 7pm.

For another splendid view, go to the **Fort de Ste-Adresse,** above Ste-Adresse, a suburb of Le Havre. On a clear day, you can see the Côte de Grace, Honfleur, and the Seine estuary. On a recent summer visit I could see the entire coast of Calvados.

In addition, Le Havre has two museums worth visiting:

ANDRE MALRAUX MUSEE DES BEAUX-ARTS, bd. J-F-Kennedy. Tel. 35-42-33-97.
This museum, sophisticated in design, brilliantly shows off a collection that includes works by Raoul Dufy, along with many of the impressionists who were drawn to the north coast, including Monet, Pissarro, Sisley, and Renoir. There is also an outstanding collection of the works of Eugène Boudin.
Admission: Free.
Open: Wed–Mon 10am–noon and 2–6pm.

MUSEE DE L'ANCIEN HAVRE, 1, rue Jérôme-Bellarmato. Tel. 35-42-27-90.
Located in a restored 17th- to 18th-century town house, this museum of ancient Le Havre has two galleries devoted to the town's planning history, two others devoted to maritime and harbor history, and one that deals with the music of the street. Some temporary exhibits are organized in a special gallery. The collections consist of china, models (especially ship models), photographs, engravings, and watercolors.
Admission: Free.
Open: Wed–Sun 10am–noon and 2–6pm. **Closed:** Bank holidays.

WHERE TO STAY

Le Monaco, listed under "Where to Dine," below, also rents pleasantly furnished guest rooms.

LE BORDEAUX, 147, rue Louis-Brindeau, 76600 Le Havre. Tel. 35-22-69-44. 31 rms (all with bath or shower). MINIBAR TV TEL
$ Rates: 290–445 F ($52.20–$80.10) single; 350–500 F ($63–$90) double. Breakfast 42 F ($7.50) extra. AE, DC, MC, V.
Though it doesn't have a restaurant, this is the leading hotel. Le Bordeaux is located in the center of the port, near the Bassin du Commerce. Your bedroom window might overlook a yacht belonging to a wealthy Londoner. The compact, soundproof bedrooms are bright and pleasantly furnished.

HOTEL ASTORIA, 13, cours de la République, 76000 Le Havre. Tel. 35-25-00-03. Fax 35-26-48-34. 37 rms (all with bath). TV TEL
$ Rates: 240 F ($43.20) single; 260 F ($46.80) double. Breakfast 30 F ($5.40) extra. AE, DC, MC, V. **Parking:** Free.

Set across from the railway station, this four-story hotel was built in the 1960s and renovated as recently as 1992. It offers clean and comfortable bedrooms, although with a minimum of frills. Its restaurant is one of the most reasonable at the port, featuring many fish dishes and offering a selection of fixed-price meals at 53 F ($9.50), 76 F ($13.60), and 120 F ($21.60).

LE MERCURE, chaussée d'Angoulême, 76600 Le Havre. Tel. 35-19-50-50. Fax 35-19-50-99. 96 rms (all with bath). TV TEL

$ **Rates:** 600 F ($108) single; 690 F ($124.20) double. Breakfast 52 F ($9.30) extra. AE, DC, MC, V. **Parking:** 30 F ($5.40).

Located near the ocean and facing the Arts Center, this hotel is a member of a nationwide hotel chain. All the well-furnished bedrooms have radios. The hotel runs one of the best restaurants in town, where fixed-price meals begin at 125 F ($22.50).

WHERE TO DINE

LE MONACO, 16, rue de Paris, 76600 Le Havre. Tel. 35-42-21-01.
Cuisine: FRENCH. **Reservations:** Required.

$ **Prices:** Appetizers 60–125 F ($10.80–$22.50); main dishes 60–150 F ($10.80–$27); fixed-price meals 145 F ($26.10), 260 F ($46.80), and 340 F ($61.20). AE, DC, MC, V.
Open: Lunch daily noon–2pm; dinner daily 7:30–9:30pm. **Closed:** Feb 15–Mar 1.

This modern restaurant attracts the bright young French, plus a large coterie of English people who visit for the weekend. The varied cuisine is often excellent and includes braised turbot in Calvados, smoked Norwegian salmon, fresh goose liver, feuilleté of snails cooked in cider, and barbue suprême with sorrel. Fresh salmon is occasionally featured, also served with sorrel, and the roast lamb is always reliable. The chef is likely to offer fresh mussels, prawns, and oysters.

The restaurant also rents nine small, pleasantly furnished bedrooms. A single costs 135–210 F ($24.30–$37.80), and a double goes for 160–260 F ($28.80–$46.80).

LA PETITE AUBERGE, 32, rue Ste-Adresse. Tel. 35-46-27-32.
Cuisine: FRENCH. **Reservations:** Required.

$ **Prices:** Appetizers 95–108 F ($17.10–$19.40); main dishes 98–138 F ($17.60–$24.80); fixed-price meals 110–185 F ($19.80–$33.30). AE, MC, V.
Open: Lunch Tues–Sun noon–2pm; dinner Tues–Sat 7–9:30pm. **Closed:** Aug 12–Sept 2.

I am especially fond of this place for its pleasing ambience, and I like the prices even better. Of course, you can dine more expensively—especially on a Saturday night, when the 110-F ($19.80) fixed-price menu isn't available. Specialties include sweetbread salad with mussels, turbot filet with zucchini-laced spaghetti, loin of lamb with sweet garlic, and filet mignon with truffles. The Dover sole with a coulis of lobster also is delectable.

20. FÉCAMP

127 miles NW of Paris, 25 miles NE of Le Havre

GETTING THERE   By Train   Six trains a day arrive in Fécamp from Le Havre (taking an hour and 15 minutes). The train station is on boulevard de la République.

By Car   If you are driving from Le Havre, take the D925 north, then continue along rue Le Borgne until you reach the town center.

ESSENTIALS   Orientation   Most of the town lies on the west side of a basin.

Information   The Maison du Tourisme 113R is at 113, rue Alexandre-Le-Grand (tel. 35-28-51-01).

This cod-fishing port is where the popular Benedictine liqueur is distilled. At the mouth of the Fécamp River, this town is squeezed between two high cliffs. De Maupassant once lived here, using it as the setting in some of his stories.

According to legend, the "True Blood" of Christ drifted to Fécamp from Palestine in the trunk of a fig tree. That relic is today the precious Treasury in the **Eglise de la Trinité,** which dates mostly from 1175 to 1225. It is located just off boulevard de la République. From its central tower, 210 feet high, you'll have a good view of this seaside resort and the English Channel. The venerated relic of the True Blood is housed in a 16th-century tabernacle. The former abbey church's length of 416 feet almost rivals that of Notre-Dame in Paris, which extends 10 feet more. In the transept is an interesting *Assumption* from the late 15th century, and from the next century there are some splendid carved screens. The church is open daily 8am to 7pm.

The **Musée Bénédictine,** 110 rue Alexandre-Le-Grand (tel. 35-10-26-10), owes its inception to Alexandre Le Grand, who rediscovered and renovated the elixir invented by Dom Bernardo Vincelli, a Benedictine monk who distilled spices and local herbs. You can tour the Distillerie Bénédictine, with its Gothic and Renaissance buildings, and the old distilling chamber where the world-famous liqueur was first produced.

The museum is open daily from 9:30 to 11:30am and 2 to 5:30pm; admission is 25 F ($4.50) for adults and 12.50 F ($2.20) for children 10–17, and includes a tasting of a Benedictine specialty.

WHERE TO STAY

Most visitors drive on to Le Havre or Dieppe for the night, but if you're going to stay in Fécamp, I recommend the following. Auberge de la Rouge, listed under "Where to Dine," below, also offers accommodations.

HOTEL-RESTAURANT D'ANGLETERRE, 91-93, rue de la Plage, 76400 Fécamp. Tel. 35-28-01-60. Fax 35-28-62-95. 30 rms (25 with bath or shower). TV
$ Rates: 150–200 F ($27–$36) single or double without bath, 190–300 F ($34.20–$54) single or double with bath. Breakfast 26 F ($4.60) extra. AE, DC, MC, V. **Parking:** Free.
Already flourishing in 1900, this hotel was modernized between the wars. It lies one block from the elevated promenade opening onto the sea. The hotel was designed along traditional Mansard-inspired lines. The year-round hotel has modestly furnished rooms and is popular with the English who cross the Channel for a holiday in France.

WHERE TO DINE

AUBERGE DE LA ROUGE, route du Havre, St-Léonard, 76400 Fécamp. Tel. 35-28-07-59.
Cuisine: FRENCH. **Reservations:** Required. **Directions:** Take the D925 south one mile.
$ Prices: Appetizers 85–130 F ($15.30–$23.40); main dishes 135–210 F ($24.30–$37.80); fixed-price menus 105 F ($18.90), 190 F ($34.20), and 260 F ($46.80). AE, DC, MC, V.
Open: Lunch Tues–Sun noon–2:30pm; dinner Tues–Sat 7:15–9:30pm. **Closed:** Feb.
The best restaurant in town is also a small hotel. You're welcomed by M and Mme

Claude Guyot in what was built in 1894 as a relay station for the French postal service. The owners prepare consistently fine dishes, such as lobster à l'armoricaine and sole normande. Game dishes are a specialty in season, and at all times they offer caneton (duck) rouennais.

The Auberge also rents eight air-conditioned rooms with private baths or showers, TVs, and telephones. A single costs 280 F ($50.40); a double, 350 F ($63).

LE MARITIME, 2, place Nicolas-Selles. Tel. 35-28-21-71.
    Cuisine: FRENCH. **Reservations:** Recommended.
$ Prices: Appetizers 45–110 F ($8.10–$19.80); main dishes 110–175 F ($19.80–$31.50); fixed-price meals 105 F ($18.90); 145 F ($26.10), 175 F ($31.50), and 210 F ($37.80). MC, V.
    Open: Lunch daily noon–2:15pm; dinner daily 7–9:30pm.

This restaurant, housed in a corner building between the old town and the harbor, has become a local favorite. The upstairs dining room has a view; the downstairs dining room is less formal and very nautical. Tempting fish dishes and daily changing specials are the features of the enjoyable menu. Typical menu items include salmon-stuffed blinis, a platter of fresh shellfish, grilled beef with béarnaise sauce, mussels marinara, and grilled andouillette (chitterling) sausages served with mustard.

21. DIEPPE

104 miles NW of Paris, 65 miles NE of Le Havre

GETTING THERE   By Train   Dieppe is easily reached from Paris (Gare St-Lazare) or Rouen.

ESSENTIALS   Orientation   The main business center of town is the Grande Rue. Boulevard de Verdun is the more elegant promenade, with the casino and a grassy area separating it from the seafront and boulevard du Maréchal-Foch.

Information   The Office de Tourisme is at Pont Jehan-Ango, quai du Carenage (tel. 35-84-11-77).

In a valley bordered by steep white cliffs reminiscent of those at Dover (England), Dieppe on the Channel coast has long been popular as a seaside resort, in spite of its pebbly beach. In fact it is one of the oldest seaside resorts in France, as it is the nearest beach to Paris, 104 miles away and easily reached by rail. Dieppe has enjoyed favor with the English too, including Oscar Wilde, many of the British preferring it to their own Brighton in Sussex.

Badly shattered during World War II, Dieppe is now a progressive, modern town, the fourth-largest passenger port in the country. The cross-Channel steamer arrives from Newhaven, near Brighton on England's south coast, dispensing the daily trippers seeking a "holiday on the continent."

WHAT TO SEE & DO

Dieppe is one of the safest and deepest harbors in the English Channel. It was the subject of a daring but unsuccessful Canadian commando raid in 1942. The outer port, the **Port de Voyageurs,** is where the Channel ferryboats dock. You can attend a lively fish market under the arcades, but the fishing port itself, **Port de Pêche,** has more local color. The commercial harbor, **Port de Commerce,** lies beyond and does a thriving banana trade with the West Indies.

Take a walk through **place du Puits-Salés,** the heart of Dieppe, where six streets meet. From this small square you can walk up rue St-Jacques to the **Eglise St-Jacques** (St. James), founded in the 13th century. Supporting the more modern central tower, the transept is the oldest part of the church. St-Jacques has some lovely portals and is elegantly decorated. It's open daily from 8am to 6pm.

West of the harbor, which has a casino and a bathing beach, you reach the **Château-Musée de Dieppe** (tel. 35-84-19-76), on a high chalk cliff. It dates from 1435 and has been much altered over the years. The château houses a museum that contains an excellent collection of Dieppe ivories, medieval and Renaissance sculpture, a large collection of 19th-century European paintings including works by the impressionists, and other souvenirs of the seaport. See also the prints by Georges Braque. Charging 12 F ($2.10) for adults, 8 F ($1.40) for children, the museum is open June through September, daily from 10am to noon and 2 to 6pm; October to May, it's open Wednesday through Monday from 10am to noon and 2 to 5pm.

The **Château de Miromesnil**, 76550 Tourville sur Arques (follow the N27 to the junction with the D915 from which the château is signposted) (tel. 35-04-40-30), is in a wooded park with a garden in an ancient beech forest. Built just after the Battle of Arques in 1589, it has two contrasting facades: rosy brick on the south and majestic classicism on the north.

Guy de Maupassant was born here in 1850, and a few souvenirs of the author can be seen, as well as a collection of historical objects and documents from the families of the present owner, Countess Bertrand de Vogue. A little 15th-century chapel is the only relic of an earlier château. Guided tours are given May through mid-October, daily from 2 to 6pm. Admission is 25 F ($4.50) for adults, 15 F ($2.70) for children under 13. The château lies near the hamlet of St-Aubin-sur-Scie.

WHERE TO STAY

HOTEL WINDSOR, 18, bd. de Verdun, 76200 Dieppe. Tel. 35-84-15-23.
48 rms (43 with bath). TV TEL
$ Rates: 130–175 F ($23.40–$31.50) single or double without bath, 265–315 F ($47.70–$56.70) single or double with bath. Breakfast 35 F ($6.30) extra. AE, DC, MC, V. **Parking:** Free. **Closed:** Dec 17–Jan 23.
One of the best values in town, the Hôtel Windsor is known for its panoramic restaurant, Le Haut Gallion. Originally constructed in 1870 as a private house for the paymaster of Napoléon's army, this became a hotel in 1930 and was renovated in 1991. It opens onto a seafront promenade, and the bedrooms are conservatively modern and comfortable. The rates depend on the bath and the view.

The restaurant is open from noon to 2:30pm and 7 to 9:30pm; it's closed Sunday night from October to May. Fixed-price meals cost 100–280 F ($18–$50.40).

LA PRESIDENCE, 1, bd. de Verdun, 76200 Dieppe. Tel. 35-84-31-31. Fax 35-84-86-70. 88 rms (all with bath). A/C TV TEL
$ Rates: 340 F ($61.20) single; 560 F ($100.80) double. Breakfast 50 F ($9) extra. AE, DC, MC, V. **Parking:** Free.
The town's best hotel, La Présidence opens onto the sea and stands right next to the Municipal Casino. It's modern and functional and has well-planned bedrooms. Le Queiros is a good grill room, featuring French cuisine with plenty of fresh oysters and scallops. The chef also prepares meat dishes well, including the choice beef cut, onglet, which is grilled and occasionally served with shallots. More exotic specialties include calves' head in vinaigrette sauce and skate in black butter. A fixed-price meal is offered for 150 F ($27). The restaurant is open daily from noon to 3pm and 7:30pm to 1am. A parking garage is available.

WHERE TO DINE

Both of the hotels listed above also have fine restaurants.

A LA MARMITE DIEPPOISE, 8, rue St-Jean. Tel. 35-84-24-26.
   Cuisine: FRENCH. **Reservations:** Required.
$ Prices: Appetizers 45–110 F ($8.10–$19.80); main dishes 110–175 F ($19.80–$31.50); fixed-price meals 85 F ($15.30) (lunch only), 135 F ($24.30), 160 F ($28.80), and 210 F ($37.80). MC, V.
   Open: Lunch Tues–Sun noon–2pm; dinner Tues–Wed and Fri–Sat 7:30–9:15pm.
   Closed: June 21–July 5.

Located in town, this cheerfully decorated restaurant has a varied and moderately priced menu. The service is prompt and friendly. The owner and chef, Jean-Pierre Toussat, offers (naturally) la marmite dieppoise as his specialty. I also recommend the mussels marinière, an assiette of fresh seafood, and a fisherman's-style sauerkraut.

LE PORT, 99, quai Henri-IV. Tel. 35-84-36-64.
  Cuisine: FRENCH. **Reservations:** Recommended.
$ **Prices:** Appetizers 40–92 F ($7.20–$16.60); main courses 85–120 F ($15.30–$21.60); fixed-price menus 98 F ($17.60), 145 F ($26.10), and 180 F ($32.40). AE, MC, V.
  Open: Lunch Fri–Wed noon–2pm; dinner Fri–Wed 6–9:30pm. **Closed:** Jan 10–Feb 15.

Le Port's harborside location is appropriate to the seafood that is this establishment's specialty. Within an elegantly conservative dining room in a much restored 19th-century building, you can enjoy some of the freshest fish in town. Menu items include a thick slice of monkfish with fresh fennel, roast shank of rabbit with a mustard sauce, several preparations of mussels, and an array of sole dishes. There's also a limited selection of meat dishes.

NEARBY DINING

LA BÛCHERIE, at Vertus. Tel. 35-84-83-10.
  Cuisine: FRENCH. **Reservations:** Required. **Directions:** From Dieppe, take the N27 south for two miles.
$ **Prices:** Appetizers 110–165 F ($19.80–$29.70); main dishes 150–230 F ($27–$41.40); fixed-price meals 160–240 F ($28.80–$43.20).
  Open: Lunch Tues–Sun 12:15–2pm; dinner Tues–Sat 7:30–9:30pm. **Closed:** June 25–July 2.

The food you'll find at La Bûcherie is even better than the food served in town. Named for the log-burning fireplace at one end of the elegant bar, this restaurant is run by the Delaunay family and lies in a farming hamlet. It draws a distinguished clientele who appreciate good food and service. Specialties include terrine of duck, fresh lobster, wild salmon, marmite dieppoise, and a blanquette of sole, turbot, brill, and fresh salmon. The decor is elegantly provincial.

CHAPTER 14
BRITTANY

The old people may be fading away, but while they live, so will the past. In the northwestern corner of France, in the ancient province and duchy of Brittany, the Bretons—at least some of them—stubbornly hold onto their traditions. True, the young people head for Paris for "a better life," and the men who returned from World War II brought "alarming" new ideas. Nevertheless, deep in the heart of the interior, called l'Argoat, the old folks quietly live in stone farmhouses, with much the same ideas their grandparents had. The older women, at least on special occasions, still can be seen wearing their starched-lace headdresses.

The Breton language is still spoken, better understood by the Welsh and the Cornish folk than by the French. Sadly, it may die out altogether, in spite of attempts by folklore groups to keep it alive. In that sense, Brittany is the Wales of France.

Conquered by Caesar in 56 B.C., the land was once called Armorica. However, the Celtic inhabitants of the British Isles, the Britons, crossed the Channel in A.D. 500, fleeing from the invading Angles and Saxons.

The true Bretons—except those whose parents married "foreigners" from Paris—are generally darker and shorter than their compatriots in France. These characteristics reflect their Celtic origin, which still lives on in superstition, folklore, and fairy tales. Breton *pardons* are famous. These are religious festivals, sometimes attracting thousands of pilgrims who turn up in traditional dress.

Nearly every hamlet has its own *pardon*. These observances are major attractions, drawing the French from as far away as Marseille and Scots from the north. The best-known ones are on May 19 at Treguier (honoring St. Yves, who consoled the poor and righted wrongs), on the second Sunday in July at Locronan (in the footsteps of St. Ronan), on July 26 at St-Anne-d'Auray (honoring the "mothers of Bretons"), and on September 8 at Le Folgoet (commemorating *ar foll coat*, or that "idiot of the forest").

Many Bretons consider themselves a nation within a nation. Movements for independence—particularly strong in the 19th century—come and go. Brittany was joined with the crown of France through Anne of Brittany's marriages to Charles VIII and later to Louis XII.

Traditionally, the province is divided into Haute-Bretagne and Basse-Bretagne. The rocky coastline, some 750 miles long, is studded with promontories, coves, and occasional beaches. Like the prow of a ship, Brittany projects into the sea. Hence, the province gives France its best sailors. The interior, however, is a land of sleepy hamlets, stone farmhouses, and moors covered with yellow broom and purple heather.

WHAT'S SPECIAL ABOUT BRITTANY

Beaches

☐ 750 miles of grand rocky coastline, studded with sandy coves, white beaches, bays, and little fishing villages.

☐ La Baule, along the Côte d'Amour (Coast of Love), the premier beach resort of Brittany, with miles of crescent-shaped white-sand beach.

Islands

☐ Atlantic islands, to the west of France: 12 belong to Brittany, lying halfway between the mainland and the high seas.

Great Towns/Villages

☐ Ville-Close, Concarneau, an ancient hamlet surrounded by ramparts, some dating from the 14th century.

☐ Old Town, Dinan, a 1½-mile circuit of walls, with steep cobbled streets of medieval houses.

Ancient Monuments

☐ Field of Megaliths at Carnac, hundreds of huge stones, the most important prehistoric find in northern France.

☐ Château de la Duchesse Anne at Dinan, a 14th-century dungeon and a 15th-century tower.

Architectural Highlights

☐ Cathedral of St. Peter at Nantes, begun in 1434 and containing the tomb of François II, duc de Bretagne.

☐ Château des Ducs de Bretagne, also at Nantes, where the Edict of Nantes was signed.

Events/Festivals

☐ Brittany is the site of pilgrimage festivals, called *pardons,* organized usually from May to September.

First-time visitors to the craggy peninsula would be better advised to stick to the coastline, where salt-meadow sheep can be seen grazing along pasture land whipped by sea breezes. Those leaving Mont Saint-Michel can center at the trio of tourist towns, St-Malo, Dinan, or Dinard. Coming from the château country, visitors can explore the south Brittany coastline.

SEEING BRITTANY

GETTING THERE Brittany boasts several airports (serviced by Air Inter), including those at Rennes, Dinard, Quimper, and Nantes. Railway connections from Paris to the main stations of Brittany are fast and efficient. TGV rail links Paris to Rennes, for example, in just two hours. About six trains daily leave Gare Montparnasse in Paris for Rennes, where you can make connections to other parts of Brittany. The French National Railway also runs regular bus service to the major holiday resorts.

From late spring until early autumn Brittany is best visited by car. The 217-mile drive from Paris to the outskirts of Brittany takes about six hours. Ferries also take passengers from Portsmouth (England) to St-Malo. Brittany is also ideal country for cycling, hiking, and riding.

Hotel rooms are hard to come by in July and August unless you make reservations far in advance. Many places close in the off-season (mid-October to mid-March).

A SUGGESTED ROUTE Tie in your tour of Brittany with a visit to Normandy (see Chapter 13). Make either St-Malo, Dinan, or Dinard your north-coast base, where you'll need at least two days. The next center for touring would be Quimper, on the west coast. Spend two or three days seeing Quimper itself and taking trips to explore Locronan; Concarneau, with its Ville-Close; and Pont-Aven, with its colony of artists made famous by Gauguin.

Then move on to La Baule on the southern coast, especially in summer. It's a first-class, but pricey, beach resort, and from there you can visit Nantes, about 45 miles east on a day trip.

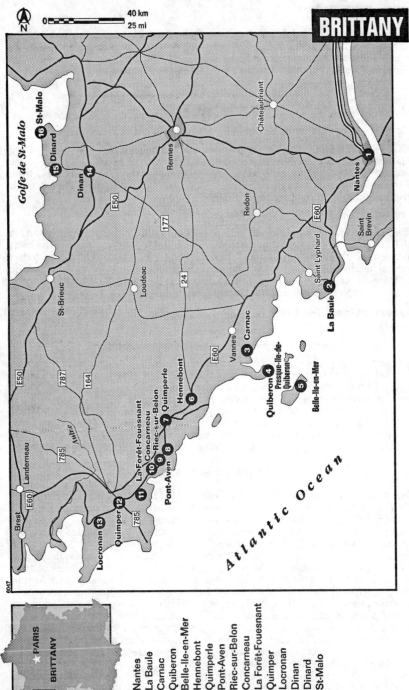

BRITTANY

40 km
25 mi

N

Golfe de St-Malo

Atlantic Ocean

St-Malo 16
Dinard 15
Dinan 14

Rennes

Châteaubriant

Nantes 1

Saint Brevin

St-Brieuc

Loudéac

Redon

Saint Lyphard

La Baule 2

Landerneau

Brest

Carnac 3

Vannes

Quiberon 4
Presque-Île-de-Quiberon

Belle-Île-en-Mer 5

Quimperle 6
Hennebont

Riec-sur-Belon 7
Quimperle

La Forêt-Fouesnant
Concarneau 10
9
Pont-Aven 8

Quimper 12
11

Locronan 13

E50
E60
E50
787
164
177
24
E60
E60
785
785

Aulne

8047

PARIS

BRITTANY

1 Nantes
2 La Baule
3 Carnac
4 Quiberon
5 Belle-Île-en-Mer
6 Hennebont
7 Quimperle
8 Pont-Aven
9 Riec-sur-Belon
10 Concarneau
11 La Forêt-Fouesnant
12 Quimper
13 Locronan
14 Dinan
15 Dinard
16 St-Malo

For the most delightful trip of all, take a 45-minute boat trip from Quiberon (on the south coast) to Belle-Ile, beloved by legendary stage actress Sarah Bernhardt. It's one of the most charming islands in the Atlantic. On the way back to Paris, save some time—once you're in mainland Brittany—to explore Carnac.

---

1. NANTES

239 miles SW of Paris, 202 miles N of Bordeaux

GETTING THERE   By Train   About a dozen trains leave Paris, usually from Gare Montparnasse, for Nantes every day, taking three to six hours, depending on the number of stops. The world's fastest train (300 m.p.h.) the TGV *Atlantique,* from Paris to Rennes and Nantes, is the best connection. Trains also make the four-hour trip to Bordeaux at least five times a day.

By Car   The A11 links Paris to Nantes.

ESSENTIALS   Orientation   Originally built on the largest of three islands in the Loire, the city expanded in the Middle Ages to the northern edge of the river, where its center lies today. The most visible building is the Château Ducal, which rises several hundred feet from a wide boulevard, the main artery of Nantes—the quai de la Fosse. At one end of this long, busy boulevard lies the train station; at the other, the waterside promenades beside the Loire.

Information   The Office de Tourisme is on place du Commerce (tel. 40-47-04-51).

In western France, Nantes is the largest town of Brittany, although in spirit it seems to belong more to the château country along the Loire. The mouth of the Loire is about 30 miles away, and at Nantes the river divides into several branches. Nantes spreads itself over these Loire islands, but it lies mostly on the north bank. A commercial and industrial city, it is a busy port that suffered great damage in World War II. The city is known for the Edict of Nantes, sponsored by Henri IV in 1598, guaranteeing religious freedom to Protestants (it was later revoked). Many famous people have lived here, from Molière to Madame de Sévigné to Stendhal to Michelet.

WHAT TO SEE & DO

The **Cathédrale de St-Pierre (Cathedral of St. Peter),** place St-Pierre (tel. 40-47-84-64), begun in 1434, wasn't finished until the closing years of the 19th century, yet it remained harmonious architecturally—a rare feat of which few European cathedrals can boast. The facade is characterized by two square towers, but the 335-foot-long interior is more impressive. Its pièce de résistance, however, is the Renaissance masterpiece of Michel Colomb—the tomb of François II, duc de Bretagne, and his second wife, Marguerite de Foix. Another impressive work of art is the tomb of Gen. Juchault de Lamoricière, a native of Nantes and a great African campaigner; sculptor Paul Dubois completed the tomb in 1879. After a fire totally destroyed the roof in January 1972 (rebuilt in 1975), the interior of the cathedral was completely restored. The white walls and pillars contrast with the rich colors of the stained-glass windows. The crypt, which dates from the 11th century, shelters a museum of religions. The cathedral is open daily from 8:45am to noon and 2 to 7pm.

Between the cathedral and the Loire stands the second major sight of Nantes, the **Château des Ducs de Bretagne,** 1, place Marc-Elder (tel. 40-41-56-56), once the seat of the dukes of Brittany. It was here that the Edict of Nantes was discussed. The castle was founded in the 9th or 10th century, and François II, duc de Bretagne, began its reconstruction in 1466. It is flanked by large towers and a bastion. The duchesse du Berry was imprisoned here, as was Gilles de Retz, known as "Bluebeard," who confessed to more than 100 murders.

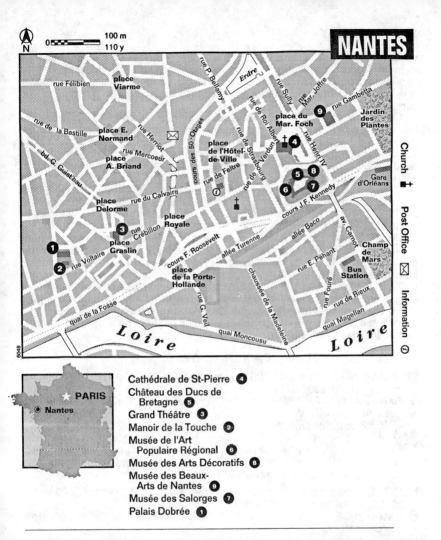

Behind its walls the castle has installed three museums. The **Museum of Decorative Arts,** in a room in the Tour du Fer à Cheval (Horseshoe Tower), is dedicated to contemporary textile art. The **Museum of the Salorges** was created by Nantes industrialists in 1928 and offers exhibits on the different aspects of commercial, colonial, and industrial activities of the city since the 18th century, including the slave trade. Ship models are especially interesting, including fishing boats of Brittany. The **Museum of Popular Regional Art** (in the Grand Gouvernement building) presents many aspects of costumes, furniture, and handcrafts of the Breton people. All three museums can be visited for 20 F ($3.60) for adults, 10 F ($1.80) for children. In July and August they are open daily from 10am to noon and 2 to 6pm; the rest of the year they are open the same hours but only Wednesday through Monday.

If time remains, you might want to visit the **Musée des Beaux-Arts de Nantes,** 10, rue Georges-Clemenceau (tel. 40-41-65-65), east of place du Maréchal-Foch. This is one of the most interesting provincial galleries of art in western France; it contains an unusually fine collection of sculptures and paintings that accent the French modern schools. Sculpture and temporary exhibitions are displayed on the ground floor. See Ingres's portrait of Madame de Senonnes, a painting by Courbet, works by Delacroix and Georges de La Tour, *Two Saints* by Bergognone, and examples from the Italian school. See also the collection of modern paintings, including works by Kandinsky, Hartung, Poliakoff, and Gorin. The museum, charging an admission of 20 F ($3.60) for adults and 10 F ($1.80) for children, is open Monday and Wednesday through Saturday from 10am to noon and 1 to 5:45pm, and on Sunday from 11am to 5pm.

Of minor interest, the **Musée Dobrée,** place Jean-V (tel. 40-69-76-08), is a town mansion from the 19th century that was built by an important collector in Nantes, from whom the palace takes its name. It stands alongside the manor of Jean de la Touche from the 15th century, where the bishops of Nantes occasionally lived. Both buildings are museums and contain a varied collection gathered by Monsieur Dobrée, including prehistoric and medieval antiquities, Flemish paintings from the 15th century, and many ecclesiastical relics. The museum is in the vicinity of place Graslin and the attractive cours Cambronne. It charges admission of 20 F ($3.60) for adults and 10 F ($1.80) for children, and is open Wednesday through Monday from 10am to noon and 2 to 6pm.

Jules Verne, the French novelist (*Around the World in Eighty Days*), was born in Nantes in 1828, and literary fans like to seek out his house at 4, rue de Clisson in the Ile-Feydeau. However, the **Musée Jules Verne de Nantes,** at 3, rue de l'Hermitage (tel. 40-69-72-52), is filled with memorabilia of the writer. Verne was one of the most translated of all French writers, and the museum displays any number of objects his writings inspired, ranging from inkpots to a "magic" lantern with glass slides. The museum is open Wednesday through Saturday from 10am to noon and 2 to 5pm, and on Sunday from 2 to 5pm, charging 8 F ($1.40) for adults and 4 F (70¢) for children and senior citizens.

WHERE TO STAY

GRASLIN, 1, rue Piron, 44000 Nantes. Tel. 40-69-72-91. Fax 40-69-04-44.
    47 rms (all with bath). TV TEL
$ Rates: 290–360 F ($52.20–$64.80) single or double. Breakfast 38 F ($6.80) extra. AE, DC, MC, V.

In the center of town facing the Graslin et Théâtre, the Graslin lies on a steep old street near the harbor. The owners, Monsieur and Madame Cassard, have given it many homelike touches, and it now offers more for the money than almost any hotel in its price category in Nantes. The comfortable bedrooms have radios and are decorated with functional simplicity. Eight contain minibars.

L'HOTEL, 6, rue Henry-IV, 44000 Nantes. Tel. 40-29-30-31. Fax 40-29-00-95. 31 rms (all with bath). TV TEL
$ Rates: 360 F ($64.80) single; 400 F ($72) double. Breakfast 37 F ($6.60) extra. AE, DC, MC, V.

Located at the top of place de la Duchesse-Anne, this comfortable hotel sits across the street from the moat surrounding the Château des Ducs de Bretagne—within easy access of the dining and entertainment facilities of Nantes. A scattering of 19th-century antiques stands in the tile reception area, and nearby are the paneled walls and deep modern sofas and chairs of the sitting room. The rooms are decorated differently in coordinated colors that complement the bentwood and rattan furnishings.

MERCURE NANTES, Ile-Beaulieu, 44000 Nantes-Beaulieu. Tel. 40-47-61-03. Fax 40-48-23-83. 98 rms (all with bath). A/C MINIBAR TV TEL
$ Rates: 480 F ($86.40) single; 530 F ($95.40) double. Breakfast 50 F ($9) extra. AE, DC, MC, V. **Parking:** 20 F ($3.60).

On an island surrounded by the Loire, two miles from the center of town and the railway station, the Mercure Nantes offers well-furnished, soundproof chambers that are a model of efficient hotel planning. In fact, this chain hotel is the best place to stay in town for those seeking the most up-to-date amenities. The restaurant and bar, Le Tilbury, offers a wide choice of seafood and fish dishes, with meals costing 110–140 F ($19.80–$25.20). There is a heated outdoor swimming pool with a lounging terrace, plus tennis courts.

WHERE TO DINE

LA CIGALE, 4, place Graslin. Tel. 40-69-76-41.
  Cuisine: FRENCH. **Reservations:** Recommended. **Bus:** 11 or 34.
$ Prices: Appetizers 35–40 F ($6.30–$7.20); main dishes 65–80 F ($11.70–$14.40); fixed-price meals 69–130 F ($12.40–$23.40). MC, V.
  Open: Lunch daily 11:45am–2:30pm; dinner daily 6:45pm–12:30am.

By anyone's estimate, this is the most famous and historic brasserie in Nantes, outfitted in a museum-quality Belle Epoque style that has changed very little since the place was established in 1895. Located in the monumental heart of Nantes, across from the most visible theater in town (Le Théâtre Graslin), it offers old-world service, ample portions, and numerous nooks and semi-concealed crannies amid a large, bustling, and endlessly interesting background. (Past clients have included virtually every artist, writer, or politician visiting Nantes, and such world-class names as the Soviet-born ballet dancer Baryshnikov.)

Menu items might include heaping platters of fresh shellfish, zander in beurre-blanc sauce, a confit des cuisses de canard, an array of grilled steaks, steak tartare, and specialties that change with the seasons and the availability of the ingredients.

COQ HARDI, 22, allée du Commandant-Charcot. Tel. 40-74-14-25.
  Cuisine: FRENCH. **Reservations:** Required.
$ Prices: Appetizers 40–85 F ($7.20–$15.30); main dishes 95–135 F ($17.10–$24.30); fixed-price lunch 93–138 F ($16.70–$24.80). AE, MC, V.
  Open: Lunch Sun–Fri noon–2pm; dinner Sun–Thurs 7–10pm.

Located near the railway station, Le Coq Hardi is in an 18th-century house on a busy promenade near the river. In honor of its namesake, there are a number of roosters in various shapes and forms scattered throughout the comfortable interior. Landscapes of Brittany adorn the walls. This top-grade restaurant offers a refined modern atmosphere and polite service. It specializes in fresh fish, such as sea bass in beurre blanc (white butter); also, the chef prepares a superb canard (duck) du muscadet.

MON REVE, route des Bords de Loire. Tel. 40-03-55-50.
  Cuisine: FRENCH. **Reservations:** Required. **Directions:** Take the N751 five miles east of Nantes.
$ Prices: Appetizers 60–120 F ($10.80–$21.60); main dishes 98–148 F ($17.60–$26.60); fixed-price meals 150 F ($27) at lunch, 190–286 F ($34.20–$51.40) at dinner. AE, DC, MC, V.
  Open: May–Aug, lunch daily 12:15–2pm; dinner daily 7:30–9:30pm. Sept–Apr, lunch Wed–Mon 12:15–2pm; dinner Thurs–Mon 7:30–9:30pm. **Closed:** 15 days in late Oct and early Nov (dates vary).

The people of Nantes have been dining in this parklike setting with a rose garden for years. The chef, Gérard Ryngel, and his wife, Cécile, took over operation of Mon Rêve in 1979. Monsieur Ryngel produces such dishes as the fresh Loire salmon steak, wild duck with Bourjeuil sauce, and light, airy pastries; he also makes the famous beurre-blanc (white-butter) sauce. His repertoire includes both regional specialties and those of his own creation—a delectable dish of sweetbreads with crayfish, turbot with lobster, and a coquilles St-Jacques (scallops) en chemise that deserves a prize. His fixed-price dinner is among the most outstanding dinners in the area. However, if you're rushed, ask for his *déjeuner rapide,* a quickly served fixed-price lunch.

---

2. LA BAULE

281 miles SW of Paris, 49 miles NW of Nantes

GETTING THERE By Train The train from Nantes is about a one-hour ride. Get off at the most central inner-city station, La Baule–Escoublac, or the more easterly and remote La Baule–Les Pins.

ESSENTIALS Orientation The town is north of a long, popular stretch of beachfront. The two main boulevards run roughly parallel to one another through the long, narrow town. The one closer to the ocean changes its name six different times, although at its most famous point it's called boulevard de l'Océan.

Information For information, go to the Office de Tourisme, 8, place Victoire (tel. 40-24-34-44).

Founded in the heyday of the Victorian seaside craze of 1879, La Baule remains as inviting as the Gulf Stream that warms the waters of its wide, five-mile-long, crescent-shaped, white-sand beach, considered by many the finest in Europe. Occupying a strip known as the Côte d'Amour ("Coast of Love"), it competes with Biarritz for being the most fashionable resort on the Atlantic coast. This south Breton resort is still essentially French and draws only a nominal string of sun-seeking foreigners.

That "Prince of Gamblers," François André, founded the casino and the major resort hotels. Pines grow on the dunes, and on the outskirts, villas draw the wealthy chic in season (late June to mid-September); should you arrive at any other time, you might have La Baule to yourself. While the movie stars go to Deauville or Cannes, La Baule draws a more middle-class clientele; but the quieter wealthy still come here—as the yachts in the harbor testify. Tennis, golf, and sailing are popular along the coast, and, of course, there's the inevitable casino, which often books top talent.

WHERE TO STAY

Expensive

CASTEL MARIE-LOUISE, 1, av. Andrieu, 44504 La Baule. Tel. 40-42-72-10. Fax 40-42-72-10. 29 rms (all with bath). MINIBAR TV TEL
$ Rates (including half board): 1,070–1,730 F ($192.60–$311.40) per person. AE, DC, MC, V. **Parking:** Free.

This Breton manor house provides grand living in a pine-park estate along the oceanfront. Seemingly created as an overscale private villa for some wealthy person, the gabled stone castle now offers plush living for vacationers all year-round. The public rooms, including a salon for drinks, are furnished tastefully in the French provincial style; wall tapestries depict stylized animals in brown and green. Most of the renovated accommodations on the upper floors come with private balcony; two rooms are in a tower. Furnishings reflect several styles, including Louis XV, Directoire, and rustic.

The excellent chef is reason enough to stay here, and even if you aren't a guest, you may want to reserve a table for a meal. Specialties include lobster and home-smoked salmon. Many diners prefer to begin their meal with Breton oysters, perhaps followed by turbot. A fixed-price luncheon is offered for 195 F ($35.10), and table d'hôte dinners go for 295 F ($53.10).

HERMITAGE, 5, esplanade Lucien-Barrière, 44504 La Baule CEDEX. Tel. 40-11-46-46. Fax 40-11-46-45. 215 rms (all with bath), 9 suites. A/C MINIBAR TV TEL
$ Rates: 2,135 F ($384.30) single; 2,420 F ($435.60) double; from 3,670 F ($660.60) suite. Breakfast 85 F ($15.30) extra. Half board 2,260–2,670 F ($406.80–$480.60) per person. AE, DC, MC, V. **Parking:** 100 F ($18). **Closed:** End of Oct to the first part of Apr.

Impressively built seven stories high and studded with five balconies, this regal palace occupies a dominant position on the beach and maintains high standards. The upper three floors, with green timbers, are a melange of gables and dormers. The interior is ornate and plush, and the bedrooms are furnished with reproductions of English and French antiques. The main drawing room is conservatively modern.

The Hermitage offers a choice of three restaurants with excellent cuisine: a beach terrace, a grill, and a main dining room with arched windows, paneled ceilings, and glittering chandeliers. Facilities include an 18-hole golf course, 28 tennis courts, and a heated seawater pool.

Moderate

ALEXANDRA, 3, bd. René-Dubois, 44500 La Baule. Tel. 40-60-30-06.
Fax 40-24-57-09. 36 rms (all with bath). TV TEL
$ Rates: 480–580 F ($86.40–$104.40) single or double. Breakfast 42 F ($7.50) extra. Half board 600 F ($108) per person. AE, DC, MC, V. **Parking:** Free. **Closed:** Oct–Mar.

This is one of the best of the modern hotels in the center of La Baule. Right on the oceanfront, the Alexandra boasts eight floors of modern bedrooms with glass doors opening onto private balconies facing the beach. There's an open-air terrace with umbrellas and sidewalk tables, plus planters of flowers and greenery. The ninth-floor solarium, where guests sit under parasols, is a popular spot for drinks and coffee. Although the second-floor dining room has a view of the ocean, and the drinking lounge is *intime,* the bedrooms are the best feature.

BELLEVUE PLAGE, 27, bd. de l'Océan, 44500 La Baule. Tel. 40-60-28-55. Fax 40-60-10-18. 35 rms (all with bath). A/C TV TEL
$ Rates: 480–780 F ($86.40–$140.40) single or double. Breakfast 50 F ($9) extra. AE, DC, MC, V. **Parking:** Free. **Closed:** Mid-Nov to Feb.

This hotel occupies a prominent yet peaceful position in the center of the shoreline curving around the bay. The decor is contemporary, with a rooftop solarium where many guests gravitate during their stay, plus a garden and a restaurant with a sweeping view of the water. Each of the bedrooms is pleasant. You'll find a beach, sailboats for rent, and access to spa facilities.

Inexpensive

HOTEL FLEPEN, 145, av. de Lattre-De-Tassigny, 44500 La Baule. Tel. 40-60-29-30. Fax 40-60-74-07. 25 rms (20 with bath). TV TEL
$ Rates: 210 F ($37.80) single without bath; 430 F ($77.40) double with bath. Breakfast 45 F ($8.10) extra. AE, MC, V. **Parking:** Free. **Closed:** Nov 25–Jan 5.

When the original owners of this villa commissioned its construction, they selected a site within a short walk of the beach and the casino. Today, after a renovation of the old building, the establishment attracts beach-lovers who congregate on its outdoor terrace and garden. Bedrooms are simply but comfortably furnished.

WHERE TO DINE

In addition to the following, many of the hotels listed above have superb restaurants.

LA MARCANDERIE, 5, av. d'Agen. Tel. 40-24-03-12.
Cuisine: FRENCH. **Reservations:** Required.
$ Prices: Appetizers 75–110 F ($13.50–$19.80); main dishes 110–210 F ($19.80–$37.80); fixed-price menus 145 F ($26.10) (Mon–Fri only), 220 F ($39.60), 270 F ($48.60), and 370 F ($66.60).
Open: Lunch Tues–Sun noon–2:30pm; dinner Tues–Sat 7–9:30pm. **Closed:** Feb 1–15.

An award-winning chef, Jean-Luc Giraud, has transformed this street-level building—once a private residence—into one of the finest restaurants at La Baule. The dining room is decorated in harmonious pastels, and the cuisine is savory and well prepared, using only the freshest ingredients. Try, for example, scallops and endive in a light cream sauce or an elegant marmite of shellfish served with caramelized scalloped potatoes. The welcome is warm, and the wine cellar is carefully chosen.

3. CARNAC

302 miles SW of Paris, 23 miles SE of Lorient, 62 miles SE of Quimper

GETTING THERE Most trains stop in nearby Auray, but the scattered monuments in rural areas make a car your best bet.

ESSENTIALS Orientation The center of Carnac is about a half mile from the sea. From the main square, where the Eglise St-Cornely is, rue du Tumulus leads out of town toward the Tumulus St-Michel, a Celtic burial chamber. The beach area, Carnac-Plage, lies beside the ocean, alongside the waterfront boulevard de la Plage.

Information The Office de Tourisme, avenue des Druides (tel. 97-52-13-52), is open all year.

In May and June the fields of Carnac are resplendent with golden broom; sometimes the good weather at this seaside resort continues into October. Aside from "sea and sail," Carnac is one of the most important centers in the world for seeing evidence of prehistoric history. For here lies the ✪ **Field of Megaliths,** huge stones numbering in the hundreds, considered the most important prehistoric find in northern France. Their arrangement and placement remain a mystery. At **Carnac Ville,** the Musée de Préhistoire, 10, place de la Chapelle (tel. 97-52-22-04), is the third such museum in Europe. The collections are from 350,000 B.C. to the 8th century A.D. The museum, charging 28 F ($5) for adults and 10 F ($1.80) for children, is open Wednesday through Monday from 10am to noon and 2 to 6pm.

Even if Carnac didn't possess prehistoric monuments, its pine-studded sand dunes would be worth the trip. Protected by the Quiberon Peninsula, **Carnac-Plage** is a family resort.

WHERE TO STAY & DINE

LA DIANA, 21, bd. de la Plage, 56340 Carnac. Tel. 97-52-05-38. Fax 97-52-87-91. 30 rms (all with bath or shower), 3 suites. MINIBAR TV TEL
$ Rates: 850 F ($153) single; 1,100 F ($198) double; from 1,400 F ($252) suite. Breakfast 80 F ($14.40) extra. DC, MC. **Parking:** Free. **Closed:** Oct 4–Apr 8.
On the most popular beach in town, Le Diana offers a terrace where you can sip drinks and watch the crashing waves. The contemporary bedrooms are fairly spacious and have balconies facing the sea; they also have radios. Fixed-price meals in the restaurant cost 240–300 F ($43.20–$54).

HOTEL LES ALIGNEMENTS, 45, rue St-Cornély, 56340 Carnac. Tel. 97-52-06-30. Fax 97-52-76-56. 27 rms (all with bath). TV TEL
$ Rates: 260–360 F ($46.80–$64.80) single or double. Breakfast 39 F ($7) extra. MC, V. **Parking:** Free. **Closed:** Oct–Easter.
Set at the edge of Carnac village, about 200 yards from the prehistoric megaliths that make the town famous, this four-story hotel was built in 1972 and completely renovated in 1991. The back looks onto a garden, and inside, everything is clean and efficient. On the second and third floors the rooms have balconies or loggias; those facing the street have double windows to keep down the noise. For decoration, there are wall tapestries, and fabrics have been color coordinated. Nonresidents are welcome to dine in the modern, rustic restaurant, where fixed-price meals run 99–245 F ($17.80–$44.10).

LANN-ROZ, 36, av. de la Poste, 56340 Carnac. Tel. 97-52-10-48. Fax
97-52-03-69. 14 rms (all with bath or shower). TV TEL
$ **Rates** (including half board): 330–350 F ($59.40–$63) per person. AE, DC, MC,
V. **Closed:** Jan 5–Feb 10.

Within walking distance of the water is this good oasis for the budget-minded,
built in the Breton manner and surrounded by a private garden of flowers and
lawns. Family-owned and -operated, the Lann-Roz is managed by the friendly
Madame Le Calvez, who invites guests to have a drink on the veranda. Also fronting
the garden is a typical Breton living room, where the chef serves generous portions of
regional dishes. You don't have to be a guest of the hotel to enjoy a meal here, which
costs 95–250 F ($17.10–$45).

**NOVOTEL CARNAC PLAGE, av. de l'Atlantique, 56340 Carnac. Tel.
97-52-53-00.** Fax 97-52-53-55. 110 rms (all with bath). A/C MINIBAR TV TEL
$ **Rates:** 470–710 F ($84.60–$127.80) single or double. Breakfast 55 F ($9.90)
extra. AE, DC, MC, V. **Parking:** Free. **Closed:** Jan.

The spacious and well-furnished accommodations here are in cheerfully decorated
rooms in a modern setting near the ocean. Guests have access to a spa facility and an
indoor saltwater swimming pool. A restaurant on the premises serves a fixed-price
menu for 180 F ($32.40).

4. QUIBERON

311 miles SW of Paris, 30 miles SE of Lorient

GETTING THERE By Train Most trains from the rest of Brittany and Paris
stop in nearby Auray and depart frequently throughout the day.

By Car Roads are good, and many visitors arrive by car, taking the D768 south
from Carnac.

ESSENTIALS Orientation Set beside the sea, Quiberon's most visible
harborfront is the Port Maria, a ferryboat terminus, near most of the hotels and
restaurants.

Information The Office de Tourisme is at 14, rue Verdun (tel. 97-50-07-84).

A sardine-fishing port, Quiberon is also a noted south Breton resort with a large
white-sand beach. It's on a peninsula (formerly an island) connected to the
mainland by a narrow strip of alluvial deposits. Aside from the beach, the best local
sight is the rugged Breton fishers hauling in their sardine catch.

The entire coast—the **Côte Sauvage (Wild Coast)**—is rugged; the ocean
breaks with fury against the reefs. Fierce northern winds, especially in winter, lash
across the sand dunes, shaving the short pines that grow here. On the landward side,
however, the beach is calm and relatively protected.

WHERE TO STAY

KER NOYAL, rue de St-Clément, 56170 Quiberon. Tel. 97-50-08-41. Fax
97-30-58-20. 102 rms (all with bath or shower). TV TEL
$ **Rates:** 470–550 F ($84.60–$99) single or double. Breakfast 50 F ($9) extra. AE,
DC, MC, V. **Parking:** Free. **Closed:** Nov–Feb.

This hotel, which has an intimate country-club atmosphere, lies in a well-planned
garden a short walk from the beach. Gravel paths are bordered by brilliantly colored
flowers, the grounds are studded with pine trees, and white garden furniture is set

under parasols. The rooms in the main building of the older annex overlook the sea or the garden. The newer building has sun balconies with wrought-iron furniture. Each comfortable accommodation, tastefully contemporary, is kept light and airy. Meals are served in one of two dining rooms, which have a view of a garden; fixed-price meals begin at 190 F ($34.20).

SOFITEL THALASSA, pointe de Goulvars, 56170 Quiberon. Tel. 97-50-20-00. Fax 97-50-46-32. 117 rms (all with bath), 16 suites. MINIBAR TV TEL
$ Rates (including half board): 1,380 F ($248.40) single; 1,520 F ($273.60) double; from 3,020 F ($543.60) suite for two. AE, DC, MC, V. **Parking:** Free. **Closed:** Jan.

This leading beachside hotel is part of a well-run chain. Built in the 1970s, it sits at the edge of the sea, a half mile east of the town center. Bedrooms have private balconies facing the sea or the rear plaza and are tastefully decorated in muted colors. The lounge is sun-drenched and carpeted, and a bar/lounge serves cocktails before dinner. If you don't want to swim in the Atlantic, there is a covered Olympic-size pool with an all-glass wall facing the sea. The Restaurant Thalassa, which overlooks the water, combines a sophisticated decor with the best of the viands at the resort. Specialties include fines belons (oysters), palourdes farcies (stuffed clams), and grilled brill. Meal prices are 230–330 F ($41.40–$59.40).

WHERE TO DINE

LA GOURSEN, 10, quai d l'Océan à Port Maria. Tel. 97-50-07-94.
Cuisine: FRENCH. **Reservations:** Required.
$ Prices: Appetizers 35–110 F ($6.30–$19.80); main dishes 85–175 F ($15.30–$31.50). MC, V.
Open: July–Aug, lunch daily 12:30–2pm; dinner daily 7–9:30pm. May–June and Sept–Oct, lunch Wed–Mon 12:30–2pm; dinner Wed–Mon 7–9:30pm. **Closed:** Nov–Apr.

This turn-of-the-century bistro is one of the most charming places in town. The service is friendly, and the fish dishes are inviting. Michel Lucas, owner and chef, offers such specialties as filet of bar with mustard sauce, garlic-flavored fish sausages, mariner-style sauerkraut, and John Dory with baby vegetables.

LE RELAX, 27, bd. Castero, Plage de Ker Morvan. Tel. 97-50-12-84.
Cuisine: FRENCH. **Reservations:** Recommended.
$ Prices: Appetizers 42–78 F ($7.50–$14); main dishes 65–105 F ($11.70–$18.90); fixed-price menus 62 F ($11.10), 95 F ($17.10), and 130 F ($23.40). DC, MC, V.
Open: July–Aug, lunch daily noon–2pm; dinner daily 7–10pm. Feb–June and Sept–Dec, lunch Tues–Sun noon–2pm; dinner Tues–Sat 7–10pm. **Closed:** Jan.

With a magnificent view of the bay, Le Relax offers a pub-style atmosphere. A generously portioned menu specializing in seafood is served in the round dining room. Try the John Dory with sorrel or grilled lobster.

5. BELLE-ILE-EN-MER

10 miles W of Brittany's shoreline

GETTING THERE   By Ferry Depending on the season, 4–12 ferries depart every day for Belle-Ile from Port Maria, in Quiberon. The trip takes 45 minutes. In summer you must reserve space on board for your car.

ESSENTIALS   Orientation The ferry docks at Le Palais, a fortified port dating from the 16th century. A drive around the periphery is about 35 miles.

Information The Office de Tourisme is on quai Bonnelle, Le Palais (tel. 97-31-81-93).

From Quiberon, you can take a steamer (several run daily) to **Belle-Ile,** the largest island off the coast of southern Brittany; cars can also be transported.

About 10 miles off the coast, this storm-wracked island is eerie with its rocky cliffs, its reef-fringed west coast, its **Grotte de l'Apothicairerie,** and its general sense of isolation from the world. Valleys cut through the ravines, wending their way to such small ports as **Le Palais,** the point at which you dock.

In the days before he was overthrown for making the Sun King jealous, Fouquet, the finance minister, erected a château on the island. Much later, the great actress Sarah Bernhardt enjoyed spending her summers at Belle-Ile, as did Marcel Proust, Flaubert, Manet, and Courbet.

WHERE TO STAY & DINE

Port de Goulphar

If you'd like to stay on the island to explore it in more depth, you'll find excellent accommodations at Port de Goulphar, one of the most charming spots on Belle-Ile-en-Mer. This port lies on the southern shores, on a narrow inlet framed by cliffs. Boats dock at Le Palais, to the north.

CASTEL CLARA, port de Goulphar, 56360 Le Palais. Tel. 97-31-84-21.
Fax 97-31-51-69. 43 rms (all with bath). TV TEL
$ Rates (including half board): 710–845 F ($127.80–$152.10) per person. MC, V.
Parking: Free. **Closed:** Nov 15–Feb 15.

⭐ This is a warm and colorful Relais & Châteaux, built in 1970 two miles from the village of Bangor. At an enchanting spot, the complex seems to extend to the Côte Sauvage. There are few places along the coast where guests can enjoy such peace along with ideal service and a first-class cuisine. Under paneled ceilings, the

---

IN THEIR FOOTSTEPS

Sarah Bernhardt (1844–1923) Known as "the Divine Sarah" or "Madame Sarah," Henriette-Rosine Bernard was a tempestuous Frenchwoman considered by many critics "the greatest actress who ever lived." She enjoyed a long and glorious career in the theater, appearing in such classics as Racine's *Phedre* and in the perennial revivals of Dumas fils' *La Dame aux Camélias*.

- **Birthplace:** Paris, on October 23, 1844, but the exact address is still a subject of controversy. She was the illegitimate daughter of a milliner.
- **Residences:** Her best-known residence was a 17th-century fortress at Belle-Ile, off the southern coast of Brittany, which was "always swarming with guests."
- **Favorite Haunts:** Comédie Française in Paris, where, in her words, "it was the curtain of my life which was rising." Eventually she found it filled with people who were "stilted, gossipy, and jealous," and she fled to the "second Comédie Française," the Left Bank Théâtre de l'Odéon, where she scored her first hit playing a boy in Racine's *Athalie*. Her adored restaurant in Paris, Escargot-Montorgueil, is still going today.
- **Resting Place:** Père-Lachaise Cemetery, Paris. She used to sleep in a rosewood coffin lined with white satin, "to get used to it." Upon her death on March 26, 1923, the government refused her a state funeral. Her monument bears the single name: BERNHARDT.

guest rooms are well furnished and have private balconies facing the sea. The fixed-price meals in the restaurant begin at 245 F ($44.10), and à la carte orders average 350 F ($63). The hotel also offers a large terrace with a solarium around a heated seawater swimming pool. The cozy bar is *très intime;* there's even a playroom for children and a billiard table.

MANOIR DE GOULPHAR, port de Goulphar, 56360 Le Palais. Tel. 97-31-80-10. Fax 97-31-80-05. 65 rms (all with bath). TV TEL
$ Rates (including half board): 500–515 F ($90–$92.70) single; 900–975 F ($162–$175.50) double. MC, V. **Parking:** Free. **Closed:** Nov 1–Mar 15.
This creamy-colored building with a blue roof and a round tower lies on the Goulphar Harbor, which many have compared to a fjord in Norway. The rocky landscape on the wild coast makes for a tranquil setting for "Le Manoir," which, although modern, looks from a distance like a country estate. A first-class hotel built in the 1970s, it offers stylish bedrooms with sunny balconies opening onto the Atlantic and the harbor at Goulphar. The restaurant offers excellent food and service.

Sauzon

Port de Goulphar has long had a monopoly on the desirable accommodations on the island, but the following recommendation is a serious challenger:

LE CARDINAL, à la Pointe du Cardinal, Sauzon, 56360 Le Palais. Tel. 97-31-61-60. Fax 97-31-66-87. 75 rms (all with bath). TV TEL
$ Rates (including half board): 485–545 F ($87.30–$98.10) single; 835–975 F ($150.30–$175.50) double. MC, V. **Parking:** Free. **Closed:** Oct 15–Apr 1.
One of the more attractive modern hotels in the region, Le Cardinal is situated amid low-lying heath on a peninsula extending into the ocean. Water sports–lovers will appreciate the facilities available, as well as the view of the harbor. The earth-tone color scheme is relaxing and pleasant, and the attractively furnished bedrooms contain all the modern comforts. Half board is required.

Bangor

You might want to plan your tour of the island so you can stop off at the following recommendation for a meal:

LA FORGE, route de Port-Goulphar. Tel. 97-31-51-76.
  Cuisine: FRENCH. **Reservations:** Recommended.
$ Prices: Appetizers 45–90 F ($8.10–$16.20); main dishes 110–170 F ($19.80–$30.60); fixed-price lunch 120 F ($21.60). AE, DC, MC, V.
  Open: July–Aug, lunch 12:30–2pm; dinner 7–10pm. Easter–June and Sept to mid-Nov, lunch 12:30–2pm; dinner 7–9pm. **Closed:** Mid-Nov to Easter.
Aptly named, La Forge occupies a converted blacksmith's shop. The owner, Odile Mulon, is firmly in charge of the dining room, and makes sure that customers are well looked after. The room is about as charmingly rustic as any you'll find in Brittany; it's constructed from blocks of local granite. The kitchen turns out such specialties as a corille of mussels and oysters, turbot and a shallot purée, crab with grilled scallops, local lamb, and lobsters in puff pastry. In summer you can enjoy your repast either in the main dining room or on the flowery outdoor terrace.

---

6. HENNEBONT
301 miles W of Paris, 29 miles NW of Vannes

GETTING THERE By Car From Nantes, head northwest into Brittany along E13, via Vannes; Hennebont will be signposted 29 miles northwest of Vannes.

ESSENTIALS Orientation The major hotel is three miles south of Hennebont, on a private road off the N781.

Information There is no tourist office in Hennebont. The nearest information center is in Vannes at 1, rue Thiers (tel. 97-47-24-34).

On the outskirts of this once-fortified town split by the Blavet River is one of the most delightful accommodations in all of south Brittany. It lies three miles south of the town, on a private road off the N781; called the Château de Locguénolé, it is previewed below.

WHERE TO STAY & DINE

CHATEAU DE LOCGUENOLE, route de Port-Louis, 56700 Hennebont. Tel. 97-76-29-04. Fax 97-76-39-47. 20 rms (all with bath), 4 suites. TV TEL

$ Rates (including half board): 1,094 F ($196.90) single; 1,688–2,248 F ($303.80–$404.60) double; 2,360–3,000 F ($424.80–$540) suite for two. AE, DC, MC, V. **Parking:** Free. **Closed:** Jan.

This 900-acre hilltop estate overlooking the tree-covered Blavet River valley has been owned by the same family for more than 500 years. Now a Relais & Châteaux, it's filled with antiques, tapestries, and paintings accumulated over the centuries. Discriminating clients, such as writers, painters, and statesmen, frequent the château. The drawing rooms and the petits salons are furnished with old pieces. The bedchambers vary widely in size and furnishings, but each has decorative floral sprays and harmonious colors. While the second floor has great old bedrooms, the upper-floor accommodations—the converted maids' rooms—also are charming. Some of the rooms are in a converted Breton cottage.

Even if you can't stay here, consider reserving a meal in the dining hall, which is decorated with a room-wide Aubusson tapestry. While sitting on Louis XVI red-velvet-and-cane chairs, you can order such specialties as filet de boeuf poêle au foie gras frais, suprême de barbue (brill) with cider and leeks, and grilled salmon. Meals cost 190–600 F ($34.20–$108). Facilities include tennis courts and an outdoor swimming pool.

7. QUIMPERLE

317 miles W of Paris, 28½ miles SE of Quimper

GETTING THERE By Train There is train service to Quimperlé.

By Car From Lorient or Quimper, take the N165.

ESSENTIALS Orientation At the junction of the Ellé and Isole rivers, the town is bisected by many bridges. Its two main centers are place St-Michel and place Charles-de Gaulle, near the Église de la Sainte-Croix. Both the upper and lower sections of town have interesting buildings.

Information The Office de Tourisme, pont Bourgneuf (tel. 98-96-04-32), is open year round.

Built on a hillside, Quimperlé, about 28½ miles from Quimper, offers a refreshing sojourn into the charm of a former age. Because of its unique situation—where two rivers, the Isole and the Ellé, meet to form the Laïta—it is called a paradise for anglers. The salmon and trout are fairly abundant.

In the lower town, the Basse-Ville, is **Eglise de la Ste-Croix,** a unique Romanesque church with an 11th-century crypt. Its Greek-cross plan is based on that of the Holy Sepulchre in Jerusalem. The hill overhanging the town like a sugarloaf gives it the nickname "Mont St-Michel of the land."

About a mile away, the **Carnoët State Forest** is a setting for horseback riding, with its towering trees re-creating the mood of the legends of the Breton Bluebeard and of St. Maurice, that charmer of birds. Only 6½ miles away you can explore the beaches with their hidden coves, enjoying the adventure of the sea and practicing sailing at the school at **Le Pouldu.**

WHERE TO STAY

HOTEL DE L'HERMITAGE, au Manoir de Kerroch, route du Pouldu,
29130 Quimperlé. Tel. 98-96-04-66. Fax 98-39-23-41. 28 rms (all with bath or shower). MINIBAR TV TEL **Directions:** Take the D49 1½ miles south of town.
$ Rates: 310–390 F ($55.80–$70.20) single or double. Breakfast 30 F ($5.40) extra. AE, DC, MC, V. **Parking:** Free.

Located at the edge of a forest, the Hôtel de l'Hermitage stands in a five-acre garden and is enclosed by an old stone wall and a manor house from 1900. You'll drive along the Laïta River, passing under a Romanesque bridge, until you reach a creaky iron gate and a most tranquil setting. The Hermitage is a complex of three buildings and has a heated swimming pool. The rooms come in many shapes and sizes, and the furnishings are a mixture of antiques, reproductions, and modern.

WHERE TO DINE

RELAIS DU ROCH, route du Pouldu, at Kerroch. Tel. 98-96-12-97.
Cuisine: FRENCH. **Reservations:** Required. **Directions:** Take the D94 one mile south of Quimperlé.
$ Prices: Appetizers 50–90 F ($9–$16.20); main dishes 85–125 F ($15.30–$22.50). MC, V.
Open: July–Aug, lunch daily noon–2:30pm; dinner daily 7–9pm. Feb–June and Sept–Dec, lunch Tues–Sun noon–2:30pm; dinner Tues–Sat 7–9pm. **Closed:** Jan.

This restaurant has filled its contemporary premises with antiques and rustic accessories. It offers a seafood menu that includes shellfish, monkfish with sorrel, many kinds of ocean fish, and a variety of grilled meats.

---

8. PONT-AVEN

324 miles W of Paris, 20 miles SE of Quimper

GETTING THERE   By Car   From Quimperlé, motorists can continue west along D783 in the direction of Concarneau.

ESSENTIALS   Orientation   The town lies between a portside promenade, loaded with galleries and shops, and the upper Bois d'Amour, a manicured forest that has hosted generations of visiting artists.

Information   Contact the Office de Tourisme, place de l'Hôtel-de-Ville (tel. 98-06-04-70).

Paul Gauguin loved this village with its little white houses along the gently flowing Aven. In the late 19th century a school of painters followed in his trail, led by Maurice Denis, Sérusier, and Émile Bernard. The colony of artists became known as the School of Pont-Aven.

Before departing for Tahiti, Gauguin painted *The Golden Christ* and *The Beautiful Angela* here. People can admire the crucifix that inspired *The Golden Christ* in the Chapelle de Trémalo, not a mile away from the little town. Every year the

Société de Peinture organizes an exhibition of paintings by other members of the School of Pont-Aven, including Sérusier, Bernard, and Delavellée.

Another resident of Pont-Aven was Théodore Botrel, who won his fame composing patriotic French songs during World War I.

Pont-Aven, ten miles south of Concarneau, is quiet and peaceful today, a Breton market village with a good and beautifully situated restaurant, described below.

WHERE TO STAY & DINE

LE MOULIN DE ROSMADEC, 29123 Pont-Aven. Tel. 98-06-00-22. Fax 98-06-18-00.
  Cuisine: FRENCH. **Reservations:** Recommended.
$ Prices: Fixed-price menus 170–290 F ($30.60–$52.20). MC, V.
  Open: Lunch Thurs–Tues 12:30–2pm; dinner Thurs–Tues 7:30–9pm. **Closed:** Oct 15–30, Sun evening in winter.

★ When it comes to a charming setting, this 15th-century reconstructed stone mill has no comparison in Brittany. Regional meals are served in a two-level dining room, where you're surrounded by antique furniture and decorative accessories. In addition (and this is preferable in good weather), you can enjoy your meal on an "island" terrace filled with flowers, while listening to the water from the nearby flowing river. Owners Monsieur and Madame Sebilleau serve some of the finest viands along the southern coast of Brittany; specialties include trout with almonds, homard (lobster) grille à l'estragon, suprême of sole with champagne, and duck breast with cassis.

The Moulin also rents four comfortably furnished bedrooms, costing 400–470 F ($72–$84.60) for a double, plus 45 F ($8.10) for breakfast.

---

9. CONCARNEAU

335 miles W of Paris, 58 miles SE of Brest

GETTING THERE By Car You'll have to drive since local rail service is limited to freight.

ESSENTIALS Orientation The town is built on three sides of a natural harbor whose innermost sheltered section is the Nouveau Port. In the center of the harbor, connected to its westernmost edge by a bridge, is the heavily fortified Ville-Close.

Information The Office de Tourisme is on quai d'Aiguillon (tel. 98-97-01-44).

This port is a favorite of painters, who never tire of capturing on canvas the changes and subtleties of the fishing fleet in the harbor. It's my favorite of the south Breton coastal communities—primarily because it doesn't depend on tourists for its livelihood. In fact its canneries produce nearly three-quarters of all the "tunny" fish consumed in France. Walk along the quays here, especially in the late evening, and watch the rustic Breton fishers unload their catch; later, join them for a pint of potent cider in their local taverns.

Of course, all tourists visit Concarneau to explore its **Ville-Close,** an ancient hamlet surrounded by ramparts, some of which date from the 14th century. From the quay, cross the bridge and descend into the isolated old town. Admittedly, the souvenir shops have taken over, but don't let that spoil it for you. You can easily spend an hour wandering the narrow, winding alleys, gazing up at the towers, peering at the stone houses, and pausing for a moment in the secluded squares. For a splendid view of the port, walk the ramparts; the cost is 5 F (90¢) for adults, half price for children.

Also in the old town is a fishing museum, the **Musée de la Pêche,** rue Vauvan, Ville-Close (tel. 98-97-10-20). In a 17th-century building, it displays ship models and exhibits tracing the development of the fishing industry throughout the world. The preserved ship *Hemerica* can be viewed. Admission is 30 F ($5.40) for adults and 20 F

($3.60) for children. You can visit in July and August daily from 9:30am to 7pm; in other months, hours are 9:30am to 12:30pm and 2 to 6pm.

WHERE TO STAY

After sightseeing, repair to one of the nearby beaches of Les Sables Blancs. Or check into one of the hotels of this port town and enjoy the boating, coastal fishing, tennis, golf, horseback riding, and canoeing. In addition to the following, two of the restaurants listed under "Where to Dine," below, have guest rooms.

GRAND HOTEL, 1, av. Pierre-Guéguen, 29110 Concarneau. Tel. 98-97-00-28. 33 rms (18 with bath). TEL

$ Rates: 155 F ($27.90) single or double with hot and cold running water, 300 F ($54) single or double with bath. Breakfast 29 F ($5.20) extra. MC, V. **Parking:** Free. **Closed:** Oct 11–Apr 9.

This is the best budget choice in the center of the port. Directly on the quay, across from La Ville-Close, the Grand Hôtel overlooks the fishing fleet and the marketplace and has open stalls selling fresh vegetables, fruit, fish, and even clothing. Bedrooms are simply but comfortably furnished. Only breakfast is served.

WHERE TO DINE

LA COQUILLE, 1, rue du Moros, at Nouveau Port. Tel. 98-97-08-52.
Cuisine: FRENCH. **Reservations:** Required Sat–Sun and in summer.
$ Prices: Appetizers 55–120 F ($9.90–$21.60); main dishes 100–140 F ($18–$25.20); fixed-price meals 190–390 F ($34.20–$70.20). AE, DC, MC, V.
Open: Lunch Tues–Sun 12:30–1:30pm; dinner Tues–Sat 7:30–9:30pm.
Closed: Jan.

This 30-year-old restaurant occupies one end of a stone-sided harborfront building that was a fish-processing plant a century ago. At this pleasant Breton restaurant you can admire the fishing boats that bring in the catch you may find on your plate. It contains a trio of dining rooms with exposed stone walls and a scattering of ceiling beams. Set directly on the port, La Coquille serves primarily seafood, particularly lobster. The small outdoor terrace offers a view of the port during warm weather.

LE GALION, 15, rue St-Guenole, in La Ville-Close. Tel. 98-97-30-16.
Cuisine: FRENCH. **Reservations:** Required.
$ Prices: Appetizers 70–130 F ($12.60–$23.40); main dishes 100–150 F ($18–$27); fixed-price meals 150 F ($27), 180 F ($32.40), 240 F ($43.20), and 340 F ($61.20). AE, DC, MC, V.
Open: Lunch Tues–Sun 12:30–2:30pm; dinner Tues–Sat 7:30–9:30pm.
Closed: Jan 15–Mar 1.

Ringed with granite walls and massive timbers, this is one of the best examples of a country inn in Brittany. In the heart of the old city, the cozy, rustic dining room has a massive fireplace. The hosts who welcome guests into the dining room and prepare the tasty dishes are proudly Breton and the spelling of their name proves it—Gaonac'h. Specialties include a blanquette of lobster with fresh asparagus (April to mid-June only), John Dory flavored with rhubarb, and a paupiette of sole.

Just across the street, in a renovated old granite house, Monsieur and Madame Gaonac'h rent five comfortable rooms at La Résidence des Iles, with double or twin beds, private bath, and kitchenette. The rate is 400 F ($72), plus 40 F ($7.20) for breakfast.

HOTEL DES SABLES-BLANCS, plage des Sables-Blancs, 29181 Concarneau CEDEX. Tel. 98-97-01-39. Fax 98-50-65-88.
Cuisine: FRENCH. **Reservations:** Not required.
$ Prices: Appetizers 45–55 F ($8.10–$9.90); main dishes 100–160 F ($18–$28.80); fixed-price menus 77–169 F ($13.80–$30.40). AE, DC, V.
Open: Lunch daily 12:30–2pm; dinner daily 7–9:30pm. **Closed:** Second week in Nov to mid-Apr.

Owned and directed by the Chabrier family, this leading hotel and seaside restaurant serves standard French specialties, usually on a terrace with a view. It lies one mile south of the center. You might begin your meal with a helping of crab with mayonnaise or marinated mussels.

The Chabriers also rent 48 comfortable bedrooms, 42 with private bath. Rooms range from 180 F ($32.40) in a single without bath to 250 F ($45) in a single with bath; a double without bath costs 190 F ($34.20), rising to 298 F ($53.60) in a double with bath. Breakfast is 32 F ($5.70) extra.

10. LA FORET-FOUESNANT

336 miles W of Paris, 5 miles NW of Concarneau, 8 miles from Quimper

GETTING THERE **By Car** Take the N783 and turn off at the clearly indicated sign.

ESSENTIALS **Orientation** Its center lies between place de l'Eglise and the old port. Its most important hotel (see below) is one mile north of town—follow the N783 and turn at the sign.

Information The Office de Tourisme is at 2, rue du Port (tel. 98-56-94-09).

Set in an orchard district of southern Brittany, La Forêt-Fouesnant produces the best cider in the province. One of Brittany's finest manor houses—open to the public for both rooms and meals—lies in this sleepy village.

WHERE TO STAY & DINE

MANOIR DU STANG, 29940 La Forêt-Fouesnant. Tel. 98-56-97-37. 26 rms (all with bath). TEL
$ Rates (including continental breakfast): 515 F ($92.70) single; 570–840 F ($102.60–$151.20) double. Breakfast 35 F ($6.30) per person extra. No credit cards. **Parking:** Free. **Closed:** Oct to early May. **Directions:** Lies 1 mile north of the village center, signposted from the N783; access is by private road.

To get to the graveled courtyard that leads to the entrance of this ivy-covered, 16th-century manor house, you travel down a long, tree-lined avenue and under a stone tower gate. On your right is a formal garden, and raised stone terraces lead to 25 acres of rolling woodland. The Manoir du Stang is the domain of M and Mme Guy Hubert, who provide gracious living in period drawing rooms, studies, lounges, and a dining room furnished with Breton antiques. One salon features Breton paneling, a fireplace, crystal, and Louis XIII chairs. Guests are lodged either in the main building or in the even older annex; the latter has a circular stone staircase. Your bedroom is likely to be furnished with silk and fine antiques. A maid in a starched lacy Breton cap will bring a breakfast tray to your room each morning.

In the restaurant, the chef's specialties are grilled lobster with tarragon, mousseline de turbot, côte de boeuf au poivre vert, fruits de mer (seafood), and oysters in the style of the house. Fixed-price meals begin at 170 F ($30.60).

11. QUIMPER

342 miles W of Paris, 127 miles NW of Rennes

GETTING THERE **By Train** From Paris, change trains in Rennes. Other connections can be made on the busy rail routes between Brest and Nantes.

ESSENTIALS **Orientation** Quimper is set on both banks of the Odet River, but its older and more interesting side lies on the northern bank, around the Cathédrale de St-Corentin, place St-Corentin.

Information For information, contact the Office de Tourisme, place de la Résistance (tel. 98-53-04-05).

The town that pottery built, Quimper is the historic capital of Brittany's most traditional region, La Cornouaille. Its faïence decorates tables from Europe to America. Skilled artisans have been turning out the Quimper-ware since the 17th century, using bold provincial designs. You can tour one of the factories receiving visitors during your stay at Quimper; inquire at the tourist office above.

Located at the meeting of the Odet and Steir Rivers in southwestern Brittany, Quimper was the medieval capital of Cornouailles. In some quarters it still maintains its old-world atmosphere, and charming footbridges span the rivers. At place St-Corentin, the **Cathédrale de St-Corentin** (tel. 98-95-06-19) is the town landmark, characterized by two towers that climb 250 feet. Considered the oldest example of Gothic architecture in Brittany, the cathedral was built between the 13th and 15th centuries; the spires weren't added until the 19th century. Inside, the 15th-century stained glass is exceptional. It's open daily from 9am to 6:30pm.

Also on the square is the **Musée des Beaux-Arts,** 40, place St-Corentin (tel. 98-95-45-20). Its collection includes works by Rubens, Boucher, Fragonard, Oudry, Chasseriau, Corot, and Marquet. There's an exceptionally good exhibition from the northern schools and the Pont-Aven School (Bernard, Sérusier, Lacombe, Maufra, Denis, Meyer de Haan). See also the works of artist Eugène Boudin, known for his 19th-century views of Quimper. Charging 20 F ($3.60) for admission, the gallery is open Wednesday through Monday from 10am to noon and 2 to 6pm.

WHERE TO STAY

GRIFFON, 131, route de Bénodet, 29000 Quimper. Tel. 98-90-33-33. Fax 98-53-06-67. 49 rms (all with bath), 1 suite. TV TEL
$ Rates: 370 F ($66.60) single; 450 F ($81) double; from 550 F ($99) suite. Breakfast 47 F ($8.40) extra. AE, DC, MC, V. **Parking:** Free.
The Griffon lies in a peaceful setting 1¼ miles south of the center in verdant surroundings that are augmented by a covered and heated swimming pool. The public rooms of this 1970 hotel are quite comfortable. The bedrooms are spacious and clean and have radio/alarms. There's a restaurant on the premises, Creach Gwenn, where you can dine reasonably if you order the 95-F ($17.10) fixed-price menu; it's closed Saturday night and on Sunday in winter.

NOVOTEL, 17, rue Dupoher, pont de Poulguinan, 29000 Quimper. Tel. 98-90-46-26. Fax 98-53-01-96. 92 rms (all with bath). A/C MINIBAR TV TEL
$ Rates: 420 F ($75.60) single; 470 F ($84.60) double. Breakfast 50 F ($9) extra. AE, DC, MC, V. **Parking:** Free.
Set in a garden in a labyrinth of access roads about a mile to the southwest of the town center, this Novotel opened in 1984. It's the best business-oriented hotel in the region and is also ideal for motoring families in summer. The hotel has a modern, black-slate facade, and each of its Novotel-style bedrooms has lots of space, including a large writing desk, a single bed, and a double bed. When staying with the family, free accommodations and breakfast are offered for two children up to the age of 16 who share a room with their parents. A modern bar and a good grill restaurant serves daily from 6am to midnight. Meals cost 85–115 F ($15.30–$20.70). The heated swimming pool on the grounds is a magnet in summer.

TOUR D'AUVERGNE, 13, rue Reguaires, 29000 Quimper. Tel. 98-95-08-70. Fax 98-95-17-31. 43 rms (38 with bath or shower). TEL
$ Rates: 245 F ($44.10) single without bath; 410–490 F ($73.80–$88.20) double with bath. Breakfast 44 F ($7.90) extra. AE, MC, V.
Although centrally located a short block from the Odet, this modern hotel is quiet. Inside is a little salon featuring a wall-size mural—a blow-up of an engraving of a battle scene. One of the principal reasons for staying here is the

food, because the kitchen features Breton specialties. Fixed-price meals are offered for 135 F ($24.30), 175 F ($31.50), and 230 F ($41.40). The less expensive menu is invariably good, including, on one recent occasion, spider crabs with mayonnaise and a saddle of rabbit with mustard sauce.

WHERE TO DINE

In addition to the following suggestions, all the hotels listed above have fine restaurants.

LE CAPUCIN GOURMAND, 29, rue des Réguaires. Tel. 98-95-43-12.
   Cuisine: FRENCH. **Reservations:** Required in summer.
$ **Prices:** Appetizers 80–160 F ($14.40–$28.80); main dishes 120–180 F ($21.60–$32.40); fixed-price meals 160–200 F ($28.80–$36), 250 F ($45), and 350 F ($63). DC, MC, V.
   Open: Lunch Mon–Fri 12:15–2pm; dinner Mon–Sat 7:15–10pm.

This popular restaurant, run by Soisik and Christian Conchon, is known throughout town as a place to get a filling and well-prepared meal without ruining a budget. Your repast might include any of the fresh seafood specialties. To begin, you might have scallops, scampi, oysters, or gravlax, as well as homemade duck liver or snail ravioli. You might try a seafood pot-au-feu, including scallops, scampi, turbot, sole rouget (red mullet), John Dory with ginger sauce, and assorted vegetables, or else a sole meunière or lobster and scallops with morels. Meat dishes include beef filet in garnay de Touraine sauce or breast of duck with sherry-vinegar sauce. A crème brûlée or a warm apple tart with vanilla ice cream and Calvados makes a fitting finish.

LE PARISIEN, 13, rue Jean-Jaurès. Tel. 98-90-35-29.
   Cuisine: FRENCH. **Reservations:** Recommended.
$ **Prices:** Appetizers 50–100 F ($9–$18); main dishes 60–200 F ($10.80–$36); fixed-price menus 98–185 F ($17.60–$33.30). MC, V.
   Open: Lunch Mon–Sat noon–1:30pm; dinner Mon–Sat 7:15–9pm.

Decorated in the English style with mahogany accessories and well-set tables, this is one of the best restaurants in the center. The staff offers refined meals, including salmon and lobster with zucchini, trout in a sorrel cream sauce, and filet of beef with a confit of onions.

12. LOCRONAN

354 miles W of Paris, 11 miles N of Quimper

GETTING THERE   By Car   From Quimper, motorists can head north for 11 miles along D39 and D63, from which Locronan is clearly signposted.

ESSENTIALS   Information   The Syndicat d'Initiative (tourist office), place de la Mairie (tel. 98-91-70-14), is open June 15 to September 15.

A gem among Breton villages, Locronan was once known as the City of Weavers, earning its fame in the 17th century when 300 workers labored seven days a week weaving sails for the Royal Navy. Today two weaving concerns continue the tradition, but the village is mostly noted for its old bearded woodcarvers.

The Renaissance core of Locronan, the **Place,** is remarkably preserved, standing virtually intact from the 16th and 17th centuries, with granite houses, old beams, delicate cut stone, and open well. The church on the stone square is from the 15th century, containing an interesting Chapel of Pénity in which is the tomb of St. Ronan, the patron saint of Locronan. The hermit Ronan was driven from Ireland in the 5th century. In penitence he ran four miles every day of his life, 7½ miles on Sunday. Every six years his memory is revived in a **Grand Troménie,** a pageant considered one of the most extraordinary in France. A procession covers the 7½ miles, gathering numerous of the faithful along the way. The neighboring parishes display the relics of their patron saints.

WHERE TO STAY & DINE

HOTEL BOIS DU NEVET, route du Bois-de-Nevet-Locronan, 29180, Locronan. Tel. 98-91-70-67. Fax 98-91-83-12. 24 rms (all with bath), 11 suites.

$ Rates: 220 F ($39.60) single; 280 F ($50.40) double; 380–500 F ($68.40–$90) suite. Breakfast 30 F ($5.40) extra. Half board 290 F ($52.20) per person. AE, DC, MC, V. **Parking:** Free.

Although built in a contemporary style in 1973, this hotel fits in well with the landscape half a mile west of Locronan. In a large lounge, bay windows open onto the countryside. The decoration, although modern, preserves some rustic elements, including tile floors and a large fireplace of white stone. Some of the bedrooms have mezzanines reached by a stairway. The accommodations are quiet and spacious, with large windows.

MANOIR DE MOËLLIEN, 29550 Plonevez-Porzay. Tel. 98-92-50-40. Fax 98-92-55-21. 10 rms (all with bath). TEL

$ Rates: 320 F ($57.60) single or double. Breakfast 38 F ($6.80) extra. Half board 335 F ($60.30) single; 670 F ($120.60) double. AE, DC, MC, V. **Parking:** Free. **Closed:** Jan 2–Mar.

Set in the hamlet of Plonevez-Porzay, about a mile south of Locronan, this solidly built stone-sided manor house dates from the 1600s, but was completely restored in the 1960s into a comfortable and well-managed hotel. Many French urbanites check in for the peace, quiet, and good cuisine. Most of the accommodations are in a 19th-century barn, richly restored in the 1980s, which contains all the modern comforts. Each bedroom has its own panoramic terrace and imaginative decor, and the main building retains the enormous fireplace and massive ceiling beams of its original construction.

Nonresidents are welcome in the antique dining room, where fixed-price meals begin at 124 F ($22.30) and à la carte meals begin at around 250 F ($45). The last meal served is at 9pm. The restaurant (but not the hotel) is closed on Wednesday from October through March.

13. DINAN

246 miles W of Paris, 32 miles NW of Rennes

GETTING THERE By Train There's daily train service from many of Brittany's railway junctions.

By Ferry Ferry service is daily from Dinard and St-Malo.

ESSENTIALS Orientation The fortified Vieille Ville, on the western bank of the Rance River, is Dinan's most memorable attraction. The largest monument, the Château de Dinan, is on the southernmost edge of the fortifications. In the old town's center is the Tour de l'Horloge.

Information The Office de Tourisme is at 6, rue de l'Horloge (tel. 96-39-75-40).

Once a stronghold of the ducs de Bretagne, Dinan is still one of the best-preserved towns of Brittany, characterized by houses built on stilts over the sidewalks. The 18th-century granite dwellings contrast with the medieval timbered houses in this walled town with a once-fortified château.

For orientation and a panoramic view, head first for the **Jardin Anglais (English Garden),** a terraced garden huddling up to the ramparts where you can look out over the valley. Spanning the Rance River is a Gothic-style bridge that was damaged in World War II but has been restored.

The most typical street of Dinan is the sloping **rue du Jerzual,** flanked with old buildings, some of which date from the 15th century. The street ends at **La Porte du Jerzual,** an ancient gate. **Rue du Petit-Fours** also contains a number of 15th-century maisons.

Dominating the old city's medieval ramparts, the **Château de Dinan,** rue du Château (tel. 96-39-45-20), contains a 14th-century keep and a 15th-century tower, both built for military purposes and designed to withstand lengthy sieges. Within the stones you'll see the space for the portcullis and the drawbridge. In the interior, visitors can see an exhibition of the art and architecture of the city, including a collection of locally carved sculpture dating from the 12th to the 15th century. There is an entrance fee of 20 F ($3.60) for adults, 10 F ($1.80) for children; the castle is open daily from 10am to 6:30pm.

Built in the heart of the old city, the clock tour, **la Tour de l'Horloge,** rue de l'Horloge, now classified a historical monument, contains a clock made in 1498 and a great bell donated by Anne of Brittany in 1507. There is a great view of medieval Dinan from the 75-foot-high summit. Charging 10 F ($1.80) for admission, the belfry is open Monday through Saturday from 10:45am to 1:15pm and 3 to 6pm, and on Sunday from 3 to 6pm.

The heart of Bertrand du Guesclin, who successfully defended the town when the Duke of Lancaster threatened in 1359, was entombed in a position of honor in the **Basilica St-Sauveur,** place St-Sauveur, which is characterized by its Romanesque portals and ornamented 16th-century chapels. It's open daily from 8am to 6pm.

WHERE TO STAY

Many visitors prefer to use Dinan as a base for exploring St-Malo, Dinard, and Mont St-Michel. The accommodations here are limited, but they are quite good and are moderately priced. La Caravelle, listed under "Where to Dine," below, also rents 11 guest rooms.

D'AVAUGOUR, 1, place du Champs-Clos, 22100 Dinan. Tel. 96-39-07-49. Fax 96-85-43-04. 27 rms (all with bath). MINIBAR TV TEL **Bus:** 34, 36, or 96.
$ Rates: 350 F ($63) single; 450–500 F ($81–$90) double. Breakfast 45 F ($8.10) extra. AE, DC, MC, V. **Parking:** Free.

Madame Quinton gutted an old building and turned it into the most up-to-date accommodation in Dinan. Though small, it's the best hotel in town. The bedrooms are furnished with reproductions and contemporary pieces. Half of them overlook the square; the others face the tiny rear garden filled with birdcages, flowers, and a large stone fountain. The stylish front lounge has a lot of natural stone and modern furnishings.

The restaurant d'Avaugour has efficient service, and chef Monsieur Quinton offers excellent food. It's located in the garden overlooking the ramparts and is open every day of the year. Another summertime restaurant (which closes on Sunday) is located in a former guard's room in a 15th-century tower at the rear of the garden. It specializes in grilled meats prepared on a wood-burning fireplace; the fixed-price meals cost 85 F ($15.30) (lunch only) to 250 F ($45).

HOTEL DE BRETAGNE, 1, place Duclos, 22100 Dinan. Tel. 96-39-46-15. Fax 96-85-44-03. 46 rms (all with bath or shower). TEL **Bus:** 34, 36, or 96.
$ Rates: 190 F ($34.20) single; 280 F ($50.40) double. Breakfast 25 F ($4.50) extra. AE, DC, MC, V.

In the center of town, the Bretagne is mainly a hotel, and it offers bedrooms of good standard. But this also has what may be the most popular brasserie in town—it's usually crowded with people stepping in for a quick glass of wine or a full but informal meal. The fixed-price meals, costing 150–250 F ($27–$45), contain the standard favorites you'd expect in Brittany.

MARGUERITE, 29, place du Guesclin, 22100 Dinan. Tel. 96-39-47-65. 19 rms (all with bath). TEL **Bus:** 34, 36, or 96.
$ Rates: 190–270 F ($34.20–$48.60) single or double. Breakfast 40 F ($7.20) extra. AE, DC, V. **Closed:** Nov–Feb.

This traditional turn-of-the-century hotel is located behind the château. A cozy inn, it offers bedrooms of good standard, some with TVs. The satisfying meals in the restaurant consist of local produce whenever possible. The restaurant is closed Sunday night and Monday in winter. Fixed-price menus cost 70–170 F ($12.60–$30.60).

WHERE TO DINE

The cuisine in Dinan is superb. In addition to the following, all the hotels listed above have excellent restaurants.

LA CARAVELLE, 14, place Duclos, 22100 Dinan. Tel. 96-39-00-11.
   Cuisine: FRENCH. **Reservations:** Required. **Bus:** 34, 36, or 96.
$ Prices: Appetizers 80–180 F ($14.40–$32.40); main dishes 135–240 F ($24.30–$43.20); fixed-price meals 120 F ($21.60), 170 F ($30.60), 260 F ($46.80), and 350 F ($63). AE, DC, MC, V.
   Open: Lunch daily noon–2pm; dinner daily 7–9:30pm. **Closed:** Nov 12–Dec 3.
Jean-Claude Marmion, the inventive chef here, is passionately devoted to using whatever ingredients are in season. Some of his specialties include warm oysters with shallots, civet of lobster à la fleur de Bretagne, paupiette de perch fourré with crayfish, John Dory with green mustard and a red-pepper/cream sauce, and veal kidneys in cider. In season Marmion prepares the finest game dishes in town, including jugged hare or rabbit. When the first of the spring turnips come in, he uses them in a veal filet often served with an onion compote. The reception and the service are flawless.

CHEZ LA MERE POURCEL, 3, place des Merciers. Tel. 96-39-03-80.
   Cuisine: FRENCH. **Reservations:** Recommended. **Bus:** 34, 36, or 96.
$ Prices: Appetizers 90–120 F ($16.20–$21.60); main dishes 105–140 F ($18.90–$25.20); fixed-price meals 85 F ($15.30), 145 F ($26.10), 200 F ($36), and 260 F ($46.80). AE, DC, MC, V.
   Open: Lunch Tues–Sun noon–2pm; dinner Tues–Sat 7:15–10pm. **Closed:** Jan 20–Mar 15.
This 15th-century restaurant is located in the heart of Old Dinan. It's filled with old beams and leaded-glass windows and enjoys an outstanding reputation for regional food. Most diners seem to prefer the à la carte menu, which offers such specialties as a consommé with ravioli stuffed with ham and duckling and mushrooms from the forest with lobster and green butter. For a main course, try a pastry encased with pigeon, filet of red mullet with a coulis of oysters, or chicken suprême with foie gras. Desserts are excellent, including a cold chocolate soufflé.

14. DINARD

259 miles W of Paris, 14 miles N of Dinan

GETTING THERE   **By Ferry**   Between May and September, a ferry makes one daily trip from Dinan.

By Bus   Buses arrive from many large cities in Brittany, including Rennes.

ESSENTIALS   **Information**   The Office de Tourisme is at 2, bd. Féart (tel. 99-46-94-12).

Dinard sits on a rocky promontory at the top of the Rance River, opposite St-Malo; ferryboats ply the waters between the two resorts. Turn-of-the-century Victorian-Gothic villas, many now converted into hotels, overlook the sea. Gardens and parks abound. Today the tourists in Dinard tend to be French and German, rather than British and American.

One of the best-known seaside resorts in France, Dinard offers safe, well-sheltered bathing in **La Manche.** Its origins as a resort go back to the heyday of Queen Victoria, when it became popular with the Channel-crossing English, who wanted a continental holiday but one "not too foreign." Dinard offers a trio of beaches: The main one is **La Grande Plage,** which tends to get crowded in July and August; another, facing a backdrop of towering cliffs, is **Saint-Enogat;** the third, the **Prieuré,** honors a priory that stood nearby in the Middle Ages.

From June to September there is *musique et lumière* along the floodlit seafront **promenade du Clair-de-Lune.** The **New Municipal Casino** in the Palais d'Emeraude is open year-round. And about five miles from Dinard is the 18-hole golf course at **Saint-Briac;** it's one of the finest in Brittany.

WHERE TO STAY

In addition to the following, both restaurants listed under "Where to Dine," below, rent guest rooms.

Expensive

LE GRAND HOTEL DE DINARD, 46, av. George-V, 35801 Dinard. Tel. 99-88-26-26. Fax 99-88-26-27. 63 rms (all with bath), 3 suites. MINIBAR TV TEL
$ Rates: 980–1,200 F ($176.40–$216) single or double; from 2,400 F ($432) suite. Breakfast 60 F ($10.80) extra. AE, DC, MC, V. **Parking:** Free. **Closed:** Oct–Easter.

Dinard's leading hotel, built in 1859, commands an excellent view of the harbor, and lies within a two-minute walk from the center of town. Most of the five floors of this substantial brick structure have balconies and tall French windows. Most of the bedrooms were renovated in 1989, and those few that were not renovated, at least at press time, were not available for rentals. Most bedrooms are decorated with traditional pieces, including some in the Louis XVI style.

Decorated invitingly, the bar is a popular spot before and after dinner. Fine meals, with rather generous portions, are offered in the dignified in-house restaurant, the George V, where fixed-price menus begin at 180 F ($32.40) each.

REINE HORTENSE, 19, rue de la Malouine, 35800 Dinard. Tel. 99-46-54-31. Fax 99-88-15-88. 8 rms (all with bath), 2 suites. TV TEL
$ Rates: 1,300 F ($234) single or double; 1,600–2,300 F ($288–$414) suite. Breakfast 60 F ($10.80) extra. DC, MC, V. **Parking:** Free.

The hotel was built in 1860 as a retreat for one of the Russian-born courtiers of the Holland-based queen, Hortense de Beauharnais, mother of Napoléon III. Located on the beach, it offers public salons glamorously outfitted with luxurious accessories. Many of the bedrooms are decorated in either the Louis XV or the Napoléon III style. One high-ceilinged room even has the silver-plated bathtub of Queen Hortense, which dates from the early 19th century. Breakfast is the only meal served.

Under the same umbrella, Le Castel Eugénie, which contains six rooms, lies next door and charges the same rates. Modern, it's is about a decade old, but well appointed and comfortable. It's owned by the same management.

Moderate

BALMORAL, 26, rue du Maréchal-Leclerc, 35800 Dinard. Tel. 99-46-16-97. Fax 99-88-20-48. 31 rms (all with bath). TEL
$ Rates: 260–280 F ($46.80–$50.40) single; 320–360 F ($57.60–$64.80) double. Breakfast 32 F ($5.70) extra. AE, DC, MC, V. **Parking:** Free. **Closed:** Jan.

Built between the two world wars, this hotel is studded with balconies and vaguely reminiscent of something along the Scottish coast. Within walking distance of the beaches and the casino, the hotel has an inviting communal TV room and bar. Rooms are comfortably furnished and well kept. There is no restaurant.

HOTEL-RESTAURANT EMERAUDE PLAGE, 1, bd. Albert-1er, 35802 Dinard CEDEX. Tel. 99-46-15-79. Fax 99-46-15-79. 65 rms (all with bath or shower). TV TEL
$ Rates: 300 F ($54) single; 520 F ($93.60) double. Breakfast 35 F ($6.30) extra. No credit cards. **Closed:** Oct 3–Apr 7.

This well-run hotel is located about 55 yards from the main beach and town center. A corner building, it was constructed in a turn-of-the-century style typical of northern Brittany. Claude Luyer, a native of the area, speaks English and makes his guests feel welcome. Many of the well-furnished and spacious bedrooms overlook the water. Chef Madame Luyer produces excellent breakfasts and dinners, the latter costing 105–135 F ($18.90–$24.30)—a good value considering the quality. The hotel has an elevator.

PRINTANIA, 5, av. George-V, 35800 Dinard. Tel. 99-46-13-07. Fax 99-46-26-32. 59 rms (all with bath). TV TEL
$ Rates (including half board): 270–320 F ($48.60–$57.60) per person single or double. AE, MC, V. **Closed:** Nov 15–Easter.

On August 15, 1944, this old-world Breton hotel was damaged during a bombing raid, but the debris was removed in time for the Allied victory celebration. The Printania draws many repeat guests, among them writers and artists. Everybody has stayed here, from Edward Heath to Sinclair Lewis. The antique-jammed sitting room has dark, carved-oak furniture, old clocks, and provincial chairs. The main villa stands eight stories high with terraces and a glassed-in veranda with potted palms, Breton cupboards, and ceramic pottery. Dinner at Printania combines superb cookery with a view of the coastline. The restaurant specializes in seafood and various shellfish, offering fixed-price menus to nonresidents for 90–230 F ($16.20–$41.40)— the latter price for a *menu gastronomique*. Bedrooms are furnished with antiques and Breton decorations.

Inexpensive

LES DUNES, 5, rue Georges-Clemenceau, 35800 Dinard. Tel. 99-46-12-72. Fax 99-88-14-90. 38 rms (all with bath or shower). TV TEL
$ Rates (including half board): 420 F ($75.60) single; 640 F ($115.20) double. AE, DC, MC, V. **Closed:** Nov–Mar 15.

Located high on a cliff, this hotel has tall French windows and balustraded balconies. The front terrace has garden furniture under parasols, and the bedrooms have comfortable furnishings. A dining room and lounge overlook the front garden terrace.

WHERE TO DINE

ALTAIR, 18, bd. Féart, 64200 Dinard. Tel. 99-46-13-58. Fax 99-88-20-49.
Cuisine: FRENCH. **Reservations:** Recommended.
$ Prices: Appetizers 39–95 F ($7–$17.10); main dishes 95–250 F ($17.10–$45); fixed-price meals 90–310 F ($16.20–$55.80). AE, DC, MC, V.
Open: Lunch daily noon–2pm; dinner daily 7–9:30pm. **Closed:** Mon in winter.

Patrick Leménager operates this small, intimate restaurant housed in a somewhat old-fashioned building. His excellent cuisine includes sea scallops in puff pastry with a coriander sauce, fresh salmon with herbs, and breast of duck with an apple-and-honey sauce, followed by a gratin of red fruits for dessert. In warm weather you may prefer to dine al fresco on the terrace.

The Altaïr also rents 21 bedrooms with private baths or showers and TVs. Two guests pay 280–380 F ($50.40–$68.40).

LE PETIT ROBINSON, 38, rue de la Gougeonnais, 35780 La Richardais. Tel. 99-46-14-82.
Cuisine: FRENCH. **Reservations:** Required.
$ Prices: Appetizers 30–80 F ($5.40–$14.40); main dishes 70–120 F ($12.60–$21.60); fixed-price menus 85 F ($15.30) and 160 F ($28.80). AE, DC, MC, V.
Open: July–Aug, lunch Tues–Sun noon–1:45pm; dinner Mon–Sat 7–9:30pm. Sept–June, lunch Tues–Sun noon–1:45pm; dinner Tues–Sat 7–9:30pm.

S Set about two miles southeast of Dinard in the hamlet of La Richardais, this tastefully decorated hotel and restaurant is in a rambling turn-of-the-century seaside manor house built, like many others nearby, in the English colonial style.

The conservative and well-presented cuisine includes many kinds of shellfish, filet of John Dory in either a sage or a beurre-blanc sauce, a civet of monkfish with sherry-and-raspberry vinegar, salmon with two sauces (both tomato-based and beurre blanc), grilled sea bass with fennel, and many different preparations of lobster. Patrice Nicolle and his family are the well-informed chefs and directors.

In addition to the excellent cuisine, they rent seven comfortably furnished bedrooms suitable for either one or two occupants, each with private bath or shower, color TV, and phone. Singles cost 250 F ($45) and doubles are 270 F ($48.60), with breakfast priced at an additional 30 F ($5.40).

15. ST-MALO

257 miles W of Paris, 43 miles W of Rennes, 8 miles E from Dinard

GETTING THERE   By Train   Take the train from Rennes or Dinan.

ESSENTIALS Orientation   The town is on a peninsula, curving like a boomerang around a natural harbor whose interior has been subdivided into several smaller basins. The walled city, with its château and its central monument, the Cathedral of St-Vincent, is on the peninsula's westernmost (most distant) tip.

Information   The Office de Tourisme is on esplanade St-Vincent (tel. 99-56-64-48). A passport is necessary for the hydrofoil or car-ferry trips and tours to the Channel Islands.

Built on a granite rock in the English Channel, St-Malo is joined to the mainland by a causeway. Popular with the English, especially those from the Channel Islands, it makes a modest claim to be a bathing resort.

For the best view of the bay and the offshore islets at the mouth of the Rance, walk along the ramparts dating from the Middle Ages. These walls were built over a period of centuries, some parts of them dating from the 14th century. However, they were mainly rebuilt in the 17th century, then vastly restored in the 19th. You can begin your tour at the 15th-century **Gate of St. Vincent.**

At the harbor, you can book tours for the **Channel Islands.** Hydrofoils leave for the English island of Jersey; a passport, of course, is necessary.

At low tide, you can take a 25-minute stroll to the **Ile du Grand Bé,** the site of the lonely tomb of Chateaubriand, "deserted by others and completely surrounded by storms." The tomb—marked by a cross—is simple, unlike the man it honors, but the view of the Emerald Coast from here makes up for it.

Called the "Bastille of the West," **St-Malo Castle,** Porte St-Vincent (tel. 99-40-71-11) and its towers shelter a historic museum with souvenirs of Duguay-Trouin (1673–1736) and Surcouf (1773–1827), the most famous of the St-Malo privateers. The **Museum of St-Malo** is in the donjon (inner tower or keep). You can visit Wednesday through Monday from 9:40am to noon and 2 to 6pm; admission is 10 F ($1.80). Guided tours are available only in July and August.

The museum also contains memorabilia of the celebrated native sons of St-Malo. The most famous, of course, was Chateaubriand, the romantic French writer and statesman who created the melancholy hero. However, as well known was Jacques Cartier, the French explorer and navigator who discovered the St. Lawrence River in 1536, thus establishing a French claim on North America. He named the country Canada. The third great son was the morbid Lamennais, the French priest and philosophical and political writer born in St-Malo, who wrote *Paroles d'un croyant* (Words from a Believer) in 1834, which was widely read throughout Europe.

After the castle and ramparts tour, you may have time to explore the cobbled plazas, the flagstone courtyards, the narrow streets, the fish market, the cathedral with a 12th-century nave, and the tall gabled houses. One of the most important of the Breton *pardons* is held at St-Malo in February: the **Pardon of the Newfoundland Fishing Fleet.**

In the resort of **St-Servan,** adjoining St-Malo, you can visit the **Musée**

International du Long-Cours Cap-Hornier in the Tour Solidor (tel. 99-40-71-11), a tower built in 1382, commanding the Rance estuary. Here a history of voyages around the world by way of Cape Horn is depicted in exhibits from the 16th to 20th centuries. Maps, manuscripts, ship models, and nautical instruments are on display. It's open from Easter to September, daily from 10am to noon and 2 to 6pm. Admission is 10 F ($1.80).

WHERE TO STAY

BRISTOL UNION, 4, place de la Poissonnerie, 35400 St-Malo. Tel. 99-40-83-36. 27 rms (all with bath or shower). TV TEL **Bus:** 1, 2, or 3.
$ Rates: 220–330 F ($39.60–$59.40) double. Breakfast 30 F ($5.40) extra. AE, DC, MC, V. **Closed:** Mid-Nov to Jan.
This comfortable hotel, near the railway station, is about five minutes from the departure quay for Great Britain and the Channel Islands. The owners offer individualized bedrooms, 15 of which contain minibars. Breakfast is the only meal served.

CENTRAL, 6, Grand Rue, 35400 St-Malo. Tel. 99-40-87-70. Fax 99-40-87-70. 44 rms (all with bath). MINIBAR TV TEL **Bus:** 1, 2, or 3.
$ Rates: 425 F ($76.50) single; 630 F ($113.40) double. Breakfast 55 F ($9.90) extra. AE, DC, MC, V. **Parking:** 45 F ($8.10).
Located on a street near the harbor, this leading hotel has been entirely renovated. It's provincial but in a sophisticated way. The furnishings are contemporary and color coordinated. One of the best reasons for staying here is the food; meals cost 130–190 F ($23.40–$34.20) in La Frégate. Before dinner, you can have a drink in the bar.

ELISABETH, 2, rue des Cordiers, 35400 St-Malo. Tel. 99-56-24-98. Fax 99-56-39-24. 17 rms (all with bath). TV TEL **Bus:** 1, 2, or 3.
$ Rates (including breakfast): 492–572 F ($88.50–$102.90) single; 539–619 F ($97–$111.40) double. AE, DC, MC, V. **Parking:** 45 F ($8.10).
This hotel has a 16th-century facade and a well-furnished, fairly modern interior. There's a view of the port from many of the comfortable bedrooms. Breakfast is the only meal served.

WHERE TO DINE

A LA DUCHESSE-ANNE, 5, place Guy-La-Chambre. Tel. 99-40-85-33.
Cuisine: FRENCH. **Reservations:** Required. **Bus:** 1, 2, or 3.
$ Prices: Appetizers 60–120 F ($10.80–$21.60); main dishes 125–175 F ($22.50–$31.50). MC, V.
Open: Lunch Thurs–Tues 12:15–1:30pm; dinner Thurs–Tues 7:15–9:15pm. **Closed:** Nov–Feb.
This leading restaurant, located near the château, was built into the ramparts. The atmosphere is mellow, with a white-and-gold-paneled ceiling. In summer, tables are placed under a large canopy amid hydrangeas. Try the fish specialties—the fish soup made with chunks of freshly caught seafood, spiced and cooked in an iron pot, is excellent, as are the oysters from Cancale. Main courses include grilled turbot with beurre blanc or a pepper steak. Desserts are equally tempting.

LE CHALUT, 8, rue de la Corne-de-Cerf. Tel. 99-56-71-58.
Cuisine: FRENCH. **Reservations:** Required. **Bus:** 1, 2, or 3.
$ Prices: Appetizers 45–95 F ($8.10–$17.10); main dishes 90–150 F ($16.20–$27); fixed-price meals 95–250 F ($17.10–$45). AE, MC, V.
Open: Lunch Tues–Sun 12:30–2pm; dinner Tues–Sun 7:30–10pm. **Closed:** Last two weeks of Oct.
The decor in this restaurant is nautical—with green and blue throughout. It lies in the heart of town, within the medieval walls of the old city. Jean-Philippe Foucat's flavorful cuisine is based on fresh, natural ingredients and includes braised sweetbreads with baby vegetables in a tarragon sauce, a terrine of scallops, and crayfish in a

sage-flavored sauce; for dessert there's a gâteau of bitter chocolate served with almond paste and a sorbet of mandarin oranges, or try a feuilleté of red seasonal berries.

DELAUNAY, 6, rue Ste-Barbe. Tel. 99-40-92-46.
   Cuisine: FRENCH. **Reservations:** Required. **Bus:** 1, 2, or 3.
$ Prices: Appetizers 50–105 F ($9–$18.90); main dishes 98–160 F ($17.60–$28.80); fixed-price lunches 98–160 F ($17.60–$28.80). AE, DC, MC, V.
   Open: Lunch Mon–Sat noon–2pm; dinner Mon–Sat 7:30–9:30pm. **Closed:** Nov 15–Dec 15.

Delaunay lies in the heart of the historic town, just off the most heavily trafficked (by pedestrians) inner street, rue de la Soif (Street of Great Thirst). The decor in this small bistro includes paintings and watercolors. The chef de cuisine, J. P. Delaunay, changes the menu according to the ingredients available that morning at market. You may begin your meal with half a dozen oysters; then try, if featured, turbot roasted au naturel. I also recommend the perfectly cooked panache of fish, the sweetbreads in a cider sauce, and the lobster in a "bath" of white wine sauce.

REIMS & THE CHAMPAGNE COUNTRY

In about three days a visitor traveling from Paris on the N3—the Autoroute de l'Est—can encompass a world of old cathedrals, battlefields, fantastic food, and some of France's most famous vineyards, topping the exploration with a heady glass of champagne.

On the "champagne trail," you can go first to the wine-producing center of Épernay, and then on to Reims, which lies some 90 miles to the northeast of Paris. After visiting Reims and its cathedral, you can leave on Rte. 31 east, heading in the direction of Verdun.

Old Roman roads crisscrossed Champagne, and the region has always stood in the pathway of invaders. The clashes here have gone on for two millennia. Even today, names such as Reims evoke ghastly memories of some of the worst fighting of World War I.

SEEING REIMS & THE CHAMPAGNE COUNTRY

The region deserves at least three days, more if you have time. A car allows you to explore remote, out-of-the-way places. If you're confined to public transportation, you should concentrate on Reims, famous for its great cathedral and champagne cellars.

Ideally, you should tie in a visit to the Champagne district with a trip to the Ardennes and the northern beaches, including Calais (see Chapter 16). Many visitors come here just to take the "champagne trail," beginning at Epernay and going on to Reims—budget at least two days to do this. It's best to visit from Easter through October.

GETTING THERE The drive to Reims and the champagne country from Paris is an easy trip on motorways A31, A4, and A203. Or you can take a train from Paris (Gare de l'Est) to Reims and eastern France. There are no scheduled flights to the area—the nearest airport is in Paris.

Champagne–Ardennes is crisscrossed by 403 miles of waterways, with many lakes; *bateaux-mouches* (panoramic boats) cover the whole area.

Ballooning is the latest craze in seeing Champagne; consult Champagne Air Show, 15 bis, place St-Niçaise, Reims (tel. 26-82-59-60), for all the details.

WHAT'S SPECIAL ABOUT REIMS & THE CHAMPAGNE COUNTRY

Great Towns/Villages
- [ ] Reims, an ancient city where French kings came to be crowned.
- [ ] Châlons-sur-Marne, crisscrossed by canals.
- [ ] Troyes, an architectural gem and capital of the southern champagne country.

Ancient Monuments
- [ ] Cathédrale de Notre-Dame at Reims, one of the most famous in the world.

Castles
- [ ] Castle of Condé, home of the Marquis de Sade, after whom the word *sadism* was coined.

Architectural Highlights
- [ ] Abbaye d'Hautvillers at Epernay, a gracious old abbey dating from the 12th century, and the burial place of Dom Pérignon, synonymous with great bubbly.
- [ ] Church of St-Rémi, with a grand Romanesque nave and 13th-century stained glass.

Battlefields
- [ ] Basilica of St-Urbain at Troyes, "the Parthenon of Champagne," in Gothic style.

Battlefields
- [ ] Belleau Wood, site of the second major clash of World War I, now the site of an American cemetery.

Outstanding Museums
- [ ] Musée d'Art Moderne, at Troyes, one of France's greatest collections of modern art.

Champagne Cellars
- [ ] Moët et Chandon Champagne Cellars at Epernay, where you can learn the art of making champagne.
- [ ] Reims, site of such champagne cellars as the Houses of Pommery, Taittinger, and Piper-Heidsieck.

Events/Festivals
- [ ] *Son-et-lumière* (sound-and-light) shows, June to September, with illuminations at Reims and Troyes.

1. EPERNAY

87 miles E of Paris, 16 miles S of Reims

GETTING THERE By Train Epernay is set on the main rail lines between eastern France and Paris; train service is frequent.

By Bus Those buses traveling to nearby small towns usually stop at place Notre-Dame, Epernay.

ESSENTIALS Orientation Epernay's main boulevards include the elegantly residential avenue de Champagne, rue Mercier, and rue de Reims, all radiating from place de la République. Two important squares within the narrow streets of the commercial district are place Hughes-Plomb and place des Arcades.

Information Contact the Office de Tourisme, 7, av. de Champagne (tel. 26-55-33-00), for information about the region and the best ways to visit the champagne cellars.

On the left bank of the Marne, Epernay rivals Reims as a center for champagne. With only one-sixth of Reims's population, Epernay produces nearly as much champagne as does its larger sister.

Although the town is a rather pedestrian modern one, Epernay has an estimated 200 miles or more of cellars and tunnels, a veritable rabbit warren, for storing champagne. These caves are vast vaults cut in the chalk rock on which the town is built. Represented in Epernay are such champagne companies as Moët et Chandon (the largest), Pol Roger, Mercier, and de Castellane.

Epernay has been either destroyed or burned nearly two dozen times, since it lay in the path of invading armies, particularly the Germans. Therefore, few of its old buildings are left. However, try to visit avenue de Champagne, with its neoclassical villas and Victorian town houses.

WHAT TO SEE & DO

MOET ET CHANDON CHAMPAGNE CELLARS, 18, av. de Champagne. Tel. 26-54-71-11.

An expert member of the staff gives guided tours in English and describes the champagne-making process. You'll see the *remueurs* at work, twisting each bottle a quarter turn. At the end of the tour, each visitor is given a complimentary glass of the bubbly.

Admission: Free.

Open: Apr–Oct, daily 9:30–11:30am and 2–4:45pm; Nov–Mar, Mon–Fri 9:30–11:30am and 2–4:45pm. **Closed:** National holidays.

MUSEE MUNICIPAL, 13, av. de Champagne. Tel. 26-51-90-31.

This museum exhibits collections on the ethnography of Champagne and the archeology of the region.

Admission: 8 F ($1.40).

Open: Apr–Nov, Wed–Mon 10am–noon and 2–6pm. **Closed:** Dec–Mar.

ABBAYE D'HAUTVILLERS, on the D386, signposted just north of Epernay.

This abbey, owned by Moët et Chandon, contains the tomb of the blind monk Dom Pérignon, the cellar-master at the abbey from 1670 to 1715, who is credited with inventing the process for turning the still wines of the region into sparkling champagne. Upon drinking champagne for the first time, Pérignon is reported to have said, "I am drinking stars!"

The old abbey has been rebuilt several times since it was founded in the 12th century. When the monks were evicted during the French Revolution, the abbey was purchased by the Moët family. However, today it's a church again and can be visited anytime. A representative of the Moët company can arrange for you to see the beautiful interior gardens with their incomparable view of the champagne vineyards and the Marne Valley. The Marne River was extolled in verse by La Fontaine and glorified by Corot in his landscapes.

Admission: Free.

Open: Visits by appointment; call Moët et Chandon (tel. 26-54-71-11).

WHERE TO STAY

Les Berceaux, listed under "Where to Dine," below, also rents guest rooms.

CHAMPAGNE, 30, rue Eugène-Mercier, 51200 Epernay. Tel. 26-55-30-22. Fax 26-55-10-36. 35 rms (all with bath). TV TEL

$ Rates: 255 F ($45.90) single; 390 F ($70.20) double. Breakfast 38 F ($6.80) extra. AE, DC, V. **Parking:** Free.

This relatively simple little inn is one of the best of a modest lot in the town itself (the luxurious accommodations are on the outskirts). However, it offers good prices for its clean, well-maintained, functional bedrooms. Each room has a direct-dial phone and a color TV set. A generous buffet breakfast is served every morning, and parking is available on the grounds.

WHERE TO DINE

LES BERCEAUX, 13, rue Berceaux, 51200 Epernay. Tel. 26-55-28-84. Fax 26-55-10-36.

Cuisine: FRENCH. **Reservations:** Recommended.

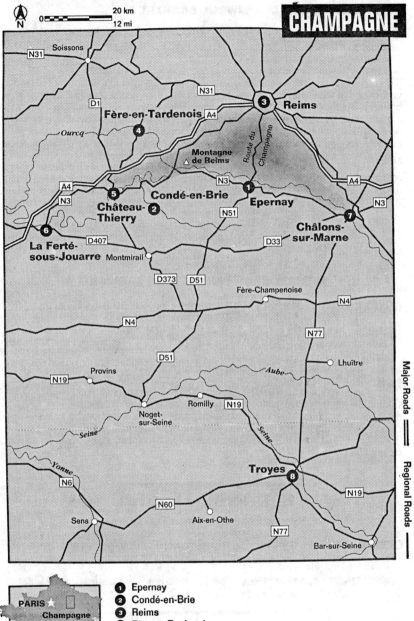

CHAMPAGNE

N

0 20 km
   12 mi

N31 Soissons

N31

D1

Fère-en-Tardenois ❹ A4

Ourcq

Montagne
de Reims

❸ Reims

Route du Champagne

A4

N3

A4

N3

N3

Château-
Thierry ❷

Condé-en-Brie

❺

❶ Epernay

Châlons-
sur-Marne ❼

N51

N3

❻
La Ferté-
sous-Jouarre

D407

D33

Montmirail

D373 D51

Fère-Champenoise

N4

N4

N77

D51

Lhuître

N19 Provins

Aube

Romilly N19

Noget-
sur-Seine

Seine

Seine

Yonne

N6

Troyes ❽

N19

N60

N19

Sens

Aix-en-Othe

N77

Bar-sur-Seine

Major Roads ═══

Regional Roads ▬▬▬

PARIS ⭐ ☐
         Champagne

FRANCE

❶ Epernay
❷ Condé-en-Brie
❸ Reims
❹ Fère-en-Tardenois
❺ Château-Thierry
❻ La Ferté-sous-Jouarre
❼ Châlons-sur-Marne
❽ Troyes

$ Prices: Appetizers 65–125 F ($11.70–$22.50); main dishes 110–185 F ($19.80–$33.30); fixed-price meals 140 F ($25.20), 190 F ($34.20), and 300 F ($54). AE, DC, MC, V.
Open: Lunch daily noon–2:30pm; dinner Mon–Sat 7–9:30pm.

This is the best bet in Epernay for both food and lodgings. Luc Maillard is the owner and chef; his wife, Jill, is English. Monsieur Maillard serves superior Champenois cookery—truly some of the best in the area. The portions, incidentally, are huge, so plan to make an evening meal here an event, and if you can afford it, wash everything down with libations of champagne. The restaurant has an aquarium on display with live lobsters and crayfish to choose from. One specialty is turbot au champagne, or you can have sole au Berceaux and pâté de foie gras of the house.

The Maillards also operate a wine bar located in the hotel, with a bistro where customers can order meals for 110 F ($19.80) and up; or you can sample good French wines by the glass, without having to buy a whole bottle. Staff members at Les Berceaux speak English and can arrange your visits to the champagne houses in the area.

The Maillards rent 29 guest rooms, all with telephones; a double with shower costs 330 F ($59.40), while a double with bath costs 440 F ($79.20), plus 35 F ($6.30) for breakfast.

NEARBY ACCOMMODATIONS & DINING

ROYAL CHAMPAGNE, 51160 Champillon. Tel. 26-52-87-11. Fax 26-52-89-69. 30 rms (all with bath or shower), 3 suites. TV TEL
$ Rates: 700–1,200 F ($126–$216) single or double; 1,200–1,500 F ($216–$270) suite. Breakfast 80 F ($14.40) extra. AE, DC, MC, V. **Parking:** Free. **Closed:** Jan.

⭐ This is the best hotel in the area, and is certainly the most scenic. A Relais & Châteaux, it's four miles from Epernay in the hamlet of Champillon, toward Reims on route du Vignoble (RN2051). This posting house dates from the 18th century; windows open onto views of the champagne vineyards. The food is exceptional, including such specialties as a lobster ragoût, salt cod with a mousseline of truffles, and roast lamb with garlic. The fixed-price menus cost 250 F ($45), 300 F ($54), 350 F ($63), and 400 F ($72); you can expect to spend 400 F ($72) for an à la carte meal.

2. CONDE-EN-BRIE

55 miles E of Paris, 15 miles W of Epernay

GETTING THERE   By Car Traveling between Château-Thierry and Epernay on Rte. 3, head South at Dormans and follow the signs to Condé-en-Brie.

ESSENTIALS   Information For information on the castle, contact Château de Condé, 02330 Condé-en-Brie (tel. 23-82-42-25).

Located west of Epernay, the **Castle of Condé,** 02330 Condé-en-Brie (tel. 23-82-42-25), was inherited in 1814 by the comte de Sade, and it remained in the Sade family until 1983. The Sade family name was besmirched by the infamous Marquis de Sade, an innovative writer whose sexual practices as described in his writing led to the word *sadism.*

The castle was constructed, probably on the ruins of a Gallo-Roman fortress, in the late 12th century by Enguerran of Coucy. A part of the old keep still remains—two big rooms with great chimneys and thick walls. The castle was entirely rebuilt in the Renaissance style at the beginning of the 16th century by the Cardinal of

Bourbon, a member of the French royal family. His nephew, Louis of Bourbon, who was the leader of the Protestant party in France and the uncle of the future King Henry IV, called himself "Prince of Condé," probably because he had many fond childhood memories of the place and liked to go there to hunt.

The castle was heavily damaged at the beginning of the 18th century and was again rebuilt by a private secretary of King Louis XIV, John Francis Leriget, marquis de La Faye. He called in the Italian architect Servandoni, who designed it. Servandoni invited the most fashionable painters to paint frescoes and paintings (which can still be seen today) inside the castle—among them, Lemoyne and his disciple, Boucher, and Watteau, Lancret, and Jean-Baptiste Oudry. Servandoni himself decorated the biggest room, making it a sort of theater hall for music and entertainment. The present castle is an exceptional ensemble of the 18th century, with its paintings, woodwork, chimneys, and so-called Versailles floor.

Admission is 26 F ($4.60) for adults and 13 F ($2.30) for children under 15. The castle is open from June through August, daily at 2:30, 3:30, and 4:30pm; in May and September, on Sunday at 2:30, 3:30, and 4:30pm; closed in other months.

3. REIMS

89 miles E of Paris, 28 miles NW of Châlons-sur-Marne

GETTING THERE   By Train   Trains leave daily to Reims from Gare de l'Est in Paris; the ride takes about an hour and a half. There are also two trains daily from Luxembourg.

ESSENTIALS   Orientation   Three important buildings (the train station, the world-famous cathedral, and the Basilica of St-Rémi) lie along a straight northwest-to-southeast line. The city lies roughly in an oval on either side of this line. One interesting street connects every neighborhood, rue Chanzy/rue Gambetta.

Information   The Office de Tourisme is located at 2, rue Guillaume-de-Machault (tel. 26-47-25-69).

Reims (pronounced Rans) is an ancient city, a Roman-era town. It was important at the time Caesar conquered Gaul. French kings came here to be crowned, and it is said that the French nation was born here in A.D. 498. Joan of Arc escorted Charles VII here in 1429, kissing the feet of the silly man. But don't let all this ancient background mislead you. The approach to Reims through prefabricated suburbs evokes the worst of apartment house blocks in Eastern Europe. There are gems in Reims, including the cathedral (see below), of course, but you must seek them out.

Aside from its historical monuments (of which there are many), Reims is visited chiefly because it is the center of a wine-growing district that gives the world a bubbly with which to make toasts. The champagne bottled in this district, of course, is said to be "the lightest and most subtle in flavor of the world's wines." Those planning more than a quick one-day trip can linger in the region, exploring the vineyards and wine cellars, the Gothic monuments, the World War battlefields. The Germans occupied Reims in 1870, 1914, and again in 1940.

WHAT TO SEE & DO

SALLE DE REDDITION, 10, rue Franklin-Roosevelt.

On May 7, 1945, the Germans surrendered to General Eisenhower in this brick building, once a little schoolhouse, near the railroad tracks. The walls of the room are lined with maps of the rail routes, exactly as they were on the day of surrender.

Admission: 10 F ($1.80) adults, 5 F (90¢) children.

Open: Apr–Sept, Wed–Mon 10am–noon and 2–6pm; Oct–Mar, Wed–Mon 2–6pm.

CATHEDRALE NOTRE-DAME, place du Cardinal-Luçon. Tel. 26-47-49-37.

⭐ This is one of the most famous cathedrals in the world. After World War I, the cathedral, which has suffered more bombardments than most fortresses, was restored largely with U.S. contributions; mercifully, it escaped World War II relatively unharmed. Built on the site of a church burned to the ground in 1211, it was intended as a sanctuary where French kings would be anointed—St. Rémi, the bishop of Reims, baptized Clovis, the pagan king of the Franks, here in 496. Kings of France from Louis VII in 1137 to Charles X in 1825 were crowned here.

Laden with statuettes, its three portals on the western facade are spectacular. A rose-colored window is above the central portal, which is dedicated to the Virgin. The right portal portrays the Apocalypse and the Last Judgment; the left, Martyrs and Saints. At the northern door of the western facade is a smiling angel. Lit by lancet window, the nave is immense, with many bays.

Located beside the cathedral is the treasury, which contains a 12th-century chalice for the communion of French monarchs and a talisman, supposedly containing a relic of the True Cross that Charlemagne is said to have worn.

Admission: Free.
Open: Daily 9:30am–7:30pm.

BASILIQUE ST-REMI, 53, rue St-Simon. Tel. 26-85-23-36.

Though sometimes unfavorably compared to the Reims's Cathedral of Notre-Dame, this church is an outstanding achievement. Once a Benedictine abbey church, it contains a grand Romanesque nave leading to a magnificent choir crowned with massive pointed arches. The nave, the transepts, one of the towers, and the aisles date from the 11th century. The portal of the south transept is in the flamboyant style of the early 16th century. The apse is made of stained glass, some from the 13th century.

The tomb of St. Rémi is elaborately carved with Renaissance figures and columns. The former abbey, rebuilt in the 18th century, has been turned into a historical and lapidary museum. In the cloister is a Gallo-Roman sarcophagus said to be that of the consul Jovin, who died in 412. There is also a collection of medieval sculpture, mostly Romanesque.

Admission: Free.
Open: Wed–Mon 10am–noon and 2–6pm.

MUSEE DES BEAUX-ARTS, 8, rue Chanzy. Tel. 26-47-28-44.

Housed in the 18th-century buildings belonging to the old abbey of St. Denis, this fine provincial art gallery has more than a dozen portraits of German princes of the Reformation by both "the Elder" and "the Younger" Cranach in the Salle Monthelon; the museum has owned this remarkable collection since it first opened in 1795. In the same hall, the Toiles Peintes (light painting on rough linen) date from the 15th and 16th centuries and depict the *Passion du Christ* and *Vengeance du Christ*.

Paintings and fine furniture from the 17th and 18th centuries, including paintings by van Moll, the Le Nain brothers, Le Brun, Poussin, Mignard, Ph. de Champaigne, and Boucher, are in the Salles Diancourt and Jamot-Neveux. In the next room is an excellent series of 26 of Corot's tree-shaded walks. The museum also exhibits in four salons paintings by David, Delacroix, Millet, Courbet, Daumier, Gericault, Jongkind, Lepine, Pissarro, Sisley, Monet, Renoir, Gauguin, Bonnard, Matisse, Dufy, Vuillard, Marquet, Puy, Vieira da Silva, and Sima.

Admission: 10 F ($1.80).
Open: Wed–Mon 10am–noon and 2–6pm.

Champagne Cellars

⭐ Many of the vast wine cellars extend for miles through chalky deposits. In fact, during the German siege of 1914 and throughout the war, people lived in them and even published a daily paper.

Although the champagne cellars are open all year, they're most interesting during

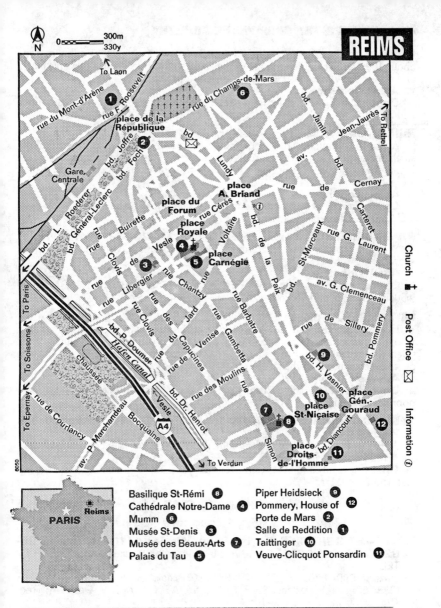

REIMS

0 300m
330y
N

To Laon

rue du Mont-d'Arène

1

place de la République

rue F. Roosevelt

rue du Champs-de-Mars

6

bd. Jamin

Jean-Jaurès
To Rethel

Gare Centrale

2

bd. Joffre
bd. Foch

bd.

Lundy

av.

bd.

Cernay

L. Roederer

bd. Général-Leclerc

Buirette

place A. Briand

rue Cérès

rue de

rue

Carteret

place du Forum

Voltaire

(i)

place Royale

bd.

St-Marceaux

rue G. Laurent

rue Clovis

Vesle

4 †

de

de la

av. G. Clemenceau

de

Sillery

place Carnégie

5

3

Libergier

rue

rue Chantzy

rue

Paix

bd.

rue Barbâtre

rue

bd. Pommery

rue

des

Jard

Venise

Gambetta

bd. H. Vasnier

9

rue Clovis

du

Capucines

rue des Moulins

rue

place Gén.-Gouraud

bd. P. Doumer

Halen Canal

rue de

10

place St-Nicaise

To Paris

To Soissons

Chaussée

Vesle

bd. Dr. Henrot

7

place

12

To Epernay

rue de Courlancy

av. P. Marchandeau

Bocquaine

A4

Simon

8 †

bd. Diancourt

11

place Droits-de-l'Homme

To Verdun

6050

Church ∎ †

Post Office ✉

Information (i)

PARIS ★ Reims

Basilique St-Rémi **8**	Piper Heidsieck **9**
Cathédrale Notre-Dame **4**	Pommery, House of **12**
Mumm **6**	Porte de Mars **2**
Musée St-Denis **3**	Salle de Reddition **1**
Musée des Beaux-Arts **7**	Taittinger **10**
Palais du Tau **5**	Veuve-Clicquot Ponsardin **11**

the fall grape harvest. After the harvest, the wine is stored in vats in the caves. While in the chalk caves, a second fermentation of the wine takes place. The wine-growers wait until the sparkle has "taken," as they say, before they remove the bottles to racks or pulpits. For about three months a turner is paid just to move them a fraction every day, which brings down impurities on the cork. After aging for a few years, the wines are mixed with a liqueur (wine and sugar), which determines the sweetness of the champagne. The entire process takes four or five years, and it takes place in caves that are usually 100 feet deep and are at a constant temperature of 50°F.

HOUSE OF POMMERY, 5, place Général-Gouraud. Tel. 26-61-62-55.

Among the most visited cellars are those found under the Gothic-style buildings and spacious gardens of the House of Pommery. A magnificent 116-step stairway leads to a maze of galleries dug into the chalk that are more than 11 miles long and about 100 feet below the ground. Various stages of champagne-making are shown, and a slide show in English is given at the end of the tour.

Admission: Free.

Open: Mar 15–Oct, daily 10am–5:30pm; Nov–Mar 15, Mon–Fri 10am–noon and 2–5pm.

MUMM, 34, rue du Champ-de-Mars. Tel. 26-49-59-70.

A visit to Mumm includes a video show and a tour of the cellars. There is also a small museum exhibiting ancient tools of a vintner and casks. This is the only cellar in Reims offering a taste of their product; you can also purchase their champagne in their gift shop.

Admission: Free.

Open: Easter–Oct, daily 9–11am and 2–5pm; Nov–Easter, Mon–Fri 9–11am and 2–5pm. **Closed:** Holidays.

PIPER-HEIDSIECK, 51, bd. Henri-Vasnier. Tel. 26-85-01-94.

You can explore these cellars in an electric train. The visit includes a video showing.

Admission: Free.

Open: Apr–Nov, daily 9:30–11:30am and 2–5:30pm; Dec–Mar, Mon–Fri 9:30am–11:30am and 2–5:30pm.

TAITTINGER, 9, place St-Niçaise. Tel. 26-85-45-35.

Here you can also visit the home of some of the most famous champagne makers, whose underground caverns once formed part of the crypt of an abbey. Guided tours given through five miles of galleries are accompanied by a slide show. You can purchase champagne in the gift shop.

Admission: 15 F ($2.70).

Open: Mar–Nov, daily 9:30am–1pm and 2–5:30pm; Dec–Feb, Mon–Fri 9am–noon and 2–6pm.

VEUVE-CLICQUOT PONSARDIN, 1, place des Droits-de-l'Homme. Tel. 26-85-24-08.

A part of the 16 miles of underground galleries can be visited on guided tours.

Admission: Free.

Open: Apr–July and Sept–Oct, Mon–Sat 9am–12:30pm and 2–6pm. **Closed:** Aug and Nov–Mar.

WHERE TO STAY

Very Expensive

BOYER-LES-CRAYERES, 64, bd. Henry-Vasnier, 51100 Reims. Tel. 26-82-80-80. Fax 26-82-65-52. 16 rms (all with bath), 3 suites. A/C MINIBAR TV TEL

$ Rates: 990–1,760 F ($178.20–$316.80) single or double; from 1,860 F ($334.80) suite. Breakfast 89 F ($16) extra. AE, DC, MC, V. **Parking:** Free. **Closed:** Christmas to mid-Jan.

This elegant hotel is housed in one of the finest châteaux in eastern France. It's richly decorated with 18-foot ceilings, burnished paneling, potted palms, and elegant furnishings. It is located in a 14-acre private park—an oasis surrounded by one of the leading industrial cities of northern France. The bedrooms are individually decorated and are usually available whenever a champagne mogul is not in residence. Each room has a terrace and all the amenities. The restaurant here is superb and is recommended separately under "Where to Dine," below.

Expensive

L'ASSIETTE CHAMPENOISE, 40, av. Paul-Vallant-Couturier, 51430 Tinqueux. Tel. 26-04-15-56. Fax 26-04-15-69. 60 rms (all with bath), 2 suites. MINIBAR TV TEL

$ Rates: 505–770 F ($90.90–$138.60) single; 545–770 F ($98.10–$138.60) double; 760–1,110 F ($136.80–$199.80) suite. Breakfast 70 F ($12.60) extra. AE, DC, MC, V. **Parking:** Free.

About four miles from the center of Reims, this is the second-best hotel and restaurant in the area (see "Where to Dine," below, for restaurant information). The accommodations, with radios, are luxuriously furnished. Set among century-old trees, this is a former private Norman estate. Some of the present structure dates from 1896, although most of it was constructed in the 1980s.

Moderate

ALTEA CHAMPAGNE, 31, bd. Paul-Doumer, 51100 Reims. Tel. 26-84-49-49. Fax 26-84-49-84. 113 rms (all with bath), 9 suites. A/C MINIBAR TV TEL **Bus:** G or H.
$ Rates: 430 F ($77.40) single; 465 F ($83.70) double; 550 F ($99) suite. Breakfast 50 F ($9) extra. AE, DC, MC, V. **Parking:** 40 F ($7.20).

On the banks of the Marne Canal, a five-minute walk from the town center, this hotel is a member of a national chain with a good reputation. It's near the entrance of the autoroute, so it's easy to find. The good-sized bedrooms have all the modern conveniences, and some have views of a scenic waterway dotted with river barges. Les Ombrages, the restaurant, serves French specialties nightly until 10pm. The fixed-price menus cost 95 F ($17.10), 140 F ($25.20), 165 F ($29.70), and 260 F ($46.80). A la carte meals average 300 F ($54).

GRAND HOTEL CONTINENTAL, 93, place Drouet-d'Erlon, 51100 Reims. Tel. 26-40-39-35. Fax 26-47-51-12. 50 rms (all with bath or shower). MINIBAR TV TEL **Bus:** G or H.
$ Rates: 300 F ($54) single; 380–450 F ($68.40–$81) double. Breakfast 37 F ($6.60) extra. AE, DC, MC, V.

Opening onto a formal park opposite the train station, this hotel is in a long, low corner building with a mansard roof and comfortable rooms. In addition to old reception lounges with antiques, there are two traditional French dining rooms.

LA PAIX, 9, rue Buirette, 51100 Reims. Tel. 26-40-04-08. Fax 26-47-75-04. 105 rms (all with bath), 1 suite. MINIBAR TV TEL **Bus:** G or H.
$ Rates: 370–420 F ($66.60–$75.60) single; 400–500 F ($72–$90) double; 520–700 F ($93.60–$126) suite. Breakfast 45 F ($8.10) extra. AE, DC, MC, V. **Parking:** 45 F ($8.10).

The rooms in this contemporary hotel (located between the train station and the cathedral) have comfortable beds, and some have views of the garden, which has a swimming pool and a chapel. The hotel also has a brasserie/taverne, which serves excellent dishes including sauerkrauts, fish, grills, oysters, and seafood; the restaurant is open daily from noon to midnight; meals begin at 85 F ($15.30). The staff can advise you on champagne cave tours.

Inexpensive

GRAND HOTEL DU NORD, 75, place Drouet-d'Erlon, 51100 Reims. Tel. 26-47-39-03. Fax 26-40-92-26. 50 rms (all with bath). MINIBAR TV TEL **Bus:** G or H.
$ Rates: 265–275 F ($47.70–$49.50) single; 285–320 F ($51.30–$57.60) double. Breakfast 30 F ($5.40) extra. AE, DC, MC, V.

Accessible by the A4 motorway (exit at "Reims-Centre"), this hotel offers calm and comfort in its comfortably decorated and personalized bedrooms. Each contains a private bath along with direct-dial phone, minibar, and color TV. A TV lounge with a cozy atmosphere is available for guests. Two steps from the hotel entrance, the liveliness of place Drouet-d'Erlon, with its boutiques, café terraces, and cinemas, unfolds. You're also near such attractions as the cathedral, the Basilique Saint-Rémi, and various museums.

WHERE TO DINE

In addition to the hotel restaurants listed above, I recommend the following:

L'ASSIETTE CHAMPENOISE, 40, av. Paul-Vaillant-Couturier, in Tinqueux. Tel. 26-04-15-56.
   Cuisine: FRENCH. **Reservations:** Recommended.
$ **Prices:** Appetizers 100–290 F ($18–$52.20); main dishes 135–185 F ($24.30–$33.30); fixed-price menus 320–495 F ($57.60–$89.10). AE, DC, MC, V.
   Open: Lunch daily noon–2pm; dinner daily 7–10:30pm.

⭐ L'Assiette Champenoise is the second-best restaurant and hotel and is located less than a mile from town (see "Where to Stay," above, for the hotel listing). Set among century-old trees, this was a former private Norman estate. Now the big champagne makers come to enjoy the cooking of Jean-Pierre Lallement, who is assisted by his wife, Colette. In their elegant country dining room, you'll be sure to enjoy yourself. The cuisine is both classical and innovative. Order the veal kidneys and sweetbreads flavored with star anise, grilled duck liver with a fondue of tomatoes, or the herb-flavored scallops. The wine list features champagne (naturally) and some excellent bottles of Bouzy, made from black grapes.

BOYER-LES-CRAYERES, 64, bd. Henry-Vasnier. Tel. 26-82-80-80.
   Cuisine: FRENCH. **Reservations:** A few days in advance for weekday dinners, at least one month in advance for weekend dinners.
$ **Prices:** Appetizers 98–430 F ($17.60–$77.40); main dishes 190–254 F ($34.20–$45.70); *menu gastronomique*, including champagne, from 800 F ($144) (price varies). AE, DC, MC, V.
   Open: Lunch Wed–Sun noon–2:30pm; dinner Tues–Sun 7:30–10:30pm.
   Closed: Christmas to mid-Jan.

⭐ Considered one of the greatest restaurants in eastern France, it lies in a château built in 1904 by the founding members of the Pommery champagne fortune. In 1991, both the château and the restaurant within were acquired by B.S.N., a French-based food distributor, which retained Gérard Boyer as the world-famous resident chef. Many guests stay overnight, just so they can enjoy a meal in the restaurant (see "Where to Stay," above, for the hotel listing). A masterpiece is the salade du Père-Maurice, made with green beans, artichoke hearts, lemon, foie gras, truffles, and lobster. Other outstanding dishes are turbot with wild mushrooms and pigeon with foie gras and truffles.

RESTAURANT LE FLORENCE, 43, bd. Foch. Tel. 26-47-12-70.
   Cuisine: FRENCH. **Reservations:** Required. **Bus:** G or H.
$ **Prices:** Appetizers 82–210 F ($14.70–$37.80); main dishes 120–180 F ($21.60–$32.40); fixed-price menus 210 F ($37.80), 290 F ($52.20), and 440 F ($79.20). AE, DC, MC, V.
   Open: Lunch Mon–Sat noon–2pm; dinner Mon–Sat 7–9:30pm. **Closed:** Aug 1–19.

⭐ This outstanding restaurant, located in an 1880 building that was once an elegant town house, is run by Jean-Pierre and Denise Maillot. Le Florence has some of the best food in the city. The service is superb, and you can look forward to a changing menu; try the crayfish salad, suprême of duckling, braised turbot in champagne sauce, or Bresse pigeon in terrine. Desserts might include caramelized pears in puff pastry—an elegant conclusion.

LE VIGNERON, place Paul-Jamot. Tel. 26-47-00-71.
   Cuisine: FRENCH. **Reservations:** Recommended. **Bus:** G or H.
$ **Prices:** Appetizers 45–95 F ($8.10–$17.10); main dishes 95–145 F ($17.10–$26.10). V.
   Open: Lunch Sun–Fri 11:30am–2:30pm; dinner Mon–Sat 5:30–10pm. **Closed:** Dec 23–Jan 2.

This bistro dedicated to champagne and good food is run by Hervé Liegent. The interior of the 17th-century house, located behind the cathedral, is filled with old champagne posters, vineyard tools, and antique champagne barrels. The food that accompanies the dozens of available brands of champagne includes baked duckling in champagne sauce, garlic sausages (andouillette) with champagne, and champagne-flavored sorbets.

4. FERE-EN-TARDENOIS

12 miles NE of Paris, 29 miles W of Reims

GETTING THERE By Car Take the N31 northwest of Reims, pass through Fismes, then turn southwest onto the N367.

ESSENTIALS Information The Syndicat d'Initiative is located at rue Moreau-Nélaton (tel. 23-82-31-57).

For the most superb restaurant in the champagne area—in fact, one of France's greatest—head for Château de Fère on the D967 (previewed below). At a point a mile and a half north of this hamlet lies the ruins of a fortified castle dating from the 12th century—also called Château de Fère. There is, as well, a Renaissance viaduct erected in 1560.

WHERE TO DINE

For those who want to stay overnight, these restaurants also have guest rooms for rent.

AUBERGE DU CONNETABLE, route du Château (via the D967), 02130 Fère-en-Tardenois. Tel. 23-82-24-25. Fax 23-82-37-81.
   Cuisine: FRENCH. **Reservations:** Recommended.
$ **Prices:** Appetizers 72–110 F ($12.90–$19.80); main dishes 85–105 F ($15.30–$18.90); fixed-price menus 135–185 F ($24.30–$33.30) Mon–Fri, 150–200 F ($27–$36) Sat–Sun. MC, V.
   Open: Lunch Tues–Sun noon–2pm; dinner Tues–Sat 7–9pm. **Closed:** Jan–Feb.

This is the bargain in the area. It was built during the 19th century as a relay station for the French postal service. Today, sheathed in ivy, it's the cost-conscious alternative to the expensive Hostellerie du Château next door. Though it's mainly a restaurant, with a dining room affording a view of the surrounding forest, it also offers three rooms to rent. Owner and chef Jean-François Santilli derives his cuisine from several major French culinary regions. Try the fricassée of sole with baby freshwater shellfish cooked in a champagne sauce, tongue of baby lamb braised with carrots and onions, or a petit ragoût of offal prepared with wild honey. For dessert, try the raspberry charlotte.

The three bedrooms, all doubles with TVs and telephones, run 170–250 F ($30.60–$45) nightly, plus another 30 F ($5.40) for breakfast.

CHATEAU DE FERE, route Forestière (D967), 02130 Fère-en-Tardenois. Tel. 23-82-21-13. Fax 23-82-37-81.
   Cuisine: FRENCH. **Reservations:** Required.
$ **Prices:** Appetizers 110–250 F ($19.80–$45); main dishes 160–260 F ($28.80–$46.80); fixed-price menus 290–480 F ($52.20–$86.40). AE, DC, MC, V.
   Open: Lunch daily noon–2:30; dinner daily 7–9:30pm.

Near the ruins in a park, this fabulous restaurant is in a restored 16th-century crenellated château with turrets. During the summer, begin your elegant repast in the sunny garden, sipping an apéritif or a glass of champagne with juice from freshly crushed raspberries. The owners of this imposing Renaissance hostelry oversee every detail and serve imaginative and original dishes. Of course, the turbot cooked in champagne may be more familiar than the paupiette of truffles and calves' kidneys. Other specialties include dégustation des trois mignons (a platter of three meats: beef, lamb, and veal). The desserts are mouth-watering, but I prefer to skip them in favor of the boulette d'Avesnes, a cone of cheese flecked with herbs and crushed peppercorns and coated with paprika.

Also available here are 14 guest rooms and nine suites—each luxuriously furnished with private bath, minibar, TV, and telephone. Single or double rooms rent for 970–1,130 F ($174.60–$203.40), while suites cost 1,300–1,900 F ($234–$342), plus another 90 F ($16.20) per person for breakfast.

EN ROUTE TO PARIS

If, after your tour of the champagne country, you have a full day left, you can return to Paris leisurely, exploring battlefields and sampling the food along the way. From Fère-en-Tardenois, head southwest to Château-Thierry.

---

5. CHATEAU-THIERRY

56 miles E of Paris, 6 miles SW of Reims

GETTING THERE By Train There are frequent local trains from Paris and Reims.

By Car Take the N367 southwest from Reims.

ESSENTIALS Orientation The town was originally built on the Marne's northern bank, and on an island in its center. The most visible monument is the ruined château, on a wooded hilltop on the river's northern edge. Some of the important streets of the old town, including the Grande Rue, curve around the base of the château.

Information Contact the Office de Tourisme, 12, place de l'Hôtel-de-Ville (tel. 23-83-10-14), for information.

An industrial town on the right bank of the Maine, **Château-Thierry** contains the ruins of a castle that is believed to have been constructed for the Frankish king, Thierry IV. Château-Thierry gained fame for being the farthest point reached by the German offensive in the summer of 1918. Under heavy bombardment, French forces were aided by the Second and Third Divisions of the American Expeditionary Force. Battlefields of the Marne are located a mile west of town; here, thousands of Allied soldiers who died fighting World War I are buried. Atop Hill 204 stands a monument honoring the American troops who lost their lives.

WHAT TO SEE & DO

Château-Thierry is also where Jean de la Fontaine, the French poet and fable writer, was born in a 16th-century home. The **Musée Jean-de-la-Fontaine,** 12, rue de la Fontaine (tel. 23-69-05-60), contains a small collection of his mementos, including many editions of his works from the Charles-Henri Genot collection, along with paintings and engravings from the 17th to the 20th century.

The museum is open July to September, Wednesday through Monday from 10am to noon and 2:30 to 6:30pm; October to March, Wednesday through Monday from 2 to 5pm; April to June, Wednesday through Monday from 10am to noon and 2 to 6pm. Admission is 10 F ($1.80).

Nearby Attractions

If you're interested in seeing some World War I relics, head for **Bois de Belleau (Belleau Wood).** The Battle of Belleau Wood marked the second clash between American and German troops in World War I and demonstrated the bravery of the U.S. soldiers in modern warfare. The battle site is five miles northwest of Château-Thierry.

After a struggle that lasted for two weeks of bitter fighting, the woods were finally taken by the Second Division of the U.S. Expeditionary Force under Maj.-Gen. Omar Bundy. Although the Germans suffered many losses, and some 1,650 prisoners were taken, the U.S. casualties were appalling. Nearly 7,585 soldiers and 285 officers were wounded, killed, or missing in action.

In 1923 the battleground was dedicated as a memorial to the men who gave their lives there. The **American cemetery** contains 2,288 graves. You'll also see a chapel that was damaged in World War II, and the rusted weapons you'll see along the scorched road are a gruesome sight.

WHERE TO STAY

HOTEL ILE-DE-FRANCE, route de Soissons, 02400 Château-Thierry. Tel. 23-69-10-12. Fax 23-83-49-70. 56 rms (50 with bath or shower). TEL
$ Rates: 280 F ($50.40) single without bath; 330 F ($59.40) single or double with bath or shower. Breakfast 40 F ($7.20) extra. AE, DC, MC, V. **Parking:** Free.
The elegant Hôtel Ile-de-France is the leading choice of the hotels in the area. Located in a park and overlooking the green Marne Valley, the four-story house has balconies and dormers and a view of the town. Part of the Inter-Hôtel chain, the hotel has well-furnished bedrooms and an excellent restaurant, where fixed-price meals begin at 98 F ($17.60)—although you can spend 250 F ($45) à la carte.

WHERE TO DINE

Even if you don't spend the night, chances are you'll be in Château-Thierry for lunch. Try the following:

AUBERGE JEAN-DE-LA-FONTAINE, 10, rue des Filoirs. Tel. 23-83-63-89.
   Cuisine: FRENCH. **Reservations:** Required.
$ Prices: Appetizers 60–110 F ($10.80–$19.80); main dishes 80–130 F ($14.40–$23.40); fixed-price menus 120 F ($21.60), 160 F ($28.80), and 350 F ($63). AE, DC, MC, V.
   Open: Lunch Tues–Sun 12:30–2pm; dinner Tues–Sat 7:30–9:30pm. **Closed:** First two weeks of Jan, first three weeks of Aug.
Originally a shoemaker's shop in the center of Château-Thierry, this restaurant is filled with engravings dedicated to the fables of Jean de la Fontaine. The menu changes every three weeks, but might include such typical dishes as foie gras maison en gelée des Sauternes, a vinaigrette of crab with salmon (accompanied by asparagus and a coulis of tomatoes), roasted and deboned pigeon with patissons (a kind of turnip) and mustard sauce, or a fisherman's salad with several kinds of filet of grilled fish with fresh herbs.

6. LA FERTE-SOUS-JOUARRE

41 miles E of Paris, 51 miles SW of Reims

GETTING THERE   By Car   Take the N3 along the Marne.

ESSENTIALS   Orientation   The town lies on the north bank of the Marne, around place de l'Hôtel-de-Ville. The town's most visited historic monument, the crypt of the Abbey, is two miles south of town, along the D402, toward Jouarre and Coulommiers.

Information   The Syndicat d'Initiative (tourist office) is located at 26, place de l'Hôtel-de-Ville (tel. 60-22-63-43).

At the hamlet of Jouarre, you can visit a Benedictine abbey dating from the 12th century and explore one of the oldest crypts in France, going back to the 7th century.

At the **Musée de la Tour de l'Abbaye,** 6 rue Montmorin (tel. 60-22-06-11), medievalists will appreciate the documents preserved here, referring to the history of the Royal Abbey of Jouarre. In its Merovingian crypt, stones evoke the 7th century.

There's also a collection of prehistoric artifacts, remnants of the Roman occupation, and a handful of sculptural fragments. The crypt and the towers are open to visitors Wednesday to Monday from 10am to noon and 2:30 to 5pm.

WHERE TO DINE

AUBERGE DE CONDE, 1, av. de Montmirail. Tel. 60-22-00-07.
   Cuisine: FRENCH. **Reservations:** Required.
$ **Prices:** Appetizers 90–190 F ($16.20–$34.20); main dishes 140–220 F ($25.20–$39.60); fixed-price menus 310–450 F ($55.80–$81). AE, DC, MC, V.
   Open: Lunch Wed–Mon noon–2pm; dinner Wed–Sun 7–9pm.

This is one of the best restaurants in "the ring around Paris," and it's a mile and a half from the abbey. The furnishings aren't luxurious—in fact, the inn is old-fashioned, with lots of provincial character. However, it serves delectable dishes and regional specialties worthy of its two-star rating. Pascal Tingaud, manager and chef de cuisine, is the grandson of the famous founding father, Emile Tingaud. You might begin with a feuilleté de truffes et foie gras, then order sweetbreads "des gourmets" or filet of sole Vincent-Bourrel. Another specialty is the poulet briarde, which is Bresse chicken poached in a rich stock and served with a sauce of cream, butter, and the grainy mustard of Meaux; the platter is served alongside the tender baby carrots of Crécy. The grand traditional cooking is accompanied by the best champagne.

7. CHALONS-SUR-MARNE

GETTING THERE   By Train   Since Châlons-sur-Marne is on the main railway line between Strasbourg and Paris, train connections are easy and frequent.

ESSENTIALS   Orientation   The railway station lies on the western edge of the city, across the Marne River from the old town. The city's old town is centered around two churches, the Cathédrale de St-Etienne and the Eglise Notre-Dame-en-Vaux. Both are connected by a main thoroughfare called rue de la Marne.

Information   The Office de Tourisme is at 3, quai des Arts (tel. 26-65-17-89).

Intersected by canals of the Marne River, Châlons-sur-Marne is a city of art and churches. Famous names of history, including Marie Antoinette, have passed through (her visit is commemorated by a triumphal arch, the Porte Dauphine). An important crossroads, Châlons lies between Reims and Troyes and Paris and Nancy, in the heart of the champagne country.

WHAT TO SEE & DO

The Romanesque and Gothic **Church of Notre-Dame-en-Vaux,** place Tissier (tel. 26-65-63-17), was, to Victor Hugo, "extremely stately and complete." The church is graced with spires reflected in the canals of the city. Launched in 1170, Notre-Dame is considered to have one of the greatest chimes on the Continent, with 56 bells; it's also known for its 16th-century stained-glass windows. The church is open Monday through Saturday from 10am to noon and 2 to 6pm; admission is free.

While you're there, you can also explore the **Musée du Cloître,** rue Nicholas-Durand (tel. 26-64-03-87). The cloister, like the church, dates from 1170, but it was destroyed during the French Revolution and many of its sculptures were "decapitated." However, with the help of recent excavations, the heads and many of the pieces have been restored. The capitals displayed in the museum are richly decorated, some with grotesque scenes. A 12th-century collection, the *Four Evangelists,* the *Marriage in Cana,* and the *Washing of the Feet,* form one of the most enduring works of art left from 12th-century France. The museum is open Wednesday through Monday from 10am to noon and 2 to 6pm (to 5pm from October to March 3). Admission is 20 F ($3.60) for adults, 6 F ($1) for children.

Though consecrated by Pope Eugene III in the 12th century, the **Cathédrale de St-Etienne,** rue de la Marne (tel. 26-64-18-30), wasn't completed until the 13th century, and it was enlarged in the 17th century. Unfortunately, it stood in the way of invading armies—most recently during World Wars I and II. After aerial bombardments, only the north tower remains from the Romanesque era. Some rare 12th-century stained-glass windows are in a vaulted room. The dark, bottle-green glass is as celebrated in eastern France as much as Chartres blue is in the Ile de France. Other stained glass you'll see is from the 13th through the 16th century. You can visit daily from 9am to dusk.

The third memorable church of Châlons-sur-Marne is the **Church of St-Alpin,** right off place Foch. Named for a bishop in Attila's time, it is Romanesque, although much was altered in the 15th and 16th centuries. It is known for its beautiful stained-glass windows—called *en grisaille*—from the 16th century.

The city is filled with mansions—called *hôtels particuliers*—that date from the 17th and 18th centuries. You may want to wander on your own and explore their facades; or the tourist office sponsors a guided tour in French.

Beside the town hall, which dates from 1772, is the 17th-century **Hôtel des Dubois de Crance,** which houses the **Bibliothèque Municipale** (tel. 26-68-54-44). Some of its manuscripts are from the 12th century. Its most prized and controversial possession is a prayerbook that may have belonged to Marie Antoinette, in which she wrote her famous "My poor children, adieu, adieu." Some scholars doubt the authenticity of her signature. Open Tuesday through Sunday from 9am to noon and 1:30 to 6pm; admission is free.

The **Musée Municipal,** place Godart (tel. 26-68-54-44), exhibits a rich collection of prehistoric Gallo-Roman and Merovingian objects from the surrounding area. Many interesting pieces rescued from the town's churches are in its sculpture section. It's open Wednesday through Monday from 2 to 6pm; admission is free.

WHERE TO STAY & DINE

HOTEL ANGLETERRE ET RESTAURANT JACKY-MICHEL, 19, place Monseigneur Tissier, 51000 Châlons-sur-Marne. Tel. 26-68-21-51.
Fax 26-70-51-67. 18 rms (all with bath or shower). MINIBAR TV TEL
$ Rates: 430–450 F ($77.40–$81) single; 450–490 F ($81–$88.20) double. Breakfast 50 F ($9) extra. AE, DC, MC, V. **Parking:** Free.

This is both the leading restaurant and the leading hotel, set near the center of town in a stone-fronted re-creation of a building destroyed in a World War II bombing raid. The pastel bedrooms are furnished in a "decorator style." Chef Jacky Michel is a culinary artist—try his warm salad of lobster with baby leeks, the ragoût of shellfish with fresh baby herbs, or his veal kidneys with red wine sauce and garlic croquettes. The dishes will go well with some of the grand wines of France, including bordeaux, burgundy, and champagne. Monday through Friday an excellent fixed-price menu is offered for only 170 F ($30.60). Otherwise, fixed-price meals cost 240–400 F ($43.20–$72). The restaurant is open for lunch Monday through Friday from 12:30 to 2pm, and for dinner Monday through Saturday from 7:30 to 9:30pm. The restaurant is closed July 16 to August 9.

NEARBY ACCOMMODATIONS & DINING

AUX ARMES DE CHAMPAGNE, 51460 L'Epine, 51460 Courtisols. Tel. 26-69-30-30. Fax 26-66-92-31. 35 rms (all with bath), 2 suites. MINIBAR TEL
$ Rates: 450–780 F ($81–$140.40) single or double; 1,250 F ($225) suite. Breakfast 55 F ($9.90) extra. MC, V. **Parking:** Free. **Closed:** Jan 10–Feb 16.

Jean-Paul Pérardel operates this outstanding restaurant and hotel, which makes a worthy detour. It's located five miles from Châlons-sur-Marne, and it opens onto the overpowering facade of the historic church, "Our Lady of the Thorn."

This has become one of the most important restaurants in the region; much care and money went into the improvement of this place, which now has an entrance hall and a garden. The food is delivered straight from the wholesale food market at Rungis twice a week. The cuisine is of simplified classicism; actual dishes change from week to week. Tables are richly set with ornaments and crystal. Fixed-price menus cost 195 F ($35.10), 270 F ($48.60), and 480 F ($86.40). Service is daily from 12:30 to 2pm and 7:30 to 9:30pm.

8. TROYES

102 miles SE of Paris, 94 miles NW of Dijon

GETTING THERE By Train Because French rail lines radiate outward from Paris, you might have to transfer in the capital if you're coming from, say, Reims or Lille. Once you're in Paris, however, service is frequent and fast from the Gare de l'Est.

ESSENTIALS Orientation Most of the old section, which is neatly bisected by a canal, is on the west bank of the Seine. A model of city planning, the old town is neatly encircled by wide boulevards, which funnel much of the traffic away from the historic core. The old town stretches roughly in an oval between three historic churches: the Cathédrale de St-Pierre et St-Paul, Eglise St-Pantaléon, and Eglise Ste-Madeleine.

Information The Office de Tourisme is at 16, bd. Carnot (tel. 25-73-00-36).

The capital of the southern champagne country, Troyes is filled with architectural glories of the Renaissance period. The comtes de Champagne acquired the town in the 10th century. The historic core of the city, called Bouchon de Champagne, means "champagne cork," to which it bears a faint resemblance. However, don't come here for champagne caves—there aren't any.

The town was rebuilt in the Renaissance style after a 1524 fire wiped out much of it, and it was destroyed again in World War II. By 1745, Troyes had become the capital of the French knitware industry. The old city lies on the River Seine, but it is the capital of the département of Aube, named for the River Aube.

WHAT TO SEE & DO

Churches

The city has at least nine churches that merit exploration (the tourist office will provide a map). Visiting hours for churches are 10am to noon and 2 to 6pm daily.

Begin your tour at place de la Liberation where you'll have a view of the Gothic **Cathédrale de St-Pierre et St-Paul**, 1, place St-Pierre (tel. 25-80-90-12), built primarily in the 13th and 17th centuries. The architecture is remarkably elegant, and the detail in the high stained-glass windows and the two rose windows provides a particularly striking example of the skill of 13th-century stained-glass artists. Above the elegant, richly decorated facade rises the 200-foot-high St. Peter's Tower. The sumptuous treasury includes enamel work, relics, and alms boxes from the comtes de Champagne and others. From June to September, there is a *son-et-lumière* (sound-and-light) show in the interior. At night, the facade is floodlit.

The cathedral is open daily from 10am to noon and 2 to 6pm; the *son-et-lumière* program is held on Tuesday, Friday, and Saturday at 10:30pm, costing 30 F ($5.40) for adults and 15 F ($2.70) for children. The treasury is open only in summer, Tuesday through Sunday from 2 to 6pm, costing 8 F ($1.40).

Eglise Ste-Madeleine, rue de la Madeleine (tel. 25-73-02-98), is the city's oldest church and dates from the mid-12th century. It was built in the late Roman and early Gothic style, with many changes occurring in the 1500s. The tower is from the 16th and 17th centuries. A charnel house dates from 1525, and its triple-arched rood screen, unique in France, was carved in 1508–15 by Jean Galide; it's a fine example of stone tracery. Brightly colored stained-glass windows are among the most beautiful examples left from the Champagne school of artisans.

Another church worth mentioning is the consummate Gothic **Basilica de St-Urbain,** rue Clemenceau (tel. 25-73-02-98). Called "the Parthenon of Champagne," the church was founded by Troyes-born Pope Urban IV; construction began in the 13th century. The bold architecture with pillars and tapered mullion windows, harmonious proportions, and elegant sculptures combine to make this the greatest monument in Troyes. The exterior is decorated with sculpted gargoyles. It's open July 1 to September 15.

Visit the **Eglise St-Jean,** rue Champeaux (tel. 25-73-02-98), noted for its landmark clock tower. Here, in 1420, the marriage of Catherine of France to the warrior king, Henry V of England, took place after the signing of the Treaty of Troyes. The treaty, incidentally, led to an English invasion and the Hundred Years' War.

Note: The three churches cited above all have the same phone number because they share the same presbytery.

More Sights

Troyes is also richly endowed with many fine museums, including the **Musée d'Art Moderne,** place St-Pierre (tel. 25-80-57-30), to the right of the cathedral. Housed in a restored bishop's palace from the 16th and 17th centuries, this is considered one of the finest modern-art collections in France, from the Pierre and Denise Lévy donation, which was one of the largest private art collections ever given to France.

The museum owns 350 paintings, some 1,300 drawings and sketches, and more than 100 sculptures. A host of famous names in art—Gauguin, Matisse, Modigliani, Picasso, Derain, Rouault, Dufy, Cézanne, Degas, and Bonnard—are on display. See, in particular, works by Fauve artists (the movement that followed impressionism at the dawn of the 20th century). Hours are Wednesday through Monday from 11am to 6pm; admission is 15 F ($2.70).

The **Musée St-Loup,** 1, rue Chrétien-de-Troyes (tel. 25-42-33-33), which is actually two museums, stands on the far side of the cathedral square. The museums are housed in the former abbey of St-Loup, and part of the cloisters can still be seen. One section is devoted to a large natural-history museum and has an outstanding bronze Gallo-Roman statue of Apollo, a collection of Merovingian weapons, gold and garnet jewelry from Attila's time, and medieval sculpture from the 12th to the 15th century. Another section displays paintings from the 15th to the 20th century, including works by Boucher, Fragonard, David, and Watteau. The museum, open Tuesday through Sunday from 10am to noon and 2 to 6pm, costs 15 F ($2.70) for adults and 10 F ($1.80) for children.

The magnificent Hôtel-Dieu (hospital) of Troyes, quai des Comtes de Champagne, has been recently converted into a university. But it's still possible for the public to visit the **Pharmacie Musée de l'Hôtel-Dieu** (tel. 25-80-98-97), which has been turned into a museum. It's one of the most unusual apothecary dispensaries open to the public in France. The comtes de Champagne founded the hospital in the 12th century, and it was rebuilt in the 18th century. The old laboratory contains ancient documents, a collection of pewter in all shapes and sizes, and such items as reliquaries from the 16th century. Painted wooden boxes and pots still hold herbs and other medicines. The museum is open Wednesday through Monday from 10am to noon and 2 to 6pm. Admission is 10 F ($1.80).

Rue Urbain-IV leads to the principal plaza of Troyes, place du Maréchal-Foch, named after the famed World War I French general. Here you can enjoy coffee and crêpes at numerous cafés and restaurants while you admire the **Hôtel de Ville** (town hall); dating from 1624, it is one of the few Louis XIII–style buildings in the region.

WHERE TO STAY

GRAND HOTEL/PATIOTEL, 4, av. Joffre, 10000 Troyes. Tel. 25-79-90-90. Fax 25-78-48-93. 102 rms (all with bath or shower), 2 suites. TV TEL

$ Rates: Grand Hotel, 365 F ($65.70) single; 435 F ($78.30) double; from 750 F ($135) suite. Patiotel, 270 F ($48.60) single; 320 F ($57.60) double. Breakfast 38 F ($6.80) extra. MC, V. **Parking:** 38 F ($6.80).

The core of this hotel and restaurant complex was originally built on a downtown street corner near the railway station in the 1930s, and gained a reputation for provincial comfort and respectability in the years which followed. In 1987, a U-shaped wing was added on the side, and a cost-conscious satellite hotel, the Patiotel, was added. Today, the Grand Hôtel and its less-expensive sibling share a common lobby, breakfast room, covered swimming pool, and garden, but maintain completely different price structures.

Rooms at the Grand are comfortingly traditional, with high ceilings, conservative furniture, and minibars. Rooms at the Patiotel are chain-hotel modern and somewhat more cramped, and always have views and windows opening onto the garden. On the premises of the two hotels are no fewer than five different restaurants. The most elegant is Le Champagne, serving fixed-price meals priced at 110–170 F ($19.80–$30.60). Less expensive are Le Jardin de la Louisiane, the Grill Aquarius, Le Croco (a brasserie), and a rustic and pleasant enclave of unpretentious food, La Taverne de l'Ecailler.

HOTEL DE LA POSTE, 35, rue Emile-Zola, 10000 Troyes. Tel. 25-73-05-05. Fax 25-73-80-76. 28 rms (all with bath). MINIBAR TV TEL
$ Rates: 395 F ($71.10) single; 550 F ($99) double. Breakfast 50 F ($9) extra. AE, V.

Another good choice, this four-star hotel offers not only comfortable accommodations but also some of the city's finest dining. The rooms, though, are quite small.

In addition to a modern bar, the hotel has three restaurants, including La Pizzeria and La Marée, which features seafood. Its prestigious dining room is La Table Gourmande, where diners enjoy outstanding classical French cooking and the lavish wine menu. The restaurant is closed Sunday night and on Monday.

WHERE TO DINE

In addition to the hotel restaurants listed above, I recommend the following:

LE BOURGOGNE, 40, rue du Général-de-Gaulle. Tel. 25-73-02-67.
Cuisine: FRENCH. **Reservations:** Required.
$ Prices: Appetizers 60–125 F ($10.80–$22.50); main dishes 85–190 F ($15.30–$34.20). MC, V.
Open: Lunch Mon–Sat 12:15–1:30pm; dinner Tues–Sat 7:15–9:15pm. **Closed:** Aug.

The Dubois brothers, the owners of this restaurant, are from Bresse, which is said to have the finest poultry in France. Their refined cuisine is made with very fresh ingredients, and their wine cellar contains several treasures that have been carefully amassed over the decades. Try the grilled turbot in a beurre-blanc sauce, sweetbreads Florentine style in puff pastry, or rack of roebuck grand veneur.

LE VALENTINO, cour de la Rencontre. Tel. 25-73-14-14.
Cuisine: FRENCH. **Reservations:** Not required.
$ Prices: Appetizers 90–150 F ($16.20–$27); main dishes 110–180 F ($19.80–$32.40); fixed-price menus 155–340 F ($27.90–$61.20). AE, DC, MC, V.
Open: Lunch Tues–Sun 12:30–1:45pm; dinner Tues–Sat 7:30–9:45pm. **Closed:** Aug 15 to the first week in Sept; some time in Feb.

Chef Alain Vattier operates a distinguished art deco dining room across from the town hall in the medieval sector of the old town. Some say that this is the finest restaurant in town. He serves his *cuisine du marché* (based on market-fresh ingredients) on two terraces. Among all the restaurateurs of Troyes, Monsieur Vattier is the expert in seafood, and he personally attends the fish market every morning. Try his lobster with butter sauce flavored with orange juice or salmon cut into ravioli-like pieces and served with caviar and a butter sauce flavored with shallots. He also cooks a young pigeon with candied onions, champagne vinegar, and apples. Menus vary according to the season.

CHAPTER 16

THE ARDENNES & THE NORTH

Many motorists seemingly speed through the north of France, heading south for Paris or more attractive destinations on the French Riviera. However, the region of the north, right on the edge of industrial Europe, also has immense stretches of calm and restful countryside and such cathedral cities as Amiens. Hugging the Belgian border, the terrain is usually low lying, with mills, canals, and factories. From such a landscape came the great artist Henri Matisse.

If you're traveling through the region from July through September, you may want to stop off at one of the Channel beach resorts, such as the most sophisticated, Le Touquet-Paris-Plage. But anytime of the year port aficionados will want to explore a trio of major ones—Dunkerque, Calais, and Boulogne—which, although badly destroyed in World War II, still have much to offer.

For those who have more time, a day or two spent driving through the Ardennes can be a rewarding adventure. Although its name still conjures up modern warfare—in the "Battle of the Bulge" an American general internationalized the term "Nuts!"—the region is one of lakes and an almost impenetrable forest, which gives it a unique character. It is crossed only by a few narrow roads running through gorges. In the section are little villages, such as Fossé, which have harmony and beauty, places of simple charm. However, I'll highlight the two most important centers—at Charleville-Mézières and Sedan.

SEEING THE ARDENNES & THE NORTH

GETTING THERE Paris's Gare de l'Est is the starting point for all **trains** to eastern France. The Paris–Basel line, for example, has stops at Charleville-Mézières. Calais–Basel lies on the north-south rail links.

By **car**, motorways A31, A4, and A203 cross the region and also allow easy driving to Champagne-Ardennes from England, Germany, the Benelux nations, Paris, Dijon, and the south of France. Those who want to learn about *itineraires ardennais* and plan a motor trip should contact the Comité Départemental de Tourisme des Ardennes, Résidence Arduinna, 18, av. Georges-Corneau, 08000 Charleville-Mézières (tel. 24-59-19-20), requesting a map.

To see it all, a car is essential, especially in the Ardennes. If you're confined to **public transportation,** use Laon, Ameins, Arras, and Lille as your bases.

A SUGGESTED ROUTE It takes a minimum of four or five days to tour the area and get to know Flanders. Start with Laon (Day 1), which will require a day to reach and explore, followed by Amiens (Day 2), the battlefields of Arras (Day 3), and the old border city of Lille (Day 4). Those with more time can spend Days 5 and 6 exploring the old ports of Dunkerque and Calais, facing the Strait of Dover. On Day 7, visit

WHAT'S SPECIAL ABOUT THE ARDENNES & THE NORTH

Beaches
- ☐ Le Touquet–Paris-Plage, "Paris by the sea," with a 1½-mile sandy beach.
- ☐ Calais, on the English Channel opposite Dover, boasting one of the best beaches in northern France.

Great Towns/Villages
- ☐ Laon, called a "crowded mountain," with more historic charm than all other towns of the north; tour the old ramparts.

Great Forests
- ☐ The Ardennes, deep forests that frightened the legions of Caesar but were penetrated by the Nazis in a last-ditch attempt.

Architectural Highlights
- ☐ The Citadel, at Lille, one of Vauban's finest works.

Ancient Monuments
- ☐ Cathédrale de Notre-Dame at Amiens, launched in 1220; at 469 feet, it's the largest church in France, and a crowning example of French Gothic.

Literary Pilgrimages
- ☐ Charleville-Mézières, hometown of poet Arthur Rimbaud; he composed "Le bateau ivre" here.

Outstanding Museums
- ☐ Musée des Beaux-Arts, in Lille, considered one of the finest art museums in the country.

Battlefields
- ☐ War cemeteries surround Arras, home of Robespierre and site of the 1917 Battle of Arras, between German and British forces.

Boulogne-sur-Mer, before staying overnight in Le Touquet–Paris-Plage, a beach town within easy commute of Paris.

1. THE ARDENNES

Charleville-Mézières: 140 miles NE of Paris, 105 miles NW of Metz Sedan: 148 miles NE of Paris, 90 miles NW of Metz

GETTING THERE **By Train** Both towns have good railway service from Paris and Reims.

ESSENTIALS **Orientation** Charleville-Mézières is actually a pair of twin cities on opposite banks of the River Meuse. Mézières, the older city, is set mostly on an island. Its centerpiece is Notre-Dame-d'Espérance. Avenue d'Arches traverses the Meuse and leads to Charleville's 17th-century place Ducale.

Sedan was originally built on the eastern bank of the river, although the modern city extends to the western bank as well. The city is dominated by its Château Fort.

Information For information on the twin cities, contact the Office du Tourisme, 4, place Ducale, 08000 Charleville-Mézières (tel. 24-38-44-80).

Little explored by most North Americans, the Ardennes in northern France— bounded by Belgium—is heavily forested. Nature-lovers seek it out. It also attracts lovers of French poetry, as it was the land of Rimbaud. Victor Hugo, George Sand, and Alexandre Dumas wrote of its beauty.

In spite of its terrain, the Ardennes has been the scene of much bitter fighting. In the Franco-German War, Napoléon III surrendered at Sedan in 1870. In World War I the Americans and Germans bitterly fought in the Argonne. Again in World War II the German breakthrough near Sedan came in the spring of 1940 in the Battle of France.

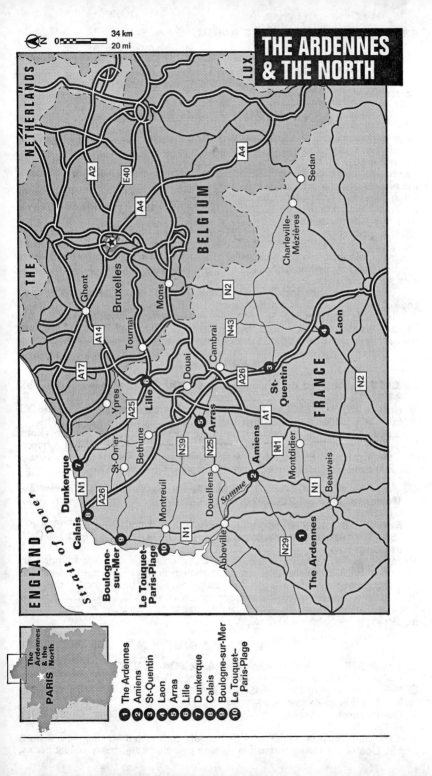

The last offensive action of the Germans occurred in the Ardennes, as they made a short-lived penetration there in December 1944.

The two chief bases for motorists planning to explore the Ardennes are Charleville-Mézières and Sedan.

CHARLEVILLE-MEZIERES

Sister towns separated by the Meuse, these twins now make a single agglomeration. Arthur Rimbaud was born at Charleville in 1854 at 12 rue Thiers. From 1869 to 1875 he lived at no. 7 on the Quai Rimbaud, now named in his honor. He composed "Le Bâteau ivre" near the old moulin still standing over the Meuse. This poem is hailed as the pioneer of the symbolist movement in French literature. Although the brilliant youth didn't fare very well in Charleville when he lived there (the son of a captain in the French army who later abandoned his family), the town in 1901 unveiled a statue to their by-then favorite son.

At the centenary of his birth, in 1954, the **Musée Municipal,** Vieux-Moulin, quai Arthur-Rimbaud (tel. 24-33-31-64), devoted a room to Rimbaud. Souvenirs of the great poet include a piece of his luggage, some drawings, even business papers relating to his long exile in Abyssinia, plus rare editions of his poems and letters, along with some portraits.

The museum is open Tuesday through Saturday from 10am to noon and 2 to 6pm, and on Sunday from 2 to 6pm. Admission is 10 F ($1.80).

Charleville, founded in 1606 by Charles de Gonzague, is noted for its admirable **Place Ducale.** This is a large rectangular square bounded by brick pavilions, uniform in design, evoking the Place des Vosges in Paris.

WHERE TO STAY

LE CLEVES, 43, rue de l'Arquebuse, 08000 Charleville-Mézières. Tel. 24-33-10-75. Fax 24-59-01-25. 48 rms (all with bath). TV TEL **Bus:** 2.
$ **Rates:** 235 F ($42.30) single; 370 F ($66.60) double. Breakfast 35 F ($6.30) extra. AE, DC, MC, V. **Parking:** 18 F ($3.20).
On a quiet city street, just steps from the house where Rimbaud was born, this hotel has an angular modern facade. Public rooms are warmly upholstered and comfortable; the bedrooms are pleasant and well illuminated, with six containing minibars. The well-managed restaurant has a central fireplace open on all sides.

LE RELAIS DU SQUARE, 3, place de la Gare, 08000 Charleville-Mézières. Tel. 24-33-38-76. Fax 24-33-56-66. 49 rms (42 with bath). MINIBAR TV TEL
$ **Rates:** 220 F ($39.60) single or double without bath, 260–280 F ($46.80–$50.40) single or double with bath. Breakfast 30 F ($5.40) extra. AE, DC, MC, V. **Parking:** Free.
Set in the heart of town, this is the largest, and probably the best-known, hotel. Its core dates from late in the 19th century, although in the 1980s another wing was added which contains many of the comfortable but simple bedrooms. On the street level, under a completely separate management, is a restaurant, Le Médicis, open for lunch and dinner every day except Sunday night and Saturday at lunch, where fixed-price menus begin at 89 F ($16).

WHERE TO DINE

LA CIGOGNE, 40, rue Dubois-Crancé. Tel. 24-33-25-39.
  Cuisine: FRENCH. **Reservations:** Required. **Bus:** 2.
$ **Prices:** Appetizers 35–60 F ($6.30–$10.80); main dishes 80–115 F ($14.40–$20.70); fixed-price menus 98–140 F ($17.60–$25.20). MC, V.
  Open: Lunch Tues–Sun noon–2pm; dinner Tues–Sat 7–9:30pm. **Closed:** Aug 4–12.
This two-floor restaurant is situated in a solidly constructed building with a stone facade. One of the dining rooms has massive oak chairs and heavy ceiling beams,

while the other is decorated with fabric stretched tightly over the walls. The skillful chef is also the owner. Some of his most popular dishes are raw saltwater salmon marinated with lime juice, game dishes (in season), pâté of trout in brioche, poached turbot with hollandaise, and duck breast Norman style.

SEDAN

This frontier town near the Luxembourg border is a manufacturing center for woolen goods. It was the birthplace of the vicomte de Turenne in 1611, the popular and heroic French military leader who fought in the Thirty Years' War. The Meuse flows through this ancient fortress town at the foot of the Ardennes.

Sedan's **Château Fort,** place du Château (tel. 24-27-73-75), dates from the 15th and 16th centuries and is the largest fort in Europe. It's open March 15 through September 14, daily from 10am to 6pm; off-season, daily from 1:30 to 5:30pm. Admission is 28 F ($5) for adults and 14 F ($2.50) for children.

Outside town on the N64 is the private **Château de Bellevue,** where Napoléon III surrendered to the Prussians. At the capitulation of the French army on September 2, 1870, he turned over his sword to the Germans.

WHERE TO STAY

L'EUROPE, 5, place de la Gare, 08200 Sedan. Tel. 24-27-18-71. Fax 24-29-32-00. 25 rms (all with bath or shower). TV TEL
$ Rates: 190–260 F ($34.20–$46.80) single or double. Breakfast 40 F ($7.20) extra. AE, DC, MC, V.

This traditional 19th-century hotel is well maintained and inviting. Rooms are simply furnished but comfortable. The restaurant, Pierre Mouric, is one of the town's most distinguished. Specialties include warm shellfish and scallops in a salad, langoustines, and turbot en papillote. The wine list is superb. Fixed-price meals run 100–160 F ($18–$28.80). The restaurant is open for lunch daily from noon to 1:30pm and for dinner Monday through Saturday from 7:30 to 9pm.

WHERE TO DINE

If you're touring the Ardennes, it would be wise to make Sedan a lunch stopover, as it has the best restaurants in the area, including, in addition to the recommendation that follows, the Pierre Mouric, in the Hôtel L'Europe, listed under "Where to Stay," above.

AU BON VIEUX TEMPS, 1-3, place Halle. Tel. 24-29-03-70.
Cuisine: FRENCH. **Reservations:** Recommended.
$ Prices: Appetizers 65–220 F ($11.70–$39.60); main dishes 56–225 F ($10–$40.50); fixed-price menus 150 F ($27), 220 F ($39.60), and 295 F ($53.10). AE, DC, MC, V.
Open: Lunch Tues–Sun noon–2pm; dinner Tues–Sat 7–9pm. **Closed:** Jan 25–Mar 1.

Chef Alain Leterme enjoys an enviable reputation as having the best restaurant in the town center. You can dine here expensively or inexpensively, depending on your choice of menu items. The 150-F ($27) fixed-price menu represents good value, or you can order à la carte, even asking for the expensive appetizers such as fresh caviar, followed by grilled lobster with white butter sauce. Some specialties include suprême of turbot with sorrel, minced veal kidney with Bouzy wine, or roast lamb with flap mushrooms (prepared only for two diners).

---

2. AMIENS

75 miles N of Paris, 71 miles SW of Lille

GETTING THERE By Train and Bus There are rail and bus connections from Lille, Paris (Gare du Nord), and most major towns in between.

ESSENTIALS Orientation Amiens is set on the south bank of the river Somme, where it subdivides into a complex series of canals and irrigation networks. The city's focal point is its world-famous cathedral. The edge of the modern town begins several blocks south of the cathedral, around the Tour Perret.

Information The Office de Tourisme is on rue Jean-Catelas (tel. 22-91-79-28).

Due north of Paris about 75 miles, Amiens has one of the finest Gothic cathedrals in France. On the Somme River, a major textile center since medieval days, Amiens was the ancient capital of Picardy. Its old town—a jumble of narrow streets crisscrossed by canals—is worth exploring, although it is very rundown and seedy.

The **Cathédrale de Notre-Dame,** place Notre-Dame (tel. 22-91-27-31), was begun in 1220 to the plans of Robert de Luzarches and completed about 1270. Two unequal towers were added later. It is 469 feet long, the largest church in France.

Surely the Amiens cathedral is the crowning example of French Gothic architecture. In John Ruskin's rhapsodical *Bible of Amiens,* which Proust translated into French, he extolled the door arches. The three portals of the west front are lavishly decorated, important examples of Gothic cathedral sculpture. The portals are surmounted by two galleries. The upper one contains 22 statues of kings, and the large rose window is from the 16th century.

In the interior are beautifully carved stalls and a flamboyant choir screen. These stalls with some 3,500 figures were made by local artisans in the early 16th century, and they are the loveliest in all of France. The interior is held up by 126 slender pillars, perhaps the zenith of the High Gothic in the north of France. The cathedral, like St. Paul's in London, somehow managed to escape destruction in World War II, and the architecture of Europe is richer for that.

The cathedral is open daily from 7:30am to noon and 2 to 7pm. The Treasury is open Monday through Saturday from 10am to noon and 2 to 6pm, charging a separate admission of 10 F ($1.80) for adults and 5 F (90¢) for children. A *son-et-lumière* program is presented Tuesday through Saturday from mid-April to mid-October, costing 45 F ($8.10) per ticket. Call 22-91-83-83 to inquire about program times and English presentations.

Musée de la Picardie, 48, rue de la République (tel. 22-91-36-44), is dedicated to the glory of Picardy and housed in a building that was designed like a palace of the Napoleonic dynasty. It's divided into three major sections, including one devoted to archeology. The other sections include exhibits on the Roman occupation of Gaul, the Merovingian era, ancient Greece, and Egypt. One collection documents the Middle Ages with ivories, enamels, art objects, and Gothic sculptures from Picardy. The collection of sculpture and painting traces the European schools from the 16th to the 20th centuries, with works by El Greco, Quentin-Latour, Guardi, and Tiepolo. Some of the paintings are reputed to have hung in the private chambers of Louis XVI at Versailles. Fragonard's *Les Lavandières* is considered by many to be his most beautiful work. The museum is open Tuesday through Sunday from 10am to 12:30pm and 2 to 6pm; admission is 15 F ($2.70) for adults, 5 F (90¢) for children.

Finally, you may want to explore the **Hortillonnages,** the market gardens east of Amiens, where fruit and vegetables are grown and irrigated by small branches of the Somme. In the St-Leu quarter, you'll see a **water market** of boats carrying produce from these little gardens. Barge excursions leave from near the Pont de Beauville.

WHERE TO STAY

Le Prieuré (see "Where to Dine," below) also rents rooms.

GRAND HOTEL DE L'UNIVERS, 2, rue de Noyon, 80000 Amiens. Tel. 22-91-52-51. Fax 22-92-81-66. 41 rms (all with bath or shower). MINIBAR TV TEL
$ Rates: 345–427 F ($62.10–$76.80) single; 375–475 F ($67.50–$85.50) double. Breakfast 50 F ($9) extra. AE, DC, MC, V. **Parking:** 30 F ($5.40).

In the center of town, within an easy walk of the rail station and the cathedral, this century-old hotel has been renovated. Rooms are beautifully decorated, often with antique chairs and tables. Three times a week a florist decorates the rooms and hotel with fresh flowers. Room service is available throughout the day, and a laundry service is offered on request.

WHERE TO DINE

LES MARISSONS, 68, rue des Marissons (pont de la Dodane). Tel. 22-92-96-66.

Cuisine: FRENCH. **Reservations:** Recommended.

$ Prices: Appetizers 90–95 F ($16.20–$17.10); main dishes 120–150 F ($21.60–$27); fixed-price meals 135 F ($24.30) (weekdays only), and 176–235 F ($31.70–$42.30). AE, DC, MC, V.

Open: Lunch Tues–Fri and Sun noon–2pm; dinner Mon–Sat 7:30–10pm.

The town's best restaurant is accessible from a side street running off one of its oldest bridges, the Pont de la Dodane. In a wood-sided, heavily beamed building which functioned during the 15th century as a shipyard for river boats, you can enjoy the fine cuisine of chef Antoine Benoit. His cuisine is known locally as a celebration of Picardy, an homage which includes even the "national colors" of the dining room (yellow for Picardy wheat; blue for the color of the region's three rivers, with bay windows overlooking the outside view). Menu specialties include canard in puff pastry with homemade foie gras, baked crayfish with tarragon sauce, rack of lamb in puff pastry with garlic and fresh thyme, and a wide array of other sophisticated dishes whose availability depends on the seasonality of the ingredients. The restaurant, which sits within a five-minute walk of the town's famous cathedral, also has a warm-weather outdoor terrace for midsummer dining.

LE PRIEURE, 17, rue Porion, 80000 Amiens. Tel. 22-92-27-67.

Cuisine: FRENCH. **Reservations:** Required.

$ Prices: Appetizers 75–130 F ($13.50–$23.40); main dishes 95–158 F ($17.10–$28.40); fixed-price menus 120 F ($21.60), 160 F ($28.80), and 200 F ($36). AE, DC, V.

Open: Lunch Tues–Sun noon–2pm; dinner Tues–Sat 7–9:30pm. **Closed:** Aug 15–31.

This outstanding restaurant is in a charming hotel in a restored 18th-century building. The chef turns fresh ingredients into delectable modern dishes, presented with a certain flourish in the dining room, which contains a big aquarium.

The hotel also offers 21 well-furnished bedrooms, each with private bath, phone, and TV. Charges are 250 F ($45) in a single, rising to 420 F ($75.60) in a double, plus another 36 F ($6.40) per person extra for breakfast.

---

3. ST-QUENTIN

91 miles NE of Paris, 45 miles E of Amiens

GETTING THERE The town is easily reached by train, bus, or car.

ESSENTIALS Orientation Ringed with wide boulevards that carry most of the heavy traffic, the medieval city is centered around its Gothic Church of St-Quentin. Two of the most important streets radiating from the center of the city are rue Emile-Zola and rue d'Isle.

Information The Office de Tourisme is on rue de la Sellerie (tel. 23-67-05-00).

A manufacturing town 45 miles due east of Amiens, St-Quentin was largely destroyed in World War I, as it lay in the heat of battle for months. The Germans occupied it from the summer of 1914 to the fall of 1918. Now completely rebuilt, the town still has a number of interesting treasures. Once St-Quentin was assigned as the dowry of Mary Queen of Scots.

On the right bank of the Somme, the hub of the town is the Place de l'Hôtel-de-Ville with a monument erected in 1896 commemorating the Battle of 1557, when Philip II of Spain staged a siege here that threatened Paris. The ornate Gothic façade of the **Hôtel de Ville,** with its curious sculptures, is from 1509, but its origins go back to 1331. It was only slightly damaged in World War II.

To the northeast of the square stands the great collegiate **St-Quentin,** 2, rue des Chevaliers de la Barre (tel. 23-62-22-05), a Gothic building dating from the 12th to 15th centuries. Damaged in World War I, it was restored and reopened in 1920. The church has large double transepts and a choir screen from the 14th century. Under the choir is an 11th-century crypt housing the tomb of the 3rd-century martyr Saint Quentin, along with two fellow martyrs. It's open daily from 8am to 5pm.

If you're a Matisse fan, you may want to drive to his birthplace in **Le Cateau-Cambrésis,** 25 miles from St-Quentin. Considered by many the most important French painter of the 20th century, Matisse was born in this small town in the final hours of 1869. The **Musée Matisse du Cateau-Cambrésis,** Palais Fenelon (tel. 27-84-13-15), was reorganized in 1982 and housed within the 18th-century walls of this palace. The museum has the third-largest Matisse collection in France. It holds works of Matisse donated by the artist, including designs, engravings, paintings, sculptures, illustrated books, and studies for the chapel at Vence on the French Riviera. The museum also includes 26 paintings and sculptures by Auguste Herbin (1882–1960) and five paintings by Geneviève Claisse.

The museum is open in summer, Monday and Wednesday through Saturday from 10am to noon and 2 to 6pm (to 5pm in winter); on Sunday it's open from 10am to 12:30pm and 2:30 to 6pm year-round. Admission is 15 F ($2.70) for adults and 3.50 F (60¢) for children 6–18.

WHERE TO STAY & DINE

GRAND HOTEL ET RESTAURANT LE PRESIDENT, 6, rue Dachery, 02100 St-Quentin. Tel. 23-62-69-77. Fax 23-62-53-52. 24 rms (all with bath). MINIBAR TV TEL
$ Rates: 430 F ($77.40) single; 620 F ($111.60) double. Breakfast 60 F ($10.80) extra. AE, DC, MC, V.

Modern and comfortable, the Grand Hôtel is the premier place to stay in St-Quentin. It's well managed and constantly being improved; much attention is paid to the comfort of guests. The star of this provincial hotel is its restaurant, Le Président. Try the salad of crayfish with avocado, filet of roast lamb with fresh thyme, or sweetbreads prepared in an original way. The chef even adds an interesting twist to the standard turbot and sole. Special desserts depend on the fruits in season. There's also an impressive wine list. Fixed-price meals cost 160–330 F ($28.80–$59.40); à la carte meals run 350–480 F ($63–$86.40).

The restaurant is open Tuesday through Saturday from noon to 2pm and 7:15 to 10pm, and on Sunday from 7:15 to 10pm. It's closed August 2–30 and December 19–27.

LE RICHE, 10, rue des Toiles. Tel. 23-62-33-53.
   Cuisine: FRENCH/SEAFOOD. **Reservations:** Recommended.
$ Prices: Appetizers 75–200 F ($13.50–$36); main dishes 40–80 F ($7.20–$14.40); fixed-price menus 75–200 F ($13.50–$36). AE, MC, V.
   Open: Lunch daily noon–2:15pm; dinner Mon–Sat 7–11pm. **Closed:** July 12–Aug 13.

Contained in an old-fashioned building that was demolished during World War I and rebuilt after 1918, this brasserie was established in 1930. It lies midway between the town's cathedral and La Mairie (town hall), on a narrow and quiet street originally laid out during the Middle Ages. Maintained since its beginning by members of the Flamant family, it features an uncomplicated interior decor and a wide array of such fish dishes as turbot with hollandaise sauce, grilled crayfish, filet of sole in beurre-blanc sauce, steaks, and sauerkraut.

4. LAON

86 miles NE of Paris, 74 miles SE of Amiens

GETTING THERE   By Train   There is rail service to Laon from Reims, Lille, and Paris (Gare du Nord).

ESSENTIALS   Orientation   The railway station lies in the not-very-interesting lower town (*Ville Basse*). You can climb the very long flight of stairs (only if you are in good health) or take a tram up the steep hillside to the ramparts of the medieval upper town.

Information   The Office de Tourisme is on place Parvis (tel. 23-20-28-62).

This is arguably the single most intriguing town to explore in the north. Its location is 28 miles from our last stopover in St-Quentin. The capital of the Département of Aisne, Laon has had a long, turbulent history, which, frankly, had to do with its remarkable site, perched on an isolated ridge that rises 328 feet above the plain and the Ardon River.

The Romans early in life saw its strategic value and had it fortified. Laon in time was besieged by Vandals, Burgundians, Franks, whomever. German troops entered in 1870. The Germans came again in the summer of 1914, holding it until the end of World War I. The town is still surrounded by medieval ramparts.

Most visitors want to head first to the famed **Cathédrale de Notre-Dame**, 8, rue du Cloître, off place Aubry (tel. 23-20-06-54), which has suffered much war damage over the years, notably in 1870 when an engineer set off a powder magazine as the German troops entered the town. The cathedral escaped relatively unharmed in World War I, however. It stands on the same spot where an ancient basilica once stood until it was destroyed by fire in 1111. The structure has six towers, four of which are complete. Huge figures of oxen are depicted on the façade. Inside you'll find stained glass, some panels dating from the 13th century, along with an 18th-century choir grill.

The town has also the Church of St. Martin from the mid-12th century.

The **Musée Archéologique Municipal**, 32, rue Georges-Ermant (tel. 23-20-19-87), is an archeological museum. It has 1,700 artifacts from Greece, Rome, Egypt, Cyprus, and Asia Minor, as well as a collection of French painting and sculpture.

From May to October, the museum is open daily from 10am to noon and 2 to 6pm; it's open until 5pm off-season. Admission is 10 F ($1.80) for adults, free for children.

WHERE TO STAY & DINE

ANGLETERRE, 10, bd. de Lyon, 02000 Laon. Tel. 23-23-04-62. 28 rms (17 with bath). TEL
$ Rates: 170 F ($30.60) single without bath; 330 F ($59.40) single or double with bath. Breakfast 28 F ($5) extra. AE, DC, MC, V. **Parking:** Free.
The rooms in this comfortable hotel vary in quality, depending on how recently each one was renovated; 10 contain TVs. The restaurant serves meals priced at 80–150 F ($14.40–$27); it's closed for Saturday lunch and on Sunday.

HOTEL DE LA BANNIERE DE FRANCE, 11, rue Franklin-Roosevelt, 02000 Laon. Tel. 23-23-21-44. Fax 23-23-21-44. 18 rms (all with bath or shower). TV TEL
$ Rates: 220 F ($39.60) single; 360 F ($64.80) double. Breakfast 35 F ($6.30) extra. AE, DC, V. **Parking:** Free.
Dating from 1685, the town's most revered hotel has been completely modernized, although an attempt was made to maintain the ambience of a traditional French hotel. All the well-furnished and comfortable bedrooms have bath or shower, satellite TV, and a hairdryer.

A well-patronized restaurant on the premises is run by the owner, Madame Paul

Lefevre, who offers such specialties as a fricassée of sweetbreads and kidneys in a cream sauce with mushrooms. Try her salade Royale or her lemon sole à la normande. For dessert, the specialty is profiteroles au chocolat. The restaurant is open daily from noon to 2pm and 7 to 9:30pm; closed January 19, May 1, and December 20.

5. ARRAS

110 miles NE of Paris, 32 miles SW of Lille

GETTING THERE   By Train   From Paris (Gare du Nord), there is train service to Arras via Amiens. There is also train service from Lille.

ESSENTIALS   Orientation   The old town is encircled by wide boulevards, which alleviate some of the traffic from the narrow inner-city streets. The town's most important monument, the Abbaye St-Vaast, lies in the geographical center.

Information   The office de Tourisme is in the Hôtel de Ville on place des Héros (tel. 21-51-26-95).

In the 15th century Arras was a major center for tapestry weavers. In some museums of Europe, Arras is still synonymous with tapestry. Despite massive damage in two World Wars, Arras, lying between Lille and Amiens, retains some of the appearance of an ancient Flemish trading town with its squares and gabled houses. This is particularly evident in the center of town around the two arcaded and linked squares, **Grand'Place** and **Place des Héros.**

On the Place des Héros, the Gothic-style **Hôtel de Ville** and its belfry were built in the 16th century and soon surrounded by 155 houses supported on 345 columns. Badly damaged in World War I, the town hall was restored, only to be attacked in World War II. Now again restored, the building and its belfry—245 feet high—can be visited daily: May through September, from 9am to noon and 2 to 5pm; off-season, from 2 to 6pm.

To the northwest of the town hall, the vast cathedral was built in the neoclassic style. Inside are two interesting triptychs. The cathedral is entered on rue des Teinturiers. On the south side is the **Abbaye St-Vaast,** 22 rue Paul-Doumer (tel. 21-71-26-43), which has had a long and turbulent history but is now a museum, open daily except Tuesday from 10am to noon and 2 to 5:30pm in summer. Sculptures line its small cloister, and works of art are displayed in its large cloister, including an exceptional collection of porcelain, paintings (Rubens, La Hyre, Vignon, Corot, and Delacroix), and tapestries.

The museum is open Wednesday through Monday from 10am to noon and 2 to 6pm (to 5pm in winter); admission is 13 F ($2.30), rising to 16 F ($2.80) when there's a special exhibition.

The town has had many associations with famous people. Robespierre was born in a house that can be seen on rue des Rapporteurs. At 2 impasse de l'Elvoye, rue d'Amiens, is the house where Verlaine stayed after he was imprisoned in Belgium. He once came to Arras with Rimbaud. Both were arrested by police after they pretended to have committed a crime.

The Battle of Arras was the name given to operations against the Germans by British forces in the spring of 1917. Arras has some important war monuments, mainly to the north of the town. A memorial was erected to unknown soldiers who died on the battlefields of Artois in 1914 and 1915, and a British military cemetery and memorial to 200 local patriots executed in World War II were also built.

WHERE TO STAY

HOTEL DE L'UNIVERS, 3, place de la Croix-Rouge, 62000 Arras. Tel. 21-71-34-01. Fax 21-71-41-42. 33 rms (all with bath or shower). TV TEL
$ Rates: 290–300 F ($52.20–$54) single; 290–380 F ($52.20–$68.40) double. Breakfast 40 F ($7.20) extra. AE, MC, V. **Parking:** Free.

One of the most historic buildings in town, this hotel was built around 1590, and functioned until the French Revolution as a monastery, a hospital, and a Jesuit-run school. After 1789, it became an inn, welcoming travelers in a tradition it continues today. Although renovations have gradually improved the look of this place and its facilities, many of the details have remained virtually unchanged since the early 1960s. Set in the town center, it features a pleasant garden, and a well-managed restaurant where fixed-price meals cost 90–160 F ($16.20–$28.80). Meals are served every day of the week from noon to 2:30pm and from 7:30 to 9:30pm, and usually include some kind of fish dish, such as turbot with hollandaise sauce, grilled monkfish, scallops in beurre-blanc sauce, and salmon with sage sauce.

WHERE TO DINE

LA COUPOLE ARRAS, 26, bd. Strasbourg. Tel. 21-71-88-44.

Cuisine: FRENCH. **Reservations:** Recommended.
$ Prices: Appetizers 42–90F ($7.60–$16.20); main dishes 85–200 F ($15.30–$36); fixed-price menus 98 F ($17.60) Mon–Fri and 190 F ($34.20) anytime. AE, DC, MC, V.
Open: Lunch Sun–Fri noon–2:30pm; dinner daily 7:30–11pm.

Set a short walk from the railway station, this well-known brasserie opened in the mid-1980s amid a carefully contrived decor which some visitors think might be a lot older. Dishes are served with an old-world flourish amid an art deco *bistro de gare*-kind of format, and might include such specialties as platters of shellfish, many different kinds of fish, grilled steaks, and sauerkraut.

LA FAISANDERIE, 45, Grand' Place. Tel. 21-48-20-76.

Cuisine: FRENCH. **Reservations:** Required.
$ Prices: Appetizers 105–145 F ($18.90–$26.10); main dishes 125–200 F ($22.50–$36); fixed-price menus 175 F ($31.50), 255 F ($45.90), 280 F ($50.40), and 375 F ($67.50). AE, DC, MC, V.
Open: Lunch Tues–Sun 12:30–2pm; dinner Tues–Sat 7–9pm. **Closed:** Two weeks in Feb and three weeks in Aug (dates vary).

The most cultivated cuisine in Arras can be found in this elegant 17th-century Flemish house on the most important and historic square. Jean-Pierre Dargent owns this retreat in a restored cellar, which has stone columns and vaults. It was originally designed as a stable for horses and the original feeding troughs and ramps have been preserved as part of the decor. The fine cuisine seems to be a "polished" version of country dishes. Ingredients arrive from all over France—the best fish from small fishing fleets off the French coast, chicken from Bresse, lamb from Pauillac, and foie gras from Maubourguet. Menus change with the season.

6. LILLE

136 miles NE of Paris, 72 miles W of Brussels

GETTING THERE Lille can be reached by air, train, and bus service from all parts of Europe.

By Train The French National TGV North train from Paris to Lille inaugurated the French-Belgium-British Eurostar service in 1993; trip time for the 136-mile train ride from Paris has been reduced to about an hour.

ESSENTIALS Orientation Ignore the industrial suburbs and concentrate on Lille's innermost core, where many of the streets are for pedestrians only. The central square is place Rihour, from which many narrow streets radiate. Looming above the old city is the town's most imposing monument, La Citadelle, still controlled by the French army.

Information The Office de Tourisme is in the Palais Rihour on place Rihour (tel. 20-30-81-00).

Near the Belgian frontier, Lille is the largest city in French Flanders and is famous for its breweries. One of the world's major textile centers, it is industrial, known for its spinning and weaving. In World War I the Germans occupied it from October 1914 until October 1918. German officers at the time often came to Lille on leave, enjoying a holiday since the city wasn't shelled by the Allies.

Once Lille was the capital of the counts of Flanders, but with the Treaty of Utrecht in 1713, it became a French possession. A few of its medieval buildings remain, and the most elegant part of the old town is the district of St-André, to the north, but essentially Lille is a busy, modern city, with office blocks and wide boulevards.

Public gardens surround the pentagonal **Citadel,** one of Vauban's finest works. It lies west of town and contains barracks and an arsenal.

The ✪ **Musée des Beaux-Arts,** place de la République (tel. 20-57-01-84), located in a 19th-century building in the city center, is considered by many art critics second only to the Louvre. Its collection of paintings by old masters alone justifies a visit to Lille. The Flemish and Dutch schools are particularly well represented, including works by Bouts, Rubens, Jordaens, van Dyck, Codde, de Witte, and van Ruisdael. Spanish paintings include two of Goya's major works, *Les Jeunes* and *Les Vieilles,* and a masterpiece by El Greco, *Saint François en Extase.* The Italian school offers paintings by Titian, Veronese, and Tintoretto. The French paintings offer a comprehensive view from the 17th to the 20th century, including works by David, Delacroix, Monet, and Renoir.

The rich graphic-art room, with 4,000 drawings—including works by Raphael, Dürer, and Poussin—can be visited only by special request.

The sculpture section covers antiquity through the 20th century, with works by Donatello and Rodin. In the decorative-arts department, you can see rare medieval ivory carvings, rich enamels, and fine gold and silver ornamental objects.

The museum is open Wednesday through Monday from 9:30am to 12:30pm and 2 to 6pm; it's closed on holidays. Admission is 10 F ($1.80).

WHERE TO STAY

CARLTON, 3, rue de Paris, 59000 Lille. Tel. 20-55-24-11. Fax 20-51-48-17. 53 rms (all with bath or shower), 7 suites. MINIBAR TV TEL **Métro:** Place Rihour.
$ Rates: 690–750 F ($124.20–$135) single; 720–790 F ($129.60–$142.20) double; from 980 F ($176.40) suite. Breakfast 65 F ($11.70) extra. AE, DC, MC, V. **Parking:** 60 F ($10.80).
Located in the city center near the railroad station, this much improved hotel was built in 1920 opposite the opera house of Lille. It was completely renovated in 1992, its bedrooms decorated with either Louis XV or Louis XVI furnishings. Rooms have harmonious styling and are soundproof. The hotel is sited near several restaurants, but also contains two well-recommended dining choices on the premises, including Brasserie Jean and Le Bistro de l'Opéra.

HOTEL BELLEVUE, 5, rue Jean-Roisin, 59800 Lille. Tel. 20-57-45-64. Fax 20-40-07-93. 60 rms (all with bath or shower), 3 suites. MINIBAR TV TEL **Métro:** Place Rihour.
$ Rates: 430–495 F ($77.40–$89.10) single; 465–530 F ($83.70–$95.40) double; 760 F ($136.80) suite. Breakfast 45 F ($8.10) extra. **Parking:** 50 F ($9).
The building containing this hotel was originally built in 1730. Some 200 years later, the interior was remodelled into an art deco–inspired design, and in 1992, many of the upstairs bedrooms were renovated and improved. Today, boasting an unusual mixture of architectural designs one atop the other, and large, somewhat severe bedrooms, the hotel sits adjacent to the city's tourist office. It contains a small bar, and recorded music floats through the public rooms. No meals are served other than breakfast, but many worthwhile restaurants are nearby.

WHERE TO DINE

ALCIDE, 5, rue Débris-St-Etienne. Tel. 20-12-06-95.
    Cuisine: FRENCH. **Reservations:** Recommended. **Métro:** Place Rihour.
$ Prices: Appetizers 28–74 F ($5–$13.30); main dishes 65–125 F ($11.70–$22.50); fixed-price menu 78 F ($14). AE, DC, MC, V.
    Open: Lunch daily noon–3pm; dinner daily 7–11pm.

    For one of the best dining values in the city center, you can patronize this typical *brasserie lilloise* with its reasonably priced dishes from the north of France. Specialties are a pot-au-feu, mussels marinara, and aiguillettes de canard (duckling). You might begin with a selection of three terrines (served as an appetizer) or rillettes of salmon. For a main course, try one of the selections of the day, including such dishes as roast lamb flavored with herbs or sauerkraut royale. The chef always offers fresh oysters, foie gras, and grills such as entrecôte béarnaise.

A L'HUITRIERE, 3, rue des Chats-Bossus. Tel. 20-55-43-41.
    Cuisine: FRENCH. **Reservations:** Required. **Métro:** Place Rihour.
$ Prices: Appetizers 90–190 F ($16.20–$34.20); main dishes 96–180 F ($17.20–$32.40); fixed-price seven-course "tasting menu" 480 F ($86.40). AE, DC, MC, V.
    Open: Lunch daily noon–2:30pm; dinner Mon–Sat 7–9:30pm. **Closed:** Holidays and July 22–Sept 1.

    On the "Street of Hunchback Cats," this restaurant run by Jean Proye offers the finest seafood in Lille. The oysters from Holland taste fresh, and the catch of the day always inspires the chef to turn out a spectacular fish dish. You usually can't go wrong by ordering the *plat du jour*. Other specialties include monkfish cooked with green beans lightly flavored with garlic and tomato, coquilles St-Jacques à la Bercy, assiette d'homard (stewed lobster, carrots, onions, leeks, and celery with a butter sauce), and turbot in a mustard sauce. The menu changes four times a year, according to the season. In addition, you might try his menu of discovery ("tasting" menu), which changes every month. À l'Huîtrière has a bountiful wine cellar—Jean Proye was once honored with the title of Wine-Butler of France.
    The entrance of the restaurant is through one of the most beautiful fish shops in France, built in 1928, where all kinds of seafood is sold, as well as other edibles such as Bresse poultry, Pauillac lamb, goose-liver pâté, and cooked dishes.

BISTROT TOURANGEAU, 61, bd. Louis-XIV. Tel. 20-52-74-64.
    Cuisine: FRENCH. **Reservations:** Required. **Métro:** Foire Commerciale.
$ Prices: Appetizers 35–90 F ($6.30–$16.20); main dishes 60–105 F ($10.80–$18.90); fixed-price meals 100–195 F ($18–$35.10). AE, MC, V.
    Open: Lunch Mon–Sat noon–2:30pm; dinner Mon–Sat 7:30–10:30pm.

Set within a 15-minute walk southeast of the town center, near the city entrance which leads from Lille to Paris, this well-managed restaurant occupies an antique house whose interior has been gracefully renovated into the art deco style. Inside, amid mirrors, bouquets of flowers, and comfortable banquettes, you'll find an intimate (30-seat) restaurant with some of the most authentic regional cuisine in Lille. Menu items vary with the seasons, but are likely to include a platter of rillettes et rillons de Touraine, l'oeuf à la moelle avec son pain au lard, tête de veau, sauvegeon (duckling) à la crème, a gallette of stuffed pigs' feet, and filet of zander with sage butter. Service is polite and well informed, and a limited array of less regional (i.e., more international) dishes are also available.

BRASSERIE LE QUEEN [L'ECUME DE MER], 10, rue de Pas. Tel. 20-54-95-40.
    Cuisine: FRENCH. **Reservations:** Recommended.
$ Prices: Appetizers 40–60 F ($7.20–$10.80); main dishes 40–120 F ($7.20–$21.60); fixed-price lunch 90 F ($16.20). AE, DC, MC, V.
    Open: Lunch daily noon–2:30pm; dinner Sun–Fri 7pm–midnight.

Occupying the once-battered premises of a recently departed English pub, across from the Palais de la Musique, this brasserie (whose name translates as "sea foam") deliberately retained part of the name of the previous occupant (Queen Victoria Pub). Increasingly popular since 1992, the Queen is outfitted in Atlantic-inspired colors of sea green and blue, and serves a classic brasserie-style menu. Items might include an array of shellfish, many different preparations of fish, and sauerkraut prepared in both the traditional (sausage and pork) version as well as a marine version made with fish. Some visitors compare its decor and service rituals to something they might have found in Boston, Massachusetts.

LA PORTE DE GAND [RESTAURANT LE FLAMBARD], rue de Gand. Tel. 20-74-28-66.
   Cuisine: FRENCH. **Reservations:** Recommended. **Métro:** Place Rihour.
$ **Prices:** Appetizers 40–80 F ($7.20–$14.40); main dishes 45–130 F ($8.10–$23.40). AE, DC, MC, V.
   Open: Lunch Tues–Sun noon–2pm; dinner Wed–Sat 7–9:30pm.
Robert Bardot's restaurant occupies part of the historic fortifications that surround medieval Lille. As part of a much-discussed restoration of the city walls, the restaurant occupies two floors (reachable via a carefully sited elevator in one of the medieval guard rooms) of the Porte de Gand (Ghent). Amid a conservative decor which was endorsed by historically conscious city planners, the setting acts as a suitable foil for the fine cuisine which the Bardot family made famous in earlier years at another location in Lille. During clement weather, outdoor tables are placed on top of the ramparts for additional dining. Cuisine is not traditional, but inventive, creative, and always skillfully prepared. Specialties include pressed foie gras of goose, sole with crayfish tails and leeks, chicken fricassée with stuffed spring turnips, and a savarin of sole with turbot.

---

7. DUNKERQUE

180 miles N of Paris, 27 miles E of Calais

GETTING THERE   By Train   Trains arrive daily from Paris, Lille, and Arras.

By Ferry   Ferryboats arrive from and depart for England every two hours during daylight.

ESSENTIALS   Orientation   The town center, near the railway station, is a commercial area; most visitors congregate in the beachside suburb of Malo-les-Bains. The heart of downtown lies near place Bollaert, a short walk from the town's port.

Information   The Office de Tourisme is on place du Beffroi (tel. 28-66-79-21).

On the coast of the North Sea only nine miles from the Belgian frontier, Dunkerque (Dunkirk in English) captured the attention of the world from May 26 to June 3, 1940. In a heroic evacuation, a British expeditionary force of 233,000 men and some 112,500 Allied troops were taken across the Strait of Dover to England just before the port was occupied by the Germans. These men were transported in every conceivable craft—motorboats, yachts, even fishing boats.

Dunkerque was nearly destroyed in that war, and it was the last French town to be liberated by the Allies, May 10, 1945. Rebuilt, Dunkerque today is the third port of France. There is daily train-ferry service to Dover.

The heart of town is the Place Jean-Bart, where the major thoroughfares converge. There stands a David d'Angers statue of Admiral Jean Bart, the noted seafarer who was born in Dunkerque in 1650.

The harbor is impressive, with its lock gates, docks, and cranes, as well as several miles of quays. It can be visited in season by a boat embarking from Place du Minck. Boat schedules vary according to the season, the trip taking about one hour.

   Musée des Beaux-Arts, place du Général-de-Gaulle (tel. 28-66-21-57), east of the Gothic church of St-Eloi, presents an interesting collection of Flemish, Italian, and French paintings. The most important works include a triptych by Pourbus, an

Adoration of the Magi by Magnasco, and a work by Hubert Robert. One entire gallery is devoted to World War II.

The museum is open Wednesday through Monday from 10am to noon and 2 to 6pm, and on Tuesday from 2 to 6pm. Admission is 6 F ($1) for adults, free for children.

Dunkerque also has another art museum worthy of your attention. It's the **Musée d'Art Contemporain,** lying off the rue des Bains (tel. 28-59-21-65). The modern collection is filled with lithographs, paintings, and sculptures, and the building is so avant-garde that it, too, attracts attention, like a frame competing with the picture it holds. For 6F ($1), the collection can be viewed Wednesday through Monday from 10am to 7pm (to 6pm in winter).

WHERE TO STAY

EUROP HOTEL, 13, rue de Leughenaer, 59140 Dunkerque. Tel. 28-66-29-07. Fax 28-63-67-87. 120 rms (all with bath). MINIBAR TV TEL
$ Rates: 330 F ($59.40) single; 380 F ($68.40) double. Breakfast 46 F ($8.20) extra. AE, DC, MC, V. **Parking:** 30 F ($5.40).

Considering that many visitors regard this hotel as the best in town, the rates are very reasonable. It's a modern structure offering spacious bedrooms with many comforts, including radio alarms. For quick meals, there's an informal grill with a self-service hors d'oeuvres table. The elegant brasserie, Le Mareyeur, specializes in fish and crustaceans; meals run 85–240 F ($15.30–$43.20). The hotel also contains the Europ Grill, where meals begin at 110 F ($19.80).

HOTEL BOREL, 6, rue l'Hermitte, 59140 Dunkerque. Tel. 28-66-51-80. Fax 28-59-33-82. 48 rms (all with bath). TV TEL
$ Rates: 340 F ($61.20) single; 400 F ($72) double. Breakfast 36 F ($6.40) extra. AE, DC, MC, V.

A few of the rooms in this family-run hotel have a view of the port. The accommodations are functionally furnished, clean, and comfortable. There is no restaurant.

MERCURE-ALTEA REUZE, 2, rue Jean-Jaurès, 59140 Dunkerque. Tel. 28-59-11-11. Fax 28-63-09-69. 122 rms (all with bath or shower). MINIBAR TV TEL
$ Rates: 355 F ($63.90) single; 600 F ($108) double. Breakfast 47 F ($8.40) extra. AE, DC, MC, V.

This modern chain hotel, one of the best in the port, attracts many weekend travelers from England. Rooms are well equipped, with radios, electric razor outlets, and safes. Hotel services include laundry and dry cleaning, currency exchange, and automatic morning calls. Breakfast is the only meal served. The hotel is located near the Bassin du Commerce.

WHERE TO DINE

LE RICHELIEU, place de la Gare. Tel. 28-66-52-13.
Cuisine: FRENCH. **Reservations:** Not required.
$ Prices: Appetizers 25–80 F ($4.50–$14.40); main dishes 60–125 F ($10.80–$22.50); fixed-price menus 100–125 F ($18–$22.50). AE, DC, MC, V.
Open: Lunch daily noon–3pm; dinner Tues–Sat 7–9pm.

Next to hotel dining, the best restaurant is at the railway station. This buffet gare offers three choices: a café, an informal brasserie, and a relatively elegant restaurant. Le Richelieu is without doubt the busiest all-purpose eatery in town, and it has a meal for every budget. Especially budget conscious diners head for the street-level brasserie, where no one minds if you order only a well-prepared *plat du jour*. More formal meals, in a more elegant setting of rich curtains and comfortable upholstery, are available in the adjacent restaurant. There you can dine more leisurely on such dishes as turbot in hollandaise, filet of sole, and veal kidneys flambé. The cuisine is superb, and the service is excellent.

NEARBY ACCOMMODATIONS & DINING

Motorists might want to leave Dunkerque altogether and head for Téteghem, about four miles east on the N40 and a switch off onto the D204.

LA MEUNERIE, 174, rue Pierres, 59229. Tel. 28-26-14-30. Fax 28-26-17-32. 9 rms (all with bath or shower), 1 suite. MINIBAR TV TEL
$ Rates: 500–800 F ($90–$144) single or double; from 1,300 F ($234) suite. Breakfast 55 F ($9.90) extra. AE, DC, MC, V. **Parking:** Free.

The soundproof rooms at La Meunerie are decorated in styles ranging from Louis XV to Restoration, 19th-century romantic, and Roaring '20s. The elegant restaurant in an old mill treats you to the savory cooking of Jean-Pierre Delbé. The featured seafood comes from the North Sea, and meat and poultry dishes change with the season. The combination of flavors is often intriguing, and the tables are kept immaculate. Menus begin at 260 F ($46.80); à la carte dinners could easily reach 500 F ($90). Lunch is served Tuesday through Sunday from noon to 2pm; dinner is served Tuesday through Saturday from 7:30 to 9:30pm.

---

8. CALAIS

181 miles N of Paris, 27 miles W of Dunkerque,
21 miles from Dover (across the Channel)

GETTING THERE By Train Because of Calais's importance as a gateway to England, there are many daily trains to and from Paris (Gare du Nord). There is also service from Lille, Dunkerque, and Boulogne.

Calais has two train stations, Gare Calais-Maritime (near the hovercraft and ferryboat terminals) and Gare Calais-Ville (close to the center of town).

ESSENTIALS Orientation The canals of the city's port encircle the historic center, Calais-Nord, on all sides. The centerpiece of Calais-Nord is place d'Armes. The relatively modern Calais-Sud radiates outward from the Hôtel de Ville and the town's main commercial streets, boulevard Lafayette and boulevard Jacquard.

Information The Office de Tourisme is located at 12, bd. Georges-Clemenceau (tel. 21-96-01-92).

This is the closest Channel port to England, a distance of 21 miles to the "white cliffs" of Dover. The bombs of World War II destroyed most of Vieux Calais, the old town with its citadel of 1560. In its place, a new quarter was built on an island bordered by the harbor basins and a canal. To the south lies the larger quarter of St-Pierre, an industrial area with its tulle and lace factories.

Originally a fishing village, Calais is today the second most important passenger port in France. It is, of course, in front-ranking position for passenger traffic with England. Several daily cross-Channel sea services operate, not only to Dover but to Folkestone as well, taking both passengers and automobiles.

In history, England's Edward III had reduced the seaport to famine in 1346, until the six burghers of Calais turned themselves over as hostages, an event commemorated by Auguste Rodin's world-renowned monument. The monument stands in the center of town, the Place du Soldat-Inconnu, with its Hôtel de Ville, a town hall built in the Flemish-Renaissance style.

WHERE TO STAY

GEORGE V, 36, rue Royale, 62100 Calais. Tel. 21-97-68-00. Fax 21-97-34-73. 45 rms (all with bath or shower). TV TEL
$ Rates: 190 F ($34.20) single; 340 F ($61.20) double. Breakfast 38 F ($5) extra. AE, DC, MC, V. **Parking:** Free.

Ⓢ Conveniently located in the city center, near one of the most popular beaches, this restored hotel is run by the Beauvalot family. Bedrooms are done in a simple, functional modern. The hotel has a gastronomic restaurant, where meals cost 155–250 F ($27.90–$45). There's also the Petit George where a simple menu is priced at 80 F ($14.40). Hotel guests can also avail themselves of a private lounge bar.

MEURICE, 5, rue Edmond-Roche, 62100 Calais. Tel. 21-34-57-03. Fax 21-34-14-71. 40 rms (all with bath). TV TEL
$ **Rates:** 310 F ($55.80) single; 435 F ($78.30) double. Breakfast 38 F ($6.80) extra. AE, DC, MC, V.

This comfortable hotel, located at the center of town, blends old-world elegance with modern amenities. It carries on the tradition of Monsieur Augustin Meurice, who in 1772 owned the stagecoach express line, Le Chariot Royale. He opened his first inn in Calais and by 1816 had a chain of accommodations—all called Meurice—for overnight travelers from London to Paris. Rooms are well furnished and well maintained, and some have views of Richelieu Park. You can rest in the interior garden between Channel crossings.

WHERE TO DINE

LE CHANNEL, 3, bd. de la Résistance. Tel. 21-34-42-30.
Cuisine: FRENCH. **Reservations:** Required in summer.
$ **Prices:** Appetizers 70–110 F ($12.60–$19.80); main dishes 85–130 F ($15.30–$23.40); fixed-price menus 80 F ($14.40) (Mon–Sat), 130 F ($23.40), 180 F ($32.40) and 300 F ($54). AE, DC, MC, V.
Open: Lunch Wed–Mon noon–2:30pm; dinner Mon and Wed–Sat 7–9:30pm.
Closed: June 8–16 and Dec 21–Jan 17.

Ⓢ A family owns this rustic restaurant where fresh fish is the specialty and where you can find the best dinner value in Calais. Specialties include grilled salmon, confit of duck, and filet of turbot with asparagus.

LA SOLE MEUNIERE, 1, bd. de la Résistance. Tel. 21-34-43-01.
Cuisine: FRENCH. **Reservations:** Required.
$ **Prices:** Appetizers 40–100 F ($7.20–$18); main dishes 80–120 F ($14.40–$21.60); fixed-price menus 80 F ($14.40), 120 F ($21.60), 160 F ($28.80), and 250 F ($45). AE, DC, V.
Open: Lunch daily 11:30am–2:30pm; dinner Wed–Mon 6–10:30pm.

This restaurant is a veritable Calais institution, offering an impressive array of fish and fresh shellfish at moderate prices. Its big windows overlook a yacht-filled marina and Port Plaisance.

9. BOULOGNE-SUR-MER

152 miles N of Paris, 21 miles SW of Calais

GETTING THERE By Train Because of its importance as a maritime depar-ture point for Britain, a network of trains links Boulogne to Paris (Gare du Nord), Lille, and Calais. The town has two railway stations. The Gare Maritime, used less frequently, times its departures to Paris for the arrivals of the ferryboats from Britain. The Gare Boulogne-Ville deposits passengers in the center of the town.

ESSENTIALS Orientation The historic core of Boulogne lies east of the port on a once-fortified hilltop called Ville Haute. Its most visible attraction is the Hôtel de Ville, whose 13th century tower lies near the center of the rectangular fortifications.

Information The Office de Tourisme is on quai de la Poste (tel. 21-31-68-38).

By ship and hovercraft the English for years have been streaking over to Boulogne, less than two hours away, to savor a bit of the continent. On the English Channel,

Boulogne is about 30 miles from Dover and Folkestone. One of France's busiest commercial ports, it boasts a modern fishing fleet, with many vessels in active pursuit of herring and mackerel.

Boulogne started as a Roman city from which Julius Caesar and his men sailed in 800 boats to conquer England. In 1803 Napoleon had the same plan, but Admiral Nelson had a different idea. American bombers after D-Day destroyed Caligula's Tower, which celebrated Caesar's role in developing Boulogne as an important Channel port. However, Napoleon's thwarted dream is still commemorated in a **Column of the Grande Armée,** rising 174 feet over Boulogne. A statue of the French emperor tops the column, which lies about 1¼ miles out the N1. It can be visited daily from 9am to noon and 2 to 6pm; in winter and on Tuesday during October it closes at 4pm. Admission is 18 F ($3.20) for adults, 5 F (90¢) for children.

In World War II Boulogne was one of the most bombed and damaged cities along the English Channel, but it has been impressively rebuilt. The port's old or upper town, **Haute Ville,** is worth exploring, as it is enclosed by 13th-century ramparts and four gateways that miraculously escaped the bombs of 20th-century war. The **Hôtel de Ville** was constructed in the upper town in 1734, but its 155-foot-high belfry is from the 13th and 17th centuries. The old citadel has a certain medieval charm, and it was known to both Charles Dickens and Sir Arthur Conan Doyle, who each lived in Boulogne for a short time.

The town has memorials to both Gen. John J. Pershing, who landed here as the head of the American Expeditionary Force of World War I, and the late President John F. Kennedy.

The principal church of Boulogne is the **Basilica of Notre-Dame,** 2, Parvis-Notre-Dame (tel. 21-80-44-04). It was built from 1827 to 1866 in the neoclassic style, with a dome. It has an 11th-century crypt, all that is left from the original church that stood on this spot. The crypt is open Tuesday through Sunday from 2 to 5pm. Admission to the crypt is 12 F ($2.10) for adults, 6 F ($1) for children.

In addition, the port of Boulogne has some good beaches nearby, and even boasts a casino, offering an indoor swimming pool and miniature golf.

WHERE TO STAY

IBIS, bd. Diderot, 62200 Boulogne-sur-Mer. Tel. 21-30-12-40. Fax 21-87-48-98. 80 rms (all with bath). TEL
$ Rates: 275 F ($49.50) single; 305 F ($54.90) double. Breakfast 32 F ($5.70) extra. MC, V.
A member of a nationwide hotel chain, the Ibis offers simple, comfortable rooms with functional furniture. Its informal restaurant offers fixed-price meals reasonably priced at 65 F ($11.70) and 83 F ($14.90). Ibis is conveniently located near the port, the train station, and the ferryboat dock.

METROPOLE, 51, rue Thiers, 62200 Boulogne-sur-Mer. Tel. 21-31-54-30. Fax 21-30-45-72. 25 rms (all with bath). TV TEL
$ Rates: 310 F ($55.80) single; 390 F ($70.20) double. Breakfast 40 F ($7.20) extra. AE, MC, V.
Although it's far from luxurious, the Metropole, located in the center of the port, is considered the best hotel in Boulogne. Rooms are comfortably furnished, 10 with minibars. Breakfast is the only meal served.

WHERE TO DINE

LE LIEGEOISE, 10, rue Monsigny. Tel. 21-31-61-15.
Cuisine: FRENCH. **Reservations:** Required.
$ Prices: Appetizers 65–115 F ($11.70–$20.70); main dishes 95–155 F ($17.10–$27.90); fixed-price menus 160 F ($28.80), 210 F ($37.80), and 310 F ($55.80). DC, MC, V.
Open: Lunch Thurs–Tues noon–2:30pm; dinner Mon–Tues and Thurs–Sat 7–9:30pm. **Closed:** July 26–Aug 9.
The chef at La Liègeoise, Alain Delpierre, was trained at one of Lille's best

restaurants, and he changes the menu frequently, based on whatever is available at the local markets. Specialties include braised brill in mustard sauce, Boulogne-style cucumber soup, salmon salad, foie gras of duckling, and turbot stuffed with mussels.

LA MATELOTE, 80, bd. Ste-Beuve. Tel. 21-30-17-97.
   Cuisine: FRENCH. **Reservations:** Required.
$ **Prices:** Appetizers 86–120 F ($15.40–$21.60); main dishes 110–135 F ($19.80–$24.30); fixed-price menus 160 F ($28.80), 210 F ($37.80), and 345 F ($62.10). MC, V.
   Open: Lunch daily noon–2pm; dinner Mon–Sat 7:30–10pm. **Closed:** Dec 23–Jan 15.

⭐ This modern, sunny restaurant is the best restaurant in Boulogne. Chef Tony Lestienne makes a warm salmon salad that's a local favorite. Other specialties include oyster-and-winkle soup, turbot cooked in a court bouillon, and delectable grilled crayfish. My favorite dessert is a sugared apple tart with apricot essence.

NEARBY ACCOMMODATIONS & DINING

You can drive to Wimereux, about 3½ miles north of Boulogne, along the CD940.

HOTEL ATLANTIC, Digue de Mer, 62930 Wimereux. Tel. 21-32-41-01.
   Fax 21-87-46-17. 11 rms (all with bath). TV TEL
$ **Rates:** 270–350 F ($48.60–$63) single; 320–400 F ($57.60–$72) double. Breakfast 35 F ($6.30) extra. V. **Parking:** Free. **Closed:** Dec–Feb.
The Hôtel Atlantic offers comfortably furnished bedrooms overlooking the beach. On the premises is an excellent restaurant offering elaborately prepared dishes—but not so elaborately that the natural taste has been destroyed. I recently started a meal with an omelet made with fresh crab, then followed that with trout and sea bass in the beurre-blanc sauce that is so acclaimed in the Loire Valley. The chef also does a superb turbot pâté in gelatin and a lobster salad with truffles and celeriac. Only the best-tasting sole and lobster are sold here. Fixed-price meals run 110–190 F ($19.80–$34.20). The restaurant is open Tuesday through Sunday from noon to 2:30pm and 7 to 9:30pm; in July and August it's open daily.

10. LE TOUQUET–PARIS-PLAGE

GETTING THERE   By Car-Ferry   The airport provides car-ferry service to and from Lydd, near Hythe, in England; the trip takes 20 minutes.

By Train and Bus   There is train service to nearby Etaples, where you can take a bus to Le Touquet–Paris-Plage.

ESSENTIALS   Orientation   The centerpiece of this resort is the casino and the adjacent Palais de l'Europe, located about a quarter of a mile inland from the beachfront facing the English Channel.

Information   The Office de Tourisme is in the Palais de l'Europe (tel. 21-05-21-65).

Stretched out along the English Channel are many French resort towns, in all shapes and sizes and of distinctively different character. The most fashionable and the best equipped of all these is Le Touquet–Paris-Plage, just south of Boulogne. In addition to a very good golf course, the resort has a casino, the **Casino de la Plage,** and a sandy beach that stretches for 1½ miles. There is as well a racetrack near the Canache River. All this helps to explain why Le Touquet–Paris-Plage was known as the "playground of kings" in the days before World War II.

WHERE TO STAY

LE MANOIR, av. du Golf, 62520 Le Touquet. Tel. 21-05-20-22. Fax 21-05-31-26. 41 rms (all with bath). TV TEL
$ Rates: 730 F ($131.40) single; 1,110 F ($199.80) double. Half-board 650–745 F ($117–$134.10) per person. AE, MC, V. **Parking:** Free.

Le Manoir looks like an English manor house with its steep gables, prominent chimneys, and thick ivy. But inside, the allure of this tranquil retreat is unreservedly French. It lies within the forest of Le Touquet and attracts Parisians on the weekend. Rooms are luxuriously furnished with a conservative decor. In addition to regular hotel rooms, there are six outlying bungalows. The hotel offers a heated outdoor swimming pool and an 18-hole golf course; tennis courts and the largest horseback-riding center in the north of France are nearby.

NOVOTEL THALASSA, Front de Mer, 62520 Le Touquet. Tel. 21-09-85-00. Fax 21-09-85-10. 146 rms (all with bath), 3 suites. MINIBAR TV TEL
$ Rates: 450–540 F ($81–$97.20) single; 500–610 F ($90–$109.80) double; 950 F ($171) suite. Breakfast 55 F ($9.90) extra. AE, DC, MC, V. **Parking:** 50 F ($9).

Set about a 20-minute walk south of Touquet's commercial center, between the sea and a heath-studded expanse of sand dunes, this hotel was built in an upscale chain-hotel format in the 1980s. It's the better of two hotels linked architecturally to a spa facility, where seawater, massage, and relaxation therapies are available to stressed-out urbanites looking for a cure. Bedrooms are sunny, modern, and monochromatic, with views overlooking either the sea or the dunes, and sometimes with private balconies. Fixed-price menus are available for 145 F ($26.10) each, in a modern restaurant with big windows overlooking the sea. The restaurant remains open throughout most of every afternoon for anyone wanting midafternoon coffee or tea.

WESTMINSTER HOTEL, av. du Verger, 62520 Le Touquet. Tel. 21-05-48-48. Fax 21-05-45-45. 115 rms (all with bath), 2 suites. MINIBAR TV TEL
$ Rates: 600–980 F ($108–$176.40) single; 750–1,150 F ($135–$207) double; from 1,800 F ($324) suite. Breakfast 70 F ($12.60) extra. AE, DC, MC, V. **Parking:** Free.

This antique palace near the casino has long been a favorite of the British, and now it's open year-round. Rooms, which have views of either the forest or a small estuary of the Canache, are beautifully maintained and have many amenities. For recreation, the hotel offers a heated covered pool, a sauna, a Jacuzzi, a solarium, and a snooker room. The deluxe hotel has two well-run restaurants, one providing light meals and the other offering gastronomic menus for 250–350 F ($45–$63).

WHERE TO DINE

FLAVIO-CLUB DE LA FORET, 1-2, av. du Verger. Tel. 21-05-10-22.
Cuisine: FRENCH. **Reservations:** Required.
$ Prices: Appetizers 95–160 F ($17.10–$28.80); main dishes 160–280 F ($28.80–$50.40); fixed-price menus 150 F ($27), 250 F ($45), 420 F ($75.60), and 720 F ($129.60). AE, DC, MC, V.
Open: Lunch Thurs–Tues 12:30–2pm; dinner Thurs–Mon 7–9:30pm. **Closed:** Jan–Feb.

The best food to be had is near the casino and the Westminster Hôtel, recommended above. The cuisine of Guy Delmotte is inventive and modern; the menu includes steamed fresh salmon, a bass served with crispy vegetables, and a savory stew of red mullet with cucumbers. His mousseline of lobster and salmon is available from mid-May to mid-October, and his grilled lobster with tarragon butter is delicious but expensive. He is also known for his excellent foie gras made with livers from Les Landes in southwestern France. For dessert, try the salad of strawberries and rhubarb with Bouzy from the champagne country—it's spectacular!

LE JARDIN COTE DE LA MER, 7, bd. Dr-Jules-Pouget. Tel. 21-05-22-55.
Cuisine: SEAFOOD. **Reservations:** Recommended.

\$ Prices: Appetizers 38–88 F (\$6.80–\$15.80); main dishes 43–175 F (\$7.70–\$31.50); fixed-price menus 88–139 F (\$15.80–\$25). AE, DC, V.

Open: Lunch Tues–Sun noon–2pm; dinner Tues–Sat 7:30–10pm.

Your best dining value can be found in this comfortable dining room, which extends into a covered terrace ideal for warm-weather meals. Specialties are fish and shellfish, which are always fresh, prepared to order, and never too dry. The menu depends on the catch of the day. For a main course, try the monkfish with fennel, the roast crayfish, or sea bass Agadir style.

CHAPTER 17
ALSACE-LORRAINE & THE VOSGES

Old Germans still speak of it as "the lost provinces," a reference to Alsace-Lorraine, whose ancient capitals are Strasbourg and Nancy. Alsace, for example, has been called "the least French of French provinces," perhaps more reminiscent of the Black Forest facing it across the Rhine.

This territory has been much disputed by Germany and France. In fact it became German from 1870 until after World War I, and again, it was ruled by Hitler from 1940 to 1944. But now both of the old provinces are happily back under French control, although they are somewhat independent, remembering the days when they ruled themselves.

In the Vosges you can follow the Crest Road or skirt along the foothills, visiting the wine towns of Alsace.

In its old cities and cathedrals, the castle-dotted landscape evokes memories of a great past, and in battle monuments or scars, sometimes of military glory or defeat. Lorraine is Joan of Arc country too, and many of its towns still suggest their heritage from the Middle Ages.

SEEING ALSACE-LORRAINE

If you want to explore Alsace at its best, go any time from early May until October.

GETTING THERE   By Plane   The fastest way to go is on Air Inter, which has six 60-minute flights daily from Orly Airport in Paris to Strasbourg.

By Train   Figure on about 4½ hours from Gare de l'Est in Paris to Strasbourg, with 10 departures daily. You can reach Colmar by rail, with about 14 trains a day departing from Gare de l'Est, Paris.

By Car   In Strasbourg and Colmar, you can rent a car at the rail station or airport. Frankly, the only way to explore the region in any depth—especially the Wine Road of Alsace—is by car.

By Public Transportation   If you're limited to public transportation, you may want to confine your visit to Strasbourg and Colmar because of their superior transportation networks.

A SUGGESTED ROUTE   If you're touring Alsace, allow at least a day in each major town on the grand wine route of eastern France: Strasbourg (Day 1), Colmar (Day 2), and Mulhouse (Day 3). The final day (Day 4) could be spent exploring the Wine Road of Alsace.

Lorraine's canal network is particularly extensive, with 435 miles of waterways, including the Marne-Rhine Canal and the Moselle. A journey through this region might begin with an overnight stop in Verdun (Day 1) with a tour of its battlefields. Then the historic city of Metz (Day 2) for another overnight, and Nancy (Day 3),

WHAT'S SPECIAL ABOUT ALSACE-LORRAINE

Great Towns/Villages
☐ Nancy, capital of old Lorraine, full of serene beauty, history, and tradition.
☐ Strasbourg, capital of Alsace and one of the great cities of France (also capital of pâté de foie gras).
☐ Colmar, one of the gems of Alsace, filled with medieval and Renaissance buildings.

Ancient Monuments
☐ Strasbourg Cathedral, an outstanding example of French Gothic architecture.
☐ Cathédrale de St-Etienne at Metz, begun in 1240 in high-soaring Gothic style, with stained-glass windows by Chagall.

Architectural Highlights
☐ Place Stanislas in Nancy, which some critics claim is the grandest square in the world.
☐ Palais Rohan at Strasbourg, a palace from 1732, one of the crowning design achievements in eastern France.

Outstanding Museums
☐ Musée d'Unterlinden, acclaimed for an immense altar screen, the Issenheim Altarpiece.
☐ Musée de l'Automobile at Mulhouse, the greatest automobile museum in the world.

Wine Routes/Scenic Drives
☐ The Wine Road of Alsace, 60 miles through charming villages illuminated on summer nights, past medieval towers, feudal ruins, and acres of vineyards.
☐ The Crest Road, running 150 miles, cutting through the Vosges mountain range.

Battlefields
☐ A tour of Circuit des Forts, outside Verdun, which evokes the bloodiest fighting of World War I.

Pilgrimage Sites
☐ Domrémy-la-Pucelle, the little hamlet that gave the world Joan of Arc.

followed by pilgrimages to Domrémy-la-Pucelle, birthplace of Joan of Arc, and a cross-country drive to Luneville and Baccarat, of crystal fame.

Those with a fifth night might drive southeast through the Vosges mountains to Mulhouse. From there, instead of going back to Paris, you can easily drive to the airport Mulhouse shares with the Swiss city of Basel.

1. VERDUN

162 miles E of Paris, 41 miles W of Metz

GETTING THERE   By Train   Four trains (sometimes fewer) arrive from Paris's Gare de l'Est daily, after a transfer at Châlons-sur-Marne. Several daily trains also arrive from Metz, after a change at Conflans.

By Car   Driving is easy since Verdun is several miles north of the Paris–Strasbourg autoroute (the A4).

ESSENTIALS   Orientation   Built on both banks of the Meuse and intersected by a complicated series of canals, Verdun's oldest section is the Ville Haute, on the east bank, which includes the cathedral and the episcopal palace. Most visitors, however, come to see the infamous battlefields of World War I, some of which lie two miles east of the town center, off the N3 highway toward Metz.

Information   The Office de Tourisme, place de la Nation, 55100 Verdun (tel. 29-86-14-18), is closed from mid-December to mid-January.

At this garrison town in eastern France Maréchal Pétain said, "They shall not pass!"—and they didn't. Verdun, where the Allies held out against a massive assault by the German army in World War I, evokes tin-helmeted soldiers in *All Quiet on the Western Front*. In the closing years of World War I an estimated 600,000 to 800,000 French and German soldiers died battling over a few miles of territory.

Today stone houses clustered on narrow, cobblestone streets give Verdun a medieval appearance. It lies on the muddy Meuse between Paris and the Rhine. Two monuments commemorate these tragic events: Rodin's *Defense* and Boucher's *To Victory and the Dead.*

A tour of the battlefields is called **Circuit des Forts,** covering the main fortifications. On the right bank of the Meuse, this is a good 20-mile run, taking in **Fort Vaux,** where Raynal staged his heroic defense after sending his last message by carrier pigeon. After passing a vast French cemetery of 16,000 graves, an endless field of crosses, you arrive at the **Ossuaire de Douaumont.** Here, the bones of those killed in battle—literally blown to bits—were embedded. Nearby at the mostly underground **Fort de Douaumont** the "hell of Verdun" was unleashed. From the roof you can look out at a vast field of corroded tops of "pillboxes." Then on to the **Trench of Bayonets.** Bayonets of French soldiers instantly entombed by a shellburst form this unique memorial.

The other tour, the **Circuit Rive Gauche,** is about a 60-mile run and takes in the **Hill of Montfaucon,** where the Americans erected a memorial tower, and the **American Cemetery at Romagne,** with some 15,000 graves.

WHERE TO STAY

LE COQ HARDI, 8, av. de la Victoire, 55100 Verdun. Tel. 29-86-36-36.
Fax 29-86-09-21. 40 rms (30 with bath or shower), 5 suites. TV TEL
$ Rates: 380–520 F ($68.40–$93.60) single with bath or shower; 220 F ($39.60) double without bath; 390–650 F ($70.20–$117) double with bath; from 900 F ($162) suite. Breakfast 50 F ($9) extra. AE, DC, MC, V. **Parking:** 50 F ($9).
Le Coq Hardi is my favorite hotel in Verdun. It's composed of four attached 18th-century houses, centrally located near the riverbanks of the Meuse. The stone interior contains church pews and antiques, as well as a Renaissance fireplace crowned with a salamander, symbolizing François I. The dining room serves the best food in town (see "Where to Dine," below).

HOTEL BELLEVUE, 1, Rond-point du Maréchal-de-Lattre-de-Tassigny, 55100 Verdun. Tel. 29-84-39-41. Fax 29-86-09-21. 72 rms (51 with bath), 1 suite. TV TEL
$ Rates: 170 F ($30.60) single; 360 F ($64.80) double; from 650 F ($117) suite. Breakfast 38 F ($6.80) extra. AE, DC, MC, V. **Parking:** Free. **Closed:** Mid-Oct to Easter.
Located across from the botanical gardens, the Hôtel Bellevue is a family-run hotel with a wrought-iron and glass canopy covering the formal entrance. A side courtyard displays a small cherub carving. The rooms are comfortable, and the hotel's restaurant is known for its wine cellar, with some vintages dating from the 19th century. Only dinner is served, usually starting at 115 F ($20.70).

HOTEL DE LA POSTE ET RESTAURANT PERGOLA, 8, av. Douaumont, 55100 Verdun. Tel. 29-86-03-90. TEL
$ Rates: 125 F ($22.50) single; 200 F ($36) double. Breakfast 35 F ($6.30) extra. MC, V. **Closed:** Jan 20–Mar 15.
⑤ The Hôtel de la Poste is a member of Logis de France, a nonprofit national association that offers financial support to innkeepers who preserve the regional characteristics of their establishments. At the Hôtel de la Poste, well-equipped accommodations contain spacious closets, writing tables, and, in some cases, sofas. A continental breakfast is available from room service. La Pergola restaurant offers fine

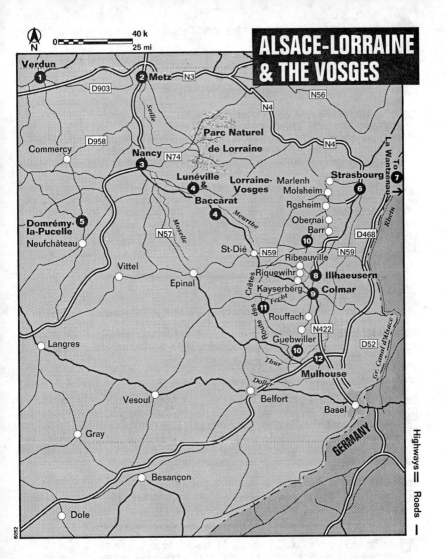

ALSACE-LORRAINE & THE VOSGES

N

0 ⌐40 k
⌐25 mi

Verdun ①

Metz ② N3

D903

N56

N4

D958

Parc Naturel

Commercy

de Lorraine

Nancy ③ N74

N4

Lunéville ④ **Strasbourg** ⑥

& Vosges Marlenh

Baccarat Molsheim

④ Rosheim

Domrémy- ⑤

la-Pucelle Obernai

Neufchâteau Barr

N57 ⑩ D468

St-Dié N59 N59

Vittel Ribeauville

Riquewihr

Epinal ⑧ **Illhaeusern**

Kayserberg ⑨ **Colmar**

⑪ Rouffach

Langres N422

Guebwiller D52

⑩ ⑫

Mulhouse

Vesoul Belfort

Gray Basel

GERMANY

Besançon

Dole

Highways ═ Roads ▬

PARIS

Alsace Lorraine
& The Vosges

① Verdun   ⑦ La Wantzenau

② Metz   ⑧ Illhaeusern

③ Nancy   ⑨ Colmar

④ Lunéville & Baccarat   ⑩ The Wine Road of Alsace

⑤ Domrémy-la-Pucelle   ⑪ Route des Crêtes
       (the Crest Road)

⑥ Strasbourg   ⑫ Mulhouse

dining; meals cost 90–165 F ($16.20–$29.70). The restaurant is open daily from noon to 2pm and 7 to 9:30pm.

WHERE TO DINE

LE COQ HARDI, 8, av. de la Victoire. Tel. 29-86-36-36.
   Cuisine: FRENCH. **Reservations:** Required.
$ Prices: Appetizers 65–160 F ($11.70–$28.80); main dishes 90–160 F ($16.20–$28.80); fixed price menus 195–440 F ($35.10–$79.20). AE, DC, MC, V.
   Open: Lunch Sat–Wed noon–2pm; dinner Sat–Wed 7:30–9:30pm. **Closed:** Jan.

⭐ This elegant dining room serves the best food in town. The restaurant has a painted ceiling, Louis XIII chairs with needlepoint upholstery, and two deactivated bombshells from World War I at its entrance. Menu specialties include a salade Coq Hardi with green mustard and pine nuts, duck from Challons, stuffed cabbage with turbot, a cassolette of snails in champagne, and foie gras from Landes. The hotel is the best in Verdun (see "Where to Stay," above).

2. METZ

217 miles E of Paris, 100 miles NW of Strasbourg

GETTING THERE   By Train   Metz is an important regional railway junction; many trains arrive every day from Strasbourg, Lyon, Mulhouse, and Nancy.

By Bus   Smaller towns nearby, including Verdun, are serviced by buses, which arrive at and depart from place Coislin in Metz.

ESSENTIALS   Orientation   The city was originally built on a handful of islands formed by the Moselle and the Seille Rivers. The eastern entrance to the city is appropriately named La Porte des Allemands (the Gate of the Germans). The western approach is named La rue du Pont-des-Morts (Street of the Bridge of the Dead), and one of the most central squares is place d'Armes. The most important of the town's monuments, the Cathédrale de St-Etienne, lies slightly northwest of the city center.

Information   The Office de Tourisme is on place d'Armes, 57000 Metz (tel. 87-75-65-21). It's open Monday through Friday from 9am to 7pm, on Saturday from 9am to 6:30pm, and on Sunday from 10:30am to 5pm.

Metz has had many faces. Caesar called it one of the great towns of Gaul. In time it became an important Roman city and later the cradle and heart of the Carolingian empire, until it stood alone as an independent republic before it was annexed to France. The Germans took the town in 1870, and it was ceded to them the following year, becoming the capital of Lorraine. However, it reverted to France in 1918.

Metz lies in a valley where the waters of the Moselle meet those of the Seille, forming several islands. In spite of much war damage, Metz still contains many quaint old streets, alleys, and houses. It has ten city gates still existing, two of them interesting. The **Porte des Allemands** on the eastern side of town is a castellated structure from 1445, and the **Porte Serpenoise** on the south is flanked by turrets belonging to old ramparts that once encircled Metz.

At the southwestern edge of the city is a beautiful terrace, known as the **Esplanade,** which commands a view of the Moselle Valley. It's a fashionable place for promenading as in olden days, following in the footsteps of the poet Paul Verlaine, who was born here.

The **Cathédrale St-Etienne,** place d'Armes (tel. 87-75-54-61), with its two tall spires, is among the greatest in France. Begun in 1240, it was finished in 1520 in yellow limestone. Along with those at Amiens and Beauvais, its 140-foot-tall nave is a daring example of high-soaring Gothic art. In fact, with its slender columns and flying buttresses the cathedral belongs to the second period of the Gothic style.

Go here to see its magnificent stained-glass windows, some by Marc Chagall, others from the 13th century. Perhaps you'll arrive on a clear day and can appreciate why the edifice has been called "the very apotheosis of light."

Ask permission to see the treasury, which contains what is reputed to be the cloak of Charlemagne, with its Byzantine embroidery and incrustation.

The cathedral is open from May through September, daily from 9:15am to 6:45pm; October through April, daily from 9:30am to noon and 2 to 5pm. You can visit its Tour de Mutte (Tower of Mutte) for 10 F ($1.80), its interior for 5 F (90¢), and its crypt and treasury for 12 F ($2.20).

Next to the cathedral, the **Musée d'Art et d'Histoire,** 2, rue du Haut-Poirier (tel. 87-75-10-18), part of which is housed in the old Roman baths, has a splendid Gallo-Roman collection. See, in particular, a cluster of funeral and votive sculpture which was unearthed in the foundations of the building. The other part of the complex is occupied by the **La Cour d'Or,** which has some impressive works by Dutch masters of the 17th century and some fine French portraits, including Nattier's *Young Woman,* plus works by Delacroix and Corot.

Entrance to both museums is 15 F ($2.70) for adults and 7.50 F ($1.40) for children. They are open Wednesday through Monday from 10am to noon and 2 to 6pm (to 5pm off-season).

The **Church of St-Pierre-aux-Nonnains** is said to be the oldest church in France, with one wall dating from the 4th century. Records say that the original church was incorporated into a Benedictine abbey in the 7th century. The best-preserved section is the 10th-century nave, which has been restored. Archeological excavations have uncovered the foundations of a 4th-century building to one side, which might have been used as a baptistery or more likely (the experts are uncertain) as a private bath during the last days of the Roman Empire.

The church is open April to September, Tuesday through Saturday, from 2 to 7pm; off-season, on Saturday and Sunday from 2 to 6pm. Admission is 10 F ($1.80).

Near the church is a cultural complex, **Arsenal** (call for more information, tel. 87-39-92-00). It's a center for music, dance, and the arts, including a restaurant, two concert halls, and an exhibition hall.

WHERE TO STAY

HOTEL METROPOLE, 5, place du Général-de-Gaulle, 57000 Metz. Tel. 87-66-26-22. Fax 87-66-29-91. 80 rms (63 with bath). TEL **Bus:** 5, 9, or 25.

$ Rates: 205 F ($36.90) double without bath. 220 F ($39.60) double with bath. Breakfast 23 F ($4.10) extra. AE, MC, V.

The Hôtel Metropole, right across from the train station, is a turn-of-the-century structure with well-furnished bedrooms, each a double. Some are more up-to-date than others, but each is still comfortable and well maintained. Breakfast is the only meal served.

HOTEL ROYAL CONCORDE, 23, av. Foch, 57000 Metz. Tel. 87-66-81-11. Fax 87-56-13-16. 75 rms (all with bath), 11 suites. MINIBAR TV TEL

$ Rates: 520 F ($93.60) single; 600 F ($108) double; from 800 F ($144) suite. Breakfast 65 F ($11.70) extra. AE, DC, MC, V.

Located across from the train station in the center of town, the Royal Concorde's 1906 stone facade looks like a mixture of Romanesque and art nouveau. Most of the rooms are contemporary, although several offer copies of cabriole-legged beds and armchairs, with flocked wallpaper and deluxe accessories. Beamed ceilings run throughout the public rooms; the bar in the basement has exposed stone, and the sitting room has copies of Louis XIII furniture.

Guests can dine in the art deco Royal Restaurant or enjoy regional dishes in Le Caveau. Dinner in the Royal Restaurant costs around 220 F ($39.60); a meal at Le Caveau costs 160 F ($28.80).

NOVOTEL, place des Paraiges, 57000 Metz. Tel. 87-37-38-39. Fax 87-36-10-00. 117 rms (all with bath), 3 suites. A/C MINIBAR TV TEL **Bus:** 5, 9, or 25.

$ Rates: 480 F ($86.40) single; 520 F ($93.60) double; from 820 F ($147.60) suite. Breakfast 49 F ($8.80) extra. AE, DC, MC, V. **Parking:** 30 F ($5.40).

Centrally located at the Centre St-Jacques, the Novotel is the best place to stay in Metz. Formerly a Sofitel, it came under the Novotel banner in 1988. Within walking distance of many of the attractions, the well-run and streamlined hotel has lots of amenities and facilities, including a swimming pool. The hotel operates a grill, open from 6am to midnight. Meals begin at 150 F ($27).

WHERE TO DINE

In addition to the hotel restaurants mentioned above, I recommend the following:

A LA VILLE DE LYON, 7, rue des Piques. Tel. 87-36-07-01.
   Cuisine: FRENCH. **Reservations:** Required. **Bus:** 5, 9, or 25.
$ Prices: Appetizers 65–115 F ($11.70–$20.70); main dishes 90–150 F ($16.20–$27); fixed-price menus 100–290 F ($18–$52.20). AE, DC, MC, V.
   Open: Lunch Tues–Sun 11:45am–2pm; dinner Tues–Sat 7–10pm. **Closed:** July 27–Aug 25.

One of the most unusual restaurants in the region lies in the heart of the historic center of Metz, beneath the soaring ogival vaults of what was originally built during the 14th century as a chapel. Functioning as one of the most famous restaurants in Metz since 1880, it has attracted a regular clientele of Lyon-born diners who appreciated its conservative cuisine and who eventually gave it its present name. Classified as a historic monument by the French government, the restaurant serves such dishes as zander with cumin sauce, pigeon with bordeaux wine, salmon in anise, and tournedos Rossini with foie gras.

LA DINANDERIE, 2, rue de Paris. Tel. 87-30-14-40.
   Cuisine: FRENCH. **Reservations:** Required.
$ Prices: Appetizers 75–125 F ($13.50–$22.50); main dishes 105–170 F ($18.90–$30.60); fixed-price menus 170 F ($30.60), 240 F ($43.20), and 350 F ($63). AE, MC, V.
   Open: Lunch Tues–Sat 11:45am–2pm; dinner Tues–Sat 6:45–9:45pm. **Closed:** Feb and Aug 10–31.

This place lies within a 10-minute walk north of the cathedral, on the outskirts of town, and was built during the 17th century as housing for army officers. La Dinanderie is a sophisticated restaurant where Claude Piergiorgi concocts such specialties as ravioli with crayfish, filet of red mullet in vinaigrette, filet of beef with marrow, and foie gras. The cuisine is based on fresh market ingredients.

3. NANCY

230 miles SE of Paris, 92 miles W of Strasbourg

GETTING THERE   By Train   Trains arrive frequently from Paris's Gare de l'Est and from Strasbourg and Dijon.

ESSENTIALS   Orientation   The city was originally built around a fortified castle on a rock in the swampland near the Meurthe River. The important canal a few blocks east of the historic center connects the Marne to the Rhine. In the city's heart is its most visible monument, place Stanislas. Within a brisk walk in three directions, large inner-city parks and gardens provide lots of breathing space.

Information The Office de Tourisme is located at 14, place Stanislas (tel. 83-35-22-41).

In the northeastern corner of France, about 230 miles from Paris, Nancy was the capital of old Lorraine. On the Muerthe River, it is serenely beautiful, with a historical tradition, a cuisine, and an architecture all its own. It was once the rival of Paris as a center for art nouveau. Nancy has a kind of triple face: the medieval alleys and towers around the old Ducal Palace where Charles II received Joan of Arc, the golden gates and frivolous fountains of the rococo period, and the constantly spreading modern sections with their widely known university and industry.

WHAT TO SEE & DO
A Stroll Through the City

The heartbeat of the city, however, is the **Place Stanislas,** to which you may want to head first. It was named for Stanislas Leczinski, the last of the dukes of Lorraine, the ex-king of Poland, and the father-in-law of Louis XV. Stanislas turned Nancy into one of the palatial cities of Europe. The square stands between the two major sectors of the city—the **Ville-Vieille** in the northwest, with its narrow, winding streets, and the **Ville-Neuve** in the southeast, dating from the 16th and 18th centuries when the streets were made broad and straight.

Imposing buildings rise on all sides of the Place Stanislas, which was laid out in 1752–1760 to the designs of Emmanuel Héré. The ironwork gates of the square are magnificent. The grilles stand at each of the four corners, and two enclose fountains, the Neptune and the Amphitrite.

The most imposing building on the square is the **Hôtel de Ville.** See its magnificent inner staircase and the 80-foot-long, forged-iron balustrade with a handrail in a single piece, the masterpiece of Jean Lamour, who designed the screens and fountains of the square.

On the eastern side, the **Musée des Beaux-Arts** (see below).

The **Arc de Triomphe,** constructed in 1754–1756 by Stanislas to honor Louis XV, brings you to the long rectangular **Place de la Carrière,** a beautiful, tree-lined promenade leading to the **Palais du Gouvernement,** built in 1760.

This governmental palace adjoins the already mentioned **Ducal Palace,** built in 1502 in the Gothic style with flamboyant balconies. The much-restored palace contains the **Musée Lorrain** (see below).

Alongside the Ducal Palace stands the **Church of Cordeliers** with its round chapel based on a design for the Medici in Florence (see below).

The **Musee de l'Ecole de Nancy,** 38, rue Sergent-Blandan, attracts art nouveau devotees from all over the world (see below).

Finally a short walk from this art museum leads to the **Porte de la Craffe,** the oldest building in Nancy, dating from 1360. The interior was a prison during the Revolution and may be visited July to mid-September, Wednesday through Monday from 10am to noon and 2 to 6pm. Admission is 8 F ($1.40).

More Attractions

CHURCH OF THE CORDELIERS, 66, Grande Rue. Tel. 83-35-26-03.
The Church of the Cordeliers, with a round chapel based on a design for the Medici in Florence, contains the burial monuments of the dukes of Lorraine. The two most notable are those of René II (1509) by Mansuy Gauvain and the duke's second wife, Philippa of Gueldres, by Ligier Richier. The octagonal ducal chapel, built in 1607, holds the baroque sarcophagi. The convent houses the Musée des Arts et Traditions Populaires, which has a collection of antiques, porcelain, and reconstructed interiors of regional maisons.
Admission: 10 F ($1.80) adults, 7 F ($1.30) children.
Open: Mon–Sat 10am–noon and 2–5pm, Sun 10am–noon and 2–6pm.

MUSEE DE L'ECOLE DE NANCY, 38, rue Sergent-Blandan. Tel. 83-40-14-86.

Appropriately housed in a stunning turn-of-the-century building, this museum attracts art nouveau devotees from all over the world. Here you can see the work of Emile Gallé, the greatest artist of the Nancy style. See, in particular, Gallé's celebrated "Dawn and Dusk" bed and, my favorite, the well-known "mushroom lamp." Works by Eugène Vallin, another outstanding artist, are also on display.

Admission: 20 F ($3.60) adults, 15 F ($2.70) children.

Open: Apr–Sept, Wed–Mon 10am–noon and 2–6pm; Oct–Mar, Wed–Mon 10am–noon and 2–5pm.

MUSEE DES BEAUX-ARTS, 3, place Stanislas. Tel. 83-85-30-72.

Built in the 1700s, the Musée des Beaux-Arts contains one of Manet's most remarkable portraits, plus works by Delacroix, Dufy, Utrillo, Bonnard, Modigliani, Boucher, and Rubens. The Italian artists, such as Perugino, Caravaggio, Ribera, and Tintoretto, also are represented, as is Claude Gellée, who changed his name to Lorrain. In addition to the paintings, the museum exhibits Daum crystal vases and lamps.

Admission: 20 F ($3.60) adults, free for children.

Open: Wed–Sun 10:30am–6pm, Mon 1:30–5:45pm.

MUSEE LORRAIN, in the Ducal Palace, 64, Grande Rue. Tel. 83-32-18-74.

Housed in the Ducal Palace, the Musée Lorrain is one of the great museums of France; it depicts close to 2,000 years of European history. The first floor devotes an entire room to the work of Jacques Callot, the noted engraver who was born in Nancy in 1592. The Galerie des Cerfs displays excellent tapestries, including the first French flag, representing the reign of Henri II. There is a comprehensive collection of 17th-century Lorraine masterpieces, from when the duchy was known as a cultural center. The museum also has three pictures by Georges de La Tour, as well as a room portraying Jewish history in eastern France. Wrought ironwork, antiques, chinaware, glassware, costumes, and pharmaceutical items are on display as well.

Admission: 20 F ($3.60) adults, 15 F ($2.70) children.

Open: Wed–Mon 10am–noon and 2–5pm.

WHERE TO STAY

ALBERT 1ER–ASTORIA, 3, rue de l'Armée-Patton, 54000 Nancy. Tel. 83-40-31-24. Fax 83-28-47-78. 126 rms (120 with bath or shower). TV TEL

$ Rates: 285 F ($51.30) single or double without bath or shower, 400 F ($72) single or double with bath or shower. Breakfast 30 F ($5.40) extra. AE, DC, MC, V.

Parking: 30 F ($5.40).

The centrally located Albert 1er–Astoria contains an interior garden, a solarium, a sauna, and an English bar called L'Astor. Located across from the railway station, the well-equipped hotel is run in a businesslike manner, and the bedrooms are soberly furnished with built-in units.

GRAND HOTEL DE LA REINE, 2, place Stanislas, 54000 Nancy. Tel. 83-35-03-01, or toll free 800/777-4182 in the U.S. and Canada. Fax 83-32-86-04. 48 rms (all with bath), 7 suites.

$ Rates: 600 F ($108) single; 730–1,350 F ($131.40–$243) double; 2,000 F ($360) suite. Breakfast 75 F ($13.50) extra. AE, DC, MC, V.

In the center of the city, this 18th-century mansion opens onto one of the great squares of France. This is an exceptional residence, offering classically designed bedrooms, with draped testers over the beds, Venetian-style chandeliers, and gilt-framed mirrors; the bathrooms, however, have been modernized. The salons are decorated with antique wainscoting, and there is a grand stairway. The restaurant, called the Stanislas, serves both classic and modern dishes, and the waiters are formal and considerate. Meals cost 230–410 F ($41.40–$73.80).

HOTEL CHOLEY, 28, rue Gustave-Simon, 54000 Nancy. Tel. 83-32-31-98. Fax 83-37-47-73. 20 rms (8 with bath).

$ Rates: 140 F ($25.20) single or double without bath; 230–280 F ($41.40–$50.40) double with bath. Extra bed in room 45 F ($8.10) per person. Breakfast 30 F ($5.40) extra. MC, V.

This unusual hotel is worth looking into before you head to the more expensive hotels in Nancy. It is the domain of an Alsatian family whose ancestors escaped to Lorraine in 1875 to avoid living under German occupation. Today the third generation of the Choley family lives in this early 18th-century building, which they have transformed into a kind of rustic folk-art museum. Each of the bedrooms is different, often with turn-of-the-century antiques, fresh wallpaper, and wood structures. There is an ornate billiard table that was rescued from World War II bombings and a collection of old musical instruments surrounding the stone fireplace in the public room.

The restaurant's nine dining room tables are centered around a magnificent pair of sideboards (ca. 1900) made by a Nancy cabinetmaker, Majorelle, whose works are considered among the most valuable of their period. The well-prepared cuisine is described by the Choleys as "family style." The fixed-price menu costs 140–160 F ($25.20–$28.80).

MERCURE ALTEA THIERS, 11, rue Raymond-Poincaré, 54000 Nancy. Tel. 83-39-75-75. Fax 83-32-78-17. 178 rms (all with bath). MINIBAR TV TEL

$ Rates: 475 F ($85.50) single; 625 F ($112.50) double. Breakfast 52 F ($9.40) extra. AE, DC, MC, V.

The Mercure Altéa Thiers is an efficient, streamlined hotel for executives and tourists alike. The rooms are first class, and its restaurant, La Toison d'Or, offers excellent dishes. The hotel also operates a popular brasserie.

WHERE TO DINE

CAFE FOY, 1, place Stanislas. Tel. 83-32-21-44.
   Cuisine: FRENCH. **Reservations:** Recommended.
$ Prices: Appetizers 45–85 F ($8.10–$15.30); main dishes 85–145 F ($15.30–$26.10); fixed-price menus 120 F ($21.60), 150 F ($27), and 185 F ($33.30). V.
   Open: Lunch Thurs–Tues noon–2pm; dinner Thurs–Tues 7–9:30pm. **Closed:** Jan.

A Regency room with ornate ceilings, crystal chandeliers, marble- and brass-trimmed floors, and enormous windows overlooking the square, the Café Foy is the most prominent café in town. In summer the outdoor tables offer the best view of the square; also, the atmosphere becomes more formal, and string music is sometimes played. Off-season, the clientele is blue collar. If you're interested in more than a drink, the Restaurant Le Foy upstairs is accessible by a separate staircase opening directly onto the square.

LE CAPUCIN GOURMAND, 31, rue Gambetta. Tel. 83-35-26-98.
   Cuisine: FRENCH. **Reservations:** Required.
$ Prices: Appetizers 75–125 F ($13.50–$22.50); main dishes 120–225 F ($21.60–$40.50). AE, V.
   Open: Lunch Tues–Sun 12:30–2pm; dinner Tues–Sat 7:30–10pm. **Closed:** Aug 1–16.

In an old house near place Stanislas, Gérard Veissière treats his guests to excellent service and regional cuisine that is favored by visiting connoisseurs. In homage to Nancy's art nouveau tradition, the restaurant, in an old house, integrates Gallé and Daum glass with Louis Majorelle furniture. You can always order the classic quiche Lorraine here, but don't overlook the sole cooked with vermouth, the duck soup with lentils, the fresh foie gras, the pigeon casserole, or the pêche mignon du Capucin. The featured wine is Gris de Toul.

LA GENTILHOMMIERE, 29, rue des Maréchaux. Tel. 83-32-26-44.
   Cuisine: FRENCH. **Reservations:** Required.
$ **Prices:** Appetizers 70–130 F ($12.60–$23.40); main dishes 105–180 F ($18.90–$32.40); fixed-price menu 160 F ($28.80). AE, MC, V.
   Open: Lunch Mon–Fri noon–2pm; dinner Mon–Sat 7–10pm. **Closed:** Mid-Aug to early Sept.

Housed in the former residence of Victor Hugo's father, this restaurant is filled with Oriental rugs, dark-wood antiques, and two arched, tinted windows with a streetside view. The place is run by Madame Bouillier, whose meals are considered by many to be the best in Nancy. Dishes include pigeon with a garlic confit, stuffed morels, and poached eggs with lobster and a tarragon vinaigrette. The featured wine is Gris de Toul. After May, you can dine on a shaded terrace.

4. LUNEVILLE & BACCARAT

Lunéville: 208 miles SE of Paris, 22 miles SE of Nancy
Baccarat: 223 miles SE of Paris, 37 miles SE of Nancy

GETTING THERE   By Train   Both towns are connected with local train service from Nancy and Strasbourg.

ESSENTIALS   Information   In Lunéville, contact the Office de Tourisme, au Château, Lunéville (tel. 83-74-06-55). In Baccarat, the Syndicat d'Initiative is at place des Arcades, Baccarat (tel. 83-75-13-37), which is open only from June to September.

If chandeliers and decanters, along with wine glasses, evoke glamour and glitter for you and you've come this deep into Lorraine, you might spend one of the most enjoyable days of your trip to eastern France by visiting Lunéville and Baccarat.

LUNEVILLE

Lying some 21 miles from Nancy, Lunéville was a walled town in medieval days. After a decline brought on by war, plague, and famine, it rose again under the dukes of Léopold and Stanislas.

Lunéville contains factories that produce some of France's best-known porcelain, painted in patterns easily recognizable for their vivid colors and whimsical designs. For many years in the early 18th century this town was the preferred residence of Léopold, the duke of Lorraine who admired Louis XIV so much (and perhaps to flatter the Sun King) that he erected a château that in some ways, particularly the chapel, is a replica of the one at Versailles.

The **Musée du Château,** au Château (tel. 83-76-23-57) is rich in old porcelain, drawings, and paintings, as well as various military weapons. It is open Wednesday through Monday from 10am to noon and 2 to 6pm (to 5pm in winter). Admission is 10 F ($1.80).

There's also a baroque church whose construction ended around 1750, **Eglise St-Jacques.** It contains a 15th-century pietà of polychrome stone and wood panels carved into Régence detailings. The church is open daily from 8am to 5pm.

On a more recent note, automobile buffs will enjoy the more than 100 antique two- or three-wheeled vehicles, a few of which were designed with engines, displayed in the **Musée de la Moto et du Vélo,** place de la 2e D.C. (tel. 83-74-10-56). Just opposite the château, the museum is open Tuesday through Sunday from 9am to noon and 2 to 6pm; closed holidays. Admission costs 16 F ($2.90).

Shops everywhere sell modern examples of the famed dinnerware, which—if you can pack it properly—can become a treasured souvenir of your visit.

WHERE TO STAY

The Château d'Adomenil, listed under "Where to Dine," below, also has rooms for rent.

HOTEL DES PAGES, 5, quai des Petits-Bosquets, 54300 Lunéville. Tel. 83-74-11-42. Fax 83-74-11-42. 32 rms (all with bath), TV TEL
$ Rates: 200–210 F ($36–$37.80) single; 220–240 F ($39.60–$43.20) double. AE, DC, MC, V.
Built in 1973, this three-story hotel enjoys a central location beside the Château of Lunéville. Inside, comfortable rooms are simply furnished with functional furniture. There's a cost-conscious restaurant, Le Petit Comptoir, where fixed-price menus begin at 95 F ($17.10).

HOTEL OASIS, 3, av. Voltaire, 54300 Lunéville. Tel. 83-74-11-42. Fax 83-73-46-63. 32 rms (all with bath or shower). TV TEL
$ Rates: 220–255 F ($39.60–$45.90) single; 240–285 F ($43.20–$51.30) double. Breakfast 30 F ($5.40) extra. AE, DC, MC, V. **Parking:** Free.
Set about a 10-minute walk from the town center, this two-story concrete-sided hotel opened in 1990 and has been considered ever since as one of the best hotels in town. It contains a bar and breakfast room, but no restaurant. Bedrooms have modern furnishings and big windows. The hotel is owned by the same family as the Hôtel des Pages (see above), with which it shares some of its administrative functions.

WHERE TO DINE

CHATEAU D'ADOMENIL, Rehainviller, 54300 Lunéville. Tel. 83-74-04-81. Fax 83-74-21-78.
Cuisine: FRENCH. **Reservations:** Required.
$ Prices: Appetizers 110–150 F ($19.80–$27); main dishes 115–175 F ($20.70–$31.50); fixed-price menus 220 F ($39.60), 310 F ($55.80), 360 F ($64.80), and 430 F ($77.40). AE, MC, V.
Open: Lunch Tues–Sun noon–2pm; dinner Tues–Sat 7–9:30pm. **Closed:** Feb.
Set on 16 lovely acres of parkland, containing a 17th-century wine press, the Château d'Adomenil lies about 2½ miles south of Lunéville. While there are seven rooms for rent—a double costs 550–1,200 F ($99–$216)—all with TVs and telephones, most people visit the 19th-century château for the food. Guests may begin with cocktails and miniature versions of quiche Lorraine in the oak-beamed salon. Dinner is served in an elegant dining room, with a view of expansive lawns, reflecting pools, and peacocks.

The owner, Michel Million, is one of the most outstanding chefs in the province. He will often help with menu selections, suggesting such delectable fare as quail wrapped in cabbage leaves, a salad of frogs' legs with peppered mint, lobster in court bouillon with saffron, filet of lamb en croûte with thyme, filet of John Dory with rhubarb, and pigeon stuffed with chanterelles (mushrooms). His wife, Bernadette, greets guests cheerfully and sees that they receive impeccable service. There is both terrace and indoor dining.

BACCARAT

This small town owes its fame, of course, to Baccarat crystal. The company, founded in 1764, was originally a glass manufacturer called La Verrerie Sainte-Anne. In 1817, however, it switched to crystal and became known as the Compagnie des Cristalleries de Baccarat.

WHAT TO SEE & DO

In addition to displaying some of the factory's oldest and most noteworthy pieces, the **Musée du Cristal** (tel. 83-75-10-01) has a video in English about crystal manufacturing. You'll learn how lead, potassium, and silica combine to form crystal. The museum is open May through September, daily from 10am to noon and 2 to 6:30pm; off-season, on Saturday and Sunday from 10am to noon and 2 to 6pm. Admission is 10 F ($1.80).

A Baccarat shop on the square near the museum is housed in a futuristic rectangular building where the walls are made, appropriately, almost entirely of glass. It's loaded with crystal.

WHERE TO STAY & DINE

RENAISSANCE, 31, rue des Cristalleries, 54120 Baccarat. Tel. 83-75-11-31. 19 rms (all with bath). TEL
$ Rates: 150–250 F ($27–$45) single or double. Breakfast 25 F ($4.50) extra. AE, DC, MC, V. **Parking:** Free. **Closed:** Jan 15–Feb 15.
This is a provincial hotel catering to many visitors and businesspeople in town who deal with the local glass companies. A conventional, not particularly exciting hotel, it was built after World War II and was partially renovated in 1993. Rooms are functional but well kept. The hotel restaurant does a good business and is open daily in summer; from October through March it closes on Friday night and all day Saturday. Menus cost 60 F ($10.80), 75 F ($13.50), 100 F ($18), and 180 F ($32.40).

5. DOMRÉMY-LA-PUCELLE

A pilgrimage center attracting flocks of tourists from all over the world, Domrémy is a plain hamlet that would be overlooked by visitors except for one event: Joan of Arc was born here in 1412. Here she saw the visions and heard the voices that led her to play out her historic role as the heroine of France. The Lorraine village lies 6½ miles from Neufchâteau, 35½ miles from Nancy.

A residence traditionally considered the Arc family house, near the church, is known as the **Maison Natale de Jeanne d'Arc** (tel. 29-06-95-86). Here you can see the bleak *chambre natale* where she was born. A museum beside the house shows a film depicting the life of Joan of Arc.

The house can be visited April to September 15, daily from 9am to 12:30pm and 2 to 7pm; off-season, daily from 9:30am to noon and from 2 to 5pm. Admission costs 6 F ($1.10) for adults, 3 F (50¢) for children 10–16, free for children under 10.

Only the tower remains of the church where Joan was baptized. However, above the village, on a slope of the Bois-Chenu, the **Basilique du Bois-Chenu** was commenced in 1881 and consecrated in 1926. The tree that in spring was "lovely as a lily" and believed to be haunted by "faery ladies" no longer exists.

WHERE TO STAY & DINE

HOTEL DE LA BASILIQUE, Le Bois-Chenu, 88630 Domrémy-la-Pucelle. Tel. 29-06-84-07. Fax 29-06-84-08. 11 rms (all with bath).
$ Rates: 180 F ($32.40) single; 200 F ($36) double. Breakfast 30 F ($5.40) extra. MC, V. **Parking:** Free. **Closed:** Jan–Mar 15; Sun night and Mon Mar 16 through June and Oct–Dec.
This modest but rustically accommodating hotel, run by members of the Vaudron family since 1993, was built adjacent to the 19th-century Basilique St-Jeanne-d'Arc, about a mile north of the village center. Built around 1970, and rated one star by the

French government, it contains simple bedrooms which share a communal telephone near the reception desk. Most of the establishment's business derives from its restaurant, where fixed-price meals cost 70–230 F ($12.60–$41.40) each. The restaurant is open for lunch from noon to 2pm and for dinner from 7 to 9pm.

RELAIS DE LA PUCELLE, 88630 Domrémy-la-Pucelle. Tel. 29-06-95-72.
12 rms (6 with bath).

$ Rates: 110 F ($19.80) single or double without bath, 150–160 F ($27–$28.80) single or double with bath. Breakfast 25 F ($4.50) extra. AE, DC, MC, V. **Parking:** Free. **Closed:** Mon Nov–Mar.

Facing the house of Joan of Arc, the restaurant at Relais de la Pucelle is known for its superb Lorraine pâté and generous portions. Full meals cost 68 F ($12.20), 90 F ($16.20), and 115 F ($20.70). The restaurant is open for lunch from noon to 2pm and for dinner from 8 to 10pm. No bedroom contains a TV or phone. Rooms are very modest, but clean and old-fashioned.

---

6. STRASBOURG

303 miles SE of Paris, 135 miles SW of Frankfurt

GETTING THERE By Plane The city's airport, Strasbourg-Entzheim, seven miles southwest of the city center, receives daily flights from most European political and financial centers—including, of course, Paris and Frankfurt.

By Train Strasbourg is a major rail junction in Europe, with trains arriving from Paris every two hours (trip time 4½ hours).

By Car The N83, a giant highway with many lanes, crosses the plain of Alsace, becoming at times the A35 expressway. It links Strasbourg with Colmar and Mulhouse.

ESSENTIALS Information The Office de Tourisme is on place de la Cathédrale (tel. 88-52-28-28).

Orientation With its eastern border on the banks of the Rhine, Strasbourg is intersected in dozens of places by two branches of the Ill River and by many canals—the most famous of which is an artificial waterway connecting the Marne with the Rhine. Most of the historic monuments lie on or near a circular island created by the two branches of the Ill.

SPECIAL EVENTS The International Music Festival is held each year in June at the cathedral, the Palais de la Musique et des Congrès, and the courtyard of the Château des Rohan.

RIVER CRUISES One of the most romantic ways to spend your time in Strasbourg is to take an excursion on the Ill River, leaving from the Château des Rohan near the cathedral. Day excursions operate year-round, and night excursions are offered only from May through October.

Those with more time may want to take excursions on the Rhine, which cross the Strasbourg lock. These three- to four-hour cruises on a 300-passenger ship leave from promenade Dauphine May through September only. Meals and cocktails are served on board.

Longer excursions along the Rhine can also be booked. Information is provided by the Strasbourg Port Authority, 25, rue de la Nuée-Bleue (tel. 88-21-74-74).

Capital of Alsace, Strasbourg is one of France's greatest cities. It is also the capital of pâté de foie gras. It was in Strasbourg that Rouget de Lisle first sang the

"Marseillaise." In June of every year the artistic life of Strasbourg reaches its zenith at the **International Music Festival** held at the cathedral, the Palais de la Musique et des Congrès, and in the courtyard of the Château des Rohan.

Strasbourg is not only a great university city, the seat of the Council of Europe, but one of France's most important ports, lying two miles west of the Rhine. In addition to hosting the Council of Europe, Strasbourg is also the meeting place of the European Parliament, which convenes at the **Palais de l'Europe.**

Despite war damage, much remains of old Strasbourg. It still has covered bridges and the old towers of its former fortifications, and many 15th- and 17th-century dwellings with painted wooden fronts and carved beams.

In 1871 Strasbourg became German and was made the capital of the imperial territory of Alsace-Lorraine, reverting back to France in 1918. Germans continue to invade it, but today's visitors are friendly ones, pouring over the border on the weekends to sample the fine food, wine, and beer of Alsace.

One street alone illustrates Strasbourg's identity crisis. More than a century ago it was called the Avenue Napoléon. In 1871 it became the Kaiser Wilhelmstrasse, turning into the Boulevard de la République in 1918. In 1940 it underwent another change, becoming Adolf Hitler Strasse, before ending up as the Avenue du Général-de-Gaulle in 1945.

WHAT TO SEE & DO

The traffic hub of Strasbourg is the **Place Kléber,** which dates from the 15th century. Sit here with a tankard of Alsatian beer and slowly get to know Strasbourg. Eventually everybody seems to cross this square. The bronze statue in the center is of J. B. Kléber, born in Strasbourg in 1753. He became one of Napoleon's most noted generals, and was buried under this monument. Apparently his presence offended the Nazis, who removed the statue in 1940. However, this Alsatian bronze was restored to its proper place in 1945 at the liberation.

From Kléber Square, you can take rue des Grandes-Arcades to the **Place Gutenberg,** one of the oldest squares of Strasbourg. It was formerly a *marché aux herbes*. The statue in the center is by David d'Angers, dated 1840. It is of Gutenberg, who perfected his printing press in Strasbourg in the winter of 1436–1437. The former town hall, now the **Hôtel du Commerce,** was built in 1582, and is considered one of the most significant Renaissance buildings in all of Alsace.

With this small orientation, you can now make your way along rue Mercière to the Place de la Cathédrale to see the crowning glory of Strasbourg.

The **Cathédrale Notre-Dame** (tel. 88-32-37-92), which inspired the poetry of Goethe, was built on the site of a Romanesque church of 1015. Today it stands proudly, one of the largest churches of Christianity, one of the most outstanding examples of Gothic, representing a harmonious transition from the Romanesque. Construction began on it in 1176. The pyramidal tower in rose-colored stone was completed in 1439, and is the tallest such one dating from medieval times, soaring to a height of 469 feet.

You can ascend the tower daily from 8:30am to 7pm in July and August; from April to June and in September hours are 9am to 6:30pm; in March and October, 9am to 5:30pm; and November through February, 9am to 4:30pm. Because of certain structural problems and renovations, visitors are allowed to climb only 329 steps to the platform for a panoramic view—climbing all the way to the spire is forbidden. To make the climb will cost 8 F ($1.40).

On the main façade, four large counterforts divide the front into three vertical parts and two horizontal galleries. Note the great rose window, which looks like real stone lace. The façade is rich in sculptural decoration. On the portal of the south transept, the "Coronation and Death" of the Virgin in one of the two tympana is considered one of the finest such medieval works. In the north transept, see also the face of St. Lawrence Chapel, a stunning achievement of the late-Gothic German style.

A Romanesque crypt lies under the chancel, which is covered with a square of stonework. The stained-glass window in the center is the work of Max Ingrand. The nave is vast and majestic, with windows depicting emperors and kings on the north

Cathédrale Notre-Dame **8**
Château des Rohan **9**
Hôtel du Commerce **7**
La Petite France quarter **3**
Musée Alsacien **13**
Musée Historique **11**
Musée de l'Oeuvre
    Notre-Dame **10**

Place du Château **10**
Place Gutenberg **6**
Place Kléber **5**
St-Jean-Baptiste **1**
St-Paul **14**
St-Pierre-le-Jeune **4**
St-Pierre-le-Vieux **2**
St-Thomas **12**

aisle. Five chapels are grouped around the transept, including one built in 1500 in the flamboyant Gothic style. In the south transept stands the Angel Pillar, illustrating the Last Judgment, with angels lowering their trumpets.

The astronomical clock was built between 1547 and 1574. However, it stopped working during the Revolution, and from 1838 to 1842 the mechanism was replaced. The clock is wound once a week. People flock to see its 12:30pm show of allegorical figures. On Sunday Apollo appears driving his sun horses; on Thursday you see Jupiter and his eagle, and so on. The main body of the clock has a planetarium according to Copernicus.

The public is welcome to get a closer view of the clock between noon and 12:30pm. Tickets costing 4 F (70¢) are on sale daily in the south portal at 11:30am.

On the south side of the cathedral, at 2 place du Château, the **Palais Rohan** (tel. 88-32-48-95), built from 1732 to 1742, is an architectural example of supreme elegance and perfect proportions. It is considered one of the crowning design achievements in eastern France in the 18th century, and is noted in particular for its façades and its beautiful rococo interior decoration. On the first floor is a fine-arts museum, with works by Rubens, Rembrandt, Van Dyck, El Greco, Goya, Watteau (*The Copper Cleaners*), Renoir, and Monet. There is also a museum devoted to decorative arts, including ceramics and the original machinery of the first astronomical clock of the cathedral.

The museum, charging 15 F ($2.70) for adults (free for children), is open Wednesday through Monday from 10am to noon and 2 to 6pm.

On the southwest corner of the Place du Château, at no. 3, the **Musée de l'Oeuvre Notre-Dame** (tel. 88-32-06-39) is located in a collection of ancient houses with wooden galleries. Inside is a museum illustrating art of the Middle Ages and the Renaissance in Strasbourg and surrounding Alsace. The original building dates from 1347, although there have been many later additions. Some of the pieces of art were formerly displayed in the cathedral, where copies have been substituted. The most celebrated prize is a stained-glass head of Christ from a window said to have originally been at Wissembourg, dating from about 1070, one of the oldest known. There is also a stained-glass window depicting an emperor from about 1200. The medieval sculpture is of much interest, as are the works from the Strasbourg goldsmiths from the 16th through the 17th centuries. The museum's winding staircase and interior are in the pure Renaissance style. The 13th-century hall contains the loveliest sculptures from the cathedral, including the wise and foolish virgins from 1280.

The museum is open Wednesday through Monday from 10am to noon and 2 to 6pm. Admission costs 12 F ($2.20) for adults, 6 F ($1.10) for children.

Musée Alsacien, 23, Quai St-Nicolas (tel. 88-35-55-36), occupies three mansions dating from the 16th and 17th centuries. It is like a living textbook of the folklore and customs of Alsace, containing arts, crafts, and tools of the old province.

The museum is open Wednesday through Monday from 10am to noon and 2 to 6pm. Admission is 15 F ($2.70) for adults, free for children.

The **Church of St. Thomas,** rue Martin-Luther, built between 1230 and 1330, is peculiar in that it has five naves. A Protestant church, it is the most interesting one in Strasbourg after the cathedral. It contains the mausoleum of Maréchal de Saxe, a masterpiece of French art by Pigalle, dating from 1777. The church lies along rue St-Thomas, near the Bridge of St. Thomas. Open daily from 10am to noon and 2 to 6pm (until 5pm in winter).

La Petite France, a long walk from the church down the colorful rue des Dentelles, is the most interesting quarter of Strasbourg. Its houses from the 16th century are mirrored in the waters of the Ill. In "Little France," old roofs with gray tiles have sheltered families for ages, and the crossbeamed façades with their roughly carved rafters are in the typical Alsatian style. Rue du Bain-aux-Plantes is of particular interest. An island in the middle of the river is cut by four canals. For a view, walk along rue des Moulins, branching off from rue du Bain-aux-Plantes.

WHERE TO STAY

Strasbourg has a wide range of hotels in several price brackets. Because of its popularity in summer, many of these fill up quickly—so it's best to arrive with a reservation.

Very Expensive

HILTON INTERNATIONAL STRASBOURG, av. Herrenschmidt, 67000 Strasbourg. Tel. 88-37-10-10, or toll free 800/445-8667 in the U.S. and Canada. Fax 88-36-83-27. A/C MINIBAR TV TEL **Bus:** 6, 16, or 26.

$ **Rates:** 990 F ($178.20) single; 1,090 F ($196.20) double; from 3,000 F ($540) suite. Breakfast 90 F ($16.20) extra. AE, DC, MC, V. **Parking:** Free.

Opened in 1981, the Hilton International was designed by a local architect to include every luxury associated with its name. The hotel is just a five-minute drive from the center of town—take the Strasbourg-Centre exit from the autoroute and follow signs to the Wacken, Palais des Congrès, and the Palais de l'Europe. The seven-story glass hotel looms over a university complex and is just opposite the Palais des Congrès. Five kinds of Iberian marble were used in the decor—much of it chosen to resemble the same ruddy sandstone used in the city's famous cathedral, which is visible from the hotel. Bedrooms contain tasteful artwork, spacious marble-trimmed bathrooms, radios, and all the extra services you'd expect to find in a luxury hotel.

Dining/Entertainment: Live music and guests ranging from heads of state to international tourists make the Bugatti Bar the social center of Strasbourg. The bar, named for Ettore Bugatti, opened on the 100th birthday of the Alsatian car manufacturer and is decorated with comfortable leather furniture and automobile memorabilia. There is also a moderately priced restaurant, Le Jardin, which offers a buffet not only at breakfast, but at lunch and dinner too. Some evenings are devoted to special themes such as seafood, Italian, or even vegetarian. The hotel's gastronomic restaurant, Maison du Boeuf, is recommended separately (see "Where to Dine," below).

Services: 24-hour room service, laundry, dry cleaning.

Facilities: Sauna, health club, massage facilities, boutiques, security system, an impressive array of interpretive and secretarial facilities.

Expensive

BEAUCOUR, 5, rue Bouchers, 67000 Strasbourg. Tel. 88-76-72-00. Fax 88-76-72-60. 49 rms (all with bath), 3 suites. A/C TV TEL **Bus:** 10, 20, or 36.

$ Rates: 550 F ($99) single; 750 F ($135) double; from 850 F ($153) suite. Breakfast 60 F ($10.80) extra. AE, DC, MC, V. **Parking:** 30 F ($5.40).

A three-star hotel, this establishment was geared mainly to business travelers to the city, although many tourists will find it ideal as well. Lying at the end of a private street a few blocks east of the cathedral, it is installed in a 17th century building with lots of timbered ceilings. Both the bedrooms and suites harmoniously blend modern and traditional styling and furnishings. Every bedroom has whirlpool bathtubs, fax hookups, and computer connections. The best chambers are a trio of Alsatian suites. The hotel has a cozy public bar, and maintains an affiliation with three restaurants which are just a short walk from the hotel. The helpful concierge, who seems to know "all the city's secrets," will gladly make reservations for you.

HOTEL MONOPOLE-METROPOLE, 16, rue Kuhn, 67000 Strasbourg. Tel. 88-32-11-94. Fax 88-32-82-55. 94 rms (all with bath). MINIBAR TV TEL **Bus:** 10, 20, or 36.

$ Rates: 360–460 F ($64.80–$82.80) single; 440–520 F ($79.20–$93.60) double. Breakfast 60 F ($10.80) extra. AE, DC, MC, V. **Parking:** 35 F ($6.30).

Housed in a red-brick and stone building covered with turn-of-the-century detailing, the Hôtel Monopole-Métropole is located on a quiet street corner near the train station and contains a modernized lobby with a scattering of antiques, among them a 17th-century carved armoire and a bronze statue of a night watchman. An extension of the salon displays oil portraits of 18th-century Alsatian personalities and glass cases filled with pewter tankards and brass candlesticks. Breakfast only is served in the high-ceilinged and spacious Alsatian-style dining room. Each bedroom is unique— many contain Louis-Philippe antiques and high ceilings. Léon and Monique Siegel are the proprietors; members of their family have owned this establishment since 1919.

SOFITEL STRASBOURG, place St-Pierre-le-Jeane, 67000 Strasbourg. Tel. 88-32-99-30. Fax 88-32-60-67. 158 rms (all with bath), 5 suites. MINIBAR TV TEL **Bus:** 10 or 20.

$ Rates: 780 F ($140.40) single or double; from 900 F ($162) suite. Breakfast 75 F ($13.50) extra. AE, DC, MC, V. **Parking:** 60 F ($10.80).

Situated next to one of the city's oldest churches, the Sofitel Strasbourg is a contemporary hotel on a tree-shaded square in the center of town. The atmosphere, the architecture, and the furnishings—French traditional combined with modern— are light and airy. A basement garage has direct elevator access to the marble lobby, the lounges, and the bar, as well as the carpeted bedrooms, which have soundproof windows.

The hotel restaurant, L'Alsace Gourmande, opens onto a little plaza with beds of seasonal flowers. The food is international, including sauerkraut alsacienne, roast lamb flavored with the herbs of Provence, and pike perch suprême with riesling. Dinner begins at 200 F ($36).

TERMINUS PLAZA, 10, place de la Gare, 67000 Strasbourg. Tel. 88-32-87-00. Fax 88-32-16-46. 78 rms (70 with bath or shower), 12 suites. MINIBAR TV TEL **Bus:** 1, 10, 11, or 20.

$ Rates: 400 F ($72) single without bath, 460 F ($82.80) single with bath; 450 F ($81) double without bath, 530 F ($95.40) double with bath; from 700 F ($126) suite. Breakfast 58 F ($10.40) extra. AE, DC, MC, V. **Parking:** 50 F ($9).

This leading modern hotel by the railway station has a streamlined facade that contradicts its traditional interior. Inside, comfortable bedrooms have French furnishings and immaculate bathrooms. The hotel also offers two restaurants—Le Salon des Aubussons, frequented mostly by executives at lunchtime, and the luxurious La Cour de Rosemont. The latter restaurant has very good food, including such Alsatian specialties as snails and choucroute garnie (sauerkraut with pork products). In season the chef specializes in game dishes, such as roast pheasant; his fish dishes, such as a turbot soufflé, are works of art. A la carte dinner at La Cour de Rosemont costs 220 F ($39.60), and a fixed-price menu costs 170 F ($30.60) at lunch. Meals at the informal brasserie begin at 100 F ($18).

Moderate

FRANCE, 20, rue du Jeu-des-Enfants, 67000 Strasbourg. Tel. 88-32-37-12. Fax 88-22-48-08. 56 rms (all with bath), 10 suites. MINIBAR TV TEL **Bus:** 10, 13, 20, or 36.

$ Rates: 385–420 F ($69.30–$75.60) single; 420–460 F ($75.60–$82.80) double; 595–620 F ($107.10–$111.60) suite. Breakfast 50 F ($9) extra. AE, MC, V.

The France, near the railway station and the town center, has practical rooms, with soft beds and fruitwood and Formica furnishings. This six-story concrete-sided structure was constructed in the 1970s and renovated as recently as 1992. Windows in the breakfast room open onto the plaza. Breakfast is the only meal served, although the hotel has a bar.

Inexpensive

GUTENBERG, 31, rue des Serruriers, 67000 Strasbourg. Tel. 88-32-17-15. Fax 88-75-76-67. 50 rms (42 with bath). TEL **Bus:** 1, 11, or 21.

$ Rates: 195 F ($35.10) single without bath; 295 F ($53.10) double without bath, 350 F ($63) double with bath. Breakfast 36 F ($6.50) extra. MC, V.

Located near place Gutenberg, the Gutenberg occupies a mansion built in 1745. Madame Lette offers a warm atmosphere with plenty of old furniture and pictures and serves only breakfast.

HOTEL DE L'ILL, 8, rue des Bateliers, 67000 Strasbourg. Tel. 88-36-20-01. 20 rms (all with shower). TV TEL **Bus:** 10, 20, or 36.

$ Rates: 140–205 F ($25.20–$36.90) single; 165–260 F ($29.70–$46.80) double. Breakfast 22 F ($4) extra. No credit cards.

This two-star hotel was completely renovated in 1990, turning it into one of the good-value hotels of Strasbourg. A well-maintained and inviting little place, it offers comfortably furnished and quiet bedrooms located on a side street. Behind the hotel is a yard, with both a terrace and a garden. The site is about a five-minute walk from the cathedral. The least expensive bedrooms offer a shower and a double bed but no toilet, whereas the most expensive units are equipped with shower and toilet. All the accommodations have double beds. There is also a breakfast lounge.

HOTEL DES PRINCES, 33, rue Geiler, Conseil de l'Europe, 67000 Strasbourg. Tel. 88-61-55-19. Fax 88-14-10-92. 43 rms (all with bath). TEL **Bus:** 15 or 20.

$ Rates: 405 F ($72.90) single; 415–490 F ($74.70–$88.20) double. Breakfast 42 F ($7.60) extra. AE, MC, V.

A 15-minute walk from the center of town, the Hôtel des Princes has received a three-star government rating and is one of the best values in the city. The management is helpful, and the rooms are well furnished. A continental breakfast is the only meal served.

HOTEL DU DRAGON, 2, rue de l'Ecarlate, 67000 Strasbourg. Tel. 88-35-79-80. Fax 88-25-78-95. 32 rms (all with bath). TV TEL **Bus:** 21.

$ Rates: 420–550 F ($75.60–$99) single; 460–590 F ($82.80–$106.20) double. Breakfast 52 F ($9.40) extra. MC, V. **Parking:** Free.

This is only a five-minute walk from the historic center, la Petite France. Since 1987 the Hôtel du Dragon has been one of the finest small hotels in Strasbourg. Once a collection of private apartments annexed to the Dragon family's 17th-century dwelling, the hotel today offers well-furnished, modern accommodations. The hotel serves breakfast only, and it has a bar. There are many restaurants nearby.

VENDOME, 9, place de la Gare, 67000 Strasbourg. Tel. 88-32-45-23.
Fax 88-32-23-02. 48 rms (all with bath). TV TEL **Bus:** 10, 20, or 36.
$ Rates: 250–300 F ($45–$54) single; 280–330 F ($50.40–$59.40) double. Breakfast 30 F ($5.40) extra. AE, DC, MC, V. **Parking:** 30 F ($5.40).

Just opposite the railway station in a relatively new building, the Vendôme tends to shelter Eurailpass travelers, among others. Comfortable, modern rooms have either provincial or contemporary furnishings. The hotel has a lounge bar and serves only breakfast.

WHERE TO EAT
Very Expensive

AU CROCODILE, 10, rue de l'Outre. Tel. 88-32-13-02.
Cuisine: ALSATIAN. **Reservations:** Required. **Bus:** 10, 20, or 36.
$ Prices: Appetizers 85–295 F ($15.30–$53.10); main dishes 190–285 F ($34.20–$51.30); fixed-price menu 280 F ($50.40), 380 F ($68.40), and 590 F ($106.20). AE, DC, MC, V.
Open: Lunch Tues–Sat noon–2pm; dinner Tues–Sat 7–9:30pm. **Closed:** July 11–Aug 2 and Dec 24–Jan 3.

A beautiful, old, skylit restaurant, Au Crocodile serves some of the most inventive food in Strasbourg. Chef Emile Jung offers a wide array of dishes, including a boned quail stuffed with foie gras, braised slowly in goose fat, and chilled in a meat gelatin. There is also a remarkable flan of watercress and frogs' legs, endive salad with hot goose liver, turbot with thin strips of vegetables, a timbale of sole and lobster, and crayfish in a tarragon gelatin. In addition to the fine cuisine, the restaurant stocks the best Alsatian wines.

BUEREHIESEL, 4, parc de l'Orangerie. Tel. 88-61-62-24.
Cuisine: FRENCH. **Reservations:** Required. **Bus:** 6, 16, or 26.
$ Prices: Appetizers 138–186 F ($24.80–$33.50); main dishes 146–286 F ($26.30–$51.50); fixed-price meal 280 F ($50.40) at lunch, 300 F ($54) at dinner; seven-course *menu dégustation* 530 F ($95.40). AE, DC, MC, V.
Open: Lunch Thurs–Tues noon–2:30pm; dinner Thurs–Mon 7–9:30pm. **Closed:** Feb 23–Mar 9, Aug 11–26, and Dec 23–Jan 5.

Also known as "Chez Westermann," Buerehiesel is famous for Antoine Westermann's *cuisine moderne,* as well as the restaurant's prime location. L'Orangerie, which is a beautiful park at the end of the allée de la Robertsau, near the Council of Europe, was planned by the landscape artist Le Nôtre and was offered to the Empress Joséphine. Main courses are likely to include a sole and lobster à la nage (cooked in court bouillon and flavored with herbs), salmis de pigeon au Bourgogne, steamed spring chicken with cabbage, and braised sweetbreads with truffles.

Expensive

LA MAISON DU BOEUF, in the Hilton International Strasbourg, av. Herrenschmidt. Tel. 88-37-10-10.
Cuisine: FRENCH. **Reservations:** Recommended. **Bus:** 6, 16, or 26.
$ Prices: Appetizers 95–145 F ($17.10–$26.10); main dishes 110–180 F ($19.80–$32.40); fixed-price lunch 170 F ($30.60); *menu dégustation* 280 F ($50.40). AE, DC, MC, V.
Open: Lunch Mon–Fri noon–2:30pm; dinner Mon–Sat 7–10:30pm.

Housed in the most luxurious hotel in Alsace, La Maison du Boeuf spared no expense in becoming one of Strasbourg's best restaurants. The Belle Epoque decor includes brass-trimmed doors, dark paneling, etched glass, peacock-blue chairs, and scarlet carpeting. The restaurant—winner of a national wine list competition—serves an array of Alsatian and international dishes. Specialties include U.S. rib of beef roasted in a salt crust. Other dishes to tempt include duck-liver terrine, Caesar salad with chunks of lobster, kidneys flambéed in cognac, and various versions of fresh pasta. The dessert specialty is crêpes Suzette flambéed in Grand Marnier. The wine list, in addition to its impressive array of classical French vintages, offers a wide variety of Alsatian wines.

Moderate

MAISON KAMMERZELL, 16, place de la Cathédrale. Tel. 88-32-42-14.
   Cuisine: FRENCH. **Reservations:** Required. **Bus:** 21.
$ **Prices:** Appetizers 39–109 F ($7–$19.60); main dishes 94–160 F ($16.90–$28.80); fixed-price menus 190 F ($34.20) and 260 F ($46.80). AE, DC, MC, V.
   Open: Lunch daily noon–3pm; dinner daily 7pm–1am.
Dating from 1467, the gingerbread-style Maison Kammerzell, across from the cathedral, is a sightseeing attraction as well as one of the best restaurants in Strasbourg. The carved-wood framework was constructed during the Renaissance; the overhanging stories were built in 1589 by a cheese dealer known as Martin Braun.
   I suggest la choucroute formidable (for two people), the Alsatian specialty prepared with goose fat and riesling wine, and Strasbourg sausages, pork cutlets, and smoked breast of pork. Owner Guy-Pierre Baumann also offers guinea hen with mushrooms, medallion of young wild boar, filet of beef Vigneronne with vegetables, and such regional specialties as baeckeoffe (boulangère potatoes with meat).

LA MAISON DES TANNEURS, 42, rue du Bain-aux-Plantes. Tel. 88-32-79-70.
   Cuisine: FRENCH. **Reservations:** Required. **Bus:** 21.
$ **Prices:** Appetizers 48–130 F ($8.60–$23.40); main dishes 100–135 F ($18–$24.30); fixed-price menus 235 F ($42.30) and 275 F ($49.50). AE, DC, MC, V.
   Open: Lunch Tues–Sat noon–2:15pm; dinner Tues–Sat 7:15–9:30pm. **Closed:** Dec 22–Jan 22 and July 15–31.
Established in 1572, La Maison des Tanneurs stands on a typical old street in the Petite France quarter. Inside, flowers and Alsatian antiques create a warm atmosphere, while the dining terrace opens onto the canal. The restaurant has been called "La maison de la choucroute," as the sauerkraut-and-pork platter is a specialty of the house. But the chef prepares many other dishes equally as well, including the extravagant parfait of foie gras with fresh truffles. Main courses I recommend include crayfish tails à la nage, and poulet—known as coq au riesling—cooked in white wine and served with noodles. Other dishes to sample include lobster bisque, duck with black pepper, and smoked salmon.

VALENTIN-SORG, 6, place Homme-de-Fer. Tel. 88-32-12-16.
   Cuisine: FRENCH. **Reservations:** Required. **Bus:** 10, 20, or 36.
$ **Prices:** Appetizers 65–120 F ($11.70–$21.60); main dishes 95–200 F ($17.10–$36); fixed-price menus 150 F ($27), 170 F ($30.60), 280 F ($50.40), and 380 F ($68.40). AE, DC, MC, V.
   Open: Lunch Mon–Sat noon–2pm; dinner Mon–Sat 7–9:30pm. **Closed:** Aug 1–15.
Ever since it was located on "the old winemarket street," Valentin-Sorg has been a favorite of mine. Today, as it sits atop a building called "the Tower" overlooking the "Square of the Iron Man," the restaurant offers a panoramic view as well as some of the finest cuisine in the city. Here you can order the classic French dishes—sole Pyramide, frogs' legs with riesling, tournedos Rossini, duck in orange sauce, and even beef Wellington if it's ordered 24 hours in advance. The chef is proudest of his filet of turbot gratiné au Viennoise, pigeon en croûte with a truffle sauce, and crêpes au kirsch.

Inexpensive

L'ARSENAL, 11, rue de l'Abreuvoir. Tel. 88-35-03-69.
   Cuisine: FRENCH. **Reservations:** Required. **Bus:** 10.
$ **Prices:** Appetizers 45–95 F ($8.10–$17.10); main dishes 75–130 F ($13.50–$23.40); fixed-price meal 130 F ($23.40) at lunch, 175 F ($31.50) at dinner. AE, DC, MC, V.

Open: Lunch daily noon–2pm; dinner daily 7–11pm. **Closed:** July 28–Aug 15.
This pleasant, typically Alsatian restaurant is located in a historic building and often
counts members of the European Parliament among its clientele. The inventive
regional menu changes every few weeks, but it often includes breaded pigs' trotters,
homemade goose liver, calf's head with beer sauce, and matelote of eel.

BRASSERIE DE L'ANCIENNE DOUANE, 6, rue de la Douane. Tel. 88-32-42-19.
  Cuisine: FRENCH. **Reservations:** Recommended. **Bus:** 21.
$ **Prices:** Appetizers 29–98 F ($5.20–$17.60); main dishes 37–122 F ($6.70–$22); fixed-price menus 65–99 F ($11.70–$17.80). AE, DC, MC, V.
  Open: Daily 11:30am–11pm. **Closed:** Jan 8–22.

In a building which functioned during the Middle Ages as the toll house for
river traffic on the River Ill, this is the largest, and probably the noisiest, and
most colorful dining spot in Strasbourg. Established in 1965 as part of a
historic renovation, it offers 600 indoor seats, and an additional 200 seats available
during clement weather on an outdoor terrace. The closest thing to a Teutonic
beerhall and winehouse in town, it serves bountiful portions in a historic setting.
From the outside, along a street in the oldest part of town, you'll see the arcades of the
lower floor and the small windows of the stone facade. Inside, the high-ceilinged
rooms are somewhat formal, with Teutonic chairs and heavily timbered ceilings.
Among the Alsatian specialties are the well-known "sauerkraut of the Customs
officers" and the foie gras of Strasbourg; chicken in riesling with Alsatian noodles,
onion pie, and ham knuckle with potato salad and horseradish also are popular dishes.
  Next to the brasserie is an old tavern which has been renovated and turned into the
Quai des Bières, featuring 30 different kinds of beers.

7. LA WANTZENAU

Instead of dining in Strasbourg, many motorists prefer to head north for 7½ miles to
the village of La Wantzenau, which has very good restaurants and lots of regional
specialties. From Strasbourg, go northeast on the D468, which runs along the west
bank of the Rhine, if you'd like to follow their example.

WHERE TO DINE

A LA BARRIERE, 3, route de Strasbourg. Tel. 88-96-20-23.
  Cuisine: FRENCH. **Reservations:** Required.
$ **Prices:** Appetizers 65–195 F ($11.70–$35.10); main dishes 110–175 F ($19.80–$31.50); fixed-price menus 150–250 F ($27–$45). AE, DC, MC, V.
  Open: Lunch Thurs–Tues noon–2:30pm; dinner Thurs–Mon 7–9:30pm.
  Closed: Feb and Aug 7–30.
Established just before World War II, and famous throughout Alsace as a refuge for
gastronomes, this restaurant lies a five-minute walk from the center of La Wantzenau.
Within a restrained art deco interior, Claude Sutter, former pupil of the recently
retired master chef and original founder of the place, prepares a sophisticated cuisine
based on classic French principles. The menu might include filet of sole with scallops
and scampi bound together in a ginger sauce; rack of roasted lamb with gratin
dauphinois and garlic en chemise; roasted dorado with fennel, celery, and tomatoes;
zander in riesling; and salmon steaks with sorrel. In autumn, the game dishes
(especially the pheasant and venison) are excellent.

LE MOULIN DE LA WANTZENAU, 27, route de Strasbourg, 67610 La Wantzenau. Tel. 88-96-27-83. Fax 88-96-68-32.
  Cuisine: FRENCH. **Reservations:** Required.
$ **Prices:** Appetizers 52–135 F ($9.40–$24.30); main dishes 75–175 F ($13.50–$31.50); fixed-price menus 140 F ($25.20), 225 F ($40.50), and 325 F ($58.50). AE, MC, V.

Open: Lunch Thurs–Tues noon–2pm; dinner Mon–Tues and Thurs–Sat 7:15–9:15pm. **Closed:** Dec 24–Jan 2.

Le Moulin de la Wantzenau, set in a garden, is another favorite. It's a large house where owners Charles and Philippe Clauss serve diners in a traditional setting. Not only is the cooking exceptional, but also the wine is rewarding, including riesling, Pinot Noir, and Tokay. German diners from across the border come here with their list of dishes to order: specialties such as foie gras frais maison, matelote with white wine, poussin (pullet) Mère Clauss, and carré d'agneau (loin of lamb with ribs).

The old mill, opposite the restaurant, was transformed into a small hotel decorated with taste. The 20 rooms have private baths or showers, alarm clocks, radios, TVs, and telephones. A double costs 310–410 F ($55.80–$73.80); continental breakfast is 45 F ($8.10) extra.

ZIMMER, 23, rue des Héros. Tel. 88-96-62-08.
  Cuisine: FRENCH. **Reservations:** Recommended.
$ Prices: Appetizers 85–150 F ($15.30–$27); main dishes 100–150 F ($18–$27); fixed-price menus 135 F ($24.30), 220 F ($39.60), and 330 F ($59.40). AE, DC, MC, V.
  Open: Lunch Tues–Sun noon–2pm; dinner Tues–Sat 6:45–9:15pm. **Closed:** Jan 17–Feb 3 and July 18–Aug 11.

Under the watchful eye of Monsieur and Madame Jean-Pierre Bengel, this restaurant serves large portions of excellent regional specialties. Connoisseurs drive from Germany just to sample the restaurant's poussin à la Wantzenau, the village's famous chicken dish. Other draws include matelote with riesling, salmon stewed with mushrooms, and breast of duck with vegetables. Featured wines include Pinot Noir and Edelzquicker.

8. ILLHAEUSERN

Gourmets from all over the world flock to this sleepy village, 11 miles from Colmar, 38 miles south of Strasbourg, for one important reason—to dine at L'Auberge de l'Ill, one of the greatest restaurants in France. The farm village of Illhaeusern is located east of Rte. N83. The signs for the restaurant, besides the village's main highway, are difficult to miss.

WHERE TO DINE

L'AUBERGE DE L'ILL, route de Collonges. Tel. 89-71-83-23.
  Cuisine: FRENCH. **Reservations:** Required, sometimes six weeks in advance on midsummer weekends.
$ Prices: Appetizers 110–400 F ($19.80–$72); main dishes 190–250 F ($34.20–$45); fixed-price menus 570 F ($102.60) at lunch, 640 F ($115.20) at dinner. AE, DC, MC, V.
  Open: Lunch Wed–Mon noon–2pm; dinner Wed–Sun 7–9pm. **Closed:** Feb and one week in July.

Run by the Haeberlin brothers in what used to be their family's 19th-century farmhouse, L'Auberge de l'Ill combines the finest-quality Alsatian specialties with *cuisine moderne* and other classic offerings. In a scene that could have been painted by Watteau, there is a beautiful garden where you can take your apéritif or coffee under the weeping willows, with a view of the Ill. Inside, the house is furnished with antiques, highly polished silver hollowware, and paintings by Bernard Buffet.

Jean-Pierre Haeberlin, a talented painter and the restaurant's designer, is in charge of the dining room. Paul Haeberlin, the chef, first learned cuisine from his mother and aunt. Soon he was taking dishes of Alsatian origin and making them into grande cuisine, as represented by matelote au riesling, eel stewed in riesling wine, and his inventive foie gras. The partridge, pheasant, and duckling are among the best in Europe. Sometimes braised slices of pheasant and partridge are served together with a winey game sauce, chestnuts, and an unexpected addition of wild mushrooms and light Breton cornmeal. The salmon soufflé is unsurpassed in all of France. Some dishes require 24-hour advance notice.

---

9. COLMAR

273 miles SE of Paris, 87 miles SE of Nancy, 44 miles SW of Strasbourg

GETTING THERE   By Train   Railway lines link Colmar to Nancy, Strasbourg, and Mulhouse, as well as to Germany via Freiburg, just across the Rhine.

By Car   Take the N83 from Strasbourg. Because of Colmar's narrow streets, many motorists park northeast of the railway station, in the Champ-de-Mars, before walking a few blocks east to the heart of the old city.

ESSENTIALS   Orientation   The Musee d'Unterlinden is in the north end, at the terminus of avenue de la République, which passes in front of the railway station.

Information   The Office de Tourisme is at 4, rue d'Unterlinden, 68000 Colmar (tel. 89-20-68-92).

Wine Tours   For information about free winery tours in the district, contact CIVA (Alsace Wine Committee), Maison du Vin d'Alsace, 12, av. de la Foire-aux-Vins (tel. 89-24-09-45). The CIVA office is usually open Monday through Saturday from 9am to noon and 2 to 5pm. Arrangements should be made as far in advance as possible.

One of the most attractive towns in Alsace, Colmar is filled with many old medieval and early Renaissance buildings, with half-timbered structures, sculptured gables, and gracious loggias. Little gardens and wash houses surround many of the old homes. Its old quarter looks more German than French, filled as it is with streets of unexpected twists and turns. As a gateway to the Rhine country, Colmar is a major stopover south from Strasbourg, 44 miles away. On the Ill River, Colmar is the third-largest town in Alsace, lying near the vine-covered slopes of the southern Vosges.

WHAT TO SEE & DO

The city's major attraction is the **Musée d'Unterlinden** (Under the Linden Trees), Place d'Unterlinden (tel. 89-41-89-23), one of the most visited and most famous of all French provincial museums. The museum is housed in a former Dominican convent built in 1232. The convent was the chief seat of Rhenish mysticism in the 14th and 15th centuries. Converted to a museum around 1850, it has been a treasure house of art and history of Alsace ever since.

The jewel of its collection is an immense altar screen with folding, two-sided wing pieces. It was designed that way to show first the Crucifixion, then the Incarnation, framed by the Annunciation and the Resurrection. The carved altar screen depicts St. Anthony visiting the hermit St. Paul. It also reveals the Temptation of St. Anthony, the most soothing and beguiling part of a work, which has some ghastly scenes of misshapen birds, weird monsters, and loathsome animals. The demon of the plague, for example, is depicted with a swollen belly and purple skin, his body blotched with boils, a diabolical grin spread across his horrible face. He stands on webbed feet, his hands rotting stumps reaching out to seize the hermit's breviary. One of the most exciting works in the history of German art, the *Issenheim Altarpiece* was created by the Würzburg-born Matthias Grünewald (1460–1528), called "the most furious of realists." His colors glow, his fantasy overwhelms you.

The museum has other attractions as well, including the magnificent altarpiece of Jean d'Orlier by Martin Schongauer from around 1470. Also displayed are other works of artists from the 14th to the 15th centuries who were painting in Colmar. In religious art, the former convent has a large collection of woodcarvings and stained glass from the 14th to the 18th centuries, plus some lapidary collections of the Gallo-Roman period, including funeral slabs. Its armory collection includes ancient arms from the Romanesque to the Renaissance periods, featuring halberds and crossbows.

Charging 25 F ($4.50) for adults and 15 F ($2.70) for children 12–17 (free for children under 12), the museum is open November to March, Wednesday through Monday from 9am to noon and 2 to 5pm; April through October, daily from 9am to noon and 2 to 6pm.

Eglise St-Martin (St. Martin's Church), in the heart of Old Colmar at 1, cours St-Martin, is a collegiate church begun in 1230 on the site of a Romanesque church. It has a notable choir erected by William of Marburg in 1350. The church is crowned by a steeple rising to a height of 232 feet. Open daily from 8am to 5pm.

About two blocks away, opening onto the place des Dominicains, is the **Eglise des Dominicains,** which contains one of the most famous artistic treasures of Colmar, Martin Schongauer's painting *Virgin of the Rosebush,* all gold, red, and white, with fluttering birds. Look for it in the choir.

Visiting hours are 10am to 6pm daily; closed November to March. Admission is 10 F ($1.80) for adults, 5 F (90¢) for children.

One of the most beautiful houses in Colmar is the **Maison Pfister,** 11 rue des Marchands (tel. 89-41-33-61), a civic building erected in 1537 with wooden balconies. It stands at the corner of rue Mercière. On the ground floor is a wine boutique (wineshop) which presents a vast array of wines. The shop is owned by a major Alsace wine grower, Mure, proprietor of the vineyard Clos St-Landelin.

If you take St. Peter's Bridge over the Lauch River, you'll have an excellent view of Old Colmar and can explore the section known as **Petite Venice** because it is riddled with canals.

Because of the Statue of Liberty in New York, interest continues in Auguste Bartholdi, who was born in Colmar in 1834. This sculptor enjoys world fame as the creator of the Statue of Liberty. **Musée Bartholdi,** 30, rue des Marchands (tel. 89-41-90-60), is a small memento-filled museum of the artist. There are Statue of Liberty rooms containing plans and scale models of the statue, as well as documents in connection with its construction and other works regarding U.S. history. The Paris apartment of Bartholdi, with furniture and memorabilia, has been reconstructed here. The museum supplements its exhibits with displays tracing the history of Colmar.

The museum is open March through December, daily from 10am to noon and 2 to 6pm. Admission is 20 F ($3.60) for adults, 10 F ($1.80) for children ages 8–18.

WHERE TO STAY

LA FECHT, 1, rue de la Fecht, 68000 Colmar. Tel. 89-41-34-08. Fax 89-23-80-28. 39 rms (all with bath). MINIBAR TV TEL
$ Rates: 290 F ($52.20) single; 400 F ($72) double. Breakfast 37 F ($6.70) extra. AE, DC, MC, V.

Conveniently set at the edge of the old city, La Fecht is a small hotel with a garden and outdoor terrace. The well-designed rooms include clock radios. The hotel's restaurant serves well-prepared meals costing 92–250 F ($16.60–$45).

HOSTELLERIE LE MARECHAL, 4-5, place des Six-Montagnes-Noires, 68000 Colmar. Tel. 89-41-60-32. Fax 89-24-59-40. 30 rms (all with bath), 6 suites. MINIBAR TV TEL
$ Rates: 450 F ($81) single; 550 F ($99) double; 1,000–1,400 F ($180–$252) suite. Breakfast 60 F ($10.80) extra. AE, MC, V. **Parking:** Free.

This hotel was formed when three 16th-century houses were joined. The Lauch River is visible from the rear windows, as are the rows of narrow houses. Guests climb a wide staircase to reach the bedrooms, most of which are air-conditioned. In the east wing there's a small, partially timbered room with a sloping ceiling.

When Gilbert Bomo set up this hostelry in 1972, he created a winter restaurant with a welcoming fireplace. In summer the restaurant is moved to another part of the complex, so that diners have a water view. You can feast on such specialties as stuffed quail, good beef and veal dishes, and lamb provençal—accompanied by Tokay and Alsatian wines. Fixed-price menus cost 180 F ($32.40), 220 F ($39.60), 320 F ($57.60), and 450 F ($81).

HOTEL TURENNE, 10, route de Bâle, 68000 Colmar. Tel. 89-41-12-26.
Fax 89-41-27-64. 83 rms (all with bath). TV TEL
$ Rates: 280 F ($50.40) single; 350 F ($63) double. Breakfast 36 F ($6.50) extra. AE, DC, MC, V. **Parking:** Free.

Relatively modern, and built in the traditional Alsatian style with pointed roofs and wooden shutters, this hotel has a warm interior with wood furnishings and an informal lounge. Rooms are simply but comfortably furnished. A continental breakfast is the only meal served.

TERMINUS-BRISTOL, 7, place de la Gare, 68000 Colmar. Tel. 89-23-59-59.
Fax 89-23-92-26. 70 rms (all with bath). MINIBAR TV TEL
$ Rates: 400–450 F ($72–$81) single; 500–750 F ($90–$135) double. Breakfast 50 F ($9) extra. AE, DC, MC, V. **Parking:** Free.

The red sandstone Terminus-Bristol is the traditional first choice, housing Rendezvous de Chasse, one of the finest restaurants and bars in Colmar. Right at the busy railway station, the hotel provides bedrooms with both modern and provincial decor.

WHERE TO DINE

In addition to the following, some of the hotels listed above have restaurants.

AU FER ROUGE, 52, Grand'Rue. Tel. 89-41-37-24.
Cuisine: FRENCH. **Reservations:** Required.
$ Prices: Appetizers 145–180 F ($26.10–$32.40); main dishes 150–240 F ($27–$43.20); fixed-price menus 210–470 F ($37.80–$84.60) Mon–Fri, 350–470 F ($63–$84.60) Sat–Sun. AE, DC, MC, V.
Open: Lunch Tues–Sun noon–2pm; dinner Tues–Sat 7–9:30pm. **Closed:** Jan and Aug 1–2.

In a black-and-white-timbered building that opens onto a small cobblestone square, Au Fer Rouge has stained- and bottle-glass windows and outside boxes that overflow with geraniums in summer. Inside, carved oak beams and brass and copper decorations provide both floors of dining with a traditional setting.

Owner Patrick Fulgraff has departed from the typical Alsatian fare in favor of the more inventive styles of the legendary Paul Bocuse of Lyon and Monsieur Peyrot of Paris. Specialties include noisettes of lamb with tarragon, quail with shredded cabbage and truffles, roast suckling pig, filet of beef with marrow, wild duck cooked in its own juice, and, for dessert, apples and cinnamon in puff pastry. Overall, the restaurant provides good service and a variety of selections.

LA MAISON DES TETES, 19, rue des Têtes. Tel. 89-24-43-43.
Cuisine: FRENCH. **Reservations:** Required.
$ Prices: Appetizers 40–119 F ($7.20–$21.40); main dishes 76–195 F ($13.70–$35.10); fixed-price menus 130 F ($23.40), 168 F ($30.20), 176 F ($31.70), 198 F ($35.60), and 300 F ($54). AE, DC, MC, V.
Open: Lunch Tues–Sun noon–1:45pm; dinner Tues–Sat 7–9:30pm. **Closed:** Jan 15–Feb.

La Maison des Têtes, or the "House of Heads," is a Colmar monument named for the sculptured heads on its stone facade. The building itself, reached by way of a covered cobblestone driveway and open courtyard, dates from 1609. The two dining rooms are decorated with aged-wood beams and paneling, art nouveau lighting fixtures in clusters of glass grapes, and stained-glass and leaded windows. Details, such as an elaborate hand-carved wooden clock and a free-standing stove with decorative tiles, provide a cozy atmosphere.

The food is excellent, including the traditional foie gras with truffles, choucroute, seasonal roebuck served with morels, and fresh trout or Rhine salmon braised in riesling wine. There is also a young chicken dish flavored with tarragon sauce, as well as a specially prepared crayfish. The Alsatian wines are superb.

RENDEZ-VOUS DE CHASSE, in the Hôtel Terminus-Bristol, 7, place de la Gare. Tel. 89-41-10-10.
  Cuisine: FRENCH. **Reservations:** Recommended.
$ **Prices:** Appetizers 95–150 F ($17.10–$27); main dishes 110–190 F ($19.80–$34.20); fixed-price menus 180–390 F ($32.40–$70.20). AE, DC, MC, V.
  Open: Lunch Wed–Mon noon–2:30pm; dinner Wed–Mon 7–10pm.

Located in the previously recommended Hôtel Terminus-Bristol, this first-class restaurant offers fine food, a plushly upholstered sense of calm, and an elegant setting. In a pale green setting, with a monumental fireplace and three bay windows, you can order meals which might begin with a terrine of duckling foie gras with a small celery-and-apple salad, then go on to roast pike perch or young rabbit pie with tender turnips and prunes; a specialty is boned pigs' trotters. Tarts are based on seasonal fresh fruit.

SCHILLINGER, 16, rue Stanislas. Tel. 89-41-43-17.
  Cuisine: FRENCH. **Reservations:** Required.
$ **Prices:** Appetizers 120–330 F ($21.60–$59.40); main dishes 150–320 F ($27–$57.60); fixed-price menus 360 F ($64.80) and 500 F ($90). AE, DC, MC, V.
  Open: Lunch Tues–Sun noon–2:15pm; dinner Tues–Sat 7–9:15pm. **Closed:** July 5–26.

Schillinger is a *belle maison,* with Louis XVI–style decor. The talented chef, Jean Schillinger, prepares such specialties as foie gras maison, foie d'oie chaud au vinaigre, and duckling in lemon sauce (for two). This is the most acclaimed restaurant in Colmar.

NEARBY ACCOMMODATIONS & DINING

L'AUBERGE DU PERE-FLORANC, 9, rue Herzog, 68920 Wettolsheim.
  Tel. 89-80-79-14. Fax 89-79-77-00. 31 rms (all with bath), 1 suite. TV TEL
  Directions: Head westward from Colmar for 2½ miles on the RN83.
$ **Rates:** 295–345 F ($53.10–$62.10) single or double; 510 F ($91.80) suite. Breakfast 50 F ($9) extra. AE, DC, MC, V. **Parking:** Free. **Closed:** Mon all year, Sun night Nov to mid-July, two weeks in July, and mid-Nov to mid-Dec.
Contained in a complex of modern and 1920-era buildings in the agrarian hamlet of Wettolsheim, west of Colmar, this establishment dates from before World War II. It's directed by René Floranc, whose two sons, Daniel (the chef de cuisine) and Patrick (maître d'hôtel of the excellent dining room), work here with their wives. Bedrooms are well upholstered, traditionally styled, and very comfortable; some are located in an outlying annex known as the Pavilion.

Almost every overnight guest opts for an evening meal in the dining room. Menu specialties include an appetizer containing four different preparations of foie gras in the style of the house, a cassolette of snails with flap mushrooms, stuffed pike en croûte, an excellent version of tournedos, and autumnal game dishes. One touch I like—one of the dessert cakes is named after Albert Schweitzer, who was born nearby. Service is efficient and courteous. Fixed-price meals cost 95–375 F ($17.10–$67.50).

10. THE WINE ROAD OF ALSACE

From Strasbourg, motorists heading south to the sights of Colmar, 42 miles away, can take the N83, a direct route. However, if you've got the time, the famous wine road of Alsace is one of the most rewarding sightseeing targets in eastern France. For some 60 miles the road goes through charming villages, many of which are illuminated on summer nights for your viewing pleasure. Along the way are country inns if you'd like to stop and sample some of the wine, perhaps take a leisurely lunch or dinner or a room for the night. The wine road runs along the foothills of the Vosges. Medieval towers and feudal ruins evoke the pageantry of a faded time.

Of course, the slopes are covered with vines, as there are an estimated 50,000 acres of vineyards along this road, sometimes reaching a height of 1,450 feet. Some 30,000 families earn their living tending the grapes. The best time to go is for the vintage in September and October.

Riesling is the king of Alsatian wine, with its exquisitely perfumed bouquet. Other wines include Chasselas, Knipperle, Sylvaner, Pinot Blanc (one of the oldest of Alsatian wines), Muscat (a dry fruit wine), Pinot Auxerrois, Pinot Gris, Traminer, and Gewürztraminer.

The traditional route starts at—

MARLENHEIM   This agreeable wine town—noted for its Vorlauf red wine—lies 13 miles due west of Strasbourg on the N4. You might want to visit it even if you can't take the complete route, as it offers an excellent inn, Hostellerie du Cerf.

Where to Stay and Dine in Marlenheim

HOSTELLERIE DU CERF, 30, rue du Général-de-Gaulle, 67520 Marlenheim. Tel. 88-87-73-73. Fax 88-87-68-08. 15 rms (all with bath or shower), 2 suites. TEL

$ Rates: 450–550 F ($81–$99) single or double; 600 F ($108) suite. Breakfast 55–80 F ($9.90–$14.40) extra. AE, MC, V. **Parking:** 10 F ($1.80).

Set in the heart of the medieval village, in a half-timbered building at least 300 years old, this establishment offers 15 pleasantly furnished bedrooms which adjoin an excellent restaurant (10 of the rooms contain TV and minibar).

Robert Husser and his son, Michel, will feed you such specialties as fresh foie gras, a cassolette of lobster, a ballotine of quail (in autumn only) with sweetbreads, oysters cooked in court bouillon and flavored with herbs, and roast turbot served with small strips of vegetables. One of the most charming offerings is an all-Alsatian fixed-price meal, featuring the region's culinary bounty and traditions for 380 F ($68.40) per person. Other fixed-price meals begin at 295 F ($53.10) at lunch during the week. Regular fixed-price menus cost 325–450 F ($58.50–$81). The restaurant is closed every Tuesday and Wednesday; other days, hours are noon to 2:15pm and 6:15 to 9pm.

WANGEN   One of the many jewels along the route, Wangen contains narrow, twisting streets. A city gate is crowned by a tower. It's one of the most typical of the Alsatian wine towns. The road from Wangen winds down to—

MOLSHEIM   This is one of the ten free cities of Alsace, called the "Decapolis." It retains its old ramparts and has a Gothic and Renaissance church built in 1614–1619, plus a large fountain. Its Alte Metzig, or town hall, was erected by the Guild of Butchers and is a most interesting sight, with its turret, gargoyles, loggia, and a belfry housing a clock with allegorical figures striking the hour.

ROSHEIM   Nestled behind medieval fortifications, this old wine-growing town— another of the ten free Alsatian cities of the empire—has a Romanesque house of the 12th century and the Church of Sts. Peter and Paul, also Romanesque, from two centuries later, which is dominated by an octagonal tower. Medieval walls and gate towers evoke its past.

OBERNAI   The patron saint of Alsace, Obernai, was born here. With its old timbered houses and colorful marketplace, the Place du Marché, it is one of the most interesting stopovers along the wine route. Its walls are partially preserved. The Place de l'Etoile is decked out in flowers, and the Hôtel de Ville of 1523 has a delightful loggia (inside you can view the council chamber). An old watchtower, the Tour de la Chapelle, is from the 13th and 16th centuries. The town's six-pail fountain is one of the most spectacular in Alsace.

The **Office de Tourisme** is located at Chapelle du Beffroi, 67210 Obernoi (tel. 88-95-64-13).

Where to Stay and Dine in Obernai

LE PARC, 169, rue du Général-Gourand, 67210 Obernai. Tel. 88-95-50-08. Fax 88-95-37-29. 50 rms (all with bath). TV TEL

$ Rates: 380 F ($68.40) single; 450–570 F ($81–$102.60) double. Half board (required in high season) 650 F ($117) single; 970 F ($174.60) double; three-day minimum stay. Breakfast 55 F ($9.90) extra. AE, MC, V. **Parking:** Free. **Closed:** Dec 5–Jan 6 and June 28–July 10.

I recommend Le Parc if you're looking for either meals or lodging. The establishment, which is surrounded by a park, contains three dining rooms, each in a different decor. The fresh food depends on what's available in the local markets and might include monkfish with mushrooms, duckling with apples and cèpes (flap mushrooms), a salad of foie gras, salmon in red wine sauce, and rich fruit desserts. À la carte dinners cost 300–350 F ($54–$63); fixed-price menus are 190 F ($34.20), 280 F ($50.40), and 335 F ($60.30). The dining rooms are closed Sunday night and Monday.

On the premises, owner Marc Wucher rents spacious and well-furnished rooms. Additional facilities include a hot tub, a sauna, and a fitness center.

BARR The grapes for some of the finest Alsatian wines, Sylvaner and Gewürtztraminer, are harvested here. The castles of Landsberg and Andlau stand high above the town. Barr has many pleasant old timbered houses and a charming Place de l'Hôtel-de-Ville with a town hall from 1640.

MITTELBERGHEIM Perched like a stork on a housetop, this is a charming village. Its Place de L'Hôtel-de-Ville is bordered with houses in the Renaissance style.

Where to Stay and Dine in Mittelbergheim

WINSTUB GILG, 1, route du Vin, Mittelbergheim, 67140 Barr. Tel. 88-08-91-37. Fax 88-08-45-17. 10 rms (all with bath or shower). TV TEL

$ Rates: 250–360 F ($45–$64.80) single or double. Breakfast 30 F ($5.40) extra. AE, DC, MC, V. **Parking:** Free.

The Winstub Gilg is an excellent inn set in the heart of the village. Although parts of the building date from 1614, its architectural showpiece is a two-story stone staircase, classified as a historic monument, which was carved by the medieval stonemasons who worked on the cathedral at Strasbourg. Bedrooms are comfortably and attractively furnished. Georges Gilg, the old-time chef, attracts a loyal following with his regional specialties, including onion tart, sauerkraut, and foie gras en broche. Main dishes include stewed kidneys and sweetbreads and duck with oranges nantaise. In the shooting season, he is likely to offer roast pheasant with grapes and filets of roebuck. Fixed-price menus run 125–325 F ($22.50–$58.50). The restaurant is closed Tuesday night, Wednesday, from January 5 to February 21, and for 15 days at the end of June.

ANDLAU This garden-like summer resort was once the site of a famous abbey dating from 887, founded by the disgraced wife of the emperor, Charles the Fat. It has now faded into history, but a church remains which dates from the 12th century. In the tympanum are noteworthy Romanesque carvings.

Where to Dine in Andlau

AU BOEUF ROUGE, 6, rue du Dr-Stoltz. Tel. 88-08-96-26.
Cuisine: FRENCH. **Reservations:** Recommended.
$ Prices: Appetizers 55–120 F ($9.90–$21.60); main dishes 85–155 F ($15.30–$27.90); fixed-price menus 160–240 F ($28.80–$43.20). AE, DC, MC, V.
Open: Lunch Fri–Wed 11:30am–2pm; dinner Fri–Tues 6:30–9:30pm. **Closed:** Last week in June to the first week in July.

Once a 16th-century relay station for the French postal services, this structure is now occupied by a rustic, ground-floor dining room and bar. The popular restaurant, which has been owned by the Kieffer family for 100 years, offers such classic specialties as homemade terrines, gamecock, fresh fish, a wide array of meats, and a tempting dessert cart.

DAMBACH In the midst of its well-known vineyards, Dambach is one of the delights of the wine route. Its timbered houses are gabled with galleries, and many contain oriels. Wrought-iron shop signs still tell you if a place is a bakery or a butcher shop. The town has ramparts and three fortified gates. A short drive from the town leads to the Saint Sebastian chapel, with a 15th-century ossuary.

Going through Chatenois, you reach—

SELESTAT   This was once a free city, a center of the Renaissance, and the seat of a great school. Its **Bibliothèque Humaniste,** 1, rue de la Bibliothèque (tel. 88-92-03-24), contains a rare collection of manuscripts including Sainte-Foy's *Book of Miracles.* This library is open Monday through Friday from 9am to noon and 2 to 6pm, and on Saturday from 9am to noon. Admission is 8 F ($1.40) for adults, 5 F (90¢) for children.

The gothic **Church of St-George** contains some fine stained glass and a stone pulpit that was gilded and painted. Finally, see the **Church of Ste-Foy,** built of red sandstone from the Vosges in the Romanesque style in the 12th century. One of the town's most noteworthy Renaissance buildings is the **Maison de Stephan Ziegler.** Towered battlements enclose the town.

The **Office du Tourisme** is located in La Commanderie, boulevard du Général-Leclerc, 67600 Sélestat (tel. 88-92-02-66).

Where to Dine in Selestat

LA COURONNE, 45, rue de Sélestat. Tel. 88-85-32-22.

Cuisine: FRENCH. **Reservations:** Required. **Directions:** From Sélestat, go 5½ miles east on the D21, and when the road forks, take the right-hand turn, the D209, to the village of Baldenheim.

$ Prices: Appetizers 75–135 F ($13.50–$24.30); main dishes 90–160 F ($16.20–$28.80); fixed-price menus 150–395 F ($27–$71.10). AE, MC, V.

Open: Lunch Tues–Sun noon–2pm; dinner Tues–Sat 7–9pm. **Closed:** First week in Jan and the last week in July.

When it was established in the 1930s, this family-run establishment functioned as an unpretentious bistro. Today, its cuisine reflects the bounty of Alsace, prepared with considerable finesse. A flower-filled vestibule near the entrance, where you're greeted, leads to a trio of pleasant dining rooms linked together like railway cars. Menu specialties change with the seasons, but are likely to include noisettes of roebuck (from midsummer until Christmas), frogs' legs in garlic, foie gras, l'omble chevalier (the elusive fish from Lake Geneva) prepared with sauerkraut and cumin-laced potatoes, and a traditional Alsatian dish known as matelote ride, a combination of zander, brochet, and eel poached together in riesling.

HAUT-KOENIGSBOURG CASTLE   From Sélestat, you can make an excursion to Château Haut-Koenigsbourg, 67600 Orschwiller (tel. 88-82-50-60). Standing 2,500 feet up on an isolated peak, this 15th-century castle—the largest in Alsace—treats you to an eagle's nest view. From its platforms, a panoramic view of the Vosges unfolds. It once belonged to the Hohenstaufens. During the Thirty Years' War, the Swedes dismantled the château, but it was rebuilt in 1901 after it was presented as a gift to Kaiser Wilhem II.

It's open daily: June 1 to September, from 9am to 6pm; in April and May, 9am to noon and 1 to 6pm; in March and October, 9am to noon and 1 to 5pm; and November to February, 9am to noon and 1 to 4pm. Admission is 31 F ($5.60) for adults, 6 F ($1.10) for children 7–17.

BERGHEIM   Renowned for its wines, this town has kept part of its 15th-century fortifications. There are many timbered Alsatian houses and a Gothic church.

RIBEAUVILLE   In September a fair is held here known as the "Day of the Strolling Fiddlers." At the foot of vine-clad hills, the town is charming, with old shop signs, pierced balconies, turrets, and flower-decorated houses. See its Renaissance fountain and its Hôtel-de-Ville which has a collection of Alsatian tankards known as "hanaps." Of interest also is the Tour des Bouchers, a "butchers' tower" of the 13th and 16th centuries. The town is also noted for its riesling and Traminer wines.

The Office de Tourisme is at Grand' Rue 68150 Ribeauvillé (tel. 89-73-62-22).

Where to Stay and Dine in Ribeauvillé

CLOS ST-VINCENT, route de Bergheim, 68150 Ribeauvillé. Tel. 89-73-67-65. Fax 89-73-32-20. 12 rms (all with bath or shower), 3 suites.

$ Rates: 600 F ($108) single; 680–840 F ($122.40–$151.20) double; from 970 F ($174.60) suite. MC, V. **Parking:** Free.

Clos St-Vincent, a Relais & Châteaux, is one of the most elegant dining and lodging choices along the Alsatian wine road. Guests here will get much more than a lovely view of the Haut-Rhin landscape of vineyards and summertime roses. Most of the accommodations have a private balcony or terrace overlooking the plain of Alsace.

Bertrand Chapotin's food is exceptional—hot duck liver with nuts, turbot with sorrel, roebuck (in season only) in a hot sauce, and veal kidneys in Pinot Noir. Of course, the wines are smooth, especially the riesling and Gewürztraminer, which seems to be the popular choice. Fixed-price menus cost 250 F ($45).

RIQUEWIHR   This town, surrounded by some of the finest vineyards in Alsace, appears much as it did in the 16th century. With its well-preserved walls and towers, its great wine presses and old wells, it is one of the most rewarding targets along the route. The town has many houses in the Gothic and Renaissance styles, with wooden balconies, voluted gables, and elaborately carved doors and windows. Its most interesting houses are the Maison Liebrich, built in 1535; the Maison Preiss-Zimmer, from 1686; and Maison Kiener, from 1574. If possible, try to peer into some of the galleried courtyards, where centuries virtually have stopped. The High Gate of Dolder, straddling an arch through which you can pass, is from 1291. Nearby, the pentagonal Tower of Thieves (sometimes called "the robbers' tower") contains a torture chamber. The château, from 1539, offers a minor museum devoted to the history of Alsace.

Where to Stay and Dine in Riquewihr

LE RIQUEWIHR, route de Ribeauvillé, 68340 Riquewihr. Tel. 89-47-83-13. Fax 89-47-99-76. 49 rms (all with bath). TEL

$ Rates: 240–280 F ($43.20–$50.40) single; 255–315 F ($45.90–$56.70) double. Breakfast 38 F ($6.80) extra. AE, DC, MC, V. **Parking:** Free.

For an overnight stay, you might try Le Riquewihr, just outside of town. There's a late-night bar in this establishment, but it has no restaurant. That doesn't seem to prevent this place from doing a brisk business, especially in summer. Each of the bedrooms has a view over the vineyards.

AUBERGE DU SCHOENENBOURG, 2, rue de la Piscine. Tel. 89-47-92-28.
Cuisine: FRENCH. **Reservations:** Required.

$ Prices: Appetizers 88–130 F ($15.80–$23.40); main dishes 110–145 F ($19.80–$26.10); fixed-price menus 160 F ($28.80) Mon–Fri, 205–340 F ($36.90–$61.20) Sat–Sun. MC, V.

Open: Lunch daily noon–2pm; dinner daily 7–9:30pm. **Closed:** Nov.

A good place to dine is this auberge, where meals are served in a garden setting completely surrounded by vineyards at the edge of the village. The cuisine of Francois Kiener, who used to live in San Francisco, offers a delectable array of tantalizingly prepared dishes—foie gras maison you expect, but salmon soufflé with sabayon truffles is an elegant touch. Perhaps you'll order the panache of fish with sorrel or raviloi of snails with poppy seed. There are no accommodations here.

KIENTZHEIM   Known for its wine, Kientzheim is one of the three towns to explore in this valley of vineyards, ranking along with Kaysersberg and Ammerschwihr. Two castles, timber-framed houses, and walls that date from the Middle Ages make it an appealing choice for a visit. After you have passed through, it is just a short drive to—

KAYSERSBERG   Once a Free City of the empire, Kaysersberg lies at the mouth of the Weiss Valley, built between two vine-covered slopes and crowned by a feudal castle that was ruined in the Thirty Years' War. Kaysersberg rivals Riquewihr as one of the most visited towns along the wine route.

Nestled in a valley between two low hills, the town stretches snake-like along either side of a rushing stream. From one of the many ornately carved bridges, you can see the city's medieval fortifications stretching along the top of one of the nearby hills. Many of the houses are from the Gothic and Renaissance eras, and most of them have prominent half-timbering, lots of wrought-iron accents, small leaded windows, and multiple designs carved into the reddish sandstone that seems to have been the principal building material.

In the cafés you'll hear a confusing combination of French and Alsatian. The language spoken is usually determined by the age of the speaker, the older ones remaining faithful to the dialect spoken by their grandfathers.

Dr. Albert Schweitzer was born in this pleasant town in 1875. His house stands near the fortified bridge over the Weiss. You can visit the **Albert Schweitzer Cultural Center** June to October, daily from 10am to noon and 2 to 6pm.

Where to Stay and Dine in Kaysersberg

CHAMBARD, 9-13, rue du Général-de-Gaulle, 68240 Kaysersberg. Tel. 89-47-10-17. Fax 89-47-35-03.
   Cuisine: FRENCH. **Reservations:** Required.
$ **Prices:** Appetizers 85–110 F ($15.30–$19.80); main dishes 100–200 F ($18–$36); fixed-price menus 300 F ($54), 380 F ($68.40), and 450 F ($81). AE, MC, V.
   Open: Lunch Wed–Sun noon–2pm; dinner daily 7–9:30pm.
   Closed: Mar 1–21 and the Christmas holidays.

Chambard is the domain of a chef of unusual versatility and imagination. His restaurant, with an adjoining hotel, is at the bottom of the main street of town, a thoroughfare lined with half-timbered houses, each of which seems to be at least 300 years old.

You'll recognize the establishment—the finest in town—by the gilded wrought-iron sign hanging above the cobblestones. Inside you'll find a renovated but rustic ambience, with exposed stone and polished wood. The regional cuisine is so good that it's well worth planning your wine tour to include a stopover. Also, try Monsieur Irrmann's foie gras, turbot in ginger, Bresse chicken sautéed with crayfish tails, or chicken sautéed with riesling. Riesling and Tokay are the natural wines to order.

If you decide to spend the night, the Chambard offers an annex constructed in 1981 to match the other buildings on the street. Separated from the restaurant by a stone wall with an antique wine press, the hotel has a massive Renaissance fireplace that was transported from another building. There are 20 rooms; a single costs 650 F ($117) and a double is 850 F ($153), plus 60 F ($10.80) for breakfast.

AU LION D'OR, 66, rue du Général-de-Gaulle. Tel. 89-47-11-16.
   Cuisine: FRENCH. **Reservations:** Required.
$ **Prices:** Appetizers 48–110 F ($8.60–$19.80); main dishes 60–130 F ($10.80–$23.40); fixed-price menus 98 F ($17.60), 145 F ($26.10), 160 F ($28.80), 200 F ($36), and 280 F ($50.40). MC, V.
   Open: Lunch Thurs–Tues noon–2pm; dinner Thurs–Mon 7–9:30pm. **Closed:** Jan–Feb 15.

This restaurant, conveniently situated on the cobblestone main street of town, presents an exceptionally beautiful decor. A carved lion's head is set into the oak door leading into the restaurant where beamed ceilings, stone detailing, brass chandeliers, and the room's focal point, a massive fireplace, are grouped attractively. The building dates from 1521. If you eat at one of the outdoor tables, you'll have a view of one of the prettiest streets of Alsace. There are no accommodations here.

ROUFFACH   One vineyard worth exploring is **Clos St-Landelin** (tel. 89-49-62-19), route du Vin (carrefour RN 83/route de Soultzmatt), lying 10½ miles south of Colmar. Here the vines grow on little hills at the foot of the Vosges. Rouffach is sheltered by one of the highest of the Vosges mountains, the Grand Ballon, which stops the winds that bring rain. That makes for a dry climate and a special grape. Since

1630 the Muré family has owned the vineyards. In their cellar is the oldest wine press in Alsace, dating from the 13th century. They welcome visitors, and English is spoken.

AMMERSCHWIHR Finally, to cap the wine road tour, as you move near the outskirts of Colmar, you'll come to Ammerschwihr. Once an old Free City of the empire, it was almost completely destroyed in 1944 in World War II battles, but has been reconstructed in the traditional style. Motorists stop off here in increasing numbers to drink the wine, especially Käferkopf. A trio of gate towers, a 16th-century parish church, and remains of its early fortifications evoke yesterday.

Where to Stay and Dine in Ammerschwihr

A L'ARBRE VERT, 7, rue des Cigognes, 68770 Ammerschwihr. Tel. 89-47-12-23. Fax 89-78-27-21. 17 rms (all with bath). TV TEL

$ Rates: 220 F ($39.60) single; 370 F ($66.60) double. Half board 270–360 F ($48.60–$64.80) per person. Breakfast 36 F ($6.50) extra. AE, DC, MC, V.
Parking: Free. **Closed:** Tues year round, Feb 15–Mar 25, and Nov 25–Dec 6.

If you don't want to go to Colmar, A l'Arbre Vert is a charming place to stay. Near an old fountain, it's delightfully decorated. The inn also serves very good Alsatian specialties in its restaurant, which is open to the public. Meals go for 95–310 F ($17.10–$55.80).

AUX ARMES DE FRANCE, 1, Grande'Rue, 68770 Ammerschwihr. Tel. 89-47-10-12. Fax 89-47-38-12.
Cuisine: FRENCH. **Reservations:** Required.

$ Prices: Appetizers 115–225 F ($20.70–$40.50); main dishes 150–280 F ($27–$50.40); fixed-price menus 350–450 F ($63–$81). AE, DC, MC, V.
Open: Lunch Fri–Tues noon–2pm; dinner Thurs–Tues 7–9pm. **Closed:** Jan.

While there are accommodations at Aux Armes de France, the real reason to come here is the food—this is the most superb restaurant I've ever found along the Alsatian wine route. In a lovely flower-filled setting, Philippe and François Gaertner receive the finest gourmets of France and Germany. A specialty of the popular restaurant is fresh foie gras served in its own golden aspic. Main dishes include classic cuisine with imaginative variations: roebuck in season in a hot sauce, sole cooked with vermouth, and lobster fricassée with cream and truffles.

There are rooms for rent, each with a telephone; a single or double costs 310–470 F ($55.80–$84.60)—plus 35 F ($6.30) for breakfast.

11. ROUTE DES CRETES (THE CREST ROAD)

From Basel to Mainz, a distance of some 150 miles, the Vosges mountain range stretches along the west side of the Rhine Valley. It bears many similarities to the Black Forest of Germany. Many German and French families spend their entire summer vacation exploring the Vosges. However, those with less time may want to settle back for a quick look at these ancient mountains that once formed the boundary between France and Germany.

The Vosges are filled with tall hardwood and fir, and traversed by a network of narrow, twisting roads with hairpin curves. Deep in these mountain forests is the closest that France comes to having a wilderness.

You can penetrate the mountains by heading due west from Strasbourg. But one of the more interesting routes is picked up from Colmar. From that ancient Alsatian town, you can explore some of the highest of the southern Vosges with their remarkable beauty. The **Route des Crêtes,** or the crest road, begins at **Col du Bonhomme,** to the west of Colmar. The road was devised by the French High Command in World War I to carry supplies over the mountainous front. From Col du

Bonhomme you can strike out along this magnificent road, once the object of such bitter fighting but today a series of panoramic vistas, including one of the Black Forest.

At **Col de la Schlucht** you will have risen a distance of 4,905 feet. Schlucht is both a winter and a summer resort, and it is considered one of the best-known beauty spots of the Vosges—with a panoramic vista unfolding of the Valley of Munster and the slopes of Hohneck. As you skirt along the edge of this splendid, glacier-carved valley, you'll be in the midst of a land of pine groves with a necklace of lakes. You may want to turn off the main road and go exploring in several directions, the scenery is that tempting. But if you're still on the crest road, you can circle **Hohneck,** which is one of the highest peaks of the Vosges, rising 5,300 feet, dominating the Wildenstein Dam of the Bresse winter sports station.

At **Markstein** you'll come into another pleasant summer and winter resort. From there, you can take the N430, then the D10 to **Munster,** where the savory cheese is made. You go via the **Petit-Ballon,** a landscape of forest and mountain meadows with lots of grazing cows.

Finally, at **Grand-Ballon** you will have reached the highest point you can go by road in the Vosges, 4,662 feet. From there you can get out of your car and go for a walk. If it's a clear day, you'll be able to see the Jura, the French Alps beyond, and can gaze upon a panoramic vista of the Black Forest.

Where to Stay and Dine in Munster

AU CHENE VOLTAIRE, route au Chêne-Voltaire, at Luttenbach, 68140 Munster. Tel. 89-77-31-74. 19 rms (15 with bath). TV **Directions:** Take the D10 less than two miles southwest from the town center of Munster.
$ Rates: 175 F ($31.50) single without bath; 225 F ($40.50) double with bath. Breakfast 30 F ($5.40) extra. Half board 165–205 F ($29.70–$36.90) per person. AE, MC. **Parking:** Free.

This chalet-style inn is in the midst of an isolated section of the forest. The modern bedrooms are in a separate building from the rustic restaurant. Unfortunately, you can't dine here unless you're a resident of the hotel. Facilities include a sauna and a solarium.

LA CIGOGNE, 4, place du Marché. Tel. 89-77-32-27. Fax 89-77-28-64.
Cuisine: FRENCH. **Reservations:** Not required.
$ Prices: Appetizers 35–60 F ($6.30–$10.80); main dishes 55–85 F ($9.90–$15.30); fixed-price menus 120–180 F ($21.60–$32.40). MC, V.
Open: Lunch Tues–Sun noon–2pm; dinner Tues–Sat 7:30–9pm. **Closed:** June 24–30 and Nov 18–Dec 15.

This historic inn, set on the village's main square, was established in the 1870s. Today, it retains its old-fashioned Alsatian rusticity, despite a well-conceived remodelling in the 1960s and again in 1990. Meals are served in either the Restaurant or less formally in the Brasserie, where simple platters of Alsatian food comprise meals priced at about 100 F ($18) each.

On the premises, for the most part in a comfortable new wing built in the 1990s, are 22 bedrooms, each with telephone, which rent for 300–350 F ($54–$63) each, with breakfast priced at an additional 38 F ($6.80) each.

12. MULHOUSE

334 miles SE of Paris; 71 miles SW of Strasbourg;
21 miles NW of Basel, Switzerland

GETTING THERE By Plane Mulhouse has an airport, 17 miles southwest of the city center, which it shares with the Swiss city of Basel, 22 miles away.

By Train Mulhouse is well connected by rail to every other city in the region, and to Paris's Gare de l'Est.

ESSENTIALS Orientation The main square, from which many busy streets radiate, is place de la République; place de la Réunion is the old town's central square. Some of the most interesting museums are quite a distance from the center.

Information The Office de Tourisme is at 9, av. Maréchal-Foch (tel. 89-45-68-31).

Called Mülhausen by the Germans, this industrial city is topped in size only by Strasbourg in Alsace. Between the Vosges and the Black Forest, it lies about 56 miles south of Strasbourg, but only some 21 miles northwest of Basel if you're taking the train from Switzerland. On the same Ill River that flows through Strasbourg, it is the capital of an arrondissement in the département of Haut-Rhin.

If Mulhouse has an identity problem, it is to be forgiven. From 1308 until 1515 it was a free imperial city, but in 1648 it was added to the Swiss confederation. It remained with Switzerland until 1798 when it joined France. However, from 1871 to 1918 it was under German control. It is a totally bilingual city; both German and French are spoken today.

For a look at the old town, head for the marketplace, called Place de la Réunion. The town hall, the **Hôtel de Ville,** dates from the 16th century, and is the much-photographed, most interesting structure in town. Its walls are frescoed, and it has a covered outside stairway, an example of Rhenish-Renaissance style.

Those with time to explore will find some interesting museums in Mulhouse.

WHAT TO SEE & DO

MUSEE DE L'AUTOMOBILE, 192, av. de Colmar. Tel. 89-42-29-17.
The Musée de l'Automobile displays the combined collections of the Schlumpf brothers, including more than 400 vintage cars, covering the most important keystones of the European automobile industry. Some of the displays, most of which are in working order, are the steam-powered Jacquot (1878), custom-made Ferraris, more than 100 Bugattis (including two of the most expensive ever made), Rolls-Royces, and many more. Opened in 1989, one section of the museum, Espace Découverte, shows visitors how a car works.
Admission: 52 F ($9.40) adults, 23 F ($4.10) children 6–18.
Open: May–Sept, daily 10am–6pm; Oct–Apr, Wed–Mon 10am–6pm.

MUSEE DE L'IMPRESSION SUR ETOFFES, 3, rue des Bonnes-Gens. Tel. 89-45-51-20.
Containing more than 10 million swatches of cloth, this museum traces the development of printed fabrics from the 1700s. Upstairs you'll find preserved the machines that once were used to print cloth, as well as a collection of old clothing, cloth, and drawings from Alsace and the rest of France, the Far East, and Persia. From June through August printing machines are demonstrated every Monday, Wednesday, and Friday at 3pm.
Admission: 25 F ($4.50) adults, 7 F ($1.30) children.
Open: May–Sept, daily 10am–noon and 2–6pm; Oct–Apr, Wed–Mon 10am–noon and 2–6pm.

MUSEE FRANÇAIS DU CHEMIN DE FER, 2, rue Alfred-de-Glehn. Tel. 89-42-25-67.
Assembled over approximately a dozen railroad tracks, this museum offers a noteworthy collection of train engines and cars. Included are a cutaway section of a steam engine—with diagrams explaining how it works—and steam-powered trains that include the car used by Napoléon III's aides-de-camp in 1856; the interior decor is by Viollet-le-Duc. There is also a collection of 18th-century fire engines and pumps, some of them made from wood.
Admission: 38 F ($6.80) adults, 17 F ($3.10) children.
Open: Apr–Sept, daily 9am–6pm; Oct–Mar, daily 10am–5pm.

WHERE TO STAY

LA BOURSE, 14, rue de la Bourse, 68100 Mulhouse. Tel. 89-56-18-44.
Fax 89-56-60-51. 50 rms (all with bath). TV TEL **Bus:** 4.
$ Rates: 340 F ($61.20) single; 480 F ($86.40) double. Breakfast 42 F ($7.60)
extra. AE, DC, MC, V.

La Bourse offers quiet rooms in a convenient location near the stock exchange, train
station, and place de la République. Bathrooms are usually modern, even if the decor
of the rooms ranges from old-fashioned to contemporary. About half the rooms
overlook an inner courtyard.

**HOTEL ALTEA, 4, place Charles-de-Gaulle, 68100 Mulhouse. Tel. 89-46-
01-23.** Fax 89-56-59-98. 96 rms (all with bath). MINIBAR TV TEL **Bus:** 4.
$ Rates: Mon–Fri, 450 F ($81) single; 495 F ($89.10) double. Sat–Sun, 360 F
($64.80) single or double. Breakfast 50 F ($9) extra. AE, DC, MC, V. **Parking:**
50 F ($9).

Set across from the railway station in the heart of town, this five-story hotel was built
in 1969 and today is known as a middle-bracket favorite of visiting business travelers
from Germany and the rest of France. Part of a nationwide chain, it contains a bar and
a breakfast room, but no restaurant. Bedrooms are comfortable, uncomplicated, and
modern, usually outfitted in monochromatic tones of blue or beige-pink.

**HOTEL DU PARC, 26, rue de la Sinne, 68100 Mulhouse. Tel. 89-66-12-
22.** Fax 89-66-42-44. 73 rms (all with bath or shower), 3 suites. A/C MINIBAR TV
TEL **Bus:** 4.
$ Rates: 700 F ($126) single; 990 F ($178.20) double; from 1,200 F ($216) suite.
Breakfast 70 F ($12.60) extra. AE, DC, MC, V. **Parking:** 80 F ($14.40).

The Hôtel du Parc is, without argument, the leading address of Mulhouse. The
beautifully renovated building was designed to recapture the glamour of the 1930s
and to provide tasteful accommodations. Live music at teatime is one of the house's
time-honored traditions. There is a sleek art deco bar called Charlie's, and the
restaurant, Park's, offers quality luncheons, dinners, and after-theater suppers.

**INTER HOTEL SALVATOR, 29, passage Central, 68070 Mulhouse
CEDEX. Tel. 89-45-28-32.** 39 rms (all with bath). A/C TV TEL **Bus:** 4.
$ Rates: 260 F ($46.80) single; 300 F ($54) double. Breakfast 35 F ($6.30) extra.
AE, DC, MC, V. **Parking:** 25 F ($4.50).

The Inter Hôtel Salvator is a peaceful hotel in the center of the town's entertainment
district, near the Musée de l'Automobile. Rooms are comfortably furnished, and the
hotel has a private garage and an elevator. The reception staff speaks English.

WHERE TO DINE

**LE BELVEDERE, 80, av. de la Première-Division-Blindée. Tel. 89-44-
18-79.**
Cuisine: FRENCH. **Reservations:** Recommended. **Bus:** 4.
$ Prices: Appetizers 65–120 F ($11.70–$21.60); main dishes 100–120 F ($18–
$21.60); fixed-price menus 100 F ($18), 150 F ($27), 240 F ($43.20), and 300 F
($54). AE, DC, MC, V.
Open: Lunch Wed–Mon 11:45am–2pm; dinner Wed–Sun 7–9:45pm. **Closed:**
Aug 1–15.

Le Belvédère is an intimate, family-run restaurant, complete with candles, fireplace,
and ceremoniously delivered silver platters. Menu items include a three-fish platter in
riesling, salmon tartare in puff pastry, a filet of pike perch in a parsley-cream sauce,
and, when available, a well-prepared sole meunière or amandine. The restaurant offers
both fixed-price and à la carte listings.

LE RELAIS DE LA TOUR, 3, bd. de l'Europe. Tel. 89-45-12-14.
Cuisine: FRENCH. **Reservations:** Required. **Bus:** 14.
$ Prices: Appetizers 39–95 F ($7–$17.10); main dishes 77–105 F ($13.90–
$18.90); fixed-price menus 120–144 F ($21.60–$25.90). AE, DC, MC, V.
Open: Lunch daily 11:45am–2:30pm; dinner daily 7–9:30pm.

This restaurant, set on the 31st floor of the tallest office and apartment building in town, is the only one of its kind in eastern France. Built in 1973, and a tourist attraction in its own right, it pivots on its base and usually makes a complete panoramic turn every 75 minutes. As you dine, sweeping views will unfold over the Vosges, the Jura, and the Black Forest of Germany. Menu specialties cover a wide French-inspired base, and include quail stuffed with foie-gras mousse, a gratin of seafood, veal in the Zurich style, and well-flavored filets of duck, beef, and veal.

THE FRENCH ALPS

No part of France is more dramatically scenic than the Alps. The western ramparts of the Alps and their foothills is a majestic section of grandeur. From the Mediterranean to the Rhine in the north, they stretch along the southeastern flank of France.

The skiing here has no equal in Europe, not even in Switzerland. Some of the resorts are legendary, including Chamonix-Mont Blanc, the historic capital of alpine skiing, with its 12-mile Vallée Blanc run. Mont Blanc, of course, is the highest mountain in Western Europe, rising 15,780 snowy feet.

Most of my recommendations will fall in the area known as Savoy, taking in the French lake district, including the largest alpine lake, which the French share with Switzerland. The French call it Lac Léman, but it is known as Lake Geneva in English.

SEEING THE FRENCH ALPS

GETTING THERE Winter attracts skiers to Chamonix–Mont Blanc, Megève, and Courchevel 1850; summer brings spa devotees to Evian-les-Bains and Aix-les-Bains. The ideal times to visit, then, are January through March for winter sports and July through September for lakeside and mountain touring.

Grenoble, the capital of the French Alps, is the gateway. It's just 30 minutes by car from the Grenoble–Saint Geoirs airport, 40 minutes from the Lyon-Satolas international airport, and 90 minutes from the Geneva–Cointrin airport. Grenoble is also a major rail hub; trains from Paris take 3⅓ hours. The city is also connected with the Paris–Lyon–Marseille motorway on the west, and to the Chambéry–Geneva motorway on the east.

A SUGGESTED ROUTE Many visitors don't "tour" the area, skipping from one town to another. Instead, they usually select a resort and branch out for day excursions. In both winter and summer, Chamonix–Mont Blanc and Megève make ideal bases; or if you're interested in art and history, make Grenoble your center.

For a summer lakeside tour, drive along Lac d'Annecy, staying overnight in Talloires or Annecy. I'd recommend taking the road from Annecy to Faverges via Duingt; on the return trip, take the road from Faverges to Annecy along Col de la Forclaz. The 35-mile trip takes about three hours, with many stops along the way.

Another interesting alpine tour begins at Grenoble (Day 1), then Chambéry (Day 2), stopping off in the mountains at Courchevel 1850 (Day 3), with final nights and visits to Megève (Day 4) and Chamonix–Mont Blanc (Day 5).

WHAT'S SPECIAL ABOUT THE FRENCH ALPS

Great Ski Resorts

- ☐ Chamonix–Mont Blanc, the best of all the French ski resorts, at an altitude of 3,422 feet, opening onto Mont Blanc.
- ☐ Courchevel 1850, a chic enclave in the ski world, and part of Les Trois Vallées, with spectacular ski runs.
- ☐ Megève, *capitale du ski*—its ski school is one of the best in Europe.

Great Towns/Villages

- ☐ Talloires, a gastronomic village of eastern France.
- ☐ Chambéry, ancient capital of the Duchy of Savoy, with many buildings from the 15th and 16th centuries.
- ☐ Grenoble, capital of Dauphine, with excursions to the old monastery where Chartreuse liqueur is made.

Premier Spas

- ☐ Evian-les-Bains, the leading spa of eastern France, famed for its still waters.

- ☐ Annecy, on Lac d'Annecy, the jewel of the Savoy Alps and capital of Haute-Savoie.

Scenic Vistas

- ☐ Cable cars to the belvederes at Chamonix–Mont Blanc, considered among the most spectacular in the world.
- ☐ Megève, offering a chair hoist to Mont d'Arbois at 6,000 feet for a panorama of Mont Blanc.

Lake Excursions

- ☐ Annecy offers the best, across a body of water called "The Jewel of the Savoy Alps."

Literary Pilgrimages

- ☐ Les Charmettes, outside Chambéry, a 17th-century manor where Rousseau lived (read his *Confessions*).

1. EVIAN-LES-BAINS

358 miles SW of Paris, 26 miles NE of Geneva

GETTING THERE Evian-les-Bains is easily reached from Geneva, by train, car, or ferry.

ESSENTIALS The city sprawls in a long, narrow strip along the southern coast of **Lac Léman (Lake Geneva).** Its most prominent building, the casino, is in the center of town, separated from the lake by a swath of greenery and a waterfront promenade. The **Office de Tourisme** is on place d'Allinges (tel. 50-75-04-26).

On the château-dotted southern shore of Lac Léman, Evian-les-Bains is one of the leading spas and resorts in eastern France. Its lakeside promenade lined with trees and sweeping lawns has been fashionable since the 19th century. In the 16th century Evian was ruled by Switzerland, but it passed to France in 1860.

The waters of Evian became famous in the 18th century, and the first spa buildings were erected in 1839. Bottled Evian, one of the great French table waters, is considered beneficial for everything from baby's formula and salt-free diets to treating gout and arthritis.

In the town center is the Hôtel de Ville and the **Casino Royal,** Château de Blonay, rive Sud du Lac (tel. 50-21-25-10), patronized heavily by the Swiss from across the lake. The casino, charging an entrance fee of 60 F ($10.80), offers blackjack, baccarat, and roulette, among other games, and has floor shows in the Cabaret-Discothèque Le Régent five nights a week from February to mid-December. There's no fee for the show, but you must order a minimum number of drinks.

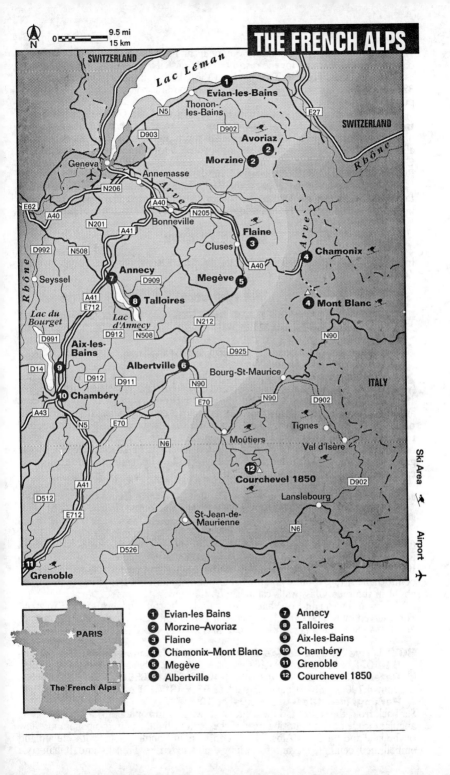

THE FRENCH ALPS

0 — 9.5 mi
0 — 15 km
N

SWITZERLAND

Lac Léman

1 Evian-les-Bains

Thonon-les-Bains

N5

D902

E27

SWITZERLAND

D903

Avoriaz **2**

Geneva

Morzine **2**

Rhône

Annemasse

N206

Arve

A40

E62

A40

N205

N201

A41

Bonneville

Flaine **3**

Arve

D992

N508

Cluses

Chamonix ⛷

Annecy **7**

A40

Seyssel

D909

Megève **5**

A41

E712

8 Talloires

Mont Blanc ⛷ **4**

Lac du Bourget

Lac d'Annecy

N212

Rhône

D912

N508

N90

D991

D925

Aix-les-Bains

D14

9

Albertville **6**

Bourg-St-Maurice

ITALY

10 Chambéry

D912

D911

N90

N90

D902

A43

E70

Tignes

N5

E70

Moûtiers

Val d'Isère

N6

D512

A41

12

Courchevel 1850

D902

Lanslebourg

St-Jean-de-Maurienne

E712

N6

D526

11

Grenoble

Ski Area ⛷

Airport ✈

PARIS ★

The French Alps

1 Evian-les Bains
2 Morzine–Avoriaz
3 Flaine
4 Chamonix–Mont Blanc
5 Megève
6 Albertville

7 Annecy
8 Talloires
9 Aix-les-Bains
10 Chambéry
11 Grenoble
12 Courchevel 1850

In addition to its spa buildings, Evian offers an imposing **Ville des Congrès,** or convention hall, earning for the resort the title of "city of conventions."

In summer the **Nautical Center** on the lake is a popular attraction; it has a 328-foot pool with a diving stage, solarium, restaurant, bar, and children's paddling pool.

The major excursion in Evian is a boat trip on Lake Geneva offered by the **Compagnie Générale de Navigation.** Go to the Office du Tourisme (see "Essentials," above) to pick up a schedule of tariffs and hours—in summer there are also night cruises. If you want to see it all, you can tour both the Haut-Lac and the Grand-Lac. The quickest and most heavily booked of all trips is the crossing from Evian to Ouchy-Lausanne, Switzerland, on the north side.

Crescent-shaped Lake Geneva is the largest lake in central Europe: the name Lac Léman was revived in the 18th century. Taking in an area of approximately 225 square miles, the lake is formed by the Rhône, and it is noted for its unusual blueness.

WHERE TO STAY

In addition to the choices that follow, the Hôtel-Restaurant Le Bourgogne (see "Where to Dine," below) also offers rooms for rent.

Expensive

HOTEL DE LA VERNIAZ ET SES CHALETS, av. Verniaz, à Neuvecelle, 74500 Evian-les-Bains. Tel. 50-75-04-90. Fax 50-70-78-92. 35 rms (all with bath), 5 suites. MINIBAR TV TEL

$ Rates (including half board): 750–850 F ($135–$153) per person. AE, DC, MC, V. **Parking:** Free. **Closed:** Nov–Jan.

This glamorous and sophisticated place has attracted a host of celebrated people, including the Aga Khan and Elizabeth Taylor. Up from the lake, the country house stands on a hillside, with a panoramic view of woods, waters, and the Alps. It is perhaps the most self-contained establishment in the area and is beautifully run and managed. The rustic central building has balconies, beams, and plaster or stone construction. The guest rooms are either here in the main house or in one of the separate chalets, such as "Le Cyclamen." The chalets have their own gardens and total privacy, but they're pricey. The hotel offers suites and bedrooms, each well furnished with many amenities.

LES PRES FLEURIS, route de Thollon, 74500 Evian-les-Bains. Tel. 50-75-29-14. Fax 50-70-77-75. 12 rms (all with bath). MINIBAR TV TEL

$ Rates: 850–1,300 F ($153–$234) single or double. Breakfast 75 F ($13.50) extra. AE, MC, V. **Parking:** Free. **Closed:** Mid-Oct to mid-May

One of the best and most scenic places to stay in the environs, this Relais & Châteaux is a casual, white-painted, attractive little villa on a lake 4½ miles east of Evian. Each bedroom is richly furnished, often with antiques or reproductions. There's a comfortable sitting room with armchairs, and many vases of fresh flowers are placed about in summer. Glass walls capitalize on the view.

Tables and wrought-iron chairs are set under the trees for meals in fair weather. Food served by M and Mme Roger Frossard is exceptional: A fixed-price menu costs 260 F ($46.80), and à la carte meal offerings average 400 F ($72).

ROYAL, rive Sud du Lac-de-Génève, 74500 Evian-les-Bains. Tel. 50-26-85-00. Fax 50-75-61-00. 127 rms (all with bath), 29 suites. MINIBAR TV TEL

$ Rates: 1,560 F ($280.80) single; 3,120–3,560 F ($561.60–$640.80) double; from 4,700 F ($846) suite. Breakfast 95 F ($17.10) extra. AE, DC, MC, V. **Parking:** Free. **Closed:** Dec 10–Feb 10.

Set back from the resort and the center of town and surrounded by a large park, the angular facade of this imposing turn-of-the-century building offers a panoramic view of the lake and the Swiss Alps. The interior contains public rooms with vaulted and embellished ceilings, elegant furnishings, and extensive French- and Italian-style murals. Each of the bedrooms has its own balcony or loggia. Rates are complicated, with about nine separate tariffs offered, ranging from tennis and golf programs to "super dietetic."

Dining/Entertainment: The club has six different restaurants, the most traditional in cuisine being the Café Royal, done in a sumptuous decor that includes frescoes and murals by well-known artist Gustave Jaulmes. The menus change daily, based on fresh seasonal produce. Another restaurant, La Toque Royale, is listed separately under "Where to Dine," below.

Services: 24-hour room service, laundry, dry cleaning.

Facilities: Three heated swimming pools, hotel gym, exercise and fitness programs, golf, tennis, archery, aerobic jogging trail, children's club.

Inexpensive

LES CYGNES, Grande-Rive, 74500 Evian-les-Bains. Tel. 50-75-01-01. 40 rms (25 with shower but no toilet, 15 with bath). TEL

$ Rates (including breakfast): 200 F ($36) single with shower, no toilet; 255 F ($45.90) single with bath; 290 F ($52.20) double with shower, no toilet; 300–320 F ($54–$57.60) double with bath. V. **Closed:** Sept 16–June 14.

This is one of the bargains at the spa, although it's not centrally located. It was custom-built as a hotel in 1926. The Norman-style villa opens onto a lake port and is characterized by dormer windows, a conical tower, a decorative beam-and-plaster facade, a mansard roof, an entrance courtyard surrounded by flowers and shrubs, and a waterside terrace with a grape arbor and a pier extending into the lake. This homelike hotel, family run, is convenient to use as a base from which to explore Lake Geneva. Bedrooms are pleasant but old-fashioned.

WHERE TO DINE

DA BOUTTAU, quai Baron de Blonay. Tel. 50-75-02-44.
  Cuisine: FRENCH. **Reservations:** Required.
$ Prices: Appetizers 75–135 F ($13.50–$24.30); main dishes 125–195 F ($22.50–$35.10); fixed-price menu 180 F ($32.40). AE, DC, MC, V.
  Open: Lunch Wed–Mon noon–2pm; dinner Wed–Sun 7:30–9:30pm. **Closed:** Jan–Feb.

Originally founded in Nice in 1860, this has been a good two-fork restaurant in Evian for many years. Even though it's in the Alps, Da Bouttau retains its Mediterranean provincial decor with an elaborate use of copper pots. The restaurant is right near the casino, and its terrace fronts the lake; in fair weather you can request a dining table outside. The classic cuisine offers such dishes as a petite marmite of seafood, filet of turbot in a "chemise," and young rabbit gratinée with mushrooms.

HOTEL-RESTAURANT LE BOURGOGNE, place Charles-Cottet, 74500 Evian-les-Bains. Tel. 50-75-01-05.
  Cuisine: FRENCH. **Reservations:** Required.
$ Prices: Restaurant, appetizers 75–140 F ($13.50–$25.20); main dishes 88–145 F ($15.80–$26.10); fixed-price menus 145–300 F ($26.10–$54). Brasserie, fixed-price menus 69–95 F ($12.40–$17.10). AE, DC, MC, V.
  Open: Apr–Nov, lunch daily noon–2pm; dinner daily 7:30–9:30pm. Dec–Mar, lunch Tues–Sun noon–2pm; dinner Tues–Sat 7:30–9:30pm.

The establishment's core was originally built as a private home in the 1840s, but was enlarged twice in the 1980s. This charming inn located near the Congress Hall has many appealing decorative touches. Come here if you want a delectable meal, irreproachable service, an attractive setting, and excellent wine—regional wines featured are Crépy and Rousette. Dishes are likely to include veal sweetbreads "des gourmets," filet of beef in a poivrade sauce, and émincé of duckling with caramelized peaches. You have a choice of formal dining in the restaurant or you can dine informally in the brasserie. Only the restaurant is closed in November, and both the hotel and the brasserie remain open.

The inn also offers 31 well-furnished and comfortable bedrooms, all with baths, TVs, and phones. Rates are 480 F ($86.40) in a single, 520 F ($93.60) in a double, plus 39 F ($7) for breakfast and 40 F ($7.20) for parking. Other facilities of the hotel include a sauna, sun terrace, and solarium.

LA TOQUE ROYALE, Casino Royal, Château de Blonay, rive Sud du Lac. Tel. 50-75-03-78.
   Cuisine: FRENCH. **Reservations:** Required.
$ **Prices:** Appetizers 85–185 F ($15.30–$33.30); main dishes 145–215 F ($26.10–$38.70); fixed-price menus 185–550 F ($33.30–$99). AE, DC, MC, V.
   Open: Lunch daily noon–2pm; dinner daily 7:30–10:50pm.

The gourmet restaurant of the Royal Hotel (see "Where to Stay," above) is the most elegantly appointed place to eat in Evian, lying one floor above ground level with a view of the lake. Patrick Frenot, a leader in a new generation of French chefs, welcomes you with fixed-price menus plus an à la carte listing. Service is courteous and efficient. The cuisine is classic French, with many specialties from the Savoy region. Order the famed lake fish, l'omble chevalier, along with sweetbreads with flap mushrooms, Bresse pigeon with chanterelles, or a côte of beef with shallots.

2. MORZINE–AVORIAZ

370 miles SE of Paris, 25 miles S of Evian

GETTING THERE   Morzine and Avoriaz are the last stops on an ascending road that leads from Lake Geneva to a dead-end near the Swiss border. Most visitors drive to Morzine, but there is also bus service from Geneva, depositing passengers near the center of town.

To reach Avoriaz, drive along a nine-mile winding road northeast from Morzine, or take an aerial téléphérique from the cable-car station three miles east of the center of Morzine. Since cars are usually not allowed on many of Avoriaz's innermost streets, many visitors prefer to park at the base of the téléphérique and enjoy the alpine views during their ascent.

ESSENTIALS   In Morzine, the **Office de Tourisme** is on place Crusaz (tel. 50-79-03-45). In Avoriaz, a tourist office (tel. 50-74-02-11) is found at the last stop on the road before the real mountains begin.

MORZINE

The tourist capital of the Haut-Chablais district, Morzine stands in the middle of foothills and forest. The most northerly of the French alpine resorts, it offers such attractions as sleigh rides, beautiful pine forests, ice shows, and more than a dozen cabarets. For years it was known as a summer resort, but now it's also acclaimed for being a winter ski center.

From Morzine, you can visit **Lac de Montriond,** at an altitude of 3,490 feet. An 18-mile tour of this famous and beautiful lake takes about two hours.

WHERE TO STAY

LA CARLINA, av. Joux-Plane, 74110 Morzine. Tel. 50-79-01-03. Fax 50-75-94-11. 18 rms (all with bath). TEL
$ **Rates:** 340 F ($61.20) single; 450 F ($81) double. Breakfast 58 F ($10.40) extra. AE, DC, MC, V. **Closed:** Nov 15–Dec 15.
This informal village chalet has maintained a high respect among its skiing habitués. Its interior is rustic, with several lounges—from the library to the inglenook

parlor—containing open fireplaces. The decor accent is alpine, with beamed ceilings and flagstone floors. While not fashion-setting, its bedrooms are pleasantly decorated and comfortable. In summer, there's a refreshment terrace with umbrella tables at street level. In the evening, life gravitates around the Carlina Club, where you can either dance or join in the folk music. The least expensive fixed-price menu, which I heartily recommend, costs 145 F ($26.10).

LA CHICANE, 74110 Morzine. Tel. 50-79-05-99. Fax 50-79-27-13. 14 rms (all with bath or shower). TEL

$ **Rates:** 280 F ($50.40) single; 460 F ($82.80) double. Breakfast 34 F ($6.10) extra. MC, V. **Closed:** May–June 14 and Sept 16–Dec 14.

Set at the base of pine-forested hills, this hotel has a wood-trimmed exterior that looks like a cozy modern chalet, with a sloped roof and sun umbrellas outdoors in summer. Each of the bedrooms contains a kitchenette and a balcony; rooms are designed like small studio apartments. Breakfast is the only meal served.

LE DAHU, les Mas Metout, 74110 Morzine. Tel. 50-75-92-92. Fax 50-75-92-50. 40 rms (all with bath or shower). TV TEL

$ **Rates:** 480 F ($86.40) single; 850 F ($153) double. Half board 575–860 F ($103.50–$154.80) per person. MC, V. **Parking:** Free. **Closed:** Apr 11–June 18 and Sept 19–Dec 17.

This four-story modern structure built on the side of a hill offers panoramic views. Its white plaster facade is relieved by wooden balconies and picture windows opening onto the village and alpine range. Although sleekly contemporary, the hotel has some old-fashioned touches, such as stone fireplaces around which guests gather to talk after a session on the slopes in winter. In summer, the wide terraces and the open swimming pool with bar, barbecue, and poolhouse become the social center. There's also a shady lawn with flower gardens. The owner is pleased to teach climbing, in summer or winter, on the artificial climbing wall behind the hotel. Meals are served in a provincial-style dining room. Many of the up-to-date bedrooms have been given homelike touches; nearly all have south-exposure balconies.

HOTEL CHAMPS-FLEURIS, 74110 Morzine. Tel. 50-79-14-44. Fax 50-79-27-75. 45 rms (all with bath). TEL

$ **Rates** (including half board): 490–750 F ($88.20–$135) per person. V. **Parking:** Free. **Closed:** Apr 14–June 18 and Sept 6–Dec 17.

Surrounded by the ski country of the high Savoy, this hotel is as popular in summer as it is in winter. Set against a backdrop of forested mountains, it rises a few paces from T-lifts and gondolas. Visitors can sit amid lots of exposed wood softened with earth-toned carpeting and curtains and enjoy the view of the slopes. In summer, hill-climbers appreciate the walking trails that begin nearby. There's also a heated swimming pool near the flowerbeds of the garden, plus an indoor weight-lifting room with an adjacent sauna, bar, billiard room, café, and restaurant. The earth-toned bedrooms are modern and comfortable.

AVORIAZ

One of the most modern and sophisticated **ski centers** of Europe has been developed at Avoriaz. Tucked away above Morzine, it's a village of pine-and-shingle buildings, most of them less than 25 years old, in the midst of an extensive ski terrain set 6,000 feet up in the mountains. The 390 miles of ski trails, reached by some 70 lifts, can usually be used until the third week in April. Astride a series of peaks and valleys called Portes du Soleil (Gates of the Sun), Avoriaz is most easily reached by cable car, and in the village the only transportation is by foot, on skis, or by horse-drawn sleigh. Even if you don't want to stay in one of the hotels in Avoriaz, you may want to take a cable car up for a look and perhaps a meal.

The village of Avoriaz is an interesting outgrowth of the intention of young architects to create a ski-resort community above the Valley of the Slate Quarries (Vallée des Ardoisières) in a style "not defacing the mountains." Their accomplishment is notable in the stepped rooflines and geometrically shaped balconies on cylindrical buildings, designed to reflect the sharp lines of the cliffs.

An accredited branch of the French Ski School Federation, the local ski school has around 100 experienced instructors, many proficient in English. Both downhill and cross-country skiing are offered, as well as snowshoeing and indoor activities, such as aerobic dancing and squash. A feature of this family-oriented ski resort is the Village des Enfants, where children as young as 3 are taught skiing.

By cable car or bubble car you can also go to **Le Pléney,** at 5,367 feet, and enjoy a view from its belvedere looking out on Mont Blanc. Through the Dranse Gap a vista of Lake Geneva unfolds.

WHERE TO STAY

HOTEL DES DROMONTS, Avoriaz 1800, 74110 Morzine. Tel. 50-74-08-11. Fax 50-74-08-87. 37 rms (all with bath or shower). TV TEL
$ Rates (including half board): 1,100–1,210 F ($198–$217.80) single; 1,560–1,700 F ($280.80–$306) double. AE, DC, MC, V. **Parking:** 30 F ($5.40) outside, 70 F ($12.60) inside. **Closed:** Apr 16–Dec 15.

Standing on the crest of an Alp, this was the first building erected in Avoriaz. With cantilevered architecture, it spreads out to include luxurious apartment villas, a cluster of boutiques, restaurants, a nightclub, and, of course, elaborate playtime facilities. Natural shingles cover the facade, and both the public and the private rooms are oddly shaped. Long, winding ramps lead you past intimate fireplace nooks, boutiques, drinking bars, and restaurants. Every possible facility is here for *le weekend*—Le Solarium, La Taverne, Le Drugstore, Le Roc-Club Disco. Most of the bedrooms are bright with a modern design and natural wood. The hotel is usually filled with a young crowd, and ski runs and lifts are right at the door.

HOTEL DES HAUTS FORTS, Avoriaz 1800, 74110 Morzine. Tel. 50-74-09-11. 48 rms (all with bath or shower). TV TEL
$ Rates (including half board): 780–850 F ($140.40–$153) per person. V. **Parking:** 30 F ($5.40) outside, 70 F ($12.60) inside. **Closed:** May–July 1.

Named after its clear view across the valley to the Hauts Forts peaks, this hotel has the same cantilevered architecture as Des Dromonts (above) and offers most of the same attractions. Each of the modern bedrooms, often irregularly shaped, includes a radio. It also has a good restaurant, with fixed-price meals beginning at 150 F ($27). Facilities include a cinema, many recreational items, a solarium, a sauna, a massage room, and a gallery of boutiques. Ski lifts are virtually at your doorstep.

---

3. FLAINE

374 miles SE of Paris, 49 miles E of Annecy,
30 miles from Megève and Morzine

GETTING THERE Flaine is the last stop on a dead-end mountain road leading into a high alpine valley. The nearest train station is at Les Cluses, 19 miles northwest. From there, you can transfer to a bus. Most visitors, however, particularly those with ski equipment, come by car.

ESSENTIALS The hotels and chalets are centered around the main square, which contains the tourist office. The téléphérique stations and many of the parking lots are a short walk from the village center. For information, contact the **Office de Tourisme,** Galerie des Marchands (tel. 50-90-80-01).

With its superb location, Flaine boasts deep powder snow from November through April. The chalets of Flaine, at 5,412 feet, are above the valley of the Arve and the Carroz-d'Araches.

From the cable-car station, inaugurated in 1969, you are whisked up to Les Grandes Platières. There you can admire the Désert de Platé and look out on a magnificent view of Mont Blanc. Skiers have a choice of downward trails—a thrilling descent in a 4-minute run on the Diamant Noir ski trail or a 60-minute run via the Serpentine trail.

WHERE TO STAY & DINE

GRAND HOTEL LE FLAINE, Flaine, 74300 Cluses. Tel. 50-90-80-30. Fax 50-90-84-59. 60 rms (all with bath). TV
$ Rates (including half board): 405–600 F ($72.90–$108) per person. AE, MC, V. **Parking:** 50 F ($9). **Closed:** May to mid-Dec.
In the heart of the resort, this modern hotel offers the most beautiful views in Flaine. All rooms are equipped with a balcony to absorb the view. After dark, residents gather for drinks in the lounge with its open fireplace. Bedrooms are furnished in bright, modern colors. Guests often indulge in ski competitions on the slalom stadium near the hotel.

LE TOTEM, Flaine, 74300 Cluses. Tel. 50-90-81-10. Fax 50-90-84-59. 95 rms (all with bath). TEL
$ Rates (including half board): 570–840 F ($102.60–$151.20) single; 960–1,440 F ($172.80–$259.20) double. AE, MC, V. **Closed:** Apr 17–July 9 and Sept–Dec 17.
This is probably the most comfortable hotel in town, composed of the architectural unification of two four-story hotels, both of which were built in the 1970s. In 1990, they were renovated, linked with a covered corridor, and today function as a coherent whole. On the premises is a restaurant, a bar, a series of sun terraces, a well-prepared cuisine, and rows of bay windows offering a panoramic view. An indoor swimming pool and tennis courts are within easy reach.

4. CHAMONIX–MONT BLANC

381 miles SE of Paris, 58 miles E of Annecy

GETTING THERE By Train Trains arrive frequently from nearby St-Gervais, where there are frequent connections from Aix-les-Bains, Annecy, Lyon, and Chambéry.

By Bus In any season, there's at least one daily bus from Annecy and Grenoble. Within Chamonix, a local bus makes frequent runs to many of the téléphériques and villages up and down the valley.

ESSENTIALS Chamonix sprawls in a narrow strip along both banks of the Arve River. Its casino, railway and bus stations, and most of its restaurants and nightlife are in the town center. Cable cars stretch into the mountains from the town's edge. Locals refer to Les Praz, Les Bossons, Les Moussoux, and Les Pélerins as satellite villages within **Greater Chamonix,** though technically Chamonix refers to only a carefully delineated section around its place de l'Eglise. The **Office de Tourisme** is on place du Triangle-de-l'Amitié (tel. 50-53-00-24).

At an altitude of 3,422 feet, Chamonix is the historic capital of alpine skiing. The site of the first winter Olympic games, in 1924, Chamonix lies huddled in a valley almost at the junction of France, Italy, and Switzerland. Dedicated skiers all over the world know of its 10-mile **Vallée Blanche** run, considered one of the most rugged in Europe, and certainly the longest. Daredevils also flock here for mountain climbing and hang-gliding.

A charming, old-fashioned mountain town, Chamonix has a most thrilling backdrop—**Mont Blanc,** Western Europe's highest mountain, rising to a peak of 15,780 feet. When two Englishmen, Windham and Pococke, first visited Chamonix in 1740, they were thrilled with its location and later wrote a travel book making the village known around the world. When their guide was published, it was believed that no human foot had yet trod on Mont Blanc. On August 7, 1786, Jacques Balmat became the first man to climb the mountain, destroying the myth that no one could spend a night high on the mountain and survive. In the old quarter of town a memorial to this brave pioneer stands in front of the village church.

With the opening of the seven-mile miracle **Mont Blanc Tunnel** (tel. 50-53-06-15), Chamonix became a major stage on one of the busiest highways in Europe. By literally going under the mountains, the tunnel provides the easiest way to get past the mountains to Italy. Motorists now stop at Chamonix even if they aren't interested in winter skiing or summer mountain climbing. Toll rates for the tunnel depend on the distance between the axles of the vehicle being taken through. Prices for a one-way transit through the tunnel for the average car is 125 F ($22.50), or 155 F ($27.90) round-trip; a car with a camping caravan or trailer is 165 F ($29.70) one way, or 210 F ($37.80) round-trip.

Because of its exceptional equipment, including gondolas, cable cars, and chair lifts, Chamonix is one of the major sports resorts of Europe, attracting an international crowd.

WHAT TO SEE & DO

The belvederes that can be reached from Chamonix by ✪ **cable car** or **mountain railway rides** are famous. For information about all these rides, contact the **Société Touristique du Mont-Blanc,** P.O. Box 58, 74402 Chamonix CEDEX (tel. 50-53-30-80).

In the heart of town you can board a cable car heading for the Aiguille du Midi and on to Italy—a harrowing journey. The first stage of the trip, a nine-minute run to the **Plan des Aiguilles** at an altitude of 7,544 feet, isn't so alarming. But the second stage, to an altitude of 12,602 feet, the **Aiguille du Midi** station, may make your heart sink, especially when the car rises 2,000 feet between towers.

At the summit you're 1,110 yards from the peak of Mont Blanc. From the belvedere you have a commanding view of the Aiguilles of Chamonix and Vallée Blanche, the largest glacier in Europe (9.3 miles long and 3.7 miles wide). You also have a 125-mile panoramic view of the Jura and the French, Swiss, and Italian Alps.

You leave the tram station along a chasm-spanning narrow bridge leading to the third cable car and the glacial fields that lie beyond. Or you can end your journey at Aiguille du Midi and return to Chamonix. Generally the cable cars operate all year: in summer, daily from 6am to 5pm, leaving at least every half hour; in winter, daily from 8am to 4pm, leaving every hour. The first stage of the trip, to Plan des Aiguilles, costs 50 F ($9) round-trip, increasing to 120 F ($21.60) per person for a round-trip to Aiguille du Midi.

For the final lap of the trip, you cross over high mountains and pass jagged needles of rock and ice bathed in a dazzling light. The final trip to **Pointe Helbronner** in Italy—at an altitude of 11,355 feet—requires a passport if you wish to leave the station and descend on two more cable cars to the village of Courmayeur. From there you can go to nearby Entrèves to dine at La Maison de Filippo, called a "chalet of gluttony," the Chamonix visitor's favorite restaurant across the border in Italy. The round-trip from Chamonix to Pointe Helbronner is 184 F ($33.10); the cable car operates only in summer.

Another aerial cableway takes you up to **Brévent** at an altitude of 8,284 feet. From here you'll have a first-rate view (frontal) of Mont Blanc and the Aiguilles de Chamonix. The trip takes about 1½ hours round-trip. Cable cars operate from December 16 to October 31, beginning at 8am and shutting down at 5pm. In summer, departures are at least every half hour. A round-trip ticket costs 64 F ($11.50).

Yet another aerial journey is to **Le Montenvers,** at an altitude of 6,276 feet. Here, from the belvedere at the end of the cable-car run, you'll have a view of the Mer de Glace (Sea of Ice, or glacier), which is four miles long. The Aiguille du Dru is a rock climb notorious for its difficulty. The trip takes 1½ hours, including a return by rail. Departures are 8am to 6pm in summer, until 4:30pm off-season. Round-trip fare is 47 F ($8.50) per person, and service is usually from May to November.

You can also visit a cave hollowed out of the Mer de Glace; a cable car connects it with the upper resort of Montenvers, and the trip takes just three minutes. Entrance to the cave costs 11 F ($2).

WHERE TO STAY

Chamonix doesn't have the chic and sophisticated ski resorts that Courchevel 1850 possesses; inns, with a few exceptions, tend to be plain and often cater to tour groups in summer and winter.

Expensive

HOTEL ALBERT-1ER ET DE MILAN, 119, impasse Montenvers, 74400 Chamonix–Mont Blanc. Tel. 50-53-05-09. Fax 50-55-95-48. 17 rms (all with bath or shower). TV TEL

$ Rates: 650 F ($117) single; 850 F ($153) double. Breakfast 65 F ($11.70) extra. AE, DC, MC, V. **Closed:** May 10–27 and Oct 25–Dec 3.

This establishment received its name in 1905 when King Albert of Belgium stayed here on a holiday. Today, it's an enlarged and solid alpine chalet located at the commercial edge of town, ringed by a flower garden and private residences. A stone-sided fireplace fronted with comfortable settees is enjoyed by guests. Each of the well-furnished bedrooms offers a view of the mountains; several also feature private balconies.

Dining/Entertainment: The hotel is known for its restaurant—see "Where to Dine," below. A copper-topped bar is in the lobby.

Facilities: Outdoor swimming pool, tennis court, Jacuzzi.

HOTEL ALPINA, 79 av. de Mont-Blanc, 74400 Chamonix–Mont Blanc. Tel. 50-53-47-77. Fax 50-55-98-99. 136 rms (all with bath), 9 suites. MINIBAR TV TEL

$ Rates (including continental breakfast): 454–623 F ($81.70–$112.10) single; 1,008–1,346 F ($181.40–$242.30) double; from 1,346 F ($242.30) suite. AE, DC, MC, V. **Parking:** 35 F ($6.30).

Set at the edge of town near a flowing stream, this is the largest and, architecturally, the most modern hotel in town. It was built in the early 1970s. Most of its balconies are angled toward the south, and the rooms are well furnished.

Dining/Entertainment: One of the most attractive places in the hotel is a panoramic restaurant on the top floor, which opens onto sweeping views of Mont Blanc.

Facilities: Fitness center, with hydrotherapy, massage, sauna, and a beauty institute.

HOTEL MONT-BLANC, 62, allée du Majéstic, 74400 Chamonix–Mont Blanc. Tel. 50-53-05-64. Fax 50-53-41-39. 43 rms (all with bath), 18 suites. MINIBAR TV TEL

$ Rates (including continental breakfast): 533–767 F ($95.90–$138.10) single; 826–1,294 F ($148.70–$232.90) double; from 1,694 F ($304.90) suite. AE, DC, MC, V. **Parking:** 35 F ($6.30). **Closed:** Oct 15–Dec 17.

This is a salmon-colored turn-of-the-century hotel whose Belle Epoque lines have been only slightly marred by the addition of a corkscrew staircase required by fire codes. It sits on a relatively quiet edge of town, sheltered by its gardens. Double-decker sun terraces look south onto Aiguille du Midi and Mont Blanc. The five-story hotel offers renovated and comfortable bedrooms with pinewood paneling and, in most cases, a view of the mountains.

Dining/Entertainment: Guests can drink the night away in the piano bar until 1am, and one of the town's finest restaurants, Matafan, is located here.

Facilities: Heated outdoor swimming pool.

NOVOTEL CHAMONIX, vers le Nant, Les Bossons, 74400 Chamonix–Mont Blanc. Tel. 50-53-26-22. Fax 50-53-31-31. 89 rms (all with bath), 1 suite. TV TEL

$ Rates: 470 F ($84.60) single or double; from 650 F ($117) suite for five people. Breakfast 48 F ($8.60) extra. AE, DC, MC, V. **Parking:** 40 F ($7.20).

Part of a nationwide chain, this efficient and well-managed hotel just 2½ miles east of the center of Chamonix in Les Bossons combines a mass-market design with a warm ambience; the result is a very comfortable hotel with spacious bedrooms. Accommodations are each equipped with both a single and a double bed, and some rooms open onto Mont Blanc. Most units have minibars. The staff is helpful.

Dining/Entertainment: There's a dining room with a big window, as well as a cozy bar.

Moderate

AU BON COIN, 80, av. de l'Aiguille-du-Midi, 74400 Chamonix–Mont Blanc. Tel. 50-53-15-67. Fax 50-53-51-51. 20 rms (16 with bath). TEL

$ Rates (including continental breakfast): 220 F ($39.60) single without bath, 330 F ($59.40) single with bath; 260 F ($46.80) double without bath, 380 F ($68.40) double with bath. MC, V. **Parking:** Free. **Closed:** May–June and Oct–Dec 18.

ⓢ This two-star hotel is very French and very alpine. It has modern, comfortable, clean, and well-kept rooms, often with views of the surrounding mountainside—in autumn, the colors are spectacular. The bedrooms also contain terraces where you can soak up the sun, even in winter. The chalet is tranquil, and the owner provides private parking as well as a garden.

Inexpensive

HOTEL ROMA, 289, rue Ravanel-le-Rouge, 74402 Chamonix. Tel. 50-53-00-62. Fax 50-53-50-31. 30 rms (25 with bath or shower). TEL

$ Rates (including breakfast): 310 F ($55.80) single with shower; 325 F ($58.50) double without bath or shower, 406–446 F ($73.10–$80.30) double with bath or shower. AE, DC, MC, V. **Parking:** Free. **Closed:** Three weeks in June and Oct 15–Dec 20.

ⓢ Established in 1907, this was one of the first hotels in Chamonix. Despite an ongoing renovation that was more or less completed in 1992, the Roma retains an old-fashioned feeling of alpine charm and uncluttered simplicity. The English- and Italian-speaking owners, the Quaglia family, welcome guests to their establishment. The only meal served is breakfast. You'll find this cozy two-star hotel about a five-minute walk south of the town center.

WHERE TO DINE

Expensive

HOTEL ALBERT-1ER ET DE MILAN, 119, impasse de Montenvers. Tel. 50-53-05-09.
Cuisine: FRENCH. **Reservations:** Required.

$ Prices: Appetizers 92–165 F ($16.60–$29.70); main dishes 130–240 F ($23.40–$43.20); fixed-price menus 175 F ($31.50), 195 F ($35.10), 275 F ($49.50), 320 F ($57.60), and 410 F ($73.80). AE, DC, MC, V.

Open: Lunch Thurs–Tues 12:30–1:30pm; dinner daily 7:30–9:30pm. **Closed:** May 13–June 1 and Oct 20–Dec 5.

According to some, this restaurant serves the finest food in town. You dine in a trio of elegantly paneled rooms, where Oriental carpets and 18th-century chests create a richly conservative milieu. Dishes include suprême of duckling in puff pastry with lentils, ravioli of truffles with duck fat, and sea bass roasted with endive.

RESTAURANT MATAFAN, in the Hôtel Mont-Blanc, 62, allée du Majéstic. Tel. 50-53-05-64.
Cuisine: FRENCH. **Reservations:** Required.

$ Prices: Appetizers 78–130 F ($14–$23.40); main dishes 118–180 F ($21.20–

$32.40); fixed-price menus 200 F ($36), 260 F ($46.80), and 360 F ($64.80). AE, DC, MC, V.

Open: Lunch daily 12:30–2pm; dinner daily 7:30–9:30pm. **Closed:** Oct 15–Dec 19.

This has a reputation as a stellar restaurant, with a decor of soft pastel colors and hand-woven tapestries on the walls. Staffed by a battalion of uniformed employees, the restaurant is arranged around a pentagonal fireplace set in the center of the room, with dozens of impeccably accessorized tables. Specialties change with the season, but typical offerings are likely to include omble chevalier meunière, a rack of lamb roasted with herbs (for two), and succulently sinful desserts. In the excellent cellar are more than 500 different wines. In summer, you can lunch next to the swimming pool in the garden.

Inexpensive

LE CHAUDRON, 79, rue des Moulins. Tel. 50-53-40-34.
Cuisine: FRENCH. **Reservations:** Recommended.
$ Prices: Appetizers 32–74 F ($5.80–$13.30); main dishes 65–125 F ($11.70–$22.50); fixed-price menus 98–130 F ($17.60–$23.40). AE, DC, MC, V.
Open: Dinner only, daily 7pm–midnight. **Closed:** June and Oct–Nov.

Le Chaudron is housed in a very old wood structure in Chamonix, just in front of the nightclub Le Pèle. Chef Pierre Osterberger cooks right in front of you, and you are sure to appreciate his specialties, which include house-style sweetbreads, several robust beef dishes, and fondues, as well as lots of salads and desserts. The cellar is filled with good wines, including Château Mouton Rothschild and Château Latour.

BARTAVEL, impasse du Vox. Tel. 50-53-26-51.
Cuisine: ITALIAN. **Reservations:** Not required.
$ Prices: Pizzas 35–45 F ($6.30–$8.10); main dishes 48–55 F ($8.60–$9.90). AE, MC, V.
Open: Daily noon–midnight.

Warmly decorated, much like a tavern you'd expect to find in Italy, this pizzeria is the domain of Treviso-born Valerio Commazzetto, who prepares 20 kinds of pizza and a wide range of pastas for his hungry guests. You'll find it near the post office in the center of the resort. Other menu items include grilled steaks and chops, escalopes milanese or pizzaiola, and an array of simple desserts. Beer and wine flow liberally, and the place attracts a goodly share of outdoor enthusiasts who appreciate its copious portions and reasonable prices.

L'IMPOSSIBLE, route des Pélerins. Tel. 50-53-20-36.
Cuisine: FRENCH. **Reservations:** Recommended.
$ Prices: Appetizers 35–65 F ($6.30–$11.70); main dishes 75–170 F ($13.50–$30.60); fixed-price menus 98 F ($17.60) and 169 F ($30.40). MC, V.
Open: Dinner only, daily 7pm–1am. **Closed:** Nov.

The building housing this restaurant was a barn in 1754. It's located near the Chamonix Sud and Aiguille du Midi cable station. Climb to the second floor where drafts from the soaring barnlike ceiling are offset by a fire in a large masonry fireplace; the ambience is rustic. Many cheese dishes are served, including raclette and a Savoyard fondue made from four kinds of cheese. You can also order entrecôte flambéed with Armagnac, tournedos with roquefort, and grilled varieties of beef.

RISTORANTE LE COQUELICOT, 88, rue du Lyret. Tel. 50-55-93-40.
Cuisine: ITALIAN. **Reservations:** Recommended.
$ Prices: Appetizers 42–65 F ($7.60–$11.70); main dishes 75–125 F ($13.50–$22.50); fixed-price menus 75–150 F ($13.50–$27).
Open: July–Apr, lunch daily noon–2:30pm; dinner daily 7–10:45pm. May–June, lunch Thurs–Tues noon–2:30pm; dinner Thurs–Tues 7–10:45pm.

Here, you pass beside a richly textured wooden bar before reaching the handsomely decorated restaurant set at the rear of the room on a small dais. Full meals are served with Mediterranean panache; you can order from an array of pastas, risotto with flap mushrooms, osso bucco, minestrone, cannelloni, and veal kidneys flambé.

LA TARTIFFLE, 87, rue des Moulins. Tel. 50-53-20-02.
Cuisine: FRENCH. **Reservations:** Recommended.
$ Prices: Appetizers 30–38 F ($5.40–$6.80); main dishes 68–75 F ($12.20–$13.50); fixed-price menus 68 F ($12.20), 90 F ($16.20), and 120 F ($21.60). AE, DC, MC, V.
Open: Lunch Wed–Mon noon–2:30pm; dinner Wed–Mon 7–11pm.

⑤ La Tartiffle is on the site of an old barn on one of the most rustic streets of Chamonix. Today it's the best choice in town for Savoyard specialties, including two types of fondue, raclette royale, feuilleté of trout with a beurre-blanc sauce, a cassoulet of snails Burgundy style, and many forms of grilled meat. The centuries-old poem associated with the name of the restaurant reflects the Savoy's mountain-bred independence—*tartiffle* means "potato" in dialect. As the poem goes, "I would prefer to be free rather than to eat the government's potatoes."

EVENING ENTERTAINMENT

LE CHOUCAS, rue du Dr-Paccard. Tel. 50-53-03-23.
Loud, animated, and convivial, this is the most popular après-ski hangout in Chamonix. Owned and managed with sophisticated savvy by Eric Durandard (who grew up in Courchevel), the place combines recorded music with multiple video screens, alpine accessories, and flowing beer and wine. Historians and sports fans will appreciate the dozens of photographs, dating from the 1950s, of the Olympic-grade athletes who have made this bar their favorite. Named after an alpine blackbird (whose effigy sits, stuffed, above the banks of electronic video and music equipment), Le Choucas enjoys its status as the establishment with the highest annual consumption of beer anywhere in the Savoy. It's open daily from 4pm to 4am; closed October and November.Come early—by 11pm there's little room to move. Drinks run 39 F ($7); beer goes for 15 F ($2.70).

---

5. MEGÈVE

372 miles SE of Paris, 43 miles SE of Geneva

GETTING THERE Megève is easy to reach, owing to its proximity to the Geneva airport. On weekends, the high-speed train—the Paris–Sallanches run—delivers passengers to Megève. On weekdays, the Paris–Bellegarde train makes the same connections.

ESSENTIALS Orientation The interesting and commercial center contains **place de l'Eglise** and its famous hotel, the Mont-Blanc, south of the main arteries that cut through the valley. Some of the resort's hotels and one of its most important cable-car depots are in the peripheral village of **Mont d'Arbois,** about a mile east of the center of Megève, at the end of a steep, narrow, and winding road. In winter, it's unwise to drive up that road without chains on your snow tires.

Information Contact the **Office de Tourisme,** rue de la Poste (tel. 50-21-27-28).

Called a *cité verte*, Megève is famous as a summer resort set amid pine forests, foothills, and mountain streams. But it's even better known as a charming cosmopolitan town, referred to as a *capitale du ski*. The old village with its turreted houses gathered around the church, which dates from the 17th century, suggests what Megève looked like at the turn of the century. However, after 1920 the new town came along and started attracting people who like to go to the mountains for fun—especially skiers. Megève was made popular by the baronne de Rothschild.

Tennis, horseback riding, and cable railways add to the attractions. There are wide views of the Mont Blanc area from the top of each ski lift. The range of amusements includes a casino, nightclubs, discos, dancing, and shows. At the foot of Mont Blanc,

Megève is actually one of the best equipped of the French winter-sports resorts and is a social center of international status.

WHAT TO SEE & DO

In the environs you can take a chair hoist to **Mont d'Arbois,** at an altitude of 6,000 feet. Here a magnificent panorama unfolds, including not only Mont Blanc but the Fis and Aravis Massifs. Cable service operates from July 1 to October 1 every half hour from 9am to 6pm. To reach the station, take the route du Mont-d'Arbois from the center of the resort, going past the golf course. But remember that snow chains are almost always mandatory for midwinter driving. The mountain was originally developed in the 1920s by members of the Rothschild family, whose search for solitude led them here to this scenic outpost, a mile west of the center of Megève. Today Mont d'Arbois is considered a pocket of posh in an already-posh resort.

From 11am to 6am the center of the old village is closed to traffic, except the pedestrian variety and sledges. You can shop at leisure (some 200 tradespeople await your service, ranging from a cobbler to an antiques dealer, along with many boutiques).

The **Ski School,** 70, impasse du Chamois (tel. 50-21-00-97), is one of the foremost in Europe, with 197 instructors for adults and 32 for children. Collective courses include the complete French skiing method, modern ski techniques, monosurf-acrobatic skiing, cross-country skiing, and ski touring. The school is open December 20 until the end of April, daily from 8:45am to 7pm. Much improvement has been made in recent years in sports facilities, including a Chamois gondola, which takes skiers to the mountain from the center of town; the Rocharbois cable car, linking the two major ski areas of Mont d'Arbois and Rochebrune; and the addition of a gondola and chair lift at the Rochebrune massif.

The **Megève Palais des Sports et des Congrès (Sports Palace and Assembly Hall),** 74120 Megève (tel. 50-21-15-71), is for ice sports, swimming, tennis, meetings, and often shows and gala festivals. It's a complex of two swimming pools with a solarium, saunas, an Olympic-size skating rink, a curling track, a body-building room, a dance salon, a bar, a restaurant, a gymnasium, tennis courts, an auditorium, conference rooms, and an exhibition gallery. It's open daily from 9am to 7pm.

WHERE TO STAY
Very Expensive

CHALET DE MONT-D'ARBOIS, route du Mont-d'Arbois, 74120 Megève. Tel. 50-21-25-03. Fax 50-21-24-79. 20 rms (all with bath). TV TEL
$ Rates (including half board): 1,130–1,180 F ($203.40–$212.40) per person. AE, DC, MC, V. **Closed:** May–June 19 and Oct 4–Dec 17.

Originally built in 1928 by a matriarch of the Rothschild family, this chalet houses the best resort on the mountain, with the most beautiful and elegant accommodations. Each room is furnished with bleached pine and has a radio. The chalet's public rooms are the grandest in Megève, outfitted rustically with roaring fireplaces, beamed ceilings, alpine antiques, mounted stag horns, and silver-plated replicas of alert deer. During some part of the season the hotel might be partially filled with friends of Mme Nadine de Rothschild, whose richly anecdotal advice on how a woman should treat her husband became a bestseller in France. This charming hotel lies at the bottom of a meadow dotted with expensive condos and privately owned apartments.

HOTEL DU MONT-BLANC, place de l'Eglise, 74120 Megève. Tel. 50-21-20-02. Fax 50-21-45-28. 41 rms (all with bath), 3 suites. MINIBAR TV TEL
$ Rates: 1,000 F ($180) single; 1,940 F ($349.20) double; from 2,100 F ($378) suite. Breakfast 80 F ($14.40) extra. AE, DC, MC, V. **Parking:** 40 F ($7.20). **Closed:** Sept.

This is the elegant first choice for clients from as far away as Paris, who have to scheme to get a room here during the high winter season. Located at the departure point for the Chamois-Rocharbois cable car, in the town center near the church, the hotel was built in 1970. Its elaborate chalet balconies are recognizable from a distance; the warmly patterned interior offers comfortable, velvet-covered chairs amid Oriental rugs, modern sculptures, attractive accessories, and small-scale charm. All the well-furnished and soundproof bedrooms and suites have balconies.

Dining/Entertainment: See "Where to Dine," below, for my recommendation of the hotel's restaurant, Les Enfants Terribles.

Services: Room service, laundry, dry cleaning.

Facilities: Swimming pool, sauna, massages, heated garage.

PARC DES LOGES, 100, rue d'Arly, 74120 Vieux-Megève. Tel. 50-93-05-03. Fax 50-93-09-52. 40 rms (all with bath or shower), 13 suites. A/C MINIBAR TV TEL

$ Rates (including half board): 980–1,280 F ($176.40–$230.40) per person. AE, DC, MC, V. **Parking:** 40 F ($7.20). **Closed:** Apr 15–July 9 and Oct 16–Dec 14.

In the center of old Megève, 200 yards from the cable-car station, this is a sleekly modern four-star hotel. The Parc des Loges is a good choice for a holiday and has beautiful gardens. Each accommodation is equipped with a radio, video, a safe, and, in some cases, a private balcony or terrace and a fireplace.

Dining/Entertainment: Famous chefs in France take their turns supervising the menus at La Rotonde, the gourmet restaurant of the hotel. Le Grand Café has a patio and piano bar.

Services: Room service, laundry, dry cleaning.

Facilities: Jacuzzi, video and book library, outdoor swimming pool, ski room, private garage.

Moderate

AU COIN DU FEU, route du Téléphérique de Rochebrune, 74120 Megève. Tel. 50-21-04-94. Fax 50-21-20-15. 23 rms (all with bath or shower). TV TEL

$ Rates (including half board): 870 F ($156.60) single; 1,110–1,400 F ($199.80–$252) double. AE, MC, V. **Closed:** Apr 11–July 9 and Sept–Dec 19.

This modern, grand chalet is one of the best of the middle-bracket hotels. It offers a lot of amenities, including an American bar and table tennis. Connections are easily made to the Rochebrune téléphérique (cable car). Rooms are well furnished and beautifully maintained, and the hotel is most comfortable. The hotel's excellent restaurant is Le Saint Nicolas.

AU VIEUX MOULIN, av. Ambroise-Martin, 74120 Megève. Tel. 50-21-22-29. 33 rms (all with bath or shower). TV TEL

$ Rates (including half board): 700–815 F ($126–$146.70) single; 950–1,200 F ($171–$216) double. MC, V. **Closed:** Mid-Apr to early June and late Sept to mid-Dec.

Named after an old mill that no longer exists, the establishment today is a four-story stucco and wood-trimmed building separated from the street by a tiny pool, a lawn, and wrought-iron gates. The bedrooms and the lobby, with its coffered ceilings and black slate floors, are well maintained, and the hotel also has a swimming pool and a terrace.

LE FER A CHEVAL, 36, route du Crêt-d'Arbois, 74120 Megève. Tel. 50-21-30-39. Fax 50-93-07-60. 30 rms (all with bath). TV TEL

$ Rates (including half board): 675–850 F ($121.50–$153) per person. MC, V. **Parking:** Free. **Closed:** Apr 11–June and Sept 11–Dec 24.

⭐ Le Fer à Cheval appeals to the traditionalist seeking an authentic Savoy atmosphere. With its three-star classification, it's perhaps the finest in the center of the village and is filled with skiers in winter and mountain motorists in summer. The management offers well-decorated bedrooms. The hotel's restaurant, decorated with wood to evoke an old-fashioned Savoy atmosphere, is open also to nonresidents, with meals costing from 230 F ($41.40). In summer, a swimming pool draws guests to the beautiful garden of the hotel, whereas a sauna and Jacuzzi are winter lures. Guests often gather for tea around a wood-and-stone fireplace, where they also can enjoy good-tasting meals.

WHERE TO DINE

In addition to the following, see "Where to Stay," above, for some hotel restaurants.

Expensive

CHALET DU MONT-D'ARBOIS, route du Mont-d'Arbois. Tel. 50-21-25-03.
Cuisine: FRENCH. **Reservations:** Required.
$ **Prices:** Appetizers 80–180 F ($14.40–$32.40); main dishes 120–185 F ($21.60–$33.30). AE, DC, MC, V.
Open: Lunch daily noon–2pm; dinner daily 7:30–10pm. **Closed:** May–June 19 and Oct 4–Dec 17.

Elegant and richly accessorized, this hotel restaurant lies one floor below lobby level (see my hotel recommendation under "Where to Stay," above) and has a wood-burning grill. Accumulated mementos of the restaurant's owners, the Rothschild family, and wood paneling are part of the decor. As might be expected from a family connected with some of the greatest vineyards of France, the wine list is overwhelming—it's almost a library reference. Some of the menu items seem to have been named after the Rothschild image, such as vol-au-vent financière; another dish is spit-roasted Bresse chicken.

LES ENFANTS TERRIBLES, in the Hôtel du Mont-Blanc, place de l'Eglise. Tel. 50-21-20-02.
Cuisine: FRENCH. **Reservations:** Required.
$ **Prices:** Appetizers 70–205 F ($12.60–$36.90); main dishes 120–250 F ($21.60–$45); fixed-price menu 180 F ($32.40). AE, DC, MC, V.
Open: Lunch daily noon–3pm; dinner daily 7–11pm.

This is the acclaimed restaurant with an adjoining bar where Jean Cocteau painted the wall frescoes that gave the place its name. Today this well-decorated restaurant serves a refined menu to a faithful crowd. The decor is like a supper club, with pine lampshades and tones of burgundy and mauve. Menu items are often prepared with expensive extras such as truffles, foie gras, and fine wines. Try, for example, the steak Enfants Terribles. Locally inspired Savoy dishes are popular. Dinner is served either indoors or on a covered terrace in warm weather. See "Where to Stay," above, for my hotel recommendation.

LE PRIEURE, place de l'Eglise. Tel. 50-21-01-79.
Cuisine: FRENCH. **Reservations:** Required.
$ **Prices:** Appetizers 50–100 F ($9–$18); main dishes 75–160 F ($13.50–$28.80); fixed-price meal 140 F ($25.20) at lunch, 180 F ($32.40) at dinner. AE, DC, MC, V.
Open: Lunch daily noon–2:30pm; dinner daily 7–10pm. **Closed:** June 12–July 10 and Nov 3–Dec 1.

The Prieuré lies in the center of town beside the major church, offering typical and traditional French cooking, with such specialties as foie gras de canard (duckling) and a fish salad made from crab, mussels, and lake fish. You might begin with fresh melon with locally cured ham, then follow with grilled bass filet with fennel or magrét of duckling flavored with peaches. For dessert, try the apple pie.

LA ROTONDE, in the Parc des Loges, 100, rue d'Arly. Tel. 50-93-05-03.
Cuisine: FRENCH. **Reservations:** Required.
$ **Prices:** Appetizers 80–135 F ($14.40–$24.30); main dishes 135–205 F ($24.30–$36.90). AE, DC, MC, V.
Open: Lunch daily 12:30–2pm; dinner daily 8–10pm.

This is the gourmet restaurant of the Parc des Loges (see "Where to Stay," above); five chefs, known throughout France, take turns preparing the delectable cuisine of this elegant restaurant, where you'll enjoy grand service. Menus change with the season and the inspirations of the various chefs. You can order such dishes as roasted and boneless rack of rabbit, roast pigeon with onions and mushrooms, and red mullet with small lobsters and John Dory just roasted and served with a garlic-laced mayonnaise.

Moderate

LA TAVERNE DU MONT-D'ARBOIS, route du Mont-d'Arbois. Tel. 50-21-03-53.

Cuisine: FRENCH. **Reservations:** Required.

$ Prices: Appetizers 48–82 F ($8.60–$14.80); main dishes 82–140 F ($14.80–$25.20). V.

Open: Lunch daily 12:15–2pm; dinner daily 7:15–10pm. **Closed:** May 28–June 15.

This is the most visible restaurant in the satellite community of Mont d'Arbois, located near a series of ski lifts. Owned by the Rothschild family (and eager to promote the produce of the family's vineyards), the place offers a rustic ambience of blackened timbers and weathered planking. It's so popular that getting a table might be difficult in midwinter. You'll be faced with an array of Savoyard-inspired mountain specialties, including at least three different kinds of cheese dishes.

6. ALBERTVILLE

362 miles SE of Paris, 30 miles E of Chambéry, 28 miles S of Annecy

GETTING THERE   By Car   Motorists leaving Megève (our last stopover, see above) should continue along Route 212 southwest to Albertville. Two important highways, the N90 and the A430, meet just southwest of the city center.

ESSENTIALS   Orientation   The city's 19th-century charm is found around the Eglise St-Jean Baptiste and place de la Liberté. The much older and smaller village of Conflans lies across the river and the highway from Albertville.

Information   The Syndicat d'Initiative (tourist office) is located at 1, rue Bugeaud (tel. 79-32-04-22).

Albertville is one of the gourmet centers of the Savoy and it attracted world attention as a seat of the 1992 Olympic games. It is conveniently situated near main roads leading to the northern Alps. A town full of history, it developed from the medieval city of Conflans. Today, it's filled with the buzz of life. Its Olympic ice rink, dome-shaped theater, and superb sports facilities make it a first-class sports and cultural resort.

The origins of the town date from centuries ago, with a city called Conflans, whose confines are surrounded by the modern settlement of Albertville. On its narrow streets, where traffic is prohibited in winter, lie a church, a Grande Place with an 18th-century fountain, a collection of medieval buildings occupied by artisans and craftspeople, and a municipal museum, the **Musée des Conflans** (tel. 79-32-57-42), which is in the Maison Rouge. Displays include old utensils, local carvings, prehistoric mementos, and furniture. The Maison Rouge was a 13th-century convent later transformed into a military arsenal. From June through September it's open daily from 10am to noon and 2 to 7pm; from Easter through May, daily from 2 to 7pm. Admission is 10 F ($1.80) for adults, 5 F (90¢) for children.

WHERE TO DINE

CHEZ UGINET, 8, place Charles-Albert. Tel. 79-32-00-50.

Cuisine: FRENCH. **Reservations:** Required.

$ Prices: Appetizers 70–130 F ($12.60–$23.40); main dishes 90–130 F ($16.20–$23.40); fixed-price menus 115–340 F ($20.70–$61.20). AE, DC, MC, V.

Open: Lunch Wed–Mon noon–2pm; dinner Wed–Mon 7–9:30pm. **Closed:** June 25–July 5 and Nov 12–Dec 5.

Under the direction of Eric and Josie Guillot, the chefs at the elegant Chez Uginet prepare delicate combinations of food that merit a stop in Albertville for at least one meal. You'll dine in a stone building high on a bank above the river, connected to the quiet road with a long causeway. The 60 seats hold a varied collection of diners, including ski champions. Specialties include duckling foie gras, cassolette of lobster with pink peppercorns and baby vegetables, and escalope of roebuck with apple marmalade and cinnamon. There's a terrace, which has a view of the rushing river, where you can enjoy a leisurely dinner in warm weather.

HOTEL MILLION, 8, place de la Liberté, 73200 Albertville. Tel. 79-32-25-36. Fax 79-32-25-36.
   Cuisine: FRENCH. **Reservations:** Required.
$ Prices: Appetizers 95–160 F ($17.10–$28.80); main dishes 140–205 F ($25.20–$36.90); fixed-price menus 150 F ($27), 180 F ($32.40), 280 F ($50.40), and 500 F ($90). AE, V.
   Open: Lunch Tues–Sun noon–2:30pm; dinner Tues–Sat 7–9:30pm.

Set back from the main road through town, the year-round Hôtel Million was established in 1770 by an ancestor of Philippe Million, the current owner and chef whose cuisine did much to put Albertville on the gourmet map. The operation is in a white building with strong horizontal lines and gables on a flagstone-covered square. The spacious public rooms include an elegant salon and a peach-colored dining room; there's also a pleasant outdoor terrace for summer dining. Some of the chef's dishes were inspired by the chef of the Duke of Savoy in the 19th century. Specialties are rooster's comb and kernels in a balsamic vinegar sauce, cold frogs' legs in a herb-flavored cream sauce with smoked salmon, and sautéed lobster served with a hot chutney and sweetbreads.

Each of the 28 attractive bedrooms contains a private bath, minibar, TV, telephone, and lots of space (a dozen rooms offer air conditioning). Rates are 420 F ($75.60) in a single and 590 F ($106.20) in a double, plus 60 F ($10.80) for breakfast.

7. ANNECY

334 miles SE of Paris, 35 miles SE of Geneva, 85 miles E of Lyon

GETTING THERE   Annecy has railway and bus service from Geneva, Grenoble, and Lyon. It's also near a network of highways, and many people drive there.

ESSENTIALS   The city was built at the point where the River Thiou drains the waters of the Lake of Annecy. Its cathedral and its **château,** both landmarks, face one another from opposite banks of the river, which is traversed by several old and charming bridges, some of which are limited to pedestrians. The **Office de Tourisme** is at 1, rue Jean-Jaurès (tel. 50-45-00-33).

On Lac d'Annecy, the jewel of the Savoy Alps, the resort of Annecy makes the best base for touring Haute-Savoie, of which it is the capital. The former seat of the counts of Geneva, and before that a Gallo-Roman town, Annecy opens onto one of the best views of lakes and mountains in the French Alps.

WHAT TO SEE & DO

The resort is dominated by the **Château d'Annecy** (tel. 50-45-29-66). Its Queen's Tower dates from the 12th century, and it was in this castle that the counts of Geneva took refuge in the 13th century. Go up in the castle and look out on the town's roof and belfries. The museum of regional artifacts is open Wednesday through Monday from 10am to noon and 2 to 6pm. Admission is 15 F ($2.70) for adults, free for children under 10.

Built around the River Thiou, Annecy has been called "the Venice of the Alps" because of the **canals** cut through the old part of town, **Vieil Annecy.** You can explore the arcaded streets of the old town where Jean-Jacques Rousseau arrived in 1728.

After exploring Annecy, I suggest a visit to **Les Gorges du Fier,** six miles from Annecy, 12 minutes by train from the Lovagny station (Aix-les-Bains line). For the latest schedule of daily motorcoach trips offered, go to the Office de Tourisme (see "Essentials," above). This striking gorge is considered one of the most interesting sights in the French Alps. A gangway takes visitors through a winding gully, varying from 10 to 30 feet wide. The gully was cut by the torrent through the rock and over breathtaking depths. You'll hear the roar of the river at the bottom. Emerging from this labyrinth, you'll be greeted by a huge expanse of boulders. The gorge is open Easter to October, daily from 9am to 6pm (to 7pm in July and August). The tour takes less than an hour and costs 22 F ($4). Call 50-46-23-07 for more information.

In the area, you can also visit the 13th- and 14th-century **Château de Montrottier,** 74330 Lovagny (tel. 50-23-68-80), with a spectacular view of Mont Blanc from its tower. The château contains pottery, Oriental costumes, armor, tapestries, and antiques, as well as some bronze bas-reliefs by Peter and Hans Vischer of Nürnberg—their art dates from the 16th century. The castle is open from the Sunday before Easter to mid-October, daily from 9am to noon and 2 to 6pm (closed Tuesday in June, July, and August). Admission is 25 F ($4.50) for adults and 15 F ($2.70) for children.

Of course, a most interesting excursion is a tour of **Lac d'Annecy,** available from Easter until the end of September. Inquire at the tourist office (see above) about various possibilities. In July and August there are at least 12 steamers leaving from Annecy. Call 50-46-23-07 for more information.

WHERE TO STAY
Expensive

DEMEURE DE CHAVOIRE, 71, route d'Annecy, 74290 Veyrier-du-Lac. Tel. 50-60-04-38. Fax 50-60-05-36. 13 rms (all with bath). MINIBAR TV TEL
$ Rates: 750 F ($135) single; 1,000 F ($180) double. Breakfast 60 F ($10.80) extra. AE, DC, V.
One of the most charming and elegant accommodations lies at Chavoires, about two miles west of Annecy. Small, intimate, and cozy, it's brightly decorated and homelike. The little hotel is decorated with well-chosen Savoy antiques. Through large doors you can walk down to the gardens which overlook the lake. Bedrooms aren't numbered, but have names, and each one is uniquely decorated. Thoughtful extras such as chocolates by the bed make this a deserving choice. It's a more tranquil choice than the accommodations in the center of Annecy. The helpful staff will direct you to nearby restaurants.

Moderate

HOTEL L'ABBAYE, 15, chemin de l'Abbaye, 74940 Annecy-le-Vieux. Tel. 50-23-61-08. Fax 50-27-77-65. 15 rms (all with bath), 3 suites. MINIBAR TV TEL **Bus:** 6 or 21.
$ Rates: 450–650 F ($81–$117) single or double; 800–1,200 F ($144–$216) suite. Breakfast 45 F ($8.10) extra. AE, DC, MC, V.
Well known both for the charm of its accommodations and the quality of its cuisine, this graceful hotel occupies the premises of a 15th-century Dominican convent and is set in the midst of gardens. Most visitors come here just for the restaurant—see my recommendation under "Where to Dine," below.

AU FAISAN DORE, 34, av. d'Albigny, 74000 Annecy. Tel. 50-23-02-46. Fax 50-23-11-10. 40 rms (all with bath or shower). TV TEL **Bus:** 2 or 21.
$ Rates (including half board): 300–380 F ($54–$68.40) per person. MC, V. **Parking:** 45 F ($8.10). **Closed:** Oct 31–Nov 7 and Dec 12–Jan 24.
Located near the casino at the end of avenue d'Albigny, a tree-lined lakefront boulevard, this hotel stands in front of a Catholic church, Sainte-Bernadette. It lies only two minutes by foot from the lake and Imperial Park. A three-star hotel since 1992, it is a member of the chain Logis de France, a value-oriented hotel catering to the family trade. The hotel has been owned and run by the Clavel family since 1919.

The public and private rooms follow the decor of the Haute Savoy. Each bedroom is well furnished. The chef proposes three fixed-price menus at 120 F ($21.60), 160 F ($28.80), and 190 F ($34.20).

DU NORD, 24, rue Sommeiller, 74000 Annecy. Tel. 50-45-08-78. Fax 50-51-22-04. 35 rms (all with bath or shower). TV TEL

$ Rates: 250 F ($45) single; 300 F ($54) double. Breakfast 32 F ($5.80) extra. V.

A two-star hotel in the center of Annecy, near the old city and lake, the newly renovated Du Nord is one of the better bargains at the resort. The staff is extremely helpful, and they speak English. Guests appreciate the cleanliness and the modernity of the well-maintained bedrooms. Rooms have such amenities as soundproofing and direct-dial phoning. Breakfast is the only meal served, but the staff will direct you to nearby reasonably priced and typical restaurants of the region.

SUPER PANORAMA, route de Semnoz, 74000 Annecy. Tel. 50-45-34-86. 5 rms (all with bath). TV TEL

$ Rates: 250–400 F ($45–$72) double. Breakfast 40 F ($7.20) extra. MC, V. **Closed:** Tues and Dec 22–Jan 27.

Bargain seekers may also be drawn to this location, 1½ miles south of Annecy, where they can enjoy the splendid vista of lake and mountain while sitting on the terrace. The bedrooms are modestly furnished. The Super Panorama is one of the best values offered at this lakeside resort, considering that the alpine food is good and hearty and the portions are of generous size. Meals begin at 120 F ($21.60).

WHERE TO DINE

In addition to the following, see the hotel restaurants listed above.

AUBERGE DE L'ERIDAN, 13, vieille route des Pensières, 74290 Veyrier-du-Lac. Tel. 50-60-24-00. Fax 50-60-23-63.
Cuisine: FRENCH. **Reservations:** Required.
$ Prices: Appetizers 198–400 F ($35.60–$72); main dishes 200–400 F ($36–$72); fixed-price meals 490–950 F ($88.20–$171). AE, DC, MC, V.
Open: Lunch Thurs–Tues noon–2:30pm; dinner Mon–Tues and Thurs–Sat 7 9:30pm. **Closed:** Jan–Feb.

Famous throughout France because of the excellent and unusual cuisine of its owner, Marc Veyrat-Durebex, this world-class establishment moved into new premises in 1992. Today, it occupies a romanticized version of a château which lies at the edge of the lake in the alpine village of Veyrier-du-Lac, about a mile from the heart of Annecy. Built in the 1930s, the building was radically altered for its new tenants, with the addition of nine bedrooms and two suites, marble-sheathed bathrooms, a pier jutting into the lake, and an elegantly glossy dining room whose ceiling frescoes and blue-and-white color scheme have been compared by locals to something they might have found in Hollywood, California.

Menu items include a ravioli of vegetables flavored with rare alpine herbs which are carefully gathered by Mr. Veyrat-Durebex and his team in the high mountains. Also well recommended are a sausage of pike perch, crayfish poached with bitter almonds, a rack of lamb infused with alpine herbs and flowers, and poached sea bass with caviar.

Bedrooms rent for 1,500–4,000 F ($270–$720), with suites going for 4,500 F ($810) each. Breakfast costs an additional 180 F ($32.40) per person. Parking, at least, is free. Mr. Veyrat-Durebex is assisted by his wife, Annick.

LE BELVEDERE, 7, chemin du Belvédère, 74000 Annecy. Tel. 50-45-04-90.
Cuisine: FRENCH. **Reservations:** Recommended.
$ Prices: Appetizers 65–135 F ($11.70–$24.30); main dishes 135–200 F ($24.30–$36); fixed-price menus 200–350 F ($36–$63). MC, V.
Open: July–Aug, lunch daily 12:30–2pm; dinner daily 8–9:30pm. Mid-Dec to June and Sept–Oct, lunch Tues–Sun 12:30–2pm; dinner Tues–Sat 8–9:30pm. **Closed:** Nov to mid-Dec.

This restaurant lies in an early 20th-century house set just on the periphery of Annecy, with sweeping views over both the lake and the town. Born and raised in La Rochelle, near the sea, owner Jean-Louis Aubeneau serves the finest seafood cuisine in all of Annecy; he invents dishes instead of relying on classic methods of preparation. Call for a table at lunch or dinner to get a good view of the lake. I recommend his pot-au-feu of the ocean, a marvelous meal, or perhaps his turbot sautéed with three different kinds of pepper. He also makes a soup of scallops with little strips of vegetables, and stuffed brill with red-mullet mousse and a caviar-laced sauce.

Monsieur Aubeneau also rents 10 simply furnished bedrooms, which have telephones and views of the lake (3 contain private baths). These rooms are available only from May through October, costing 190–230 F ($34.20–$41.40) single or double, with breakfast going for 35 F ($6.30) per person extra.

HOTEL L'ABBAYE, 15, chemin de l'Abbaye, Annecy-le-Vieux. Tel. 50-23-61-08.
   Cuisine: FRENCH. **Reservations:** Recommended. **Bus:** 6 or 21.
$ Prices: Appetizers 40–110 F ($7.20–$19.80); main dishes 80–120 F ($14.40–$21.60). AE, DC, MC, V.
   Open: Dinner only, Tues–Sun 8pm–midnight.
Beneath some vaulting and within view of a medieval fresco, enjoy this high-quality, classic French cuisine where the menu changes depending on what's available and very fresh at the market every day. Or, in clement weather, dine on the outdoor terrace and enjoy the view of the gardens. This restaurant and hotel (see "Where to Stay," above) is housed in a 15th-century Dominican convent. Only dinner is served.

8. TALLOIRES

342 miles SE of Paris, 20 miles N of Albertville, 8 miles S of Annecy

GETTING THERE By Car After leaving Annecy (see above), motorists can continue south along Route N508 (on the eastern shore of Lac d'Annecy) for 8 miles to reach Talloires.

ESSENTIALS Orientation The focal point of the town is the chestnut-lined promenade beside the water. The glamour of the real estate increases as you approach the lake. Signs indicate the location of virtually every commercial establishment in town.

Information The Office de Tourisme is on rue André-Theuriet (tel. 50-60-70-64).

The charming village of Talloires is old enough to appear on lists of territories controlled by Lothar II, great-grandson of Charlemagne—it dates back to 866. Chalk cliffs surround a pleasant bay. At the lower end a wooden promontory encloses a small port. An 18-hole golf course and water sports such as skiing, boating, swimming, and fishing make this a favorite spot with French holiday makers.

Talloires is a gourmet citadel, containing one of France's great restaurants (the Auberge du Père Bise, previewed below) and a Benedictine abbey founded here in the 11th century but now transformed into a deluxe hotel (Hotel de l'Abbaye, also previewed below).

WHERE TO STAY

In addition to the following hotel, several of the restaurants under "Where to Dine," below, rent luxurious rooms and suites.

HOTEL DE L'ABBAYE, route du Port, 74290 Talloires. Tel. 50-60-77-33.
   Fax 50-60-78-81. 28 rms (all with bath). TEL
$ Rates (including half board): 690–995 F ($124.20–$179.10) per person. AE, DC, MC, V. **Parking:** Free. **Closed:** Mid-Dec to mid-Jan.

This former Benedictine abbey is now a Relais & Châteaux. Many famous guests have stayed here, including Walter Cronkite and "Baby Doc" Duvalier, who fled here in 1986 after his abdication as "President-for-Life" (dictator) of Haiti. Reconstructed in the 17th century, the abbey was used as a rest camp for the army in World War II, and was turned into a hotel in 1945. To enter the abbey, walk through the iron gateway and stroll along shaded walks, bypassing the formal French gardens. The secluded hotel is richly outfitted with beamed ceilings, antique portraits, thick walls, modern deep leather chairs, and richly carved balustrades. The great corridors lead to converted bedchambers—no two alike—and suspended wooden balconies lead to a second level of bedrooms. The furnishings are distinguished, and some chambers have frescoed ceilings. The dining room, once the monks' dining hall, has large wooden chandeliers. In summer, guests can also dine outside under the shade trees and enjoy a view of the lake.

WHERE TO DINE

AUBERGE DU PERE-BISE, Bord du Lac, 74290 Talloires. Tel. 50-60-72-01. Fax 50-60-73-05.
   Cuisine: FRENCH. **Reservations:** Required.
$ **Prices:** Appetizers 150–350 F ($27–$63); main dishes 190–300 F ($34.20–$54); fixed-price menus 480–680 F ($86.40–$122.40). AE, DC, MC, V.
   Open: Lunch Thurs–Tues noon–2pm; dinner daily 7–9pm. **Closed:** Tues Oct 10–May 1 and Nov 11–Jan 15.

This elegant chalet, located in a private park at an enchanting spot on the lake, opened in 1901 as a simple country tavern. Père Bise's heirs inherited his secret recipes and carry on his great tradition. The kitchen has glistening copper pots and pans, and the dining room has sparkling silverware and bowls of fresh flowers. In fair weather guests can dine under a vine-covered pergola and enjoy the view of the lake. The cuisine, popular with everybody from the Duke of Windsor to the Rothschilds, is under the direction of Sophie Bise, the only female three-star chef in France. She offers classic dishes, such as mousse of goose foie gras, young lamb (most delicate), and braised pullet with fresh morels.

The inn also offers three suites and 31 well-furnished bedrooms, each with private bath or shower, minibar, TV, and phone; accommodations are spread across four buildings. Most guests book on half-board terms, which cost 1,200–1,900 F ($216–$342) per person. Some rooms, which have French provincial decor, are over the restaurant in the main building, but a particular favorite is the Villa Les Roses, a lovely three-story country house. It's wise to make reservations at least two months in advance, especially in summer.

LE COTTAGE FERNAND BISE, Bord du Lac, 74290 Talloires. Tel. 50-60-71-10. Fax 50-60-77-51.
   Cuisine: FRENCH. **Reservations:** Recommended.
$ **Prices:** Appetizers 75–190 F ($13.50–$34.20); main dishes 100–205 F ($18–$36.90); fixed-price menus 180 F ($32.40), 280 F ($50.40), and 380 F ($68.40). AE, DC, MC, V.
   Open: Lunch daily noon–2pm; dinner daily 7:15–9:45pm. **Closed:** Nov–Mar.
The brother of Père Bise, Georges Bise, founded this establishment around 1920; nowadays, family member Jean-Claude Bise carries on the tradition. Georges once entertained Sir Winston Churchill here, and after World War I, the chef cooked a banquet for French President Aristide Briand. At this terraced restaurant, the chef offers such dishes as a mousse of chicken livers, wild young duck plain roasted with fresh green pepper, and a warm strawberry soufflé. Omble chevalier from Lake Geneva is another specialty.

The Cottage also offers 35 elegantly furnished and comfortable bedrooms with TVs and telephones; the luxurious doubles with baths rent for 700–1,000 F ($126–$180), plus 65 F ($11.70) extra for breakfast.

VILLA DES FLEURS, route du Port, 74290 Talloires. Tel. 50-60-71-14. Fax 50-60-74-06.

Cuisine: FRENCH. **Reservations:** Required.

$ Prices: Appetizers 58–130 F ($10.40–$23.40); main dishes 85–185 F ($15.30–$33.30); fixed-price menus 140 F ($25.20), 198 F ($35.60), and 270 F ($48.60). MC, V.

Open: Lunch daily 12:15–2:30pm; dinner daily 7:15–9:30pm. **Closed:** Nov 15–Dec 15 and Mon Nov–May.

⑤ This attractive *restaurant avec chambres* should be better known—it's the best establishment in Talloires in this price range. Proprietors Marie-France and Charles Jaegler transformed the 1895 structure after they moved to Talloires from the Vosges. The hard-working Jaeglers serve perfectly prepared meals, which often include veal kidneys, a salade landaise with foie gras, and filet of fera, which live only in Lake Geneva. The dining room overlooks the water. The most expensive fixed-price menu is a *menu des poissons du lac,* featuring only lakefish in rather sophisticated preparations.

If you want to spend the night, stay in one of the eight bedrooms, which are outfitted with modern private baths, minibars, telephones, and rustic Victorian-era decor. Singles or doubles cost 310–440 F ($55.80–$79.20); they're at the top of a winding stair—there's no elevator. Breakfast is 45 F ($8.10) extra.

9. AIX-LES-BAINS

332 miles SE of Paris, 21 miles SW of Annecy, 10 miles N of Chambéry

GETTING THERE The town has a railway station and bus depot, both linked to most of the important cities of the region.

ESSENTIALS Set on the eastern edge of the Lac du Bourget, modern Aix-les-Bains is still focused on the **hot-water springs** first publicized by the ancient Romans. These "Thermes Nationaux" lie in the center of town, more than two miles from the lakeshore, near the casino, the Temple of Diana, and the Hôtel de Ville. Closer to the lake, a long string of flowerbeds and ornamental shrubs border the town's famous waterside promenades. For information, inquire at the **Syndicat d'Initiative** (tourist office), place Maurice-Mollard (tel. 79-35-05-92).

Aix-les-Bains is the most fashionable spa of eastern France and also one of the largest. The hot springs, which offered comfort to the Romans, are said to be useful in the treatment of rheumatism. The spa is well equipped for visitors: It contains flower gardens, a casino (the Palais de Savoie), a race course, a golf course, and Lac du Bourget, which has a beach.

It was at Aix-les-Bains that Lamartine, the early 19th-century French poet (author of *Poetic Meditations*), met the doctor's wife, Julie Desherettes, the "Elvire" of his early poems and the inspiration for his most famous piece, "Le Lac." Balzac also described the lake in his novel *Peau de Chagrin.*

Regular steamer service takes you on a four-hour **boat ride** on Lac du Bourget—it's a beautiful trip. For information about departure times (which change seasonally), consult the Syndicat d'Initiative (see "Essentials," above). Boats depart from the landing stage at Grand Port.

You can also take a bus ride from Aix to the small town of **Revard,** at an altitude of 5,080 feet, where you'll be rewarded with a panoramic view of Mont Blanc.

WHAT TO SEE & DO

ABBAYE D'HAUTECOMBE, 73310 Chindrieux. Tel. 79-54-26-12.

The abbey, which has been called the St-Denis of Savoy, is the mausoleum of many of the princes of the House of Savoy. Standing on a promontory jutting out into the lake, the church was rebuilt in the 19th century in what is called the "Troubadour Gothic" style. There is an English guided tour of the church offered free to the public, who are also welcome to participate in the mass which is celebrated daily at noon (on

Sunday at 9:15am). The Christian community that lives in the abbey organizes religious seminars, and perpetuates the tradition of worship maintained on this site since the 12th century. From April to October the abbey inn serves a lunch for 80 F ($14.40).

The abbey can also be reached by boat, with two to five steamers leaving daily from Easter until September 30. To board, go to the landing stage at Aix-les-Bains. The price is 40 F ($7.20) for the 2½-hour trip.

Admission: Free.
Open: Wed–Mon 10am–noon and 2–5:30pm.

MUSEE FAURE, bd. des Côtes. Tel. 79-61-06-57.

This is the spa's most interesting museum, with its modern-art collection, including sculptures by Rodin plus works by Degas, Corot, and Cézanne.

Admission: 15 F ($2.70).
Open: Wed–Mon 9:30am–noon and 2–6pm.

LES THERMES NATIONAUX D'AIX-LES-BAINS, place Maurice-Mollard. Tel. 79-35-38-50.

The original structure was begun in 1857 by Victor Emmanuel II; the New Baths, launched in 1934, were later expanded and renovated in 1972. To visit, go to the caretaker at the entrance opposite the Hôtel de Ville, the former château of the marquises of Aix in the 16th century. Before you enter the baths, you can visit the thermal caves. In the center of the spa are two Roman remains—a Temple of Diana and the 30-foot-high triumphal Arch of Campanus.

Admission: 10 F ($1.80).
Open: Apr–Oct, Mon–Sat 3–9pm. **Closed:** Holidays.

WHERE TO STAY

The restaurants listed under "Where to Dine," below, also have rooms for rent.

HOSTELLERIE LE MANOIR, 37, rue Georges-1er, 73100 Aix-les-Bains. Tel. 79-61-44-00. Fax 79-35-67-67. 73 rms (all with bath). TV TEL

$ Rates: 300 F ($54) single; 545 F ($98.10) double. Breakfast 48 F ($8.60) extra. DC, MC, V. **Parking:** Free. **Closed:** Dec 20–Jan 7.

This charming old building with a rustic decoration, within walking distance of the thermal center, is in the Parc du Splendide-Royal. The white-stucco hotel has shutters and an overhanging roof, and pathways weave through the old-world gardens in which outdoor furniture has been placed under shade trees. Guests order breakfast or dinner, weather permitting, on an attractive terrace bordering the garden. Most of the public rooms, as well as the bedrooms, open onto terraces and flowering shrubbery. The decor is traditional, with antique and provincial furniture in the comfortable bedrooms. The dining hall has large wooden beams; a tall, open fireplace; and a center that opens onto a wooden mezzanine. Meals begin at 135 F ($24.30).

HOTEL ARIANA, av. de Marlioz, à Marlioz 73100 Aix-les-Bains. Tel. 79-88-08-00. Fax 79-88-87-46. 60 rms (all with bath or shower). TV TEL

$ Rates: 550 F ($99) single; 850 F ($153) double. Breakfast 65 F ($11.70) extra. AE, DC, MC, V. **Parking:** Free.

The most up-to-date hotel in town, the Ariana caters to a spa-oriented clientele who enjoy taking quiet walks through the surrounding park. The hotel was built in 1983 next to the baths of the Marlioz Institute, on the outskirts of town. The stylized glass and loggia-dotted exterior opens into a modernized art deco interior highlighted by contrasting shades of metal, wood, and fabrics, and plenty of white marble and carpeting. Tunnellike glass walkways connect it to the therapeutic outbuildings. All accommodations have radios, and some have loggias.

WHERE TO DINE

HOTEL RESTAURANT DAVAT, au Grand Port, 73100 Aix-les-Bains. Tel. 79-63-40-40.

Cuisine: FRENCH. **Reservations:** Required.

$ Prices: Appetizers 55–110 F ($9.90–$19.80); main dishes 115–175 F ($20.70–$31.50); fixed-price menus 100 F ($18), 130 F ($23.40), 190 F ($34.20), and 250 F ($45). MC, V.

Open: Lunch Wed–Mon noon–2pm; dinner Wed–Sun 7:30–9:30pm. **Closed:** Nov–Mar 20.

Diners here enjoy the robust cooking, the gracious service, and the selection of regional wines. This is not only a leading restaurant, but also an excellent, moderately priced place to stay. It was originally a lakeside family home in the 19th century. The chief attraction here is the beautiful flower garden. The 20 bedrooms with telephones are simply furnished and cost from 360 F ($64.80) for a double, including breakfast.

LILLE, au Grand Port, 73100 Aix-les-Bains. Tel. 79-63-40-00. Fax 79-34-00-30.

Cuisine: FRENCH. **Reservations:** Required.

$ Prices: Appetizers 110–205 F ($19.80–$36.90); main dishes 140–255 F ($25.20–$45.90); fixed-price menus 140 F ($25.20), 260 F ($46.80), and 360 F ($64.80). AE, DC, MC, V.

Open: Lunch Thurs–Mon noon–2pm; dinner Thurs–Mon 7:30–9pm. **Closed:** Jan.

Near the landing stages where the lake steamers of Lac du Bourget depart is one of the best restaurants in Aix-les-Bains. It's housed in what was originally built in the 19th century as a private lakeside villa. The main dishes include pâté en croûte with foie gras, a cassolette of crayfish, and grilled lobster flambé.

It's also possible to stay overnight in one of 18 simply furnished, comfortable bedrooms, each with private bath or shower, direct-dial phone, and TV. Singles cost 290 F ($52.20); doubles, 350 F ($63). Breakfast is 35 F ($6.30) per person extra. Parking is free.

---

10. CHAMBERY

33 miles SE of Paris, 34 miles N of Grenoble, 61 miles SE of Lyon

GETTING THERE Chambéry has excellent bus and rail service from major cities in eastern France; both depots lie on the western edge of the old city. The nearby junction of many highways makes driving to Chambéry easy.

ESSENTIALS The most important (and biggest) monument is the **Château des Ducs de Savoie,** in the southwest corner of the old town. From its base, **rue de Boigne** leads past arcades and historic buildings to the Fontaine des Eléphants. The **Office de Tourisme** is located at 24, bd. de la Colonne (tel. 79-33-42-47).

Chambéry used to be the capital of an ancient sovereign state, the Duchy of Savoy. It is not as important a resort as most nearby towns, but with its handsome streets, good food, and its château, it has much to lure visitors. Everywhere you look are reminders of the 15th and 16th centuries.

WHAT TO SEE & DO

The residence of the former dukes, the **Château des Ducs de Savoie,** rue Basse du Château, which towers over the city, is best visited on a guided tour. The château was founded in the 14th century and partly rebuilt in the 18th and 19th centuries. Its Sainte-Chapelle contained the Holy Shroud for most of the 16th century, until it was moved to the Cathedral of Turin in Italy. Construction of the Gothic chapel began in 1408. If you're willing to climb nearly 200 steps to the top of Round Tower, you'll have a great view. The underground chambers, which used to be barracks, can also be explored. Guided tours are obligatory. Five per day are offered in July and August, two per day in June and September. Times vary depending on demand. From March to May and in October and November, tours are conducted on Saturday at 2:15pm and on Sunday at 3:30pm. Admission is 20 F ($3.60) for adults, 10 F ($1.80) for children. For more information, call the tourist office (see "Essentials," above).

From the château, you can take **rue de Boigne,** lined with porticoes, which will lead you to the Fontaine des Eléphants, erected in memory of native son General de Boigne (1751–1830), who left to his hometown some of the fortune he acquired in India.

In the environs, going up the steep chemin des Charmettes leads to the **Musée des Charmettes** (tel. 79-33-44-48), the handsome 17th-century country house where Jean-Jacques Rousseau lived with Madame de Warens between 1738 and 1740. The property lies 1¼ miles southeast of Chambéry—head out rue de la République, which becomes rue J-J-Rousseau. The bedroom of Rousseau contains the original furniture, and in the drawing room you can see Madame de Warens's clavichord. Wander in the beautiful garden and enjoy the view of the Chambéry valley from the terrace. Rousseau praised the country house in his *Confessions.* The house is open April to September, Wednesday through Monday from 10am to noon and 2 to 6pm; off-season, Wednesday through Monday from 10am to noon and 2 to 4:30pm. Admission is 10 F ($1.80).

WHERE TO STAY

HOTEL DES PRINCES, 4, rue de Boigne, 73000 Chambéry. Tel. 79-33-45-36. Fax 79-70-31-47. 45 rms (all with bath). TV TEL
$ Rates: 260 F ($46.80) single; 400 F ($72) double. Breakfast 33 F ($5.90) extra. AE, DC, MC, V.

Set in the grandest section of the old town, beneath 18th-century arcades, this is one of the most pleasant hotels in Chambéry. You register in an elegantly old-fashioned lobby capped with ceiling beams, then are escorted to your comfortably furnished, art decoish bedroom. In addition to the bar and lounge, the hotel also has one of the city's most attractive restaurants.

HOTEL RESIDENCE LE FRANCE, 22, faubourg Reclus, 73000 Chambéry. Tel. 79-33-51-18. Fax 79-85-06-30. 48 rms (all with bath or shower). A/C MINIBAR TV TEL
$ Rates: 320 F ($57.60) single; 440 F ($79.20) double. Breakfast 45 F ($8.10) extra. AE, DC, MC, V.

The streamlined and well-furnished bedrooms in this modern hotel have balconies and also radios. The hotel has a contemporary lobby, with seats clustered around a small bar. Breakfast is the only meal served.

NOVOTEL CHAMBERY, La Motte Servolex, 73000 Chambéry. Tel. 79-69-21-27. Fax 79-69-71-13. 103 rms (all with bath). A/C MINIBAR TV TEL
$ Rates: 445 F ($80.10) single; 480 F ($86.40) double. Breakfast 52 F ($9.40) extra. AE, DC, MC, V. **Parking:** Free.

This Novotel is located 1½ miles north of Chambéry center near La Motte Servolex exit from the autoroute between Chambéry and Lyon. For motorists who prefer ease of access to a position in the heart of the city, this chain hotel might be the perfect choice. All the spacious bedrooms are exactly and efficiently alike and contain a comfortable collection of practical accessories. Guests also enjoy the bar and the grill restaurant, where they can order good food daily from 6am to midnight. Meals begin at 130 F ($23.40). Parking is available (the area is closed in by an electronic gate at night).

WHERE TO DINE

In addition to the following, see "Where to Stay," above, for the hotel restaurants.

LA CHAUMIERE, 14, rue Denfert-Rochereau. Tel. 79-33-16-26.

Cuisine: FRENCH. **Reservations:** Required.
$ Prices: Appetizers 38–65 F ($6.80–$11.70); main dishes 52–95 F ($9.40–$17.10); fixed-price menus 80–170 F ($14.40–$30.60). MC, V.
Open: Lunch Mon–Sat noon–2pm; dinner Mon–Sat 7–10:30pm. **Closed:** Aug.

If you want a reasonably priced meal in a cozy room, visit La Chaumière (Thatched Hut) for the best fixed-price dinner in town. The restaurant lies near the Théâtre Dullin on a street with limited traffic access, which makes the outdoor terrace in front more desirable. Quality products are used, and the chef is skilled in cooking traditional French dishes. Foie gras and duck breast are his specialties, but you might prefer fish, either grilled or steamed in a light sauce. The cellar contains a good range of reasonably priced local wines, including some inexpensive ones served in cafés.

L'ESSENTIEL, 183, place de la Gare. Tel. 79-96-97-27.
Cuisine: SAVOYARD/FRENCH. **Reservations:** Recommended.
$ Prices: Appetizers 45–100 F ($8.10–$18); main dishes 45–100 F ($8.10–$18); fixed-price menus 90–235 F ($16.20–$42.30). AE, MC, V.
Open: Lunch Sun–Fri 12:30–3pm; dinner daily 7–10:30pm.

Beneath a soaring greenhouse-style ceiling, adjacent to the Hôtel Mercure and across from the railway station of Chambéry, this is the newest and most talked-about restaurant in town. Established late in 1991, it's the domain of one of the best-trained chefs in the region, Jean-Michel Bouvier. Ably assisted in the ocher-colored dining room by members of his family (especially his wife, Catherine, and his sister, Elisabeth), he prepares unusual dishes based strictly on seasonal ingredients. These might include scallops in a herb-flavored bouillon, ravioli stuffed with snails, frogs' legs with a purée of fresh peas, seafood ravioli with flap mushrooms and ginger, a fricassée of crayfish with thyme, caramelized duckling with pine-flavored honey and a mignonnette of pepper, suprême of roast pigeon served with its thighs stuffed with foie gras, and omble chevalier prepared meunière style with walnut oil.

NEARBY ACCOMMODATIONS & DINING

AUX PERVENCHES, aux Charmettes, 73000 Chambéry. Tel. 79-33-34-26. Fax 79-60-02-52. 13 rms (all with bath). TEL **Directions:** Take the D4 1¼ miles southeast.
$ Rates: 110 F ($19.80) single; 160 F ($28.80) double. Breakfast 25 F ($4.50) extra. MC, V. **Closed:** Jan 18–24 and Aug 10–31.

If you have a car, you might want to stay at this charming stone chalet outside town. Rooms are furnished in typical French-inn style, with flowered wallpaper and simple furniture. The house, which stands near the Rousseau home, has a warm and inviting restaurant with meals for 110 F ($19.80). It's open for lunch Thursday through Tuesday from noon to 2pm, and for dinner on Monday, Tuesday, and Thursday through Saturday from 7:30 to 9:30pm.

11. GRENOBLE

352 miles SE of Paris, 34 miles S of Chambéry, 64 miles SE of Lyon

GETTING THERE An important rail and bus junction, Grenoble is easily accessible from Paris and all the cities recommended in this chapter. Its airport is 18 miles northwest of the city center.

ESSENTIALS Orientation Grenoble lies near the junction of the Isère and Drac Rivers. Most of the city is on the south bank of the **Isère,** although its most impressive monument, **Fort de la Bastille,** stands in relative isolation on a rocky hilltop on the river's north bank. A cable car will carry you from the south bank's quai Stephane-Jay across the river to the top of the fort. The center of Grenoble's historic section is the **Palais de Justice** and **place St-André.** The more modern part of town lies southeast, and is centered around the contemporary **Hôtel de Ville,** and the nearby Tour Perret.

Information   The **Office de Tourisme** is located at 14, rue de la République (tel. 76-54-34-36).

Because this city, the ancient capital of Dauphine, is the commercial, intellectual, and tourist center of the alpine area, it's a major stopover for those exploring the French Alps and for motorists traveling between the Riviera and Geneva. A sports capital in both winter and summer, it also attracts many foreign students—its university has the largest summer-session program in Europe. The university occupies a modern campus on the outskirts of the city, and many buildings erected for the 1968 Olympics have been put to creative use.

WHAT TO SEE & DO

First, head for **place Grenette,** a lively square filled with beautiful flowers in late spring and early summer, where you can enjoy a drink or a cup of espresso. This square enjoys many associations with Grenoble-born Stendhal, who wrote such masterpieces as *The Red and the Black* and *The Charterhouse of Parma.* It was here that Antoine Berthet, supposedly the model for Stendhal's Julien Grel, was executed for attempted murder in 1827.

Next, I suggest a ride on the **Téléférique de la Bastille.** These high-swinging cable cars take you over the Isère River. Most of the year it operates from 9am to midnight, except in winter, when service stops at 7:30pm; a round-trip costs 30 F ($5.40) for adults, 16 F ($2.90) for children. For information about the service, phone 76-44-33-65. From the belvedere where you land you'll have a panoramic view of the city and the surrounding mountains. If you want to walk, you can return on foot. Signs point the way to the Parc de la Bastille and the Parc Guy-Pape, and eventually lead you to the **Jardin des Dauphins,** which is open daily in summer from 9am to 7:30pm.

If you prefer, from the Belvédère de Grenoble you can take the **Télésiège Bastille–Mont-Jalla** for an even loftier view of the environs. To board the car in Grenoble, head for the Gare de Départ on quai St-Stéphane-Jay, facing the Jardin de Ville.

The **Musée des Beaux-Arts,** place de Verdun (tel. 76-54-09-82), is one of the best art galleries in provincial France, with a fabulous collection of modern art, including Matisse's *Intérieur aux Aubergines,* Léger's *Le Remorqueur,* a Delaunay, a Bonnard, a Klee, a Max Ernst, and a Gonzalez. Contemporary works include a 1968 Martial Raysse and Jean Dubuffet's *Mire G. 137:Kowloon,* 1983. Upstairs, you'll find works by Gustave Doré, Boudin, Monet, Gauguin, Matisse, Rouault, and some works by Grenboblois Fantin-Latour (1836–1904); there's also a fine Egyptian collection. More works displayed in the gallery are by Veronese, Tintoretto, Philippe de Champaigne, Le Lorrain, and Georges de La Tour. Ruben's *Saint Grégoire Entouré de Saints* is exhibited here. The museum is open Wednesday through Monday from 10am to noon and 2 to 6pm; admission is 15 F ($2.70) for adults, 10 F ($1.80) for children 10–16.

If you have time, visit the **Musée Dauphinois,** 30, rue Maurice-Gignoux (tel. 76-87-66-77), housed in a 17th-century convent and enhanced by the cloister, gardens, and baroque chapel. A collection of ethnographical and historical mementos of Dauphine are displayed here, along with folk arts and crafts. The museum lies across the Isère in the Ste-Marie-d'en-Haut section. It's open Wednesday through Monday from 9am to noon and 2 to 6pm (closed January 1, May 1, and December 25); admission is 15 F ($2.70) for adults, 10 F ($1.80) for children 10–16.

Designed by the architect A. Wogenscky and constructed in 1968, the **Maison de la Culture** lies in the new quarter of Malherbe. At the Office de Tourisme (see

"Essentials," above), you can pick up a calendar listing the events of the month—they range from impressionist exhibitions to cinema showings, from orchestral concerts to dance. The center is open Tuesday through Saturday from 1 to 6pm and on Sunday from 1 to 7pm; it's closed part of August.

WHERE TO STAY

HOTEL BELALP, 8, av. Victor-Hugo, 38170 Seyssinet-Grenoble. Tel. 76-96-10-27. Fax 76-48-34-95. 30 rms (all with bath or shower). TV TEL
Directions: Take the N531 one mile from the town center.
$ Rates: 220 F ($39.60) single; 280 F ($50.40) double. Breakfast 25 F ($4.50) extra. MC, V. **Parking:** Free.

This tastefully contemporary hotel with sunny and well-maintained accommodations sits one floor above ground level in a combination apartment/office building. There's no restaurant on the premises, but you can order drinks in a tiny bar. I recommend this hotel for motorists who don't want to drive into the center of Grenoble.

HOTEL D'ANGLETERRE, 5, place Victor-Hugo, 38000 Grenoble. Tel. 76-87-37-21. Fax 76-50-94-10. 70 rms (all with bath). A/C MINIBAR TV TEL
$ Rates: 460 F ($82.80) single; 540 F ($97.20) double. Breakfast 45 F ($8.10) extra. AE, DC, MC, V.
Behind a classic facade with tall, graceful windows and wrought-iron balconies, this hotel has a sparkling contemporary interior. The hotel opens onto a pleasant square with huge chestnut trees in the center of Grenoble. The salons have wood-grained walls and ceilings, tropical plants, and stylish furnishings. Most of the bedrooms have radios, soundproofing, and dressing tables. Breakfast is the only meal served.

HOTEL LESDIGUIERES, 122, cours de la Libération, 38000 Grenoble. Tel. 76-96-55-36. Fax 76-48-10-13. 36 rms (all with bath or shower). TV TEL
$ Rates: 315 F ($56.70) single; 490 F ($88.20) double. Breakfast 39 F ($7) extra. AE, DC, MC, V. **Parking:** 30 F ($5.40). **Closed:** Aug and Dec 18–Jan 14.
Named after the Renaissance lord of Grenoble who, under Henri IV, fortified and embellished the city, this facility serves as a training ground for the local hotel school. Everyone—including the receptionist, the bellboys, and the restaurant staff—is a member of the most recent graduating class. The hotel, located at the edge of the city, is surrounded by a spacious lawn. The imposing premises are fashioned from gray-brown stucco with white trim and brick accents. Inside, the sunny public rooms are filled with Louis XIII chairs, Oriental rugs, and elegant accessories; bedrooms are well furnished. Fixed-price menus in the dining room run 135–175 F ($24.30–$31.50).

PARK HOTEL, 10, place Paul-Mistral, 38000 Grenoble. Tel. 76-87-29-11. Fax 76-46-49-88. 50 rms (all with bath). 10 suites. A/C MINIBAR TV TEL
$ Rates: 595–995 F ($107.10–$179.10) single; 695–1,195 F ($125.10–$215.10) double; from 1,595 F ($287.10) suite. Breakfast 55 F ($9.90) extra. AE, DC, MC, V. **Parking:** 70 F ($12.60).

This is Grenoble's leading modern hotel. A bright place, it has contemporary lounges and bedrooms that are well kept, soundproof, and comfortably furnished with many amenities. The staff is polite and helpful; the Taverne di Ripaille, open from noon to midnight, is an attractive restaurant.

WHERE TO DINE

LE BERLIOZ, 4, rue Strasbourg. Tel. 76-56-22-39.
Cuisine: FRENCH. **Reservations:** Required.
$ Prices: Appetizers 64–100 F ($11.50–$18); main dishes 120–170 F ($21.60–$30.60); fixed-price menus 70 F ($12.60), 115 F ($20.70), 148 F ($26.60), 178 F ($32), and 298 F ($53.60). AE, V.

Open: Lunch Mon–Fri noon–2pm; dinner Mon–Sat 7:30–10:30pm. **Closed:** May 17–23 and July 25–Aug 24.

With her policy of featuring a different menu with regional specialties every month, the chef offers a gourmet tour of France. Françoise Legras has won much local acclaim with her talented kitchen staff. Try, for example, fresh codfish with green cabbage and smoked lard, side of beef with baby vegetables in a wine sauce, or perhaps braised shoulder of lamb served with eggplant "cake." If featured, roast duck in a spicy honey sauce is a winner. This salmon-pink dining room is in an 18th-century house.

POULARDE BRESSANE, 12, place Paul-Mistral. Tel. 76-87-08-90.
   Cuisine: FRENCH. **Reservations:** Required.
$ **Prices:** Appetizers 38–128 F ($6.80–$23); main dishes 78–148 F ($14–$26.60); fixed-price menus 138 F ($24.80), 180 F ($32.40), and 248 F ($44.60). AE, DC, MC, V.
   Open: Lunch Mon–Fri noon–2pm; dinner Mon–Sat 7:30–9:45pm.

Diners here enjoy superb cuisine in an elegant modern setting in the center of Grenoble. Although dishes are both classical and traditional haute cuisine, contemporary culinary delights have been mastered as well. In honor of the restaurant's namesake, poularde Bressane is the most important specialty. The chef's fish pâté also is excellent, as is his red mullet flavored with basil. The menu is very much a *cuisine du marché*—that is, based on the shopping in the market that day. Desserts are delectable, many prepared at the time of request.

NEARBY ATTRACTIONS

Monks have created some of the famous wines and liqueurs, but **Chartreuse** is not one of them, even though it was named after the Carthusians. They are, however, the custodians of the ultra-secret formula, which was given to them in 1605 by Marshal d'Estrées. It was an elixir involving the distillation of 130 herbs, and it was believed to have been originated by an anonymous alchemist.

Eventually the formula found its way to **La Grande Chartreuse** (or charterhouse), which was founded in 1084, about 20 miles north of Grenoble. The monastery was destroyed and rebuilt many times; the present buildings date from 1688. The French Revolution broke up monastic orders, but somehow the monks held on to their formula, returning to Grenoble in 1816 with the restoration of the monarchy. When they were expelled from France again in 1903 during a period of anticlericalism, they took their recipe with them to their monastery at Tarragona in Spain, where they continued making their liqueurs. They returned to La Grande Chartreuse again in 1940, shortly before the German attack on France.

The monastery is no longer open to the public, but you are allowed to visit the **Musée de la Correrie,** 38380 St-Pierre-de-Chartreuse (tel. 76-88-60-45), in a building dating from the 15th century and standing at the head of the valley about 1½ miles from the monastery. For 12 F ($2.20) for adults and 6 F ($1.10) for children, the museum can be visited April to October, daily from 9:30am to noon and 2 to 6:30pm. In this unusual museum you'll get a glimpse of a monk's life; the sound you'll hear is chanting.

For most visitors, even more interesting than visiting the museum is a trip to **Voiron,** about 20 miles away, where you can visit the distillery where the famed Chartreuse is made. The distillery lies on the main street of town, and free visits are possible Monday through Friday from 8 to 11:30am and 2 to 6:30pm. Dressed in chartreuse green, a guide will show you around, let you view the copper stills, and then take you to the cellar, which is filled with gargantuan oak casks in which the liqueur matures for several years. At the end of the tour you'll be given a free drink of the yellow or fiery green Chartreuse or of one of the new products. You can also purchase bottles at a shop on the premises. It is said that only three monks and the Father Procurator have access to the formula.

Before you head out into the Massif de la Chartreuse, where the monastery and distillery lie, obtain a good, detailed map from the tourist office in Grenoble.

NEARBY ACCOMMODATIONS & DINING

RELAIS L'ESCALE, place de la République, 38761 Varces. Tel. 76-72-80-19. Fax 76-72-92-58. 7 rms (all with bath). A/C MINIBAR TV TEL **Directions:** Take the N75 eight miles southeast of Grenoble.

$ Rates: 420 F ($75.60) single; 490 F ($88.20) double. Breakfast 60 F ($10.80) extra. MC, V. **Parking:** Free. **Closed:** Jan–Feb 5.

A Relais & Châteaux, this hotel and restaurant offers wooden chalets in a lovely garden setting and al fresco dining on a terrace where there's a view of an alpine garden. Bedrooms are well furnished and homelike. At the Restaurant l'Escale, enjoy the specialties of chef Frédéric Buntinx, including salmon tartare in herb sauce, young duckling with honey and red fruit, and fresh foie gras made in the kitchen. Hours are 12:15 to 2pm and 7:30 to 9:15pm; it's closed Tuesday in summer and on Sunday night and Monday off-season. Fixed-price meals cost 180 F ($32.40), 260 F ($46.80), and 360 F ($64.80).

---

12. COURCHEVEL 1850

393 miles SE of Paris, 32 miles SE of Albertville, 60 miles SE of Chambéry

GETTING THERE Courchevel 1850 is the last stop on a steep alpine road that dead-ends at the village center. To go any higher, you'll have to take a cable car from the center of town. Most visitors arrive by car (you'll need snow tires and chains), but some buses link the city to railway junctions farther down the mountain.

ESSENTIALS On your way up the valley, you'll pass several other "Courchevels" (for example, Courchevel 1300, Courchevel 1550, and Courchevel 1650), which have tried to capitalize on the fame of the uppermost resort. The center of town is a commercial mall called **La Croisette,** where you'll find shops, banks, the tourist office, and most of the téléphérique bases. For information, inquire at the **Office de Tourisme,** La Croisette (tel. 79-08-00-29).

Courchevel has been called a resort of "high taste, high fashion, and high profile." Skiers and geographers know of it as part of Les Trois Vallées, sometimes called "the skiing supermarket of France," thanks to its conception in 1947 as a resort exclusively for skiing. The resort's 1,400 acres of ski runs employ as many workers in summer as they do in winter, simply to manicure and maintain the top-notch ski conditions that won Courchevel the coveted role as a host of the 1992 winter Olympics.

Believe it or not, Courchevel's origins were rustic. In Savoyard dialect, the name was derived from a place where cows (*vel*) were killed, skinned, and flayed (*écorché*). But that's a forgotten memory to occupants of the chalets selling for $4 million on the pine-covered mountains.

Courchevel maintains three different ski schools, with an average staff of 450 ski instructors, a labyrinth of chair lifts, and more than 200 ski runs, which are considered excellent in both the intermediate and advanced categories. Included with Courchevel in Les Trois Vallées are the less well known resorts of Méribel, Les Menuires, and Val Thorens, which you should avoid unless you direly need to save money. Courchevel consists of four planned ski towns, each marked by its elevation in meters. Thus you have the less-fashionable Courchevel 1300 (Le Prez), 1550, and 1650. Crowning them all is Courchevel 1850.

Courchevel 1850 is the most attractive ski mecca in the French Alps, a position once held by Megève. It's also the focal point of a chair-hoist network crisscrossing the region. At the center of one of the largest ski areas in the world, Courchevel was built at the base of a soaring alpine amphitheater whose deep snowfalls last longer than those at most other resorts because it faces the north winds. This place attracts the ultra-rich international elite—and it's not cheap.

Courchevel 1850 is also distinguished by having more high-quality restaurants and hotels than any other resort in Europe—it's definitely a place for the glitterati.

WHERE TO STAY
Expensive

LE CHABICHOU, quartier Les Chenus, 73120 Courchevel 1850. Tel. 79-08-00-55. Fax 79-08-33-58. 34 rms (all with bath). TV TEL
$ Rates (including half board): 1,010–2,020 F ($181.80–$363.60) per person. AE, DC, MC, V. **Closed:** May 10–June 19 and Sept 26–Nov 8.
This is considered one of the finest hotels in town, and it's even better known for its restaurant (see "Where to Dine," below). Located uphill from the commercial center, Le Chabichou is within easy walking distance of many of the nighttime attractions. Bedrooms are plush, and facilities include a sauna, an indoor swimming pool, a Jacuzzi, and an exercise room.

HOTEL ANNAPURNA, route de l'Altiport, 73120 Courchevel 1850. Tel. 79-08-04-60. Fax 79-08-15-31. 66 rms (all with bath), 4 suites. A/C TV TEL
$ Rates (including half board): 1,152–1,600 F ($207.40–$288) per person double. AE, DC, MC, V. **Parking:** 80 F ($14.40). **Closed:** Mid-Apr to mid-Dec.
Named after one of the most inaccessible peaks of the Himalayas, this hotel sits in the very upper reaches of the resort. Its striking and modern architecture incorporates such elements as long stretches of laminated ceiling beams, rounded fireplaces in the middle of plushy comfortable lounges, and large windows overlooking the slopes. Bedrooms have wooden walls and ceilings and soft colors throughout. Superb ski conditions are just a few paces from the front door.
   Dining/Entertainment: There is an elegant restaurant and a piano bar.
   Facilities: Indoor glassed-in swimming pool.

HOTEL BELLECOTE, route de l'Altiport, 73120 Courchevel 1850. Tel. 79-08-10-19. Fax 79-08-17-16. 53 rms (all with bath), 2 suites. MINIBAR TV TEL
$ Rates (including half board): 1,225–1,725 F ($220.50–$310.50) per person. AE, DC, MC, V. **Closed:** May–Dec 10.
Beside the Jardin Alpin, this seven-story chalet of impressive proportions supported on a stone foundation is known for the quality of its construction and its collection of antiques. Bored with traditional alpine motifs, its founder, Roger Toussaint, scoured the bazaars of Afghanistan and the Himalayas for an array of fascinating objects, which lend exotic warmth to the wood-sheathed walls and ceilings of this unusual and desirable hotel. Each of the bedrooms contains plush accessories as well as exotic Far or Middle Eastern carved wooden objects.
   Dining/Entertainment: Full meals in the big-windowed and elegant dining room cost 330 F ($59.40) and up and include a cassolette of sweetbreads with flap mushrooms, frogs' legs provençal, and chicken with morels. An impressive luncheon buffet table is laden with a dazzling array of seafood, including crayfish and urchins, followed by succulent sauerkraut with pork products. The undisputed most flavorful "fondant au chocolat" in the Alps is served here. Meals are offered daily from 12:30 to 2pm and 7:30 to 11pm.
   Facilities: Indoor swimming pool.

HOTEL BYBLOS-DES-NEIGES, au Jardin Alpin, 73120 Courchevel 1850. Tel. 79-08-12-12. Fax 79-08-19-38. 78 rms (all with bath), 11 suites. MINIBAR TV TEL
$ Rates: 1,520–1,620 F ($273.60–$291.60) single; 2,040–3,460 F ($367.20–$622.80) double; from 4,640 F ($835.20) suite. Breakfast 100 F ($18) extra. AE, DC, MC, V. **Parking:** 150 F ($27). **Closed:** Apr 15–Dec 18.
This is the most impressive hotel at the resort, sweeping in a wide arc across an isolated landscape above the commercial center. Conceived in Neo-Phoenician design, this snowbound version adds roughly hewn timbers, lots of weathered planking, and an allegiance to Savoyard themes. The effect, nevertheless, is light and

airy, much to the delight of its sophisticated and glamorous clientele from around the world. With a branch of just about every chicly expensive boutique in Paris, this is one of the largest hotels in Courchevel and is also one of the best managed. Each of the bedrooms is predictably plush, if a little small, and sunlight streams through wide panoramic windows. Many units have outdoor terraces, and each comes with a radio.

Dining/Entertainment: L'Ecailler Restaurant is recommended under "Where to Dine," below.

Services: Concierge, room service, laundry, dry cleaning.

Facilities: Indoor swimming pool, heated garage.

HOTEL PRALONG 2000, route de l'Altiport, 73120 Courchevel 1850. Tel. 79-08-24-82. Fax 79-08-36-41. 68 rms (all with bath), 4 suites. MINIBAR TV TEL

$ Rates (including half board): 860–1,555 F ($154.80–$279.90) per person. AE, DC, MC, V. **Parking:** 100 F ($18). **Closed:** Mid-Apr to mid-Dec.

Set in the middle of a meadow, the Hôtel Pralong is a dramatic-looking structure of cedar shingles and prominent balconies. The elegant bedrooms are among the most alluring at the resort; accommodations facing south have sun-flooded balconies. The owners, the Parveaux family, have plenty of experience running hotels through their association with some of the most prestigious châteaux of France.

Dining/Entertainment: For information on the hotel's famous restaurant, see "Where to Dine," below.

Services: Room service, dry cleaning, laundry.

Facilities: Indoor swimming pool.

Moderate

LES DUCS DE SAVOIE, au Jardin Alpin, 73120 Courchevel 1850. Tel. 79-08-03-00. Fax 79-08-16-30. 70 rms (all with bath). TEL

$ Rates (including half board): 795–1,215 F ($143.10–$218.70) per person. V. **Parking:** 100 F ($18). **Closed:** Apr 20–Dec 19.

Located near the Hôtel Byblos-des-Neiges above the center of town, this establishment, one of the largest at Courchevel, has elaborately scrolled pinewood and often rows of icicles hanging from the protruding eaves. There's a covered garage, plus an indoor pool with walls intricately chiseled from mountain flagstones. In the lobby bar, the stone base deliberately retains its mountain lichens. Fireplaces add to the conviviality of the good food, drinks, and lively conversation. It lies a few feet from the Téléski of the Jardin Alpin, and guests can ski directly to the hotel's vestibule at the end of the day.

LA SIVOLIERE, quartier Les Chenus, 73120 Courchevel 1850. Tel. 79-08-08-33. Fax 79-08-15-73. 32 rms (all with bath). TV TEL

$ Rates: 725–1,670 F ($130.50–$300.60) single or double. Breakfast 75 F ($13.50) extra. MC, V. **Parking:** 80 F ($14.40). **Closed:** Late Apr to late Nov.

La Sivolière attracts such illustrious guests as the royal family of Spain. The secret of its success is Madeleine Cattelin, the owner, who has a rich knowledge of and appreciation for her native Savoy. Within its modern confines, 18th- and 19th-century antiques are mixed with well-chosen fabrics, comfortable sofas, and two large fireplaces. One of the many public rooms, the Salon Dolomite, is sheathed in carved pinewood. Each of the bedrooms contains tastefully elegant furnishings, lots of exposed pinewood, and all the modern conveniences. Rooms include free access to the sauna, steambath, and exercise room, as well as an invitation to a richly laden afternoon tea table. In the dining rooms there's no formal menu, and you're likely to get such dishes as filet of John Dory with watercress sauce and sea bass with essence of zucchini. Full meals, starting at 200 F ($36), also are served to nonresidents who make reservations, from noon to 2:15pm and 7 to 11pm. The Dou du Midi ski slopes are nearby.

Inexpensive

LE DAHU, près de la Station (near the bus station), 73120 Courchevel 1850. Tel. 79-08-01-18. Fax 79-08-11-98. 38 rms (all with bath). TEL

$ Rates: 500 F ($90) single; 750 F ($135) double. Breakfast 75 F ($13.50) extra. MC. V. **Closed:** Apr 26–Dec 14.

Located in the commercial center, across the street from the municipal skating rink behind a wooden chalet facade, is one of the resort's most alluring bargains, offering clean and comfortable bedrooms, a charming salon, a bar, and a restaurant. The hotel, renovated in 1987, is named after a mythical alpine goat whose capture by tourists is jokingly encouraged by local guides. The hotel's social center lies one flight above the reception. Upstairs, there is stylish furniture and a long and accommodating bar. Meals are served in the restaurant from 12:30 to 2pm and 7:30 to 8:45pm, and a full meal begins at 220 F ($39.60); nonresidents who make reservations are welcome.

WHERE TO DINE

In addition to the following restaurants, see "Where to Stay," above, for more hotel restaurants.

Expensive

LE BATEAU IVRE, in the Hôtel Pomme-de-Pin, quartier Les Chenus. Tel. 79-08-36-88.
   Cuisine: FRENCH. **Reservations:** Required.
$ Prices: Appetizers 116–204 F ($20.90–$36.70); main dishes 150–290 F ($27–$52.20); fixed-price menus 195 F ($35.10) (lunch only), 350 F ($63), and 490 F ($88.20). AE, DC, MC, V.
   Open: Lunch daily 12:30–2:15pm; dinner daily 7:30–10pm. **Closed:** Easter–Dec 19.

This is one of the very best restaurants in the resort, offering a panoramic view from its well-laid tables. Its fine reputation is the result of the dedicated efforts of the Jacob family. Their restaurant is far more exciting than the hotel that contains it. Full meals might include polenta and escalopes of foie gras in a vinaigrette, roast turbot with beignets of artichoke, fricassée of lobster and truffles, and a lasagne of oysters and crayfish; especially delectable is a succulent version of rack of lamb with black olives and artichokes. Try one of the superbly crafted desserts with one of four exotic coffees.

LE CHABICHOU, quartier Les Chenus. Tel. 79-08-00-55.
   Cuisine: FRENCH. **Reservations:** Required.
$ Prices: Appetizers 120–180 F ($21.60–$32.40); main dishes 140–250 F ($25.20–$45); fixed-price menus 200 F ($36) at lunch, 320–600 F ($57.60–$108) at dinner. AE, DC, MC, V.
   Open: Lunch daily noon–2pm; dinner daily 8–10pm. **Closed:** Easter–Dec.

Considered the best restaurant at the resort, Le Chabichou is on the lobby level of the hotel by the same name. Michel and Maryse Rochedy acquired a reputation for their cuisine at their similarly named establishment in St-Tropez. The decor includes big windows showcasing a view of the snow, a low but discreetly engineered ceiling with painted fields of geometric colors, and an elegant series of tableware accessories. The menu lists a number of superlative dishes, including oyster soup with wild mushrooms, a tempura of crayfish and rollmops of red mullet with saffron-flavored vegetables, roast pigeon on a bed of fresh green cabbage, and a succulent version of aiguillettes of duckling with peaches.

HOTEL PRALONG 2000, route de l'Altiport. Tel. 79-08-24-82.
   Cuisine: FRENCH. **Reservations:** Required.
$ Prices: Appetizers 60–100 F ($10.80–$18) at lunch, 130–215 F ($23.40–$38.70) at dinner; main dishes 120–170 F ($21.60–$30.60) at lunch, 150–275 F ($27–$49.50) at dinner. AE, DC, MC, V.
   Open: Lunch daily noon–2pm; dinner daily 7:30–9:30pm. **Closed:** Mid-Apr to mid-Dec.

This is one of the finest dining rooms at Courchevel, located on the ground level of the hotel by the same name, with lots of big windows, plush accessories, and impeccable service. Selected specialties include a thick grilled slice of turbot with a purée of sweet peppers, truffles with foie gras in puff pastry with a port sauce, and a salad of mâche and endive capped with rondelles of chive-flavored crayfish. There's also an impressive array of poultry, beef, and fish dishes.

RESTAURANT L'ECAILLER, in the Hôtel Byblos-des-Neiges, au Jardin Alpin. Tel. 79-08-12-12.

Cuisine: FRENCH. **Reservations:** Required.

$ Prices: Appetizers 130–230 F ($23.40–$41.40); main dishes 150–210 F ($27–$37.80). AE, DC, V.

Open: Dinner only, daily 8–11pm. **Closed:** Apr 15–Dec 18.

The most glamorous and sophisticated of the hotel restaurants, this restaurant is accessible from the lobby via the most impressive staircase in Courchevel (see "Where to Stay," above). It's customary to stop for an apéritif in the piano bar, where you can overlook the indoor pool; the music in the bar continues to 2am. The cuisine depends on what's available at the market. Specialties usually include seafood salad with walnut oil and cider vinegar, an escalope Cordon Rouge of salmon and lobster with truffles in puff pastry, a saddle of lamb with baby vegetables, and elaborate desserts.

Moderate

LA BERGERIE. Tel. 79-08-24-70.

Cuisine: FRENCH. **Reservations:** Required.

$ Prices: Appetizers 50–120 F ($9–$21.60); main dishes 65–170 F ($11.70–$30.60); fixed-price dinner 300 F ($54). AE, DC, V.

Open: Lunch daily noon–3pm; dinner daily 8–10pm. **Closed:** Mid-Apr to mid-Dec.

The uneven flagstone steps leading to it, the stacks of carefully split firewood, and the roughly weathered pine logs and planks on its sides testify to La Bergerie's origin in the 1830s as a shepherd's hut. Within its time-blackened vestibule you can join a long list of patrons, which has included ski and film stars, racecar drivers, and jockeys. A low-ceilinged dining room on the ground floor contains a dance floor and live entertainment. From December until the end of April, a dinner of alpine specialties is offered for 300 F ($54). Upstairs, a lunch restaurant and bar attract daytime drinkers and diners. Typical menu items include scallops in shallot butter, raclette, fondue bourguignonne, filet au poivre alpine style, and fricassée of chicken.

CHALET DES PIERRES, au Jardin Alpin. Tel. 79-08-18-61.

Cuisine: FRENCH. **Reservations:** Required.

$ Prices: Appetizers 62–190 F ($11.20–$34.20); main dishes 125–180 F ($22.50–$32.40). MC, V.

Open: Daily 11:45am–5pm. **Closed:** End of Apr to mid-Dec.

This one is the best of the several lunch restaurants scattered over the surrounding ski slopes. Built in the mid-1970s of fieldstone and weathered planking, it sits directly in the middle of the Verdon slope, a few paces from the whizzing path of skiers. Lunch is served on a sun terrace, but most visitors gravitate to the rustic two-story interior, where blazing fireplaces, a handful of hunting trophies, and "internationally hip" clients contribute to the allure and excitement. Meals often include an array of air-dried alpine meat and sausages, the best pommes frites in Courchevel, pepper steak, veal chop, rack of lamb, and *plats du jour*.

EVENING ENTERTAINMENT

From casual to sophisticated, après-ski and nighttime diversions in Courchevel are the most varied in the French Alps. Here's only a sampling of some leading places:

LE BISTROT DES CAVES, porte de Courchevel. Tel. 79-08-02-07.

Located in the commercial center, this club attracts some of the best-heeled patrons in town. Much of its allure comes from a live pianist, who can be enjoyed nightly in winter from 8pm to 1am. A mock Tyrolean facade of weathered wood hides a club evoking a medieval cloister, with stone arches and columns. Full meals in the restaurant, open nightly from 8pm to 6am, begin at 250 F ($45) and include mignon of pork with olives and frogs' legs provençal. Drinks cost 50 F ($9) and up. It's open December to April, daily from 6pm to 6am (closed May to November).

LA GRANGE, rond point des Pistes. Tel. 79-08-07-39.

This is the most rustic and informal of the resort's leading nightspots, where you can enjoy music and dancing. If a spectacle is being staged on the night of your visit, the doors may open earlier. Drinks start at 95 F ($17.10). It's open December to April, daily from 10:30pm to 5am (closed May to November).

LES PIRATES, porte de Courchevel. Tel. 79-08-12-74.

Established by a nightclub impresario, this is the most sought-after nightclub in the resort. Behind a wooden facade of weathered planking in the center, it has a theatrically wide staircase sheathed in black and plays the latest recorded music. Drinks run 100 F ($18). Open December to April, daily from 10pm until dawn (closed May to November).

Admission: Free.

SAINT NICOLAS, rond point des Pistes. Tel. 79-08-21-67.

This chalet, located on the upper reaches of the commercial center, has a fun disco. At its timbered portico, a life-size wooden statue of a crozier-carrying Saint Nicolas will encourage you to select between the disco on the left and the Bistrot on the right—the Bistrot a candlelit room filled with Belle Epoque accessories and rustic paneling, where dinner is served nightly from 8pm till "late," at prices beginning at 150 F ($27). Specialties include seafood pot-au-feu, filet of veal with kidneys and flap mushrooms, and steaks. Drinks run 70–95 F ($12.60–$17.10). It's open December to April, daily from 8pm to 6am (closed May to November).

BURGUNDY

Vineyard castles and ancient churches make La Province de Bourgogne in eastern France the land of the good life for those who savor food and drink. Once, Burgundy was as powerful as La Belle France herself, its dukes spreading their might across Europe.

The famed Valois dukes ruled Burgundy from 1363 to 1477. The splendor of their court became known throughout Europe. To maintain its shaky independence, Burgundy faced many struggles, notably under the leadership of Charles the Bold, who seemed in perpetual conflict with Louis XI. When Charles died in 1477, Louis XI invaded the duchy. The duchy became annexed to the French crown, albeit reluctantly.

Even so, the Habsburgs still maintained their claims to Burgundy. But after its reunion with France, Burgundy was still to know no peace, as it suffered many more upheavals, such as its ravaging in the Franco-Spanish wars beginning in 1636. Peace came in 1678.

At the time of the French Revolution, Burgundy disappeared as a political entity when it was subdivided into the départements of France, Yonne, Saône-et-Loire, and Côte-d'Or.

The dukes of Burgundy are but a dim memory now, but they left a legacy of vintage red and white wines to please and excite the palate. The six major wine-growing regions of Burgundy are Chablis, Côte de Nuits, Côte de Beaune, Côte de Chalon, the Mâconnais, and the Nivernais.

SEEING BURGUNDY

GETTING THERE Easily accessible, thanks to rapid TGV trains and numerous highways, Burgundy has always been at the meeting point of European civilizations.

There are daily flights to **Dijon-Bourgogne airport** from both Orly and Charles de Gaulle, and the region also is accessible by car and high-speed train from three other international airports: Lyon (Satolas), Geneva (Cointrin), and Basel-Mulhouse.

Direct **trains** leave Paris for Dijon, Montbard, and Beaune, while the Lyon line serves Le Creusot and Mâcon-Loche stations. Rapid TGV trains arrive in Dijon from Besançon, Lausanne, and Bern.

Five major **highways** (A6, A31, A36, A38, and A40) cross near Dijon, Beaune, and Mâcon. From Paris, an access road at the Pouilly-en-Auxois interchange provides direct access to Dijon, and the Dordives access road allows rapid transit to Nevers.

WHAT'S SPECIAL ABOUT BURGUNDY

Great Towns/Villages
- ☐ Vézelay, a living museum of French antiquity.
- ☐ Avallon, shielded behind ramparts with a medieval atmosphere.
- ☐ Beaune, capital of the burgundy wine country and a well-preserved medieval city.
- ☐ Dijon, the center of the Côte d'Or and ancient capital of Burgundy.

Ancient Monuments
- ☐ Basilique Ste-Madeleine at Vézelay, the largest and most famous Romanesque church in France.
- ☐ Autun, one of the oldest towns in France, called "the other Rome." Roman relics include the largest theater in Gaul.

Outstanding Museums
- ☐ Musée des Beaux-Arts at Dijon, the premier museum of Burgundy; in the former palace of the dukes of Burgundy, it's one of the oldest and richest museums in France.

Castles
- ☐ Château de Gevrey-Chambertin, a thick-walled castle dating from the 10th century.

Architectural Highlights
- ☐ Cathédrale de St-Etienne, built in the 13th century at Auxerre, in the flamboyant Gothic style.

Gastronomic Pilgrimages
- ☐ L'Espérance, outside Vézelay, considered one of the world's greatest gastronomic shrines.
- ☐ A la Côte St-Jacques at Joigny, a sumptuous Relais & Châteaux that attracts Parisians who drive down just for dinner.

Events/Festivals
- ☐ Festival International de Folklore et Fête de la Vine (International Folklore and Wine Festival), the first week in September, at Lyon.

There is probably no better way to see Burgundy than by **boat.** The province has about 745 miles of rivers and canals almost deserted by commercial navigation and available for pleasure boats. Contact the Central Reservations Office, 1-2, quai de la République, 89000 Auxerre (tel. 86-52-18-99), for a brochure and reservations.

A SUGGESTED ROUTE You need at least a week to tour Burgundy. I'd suggest that you make Auxerre, Vézelay, Beaune, or Dijon your base, especially if you're dependent on public transportation. The best way to "do" Burgundy is by car.

If you're driving from Paris, spend the first night (Day 1) at Auxerre, taking a brief excursion to Chablis. Drive the following day (Day 2) to Vézelay for a morning visit, perhaps staying overnight in Avallon. Continue on (Day 3) to Autun, scheduling a luncheon stopover at Saulieu. After Autun, head for Beaune for another night (Day 4) before finishing the trip with a visit and an overnight stay (Day 5) at Dijon, a good place to make connections for your next destination.

1. CHABLIS

113 miles SE of Paris, 12 miles E of Auxerre

GETTING THERE   By Car Because of inadequate public transportation, Chablis is most often visited by motorists on a day trip from Auxerre (take the D965 east).

ESSENTIALS Orientation The architectural centerpieces of Chablis are the Church of St-Martin and the Church of St-Pierre. From almost anywhere you stand in the village you can see vineyards sloping upward from the valley's floor.

Information For tourist information, inquire at Auxerre (see below).

A celebrated wine-making village lying 12 miles from Auxerre, Chablis is the gateway to northern Burgundy and the capital of the vineyards of Basse Bourgogne (Lower Burgundy). It is surrounded by about 20 wine villages, many of them clustered along the banks of the Serein River which flows through the town.

Chablis is not much of a tourist village, at least in the sense of having many attractions, yet its fame is so great that visitors flock here anyway. In the 16th century the region was especially prosperous, producing wines for much of what was then called France.

Incidentally, if you taste new chablis in any of the wine cellars, it's likely to be very acidic and raw. The professionals taste the wine, then spit it out.

The ideal time to go is in October, when tractors loaded with grapes freshly picked ride through the streets of the town. After aging, the wine begins to take on a delicate aroma around March of the following year.

Many wine makers in the village will allow you to visit their premises. They'll explain that the vine which produces the wine is from the chardonnay family, which locals call Beaunois. Many Parisians flock to the village to buy their chablis directly from the producer. Chablis, of course, is the most famous of all white burgundies. The finest chablis is called Grand Cru, and is produced in seven rigidly defined areas, all of them clustered on the right bank of the Serein.

Among the sightseeing attractions of the town, the 12th-century Church of St. Martin is visited, as is the Romanesque former parish Church of St. Pierre.

WHERE TO STAY & DINE

L'ETOILE, 4, rue des Moulins, 89800 Chablis. Tel. 86-42-10-50. Fax 86-42-81-21.
   Cuisine: FRENCH. **Reservations:** Recommended.
$ Prices: Appetizers 50–150 F ($9–$27); main dishes 85–155 F ($15.30–$27.90); fixed-price menus 110–150 F ($19.80–$27), 220 F ($39.60), 280 F ($50.40), and 290 F ($52.20). AE, MC, V.
   Open: Lunch Tues–Sun noon–2pm; dinner Tues–Sun 7–9:30pm. **Closed:** Feb.

L'Etoile serves regional meals that, naturally, are best accompanied by local chablis. Meals include poached eggs Chablis style, chitterling sausages, and braised ham. Its hotel offers 12 simply furnished bedrooms, 10 with private bath or shower. A single or double without bath costs 140–200 F ($25.20–$36), rising to 255 F ($45.90) with bath. Breakfast is another 32 F ($5.80) per person, and parking is free.

HOSTELLERIE DES CLOS, rue Jules-Rathier, 89800 Chablis. Tel. 86-42-10-63. Fax 86-42-17-11.
   Cuisine: FRENCH. **Reservations:** Required.
$ Prices: Appetizers 95–200 F ($17.10–$36); main dishes 115–225 F ($20.70–$40.50); fixed-price menus 160 F ($28.80), 270 F ($48.60), and 400 F ($72). AE, DC, MC, V.
   Open: Lunch Thurs and Sat–Tues noon–2pm; dinner Thurs–Tues 7–9:30pm. **Closed:** Dec 22–Jan 22.

Housed in a very old chapel and manor house, this hotel/restaurant serves the finest cuisine in Chablis. Combining traditional fare with innovative techniques, owner Michel Vignaud provides each course on the fixed-price menus with the suitable local wine. Specialties include a fricassée of snails in burgundy, zander cooked in chablis, or smoked chicken cooked in chablis.

Its 26 air-conditioned bedrooms contain private baths, phones, and radio alarms.

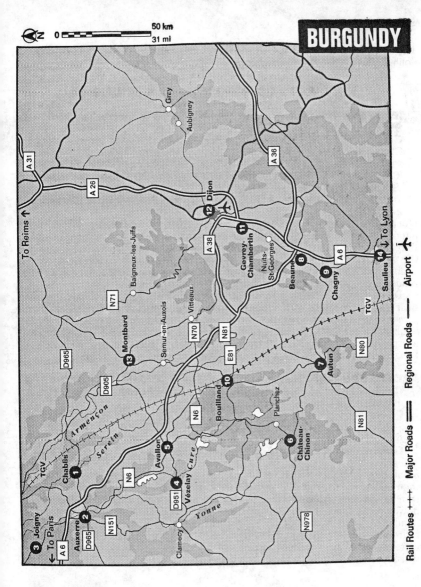

BURGUNDY

Rail Routes +++   Major Roads ═══   Regional Roads ━━━   Airport ✈

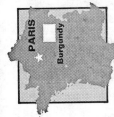

PARIS
Burgundy

1. Chablis
2. Auxerre
3. Joigny
4. Vézelay
5. Avallon
6. Château-Chinon
7. Autun
8. Beaune
9. Chagny
10. Bouilland
11. Gevrey-Chambertin
12. Dijon
13. Montbard
14. Saulieu

They rent for 240–495 F ($43.20–$89.10) single and 268–530 F ($48.20–$95.40) double, plus 50 F ($9) for breakfast.

NEARBY ACCOMMODATIONS & DINING

L'ABBAYE ST-MICHEL, route St-Michel, 89700 Tonnerre. Tel. 86-55-05-99. Fax 86-55-00-10.
Cuisine: FRENCH. **Reservations:** Required. **Directions:** Continue east from Chablis along the D965.
$ Prices: Appetizers 170–230 F ($30.60–$41.40); main dishes 170–240 F ($30.60–$43.20); fixed-price menus 300 F ($54), 480 F ($86.40), and 630 F ($113.40). AE, DC, V.
Open: Lunch Wed–Sun 12:30–2pm; dinner Tues–Sun 7–9:15pm. **Closed:** Jan 2–Feb 7.

Housed in a former 10th-century Benedictine monastery 16 miles east of Chablis, this inn overlooks the ancient Church of St-Pierre and has one of the best restaurants in Burgundy. The vaulted dining room is run by the owners' son, chef Christophe Cussac, who trained at Jamin, one of Paris's finest restaurants. Specialties include a salad of small lobsters and scallops flavored with saffron and fresh coriander, a filet of zander (a delicate, local freshwater fish), and regional meat dishes.

Daniel Cussac, formerly a Parisian engineer, and his wife, Denise, have furnished their nine guest rooms with antiques and beautiful fabrics and provided each with private bath or shower, direct-dial phone, TV, and minibar. Singles cost 750 F ($135), doubles go for 1,000 F ($180), and the six suites cost 1,300 F ($234) for two guests—plus 85 F ($15.30) for breakfast. A glassed-in reception area offers views of the gardens and village. The abbey also offers tennis and miniature golf.

AUBERGE DU BIEF, 2, av. de Chablis, Ligny-le-Châtel. Tel. 86-47-43-42.
Cuisine: FRENCH. **Reservations:** Required. **Directions:** Take the D91 seven miles north of Chablis.
$ Prices: Appetizers 55–98 F ($9.90–$17.60); main dishes 80–95 F ($14.40–$17.10); fixed-price menus 108 F ($19.40), 160 F ($28.80), and 198 F ($35.60). AE, DC, MC, V.
Open: Lunch Tues–Sun 12:15–2:15pm; dinner Tues–Sat 7:30–9pm. **Closed:** Jan.

Set at the edge of the Serein River, opposite the village church in a hamlet with about a thousand residents, this 200-year-old inn was originally built to feed horses and travelers passing through the region. Named after a narrow canal (Le Bief) which powers a still-functioning grain mill nearby, the place is run by Serge Baffet and his family. Menu items include an elegant assemblage of such dishes as a gâteau of artichokes with melted butter and fresh herbs, a hot two-fish terrine (sea trout and carrelet) served with a sauce made from a local wine (Irancy), sweetbreads with whiskey, and a tempting array of rich desserts.

2. AUXERRE

103 miles SE of Paris, 92 miles NW of Dijon

GETTING THERE   By Train   Many of the trains traveling between Paris and Lyon stop at Auxerre.

By Car   Many visitors drive since Auxerre is near the A6/E1 (Autoroute du Soleil).

ESSENTIALS   Orientation   The railway station lies at the eastern edge of town, about a mile from the historic center. Most of Auxerre is on the opposite (western) bank of the Yonne River. Its heart is between place du Maréchal-Leclerc (where you'll find the Hôtel de Ville) and the famous Cathédrale St-Etienne.

Information For information, inquire at the Office de Tourisme, 1-2, quai de la République (tel. 86-52-06-19).

This old town was founded by the Gauls and enlarged by the Romans. On a hill overlooking the Yonne River, it is the capital of Lower Burgundy and the center of vineyards, some of which produce chablis.

Joan of Arc spent several days here in 1429. Napoléon met Marshal Ney here on March 17, 1815, on the former emperor's return from Elba. King Louis XVIII had sent Ney to stop Napoléon. Instead, Ney embraced him and turned his army against the king. For that gesture, Ney was later shot in Paris.

Pay a visit to the **Cathédrale St-Étienne** (tel. 86-52-23-29), built during the 13th century but not completed until the 16th. It's a good example of the flamboyant Gothic style. The front is remarkable, with its sculptured portals. Inside, the stained glass is famous, some of it the original from the 13th century. In the crypt, all that remains of the Romanesque church that stood on this site, you can see frescoes from the 11th century. The church is open Monday through Saturday from 9am to noon and 2 to 6pm, and on Sunday from 2 to 6pm. It costs 10 F ($1.80) each to visit the crypt or treasury.

Auxerre used to be a gastronomic relay on the road between Paris and Lyon, but the Autoroute du Soleil has mostly ended that. However, **shops** display interesting regional specialties, including chocolate snails filled with almond praline, chocolate truffles with rum-soaked grapes, and garlic sausage baked in brioche, even sourdough bread from wood-fired ovens.

WHERE TO STAY

LE MAXIME HOTEL, 2, quai de la Marine, 89000 Auxerre. Tel. 86-52-14-19. Fax 86-52-21-70. 25 rms (all with bath or shower). TV TEL
$ Rates: 450–590 F ($81–$106.20) single or double. Breakfast 42 F ($7.60) extra. AE, DC, MC, V. **Parking:** 24 F ($4.30).

The 19th-century building that houses this establishment used to be a salt warehouse. Now a family-run hotel with a conservative decor, it contains an elevator and attractively decorated bedrooms, many with views of the river or of the old city. Guests can take breakfast in their bedrooms or in the quiet salon, amid Oriental rugs and polished paneling.

LE NORMANDIE, 41, bd. Vauban, 89000 Auxerre. Tel. 86-52-57-80. Fax 86-51-54-33. 47 rms (all with bath). TV TEL
$ Rates: 260–320 F ($46.80–$57.60) single or double. Breakfast 30 F ($5.40) extra. AE, DC, MC, V. **Parking:** 24 F ($4.30).

Close to Chablis (see above) and Vézelay (see below), the Hôtel Normandie offers traditional French hospitality. This 19th-century house combines antique furnishings with modern amenities. The hotel is centrally located and features tranquil and comfortably furnished bedrooms opening onto views of the garden. Each room is equipped with color TV (with English satellite programs), phone, and a clock radio. There is overnight parking for 30 cars, and other facilities include a complete gymnasium with a sauna. Visitors from around the world are welcomed at this family-run establishment.

WHERE TO DINE

LE JARDIN GOURMAND, 56, bd. Vauban. Tel. 86-51-53-52.
Cuisine: FRENCH. **Reservations:** Required.
$ Prices: Appetizers 60–150 F ($10.80–$27); main dishes 70–150 F ($12.60–$27); fixed-price menus 140 F ($25.20), 190 F ($34.20), and 270 F ($48.60). MC, V.
Open: Lunch Wed–Sun noon–2pm; dinner Tues–Sun 7:30–9:30pm. **Closed:** Dec.

Popular with residents and tourists alike, Le Jardin Gourmand serves *cuisine moderne du marché,* using the freshest ingredients from local markets. Pierre Boussereau is the experienced chef, who changes his menus seven times a year. The restaurant, with Louis XVI furnishings, has seating in the garden or on the terrace during warm weather. The wine list is composed of 330 different wines, including 50 selections of chablis, the king of wines in the area. Some good, simple, local, and reasonably priced burgundies are also featured.

---

3. JOIGNY

91 miles SE of Paris, 17 miles N of Auxerre

GETTING THERE By Train Joigny has rail connections to Paris and Auxerre, with easy transfers to Lyon and the rest of France.

ESSENTIALS Orientation The railway station is south of town, across the Yonne River. A single bridge connects both banks of the river. At its northern terminus, rue Gabriel-Cortel leads to the old town, the site of Joigny's two famous churches.

Information The Office de Tourisme is on quai Henri-Ragobert (tel. 86-62-11-05).

The most notable event that ever happened in Joigny was a revolt by the townspeople against their feudal lord, Guy de la Trémoille, in 1438. After attacking his château, they kidnapped him and killed him with blows from the mallets used at that time as vintners' tools. To this day the coat-of-arms for the city contains a depiction of a mallet, and the people of Joigny have ever since been called *les Maillotins.*

Today visitors appreciate the many winding, narrow streets leading to the Eglise St-Thibault, completed in the early 1500s, unusual because of its asymmetrical interior, and the Eglise St-Jean.

Most people, however, come to Joigny for the sole purpose of eating at A la Côte St-Jacques, which is considered one of the finest restaurants in France.

WHERE TO STAY & DINE

A LA COTE ST-JACQUES, 14, faubourg de Paris, 89300 Joigny. Tel. 86-62-09-70. Fax 86-91-49-70.
   Cuisine: FRENCH. **Reservations:** Required.
$ **Prices:** Appetizers 210–360 F ($37.80–$64.80); main dishes 180–290 F ($32.40–$52.20); fixed-price *menu gourmand* 640 F ($115.20). AE, DC, MC, V.
   Open: Lunch daily 12:15pm–2:45pm; dinner daily 7:15–9:45pm. **Closed:** Jan.
   Michel Lorain is the entrepreneur who, with his wife, Jacqueline (a noted sommelière), and their son, Jean-Michel, transformed his family's 300-year-old house into one of the most luxurious Relais & Châteaux in the region. The core of the establishment is a 19th-century building; an annex across the road dates from 1985, and the entire property was renovated in 1993. On an outdoor terrace or in one of the elegant modern dining rooms, you can enjoy such specialties as carp en gelée with spinach buds, a cassolette of morels and frogs' legs, and salmon with caviar-cream sauce, as well as an incredible array of desserts. A la Côte St-Jacques is located at the edge of town on the N6 leading to Sens.

The hotel also rents 10 beautifully furnished bedrooms and eight even more luxurious suites, each with private bath, air conditioning, TV, minibar, and phone. There's also a heated swimming pool, tennis courts, a sauna, and an underground tunnel that links the apartments across the highway with the main building.

A single or double costs 765–1,170 F ($137.70–$210.60), rising to 1,800–2,730 F ($324–$491.40) in a suite. Breakfast is another 100 F ($18) per person extra, and parking is free.

MODERN HOTEL, rue Robert-Petit, 89300 Joigy. Tel. 86-62-16-28, or toll free 800/528-1234 in the U.S. and Canada. Fax 86-62-44-33. 21 rms (all with bath). MINIBAR TV TEL
$ Rates: 320 F ($57.60) single; 520 F ($93.60) double. Breakfast 80 F ($14.40) extra. AE, DC, MC, V. **Parking:** 35 F ($6.30).
Giving A la Côte St-Jacques serious competition these days, this hotel of Jean-Claude Godard, in spite of its rather dull name, is a French residence of character. Throughout the years, the Godard family has continued to make improvements in this small hotel and today it's bright, airy, well furnished, and comfortable, in both its public and private rooms. Floral gardens enhance the setting, and there is also a summer swimming pool on the grounds, along with a half-size tennis court.
The hotel restaurant is now recognized as one of the most distinguished in the area. Jean-Claude shops for only the finest in seasonal produce available at the market. From that, he concocts delectable meals that are inventive. Everything is backed up with an excellent wine list. The dining room, decorated with flowers, opens onto a patio. Fixed-price menus cost 135–350 F ($24.30–$63).

NEARBY ACCOMMODATIONS & DINING

CHATEAU DE PRUNOY, 89120 Charny. Tel. 86-63-66-91. 13 rms (all with bath), 6 suites.
$ Rates: 600–650 F ($108–$117) single or double; 850–900 F ($153–$162) suite. Breakfast 50 F ($9) extra. AE, MC, V. **Parking:** Free. **Closed:** Feb–Mar.
In 1510, Guillaume de Crève-Coeur (William the Broken-Hearted) built a Gothic château in a 15,000-acre park, honoring the site of a major battle between the Burgundians and the forces of the Ile de France. In 1721, parts of the building were demolished and rebuilt in the 18th-century style then popular in Paris. Today, the monument welcomes diners and overnight guests into a gracious antique world of considerable charm. Surrounded by about 120 acres of forested park, the establishment is calm, quiet, and eminently respectable. The hotel lies about 2 miles north of the hamlet of Charny on the D950, 12 miles west of Joigny.

LE DAUPHIN, 12-14, rue Carnot, 89500 Villeneuve-sur-Yonne. Tel. 86-87-18-55. 11 rms (all with bath). TEL
$ Rates: 220 F ($39.60) single; 300–580 F ($54–$104.40) double. Breakfast 40 F ($7.20) extra. No credit cards. **Parking:** 30 F ($5.40). **Closed:** Hotel and Restaurant, Mar 1–20 and Nov 2–20.
About 10½ miles from Joigny and 8 miles from Sens is this small, French provincial inn with individually decorated rooms, operated by Dominique and Waltraud Chadelat. Monsieur Chadelat serves such specialties as homemade lobster bisque, escargots cooked with chablis, daurade (a fish) with five sauces, and hot sausage lyonnaise with potatoes cooked in wine. Fixed-price menus are available at 98 F ($17.60), 140 F ($25.20), 160 F ($28.80), and 240 F ($43.20). The restaurant is closed Sunday night and Monday off-season. The annual closing for the hotel and restaurant is March 1 through 20 and November 2 through 20.

4. VEZELAY

135 miles SE of Paris, 32 miles S of Auxerre

GETTING THERE   By Train and Bus   Trains travel from Auxerre to nearby Sermizelles, where an infrequent bus makes the run to Vézelay. Another bus arrives in

Vézelay late in the day from Avallon. Bus service to Vézelay is Monday through Saturday.

ESSENTIALS Orientation It's best to park near the lower periphery of the village, then continue on foot through the maze of narrow streets to the Basilique de Ste-Madeleine.

Information The Syndicat d'Initiative (tourist office) is on rue St-Pierre (tel. 86-33-23-69), open April to October.

Vézelay, about 32 miles from Auxerre, stands frozen in time, a living museum of French antiquity. For many, the town is the high point of their trip through Burgundy and Morvan. Because it contained what was believed to be the tomb of St. Mary Magdalene, that "beloved and pardoned sinner," it was once one of the great pilgrimage sites of the Christian world.

On a hill 360 feet above the surrounding countryside, the town is characterized by its ramparts and its old houses with sculptured doorways, corbelled staircases, and mullioned windows. The site of Vézelay was originally an abbey, founded by Girart de Roussillon, a Count of Burgundy (troubadours were fond of singing of his exploits). It was consecrated in 878 by Pope John VIII.

On March 31, 1146, Saint Bernard preached the Second Crusade there; in 1190 the town was the rendezvous point for the Third Crusade, drawing such personages as Richard the Lion-Hearted and King Philippe-Auguste of France. Later, Saint Louis of France came here several times on pilgrimages.

Park outside the town hall and walk through the medieval streets past flower-filled gardens. After about a quarter of a mile of climbing streets, you reach the **Basilique Ste-Madeleine** (tel. 86-33-24-36). The largest and most famous Romanesque church in France, this basilica is only 10 yards shorter than Notre-Dame de Paris. The facade was rebuilt by Viollet-le-Duc, who restored Notre-Dame. You enter the narthex, a vestibule of large dimensions, about 4,000 square feet. Look through the main door for a tremendous view of Burgundian-Romanesque glory. The high nave is built in white and beige chalk stones. It is full of light, and each capital shows a different sculpture. It's possible to visit the Carolingian crypt, where the tomb of Mary Magdalene formerly rested (today it contains some of her relics).

Afterward, you can end your walk by going alongside the ancient walls and back to place du Champ-de-Foire at the lower end of town.

Try to make it to L'Espérance for some of the finest—but expensive—cuisine in the world.

WHERE TO STAY

LE COMPOSTELLE, place du Champ-de-Foire, 89450 Vézelay. Tel. 86-33-28-63. Fax 86-33-34-34. 18 rms (all with bath) TV TEL

$ Rates: 240–290 F ($43.20–$52.20) single or double. Breakfast 32 F ($5.80) extra. MC, V. **Parking:** Free. **Closed:** Jan.

In 1991, long-time residents of Vézelay renovated an early 19th-century house and transformed it into this clean, unpretentious, and pleasant hotel. It lies in the center of town, midway up the hill leading to the famous basilica. Despite the building's modernization, many of the old ceiling beams were left intact. There's no restaurant inside; only breakfast is served.

POSTE ET LION D'OR, place du Champ-de-Foire, 89450 Vézelay. Tel. 86-33-21-23. Fax 86-32-30-92. 48 rms (9 with bath or shower). TEL

$ Rates: 250 F ($45) single or double without bath or shower, 620 F ($111.60) single or double with bath or shower. Breakfast 50 F ($9) extra. AE, MC, V. **Parking:** 50 F ($9). **Closed:** Nov 2–Apr 1.

A local monument and former post station, the Poste et Lion d'Or is a grand, fully restored, first-class establishment with reasonable fees. The food is exceptionally good—especially the escargots de Bourgogne in chablis and the stuffed trout with herbs. Fixed-priced menus cost 135–295 F ($24.30–$53.10). The restaurant is closed on Monday and Tuesday at lunch.

RESIDENCE HOTEL LE PONTOT, place du Pontot, 89450 Vézelay. Tel. 86-33-24-40. 8 rms (all with bath), 3 suites. TEL

$ Rates: 550 F ($99) single; 550–800 F ($99–$144) double; 700–900 F ($126–$162) suite. Breakfast 60 F ($10.80) extra. DC, MC, V. **Parking:** 50 F ($9). **Closed:** Nov–Easter.

Located in the upper part of the village near the basilica, this tastefully renovated, fortified medieval structure is Vézelay's other leading hotel. It has a charming walled garden for breakfast and bar service, but no restaurant. English is spoken.

WHERE TO DINE

For the hotel restaurants, see "Where to Stay," above. The following, however, is my top choice:

L'ESPERANCE, St-Père-sous-Vézelay, 89450 Vézelay. Tel. 86-33-20-45. Fax 86-33-26-15.

Cuisine: FRENCH. **Reservations:** Required. **Directions:** Take the D957 1¼ miles south of Vézelay.

$ Prices: Appetizers 290–580 F ($52.20–$104.40); main dishes 290–380 F ($52.20–$68.40); fixed-price menus 470–780 F ($84.60–$140.40). AE, DC, MC, V.

Open: May–Nov, lunch Thurs–Mon noon–2pm; dinner Wed–Mon 7:30–9:30pm. Dec–Apr, lunch Thurs–Mon noon–2pm; dinner Thurs–Mon 7:30–9:30pm.

At the bottom of the hill near the River Chur, L'Espérance is the most celebrated restaurant in Burgundy, and one of the best in the world. Marc and Françoise Meneau began their business with what had been a family bakery in a stone farmhouse. Marc Meneau is the self-taught son of a village harness maker, whose culinary experience includes creating special recipes for astronauts. Françoise Meneau helped in decorating the exquisite public rooms, the elegant marble bedrooms, and the dining room with its flagstone floors, Oriental rugs, high windows, and garden view. The complex consists of a main building (housing the restaurant) and three outbuildings, the latter containing 34 rooms, plus six suites.

In the restaurant you're offered such superb fare as cromesquis (liquefied foie gras, which you eat whole). You might follow with one of the many specialties of the house—for example, ambrosia of poultry with truffles and foie gras. In spite of such glamorous offerings, the chef notes that his food is "unpretentious, rustic, and substantial, hearty and nourishing, not just pretty to look at." As for dessert, you'll beg them for their recipe for orange soufflé pie.

Single or double rooms cost 350–1,300 F ($63–$234); however, there are only a few rooms at 350 F ($63), which—as a curiosity—cost less than the most expensive appetizers in the deluxe restaurant. Suites run 1,950–2,800 F ($351–$504).

5. AVALLON

133 miles SE of Paris, 32 miles SE of Auxerre

GETTING THERE   By Train   Avallon is connected by rail to Paris and the rest of France by about a half dozen daily trains. You may have to change trains in Laroche.

ESSENTIALS   Orientation   The railway station stands north of the town's ramparts, which surround its oldest buildings. The main street is the Grande'Rue

Aristide-Briand, which connects place du Général-de-Gaulle in the north with the Church of St-Lazarus in the south. Because of the maze of narrow one-way streets, many visitors prefer to park their cars outside the city walls and explore Avallon on foot.

Information The Office de Tourisme is located at 4-6 rue Bocquillot (tel. 86-34-14-19).

This old fortified town is shielded behind its ancient ramparts, upon which you can stroll. A medieval atmosphere still permeates the town, and you'll find many 15th- and 16th-century houses. At the town gate on the Grande'Rue is a **clock tower** from 1460. The Romanesque **Church of St-Lazarus** dates from the 12th century and has two interesting doorways. The church is said to have received the head of St. Lazarus in 1000. This turned Avallon into a pilgrimage site. Today, Avallon is used as a base for excursions to the north of the Massif du Morvan. But it is mainly visited because it's a gastronomic highlight of Burgundy, as reflected by the following recommendations.

WHERE TO STAY

CHATEAU DE VAULT-DE-LUGNY, à Vault de Lugny, 89200 Avallon. Tel. 86-34-07-86. Fax 86-34-16-36. 5 rms (all with bath), 6 suites. TV TEL **Directions:** Join the main road (D957) linking Avallon and Vézelay; turn right in the hamlet of Pontaubert and follow the signs to the château; Vault-de-Lugny is about two miles from Pontaubert.
$ Rates (including breakfast): 650–950 F ($117–$171) single; 700–1,600 F ($126–$288) double; from 1,700 F ($306) suite. AE, V. **Parking:** Free. **Closed:** Mid-Nov to Apr.

The most luxurious living is in a Relais & Châteaux property on the outskirts. A father-daughter team, Matherat Audan and Elisabeth, welcome you into their sumptuous home where you experience some of the best living in La Belle France. Lying at a point halfway between Avallon and Vézelay, the château is well located for excursions in many directions. The château dates from the 16th century and lies in a serene valley. It's encircled by a grassy moat, and estate grounds have a fortress tower and arrogant peacocks.

Personal service is a hallmark of the hotel (two staff members to every guest). Rooms and suites are often sumptuously furnished, with half-tester or canopied beds along with antique furnishings and baronial fireplaces. Elegance and taste go hand in hand. The menu offers solid Burgundian fare; drinks are ordered in an ornate salon, followed by dinner by candlelight.

HOSTELLERIE DE LA POSTE, 13, place Vauban, 89200 Avallon. Tel. 86-34-06-12. Fax 86-34-47-11. 20 rms (all with bath), 5 suites. TV TEL
$ Rates: 500 F ($90) single; 650–750 F ($117–$135) double; from 1,000 F ($180) suite. Breakfast 60 F ($10.80) extra. AE, DC, MC, V. **Parking:** Free.
The Hostellerie de la Poste is the best choice within the town center. Napoléon slept here on March 16, 1815, on his way back from Elba, and it hasn't changed much since then. As far back as 1707 this was a horse-and-buggy stopover. Today it consists of two two-story buildings along an arched cobblestone path. It's decorated with marble mantelpieces, tapestries, iron fireplace implements, and antiques.

MOULIN DES RUATS, Vallée du Cousin, 89200 Avallon. Tel. 86-34-07-14. Fax 86-31-65-47. 26 rms (all with bath or shower). TEL **Directions:** Take the D427 two miles outside town.
$ Rates: 320 F ($57.60) single; 650 F ($117) double. Breakfast 50 F ($9) extra. DC, MC, V. **Parking:** Free. **Closed:** Nov 15–Feb 15.
Situated on the banks of the Cousin in the valley, this country inn is equally as enchanting and expensive as the Hostellerie de la Poste. The serene and elegant

restaurant, which has a terrace overlooking the stream, serves freshwater fish. In addition to the excellent menu, costing 240 F ($43.20), the hostellerie offers a fine wine list. The restaurant is closed Monday and Tuesday for lunch.

LE MOULIN DES TEMPLIERS, Vallée du Cousin-Pontaubert, 89200 Avallon. Tel. 86-34-10-80. 14 rms (9 with bath). TEL **Directions:** Take the D957 in the direction of Pontaubert, about 2½ miles west of the center of Avallon.

$ Rates: 290 F ($52.20) single without bath; 340 F ($61.20) double with bath. No credit cards. **Parking:** Free. **Closed:** Nov–Mar 15.

Set at the edge of the river in an almost primeval forest, this country inn offers small bedrooms with a rural decor. Marie-Françoise Hilmoine, the genteel hostess, will have breakfast brought to your room. No other meals are served.

WHERE TO DINE

RESTAURANT LE MORVAN, 7, route de Paris (N6). Tel. 86-34-18-20.
   Cuisine: FRENCH. **Reservations:** Required. **Directions:** From the town center, follow the signs to the N6 in the direction of Auxerre.

$ Prices: Appetizers 85–110 F ($15.30–$19.80); main dishes 85–110 F ($15.30–$19.80); fixed-price menus 128 F ($23), 175 F ($31.50), and 225 F ($40.50). AE, MC, V.
   Open: Lunch Tues–Sun noon–2pm; dinner Tues–Sat 7–9pm. **Closed:** Jan 8–Feb 26.

On the edge of town, Restaurant Le Morvan is a rustic 18th-century inn with a park view. Menu specials, prepared by chef Jean Breton, may be filet of smoked duckling, veal scallop with ris de veau (sweetbreads) and sorrel, a timbale of snails with chablis, and excellent terrines, many of which are supplied to Fauchon in Paris.

6. CHATEAU-CHINON

174 miles SE of Paris, 38 miles S of Avallon

GETTING THERE   By Bus   There is bus service from nearby Autun, which has railway links to other cities, including Auxerre.

ESSENTIALS   Orientation   The promenade du Château, best negotiated with a car, encircles the base of the ruined castle and offers splendid views over the surrounding Morvan Nature Park. The town's highest point, accessible only on foot, is the Panorama du Calvaire. One of the most central points is place Gudin.

Information   For information, contact the Office de Tourisme, rue du Champlain (tel. 86-85-06-58), open June to September.

This scenic town was a natural fortress, with a feudal castle, looking out over the plains of Morvan and Nivernais.

For a remarkable view of the town and the Morvan mountains, you can climb to the 2,000-foot **Panorama du Calvaire,** where you'll find the site of a Gallic settlement. In clear weather you may even see westward to the Loire Valley and south to the summit of Haut Folin (3,000 feet). Finally, if you have a car, take the **promenade du Château,** running along the side of the hill and around the town.

WHERE TO STAY & DINE

AU VIEUX MORVAN, 8, place Gudin, 58120 Château-Chinon. Tel. 86-85-05-01. Fax 86-85-02-78. 24 rms (all with bath or shower). TV TEL

$ Rates: 240–260 F ($43.20–$46.80) single; 270–300 F ($48.60–$54) double. Breakfast 30 F ($5.40) extra. MC, V. **Parking:** Free.

Once a favorite retreat of French President François Mitterand, this centrally located country inn offers good local cooking and simply furnished bedrooms. It lies in the center of Château-Chinon, with a high view overlooking the region of the Morvan.

The dining room has a panoramic view of the Valley of the Yonne. Fixed-price menus cost 90 F ($16.20), 130 F ($23.40), and 190 F ($34.20). Main dishes are likely to include filet of monkfish à l'Américaine or pintade (guinea fowl) roasted.

LE FOLIN, route de Nevers, 58120 Château-Chinon. Tel. 86-85-00-80.
  Fax 86-85-21-29. 33 rms (all with bath). TV TEL
$ Rates: 230 F ($41.40) single; 260 F ($46.80) double. Breakfast 35 F ($6.30) extra. V. **Closed:** Nov 20–30.
This is a centrally located two-star hotel that many view as the best little inn in town. All the local hotels are modest. Bedrooms are comfortably furnished but simple. Many guests, including locals, stop here just for the good food served. You can order one of the best fixed-price menus in town for only 78 F ($14), although, if you feel like more elaborate food, you can ask for one of the fixed-price menus at 120 F ($21.60) or 180 F ($32.40).

EN ROUTE TO AUTUN

Leave Château-Chinon by the N78, heading toward Autun. At the town of **Arleuf,** take the D500 on your right, a narrow and rough road through a large, dark forest. At a fork, turn right to Glux. After Glux, follow the arrows to **Mont Beuvray** via the D18. You reach the summit through the D274, a narrow, winding, one-way road. After two miles of climbing, you're at **Oppidum of Bibracte,** home of the Éduens, a Gallic tribe. At this altitude of 2,800 feet, Vercingetorix organized the Gauls to fight Caesar's legions in A.D. 52. From here there is a splendid view of Autun and Mont St-Vincent. If the weather is clear, you can see the Jura and snowy Mont Blanc. All around are oaks and beeches, some of them more than 1,000 years old. After leaving Mont Beuvray by the D274, you'll come to St-Léger-sous-Beuvray.

---

7. AUTUN

182 miles SE of Paris, 53 miles SW of Dijon, 30 miles W of Beaune

GETTING THERE   Autun has rail and bus connections to the rest of France. By car, take the D3 from St-Léger-sous-Beuvray.

ESSENTIALS Orientation   The railway and bus stations lie on the western edge of town, just outside the ancient town walls, which still define the geographical boundaries of the village. Within Autun's eastern end is the Roman amphitheater; on its southern (and highest) end is the Cathédrale St-Lazare.

Information   The Office de Tourisme is located at 3, av. Charles-de-Gaulle (tel. 85-52-20-34).

Deep in burgundy country, Autun is one of the oldest towns in France, lying some 30 miles west of Beaune. In the days of the Roman Empire it was often called "the other Rome." Some of the Roman relics still stand, including the remains of a theater, the **Théâtre Romain,** the largest in Gaul, holding some 15,000 spectators. It was nearly 500 feet in diameter. Outside the town you can see the quadrangular tower of the **Temple of Janus** rising incongruously 80 feet over the plain.

Once, Autun was an important link on the road from Lyon to Boulogne, as reflected by the **Porte d'Arroux,** with two large archways used now for cars, and two smaller ones for pedestrians. It's in the northwest section, rising 55 feet. Also exceptional is the **Porte St-André,** or St. Andrew's Gate, about a quarter of a mile northwest of the Roman theater. Rising 65 feet high, it, too, has four doorways, and is surmounted by a gallery of 10 arcades.

The crowning achievement of Autun, however, is the **Cathédrale St-Lazare,** standing on the highest point in Autun, built in 1120 to house the relics of St. Lazarus. On the facade, the tympanum in the central portal depicts the Last Judgment—one of the triumphs of Romanesque sculpture. Some of the stone carvings are by Gislebertus, one of the few artists at that time who signed their names to their works. Inside, a painting by Ingres depicts the martyrdom of St. Symphorien, who was killed in Autun. In summer you can climb the tower and from there enjoy a good view over the town for 3 F (50¢); it's open daily from 9am to 5pm.

The **Musée Rolin,** 3, rue des Bancs (tel. 85-52-09-76), is installed in a 15th-century *maison* built for Nicolas Rolin, who became a famous lawyer in his day (born in 1380). An easy walk from the cathedral, the museum displays a fine collection of Burgundian Romanesque sculptures, as well as paintings and archeological mementos. From the original Rolin collection are exhibited the *Nativity* by the Maître de Moulins, along with a statue that's a masterpiece of 15th-century work, *Our Lady of Autun.*

It's open January to March, Monday and Wednesday through Saturday from 10am to noon and 2 to 4pm, and on Sunday from 2:30 to 5pm; April to September, daily from 9:30am to noon and 1:30 to 6pm; in October, Monday and Wednesday through Saturday from 10am to noon and 2 to 5pm, and on Sunday from 2 to 5pm; in November and December, Monday and Wednesday through Saturday from 10am to noon and 2 to 4pm, and on Sunday from 2:30 to 5pm. Admission is 12 F ($2.20) for adults and 6 F ($1.10) for children.

WHERE TO STAY & DINE

HOSTELLERIE DU VIEUX MOULIN, porte d'Arroux, 71400 Autun. Tel. 85-51-10-90. Fax 85-86-32-15. 16 rms (all with bath). TEL
$ Rates: 225 F ($40.50) single; 320 F ($57.60) double. Breakfast 37 F ($6.70) extra. AE, MC, V. **Parking:** Free. **Closed:** Mid-Dec to Mar 1.

Not only does the Hostellerie du Vieux Moulin contain the best restaurant in Autun, but it's also a good bargain for lodging. The inn has a warm ambience, with simple but clean rooms. In summer you can sit at a table overlooking the garden and a tiny millstream nearby. Most guests order the 160-F ($28.80) fixed-price menu, although a huge *gastronomique* special is featured for 250 F ($45). The dining room is open for lunch Tuesday through Sunday from noon to 2pm, and for dinner Tuesday through Saturday from 7:30 to 9pm.

HOTEL ST-LOUIS AND RESTAURANT LA ROTONDE, 6, rue l'Arbalète, 71400 Autun. Tel. 85-52-21-03. Fax 85-86-32-54. 51 rms (39 with bath or shower), 1 suite. MINIBAR TV TEL
$ Rates: 125 F ($22.50) single without bath or shower, 315 F ($56.70) single with bath or shower; 250 F ($45) double without bath or shower, 347 F ($62.50) double with bath or shower; 485 F ($87.30) suite. Breakfast 42 F ($7.60) extra. AE, DC, MC, V. **Parking:** 35 F ($6.30). **Closed:** Dec 20–Jan 25.

Built in 1696, this structure originally served as a postal inn on the main Paris–Nice route. Napoléon stayed here twice: once with his wife, Joséphine, on January 10, 1802, and again on March 15, 1815, upon his victorious return from Elba. His room, called the Napoleonic Chamber, comes with two canopied mahogany beds and an Empire fireplace. Most bedrooms have rustic furniture and floral wallpaper, and some contain brass beds. There is an American bar. The dining room, with large bay windows overlooking the courtyard (once the stables), serves good fixed-price menus for 80–200 F ($14.40–$36).

EN ROUTE TO BEAUNE

Leave Autun on the N73. After six miles, turn left onto the D326 toward **Sully.** Here you'll find the **Château de Sully,** once known as the Fontainebleau of Burgundy; unfortunately, it's closed to the public. The gardens are open from Easter to September, daily from 8am to 6pm, charging an admission of 5 F (90¢).

Leave Sully by taking the D26 until you cross the N73. Turn left toward Nolay and go through this small village. Three miles past Nolay you'll reach **La Rochepot,** with its medieval-style fortress built during the Renaissance. The attraction is open from Palm Sunday to November 1, Wednesday through Monday from 10am to noon and 2 to 6pm; admission is 15 F ($2.70).

After La Rochepot, head toward Beaune, first on the N6, then on the N74. Here you will pass through some of the best-known burgundy vineyards, including Chassagne Montrachet, Puligny-Montrachet, Meursault, Auxey Duresses, Volnay, and Pommard.

---

8. BEAUNE

196 miles SE of Paris, 24 miles SW of Dijon

GETTING THERE By Train Beaune has good railway connections from Dijon, Lyon, and Paris.

By Car Beaune is a few miles from the junction of four superhighways that fan out.

ESSENTIALS Orientation The railway station is set about a quarter of a mile east of the circular medieval ramparts, which are paralleled by modern boulevards. Near the center of these concentric circles are place Monge, with its famous belfry, and (a bit to the south, but still within the walls) the Musée de l'Hôtel-de-Dieu de Beaune.

Information The Office de Tourisme is on rue de l'Hôtel-Dieu (tel. 80-22-24-51).

This is the capital of the burgundy wine country and is also one of the best-preserved medieval cities in the district, with a girdle of ramparts. Its history goes back more than 2,000 years. Twenty-four miles south of Dijon, Beaune was a Gallic sanctuary, later a Roman town. Until the 14th century it was the residence of the dukes of Burgundy. When the last duke, Charles the Bold, died in 1447, Beaune was annexed by the crown of France.

WHAT TO SEE & DO

North of the Hôtel-Dieu, **Collégiale Notre-Dame** is a Burgundian Romanesque church that was built in 1120. Some remarkable tapestries illustrating scenes from the life of Mary are displayed in the sanctuary. They may be viewed from Easter to Christmas.

MUSEE DE L'HOTEL-DIEU, place de la Halle. Tel. 80-24-75-75.
This perfectly preserved 15th-century hospice is also one of the world's wealthiest working hospitals, since its own vineyards produce such renowned wines as Aloxe-Corton and Meursault. (On the third Sunday of November the wines are auctioned.) The Gothic building also houses Flemish-Burgundian art, such as the 1443 polyptych of *The Last Judgment* by Roger van der Weyden. In the Chambre des Pauvres (Room of the Poor) you will find painted, broken-barrel, timbered vaulting, with mostly authentic furnishings.
Admission: 25 F ($4.50) adults, 20 F ($3.60) children.
Open: Apr–Nov 17, daily 9am–6:30pm; Nov 18–Mar, daily 9–11:30am and 2–5:30pm.

MUSEE DES BEAUX-ARTS ET MUSEE MAREY, Hôtel de Ville. Tel. 80-24-56-92.
This museum contains a rich Gallo-Roman archeological section from the district, including burial stones, statuary, and pottery. The main gallery of paintings houses works from the 16th to the 19th century, including Flemish primitives. Sculptures from the Middle Ages and the Renaissance are also displayed. A larger part of the museum honors the Beaune physiologist Etienne Jules Marey (1830–1904), who discovered the principles of the cinema long before 1895.
Admission: Included with admission to Musée du Vin (see below).
Open: June–Sept, daily 9:30am–1pm and 2–6pm; Oct–Nov 21 and Apr–May, daily 2–6pm. **Closed:** Nov 22–Mar.

MUSEE DU VIN DE BOURGOGNE, rue d'Enfer. Tel. 80-22-08-19.

Housed in the former mansion of the dukes of Burgundy, this museum presents a regional history by tracing the evolution of wine making. The collection, comprised of tools, objets d'art, and documents, is contained in 15th- and 16th-century rooms. A collection of wine presses is displayed in a 14th-century press house.

Admission: 20 F ($3.60) adults, 7 F ($1.30) children.
Open: Daily 9:30am–6pm (until 5:30pm Nov–Mar).

WHERE TO STAY

HOSTELLERIE DE BRETONNIERE, 43, faubourg Bretonnière, 21200 Beaune. Tel. 80-22-15-77. Fax 80-22-72-54. 27 rms (all with bath or shower). TEL **Bus:** 1.

$ **Rates:** 295–340 F ($53.10–$61.20) single or double. Breakfast 34 F ($6.10) extra. MC, V. **Parking:** Free.

This hotel is the best bargain in town. Entered through a courtyard, it's well run, with clean and quiet rooms, 24 of which contain TVs. There's no restaurant, but a continental breakfast is available.

HOTEL DE BOURGOGNE, 27, av. du Général-de-Gaulle, 21200 Beaune. Tel. 80-22-22-00. Fax 80-22-91-74. 120 rms (all with bath). TV TEL

$ **Rates:** 405 F ($72.90) single; 440 F ($79.20) double. Breakfast 50 F ($9) extra. AE, DC, MC, V. **Parking:** Free.

Set a quarter of a mile outside the walls of the old city, the Hôtel de Bourgogne rises five floors in a residential neighborhood. Contemporary furnishings fill the bedrooms. A helpful staff is found in the dining room where fixed-price menus cost 98–165 F ($17.60–$29.70). There's an outdoor swimming pool.

HOTEL DE LA POSTE, 1, bd. Georges-Clemenceau, 21200 Beaune. Tel. 80-22-01-11. Fax 80-24-19-71. 21 rms (all with bath), 8 suites. TV TEL

$ **Rates:** 500–850 F ($90–$153) single or double; from 1,400 F ($252) suite. Breakfast 50 F ($9) extra. AE, DC, MC, V. **Parking:** 30 F ($5.40).

Located outside the town's fortifications, this rustic hotel has been completely renovated. Some bedrooms, which overlook either the ramparts or the vineyards, have brass beds, TVs, and air conditioning. Menu specialties include chicken fricassée flavored with tarragon and sole simmered in a court bouillon and served with beurre blanc. Meals begin at 160 F ($28.80).

WHERE TO DINE

BERNARD MORILLON, 31, rue Maufoux. Tel. 80-24-12-06.

Cuisine: FRENCH. **Reservations:** Recommended.
$ **Prices:** Appetizers 120–200 F ($21.60–$36); main dishes 150–250 F ($27–$45); fixed-price meals 160–420 F ($28.80–$75.60). AE, DC, MC, V.
Open: Lunch Wed–Sun noon–2:30pm; dinner Tues–Sun 7:30–10pm.

You'll dine here amid a Directoire/Louis XV decor beneath beamed and ornately decorated ceilings on such specialties as a gratin of crayfish tails, an unusual version of tournedos made with fish (les filets de bar) served with a fumet of red wine, sweetbreads with saffron seasoning, and deboned Bresse pigeon stuffed with foie gras and truffles. The restaurant is now located behind the Hospices of Beaune, but at press time, there was the possibility that it might move, so be sure to confirm the address.

RELAIS DE SAULX, 6, rue Louis-Very. Tel. 80-21-01-35.

Cuisine: FRENCH. **Reservations:** Required for large groups.
$ **Prices:** Appetizers 100–180 F ($18–$32.40); main dishes 110–190 F ($19.80–$34.20); fixed-price menus 150 F ($27) (Tues–Sat at lunch only) and 195–250 F ($35.10–$45); *menu dégustation* 360 F ($64.80). MC, V.
Open: Lunch Tues–Sun noon–2pm; dinner Tues–Sat 7:30–9:30pm. **Closed:** Dec 1–20.

On a narrow street behind Les Hospices, the Relais de Saulx is decorated with heavy timbers, velvet, and paintings. Chef Jean-Louis Monnoir prepares a sophisticated combination of traditional bourguignon cuisine and up-to-date adaptations such as salmon with endive and pigeon with foie gras.

NEARBY ACCOMMODATIONS & DINING

HOSTELLERIE DE LEVERNOIS, route de Verdun-sur-les-Doubs, Levernois, 21200 Beaune. Tel. 80-24-73-58. Fax 80-22-78-00.
Cuisine: FRENCH. **Reservations:** Required.
$ Prices: Appetizers 70–125 F ($12.60–$22.50); main dishes 160–380 F ($28.80–$68.40); fixed price menus 380–520 F ($68.40–$93.60). AE, DC, MC, V.
Open: Lunch Thurs–Mon noon–2pm; dinner Wed–Mon 7–9:30pm.

Christophe and Jean Crotet offer grand cuisine in an idyllic setting just three miles southeast of Beaune. The kitchen prepares such specialties as salmon smoked on the grounds and snails in puff pastry. Three kinds of fish en papillote are offered as a main course.

The inn rents 14 beautifully furnished rooms—each with private bath or shower, TV, and telephone—in a recently constructed pavilion reached through the gardens. Singles or doubles cost 900 F ($162). Two suites rent for 1,500 F ($270). Breakfast is another 90 F ($16.20).

9. CHAGNY

203 miles SE of Paris, 27 miles E of Autun, 11 miles SW of Beaune

GETTING THERE Chagny has rail and highway connections from Dijon and Lyon. By car, you can come from Beaune, before picking up the Burgundian wine train again.

ESSENTIALS Orientation The major inner-city thoroughfare is rue de la Liberté/rue Charles-de-Gaulle. Place d'Armes, site of my recommended restaurant, is the town center.

Information The Office de Tourisme is located at 2, rue Halles (tel. 85-87-25-95).

Although it isn't included in most sightseeing tours of Burgundy, this bustling industrial town does attract gourmets from all over the world. Its major sight is a 12th century church with a Romanesque tower.

WHERE TO STAY

AUBERGE DU CAMP-ROMAIN, Chassey-le-Camp, 71150 Chagny. Tel. 85-87-09-91. 42 rms (all with bath), 5 suites. TV TEL **Directions:** Follow the D974, then take the D109 about 3¾ miles west of Chagny.
$ Rates: 138 F ($24.80) single; 237–325 F ($42.70–$58.50) double; from 342 F ($61.60) suite. Breakfast 30 F ($5.40) extra. MC, V. **Parking:** Free. **Closed:** Jan–Feb 10.

In a secluded and peaceful spot, guests of this fairly modern hotel can relax around a swimming pool. The in-house restaurant serves well-prepared fixed-price menus for 113 F ($20.30), 126 F ($22.70), 141 F ($25.40), and 164 F ($29.50). Jean-Louis Dressinval will give you directions over the phone if necessary.

WHERE TO DINE

LAMELOISE, 36, place d'Armes, 71150 Chagny. Tel. 85-87-08-85. Fax 85-87-03-57.
Cuisine: FRENCH. **Reservations:** Required.

$ Prices: Appetizers 145–215 F ($26.10–$38.70); main dishes 175–295 F ($31.50–$53.10); fixed-price menus 350–550 F ($63–$99). AE, MC, V.
Open: Lunch Fri–Tues noon–2pm; dinner Thurs–Tues 7:30–9:30pm. **Closed:** Dec 22–Jan 27.

This outstanding *relais gourmand*, built in the 15th century, has one of the best restaurants in the country. Opened in 1920, it's now run by chef Jacques Lameloise, a third-generation family member. The service and decor in the three dining rooms are impeccable.

You might begin with his snail-stuffed ravioli with a duxelles of wild mushrooms or perhaps foie gras with herb vinaigrette. For your main dish, the chef might prepare a Bresse pigeon (considered the best in the world), cooked in a bladder and served with fettuccine laced with truffles. Lamb filet is cooked in a delicate rice crêpe with thyme and other herbs. For dessert, try the celebrated hot lemon soufflé. The restaurant also offers some of the finest wines in the region. Try, in particular, Rully and Chassagne-Montrachet.

The inn also rents 18 small but well-decorated bedrooms, all with either a shower or bath, a TV, and a phone. Doubles run 600–1,300 F ($108–$234), plus 80 F ($14.40) for breakfast.

10. BOUILLAND

202 miles SE of Paris, 27 miles SW of Dijon

GETTING THERE By Car Most visitors drive to Bouilland. Take the D2 from Beaune.

ESSENTIALS The village church and my restaurant recommendation (see below) are both easily visible in this village of only 150 inhabitants.

The drive to this village takes you through one of the most famous white wine roads of Burgundy, along the narrow valley of the Rhoin. Soon Bouilland, circled by wooded hills, comes into view. Its church is 900 years old and in remarkably good shape. Here in this secluded oasis you may wish to follow your gastronomic nose to the following recommendation:

WHERE TO STAY & DINE

HOSTELLERIE DU VIEUX-MOULIN, route de Savigny, 21420 Bouilland.
Tel. 80-21-51-16. Fax 80-21-59-90.
Cuisine: FRENCH. **Reservations:** Required.
$ Prices: Appetizers 150–280 F ($27–$50.40); main dishes 95–260 F ($17.10–$46.80); fixed-price menus 200 F ($36), 300 F ($54), and 450 F ($81). MC, V.
Open: Lunch Fri–Tues noon–2pm; dinner Thurs–Tues 7–9pm. **Closed:** Jan.
This small inn at the edge of Bouilland has one of the best restaurants in Burgundy. Its highly acclaimed owner and chef, Jean-Pierre Silva creates original recipes; his wife, Isabelle, acts as an outstanding sommelière. Monsieur Silva also gathers the wild mushrooms, which appear in many of his dishes.

You can begin with a velvety oyster flan. Perhaps you'll try his fish "confused" with wine, figs, honey, and fresh herbs. You might order his John Dory with a Provence-inspired compote, or else fresh trout *au bleu* (which is simmered in court bouillon).

The inn also offers 24 beautifully furnished bedrooms, each with a private bath or shower, TV, and phone. Singles or doubles are 400–850 F ($72–$153), plus 70 F ($12.60) for breakfast. Two suites rent for 1,300 F ($234).

EN ROUTE TO DIJON

Back on the N74, the road takes you through the wine district en route to Dijon. Along the way you'll pass through **Aloxe-Corton,** where the Emperor Charlemagne once owned vineyards. The Corton-Charlemagne is still a famous white burgundy. **Comblanchien** is known for a white stone quarried from neighboring cliffs. Wine from Nuits-St-Georges was particularly renowned during the reign of Louis XIV.

The next village is **Vougeot**, which produces an excellent red wine. Here you can visit the **Château du Clos-de-Vougeot,** 21650 Vougeot (tel. 80-62-86-09), surrounded by the most celebrated vineyards in France. The Renaissance château is associated with the Brotherhood of the Knights of Tastevin, known for its promotion of Burgundian wines. You can explore the 12th-century cellar. From April to the end of March, it's open daily from 9 to 11:30am and 2 to 5:30pm. Admission is 15 F ($2.70).

Leave the N74 for the D122. This will take you through the scenic **Chambolle Musigny,** then to **Morey St-Denis** and **Gevrey-Chambertin,** marking the beginning of the Côte de Nuits wine district.

11. GEVREY-CHAMBERTIN

194 miles SE of Paris, 17 miles NE of Beaune, 8 miles SW of Dijon

GETTING THERE   By Car   South of Burgundy lies the Côte d'Or or "golden slope," a famous wine-growing district. Leave Dijon via the D122—grandly called "Route des Grands Crus"—and follow it south until the junction with the N74 at Vougeot. Along the way the most notable wine-producing town you'll go through is Gevrey-Chambertin.

ESSENTIALS   Orientation   The most important landmark in the town center is the château.

Information   The **Office de Tourisme,** place de la Mairie (tel. 80-34-38-40), is open from May to October only.

This town eight miles south of Dijon was immortalized by the writer Gaston Roupnel. Typical of the villages of the Côte d'Or, Gevrey added Chambertin to its name, which is the name of its most famous vineyard.

In the village stands the **Château de Gevrey-Chambertin** (tel. 80-34-36-13), constructed at a high point of the village around the 10th century by the lords of Vergy. The thick-walled castle was in disrepair by the 13th century, but it was restored and expanded by the powerful order of the monks of Cluny, who retained the corkscrew staircases whose unevenly spaced steps, now polished slick by the passage of thousands of feet, sometimes prove difficult to negotiate. The great hall is impressive, with exposed ceiling beams. The guardsmen's room in the watchtower and the collections of aging wines in the vaulted cellars are part of the château's charm.

Between April 15 and November 15, half-hour guided tours are given in English, daily from 10am to noon and 2 (2:30 on Sunday) to 6pm. In winter, tours are given from 10:30am to noon and 2:30 to 6:30pm. The château is closed Sunday morning. Admission is 20 F ($3.60) for adults, 10 F ($1.80) for children 7–12.

The village church with its Romanesque doorway dates from the 14th century.

WHERE TO STAY

HOTEL LES-GRANDS-CRUS, route des Grands-Crus, 21220 Gevrey-Chambertin. Tel. 80-34-34-15. Fax 80-51-89-07. 24 rms (all with bath or shower). TEL

$ Rates: 350 F ($63) single; 430 F ($77.40) double. Breakfast 45 F ($8.10) extra. MC, V. **Parking:** Free. **Closed:** Dec–Feb 25.

This charming hotel, located near a tiny 12th-century château, opened in 1977. The hotel is run by Madame Farnier, the helpful host, who speaks English. Bedrooms, some of which have Louis XV furnishings, provide views of vineyards and a 12th-century church. The hotel does not have a restaurant but serves a continental breakfast. Regional wines also are available.

LES TERROIRS, 28, route de Dijon, 21220 Gevrey-Chambertin. Tel. 80-34-30-76. Fax 80-34-11-79. 23 rms (all with bath or shower). TV TEL

$ Rates: 330 F ($59.40) single; 380–500 F ($68.40–$90) double. Breakfast 42 F ($7.60) extra. AE, DC, MC, V. **Closed:** Dec 20–Jan 20.

Les Terroirs is a good value, offering clean and well-furnished bedrooms. There is a bar, but breakfast is the only meal served. The hotel is open all year.

WHERE TO DINE

LES MILLESIMES, 25, rue de l'Eglise and rue de Meixville. Tel. 80-51-84-24.

Cuisine: FRENCH. **Reservations:** Required.

$ Prices: Appetizers 110–205 F ($19.80–$36.90); main dishes 145–280 F ($26.10–$50.40); fixed-price menu 295 F ($53.10); *menu dégustation* 495 F ($89.10). AE, DC, MC, V.

Open: Lunch Thurs–Mon 12:30–1:30pm; dinner Wed–Mon 7:30pm. **Closed:** Jan.

Monique Sangoy and her children operate one of the most outstanding restaurants in the area, in the courtyard of what used to be a 17th-century warehouse for local wines, with an iron archway with exposed stone and ceiling vaulting. House specialties include a salad of foie gras, honey duck flavored with spices, and, for dessert, a soufflé dropped in a fruit syrup. There's a splendid wine list, with more than 1,800 references.

LA ROTISSERIE DU CHAMBERTIN, rue Chambertin. Tel. 80-34-33-20.

Cuisine: FRENCH. **Reservations:** Required.

$ Prices: Appetizers 80–135 F ($14.40–$24.30); main dishes 120–160 F ($21.60–$28.80); fixed-price menus 260–410 F ($46.80–$73.80). MC, V.

Open: Lunch Tues–Sun noon–1:30pm; dinner Tues–Sat 7–9pm. **Closed:** Feb and July 29–Aug 6.

An inconspicuous entrance, marked only with the menu, leads to this popular regional restaurant. Visitors must first pass through a museum devoted to the history of barrel-making, in honor of the owner's great-grandfather who was the town cooper on this very spot. A small section of the floor plan follows the floor plan of the 12th-century vaults, but more accurately, most of the building was restored and enlarged in the 18th century, and the building follows that form today. Once you arrive, be sure to take advantage of the inn's wines. Chambertin has been called "the wine for moments of great decision." Perhaps that's why Napoléon always took it on his campaigns—even to Moscow. Although the wine list is not extensive, it includes the best of recent vintages. The chef prepares the regional classics, including coq au vin. Perhaps you'll order a large sole grilled to perfection on an open wood fire or "winegrower's beef." Try also the herb-flavored roast lamb.

EN ROUTE TO DIJON

At **Brochon,** you're at the boundary between the Côte de Nuits district and the Côte de Dijon. Farther on, at **Fixin** you can stop to visit **Parc Noisot** for a view of the environs of Dijon. **Marsannay-la-Côte,** the next town, produces a rosé wine from black grapes. At **Chenove,** the vineyards were once owned by Autun monks and the dukes of Burgundy.

---

12. DIJON

194 miles SE of Paris, 199 miles NE of Lyon

GETTING THERE Dijon has excellent rail, air, bus, and highway connections to the rest of Europe. Five TGV trains arrive from Paris each day (trip time: 1½ hours). Trains arrive from Lyon every hour (trip time: 2 hours).

ESSENTIALS Orientation The oldest part of the city is surrounded by a pentagonal network of wide boulevards and modern access roads. Inside this ring, the old city's centerpiece is the Palais des Ducs de Bourgogne, around which all the other historic buildings seem to pay homage.

Information The Office de Tourisme is at 34, rue des Forges (tel. 80-30-35-39) and at place Darcy (tel. 80-43-42-12).

Dijon is known overseas mainly for its mustard. In the center of the Côte d'Or, it is the ancient capital of Burgundy. Here, good food is accompanied by great wine. Between meals you can enjoy Dijon's art and architecture.

The remains of the former palace of the dukes of Burgundy (**Ancien Palais des Ducs de Bourgogne**) has been turned into the **Musée des Beaux-Arts** (Fine Arts Museum), place de la Sainte-Chapelle (tel. 80-74-52-70). One of the oldest and richest museums in France, it contains exceptional sculpture, ducal kitchens from the mid-1400s (with great chimneypieces), a representative collection of European paintings from the 14th through the 19th century, and modern French paintings and sculptures. Take special note of the Salle des Gardes, built by Philip the Good. It was the banqueting hall of the old palace. The grave of Philip the Bold was built between 1385 and 1411 and is one of the best in France. A reclining figure rests on a slab of black marble, surrounded by 41 mourners.

The museum is open Wednesday through Monday from 10am to 6pm. Some rooms are closed from noon to 2pm. Admission is 10 F ($1.80).

A mile from the center of town on the N5 stands **Chartreuse de Champmol,** the Carthusian monastery built by Philip the Bold as a burial place; it is now a mental hospital. Much was destroyed during the Revolution, but you can see the Moses Fountain in the gardens designed by Sluter at the end of the 14th century. The Gothic entrance is superb.

Major churches to visit in Dijon include the **Cathédrale St-Bénigne,** a 13th-century abbey church in the Burgundian-Gothic style; the **Eglise St-Michel,** in the Renaissance style; and the **Eglise Notre-Dame,** built in the 13th century in the Burgundian-Gothic style with a facade decorated partly with gargoyles. On the Jaquemart clock, the hour is struck by a mechanical family.

WHERE TO STAY

HOSTELLERIE DU CHAPEAU-ROUGE, 5, rue Michelet, 21000 Dijon. Tel. 80-30-28-10, or toll free 800/528-1234 in the U.S. and Canada. Fax 80-30-33-89. 31 rms (all with bath), 2 suites. MINIBAR TV TEL
$ Rates: 450–545 F ($81–$98.10) single; 545–705 F ($98.10–$126.90) double; from 1,300 F ($234) suite. Breakfast 60 F ($10.80) extra. AE, DC, MC, V. **Parking:** 20 F ($3.60).
This is a Dijon landmark, partly because of its desirable location and partly because of its restaurant. Located on a quiet street behind the cathedral, the hotel is filled with 19th-century antiques, warm colors, and rooms with modern conveniences and comfortable furnishings, 10 of which are air-conditioned. Also there is a skylit, rattan-and plant-filled salon, which was originally the courtyard of the 15th-century building.

HOTEL IBIS CENTRAL, 3, place Grangier, 21000 Dijon. Tel. 80-30-44-00. Fax 80-30-77-12. 90 rms (all with shower). TV TEL
$ Rates: 295 F ($53.10) single; 345 F ($62.10) double. Breakfast 38 F ($6.80) extra. AE, DC, MC, V. **Parking:** 30 F ($5.40).
Prominently situated on a busy downtown square across from the main post office, this hotel is clean and attractive. Built in 1926, it offers "two-star" hotel comfort in its

DIJON

0 — 150 m
— 165 y

place de la Banque

To Langres

place Darcy

place Grangier

rue de la Poste

rue de la Liberté

rue Musette

place des Ducs

rue Chaudronnerie

rue Jeannin

place St-Michel

rue Vaillant

place de la Libération

place du Théâtre

rue Michelet

place St-Bénigne

rue Piron

rue Berbisey

rue Monge

rue Charrue

rue Amiral-Roussin

To Dôle

Church ■ †

Post Office ⊠

Information ⊙

Cathédrale St-Bénigne ❷
Eglise Notre-Dame ❹
Eglise St-Michel ❽
Musée Archéologique ❶
Musée des Beaux-Arts ❻

Musée Magnin ❼
Musée Perrin ❸
Palais des Ducs de Bourgogne ❺

PARIS ★
Dijon ⦿

---

soundproof bedrooms. The Central Grill Rôtisserie offers candlelit dinner and a panoramic view of Dijon. Meals begin at 165 F ($29.70).

HOTEL PULLMAN–LA CLOCHE, 14, place Darcy, 21000 Dijon. Tel. 80-30-12-32. Fax 80-30-04-15. 76 rms (all with bath), 4 suites. A/C MINIBAR TV TEL

$ Rates: 540 F ($97.20) single; 630 F ($113.40) double; from 1,300 F ($234) suite. Breakfast 62 F ($11.20) extra. AE, DC, MC, V.

This 15th-century historic monument is in the commercial center of town. The sophisticated interior has Oriental rugs and a pink-and-gray marble floor. The lobby-level bar is one of the most elegant places in town, with exposed brass, wood tones, and a view of the garden shared by an adjoining glassed-in tea room. The restaurant, Jean-Pierre Billoux, is recommended in "Where to Dine," below.

WHERE TO DINE

JEAN-PIERRE BILLOUX, in the Hôtel Pullman–La Cloche, 14, place Darcy. Tel. 80-30-11-00.
Cuisine: BURGUNDIAN/FRENCH. **Reservations:** Recommended.

$ Prices: Appetizers 120–180 F ($21.60–$32.40); main dishes 180–250 F ($32.40–$45); fixed-price meals 200 F ($36) (lunch only), 350 F ($63), and 440 F ($79.20). AE, MC, V.

Open: Lunch Tues–Sun noon–2pm; dinner Tues–Sat 7:30–9:30pm. **Closed:** Two weeks in Feb–Mar and one week in Aug.

✪ Considered one of the finest restaurants in Burgundy, this establishment lies in the heart of Dijon, beneath the soaring stone vaults of an underground wine cellar originally built around 1870. Its chef and owner, the Billoux family, prepare honest, straightforward, deceptively simple food which has won acclaim throughout Burgundy for its reliance on natural local ingredients and country-rustic finesse. Menu items might include roast chicken steeped in liquefied almonds, terrine of pigeon, guinea fowl with capers, steamed frogs' legs served with watercress crêpes, or thick-sliced filet of sole served on a bed of tomato-infused polenta. The array of available wines has been called an oenophilic library of Burgundian wines, a joy to any connoisseur.

LE RALLYE, 39, rue Chabot-Charny. Tel. 80-67-11-55.
   Cuisine: FRENCH. **Reservations:** Required.
$ **Prices:** Appetizers 50–80 F ($9–$14.40); main dishes 80–120 F ($14.40–$21.60); fixed-price menus 90 F ($16.20), 150 F ($27), and 220 F ($39.60). AE, DC, MC, V.
   Open: Lunch Mon–Sat noon–2pm; dinner Mon–Sat 7:30–9:30pm. **Closed:** Feb 25–Mar 12 and July 29–Aug 19.

Housed in a stone building from 1750 in the center of the old city, Le Rallye has a traditional interior with beamed ceilings and old-fashioned furniture. Owners François and Monique Minot prepare such specialties as a "daisy" of artichokes, terrine of duck with pistachios, escalope of salmon flavored with ginger, filet of duck with honey and lemon, coq au vin (with a local burgundy), and steamed turbot flavored with sage.

LA TOISON D'OR, 18, rue Ste-Anne. Tel. 80-30-73-52.
   Cuisine: FRENCH. **Reservations:** Required.
$ **Prices:** Appetizers 60–150 F ($10.80–$27); main dishes 90–160 F ($16.20–$28.80); fixed-price menus 150 F ($27), 190 F ($34.20), and 240 F ($43.20). AE, DC, MC, V.
   Open: Lunch daily noon–1:30pm; dinner Mon–Sat 7–9:30pm. **Closed:** Aug 8–23.

At the end of a large stone courtyard, off a quiet street in the old part of town, this elegantly rustic restaurant offers some of the best food in Burgundy. As soon as you enter you'll be offered an English-speaking tour of the adjoining wine museum and medieval buildings. Your guide will include a grisly depiction of medieval slayings, Carolingian tortures, and a look at everything connected to the local history of wine making. The premises are part of a 15th-century house that, with its sculpted inner courtyard, was connected to the adjoining 17th-century building.
   Amid stone walls, Oriental rugs, high ceilings, and Louis XIII chairs, you'll enjoy such specialties as sautéed duck livers and sweetbreads in a spinach salad, incredibly smooth foie gras, a half-cooked filet of salmon in a delightful bitter sauce, and filet of duckling doused in liver sauce with grated truffles. The wine list is very extensive, and many of the vintages are moderately priced.

NEARBY ATTRACTIONS

Leave Dijon on the N5, heading toward Paris. For a few miles you'll take a good road in the **Vallée de l'Ouche,** alongside the Burgundy Canal. At **Pont de Pany,** keep going on the N5 toward **Sombernon.** After Aubigny, on your left lies the artificial lake of **Grosbois.** The scenery is typical of agricultural France, with isolated farms, woods, and pastures.
   You pass through Vitteaux and just before the next village, **Posanges,** stands a magnificent feudal château. You can't visit it, but it's worth a picture. Continue on the N5 for a few miles after Posanges until you come to a railroad crossing. There on your left is another old castle, now part of a farm.
   The next village you reach is **Pouillenay.** Turn right there onto the D9, heading toward Flavigny-sur-Ozerain. Park your car outside the walls and walk through the old streets.
   You leave Flavigny on the D29, crossing the D6 and turning left on the small D103

toward **Alise-Ste-Reine.** This was the site of the camp of Alesia, where, in 52 B.C., Caesar overcame Gallic forces. Here, Millet sculpted a bronze statue of the leader of the Gauls, Vercingetorix.

Visitors can explore the excavated ruins of a Roman-Gallic town and visit the **Musée Alesia,** rue de l'Hôpital (tel. 80-96-10-95), daily from 9am to 7pm July 1 to September 15; off-season hours are 10am to 6pm; it's closed from November to March. Admission (including the excavations and the museum) is 20 F ($3.60) for adults and 16 F ($2.90) for children.

Alise-Ste-Reine honors a Christian girl who was decapitated for refusing to marry a Roman governor, Olibrius. As late as the 17th century, a fountain at the site of the beheading was said to have curative powers.

After Alise-Ste-Reine, you can head back toward the village of **Les Laumes,** a railroad center. Before entering the village, make a U-turn to the right, taking the N454 to **Baigneux-les-Juifs.** After the village of **Grésigny,** on your left there is a farm-fortress surrounded by water.

One mile farther, turn right toward the **Château de Bussy-Rabutin.** Roger de Rabutin, the cousin of Madame de Sévigné, ridiculed the court of Louis XIV, for which he spent six years in the Bastille. The château, which has two round towers, has survived mostly intact, including the interior decoration ordered by the count. The gardens and park are attributed to Le Nôtre. It's open April to September, Wednesday through Monday from 9am to noon and 2 to 6pm; the rest of the year, Wednesday through Monday from 10am to noon and 2 to 5pm. Admission is 20 F ($3.60).

Going back to Grésigny, turn right before the farm-fortress, then turn left. Outside the village, turn right again toward **Menetreux Le Pitois.** You're now off the main road and into the real countryside.

Once back on the N5, head on to **Montbard.** After six miles you reach the village of Marmagne. There you can turn left on the D32 toward the **Abbaye de Fontenay** (tel. 80-92-15-00). Isolated in a small valley, Fontenay is one of the most unspoiled examples of a 12th-century Cistercian abbey. It was classed a "Universal Heritage" by UNESCO in 1981. The church, dating from 1139, is one of the oldest Cistercian houses of worship in the country. A private historical monument, the abbey charges an admission of 34 F ($6.10) for adults, 16 F ($2.90) for children. It's open daily from 9am to noon and 2 to 6pm (to 5pm in winter).

NEARBY ACCOMMODATIONS

NOVOTEL DIJON SUD, route de Beaune, 21160 Marsannay-la-Côte. Tel. 80-52-14-22. Fax 80-51-02-28. 122 rms (all with bath). A/C MINIBAR TV TEL
Directions: From Lyon, exit at Dijon Sud; it's beside Rte. 74, 3½ miles southwest of Dijon's center (look for the blue-and-white Novotel signs). **Bus:** 60.
$ Rates: 390 F ($70.20) single; 460 F ($82.80) double. Breakfast 48 F ($8.60) extra. AE, DC, MC, V. **Parking:** Free.
Novotel has a commercially successful format of standardized bedrooms each containing one single bed (which serves, thanks to bolster pillows, as a couch) and one double bed. The hotel also contains one of the better restaurants in the entire chain, open daily from 6am to midnight, serving full meals for 165 F ($29.70).

NEARBY DINING

JOEL PERREAUT'S RESTAURANT DES GOURMETS, 8, rue Puits-de-Têt, Marsannay-la Côte. Tel. 80-52-16-32.
Cuisine: FRENCH. **Reservations:** Required. **Directions:** Drive four miles south of Dijon, to the first village on Burgundy's Wine Road.
$ Prices: 96–142 F ($17.30–$25.60); main dishes 136–178 F ($24.50–$32); fixed-price menus 215 F ($38.70), 350 F ($63), and 450 F ($81). AE, DC, MC, V.
Open: Lunch Tues–Sun 12:15–2pm; dinner Tues–Sat 7–9:30pm. **Closed:** Jan.
This restaurant provides ample justification for a journey outside Dijon. Situated in a charming stone village, the restaurant is housed in an 18th-century masonry building that originally served as a shepherd's barn. After Jöel and Nicole Perreaut added an

annex, modern kitchens, and a dining room, the place became well known as one of Burgundy's best restaurants. One dining room opens onto a garden. Amid fresh flowers, candles, and original watercolor paintings, enjoy such excellent dishes as Burgundy snails, filet of John Dory in a balsamic vinegar sauce, and filet of roast pigeon. The roast lamb also is marvelous.

13. MONTBARD

146 miles SE of Paris, 50 miles NW of Dijon

GETTING THERE **By Train** Montbard has rail service from Dijon and Paris.

ESSENTIALS **Orientation** Montbard is located between the Burgundy Canal and the Brenne River. Place Buffon lies close to the town's most important monuments: Buffon's house and the Parc Buffon.

Information The Office du Tourisme is on rue Carnot (tel. 80-92-03-75).

On the Burgundy Canal, this busy port was the birthplace of Comte George Louis Leclerc de Buffon. Born in 1707, the French naturalist was the author of the monumental *Histoire Naturelle,* published from 1749 to 1804 in 44 volumes. In spite of his international fame, he remained simple in his tastes, preferring to live in Montbard rather than in Paris.

Buffon died in Paris in 1788, and he was buried in Montbard in a small chapel next to the Church of St-Urse. The **Parc Buffon** was laid out by the great master. You can visit **Tour St-Louis,** where mementos of Buffon are displayed; it's open Thursday through Tuesday from 10am to noon and 3 to 6pm. Buffon's study, **Cabinet de Travail de Buffon,** where he wrote his many volumes, also is open to the public during the same hours.

WHERE TO DINE

HOTEL DE L'ECU, 7, rue Auguste-Carré, 21500 Montbard. Tel. 80-92-11-66. Fax 80-92-14-13.

　Cuisine: FRENCH. **Reservations:** Recommended. **Directions:** From the A6, exit at Bierre-les-Semur and continue about 15½ miles.

$ **Prices:** Appetizers 50–110 F ($9–$19.80); main dishes 90–130 F ($16.20–$23.40); fixed-price menus 95 F ($17.10), 135 F ($24.30), 180 F ($32.40), and 250 F ($45). AE, DC, MC, V.

　Open: Lunch daily noon–2pm; dinner daily 7–9pm.

The Hôtel de l'Ecu is a sure bet for an excellent meal and a comfortable bed. It was originally a relay station for postal carriages, horses, and passengers in the 1700s. Owner Bernard Coupat maintains the rustically 18th-century-style dining rooms, serving such dishes as meurette of beef and a full range of local specialties, which might include breast of duckling beaunoise, coq au vin, and Burgundian snails.

If you'd like to stay over, you'll find 25 bedrooms with private baths or showers, direct-dial phones, TVs, and minibars. Singles go for 230–260 F ($41.40–$46.80) and doubles cost 330–400 F ($59.40–$72), plus 35 F ($6.30) for breakfast. Parking is free.

EN ROUTE TO SAULIEU

Leaving Montbard, cross the Burgundy Canal and take the N80 toward Semur-en-Auxois. A few miles away from the city on the right are the ruins of the feudal **Château de Montfont.** In Semur you can visit the **Eglise Notre-Dame,** rebuilt in the 13th and 14th centuries. You can also spend an hour or so touring the ramparts of the old château.

The N80 carries you toward Saulieu. At the crossroads with the N70, turn left toward the ruins of **Thil,** a collegiate church founded in the 14th century. The ruins of the 12th-century château nearby can't be visited without a guide. It was built on the site of a Roman *oppidum,* and some of the walls date back to the 9th century.

At the village of Precy-sous-Thil, join the N80, which passes through a forest.

14. SAULIEU

155 miles SE of Paris, 47 miles NW of Beaune

GETTING THERE By Train Saulieu has a railway station (northeast of the town center) linked to the French railway network.

By Car Take the N80 from Montbard.

ESSENTIALS Orientation Set on a hilltop, the town is built around the 12th-century Basilique St-Andoche, located on place de la Fontaine with the town's most important museum.

Information For information, contact the Maison du Tourisme, 24, rue d'Argentine (tel. 80-64-00-21).

Although the town is fairly interesting, its gastronomy has given this small place international fame. On the boundaries of Morvan and Auxois, the town has enjoyed a reputation for cooking since the 17th century. Even Madame de Sévigné praised it in her letters. So did Rabelais.

The main sight is **Basilique St-Andoche** on place de la Fontaine, which has some interesting decorated capitals. In the art museum, **Musée François-Pompon,** place de la Fontaine (tel. 80-64-09-22), you can see many works by François Pompon, the well-known sculptor of animals. His bull, considered his masterpiece, stands on a plaza off the N6 at the entrance to Saulieu.

The museum is open Wednesday through Sunday from 10am to 4pm, charging 15 F ($2.70) for adults and 10 F ($1.80) for children; it's closed from November to March.

WHERE TO STAY & DINE

HOTEL DE LA COTE D'OR, 2, rue d'Argentine, 21210 Saulieu. Tel. 80-64-07-66. Fax 80-64-08-92. 15 rms (all with bath or shower), 7 suites. TV TEL

$ Rates: 310–980 F ($55.80–$176.40) single or double; 1,600–1,900 F ($288–$342) suite. Breakfast 95 F ($17.10) extra. AE, DC, MC, V. **Parking:** Free.

This former stagecoach stopover is an excellent choice—one of the finest in France. Although chef Alexandre Dumaine, the man who made this a world-famous restaurant, is long gone, today inventive chef Bernard Louiseau works hard to maintain his standards. Actually, according to most critics, chef Louiseau has surpassed all previous standards, becoming one of the grand culinary stars of Europe. This establishment is ranked among the 20 great restaurants of France. The cooking is less traditional, leaning away from heavy sauces, toward *cuisine légère.* All the great burgundies are on the wine list. Fixed-price menus cost 320–690 F ($57.60–$124.20), with à la carte meals averaging 650 F ($117).

If you want to stay overnight, or if you've had a little too much burgundy, you'll find recently renovated rooms with everything from Empire to Louis XV decor. Your bed will be comfortable, although it's likely to be 200 years old.

HOTEL DE LA POSTE, 1, rue Grillot, 21210 Saulieu. Tel. 80-64-05-67. 48 rms (40 with bath). A/C MINIBAR TV TEL

$ Rates: 285 F ($51.30) single without bath, 335 F ($60.30) single with bath; 350 F ($63) double without bath, 485 F ($87.30) double with bath. Breakfast 35 F ($6.30) extra. AE, DC, V. **Parking:** Free.

Originally a 17th-century postal relay station, the Hôtel de la Poste has been completely renovated by Guy Virlouvet. Bedrooms are comfortably upholstered and sometimes have courtyard views. The Belle Epoque dining room is open to nonresidents as well as to guests. Specialties include escalope of sea perch with baby vegetables, shrimp with saffron and asparagus tips, filet of Charolais beef with a marrow sauce, and kidneys in a sauce of aged mustard. Meals cost 130–300 F ($23.40–$54). Service is daily from noon to 2:30pm and 7 to 10:30pm.

NEARBY ACCOMMODATIONS & DINING

AUBERGE DU VIEUX MOULIN, porte de la Bourgogne, Aubigney, 70140 Pesmes. Tel. 84-31-61-61. Fax 84-31-21-75.

    Cuisine: FRENCH. **Reservations:** Recommended. **Directions:** Drive about 9 miles from Gray, 27 miles east of Dijon, to the southwestern corner of Haute-Saône.

$ **Prices:** Appetizers 55–95 F ($9.90–$17.10); main dishes 115–205 F ($20.70–$36.90); fixed-price menus 100 F ($18), 200 F ($36), and 400 F ($72). AE, DC, V.

    Open: Lunch daily noon–2pm; dinner daily 7:30–9pm. **Closed:** Dec 15–Feb 15.

Aubigney would have little to recommend it if it weren't for the Auberge du Vieux Moulin, whose hospitality and good food alone are enough to justify the excursion. The property has been in the Mirbey family since the end of the 18th century, serving first as a wheat mill and later as a wood mill. Today you'll find elegant antiques, gilt-rimmed mirrors, and sparkling table settings throughout the establishment. Elisabeth Mirbey is one of France's outstanding *dames cuisinières*. Elisabeth, with two other chefs, was the first woman to prepare a meal in the Elysée Palace, where President Mitterrand and Françoise Sagan had her crêpes de la chandeleur en aumonière à la crème de Grand Marnier.

The menu has a regional section, including chicken suprême in a sauce flavored with Savagnin and a cassolette of Burgundy snails. The terrines are excellent, as are the duckling dishes, veal kidneys, rabbit, and sweetbreads. The homemade desserts are light and delicious.

The auberge is also a good place to stay if you prefer to be away from the crowds of Dijon and other tourist centers. There are seven bedrooms with phones, five of which contain private baths or showers. A single or double costs 350–400 F ($63–$72), plus 50 F ($9) for breakfast.

CHAPTER 20

THE RHONE VALLEY

Le Rhône, just as mighty as the Saône is peaceful, is celebrated for the excellence of its table. These two great rivers form a part of the French countryside that is often glimpsed only briefly by motorists rushing south to the Riviera on the thundering Mediterranean Express. But this land of mountains and rivers, linked by a good road network, invites more exploration than that: It's the home of the beaujolais country; France's gastronomic center, Lyon; Roman ruins, charming villages, and castles.

It was from the Valley of the Rhône that Greek art and Roman architecture made their way to the Loire Valley, the château country, and finally to Paris. The district abounds in pleasant old inns and good restaurants, offering a regional cuisine that's among the finest in the world.

I'll start our exploration in the north, which is really the southern part of Burgundy, ending our itinerary in the northern sector of Provence.

SEEING THE RHONE VALLEY

GETTING THERE The Rhône Valley in southeastern France is easily accessible by **plane.** There are five flights weekly from New York to Lyon's Satolas Airport and also frequent domestic links to Paris.

The high-speed **train,** the TGV, takes passengers from Paris to Lyon in two hours. Direct service also operates from Paris to Bourg-en-Bresse, also taking two hours. Lyon is also on the European **motorway** network linking Germany and the north of France to the Mediterranean and the Alps.

Lyon's **bateaux mouches** operate regular boat services on the Rhône and Saône, with spectacular views of Lyon's old quarters and historic monuments. For more information, contact Navig'Inter, 13 bis, quai Rimbaud, Lyon (tel. 78-42-96-81).

The region is best toured by car. If that's not possible, make Lyon your base because of its superior transportation network.

A SUGGESTED ROUTE A driving tour might begin at Bourg-en-Bresse (Day 1), with another night spent in the medieval city of Pérouges (Day 2). I'd suggest three nights (Days 3–5) in Lyon. Or on the third day head north, while still based in Lyon, to the Beaujolais Wine Route. For a final night along the Rhône, drive south to Vienne (Day 6) for an overnight stay after exploring its old attractions.

---

1. BOURG-EN-BRESSE

264 miles SE of Paris, 21 miles from Mâcon, 38 miles NE of Lyon

GETTING THERE The town is linked by rail and autoroute to Lyon, Dijon, and Geneva.

WHAT'S SPECIAL ABOUT THE RHONE VALLEY

Great Towns/Villages

- ☐ Lyon, the gastronomic capital of France.
- ☐ Pérouges, a virtual living medieval museum.
- ☐ Vienne, a wine center with Roman ruins and medieval monuments.

Ancient Monuments

- ☐ Church of Brou at Bourg-en-Bresse, built in the flamboyant Gothic style and known for its royal tombs.
- ☐ Théâtre Romain, a Roman theater at Lyon, the most ancient in France, built by order of Augustus Caesar in 15 B.C.
- ☐ Church of St-Pierre at Vienne, originating in the 5th century, one of the oldest medieval churches of France.

Events/Festivals

- ☐ The Biennale Internationale de la Danse, a dance festival held every two years during the first three weeks of September, in Lyon.

Architectural Highlights

- ☐ Vieux Lyon, one of the finest collections of medieval and Renaissance buildings in Europe.

Gastronomic Shrines

- ☐ Paul Bocuse, a restaurant outside Lyon, home to one whom many consider the world's greatest chef.
- ☐ Hôtel des Frères-Troisgros, at Roanne, one of the major hotel dining rooms of France and part of the nation's culinary lore.
- ☐ Restaurant Pic, at Valence, one of the premier three-star restaurants of France.

Wine Routes

- ☐ The beaujolais country, 25 miles north of Lyon, with vineyard after vineyard on sunlit hillsides.

Film Locations

- ☐ Pérouges, setting for *The Three Musketeers* and *Monsieur Vincent*.

ESSENTIALS Orientation Boulevard de Brou is the main north-south artery through town. On either side, you'll pass some of the town's famous restaurants and the landmark Church of Brou.

Information The Office de Tourisme is at 15, av. Alsace-Lorraine (tel. 74-22-43-11).

The ancient capital of Bress, this farming and business center lies on the border between Burgundy and the Jura. It is considered a gastronomic center in the region.

Art lovers are attracted to the **Church of Brou,** 63, bd. de Brou (tel. 74-22-26-55), for its magnificent tombs. One of France's greatest artistic heritages, this flamboyant Gothic church was built between 1506 and 1532 by Margaret of Austria, the ill-fated daughter of the Emperor Maximilian. Over the ornate Renaissance doorway the tympanum depicts Margaret and her "handsome duke," Philibert, who died when he caught cold on a hunting expedition. The initials of Philibert (sometimes known as "the Fair") and Margaret are linked by love-knots.

Inside, the nave and its double aisles are admirable. Look for the rood screen, which is ornately decorated with basket-handle arching. Ask a guide for a tour of the choir. Rich in decorative detail, the choir stalls, 74 in all, were made out of oak, the work completed in just two years by the local craftsmen.

The tombs form the church's greatest treasure. In Carrara marble, the statues are of Philibert, who died in 1504, and of Margaret of Austria, who remained faithful to his memory until her own death in 1530. Another tomb is that of Margaret of Bourbon, the grandmother of François I, who died in 1483. See also the stained-glass

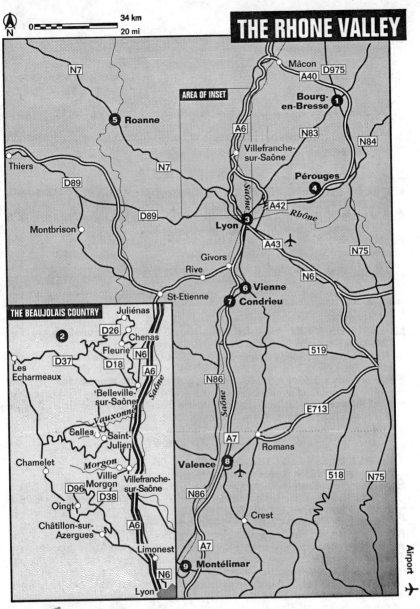

THE RHONE VALLEY

N

0 — 34 km
0 — 20 mi

AREA OF INSET

N7

● 5 Roanne

Thiers

D89

Montbrison

Mâcon
D975
A40

Bourg-en-Bresse ● 1

A6

N83

N84

Villefranche-sur-Saône

Pérouges
● 4

D89

A42

Rhône

Lyon ● 3

A43 ✈

N75

Givors

Rive

N6

St-Etienne

● 6 **Vienne**
● 7 **Condrieu**

519

N86

Saône

E713

A7

Romans

Valence ● 8 ✈

518 N75

N86

Crest

A7

● 9 **Montélimar**

Airport ✈

THE BEAUJOLAIS COUNTRY

Juliénas

● 2

D26

Chenas

Fleurie

D37

D18 N6

A6

Les Echarmeaux

Saône

Belleville-sur-Saône

Vauxonne

Salles

Saint-Julien

Chamelet

Morgon

Villié-Morgon

Villefranche-sur-Saône

D96

D38

Oingt

A6

Châtillon-sur-Azergues

Limonest

N6

Lyon

★ PARIS

The Rhône Valley

1 Bourg-en-Bresse
2 The Beaujolais Country
3 Lyon
4 Pérouges
5 Roanne

6 Vienne
7 Condrieu
8 Valence
9 Montélimar

windows, inspired by a Dürer engraving, and a retable depicting *The Seven Joys of the Madonna*.

The church is open between April and September, daily from 8:30am to noon and 2 to 6pm; between October and March, Monday through Friday from 10am to noon and 2 to 4:30pm, Saturday and Sunday from 10am to 12:30pm and 2 to 5pm. Admission is 25 F ($4.50) for adults, 15 F ($2.70) for children.

If time remains, see the **Church of Notre-Dame,** off place Carriat. Begun in 1505, it contains some finely carved stalls dating from the 16th century. There are some 15th-century houses on rue du Palais and rue Gambetta, if you'd like to wander around town.

WHERE TO STAY

HOTEL DU PRIEURE, 49-51, bd. de Bourg-en-Bresse. Tel. 74-22-44-60. Fax 74-22-71-07. 14 rms (all with bath or shower), 1 suite. TV TEL

$ Rates: 400–550 F ($72–$99) double; 720 F ($129.60) suite. Breakfast 45 F ($8.10) extra. AE, DC, MC, V. **Parking:** 60 F ($10.80).

Established in 1982 by two French sisters, Mesdames Alby and Guerrin, this is the most charming and gracious oasis in Bourg-en-Bresse. Its angled exterior is surrounded by an acre of carefully planned gardens and 400-year-old stone walls. The place is especially alluring in spring, when forsythia, lilacs, roses, and Japanese cherries literally flood the public rooms with perfumes. All the bedrooms are large and tranquil, and each is outfitted in Louis XV, Louis XVI, or French country rustic. The hotel is a minute's walk from the town's famous church.

LE LOGIS DE BROU, 132, bd. de Brou, 01000 Bourg-en-Bresse. Tel. 74-22-11-55. Fax 74-22-37-30. 30 rms (all with bath). TV TEL

$ Rates: 260 F ($46.80) single; 380 F ($68.40) double. Breakfast 35 F ($6.30) extra. AE, DC, MC, V. **Parking:** 50 F ($9).

This is actually a much better hotel than its boxlike exterior suggests. Built in 1968, the four-story building has landscaped grounds and is near the busy road running in front of the town church. You register in a lobby that has a raised hearth. Each of the rooms contains well-crafted reproductions of antique furniture.

WHERE TO DINE

AUBERGE BRESSANE, 166, bd. de Brou. Tel. 74-22-22-68. **Cuisine:** FRENCH. **Reservations:** Recommended.

$ Prices: Appetizers 140–460 F ($25.20–$82.80); main dishes 140–230 F ($25.20–$41.40); fixed-price menus 120 F ($21.60), 160 F ($28.80), 290 F ($52.20), and 340 F ($61.20). AE, DC, MC, V.

Open: Lunch Wed–Mon noon–1:30pm; dinner Wed–Sun 7:15–9:45pm.

Bresse poultry is considered the best in France, and chef Jean-Pierre Vullin appropriately specializes in the succulent volaille de Bresse, served five different ways. The chicken is bathed in milk, giving it a pearly color. Of course the chef of this old, rustic maison across from the Church of Brou knows how to prepare other dishes equally well. You may enjoy a gâteau of chicken liver, crayfish gratin, or sea bass flavored with fresh basil. You can accompany all of these with regional wines, such as Seyssel and Montagnieu.

AU CHALET DE BROU, 168, bd. de Brou. Tel. 74-22-26-28. **Cuisine:** FRENCH. **Reservations:** Recommended.

$ Prices: Appetizers 40–80 F ($7.20–$14.40); main dishes 70–130 F ($12.60–$23.40); fixed-price menus 90 F ($16.20), 120 F ($21.60), and 220 F ($39.60). MC, V.

Open: Lunch Sat–Wed noon–2pm; dinner Sat–Wed 7–9:30am. **Closed:** 15 days in June and Dec 23–Jan 20.

If you'd like to spend less money, you'll find good food in this restaurant across from the Church of Brou. The chef's specialties include several tasty poultry dishes, and regional products and fresh ingredients are emphasized. Try, if featured, poulet de Bresse prepared with morels and a chardonnay-cream sauce, terrine of artichoke hearts, and crêpes with mussels.

HOTEL RESTAURANT DU MAIL, route de Trevoux (46, av. du Mail). Tel. 74-21-00-26. Fax 74-21-29-55.
   Cuisine: FRENCH. **Reservations:** Recommended.
$ **Prices:** Appetizers 85–120 F ($15.30–$21.60); main dishes 90–110 F ($16.20–$19.80); fixed-price menus 120–300 F ($21.60–$54). AE, DC, V.
   Open: Lunch Tues–Sun noon–2pm; dinner Tues–Sat 7:30–9:30pm. **Closed:** July 12–27 and Dec 22–Jan 12.

Built in the 1950s, this is one of the most popular restaurants in the region. It's most crowded on weekends, especially on Sunday at noon, when guests enjoy such conservative specialties as sautéed frogs' legs, roast Bresse chicken, warm salad of sea bass (loup de mer), and an array of fruited dessert tarts. Roger Charolles is the chef of this unchanging but sure-bet institution.

This inn is also a reasonable place to stay, renting nine well-furnished bedrooms, each with private bath, TV, and phone. A single or double costs 160–250 F ($28.80–$45), plus another 25 F ($4.50) for breakfast. Covered parking is 20 F ($3.60); outside parking is free.

2. THE BEAUJOLAIS COUNTRY

The vineyards of beaujolais start about 25 miles north of Lyon. This wine-producing region is small—only 40 miles long and less than 10 miles wide—yet it's one of the most famous areas in the nation and has become increasingly known throughout the world because of the "beaujolais craze" that began in Paris some 30 years ago. The United States is now one of the three big world markets for beaujolais. In an average year this tiny region produces some 30 million gallons of the wine, more than 190 million bottles.

Léon Daudet once wrote, "Lyon has three rivers, the Rhône, the Saône, and the Beaujolais." Most people don't come to the beaujolais country to visit specific sites but rather to drink the wine. There are some 180 châteaux scattered throughout this part of France. At many of these, a wine devotee can stop and sample the beaujolais or buy bottles of it.

Villefranche, Capital of Beaujolais

Unlike the wine road of Alsace, the beaujolais country does not have a clearly defined route. Motorists seem to branch off in many directions, stopping at whatever point or wine cellar intrigues or amuses them. I can't think of a way to improve on that system.

However, in the capital of beaujolais, Villefranche, it would be wise to go to the **Office du Tourisme,** 290 rue de Thizy, 69400 Villefranche-sur-Saône (tel. 74-68-05-18), not far from the marketplace. There you can pick up a booklet on the beaujolais country containing a map of the region and giving many itineraries. The booklet lists some 30 villages and the wine-tasting cellars open to the public.

In Le Beaujolais—the countryside, not the wine—you'll find a colorful part of France: not only vineyards on sunlit hillsides but pleasant golden cottages where the vine growers live, as well as historic houses and castles. It has been called the "Land of the Golden Stones."

Saint-Julien-sous-Montmelas

The charming village of Saint-Julien-sous-Montmelas is 6½ miles northwest of Villefranche. This village was the home of Claude Bernard, the father of physiology, who was born here in 1813. The small stone house in which he lived—now the **Musée Claude-Bernard** (tel. 74-67-51-44)—contains mementos of the great scholar, including instruments and books that belonged to him. The museum is open Tuesday through Sunday from 9am to noon and 2 to 6pm. Admission is 10 F ($1.80) for adults, 8 F ($1.40) for children.

Salles

If you want specific sites to visit, I suggest the monastery, **Le Prieuré**, at Salles (tel. 74-67-57-39), the church and the Romanesque cloister built in the 11th and 12th centuries out of mellow golden stones, plus **Le Chapitre des Chanoinesses,** the chapter house of the canonesses erected in the 18th century. The tour through the complex takes about 1½ hours. Call ahead to request a guide. Admission is free. Salles lies northwest of Villefranche.

Juliénas

Juliénas is a village that produces a full-bodied, robust wine. In this village people go to the **Cellier dans l'Ancien Eglise,** the old church cellar, to sip the wine. A statue of Bacchus with some scantily clad and tipsy girlfriends looks on from what used to be the altar. It's open daily from 9:45am to noon and 2:30pm to 6:30pm (closed Tuesday from October 1 to June 1).

Chenas

At Chenas, three miles south of Juliénas, you might want to schedule a luncheon stopover. A popular eating place and one of the best dining rooms in the beaujolais country, Robin is previewed below.

ROBIN, aux Deschamps, Chenas (three miles south of Juliénas). Tel. 85-36-72-67.
Cuisine: FRENCH. **Reservations:** Required Sun.
$ Prices: Appetizers 60–120 F ($10.80–$21.60); main dishes 90–150 F ($16.20–$27); fixed-price menus 140 F ($25.20), 190 F ($34.20), 240 F ($43.20), 290 F ($52.20), and 340 F ($61.20). AE, DC, MC, V.
Open: Lunch Thurs–Tues noon–2pm; dinner Fri–Sat 7–9:30pm. **Closed:** Feb.
Contained in a stone-sided farmhouse from the 19th century, this restaurant is completely surrounded by the famous vineyards of the region. (As you sip one of the local vintages, either in the dining room or on the terrace in front, you can look out over some of the most famous grapes in Europe.) Especially popular at lunchtime and on weekends, the restaurant is the domain of Daniel Robin, who trained for several years with the great Alain Chapel. He prepares superb regional dishes, including a Bresse chicken cooked in beaujolais and some of the finest andouillette (chitterling sausage) I've ever sampled. If you prefer, you can dine more elegantly on foie gras of duckling. His gratin of crayfish and his Charolais bourguignon have drawn the praise of connoisseurs.

Villié-Morgon

Heading south, you reach this village, which produces one of the greatest beaujolais wines. In the basement of the Hôtel de Ville, the Caveau de Morgon (tel. 74-04-20-99) is open daily from 9am to noon and 2 to 7pm; closed in January. Admission is free.

Belleville-sur-Saone

If you'd like another dining choice in the beaujolais country, I suggest driving south from Villié-Morgon to the junction with the D37. Head due east to Belleville-sur-Sâone; Le Rhône au Rhin, with a chef whom many locals consider the finest in town, is previewed below.

LE RHONE AU RHIN, 10, av. du Port. Tel. 74-66-16-23.
Cuisine: FRENCH. **Reservations:** Required.
$ Prices: Fixed-price menus 110 F ($19.80), 145 F ($26.10), 185 F ($33.30), 210 F ($37.80), and 260 F ($46.80). AE, V.
Open: Lunch Tues–Sun noon–2pm; dinner Tues–Sat 7–9:30pm.

In an attractive setting, chef Michel Debize operates a restaurant where the service and food are impressive. A special feature of the establishment is his wide selection of fixed-price menus, beginning inexpensively and climbing the scale for those who want to dine more elaborately. Specialties include raw salmon terrine or an assiette of "fruits of the sea" for openers, or perhaps fresh foie gras. For a main dish, favored choices include ris de veau (sweetbreads) au Saint-Véran.

3. LYON

268 miles SE of Paris, 193 miles N of Marseille

GETTING THERE By Train There are three train stations in Lyon. If you're arriving from the north, don't get off at the first station, Gare La Part-Dieu, continue on to Gare de Perrache, where you can begin sightseeing. The high-speed TGV (*train à grande vitesse*), takes only two hours from Paris. Lyon makes a good stopover en route to the Alps or the Riviera.

By Plane It takes 45 minutes from Paris.

ESSENTIALS Orientation Lyon was founded on the long, narrow strip of land between the Rhône and Saône Rivers. Today, the city sprawls over many square miles, divided, like Paris, into arrondissements. The historic heart of the old city lies on both banks of the Saône, around the east bank's place Bellecour and the west bank's Primatiale St-Jean. The most central of Lyon's three railway stations is the Gare de Perrache, which deposits passengers at the frenetically busy **place Carnot,** three-quarters of a mile south of place Bellecour. The other railway stations (Gare des Brotteaux and the Gare La Part-Dieu) are in Lyon's commercial and industrial east end.

Information Contact the Office de Tourisme, place Bellecour (tel. 78-42-25-75).

At the junction of the turbulent Rhône and the tranquil Saône, a crossroads of western Europe, Lyon is the third-largest city in France. It's a leader in book publishing and banking and is the world's silk capital. It's also the gastronomic capital of France. Some of the most highly rated restaurants in the country, including Paul Bocuse (see "Where to Dine," below), are found in and around Lyon. Such dishes as Lyon sausage, quenelles (fish balls), and tripe lyonnais are world famous. The region's succulent Bresse poultry is the best in France.

Founded in 43 B.C., the city became known as Lugdunum, capital of Gaul, a cornerstone of the Roman Empire. Although its fortunes declined with those of Rome, the city revived during the French Renaissance.

A seat of learning, Lyon has a university that is second only to the Sorbonne of Paris. Incidentally, the university has a veterinary school founded in 1762, the oldest in the world.

WHAT TO SEE & DO

Begin your tour of Lyon at **place Bellecour,** one of the largest and most charming squares in France. A handsome equestrian statue of Louis XIV looks out on the encircling 18th-century buildings. Going down rue Victor-Hugo, south of the square, you reach the **Basilique Romane de St-Martin-d'Ainay,** rue Bourgelat (tel. 78-37-48-97), the oldest church in Lyon, dating from 1107. Admission free, it's open Sunday through Friday from 8:30 to 11:30am and 3 to 6pm; closed in August.

Nearby are two of the city's most important museums: the **Musée des Arts-Décoratifs** (Museum of Decorative Arts) and the **Musée Historique des Tissus** (Museum of the History of Fabric); see below for details.

Back at place Bellecour, head north along rue de l'Hôtel-de-Ville, which leads to **place des Terreaux.** The Hôtel de Ville, one of the most beautiful town halls in

Europe, dominates the square. It dates from 1746 and the outside is dark and rather severe, but the inside is brilliant.

If there's still time, visit the Musée des Beaux-Arts (on the south side of the square) and the nearby Musée de l'Imprimerie et de la Banque. (See below for details.)

MUSEE DES ARTS-DECORATIFS, 30, rue de la Charité. Tel. 78-37-15-05.

Located in the Lacroix-Laval mansion built by Soufflot in 1739 (he was the architect of the Panthéon in Paris), it contains furniture and objets d'art, mostly from the 17th and 18th centuries. The medieval and Renaissance periods also are represented. The collection includes a little bit of everything, from ivory-decorated rifles to four-posters draped in red velvet. One room, hung with Aubusson tapestries, displays Louis XIV furnishings. Look for a rare five-octave clavecin by Donzelague of Lyon, the great creator of musical instruments in France in the 18th century.

Admission: 20 F ($3.60) adults, 10 F ($1.80) children; also good for the Musée Historique des Tissus (see below).

Open: Tues–Sun 10am–noon and 2–5:30pm.

MUSEE DES BEAUX-ARTS, 20, place des Terreaux. Tel. 78-28-07-66.

On the south side of the square stands the Palais des Arts (also called the Palace of St-Pierre). This former Benedictine abbey was built between 1659 and 1685 in the Italian baroque style. Today it contains the Musée des Beaux-Arts with its outstanding collection of paintings and sculpture. You enter through the most charming courtyard in Lyon, graced with statuary, chirping birds, and shade trees. On the ground floor is a display of Quattrocento paintings. The collection also includes Etruscan, Egyptian, Phoenician, Sumerian, and Persian art. See, in particular, Perugino's altarpiece. The top floor is devoted to works by artists ranging from Veronese, Tintoretto, and Rubens to Braque, Bonnard, and Picasso, with one of the richest 19th-century collections in France. Represented are Géricault, Delacroix, Corot, Daumier, Courbet, Manet, Degas, Renoir, Gauguin, and Rodin, among others, including the Lyonnese Puvis de Chavannes. Of the 90 galleries, many were filled with treasures sent here by Napoléon when he dispersed the royal collections. See Joseph Chinard's bust of Madame Récamier, the captivating beauty from Lyon who charmed Napoleonic Paris. Also seek out the Fantin-Latour masterpiece *Reading* and see *La Maraichère,* a mysterious painting of a vegetable peddler, a celebration of the working class. The museum also has a fine-arts department and shows in rotation its important drawings and prints collection.

Admission: 20 F ($3.60) adults, free for children.

Open: Wed–Sun 10:30am–6pm.

MUSEE DE L'IMPRIMERIE ET DE LA BANQUE, 13, rue de la Poulaillerie. Tel. 78-37-65-98.

This museum is in a 15th-century mansion that was the Hôtel de Ville of Lyon in the 17th century. It is devoted to mementos of Lyon's role in the world of printing and banking. Printing exhibits include a page of a Gutenberg Bible, 17th- to 20th-century presses, manuscripts, 16th- and 18th-century woodcuts, and many engravings. This is one of the most important printing museums in Europe, ranking with those at Mainz and Antwerp. It has a collection of books dating from "all epochs," including incunabula, books printed before Easter 1500. It also contains the first book printed in Lyon, as well as the first book printed in French. The exhibits continue until you reach the birth of the modern press. The banking section depicts Lyonnais banking from the 16th century to the present. In addition to this general sweep of Lyon banks, you can see such details as the quotation of industrial shares in 1875.

Admission: 20 F ($3.60) adults, 10 F ($1.80) children.

Open: Wed–Sun 9:30am–noon and 2–6pm.

MUSEE HISTORIQUE DES TISSUS, 34, rue de la Charité. Tel. 78-37-03-92.

Your ticket to the Musée des Arts-Décoratifs also admits you to this even more interesting museum next door. On display is a priceless collection of fabrics from all over the world and spanning 2,000 years—a woven record of civilization. It's one of

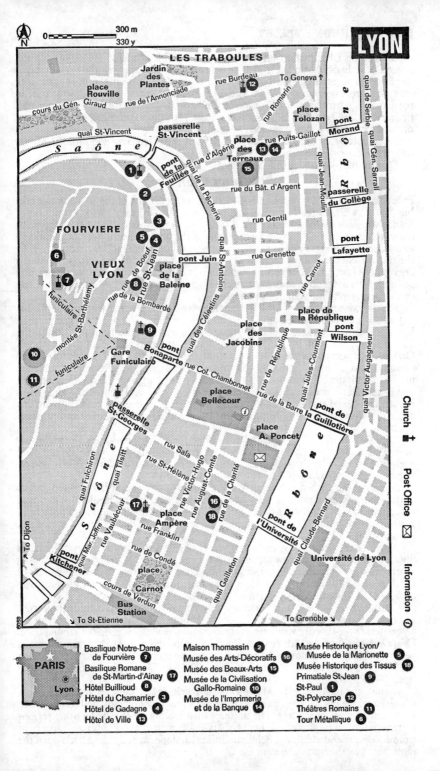

the most unusual attractions in Lyon and is located in the 1730 Palace of Villeroy. Some of the finest fabric made in Lyon from the 17th century to the present day is displayed. The textiles embroidered with religious motifs in the 15th and 16th centuries are noteworthy, as are the 17th-century Persian carpets. Seek out, in particular, a partridge-motif brocade by Philippe de la Salle for Marie Antoinette's bedroom, as well as a brocaded satin woven of 150 colors with birds of paradise and orchids for Queen Victoria.

Admission: 20 F ($3.60) adults, 13 F ($2.30) children; also good for the Musée des Arts-Décoratifs (see above).

Open: Tues–Sun 10:30am–5:30pm.

Vieux Lyon

From place Bellecour, cross pont Bonaparte to the right bank of the Saône or else take bus no. 1 or 31 to reach the attractions below. You'll be in Vieux Lyon, one of France's leading tourist attractions and the result of massive urban renewal. Covering about a square mile, Old Lyon contains one of the finest collections of medieval and Renaissance buildings in Europe. Many of these houses were built five stories high by thriving merchants to show off their newly acquired wealth. After years as a slum, the area is now fashionable, attracting antiques dealers, artisans, weavers, sculptors, and painters, who never seem to tire of scenes along the characteristic **rue du Boeuf,** one of the best streets for walking and exploring.

First, however, stop to see the **Primatiale St-Jean,** place St-Jean (tel. 78-42-11-04), a cathedral built between the 12th and 15th centuries. Its apse is a masterpiece of Lyonnais Romanesque. Exceptional stained-glass windows are from the 12th to the 15th century. Seek out, in particular, the flamboyant Gothic chapel of the Bourbons. On the front portals are medallions depicting the signs of the zodiac, the story of the Creation, and the life of St. John, which number among the finest examples of French medieval sculpture. The cathedral's 16th-century Swiss astronomical clock is intricate and beautiful; it announces the hour daily at noon, 2pm, and 3pm—in grand style a rooster crows and angels herald the event. On the right side of the cathedral, you can enter the treasury where rare pieces are exhibited, including jewels and precious Lyonnais silk.

Admission is 16 F ($2.90) for adults, 5 F (90¢) for children under 18. The treasury is open Wednesday through Sunday from 9:30am to noon and 2 to 6pm. The cathedral itself is open Monday through Friday from 7:30am to noon and 2 to 7:30pm, and on Saturday and Sunday from 2 to 5pm. Admission is free.

South of the cathedral is the **Manécenterie,** 70, rue St-Jean, noted for its 12th-century Romanesque facade. The boys who sang in the medieval choir lived here, making it the oldest residence in Lyon. It's open Monday through Friday from 7:30am to noon and 2 to 7:30pm, and on Saturday and Sunday from 2 to 5pm. Admission is 10 F ($1.80).

North of the cathedral is the major sector of Old Lyon. It's a true *musée vivant* (living museum), with narrow streets, courtyards, spiral stairs, hanging gardens, and soaring towers. The most outstanding of these courtyards is the overhanging gallery of the **Hôtel Buillioud,** built in 1536 for a bureaucrat by Philibert Delorme, who designed the Tuileries Palace in Paris.

On rue de Gadagne (no. 14) stands the Hôtel de Gadagne, an early 16th-century residence. Rabelais described its rich decor. It houses the **Musée Historique de Lyon** (tel. 78-42-03-61), with interesting Romanesque sculptures on the ground floor. Other exhibits include 18th-century Lyon furniture and pottery, Nevers ceramics, a pewter collection, and numerous paintings and engravings of Lyon vistas. Admission is 20 F ($3.60) for adults, free for children. It's open Wednesday through Monday from 10:45 to 8:30pm.

In the same building is the **Musée de la Marionette** (same telephone number), which has three puppets by Laurent Mourguet, creator of Guignol, best known of all French marionette characters. The museum also has marionettes from other regions of France (including Amiens, Lille, and Aix-en-Provence) and important collections from around the world (Italy, Belgium, Turkey, Indonesia, and Russia). It's open the same hours as the history museum.

While still in Vieux Lyon, make an attempt to see the exceptional Gothic arcades of the 16th-century **Maison Thomassin,** place du Change; also the 16th-century **Hôtel du Chamarier,** 37, rue St-Jean, where the marquise de Sévigné lived; and, finally, the **Church of St-Paul,** with its octagonal lantern tower from the 12th century. The church has been rebuilt, but it traces its history back to the 6th century.

Fourvière Hill and Basilica

Rising to the west of Vieux Lyon on a hill on the west bank of the Saône is Fourvière Hill and Basilica. This richly wooded hill—on which numerous convents, colleges, hospitals, two Roman theaters, and a superb Gallo-Roman museum have been established—affords a panoramic vista of Lyon, with its many bridges across two rivers, the rooftops of the medieval town, and in clear weather a view of the surrounding countryside extending to the snow-capped Alps.

Enthroned on its summit is the gaudiest of the 19th-century churches, the **Basilique Notre-Dame de Fourvière** (Basilica of Our Lady of Fourvière) 8, place de Fourvière (tel. 78-25-51-82). It rises fortresslike with four octagonal towers and crenellated walls. Its interior is covered with richly colored mosaics. Adjoining is an ancient chapel, dating from the 12th to the 18th century. The belfry is surmounted by a gilded statue of the Virgin. Admission is free. It's open daily from 6:30am to 7pm.

The **Gardens of the Rosary** extend on the hillside between the basilica and the 13th-century **Cathédrale St-Jean.** They're open daily between 8am and 6pm, and provide a pleasant walk. A vast shelter for up to 200 pilgrims is found here. An elevator takes visitors to the top of the towers. Two funiculars service the hill.

In a park south of the basilica are the excavated **Théâtres Romains,** Montée de Fourvière, a Roman theater and odeum at 6, rue de l'Antiquaille. The theater is the most ancient in France, built by order of Augustus Caesar in 15 B.C. and greatly expanded during the reign of Hadrian. It had a curtain that was raised and lowered during performances. The odeum, which was reserved for musical performances, apparently was once sumptuously decorated. Its orchestra floor, for example, contains mosaics of such materials as brightly colored marble and porphyry. The third remaining building in the sanctuary was dedicated in A.D. 160 to the goddess Cybele, or Sibella, whose cult originated in Asia Minor. All that remains are the foundations, although they almost seem to dominate the theater (175 feet by 284 feet). An altar dedicated to a bull cult and a monumental statue in marble of the goddess are exhibited in the **Musée de la Civilisation Gallo-Romaine,** 17, rue Cléberg (tel. 78-25-94-68), which is a few steps from the archeological site. Admission is free. The site is open March to October, Monday through Saturday from 9:30am to noon and 2 to 6pm, and on Sunday from 2 to 6pm. Guides are available on Sunday and holidays from 3 to 6pm. Performances are given at both theaters in summer.

Croix-Rousse

North of Lyon's downtown district lies Colline de la Croix-Rousse, crowned by the baroque **Church of St-Bruno-les-Chartreux,** 9, impasse des Chartreux (tel. 78-28-41-68). This sector has been the center of the French silk industry since the 15th century. Until fairly recently the old houses along the hill were still inhabited by weavers who both lived and worked there. *Traboules* (covered passages) run from street to street. They form a network used by the French Resistance trying to escape the "butcher of Lyon" in World War II. You can visit a workshop at **Musée des Canutes,** 10-12, rue d'Ivry (tel. 78-28-62-04), where weavers work at their age-old craft. Lyon is famed for its renewed silk industry. Admission is 6 F ($1.10). The museum is open Monday through Friday from 8:30am to noon and 2 to 6:30pm, and on Saturday from 9am to noon and 2 to 6pm. Take bus no. 13 or 18 to reach the site.

Nearby Attractions

The **Amphithéâtre des Trois-Gauls** is built on the slope of Croix-Rousse, near Condate, a Gallic village at the meeting of the Rhône and Saône Rivers. This partly excavated amphitheater is known to have existed several centuries before the Romans arrived. Delegates from 60 tribes from all over Gaul met here in the earliest known example of a French parliamentary system—in fact, it's sometimes referred to as the world's first parliament. For this reason the 2,000th anniversary of France, its bimillennium, was celebrated in Lyon in 1989.

Across the Rhône, the 290-acre **Parc de la Tête** is the setting for a *son-et-lumière* program from June to October. The tourist office (see "Essentials," above) will supply details. Surrounded by a wealthy residential quarter, the park has a lake, illuminated fountains, a little zoo, a botanical garden with greenhouses, and a rose garden with some 100,000 plants.

In the tiny village of **Hauteville** near Lyon stands one of the strangest pieces of architecture in the world. It represents the lifelong avocation of a French postman, Ferdinand Cheval, and is a palace of fantasy in a high-walled garden. One is reminded of Simon Rodia, who built the unique Watts Towers in Los Angeles. During his lifetime Monsieur Cheval was ridiculed by his neighbors as a crackpot, but his palace has been declared a national monument. The work was finished in 1912, when Cheval was 76 years old; he died in 1925. The north end of the facade is in a massive rococo style. The turreted tower is 35 feet tall, and the entire building is 85 feet long. The elaborate sculptural decorations include animals, such as leopards, and artifacts, such as Roman vases.

At **Rochetaillée-sur-Saône,** seven miles north of Lyon on the N433, the **Musée Français de l'Automobile "Henri Malartre"** is installed in the historic Château de Rochetaillée, 645, chemin du Musée, 69270 Rochetaillée-sur-Saône (tel. 78-22-18-80). One of the earliest cars exhibited is an 1898 Peugeot. The collection also includes an 1908 Berliet and a 1900 Renault, and such later models as a 1938 Lancia-Astura delight as well. The château is surrounded by a large park. Admission to the museum and château is 20 F ($3.60) for adults, free for children under 18. Both are open daily from 9am to 5pm.

WHERE TO STAY
Expensive

COUR DES LOGES, 2468, rue du Boeuf, 69005 Vieux-Lyon. Tel. 78-42-75-75. Fax 72-40-93-61. 53 rms (all with bath), 10 suites. A/C MINIBAR TV TEL **Bus:** 1 or 31.

$ Rates: 1,000–1,700 F ($180–$306) single or double; 2,000–3,000 F ($360–$540) suite. Breakfast 105 F ($18.90) extra. AE, DC, MC, V. **Parking:** 120 F ($21.60).

★ This four-star luxury hotel in Old Lyon occupies several Renaissance houses. The latest of modern materials were blended successfully in the historic setting. The superb hotel, launched in 1989, offers beautifully furnished and well-appointed bedrooms and suites—each equipped with a color TV with foreign channels, radio, and videocassette recorder. The restaurant serves excellent food in its intimate restaurant. The hotel also offers a tapas bar, lounges, an indoor swimming pool, a Jacuzzi, a dry sauna, terraced gardens, a wine cellar, and a private garage. Services include valet and 24-hour room service.

LE GRAND HOTEL CONCORDE, 11, rue Grôlée, 69002 Lyon. Tel. 72-40-45-45. Fax 78-37-52-55. 140 rms (all with bath), 3 suites. A/C MINIBAR TV TEL **Métro:** Gare La Part-Dieu.

$ Rates: 590–850 F ($106.20–$153) single; 640–890 F ($115.20–$160.20) double; 1,850 F ($333) suite. Breakfast 60 F ($10.80) extra. AE, DC, MC, V. **Parking:** 60 F ($10.80).

Situated near the river, the Grand Hôtel is one of the leading hotels of Lyon. Built at the end of the 19th century, it was completely renovated in 1989. Beyond the traditional exterior, rooms are well furnished, with conservative decor, Oriental rugs, and marble accents.

PULLMAN PART-DIEU, 129, rue Servient, 69003 Lyon. Tel. 78-63-55-00. Fax 78-60-41-77. 245 rms (all with bath). A/C MINIBAR TV TEL **Métro:** Gare La Part-Dieu.

$ Rates: 620 F ($111.60) single; 900 F ($162) double. Breakfast 58 F ($10.40) extra. AE, DC, MC, V. **Parking:** 60 F ($10.80).

The tallest hotel in Lyon, the Pullman shares a cylindrical glass-walled tower with the Crédit Lyonnais bank in a part of the city known as La Part-Dieu Nord. The seven-story lobby is ringed with an atriumlike series of corridors leading to the guest rooms, which are functionally furnished and comfortable. Bathrooms are modern and tiled, with well-coordinated accessories.

One of the hotel's restaurants, L'Arc-en-Ciel, is on the tower's 30th floor, offering well-prepared specialties and a panoramic view. Meals begin at 250 F ($45). The restaurant is open Monday through Saturday from mid-July to mid-August, except Monday lunch. La Rapaille grill, serving meals from 115 F ($20.70), is open Sunday through Friday, except Friday night.

PULLMAN PERRACHE, 12, cours de Verdun, 69002 Lyon. Tel. 78-37-58-11. Fax 78-37-06-56. 124 rms (all with bath). A/C MINIBAR TV TEL **Métro:** Perrache.

$ Rates: 610 F ($109.80) single; 790 F ($142.20) double. Breakfast 62 F ($11.20) extra. AE, DC, MC, V.

As its name suggests, this hotel is near the Perrache train station, and it offers some of the best rooms in Lyon. They're outfitted with plush fabrics and inviting colors and open onto hallways graced with Oriental runners, 19th-century furniture, and painted jardinières. The hotel is a monument to art nouveau. Bedrooms have been redecorated in a traditional style, and many improvements, such as the installation of air conditioning, have been made.

SOFITEL LYON, 20, quai Gailleton, 69002 Lyon. Tel. 72-41-20-20. Fax 72-40-05-50. 167 rms (all with bath). A/C MINIBAR TV TEL **Métro:** Bellecour.

$ Rates: 850 F ($153) single; 1,150 F ($207) double. Breakfast 75 F ($13.50) extra. AE, DC, MC, V.

This is the leading hotel in Lyon, with a patio containing tropical plants and a panoramic restaurant, Le Sofi-Shop, where fixed-price meals start at 150 F ($27). Another restaurant, the eighth-floor Les Trois Dômes, offers meals beginning at 290 F ($52.20). The view takes in the Rhône as well as Vieux Lyon. The bar is called Le Fregoli. The restaurants and bar have warm decorative themes and picture windows. Rooms are modern and attractively furnished.

Moderate

GLOBE ET CECIL, 21, rue Gasparin, 69002 Lyon. Tel. 78-42-58-95. Fax 72-41-99-06. 65 rms (all with bath or shower). TV TEL **Métro:** Bellecour.

$ Rates: 360 F ($64.80) single; 500 F ($90) double. Breakfast 45 F ($8.10) extra. AE, DC, V.

In the heartbeat center, right near place Bellecour, this hotel is good value for Lyon, not only because of its location, but because of its helpful and attentive staff. The bedrooms have been recently renovated and are attractively furnished and comfortable. Many of the units are also generous in size. Nicole Renart, the owner, insisted that each bedroom be individually decorated, avoiding that "peas-in-a-pod" look. The public rooms are done with contemporary styling. Only breakfast is served, which can be enjoyed at the hotel or at one of the cafés along place Bellecour.

GRAND HOTEL DES BEAUX-ARTS, 75, rue Président-Edouard-Herriot, 69002 Lyon. Tel. 78-38-09-50. Fax 78-42-19-19. 79 rms (all with bath). A/C TV TEL **Métro:** Cordelier.

$ Rates: 350 F ($63) single; 600 F ($108) double. Breakfast 52 F ($9.40) extra. AE, DC, V.

In the heart of Lyon, this hotel has long been considered one of the leading moderately priced choices in the city. The lobby evokes the 1930s, but not so the bedrooms upstairs. They are done in a relatively no-nonsense modern style, although they have such amenities as air conditioning. Since this is a noisy part of the city, double glazing on the windows helps shut off the sound of much of the traffic. Breakfast is the only meal served here, although many visitors prefer a more authentic French experience: having a breakfast of croissants and café au lait at one of the cafés along the close-at-hand place Bellecour.

HOTEL CARLTON, 4, rue Jussieu, 69002 Lyon. Tel. 78-42-56-51, or toll free 800/528-1234 in the U.S. and Canada. Fax 78-42-10-71. 83 rms (all with bath or shower). A/C TV TEL **Métro:** Cordelier.

$ **Rates:** 480–600 F ($86.40–$108) single; 520–640 F ($93.60–$115.20) double. Breakfast 55 F ($9.90) extra. AE, DC, MC, V.

This elegant hotel with traces of its Belle Epoque days, including high ceilings, is near the Rhône. The lobby has a coffered ceiling of blue-gray and gold and a wrought-iron elevator set between the limestone curves of the grand staircase. The pleasantly furnished rooms are each equipped with a radio. Rooms with traditional furnishings have the most charm.

HOTEL DES ARTISTES, 8, rue Gaspard-André, 69002 Lyon. Tel. 78-42-04-88. Fax 78-42-93-76. 45 rms (all with bath). TV TEL **Métro:** Bellecour.

$ **Rates:** 320 F ($57.60) single; 410 F ($73.80) double. Breakfast 45 F ($8.10) extra. AE, DC, MC, V.

Right in the city center, this gem is home base for many singers, actors, and revue artists who appear in the Théâtre des Célestins next door. Autographed photographs are kept under glass at the reception desk. The hotel offers comfortably furnished although small bedrooms; breakfast is the only meal served.

Inexpensive

BAYARD, 23, place Bellecour, 69002 Lyon. Tel. 78-37-39-64. Fax 72-40-95-51. 15 rms (all with bath or shower). TV TEL **Métro:** Bellecour.

$ **Rates:** 280 F ($50.40) single; 310 F ($55.80) double. Breakfast 30 F ($5.40) extra. AE, V.

This reconstructed town house is opposite the Lyon Tourist Office, on the landmark place Bellecour, midway between the two rivers. Don't be put off by the entrance, which is down a narrow hallway on the second floor. Inside, you'll find special accommodations, each with a different name, price, and decor.

BELLECORDIERE, 18, rue Bellecordière, 69002 Lyon. Tel. 78-42-27-78. Fax 72-40-92-27. 45 rms (all with bath). TV TEL **Métro:** Bellecour.

$ **Rates:** 260 F ($46.80) single; 320 F ($57.60) double. Breakfast 34 F ($6.10) extra. AE, V.

If you'd like to be in the center of Lyon, near the landmark place Bellecour, then this hotel and the Bayard (see above) are your best bets for a budget holiday. A savvy gourmet traveler I know always stays here, preferring to spend her money on the restaurants of Lyon, not the bedrooms. The hotel accommodations here, often small, are of the no-frills variety, although each one is reasonably comfortable; all are well maintained. The helpful service and the politeness of the staff more than compensate. The hotel serves only breakfast, and has no restaurant, but who needs one with so many good ones within walking distance of the hotel?

HOTEL LA RESIDENCE, 18, rue Victor-Hugo, 69002 Lyon. Tel. 78-42-63-28. Fax 78-42-85-76. 65 rms (all with bath or shower). TV TEL **Métro:** Bellecour.

$ **Rates:** 280–310 F ($50.40–$55.80) single or double. Breakfast 32 F ($5.80) extra. AE, DC, MC, V.

One of my favorite budget hotels in Lyon is at the corner of a pedestrian zone in the center of Lyon. Beyond the ornate 19th-century facade, rooms are comfortably furnished. The manager speaks English. There's no bar, but drinks can be served on request in the marble lobby. Breakfast is the only meal served.

WHERE TO DINE

The food in Lyon, as already noted, is among the finest in the world. It also can be very expensive. However, I have found that a diner of moderate means can often afford the most reasonable fixed-price menu at one of the following "expensive" restaurants. For example, one such menu recently began with an escalope of foie gras with mushrooms "from the woods" and went on to other delectable dishes. Brillat-Savarin, a Lyonnese, once wrote: "You are what you eat."

Expensive

ALAIN CHAPEL, N83 Mionnay, 01390 St-André-de-Corcy. Tel. 78-91-82-02. Fax 78-91-82-37,
Cuisine: FRENCH. **Reservations:** Required.
$ **Prices:** Appetizers 165–495 F ($29.70–$89.10); main dishes 185–410 F ($33.30–$73.80); fixed-price menus 520–780 F ($93.60–$140.40). AE, DC, MC, V.
Open: Lunch Wed–Sun 12:30–2pm; dinner Tues–Sun 7:30–10:30pm. **Closed:** Jan.

I always venture 12½ miles north of Lyon along route N83 for at least one meal at Alain Chapel, one of the great restaurants of France. This three-star Relais Gourmand set in the hamlet of Mionnay is a stylish place with a flower-garden setting. The late Monsieur Chapel was one of the premier chefs of the world. I recommend, as an appetizer, the gâteau de foies blondes, a hot mousse of chicken livers and marrow, pale gold in color, covered with a pink Nantua sauce. Or perhaps a velvety-smooth eel pâté in a puff pastry with two butter sauces. Delectable dishes include pan-fried skillet of fresh mushrooms that grow in the woods and poulette de Bresse en vessie—truffled chicken poached and sewn into a pig's bladder (to retain its juices), baked and served with a cream sauce with a bit of foie gras. Menu offerings change according to seasonal ingredients. Fresh vegetables such as turnips, parsnips, and carrots cooked al dente accompany many of the main courses.

The establishment also offers 14 beautifully furnished rooms, each with private bath and phone. A single or double runs 750–875 F ($135–$157.50), plus 80 F ($14.40) for breakfast and 55 F ($9.90) for parking.

LEON DE LYON, 1, rue Pleney. Tel. 78-28-11-33.
Cuisine: FRENCH. **Reservations:** Required. **Métro:** Hôtel-de-Ville.
$ **Prices:** Appetizers 130–190 F ($23.40–$34.20); main dishes 155–250 F ($27.90–$45); fixed-price meals 250 F ($45) at lunch, 250 F ($45) and 490 F ($88.20) at dinner. AE, MC, V.
Open: Lunch Mon–Sat noon–2pm; dinner Mon–Sat 7:30–10pm. **Closed:** Dec.

It's well worth the effort to locate this two-story restaurant and bar in the style of Old Lyon. The structure, somewhat hidden on a colorful and narrow street in the center of Lyon, was built late in the 19th century as a private house. Hydrangeas are planted above the entrance in summer. Upstairs, tables are placed in a series of small rooms decorated with culinary artifacts. The atmosphere may be traditional and typical, but the food certainly isn't. Its owner, Jean-Paul Lacombe, has been called a daring challenger to the top chefs of Lyon, serving both regional and modern cuisine. Some of his Lyonnais customers claim that he serves the finest food in the city and that he ranks right after Paul Bocuse in the environs. Monsieur Lacombe prepares an inventive cuisine based on the ingredients in season. Offerings might include oysters with Pouilly-Fuissé (the dry white burgundy), pike quenelles, or lobster with asparagus. Seasonal offerings include snails bubbling in butter. Newer and more challenging fare includes a terrine of sweetbreads with spinach, and even a quenelle of hare with a purée of turnips. His sorbets made with fresh fruits are a perfect ending.

LA MERE BRAZIER, 12, rue Royale. Tel. 78-28-15-49.
Cuisine: FRENCH. **Reservations:** Required. **Métro:** Croix-Paquet.
$ **Prices:** Appetizers 55–250 F ($9.90–$45); main dishes 95–220 F ($17.10–$39.60); fixed-price menus 320–370 F ($57.60–$66.60). AE, DC, MC, V.
Open: Lunch Mon–Fri 12:30–2pm; dinner Mon–Fri 8:30–10pm. **Closed:** Aug.

Near pont Morand, this Gallic restaurant has grown from a 1921 lunchtime rendezvous for silk workers to an international target for connoisseurs. The restaurant is managed by Carmine and Jacotte Brazier—the daughter-in-law and one of the granddaughters of the founding mother, Madame Brazier. The simple decor and wood paneling make an attractive setting for a long, leisurely lunch or an outstanding supper. Here you can order some excellent regional dishes, accompanied by such local wines as Mâcon, Juliénas, Morgon, and Chiroubles. Appetizers include artichoke hearts stuffed with foie gras and also smoked Nordic salmon. Specialties are volaille demi-deuil (boiled chicken with truffles under the skin, served with vegetables, rice, and bouillon) and superbly smooth quenelles de brochet (pike). More extravagant fare includes lobster Belle Aurore or à la nage. The service is solicitous.

LA MERE GUY [ROGER ROUCOU], 35, quai Jean-Jacques-Rousseau. Tel. 78-52-65-37.

Cuisine: FRENCH. **Reservations:** Required. **Bus:** 63.
$ Prices: Appetizers 70–250 F ($12.60–$45); main dishes 80–250 F ($14.40–$45); fixed-price meals 250 F ($45) and 490 F ($88.20). AE, DC, V.
Open: Lunch Tues–Sun noon–2pm; dinner Tues–Sat 7–10pm. **Closed:** Aug.

This charming, very solicitous, and very old-world establishment is considered the most famous traditional restaurant in Lyon. Superb cooking and service are offered in this elegant domain in La Mulatière, a satellite suburb on the right bank of the Saône. Roger Roucou painstakingly supervises every platter that emerges from his kitchen. *Cuisine moderne* seems to hold little interest for him; his cooking reflects the time-tested recipes of Escoffier and others, along with his own masterful touch. Dining in La Salle Louis XV, you are likely to be presented with an array of dishes that might include foie gras de canard (duckling) au poivre vert, truffles périgourdine, sole soufflé Escoffier, and turbot with champagne. The wines in the cellar are reasonably priced. For such a deluxe restaurant, you can dine here reasonably well by sticking to one of the fixed-price menus.

NANDRON, 26, quai Jean-Moulin. Tel. 78-42-10-26.

Cuisine: FRENCH. **Reservations:** Recommended. **Métro:** Cordelier.
$ Prices: Appetizers 100–200 F ($18–$36); main dishes 150–200 F ($27–$36); fixed-price menus 190 F ($34.20), 350 F ($63), and 450 F ($81). AE, DC, MC, V.
Open: Lunch Sun–Fri noon–2pm; dinner Sun–Fri 7:30–10pm. **Closed:** July 24–Aug 23.

In a stone-fronted town house on the quays of the Rhône, this restaurant offers views of the river and the historic pont Lafayette. There's a charming salon on the street level, but most diners head for the large and airy air-conditioned dining room on the second floor. Gérard Nandron is a chef who knows how to prepare both simple and complex dishes to perfection. His sauces are light and well balanced, and he uses fresh local ingredients. Excellent regional specialties include Bresse chicken cooked in tarragon vinegar, quenelle de brochet à la lyonnaise, blanquette de volaille de Bresse, and braised sweetbreads with mussels. Some of his newer, more challenging fare, however, follows the *cuisine moderne* trend: a vegetable pâté with tomato mousse, and sole or turbot simmered in court bouillon with herbs, fresh mushrooms "of the woods," and raw salmon with citron. The waiters are helpful, and English is spoken here.

PAUL BOCUSE, pont de Collonges. Tel. 78-22-01-40.

Cuisine: FRENCH. **Reservations:** Required, as far in advance as possible.
Directions: Take the N433 5½ miles north of Lyon.
$ Prices: Appetizers 60–295 F ($10.80–$53.10); main dishes 160–360 F ($28.80–$64.80); two-course business lunch (Mon–Sat) 290 F ($52.20); fixed-price menus 420–550 F ($75.60–$99) for two courses, 590–710 F ($106.20–$127.80) for three courses. AE, DC, MC, V.
Open: Lunch daily noon–2pm; dinner daily 7–10pm.

Paul Bocuse is the most famous contemporary chef in the world, and his restaurant is on the banks of the Saône at Collonges-au-Mont-d'Or. Once called an *enfant terrible*—he has been known to dance on the tables at the end of the evening and even toss champagne glasses in the air—with the passage of years such excitement is rarely generated around here nowadays. He specializes in regional cuisine, although long ago he was the leading exponent of La Nouvelle Cuisine (he later called that "a joke"). Often he is away from Lyon on tour. The decor of his establishment has been compared to that of a steakhouse off the Connecticut Turnpike.

Begin your meal with a Burgundian apéritif, kir (champagne and crème de cassis or black-currant liqueur, or even a touch of raspberry liqueur). My favorite main course is an impeccably constructed loup en croûte. This is a sea bass on a bed of tarragon and other herbs and stuffed with lobster mousse. It's then baked in a pastry shell symbolically decorated to represent the fish inside. It is served with a light tomato-and-cream sauce called Choron ladled over it. Other delectable dishes include warm pâté of game birds becassines served with truffles and his terrines of foie gras and squab. The fruit sorbets are among the best I've ever had, particularly the strawberry.

PIERRE ORSI, 3, place Kléber. Tel. 78-89-57-68.
   Cuisine: FRENCH. **Reservations:** Required. **Métro:** Place Kleber.
$ Prices: Appetizers 80–200 F ($14.40–$36); main dishes 150–350 F ($27–$63); fixed-price *menu terrasse* (summer only, on the outside terrace) 180 F ($32.40); business person's lunch 240 F ($43.20); fixed-price menus (available anytime) 400–600 F ($72–$108). AE, MC, V.
   Open: Mid-June to mid-Sept, lunch Mon–Sat 12:15–1:30pm; dinner Mon–Sat 8–9:30pm. Mid-Sept to mid-June, lunch daily 12:15–1:30pm; dinner Mon–Sat 8–9:30pm.

✪ The dusty-rose-colored decor, pink linen, and long dresses of the waitresses give this restaurant a certain delicacy. Located on the eastern periphery of Lyon, this was once a private home, dating from the 19th century. Bouquets of flowers are scattered throughout the dining room. Pierre Orsi rises before dawn to select the freshest ingredients for the day's menus, which could include monkfish and daurade cooked with fresh basil, perfectly prepared veal kidneys, raw salmon marinated in lime juice, Bresse pigeon with garlic, lobster and wild mushrooms in puff pastry, and wild duckling with rice. Pierre Orsi usually circulates among the guests in the dining room where his charming wife, Geneviève, supervises the service.

LA TOUR ROSE, 22, rue du Boeuf. Tel. 78-37-25-90. Fax 78-42-26-02.
   Cuisine: FRENCH. **Reservations:** Recommended. **Métro:** St-Jean. **Bus:** 1, 29, or 30.
$ Prices: Appetizers 140–220 F ($25.20–$39.60); main dishes 180–270 F ($32.40–$48.60); fixed-price menus 395–625 F ($71.10–$112.50). AE, DC, MC, V.
   Open: Lunch Mon–Sat noon–2pm; dinner Mon–Sat 7:30–10:30pm.

✪ This elegant restaurant occupies a historic three-building complex in the heart of Vieux Lyon, the premises of a convent that was originally built in the 15th and 17th centuries. In the complex is a comfortable collection of bedrooms (nine rooms plus three suites, all with telephone and TV), as well as a cooking school (L'Ecole de Cuisine). The entire organization is the result of a 1991 expansion by chef-entrepreneur Philippe Chavent and his staff.

You might enjoy an apéritif in the Bar du Jeu-de-Paume before your meal. Menu items served in the elegantly antique dining rooms (which were restored in 1990) include a bisque of sea urchins, a potato salad studded with caviar, a cold fish salad with diced tomatoes and julienned cucumbers, a pot-au-feu of pigeon, and filets of red mullet with curry sauce. A well-known house specialty is duck with figs.

Bedrooms rent for 1,050–1,600 F ($189–$288) single or double, with suites priced at 1,950–2,800 F ($351–$504). Breakfast costs an additional 90 F ($16.20) per person, and parking is 100 F ($18) per night.

Moderate

BISTROT DE LYON, 64, rue Mercière. Tel. 78-37-00-62.
   Cuisine: FRENCH. **Reservations:** Not required. **Bus:** 13 or 28.
$ Prices: Appetizers 60–100 F ($10.80–$18); main dishes 70–120 F ($12.60–$21.60); fixed-price lunch 130 F ($23.40). AE, MC, V.
   Open: Lunch daily noon–2:30pm; dinner daily 7pm–1:30am.
This rendezvous place for *le tout Lyon* is lively until early in the morning. It stands on a street of bistros, with several wine bars mixed in. Bistrot de Lyon is considered the best, or at least it's the best known. The setting is elegant and traditional, evoking the

Belle Epoque days; tables are marble-topped. Many dishes are offered, but you might stick to the classic Lyonnaise fare, including poached eggs in a red wine sauce (that eternal favorite) or a pot-au-feu with fresh vegetables. Another classic dish is chicken with heaps of fresh pasta. This is a great place to people-watch.

CHEZ GERVAIS, 42, rue Pierre-Corneille. Tel. 78-52-19-13.
  Cuisine: FRENCH. **Reservations:** Recommended. **Métro:** Avenue Foche.
$ Prices: Appetizers 50–160 F ($9–$28.80); main dishes 110–160 F ($19.80–$28.80); fixed-price menus 150–185 F ($27–$33.30) (lunch only) and 185 F ($33.30). AE, MC, V.
  Open: Lunch Mon–Fri 12:15–1:30pm; dinner Mon–Fri 8–9:30pm. **Closed:** July.

The classic cuisine of this well-established restaurant is served in a fancifully green-lacquered decor. There are more tables on the second floor. After a friendly welcome, you choose among a wide selection of well-prepared specialties, including warm seasonal asparagus in three sauces, stuffed turbot in a champagne sauce, a gratin of crayfish tails, and veal kidneys with white port sauce.

LES FANTASQUES, 51, rue de la Bourse. Tel. 78-37-36-58.
  Cuisine: FRENCH. **Reservations:** Recommended. **Métro:** Cordelier.
$ Prices: Appetizers 65–120 F ($11.70–$21.60); main dishes 250–300 F ($45–$54); fixed-price menus 150 F ($27) (lunch only), 255 F ($45.90), and 280 F ($50.40). AE, DC, MC, V.
  Open: Lunch Mon–Sat noon–2pm; dinner Mon–Sat 7:30–10pm. **Closed:** Aug.

Claude Gervais offers a tempting menu at his restaurant in the shadow of the now-empty premises of what used to the be Lyon Stock Exchange. (Since its demise, an attractive park and flower garden was laid out in front.) Inside the restaurant, you'll find carefully maintained paneling and displays of fresh produce and fresh fish and shellfish. Some say that the bouillabaisse served here is as good (maybe better) than can be found along the Riviera. Filets of sole can be served with a delectable garlic mayonnaise, or you might prefer the sea bream (daurade) in fennel sauce.

QUATRE SAISONS, 15, rue de Sully. Tel. 78-93-76-07.
  Cuisine: FRENCH. **Reservations:** Recommended. **Métro:** Avenue Foche.
$ Prices: Appetizers 80–136 F ($14.40–$24.50); main dishes 122–187 F ($22–$33.70); fixed-price menus 120 F ($21.60), 180 F ($32.40), and 235 F ($42.30). AE, DC, MC, V.
  Open: Lunch Mon–Fri noon–2:30pm; dinner Mon–Sat 7–10pm. **Closed:** Aug.

An excellent restaurant, the Four Seasons is known for its impeccable service. The chef serves an imaginative cuisine based on fresh produce from the market. At the well-decorated tables, you can order such dishes as scallops in puff pastry, red snapper with fennel, a duet of foie gras (hot and cold), scallops with vegetables and truffled juice, and tournedos Rossini.

Inexpensive

CAFE DES FEDERATIONS, 8, rue Major-Martin. Tel. 78-28-26-00.
  Cuisine: FRENCH. **Reservations:** Recommended. **Métro:** Hôtel-de-Ville.
$ Prices: Appetizers 45–60 F ($8.10–$10.80); fixed-price menu 135 F ($24.30). AE, DC, V.
  Open: Lunch Mon–Fri noon–2:30pm; dinner Mon–Fri 7–9:45pm. **Closed:** Aug.

This is one of the city's best-run bistros, operated with panache by Raymond Fulchiron. The café and its owner are so popular that you may have to vie with the regulars for a table, but it's worth it to experience the true bistro ambience. A sawdust-covered tile floor and long sausages hanging from the ceiling set the tone, and the well-prepared traditional food completes the picture. The host will help you choose from the menu. Possible dishes include sliced pork sausages of Lyon with boiled potatoes and watercress; tripe such as andouillettes, or tripe marinated, breaded, and grilled; and blood sausage with sautéed apples. You can end your meal with some of the excellent cheeses or a fruit tart.

CHEVALLIER, 40, rue Sergent-Blandan. Tel. 78-28-19-83.
Cuisine: FRENCH. **Reservations:** Recommended. **Métro:** Hôtel-de-Ville.
$ Prices: Appetizers 65–98 F ($11.70–$17.60); main dishes 75–100 F ($13.50–$18); fixed-price meals 115 F ($20.70), 140 F ($25.20), and 185 F ($33.30). AE, DC, MC, V.
Open: Lunch Thurs–Mon noon–2pm; dinner Thurs–Mon 8–10pm. **Closed:** July 24–Aug 15.

Situated in a 19th-century Lyonnais house set on a cobblestone street where horsechestnuts bloom in the spring, the Chevallier lies a short walk from place Sathonay, one of the oldest and most characteristic of Lyon's squares. The comfortable and rustically pleasant dining room is filled with local pottery and 19th-century copper utensils and samovars, collected over the years by the owners. Typical dishes include a wide repertoire of traditional Lyonnais dishes, such as coq au vin, tripe, and quenelles of brochet. Also available are monkfish in a butter, herb, and vegetable sauce; a filet of berix (a local fish) with a confit of tomatoes; and filet of beef with béarnaise or pepper sauce.

LA MEUNIERE, 11, rue Neuve. Tel. 78-28-62-91.
Cuisine: FRENCH. **Reservations:** Required. **Métro:** Cordelier.
$ Prices: Appetizers 20–45 F ($3.60–$8.10); main dishes 40–85 F ($7.20–$15.30); fixed-price menus 85 F ($15.30), 95 F ($17.10), and 140 F ($25.20). AE, DC, MC, V.
Open: Lunch Tues–Sat 12:30–1:45pm; dinner Tues–Sat 7:30–9:45pm. **Closed:** July 13–Aug 16.

This is a Lyon bistro the way they used to be. The decor is of another era and the walls are faded, but fancy trappings are not why people come here. It's for the food, hearty and robust. Under the direction of Maurice Debrosse, the kitchen still serves a *saladier lyonnais* at the beginning of the meal. That's a litany of salads, everything from lentils to one of boiled beef in a garlic-flavored vinaigrette. These salads are passed around by the waiters, and diners help themselves. Of course, crusty, freshly baked French bread and a bottle of beaujolais accompany such fare. Afterward, diners can select a *plat du jour*, perhaps grilled andouillette or a veal head.

RESTAURANT LA VOUTE [Chez Léa], 11, place Antonin-Gourju. Tel. 78-42-01-33.
Cuisine: FRENCH. **Reservations:** Required. **Métro:** Bellecour.
$ Prices: Appetizers 30–45 F ($5.40–$8.10); main dishes 50–90 F ($9–$16.20); fixed-price menus 118 F ($21.20) and 160 F ($28.80). AE, DC, MC, V.
Open: Lunch Mon–Sat noon–2pm; dinner Mon–Sat 7–9:30pm.

Established around 1900, and later the domain of one of the most famous female chefs in France, Madame Léa, this restaurant continues a tradition of fine brasserie dining in the Lyonnais style. Owner Philippe Rabatel carefully maintains the paneling and the art deco accessories, and the regional flavor, serving such dishes as roasted spring goat, shoestring-potato pancakes, tender local chicken cooked in red wine vinegar, and macaroni gratin lyonnais. The preferred choice of many local sculptors and painters, the restaurant lies just off place Bellecour along the banks of the river (quai des Célestins). Be warned that, at press time, Lyon contained two other restaurants named La Voute, a source of considerable confusion for diners.

TANTE ALICE, 22, rue Remparts-d'Ainay. Tel. 78-37-49-83.
Cuisine: FRENCH. **Reservations:** Not required. **Métro:** Perrache.
$ Prices: Appetizers 65–100 F ($11.70–$18); main dishes 110–210 F ($19.80–$37.80); fixed-price menus 90 F ($16.20), 149 F ($26.80), and 194 F ($34.90). AE, MC, V.
Open: Lunch Sun–Fri noon–1:30pm; dinner Sun–Thurs 7–9:30pm. **Closed:** Mid-July to late Aug.

Annie Morel, not Aunt Alice, runs this old-fashioned bar and bistro with the flavor of a country inn. The cuisine is rich, and many of the specialties are featured on the fixed-price menus. The traditional appetizer is quenelle de brochet maison. For a main course, I'm especially fond of filet de sole Aunt Alice.

LA TASSEE, 20, rue de la Charité. Tel. 78-37-02-35.
  Cuisine: FRENCH. **Reservations:** Not required. **Métro:** Bellecour.
$ Prices: Appetizers 45–145 F ($8.10–$26.10); main dishes 80–140 F ($14.40–$25.20); fixed-price menus 120 F ($21.60), 160 F ($28.80), 190 F ($34.20), and 280 F ($50.40). DC, MC, V.
  Open: Lunch Mon–Sat noon–2pm; dinner Mon–Sat 7–10:30pm. **Closed:** Sat–Sun in July–Aug.

This is the kind of bistro that made Lyon celebrated for its cuisine. The chef here isn't interested in a lot of fancy show or frills, but believes in serving good food and plenty of it, at prices most people can afford. Huge portions are served, and you might be offered anything from strips of tripe with onions to game or perhaps sole. The owners are Roger and Jean-Paul Borgeot. On my most recent visit I arrived at the bar just as the beaujolais nouveau had come in. It's a thin, sharp wine, bearing little resemblance to the real beaujolais with its uncomplicated taste and flowery bouquet. Wine is served in the shallow metal cup used by wine tasters, known as a *tastevin*. The dining room is ringed with large and artistically noteworthy 19th-century frescoes.

4. PEROUGES

288 miles SE of Paris, 22 miles NE of Lyon

GETTING THERE   By Car   It's easiest to drive to Pérouges, although the signs for the town, especially at night, are confusing. Remember as you drive that it lies northeast of Lyon, off Rte. 84, near Meximieux.

ESSENTIALS   Orientation   Everything in town is linked by the encircling walls and ramparts. Most of the streets are crooked and narrow—perfect for the aimless strolling that invariably brings you back to your starting point. Rue du Prince and place du Tilleul are important landmarks.

Information   There is no tourist office in Perouges; the nearest office is in Lyon (see above).

The Middle Ages live on. Saved from demolition by a courageous mayor in 1909 and preserved by the government, this village of craftspeople often attracts movie crews; *The Three Musketeers* and *Monsieur Vincent* were filmed here. The town sits on what has been called an "isolated throne," atop a hill some 22 miles northeast of Lyon off Rte. 84, near Meximieux.

Follow rue du Prince, once the main business street, to **place du Tilleul** and the Ostellerie du Vieux-Pérouges, a fine regional restaurant (described below) in a 13th-century house. In the center of the square is a **Tree of Liberty** planted in 1792 to honor the Revolution. Nearby stands the **Musée de Vieux-Pérouges** (tel. 74-61-00-88), displaying such artifacts as hand-looms. It is open Thursday through Tuesday from 10am to noon and 2 to 6pm (closed in January). Admission is 15 F ($2.70). In the village's heyday in the 13th century, weaving was the principal industry, and linen merchants sold their wares in the Gothic gallery.

The whole village is a living museum, so wander at leisure. The finest house is on rue du Prince; it's the **House of the Princes of Savoy.** You can visit its watchtower. Also ask to be shown the garden planted with "flowers of love." In the eastern sector of **rue des Rondes** are many stone houses of former hand-weavers. The stone hooks on the facades were for newly woven pieces of linen.

WHERE TO STAY & DINE

OSTELLERIE DU VIEUX-PEROUGES, place du Tilleul, Pérouges, 01800
  Meximieux. Tel. 74-61-00-88. Fax 74-34-77-90. 26 rms (all with bath). TEL
$ Rates: 700–980 F ($126–$176.40) single or double. Breakfast 60 F ($10.80) extra. MC, V. **Parking:** 30 F ($5.40). **Closed:** Hotel and restaurant are closed Thurs at lunch and on Wed Nov–Mar.

★ This inn is a treasure of France, a handsome and lavishly restored group of 13th-century timbered buildings. The proprietor, Georges Thibaut, runs a museum-caliber inn furnished with polished antiques, cupboards with pewter plates, iron lanterns hanging from medieval beams, glistening refectory dining tables, stone fireplaces, and wide plank floors.

The restaurant is run in association with Le Manoir, where overnight guests are accommodated. The food is exceptional, especially when it's served with the local wine, Montagnieu, a sparkling drink that has been compared to Asti-Spumante. Specialties include terrine truffée Brillat-Savarin, écrevisses (crayfish) pérougiennes, and a dessert, galette pérougienne à la crème (a type of crêpe). After dinner, ask for a unique liqueur made from a recipe from the Middle Ages and called Ypocras, "the liqueur of the gods." Meals cost 130–390 F ($23.40–$70.20).

5. ROANNE

242 miles SE of Paris, 54 miles NW of Lyon

GETTING THERE There are trains and bus connections to nearby cities, notably Lyon.

ESSENTIALS Orientation Set on the west bank of the Loire, Roanne is centered around place de Verdun. Place de la Gare, site of train arrivals, and one of France's most famous restaurants (see below), lies about a half mile west of place de Verdun.

Information For information, inquire at the Office de Tourisme, cours de la République (tel. 77-71-51-77).

On the left bank of the Loire, this is an industrial town which is often visited from Lyon or Vichy because it contains one of France's greatest three-star restaurants, the Hôtel des Frères-Troisgros (see "Where to Stay and Dine," below). Roanne was an ancient station on the Roman road from Lyon to the sea.

In a beautiful neoclassic mansion built at the end of the 18th century by the architect de Lavoipierre, the **Musée Joseph-Déchelette,** 22, rue Anatole-France (tel. 77-71-47-41), offers an exceptional display of Italian and French earthenware from the 16th, 17th, and 18th centuries, as well as earthenware produced in Roanne from the 16th to the 19th century. Important collections of prehistoric, protohistoric, and Gallo-Roman archeology are displayed, and there is an excellent selection of ancient paintings. This is the most important privately endowed museum in this part of France. Admission is 10 F ($1.80). The museum is open Wednesday through Monday from 10am to noon and 2 to 6pm.

The major church, **St-Étienne,** dates from the 13th and 14th centuries with overhauls in the 19th century. It's off place de Verdun.

WHERE TO STAY & DINE

HOTEL DES FRERES-TROISGROS, place de la Gare, 42300 Roanne. Tel. 77-71-66-97. Fax 77-70-39-77.

Cuisine: FRENCH. **Reservations:** Required.

$ **Prices:** Appetizers 150–240 F ($27–$43.20); main dishes 165–380 F ($29.70–$68.40); fixed-price menus 490–610 F ($88.20–$109.80). AE, DC, MC, V.

Open: Lunch Thurs–Mon noon–1:30pm; dinner Wed–Mon 7:30–9:30pm.

Closed: Feb.

★ The restaurant in this railway-station hotel is one of the best in France. The dining room has been modernized and is decorated with contemporary art. Pierre and Michel Troisgros are the chefs of this French mecca that has earned a place in gastronomic lore. Appetizers include warm oysters in butter "in the style of Julia," and thin escalopes of salmon in a sorrel sauce. For a main course, I recommend legs of duck served au vinaigre, a panaché of fish, thyme-scented chops of a ewe,

Charolais beef with marrow in a red wine sauce, or a superb-tasting squab. Menus change frequently. For dessert, choose an assortment of cheese or a praline soufflé. The petits-fours with candied citrus peel may make you linger longer than you intended. The prices are high, but you're paying for acclaimed cuisine, beautiful service, and quality ingredients.

The hotel offers 19 well-furnished air-conditioned rooms, each with TV and phone, plus three suites. Rooms go for 700–1,200 F ($126–$216) single or double, with suites costing 1,400–1,850 F ($252–$333), plus another 100 F ($18) per person for breakfast.

NEARBY DINING & ACCOMMODATIONS

ARTAUD HOTEL RESTAURANT, 133, av. de la Libération, 42120 Roanne, Le Coteau. Tel. 77-68-46-44. Fax 77-72-23-50.
Cuisine: FRENCH. **Reservations:** Recommended. **Directions:** Take the N7 two miles from the center of Roanne. **Bus:** 4.
$ Prices: Appetizers 58–110 F ($10.40–$19.80); main dishes 80–115 F ($14.40–$20.70); fixed-price menus 95 F ($17.10), 158 F ($28.40), 195 F ($35.10), and 350 F ($63). MC, V.
Open: Lunch Mon–Sat noon–2pm; dinner Mon–Sat 7:30–9pm. **Closed:** July 25–Aug 8.

This is one of several restaurants in the satellite village of Le Coteau. In an elegant dining room, Nicole and Alain Artaud offer traditional French cuisine. Dishes include a salad of monkfish with saffron, a salad of sautéed foie gras with strips of smoked breast of duckling, beef from local farms, and a variety of desserts. There is also a good selection of French wines.

The hotel offers 25 comfortable and beautifully appointed rooms, each with a private shower or bath, a color TV, and a direct-dial phone. Singles are 180–290 F ($32.40–$52.20) and doubles run 180–380 F ($32.40–$68.40), plus 33 F ($5.90) for breakfast.

AUBERGE COSTELLOISE, 2, av. de la Libération, Le Coteau. Tel. 77-68-12-71.
Cuisine: FRENCH. **Reservations:** Required. **Bus:** 4.
$ Prices: Appetizers 75–110 F ($13.50–$19.80); main dishes 80–130 F ($14.40–$23.40); fixed-price menus 115 F ($20.70), 175 F ($31.50), 240 F ($43.20), and 330 F ($59.40). MC, V.
Open: Lunch Tues–Sat 12:15–2pm; dinner Tues–Sat 7:45–9pm. **Closed:** Aug 1–21 and Dec 25–Jan 3.

Chef Daniel Alex and his wife, Solange, provide just what this region needs: an attractive restaurant with fine cuisine and reasonable prices. Oil paintings are illuminated by spotlights in the dining room. Diners choose from one of the "fixed-price à la carte menus," which change weekly. Popular dishes include a gâteau of chicken livers with essence of shrimp, filet of sole with a confit of leeks, and a pavé of Charolais bordelaise. You can order fine vintages of Burgundian wines by the pitcher.

6. VIENNE

304 miles SE of Paris, 19 miles S of Lyon

GETTING THERE   By Train   Rail lines connect Vienne with the rest of France. Some trips require a transfer in nearby Lyon.

By Car   After leaving Lyon, motorists take either the N7 (which is more direct) or the A7, the latter an expressway meandering along the banks of the Rhône River.

ESSENTIALS   Orientation   Set on the east bank of the Rhône River and bounded on the north by the much smaller Gere River, Vienne is centered around its 11th-century Cathédrale St-Maurice, place St-Maurice, and its ancient Temple d'August et de Livie, on place du Palais.

Information   The Office de Tourisme is at 3, cours Brillier (tel. 74-85-12-62).

Of course, serious gastronomes know of Vienne because it contains one of France's leading restaurants, La Pyramide (see below). But even if you can't afford to partake of the haute cuisine at that deluxe citadel, you may want to visit Vienne for its sights. About 17 miles south from Lyon, on the left bank of the Rhône, it is a wine center, the most southern of the Burgundian towns.

A Roman colony founded by Caesar in about 47 B.C., Vienne contains many embellishments from its past making it a true *ville romaine et médiévale*. Near the center of town on place du Palais stands the **Temple d'Auguste et de Livie,** inviting comparisons with the Maison Carrée at Nîmes. It was ordered built by Claudius, and was turned into a temple of reason at the time of the Revolution. Another outstanding monument is the **Pyramide du Cirque,** a small pyramid that was part of the Roman circus. Rising 52 feet high, it rests on a portico with four arches and is sometimes known as the tomb of Pilate.

Take rue Clémentine to the **Cathédrale St-Maurice,** place St-Maurice, dating from the 12th century, although it wasn't completed until the 15th. It has three aisles but no transepts. Its west front is built in the flamboyant Gothic style, and inside are many fine Romanesque sculptures.

In the southern part of town near the river stands the **Church of St-Pierre,** at place Saint-Pierre, a landmark that traces its origins to the 5th century, making it one of the oldest medieval churches in France. It contains a **Musée Lapidaire** (tel. 74-85-20-35) displaying architectural fragments and sculptures found in local excavations. The museum is open April to mid-October Wednesday to Monday from 9am to 1pm and 2 to 6:30pm; off-season, Wednesday through Saturday from 10am to noon and 2 to 5pm, and on Sunday from 2 to 5pm. Admission is 8 F ($1.40).

A large **Théâtre Romain** has been excavated at the foot of Mont Pipet, east of town. Theatrical spectacles were staged here for an audience of thousands. From April to October 15, you can visit Wednesday through Monday from 9am to noon and 2 to 5:30pm; off-season, Wednesday through Saturday from 10am to noon and 2 to 5pm, and on Sunday from 1:30 to 5:30pm. Admission is 16 F ($2.90), which also entitles you to visit most of the major attractions in the city.

WHERE TO STAY & DINE

LE BEC FIN, 7, place St-Maurice. Tel. 74-85-76-72.
   Cuisine: FRENCH. **Reservations:** Required.
$ Prices: 60–140 F ($10.80–$25.20); main dishes 60–140 F ($10.80–$25.20); fixed-price menus 108 F ($19.40), 180 F ($32.40), and 240 F ($43.20). MC, V
   Open: Lunch Tues–Sun noon–2pm; dinner Tues–Sat 7–9pm.

⑤   The best-prepared and most generously served fixed-price meals in town are available in this rustic setting near the cathedral. A la carte specialties are somewhat more sophisticated, including salads laced with all the delicacies of the region (foie gras, smoked duckling, and the like), breast of duckling with a truffled sauce, filet of turbot, and monkfish with saffron.

LA PYRAMIDE FERNAND POINT, 14, bd. Fernand-Point, 38200 Vienne.
   Tel. 74-53-01-96. Fax 74-85-69-73.
   Cuisine: FRENCH. **Reservations:** Required.
$ Prices: Appetizers 120–365 F ($21.60–$65.70); main dishes 140–365 F ($25.20–$65.70); fixed-price menus 260 F ($46.80), 390 F ($70.20), 480 F ($86.40), and 600 F ($108). AE, DC, MC, V.
   Open: Lunch Fri–Tues 12:30–2:30pm; dinner Thurs–Tues 7–9:30pm. **Closed:** Feb.

⭐ This is the premier place to stay and/or eat in the area. The restaurant perpetuates the memory of one of the country's greatest chefs, the late Fernand Point, who founded it in 1923. Many of his secrets have been preserved, especially his sauces, which were touted as the best in the country. The restaurant serves traditional as well as new dishes. You may dine in the air-conditioned dining room or the summer terrace. Specialties include turbot cooked in champagne, a fat hen cooked in a bladder, and a delectable sole with morels. Pike quenelles, that classic dish of Lyon, is served to perfection here.

The hotel has been restored and enlarged, offering 21 air-conditioned rooms and four unique suites, all modern and decorated with oak and containing TVs, minibars, and direct-dial phones. Singles rent for 750 F ($135), doubles cost 850 F ($153), and suites are 1,300 F ($234), plus another 95 F ($17.10) for breakfast. Parking is free.

NEARBY ACCOMMODATIONS & DINING

HOSTELLERIE BEAU-RIVAGE, 2, rue de Beau-Rivage, 69420 Condrieu. Tel. 74-59-52-24. Fax 74-59-59-36. 20 rms (all with bath or shower). MINIBAR TV TEL

$ Rates: 550–820 F ($99–$147.60) single or double. Breakfast 60 F ($10.80) extra. AE, DC, MC, V. **Parking:** Free.

⭐ Just 11 miles from Vienne is Condrieu, a Rhône-side hamlet that's a favorite point for in-the-know Parisians driving from Paris to Avignon. Although the Rhône may be somewhat industrial around here, you are soon captivated by the charm of this establishment located in a woods. Virginia creeper covers the exterior, and the fast-flowing river passes by the dining terrace. Nearby is a weeping willow. A Relais & Châteaux, the inn offers large, well-furnished rooms decorated in an old-fashioned way. One of the accommodations is a former apartment, with lots of space and a Renaissance decor.

The cuisine is exceptional and traditional. Try tarragon chicken cooked in a pig's bladder (to seal its juices), terrine of young rabbit, smoked salmon blinis, lobster bisque, stuffed quail, matelote of eels, fry of small red mullets, or mousseline of lobster with chervil. The Côtes du Rhône wines complement the food well. Meals cost 180–435 F ($32.40–$78.30).

---

7. VALENCE

417 miles SE of Paris, 62 miles S of Lyon

GETTING THERE By Train or Car There are fast and easy rail and highway connections to Lyon, Grenoble, and Marseille.

ESSENTIALS Orientation Set on the east bank of the Rhône, Valence is centered around its place des Ormeaux, near the 11th-century Cathédrale St-Apollinaire. The Parc Jouvet, a few blocks south of the cathedral, adds some welcome breathing space.

Information The Office de Tourisme is on place du Général-Leclerc (tel. 75-43-04-88).

Valence stands on the left bank of the Rhône between Lyon and Avignon. A former Roman colony, it later became the capital of the Duchy of Valentinois, which was set up by Louis XII in 1493 for Cesare Borgia.

The most interesting sight in Valence is the **Cathédrale St-Apollinaire,** consecrated by Urban II in 1095, although it certainly has been much restored since that long-ago time. Built in the Auvergnat-Romanesque style, the cathedral is on place des Clercs in the center of town. The choir contains the tomb of Pope Pius VI, who died here a prisoner at the end of the 18th century. Open daily from 8am to 7pm.

Adjoining the cathedral is the **Musée Municipal,** 4, place des Ormeaux (tel. 75-79-20-80), noted for its nearly 100 red-chalk drawings by Hubert Robert done in the 18th century. It also has a number of Greco-Roman artifacts. It's open on Monday, Tuesday, Thursday, and Friday from 2 to 6pm; on Wednesday, Saturday, and Sunday from 9am to noon and 2 to 6pm. Admission is 12 F ($2.20) for adults, free for children under 16.

On the north side of the square, on Grand-Rue, you'll pass the **Maison des Têtes,** built in 1532 with sculpted heads of Homer, Hippocrates, Aristotle, and other Greeks.

WHERE TO STAY

NOVOTEL, 217, av. Provence, 26000 Valence. Tel. 75-42-20-15. Fax 75-43-56-29. 107 rms (all with bath). A/C MINIBAR TV TEL
$ Rates: 420 F ($75.60) single; 450 F ($81) double. Breakfast 47 F ($8.50) extra. AE, DC, MC, V. **Parking:** Free.

I recommend this Novotel on the A7 in the southern part of town. Rooms are tastefully furnished. There are a restaurant, an American bar, and swimming pool and tennis court. Meals begin at 165 F ($29.70).

WHERE TO DINE

RESTAURANT PIC, 285, av. Victor-Hugo, 26000 Valence. Tel. 75-44-15-32. Fax 75-40-96-03.
Cuisine: FRENCH. **Reservations:** Required.
$ Prices: Appetizers 180–250 F ($32.40–$45); main dishes 200–320 F ($36–$57.60); fixed-price menus 280 F ($50.40), 500 F ($90), and 600 F ($108). AE, DC, MC, V.
Open: Lunch Thurs–Tues noon–2:30pm; dinner Mon–Tues and Thurs–Sat 8–9:30pm. **Closed:** Aug.

Worth the drive from Paris, this is perhaps the least known of the great three-star restaurants of France. Not only is the cooking exceptional, but also the wine list is very good, featuring such regional selections as Hermitage and St-Péray as well as Côtes du Rhône. The restaurant was founded a generation ago by Jacques Pic's father. It was a local secret until word of its great cuisine spread to Paris. It was soon on every gourmet's list of stopovers between Lyon and Avignon. The charming villa has a flower-garden courtyard. The dining room has big tables and ample chairs. Appetizers include a ballotine of squab, pâté de foie gras en croûte, émincé of duck flecked with truffles, fresh duck liver, and breasts of small game bird. For a main course I recommend the filet of sea bass served in a velvety velouté and crowned by caviar. Don't overlook, however, the chicken cooked in a pig's bladder, the filet of sole in champagne, or the lamb stew seasoned with basil (it also includes sweetbreads and kidneys for added flavor). In season, I suggest one of the chef's masterpieces—noisettes of venison that are tender and served in a wine-dark sauce light as chiffon. The desserts are a rapturous experience, from the grapefruit sorbet to the cold orange soufflé.

Pic also rents three well-furnished doubles, each with bath, TV, and telephone, at the rate of 650–800 F ($117–$144). Two suites, suitable for two, cost 850–1,000 F ($153–$180). Reserve as far in advance as possible. Breakfast is 80 F ($14.40) extra.

LE SAINT-RUF, 9, rue Sabaterie. Tel. 75-43-48-64.
Cuisine: FRENCH. **Reservations:** Recommended.
$ Prices: Appetizers 55–90 F ($9.90–$16.20); main dishes 87–120 F ($15.70–$21.60); fixed-price menus 150–255 F ($27–$45.90). AE, MC, V.
Open: July–Aug, lunch Tues–Sat noon–1:30pm; dinner Tues–Sat 7:45–9:30pm. Sept–June, lunch Tues–Sun noon–1:30pm; dinner Tues–Sat 7:45–9:30pm. **Closed:** One week in Jan and two weeks in Aug.

Set near a convent in the historic center of Valence, in the Quartier Saint-Ruf, across from a ruined police station which was bombed during World War II and never rebuilt, this restaurant prepares fine versions of regional and French cuisine. Amid ceiling beams and century-old stone walls, you'll be welcomed by Nadine Margarit and served the culinary specialties of her husband, Hervé. The menu might include homemade versions of foie gras with white wine, lobster served with its liquefied essence and a potato galette studded with truffles, a bavet of turbot with balsamic vinegar, a bavarois of smoked salmon served with dill and a coulis of peppers, and veal kidneys with mint.

8. MONTELIMAR

376 miles SE of Paris, 29 miles S of Valence

GETTING THERE   By Train or Car   Montélimar has frequent rail links with Lyon. Motorists in Valence (our last stopover) can continue south along the D933.

ESSENTIALS   Orientation   Set between the Rhône and the E1/A7, the city is encircled by wide boulevards. The most central street in the old town is rue Pierre-Julien, which runs from south to north past several of the town's monuments.

Information   For information, inquire at the Office de Tourisme, allées Champ-de-Mars (tel. 75-01-00-20).

If you've been following the Rhône trail south from Valence, you have now reached Provence. For your gateway to this enchanting land, I suggest this ancient Provençal town, standing on the Roubion, a river that runs 2½ miles east of the Rhône. Montélimar lies on the historic route between Paris and Arles. It is famous for its nougat, which is a splendid almond confection. You can purchase nougat in one of the local shops, or visit the factory where it's made.

But don't plan to visit the 12th-century fortress château, as it is currently used as a prison. However, there are remains of the ramparts that once encircled the town and four old gates dating from the 14th, 15th, and 16th centuries.

WHERE TO STAY & DINE

HOTEL BEAUSOLEIL, 14, bd. Pêcher, 26200 Montélimar. Tel. 75-01-19-80. 16 rms (all with bath). TV TEL
$ Rates: 220 F ($39.60) single; 280 F ($50.40) double. Breakfast 32 F ($5.80) extra. MC, V. **Parking:** Free. **Closed:** Aug 7–22.
This is a small, well-maintained villa with rooms that come in a variety of sizes. There is no elevator, but an electric dumbwaiter will transport your baggage upstairs. Breakfast is the only meal served.

RELAIS DE L'EMPEREUR, 1, place Marx-Dormoy, 26200 Montélimar. Tel. 75-01-29-00. Fax 75-01-32-21. 35 rms (all with bath). MINIBAR TV TEL
$ Rates: 300–440 F ($54–$79.20) single or double. Breakfast 42 F ($7.60) extra. AE, DC, MC, V. **Parking:** 20 F ($3.60).
Just five minutes from the autoroute, this place offers some of the finest food and accommodations in the region. Rooms are decorated in either the Napoleonic campaign style or the "Malmaison" style. The owner invites you to his Napoleonic-style dining room. Specialties include terrine of lark de la Drôme, chicken tarragon, wild duck (in season), a suprême of guinea-fowl with morels, and salmon in a sorrel sauce. The food is remarkable, the service grand, and the reception fit for an emperor. For dessert, try a sorbet. Fixed-price menus cost 168–210 F ($30.20–$37.80). A la carte meals can cost as much as 380 F ($68.40).

THE MASSIF CENTRAL

In your race south to Biarritz or through the Rhône Valley to the Riviera, you will have to penetrate the Massif Central, the rugged agricultural heartland of France. The most discerning, who have ventured into this region, have often returned with tales of ancient cities, lovely valleys, and a provincial cuisine that makes one dream of going there to savor the specialties.

With its rolling farmland and highly individualistic people, its châteaux and manor houses (in many of which you can stay and dine), and its isolated countryside, this is one of the most unspoiled and untainted parts of France—your chance to see and be part of a life all too rapidly fading. This is a large, varied territory, containing the capital of the old province of Auvergne, Clermont-Ferrand, and also the old capital of Limousin, Limoges.

From the spa at Vichy to the volcanic *puys* of Auvergne, there is much of interest to the visitor and much to learn about the art of good living. We'll begin in the George Sand country in the old province of Berry, then proceed to Auvergne and motor west to Limousin.

SEEING THE MASSIF CENTRAL

GETTING THERE Most visitors will prefer to tour from spring to autumn, although downhill skiing attracts French families in winter. September, if you have a choice, is the best month for enjoying the chestnuts and wild mushrooms for which the Auvergne is famous.

From Paris, the Massif Central is a long drive. **Air Inter** takes only an hour from Orly Ouest in Paris to Clermont-Ferrand. The **train** ride from Paris's Gare de Lyon takes four hours. You can rent cars at the airport and train stations.

The old province of Limousin is also easily reached by air. The regional airport Limoges-Belegarde, 10 minutes from the center of Limoges, has three daily flights to Orly. By train the trip from Paris to Limoges takes 2½ hours. By road, the province lies at the crossroads for the large north-south highway (RN 20), linking northern Europe with Barcelona via Paris.

A SUGGESTED ROUTE Auvergne today is actually made up of four départements of France: Allier, Cantal, Haute-Loire, and Puy-le-Dôme. If you're using public transportation, make Clermont-Ferrand or Limoges your base, because of their superior transportation. However, you'll see a lot more if you're covering the region by car.

WHAT'S SPECIAL ABOUT THE MASSIF CENTRAL

Great Towns/Villages

☐ Bourges, the old capital of Aquitaine and the geographical heart of France.

☐ Clermont-Ferrand, the ancient capital of the Auvergne, a double city on the Tiretaine River.

☐ Aubusson, "Ville de la Tapisserie," celebrated for its carpets and tapestries.

☐ Limoges, the historical center of Limousin, known for its porcelain and enamel works.

Ancient Monuments

☐ Cathédrale St-Etienne, one of the most beautiful Gothic cathedrals of France, at Bourges.

☐ Montferrand at Clermont-Ferrand, northeast of the city, a district of Gothic and Renaissance buildings.

Literary Pilgrimages

☐ Château de Nohant, where novelist George Sand wrote and entertained the literati.

Special-Interest Museums

☐ Musée de Ranquet, at Clermont-Ferrand, with its exceptional collection of Gallo-Roman artifacts.

☐ Musée Départemental de la Tapisserie, at Aubusson, exploring five centuries of Aubusson carpet weaving.

☐ Musée National Adrien-Dubouche, at Limoges, the "second great" porcelain museum of France.

Events/Festivals

☐ Foire des Vins (wine fair), the last weekend in August, at Saint-Pourçain-sur-Sioule.

Architectural Highlights

☐ Parc des Sources, a promenade walk at Vichy, the most fashionable promenade in the region.

☐ Cathédrale Notre-Dame, at Clermont-Ferrand, one of the great Gothic churches of central France, from the 13th century.

Begin at the cathedral city of Bourges (Day 1); drive the next day to Clermont-Ferrand (Day 2) for an overnight stay, then head south to Le Puy (Day 3). Allow plenty of time to cross the difficult, winding road west from Le Puy to Aurillac (Day 4). Along the way, however, you'll take in some of the most beautiful scenery of the Massif Central. Those with a final day can proceed northwest to Limoges (Day 5) or head into the Dordogne and Périgord (see Chapter 22).

---

1. BOURGES

148 miles S of Paris, 43 miles NW of Nevers,
95 miles NW of Vichy, 175 miles NW of Lyon

GETTING THERE There are good road and rail connections from Tours and other regional cities. For example, 13 trains arrive daily from Paris, taking 2½ hours. Sometimes a transfer is required at nearby Vierzon. From Tours, four trains a day arrive, taking 90 minutes.

ESSENTIALS Orientation Its cathedral, on the southern edge of the old town, dominates the city. Closer to the center is the Palais Jacques-Coeur. **Rue Moyenne** connects the two.

Information The **Office de Tourisme** is at 21, rue Victor-Hugo (tel. 48-24-75-33).

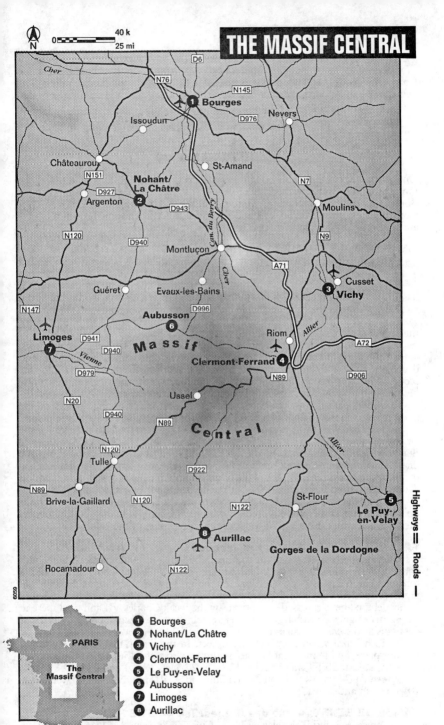

THE MASSIF CENTRAL

0 ⊢⊢⊢⊢⊣ 40 k
⊢⊢⊢⊢⊣ 25 mi

Cher

D6

N76

✈ **❶ Bourges**

N145

Issoudun

Nevers

D976

Châteauroux

St-Amand

N7

N151

**Nohant/
La Châtre
❷**

Argenton

D927

D943

Can. du Berry

Moulins

N120

D940

N9

Montluçon

Cher

A71

Guéret

Evaux-les-Bains

✈ **❸
Vichy**

Cusset

**Aubusson
❻**

D996

Riom

Allier

A72

**Limoges
❼** ✈

D941

M a s s i f

Clermont-Ferrand ❹

N147

D940

Vienne

D979

N89

D906

N20

Ussel

D940

N89

C e n t r a l

Allier

N120

Tulle

D922

N89

St-Flour

**❺
Le Puy-
en-Velay**

Brive-la-Gaillard

N120

N122

❽ Aurillac ✈

Gorges de la Dordogne

Rocamadour

N122

Highways ═══ Roads ──

6059

★ **PARIS**

**The
Massif Central**

❶ Bourges
❷ Nohant/La Châtre
❸ Vichy
❹ Clermont-Ferrand
❺ Le Puy-en-Velay
❻ Aubusson
❼ Limoges
❽ Aurillac

Once the capital of Aquitaine, Bourges lies in the geographical heart of France 95 miles northwest of Vichy, 175 miles northwest from Lyon. It can easily be visited from Orléans at the end of your eastern trek through the Loire Valley. The commercial and industrial center of Berry, this regional capital is still off the beaten path for much tourism, even though it has a rich medieval past still very much in evidence today. Its history goes back far beyond the Middle Ages. In 52 B.C. Caesar called it the finest city in Gaul. Joan of Arc spent the winter of 1429–30 here.

WHAT TO SEE & DO

On the summit of a hill dominating the town, the Cathédrale St-Etienne is one of the most beautiful Gothic cathedrals of France. If time remains, the older parts of Bourges are worth exploring. As you walk along the cobblestone streets you'll see many remains of the Middle Ages and the Renaissance, even some Roman ramparts and 13th-century fortifications that have been preserved.

CATHEDRALE ST-ETIENNE, 9, rue Molière. Tel. 48-24-07-93.

Dominating the town, this beautiful Gothic cathedral was begun at the end of the 12th century and completed a century and a half later. Subsequent additions have been made, however. Flanked by two asymmetrical towers, it has five magnificent doorways, including one depicting episodes in the life of St. Stephen, to whom the cathedral is dedicated. In harmonious splendor, with a high vaulted roof, the cathedral has five aisles and is remarkably long, 407 feet deep, one of the largest Gothic cathedrals in the country.

Mostly, the Bourges cathedral is distinguished for its stained-glass windows, among the finest in France. They are best viewed with binoculars. In rich blues and deep ruby reds, many of these windows were made between 1215 and 1225. One scene, *A Meal in the House of Simon*, is vividly colored, showing Jesus lecturing before Simon on the forgiveness of sins as Mary Magdalene repents at his feet.

To climb the north tower for a view of the cathedral and Bourges, you must obtain a ticket from the custodian, costing 20 F ($3.60) for adults and 6 F ($1.10) for children. The same ticket allows you to explore the crypt. Dating from the 12th century, it is the largest in France. In the crypt rests the tomb (built between 1422 and 1438) of Jean de Berry, who ruled this duchy in the 14th century. Fanatically dedicated to art, he directed what was called a "small army" of artisans, painters, and sculptors. The recumbent figure is the only part of the original tomb that has survived. The cathedral is open daily from 8am to 6:30pm, but the crypt cannot be visited on Sunday.

You may want to wander through the **Jardins de l'Archevêché,** the archbishop's gardens which Le Nôtre is credited with having laid out in the 17th century. In these gardens you'll have a good view of the eastern side of the cathedral.

PALAIS JACQUES-COEUR, rue Jacques-Coeur. Tel. 48-24-06-87.

Take a guided tour through the four main buildings around a central court, built about 1450 by finance minister and banker Jacques Coeur, who had amassed a fortune. The palais is considered one of the greatest secular Gothic buildings in France. Monsieur Coeur never got to enjoy the palace, however. After a trial by a jury of his debtors, he was tossed into prison by the weak Charles VII and died there in 1456. His original furnishings no longer remain, but the decoration and wealth of detail inside the palace form a remarkable and rare view of how opulent life could be in the 15th century if money were no object. In the dining hall is a monumental chimneypiece, and in the great hall are sculptures from the 15th and 16th centuries.

Admission: 20 F ($3.60) adults, 12 F ($2.20) ages 18–24 and over 60.

Open: Apr–Oct, Wed–Mon 9–11:15am and 2–5:15pm; Nov–Mar, Wed–Mon 10–11:15am and 2–4:15pm.

MUSEE DU BERRY, 4, rue des Arènes. Tel. 48-57-81-15.

The museum is inside the elegant Hôtel Cujas, built around 1515. On display is a large collection of Celtic and Gallo-Roman artifacts. Especially impressive are the 280 funerary sculptures. The second floor presents ethnography and regional stonewares of folk art. Some rooms are devoted to finds from Egyptian archeological digs, along with medieval masterpieces of sculpture dating from around 1400.

Admission: 12 F ($2.20) adults, 6 F ($1.10) children.
Open: Mon and Wed–Sat 10am–noon and 2–6pm, Sun 2–6pm.

HOTEL LALLEMANT, 6, rue Bourbonnoux. Tel. 48-57-81-17.

This Renaissance mansion north of the cathedral has been transformed into a museum of decorative art. The mansion was built for a rich textile merchant. Today its galleries display a colorful history of Bourges. Exhibits include china, objets d'art, ceramics, and a large display of antique furniture.

Admission: 14 F ($2.50) adults, 7 F ($1.30) children.
Open: Tues–Sat 10am–noon and 2–6pm, Sun 2–6pm.

WHERE TO STAY

Although Bourges has several modest hotels, it's not a major stopover point for tourists, most of whom seem to visit for lunch and then head to other destinations. However, the city does have an exceptional restaurant (see "Where to Dine," below).

LE CHRISTINA, 5, rue de la Halle, 18000 Bourges. Tel. 48-70-56-50. Fax 48-70-58-13. 76 rms (all with bath or shower).

$ Rates: 210–250 F ($37.80–$45) single; 220–275 F ($39.60–$49.50) double. Breakfast 33 F ($5.90) extra. AE, MC, V. **Parking:** 30 F ($5.40).

The rooms at Christina are comfortable and, in part, furnished with some stylish pieces. It's within an easy walk of the Palais Jacques-Coeur and the cathedral. Breakfast is the only meal served.

HOSTELLERIE DU GRAND-ARGENTIER, 9, rue Parerie, 18000 Bourges. Tel. 48-70-84-31. 14 rms (none with bath). TEL

$ Rates: 300 F ($54) single; 370 F ($66.60) double. Breakfast 34 F ($6.10) extra. AE, DC, MC, V. **Closed:** Sun–Mon Nov–May.

Some of the decor of this family-style hotel dates from the 15th century. Rooms are simply furnished but comfortable. Breakfast is the only meal served.

WHERE TO DINE

JACQUES-COEUR, 3, place Jacques-Coeur. Tel. 48-70-12-72.

Cuisine: FRENCH. **Reservations:** Required.

$ Prices: Appetizers 55–100 F ($9.90–$18); main dishes 85–125 F ($15.30–$22.50); fixed-price menus 145 F ($26.10) and 180 F ($32.40). AE, DC, MC, V.
Open: Lunch Sun–Fri noon–2pm; dinner Mon–Fri 7:15–9:15pm. **Closed:** July 24–Aug 24 and Dec 24–Jan 3.

François Bernard serves tasty traditional cuisine against the backdrop of a medieval decor in a building that was actually constructed in 1947. The restaurant is across from the Palais Jacques-Coeur. Specialties include veal kidneys berrichonne, fresh frogs' legs sautéed with herbs, scallops (available from spring to October), a head of veal with a highly seasoned white sauce, and beef stew à la mode. The desserts are all homemade and tempting, and service is politely efficient. The featured wines are Quincy and Menetou-Salon.

2. NOHANT/LA CHATRE

180 miles S of Paris, 19 miles S of Châteauroux

GETTING THERE The nearest train station is in Châteauroux; most visitors drive instead of relying on public transportation.

ESSENTIALS Orientation The château and the major hotels lie in the middle of town. St-Chartier is a separate community a short drive from the château.

Information The nearest **Office de Tourisme** is on Square George-Sand (tel. 54-48-22-64) in La Châtre, open daily year-round.

George Sand was the pen name of Ámandine Lucile Aurore Dupin, Baronne Dudevant, the French novelist born in 1804. Her memory is forever connected to this little Berry hamlet near the Indre Valley.

In her early life she wrote bucolic tales of peasants, but she also penned romantic novels in which she maintained that women were entitled to a freedom equal to men's. Among 80 novels, some of her best known were *François le champi* and *La mare au diable*. She was also known for her love affairs, her most notorious being with Alfred de Musset, who journeyed with her to Venice, and Chopin, who went with her to Majorca. At the time of her death in Nohant in 1876, George Sand had become a legend.

It was at the **Château of Nohant** (tel. 54-31-06-04) that George Sand learned the ways and thoughts of the peasants. It was to this same château that in time she would invite some of the intellectual and artistic elite of Europe—Flaubert, Balzac, Delacroix, Liszt, and Théophile Gautier. The château is an 18th-century mansion that has been turned into a museum, housing the mementos of George Sand and her admirers and friends. You can see the boudoir where she wrote *Indiana,* the novel published when she was 28 years old. You can also visit her private bedchamber and study. At Nohant, George Sand staged theatricals for her guests, dramatizing several of her novels—not very successfully, according to reports. Sometimes today, *fêtes romantiques de Nohant* are staged, with an impressive list of musical performers, perhaps in some way recapturing the glory that the château knew in its heyday.

The tour through the mansion takes about a half hour, and it's open from the first of April until the end of September, daily from 9 to 11:30am and 1:30 to 5:30pm. Admission is 24 F ($4.30) for adults, 13 F ($2.30) for children.

WHERE TO STAY & DINE

AUBERGE DE LA PETITE FADETTE, Nohant-Vic, 35400 La Châtre. Tel. 53-31-01-48. 11 rms (all with bath). TV TEL
$ Rates: 220–280 F ($39.60–$50.40) single or double. Breakfast 38 F ($6.80) extra. MC, V. **Parking:** Free.

The simply furnished rooms here are popular with literary fans who come to pay their respects to George Sand. Bathroom facilities vary from a shower to a complete bath. The inn is open all year. The food is quite good, with fixed-price menus running 78–170 F ($14–$30.60).

CHATEAU DE LA VALLEE BLEUE, route Verneuil, St-Chartier, 36400 La Châtre. Tel. 54-31-01-91. Fax 54-31-04-48. 13 rms (all with bath or shower). MINIBAR TV TEL
$ Rates: 310–550 F ($55.80–$99) single or double. Breakfast 50 F ($9) extra. MC, V.

This château was built by Dr. Pestel, who wanted to be close to his patient, George Sand. The two homes are separated only by fields and trees. The doctor's home is now a hotel and restaurant owned by Gérard Gasquet (also the chef) and his wife. It's within walking distance of the George Sand Museum in Nohant. The rooms have been named after the doctor's former guests, including Musset, Delacroix, Flaubert, Chopin, and Liszt. There is also a 10-acre wooded park with a 400-year-old oak and a swimming pool.

Excellent regional specialties are served in the two dining rooms, done in what is known as *cuisine actuelle* (halfway between *cuisine moderne* and classical cuisine, with an accent on the presentation). Regional dishes include goat cheese and smoked duck breast on salad, filet of carp stuffed with carp and mushrooms, farm-fresh rabbit with tarragon sauce and homemade fresh pasta, and for dessert, pear in a pastry crust. Fixed-price menus cost 125–375 F ($22.50–$67.50). The restaurant is open daily in summer; closed on Sunday evening and Monday from October to mid-April and also December 20–28 and in February.

3. VICHY

216 miles S of Paris, 33 miles NE of Clermont-Ferrand,
108 miles NW of Lyon

GETTING THERE   There is frequent rail and bus service from Clermont-Ferrand, and rail service to Paris and Nîmes.

ESSENTIALS Orientation   The best neighborhood for sights and people-watching is between place Charles-de-Gaulle and the Parc des Sources. There's a park on the western border of town, along the Allier River.

Information   For information, contact the Office de Tourisme, 19, rue du Parc (tel. 70-98-71-94).

This world-renowned spa on the north edge of Auvergne, in the heart of Bourbon country, noted for its sparkling waters, looks much as it did a century ago when the princes and industrial barons filled its rococo casino. From 1861, Napoléon III was a frequent visitor, doing much to add to the spa's fame throughout Europe. However, by the 1980s the clients and their tastes changed. In recent years Vichy has begun a major step in sprucing up its hotels and modernizing its baths. In that, it has been successful. It not only caters to the elderly, called the *curistes,* but it's a modern city for health and relaxation, aided in no small part by the Perrier craze that has swept not only Europe but North America and other regions.

The Perrier Company has a contract to bottle Vichy water for sale elsewhere, and it also runs the city's major attractions. The chief spa of France, Vichy lies on the Allier River. In World War II, Vichy was the seat of the collaborationist government under Marshal Pétain. But no Vichyssoise seems to want to talk about the years 1940–44.

Gardens separate the town from the Allier. The spa waters are said to alleviate liver and stomach ailments. Vichy is a sports and recreation center, with a casino, theaters, regattas, horse racing, and golf.

A promenade with covered walks, the **Parc des Sources,** is the center of the spa's fashionable life, which lasts from May to the end of September. At night the chief attraction is the brilliantly illuminated **Grand Casino,** 5, rue du Casino (tel. 70-97-93-37). Under high ceilings and immense chandeliers, gamblers come here from around the world to play at the blackjack and roulette tables set off by copper railings. In the casino theater, Diaghilev produced his last ballet and Strauss directed *Salomé.* The Hall des Sources, the Galerie Napoléon, and the Grand Etablissement Thermal (the largest treatment center of its kind in Europe) are found here. The baths can be visited June through August, on Wednesday, Thursday, and Saturday from 3 to 4:30pm.

WHERE TO STAY

ALETTI PALACE HOTEL, 3, place Joseph-Aletti, 03200 Vichy. Tel. 70-31-78-77. Fax 70-98-13-82. 54 rms (all with bath or shower). 14 suites. TV TEL

$ Rates: 780 F ($140.40) single; 1,100 F ($198) double; from 1,300 F ($234) suite. Breakfast 70 F ($12.60) extra. DC, MC, V.

This luxury hotel contains all the grand vistas and elegant accessories you'd expect. Rooms are well furnished, many with balconies overlooking the wooded park. The hotel has a good restaurant and offers a bar and a terrace with a panoramic view of Vichy. Meals begin at 180 F ($32.40).

HOTEL CHAMBORD, 84, rue de Paris, 03200 Vichy. Tel. 70-31-22-88. Fax 70-31-54-92. 32 rms (all with bath or shower). TV TEL

$ Rates: 275 F ($49.50) single; 315 F ($56.70) double. Breakfast 30 F ($5.40) extra. AE, MC, V.

This pleasantly renovated hotel is conveniently situated near the train stations. Rooms are comfortably furnished. The restaurant, Escargot qui Tête, offers good meals for reasonable prices, with fixed-price menus starting at 95 F ($17.10). The restaurant is open Tuesday through Sunday (closed Sunday night).

PAVILLON SEVIGNE, 10, place Sévigné, 03200 Vichy. Tel. 70-32-16-22. Fax 70-59-97-37. 45 rms (all with bath). MINIBAR TV TEL

$ Rates: 710 F ($127.80) single; 1,050 F ($189) double. Breakfast 75 F ($13.50) extra. AE, DC, MC, V. **Parking:** Free.

Renowned letter writer the marquise de Sévigné stayed here when she was in Vichy for "the cure." Built in the époque of Louis XIII, this "grand Petit" offers gracious, old-style living near the thermal spa. Madame de Sévigné helped popularize the resort in the 17th century—"The countryside alone could cure me," she said. She admitted that Vichy was, of course, a bore. "But that is the cure," she added. After learning that a noblewoman had been burned at the stake for poisoning her husband, she wrote, "We are all breathing her now." The Pavillon has an ivory-colored brick exterior and ceramic parquet floors. The Empire-style rooms are individually decorated in pastel hues. The salon in which Madame de Sévigné lived still evokes the 1600s, overlooking a graveled courtyard.

The restaurant is one of the finest in Vichy, with a menu in the tradition of the famous Les Frères Troisgros in Roanne. The decor is in the style of Napoléon III. Meals begin at 210 F ($37.80).

WHERE TO DINE

L'ALAMBIC, 8, rue Nicholas-Larbaud. Tel. 70-59-12-71.
   Cuisine: FRENCH. **Reservations:** Required.
$ Prices: Appetizers 75–110 F ($13.50–$19.80); main dishes 125–178 F ($22.50–$32); fixed-price menus 170 F ($30.60) and 290 F ($52.20). MC, V.
   Open: Lunch Wed–Sun noon–2pm; dinner Tues–Sun 7:30–10pm. **Closed:** Feb 4–27 and Aug 19–Sept 3.

There are only 20 places at this small restaurant, but they fill up quickly because the cuisine is the best in Vichy. Since July 1989, Jean-Jacques Barbot has run a busy place, appealing to what one food critic called "the jaded palates of Vichy." In a well-lit, pristinely elegant setting, diners can enjoy such dishes as a ravioli stuffed with frogs' legs and fresh herbs, a ragoût of crayfish with wild mushrooms, and roast pigeon. Lobster bourguignon with baby vegetables and filet of beef grilled with marrow are two other specialties. Desserts are spectacular, including a gratin of pears grilled with almonds. The 290-F ($52.20) fixed-price menu is exceptional.

BRASSERIE DU CASINO, 4, rue du Casino. Tel. 70-98-23-06.
   Cuisine: FRENCH. **Reservations:** Recommended at lunch.
$ Prices: Appetizers 35–55 F ($6.30–$9.90); main dishes 65–110 F ($11.70–$19.80); fixed-price menus 95–135 F ($17.10–$24.30). AE, MC, V.
   Open: Lunch Fri–Tues noon–1:30pm; dinner Thurs–Tues 7–10pm. **Closed:** Nov 21–Feb 28.

This has been a well-maintained and thriving brasserie since the 1920s, and it's a preferred stopover for actors and musicians visiting from Paris to perform at the casino. Its chandeliers and etched glass are authentic to the year of construction (1920). The de Chassat family are charming and especially solicitous to foreigners dining at their restaurant. The place remained open during World War II and witnessed much wartime intrigue within its paneled precincts. It's known for the beauty of its interior, which has a sheathing of copper and art deco mahogany. At lunch it's busy, but the real charm comes out at night, when a pianist entertains. The cuisine bears a fine relationship between quality and price. Specialties include sweetbreads with hazelnuts, a paupiette of rabbit with shallots, a salad of lentils and brains with a strong mustard, and a veal liver with a fondue of onions—along with good beef, such as steaks and tournedos.

4. CLERMONT-FERRAND

248 miles S of Paris, 110 miles W of Lyon

GETTING THERE   By Plane   There's an airport (Clermont-Aulnat) four miles east of town.

By Train   Rail lines converge on Clermont-Ferrand from all parts of France, including Paris's Gare de Lyon, Marseille, and Toulouse. Trains from small towns in the Auvergne usually require a connection.

ESSENTIALS   Orientation   The city was formed when Clermont merged with Montferrand under Louis XV. Most of the interesting old buildings lie in Vieux-Clermont, which has as its focal point **place de la Victoire,** site of the black-lava Cathédrale de Notre-Dame. Several blocks northeast stands the even older Notre-Dame du Port. On the northwest edge of the old city is the **Marché St-Pierre,** the biggest produce market in town. **Place de Jaude** is another important commercial square.

Information   The **Office de Tourisme** is located at 69, bd. Gergovia (tel. 73-93-30-20).

The ancient capital of Auvergne, this old double city in south-central France has looked down on a long parade of history. Situated on the small Tiretaine River, it was created in 1731 by a merger of two towns, Clermont and Montferrand. It is surrounded by hills, and in the distance lies one of the great attractions of Auvergne, Puy-de-Dôme, the volcanic mountain I'll describe later.

WHAT TO SEE & DO

To begin your tour, head for the center of Clermont, the bustling **place de Jaude,** where you can sample a glass of regional wine at a café under the shade of a catalpa tree. When you're ready, take rue du 11-Novembre, which branches off from the main plaza. This street leads to **rue des Gras,** the most interesting artery of Clermont.

Built of dark volcanic stone, the **Cathédrale de Notre-Dame,** rue de la Cathédrale (tel. 73-92-46-61), is one of the great Gothic churches of central France, dating primarily from the 13th and 14th centuries. It witnessed later additions in the 19th century. Inside, its most outstanding feature is the series of stained-glass windows from the 13th and 14th centuries. Admission is free. Open Monday through Saturday from 9:30am to noon and 2 to 5pm.

After leaving the cathedral, you can explore **Vieux-Clermont,** a small surrounding sector that contains many houses dating from the 16th and 18th centuries. See the **Maison de Savaron,** constructed in 1513, at 3, rue des Chaussetiers. It has a beautiful courtyard and a staircase tower.

One of the finest examples of the Auvergnat Romanesque style of architecture is the **Église Notre-Dame-du-Port,** rue du Port (tel. 73-91-32-94). Dating from the 11th and 12th centuries, the church rises in the northeastern part of town. It has four radiating chapels, and its transept is surmounted by an octagonal tower. The building is made of lava from volcanic deposits in the region. The crypt holds a 17th-century "black Madonna." Admission is free. Open daily from 8:30am to 6:30pm.

Between the two churches stands the Renaissance Fontaine d'Amboise, ordered built on place de la Poterne, its pyramid supporting a statue of Hercules. Nearby is the Square Pascal, commemorating the fact that Blaise Pascal was born here in 1623 in a house on rue des Gras. Regrettably, the house was demolished in 1958, but a statue in the square honors the native son, the author of *Pensées.*

MUSÉE BARGION, 45, rue de Ballainvilliers. Tel. 73-91-37-31.
The wide range of exhibits includes some prehistoric objects, as well as wooden carvings and bronzes from the Gallo-Roman era. The museum also has some

interesting stained-glass windows, plus a wide range of paintings, including works by Armand Guillaumin, Joseph Vernet, Carle van Loo, Gustave Doré, and Buffet. The Flemish, French, and Italian masters range from the 17th to the 19th century, and there are contemporary artists as well.

Admission: Free.

Open: May–Sept, Tues–Sat 10am–noon and 2–6pm, Sun 2–6pm; Oct–Apr, Tues–Sat 10am–noon and 2–5pm, Sun 2–6pm.

MUSEE DE RANQUET, 1, petite rue St-Pierre. Tel. 73-37-38-63.

This museum of Gallo-Roman artifacts and local memorabilia is in the Maison des Architects, a Renaissance landmark. The collection includes regional furniture and workaday objects, including regional pottery from the 18th century. The museum owns two "arithmetical machines" that belonged to Pascal, the only two of their kind said to exist outside of private collections in France. There's also a room devoted to France's hero of the Battle of Marengo, Général Desaix.

Admission: Free.

Open: May–Sept, Tues–Sat 10am–noon and 2–6pm, Sun 2–6pm; Oct–Apr, Tues–Sat 10am–noon and 2–5pm, Sun 2–6pm.

WHERE TO STAY

GALLIENI, 51, rue Bonnabaud, 63000 Clermont-Ferrand. Tel. 73-93-59-69. Fax 73-34-89-29. 80 rms (all with bath). MINIBAR TV TEL **Bus:** 1, 2, 4, or 9.

$ Rates: 300 F ($54) single; 340 F ($61.20) double. Breakfast 40 F ($7.20) extra. AE, DC, MC, V. **Parking:** 30 F ($5.40).

At the Gallieni, all the rooms are modern and comfortable. La Charade restaurant offers some of the best cuisine in town, with meals costing 85–250 F ($15.30–$45). The location is directly south of the historic center.

MERCURE ALTEA GERGOVIE, 82, bd. Gergovia, 63000 Clermont-Ferrand. Tel. 73-34-46-46. Fax 73-34-46-36. 124 rms (all with bath). MINIBAR TV TEL **Bus:** 1, 2, 4, or 9.

$ Rates: 395 F ($71.10) single; 550 F ($99) double. Breakfast 52 F ($9.40) extra. AE, DC, MC, V. **Parking:** 30 F ($5.40).

This modern hotel is centrally located near the Jardin Lecoq, the loveliest gardens in Clermont. Rooms are well furnished and immaculate. La Retirade restaurant is excellent, with meals beginning at 115 F ($20.70).

WHERE TO DINE

LE CLAVE, 10-12, rue St-Adjutor. Tel. 73-36-46-30.

Cuisine: FRENCH. **Reservations:** Required. **Bus:** 1, 2, 4, or 9.

$ Prices: Appetizers 80–180 F ($14.40–$32.40); main dishes 100–150 F ($18–$27); fixed-price menus 150–280 F ($27–$50.40). MC, V.

Open: Lunch Mon–Fri noon–2pm; dinner Mon–Sat 8–10:30pm.

Recently renovated, this well-known restaurant brings an urbanized, big-city aesthetic to the heart of Clermont-Ferrand. Set inside a 19th-century stone house, the establishment contains two separate dining rooms completely outfitted in monochromatic tones of gray and off-white. Menu items are both classic and contemporary, each prepared with fresh ingredients. Your meal might include foie gras en terrine or an unusual warm chiffonnade of crustaceans. If you like fish, you might try that old Mediterranean favorite, rascasse bonne femme or a filet of Atlantic perch, grilled and served with fennel and beurre blanc. If you prefer beef, try a pavé of beef with foie-gras sauce. Desserts, which are wheeled to your table on a trolley, vary with the inspiration of the chef.

JEAN-YVES BATH, place du Marché-St-Pierre. Tel. 73-31-23-23.

Cuisine: FRENCH. **Reservations:** Required. **Bus:** 1, 2, 4, or 9.

$ Prices: Restaurant, appetizers 70–150 F ($12.60–$27); main dishes 90–200 F ($16.20–$36); fixed price menus 260–320 F ($46.80–$57.60). Brasserie, platters 45–55 F ($8.10–$9.90). AE, MC, V.

Open: Restaurant, lunch Tues–Fri noon–2pm; dinner Mon–Sat 7:30–9:15pm. Brasserie, Mon–Sat noon–1am. **Closed:** Feb and Oct.

Few pretensions and lots of well-studied flavors go into the locally inspired cuisine served at Jean-Yves Bath's charming restaurant, standing one floor above street level. The dining room looks like the interior of a yacht thanks to liberal amounts of brass and mahogany. It's the perfect setting for a fish salad covered with truffles and vinaigrette. Other dishes include a salad of rabbit with orange zest, fresh thyme, and essence of tomato, and sweetbreads in puff pastry. Dessert might be strawberry ravioli.

Cost-conscious meals are served throughout the day in the street-level brasserie. Here, the menu features heaping platters of bistro-style food (steaks, fish, and local sausages) served without fuss or bother by a busy staff. The ground floor also contains a wine bar, where unusual local vintages are sold by the glass.

NEARBY ATTRACTIONS

MONTFERRAND About 1⅛ miles northeast of town is the once socially elegant and wealthy, but now shrunken and sleepy Montferrand. It contains many ancient houses with beautiful courtyards, including one dedicated to an elephant and another to Adam and Eve. Many of these Gothic and Renaissance houses are well preserved. The most notable *maisons* are on rue Jules-Guesde, where you'll find the Hôtel Fontreyde at no. 28 and the Hôtel de Lignat at no. 18.

PUY-DE-DOME The volcanic mountain, Puy-de-Dôme, is about 11 miles out of town. Its peak is at 4,800 feet, and it's considered the oldest volcano in France. Once the Gauls erected a shrine at its peak, but the Romans replaced it with a temple dedicated to Mercury. In the 19th century the foundations of this temple were discovered and the ruins excavated. Pascal came here to illustrate his theory of the barometric pressure of air. From the mountain's summit, there is a panoramic view of this whole part of France. On a clear day you can see all the way to Mont Blanc in the east. Shuttle buses run from the base to the summit, costing 18 F ($3.20) round-trip.

5. LE PUY-EN-VELAY

325 miles S of Paris, 80 miles SE of Clermont-Ferrand

GETTING THERE   By Train St-Georges-d'Aurac is the nearest railway station, with connections from Nîmes and Clermont-Ferrand. From St-Georges-d'Aurac, a local train makes a slow and infrequent run into Le Puy. Trains from Lyon or St-Etienne are more direct.

ESSENTIALS   Orientation The town is dominated by the volcanic Rocher Corneille. At its southernmost base, in the center of the old town, is the Romanesque Cathédrale de Notre-Dame.

Information The Office de Tourisme is on place du Breuil (tel. 71-09-38-41).

The site of Le Puy has been called one of the most extraordinary sights of France. The steep volcanic spires left from geological activities that ended millennia ago were capped with Romanesque churches, a cathedral, and a collection of medieval houses that rise sinuously from the plain below. The history of Le Puy is centered around the cult of the Virgin Mary, which prompted the construction of many of the city's churches.

WHAT TO SEE & DO

CATHEDRALE DE NOTRE-DAME, place du For. Tel. 73-62-11-45.
This Romanesque cathedral used to house many of the pilgrims heading toward Santiago de Compostela in Spain. Marked by a vivid Oriental and Byzantine influence,

it's worth a visit. You can also visit the adjoining cloisters; some of the carved capitals date from the Carolingian era, and many experts cite the geometric wall patterns as something derived from Arab influences. Your ticket to the cloisters also admits you to the Chapelle des Reliques et Trésor d'Art Religieux, which contains fabrics and gold and silver objects from the church treasury, as well as an unusual enameled chalice from the 12th century.

Admission: Cathedral, free; cloisters and Chapel of Relics, 20 F ($3.60) adults, 13 F ($2.30) children.

Open: Cathedral, daily 7am–6pm; cloisters and Chapel of Relics, Wed–Mon 9am–noon and 2–6pm.

CHAPELLE ST-MICHEL-D'AIGUILHE, atop the Rocher St-Michel.

It's a very long climb up rocky stairs to reach this place, but when you get here you'll be struck by the Oriental influences in the floor plan, the arabesques, and the mosaics crafted from black stone. On view are some 12th-century murals and an 11th-century wooden depiction of Christ.

Admission: 8 F ($1.40) adults, 5 F (90¢) children.

Open: Daily 9am–noon and 2–7pm (to 5pm in winter).

MUSEE CROZATIER, Jardin Henry-Vinay. Tel. 71-09-38-90.

If you appreciate handcrafts, you'll enjoy the displays of lace, some of which dates from the 16th century. Also on view is a collection of carved architectural embellishments from the Romanesque era and paintings from the 14th through the 20th century.

Admission: 11 F ($2) adults, 5.50 F ($1) children.

Open: May–Sept, Wed–Mon 10am–noon and 2–6pm; Oct–Jan and Mar–Apr, Wed–Mon 10am–noon and 2–4pm. **Closed:** Feb.

ROCHER CORNEILLE. Tel. 71-09-73-45.

You can climb one of the volcanic chimneys for a panoramic view of the town and the surrounding region. At Rocher Corneille you'll see a huge statue of the Virgin Mary, paid for by national fund-raising and erected in 1860. Hundreds of cannons seized at the Battle of Sebastopol were melted down to form the solid cast-iron statue that weighs 110 tons. You can climb an interior stairwell to reach an observation platform set into the Virgin's crown.

Admission: 9 F ($1.60) adults, 4.50 F (80¢) children.

Open: Mar–Apr, daily 9am–6pm; May–Sept, daily 9am–7pm; Oct–Nov and Feb, daily 10am–5pm. **Closed:** Dec–Jan (except Sun afternoon and during school holidays).

WHERE TO STAY

HOTEL CHRIS'TEL, 15, bd. Alexandre-Clair, 43003 Le Puy CEDEX. Tel. 71-02-24-44. Fax 71-02-52-68. 30 rms (all with bath). TV TEL

$ Rates: 260 F ($46.80) single; 390 F ($70.20) double. Breakfast 40 F ($7.20) extra. AE, DC, MC, V. **Parking:** 30 F ($5.40).

This contemporary hotel in a good location offers comfortable rooms, each with a writing desk, an easy chair, and full-length windows that open onto a balcony. The hotel has a pleasant staff and an inviting dining room, serving only breakfast. The hotel is 12 minutes from the town center and a 5-minute walk from the Jardin Henry-Vinay.

WHERE TO DINE

LE BATEAU IVRE, 5, rue Portail-d'Avignon. Tel. 71-09-67-20.

Cuisine: FRENCH. **Reservations:** Recommended.

$ Prices: Appetizers 52–95 F ($9.40–$17.10); main dishes 85–105 F ($15.30–$18.90); fixed-price menus 100–280 F ($18–$50.40).

Open: Lunch Tues–Sat noon–2:30pm; dinner Tues–Sat 7:30–10pm. **Closed:** Nov 1–15.

This intimate dining room is in a pretty 19th-century house with lots of rustic detail.

Monsieur and Madame Datessen cook and supervise the dining room. Specialties include salmon, snails, lamb cooked in wine, and a full array of other well-prepared French dishes. The cheapest fixed-price meal is not served on Friday and Saturday.

6. AUBUSSON

236 miles S of Paris, 55 miles E of Limoges,
59 miles NW of Clermont-Ferrand

GETTING THERE By Train and Bus Aubusson has bus and rail service, much of it indirect, from Clermont-Ferrand and Paris, among other cities.

ESSENTIALS Orientation The historic core lies along the north bank of the **Creuse River.** The old town has four major parallel east-west streets; **rue Vieille,** where you'll find the tourist office and several old buildings, is the northernmost of them.

Information For information, contact the **Office de Tourisme,** rue Vieille (tel. 55-66-32-12).

Deep in France is the "ville de la tapisserie." In the narrow Creuse Valley, the little market town of Aubusson enjoys world renown for its carpets and tapestries.

The town is characterized by clock towers, bridges, peaked roofs, and turrets—all of which formed the inspiration of the painter Gromaire's widely reproduced cartoon *View of Aubusson.* Against the gray granite, rainbow-hued skeins of wool hang from the windows. Ateliers, the workshops of the craftspeople, are spread throughout the town. Many are open to the public (inquire at the door).

The origin of the industry is unknown. Some credit the Arabs who settled here in 732. Others think the craft came from Flanders in the Middle Ages. For years the favorite subject was *The Lady and the Unicorn,* the original of which was discovered in the nearby Château de Boussac. Many tapestry reproductions of 18th-century painters such as Boucher and Watteau have also been made. Since World War II, designs by such painters as Picasso, Matisse, and Braque have been stressed.

WHAT TO SEE & DO

The **Musée Départemental de la Tapisserie,** Centre Culturel Jean-Lurçat, avenue des Lissiers (tel. 55-66-33-06), contains exhibits related to the six-century-long tradition of the Aubusson carpet-weaving industry. The displays also highlight the 20th-century rebirth of the Aubusson carpet and the art of tapestry weaving. It's open Friday through Wednesday from 9:30am to 12:30pm and 2 to 6pm; in summer, also on Thursday from 2 to 6pm. Admission is 18 F ($3.20) for adults and 12 F ($2.20) for children 11–16.

La Maison du Vieux Tapissier, rue Vieille (tel. 55-66-32-12), exhibits old carpets, and also displays a reconstruction of an old carpet-weaving studio.

WHERE TO STAY & DINE

HOTEL DE FRANCE, 6, rue des Déportés, 23200 Aubusson. Tel. 55-66-10-22. Fax 55-66-88-64. 21 rms (all with bath or shower). TV TEL
$ Rates: 260–300 F ($46.80–$54) single; 300–350 F ($54–$63) double. Breakfast 30 F ($5.40) extra. MC, V. **Parking:** 30 F ($5.40).
This hotel was originally built as the private home of a prominent local doctor in 1730, and it has been owned and managed as a country hotel by five generations of the Dubreuil family. Rooms are comfortable and pleasantly furnished. The restaurant

serves good food, especially fresh river trout in season and tender, white veal. Fraises des bois (wild strawberries) in season make a succulent finish to any repast. The selection from the Limousin cheese tray is delectable. Meals run 70–150 F ($12.60–$27). The restaurant is closed Sunday night and Monday from September to April.

7. LIMOGES

246 miles S of Paris, 193 miles N of Toulouse

GETTING THERE   By Train and Bus   Limoges has bus and train service from all other regional cities, with direct trains from Toulouse, Poitiers, and Paris.

ESSENTIALS   Orientation   Many motorists park in place de la République before continuing their exploration on foot. Located along an east-west line through the heart of the old city are three of the town's landmarks: place de la Cathédrale de St-Etienne, place du Présidial (with its Eglise St-Michel-des-Lions), and the Musée National Adrien-Dubouche.

Information   The Office de Tourisme is on boulevard de Fleurus (tel. 55-34-46-87).

The ancient capital of Limousin, Limoges is a town in west-central France famous for its exquisite porcelain and enamel works, the latter a medieval industry revived in the 19th century. Rising on the right bank of the Vienne, the town historically has had two parts: the Cité, its narrow streets and old *maisons* occupying the lower slope, and the town proper at the summit.

WHAT TO SEE & DO

If you'd like to see an enameler or porcelain factory, consult the list of workshops available at the tourist office (see "Essentials," above).

Or go directly to the famous **Le Pavillon de la Porcelaine,** route de Toulouse (tel. 55-30-21-86). Since 1842 the Haviland company has been exporting to the United States and elsewhere, and customers have included everybody from Ulysses S. Grant to the late Shah of Iran. Over the years the company has used the designs of such artists as Gauguin and Dalí. You can see the masterpieces produced since 1842 in a museum. Later, visit an air-conditioned room where you can follow step by step the manufacturing process with the help of a video on a giant screen. A large shop also sells the porcelain at factory prices.

Admission is free, and Le Pavillon is open April to October, daily from 8:30am to 7:30pm; November to March, daily from 8:30am to 7pm.

The **Musée National Adrien-Dubouché,** 8 bis, place Winston-Churchill (tel. 55-77-45-58), displays a beautiful collection of Limoges china. In its porcelain collection the museum is second in France, bowing only to Sèvres. Its galleries trace the entire history of chinaware, including not only that in Europe but in Japan and China as well. Entire dinner sets of noted figures are here. The main gallery also contains contemporary Limoges ware.

Admission is 15 F ($2.70) for adults, 8 F ($1.40) on Sunday; children under 18 are free. The museum is open Wednesday through Monday from 10am to noon and 1:30 to 5pm (closed holidays). The park, place du Champs-de-Foire, is nearby.

The **Cathédrale de St-Etienne,** place de la Cathédrale (tel. 55-34-17-38), was begun in 1273, but it took many years to complete. The choir, for example, was finished in 1327, but work was going on in the nave until almost 1890. The cathedral is the only one in the old province of Limousin to be built entirely in the Gothic style. The main entrance is through St. John's Portal (Portal St-Jean), which has some beautiful carved wooden doors from the 16th century. The portal was constructed at the flowering peak of the flamboyant Gothic style. The entrance is surmounted by a rose window. Inside, the nave appears so harmonious it is hard to imagine that its construction took six centuries. The rood screen is of interest, built in 1533 in the ornate style of the Italian Renaissance. The cathedral also contains some admirable bishops' tombs from the 14th to the 16th century.

Adjoining the cathedral in the **Jardins de l'Evêché**—which offer a view of the Vienne and the Bridge of St. Stephen from the 13th century—the old archbishops' palace has been turned into the **Musée Municipal,** place de la Cathédrale (tel. 55-45-61-75).

The 18th-century building, elegant in line, has an outstanding collection of Limoges enamels dating from the 12th century, as well as some enamel paintings by Leonard Limousin, who was born in 1505 in Limoges and went on to win world acclaim and the favor of four monarchs.

Limoges was also the birthplace of the impressionist painter Renoir, and the museum displays several works by this world-class artist.

From June to September, the museum is open daily (except holidays) from 10am to noon and 2 to 6pm; off-season, Wednesday through Monday until 5pm. Admission is free.

Another church of interest is the **Eglise St-Michel-des-Lions** at 11, rue Petitniauds-Beaupeyrat (tel. 55-34-18-13). Construction on this church was launched in the 14th century and work continued in the 15th and 16th centuries. The church has some late Gothic stained glass, plus relics of St. Martial, including his head. Open daily from 8am to 7pm.

WHERE TO STAY

LA CARAVELLE, 21, rue Armand-Barbès, 87000 Limoges. Tel. 55-77-75-29. Fax 55-79-27-60. 37 rms (all with bath). TV TEL
$ Rates: 260 F ($46.80) single; 370 F ($66.60) double. Breakfast 30 F ($5.40) extra. AE, DC, MC, V. **Parking:** Free.
Just north of the city center, a long block from the wooded Champ-de-Juillet, is this highly recommendable modern hotel designed to stay young for many years to come. It possesses a tranquil atmosphere. The rooms are simply furnished. Breakfast is the only meal served.

LE RICHELIEU, 40, av. Baudin, 87000 Limoges. Tel. 55-34-22-82. Fax 55-32-48-73. 32 rms (all with bath). TV TEL
$ Rates: 270–400 F ($48.60–$72) single; 290–420 F ($52.20–$75.60) double. Breakfast 40 F ($7.20) extra. MC, V. **Parking:** 40 F ($7.20).
Modern and simple, this four-story hotel was renovated and upgraded in 1989, and today provides uncomplicated accommodations about a five-minute drive south of the town center. Each of the modestly furnished bedrooms has soundproof windows. There's a bar on the premises, much favored by the business travelers checking in here, but breakfast is the only meal served.

ROYAL LIMOUSIN, place de la République, 87000 Limoges. Tel. 55-34-65-30. Fax 55-34-55-21. 70 rms (all with bath). MINIBAR TV TEL
$ Rates: 450 F ($81) single; 530 F ($95.40) double. Breakfast 48 F ($8.60) extra. AE, DC, MC, V.
This modern oasis in a place of antiquity stands near a large municipal parking lot in the center of Limoges. Rooms are well equipped and modish in the chain-hotel style. You don't get luxury, but you do get comfort and convenience.

WHERE TO DINE

PHILIPPE REDON, 3, rue Aguesseau. Tel. 55-34-66-22.
Cuisine: FRENCH. **Reservations:** Recommended.
$ Prices: Appetizers 65–90 F ($11.70–$16.20); main dishes 80–130 F ($14.40–$23.40); fixed-price meals 130–190 F ($23.40–$34.20). AE, DC, MC, V.
Open: Lunch Tues–Sat noon–2:30pm; dinner Mon–Sat 7–10pm.
Set in a 19th-century house a few steps from the produce market of Limoges, in the town center, this restaurant is maintained by a bright and youthful team of waiters headed by owner-chef Philippe Redon. Opened in 1990, the restaurant contains a

modernized art deco-inspired interior accented with exposed stone and bouquets of flowers. Menu items are the personal statement of the chef, and vary with the availability of local ingredients. Examples might include crayfish with spices, turbot with girolle mushrooms, filet of monkfish marinated in Szechuan pepper, and codfish studded with truffles in puff pastry.

SHOPPING

Two shops specialize in local products, the first in crystal and silverware and the second in porcelain and "seconds." Both are open Monday through Saturday from 9:15am to noon and 2 to 7pm.

PRESTIGE DE LIMOGES, 2-13, bd. Louis-Blanc. Tel. 55-34-44-15.

Limoges's own "unblemished crystal" is sold here, as well as crystal from Lalique, St. Louis, and Baccarat, along with silverware from Christofle and Puiforcat.

PRESTIGE DE LIMOGES, 27, bd. Louis-Blanc. Tel. 55-34-58-61.

The same company sells porcelain from Haviland, Bernardaud, Raynaud, and Lafarge. There is also a collection of slightly damaged, imperfect seconds.

NEARBY ACCOMMODATIONS & DINING
Saint-Martin-Du-Fault

LA CHAPELLE SAINT-MARTIN, 87510 Nieul. Tel. 55-75-80-17. Fax 55-75-89-50. 10 rms (none with bath), 3 suites. A/C TEL **Directions:** Take the N147 and the D35 seven miles northeast from Limoges.
$ Rates: 590 F ($106.20) single; 690–980 F ($124.20–$176.40) double; 1,300–1,500 F ($234–$270) suite. Half board 750–850 F ($135–$153) per person. V. **Closed:** Hotel, Jan–Feb. Restaurant, Mon year round. **Parking:** Free.
This is the best place to stay in the environs of Limoges if you enjoy a turn-of-the-century style of living and superb food in the tradition of the Relais & Châteaux group. The hotel is graciously situated in a private park with two ponds attracting seasonal fowl. You couldn't find a more peaceful retreat in "Greater Limoges," where the atmosphere is so sophisticated and enchanting. Your host, Monsieur Dudognon, requests that you write or call well in advance. Rooms are individually decorated and very tasteful. The food is excellent, the ingredients selected with care, and the dishes prepared with flair, in the traditional style of classic French cuisine. A swimming pool and tennis courts are available.

Nieul

CHATEAU DE NIEUL, 16270 Nieul. Tel. 45-71-36-38. Fax 45-71-46-45. 11 rms (all with bath or shower), 3 suites. TEL **Directions:** From the center of Limoges, follow the N147 and the D35 for 8 miles to Nieul. From the center of Nieul, take the route de Fontafie, following the signs for about a mile east of town.
$ Rates: 740–1,125 F ($133.20–$202.50) single; 820–1,250 F ($147.60–$225) double; 1,350–1,950 F ($243–$351) suite. Breakfast 70 F ($12.60) extra. AE, DC, MC, V. **Parking:** Free. **Closed:** Mid-Nov to late Apr.
This elegant dwelling, built during the 15th century as a hunting lodge for King François I, was transformed in 1937 into the first château-hotel created in France. Restored early in the 1800s after its destruction in the French Revolution by the comte de Dampierre, it has remained within the family of Jean-Michel Bodinaud for the past three generations. Today, 400 acres of park and forest lead up to a series of beautifully maintained gardens, the pride of the owners. On the premises are tennis courts, a swimming pool, and—in what used to be the château's stables—an art and antique gallery.
The cuisine, supervised by Mme Luce Bodinaud, is superb, focusing on classic French traditions and recipes from the region. Typical dishes include stuffed cabbage, roast lamb, tournedos, escalope of foie gras caramelized in port wine, filet of beef with a mignonnette of pepper, and salmon cooked in a court bouillon with sage. Fixed-price menus, readily served to nonresidents who telephone in advance, cost

230–300 F ($41.40–$54). Appetizers cost 70–150 F ($12.60–$27), and main courses go for 125–150 F ($22.50–$27) each.

8. AURILLAC

350 miles S of Paris, 60 miles SE of Brive-la-Gaillard

GETTING THERE   The town is serviced by bus and railway. Four trains per day arrive from Toulouse (trip time: 3½ hours) and five trains per day from Clermont-Ferrand (trip time: 3 hours). About six trains per day arrive from Paris, via Brive or Nevers, with most trips taking about 6½ hours. Many visitors prefer to drive here and park in public lots near place des Carmes and pont Rouge.

ESSENTIALS Orientation   The old town is centered around the Church of Géraud, but a more immediately visible monument is the Château de St-Etienne, about a half mile north of the historic center.

Information   The Office de Tourisme is on place Square (tel. 71-48-46-58).

Residents of Aurillac, the capital of Cantal, are proud of the fact that the first French pope came from a 9th-century abbey on the premises of what is today the commercial center of upper Auvergne. Known to Christendom as Sylvester II, his prepapal name was Gerbert. His name, of course, changed after he was named pope in time for the millennium in A.D. 999.

Gerbert is said to have introduced the pendulum-weighted clock, the navigational astrolabe, an improved musical organ, and arabic numerals into western Europe. All of this happened after he abandoned the limited confines of 10th-century Aurillac and went to study at the Arabic universities of Spain. Later, Aurillac became a center for the study of alchemy.

During the 16th century the wars of religion attracted hundreds of Protestants into the confines of the city. The Catholic authorities ordered a general massacre of the Protestants, who were later avenged.

In the 18th century, Colbert, the brilliant finance minister, encouraged lace, goldsmithing, and crafts industries in Aurillac, a few vestiges of which survive today.

The **Château de St-Etienne,** off the D35 north of town (tel. 71-48-49-09), houses a 13th-century dungeon and a Maison des Volcans in one of the castle's wings. The latter contains geological specimens, audiovisual presentations on rocks, and environmental exhibits. It's open July to mid-September, Monday through Saturday from 10am to 6:30pm; off-season, Monday through Saturday from 9am to noon and 2 to 6pm. Admission is 10 F ($1.80) for adults, 5 F (90¢) for children.

Other than possessing a rich history, Aurillac doesn't have too much to offer, although it's used as a base to explore the **Monts du Cantal.** This is one of the richest regions in France for the exploration of the unusual geological formations in which the area abounds. Ask the tourist office (see "Essentials," above) for information.

WHERE TO STAY

GRAND HOTEL DE BOURDEAUX, 2, av. de la République, 15000 Aurillac. Tel. 71-48-01-84, or toll free 800/528-1234 in the U.S. and Canada. Fax 71-48-49-93. 35 rms (all with bath or shower), 2 suites. MINIBAR TV TEL

$ Rates: 290–350 F ($52.20–$63) single; 320–450 F ($57.60–$81) double; 650 F ($117) suite. Breakfast 37 F ($6.70) extra. AE, DC, MC, V. **Parking:** 40 F ($7.20). **Closed:** Dec 20–Jan 15.

The comfortable, spacious rooms in the Grand Hôtel are one of the best bargains in town. In addition, the stylish bar here is one of the most popular places around. You'll recognize the building by its white walls and white shutters across the street from the Palais de Justice in the town center and by its Mapotel and Best Western signs out front.

LA THOMASSE, rue du Dr-Mallet, 15000 Aurillac. Tel. 71-48-26-47. 21 rms (all with bath), 1 suite. TV TEL

$ Rates: 320–370 F ($57.60–$66.60) single or double; 450 F ($81) suite. Breakfast 37 F ($6.70) extra. AE, DC, MC, V. **Parking:** Free.

One of the best hotels in town is this ivy-sheathed, tradition-inspired structure in a verdant private park about half a mile west of the town center. Built in 1970, it offers calm and restful rooms and easy access to city-run tennis courts and a public swimming pool.

Meals in the dining room are well prepared and politely served. Appetizers cost 30–70 F ($5.40–$12.60); main courses, 50–80 F ($9–$14.40).

WHERE TO DINE

LES QUATRE SAISONS, 10, rue Champeil. Tel. 71-64-85-38.
Cuisine: FRENCH. **Reservations:** Recommended.
$ Prices: Appetizers 60–70 F ($10.80–$12.60); main dishes 65–75 F ($11.70–$13.50); fixed-price meals 75–195 F ($13.50–$35.10). AE, MC, V.
Open: Lunch Tues–Sat noon–2pm; dinner Tues–Sat 7–10pm.

Set in the heart of town, this restaurant offers well-prepared food and congenial service amid a decor whose marine blue and green colors were inspired by the interior of an aquarium. Menu choices vary with the seasons, and reflect the available ingredients of the moment, but might include a feuilleté of lamb's sweetbreads bordelaise, a gâteau of fish served with a fricassée of shrimp, sole meunière with citrus-flavored butter sauce, and a succulent filet of beef with morels and morel sauce.

DORDOGNE & PERIGORD

Gastronomes seeking foie gras and truffles and nature lovers have always sought out the Périgord and Dordogne region of France. In this chapter we'll look at some old capitals of old provinces (long ago subdivided into départements of France). Périgueux, to begin our tour, was the capital of the old province of Périgord. After following the trail of the Cro-Magnon people, we will visit Cahors, the ancient capital of Quercy, to be followed by Montauban, the city of the painter Ingres.

But in Périgord and the Dordogne it is not the towns themselves that hold the fascination, but the unspoiled countryside, a rich, fertile region of much hidden charm and antique character. In some villages the Middle Ages seem to live on. It is said that there are no discoveries to be made in France, but you can defy the experts and make many discoveries for yourself if you give yourself adequate time to visit a region too often neglected by the North American.

Between the province of Limousin and the deep valleys of the Aquitaine (from which came Eleanor, the most famous woman of the Middle Ages), lies Périgord. More than 40% of it is still covered with woodland.

The Dordogne, an inland département of southwestern France, is a land of crystalline and limestone rocks. Fine medieval castles rise abruptly on the hilltops, remembering a grander day.

Once these lands were called "the undiscovered provinces," but for the French at least, that is a dated reference today. In summer the major towns seem overrun with tour buses, but in the villages off the beaten track the bucolic life still holds forth.

SEEING DORDOGNE & PERIGORD

GETTING THERE Unless you have unlimited time, a car is the only way to explore this relatively remote region, since it lacks major transportation hubs. Many of its most interesting towns, such as Montauban and Rocamadour, might be approached from Toulouse as your gateway.

Toulouse is in the Mid-Pyrénées, only an hour from Paris by plane, with 14 daily flights. From the Toulouse airport, you can rent a car, driving north along the autoroute to Bordeaux, until you see the turnoff northeast to Montauban, where you'll be within easy reach of the most interesting regional towns, including Cahors, Rocamadour, and Sarlat-la-Canéda.

Limoges, in the north, is another potential gateway city, with three flights daily from Orly in Paris. You could also take a 3½-hour train to Brive from Paris. If you're driving, the RN 20 connects northern Europe with Barcelona, Paris, Limoges, and Toulouse.

A SUGGESTED ROUTE Spend your first night (Day 1) at Montauban, then drive

WHAT'S SPECIAL ABOUT DORDOGNE & PERIGORD

Great Towns/Villages
☐ Périgueux, city of foie gras and truffles and capital of the old province of Perigord.
☐ Les Eyzies-de-Tayac, called an archeologist's dream, one of the world's richest ancient sites.
☐ Sarlat-la-Canéda, a beautifully preserved medieval town, the capital of Black Périgord.
☐ Rocamadour, another medieval town that defies gravity.

Ancient Monuments
☐ Grotte du Pech-Merle, a prehistoric cave near Cabrerets.
☐ Old Sarlat, the Vielle-Ville, now a living museum with a cathedral from 1317.

Literary Pilgrimages
☐ Château de Castel-Novel, former residence of French novelist Colette, now a Relais & Châteaux hotel.

Architectural Highlights
☐ Cathédrale de St-Front, the last of the Aquitanian domed churches at Périgueux.
☐ The "red village" of Collonges, with small mansions built of dark-red stone and a Romanesque church.

Outstanding Museums
☐ Lascaux II, at Lascaux, displaying reproductions of the Sistine Chapel of prehistoric art.
☐ Musée Ingres, at Montauban, the premier museum of the whole province, with more than a dozen paintings by Ingres, born here in 1780.

Castles
☐ The fortress castle at Les Eyzies-de-Tayac, now home to a collection of prehistoric relics.
☐ Château de Beynac, at Beynac-et-Cazenac, with a panoramic view of Dordogne.

---

north after viewing the Ingres Museum and have lunch in Cahors before heading to Rocamadour (Day 2) for the night. Continue west to Sarlat-le-Canéda (Day 3). While still based in Sarlat, you can take excursions the following day (Day 4) to Les Eyzies-de-Tayac and the cave paintings at Lascaux. Take a cross-country drive to Périgueux (Day 5), where you'll have a final dinner.

1. PERIGUEUX

301 miles SW of Paris, 53 miles SE of Angoulême,
70 miles NE of Bordeaux, 63 miles SW of Limoges

GETTING THERE By Train Trains run frequently from Paris, Lyon, and Toulouse, and many regional towns and villages. Six trains per day arrive from Paris (trip time: 6–7 hours), four trains pull in from Lyon (trip time: 7 hours), 10 trains per day from Bordeaux (trip time: 2½ hours), and seven trains arrive from Toulouse (trip time: 4 hours).

ESSENTIALS Orientation Most of the old town is on the north bank of the Isle River around the medieval Cathédrale de St-Front. The Roman amphitheater (Les Arènes) is less than half a mile west of the cathedral, near the town's administrative headquarters.

Information For information, inquire at the Office du Tourisme, 26, place Francheville (tel. 53-53-10-63).

Gastronomes speak of it as a "city of foie gras and truffles." Throughout France you'll see dishes appearing on menus with the appendage of *à la périgourdine*.

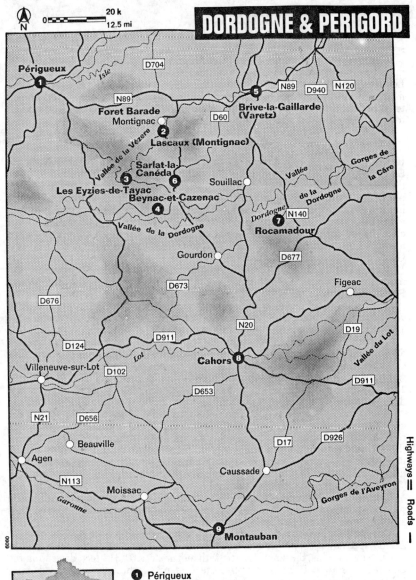

DORDOGNE & PERIGORD

20 k
12.5 mi

N

Périgueux
Isle
D704
N89
D940
N120
Forêt Barade
Montignac
Brive-la-Gaillarde (Varetz)
D60
Lascaux (Montignac)
Vallée de la Vézère
Sarlat-la-Canéda
Souillac
Gorges de la Câre
Les Eyzies-de-Tayac
Vallée de la Dordogne
Beynac-et-Cazenac
Dordogne
N140
Rocamadour
Vallée de la Dordogne
Gourdon
D677
D673
Figeac
D676
N20
D19
D124
D911
Lot
Vallée du Lot
Villeneuve-sur-Lot
D102
Cahors
D911
D653
N21
D656
D17
D926
Beauville
Agen
Caussade
N113
Moissac
Gorges de l'Aveyron
Garonne
Montauban

Highways ═══ Roads ──

PARIS

Dordogne & Périgord

❶ Périgueux
❷ Lascaux
❸ Les Eyzies-de-Tayac
❹ Beynac-et-Cazenac
❺ Brive-la-Gaillarde (Varetz)
❻ Sarlat-la-Canéda
❼ Rocamadour
❽ Cahors
❾ Montauban

That means a garnish of truffles, the tastiest fungus nature ever provided. Foie gras is sometimes added as well.

Capital of the old province of Périgord, Périgueux stands on the Isle River about 70 miles east-northeast of Bordeaux and some 63 miles south and slightly west of Limoges. In addition to its food products, the region is known for its Roman ruins and medieval churches. The city is divided into three separate sections: the old Roman town or Cité, the medieval town on the slope of the hill, and to the west, the modern town.

WHAT TO SEE & DO

In the medieval quarter, known as Le Puy St-Front, rises the **Cathédrale de St-Front,** at place de la Clautre (tel. 53-53-23-62). It was built from 1125 to 1150, the last of the Aquitanian domed churches. Dedicated to St. Fronto, a local bishop, it's one of the largest churches in southwestern France. A major reconstruction took place in the 19th century, work continuing until the dawn of the 20th. Its four-story bell tower rises nearly 200 feet, overlooking the marketplace. It is surmounted by a cone-shaped spire. With its five white domes and colonnaded turrets, it evokes memories of Constantinople. The interior, somewhat bare, is built on the plan of a Greek cross, unusual for France.

Hearty visitors can apply to the sacristan (tip expected) for a tour of the roof. On this tour, you can walk between the domes and turrets, looking out over **Vieux Périgueux** with its old houses running down to the Isle.

The cathedral is open daily from 8am to noon and 2:30 to 7:30 (closes at dusk in winter). You are admitted to the crypt and cloisters, dating from the 9th century, for 10 F ($1.80).

The other remarkable church—this one lying in the Cité area on rue de la Cité (tel. 53-53-21-35)—is the **Eglise St-Etienne-de-la-Cité** (St. Stephen's in the City). This church was a cathedral until 1669 when it lost its position to St. Front. The church was built in the 12th century, but it has been much mutilated since then. It contains a 12th-century bishop's tomb and a fine carved wooden reredos of the 17th century, depicting the Assumption of the Madonna. Open daily from 8am to 5pm.

Built on the site of an Augustinian monastery, the **Musée de Périgord,** 22, cours Tourny (tel. 53-53-16-42), contains an exceptional collection of prehistoric relics as well as sculptures, Gallo-Roman mosaics, and a lapidary collection. Many of the artifacts were recovered from digs in the Périgord region, which is rich in prehistoric remains. The museum is open Wednesday through Monday from 10am to noon and 2 to 6pm; from October through March, it closes at 5pm. Admission is 10 F ($1.80) for adults, 5 F (90¢) for children.

The **Tour de Vésone** stands 85 feet tall beyond the railway station, half a mile southwest of town. The *cella* of a Roman temple dedicated to the goddess Vesuna, it is all that remains to conjure up images of ancient rites.

Jardin des Arènes, a vast, elliptical amphitheater that once held as many as 22,000 spectators, is another reminder of the days when Périgueux was a Roman town. Now in ruins, the amphitheater, with a diameter of 1,312 feet, dates from the 2nd or 3rd century. The admission-free site is open May through August, daily from 7:30am to 9pm; off-season, daily from 8am to 6pm.

Near the arena are the remains of the **Château Barrière,** rue Turenne, which was built in the 11th or 12th century on Roman foundations.

WHERE TO STAY

HOTEL BRISTOL, 37, rue Antoine-Gadaud, 24000 Périgueux. Tel. 53-08-75-90. Fax 53-07-00-49. 29 rms (all with bath). A/C TV TEL

$ Rates: 250–310 F ($45–$55.80) single; 280–340 F ($50.40–$61.20) double. Breakfast 35 F ($6.30) extra. AE, MC, V. **Parking:** Free.

This modern angular hotel (built in 1975) is centrally located behind a small parking lot, and it offers comfortable, serviceable rooms, often with sleek contemporary styling. Breakfast is the only meal served. It's only a five-minute walk from the hotel to the town's best restaurants and major points of interest.

WHERE TO DINE

LA FLAMBEE, 2, rue Montaigne. Tel. 53-53-23-06.
  Cuisine: FRENCH. **Reservations:** Recommended.
$ Prices: Appetizers 40–100 F ($7.20–$18); main dishes 75–140 F ($13.50–$25.20); fixed-price menu 125 F ($22.50). MC, V.
  Open: Lunch Mon–Sat noon–2pm; dinner Mon–Sat 6–10pm.
This restaurant is housed in a 250-year-old building with a high beamed ceiling and a staff that's been around for at least 20 years. You'll be greeted cordially here and treated to a rich cuisine of fresh local ingredients. The Thévenet family has much experience in preparing delicious food and specializes in several foie gras dishes. Other popular choices include magrêt of duck, a variety of succulent grilled fish, tournedos Rossini, and lobster from the in-house aquarium.

L'OISON, 31, rue St-Front. Tel. 53-09-84-02.
  Cuisine: FRENCH. **Reservations:** Required.
$ Prices: Appetizers 65–105 F ($11.70–$18.90); main dishes 105–210 F ($18.90–$37.80); fixed-price menus 180 F ($32.40), 260 F ($46.80), 300 F ($54), and 420 F ($75.60). AE, DC, MC, V.
  Open: Lunch Tues–Sun noon–2pm; dinner Tues–Sat 8–10pm. **Closed:** Feb 15–Mar 1 and July 1–14.
   This is one of my favorites. It's said in Périgueux that the talented chef, Régis Chiòrozas, can do more with fresh ingredients and air than anyone else in town. His *cuisine du marché* (based on market-fresh ingredients) has an exquisite lightness. The menu might include a salad of fresh truffles, jambonnette of chicken with a fumet of truffles, panaché of fish, viennoise of John Dory with artichoke hearts, and sublime desserts. In season, young partridge, roebuck, and hare are available. Local gourmets and civic leaders have flocked to this converted warehouse since the restaurant opened in 1982.

2. LASCAUX (MONTIGNAC)

308 miles SW of Paris, 29 miles SE of Périgueux

GETTING THERE By Train Train connections to Montignac are infrequent and inconvenient (there's only one train daily, from Brive).

By Bus There are bus connections from Sarlat.

By Car By far the easiest way to reach Montignac is to drive northeast from Eyzies on the N704 for 12 miles—from Eyzies, there are lots of signs to Brive.

ESSENTIALS Orientation Most of the town's hotels and restaurants lie within Montignac, whose main square, containing the tourist office, is place Betran-de-Born. Drive southwest on a road that dead-ends into the hills to see the caves at Lascaux.

Information The Syndicat d'Initiative (tourist office) is on place Bertran-de-Born (tel. 53-51-82-60), in Montignac.

The **Caves at Lascaux,** near the Vézère River town of Montignac in the Dordogne region of southwestern France, contain the most beautiful and most famous cave paintings in the world. If you were not among the fortunate thousands who got to view the actual paintings before 1963, you may be permanently out of luck. The cave drawings have been closed to the general public to prevent deterioration, but a replica gives you a clear picture of the remarkable paintings.
   They were discovered in 1940 by four boys looking for a dog and were opened to the public in 1948, quickly becoming one of France's major tourist attractions,

drawing 125,000 visitors annually. However, it became evident that the hordes of tourists had caused atmospheric changes in the caves, endangering the paintings. Scientists went to work to halt the deterioration, known as "the green sickness."

SEEING THE CAVES

Visits to **Lascaux I** are by invitation only, and people in certain professions, including those involved in museums, science, and journalism, are qualified to visit, providing they obtain permission months in advance. If you think you might qualify, you can write to: Direction des Antiquités Préhistoriques d'Aquitaine, 6 bis, cours de Gourgue, 33074 Bordeaux CEDEX (tel. 56-51-39-06).

A short walk downhill from the caves leads to **Lascaux II** (tel. 53-51-95-03), which is an impressive reproduction in concrete, molded above ground. The 131-foot-long reproduction displays some 200 paintings so that visitors will at least have some idea of what the "Sistine Chapel of prehistory" looked like. Here you can see majestic bulls, wild boars, stags, "Chinese horses," and lifelike deer, the originals of which were painted by Stone Age hunters 15,000–20,000 years ago.

Lascaux II is open in July and August, daily from 9:30am to 7pm; off-season, Tuesday through Sunday from 10am to noon and 2 to 5:30pm. It's closed from the first week of January until February 3. Admission is 45 F ($8.10) for adults, 20 F ($3.60) for children under 12. Try to show up as close to the opening time as possible—the number of visitors per day is limited to 2,000 and tickets are usually sold out within two hours of opening.

With the same ticket you can visit a museum devoted to cave art: **Le Trot** (tel. 53-50-70-44), 4½ miles from Montignac along the D706—open April through September, daily from 9:30am to 9:30pm; off-season, Tuesday through Saturday from 10am to noon and 2 to 5pm, and on Sunday from 10am to noon and 2 to 6pm. After your visit, walk out on the terrace for a view of the Vézère Valley, the Lascaux hills, and an animal park.

Near the barricaded grotto of Lascaux, a narrow road branches off to the right and goes through woods for about half a mile until it reaches **Site Préhistorique de Regourdou** (tel. 53-51-81-23). This site, discovered only in 1954, produced such finds as a jawbone and other artifacts. It can be visited April through September, daily from 9am to noon and 2 to 6pm; off-season, daily from 10 to 11:30am and 2 to 4pm. Admission is 30 F ($5.40) for adults, 15 F ($2.70) for children.

WHERE TO STAY & DINE

CHATEAU DE PUY ROBERT, route 65, 24290 Montignac Lascaux. Tel. 53-51-92-13. Fax 53-51-80-11. 33 rms (all with bath), 5 suites. MINIBAR TV TEL

$ Rates (including breakfast): 532–882 F ($95.80–$158.80) single; 760–1,260 F ($136.80–$226.80) double; 1,640 F ($295.20) suite. AE, DC, MC, V. **Parking:** Free. **Closed:** Oct 15–May 5.

Set in a 16-acre privately owned park, about a 10-minute walk from the world-famous grottoes of Lascaux, this establishment was originally built in 1860 as the country home of a wealthy merchant. The handsomely furnished and comfortable bedrooms offer views of the Vézère Valley, and on the premises is an outdoor swimming pool; mountain bikes are available for clients who want them.

The in-house restaurant produces imaginative dishes using fresh local ingredients. Specialties change with the season, with fixed-price menus priced at 185–360 F ($33.30–$64.80). Both the restaurant and the hotel lie about half a mile west of the center of Montignac village.

SOLEIL D'OR, 16, rue du 4-Septembre, 24290 Montignac Lascaux. Tel. 53-51-80-22. Fax 53-50-27-54. 28 rms (all with bath or shower), 4 suites. MINIBAR TV TEL

$ Rates: 270 F ($48.60) single; 290–380 F ($52.20–$68.40) double; 600 F ($108) suite. Breakfast 40 F ($7.20) extra. AE, MC, V. **Parking:** Free. **Closed:** Jan 5–Feb 15.

Set in the heart of Montignac village, this solidly built structure functioned during the 1800s as a relay station for the French postal system, offering food and lodgings to both travelers and horses. Today, much renovated and improved, it offers comfortable and traditionally furnished bedrooms. Facilities include an outdoor swimming pool, a lushly landscaped garden, a pub, and two restaurants. The less formal of these (Le Bistrot) offers salads, snacks, and simple platters of food priced at around 50 F ($9) each. The Restaurant serves traditional Dordogne food (blanquettes of veal and daubes of beef) as part of fixed-price meals which cost 110–350 F ($19.80–$63) each.

3. LES EYZIES-DE-TAYAC

331 miles SW of Paris, 28 miles SE of Périgueux

GETTING THERE   By Train   Local trains run from nearby Le Buisson, which has connections from larger cities like Bordeaux. The several daily trains from Périgueux are more direct.

ESSENTIALS   Orientation   The town has only one important street, containing most of the civic monuments. The famous caves, most notably the Font-de-Gaume and the Grotte des Combarelles, begin about a mile northeast of town, on the D47.

Information   The Office de Tourisme, place de la Mairie (tel. 53-06-97-05), is open from March to October only.

When prehistoric skeletons were unearthed in 1868, the market town of Les Eyzies was launched as an archeologist's dream. This area in the Dordogne Valley was found to be one of the richest in the world in ancient sites and deposits. Little by little, more and more caves were discovered in the region. In some of these caves our early ancestors had made primitive drawings going back some 30,000 years, the most beautiful and most famous, of course, at Lascaux. Many caves around Les Eyzies are open to the public.

WHAT TO SEE & DO

For a quick orientation, visit the **Musée National de Préhistoire.** Even if your time is limited, I suggest that you see at least one of the many caves in the area. Start with the Grotte du Grand-Roc. If you plan to see several caves, you might as well stay over and become an amateur archeologist.

MUSEE NATIONAL DE PREHISTOIRE. Tel. 53-06-97-03.

Prehistoric artifacts from local excavations are on display in a fortress castle dating from the end of the 16th century. The castle is on a cliff overlooking Les Eyzies and was once inhabited by the barons de Beynac. On the terrace is a statue of Neanderthal man created by Darde in 1930. One building displays a reconstructed Magdalenian tomb containing a woman's skeleton.

Admission: 17 F ($3.10) adults, 11 F ($2) ages 18–25, free for children under 18.
Open: Wed–Mon 9:30am–noon and 2–6pm (to 5pm Dec–Mar).

The Caves

GROTTE DE FONT-DE-GAUME. Tel. 53-06-97-48.

This cave allows only a small group of visitors daily (my group contained 12). Unfortunately, some of those markings you see were not from the Magdalenian ages, but from British students on a holiday back in the 18th century. Here bison, reindeer, and horses, along with other animals, reveal the skill of the prehistoric artists. The paintings are not as well preserved as those at Lascaux. Note that unless you show up very early or in off-season, it may be impossible to get a ticket to look at these remarkable drawings. In season, demand far exceeds the supply of tickets.

Admission: 31 F ($5.60) adults, 17 F ($3.10) ages 18–25 and over 60, 6 F ($1.10) children 7–17, free for children under 7.

Open: Apr–Sept, Wed–Mon 9am–noon and 2–6pm; Oct–Mar, Wed–Mon 10am–noon and 2–4pm.

GROTTE DES COMBARELLES. Tel. 53-06-97-72.

Discovered at the turn of the century, this cave has many drawings of animals, including musk oxen, horses, bison, and aurochs. Think of it as a gallery of Magdalenian art. To get here, take the D47. Guided tours are available.

Admission: 25 F ($4.50) adults, 14 F ($2.50) ages 18–25 and over 60, 6 F ($1.10) children 7–17, free for children under 7.

Open: Apr–Sept, Wed–Mon 9am–noon and 2–6pm; Oct–Mar, Wed–Mon 10am–noon and 2–4pm.

GROTTE DU GRAND-ROC [Cave of the Big Rock]. Tel. 53-06-92-70.

This is the most interesting cave. After you enter, there is a tunnel of stalagmites and stalactites. The cave is northwest of the market town on the left bank of the Vézère (signs point the way on the D47).

Admission: 30 F ($5.40) adults, 13 F ($2.30) children.

Open: June–Sept, daily 9am–7pm; off-season, daily 9:30am–6pm. **Closed:** Nov 11–Mar 30.

WHERE TO STAY & DINE

LE CENTENAIRE, Rocher de la Penne, 24620 Les Eyzies-Tayac-Sireuil. Tel. 53-06-97-18. Fax 53-06-92-41. 22 rms (all with bath), 5 suites. MINIBAR TV TEL

$ Rates: 400 F ($72) single; 600–900 F ($108–$162) double; 1,200–1,500 F ($216–$270) suite. Breakfast 67 F ($12.10) extra. DC, MC, V. **Parking:** Free. **Closed:** Early Nov to late Mar.

Extensive renovation and smart decorating have made this a charming hotel with handsome rooms. The hotel offers a heated swimming pool, health club, and shopping gallery. The talented chef, Roland Mazère, creates a light, modern French cuisine. The menu might include fresh foie gras in a terrine; a brochette of fresh salmon (May to September only); noisettes d'agneau (lamb); young hare with a purée of onions; a ragoût of sweetbreads, brains, crayfish, and a variety of mushrooms known as mousseron; and lobster with truffles. Service is efficient. Fixed-price menus cost 230 F ($41.40), 350 F ($63), and 480 F ($86.40).

CRO-MAGNON, route de Périgueux, 24620 Les Eyzies-Tayac-Sireuil. Tel. 53-06-97-06. Fax 53-06-95-45. 18 rms (all with bath), 4 suites. TEL

$ Rates (including half board): 400–510 F ($72–$91.80) per person. AE, DC, MC, V. **Parking:** Free. **Closed:** Oct 10 to late Apr.

Modern and attractive despite its name, the Cro-Magnon contains a lovely, spacious garden with a swimming pool and a shaded dining terrace. The warmly decorated rooms, 10 of which have TVs, have modern amenities while still managing to evoke the past. The owner, Jacques Leysales, and his kitchen staff produce exceptionally good food. Even if you're not staying here, reserve a table to enjoy a fixed-price menu for 130–350 F ($23.40–$63). Specialties include a terrine of foie gras, zander with truffles, and aiguillettes of duckling. Choice wines include Callever and Clos-de-Gamot.

LES GLYCINES, route de Périgueux (D47), 24620 Les Eyzies-Tayac-Sireuil. Tel. 53-06-97-07. Fax 53-06-92-19. 25 rms (all with bath). TEL

$ Rates: 298–377 F ($53.60–$67.90) single; 340–390 F ($61.20–$70.20) double. Half board 380–420 F ($68.40–$75.60) per person. AE, MC, V. **Parking:** Free. **Closed:** Early Nov to late Mar.

Since 1862 this establishment has presented substantial regional cuisine, comfortable accommodations, and dozens of charming touches. It is named for the wisteria (*les glycines*) that fills parts of the garden. Drinks are served on an outdoor veranda with a grape arbor. Henri and Christiane Mercat are the hard-working owners of this four-acre garden inn with a swimming pool. In the restaurant, specialties include eminceé of goose en confit. Fixed-price menus go for 135 F ($24.30), 180 F ($32.40), and 270 F ($48.60).

**HOTEL DU CENTRE, place de la Mairie, 24620 Les Eyzies-Tayac-Sireuil.
Tel. 53-06-97-13.** Fax 53-06-91-63. 20 rms (all with bath). TEL
$ Rates: 265–285 F ($47.70–$51.30) single or double. Breakfast 34 F ($6.10) extra. MC, V. **Parking:** Free. **Closed:** Mid-Nov to March.

Enjoy the rustic setting and riverside garden at this hotel. Gérard Brun offers comfortable, provincial rooms. The cooking is unusually good, and Monsieur Brun probably serves the best fixed-price menus in town for 85–340 F ($15.30–$61.20). Specialties include aiguillettes of duck with cèpes (flap mushrooms), assiette périgourdine, ragoût of seafood, and soufflé aux noix. In season, enjoy your meal on a shaded terrace.

4. BEYNAC-ET-CAZENAC

341 miles SW of Paris, 39 miles E of Bergerac

GETTING THERE **By Car** From Brive le Gaillarde, head south on Rte. 20 to Souillac, then cut west along a secondary road to Sarlat-la-Canéda, where the minor road to Beynac is signposted.

ESSENTIALS **Orientation** Built high above a particularly scenic bend in the river, the village is dominated by its clifftop château.

Information The nearest tourist office is at 97, rue Neuve-d'Argenson at Bergerac (tel. 53-57-03-11).

Rising from the summit of a rocky plateau, the **Château of Beynac** dominates the village at its feet. From its terraces a panoramic view of the Dordogne Valley unfolds. The most agile can reach it by foot. Others prefer to take the road, which circles around for about a mile and a half before coming to the castle. The keep is from the 13th century. The aristocracy of Périgord used to assemble in the Grand Hall, with its ogival vaulting. In the oratory are some Gothic frescoes of *The Last Supper*—not da Vinci, but interesting nevertheless. Although the castle is a curiosity, it is really the view that makes it worth the climb.

The château is open daily from March 1 to November 15: from 10am to noon and 2:30pm to 5pm in March, to 5:30pm in April, to 6:30pm from May to September, to 5pm in October, and to 4:30pm in November. Admission is 24 F ($4.30) for adults, 10 F ($1.80) for children.

WHERE TO STAY & DINE

HOTEL BONNET, 24220 Beynac-et-Cazenac. Tel. 53-29-50-01. 21 rms (all with bath). TEL
$ Rates: 235 F ($42.30) single; 300 F ($54) double. Breakfast 30 F ($5.40) extra. MC, V. **Parking:** Free. **Closed:** Mid-Oct to Mar.

This is a secret address in the Dordogne treasured by the English for decades and also known to novelist Henry Miller. The atmosphere created by Renée Bonner is casual and relaxed, and most guests are content to do nothing. There is a salon where cards and games are sometimes played. Rooms are pleasantly furnished and comfortable. If you don't mind the traffic noise, request a front room with a river view.

The hotel also has a bar and restaurant. If you're driving through Dordogne, dine above the river on a creeper-covered terrace after you've had a stroll in the garden. I recently ordered crudités and was amazed by the appetizing selection that arrived at the table. Included were large flap mushrooms sautéed with garlic and herbs, celeriac cut julienne and served with a velvety rémoulade sauce, a bright-green artichoke in a vinaigrette sauce, plus marinated beets, green and red peppers, eggplant ratatouille, and cauliflower. Try such specialties as a confit de canard (duckling), herb-seasoned roast of lamb, tournedos gourmandine with a Périgueux sauce, and truffles en croûte. Fixed-price menus run 120 F ($21.60), 200 F ($36), and 260 F ($46.80).

5. BRIVE-LA-GAILLARDE (VARETZ)

302 miles SW of Paris, 56 miles S of Limoges

GETTING THERE   Brive has rail, bus, and highway connections from all other parts of France as it lies at the intersection of the Paris–Spain and Bordeaux–Lyon rail lines. The local airport, Laroche, is three miles west of the town center.

ESSENTIALS   Orientation   About a half mile south of the Corrèze River, the city center is built in a circular pattern around the Eglise St-Martin. A few blocks east is the beautiful Hôtel de Labenche, the town museum. Varetz is 6½ miles northwest of Brive on the D152.

Information   The Office de Tourisme is on place du 14-Juillet (tel. 55-24-08-80).

Three of the old provinces of France—Limousin, Quercy, and Périgord—met near here. At the crossroads, Brive the "bold" is an inviting town, with its memories of the renowned French novelist Colette, who lived nearby when she was the wife of Henri de Jouvenel (see the Château de Castel-Novel in "Where to Stay," below). An important gastronomic center, Brive is a land of fine fruits, truffles, vegetables, and liqueurs, and in some of its shops you can buy a uniquely flavored local mustard cherished by gastronomes.

In the town center is the **Musée de Brive,** Hôtel de Labenche, 26 bis, bd. Jules Ferry (tel. 55-24-19-05). The 16th-century residence that houses it is considered one of the most beautiful monuments of Brive. The art collections inside include objects from the prehistoric and Gallo-Roman periods, paintings, folk art, natural-history exhibits, and mementos of Brive's celebrated native daughters and sons.

The museum is open April to October, Wednesday through Sunday from 10am to 6:30pm; closed at 6pm during off-season. Admission is 24 F ($4.30) for adults, free for children under 16.

Nearby is the **Eglise St-Martin,** place de Gaulle (tel. 55-24-10-82), which is a hodgepodge of architectural styles, with a Romanesque transept and 14th-century aisles. Open daily from 9am to 5pm.

WHERE TO STAY

CHATEAU DE CASTEL NOVEL, 19240 Varetz. Tel. 55-85-00-01. 31 rms (all with bath), 5 suites. TV TEL **Directions:** Take the D901 6½ miles northwest of Brive to a location half a mile outside Varetz.

$ Rates: 460–1,230 F ($82.80–$221.40) single; 560–1,330 F ($100.80–$239.40) double; 1,480 F ($266.40) suite. Breakfast 60 F ($10.80) extra. AE, DC, MC, V. **Parking:** Free. **Closed:** Oct 17–May 15.

The spirit of Colette lives on in this isolated old château set on 25 acres of parkland. The French novelist often lived here when she was married to Henri de Jouvenel and drew many of the political and literary luminaries of her day to Varetz. The château, which stands on a broad plateau near the Vézère, was also owned by the Vicomte de Limoges. The towers once housed the lords of Aubusson. The château was built in the 1300s and enlarged into its present form just before the French Revolution.

Today this Relais & Château is run by Albert R. Parveaux. Ten new rooms are in an annex, La Borderie, each with minibar and air conditioning. Colette's library has been turned into a charming salon, and the old stables have been converted into a banqueting hall.

Dining/Entertainment: In summer, lunch is prepared on a grill near the pool. In the restaurant, the cuisine includes such temptations as three fish in a roquefort-cream sauce, duckling stuffed with sorrel, a ragoût of foie gras and truffles, and a salad made with cèpes (flap mushrooms) and gizzards. Fixed-price menus go for 155–315 F ($27.90–$56.70) at lunch and 165–370 F ($29.70–$66.60) at dinner. Reservations are required.

Facilities: Swimming pool, tennis courts, three-hole golf course, park for jogging and bicycling.

HOTEL IBIS, 32, rue Marcellin-Roche, 19100 Brive-la-Gaillarde. Tel. 55-74-34-70. Fax 55-23-54-41. 48 rms (all with bath). TV TEL
$ Rates: 275 F ($49.50) single; 300 F ($54) double. Breakfast 33 F ($5.90) extra. MC, V. **Parking:** Free.
About a five-minute walk from the town center, adjacent to the banks of the river (La Corèze), this four-story hotel was built in the 1970s. Since then, after several management changes, it has borne three different names, currently Hotel Ibis. Bedrooms are modern, chain-hotel standardized, neutrally decorated, and comfortable. Although no meals are served other than breakfast, the staff maintains a cooperative arrangement with a pleasant inn three buildings away (l'Auberge Inn) where fixed-price meals cost 72–155 F ($13–$27.90). The hotel maintains a bar on the premises.

WHERE TO DINE

LA CREMAILLERE, 53, av. de Paris, 19100 Brive. Tel. 55-74-32-47.
Cuisine: FRENCH. **Reservations:** Required.
$ Prices: Appetizers 75–110 F ($13.50–$19.80); main dishes 110–175 F ($19.80–$31.50); fixed-price menus 100 F ($18), 140 F ($25.20), 180 F ($32.40), and 220 F ($39.60). MC, V.
Open: Lunch Tues–Sun 12:30–1:30pm; dinner Tues–Sat 7:30–9:30pm.
Charles Reynal is winning increasing acclaim as a versatile and inventive chef. He knows how to take local produce and transform it into award-winning dishes. Specialties are egg in a coddler with a purée of truffles and morels, flan of flap mushrooms with a sauce of morels, sliced filet of duck with cassisberry sauce, and puff pastry with marinated prunes and plum liqueur.

Eight well-furnished rooms, all of which have a bath or shower, TV, and phone, also are available, costing 250–290 F ($45–$52.20) single or double.

NEARBY ATTRACTIONS

If you have a car, I suggest that you head south of Brive on the D38 until you reach the "red village" of **Collonges.** This tiny hamlet contains petite mansions built of dark-red stone, including one corbelled house from the 16th century dedicated to the Siren. The church nearby is Romanesque, built in the 11th and 12th centuries, with a belfry in the Limousin style.

After leaving Collonges, you can continue south, passing the Puy Rouge, until you reach **Meyssac,** which is also built of red sandstone, known as "Collonges clay." The people of the village make a pottery out of this clay. The village is charming, with wooden buildings, some with porch roofs, and antique towers.

From Meyssac, you can take the D14 which becomes the D96 until you reach the intersection with the D20. Take the D20, which becomes the D8, leading north to Brive again. On the way back, you might like to stop at the tiny village of **Turenne,** its old houses giving you a sleepy look at long-ago provincial France.

From there, continue along the D8, passing through Nazareth, until you connect with the D158 leading to **Noailles.** On a hillside, the Noailles church with its Limousin-style bell tower dominates the rolling green countryside. From Noailles, it's just a short drive back into Brive.

6. SARLAT-LA-CANEDA

334 miles SW of Paris, 32 miles SW of Brive-la-Gaillarde

GETTING THERE By Train Passengers must transfer in Souillac (from Toulouse or Brive) or Le Buisson. Connections from Souillac are more frequent and easier than from Le Buisson. Depending on the schedule, it's sometime possible to ride by SNCF bus to Sarlat from either of those connecting rail stations.

ESSENTIALS Orientation Sarlat is a well-preserved medieval gem, with the sole exception of the modern La Traverse (rue de la République), which bisects its center. One of the most picturesque streets is the rue des Consuls.

Information For information, inquire at the Office de Tourisme, place de la Liberté (tel. 53-59-27-67). The office will give you a map, detailing the most outstanding attractions. Allow about two hours (without stopovers) for a complete tour.

SPECIAL EVENTS The best time to arrive is on Saturday morning, in time for the market at place des Oies (geese). There are open-air performances in August at the Sarlat Festival, but rooms are impossible to find at that time.

The capital of "Black Périgord" (or Périgord Noir in French) is a town from the Middle Ages, beautifully preserved. Most writers who visit it always report that it's a "living museum." The townspeople have worked for the past two decades to restore their age-old houses, mostly built of ochre stone, which close in like sheets in the wind along narrow, winding cobblestone streets, which are lit by lanterns.

Old Sarlat, called Vieille-Ville, has a main street, rue de la République, which is very commercial and not of tourist interest. But don't judge Sarlat by that. Its history goes back to Gallo-Roman times. It's had a town charter since 1298, and at the time of Charlemagne it was an ecclesiastical center of some note. Its fame reached a zenith in the 14th century, when it was known in France as a bustling center of artisans, painters, and students.

The **Cathédrale de St-Sacerdos,** on place du Peyrou (tel. 53-59-03-16), is a major attraction and a good starting point for your tour. As early as 1317 it was an episcopal seat, losing that distinction in 1790. The church has a Romanesque bell tower, but most of the structure is from the 16th and 17th centuries. Much of the interior is in the late Gothic style.

Nearby on place André-Malraux is the **Maison de la Boétie,** a charming Renaissance house, the finest in Sarlat. It dates from 1525 and was once inhabited by the town's most famous son, Etienne de La Boétie, who was born five years after the house was completed. A criminal magistrate, he had a close, lifelong friendship with Montaigne. Montaigne was at La Boétie's bedside when he died in 1563, and that death inspired Montaigne's essay on "Friendship." The house is studded with mullioned windows and has a painted gable.

The Maison de la Boétie is now the seat of the Chambre de Commerce et d'Industrie; sometimes small exhibitions are staged on its ground floor.

The town has, naturally, an architectural curiosity called **Lanterne des Morts,** or lantern to the dead. A 12th-century tower, characterized by a tall cone-shaped roof, it is supposedly the oldest structure in Sarlat. Its appearance has been compared to that of a beehive.

For the most part you will not need to seek out more than the obligatory landmarks. All of Sarlat makes for an interesting tour. You can even allow yourself to get lost, as you'll invariably wind up back at place de la Liberté, the heart of town.

WHERE TO STAY & DINE

HOTEL ST-ALBERT ET MONTAIGNE, 10, place Pasteur, 24200 Sarlat-la-Canéda. Tel. 53-31-55-55. Fax 53-59-19-99. 61 rms (all with bath or shower). TV TEL

$ Rates: 230 F ($41.40) single; 310 F ($55.80) double. Breakfast 40 F ($7.20) extra. AE, DC, MC, V.

The Hôtel St-Albert is near the post office and the entrance to the old city. Built in 1850, this inn was a popular stopover on the coaching route. Since 1940 the Garrigou family has continued the tradition, attracting many motorists. Today Jean-Michel and his wife, Mireille, labor to keep regional culinary traditions alive and well. Decor is modern with a handful of regional accessories. The furniture is streamlined. The same management also runs the Hôtel Montaigne, an annex in a modernized but traditional building that once welcomed the great Montaigne. Guests at the Hôtel Montaigne dine at the St-Albert.

The hotel's restaurant offers sumptuous platters, with a homemade flavor and Périgourdine authenticity. Fresh ingredients go into such specialties as stuffed cabbage, poule au pot, truffle soufflé, five different preparations of homemade foie gras (with or without truffles), and a succulent grilled and garnished breast of duckling. Juicy beef and lamb dishes also are featured. Meals cost 110–230 F ($19.80–$41.40). The restaurant is closed Sunday night from November 1 to Easter and on Monday.

LA MADELEINE, 1, place de la Petite-Riguadie, 24200 Sarlat-la-Canéda. Tel. 53-59-10-41. Fax 53-31-03-62. 19 rms (all with bath or shower). A/C MINIBAR TV TEL
$ Rates: 325 F ($58.50) single; 400 F ($72) double. Half board 380–460 F ($68.40–$82.80) per person. MC, V. **Closed:** Nov 15–Mar 12.

This centrally located landmark of local hotels is solidly constructed, with plenty of no-nonsense charm. Most rooms are spacious. The old-world dining room is supervised by the chef and owner, Philippe Melot. He specializes in the traditional rich dishes, incorporating the abundance of local ingredients. Such dishes include ragoût of duckling with red wine, foie gras, sweetbreads with morels, and flavorful sauces, rich with truffles, cèpes, and wild mushrooms. Fixed-price menus cost 130–295 F ($23.40–$53.10). Dine on the outdoor terrace in fair weather. The restaurant closes at 9pm.

WHERE TO DINE

HOSTELLERIE MARCEL, 8, av. de Selves. Tel. 53-59-21-98.
Cuisine: FRENCH. **Reservations:** Required.
$ Prices: Appetizers 25–110 F ($4.50–$19.80); main dishes 45–120 F ($8.10–$21.60); fixed-price menus 88–210 F ($15.80–$37.80). MC, V.
Open: July–Aug, lunch daily noon–2pm; dinner daily 7–9pm. Off-season, lunch Tues–Sun noon–2pm; dinner Tues–Sun 7–9pm. **Closed:** Nov 15–Feb 15.

This restaurant was established during the closing days of World War II by M and Mme Marcel Clerot, in a simple family homestead on the northern perimeter of town. Today, along with memories of the France of long ago, you can enjoy such dishes as shish kebab with sorrel, sweetbreads Périgueux, stuffed goose neck, confit of duckling, and an unusual collection of tasty desserts.

NEARBY ACCOMMODATIONS & DINING

HOSTELLERIE DE MEYSSET, route des Eyzies, 24200 Sarlat-la-Canéda. Tel. 53-59-08-29. Fax 53-28-47-61. 22 rms (all with bath), 4 suites. TEL
$ Rates (including half board): 524 F ($94.30) single; 850 F ($153) double; 1,070 F ($192.60) suite for two. AE, DC, MC, V. **Parking:** Free. **Closed:** Oct 10–Apr 27.
Charming and comfortable, this hotel was built in a three-acre private park in 1970, in a location about two miles north of the center of Sarlat. Despite its recent construction, most visitors think it's much older than it is thanks to its respect for local architectural traditions. The traditionally furnished bedrooms, scattered over two floors, sometimes have doors leading into private gardens, or, in other cases, highly appealing views over the surrounding countryside. Meals are served either inside or on an expansive terrace outdoors. (No lunch is served on Wednesday.)

Fixed-price menus cost 165 F ($29.70) for a classic French menu, or 250 F ($45) for a *menu gastronomique* whose multiple courses elegantly represent the culinary traditions of the region.

HOTEL LA HOIRIE, route D704, 24200 Sarlat-la-Canéda. Tel. 53-59-05-62. Fax 53-59-05-62. 15 rms (all with bath or shower). TV TEL

$ Rates: 320 F ($57.60) single; 520 F ($93.60) double. Breakfast 45 F ($8.10) extra. AE, DC, MC, V. **Parking:** Free. **Closed:** Nov 15–Mar 14.

This charming, old-fashioned house about 1¼ miles south of Sarlat was originally used as a hunting lodge. Today the Sainneville de Vienne family offers comfortable accommodations and a salon with stone walls, ceiling beams, and a massive hearth. There also are a flower garden and an outdoor swimming pool. A superb restaurant serves dinners for 130–290 F ($23.40–$52.20).

---

7. ROCAMADOUR

336 miles SW of Paris, 41 miles SE of Sarlat-la-Canéda,
34 miles S of Brive, 39 miles NE of Cahors

GETTING THERE Rocamadour and neighboring Padirac share a train station that isn't really convenient to either town—it's several miles east of Rocamadour, serviced by infrequent trains from Brive in the north and Capdenac in the south. Most visitors avoid the inconvenience and drive.

ESSENTIALS Orientation Rocamadour's lower town is laid out on either side of a single street. From place de la Carreta is a stairway (Le Grand Escalier) which leads to the panoramic Parvis des Eglises.

Information The Office de Tourisme, à la Mairie (tel. 65-33-62-59), is open from March to November only.

The Middle Ages seem to live on here as they do in Sarlat. After all, Rocamadour reached the zenith of its fame and prosperity in the 13th century. Make an effort to see it even if it's out of your way. The setting is striking, one of the most unusual in Europe. Towers, old buildings, and oratories rise in stages up the side of a cliff on the right slope of the usually dry gorge of Alzou.

WHAT TO SEE & DO

The gravity-defying village, with its single street (lined with souvenir shops), is boldly constructed. It is seen at its best when approached from the road coming in from the tiny village of L'Hospitalet. Once in Rocamadour, you can take a flight of steps from the lower town to the churches halfway up the cliff. The less agile would be advised to take the elevator instead, at a cost of 10 F ($1.80) for a round-trip ticket.

The entrance to the village is through the Porte de Figuier (Fig Tree Gate), through which many of the most illustrious Europeans of the 13th century passed. One of the oldest places of pilgrimage in France, Rocamadour became famous as a cult center of the black Madonna. The village was supposedly founded by Zacchaeus who entertained Christ at Jericho. He is claimed to have come to Rocamadour with a small black wooden statue of the Virgin, although some authorities have suggested that this statue was actually carved in the 9th century.

At place de la Carreta is the entrance to the **Grand Escalier** (stairway) leading to the ecclesiastical center at the top, a climb of 216 steps. Even today, pilgrims make this difficult journey on their knees in penance. If you make it, you'll arrive at the **Parvis des Eglises,** place St-Amadour, with its seven chapels. Guided tours of the chapels are conducted daily except Sunday, June 1 to September 15 from 9am to 6pm.

The **Musée-Tresor,** Parvis du Sanctuaire (tel. 65-33-63-29), contains a gold chalice presented by Pope Pius II, among other treasures. The museum is open in July and August, daily from 9am to 6:30pm; April through June and September through

October, daily from 9am to noon and 2 to 6pm. Admission is 12 F ($2.20) for adults, 6 F ($1.10) for children.

Against the cliff, the **Basilica of St. Savior,** place St-Amadour, was built in the Romanesque-Gothic style from the 11th to the 13th centuries. It is decorated with paintings and inscriptions, recalling visits of celebrated persons, including Philippe the Handsome.

In the **Chapelle Miraculeuse,** the "holy of holies," the mysterious St. Amadour (believed to be the publican, Zacchaeus) is said to have carved out an oratory in the rock. Hanging from the roof of this chapel is one of the oldest clocks known, dating from the 4th century. Above the altar is the venerated statue of the Madonna.

The **Chapel of St-Michel** was built in the Romanesque style and is sheltered by an overhanging rock. Inside are two frescoes that are rich in coloring, dating (perhaps) from the 12th century.

Above the door leading to the **Chapelle Notre-Dame** is a large iron sword that, according to legend, belonged to Roland. Open daily from 9am to 5pm.

Built on a cliff spur and now inhabited by chaplains, the **château** was medieval before its restoration. It is reached by the curvy chemin de Croix Blanche. It was originally built for the defense of the holy sanctuaries but was unable to keep out the pillaging hordes over the centuries. The château is only of minor interest, but the view from its ramparts is spectacular. It is open July 1 until the end of August, daily from 9am to 7pm; off-season, daily from 9am to noon and 1:30 to 6pm. Admission is 6.50 F ($1.20) for adults, 4.50 F (80¢) for children under 18.

WHERE TO STAY & DINE

BEAU-SITE ET NOTRE-DAME, rue Roland-le-Preux, 46500 Rocamadour. Tel. 65-33-63-08. Fax 65-33-65-23. 42 rms (all with bath), 2 suites. TV TEL

$ Rates: 340 F ($61.20) single; 460 F ($82.80) double; 650 F ($117) suite. Breakfast 49 F ($8.80) extra. AE, DC, MC, V. **Parking:** Free. **Closed:** Nov 12–Apr 1.

The stone walls were built in the 15th century by an Order of Malta commander. Today the rear terrace provides visitors with a sweeping view of the Val d'Alzou. The reception area has heavy beams and a cavernous fireplace big enough to roast an ox. The hotel abounds with modern globe lights and medieval touches. Rooms in the main building and annex are comfortable, and four are air-conditioned.

The restaurant serves flavorful, regional cuisine prepared by members of the Menot family, who have owned the place for many generations. Specialties include sautéed lamb with mustard flowers served with an eggplant flan, duckmeat salad, raw marinated salmon with green peppercorns, a combination of sea bass with crayfish tails in an anise-flavored butter sauce, and a dessert soufflé of caramelized walnuts. Fixed-price menus run 95–250 F ($17.10–$45).

SAINTE-MARIE, place des Senahles, 46500 Rocamadour. Tel. 65-33-63-07. Fax 65-33-69-08. 22 rms (all with bath). TEL

$ Rates: 160–180 F ($28.80–$32.40) single; 240 F ($43.20) double. Breakfast 30 F ($5.40) extra. MC, V. **Parking:** Free. **Closed:** Oct 10–Apr 10.

This enchanting little house has an old-world ambience. Rooms are comfortable and charming, with modern conveniences. The restaurant serves good meals and offers an unusually fine view of Sainte-Marie from the terrace. Fixed-price menus go for 65–270 F ($11.70–$48.60).

NEARBY ACCOMMODATIONS & DINING

CHATEAU DE ROMEGOUSE, N140, Rignac, 46500 Gramat. Tel. 65-33-63-81. 14 rms (all with bath), 2 suites. MINIBAR TV TEL **Directions:** Take the N140 to Roumégouse, 2½ miles southeast of Rocamadour.

$ Rates: 520 F ($93.60) single; 790–940 F ($142.20–$169.20) double; 1,050–1,280 F ($189–$230.40) suite. Breakfast 60 F ($10.80) extra. AE, DC, MC, V. **Parking:** Free. **Closed:** Nov 9–Apr 7.

If you prefer to be away from the tourist bustle of Rocamadour, try this Relais & Château in Roumégouse. The 15th-century château overlooking the Causse is surrounded by a 12-acre wooded parkland. The ambience is private and elegant. Each room is unique, in both architecture and decor. The dining room is lovely and well preserved. Fixed-price menus cost 170–320 F ($30.60–$57.60). The restaurant is closed Tuesday at lunch and from December until the end of March.

8. CAHORS

336 miles SW of Paris, 135 miles SE of Bordeaux, 55 miles N of Toulouse

GETTING THERE Cahors is serviced by train from Toulouse, Brive, and Montauban. You may have to transfer in neighboring towns. There is infrequent bus service from some of the outlying villages, several of which are of historical interest, but it's vastly easier to drive.

ESSENTIALS Orientation The old town is surrounded on three sides by an abrupt bend in the Lot River. Most traffic enters the old town via its southernmost bridge, Pont Louis-Philippe, and heads north on boulevard Gambetta. The heavily fortified Cathédrale de St-Etienne is near the river, east of boulevard Gambetta.

Information The Office de Tourisme is on place Aristide-Briand (tel. 65-35-09-56).

The ancient capital of Quercy, Cahors was a thriving university city in the Middle Ages, and many antiquities of its illustrious past life still remain. However, Cahors is known today mainly for its almost-legendary red wine that is made principally from the Malbec grapes grown in vineyards around this old city, 55 miles north of Toulouse in central France. Firm but not harsh, Cahors is considered one of the most deeply colored of fine French wines.

The town lies on a rocky peninsula almost entirely surrounded by a loop of the Lot River. It grew up near a sacred spring, which, incidentally, still supplies the city with water. At the source of the spring, the **Fontaine des Chartreux** stands by the side of the **pont Valentré** (also called the pont du Diable), a bridge with a trio of towers, a magnificent example of medieval defensive design erected between 1308 and 1380, then much restored in the 19th century. The pont, the first medieval fortified bridge in France, is the most colorful site in Cahors, with its crenellated parapets, its battlements, and its seven pointed arches.

Dominating the old town, the **Cathédrale de St-Etienne,** 30, rue de la Chanterie (tel. 65-35-27-80), was built in 1119 but reconstructed in part between 1285 and 1500. It appears to be a fortress and was the first cathedral in the country to have cupolas, giving it a Romanesque-Byzantine look. One of the most remarkable features is its finely sculptured north portal, a Romanesque door carved about 1135 in the Languedoc style. Adjoining the cathedral are the remains of a Gothic cloister from the latter part of the 15th century.

Cahors is a starting point for an excursion to the **Célé and Lot Valleys,** a long journey that many French people are fond of taking in the summer, a round-trip of about 125 miles, lasting some two days if you have plenty of time for sightseeing. The Office du Tourisme (see "Essentials," above) provides maps giving itineraries.

WHERE TO STAY

FRANCE, 252, av. Jean-Jaurès, 46000 Cahors. Tel. 65-35-16-76. Fax 65-22-01-08. 79 rms (all with bath or shower). MINIBAR TEL
$ Rates: 210 F ($37.80) single; 360 F ($64.80) double. Breakfast 35 F ($6.30) extra. AE, DC, MC, V. **Parking:** 40 F ($7.20). **Closed:** Dec 18–Jan 4.
This hotel, conveniently located at the train station, provides the best rooms in the town center. They are well furnished and well equipped, 38 with air conditioning. Room service is efficient. Breakfast is the only meal served.

HOTEL TERMINUS, 5, av. Charles-de-Freycinet, 46000 Cahors. Tel. 65-35-24-50. Fax 65-22-06-40. 30 rms (all with bath). TV TEL
$ Rates: 255–390 F ($45.90–$70.20) single; 260–415 F ($46.80–$74.70) double. Breakfast 35 F ($6.30) extra. MC, V. **Parking:** Free in open courtyard, 25 F ($4.50) in covered garage.

In many ways, this is probably the most solidly entrenched hotel in town. Set on the avenue leading from the railway station into the heart of town, it was built in 1906 and still oozes the turn-of-the-century character of its original stone construction. Bedrooms are conservative and comfortable, and have been renovated several times since their original creation.

On the premises of the hotel, under a completely different management, is a well-recommended restaurant, Le Balandre. Even if you don't opt for one of the well-prepared meals in its art deco dining room or on its outdoor terrace, you might want to step into its 1920s-style bar for a drink. Fixed-price meals cost 130–300 F ($23.40–$54). Unlike the hotel, the restaurant accepts AE.

WHERE TO DINE

LA TAVERNE, place Escorbiac. Tel. 65-35-28-66.
   Cuisine: FRENCH. **Reservations:** Recommended.
$ Prices: Appetizers 36–120 F ($6.50–$21.60); main dishes 75–390 F ($13.50–$70.20); fixed-price menus 125 F ($22.50), 185 F ($33.30), and 250 F ($45). AE, MC, V.
   Open: Lunch Thurs–Tues noon–2pm; dinner Thurs–Tues 7–9:30pm. **Closed:** Feb 28–Mar 13.

This restaurant serves outstanding local cuisine in a rustic atmosphere. The cuisine of Quercy is featured here, along with other regional specialties. Typical dishes include truffles in puff pastry, tournedos with foie gras and truffles, duck filet, breast of chicken with morels, and fresh fish.

AN EXCURSION TO GROTTE DU PECH-MERLE

Grotte du Pech-Merle (tel. 65-31-27-05), the prehistoric cave near Cabrerets, some 21 miles east of Cahors, was once used for ancient religious rites. The wall paintings, footprints, and carvings were discovered in 1922 and are approximately 20,000 years old. The cave may be explored Easter through the end of October, daily from 9:30am to noon and 1:30 to 5pm. Admission is 42 F ($7.60) for adults, 18 F ($3.20) for children. There are two miles of chambers and galleries open to the public. Aurignacian Age art includes drawings of mammoths and bison. One cave is called the picture gallery, as it is decorated with the outlines of two horses.

9. MONTAUBAN

404 miles SW of Paris, 45 miles NW of Albi, 31 miles N of Toulouse

GETTING THERE   By Train and Bus   Montauban has bus and train connections to Toulouse, but it's easier to drive.

By Car   The RN20 (Paris–Toulouse–Andorra, Spain), the RN 113 (Bordeaux–Marseille), and the A61 motorway run through the Tarn-et-Garonne.

ESSENTIALS   Orientation   The railway and bus stations are west of the center, opposite the Tarn River from the historic old town. Place Nationale is the most central square. Two of the town's most important sights, the Musée Ingres and the Pont-Vieux, are between the railway station and place Nationale.

Information   There's an Office de Tourisme on rue du Collège (tel. 63-63-60-60).

Some 31 miles north of Toulouse, this pink-brick capital of the Tarn-et-Garonne is the city of the painter Ingres and the sculptor Bourdelle.

Montauban, on the right bank of the Tarn, is one of the most ancient of the fortified towns of southwest France. It is still dominated by the fortified **Church of St. James.** The town was the headquarters of the Huguenot rebellion in 1621. The most scenic view of Montauban is at the 14th-century brick bridge, **Pont-Vieux,** which connects the town to its satellite of **Villebourbon.** The bridge is divided by seven arches.

An admirer of Raphael and a student of David, Jean Auguste Dominique Ingres was born in 1780 in Montauban, the son of an ornamental sculptor and painter who was not well-to-do. The father recognized his son's artistic abilities early and encouraged him greatly. Ingres lived for a part of his life in Italy, seeking inspiration in classical motifs. He was noted especially for his nudes and historical paintings, all of which are today considered fine examples of neoclassicism. One of his first exhibitions of portraits in 1806 met with ridicule, but later generations have been more appreciative.

Although the Louvre in Paris owns many Ingres masterpieces, upon his death in 1867 the artist bequeathed to Montauban more than two dozen paintings and some 4,000 drawings. These are displayed at the **Musée Ingres,** 19, rue de la Mairie (tel. 63-63-18-04), in a 17th-century bishops' palace built on the site of two previous castles, one of which had been inhabited by the counts of Toulouse. One painting in the collection is *Christ and the Doctors,* painted when Ingres was 82. The *Dream of Ossian* was intended for Napoléon's bedroom in Rome. On the ground floor are works by Bourdelle (1861–1929), who was heavily influenced by Rodin. Two busts Bourdelle did, of Ingres and of Rodin, are particularly outstanding.

The museum is open Tuesday through Sunday from 10am to noon and 2 to 6pm (in July and August, daily from 9:30am to noon and 1:30 to 6pm). Admission is 15 F ($2.70) for adults, free for children.

For a final look at a masterpiece by Ingres, head for the **Cathédrale de Notre-Dame,** place Roosevelt, a classical building framed by two square towers. In the north transept is the painting the church commissioned, *Vow of Louis XIII.* Open daily from 8am to 7pm.

WHERE TO STAY

HOSTELLERIE LES COULANDRIERES, route de Castelsarrasin, 82290 Montauban. Tel. 63-67-47-47. Fax 63-67-46-45. 22 rms (all with bath or shower). MINIBAR TV TEL
$ Rates: 380 F ($68.40) single; 440 F ($79.20) double. Half board 400 F ($72) per person. AE, DC, MC, V. **Parking:** Free.
Each inn has its own charm and warmth, and this one, just two miles west of the center of Montauban, is especially nice. The lounges and dining room are traditionally furnished, and the rooms are pleasant and comfortable. It is also surrounded by three acres of parkland. Facilities include a swimming pool, volleyball court, bowling alley, and miniature-golf course.

HOTEL DU MIDI, 12, rue Notre-Dame, 82000 Montauban. Tel. 63-63-17-23. Fax 63-66-43-66. 64 rms (61 with bath). MINIBAR TEL
$ Rates: 130 F ($23.40) single without bath; 240–260 F ($43.20–$46.80) single or double with bath. Breakfast 28 F ($5) extra. AE, DC, MC, V. **Parking:** Free.
This pleasantly renovated 19th-century house contains four separate dining areas— one is antique style with vaulted ceilings, while another is contemporary with a fireplace. Located in the historic part of town near the cathedral, this hotel offers well-furnished rooms; overflow guests are accommodated at an annex across the street. During the week, order a table d'hôte for only 79 F ($14.20). However, on Sunday and holidays the fixed-price menus begin at 120 F ($21.60).

HOTEL INGRES, 10, av. Mayenne, 82000 Montauban. Tel. 63-63-36-01. Fax 63-66-02-90. 31 rms (all with bath). A/C MINIBAR TV TEL
$ Rates: 320 F ($57.60) single; 450 F ($81) double. Breakfast 40 F ($7.20) extra. AE, DC, MC, V. **Parking:** 30 F ($5.40).
Many rate the Ingres the finest place to stay in town. This contemporary hotel near the

railway station has comfortably efficient bedrooms, some of which overlook a well-tended rear garden. Breakfast is the only meal served.

WHERE TO DINE

HOTEL ORSAY ET RESTAURANT LA CUISINE D'ALAIN, face Gare (across from the train station), 82000 Montauban. Tel. 63-66-06-66.
Cuisine: FRENCH. **Reservations:** Recommended.

$ Prices: Appetizers 45–98 F ($8.10–$17.60); main dishes 95–135 F ($17.10–$24.30); fixed-price menus 150 F ($27), 170 F ($30.60), and 260 F ($46.80). AE, DC, MC, V.

Open: Lunch Tues–Sat 12:30–2pm; dinner Mon–Sat 7:30–9:30pm. **Closed:** First two weeks of Aug.

Some people consider Restaurant La Cuisine d'Alain to be the best restaurant in town. The chef, Alain Blanc, is talented and inventive. Try a terrine of lentils flavored with the neck of a fattened goose en confit, filet of beef with liver and an apple flan, or the escalope of grilled salmon within its own skin. The amazing dessert trolley offers plenty of choices.

Reasonably priced rooms also are available in the Hôtel Orsay, with radios, telephones, and baths or showers. Singles cost 250 F ($45) and doubles are 330 F ($59.40), plus 30 F ($5.40) for breakfast.

BORDEAUX & THE ATLANTIC COAST

From the historic port of La Rochelle to the bordeaux wine district, the southwest of France is too briefly glimpsed by the motorist rushing from Paris to Spain. But the area is becoming better known for its Atlantic beaches, its medieval and Renaissance ruins, its Romanesque and Gothic churches, its vineyards and charming old inns that still practice a splendid regional cuisine.

In our journey through this most intriguing part of France we will not stay entirely on the coastline, visiting such cities as Bordeaux and La Rochelle as the title of the chapter suggests, but will dip inland for a glass of cognac and trips to such nearby art cities as Poitiers and Angoulême.

Allow at least a week for this journey—just enough time to sample the wine, savor the gastronomic specialties, and see at least some of the major sights of this ancient region over which the French and English fought so bitterly for so many years.

SEEING BORDEAUX & THE ATLANTIC COAST

GETTING THERE Try to time your visit during May to September, when the region is loveliest. If you depend on public transport, make Bordeaux your center. From there, you can take organized tours of the old port and visit the wine district on a bus excursion.

Bordeaux is serviced **by plane** connections from London, Amsterdam, Brussels, Frankfurt, Geneva, Milan, Barcélona, Madrid, Pôrto, and Lisbon. The fastest way to reach the region is on a one-hour Air Inter flight from Paris, with seven departures daily from both Orly and Charles de Gaulle. TAT airlines goes from Orly Ouest in Paris to La Rochelle, the second major gateway in the region, with two flights per day Monday through Friday. Flight time is 1½ hours.

You can also take the TGV *Atlantique,* a high-speed **train** that will put you in Bordeaux in less than 3½ hours from Paris. At either La Rochelle or Bordeaux, you can rent a **car** for your tour of the Atlantic coast. Some regional towns are hard to reach by public transportation unless you have endless patience and a lot of time.

A SUGGESTED ROUTE Use Bordeaux as your gateway and spend the first day touring the city and taking a port cruise. Strike out the next morning for the Médoc vineyards. Drive north to Saintes on Day 3.

Then take an excursion east, stopping in Cognac for lunch and a tour of its warehouses, before continuing to Angoulême (Day 4) for the night. The next morning, head north to Poitiers (Day 5) and on to La Rochelle (Days 6 and 7). After touring the port, visit one of the offshore Atlantic islands.

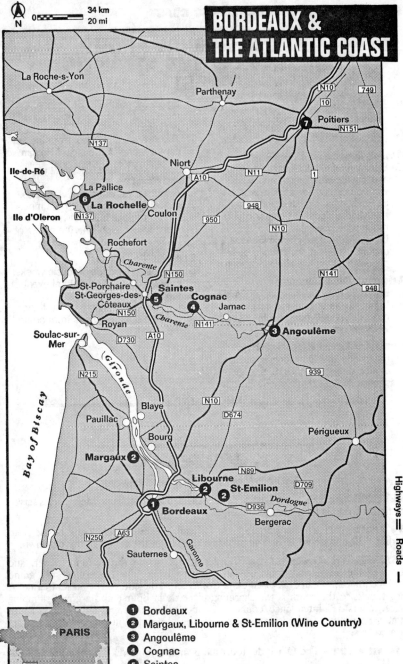

BORDEAUX & THE ATLANTIC COAST

N
0 | 34 km
20 mi

La Roche-s-Yon
Parthenay
N10
749
10
Poitiers
N151

N137
Niort
N11
1
A10
Ile-de-Ré
La Pallice
948
La Rochelle
Coulon
N137
950
N10
Ile d'Oleron
Rochefort
Charente
N150
N141
St-Porchaire
Saintes
948
St-Georges-des-
Côteaux
Cognac
N150
Jarnac
Royan
Charente
N141
Angoulême
Soulac-sur-
Mer
A10
D730
N215
Gironde
939
Blaye
N10
Pauillac
D674
Périgueux
Bourg
Margaux
N89
Libourne
D709
St-Emilion
Dordogne
Bordeaux
D936
Bergerac
N250
A63
Sauternes
Garonne

Bay of Biscay

Highways =

Roads —

PARIS

Bordeaux

1 Bordeaux
2 Margaux, Libourne & St-Emilion (Wine Country)
3 Angoulême
4 Cognac
5 Saintes
6 La Rochelle
7 Poitiers

WHAT'S SPECIAL ABOUT BORDEAUX & THE ATLANTIC COAST

Beaches
☐ Ile de Ré, an Atlantic island off the coast of La Rochelle, 19 miles long and surrounded by sandy beaches.

Great Towns/Villages
☐ Bordeaux, capital of old Aquitaine and center of the most important wine-producing area in the world.
☐ St-Emilion, an architectural gem of the Middle Ages and center of a famous wine district.
☐ La Rochelle, the "French Geneva," a historic port and ancient city of sailors, with 3½ miles of fortifications.

Ancient Monuments
☐ Eglise St-Eutrope, built in 1400s by Louis XI and considered one of the most important monuments in southwestern France.

Architectural Highlights
☐ Esplanade des Quinconces, at Bordeaux, dating from 1818, a 30-acre square, largest of its kind in Europe.

☐ Eglise Monolithe at St-Emilion, the most important underground church in France.
☐ The Arena, at Saintes, from the 1st century, one of the oldest Roman amphitheaters in the world.

Wine Routes
☐ A tour of the Bordeaux vineyards, including Médoc, one of the most visited regions in southwestern France (tour highlight: the estate of Château Mouton-Rothschild).

Events/Festivals
☐ Bordeaux, a series of music weeks in May, the leading cultural event of the region.
☐ La Rochelle, sailing week in May, drawing boat devotees from around the world.

1. BORDEAUX

359 miles SW of Paris, 341 miles W of Lyon

GETTING THERE   By Plane   The local airport, Bordeaux-Mérignac, is served by flights from as far away as London and New York.

By Train   The railway station (Gare St-Jean) lies on the west bank of the river, within a 30-minute walk (or 5-minute taxi ride) from the center of the old town.

ESSENTIALS   Orientation   Bordeaux lies beside the Garonne River, and most of the interesting sights are on the west bank. The centerpiece of "grand 18th-century Bordeaux" is place de la Comédie, at the end of rue Ste-Catherine. A few blocks to the south is the charming place de la Bourse and a grand shopping street, cours de l'Intendance/cours du Chapeau-Rouge. Several more blocks south stands Bordeaux's Cathédrale de St-André, the Hôtel de Ville, and the Musée des Beaux-Arts.

Information   The Office de Tourisme is at 12, cours du 30-Juillet (tel. 56-44-28-41).

Wine Tours   Wine exporters welcome the many guests who come to sample wines and learn about the industry. In the next section, I'll take you on a tour of the bordeaux wine country. For maps and information about the popular wine routes, go to the Maison du Vin (House of Wine), 1, cours du 30-Juillet (tel. 56-00-22-88), near

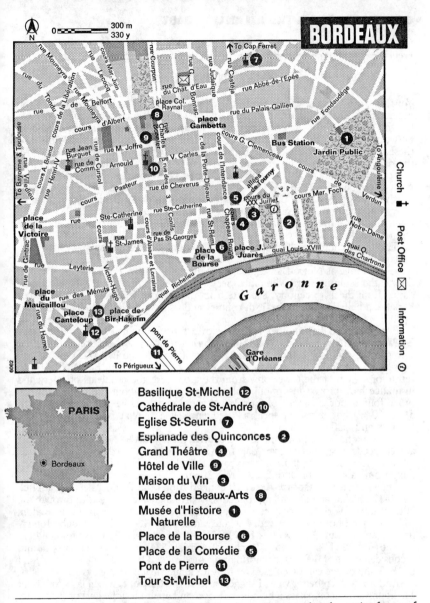

BORDEAUX

Church **✝**

Post Office ⊠

Information ⓘ

Basilique St-Michel ⑫
Cathédrale de St-André ⑩
Eglise St-Seurin ⑦
Esplanade des Quinconces ②
Grand Théâtre ④
Hôtel de Ville ⑨
Maison du Vin ③
Musée des Beaux-Arts ⑧
Musée d'Histoire ①
　Naturelle
Place de la Bourse ⑥
Place de la Comédie ⑤
Pont de Pierre ⑪
Tour St-Michel ⑬

the tourist office. To make the rounds of the vineyards, consider alternative forms of transportation to your car: bus, houseboat, or horse-drawn caravan.

The great port city of Bordeaux, on the Garonne River, the capital city of Aquitaine, struck Victor Hugo as "Versailles, with Antwerp added." As the center of the most important wine-producing area in the world, Bordeaux attracts many visitors to the offices of wine exporters here, most of whom welcome guests. (For a trip through the bordeaux wine country, refer to the next section.)

Bordeaux is a city of warehouses, factories, mansions, and exploding suburbs, as well as wide quays five miles long. Now the fifth-largest city of France, Bordeaux was for 300 years a British possession, and even today it is called the most un-French of French cities, although the same has been said of Strasbourg.

WHAT TO SEE & DO

Your tour can begin at **place de la Comédie,** which lies at the very heart of this venerated old city, a busy traffic hub that was the site of a Roman temple in olden days. On this square one of the great theaters of France, the **Grand Théâtre,** was built between 1773 and 1780. A colonnade of 12 columns graces its facade. Surmounted on these are statues of goddesses and the Muses. Apply to the porter if you'd like to visit the richly decorated interior, a harmonious setting of elegance and refinement.

From here you can walk to **esplanade des Quinconces** to the north, which was laid out between 1818 and 1828, the largest square of its kind in Europe, covering nearly 30 acres. A smaller but lovelier square is **place de la Bourse,** bounded by quays opening onto the Garonne. It was laid out between 1728 and 1755, with a fountain of the Three Graces at its center. Flanking the square are the Custom House and the Stock Exchange.

The finest church in Bordeaux is the **Cathédrale de St-André,** place Pey-Berland (tel. 56-52-68-10), standing in the south of the old town. It lacks only 20 feet of being as long as Notre-Dame in Paris. At the 13th-century Porte Royale or "royal door," the sculptures are admirable. See also the sculptures on the North Door, dating from the 14th century. Separate from the rest of the church is the Tour Pey Berland, a belfry begun in the 15th century and rising 155 feet high. The church is open daily from 8 to 11am and 2 to 6pm.

Bordeaux also has another church with a separate belfry. It's the **Basilique St-Michel** with its adjoining **Tour St-Michel.** The belfry of the church is the tallest tower in the south of France. Rising 374 feet, it was erected in 1472. Once it was possible to climb the 228 steps for a panoramic view of the port. But you'll have to settle for a view of the tower only from the ground, as the problems of safety and insurance have proved insurmountable. For information about the church, or the other four major churches of Bordeaux, you can telephone the Presbytère (tel. 56-52-50-32), but only if you speak a little French. The church is open daily from 8am to noon and 2:30 to 5:30pm.

Bordeaux has yet another interesting church, the **Eglise St-Seurin,** whose most ancient sections, such as its crypt, date from the 5th century. See the porch, which was left over from an earlier church. It has some capitals from the Romanesque era. Open daily from 8am to noon and 2:30pm to 5:30pm.

The **Musée des Beaux-Arts,** 20 cours d'Albret (Jardin du Palais Rohan) (tel. 56-10-17-49), has an outstanding collection of art ranging from the 15th through the 20th century. Works by Perugin, Titian, Rubens, Veronese, Delacroix, Gros, Redon, Marquet, and Lhote are displayed. The museum is open Wednesday through Monday from 10am to 6pm. Admission is 13.50 F ($2.40) for adults, 8 F ($1.40) for children.

The **Pont de Pierre,** with 17 arches, stretches 1,594 feet across the Garonne and is considered one of the most beautiful bridges in France. Ordered built by Napoléon I in 1813, the bridge can be crossed on foot for a fine view of the quays and the port.

And for an even better view, I suggest a **tour of the port,** which lasts for about 1½ hours and encompasses a float up the river and all around the harbor. It departs from the Embarcadères des Quinconces, on quai Louis-XVIII in the center of town.

Between April and October, tours begin Monday through Saturday at 2:30 or 3pm. The cost is 50 F ($9) for adults and 40 F ($7.20) for children under 10. For exact times, call the tourism office (see "Essentials," above) or the boat captains' office near the quai (tel. 56-52-88-88). Ask about the occasional floating concerts conducted at night. Note that tours may be cancelled without warning.

Some visitors enjoy a waterborne expedition on one of France's mightiest (and least-visited) rivers, the Garonne. During July and August, **Alienor Loisirs,** Hangar 7, quai Louis-XVIII (tel. 56-51-27-90) offers a Sunday-afternoon ride downriver from Bordeaux to the famous château town of Blaye. Boarding at the company's dock begins at around 11am before an 11:30 departure. Lunch is served on board, and between 2 and 4pm, visitors enjoy a shore excursion in Blaye. The return to Bordeaux is usually scheduled for around 6:30pm the same day. The cost of the excursion, with lunch included, is 200 F ($36) for adults and 100 F ($18) for children under 12.

The rest of the year, roughly equivalent excursions are offered, according to a flexible schedule which varies according to the number of prepaid advance reservations. For more information, call the Bordeaux tourist office or Alienor Loisirs.

WHERE TO STAY
Very Expensive

CHATEAU CHARTRONS, 81, cours St-Louis, 33300 Bordeaux. Tel. 56-43-15-00. Fax 56-69-15-21. 138 rms (all with bath), 6 suites. A/C MINIBAR TV TEL. **Bus:** 7 or 8.

$ Rates: 690–900 F ($124.20–$162) single or double; 1,200 F ($216) suites. Breakfast 65 F ($11.70) extra. AE, DC, MC, V. **Parking:** Free.

Operated by a prestigious wine exporter, La Maison Ginneste, this is probably the most visible and talked-about hotel in Bordeaux. Set near the landmark place Tourny, a five-minute walk from the historic center of town, it opened in 1991 behind the gracefully restored facade of an 18th-century mansion. (The rest of the mansion, in vital need of repair, was demolished and rebuilt in a tastefully contemporary style.)

Bedrooms are contemporary and comfortable, outfitted in shades of soft green and memorabilia of the wine trade. On the premises, you'll find a bar with an impressive array of local vintages sold by the glass, and a restaurant, Le Cabernet, where well-prepared meals begin at around 120 F ($21.60) each. A well-equipped health club a few buildings away (under separate management) opens its facilities to any guest of the hotel who wants to use them.

PULLMAN MERIADECK, 5, rue Robert-Lateulade, 33000 Bordeaux. Tel. 56-56-43-43. Fax 56-96-50-59. 192 rms (all with bath). A/C MINIBAR TV TEL **Bus:** 7 or 8.

$ Rates: 550 F ($99) single; 950 F ($171) double. Breakfast 65 F ($11.70) extra. AE, DC, MC, V.

As the leading hotel in the city, the Pullman Mériadeck offers luxury and sophistication with personalized decor. Modern comforts are provided in a setting of antiquity. Nearby, the historic place Gambetta in the center of town was called place Dauphine in the era of Louis XV. The well-furnished rooms attract vine growers and wine merchants from abroad. Le Mériadec, the hotel's main restaurant, is one of the finest in Bordeaux. Meals run 140–200 F ($25.20–$36).

Expensive

GRAND HOTEL FRANÇAIS, 12, rue du Temple, 33000 Bordeaux. Tel. 56-48-10-35. Fax 56-81-76-18. 35 rms (all with bath). TV TEL **Bus:** 7 or 8.

$ Rates: 370 F ($66.60) single; 590 F ($106.20) double. Breakfast 45 F ($8.10) extra. AE, DC, MC, V.

This restored 18th-century mansion has been elegantly upgraded; it is now one of the best moderately priced hotels in Bordeaux. The three-star hotel has attractively decorated, soundproof rooms. The predominantly business clientele gives way to tourists in the summer. Only breakfast is served.

HOTEL SOFITEL AQUITANIA, parc des Expositions, 33300 Bordeaux-le-Lac. Tel. 56-50-83-80. Fax 56-39-73-75. 211 rms (all with bath). A/C MINIBAR TV TEL **Bus:** 9.

$ Rates: 590–1,300 F ($106.20–$234) single or double. Breakfast 70 F ($12.60) extra. AE, DC, MC, V. **Parking:** Free.

Surrounded by impressive hotels, the Aquitania is the best-rated (three-star "luxe") hotel in the area; it's located west of the city center, near parc des Expositions. Beyond the white exterior is a marble and red-lacquered lobby with modern bronze sculptures. Rooms are color coordinated in warm tones. The lobby pub offers inexpensive meals, and the upstairs restaurant serves meals beginning at 150 F ($27).

NOVOTEL BORDEAUX CENTRE, 45, cours du Maréchal-Juin, 33000 Bordeaux. Tel. 56-51-46-46. Fax 56-98-25-56. 138 rms (all with bath), 2 suites. A/C MINIBAR TV TEL **Bus:** 9.
$ Rates: 490 F ($88.20) single; 550 F ($99) double; from 800 F ($144) suite. Breakfast 55 F ($9.90) extra. Children under 17 stay free in parents' room. AE, DC, MC, V. **Parking:** Free.

Opened in 1989, this first-class hotel is a short walk from the thoroughfare of Sainte Catherine, quai des Chartrons, and the cathedral, in the heart of the city near the railway station. There are nine floors and two elevators. Rooms are well decorated and comfortably furnished, with some suitable for the disabled. The hotel also offers laundry and room service.

Moderate

LE BAYONNE HOTEL, 15, cours de l'Intendance, 33000 Bordeaux. Tel. 56-48-00-88. Fax 56-52-03-79. 36 rms (all with bath or shower). A/C MINIBAR TV TEL **Bus:** 7 or 8.
$ Rates: 350 F ($63) single; 460 F ($82.80) double. Breakfast 55 F ($9.90) extra. AE, DC, MC, V. **Parking:** 55 F ($9.90).

This is a restored 18th-century building that has been turned into one of the most up-to-date three-star hotels in Bordeaux. The aura of the 1930s has been retained in decor, and many comforts have been added. The soundproof bedrooms are furnished with color-coordinated fabrics and comfortable pieces. Many attractions, including several good restaurants, are near the hotel, including the Grand Théâtre.

NOVOTEL BORDEAUX-LE-LAC, av. Jean-Gabriel-Domergue, 33300 Bordeaux-le-Lac. Tel. 56-50-99-70. Fax 56-43-00-66. 176 rms (all with bath). A/C MINIBAR TV TEL **Bus:** 9.
$ Rates: 450 F ($81) single or double. Breakfast 48 F ($8.60) extra. AE, DC, MC, V. **Parking:** Free.

Devoted primarily to business clientele, the Bordeaux is an efficient 1970s hotel located six miles north of the city center, near the commercial center of parc des Expositions. The Rôtisserie restaurant is open daily from 6am to midnight, and there's also a bar. The modern rooms are practical and comfortable, each with a desklike writing surface and both a double bed and a single bed with bolster cushions, which transforms into a couch.

Budget

ETCHE-ONA, 11, rue Mautrec, 33000 Bordeaux. Tel. 56-44-36-49. Fax 56-44-59-58. 33 rms (all with bath or shower). TV TEL **Bus:** 7, 8, or 26.
$ Rates: 230–265 F ($41.40–$47.70) single; 250–335 F ($45–$60.30) double. Breakfast 35 F ($6.30) extra. MC, V. **Parking:** 52 F ($9.40).

Small but tranquil and central, this hotel is one of the best bargains I've been able to find in Bordeaux. It's within walking distance of many of the city's major attractions, including the Grand Théâtre, the Cathédrale de St-André, place de la Bourse, and the quays. Rooms are nicely furnished. Breakfast is the only meal served.

HOTEL ATLANTIC, 69, rue Eugène-Leroy, 33800 Bordeaux. Tel. 56-92-92-22. Fax 56-94-21-42. 36 rms (all with bath). TV TEL **Bus:** 7 or 8.
$ Rates: 210 F ($37.80) single; 290 F ($52.20) double. Breakfast 30 F ($5.40) extra. AE, MC, V.

Rated only two stars, this small hotel, located near the Gare St-Jean (train station), has a welcoming staff, some of whom speak English. Most of the rooms are tasteful and comfortable; all are well lit and have adequate storage space. A continental breakfast is the only meal served.

HOTEL DE SEZE, 23, allées de Tourny, 33000 Bordeaux. Tel. 56-52-65-54. Fax 56-44-31-83. 24 rms (all with bath). MINIBAR TV TEL **Bus:** 7 or 8.
$ Rates: 300–420 F ($54–$75.60) single or double. Breakfast 35 F ($6.30) extra. AE, DC, MC, V. **Parking:** 50 F ($9).

S This three-star hotel is housed in a building classified by the French government as a historic monument. This moderately priced hotel is such a well-known value that you should make reservations as early as possible. Rooms are well furnished: the cheapest with only a bed, toilet, and shower, the most expensive with a full bath and twin beds.

WHERE TO DINE

In addition to the following, many of the hotels listed above have fine restaurants.

Very Expensive

LA CHAMADE, 20, rue des Piliers-de-Tutelle. Tel. 56-48-13-74.
   Cuisine: FRENCH. **Reservations:** Required. **Bus:** 7 or 8.
$ Prices: Appetizers 90–160 F ($16.20–$28.80); main dishes 100–180 F ($18–$32.40); fixed-price meals 180 F ($32.40) at lunch (Mon–Fri), 300 F ($54) at dinner. AE, MC, V.
   Open: Lunch Mon–Sat 12:30–2pm; dinner daily 7:30–10pm. **Closed:** Sat–Sun July–Aug.

★ Dining at La Chamade is such a delightful experience that many serious local diners even prefer it to Le Chapon Fin (described below). La Chamade is located in a vaulted 18th-century cellar of honey-colored stone. Owner Michel Carrèrc has an impressive collection of bordeaux. Try the salad of monkfish, which has been marinated and grilled and is served with leeks and Greek-style artichokes. Other dishes include roasted foie gras with a confit of leeks, and poached duck thighs served with baby vegetables. Fish dishes are steamed to precision and often served simply, sometimes with a warm vinaigrette of tomatoes and fresh basil. The fixed-price lunch is one of the dining bargains of the city, considering its quality.

LE CHAPON-FIN, 5, rue Montesquieu. Tel. 56-79-10-10.
   Cuisine: FRENCH. **Reservations:** Required. **Bus:** 7 or 8.
$ Prices: Appetizers 90–240 F ($16.20–$43.20); main dishes 135–200 F ($24.30–$36); fixed-price meals 220–400 F ($39.60–$72) at lunch, 400–420 F ($72–$75.60) at dinner. AE, DC, V.
   Open: Lunch Tues–Sat noon–2pm; dinner Tues–Sat 7:30–10pm. **Closed:** One week in Aug.

★ A chef from Barcelona has returned this famous landmark to the forefront of culinary expertise. Once compared to Maxim's in Paris, this establishment was abandoned in 1960 when the original owner died. Today, under the guidance of Francis Garcia, it's the leading restaurant in Bordeaux. His wife, Geraldine, helps manage the dining room, which has potted palms, glittering silver trolleys, elaborate latticework, and several banquettes set into artificial stone grottoes. A pivoting skylight lets in summer breezes. The elite of Bordeaux follow the trail of such artistic and political luminaries as Sarah Bernhardt, Aristide Briand, Edward VII, Winston Churchill, the Sultan of Morocco, and François Mauriac.

Wines tend to be selected from the most respected and most expensive vintages of France, and menu specialties change frequently according to the supply of ingredients. A meal might include truffle flan with essence of morels, gratin of oysters with foie gras, lobster gazpacho, and salmon steak grilled in its skin with a pepper-flavored sabayon—followed by a superb collection of cheeses and sophisticated desserts.

Expensive

LE VIEUX BORDEAUX, 27, rue Buhan. Tel. 56-52-94-36.
   Cuisine: FRENCH. **Reservations:** Recommended. **Bus:** 7 or 8.
$ Prices: Appetizers 80–100 F ($14.40–$18); main dishes 90–170 F ($16.20–$30.60); fixed-price menus 150 F ($27), 200 F ($36), and 250 F ($45). AE, V.
   Open: Lunch Mon–Fri noon–2pm; dinner Mon–Sat 8–10:15pm. **Closed:** Two weeks in Feb and three weeks in Aug.

One of the best-established restaurants in town, the Old Bordeaux is virtually a neighborhood institution; the decor is an almost-incongruous mix of exposed wood and modern accents. Specialties include a pavé of fresh salmon with warm oysters, roasted sweetbreads, turbot with a buttered truffle sauce, hare with onions, and a gratin of lobster with fresh noodles.

Moderate

L'OMBRIERE, 14, place du Parlement. Tel. 56-44-82-69.
    Cuisine: BRASSERIE-STYLE FRENCH. **Reservations:** Not required.
$ Prices: Appetizers 30–80 F ($5.40–$14.40); main dishes 55–150 F ($9.90–$27). MC, V.
    Open: Lunch Tues–Sat 11:30am–3pm; dinner Tues–Sat 6–11pm.
Considered an immovable fixture on the restaurant landscape of Bordeaux, this brasserie serves standardized portions of conservatively prepared food to a repeat clientele of local politicians, office workers, and merchants. If you try to call for reservations, you might be greeted only with a tape-recorded message announcing the establishment's open hours. This is provincial French bustle at its busiest, and the staff is likely to be overworked, but the price is more often than not relatively reasonable.

LA TUPINA, 6, rue de la Porte de la Monnaie. Tel. 56-91-56-37.
    Cuisine: FRENCH. **Reservations:** Recommended. **Bus:** 7 or 8.
$ Prices: Appetizers 55–95 F ($9.90–$17.10); main dishes 75–120 F ($13.50–$21.60); fixed-price meals 100 F ($18) at lunch, 150 F ($27) at dinner. AE, DC, MC, V.
    Open: Lunch Mon–Sat noon–2pm; dinner Mon–Sat 8–11pm.
One of Bordeaux's most talented chefs runs this small and cozy restaurant set in an 18th-century building, near quai de la Monnaie. Jean-Pierre Xiradakis's specialty is duck, so your meal might begin with croutons that have been spread with duck rillettes; shredded duck preserved in its own fat is also delicious; and his salads often use giblets, skin, and livers. The chef also prepares classic regional specialties, such as truffles and foie gras. A recent potato salad sampled here contained slices of the black truffles found in the Périgord region. The foie gras often comes steamed en papillote. Sample one of the fine wines from the cellar.

Budget

LA FORGE, 8, rue du Chai-des-Farines. Tel. 56-81-40-96.
    Cuisine: FRENCH. **Reservations:** Recommended. **Bus:** 7 or 8.
$ Prices: Appetizers 20–70 F ($3.60–$12.60); main dishes 45–130 F ($8.10–$23.40); fixed-price menus 75 F ($13.50), 100 F ($18), and 140 F ($25.20). MC, V.
    Open: Lunch Tues–Sat noon–1:30pm; dinner Tues–Sat 7:30–10:30pm. **Closed:** Mid-Aug to mid-Sept.
    Jean-Michel Pouts, a former chef on the ocean liner *France*, owns this neighborhood bistro. Well-prepared specialties include brochette of pork with gruyère, savory grilled meats, and an excellent cassoulet. The fixed-price menus are among the best in town for the price.

NEARBY ACCOMMODATIONS & DINING

RESTAURANT ST. JAMES/HOTEL HAUTERIVE, 3, place Camille-Hostein, 33270 Bouliac. Tel. 56-20-52-19. Fax 56-20-92-58.
    Cuisine: FRENCH. **Reservations:** Required.
$ Prices: Fixed-price menu 250 F ($45). AE, DC, MC, V.
    Open: Lunch Tues–Sun noon–2:30pm; dinner Tues–Sun 7–9:30pm.
    Chefs on vacation tend to dine in restaurants similar to this one, whose stone walls rise from the center of an agrarian hamlet (Bouliac), across from a 17th-century village church. Located about four miles from Bordeaux, it's the domain of Jean-Marie Amat, whose specialties are strictly based on local ingredients when they are in season. These may revolve, for example, around seasonal

abundances of cèpes (the meaty flap mushrooms of the district), game (venison and pheasant), girolles (another kind of mushroom), and fruit. Within an ultramodern dining room whose windows offer a view of some of the most famous vineyards in Europe, you can enjoy such dishes as a civet of duck, oysters from Quiberon, a tartare of salmon with olives, a salad of marinated filets of quail, grilled pigeon, Pauillac lamb, and lamprey eels à la bordelaise.

Adjacent to the restaurant is the Hotel Hautrive, whose 16 comfortably elegant rooms and two suites are scattered among a quartet of modern pavilions. Each room has a TV and telephone, and many offer views of the valley of the Garonne. Singles rent for 800 F ($144), doubles go for 850 F ($153), and suites cost 1,350 F ($243), with breakfast priced at an additional 70 F ($12.60) each.

2. THE WINE COUNTRY

Bordeaux is one of the capitals of French gastronomy. Many consider the district the equal of Lyon. Dugléré, born here, became one of the great men of classical French cookery.

The major wine districts of Bordeaux are Graves, Médoc, Sauternes, Entre-deux-Mers, Libourne, Blaye, and Bourg.

North of the city of Bordeaux, the Garonne River joins the Dordogne. This forms the Gironde, a broad estuary comprising the heart of the bordeaux wine country. More than 100,000 vineyards produce some 70 million gallons of wine a year. Some of these are among the greatest red wines in the world. The white wines are lesser known.

Wine Tours Some of the more famous vineyards are pleased to welcome visitors, providing they don't arrive at the busy harvest time. However, most vineyards are not likely to have a permanent staff to welcome you. In other words, don't just show up on the doorstep. You must call first or check with local tourist offices about appropriate times for visits.

Information The most serious visitor will contact **International Wine Tours,** 12, place de la Bourse, 33076 Bordeaux CEDEX (tel. 56-90-91-28), for information about wine tours.

Map Before heading out on this wine road, make sure you have a detailed map from the tourist office in Bordeaux, since the "trail" is not well marked and you could get lost. Head in the direction of Pauillac on the D2, the wine road, called the *Route des Grands-Crus*.

MEDOC

The Médoc, an undulating plain covered with vineyards, is one of the most visited regions in southwestern France. Its borders are marked by Bordeaux and the Pointe de Grave. In Haut-Médoc, the history of growing grapes to make wine dates from the era of Louis XIV. Throughout the region are many isolated châteaux producing grapes. Only a handful of these châteaux, however, are worthy of your time and attention. The most visited château, of course, is that of Mouton-Rothschild, said to be an attraction in southwestern France second only to Lourdes, in spite of the red tape involved in visiting it.

In Haut-Médoc, the soil is not especially fertile but absorbs much heat during the day. To benefit from this, the vines are clipped close to the ground. The French zealously regulate the cultivation of the vineyards and the making of the wine. Less than 10% of the wines from the region are called bordeaux. These are invariably red, including such famous labels as Châteaux Margaux, Château Latour, Châteaux

Mouton, and Château Lafite. Most of these labels are from grapes grown some 3,000 feet from the Gironde River.

WHAT TO SEE & DO

CHATEAU MARGAUX, 33460 Margaux, on the D2. Tel. 56-88-70-28.

Known as the Versailles of the Médoc, this Empire-style château was built in the 19th century near the village of Margaux. The estate covers more than 650 acres, of which some 187 produce Château Margaux and Pavillon Rouge du Château Margaux. Almost 30 acres are devoted to the production of Pavillon Blanc du Château Margaux. The inhabitants of the château do not allow tours, but you may admire it from the outside.

Open: Mon–Fri 9am–12:30pm and 2–5:30pm. **Closed:** Aug and during harvest. To see the vat rooms and wine cellars, make an appointment by letter or phone.

CHATEAU DE BEYCHEVELLE, St-Julien, Beychevelle, 33250 Pauillac. Tel. 56-59-23-00.

The Grand Admiral of France, the duc d'Epernon, ordered this château built in 1757 and commanded all ships to lower their sails as they passed the château. (Beychevelle means "lowered sails.") The château is located 10 miles beyond Margaux.

Open: Mon–Fri 9:30am–noon and 2–6pm; Sat 9:30am–noon. Make an appointment through the Maison du Vin in Bordeaux (see "Bordeaux," above) or by calling direct.

CHATEAU MOUTON-ROTHSCHILD, Le Pouvalet, 33250 Pauillac. Tel. 56-73-18-18.

Thousands of tourists visit this outstanding château, which is one of the many homes of Baron Philippe de Rothschild. It's located in Pauillac, a deep-water port that services the vessels that carry the region's renowned vintages. The château has more to see than any other in the Médoc. The baron's American-born wife, Pauline, contributed greatly to the restoration. The welcoming room is beautifully furnished with part of the Rothschild collection of sculpture and paintings. A 16th-century tapestry depicts the harvesting of the grape. An adjoining museum, in former wine cellars known as *chai,* contains art from many eras—much of it is related to the cultivation of the vineyards. You can see goldsmiths' work from the 15th and 16th centuries. Look, in particular, at the collection of modern art, including a statue by the American sculptor Lippold. The wine produced in the surrounding vineyards was classified as *premier cru* in 1973. Before that, it was labeled a "second growth."

Open: Mon–Thurs 9:30–11:30am and 2–5pm, Fri 9:30–11:30am and 2–4pm. Make an appointment by phone to see the cellars. **Closed:** Aug and holidays.

CHATEAU LAFITE, on the D2. Tel. 56-59-01-74.

This important château surrounded by cedars is second only to the nearby Château Mouton-Rothschild. Count on spending at least an hour here. The vinothèque contains many vintage bottles—several date from 1797. The château was purchased in 1868 by the Rothschilds.

Open: Mon–Fri 9–11am and 3–5pm. Make an appointment for a guided tour. **Closed:** Holidays and mid-Sept to late Nov.

WHERE TO STAY & DINE

Several villages in Médoc and Haut-Médoc offer inns suitable for a meal or an overnight stay.

AUBERGE ANDRE, Le Grand Port, 33880 Cambes. Tel. 56-21-31-08.

Cuisine: FRENCH. **Reservations:** Recommended.

$ Prices: Appetizers 35–100 F ($6.30–$18); main dishes 70–145 F ($12.60–$26.10); fixed-price menus 98–220 F ($17.60–$39.60). DC, MC, V.

Open: Lunch Wed–Mon 12:30–3pm; dinner Wed–Mon 7:30–10pm. **Closed:** Nov and one week in Feb.

Set at the edge of Cambes, a village with no more than 100 residents, within a century-old farmhouse whose panoramic outdoor terrace encompasses a sweeping view of the Garonne, this is considered one of the charming hideaways of the region. Maintained by the Stacchini family, whose patriarch worked in the kitchens of Paris's Ritz hotel for many years, the establishment also maintains a quartet of comfortable bedrooms upstairs. Single or double occupancy, these rent for 180 F ($32.40) each, with breakfast priced at an additional 30 F ($5.40) per person.

Menu items might include a filet of eel with parsley-butter sauce, lamprey bordelaise, foie gras, confit de canard, filet of sea bass infused with essence of laurel, and salmon cooked with port.

LIBOURNE

This is a sizable market town with a railway connection. At the junction of the Dordogne and Isle Rivers, Libourne is considered roughly the center of the St-Emilion, Pomerol, and Fronsac wine districts. In the town, a large, colonnaded square still contains some houses from the 16th century, including the **Hôtel de Ville.** In addition, you can explore the remains of 13th-century **ramparts.**

In the center of town the **Office du Tourisme,** place Abel-Surchamp, Libourne (tel. 57-51-15-04), will give you complete information on how to visit the bordeaux vineyards.

WHERE TO STAY & DINE

HOTEL LOUBAT, 32, rue Chanzy, 33500 Libourne. Tel. 57-51-17-58. 25 rms (all with bath or shower). TV TEL
$ Rates: 250–340 F ($45–$61.20) single or double. Breakfast 30 F ($5.40) extra. AE, V.

This small country inn, located across from the railway station, has a heart-warming exterior and a provincial decor. It's the leading hotel in town, with reasonable rates and good meals. The restaurant is open daily from noon to 2pm and 7 to 10pm; specialties are lamprey eels bordelaise, papillotte of salmon with crayfish, and sweetbreads with grapes and foie-gras sauce. Fixed-price menus run 95–200 F ($17.10–$36), and there's also an à la carte menu.

NEARBY ACCOMMODATIONS & DINING

LA BONNE AUBERGE, rue du 8-Mai-1945 et av. John-Talbot, 33350 Castillon-la-Bataille. Tel. 57-40-11-56. 10 rms (6 with shower but no toilet, 2 with bath).
$ Rates: 120 F ($21.60) single or double without bath, 180 F ($32.40) single or double with shower but no toilet, 230 F ($41.40) single or double with bath. Breakfast 24 F ($4.30) extra. AE, DC, MC, V. **Parking:** Free.

This family hotel is near an intersection of two busy highways, 11 miles southeast of Libourne, near the Dordogne. Rooms are simple, comfortable, and well scrubbed; the good food is plentiful. Serious diners go to the restaurant at the top of a flight of exterior stairs; there's also a brasserie on the ground level. A fixed-price menu in the downstairs brasserie costs only 53 F ($9.50), and the fixed-price menu in the restaurant goes for 68–195 F ($12.20–$35.10). Specialties include grilled salmon with shallot-flavored butter, an array of omelets, lamb with parsley, sweetbreads with flap mushrooms, and entrecôte bordelaise. The restaurant is open for lunch from noon to 2pm, and for dinner from 7:30 to 9pm. Both the brasserie and the restaurant are closed Saturday for lunch from November through March.

ST-EMILION

 Surrounded by vineyards, St-Emilion is on a limestone plateau overlooking the Valley of the Dordogne; a maze of **wine cellars** has been dug out of the limestone rock underneath the town. The wine made in this world-famous district has been called "Wine of Honor," and British sovereigns nicknamed it "King of Wines." St-Emilion was named for an 8th-century Breton saint, a former baker who became a monk. The town, made mostly of golden stone and dating from the Middle Ages, is known for its macaroons.

St-Emilion maintains the ancient tradition of La Jurade. Members of this society wear silk hats and scarlet robes edged with ermine, and the Syndicat Viticole, which watches over the quality of wine, have all been around the world to promote the wines with this appellation. St-Emilion lies 22 miles northeast of Bordeaux between Libourne (5 miles away) and Castillon-la-Bataille (7 miles away). Its **Office de Tourisme** is at place des Créneaux, St-Emilion (tel. 57-24-72-03).

Trains from Bordeaux make the 45-minute trip to St-Emilion twice per day.

WHAT TO SEE & DO

At the heart of St-Emilion is the **place du Marché,** set between two hills. An old acacia tree marks the center.

The **Eglise Monolithe** (tel. 57-24-72-03), considered to be the most important underground church in France, was carved out of limestone by the Benedictines between the 9th and 12th centuries. The facade is marked by three bay windows from the 14th century. A 14th-century sculpted portal depicts the Last Judgment and the resurrection of the dead. The church is about 37 feet high, 67 feet wide, and nearly 125 feet long. You can visit daily from 9:30am to 12:30pm and 1:45 to 6pm; admission is 30 F ($5.40) for adults and 19 F ($3.40) for children. The church is closed December 24, 25, and 31, and the first week of January.

Nearby is the **grotto** where it is believed that St. Emilion lived the quiet life of meditation and contemplation that eventually led to his canonization. The grotto, which is said to contain the saint's bed, is below the **Chapelle de la Trinité.** The chapel dates from the 13th century and is a rare structure in the southwest of France. Catacombs are nearby, and you can also view a spring of water surrounded by a 16th-century balustrade.

Finally, you may want to view the **Château du Roi,** founded by Henry III of the Plantagenet line in the 13th century. Until 1608 it was the town hall. From the top of the dungeon you can see St-Emilion, and, on a clear day, the Valley of the Dordogne. You can wander about daily from 9am to 12:30pm and 2:30 to 6:30pm. Admission is 6 F ($1.10).

WHERE TO STAY

HOSTELLERIE DE PLAISANCE, place du Clother, 33330 St-Emilion. Tel. 57-24-72-32. Fax 57-74-41-11. 12 rms (all with bath). A/C TEL

$ Rates: 490 F ($88.20) single; 775 F ($139.50) double. Breakfast 50 F ($9) extra. AE, DC, MC, V. **Parking:** Free. **Closed:** Jan.

This establishment, the best place to stay or dine in this medieval town, blends well with the surrounding antiquity. The well-styled rooms, some with views of stone monuments and towers, welcome the most sophisticated wine tasters and buyers in the world. The best doubles have sun terraces where you can enjoy breakfast.

The hotel also serves good regional cuisine with local wines; meals cost 140–280 F ($25.20–$50.40).

WHERE TO DINE

In addition to the following recommendation, the Hostellerie de Plaisance (see "Where to Stay," above) also serves good regional cuisine.

LOGIS DE LA CADENE, place Marché-au-Bois. Tel. 57-24-71-40.
   Cuisine: FRENCH. **Reservations:** Not required.
$ Prices: Appetizers 30–140 F ($5.40–$25.20); main dishes 75–160 F ($13.50–$28.80); fixed-price menus 90 F ($16.20), 130 F ($23.40), and 160 F ($28.80). No credit cards.
   Open: Lunch Tues–Sun 12:30–2pm; Dinner Tues–Sun 8–10pm. **Closed:** Jan.

$ This 19th-century house has a very pleasant, vine-covered terrace. Inside, the dining room has rustic decor. Specialties are often cooked on the grill over wood from local vineyards; many include flavorful local flap mushrooms called cèpes.

---

3. ANGOULEME

275 miles SW of Paris, 72 miles NE of Bordeaux

GETTING THERE   By Train or Bus   Angoulême is easily reached by train or bus from Poitiers, Limoges, or Bordeaux.

ESSENTIALS   Orientation   South of a bend in the Charente River, the old city is surrounded by medieval ramparts. The train and railway stations are outside the walls, on the eastern town border. The Cathédrale de St-Pierre lies near the western ramparts.

Information   The Office de Tourisme is located at 2, place St-Pierre (tel. 45-95-16-84).

On a hill between the Charente and Aguienne Rivers, Angoulême lies 72 miles north of Bordeaux. It can easily be visited on the same day as Cognac. A "Balzac town," Angoulême first saw the novelist in 1831 when he came here and much admired his host's wife, Zulma Carraud.

The hub of the town is **place de l'Hôtel-de-Ville,** with its Town Hall erected from 1858 to 1866 on the site of the old palace of the dukes of Angoulême, where Marguérite de Navarre, sister of Françoise I, was born. All that remains of the ducal palace are the Tower of Valois from the 15th century and the Tower of Lusignan from the 13th century.

The **Cathédrale de St-Pierre,** place St-Pierre (tel. 45-95-20-38), was begun in 1128, and it suffered much restoration in the 19th century. Flanked by two towers, its facade has a total of 75 statues—each in a separate niche—representing the Last Judgment. This church is one of the most startling examples of the Romanesque-Byzantine style in the country. Some of its restoration was questionable, however. The architect, Abadie (the designer of Sacré-Coeur in Paris), tore down the north tower, then rebuilt it with the original materials in the same style. In the interior you can wander under a four-domed ceiling.

Adjoining the cathedral is the former Bishops' Palace, which has been turned into the **Musée Municipal,** 1, rue Friedland (tel. 45-95-07-69), with a collection of European paintings, mainly from the 17th through the 19th century. The most interesting exhibits in the museum are the African art and ethnological collections as well as one of original comics. It is open Wednesday through Monday from 10am to noon and 2 to 6pm. Admission is 15 F ($2.70) for adults, free for children.

Finally, you can take the **promenade des Remparts,** boulevards laid down on the site of the town walls. Going along, you'll have a superb view of the valley almost 250 feet below.

WHERE TO STAY

ALTEA HOTEL DE FRANCE, 1, place des Halles, 16003 Angoulême CEDEX. Tel. 45-95-47-95. Fax 45-92-02-70. 90 rms (all with bath) TV TEL
$ Rates: 440 F ($79.20) single; 650 F ($117) double. Breakfast 50 F ($9) extra. AE, DC, MC, V. **Parking:** 35 F ($6.30).
I recommend this hotel for its spacious rooms with high ceilings and its walled garden with a very old topiary. The hotel is located inside the ramparts of the old city, near

the town hall. The limestone facade was carved in the 17th century. Guez de Balzac, who is credited with having helped to formalize French grammar, was born here in 1597.

On the same level as the lobby, a formal restaurant offers excellent food and polite service. Specialties include foie gras, local cèpes (flap mushrooms), and sole meunière and trout with almonds. Lunch is served Monday through Friday from noon to 1:30pm; dinner is served Sunday through Friday from 7 to 9:15pm. A four-course fixed-price menu costs 150 F ($27); à la carte meals start at 200 F ($36).

NOVOTEL ANGOULEME NORD, route de Poitiers, 16430 Champniers.
Tel. 45-68-53-22. Fax 45-68-33-83. 100 rms (all with bath). A/C TV TEL
Directions: Take the N10 from Angoulême about four miles toward Poitiers.
$ Rates: 395 F ($71.10) single; 420 F ($75.60) double. Breakfast 48 F ($8.60) extra. AE, DC, MC, V. **Parking:** Free.

This well-managed and dependable hotel, built in 1976, is a success. Rooms are simple and uniform, each with a double bed and a single bed that transforms into a couch. The grounds are filled with evergreens and well-maintained lawns. The sunny, pleasant, modern restaurant serves a variety of local and international specialties. Meals begin at 150 F ($27). Ample parking is available.

WHERE TO DINE

In addition to the following, the hotels listed above have fine restaurants.

LA RUELLE, 6, rue Trois-Nôtre-Dame. Tel. 45-92-94-64.
Cuisine: FRENCH. **Reservations:** Recommended.
$ Prices: Appetizers 45–140 F ($8.10–$25.20); main dishes 75–150 F ($13.50–$27); fixed-price menus 140 F ($25.20) (lunch only), 145 F ($26.10), 200 F ($36), and 240 F ($43.20). V.
Open: Lunch Mon–Fri noon–2pm; dinner Mon–Sat 7:30–10pm. **Closed:** Feb and Aug.

This first-class restaurant, located in the center of the oldest part of town, was once a pair of medieval houses separated by a narrow alleyway (a *ruelle*) that was covered over—hence the name. The ancient facade is made of stone blocks. Jean-François Dauphin is the proprietor and his wife, Véronique, is the cook. Menus change with the mood of the chef and the availability of ingredients, but you can count on classic French recipes given a modern twist. Véronique's specialties include sole with crayfish and cucumbers, a gigot of lamb au Romarin, and filet of beef with pigs' feet in a garlic-cream sauce. I especially recommend the fixed-price regional menus.

NEARBY ACCOMMODATIONS & DINING

LE MOULIN DU MAINE-BRUN, RN 141, Lieu-Dit la Vigerie, 16290
Asnières-sur-Nouère. Tel. 45-90-83-00. Fax 45-96-91-14. 18 rms (all with bath), 2 suites. MINIBAR TV TEL **Directions:** Drive seven miles west of Angoulême (turn right at Vigerie); take rte. 141.
$ Rates: 450–650 F ($81–$117) single; 550–750 F ($99–$135) double; 1,000–1,300 F ($180–$234) suite. Breakfast 60 F ($10.80) extra. AE, DC, MC, V. **Parking:** Free.

Built in the 14th century, this Relais & Châteaux was originally a flour mill. In the early 1960s, Raymond and Irene Ménager acquired the mill and 80 acres of lowlands, about half of which are now devoted to the production of cognac. The preferred brand of the maître d'hôtel is the one produced in the hotel's distillery: Moulin du Domaine de Maine-Brun. These are the most luxurious accommodations in the area and were built above the rock-sided banks of a swiftly flowing river. On one side of the inn, a bedroom wing, pool, and terrace were added. Rooms are conservative and furnished with some antiques, including Victorian (which the French call Charles X), Louis XVI, or Empire.

The restaurant serves some of the best cuisine in the area; specialties vary with the availability of ingredients but usually include foie gras perfumed with the house cognac. Fixed-price menus cost 180 F ($32.40), 280 F ($50.40), and 360 F ($64.80).

The restaurant is open from 12:30 to 2pm and 7:30 to 9pm; it's closed Monday in winter and in November and December.

4. COGNAC

297 miles SW of Paris, 23 miles NW of Angoulême, 70 miles SE of La Rochelle

GETTING THERE By Train Cognac's railway station is south of the town center, and has good service from Angoulême and Saintes, with connections from Bordeaux.

ESSENTIALS Orientation The most central square is place François Ier, which lies east of the cognac warehouses beside the Charente River. The center of the old town is the Church of St-Léger (enter from Aristide-Briand).

Information Contact the Office de Tourism, 16, rue du 14-Juillet (tel. 45-82-10-71).

Distillery Tours If you'd like to visit a distillery, go to its main office during regular business hours and request a tour. The staffs are generally receptive, and you'll see some brandies that have aged for as long as 50 or even 100 years. You can ask about guided tours at the tourist office (see "Information," above).

Cognac is a center for making brandy that has ennobled the tables of history. The world enjoys 100 million bottles a year of this nectar which Victor Hugo called "the drink of the gods." Sir Winston Churchill required a bottle a day. It's worth a detour to stop off here to visit one of the château warehouses of the great cognac bottlers. Martell, Hennessey, and Otard welcome visits from the public, and will even give you a free drink at the end of the tour.

The best distillery tour in my opinion is offered by **☯ Hennessy,** 1, rue de la Richonne (tel. 45-35-72-68). It's open June 15 to September 15, Monday through Saturday from 9am to 5:30pm; January to June 14 and September 16 until the end of December, Monday through Friday from 8:30 to 11am and 1:45 to 4:30pm.

You can also visit the **Cognac Museum,** 48, bd. Denfert-Rochereau (tel. 45-32-07-25). The collection includes local artifacts, wine-industry exhibits, paintings, sculpture, furniture, and decorative art. Cognac is also the birthplace of the postcard, and the museum has some of the rarest and oldest examples. The museum is open June to September, Wednesday through Monday from 10am to noon and 2 to 6pm; off-season, Wednesday through Monday from 2 to 5:30pm. Admission is free.

Cognac has two beautiful parks that should be visited: the **Parc François-Ier** and the **Parc de l'Hôtel-de-Ville.** The Romanesque-Gothic **Church of St-Léger** is from the 12th century, and its bell tower is from the 15th century.

François I was born in the ancient, now-dilapidated **château** in the town center; it dates from the 15th and 16th centuries and was a former residence of the House of Valois.

WHERE TO STAY

HOSTELLERIE LES PIGEONS BLANCS, 110, rue Jules-Brisson, 16100 Cognac. Tel. 45-82-16-36. Fax 45-82-29-29. 7 rms (all with bath). TV TEL
$ Rates: 280–450 F ($50.40–$81) single or double. Breakfast 40 F ($7.20) extra. AE, DC, MC, V. **Parking:** Free. **Closed:** Jan.

S I recommend this stylish hotel named after the white pigeons that nest in the moss-covered stone walls. (See "Where to Dine," below, for my restaurant recommendation.) This angular farmhouse with sloping tile roofs on a verdant slope was originally built in the 17th century as a coaching inn. For many years it was the private home of the Tachet family, until three of the entrepreneurial siblings transformed it into a hotel and restaurant in 1973. It's located a mile northwest of the center and has elegant guest rooms.

HOTEL IBIS / HOTEL URBIS, 24, rue Elisée-Mousnier, 16100 Cognac.
Tel. 45-82-19-53. Fax 45-82-86-71. 39 rms (all with bath), 1 suite. TV TEL
$ Rates: 265 F ($47.70) single; 295 F ($53.10) double; 400 F ($72) suite. Breakfast
35 F ($6.30) extra. AE, DC, MC, V. **Parking:** 15 F ($2.70).

S Clean, comfortable, and unpretentious, this hotel was built in the 1970s, but
not allied with the French hotel chain Accor until 1989. Today, it's identified by
townspeople as either the Ibis or the Urbis, depending on who you speak to,
although management suggests that the name Ibis will probably stick. It lies on the
same square as the Hôtel de Ville (Town Hall). There's a relaxed ambience in the
public rooms, and clean and pleasant bedrooms outfitted in a monochromatic and
standardized modern style which has proved popular throughout the rest of the chain.
Some rooms overlook a garden, and there's an elevator on the premises. No meals are
served other than breakfast, although in certain circumstances, simple platters can be
prepared for guests who prefer to dine in.

HOTEL LE VALOIS, 35, rue du 14-Juillet, 16100 Cognac. Tel. 45-82-76-
00, or toll free 800/528-1234 in the U.S. and Canada. Fax 45-82-76-00. 45 rms (all
with bath). A/C MINIBAR TV TEL
$ Rates: 360 F ($64.80) single; 520 F ($93.60) double. Breakfast 36 F ($6.50)
extra. AE, DC, MC, V. **Parking:** Free. **Closed:** Dec 23–Jan 2.
This boxy, modern hotel, located in the center of town near the post office, has a very
comfortable interior. The beige facade overlooks a busy commercial street, and the
carpeted rooms have radios, soundproof windows, and modern furniture. Breakfast is
the only meal served, but a stylish bar decorated with brass and glossy patches of
black is open day and night. The hotel is affiliated with Best Western.

WHERE TO DINE

HOSTELLERIE LES PIGEONS BLANCS, 110, rue Jules-Brisson. Tel.
45-82-16-36.
Cuisine: FRENCH. **Reservations:** Recommended.
$ Prices: Appetizers 55–100 F ($9.90–$18); main dishes 85–140 F ($15.30–
$25.20); fixed-price menus 128 F ($23), 165 F ($29.70), and 280 F ($50.40). AE,
DC, MC, V.
Open: Lunch daily noon–2pm; dinner Mon–Sat 7–10pm. **Closed:** Jan 8–31.
This restaurant run by the Tachet family has two elegant dining rooms with ceiling
beams and limestone fireplaces. Jacques is the chef de cuisine, Jean-Michel is the
maître d', and Catherine is the charming hostess. Menu listings depend on the
availability of ingredients, but might include warm oysters with a Vouvray-flavored
sabayon, rack of suckling pig with local wine, and filet of sole steamed in cognac. The
hotel is recommended under "Where to Stay," above.

LA MARMITE, 14, rue St-Jean-du-Perot. Tel. 46-41-17-03.
Cuisine: FRENCH. **Reservations:** Required in summer.
$ Prices: Appetizers 85–215 F ($15.30–$38.70); main dishes 150–290 F ($27–
$52.20); fixed-price menus 170 F ($30.60), 290 F ($52.20), and 360 F ($64.80).
AE, DC, MC, V.
Open: Lunch Thurs–Tues noon–2:30pm; dinner Thurs–Tues 7–9:15pm.
Closed: Feb 20–Mar 9.
Chef Louis Marzin is becoming better known all the time. His specialties are based on
modern French recipes he learned in his apprenticeships throughout the country; they
include a plate of "fruits of the sea," monkfish with wild mushrooms, and grilled
lobster. The decor is a cross between a tavern and a café. In one corner is a small salon
where you can order an apéritif.

NEARBY ACCOMMODATIONS & DINING

MOULIN DE CIERZAC, route de Barbezieux, Saint-Fort-sur-le-Né,
16130 St-Gonzac. Tel. 45-83-01-32. Fax 45-83-03-59. 10 rms (all with bath
or shower). TEL
$ Rates: 350–520 F ($63–$93.60) single or double. Breakfast 60 F ($10.80) extra.

AE, MC, V. **Closed:** Hotel closed late Jan to Feb. Restaurant closed Mon to Sun lunch but open Sun night for dinner. **Parking:** Free.

⭐ This former mill house, located at the southern edge of the village, has white shutters, strong horizontal lines, and lots of character. A stream runs beside the three-story building, which dates from the 18th century. The hotel rooms are comfortably furnished. The rustic dining room overlooks the park; specialties include steamed lobster in orange butter and filet of lamb in a garlic-cream sauce. Fixed-price menus begin at 180 F ($32.40), and à la carte dinners average 265 F ($47.70).

5. SAINTES

291 miles SW of Paris, 72 miles N of Bordeaux

GETTING THERE   By Train   Saintes is a railway junction for the surrounding region, and thanks to the nearby autoroutes, driving is easy. Seven or eight trains per day arrive from Bordeaux (trip time: 1¼ hours), and six trains per day pull in from Cognac (trip time: 20 minutes).

ESSENTIALS   Orientation   Straddling the banks of the Charente River, the two sides of Saintes are connected by a busy artery whose name changes from cours du 20-Novembre to avenue Gambetta. Most historic buildings are clustered near the Cathédrale de St-Pierre, on the west bank, but the famous Abbaye aux Dames is near the east bank's Jardin Public.

Information   For information, inquire at the Office de Tourisme, Villa Musso, 62, cours National (tel. 46-74-23-82).

The much-battered monuments of this town on the bank of the Charente River represent just about every civilization since the Roman occupation, which made it the capital of southwestern France. Today, on the tree-lined streets bordered with shops, you're likely to enjoy an unusual stopover.

The ancient Roman city was called Mediolanum Santonus, and was the place to which the Latin poet Ausone came to die at about the same time that Saint Eutrope began to Christianize the town. This latter action led to repeated attacks by barbarians. During the Middle Ages the Plantagenet rulers covered the city with religious monuments, many of which were visited by the pilgrims wending their way down to Santiago de Compostela in Spain.

During the 18th century and continuing into the 19th, the city witnessed the construction of many of its neoclassical buildings, such as the national theater and mansions erected by nobles as well as brigands. Saintes also holds the honor of being the birthplace of the 16th-century inventor of enameling, Bernard Palissy (1510–90).

WHAT TO SEE & DO

Major attractions include the **Abbaye aux Dames,** 7, place de l'Abbaye (tel. 46-74-23-82). It was founded in 1047 by Geoffroi Martel, Count of Anjou. It became a convent, attracting women from the finest families in France. Daughters of the nobility, among whom was the future Marquise de Montespan, were educated here. After the Revolution, so great was the hatred of the local people that the church was transformed into a dress shop. In 1942, after 20 years of restoration from the ravages of a more secular age, the church was reconsecrated. The style is Romanesque, although sections date from the 18th century. A festival of ancient music takes place here every summer. Open daily from 9am to 5pm.

The **Arc de Germanicus,** on esplanade André-Malraux near the tourist office, was built in A.D. 19 of local limestone. In 1842 it was moved from a position near the end of a Roman bridge the authorities were demolishing to its present location on the right bank of the Charente. It's dedicated to Germanicus and Tiberius.

The **Cathédrale de St-Pierre,** rue St-Pierre (tel. 49-41-23-76), was built on Roman foundations in the 12th century and greatly expanded in a flamboyant Gothic style in the 15th century under the direction of three bishops, all members of the aristocratic Rochechouart family. Parts were destroyed by the Calvinists in 1568, then rebuilt. The enormous organs date from the 16th and 17th centuries. Open daily from 9am to 5pm.

The **Old City** is an area of winding streets and a distinctly medieval flavor, stretching around the Cathedral of St-Pierre.

The **Eglise St-Eutrope,** rue St-Eutrope (tel. 46-72-34-58), is considered one of the most important monuments in all of southwestern France, despite the alterations to the nave that a misdirected series of architects performed in 1803. It was built in the 1400s by Louis XI, who revered St. Eutrope as his favorite holy man, believing the saint had cured him of a disease. The vast crypt is only half buried underground because of the slope of the land, and it's more a subterranean church than a crypt. The sarcophagus, said to contain the remains of St. Eutrope, dates from the 4th century. There's a very deep well, nearly 150 feet, in the crypt as well as several Roman-era baptismal fonts. Admission is free, but it costs 2 F (40¢) to have the crypt illuminated. Open daily from 9am to 5pm.

The **Arena** is accessible from rues St-Eutrope and Lacurie. To visit it, ring the bell for the custodian. Built at the beginning of the 1st century A.D., it's one of the oldest remaining Roman amphitheaters in the world, although it is medium-size in comparison to others. Many of the seats are covered today with wild shrubs and greenery. In its heyday it could hold 20,000 spectators. A fountain has been built halfway up the slope of one of the sides, marking the spot where a disciple of St. Eutrope was beheaded. Open June through September, daily from 9am to 8pm (off-season, daily from 9am to 6pm). Admission is free.

The **Musée Dupuy-Mestreau,** 4, rue Monconseil (tel. 46-93-36-71), is installed in an 18th-century palace with many rich architectural details of that period, as well as furniture, more than 200 rare postage stamps of the region, re-creations of centuries-old regional costumes, painted porcelains, 13th-century weapons, and a re-creation of an aristocratic 18th-century bedroom. Open April to October, Wednesday through Monday from 2 to 6pm; November to March, Wednesday through Sunday from 2 to 6pm. Admission is 20 F ($3.60) for adults and 12 F ($2.20) for children.

WHERE TO STAY

HOTEL DE L'AVENUE, 114, av. Gambetta, 17100 Saintes. Tel. 46-74-05-91. Fax 46-74-32-16. 15 rms (13 with bath or shower). TV TEL
$ Rates: 162 F ($29.20) single or double without bath or shower, 235–260 F ($42.30–$46.80) single or double with bath or shower. Breakfast 27 F ($4.90) extra. MC, V. **Parking:** Free.

Built in the 1970s, this hotel was richly and comfortably renovated in 1991. Today, bedrooms are cozily outfitted in tones of pink, blue, or green, and decorated with unusual lithographs and tasteful accessories. None of the bedrooms overlooks the traffic on the avenue outside, but, rather, a flowering courtyard or the garden in back. The Crozas family are the owners, who do not maintain a restaurant, but who direct guests to the adjacent Brasserie Louis (see "Where to Dine," below).

RELAIS DU BOIS ST-GEORGES, rue de Royan, 17100 Saintes. Tel. 46-93-50-99. Fax 46-93-34-93. 21 rms (all with bath), 10 suites. TV TEL
$ Rates: 500 F ($90) single; 600–750 F ($108–$135) double; from 980 F ($176.40) suite. Breakfast 70 F ($12.60) extra. MC, V. **Parking:** Free.

Conveniently situated right off the Paris–Bordeaux motorway, the Relais du Bois St-Georges is in a vast park with flower gardens. It has its own covered swimming pool and a small lake with ducks and swans. Rooms are a well-balanced combination of modern comfort and antique furnishings, some with private terraces overlooking the lake and garden. Rooms are rented in the old part of the hotel or in a newer part, which includes 10 stylish rooms and suites, each uniquely decorated.

The restaurant section is located in a renovated farmhouse, which has a view of the park and lake. The chef prepares savory specialties, including suprême of turbot in a langoustine sauce, marinated tournedos with fine cognac, and a dessert trolley filled with homemade delicacies. Fixed-price menus are offered at 160 F ($28.80), 240 F ($43.20), and 460 F ($82.80).

WHERE TO DINE

BRASSERIE LOUIS, 116, av. Gambetta. Tel. 46-74-16-85.

Cuisine: FRENCH. **Reservations:** Recommended.

$ **Prices:** Appetizers 18–64 F ($3.20–$11.50); main dishes 58–78 F ($10.40–$14); fixed-price menus 62 F ($11.20) (Tues–Fri only), and 88–160 F ($15.80–$28.80). MC, V.

Open: Lunch Tues–Sun noon–2pm; dinner Tues–Sun 7–10pm.

Named after its since-departed founder, this pleasant brasserie occupies the street level of a modern building whose interior is lined with multicolored brick. Inside, about 100 places are available for locals who look for honest, simple preparations of traditional recipes. There's an outdoor terrace overlooking a garden in back, where some of the noise from the street is obscured. Menu items include platters of shellfish, mussels prepared with either white wine or curry sauce, rack of lamb with herbs, and endless platters of entrecôte of beef with french fries.

NEARBY DINING

LA VIEILLE FORGE, route 137, vers La Rochelle. Tel. 46-92-98-30.

Cuisine: FRENCH. **Reservations:** Not required. **Directions:** Take rte. 137 to St-Georges-des-Coteaux, 3¾ miles northwest of Saintes.

$ **Prices:** Appetizers 22–45 F ($4–$8.10); main dishes 55–130 F ($9.90–$21.60); fixed-price menus 65–185 F ($11.70–$33.30). AE, DC, MC, V.

Open: Lunch daily noon–1:45pm; dinner Tues–Sat 7–9:30pm.

Despite its relative isolation midway between the villages of St-Porchaire and Saintes, this is one of the busiest restaurants in the region. It used to be a forge for a local blacksmith. The dining room in the renovated building has a high-peaked roof and is decorated with bellows and iron tools used by 19th-century blacksmiths. Typical menu items include cèpes (flap mushrooms) bordelaise, brochette of magrêt of duckling garnished with three different kinds of pepper, woodcocks with grapes, fish soup, and house-style filet of sole.

6. LA ROCHELLE

290 miles SW of Paris, 90 miles SE of Nantes,
100 miles S of Bordeaux, 88 miles NW of Angoulême

GETTING THERE By Plane The La Rochelle–Laleu airport is on the coast, north of the city.

By Train Rail connections from Bordeaux and Nantes are frequent. Six to eight trains from Bordeaux arrive daily (trip time: 2 hours), and four to five trains from Nantes (trip time: 2 hours). The TGV fast trains from Paris arrive seven to nine times per day (trip time: 3 hours).

ESSENTIALS Orientation Set on one of France's finest Atlantic harbors, the old city contains many pedestrians-only zones, making sightseeing easy. The neighborhood that runs from south to north between the Vieux-Port and place de Verdun is particularly full of old buildings.

Information The Office de Tourisme is at place Petite Sirène (tel. 46-41-14-68).

Once known as the French Geneva, La Rochelle is a historic port and ancient sailors' city, formerly the stronghold of the Huguenots. It was founded as a fishing village in the 10th century on a rocky platform in the center of a huge marshland. Eleanor of Aquitaine in 1199 gave La Rochelle a charter, freeing it from feudal dues. Becoming an independent city-state, the port capitalized on the wars between France and

England. From the port sailed the founders of Montréal and many others who helped to colonize Canada. On the Atlantic coast, the city lies 90 miles southeast of Nantes on the railway line to Bordeaux, 100 miles to the south. From the 14th to the 16th century it enjoyed its heyday as one of France's great maritime cities.

As a hotbed of Protestant factions, it armed privateers to prey on Catholic vessels. But it was eventually besieged by Catholic troops. Two strong men led the fight—Cardinal Richelieu (with, of course, his Musketeers) and Jean Guiton, formerly an admiral and then mayor of the city. Richelieu proceeded to blockade the port. Although La Rochelle bravely resisted, on October 30, 1628, Richelieu entered the city. From the almost 30,000 citizens of the proud city, he found only 5,000 survivors.

La Rochelle became the principal port between France and the colony of Canada, but the loss of Canada by France ruined its Atlantic trade.

WHAT TO SEE & DO

There are now two different aspects of La Rochelle, the old and untouched town inside the Vauban defenses and the modern and industrial suburbs. Its fortifications have a circuit of 3½ miles with a total of seven gates.

The town with its arch-covered streets will please the walker. The port is still a bustling fishing harbor and one of the greatest sailing centers in western Europe. Try to schedule a visit in time to attend a fish auction at the harbor. The best streets for strolling are **rue du Palais, rue Chaudrier,** and **rue des Merciers** with its ancient wooden houses. On the latter street, seek out in particular the houses at nos. 17, 8, 5, and 3.

HOTEL DE VILLE, place de la Mairie. Tel. 46-41-90-44.

The town hall, located in the city center, is constructed in a flamboyant 14th-century Gothic style, with battlements. Inside you can admire the Henry II staircase with canopies and the marble desk of the heroic Jean Guiton.

Admission: 14 F ($2.50) adults, 7 F ($1.30) children 4–12.

Open: Easter to late Sept, Mon–Fri 9:30–11am and 2:30–5:30pm, Sat 2:30–5pm; late Sept to Easter, Sun–Fri 2:30–4:30pm.

TOUR DE LA CHAÎNE, quai du Gabut. Tel. 46-50-52-36.

Opposite the Tower of St. Nicholas (see below), the Tour de la Chaîne is named for the large chain that was fastened to it and pulled across the harbor to close it at night. The tower dates from the 14th century.

Admission: 12 F ($2.20) adults, free for children under 16.

Open: May–Sept, daily 10am–noon and 2–6:30pm; Oct–Apr, Sat–Sun 10am–noon and 2–6:30pm.

TOUR DE ST-NICOLAS and TOUR DE LA LANTERNE, quai du Gabut. Tel. 46-41-74-13.

The oldest tower in La Rochelle is the Tower of St. Nicholas, dating from either 1371 or 1382. From its second floor you can enjoy a view of the town and harbor. However, from the top you can see only the old town and Ile d'Oléron. The Tour de la Lanterne was built between 1445 and 1476. It was once a lighthouse but was used mainly as a jail—La Rochelle sergeants were imprisoned here in 1822.

Admission: Tower of St. Nicholas only, 20 F ($3.60) adults, 6 F ($1.10) children.

Open: June–Aug, daily 9:30am–7pm; Apr–May and Sept, Wed–Mon 9:30am–12:30pm and 2–6:30pm; Oct–Mar, Wed–Mon 9:30am–12:30pm and 2–5pm.

MUSEE DES BEAUX-ARTS, 28, rue Gargoulleau. Tel. 46-41-64-65.

French paintings are displayed in this episcopal palace that was built in the mid-18th century. The art spans the 17th to the 19th century, with works by Eustache Le Sueur, Brossard de Beaulieu, Corot, and Fromentin. Some 20th-century art is by Maillol and Lagar.

Admission: 12 F ($2.20); also allows entrance to the Musée d'Orbigny-Bernon (see below).

Open: Wed–Mon 2–6pm.

MUSEE D'ORBIGNY-BERNON, 2, rue St-Côme. Tel. 46-41-18-83.

The most important artifacts pertaining to the history of La Rochelle and to the history of ceramics are displayed here. Included are painted porcelain from La Rochelle and other places throughout France.

Admission: 12 F ($2.20); also allows entrance to the Musée des Beaux-Arts (see above).

Open: Wed–Mon 10am–noon and 2–6pm.

MUSEE DU NOUVEAU-MONDE, in the Hôtel Fleuriau, 10, rue Fleuriau. Tel. 46-41-46-50.

This museum traces the port's 300-year history with the New World. Exhibits start with the discovery of the Mississippi Delta in 1682 by LaSalle and end with the settling of the Louisiana territory. Other exhibits depict French settlements in the French West Indies, including Guadeloupe and Martinique.

Admission: 12 F ($2.20) adults, free for children under 18.

Open: Fri–Wed 10:30am–12:30pm and 1:30–6pm.

MUSEE LAFAILLE, 28, rue Albert-ler. Tel. 46-41-18-25.

This ethnography and zoology museum is in a handsome 18th-century building surrounded by a flowering garden; the original paneling has been preserved. Clement de Lafaille, a former comptroller of war, assembled much of the collection, which has been enlarged since he donated it to the city. Displays include rare shellfish, an idol from Easter Island, an embalmed giraffe given to Charles X (the first such specimen to be seen in France), and a parade boat encrusted with gems that was presented as a gift from the King of Siam to Napoléon III.

Admission: 14 F ($2.50) adults, free for children.

Open: Mid-June to mid-Sept, Tues–Sat 10am–noon and 2–6pm, Sun 2–6pm; off-season, Tues–Sat 10am–noon and 2–5pm, Sun 2–5pm. **Closed:** Holidays.

WHERE TO STAY

HOTEL FRANÇOIS-I, 13, rue Bazoges, 17000 La Rochelle. Tel. 46-41-28-46. Fax 46-41-35-01. 38 rms (all with bath or shower). TV TEL

$ Rates: 170–450 F ($30.60–$81); single or double. Breakfast 35 F ($6.30) extra. MC, V. **Parking:** 30 F ($5.40).

This hotel seems to turn the clock back two centuries, but the plumbing is quite modern. Service is efficient and kind, and rooms are pleasantly furnished. Breakfast is the only meal served, and the hotel has a parking garage.

HOTEL LES BRISES, chemin de la Digne-Richelieu, 17000 La Rochelle. Tel. 46-43-89-37. Fax 46-43-27-97. 48 rms (all with bath). TV TEL

$ Rates: 325–625 F ($58.50–$112.50) single or double. Breakfast 45 F ($8.10) extra. MC, V. **Parking:** Free.

Facing the sea, this hotel is the most tranquil and scenically located; it's opposite the new port (Port des Minimes) and within view of the soaring 19th-century column dedicated to the Virgin. You can enjoy the view from the front balconies, and there is a parasol-shaded patio behind a sturdy retaining wall. The immaculate rooms have cherrywood furniture. Breakfast is the only meal served, and the hotel has a parking garage.

NOVOTEL LA ROCHELLE CENTRE, 1, av. de la Porte-Neuve, 17000 La Rochelle. Tel. 46-34-24-24. Fax. 46-34-58-32. 94 rms (all with bath). MINIBAR TV TEL

$ Rates: 455 F ($81.90) single; 630 F ($113.40) double. Breakfast 52 F ($9.40) extra. AE, DC, MC, V. **Parking:** 45 F ($8.10).

Built in 1989, this five-story hotel occupies a verdant and desirable location within the Parc Charruyer, a greenbelt about a five-minute walk from the historic port of La Rochelle. Bedrooms are monochromatic, standardized, well maintained, and comfortable, with generously proportioned writing desks and big windows overlooking the park. On the premises is an outdoor swimming pool.

An in-house restaurant serves drinks and platters throughout the day, with fixed-price meals priced at around 120 F ($21.60) each.

WHERE TO DINE

LE CLARIDGE, 1, rue Admyrault. Tel. 46-41-35-71.
  Cuisine: FRENCH. **Reservations:** Required.
$ Prices: Appetizers 75–100 F ($13.50–$18); main dishes 85–120 F ($15.30–$21.60); fixed-price menus 98–150 F ($17.60–$27). AE, MC, V.
  Open: Lunch Mon–Fri 12:30–2pm; dinner Mon–Sat 8–10pm.

The cheaper fixed-price meal here is popular with budget travelers. The restaurant is one floor above street level in a 17th-century building, which was originally used as a private house; it's located in the center of the old town. The dining room has a grand fireplace, heavy ceiling beams, thick carpeting, and attractively decorated tables with lots of space. The cuisine is traditional; a typical meal often includes half a dozen oysters, a confit of duckling house style, cheese, and dessert. The chef is particularly proud of his foie gras of duckling, his smoked salmon of the house, his feuilletté of scallops, and his assortment of fresh fish in a sauce consisting of a coulis of crayfish tails.

LES QUATRE SERGEANTS, 49, rue-St-Jean-du-Pérot. Tel. 46-41-35-80.
  Cuisine: FRENCH. **Reservations:** Required.
$ Prices: Appetizers 70–80 F ($12.60–$14.40); main dishes 80–100 F ($14.40–$18); fixed-price menus 75 F ($13.50), 108 F ($19.40), 158 F ($28.40). AE, DC, MC, V.
  Open: Lunch Tues–Sun noon–2pm; dinner Tues–Sat 7:30–10pm.

The building containing this restaurant was built around 1880, in a fanciful art nouveau–greenhouse style which some visitors compare to the framework of the Eiffel Tower in Paris. Capped with a soaring glass canopy which floods the interior with sunlight, this garden-style restaurant overlooks the town center from a position near the port of La Rochelle. Specialties include a ragoût of seafood, duxelles of turbot, mussels in curry sauce, and several regional recipes whose makeup has not changed very much in about 100 years.

RICHARD COUTANCEAU, plage de la Concurrence. Tel. 46-41-48-19.
  Cuisine: FRENCH. **Reservations:** Required.
$ Prices: Appetizers 95–130 F ($17.10–$23.40); main dishes 125–180 F ($22.50–$32.40). AE, DC, MC, V.
  Open: Lunch Mon–Sat noon–2pm; dinner Tues–Sat 7:30–9:30pm.

Delectable cuisine is served in this circular concrete pavilion built in a pine-filled park, located near the casino. Half is devoted to a tea room, the rest to an elegant and informal dining room. Mirrors opposite a bay window reflect a view of the water. Richard Coutanceau is both owner and chef; his "modernized" cuisine often includes fresh shellfish plucked from nearby waters, lobster-filled ravioli with zucchini flowers, roast bass, and Brittany lobster.

NEARBY ATTRACTIONS

LA PALLICE   Three miles to the east of La Rochelle is the commercial port of La Pallice. The Germans erected large submarine bases here in World War II, some of which can still be seen. The port was heavily bombarded by the Allies. Buses to La Pallice are available at the railway station in La Rochelle, but you may prefer a round-trip by ferry.

France's Atlantic Islands

Many of France's unusual pieces of geography have never fully reached the consciousness of North Americans because of the sheer volume of mainland attractions. Clustered just to the north of the mouth of the Gironde lie at least five sandy islands, the biggest of which are the Ile d'Oléron and the Ile de Ré. Favored by French families who flock to their beaches, the islands are filled with pines, stone buildings, seasonal restaurants serving fresh local oysters, limestone outcroppings, and the ruins of very old windmills.

ILE D'OLERON   A bridge between the mainland and the Ile d'Oléron makes access to the second-largest of France's offshore islands (Corsica is bigger) relatively easy. The bridge is at Marennes, some 35 miles south from La Rochelle. The toll is 45 F ($8.10) round-trip for a car and driver.

The Romans called Oléron Ularius, and for centuries it occupied a strategic position at the head of the Gironde estuary, lying between two of the major trading ports of the Atlantic, La Rochelle and Bordeaux. Eleanor of Aquitaine lived in the island's château in 1199, just five years before she died. Notwithstanding her banishment, she imposed legal restraints on the island, and helped to create a maritime code for it which was used centuries later as the basis for France's laws of the seas.

For more insights into her life, you can visit the **Musée de l'Ile d'Oléron Aliénor-d'Aquitaine,** 37, rue Pierre-Loti, at Saint-Pierre-d'Oléron. Open mid-June to mid-September, daily from 10am to noon and 2:30 to 6:30pm. Admission is 20 F ($3.60).

Many visitors, however, prefer simply to drive around the island's perimeter, gazing at sparkling water, the miles of oyster-laden salt flats, and the sprinkling of old churches whose spires dot the air and the wave-scoured landscapes. For more information about the Ile d'Oléron, contact the **Office du Tourisme,** place Gambetta, St-Pierre-d'Oléron (tel. 46-47-11-39). It's closed in October and every afternoon in winter.

ILE DE RE The more densely populated Ile de Ré endured the attempts for many centuries of England's imperialist yearnings, often submitting to attacks by redcoats. In 1625 more than 2,000 English soldiers were slaughtered when the armies of Louis XIII attacked them simultaneously from two sides.

One of the main products of the island today—other than tourism—is wine which French connoisseurs claim bears a subtle taste of algae.

In 1988, a bridge nearly two miles long was built to connect the Ile de Ré with the mainland. Round-trip passage costs 110 F ($19.80) per vehicle from June 1 to September 30, but only 60 F ($10.80) per vehicle off-season.

Ré has several information offices, the most convenient of which is the **Office de Tourisme,** place de la République, Rivedoux-Plage (tel. 46-09-80-62). It's open all year.

---

7. POITIERS

207 miles SW of Paris, 110 miles SE of Nantes

GETTING THERE   By Train Rail service is available from Paris, Bordeaux, and La Rochelle. Some 14 of the fast TGV trains arrive from Paris daily (trip time: 1½ hours). Eight trains arrive daily from Bordeaux (trip time: 1¾ hours), and seven trains also pull in daily from La Rochelle (trip time: 2 hours).

ESSENTIALS   Orientation Poitiers was built south of a bend in the Clain River, which defines its northern boundaries. The train station is on the southwestern edge of the old city. The old city's most important squares are place du Maréchal-Leclerc and place de Gaulle. Place de la Cathédrale, with its adjacent Cathédrale de St-Pierre and its Baptistère St-Jean, are a few blocks from the river. The triangle defined by these three squares contains many of the old town's most important sights. Outside the town center, the city grows more industrial.

Information The Office de Tourisme is at 8, rue des Grandes-Ecoles (tel. 49-41-21-24).

This city, the ancient capital of Poitou, the northern part of Aquitaine, is filled with history and memories. Everybody has passed through here from England's Black Prince to Joan of Arc to Richard the Lion-Hearted.

Some 200 miles southwest of Paris on the rail line to Bordeaux, Poitiers stands on a hill overlooking the Clain and Boivre Rivers. It was this very strategic location that tempted so many conquerors. Charles Martel proved the savior of Christendom by chasing out the Muslims in 732 and perhaps altering the course of European civilization. Poitiers was the chief city of Eleanor of Aquitaine, who discarded her pious French husband, Louis VII, in favor of England's Henry II.

For those interested in antiquity, this is one of the most fascinating towns in France. That battle we learned about in history books was fought on September 19, 1356, between the armies of Edward the Black Prince and those of King John of France. It was one of the three great English victories of the Hundred Years' War, distinguished by the use of the longbow in the skilled hands of English archers.

WHAT TO SEE & DO

In the eastern sector of Poitiers is the twin-towered **Cathédrale de St-Pierre,** place de la Cathédrale (tel. 49-41-23-76). It was begun in 1162 by Henry II of England and Eleanor of Aquitaine on the ruins of a Roman basilica. The cathedral was completed much later, but it has always been undistinguised architecturally. However, the interior, which is 295 feet long, contains some admirable stained glass from the early 13th century. Open daily from 8am to 7pm.

From the cathedral you can walk to the **Baptistère St-Jean,** rue Jean-Jaurès (no phone). This is considered the most ancient Christian monument in France. It was built as a baptistery in the first half of the 4th century on Roman foundations, then extended in the 7th century. It contains frescoes from the 11th to the 14th century and a collection of funerary sculpture. It's open in July and August, daily from 10:30am to 12:30pm and 3 to 6pm; April to June and September to October, Wednesday through Monday from 10:30am to 12:30pm and 3 to 6pm; November to March, Wednesday through Monday from 2:30 to 4:30pm. Admission is 8 F ($1.40).

A favorite place of pilgrimage in times gone by, the 11th-century **Église Ste-Radegonde,** in the eastern section of Poitiers, commemorates the patroness of Poitiers. In its crypt is her black marble sarcophagus. Radegonde, who died in 587, was the consort of Clotaire, king of the Franks.

Notre-Dame-la-Grande, place de Gaule (tel. 49-41-22-56), is from the late 11th century, built in the Romanesque-Byzantine style and considered one of the most richly decorated churches in the country. See especially its west front, dating from the mid-12th century. Surrounded by an open-air market, the facade, carved like an ivory casket, is characterized by pine-cone-shaped towers. Carvings on the doorway represent biblical scenes. Open daily from 8am to 7pm.

From place du Maréchal-Leclerc, in the center of town, you can take rue Carnot to the Romanesque **Eglise St-Hilaire-le-Grand,** rue St-Hilaire (tel. 49-41-21-57). The church dates from the 11th and 12th centuries; after much destruction, it was restored in the 19th century. Open daily from 9am to 5pm.

The **Palais de Justice,** place Lepetit (tel. 49-52-24-63), incorporates the 14th-century keep and some other parts of a ducal palace that stood here. It was here that Joan of Arc was questioned by the doctors of the university who composed the French Court of Parliament, and also here that Richard the Lion-Hearted was proclaimed comte de Poitou and duc d'Anjou in 1170. Open to the public Monday through Friday from 9am to noon and 2 to 5pm.

The **Musée St-Croix,** accessible from 61, rue St-Simplicien (tel. 49-41-07-53), was built on the site of the old abbey of St-Croix from which it takes its name. The museum has a fine-arts section devoted mainly to painting—especially Flemish art from the 16th and 17th centuries and Dutch paintings from the 16th to the 18th century. Several works by Bonnard, Sisley, and Oudot are displayed from the 19th and 20th centuries, along with a bronze, *The Three Graces,* by Maillol. A separate archeological section documents the history of Poitou, dating from prehistoric times through the Gallo-Roman era, the Renaissance, and up to the end of the 19th century. Open Wednesday through Monday from 10am to noon and 2 to 6pm; closed holidays. Admission is free.

In the environs, and drawing some one million visitors annually, **Futuroscope,** in Jaunay-Clan on the N10 (tel. 49-49-30-10), a science amusement park, lies 5½ miles north of Poitiers. It's a wonderland of technology. Whether it's for watching films or finding out about new technology, Futuroscope offers visitors a chance to experience sounds, images, and sensations new to them. The park has the most advanced film-projection techniques and the world's largest screens. It's a world devoted to the moving image. Exhibitions include "Kinemax" (a magnificent rock crystal covered with mirrors with a 400-seat cinema); "Omnimax" (films projected onto a gigantic dome via a special fish-eye lens putting you into the heart of the action); *Le Tapis Magique* (a cinema that lets you fly above a continent with a monarch butterfly to guide you), and a 3-D cinema that puts you close to the lions on a safari. One park is devoted to children. From Poitiers, bus no. 16 runs to the park. The park is open in July and August, daily from 9am to 7pm; April to June and in September, daily from 9:30am to 6:30pm; in October and November, daily from 9am to 6pm; closed December to March. Admission is 105 F ($18.90) for adults, 80 F ($14.40) for children.

WHERE TO STAY

GRAND HOTEL DE L'EUROPE, 39, rue Carnot, 86000 Poitiers. Tel. 49-88-12-00. Fax 49-88-97-30. 88 rms (all with bath). TV TEL **Bus:** 1, 2, or 9.
$ Rates: 300–480 F ($54–$86.40) single; 360–480 F ($64.80–$86.40) double. Breakfast 36 F ($6.50) extra. DC, MC, V. **Parking:** 20 F ($3.60).

Two hundred years ago this was a coaching inn, and later the stables were transformed into additional bedrooms, 35 of which contain minibars. The field where the horses were watered is now a quiet courtyard with trees and shrubbery. The isolation of this establishment enhances its sense of 1930s civility. Breakfast is served in an old-fashioned dining room, flanked with tall windows and an elaborately decorated fireplace. Many of the bedrooms received major renovations in 1989 and again in 1991 and are much more modern than the gracefully antique public rooms suggest.

HOTEL DU PLAT D'ETAIN, 7, rue du Plat-d'Etain, 86000 Poitiers. Tel. 49-41-04-80. 24 rms (21 with bath or shower). MINIBAR TV TEL **Bus:** 2A.
$ Rates: 225 F ($40.50) single or double without bath; 285 F ($51.30) single or double with bath or shower. Breakfast 35 F ($6.30) extra. AE, DC, MC, V. **Parking:** 15 F ($2.70).

One of the best bargains in Poitiers, this renovated hotel is located on a narrow alley, just a few steps from place du Maréchal-Leclerc. Many restaurants and sights are nearby. Several readers have commented on the warmth of the staff. Each room has one or two double beds. There is a guarded parking area.

WHERE TO DINE

AUX ARMES D'OBERNAI, 19, rue Arthur-Ranc. Tel. 49-41-16-33.
Cuisine: ALSATIAN. **Reservations:** Required.
$ Prices: Appetizers 48–92 F ($8.60–$16.60); main dishes 88–118 F ($15.80–$21.20); fixed-price menus 105 F ($18.90), 145 F ($26.10), and 210 F ($37.80). AE, DC, MC, V.
Open: Lunch Tues–Sun noon–1:45pm; dinner Tues–Sat 7:30–9:30pm.

This small restaurant is located in the town center near the post office. Denise Husser, one of the outstanding chefs in the region, is assisted by her husband, Louis. Specialties include lamb with thyme leaves, mignon of veal with honey and lemon, and sole with crayfish and a fondue of leeks.

MAXIME, 4, rue St-Nicolas. Tel. 49-41-09-55.
Cuisine: FRENCH. **Reservations:** Recommended.
$ Prices: Appetizers 55–110 F ($9.90–$19.80); main dishes 110–186 F ($19.80–$33.50); fixed-price menus 105 F ($18.90), 150 F ($27), 185 F ($33.30), and 235 F ($42.30). AE, V.
Open: Lunch Mon–Fri noon–2pm; dinner Mon–Sat 7:30–10pm. **Closed:** Jan 5–15, July 10–20, and Aug 10–20.

Maxime is considered the finest and most sophisticated restaurant in town. Check your coat at the street-level reception desk, then perhaps order a before-dinner drink in the salon. The upstairs dining room has bourgeois warmth and a huge reproduction of a medieval battle scene from the tapestry of Bayeux. Christian Rougier is the charming and hard-working chef. The menu varies with the seasons, but often includes ravioli with hot oysters, râble of rabbit with forcemeat and chardonnay sauce, hot goat's cheese in puff pastry, gigot of monkfish studded with garlic cloves, and a succulent array of desserts.

RESTAURANT PIERRE-BENOIST, La Croutelle. Tel. 49-57-11-52.
    Cuisine: FRENCH. **Reservations:** Required. **Directions:** Take the N10 southwest of Poitiers.
$ **Prices:** Appetizers 68–120 F ($12.20–$21.60); main dishes 115–145 F ($20.70–$26.10); fixed-price menus 160–180 F ($28.80–$32.40). AE, DC, MC, V.
    Open: Lunch Tues–Sat 12:30–2:30pm; dinner Tues–Sat 7:30–9:15pm, Sun noon–5pm. **Closed:** Jan 10–24 and Aug 1–7.

Once a farm, this establishment now serves the top-quality cuisine of Pierre Benoist. The outdoor terrace has a view over the wooded hillsides of the Clain valley. The menu includes a few regional dishes, such as rump of billygoat with green garlic. However, Benoist is mostly known for his light-textured specialties, including small lobsters with a foie-gras sauce, veal sweetbreads stuffed with morels in a vermouth-laced sauce, and a caramelized tart with a red fruit sauce.

NEARBY ACCOMMODATIONS & DINING

LE CHALET DE VENISE, 6, rue de Square (B.P.4), 86280 Saint-Benoît. Tel. 49-88-45-07. Fax 49-52-95-44. 10 rms (all with bath or shower). TEL
    Directions: Take the D88 south 2½ miles from Poitiers to Saint-Benoît, or Rte. A10 to Exit 20, "Poitiers Sud."
$ **Rates:** 200 F ($36) single; 240 F ($43.20) double. Breakfast 28 F ($5) extra. AE, MC, V. **Parking:** Free.

Those who don't want to stay in the center of town will enjoy this small, reasonably priced inn in a pleasant location near a church; surrounded by trees and shrubbery, the chalet opens onto the water. The rooms are simply furnished, clean, and comfortable, each with a distinct personality. The hotel and restaurant are warmly furnished and decorated with autumn colors.

Drinks are served on a flagstone terrace, and the restaurant has a fireplace. The food is among the best in the Poitiers area, but dieters may find the portions large. Fixed-price menus are offered at 99 F ($17.80), 159 F ($28.60), 199 F ($35.80), and 270 F ($48.60)—but for many of the specialties of Poitou you'll have to order à la carte. The restaurant is open Tuesday through Sunday from noon to 2pm and 7:30 to 9pm; closed February 1–15 and September 1–10.

NOVOTEL POITIERS NORD, route 10, 86361 Chasseneuil CEDEX. Tel. 49-52-78-78. Fax 49-52-28-04. 89 rms (all with bath). A/C MINIBAR TV TEL
    Directions: From the A10, exit at Poitiers Nord or Futuroscope, then follow the blue-and-white Novotel signs for about 1½ miles to the suburb of Chasseneuil.
$ **Rates:** 425 F ($76.50) single; 495 F ($89.10) double. Breakfast 50 F ($9) extra. AE, DC, MC, V. **Parking:** Free.

Many travelers, especially those arriving late at night, appreciate this hotel's easy-to-find location in an industrial suburb 5½ miles north of the center of Poitiers. Rooms are large, with no surprises but no disappointments; each contains a single bed (which doubles as a sofa with bolster cushions), a double bed, and a long writing desk. Built in 1976, the hotel offers a large park, terrace, and swimming pool. The restaurant serves regional and international dishes daily from 6am to midnight. Meals begin at 160 F ($28.80). There is also a bar.

CHAPTER 24

THE BASQUE COUNTRY & THE PYRENEES

The chief tourist interest in the Basque country, a land rich in folklore and old customs, is confined to a small corner of southwestern France, near the Spanish frontier. There you can visit the Basque capital at Bayonne and explore the coastal resorts, chic Biarritz and St-Jean-de-Luz. In the Roman arena at Bayonne in July and August you can see a real Spanish bullfight. The typical costume of the Basque—beret and cummerbund—isn't as plentiful as it once was, but is still evident.

Stretching the length of the Spanish frontier, the vast Pyrenean region of France is a land of glaciers, wild summits, thermal baths, subterranean grottoes and caverns, winter sports centers, and trout-filled mountain streams. Pau is a good base for excursions in the western Pyrénées; and Lourdes, of course, is the major religious pilgrimage center in all of France.

We'll begin in the west at Bayonne, working our way east across the mountain range.

SEEING THE BASQUE COUNTRY & THE PYRENEES

GETTING THERE   The most beautiful months to visit are May and September; the most crowded time is undoubtedly August, when hotel reservations are hard to come by.

If you depend on public transportation, make Biarritz your center—in the heart of the Basque coast, it has many attractions and a good transportation network. **Air Inter** flies three times daily from Orly Ouest or Charles de Gaulle outside Paris. There are also overnight **trains** from Gare d'Austerlitz in Paris, and you can rent **cars** at the train station or airport in Biarritz for a driving tour.

Many visitors prefer to make Lourdes their base, and it's easily reached on a daily flight from Paris. Or you can use Toulouse as a gateway to the Pyrénées, since there are 14 daily flights from Paris and a number of excellent roads between Toulouse and Lourdes.

A SUGGESTED ROUTE   Arrive in Biarritz (Day 1) and spend the day on the beach. While still based in Biarritz, visit St-Jean-de-Luz (Day 2) for lunch and a stroll on its long sandy beach. Pay a morning visit to Bayonne (Day 3), returning to Biarritz for a

WHAT'S SPECIAL ABOUT THE BASQUE COUNTRY & THE PYRENEES

Beaches
☐ Grand Plage and Plage de la Côte des Basques, at Biarritz, among the most fashionable in the world.
☐ St-Jean-de-Luz, the second major French Basque resort, with a long curving beach of beautiful fine sand.

Great Towns/Villages
☐ Bayonne, the leading port and yacht basin on the Côte Basque.
☐ Biarritz, the premier Basque sea resort, the stamping ground of royalty.
☐ Lourdes, the major pilgrimage center for Catholics worldwide.

Ancient Monuments
☐ Cathédrale de Ste-Marie, at Bayonne, a landmark Gothic cathedral from the early 13th century.

Castles
☐ Château de Pau, at Pau, the Renaissance center of Margaret of Navarre, known for her bawdy writings.

Architectural Highlights
☐ Hôtel du Palais, at Biarritz, built by Napoléon III for Empress Eugénie and now a deluxe hotel.
☐ Boulevard des Pyrénées, at Pau, an esplanade built by Napoléon I and offering a famous panoramic view.

Gastronomic Pilgrimages
☐ Les Prés et les Sources d'Eugénie, at Eugénie-les-Bains, center of the famous chef Michel Guérard, who gave us revolutionary *cuisine minceur*.

Spa Retreats
☐ Cauterets, site of a dozen curative thermal springs that have attracted the great.
☐ Ax-les-Thermes, center of three spas.

Events/Festivals
☐ Biarritz, the Summer Festival and regatta in July and August.

---

night at the casino. Now head deep into the Pyrénées to Pau (Day 4). Continue to Lourdes (Day 5) for another night, exploring its religious monuments. Then drive south into the mountains toward the Spanish border for an overnight stay at Cauterets (Day 6), a famous spa.

1. BAYONNE

478 miles SW of Paris, 114 miles SW of Bordeaux

GETTING THERE   By Train   Train service is available from Biarritz, Bordeaux, Paris, Toulouse, and many smaller towns nearby.

By Bus   There's bus service from Biarritz and many outlying towns not serviced by train.

ESSENTIALS   Orientation   The town was built around the junction of the Adour River and its smaller tributary, the Nive River. The older section, Grand-Bayonne, on the west bank of the Nive, contains the Cathédrale de Ste-Marie and the Château-Vieux. Petit-Bayonne lies on the east bank and contains the Château-Neuf and the town's two most important museums. Across the Adour lies the railway station, place de la République, and the neighborhood known as Esprit.

Information   The Office de Tourisme is on place des Basques (tel. 59-59-31-31).

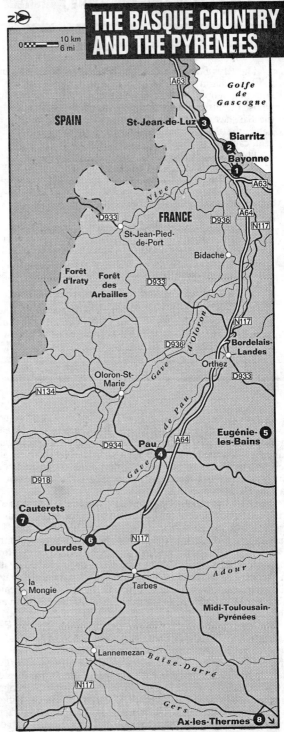

THE BASQUE COUNTRY AND THE PYRENEES

- **1** Bayonne
- **2** Biarritz
- **3** St-Jean-de-Luz
- **4** Pau
- **5** Eugénie-les-Bains
- **6** Lourdes
- **7** Cauterets
- **8** Ax-les-Thermes

PARIS

The Basque Country

0   10 km
    6 mi

SPAIN

FRANCE

Golfe de Gascogne

A63

St-Jean-de-Luz **3**

Biarritz **2**

Bayonne **1**

A63

D933

St-Jean-Pied-de-Port

Bidache

D936

A64

N117

N117

Forêt d'Iraty

Forêt des Arbailles

D933

D936

Gave d'Oloron

Bordelais-Landes

Orthez

D933

Oloron-St-Marie

Gave de Pau

N134

D934

Pau **4**

A64

Eugénie-les-Bains **5**

D918

Gave

Cauterets **7**

Lourdes **6**

N117

la Mongie

Adour

Tarbes

Midi-Toulousain-Pyrénées

Lannemezan

Baïse-Darré

N117

Gers

Ax-les-Thermes **8**

THE BASQUE PEOPLE

The *Pays Basque,* or Basque country, is home to a unique culture rich in folklore, charm, and a sense of Basque national destiny. An enterprising and seafaring people, the Basques trace their roots to a pre-Indo-European people whose origins and migratory patterns are not fully known. Fierce and warlike, the Basques resisted the incursions of both the ancient Romans and Moors. Later, the Basques became known throughout Europe for their commercial zeal, capacity for hard work, and culinary skill.

The Basque language is a linguistic riddle that has puzzled ethnologists for years; its grammar, syntax, and vocabulary are in no way related to any other European language. Depending on the dialect of Basque being spoken, the language is known as either *Uskara, Euskara,* or *Eskuara.* Although on the wane since the beginning of this century, the Basque language is now enjoying a modest renaissance.

Geographically, the Basque country straddles the western foothills of the Pyrénées mountain range, and the Basque people live in both France and Spain, the latter with greater numbers. During the Spanish Civil War (1936–39), the Basques were on the Republican side and were defeated by Franco. Oppression during the Franco years has led to deep-seated resentment against the policies of Madrid.

The Basque separatist movement ETA *Euskadi ta Azkatasuna* (Basque Nation and Liberty) and the French organization *Enbata* (Ocean Wind) engaged in guerrilla activity from 1968 in an unsuccessful attempt to secure a united Basque state. Despite the relative calm of recent years, many Basque nationalists fervently wish that the Basque people could be united into one autonomous Basque state instead of being divided between France and Spain.

The leading port and pleasure-yacht basin of the Côte Basque, Bayonne is a cathedral city and capital of the Pays Basque. It is characterized by narrow streets, quays, and ramparts. Enlivening the local scene are bullfights, pelota games (jai alai), and street dancing at annual fiestas. The town is divided by the Nive and Adour Rivers. While here you may want to buy some of Bayonne's chocolate at one of the arcaded shops along **rue du Port-Neuf,** later enjoying a coffee at one of the cafés along **place de la Liberté,** the hub of town.

The old town, **Grand Bayonne,** is within the ramparts of Vauban's fortifications, lying on the left bank of the Nive. This part of town is dominated by the **Cathédrale de Ste-Marie,** along rue d'Espagne (tel. 59-59-17-82). This is one of the most outstanding cathedrals in the southwestern part of the country, dating from the early 13th century. A Gothic building, it is characterized by two towers, one built as late as the 19th century. Incredibly beautiful, it is distinguished by its stained-glass windows in the nave. Many niches along the walls contain elaborate sarcophagi. From the 13th-century cloister you have a view of the remarkable architecture of the cathedral. It's open Monday through Saturday from 7am to 12:30pm and 2:30 to 7:30pm, and on Sunday from 8am to 12:30pm and 3:30 to 7:30pm.

An important museum worth visiting is the **Musée Bonnat,** 5, rue Jacques-Lafitte (tel. 59-59-08-52), containing a collection of artwork the painter Léon Bonnat donated to the city, including his own. Bonnat was especially fond of portraits, often of ladies in elegant 1890s dresses. In his own *Jacob Wrestling with the Angel,* the angel is so delicate and effete it's really no contest. Far greater painters whose works are represented include Degas, David, Goya, Ingres, Daubigny, Rubens, Piero della Francesca, van Dyck, Rembrandt, Tiepolo, El Greco, Ribera, Murillo, Constable, even Leonardo da Vinci. The museum is open June 15 to September 10, Wednesday through Monday from 10am to noon and 3 to 7pm (to 9pm on Friday); the rest of the year, on Saturday and Sunday from 10am to noon and 3 to 7pm. Admission costs 15 F ($2.70) for adults, 5 F (90¢) for children.

WHERE TO STAY

LE GRAND HOTEL, 21, rue Thiers, 64100 Bayonne. Tel. 59-59-14-61, or toll free 800/528-1234 in the U.S. and Canada. Fax 59-25-61-70. 62 rms (all with bath). TV TEL **Bus:** 7.
$ Rates: 360–430 F ($64.80–$77.40) single; 400–480 F ($72–$86.40) double. Breakfast 45 F ($8.10) extra. AE, DC, MC, V. **Parking:** 50 F ($9).
This hotel was built atop the ruins of a medieval Carmelite convent around 1900, a few steps from the cathedral. In 1991, after a complete renovation, it reopened in a four-star format which raised its status to one of the best hotels in town. Today, its comfortably conservative bedrooms usually contain minibars as well as plushly upholstered furnishings. On the premises is a well-managed restaurant, Les Carmes, where fixed-price meals cost 120–160 F ($21.60–$28.80) each. The hotel is a member of the Best Western reservations network.

MENDI ALDE, 8, av. du 8-Mai-1945, 64100 Bayonne. Tel. 59-42-38-44. 10 rms (all with bath). **Directions:** Take the D932 1½ miles outside town.
$ Rates: 200 F ($36) single; 240 F ($43.20) double. Breakfast 30 F ($5.40) extra. No credit cards. **Parking:** Free.
Set on the southern periphery of Bayonne, about 1½ miles from the center, near the giant Sony electronics factory, this is a simple but likable family-run hotel which serves no meals other than breakfast. The English-speaking owners might cheerfully relate stories of their Basque-born relatives in Boston. Built in 1951, the hotel's bedrooms are larger than you might have expected. The establishment's Basque name translates as "beside the mountain."

MERCURE AGORA, av. Jean-Rostand, 64100 Bayonne. Tel. 59-63-30-90. Fax 59-42-06-64. 109 rms (all with bath). A/C TV TEL **Bus:** 7.
$ Rates: 390 F ($70.20) single; 495 F ($89.10) double. Breakfast 50 F ($9) extra. AE, DC, MC, V. **Parking:** 35 F ($6.30).
This modern, chain-run hotel is the best in the area, providing well-furnished rooms with river views. Drinks are served on the terrace, by the river. The restaurant's fixed-price menus begin as low as 100 F ($18).

WHERE TO DINE

CHEVAL BLANC, 68, rue Bourgneuf. Tel. 59-59-01-33.
Cuisine: BASQUE. **Reservations:** Recommended.
$ Prices: Appetizers 60–90 F ($10.80–$16.20); main dishes 75–100 F ($13.50–$18); fixed-price menus 95–228 F ($17.10–$41). AE, DC, MC, V.
Open: July–Sept, lunch daily noon–2:15pm; dinner daily 7–9:30pm. Oct–June, lunch Tues–Sun noon–2:15pm; dinner Tues–Sat 7–9:30pm.
The finest, and most likable, restaurant in Bayonne is in a 19th-century stone and half-timbered house in the heart of the historic center, near the Musée Bonnat and the Musée Basque. In a rustically elegant interior, you can enjoy the fine cuisine of Jean-Claude Tellechea, which will be served by one of the finest maîtres d'hôtel in the Basque country, Robert Hualte. Menu items vary with the season, but might include a gazpacho of broad beans and baby peas, veal kidneys enhanced with veal drippings, and a traditional (and supremely delicious) recipe for dorado simmered in garlic and served with crépinette de marmikado (diced tuna with red and green peppers, bound together with the lining of a pig's stomach). Dessert might be a pot of bittersweet chocolate served with crème fraîche.

EUZKALDUNA, 61, rue Pannecau. Tel. 59-59-28-02.
Cuisine: BASQUE. **Reservations:** Not required. **Bus:** 7.
$ Prices: Appetizers 30–60 F ($5.40–$10.80); main dishes 50–90 F ($9–$16.20). MC, V.

Open: Lunch daily noon–2:30pm; dinner daily 7:30–9:30pm. **Closed:** Sun evening in winter.

This is the place to go for authentic Basque cuisine. The fish soup has been excellent each of the four times that I've ordered it, although the taste varies according to the catch of the day. The kitchen also prepares mussels in vinaigrette, plus an array of other Basque dishes, including omelets.

---

2. BIARRITZ

484 miles SW of Paris, 120 miles SW of Bordeaux

GETTING THERE By Train and Bus Eleven trains arrive daily from Bayonne (see above; trip time: only 10 minutes), which has rail links with Paris and other major cities in the south of France. The nearest railway station is two miles from the town center, in La Négresse. Buses carry passengers from the station to the center of Biarritz.

ESSENTIALS Orientation The original fishing village still contains the oldest buildings in town, as well as the Casino Bellevue and the Hôtel Palais (former villa of the Empress Eugénie). The old town juts out between two of the area's famous beaches, the Grande Plage and the Plage de la Côte des Basques. The old town's most visible symbols are its rocky promontories, which jut out from the coastline, one of which is connected to the mainland with a bridge (Rocher de la Vièrge). The 19th-century expansion that helped to make Biarritz famous is centered around avenue Edouard VII and avenue de l'Impératrice.

Information The Office de Tourisme is on the Square d'Ixelles (tel. 59-24-20-24).

One of the most famous seaside resorts in the world, Biarritz, in southwestern France, was once a simple fishing village near the Spanish border. Favored by the Empress Eugénie, the Atlantic village soon attracted her husband, Napoléon III, who launched it on the road to fashion. Later Queen Victoria showed up, and her son, Edward VII, visited more than once. Today, it's busy from July to September, quietly settling down for the rest of the year. Frankly, I prefer it in June, when the prices are lowered, the flowers are in bloom—especially the spectacular hydrangea—and there's space on the beach. Surfboarding is most popular here, drawing many Stateside youths.

On the fringe of the Basque country, Biarritz has good wide sandy bathing beaches (the surf can be dangerous at times on the Grand Plage). Cliff walks, forming a grand promenade planted with tamarisks, are one of the most enduring attractions of Biarritz. The most dramatic point is **Rocher de la Vièrge** (Rock of the Virgin), connected to the shore by a footbridge. Enclosed by jetties, **Port des Pêcheurs** (Port of the Fishermen) is yet another scenic spot.

WHERE TO STAY

Expensive

CHATEAU DE BRINDOS, lac de Brindos, 64600 Anglet. Tel. 59-23-17-68. Fax 59-23-48-47. 12 rms (all with bath). TV TEL
$ Rates: 950 F ($171) single; 1,350 F ($243) double. Breakfast 85 F ($15.30) extra. AE, DC, MC, V. **Parking:** Free.

With its own park and a private lake, the Château de Brindos, located near the airport about 1½ miles from Biarritz, is the most romantic stopover on the Côte Basque. Bedrooms and public rooms, one of which has a large stone fireplace, are beautifully decorated. The rooms in the annex do not overlook the lake.

The regional cuisine is superb, including a soup of foie gras, a mousseline of turbot in caviar sauce, duckling with small vegetables, and sea bass grilled with fennel. Meals cost 310–480 F ($55.80–$86.40) on the à la carte menu; call for a reservation.

CHATEAU DU CLAIR DE LUNE, 48, av. Alan-Seeger, route d'Arbonne, 64200 Biarritz. Tel. 59-23-45-96. Fax 59-23-39-13. 16 rms (all with bath). TV TEL

$ Rates: 450 F ($81) single; 700 F ($126) double. Breakfast 50 F ($9) extra. AE, DC, MC, V. **Parking:** Free.

Aficionados of French literature might be drawn to this hotel because it was lavishly praised by poet Alan Seeger in 1916 as the most magnificent place in town. It's still going strong. Constructed at the turn of the century, it has been modernized and updated with well-upholstered accommodations overlooking a garden filled with exotic trees and shrubs. There is no restaurant, and the hotel is open year-round.

HOTEL DU PALAIS, av. de l'Impératrice, 64200 Biarritz. Tel. 59-24-09-40, or toll free 800/223-6800 in the U.S. and Canada. Fax 59-41-67-99. 128 rms (all with bath), 30 suites. MINIBAR TV TEL **Bus:** 9.

$ Rates: 1,400–1,950 F ($252–$351) single; 1,800–2,650 F ($324–$477) double; from 3,000 F ($540) suite. Breakfast 100 F ($18) extra. AE, DC, MC, V. **Parking:** Free. **Closed:** Feb.

The Hôtel du Palais has been the playground for the international elite for the past century—and still is. Originally it was built in 1854 by Napoléon III for Empress Eugénie so that she wouldn't get homesick for Spain. He picked the most ideal beachfront location, in view of the rocks and rugged shoreline. It's a true palace, with grand halls and staircases, marble columns, and art nouveau decor. Edward VII of England stayed here in 1906 and 1910, Alfonso XIII (the king of Spain) in 1909, and the Duke of Windsor in the 1940s. Of course, there are elaborately furnished suites, but even the average bedrooms are decorated with period furniture, silk draperies, marquetry, and bronze hardware. Twelve rooms are air-conditioned. Guests are especially attracted to the heated seawater swimming pool on the lower terrace, with its umbrellas and lounges.

Le Grand Siècle, the gourmet restaurant, with its classic columns and crystal chandeliers, serves excellent meals. Guests also dine at La Rotonde, enjoying a typically Basque as well as international cuisine, specializing in seafood, and at the lunch-only L'Hippocampe, a buffet restaurant around the swimming pool.

HOTEL MIRAMAR, av. de l'Impératrice, 64200 Biarritz. Tel. 59-41-30-00. Fax 59-24-77-20. 109 rms (all with bath), 17 suites. MINIBAR TV TEL **Bus:** 9.

$ Rates: 1,550–2,650 F ($279–$477) single or double; from 3,000 F ($540) suite. Breakfast 100 F ($18) extra. AE, DC, MC, V. **Parking:** 50 F ($9).

A modern structure surrounded by 19th-century buildings, the Hôtel Miramar offers conservative and tasteful bedrooms that open onto views of the sea and the cliffs. On the premises are a saltwater swimming pool, piano bar, gymnasium, sauna, solarium, beauty center, hairdresser, and an adjoining spa facility—Thalassothérapie Louison Bobet, with mud baths, aerosol treatments, physiotherapy, and algae baths. The hotel's restaurant, Le Relais du Miramar, attracts the elite summer crowd. Set beside the pool, the establishment offers both outdoor and indoor dining. Open daily for lunch and dinner until 9:30pm, the restaurant charges 280 F ($50.40) and up for a fixed-price menu, with à la carte dinners averaging 400 F ($72).

Moderate

HOTEL CARLINA, bd. Prince-de-Galles, 64200 Biarritz. Tel. 59-24-42-14. Fax 59-24-95-32. 31 rms (all with bath or shower), 2 suites. MINIBAR TV TEL **Bus:** 9.

$ Rates: 500–600 F ($90–$108) single; 650–950 F ($117–$171) double; 1,100 F ($198) suite. Breakfast 45 F ($8.10) extra. AE, DC, MC, V. **Parking:** 50 F ($9). **Closed:** Nov 15–Apr 15.

This recommended hotel has an exceptional view of the Pyrénées and the Atlantic Ocean. Rooms are comfortably furnished and well maintained. Popular water sports are offered, including windsurfing. On the premises is a terrace bar and a solarium. Menus in the hotel restaurant run 80–250 F ($14.40–$45).

HOTEL PLAZA, av. Edouard-VII, 64200 Biarritz. Tel. 59-24-74-00. Fax 59-22-22-01. 60 rms (all with bath). MINIBAR TV TEL

$ Rates: 270–560 F ($48.60–$100.80) single; 620 F ($111.60) double. Breakfast 49 F ($8.80) extra. AE, DC, MC, V. **Parking:** Free.

Conveniently located near the casino in the town center, this hotel offers pleasant amenities, amid an art deco decor from 1928. This is reflected in the geometric designs of its stained-glass windows, wrought-iron mosaics, and stonework. Many of the large bedrooms have private terraces. Meals are served in a formal dining hall in summer and in a less formal pub the rest of the year.

HOTEL REGINA ET GOLF, 52, av. de l'Impératrice, 64200 Biarritz. Tel. 59-41-33-00. Fax 59-41-33-99. 60 rms (all with bath). MINIBAR TV TEL

$ Rates: 1,110 F ($199.80) single; 1,340 F ($241.20) double. Breakfast 110 F ($19.80) extra. AE, DC, MC, V. **Parking:** 60 F ($10.80). **Closed:** Nov 21–Dec 26.

A 19th-century villa set in a residential part of town, the Hôtel Régina et Golf is located midway between the ocean and the golf course, close to the Louison Bobet Institute of Thalassotherapy (seawater therapy). Each of the modernized, well-furnished rooms provides either a sea or a golf view. The hotel offers a first-class seafood restaurant, Les Jardins de l'Océan. The bar serves a before-dinner drink called the "Moby Dick." Other hotel amenities include a swimming pool.

Inexpensive

HOTEL DU FRONTON, 34-35, av. du Maréchal-Joffre, 64000 Biarritz. Tel. 59-23-09-36. 42 rms (all with bath). TV TEL **Bus:** 9.

$ Rates: 270 F ($48.60) single; 320 F ($57.60) double. Breakfast 30 F ($5.40) extra. MC, V. **Parking:** Free. **Closed:** Mar 12–26 and Oct 23–Nov 28.

Set on a street corner in the center of town, this half-timbered hotel contains a bar and restaurant on its ground floor. Bedrooms, housed in a modern white-sided annex, have tall sliding windows and built-in wood-grained furniture. The restaurant, however, provides an old French provincial ambience, with large limestone hearths and beamed ceilings. Fixed-price menus cost 68 F ($12.20), 86 F ($15.50), and 123 F ($22.10).

HOTEL DU PORT-VIEUX, 43, rue Mazagran, 64200 Biarritz. Tel. 59-24-02-84. 18 rms (all with bath). TEL

$ Rates (including continental breakfast): 236 F ($42.50) single; 250 F ($45) double. No credit cards. **Closed:** Mid-Nov to Feb.

I recommend this hotel, especially for those who would like to take their meals in the local restaurants, as it serves only breakfast. Accommodations in the "Old Port" are extremely clean.

HOTEL PALACITO, 1, rue Gambetta, 64200 Biarritz. Tel. 59-24-04-89. Fax 59-24-33-43. 30 rms (all with bath or shower). TV TEL **Bus:** 2.

$ Rates: 240–280 F ($43.20–$50.40) single; 290–340 F ($52.20–$61.20) double. Breakfast 35 F ($6.30) extra. AE, DC, MC, V.

This is a small, renovated hotel with modest bedrooms and elevator service. The hotel lies in the town center near the beach and casino. It has no restaurant but is situated near many dining establishments specializing in Basque cuisine.

OCEAN, 9, place Ste-Eugénie, 64200 Biarritz. Tel. 59-24-03-27. Fax 59-24-18-50. 24 rms (all with bath or shower). MINIBAR TV TEL **Bus:** 2.

$ Rates: 480–620 F ($86.40–$111.60) single or double. Breakfast 38 F ($6.80) extra. AE, DC, MC, V. **Closed:** Jan 3–31 and Nov 23–30.

Located in restaurant row right next to a church, this is an older, six-story corner building on the ocean side of the park. It rates highly for convenience, cleanliness, and good food. The well-tended bedrooms vary considerably in size, some overlooking the plaza and the sea. The restaurant specializes in seafood; meals cost 95 F ($17.10) and up.

WHERE TO DINE

L'AUBERGE DE LA NEGRESSE, 10, bd. de l'Aérodrome. Tel. 59-23-15-83.

Cuisine: BASQUE. **Reservations:** Required. **Bus:** 2.

$ Prices: Appetizers 15–50 F ($2.70–$9); main dishes 36–71 F ($6.50–$12.80); fixed-price menus 77 F ($13.90), 125 F ($22.50), and 135 F ($24.30). MC, V.

Open: Lunch Tues–Sun noon–2:30pm; dinner Tues–Sun 7:15–10:15pm. **Closed:** Oct.

Just 1½ miles south of Biarritz, this restaurant was named after a 19th-century slave who escaped from an American plantation by hiding in the bottom of a French ship. The inn she established on this site was used by Napoléon's army on its passage to Spain, and eventually a railway station (the Gare de la Négresse) was named in her honor. The inn doubles as a delicatessen, but the two dining rooms also serve flavorful meals to a sometimes-boisterous crowd. Typical dishes include salmon en papillotte, an array of homemade terrines, and fish.

CAFE DE PARIS, 5, place Bellevue, 64200 Biarritz. Tel. 59-24-19-53. Fax 59-24-18-20.

Cuisine: BASQUE. **Reservations:** Required. **Bus:** 2.

$ Prices: Appetizers 80–160 F ($14.40–$28.80); main dishes 90–250 F ($16.20–$45); fixed-price menus 170–400 F ($30.60–$72). AE, DC, MC, V.

Open: Lunch daily noon–2:30pm; dinner daily 7–10pm.

Originally established in 1861 as a bar for the coachmen and stablehands who transported their wealthy clients to and from Biarritz, this restaurant has evolved over the years into one of the most elegant in town. Set across from the casino, overlooking the sea, its Belle Epoque dining room is considered one of the greatest restaurants along the Côte Basque. Pierre Laporte's formally attired staff serves true haute cuisine. Specialties include a savory fish soup, followed perhaps by a vegetable pâté with a mousse made of flap mushrooms. Duckling with lime is one of the featured main dishes, as is squab with hurtleberries. If it's offered, order the tart made with fresh asparagus. Smoked fresh salmon is very good here, as is the brochette of lobster. For a fine finish, try the different types of sorbet with sauterne. Keep in mind that the menu changes constantly.

In 1992, the establishment added 19 comfortable bedrooms, each with a sea view. Decorated in a conservatively traditional style, they cost 1,050 F ($189) for a single and 1,300 F ($234) for a double, with breakfast priced at an additional 80 F ($14.40) per person. Half board in the above-mentioned restaurant is available for an additional supplement of 300 F ($54) per person.

LES FLOTS BLEUS, 41, perspective des Côtes Basques. Tel. 59-24-10-03.

Cuisine: BASQUE. **Reservations:** Recommended.

$ Prices: Appetizers 25–54 F ($4.50–$9.70); main dishes 47–80 F ($8.50–$14.40); fixed-price menus 80–164 F ($14.40–$29.50). AE, DC, MC, V.

Open: Lunch daily noon–2pm; dinner daily 7:30–9:30pm. **Closed:** One week in Nov.

Set on the rocky coastline a 10-minute walk from the town center, this restaurant lies within a turn-of-the-century house which has been the domain of Venice-born Arlette Casagrande (and a congenial colleague named Mami) for nearly 30 years. Food is served in generous portions which contain the full flavor of the Basque country. Menu choices include pâté of duck, salade basquaise, roquefort salad, marinated mussels, a richly aromatic fish soup, dorado with garlic, and filet of sole prepared according to the whims of the chef.

LE VAUDEVILLE, 5, rue du Centre. Tel. 59-24-34-66.

Cuisine: BASQUE. **Reservations:** Required. **Bus:** 2.

$ Prices: Appetizers 40–92 F ($7.20–$16.60); main dishes 78–105 F ($14–$18.90); fixed-price menus 90–145 F ($16.20–$26.10). MC, V.
Open: Lunch Thurs–Mon noon–2pm; dinner Wed–Mon 7:30–10:30pm.
Closed: Jan 1–15.

This Belle Epoque brasserie serves excellent meals. In air-conditioned comfort, sample such dishes as baby cabbage stuffed with crayfish, veal's head in a ravigote sauce, and filet of duckling in a honey-vinegar sauce. A salad of scallops and lobster is a specialty. There's also a good selection of *petits vins*.

EVENING ENTERTAINMENT

Despite the array of nightclubs that come and go with regularity in Biarritz, the favorite nocturnal activity is still gambling. Make note that, despite its name, the Casino Municipale is an exhibition and conference hall, not a gambling casino.

CASINO BELLEVUE, place Bellevue. Tel. 59-24-11-22.

Housed in a 1920s building with an art deco interior and high ceilings, this casino provides wood-and-brass roulette wheels and baccarat and blackjack tables. The gambling is on nightly from 5pm to 3am.

The Casino Bellevue also contains a first-class restaurant as well as a piano bar and disco, called La Plantation. The restaurant serves nightly from 8pm to 1am, and the disco is open from 11pm to 4am. Drinks begin at 80 F ($14.40). There is no entrance fee, unless a celebrity is performing.

Admission: Casino, presentation of a passport and a 70-F ($12.60) fee; disco, 70 F ($12.60)

---

3. ST-JEAN-DE-LUZ

491 miles SW of Paris, 9 miles S of Biarritz

GETTING THERE By Train Trains arrive several times daily from Paris, Biarritz, and other cities within Basque Country.

ESSENTIALS Orientation The old port, with its adjacent place Louis-XIV, is the focal point of St-Jean-de-Luz. Rue Gambetta, most of which is reserved for pedestrians, leads from the port to the side of the town's most famous church (Eglise St-Jean-Baptiste).

Information The Office de Tourisme is on place du Maréchal-Foch (tel. 59-26-03-16).

This Basque country tuna-fishing port and beach resort is the goal of many a person's dream of a beach vacation. About nine miles south of Biarritz moving toward the Spanish frontier, St-Jean-de-Luz lies at the mouth of the Nivelle.

In its principal church, the 13th-century **Eglise St-Jean-Baptiste,** Louis XIV and the Spanish infanta, Marie-Thérèse, were married in 1660. The interior is among the most handsomely decorated of all Basque churches, with painted wooden panels. Surmounting the altar is a statue-studded gilded retable.

At the harbor, the brick-and-stone **Maison de l'Infante,** a mansion in the Louis XIII style, sheltered the Spanish princess.

The Sun King, meanwhile, dreamed of another woman at **La Maison de Louis XIV** (also known as the **Château Lohobiague**), on place Louis-XIV, the center of the old port (tel. 59-26-01-56). The noble facade is distinguished by small towers built into each of its corners. The interior of the house is in an old Basque style, with beams and iron nails still visible. The second-floor stairwell leads to the apartments where the widow of the original builder received Louis XIV on his marriage journey. Don't miss the kitchen with its large dimensions and big fireplace.

It's open in July and August, daily from 10:30am to noon and 2:30 to 6pm; June 1–15 and in the month of September, daily from 10:30am to noon and 2:30 to 5pm; closed off-season. Admission is 15 F ($2.70) for adults and 12 F ($2.20) for children.

Many narrow streets flanked by old houses provide interesting strolls in this port town. If possible try to attend a fish auction. Livening up the resort are pelota, fandangos, and a celebration beginning on June 24 called Toro del Fuego. Highlight of the festivities is when a snorting papier-mâché bull is carried through town. The townspeople literally dance in the streets.

WHERE TO STAY

Expensive

HOTEL DE CHANTACO, golf de Chantaco, 64500 St-Jean-de-Luz. Tel. 59-26-14-76. Fax 59-26-35-97. 20 rms (all with bath), 4 suites. TV TEL
Directions: Take the D918 one mile from the town center.
$ Rates: 1,150 F ($207) single; 1,800 F ($324) double; from 2,000 F ($360) suite. Breakfast 80 F ($14.40) extra. AE, DC, MC, V. **Parking:** Free. **Closed:** Dec–Mar.

When this mansion opened at the turn of the century, it was immediately adopted by famous politicians, artists, writers, and musicians. Surrounded by an 18-hole golf course and parklands, it lies just a mile from the ocean. The hotel resembles a country château, with Moorish arches, a side patio garden, and a refined decor. The reception hall has two stone fireplaces, a wrought-iron gallery, and high-backed tapestry-covered chairs; the drawing room has a refectory table lit by silver candelabra. Bedrooms are luxuriously furnished and well equipped. Breakfast is served on a patio with wisteria-covered arches and a fountain. The hotel's restaurant, El Patio, serves excellent regional and international cuisine. Meals begin at 250 F ($45).

Moderate

LA DEVINIERE, 5, rue Loguin, 64500 St-Jean-de-Luz. Tel. 59-26-05-51. 8 rms (all with bath). TEL
$ Rates: 500 F ($90) single; 625 F ($112.50) double. Breakfast 50 F ($9) extra. V.
Originally a private town house in the center of town, La Devinière is an antique-filled, modernized hotel with elegant bedrooms. Breakfast is the only meal served, but the staff will readily direct you to nearby restaurants for other meals.

Inexpensive

LA FAYETTE, 18-20, rue de la République, 64500 St-Jean-de-Luz. Tel. 59-26-17-74. Fax 59-51-11-78. 18 rms (all with bath). TV TEL
$ Rates: 280 F ($50.40) single; 320–350 F ($57.60–$63) double. Breakfast 38 F ($6.80) extra. AE, DC, MC, V. **Parking:** 30 F ($5.40).
The four-story building that contains this hotel and restaurant was originally built in the 1700s as one of the region's first apartment buildings. Today, old-fashioned and nostalgic, it occupies a central position near place Louis-XIV. Rooms evoke the decor of a dignified (and slightly battered) earlier age, but the restaurant is considered one of the most reliable in town. Regional specialties and classic French dishes are featured, including seafood casseroles, grilled duck, sea bass with thyme and lemon-butter sauce, and roast rack of lamb. Fixed-price menus cost 98–195 F ($17.60–$35.10) each.

HOTEL MADISON, 25, bd. Thiers, 64500 St-Jean-de-Luz. Tel. 59-26-35-02. Fax 59-51-14-76. 25 rms (all with bath), 2 suites. TV TEL

$ Rates: 380 F ($68.40) single; 440 F ($79.20) double; 550 F ($99) suite. Breakfast 37 F ($6.70) extra. AE, DC, MC, V. **Parking:** 45 F ($8.10).

Near the casino and the beach, this is a conservative, tasteful hotel. Well maintained and inviting, it's decorated in a traditional French style with Basque overtones. Even though it stands in a beach resort, the hotel remains open all year.

VILLA BEL-AIR, promenade Jacques-Thibaud, 64500 St-Jean-de-Luz. Tel. 59-26-04-86. Fax 59-26-62-34. 23 rms (all with bath or shower). TV TEL

$ Rates: 360 F ($64.80) single; 375-400 F ($67.50-$72) double. Breakfast 37 F ($6.70) extra; half board 510-550 F ($91.80-$99) per person. MC, V. **Parking:** Free. **Closed:** Mid-Nov to Mar.

This hotel offers clean and comfortably furnished accommodations overlooking the sea. The restaurant serves lunch and dinner from June to October. In good weather, enjoy a meal on the terrace. Most guests stay on the half-board plan.

WHERE TO DINE

AUBERGE KAIKU, 17, rue de la République. Tel. 59-26-13-20.
   Cuisine: BASQUE. **Reservations:** Recommended.
$ Prices: Appetizers 30-125 F ($5.40-$22.50); main dishes 90-140 F ($16.20-$25.20); fixed-price menu 190 F ($34.20). AE, MC, V.
   Open: Lunch Tues-Sun noon-2pm; dinner daily 7-11pm. **Closed:** Mon Sept 15-July 15.

Centrally located on a narrow street just off place Louis-XIV Auberge Kaïku is the best restaurant in town. The structure, with hand-hewn beams and chiseled masonry, dates from 1540 and is said to be the oldest house in town. The restaurant is run by its Basque owners, Emile and Jeanne Ourdanabia, who serve a lightened, regional cuisine. You might enjoy John Dory with fresh mint, grilled shrimp, filet of beef with essence of truffles, duckling in honey, and sole with flap mushrooms.

CHEZ MAYA (PETIT GRILL BASQUE), 4, rue St-Jacques. Tel. 59-26-80-76.
   Cuisine: BASQUE. **Reservations:** Recommended.
$ Prices: Appetizers 22-75 F ($4-$13.50); main dishes 42-78 F ($7.60-$14); fixed-price menus 80 F ($14.40). MC, V.
   Open: Lunch Sat-Thurs noon-2pm; dinner Sat-Thurs 7-10pm. **Closed:** Dec 20-Jan 20.

This small auberge is highly acclaimed for both quality and value. Specialties include a delectable fish soup and paella. Its fixed-price menu is considered the best value at the resort.

RAMUNTCHO, 24, rue Garat. Tel. 59-26-03-89.
   Cuisine: BASQUE. **Reservations:** Required in summer.
$ Prices: Appetizers 30-50 F ($5.40-$9); main dishes 45-85 F ($8.10-$15.30); fixed-price menus 85 F ($15.30), 115 F ($20.70), and 160 F ($28.80). AE, MC, V.
   Open: Lunch daily noon-2pm; dinner daily 7-10pm. **Closed:** Mon Nov 11-Feb 1.

Ramuntcho is a typical Basque restaurant with exposed beams, wood tables, and a choice of well-chosen menus. Basque seafood is a specialty. Several dishes, such as the duck, show a Norman influence.

LA VIEILLE AUBERGE, 22, rue Tourasse. Tel. 59-26-19-61.
   Cuisine: BASQUE. **Reservations:** Required.
$ Prices: Appetizers 35-50 F ($6.30-$9); main dishes 75-118 F ($13.50-$21.20); fixed-price menus 75 F ($13.50), 105 F ($18.90), and 125 F ($22.50). AE, MC, V.
   Open: Lunch Thurs-Tues noon-2pm; dinner Thurs-Tues 7-10pm. **Closed:** Nov 2-Mar.

This Basque tavern specializes in seafood. Monsieur and Madame Daniel Grand offer good-value fixed-price menus, the most expensive of which is enormous. Generally, the recipes are part Basque and part Landaise, and each dish goes well with the *vin du pays*.

4. PAU

477 miles SW of Paris, 122 miles SW of Toulouse

GETTING THERE **By Plane** The local airport, Pau-Uzein, is 7½ miles north of town.

By Train There are good train connections from Biarritz (six per day taking 1¼ hours).

ESSENTIALS **Orientation** Set on the northern bank of the Gave de Pau River, Pau is most famous for its château, which stands prominently near the river at the corner of two important traffic junctions. The heart of the town's commercial district is the busy place Clemenceau, out of which radiate at least five different boulevards. Pedestrians looking for the old town should head west from place Clemenceau, where there's a large parking lot. Near the eastern base of the château is the Hédas district, centered just south of rue du Hédas, which contains many restaurants and nightclubs.

Information The Office de Tourisme is on place Royale (tel. 59-27-27-08).

High above the banks of the Gave de Pau River, the all-year resort of Pau is a good halting point in your trek through the Pyrénées. The town was once the residence of the kings of Navarre. The British discovered it back in the early 19th century, launching such innovative practices as fox hunting, a custom that has lingered.

Even if you're just passing through, go along **boulevard des Pyrénées,** an esplanade erected on orders of Napoléon I. You'll have what is perhaps the most famous panoramic view in the Pyrénées. After seeing the white-capped peaks of the Anie and Midi-de-Bigorre, the poet Lamartine said, "The landview at Pau is, like the sea-view at Naples, the finest in the world."

WHAT TO SEE & DO

CHATEAU DE PAU, 2, rue du Château. Tel. 59-82-38-00.
At the western end of town stands this château dating from the 12th century and still steeped in the Renaissance spirit of the bold Margaret of Navarre, who wrote the bawdy *Heptaméron* at 60. This collection of tales amused her brother, François I. The castle, however, has seen many builders and many tenants. Louis XV ordered the bridge that connects the castle to the town, while the great staircase hall inside was commissioned by Margaret herself. Louis-Philippe had all the apartments redecorated around 1840. Inside are many souvenirs, including a crib made of a single tortoise shell for Henry of Navarre, who was born here. There is a splendid array of Flemish and Gobelins tapestries. The great rectangular tower, Tour de Gaston Phoebus, is from the 14th century.

On the château's third floor, a **Musée Regional** contains ethnographical collections of Béarn, the old name of the country of which Pau was the capital.

Finally, you may want to walk through the beautiful **Parc National,** the gardens (or what's left of them) that used to surround the château in the 16th century.

Admission: 27 F ($4.90) adults, free for children under 18.
Open: Château and museum, daily 9:30–11:45am and 2–5:15pm.

MUSEE DES BEAUX-ARTS, rue Mathieu-Lalanne. Tel. 59-27-33-02.
The museum displays a collection of European paintings, including Spanish, Flemish, Dutch, English, and French masters, such as El Greco, Zurbarán, Degas, and Boudin.

Admission: 10 F ($1.80) adults, 5 F (90¢) children.
Open: Wed–Mon 9am–noon and 2–6pm.

WHERE TO STAY
Moderate

HOTEL CONTINENTAL, 2, rue du Maréchal-Foch, 64000 Pau. Tel. 59-27-69-31. Fax 59-27-99-84. 85 rms (all with bath). MINIBAR TV TEL **Bus:** 1.
$ Rates: 325 F ($58.50) single; 500 F ($90) double. Breakfast 40 F ($7.20) extra. AE, DC, MC, V. **Parking:** Free.

The centrally located Continental is the main hotel in the town center. Bedrooms are stylishly decorated and completely modernized. The à la carte menu begins at 135 F ($24.30). There's a garage on the premises.

HOTEL DE GRAMONT, 3, place Gramont, 64000 Pau. Tel. 59-27-84-04. Fax 59-27-62-23. 36 rms (all with bath), 2 suites. TV TEL **Bus:** 1.
$ Rates: 180–395 F ($32.40–$71.10) single; 320–420 F ($57.60–$75.60) double; 550 F ($99) suite. Breakfast 35 F ($6.30) extra. AE, DC, MC, V. **Parking:** 20 F ($3.60).

Conveniently located near the commercial center of Pau, within walking distance of nightlife, the château, and the railway station, the Hôtel de Gramont is one of the most impressive buildings in town. Originally it was a coaching inn. The four-story, châteaulike structure has street-level arcades and high-ceilinged bedrooms, 10 of which are air-conditioned.

HOTEL DE PARIS, 80, rue Emile-Garet, 64000 Pau. Tel. 59-82-58-00. Fax 59-27-30-20. 41 rms (all with bath). MINIBAR TV TEL **Bus:** 1.
$ Rates (including buffet breakfast): 410 F ($73.80) single; 490 F ($88.20) double. AE, DC, MC, V. **Parking:** Free.

The Hôtel de Paris has been completely renovated, with comfortable bedrooms facing the courtyard. It's near Beaumont Park and the center of town. Only breakfast is served.

HOTEL RONCEVAUX, 25, rue Louis-Barthou, 64000 Pau. Tel. 59-27-08-44. Fax 59-82-92-79. 40 rms (all with bath). TV TEL **Bus:** 1.
$ Rates: 320 F ($57.60) single; 400 F ($72) double. Breakfast 35 F ($6.30) extra. AE, DC, MC, V. **Parking:** 30 F ($5.40).

This hotel near the rail station offers well-maintained, soundproof rooms. Only breakfast is served. The staff will direct you to several good restaurants nearby.

NOVOTEL-PAU LESCAR, route de Bayonne, 64230 Lescar. Tel. 59-32-17-32. Fax 59-32-34-98. 89 rms (all with bath). A/C MINIBAR TV TEL
$ Rates: 415 F ($74.70) single; 455 F ($81.90) double. Breakfast 50 F ($9) extra. AE, DC, MC, V. **Parking:** Free.

The Novotel-Pau Lescar, located four miles northwest of Pau in the industrial suburb of Lescar, is part of the Novotel hotel chain. It's probably the most dollarwise and practical accommodation in town. Built in the early 1970s but renovated in 1989, the hotel has been landscaped to block out the noise from the surrounding roads. Each room contains a single bed (which, thanks to bolster cushions, doubles as a couch), a double bed, a desk, and a fully accessorized bathroom. The hotel has a high-tech bar and restaurant, serving from 6am to midnight meals that begin at 160 F ($28.80).

Budget

HOTEL-RESTAURANT CORONA, 71, av. du Général-Leclerc, 64000 Pau. Tel. 59-30-64-77. Fax 59-02-62-64. 20 rms (all with bath). TV TEL **Bus:** 1.
$ Rates: 200–250 F ($36–$45) single or double. Breakfast 28 F ($5) extra. AE, MC, V.

The French-born architect who designed this hotel in 1971 had already completed many commissions in Montréal. In honor of them, he added what were considered at the time many Canada-inspired decorative touches, especially the ample use of exposed pinewood within the rustically modern bedrooms. Set about a mile east of the center of Pau, it offers comfortable accommodations and ample portions of food in its two dining rooms. The more formal of the two is the restaurant, where fixed-price meals cost 140–180 F ($25.20–$32.40). A less expensive meal is offered in the evening, but not at lunchtime, for 80 F ($14.40). There's also a rapid-service brasserie, where *plats du jour* begin at around 41 F ($7.40) each. Both restaurants (but not the hotel) are closed Friday night, all day Saturday, and from December 20 to January 10.

LE POSTILLON, place de Verdun, 10, cours Camou, 64000 Pau. Tel. 59-72-83-00. Fax 59-72-83-13. 28 rms (all with bath or shower). MINIBAR TV TEL **Bus:** 1.

$ Rates: 195 F ($35.10) single; 225 F ($40.50) double. Breakfast 30 F ($5.40) extra. MC, V.

This is a cozy hotel, with French provincial decor and a flower-filled courtyard. Bedrooms are comfortably furnished. Breakfast is the only meal served, but there's a choice of restaurants nearby.

WHERE TO DINE

L'AGRIPAUME, 14, rue Latapie. Tel. 59-27-68-70.
Cuisine: BASQUE. **Reservations:** Required. **Bus:** 1.
$ Prices: Appetizers 45–140 F ($8.10–$25.20); main dishes 65–150 F ($11.70–$27); fixed-price menus 70 F ($12.60), 100 F ($18), 150 F ($27), and 400 F ($72). MC, V.
Open: Lunch Tues–Sun noon–2:30pm; dinner Mon–Sat 7–10:30pm.

Amid the pastel decor and regional landscape paintings, the chef prepares such specialties as roast salmon with red wine sauce, roast lamb with herbs, foie gras in gelatin, filet of sole with flap mushrooms, and magrêt of duckling flavored with honey and thyme.

AU FIN GOURMET, 24, av. Gaston-Lacoste. Tel. 59-27-47-71.
Cuisine: BASQUE. **Reservations:** Recommended. **Bus:** 1.
$ Prices: Appetizers 85–95 F ($15.30–$17.10); main dishes 70–120 F ($12.60–$21.60); fixed-price menus 85–160 F ($15.30–$28.80). AE, DC, MC, V.
Open: Lunch Tues–Sun noon–2:15pm; dinner Tues–Sun 7–10pm.

Well established and well recommended, this restaurant is maintained by the three sons (Christian, Laurent, and Patrick) of the since-retired original founder, Clément Ithuriague. Located across from the town's railway station, it offers an outdoor terrace for warm-weather dining, and a cuisine based almost exclusively on regional ingredients. Menu items include marinated codfish with herbs "from the kitchen garden" and bouillon-flavored potatoes, a rack of lamb flavored with herbs from the Pyrénées served in a parsley-enriched crust, sliced and sautéed foie gras, and braised stuffed trout.

CHEZ PIERRE, 16, rue Louis-Barthour. Tel. 59-27-76-86.
Cuisine: BEARNAISE. **Reservations:** Required. **Bus:** 1.
$ Prices: Appetizers 65–125 F ($11.70–$22.50); main dishes 115–205 F ($20.70–$36.90). AE, DC, MC, V.
Open: Lunch Mon–Fri noon–2:30pm; dinner Mon–Sat 7–10pm. **Closed:** Feb 14–28.

Housed in a restored, mid-19th-century home, Chez Pierre turns regional products into extraordinary, creative dishes. In air-conditioned comfort, choose to sit at one of the eight downstairs tables amid the hunting motif or upstairs in one of three tiny salons. Chef Raymond Casau is among the finest in Béarn, where, according to *Larousse Gastronomique,* "the art of cookery has never ceased to be honored and practiced." Casau's specialties include sole with white mushrooms and small new cucumbers, as well as fresh salmon braised with Jurançon, a rather sweet, golden Pyrenean wine favored by Henri IV. The cassoulet with white beans at Pierre's is also recommended.

LA GOUSSE D'AIL, 12, rue du Hédas. Tel. 59-27-31-55.
Cuisine: BASQUE. **Reservations:** Not required. **Bus:** 1.
$ Prices: Appetizers 45–95 F ($8.10–$17.10); main dishes 75–105 F ($13.50–$18.90). MC, V.

Open: Lunch Mon–Fri noon–1:30pm; dinner Mon–Sat 7–10:30pm.

Situated a few blocks from the château, in a neighborhood filled with colorful bars and bistros, this pleasant restaurant has a stone, brick, and stucco interior with ceiling beams and a fireplace. Meals might include a gâteau of shellfish with essence of crab; a tart of puff pastry with gruyère, tomato, and basil; a mixture of monkfish with salmon and wild mushrooms; cream of mussel soup; and an onglet of beef with mustard grains and a marmalade of shallots.

5. EUGENIE-LES-BAINS

453 miles SW of Paris, 33 miles N of Pau

GETTING THERE   By Car   Most people visit Eugénie-les-Bains only for a meal at its famous restaurant (see below), and few would consider arriving in anything less than an expensive car.

By Train   Eugénie-les-Bains has no railway station, but you could take an overnight train from Paris, stopping at Pau, where you can arrange for Eugénie's only taxi to pick you up.

ESSENTIALS   Orientation   As you approach the town, discreet but very readable signs will direct you to the famous restaurant.

Information   Information is available at the Syndicat d'Initiative, 40320 Eugénie-les-Bains (tel. 58-51-13-16).

A century ago the Empress Eugénie came here to "take the cure." Now some of the most discerning people in the world are following in her footsteps, but for a slightly different attraction. In the Landes section of France, in the foothills of the Pyrénées, about 33 miles from Pau, this spa village is better known today than it ever was because of—

WHERE TO DINE

LES PRES D'EUGENIE [Michel Guérard], Eugénie-les-Bains, 40320 Béaune. Tel. 58-05-06-07. Fax 58-51-13-59.
   Cuisine: BASQUE. **Reservations:** Required.
$ Prices: Appetizers 160–280 F ($28.80–$50.40); main dishes 190–355 F ($34.20–$63.90); fixed-price menus 380–580 F ($68.40–$104.40). AE, MC, V.
   Open: Lunch Fri–Tues 12:30–2pm; dinner Thurs–Tues 7:30–10pm.
Fashionable, and praised by the French in terms that sometimes approach poetry, this Relais & Châteaux is the creation of Michel Guérard, the master chef whose *cuisine minceur* started a culinary revolution in the early 1970s. Originally built during the 19th century as a spa where the Empress Eugénie reportedly drank a glass of mineral water during one of her rest cures, it now attracts a swelling stream of clients who appreciate the calm, the much-publicized cooking, and the endless business expansions of its owner.

   Two kinds of cuisine are offered: *cuisine minceur,* in which calorie counters can still enjoy well-seasoned flavors and fresh ingredients; and the heartier *cuisine gourmand,* whose traditions are influenced by both Basque and classic French recipes. Specialties include cream of crayfish soup, whiting in white wine sauce, mullet steamed with seaweed and oysters, lamb steamed with fennel, and a wide variety of simply steamed fish with fresh vegetables.

   Partly because of the success of his other ventures, Mr. Guérard continues to expand the complex of buildings that surround his establishment's 19th-century core. (Unfortunately, this is sometimes at the risk of the personalized attention and the elegant sense of intimacy which guests here seem to crave.) In addition to the original 28 bedrooms and seven suites in the main building, an additional eight accommodations are in an outlying annex, La Couvent des Herbes. Originally built in the 18th century as a convent, both it and the main building charge 1,650 F ($297) for either a single or double, and 1,800–2,000 F ($324–$360) for a suite. Breakfast costs an extra 90 F ($16.20) per person.

Less expensive are the 27 rooms and five apartments in La Maison Rose, where half board—priced at 700–800 F ($126–$144) per person—focuses almost exclusively on *cuisine minceur* and its dietary benefits. Decors throughout each of the three annexes are inspired by what you might find in an chintz-laden English country house.

Travelers unwilling to pay the stratospheric prices in the main restaurant sometimes select a table in a satellite restaurant operated by Mr. Guérard, La Ferme aux Grives. Inside, cuisine focuses on specialties of the region as part of fixed-price menus costing 160–180 F ($28.80–$32.40). Comfortable and rustically elegant, La Ferme aux Grives is open for lunch and dinner daily except Tuesday at lunchtime and all day Monday.

6. LOURDES

497 miles SW of Paris, 25 miles SE of Pau

GETTING THERE By Train Train passengers headed for Lourdes from Bayonne or Biarritz must transfer in Pau. There are also connections from Toulouse and Paris.

ESSENTIALS Orientation Set on the eastern end of a tight bend in the Gave de Pau River, Lourdes is neatly bisected by avenue du Maréchal-Foch. The railway station lies at the northern end of town. In its center, clustered between the river and the Church of Sacré-Coeur, is the Cité-Réligieuse. Signposts throughout the town direct you to the most important pilgrimage sites.

Information For information, inquire at the Office de Tourisme, place du Champs-Commun (tel. 62-94-15-64).

Muslims turn to Mecca, Hindus to the waters of the Ganges, but for Catholics Lourdes is the world's most beloved shrine. Nestled in a valley in the southwestern part of the Hautes-Pyrénées, it is the scene of pilgrims gathering from all over the world. Nail down your hotel reservation in overcrowded August.

On February 11, 1858, the Virgin is believed by the Roman Catholic world to have revealed herself to a poor shepherd girl, Bernadette Soubirous. Eighteen such apparitions were reported. Bernadette, subject of the film *Song of Bernadette,* died in a convent in 1879. She was beatified in 1925, then canonized in 1933.

Her apparitions literally put Lourdes on the map. The town has subsequently attracted millions of visitors from all over the world, the illustrious and the poverty-stricken. Many of the truly devout are often disheartened at the tawdry commercialism that hangs over Lourdes today. And some holiday-seekers are acutely disturbed by the human desperation of victims of various afflictions spending their hard-earned savings of a lifetime seeking a "miracle," then having to return home without a cure. However, the church has recognized many "cures" which took place after patients bathed in the springs, labeling them "true miracles."

WHAT TO SEE & DO

Exploring the Town

From July 1 to September 20, tourists and pilgrims can join the ✪ **Day Pilgrims,** a pilgrimage conducted in English that gathers at 9am at the statue of the Crowned Virgin for a prayer meeting in the meadow facing the Grotto. Parts of these services include a 9:30am Stations of the Cross and an 11am mass. In the afternoon, assembling at the same spot at 2:30pm, pilgrims are taken on a guided visit to the Sanctuaries, or places associated with Bernadette. At 4:30pm there is a Procession of the Blessed Eucharist, starting from the Grotto. The 8:45pm Marian celebration, rosary, and torchlight procession all start from the Grotto as well.

In the Sanctuaries you'll be told the Story of Lourdes and of Bernadette, complete with a free slide show (in English) that runs about 15 minutes.

At the **Grotto of Massabielle** the Virgin is said to have appeared 18 times to Bernadette between February 11 and July 16, 1858. This venerated site is accessible to pilgrims both day and night, and a Holy Mass is celebrated there every day.

The Statue of Our Lady depicts the Virgin in the posture she is said to have taken and in the place she reputedly appeared when she made herself known to Bernadette, saying to her in Pyrenean dialect, "I am the Immaculate Conception."

At the back of the Grotto, on the left of the altar, is the **Miraculous Spring** that reportedly welled up on February 25, 1858, during the ninth apparition, when Bernadette scraped the earth as instructed. The Virgin is said to have commanded her, "Go and drink at the spring and wash there." The water from this spring is collected in several big reservoirs, from which one can drink it.

Other sanctuaries associated with St. Bernadette include the crypt, the first chapel built on top of the Grotto, the Basilica of the Immaculate Conception, the Rosary Basilica, and the underground Basilica of St. Pius X. In town, there are the house where Bernadette lived, the Cachot, the baptismal font in the parish church, and the hospital chapel where she made her first communion.

The **Upper Basilica,** at place du Rosaire, was built in the 13th-century ogival style, but it was not consecrated until 1876. It contains one nave split into five equal bays. Lining its interior are votive tablets. On the west side of the square is the **Rosary Basilica,** with two small towers. It was built in 1889 in the Roman-Byzantine style and holds up to 4,000 people. Inside, 15 chapels are dedicated to the "mysteries of the rosary."

The oval **Basilica of Pius X** was consecrated in 1958. An enormous underground chamber covered by a concrete roof, it is 660 feet long and 270 feet wide, holding as many as 20,000 pilgrims. After St. Peter's in Rome, it is the world's largest church.

Nearby, the **Musée Bernadette** (tel. 62-94-13-15) contains scenes representing the life of the saint. It is open daily from 9am to noon and 2 to 6pm. The true Bernadette devotee will also seek out the **Moulin de Boly,** rue Bernadette-Soubirous (tel. 62-94-23-53), where the saint was born on January 7, 1844, the daughter of a miller. Her former home is open Easter through October, daily from 8am to 7:30pm. This was actually her mother's house. Bernadette's father, François Soubirous, had his family home in another mill, **Moulin Lacadé,** at 2, rue Bernadette-Soubirous (tel. 62-96-22-51). Visiting hours are from 9am to 12:15pm and 2:15 to 7pm. None of these attractions charges admission.

You can visit the impressive wax museum, **Musée Grévin,** 87, rue de la Grotte (tel. 62-94-33-74), where displays retrace not only Bernadette's life but also the life of Christ. There is a reproduction of Leonardo da Vinci's *The Last Supper*. This museum is in the center of Lourdes. It is open April to November, daily from 9 to 11:30am and 1:30 to 6:30pm. Admission is 28 F ($5) for adults, 12 F ($2.20) for children.

Visitors looking for a panoramic view of Lourdes should take an elevator up to the terrace of the **Château-Fort de Lourdes,** an excellent example of medieval military architecture. The castle contains the **Musée Pyrénéen,** 25, rue du Fort (tel. 62-94-02-04), with its collection of regional handcrafts and costumes, including a collection of dolls in nuns' habits. In the courtyard are scale models of different styles of regional architecture. Both the château and the museum may be visited April through mid-October, daily from 9 to 11am and from 2 to 6pm; off-season, it closes at 5pm; and is also closed Tuesday. Admission is 24 F ($4.30) for adults, 12 F ($2.20) for children 6–12.

Exploring the Pyrénées

Lourdes is one of the finest bases for exploring the Pyrénées. You can take tours into the snowcapped mountains across the border to Spain or go horseback-riding near **Lac de Lourdes,** two miles northwest of the town.

Outstanding sites include **Bagnères-de-Bigorre,** a renowned thermal spa; **Pic du Jer,** for a magnificent vista; **Béout,** for a panoramic view and an underground cave where prehistoric implements have been found (reached by funicular); **Pibeste,** for another sweeping view of the Pyrénées; the **Caves of Medous,** an underground river with stalactites; and for a full-day tour, the **Heights of Gavarnie,** at 4,500 feet, one of France's great natural wonders.

WHERE TO STAY

Expensive

GALLIA ET LONDRES, 26, av. Bernadette-Soubirous, 65100 Lourdes. Tel. 62-94-35-44. Fax 62-94-53-66. 90 rms (all with bath or shower). A/C TV TEL **Bus:** 2.
$ Rates (including breakfast): 600 F ($108) single; 700 F ($126) double. AE, V. **Parking:** 50 F ($9). **Closed:** Oct 20–Mar 28.
This old-fashioned four-star hotel was built around 1900, and has since endured a handful of partial modernizations. It's among the most patronized in Lourdes, retaining its provincial flavor for many religious groups which seem to check in en masse. Its restaurant is solidly reliable throughout the year, serving fixed-price menus beginning at 130 F ($23.40) each.

Moderate

GALILEE ET WINDSOR, 10, av. Peyramale, 65100 Lourdes. Tel. 62-94-21-55. 168 rms (all with bath or shower). A/C **Bus:** 2.
$ Rates (including breakfast): 450–550 F ($81–$99) single or double. V. **Closed:** Oct 20–Feb 15. **Parking:** Free.
The Galilée et Windsor is a traditional structure with a modernized interior. Rooms are pleasant, although they often contain plastic furnishings. The hotel's restaurant offers meals for 85 F ($15.30) and up.

GRAND HOTEL DE LA GROTTE, 66-68, rue de la Grotte, 65000 Lourdes. Tel. 62-94-58-87. Fax 62-94-20-50. 81 rms (all with bath). A/C TEL **Bus:** 2.
$ Rates: 380–600 F ($68.40–$108) single or double. Half board 345–420 F ($62.10–$75.60) per person. AE, DC, MC, V. **Parking:** 50 F ($9). **Closed:** Oct 25–Easter.
Built in 1872, five minutes from the Sanctuaries, the Grand Hôtel de la Grotte is an old favorite, well furnished with a typical upper-bourgeois French decor. Its restaurant, open to the public, offers meals at 150 F ($27).

Inexpensive

HOTEL ADRIATIC, 4, rue Baron-Duprat, 65100 Lourdes. Tel. 62-94-31-34. Fax 62-42-14-70. 85 rms (all with bath). TEL **Bus:** 2.
$ Rates: 300–360 F ($54–$64.80) single; 340–420 F ($61.20–$75.60) double. Breakfast 35 F ($6.30) extra. MC, V. **Parking:** Free.
Built in the 1950s, and staffed with a bright, English-speaking staff, this hotel offers comfortable and traditionally decorated bedrooms. Each contains a telephone, and about 23 of them also contain televisions and minibars. The in-house restaurant serves fine regionally inspired cuisine where meals cost around 130 F ($23.40) each. The hotel lies close to the shrines, the home of St. Bernadette, the parish church, and the town's fortified castle.

NOTRE-DAME DE FRANCE, 8, av. Peyramale, 65100 Lourdes. Tel. 62-94-91-45. Fax 62-94-57-21. 76 rms (all with bath or shower). A/C TEL **Bus:** 2.
$ Rates: 260 F ($46.80) single; 370 F ($66.60) double. Half board 295 F ($53.10) per person. AE, MC, V. **Closed:** Oct 13–Apr 6.

Next to the Windsor, the Notre-Dame de France is another good budget hotel, with clean rooms and simple furnishings. Meals are a good buy, beginning at 85 F ($15.30).

WHERE TO DINE

L'ERMITAGE, bd. de la Grotte et place Monseigneur-Laurence. Tel. 62-94-08-42.
　Cuisine: BASQUE. **Reservations:** Recommended. **Bus:** 2.
$ **Prices:** Appetizers 28–60 F ($5–$10.80); main dishes 60–85 F ($10.80–$15.30); fixed price menus 68 F ($12.20), 138 F ($24.80), and 198 F ($35.60). AE, DC, MC, V.
　Open: Lunch only, daily noon–2pm. **Closed:** Oct 10–May 1.
With its exposed-wood interior, this luncheon-only restaurant has the feel of an English club. Chef Pierre Chaubon serves an array of classic French and regional dishes, including a curried-mussel flan, confit of duckling, braised salmon in Jurançon wine, and filet of beef braised in madeira wine.

RELAIS DE SAUX, route de Tarbes (N21), 65100 Lourdes. Tel. 62-94-29-61. Fax 62-42-12-64.
　Cuisine: BASQUE. **Reservations:** Recommended.
$ **Prices:** Fixed-price menus 140 F ($25.20) (lunch only); and 180–310 F ($32.40–$55.80). AE, DC, MC, V.
　Open: Lunch daily noon–1:45pm; dinner daily 7:15–9:30pm.
This is the best restaurant in the area, located about 1½ miles northeast of Lourdes in the village of Saux. It's housed in an ivy-covered manor house, originally built in the late 1400s, which was rebuilt and enlarged after World War II, and then completely renovated again in 1992. Inside, a collection of carved-wood fireplaces from the age of Louis XIV complements a decor of silk-upholstered walls, beamed ceilings, and rustic artifacts. Most visitors come only for the meals, supervised by innkeeper Madeleine Heres and her husband, Bernard. Menu specialties include a warm seafood salad with marjoram, escalope of duck liver with caramelized pears, filet of beef with flap mushrooms, and roast lobster with butter mousse.

Upstairs are seven bedrooms, all with bath and, in some cases, oversize windows overlooking the garden. Singles cost 400–500 F ($72–$90); doubles, 500–600 F ($90–$108). Breakfast is priced at 45 F ($8.10) per person. Parking is free.

TAVERNE DE BIGORRE ET HOTEL D'ALBRET, 21, place du Champs-Commun, 65100 Lourdes. Tel. 62-94-75-00. Fax 62-94-78-45.
　Cuisine: BASQUE. **Reservations:** Recommended. **Bus:** 2.
$ **Prices:** Fixed-price menus 64 F ($11.50), 87 F ($15.70), 125 F ($22.50), and 160 F ($28.80). AE, MC, V.
　Open: Lunch daily noon–1:30pm; dinner daily 7–9pm. **Closed:** Jan 6–Feb 7.
　　This restaurant has some of the best food in town, with tournedos with flap mushrooms a specialty. The Hôtel d'Albret is also one of the best budget hotels in Lourdes, offering a total of 27 comfortably furnished bedrooms, each with shower or bath and telephone. Half-board rates are 184–255 F ($33.10–$45.90) per person.

7. CAUTERETS

515 miles SW of Paris, 31 miles SW of Tarbes, 18½ miles S of Lourdes

GETTING THERE   By Car   The road that winds up the Pyrenean valley from Lourdes grows narrow and very difficult after Cauterets, and eventually ends altogether at Pont d'Espagne, 10 miles south of town.

By Bus   Unless you have a car, the only option is to take one of the four or five daily SNCF buses that run from Lourdes (trip time: 1 hour).

ESSENTIALS   Orientation   Cauterets lies at the junction of two streams, the

Gave de Cambasque and the Gave de Cauterets. A cable-car station to the left of the main road as you enter the village carries sightseers up toward Pont d'Espagne.

Information The Office de Tourisme is on place de l'Hôtel-de-Ville (tel. 62-92-50-27).

The souvenir peddling and the aggressive commercial atmosphere of Lourdes offends many visitors. If you are among them, I suggest that you strike out for the mountains. One sylvan retreat, 18½ miles south from Lourdes, is Cauterets. The site of a dozen curative thermal springs, this hamlet composed mainly of hotels has been famous since Margaret of Navarre, arriving with her court, put it on the map. Even George Sand and Victor Hugo came this way, seeking cures for various ailments. The local folk will tell you, "You can be cured of whatever ails you at Cauterets, and that means everything."

Cauterets is also a center for touring some of the most majestic sights of the Pyrénées. The most popular tour is to **Pont d'Espagne** and the **Lac de Gaube**, south of Cauterets. The road goes along for about 10 miles to Pont d'Espagne. After that, only the hearty continue on foot. The **Cascade du Pont-d'Espagne** is considered the most dazzling of the waterfalls in and around Cauterets. If you're willing to walk for about an hour, you can take the path that leads to the Lac de Gaube. This lake occupies a magnificent setting, extolled by such visitors as Chateaubriand and Vigny. It has been used to illustrate almost every guide written about the Pyrénées since the Romantic period.

WHERE TO STAY & DINE

HOSTELLERIE LA FRUITIERE, Vallée de Lutour, 65110 Cauterets. Tel. 62-92-52-04. 8 rms (2 with bath). **Directions:** Take the N21C four miles from Cauterets.

$ Rates: 130 F ($23.40) single or double without bath, 180 F ($32.40) single or double with bath. Breakfast 28 F ($5) extra. No credit cards. **Parking:** Free. **Closed:** Oct–May 14.

If you'd like to be truly remote, I suggest that you journey to La Fruitière, which is located at the end of a narrow tar road in the middle of a national park. La Fruitière means a place where cheese is made by shepherds in the mountains. Untouched by commercialism, the simple, comfortable inn is tranquil and decorated with antlers, open stone fireplaces, and blackened-beamed ceilings. The restaurant serves good food, with an emphasis on regional dishes such as confit, game, mushrooms from the forest, and trout. Fixed-price menus, costing 77 F ($13.90) and 180 F ($32.40), are served daily (except Sunday evening) for both guests and nonguests.

HOTEL ALADIN/RESTAURANT LES MARMOTTES, 11, av. du Général-Leclerc, 65110 Cauterets. Tel. 62-92-60-00. Fax 62-92-63-30. 70 rms (all with bath). TEL TV

$ Rates: 430 F ($77.40) single; 610 F ($109.80) double. Breakfast 52 F ($9.40) extra. MC, V. **Parking:** 40 F ($7.20).

Begun in 1987, this is the largest hotel in town, and one of the largest commercial complexes in the Pyrénées. Rising from the town center, the complex contains a 70-room hotel (L'Hôtel Aladin), a restaurant (Les Marmottes), 56 apartment units (La Résidence Aladin; usually rented out for periods of a week or more), two banks, and half a dozen boutiques. Most readers of this guide gravitate toward the six-story Hôtel Aladin—where rooms are cozy, modern, and offer views of the mountains—and the restaurant. On the hotel's premises is a sauna, health club, and squash courts.

In the restaurant, amid bouquets of flowers and a decor of pink, blue, green, and oversize bay windows, you can enjoy well-prepared French and Basque meals priced at 36–99 F ($6.50–$17.80) for appetizers, 78–110 F ($14–$19.80) for main courses, and around 150 F ($27) for full fixed-price meals.

8. AX-LES-THERMES

512 miles SW of Paris, 64 miles S of Carcassone

GETTING THERE **By Car** A winding highway leads into town from the north and south. Allow extra time to negotiate the mountain roads.

By Bus In summer, there's daily bus service between Toulouse and Barcelona, via Ax-les-Thermes and Andorra.

ESSENTIALS **Orientation** Le Bassin des Ladres lies in the center of town.

Information The **Office de Tourisme** is at place du Brielh (tel. 61-64-20-64).

In the Valley of the Ariege, Ax is at the same time a thermal spa, a summer retreat, and a winter sports station. Some 80 springs feed it, supplying three spas: le Couloubret, le Modèle, and le Teich. Saint Louis ordered the construction of the **Bassin des Ladres,** which serves as a public washing spot. Originally its purpose was to care for leprous soldiers who returned from the Crusades. The 19th-century Hôpital St-Louis, built in 1846, is a thermal bath dating from the grand days of spas.

Several outings are possible through the Pyrénées' rocky masses, with splendid views on many sides of gushing springs, mountainous rivers, and craggy peaks. Many visitors might also want to go to Andorra, that tiny principality in the Pyrénées.

WHERE TO STAY & DINE

LE CHALET, av. Adolphe-Turrel, 09110 Ax-les-Thermes. Tel. 61-64-24-31. 10 rms (all with bath). TEL

$ Rates: 220 F ($39.60) single; 250 F ($45) double. Breakfast 24 F ($4.30) extra. V. **Closed:** Nov 12–Dec 20.

Le Chalet is a comfortable inn located across from the park surrounding one of the town's spa facilities. Each room has its own balcony. If you just want to stop for a meal, prices begin at 75 F ($13.50).

NAPOTEL ROYAL THERMAL, esplanade du Couloubret, 09110 Ax-les-Thermes. Tel. 61-64-22-51. Fax 61-64-37-77. 46 rms (all with shower or bath). TV TEL

$ Rates: 330 F ($59.40) single; 360 F ($64.80) double. Breakfast 38 F ($6.80) extra. Half board 310 F ($55.80) per person. AE, DC, MC, V. **Closed:** Oct 31–Dec 1.

This modern chain hotel is the best in the area. Most of the well-maintained bedrooms have private balconies or terraces, with views over the mountains. The hotel runs a good restaurant, and many guests opt for the half-board terms.

ROY RENE, 11, av. Dr-Gomma, 09110 Ax-les-Thermes. Tel. 61-64-22-28. Fax 61-64-32-54. 29 rms (20 with bath or shower). TEL

$ Rates (including breakfast): 178 F ($32) single without bath, 275 F ($49.50) single with bath; 198 F ($35.60) double without bath, 300 F ($54) double with bath. AE, MC, V. **Parking:** Free. **Closed:** Nov–Jan.

Built in a five-story format in 1970 in the heart of town, this is the newest hotel, and one of the tallest buildings, in town. Bedrooms are clean, contemporary, and comfortable, with a dozen of them offering a TV set. An in-house restaurant serves family-style French food, costing 98–260 F ($17.60–$46.80) for full fixed-price meals.

CHAPTER 25
LANGUEDOC, ROUSSILLON & THE CAMARGUE

Languedoc, one of the great old provinces of southern France, is a loosely defined area encompassing such cities as Nîmes, Toulouse, and Carcassonne. It's one of the leading wine-producing areas of France, and is fabled for its art treasures.

The coast of Languedoc might be called France's "second Mediterranean," first place going of course to the Riviera. This second coast essentially runs from Montpellier to the Spanish frontier. A land of ancient cities and a generous sea, it is less spoiled than the Côte d'Azur and therefore more attractive as a destination. An almost-continuous strip of sand stretches west from the Rhône curving snakelike toward the Pyrénées. Back in the days of de Gaulle, the French government began an ambitious project to develop the Roussillon-Languedoc coastline, and it has become a booming success, as the miles and miles of bodies in July and August testify.

Ancient Roussillon is a small region of greater Languedoc, forming the département of Pyrénées Orientales. It is French Catalonia, turning more to Barcelona in neighboring Spain for inspiration than to remote Paris. Once it was part of the Roman province of Narbonensis, eventually being absorbed by the Visigoths. Over its long and colorful history it has known many rulers. Legally part of the French kingdom until 1258, it was surrendered to James I of Aragón. Until 1344 it was part of the ephemeral kingdom of Majorca, with Perpignan as the capital. By 1463 Roussillon was annexed to France again. Ferdinand of Aragón won it back, but by 1659 France had it again. In spite of local sentiment for reunion with the Cataláns of Spain, France still firmly controls the land today.

The Camargue is a marshy delta lying between two arms of the Rhône. South of Arles, this is cattle country. The strong wild black bulls are bred here for the arenas of Arles and Nîmes. The small white horses, most graceful animals, were said to have been brought to the Camargue by the Saracens. They are ridden by *gardians,* French cowboys, who can usually be seen in black wide-brimmed hats. The whitewashed houses, the plaited-straw roofs, the pink flamingos who inhabit the muddy marshes, the vast plains, the endless stretches of sandbars—all this qualifies as Exotic France.

WHAT'S SPECIAL ABOUT LANGUEDOC, ROUSSILLON & THE CAMARGUE

Great Towns/Villages

☐ Toulouse, ancient capital of Languedoc and the major city of southwestern France.

☐ Cordes, built like an eagle's nest, a
town of arts and crafts.

☐ Carcassonne, a great fortress city
set against the Pyrénées.

☐ Perpignan, the "second capital" of
Catalonia, an ancient city of monuments and attractions.

☐ Montpellier, an ancient university
city and capital of Mediterranean
Languedoc.

Beaches

☐ The coast of Languedoc, a second
Mediterranean and one of the great
European beaches, running from
Montpellier to the Spanish frontier.

Architectural Highlights

☐ The entire monumental core of the
ancient duchy of Uzès, one of the
major *villes d'art* of the province.

☐ Palais de Rois de Majorque, former
palace of the kings of Majorca, at
Perpignan.

Ancient Monuments

☐ Cathédrale de Ste-Marie, at Auch,
from the 15th century, one of the
handsomest Gothic churches in the
south of France.

☐ Maison Carrée, at Nîmes, one of
the best-preserved Roman temples
in Europe.

Outstanding Museums

☐ Musée Toulouse-Lautrec, at Albi, the
most important collection of his
paintings.

☐ Musée Fabre, at Montpellier, one of
the most acclaimed provincial art
galleries of France, filled with masterpieces.

Events/Festivals

☐ Nîmes, in July, a Jazz Festival.

SEEING LANGUEDOC, ROUSSILLON & THE CAMARGUE

GETTING THERE This is a large territory to cover but is one of the most
interesting regions of France. Many people prefer the western Mediterranean coast to
the overrun French Riviera in the east.

You can begin your journey north in Toulouse or fly to one of the cities closer to
the coast, including Montpellier, Nîmes, and Perpignan. The airport at Toulouse
(Toulouse-Blagnac) has direct flights from Bordeaux, London, Madrid, Milan, and
Nice, and 14 daily flights from Paris. There is also train service from Paris to Toulouse.

Driving along National Road 20 from Paris takes about eight hours. The ideal way
to explore the region is by car, but if you depend on public transportation, use
Toulouse, Montpellier, and Nîmes as your bases.

A motorway network links northern Europe to the Languedoc–Roussillon area.
The highways run by Paris, down to the south of France (on the Autoroute du Soleil),
then on to Languedoc and Roussillon. Autoroute des Deux-Mers links Bordeaux and
Narbonne.

A SUGGESTED ROUTE Start in Toulouse (Day 1) and drive northeast to Albi
(Day 2). Allow time in the late afternoon or the next morning for a short side trip
northwest to Cordes. Continue to Carcassonne (Day 3), with a stopover at Castres.
Then take the autoroute to the coast, spending the night at Perpignan (Day 4). Now
head toward the Spanish frontier, stopping at Collioure for lunch. After that, many

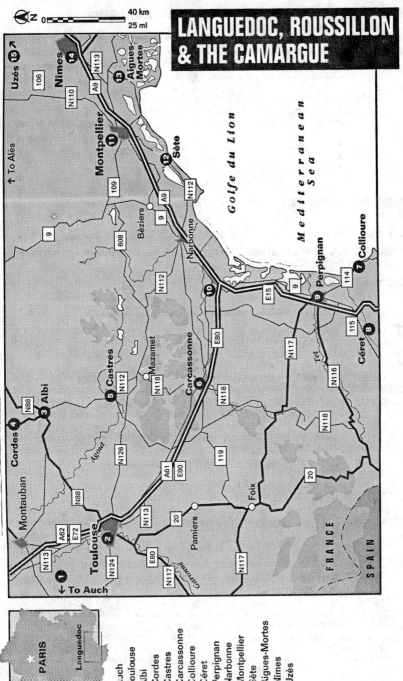

LANGUEDOC, ROUSSILLON & THE CAMARGUE

0 40 km
25 mi

N

↑ To Alès
↓ To Auch

Uzès **15**
Nîmes **14**
Aigues-Mortes **13**
Montpellier **11**
Sète **12**
Béziers
Narbonne **10**
Perpignan **9**
Collioure **7**
Céret **8**
Castres **5**
Mazamet
Carcassonne **6**
Albi **3**
Cordes **4**
Montauban
Toulouse **2**
Auch **1**
Pamiers
Foix

106
N113
A9
N110
109
9
608
N112
A9
9
N112
E15
9
114
N117
115
N116
N118
E80
N118
119
N126
Agout
A61
E80
N88
N88
A62
E72
N113
N124
N113
20
E80
N117
Garonne
N117
20
Tet

Golfe du Lion

M e d i t e r r a n e a n   S e a

F R A N C E

S P A I N

PARIS

Languedoc

1 Auch
2 Toulouse
3 Albi
4 Cordes
5 Castres
6 Carcassonne
7 Collioure
8 Céret
9 Perpignan
10 Narbonne
11 Montpellier
12 Sète
13 Aigues-Mortes
14 Nîmes
15 Uzès

motorists head along the Costa Brava in Spain. Others turn back and take the same autoroute east into France, overnighting in Narbonne (Day 5). Continue east to Montpellier (Day 6), then turn south from the autoroute to the coast for a look at the Camargue district and have a late lunch at Aigues-Mortes. Continue to Nîmes (Days 7 and 8).

Finally, if you have more time, it's an easy drive to Avignon for a tour of Provence (see Chapter 26). Instead of taking the fast autoroute into Avignon, veer off northwest to Uzès, where you can have lunch and take a walking tour before heading to Avignon.

---

1. AUCH

451 miles SW of Paris, 126 miles SE of Bordeaux

GETTING THERE By Train Six trains per day run between Toulouse and Auch (trip time: 1½ hours).

By Bus Eight to ten SNCF buses arrive in Auch daily from Agen.

ESSENTIALS Orientation Set on the west bank of the Gers River, Auch is centered around the Cathédral de Ste-Marie.

Information Contact the Office de Tourisme, place de la Cathédrale (tel. 62-05-22-89).

On the west bank of the Gers, in the heart of the ancient duchy of Gascony, of which it was the capital, the town of Auch in southwestern France is divided into an upper and lower quarter, each connected by several flights of steps. In the old part of town the narrow streets are called *pousterles*.

These streets center on **place Salinis,** from which there is a good view of the Pyrénées. Branching off from here, the **Escalier Monumental** leads down to the river, a monumental descent of 232 steps.

On the north of the square stands the **Cathédrale de Ste-Marie,** at place de la Cathédrale (tel. 62-05-04-64). Built from the 15th to the 17th century, it is one of the handsomest Gothic churches in the south of France. It has 113 Renaissance choir stalls made of carved oak, and a custodian will let you in for a look in exchange for 5 F (80¢). The stained-glass windows, also from the Renaissance era, are impressive. Its 17th-century organ was considered one of the finest in the world at the time of Louis XIV. The cathedral is open daily from 7:30am to noon and 2 to 7pm (closes at 5:30pm in winter).

Next to the cathedral stands an 18th-century archbishop's palace with a 14th-century bell tower, the **Tour d'Armagnac,** which was once a prison.

WHERE TO STAY & DINE

HOTEL DE FRANCE (Restaurant André-Daguin), place de la Libéra-tion, 32003 Auch CEDEX. Tel. 62-61-71-84. Fax 62-61-71-81. 27 rms (all with bath), 2 suites. MINIBAR TV TEL

$ Rates: 290–690 F ($52.20–$124.20) single; 600–970 F ($108–$174.60) double; 1,500–2,500 F ($270–$450) suite. Breakfast 80 F ($14.40) extra. AE, DC, MC, V. **Parking:** Free.

If, during your promenade through the region, you can spend only one night in a sleepy provincial town, André Daguin's establishment would be a very fine choice. Built around the much-modernized 16th-century core of an old inn, it lies in the center of town, close to the cathedral. Today the establishment offers comfortable and conservatively furnished bedrooms, about 14 of which are air-conditioned, and one of the most famous restaurants in France.

The cuisine served is defined by the restaurant itself as "innovative within traditional boundaries." Examples of specific dishes include an assortment of different preparations of foie gras from Gascony, all arranged on the same decorative platter; a brochette of oysters with foie gras; a duo of magrêts de canard cooked in a rock-salt shell and served with a papillotte of vegetables; and stuffed pigeon roasted with spiced honey. Desserts include a platter of four types of chocolate dishes or a café au café, a presentation of mousses and pastries unified only by their consistent permeation with coffee. The restaurant is open for lunch Tuesday through Sunday, and for dinner Tuesday through Saturday. It's closed in January.

LE RELAIS DE GASCOGNE, 5, av. de la Marne, 32000 Auch. Tel. 62-05-26-81. Fax 62-63-30-22. 38 rms (all with bath). A/C TV TEL
$ **Rates:** 240 F ($43.20) single; 320 F ($57.60) double. Breakfast 30 F ($5.40) extra. MC, V. **Parking:** 30 F ($5.40). **Closed:** Dec 18–Jan 9.

This hotel offers economical accommodations and meals. The modernized rooms are comfortably furnished and well maintained. Good meals begin at 95 F ($17.10). Try the salad of duck breast, grilled beef, or head of veal.

2. TOULOUSE

438 miles SW of Paris, 152 miles SE of Bordeaux,
60 miles W of Carcassonne

GETTING THERE By Plane Toulouse's airport, Toulouse-Blagnac, lies in the city's northwestern suburbs.

By Train Nine trains per day arrive from Paris (trip time: 8 hours), 10 from Bordeaux (trip time: 2¾ hours), and 11 from Marseille (trip time: 4½ hours).

By Boat The Canal du Midi links many of the region's cities with Toulouse by waterway.

ESSENTIALS Orientation The city was originally built on and around a cluster of marshy islands in the Garonne River, but today it sprawls over many square miles. The most interesting and historic neighborhood is patterned like an irregular rectangle on the river's east bank. Its borders begin at the river and extend east to the busy boulevard de Strasbourg/boulevard allée F-Verdier. Its major squares are place du Capitole, place Wilson, place Occitane, and place du Salin.

Information The Office de Tourisme is at Donjon du Capitole, rue Lafayette (tel. 61-11-02-22).

The old capital of Languedoc, France's fourth-largest city, "La Ville Rose" is cosmopolitan in flavor. The major city of the southwest, it is the gateway to the Pyrénées. A distinctive landscape of gardens and squares, it is especially noted for its red-brick buildings.

Built on both sides of the Garonne River at a wide bend, Toulouse is an artistic and cultural center. It's had a stormy history, playing many roles—once it was the capital of the Visigoths and later the center of the counts of Toulouse.

WHAT TO SEE & DO

The city's major monument is the **Basilique St-Sernin,** 13, place St-Sernin (tel. 61-21-80-45). Consecrated in 1096, this is the largest and finest Romanesque church extant. One of its most outstanding features is the Porte Miègeville, opening onto the south aisle and decorated with 12th-century sculptures. The door opening into the south transept is called Porte des Comtes, and its capitals depict the story of Lazarus. Nearby are the tombs of the counts of Toulouse. Entering by the main west door, you can see the double side aisles, giving the church five naves, an unusual feature in Romanesque architecture. An upper cloister forms a passageway around the interior. Look for the Romanesque capitals surmounting the columns. In the axis of the basilica, 11th-century bas-reliefs depict "Christ in his Majesty." The ambulatory leads to the crypt (ask the custodian for permission to enter), containing the relics of

128 saints, plus a thorn said to be from the Crown of Thorns. In the ambulatory, the old baroque retables and shrine have been reset and the preservation of the relics in the crypt artistically remade. The relics are those of the Apostles and the first bishops of Toulouse. The ambulatory and crypt may be visited July to September, Monday through Saturday from 10am to 5:30pm, and on Sunday from noon to 5:30pm. The basilica may not be visited during services. Admission is 8 F ($1.40).

Opposite St-Sernin is the **Musée St-Raymond,** place St-Sernin (tel. 61-22-21-85), housed in a college reconstructed in 1523. It contains one of the finest collections of Imperial busts outside Rome. Open Monday and Wednesday through Saturday from 10am to noon and 2 to 6pm, and on Sunday from 10am to noon. Admission is 10 F ($1.80) for adults, 5 F (90¢) for children.

Another important museum is the **Musée des Augustins,** 21, rue de Metz (tel. 61-22-21-82). In its 14th-century cloisters is the most important collection of Romanesque capitals in the world. The sculptures or carvings are magnificent, and there are some fine examples of early Christian sarcophagi. On the upper floors is a large painting collection, with works by Murillo, Toulouse-Lautrec, Guardi, Gérard, Delacroix, Rubens, and Ingres. The museum also contains several portraits by Antoine Rivalz (1667–1735), a home-grown artist of major talent. The museum is open Thursday through Monday from 10am to noon and 2 to 6pm, and on Wednesday from 10am to noon and 2 to 10pm. Admission is 8 F ($1.40) for adults, free for children.

The other major ecclesiastical building is the **Cathédrale de St-Étienne,** at the east end of rue de Metz (tel. 61-52-03-82). It has a bastardized look (probably because it was built between the 11th and 17th centuries). The rectangular bell tower is from the 16th century. It has a unique ogival nave to which a Gothic choir has been added.

One final church worthy of attention is **Eglise des Jacobins,** in Old Toulouse, west of place du Capitole along rue Lakanal (no phone). A Gothic brick church, it dates from the 13th century. The convent, daring in its architecture, has been restored and forms the largest block of buildings in France in use as a monastery. Visiting hours are erratic.

In civic architecture, the **Capitole,** place du Capitole (tel. 49-52-24-63), is outstanding. Built in 1753, it houses the Hôtel de Ville, or city hall, plus a theater in its right wing. Open Monday through Friday from 8:30pm to 5pm and on Saturday from 8:30am to noon; closed holidays. Admission is free.

Toulouse has a number of fine old mansions. More than 50 survive, most of them dating from the Renaissance when Toulouse was one of the richest cities of Europe. The finest is the **Hôtel d'Assézat,** on rue de Metz. It contains a 16th-century courtyard. The mansion houses the Académie des Jeux-Floraux, which since 1323 has presented flowers made of wrought metal to poets.

After all that sightseeing activity, head for the oval **place Wilson,** a 19th-century square sheltering the most fashionable cafés of Toulouse.

WHERE TO STAY
Very Expensive

GRAND HOTEL DE L'OPERA, 1, place du Capitole, 31000 Toulouse. Tel. 61-21-82-66. Fax 61-23-41-04. 40 rms (all with bath), 9 suites. A/C TV TEL **Bus:** 5 or 10.

$ Rates: 850–1,000 F ($153–$180) single; 1,000–1,300 F ($180–$234) double; 1,350–1,500 F ($243–$270) suite. Breakfast 82 F ($14.80) extra. AE, DC, MC, V.

This dramatic and opulent hotel dates from the 17th century when it was a convent. It has also been a theater and a school for classical dance. The owners have won several prestigious awards for transforming an antique building into a sophisticated new ensemble. The public rooms contain early 19th-century antiques and Napoleonic-inspired tenting over the bars. Overall, the feeling is that of being in an elegant Italian villa. Some rooms have urn-shaped balustrades overlooking formal squares. All rooms have color harmony, high ceilings, modern amenities, and radio alarms. The hotel runs the most prestigious restaurant in town (see "Where to Dine," below). Facilities include an indoor pool, a Jacuzzi, and a health club.

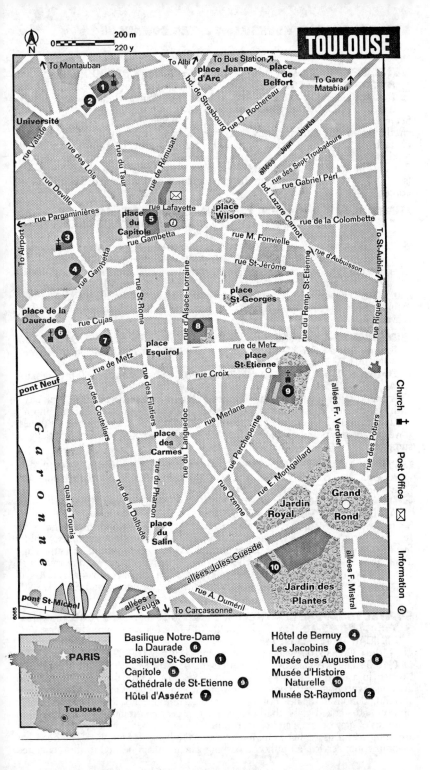

TOULOUSE

N

0 ——— 200 m
——— 220 y

To Montauban

To Albi

To Bus Station

place Jeanne-d'Arc

place de Belfort

To Gare Matabiau

Université

rue Valate

rue des Lois

rue Deville

rue du Taur

rue de Rémusat

bd. de Strasbourg

rue D. Rochereau

allées Jean Jaurès

rue des Sept-Troubadours

rue Gabriel Péri

bd. Lazare Carnot

rue Pargaminières

rue Lafayette

place du Capitole

place Wilson

rue Gambetta

rue M. Fonvielle

rue de la Colombette

rue d'Aubuisson

To St-Aubin

To Airport

rue Gambetta

rue St-Jérôme

rue St-Rome

place St-Georges

rue d'Alsace-Lorraine

place de la Daurade

rue Cujas

rue de Metz

place St-Etienne

rue du Remp. St-Etienne

pont Neuf

rue des Coutellers

rue des Filatiers

place Esquirol

rue Croix

rue de Metz

rue Merlane

allées Fr. Verdier

Garonne

rue du Languedoc

place des Carmes

rue Perchepinte

rue E. Montgaillard

rue Ozenne

Jardin Royal

Grand Rond

allées des Potiers

quai de Tounis

rue du Pharaon

rue de la Dalbade

place du Salin

allées Jules-Guesde

Jardin des Plantes

allées F. Mistral

pont St-Michel

allées P. Feuga

rue A. Duméril

To Carcassonne

Church ✛

Post Office ✉

Information ⓘ

Moderate

HOTEL DES BEAUX-ARTS, 1, place du Pont-Neuf, 31000 Toulouse. Tel. 61-23-40-50. Fax 61-22-02-27. 20 rms (all with bath or shower). A/C TV TEL
$ Rates: 330–560 F ($59.40–$100.80) single or double. Breakfast 45 F ($8.10) extra. AE, DC, MC, V. **Parking:** 50 F ($9).

Set in a richly dignified pink-brick villa which was originally built 250 years ago on the riverbanks of the Garonne, this is a charming and tastefully decorated hotel of character in the heart of town. Despite the historic facade, bedrooms are somberly modern, monochromatic (in tones of salmon and gray) and neutrally comfortable. The only meal served is breakfast; diners often head for the Brasserie des Beaux-Arts (see "Where to Dine," below), in the same building, whose entrance lies around the corner.

MERCURE ALTEA WILSON, 7, rue Labéda, 31000 Toulouse. Tel. 61-21-21-75. Fax 61-22-77-64. 94 rms (all with bath), 4 suites. A/C MINIBAR TV TEL **Bus:** 5, 10, 14, or 16.
$ Rates: 560 F ($100.80) single; 720 F ($129.60) double; from 900 F ($162) suite. Breakfast 58 F ($10.40) extra. AE, DC, MC, V. **Parking:** 30 F ($5.40).

This hotel in the town center is a favorite with business travelers. It doesn't have a restaurant, but room-service dinners are available from 7 to 10pm, and there is a piano bar. The rooms are attractive, soundproof, and contemporary. Amenities include radios and alarms, hairdryers, and private safe-deposit boxes. Garage parking is available.

MERCURE ST-GEORGES, rue St-Jérôme (place Occitaine), 31000 Toulouse. Tel. 61-23-11-77. Fax 61-23-19-38. 170 rms (all with bath or shower). MINIBAR TV TEL **Bus:** 5, 10, 14, or 16.
$ Rates: 530–650 F ($95.40–$117) single or double. Breakfast 50 F ($9) extra. AE, DC, MC, V.

This comfortable hotel is centrally located in the historic section of this "pink city," with its quartier des Fontaines. The hotel offers a gourmet restaurant, another restaurant, and a bar, where Le Fronton is the delightful local wine served. Business travelers are the prime clientele, but it's a good choice for tourists, especially in summer.

NOVOTEL TOULOUSE CENTRE, 5, place Alfonse-Jourdain, 31000 Toulouse. Tel. 61-21-74-74. Fax 61-22-81-22 125 rms (all with bath). A/C MINIBAR TV TEL **Bus:** 5, 10, 14, or 16.
$ Rates: 560 F ($100.80) single; 600 F ($108) double. Breakfast 48 F ($8.60) extra. AE, DC, MC, V. **Parking:** 30 F ($5.40).

Set in the most verdant part of Toulouse's center, this modern and efficient hotel is a few paces from the city's Japanese gardens. The Matabiau train station is within a five-minute walk, and the nerve center of the old city, place St-Sernin, is less than half a mile away. All rooms are alike, each with a single bed (which can be converted into a couch), a double bed, a long writing desk, and a fully equipped bathroom. A grill restaurant serves meals daily from 6am to midnight, beginning at 160 F ($28.80). There's also a bar.

SOFITEL TOULOUSE CENTRE, 84, allées Jean-Jaurès, 31000 Toulouse. Tel. 61-10-23-10. Fax 61-10-23-20. 105 rms (all with bath), 14 suites. A/C MINIBAR TV TEL. **Bus:** 148.
$ Rates: 600 F ($108) single or double Mon–Thurs, 520 F ($93.60) Fri–Sun; 900 F ($162) suite. Breakfast 60 F ($10.80) extra. AE, DC, MC, V. **Parking:** 50 F ($9).

Erected in a soaring, 18-story format in 1989, this is probably the best hotel in Toulouse, the preferred choice of anyone seeking well-designed and convenient accommodations in the heart of town. Set adjacent to place Wilson, behind a facade of steel and smoked glass, the hotel employs a charming bilingual staff dressed in uniforms of gray or green and offers rooms for handicapped travelers, and suites that are outfitted for use either as mini-offices or as lodgings for families. The hotel has 24-hour room service, an in-house parking garage (much needed in this congested neighborhood), a bar, and a pleasant brasserie where full meals begin at around 180 F ($32.40) each. Service is youthful and alert.

Inexpensive

HOTEL RAYMOND-IV, 16, rue Raymond-IV, 31000 Toulouse. Tel. 61-62-89-41. Fax 61-61-38-01. 38 rms (all with bath). MINIBAR TV TEL **Bus:** 5, 10, 14, or 16.

$ Rates: 310–340 F ($55.80–$61.20) single; 350–380 F ($63–$68.40) double. Breakfast 40 F ($7.20) extra. AE, DC, MC, V. **Parking:** 25 F ($4.50).

⑤ Located on a quiet street close to the town center and the rail station, this antique building contains pleasantly decorated rooms. The central location means that you're within walking distance of the historic quarter, with its theaters, shops, and nightclubs. Although only breakfast is served, the English-speaking staff will direct you to a nearby restaurant that fits your pocketbook.

LE ROYAL, 6, rue Labéda, 31000 Toulouse. Tel. 61-23-38-70. Fax 61-22-03-90. 31 rms (all with bath or shower), 1 suite. A/C MINIBAR TV TEL **Bus:** 5, 10, 14, or 16.

$ Rates: 360–550 F ($64.80–$99) single or double; from 650 F ($117) suite. Breakfast 50 F ($9) extra. AE, DC, MC, V. **Parking:** 40 F ($7.20).

This charming and traditional brick hotel is in the heart of the most active midtown district of Toulouse, near shops and restaurants. It's a very popular choice in the city. The rooms are individually decorated and face an interior courtyard.

WHERE TO DINE

Very Expensive

VANEL, 22, rue Maurice-Fonvieille. Tel. 61-21-51-82.
   Cuisine: FRENCH. **Reservations:** Required. **Bus:** 5, 10, 14, or 16.
$ Prices: Appetizers 80–150 F ($14.40–$27); main dishes 130–190 F ($23.40–$34.20); fixed-price menus 250 F ($45), 350 F ($63), and 400 F ($72). AE, MC, V.
   Open: Lunch Mon–Sat 12:15–1:30pm; dinner Mon–Sat 7:30–10pm. **Closed:** Aug 1–15, and Sat lunch July–Aug.

Locals commonly fill this well-known restaurant, which lies in a modern building in the commercial heart of Toulouse. The chef uses his culinary magic to create scrumptious meals, giving new meaning to regional dishes and often discovering new taste sensations. An endless variety of quality meats and produce, skillfully and creatively prepared, are presented for your selection: stuffed pigeon or pigeon roasted with spices and honey, pigs' feet stuffed with sweetbreads and foie gras, and sea bass with baby vegetables. The wine list is imaginative, with many interesting selections, including Cahors and Côtes de Duras. The service is impeccable.

Expensive

LES JARDINS DE L'OPERA, 1, place du Capitole. Tel. 61-23-07-76.
   Cuisine: FRENCH. **Reservations:** Required. **Bus:** 5, 10, 14, or 16.
$ Prices: Appetizers 130–220 F ($23.40–$39.60); main dishes 150–240 F ($27–$43.20); fixed-price menus 300 F ($54) and 480 F ($86.40). AE, DC, MC, V.
   Open: Lunch Mon–Sat noon–2pm; dinner Mon–Sat 8–10pm. **Closed:** Jan 2–6 and Aug 11–31.

✪ The entrance to the city's best restaurant is in the 18th-century courtyard of the Grand Hôtel de l'Opéra, across from one of the best-known theaters of Toulouse. The dining area is a series of intimate salons, several of which face a winter garden and a reflecting pool. You'll be greeted by the graciously articulate Maryse Toulousy, whose husband, Dominique, prepares what critics have called the perfect combination of modern and old-fashioned French cuisine. Menu listings change with the availability of the ingredients. Outstanding dishes are likely to include rack of lamb with garlic croquettes and a "cake" of eggplant and anchovies, shellfish salad with artichoke hearts, and blond chicken livers served with a caramelized port wine sauce. Perhaps you'll prefer ravioli stuffed with foie gras and a distillation of truffles, a tartare (raw) of salmon and oysters served with potato blinis and sour cream, or even a warm pâté of frogs' thighs with ginger.

Moderate

BRASSERIE DES BEAUX-ARTS, 1, quai de la Daurade. Tel. 61-21-12-12.
   Cuisine: FRENCH. **Reservations:** Recommended. **Bus:** 5, 10, 14, or 16.
$ Prices: Appetizers 24–89 F ($4.30–$16); main dishes 65–120 F ($11.70–$21.60); fixed-price menus 135–400 F ($24.30–$72). AE, DC, MC, V.
   Open: Lunch daily noon–3:30pm; dinner daily 7pm–1am.

This turn-of-the-century brasserie is near one of the city's famous old bridges, Pont-Neuf. It was opened in 1988 by entrepreneur Jean-Paul Bucher, who has made a career of restoring old-fashioned brasseries. His enterprises in Paris—including Brasserie Flo, Julien, and La Coupole—have already been recommended. The decor includes walnut paneling and many mirrors, and the cuisine emphasizes fresh and well-prepared fish and seafood, along with a scattering of regional dishes. Try the foie gras or the country-inspired sauerkraut. I also recommend the house riesling, served in a pitcher. During warm weather, eat on the terrace.

CHEZ EMILE, 13, place St-Georges. Tel. 61-21-05-56.
   Cuisine: TOULOUSIEN. **Reservations:** Recommended.
$ Prices: Appetizers 80–100 F ($14.40–$18); main dishes 110–180 F ($19.80–$32.40); fixed-price menus 115–150 F ($20.70–$27) at lunch, 180–210 F ($32.40–$37.80) at dinner. AE, DC, MC, V.
   Open: Lunch Tues–Sat noon–2:30pm; dinner Tues–Sat 7–9:30pm.
In an old-fashioned house on one of the quietest and most beautiful squares of Toulouse (place St-Georges), this restaurant offers the culinary specialties of chef Francis Ferrier. The format changes according to the season: In winter, meals are served one floor above street level in a warmly decorated and cozy enclave overlooking the square; in summer, the venue moves downstairs to the street-level dining room because of its easy accessibility to a flowering outdoor terrace. Menu specialties include a cassoulet toulousain, a magrêt de canard prepared in the traditional style, and a parillade of grilled fish served with a pungently aromatic cold sauce composed of sweet peppers and olive oil.

LE GRAND CAFE DE L'OPERA, in the Grand Hôtel de l'Opéra, 1, place du Capitole. Tel. 61-21-37-03.
   Cuisine: FRENCH. **Reservations:** Recommended. **Bus:** 5, 10, 14, or 16.
$ Prices: Appetizers 40–125 F ($7.20–$22.50); main dishes 80–160 F ($14.40–$28.80). AE, DC, MC, V.
   Open: Daily 9am–12:30am. **Closed:** Aug 1–15.
Le Grand Café, in the most prestigious hotel in the city, evokes memories of the old Brasserie Lipp in Paris. It is warmly decorated with rich cove moldings, lots of burnished hardwood, shimmering glass, and cut flowers. This brasserie and café features fresh shellfish. Other specialties include calf's head ravigotte, steak tartare, "butterfly oysters," and an array of *plats du jour,* based on traditional brasserie cuisine. Seasonal ingredients are used "with respect," in the words of one food critic.

NEARBY ACCOMMODATIONS & DINING

LA FLANERIE, route de Lacroix-Falgarde, 31320 Vieille-Toulouse. Tel. 61-73-39-12. Fax 61-73-18-56. 12 rms (all with bath). MINIBAR TV TEL
   Directions: Take the D4 5½ miles south of Toulouse. **Bus:** R.
$ Rates: 260 F ($46.80) single; 600 F ($108) double. Breakfast 40 F ($7.20) extra. AE, DC, MC, V. **Parking:** Free. **Closed:** Dec 23–Jan 6.
This peaceful hotel is worth the drive or bus ride. The ancient residence is surrounded by a six-acre garden overlooking the Garonne. The room furnishings have been well selected, setting a high level of style. Some of the rooms are outfitted with rich, tasteful antiques, including canopied beds, fine marquetry desks, and bronze lighting fixtures. Reservations are important for both the rooms and the light supper. The hotel has a swimming pool.

HOTEL DE DIANE, 3, route de St-Simon, or 296, chemin de Tucaut, 31100 Le Mirail. Tel. 61-07-59-52, or toll free 800/528-1234 in the U.S. and Canada. Fax 61-68-38-96. 35 rms (all with bath). MINIBAR TV TEL **Directions:** Take the D23 five miles from Toulouse to Exit 27.
$ Rates: 380–440 F ($68.40–$79.20) single; 440–500 F ($79.20–$90) double. Breakfast 45 F ($8.10) extra. AE, DC, MC, V. **Parking:** Free.

This hotel/restaurant complex surrounded by a park is the most tranquil retreat near Toulouse. The turn-of-the-century villa offers well-decorated rooms with wide windows, 13 of which are air-conditioned. Facilities include tennis courts and an outdoor pool. The establishment, owned by Sofia and André Antoine, is affiliated with the Mapotel and Best Western chains.

The restaurant, Saint-Simon, is in a rustic yet modern building and offers a choice of meals in the garden or inside the imaginatively decorated dining room. The fixed-price menu, at 150 F ($27), seems to offer the best value. The restaurant serves lunch Monday through Friday and dinner Monday through Saturday until 9:30pm.

AN EASY EXCURSION TO ARMAGNAC COUNTRY

Some 20 miles from Toulouse lies Armagnac, where the famous Armagnac brandies are produced. In the foothills of the Pyrénées, Armagnac is made up of three districts: **Haut-Armagmac, Ténarèze,** and **Bas-Armagnac.** Most of the brandies come from the flat, sandy Bas-Armagnac, the remainder being produced in Ténarèze, where vineyards grow on chalky hills. Haut-Armagnac is not a great grape area, although it does produce some alcohol used for flavoring and preserving fruits. Well-maintained country roads will take you into this country of D'Artagnan and the Three Musketeers, where you can visit a number of the cellars of the region, whose center is at Eauze.

Records show that brandy has been produced in Armagnac at least since 1422, making it older than cognac, which didn't enter the commercial world until some 200 years later. For the history of Armagnac and information about tours of the cellars and tasting the brandies, request the free booklet from **Food and Wines from France,** 215 Park Ave. S., Room 1600, New York, New York 10003 (tel. 212/477-9800). Information is also available from the **Bureau National Interprofessionnel de l'Armagnac,** place de la Liberté, 32800 Eauze (tel. 62-09-82-33).

If you prefer, you can arrange your own visits with some of the following cellars: Marquis de Caussade, 32800 Eauze; Marquis de Montesquiou, route de Cazaubon, 32800 Eauze; Janneau, 32100 Condom; Larressingle, 32100 Condom; Samalens, 32110 Laujuzan; Clés des Ducs, Panjas 32110 Negaro; Château de Mailliac, 32250 Montréal; and Sempé, 32290 Aignan.

---

3. ALBI

433 miles SW of Paris, 47 miles NE of Toulouse

GETTING THERE   By Plane   Air Inter flights from Paris are available to Albi.

By Train   Fourteen trains per day link Toulouse with Albi (trip time: 1 hour). There is also a direct Paris–Albi night train.

By Car   Motorists from Paris can take the RN20 via Cahors and Caussade; and from Bordeaux, it's the Autoroute des Deux Mers, exiting at Montauban.

ESSENTIALS   Orientation   Built on the southwestern bank of the Tarn River, Albi's historic center lies a few blocks south of Pont-Vieux. At its western edge is the fortresslike Cathédrale de Ste-Cécile.

Information   The Office de Tourisme is located at Palais de la Berbie, place Ste-Cécile (tel. 63-54-22-30).

The "red city" (for the color of the building stone) of Albi straddles both banks of the Tarn River, and is dominated by its brooding, fortified **Cathédrale de Ste-Cécile** (tel. 63-54-15-11), dating from 1282 and lying near place du Vigan, the medieval center of town. After viewing the cathedral, one writer claimed that if it were in Italy, "the French would spend a day in the train to go and see it and that stupendous view." Fortified with ramparts and parapets outside, and containing transepts or aisles inside, it was built by local bishops during a struggle for power with the counts of Toulouse. Inside, look at the 16th-century rood screen. It's exceptional. Open daily from 8:30 to 11:45am and 2:30 to 5:30pm; admission is 2 F (40¢).

Opposite the northern side of the cathedral is the Archbishop's Palace, or **Palais de la Berbie,** another fortified structure dating from the late 13th century. Inside, the **Musée Toulouse-Lautrec** (tel. 63-54-14-09) contains the world's most important collection of that artist's paintings, more than 600 specimens of his work. His family bequeathed the works remaining in his studio. Toulouse-Lautrec was born at Albi on November 24, 1864. Crippled in childhood, his legs permanently deformed, he lived in Paris most of his life and produced posters and sketches of characters in music halls and circuses. His satiric portraits of the demi-monde at the turn of the century were both amusing and affectionate. The museum also owns paintings by Degas, Bonnard, Vuillard, Matisse, Dufy, Utrillo, and Rouault. Open June 15 to September, daily from 9am to noon and 2 to 6pm; off-season, Wednesday through Monday from 10am to noon and 2 to 5pm. Admission is 18 F ($3.20) for adults, 9 F ($1.60) for children.

WHERE TO STAY

HOSTELLERIE ST-ANTOINE, 17, rue St-Antoine, 81000 Albi. Tel. 63-54-04-04. Fax 63-47-10-47. 47 rms (all with bath). A/C TV TEL
$ **Rates:** 380 F ($68.40) single; 950 F ($171) double. Breakfast 60 F ($10.80) extra. AE, DC, MC, V. **Parking:** Free.
This 250-year-old hotel has been owned by the same family for five generations; today it is managed by Jacques and Jean-François Rieux. Their mother focused on Toulouse-Lautrec when designing this hotel. Her grandfather was a close friend of the painter and was given a few of his paintings, sketches, and prints. Several are in the lounge, which opens onto a rear garden with fig trees and flagstone paths. The atmosphere evokes a private country estate. The rooms have been delightfully decorated, with a sophisticated use of color, good reproductions, and occasional antiques. Many have color TVs. The restaurant offers three fixed-price menus for 150 F ($27), 200 F ($36), and 206 F ($37.10).

HOTEL CHIFFRE, 50, rue Séré-de-Rivières, 81000 Albi. Tel. 63-54-04-60. Fax 63-47-20-61. 40 rms (all with bath). TV TEL
$ **Rates:** 360–460 F ($64.80–$82.80) single or double. Breakfast 38 F ($6.80) extra. AE, DC, MC, V. **Parking:** Free.
This well-maintained establishment in the city center has been directed by the Chiffre family since 1918. Rooms are decorated with style, some with views of the quiet inner courtyard. The hotel restaurant is popular among the locals for its fixed-price menus starting at 100 F ($18). Specialties include daube Albi style, snails or roquefort in puff pastry, and breast of duckling. Dessert might be an ice-cream dish named coupe Lautrec. No meals are served on Sunday November through March. Garage parking is available.

MERCURE ALTEA HOTEL, 41, rue Porta, 81000 Albi. Tel. 63-47-66-66. Fax 63-46-18-40. 56 rms (all with bath). MINIBAR TV TEL
$ **Rates:** 375 F ($67.50) single; 580 F ($104.40) double. Breakfast 55 F ($9.90) extra. AE, DC, MC, V. **Parking:** Free.
When it opened in 1987, the modern Altéa Hôtel was immediately recognized as one of the best places to stay in Albi. It was built in an 18th-century mill, of which the facade and huge entryway were preserved. Rooms are well equipped, with 28

containing air conditioning. The first-class restaurant serves superb meals starting at 150 F ($27). Tables are set on the terrace in summer. The hotel is located in the city center, facing the cathedral.

LA RESERVE, route de Cordes à Fonviane, 81000 Albi. Tel. 63-47-60-22. Fax 63-47-63-60. 24 rms (all with bath or shower), 4 suites. MINIBAR TV TEL
$ Rates: 500–600 F ($90–$108) single; 850 F ($153) double; from 1,000 F ($180) suite. Breakfast 70 F ($12.60) extra. AE, DC, MC, V. **Parking:** Free. **Closed:** Nov–Apr.

This country-club villa on the outskirts of Albi is managed by the Rieux family, who for generations have run the Hostellerie St-Antoine (see above). It was built in the Mediterranean style, with a swimming pool and a fine garden in which you can dine. Step terraces lead to the banks of the Tarn River. The upper-story rooms have sun terraces and French doors. Rooms, well furnished and color coordinated, contain imaginative decorations.

In the restaurant, specialties include pâté de grives (thrush), carré d'agneau (lamb) aux cèpes (flap mushrooms), and tournedos Périgueux. Meals cost 170–320 F ($30.60–$57.60).

WHERE TO DINE

In addition to the following recommendation, many of the hotels listed above have fine restaurants.

JARDIN DES QUATRE SAISONS, 19, bd. de Strasbourg. Tel. 63-60-77-76.
Cuisine: FRENCH. **Reservations:** Recommended.
$ Prices: Appetizers 38–82 F ($6.80–$14.80); main dishes 95–142 F ($17.10–$25.60); fixed-price menus 120 F ($21.60) and 150 F ($27). AE, MC, V.
Open: Lunch Tues–Sun 12:30–2pm; dinner Tues–Sun 7:30–10pm.

The best food in town is served by Georges and Martine Bermond. They believe that menus, like life, should change with the seasons—and that's how the restaurant got its name. Service is always competent and polite in a winter-garden setting much appreciated by local residents who dine here on special occasions. Visitors are always welcome. You might enjoy a gratinée of mussels in a compote of fish, anchovy ravioli with an essence of anise-scented tomatoes, or a paupiette of chicken stuffed with foie gras.

---

4. CORDES

421 miles SW of Paris, 15½ miles NW of Albi

GETTING THERE **By Train** You'll have to get off in nearby Vindrac and either rent a bicycle or take a taxi the remaining two miles to Cordes.

ESSENTIALS **Orientation** Set atop a hilltop, the town is surrounded by medieval walls, which used to protect the Cathars. The town's main street is rue Droite, and its most visible monument is the Eglise St-Michel.

Information The Syndicat d'Initiative (tourist office) is in the Maison du Grand-Fauconnier (tel. 63-56-00-52).

The site is remarkable, like an eagle's nest on a hilltop, opening onto the valley of the Cérou 15 miles from Albi. The name Cordes is derived from the textile and leather industries that thrived here during the 13th and 14th centuries. It became a fortified Protestant refuge during the wars of religion.

In the 14th century when the town's troubles eased, artisans working with linen and leather prospered. It also became known throughout France for its brilliantly colored silks. In the 15th century, however, plagues and religious massacres reduced the city to a minor role. A brief renaissance occurred in the 19th century when automatic weaving machines were introduced.

Today Cordes is an arts-and-crafts city, and many of the ancient houses on the narrow streets contain artisans plying their skills—blacksmiths, enamelers, graphics artists, weavers, engravers, sculptors, and painters. You park outside, then go under an arch leading to the old town.

WHAT TO SEE & DO

Often called "the city of a hundred Gothic arches," Cordes contains numerous old houses built of pink sandstone. Many of the doors and windows are fashioned of pointed (broken) arches that still retain their 13th- and 14th-century grace. Some of the best-preserved ones line the **Grande-Rue,** also called rue Droite.

The **Musée Charles-Portal,** le Portail-Peint (tel. 63-56-00-40), is named after the archivist of the Tarn region and an avid historian of Cordes. It contains everyday artifacts of the textile industry of long ago, old farming measures, samples of local embroidery, a reconstructed peasant home interior, and other medieval memorabilia. Open in July and August, daily from 2 to 6pm; off-season, Sunday only, from 2 to 5pm; closed November through April. Admission is 10 F ($1.80) for adults, 5 F (90¢) for children.

The **Maison du Grand-Fauconnier (House of the Falcon Master)** is named for the falcons carved into the stonework of the wall. A grandly proportioned staircase in the building leads to the **Musée Yves-Brayer,** Grande-Rue (tel. 63-56-00-40). Yves Brayer came to Cordes in 1940 and became a well-known figure. After watching Cordes fall gradually into decay, he renewed interest in its restoration. Open in July and August, daily from 10am to noon and 2 to 6pm; April to June and September to November, Monday through Friday from 8:30am to noon and 1:30 to 6pm, and on Sunday and holidays from 2 to 6pm; off-season, daily from 8:30am to noon and 1:30 to 6pm. Admission is 5 F (90¢).

The **Eglise St-Michel,** Grande-Rue (no phone), dates from the 13th century, although many alterations have been made since then. The view from the top of the tower encompasses much of the surrounding area. Much of the lateral design of the side chapels probably comes from the cathedral at Albi. The organ dates from 1830. Before being shipped here, it was in Notre-Dame de Paris. Hours are erratic. If the church is closed, ask at the *tabac* (tobacco shop) across the street from the front entrance.

WHERE TO STAY & DINE

HOSTELLERIE DU PARC, Les Cabannes, 81170 Cordes. Tel. 63-56-02-59. Fax 63-56-18-03.
   Cuisine: FRENCH. **Reservations:** Recommended.
$ **Prices:** Appetizers 50–100 F ($9–$18); main dishes 95–170 F ($17.10–$30.60); fixed-price menus 110 F ($19.80), 145 F ($26.10), 170 F ($30.60), and 260 F ($46.80). AE, DC, V.
   Open: Lunch daily noon–2pm; dinner Mon–Sat 7–10pm. **Closed:** Sun night and Mon Nov–Mar.
About a mile west of the town center, on route de St-Antonin (D600), this century-old stone house offers generously portioned meals in the wooded garden or the paneled dining room. The fireplace has an elegantly proportioned mantelpiece. The well-prepared specialties include homemade foie gras, duckling, poularde occitaine, calf's sweetbreads with morels, and rabbit with cabbage leaves. Claude Izard is the amiable director.

The hotel offers 14 bedrooms, each with phone and private bath or shower. A double goes for 220–240 F ($39.60–$43.20).

MAISON DU GRAND ECUYER, rue Voltaire, 81170 Cordes. Tel. 63-56-01-03. Fax 63-56-16-99.
   Cuisine: FRENCH. **Reservations:** Required.
$ **Prices:** Appetizers 65–110 F ($11.70–$19.80); main dishes 110–210 F

($19.80–$37.80); fixed-price menus 280 F ($50.40), 340 F ($61.20), and 380 F ($68.40). AE, DC, MC, V.
Open: Lunch Tues–Sun noon–2pm; dinner Tues–Sun 7–9:30pm. **Closed:** Mar 16–Oct 20.

The restaurant of this ancient hotel is a national historic monument. Chef Yves Thuriès began his career as a pastry maker and advanced to the well-prepared platters that have made his restaurant an almost mandatory stop during a visit to Cordes. Specialties include three confits of lobster, a salad of red mullet with fondue of vegetables, and noisette of lamb in an orange sauce. You can be assured that, because of Monsieur Thuriès's background, the dessert selection is about the grandest and the most overwhelming in this part of France.

The hotel is in a former hunting lodge of Raymond VII, comte de Toulouse. There are 11 rooms, all with many antiques, private baths, minibars, TVs, and telephones. Singles or doubles cost 590–850 F ($106.20–$153), plus 65 F ($11.70) for breakfast. The most-desired room, honoring former guest Albert Camus, contains a four-poster bed and a fireplace.

5. CASTRES

GETTING THERE By Bus Several times a day buses run to Castres from Carcassonne and Toulouse.

ESSENTIALS Orientation Set beside the Agout River, the town is built around a central square, appropriately named after its native son, Jean Jaurès.

Information The Syndicat d'Initiative (tourist office) is located in the Théâtre Municipal, place de la République (tel. 63-71-56-58).

Built on the bank of the Agout River, Castres is the point of origin of trips to the Sidobre, the mountains of Lacaune, and the Black Mountains. Today the wool industry, whose origins go back to the 14th century, has made Castres one of the two most important wool-producing areas of France. The town was formerly a Roman military installation. A Benedictine monastery was founded here in the 9th century, and the town fell under the comtes d'Albi in the 10th century. During the wars of religion, it was Protestant.

Jean Jaurès, leader of the unified Socialist party in France, was born here in 1859. Along with Emile Zola, he defended Dreyfus in the celebrated trial. He was assassinated in Paris in 1914.

WHAT TO SEE & DO

The ✪ **Musée Goya,** in the Hôtel de Ville, Jardin de l'Evêché (tel. 63-71-59-28), is in the town hall, a former archbishop's palace designed by Mansart in 1669. Some of the spacious public rooms have ceilings supported by a frieze of the archbishop's coats-of-arms. The collection includes 16th-century tapestries and the works of Spanish painters from the 15th through the 20th century.

Most notable, of course, are the paintings of Francisco de Goya y Lucientes, all of which were donated to the town in 1894 by Pierre Briguiboul, son of the Castres-born artist Marcel Briguiboul. *Les Caprices* is a study of figures created in 1799, after the illness that left Goya deaf. Filling much of an entire room, the work is composed of highly symbolic images of demons and monsters, a satire of Spanish society.

The museum is open in July and August, daily from 9am to noon and 2 to 6pm; September to June, Tuesday through Saturday from 9am to noon and 2 to 6pm, and on Sunday from 10am to noon and 2 to 6pm. Admission is 10 F ($1.80) for adults, 5 F (90¢) children 14–18; free for children under 14.

A few rooms of the former archbishop's palace are reserved for the **Musée Jean-Jaurès**, 2, place Pelisson (tel. 63-72-01-01). This museum is dedicated to the workers' movements of the late 19th and early 20th centuries. It gathers together printed material issued by various Socialist factions in France during this era. See, in particular, an issue of *L'Aurore*, containing Zola's famous "J'accuse" article from the Dreyfus case. Paintings, sculptures, films, and slides round out the collection. The museum is open in July and August, daily from 9am to noon and 2 to 6pm; April to September 21, Tuesday through Sunday from 9am to noon and 2 to 6pm; September 22 to March, Tuesday through Sunday from 9am to noon and 2 to 5pm. Admission is 10 F ($1.80) for adults, free for children.

Architect Caillau began construction of the **Eglise St-Benoît**, place du 8-Mai-1945 (tel. 63-59-05-19), in 1677, on the site of the 9th-century Benedictine abbey. The baroque structure was never completed according to its original plans, however. The painting at the far end of the church above the altar was executed by Gabriel Briard in the 18th century. Open daily from 9am to 5pm.

WHERE TO STAY

LE GRAND HOTEL, 11, rue de la Libération, 81103 Castres CEDEX. Tel. 63-59-00-30. Fax 63-59-98-05. 40 rms (all with bath). MINIBAR TV TEL **Bus: 10.**

$ **Rates:** 180–260 F ($32.40–$46.80) single; 210–280 F ($37.80–$50.40) double. Breakfast 30 F ($5.40) extra. AE, DC, MC, V. **Parking:** 20 F ($3.60). **Closed:** Dec 15–Jan 15.

This traditional hotel is one of the best of the moderately priced establishments in town. Three generations of the same family have owned the hotel since it was built in 1860. Half its comfortably furnished bedrooms open onto the river. The restaurant, La Caravelle, is open daily from June 15 to September 15. It has a terrace overlooking the river. Fixed-price menus cost 90 F ($16.20), 120 F ($21.60), and 180 F ($32.40).

WHERE TO DINE

LA MANDRAGORE, 1, rue Malpas. Tel. 63-59-51-27.
   Cuisine: LANGUEDOCIEN. **Reservations:** Recommended.

$ **Prices:** Appetizers 90–125 F ($16.20–$22.50); main dishes 90–125 F ($16.20–$22.50); fixed-price menus 70 F ($12.60) (with wine, served at lunchtime only), and 80–240 F ($14.40–$43.20). AE, DC, MC, V.

   Open: Lunch Tues–Sat noon–2pm; dinner Mon–Sat 7–10pm.

On a narrow and easily overlooked street in the historic center of town, this restaurant occupies a small section of one of the many wings of the medieval château-fort of Castres. The decor is consciously simple, perhaps as an appropriate foil for the stone walls and overhead beams. Sophie (in the dining room) and Jean-Claude (in the kitchens) Belaut prepare a regional cuisine which some visitors say is among the very best in town. Served with charm and tact, it might include a lasagne of foie gras, roast pigeon stuffed with foie gras and served with a gâteau of potatoes and flap mushrooms, des petits encornets (a local squid) stuffed with tomatoes and saffron, and several types of attractively grilled fresh fish. The Belgian-born wine steward speaks English. The establishment's name, incidentally, derives from a local plant (*le mandragore*) used by medieval alchemists, according to legend, as an aphrodisiac.

6. CARCASSONNE

495 miles SW of Paris, 57 miles SE of Toulouse

GETTING THERE There are plane, train, and bus connections from the rest of France. Carcassonne is a major rail stopover with 11 trains per day arriving from

Toulouse (50-minute trip) and 10 trains arriving from Montpellier (two-hour trip). Two planes fly in daily from Paris in just 90 minutes.

ESSENTIALS Orientation The town is divided into the Ville-Basse, which is the modern city, and the medieval and highly atmospheric Cité, which is southeast of the modern town, on the opposite bank of the Aude River. Since parking within the Cité is complicated, you should park in one of the many public lots outside the gates.

Information The Office de Tourisme is located at 15, bd. Camille-Pelletan (tel. 68-25-07-04).

Evoking bold knights, fair damsels, and troubadours, the greatest fortress city of Europe rises against a background of snow-capped Pyrénées. Floodlit at night, it captures fairytale magic, but back in its heyday in the Middle Ages, all wasn't so romantic. Shattering the peace and quiet were battering rams, grapnels, a mobile tower (inspired by the Trojan horse), quicklime, catapults, flaming arrows, and the mangonel.

Carcassonne consists of two towns, the **Ville Basse** ("Lower City") and the medieval **Cité.** The former has little interest, but the latter is among the major attractions in France, the goal of many a pilgrim. The fortifications consist of the inner and outer walls, a double line of ramparts.

The inner rampart was built by the Visigoths in the 5th century. Clovis, the king of the Franks, attacked in 506, but he failed. The Saracens overcame the city in 728, until Pepin the Short (father of Charlemagne) drove them out in 752. During a long siege by Charlemagne, the populace of the walled city was starving and near surrender until a woman named Dame Carcas came up with an idea. According to legend, she gathered up the last remaining bit of grain, fed it to a sow, then tossed the pig over the ramparts. It is said to have burst, scattering the grain. The Franks concluded that Carcassonne must have unlimited food supplies and ended their seige.

The walls were further fortified by the viscounts of Trencavel in the 12th century and by Louis IX and Philip the Bold in the following century. However, by the mid-17th century Carcassonne's position as a strategic frontier fort was over. The ramparts decayed. In the 19th century the builders of the lower town began to remove the stone for use as material in new construction. But interest in the Middle Ages revived, and the French government ordered Viollet-le-Duc (who restored Notre-Dame in Paris) to repair and where necessary rebuild the walls. Reconstruction continued until recently.

Enclosed within the walls is a small populace. The **Cathédrale de St-Nazaire,** La Cité (tel. 68-25-27-65), dates from the 11th and 12th centuries, containing some beautiful stained-glass windows and a pair of rose medallions. The nave is in the Romanesque style, but the choir and transept are Gothic. The organ, one of the oldest in southwestern France, is from the 16th century. The tomb of Bishop Radulph is well preserved, dating from A.D. 1266. Open daily from 9am to noon and 2 to 6pm. Admission is free.

WHERE TO STAY

I urge you to experience the romance of living within the once-fortified walls of the Cité. You may also choose to stay in the lower city.

In the Cité

CITE, place de l'Eglise, 11000 Carcassonne. Tel. 68-25-03-34. Fax 68-71-50-15. 23 rms (all with bath), 3 suites. A/C TV TEL **Bus:** 4.
$ Rates: 820 F ($147.60) single; 1,100 F ($198) double; from 1,600 F ($288) suite. Breakfast 80 F ($14.40) extra. AE, DC, MC, V. **Parking:** 40 F ($7.20).

This has long been the most desirable place to stay within the walls of the old city. Massively renovated, it is now the luxurious choice for Carcassonne, built within the actual walls itself, adjoining the cathedral. Many of the rooms open onto the ramparts and a garden and feature either antiques or reproductions. Modern equipment has been discreetly installed without spoiling the antique style. An adaptation of a church palace, the inn maintains the same medieval architectural heritage of thick stone walls and leaded Gothic windows. You enter into a long Gothic corridor and gallery leading to the lounge. The staff is gracious.

HOTEL DES REMPARTS, 3-5, place du Grand-Puits, 11000 Carcassonne. Tel. 68-71-27-72. 18 rms (all with bath). TEL **Bus:** 4.
$ Rates: 280 F ($50.40) single; 280–330 F ($50.40–$59.40) double. Breakfast 30 F ($5.40) extra. MC, V. **Parking:** 20 F ($3.60).

Built as an abbey in the 12th century, this building was heavily damaged by fires, floods, and dilapidation. In 1983 it was converted into a charming hotel after major repairs were made to the masonry and roof. Rooms contain no-frill furniture. The owners are most proud of the massive stone staircase that twists around itself. Parking is available in back. The hotel is located in the town center, at the edge of a stone square, near a fountain. Make reservations early, at least two months ahead if you plan to stay here during the summer.

Entrance to the Cité

HOTEL DU DONJON, 2, rue du Comte-Roger, 11000 Carcassonne. Tel. 68-71-08-80, or toll free 800/528-1234 in the U.S. and Canada. Fax 68-25-06-60. 36 rms (all with bath or shower), 2 suites. MINIBAR TV TEL **Bus:** 4.
$ Rates: 300–390 F ($54–$70.20) single; 375–505 F ($67.50–$90.90) double; 650–850 F ($117–$153) suite. Breakfast 50 F ($9) extra. AE, DC, MC, V. **Parking:** 40 F ($7.20).

This little, well-positioned hotel is big on charm, the best value in the moderate range. It even has a garden. Built in the style of the old Cité, it has a honey-colored stone exterior with iron bars on the windows. The interior is a jewel, reflecting the taste and sophistication of its owner, Christine Pujol. Rather elaborate Louis XIV–style furniture graces the reception lounges. The chairs are gilt and covered with tapestry. A newer wing contains additional rooms in a medieval architectural style, and the older rooms have been renewed. Twenty-two rooms are air-conditioned. A continental breakfast is served. The hotel also runs a restaurant nearby, the Brasserie du Donjon.

MERCURE LA VICOMTE, 18, rue Camille-Saint-Saens, 11000 Carcassonne. Tel. 68-71-45-45. Fax 68-71-11-45. 58 rms (all with bath), 3 suites. A/C TV TEL **Bus:** 4.
$ Rates: 375 F ($67.50) single; 490 F ($88.20) double; 520–600 F ($93.60–$108) suite. Breakfast 50 F ($9) extra. AE, DC, MC, V. **Parking:** Free.
From the nearby Porte Narbonnaise, this hotel looks like a sprawling network of Mediterranean houses, each with a red-tile roof and a belt of greenery. Many rooms have a view of the city's fortifications. Rooms are comfortable and modern with conservative furnishings, radios, and personal safes. The hotel offers a swimming pool and parking. The cooperative staff can advise you about tours of the ancient city.

Ville-Basse

HOTEL DU PONT-VIEUX, 32, rue Trivalle, 11000 Carcassonne. Tel. 68-25-24-99. Fax 68-47-62-71. 20 rms (all with bath). TV TEL **Bus:** 4.
$ Rates: 290–390 F ($52.20–$70.20) single or double. Breakfast 35 F ($6.30) extra. AE, MC, V. **Parking:** 30 F ($5.40).
This cozy and intimate French inn offers comfort, value, and a certain charm. It's off a cobble-covered road in bottomland dotted with 19th-century houses, between commercial Carcassonne and the walled medieval Cité. Behind its stucco facade lie

modern and comfortable public rooms and a handful of pleasantly decorated bedrooms, each with soundproof windows. There's a quiet garden in back. Underground garage parking is available.

HOTEL MONTSEGUR, 27, allée d'Iéna (route de Pamiers), 11000 Carcassonne. Tel. 68-25-31-41. Fax 68-47-13-22. 21 rms (all with bath). TV TEL **Bus:** 4.
$ Rates: 290 F ($52.20) single; 450 F ($81) double. Breakfast 48 F ($8.60) extra. AE, DC, MC, V. **Parking:** Free.

This stately old town house with a mansard roof and dormers has a front garden that's screened from the street by trees and a high wrought-iron fence. Monsieur and Madame Faugeras have furnished the hotel with antiques, avoiding that institutional look. Modern amenities include an elevator. Rooms are cheaper than you'd imagine from the looks of the place; seven are air-conditioned. A continental breakfast is available, and the highly recommended Le Languedoc restaurant (see "Where to Dine," below) is nearby. The hotel is open all year.

HOTEL TERMINUS, 2, av. du Maréchal-Joffre, 11001 Carcassonne. Tel. 68-25-25-00. Fax 68-72-53-09. 110 rms (all with bath). TEL **Bus:** 4.
$ Rates: 290 F ($52.20) single; 450 F ($81) double. Breakfast 35 F ($6.30) extra. AE, DC, MC, V. **Parking:** 30 F ($5.40).

Built in 1914, this old-style, very grand hotel has many antique furnishings. The hotel was Nazi headquarters from 1941 to 1943, but that has been happily forgotten. Most rooms are spacious, with views of the mountains, the Old City, or the river. The restaurant, Relais de l'Ecluse, offers good meals in a grand setting. Fixed-price menus are reasonably priced at 85–180 F ($15.30–$32.40). The hotel is near the train station. An air-conditioned minibus shuttle takes guests to the Old City twice a day.

WHERE TO DINE

In addition to the following recommendations, several hotels offer dining choices (see "Where to Stay," above).

AUBERGE DU PONT-LEVIS, La Cité. Tel. 68-25-55-23.
   Cuisine: FRENCH. **Reservations:** Recommended. **Bus:** 4.
$ Prices: Appetizers 80–130 F ($14.40–$23.40); main dishes 130–150 F ($23.40–$27); fixed-price menus 160–300 F ($28.80–$54). AE, DC, MC, V.
   Open: Lunch Tues–Sun noon–1:30pm; dinner Tues–Sat 8–9:30pm. **Closed:** Dec 20–Jan 20.

The Auberge du Pont-Levis is at the entrance to the medieval city near Porte Narbonnaise. Its foundations are almost as old as the city. Dine either in a dining room one floor above street level or on an outdoor terrace ringed with flowers. Henri Pautard, the owner and chef, is aided by his wife, Andrée. They serve generous portions of roast pigeon in a garlic purée, filet of sole with a velouté of lobster, filet of sea bass with cabbage and smoked salmon, and a hearty cassoulet.

AU JARDIN DE LA TOUR, 11, rue Porte-d'Aude, Cité de Carcassonne. Tel. 68-25-71-24. Bus: 4.
   Cuisine: FRENCH. **Reservations:** Recommended in summer.
$ Prices: Appetizers 50–70 F ($9–$12.60); main dishes 75–250 F ($13.50–$45); fixed-price menus 130–280 F ($23.40–$50.40). AE, DC, MC, V.
   Open: Lunch daily noon–2pm; dinner daily 8–10pm. **Closed:** Tues Nov–Easter.

A culinary team labors to create an authentic and classic French cuisine. This restaurant is in the oldest part of the Cité, a few paces from the Donjon Hôtel. It's at the end of a long corridor. Dishes include a large selection of salads, stuffed chicken, onglet of beef with shallots, confit of duckling, and steak tartare.

LE LANGUEDOC, 32, allée d'Iéna. Tel. 68-25-22-17.
   Cuisine: FRENCH. **Reservations:** Recommended. **Bus:** 4.
$ Prices: Appetizers 50–110 F ($9–$19.80); main dishes 90–140 F ($16.20–$25.20); fixed-price menus 130 F ($23.40), 175 F ($31.50), and 220 F ($39.60). AE, DC, MC, V.

Open: Lunch Tues–Sun noon–2:30pm; dinner Tues–Sat 7:30–9:30pm. **Closed:** Dec 10–Jan 15.

Monsieur Lucien Faugeras and his son, Didier, are both excellent chefs. They also own the previously recommended 19th-century Montségur Hôtel. The dining room has a warm Languedoc atmosphere, the proper setting for their culinary repertoire. The inviting ambience is achieved by rough plaster walls, ceiling beams, an open brick fireplace, and provincial cloths draped over peasant tables. It's a real country tavern. The house specialty is cassoulet au confit de canard (the world-famous stew made with duck cooked in its own fat). The pièce de résistance is tournedos Rossini, served with foie gras truffé and madeira sauce. A smooth dessert is crêpes flambées Languedoc. In summer, dine on a pleasant patio or inside the air-conditioned restaurant.

NEARBY ACCOMMODATIONS & DINING

CHATEAU SAINT-MARTIN [Logis de Trencavel], Montredon. Tel. 68-71-09-53.
Cuisine: FRENCH. **Reservations:** Recommended.
$ Prices: Appetizers 75–110 F ($13.50–$19.80); main dishes 112–205 F ($20.20–$36.90); fixed-price menus 170 F ($30.60), 210 F ($37.80), and 270 F ($48.60). AE, DC, MC, V.
Open: Lunch Thurs–Tues noon–2pm; dinner Thurs–Tues 7:30–9:30pm.

One of the most successful chefs of Languedoc operates out of this historic 16th-century château at Montredon, 2½ miles northeast of Carcassonne. Ringed by a wooded park, the restaurant is graced with the superb cuisine of co-owners Jean-Claude and Jacqueline Rodriguez. Dine inside or on the outdoor terrace. The bar has a fireplace. Menu items that have proven successful include turbot with a fondue of baby vegetables, sea bass with a mousseline of scallops, sole in tarragon, and a richly flavorful confit d'oie carcassonnaise, which is goose meat delicately cooked in its own fat and kept in earthenware pots.

DOMAINE D'AURIAC, route St-Hilaire, 11000 Carcassonne. Tel. 68-25-72-22. Fax 68-47-35-54. 23 rms (all with bath or shower). MINIBAR TV TEL
Directions: Take the D104 about two miles from Carcassonne.
$ Rates: 660–1,300 F ($118.80–$234) single or double. Breakfast 80 F ($14.40) extra. AE, DC, MC, V. **Parking:** Free. **Closed:** Jan 24–Mar 1.

The premier place for food and lodging is just outside Carcassonne. This ivy-covered 19th-century manor was originally a family home. The gardens are dotted with reflecting pools and flowered terraces. The rooms in this Relais & Châteaux have a certain type of photo magazine glamour. Each is uniquely decorated. Some are within an older building with high ceilings, and others have a more modern decor. Several have small salons.

Bernard Rigaudis sets a grand table. The dining room is lovely, with a cameolike decor of rosy beige and elegant table settings. In summer, meals are served beside the swimming pool on the terraces overlooking the gardens. There is a golf course nearby. The menu changes about five or six times yearly. The choice of offerings is determined not only by the seasons but also by regional tradition. For example, try the truffles and purple artichokes served with essences of pears and olives. Meals cost 170–370 F ($30.60–$66.60). The restaurant is open for lunch Tuesday through Sunday from 12:30 to 2pm, and for dinner Monday through Saturday from 7:30 to 9:15pm. Reservations are required.

---

7. COLLIOURE

577 miles SW of Paris, 17 miles SE of Perpignan

GETTING THERE Collioure is serviced by frequent train and bus connections, especially from Perpignan. Many visitors drive along the coastal road (N14) leading to the Spanish border.

ESSENTIALS Orientation Shaped like a half-moon, the town lies between its château and the Eglise Notre-Dame des Anges, which stand at opposite ends of the old town.

Information The Office de Tourisme is at place du 18-Juin (tel. 68-82-15-47); it is closed in January.

You may recognize this port and its sailboats in the Fauve paintings of Lhote and Derain. It's said to resemble St-Tropez before it was spoiled, attracting, in days of yore, Matisse, Picasso, and Dalí. Collioure is considered the most authentically alluring port of Roussillon, a gem with a vivid Spanish and Catalán image and flavor. Some visitors say it's the single most charming village on the Côte Vermeille.

The most memorable geography consists of a pair of curving ports separated from one another by the heavy masonry of the 13th-century **Château Royale,** place du 8-Mai-1945 (tel. 68-82-06-43). The château, now a museum of modern painting and sculpture, is open June 20 to September, Wednesday through Monday from 10:30am to 6:30pm; March to June 19 and in October and November, Wednesday through Monday from 2 to 6pm (closed other months). Admission is 20 F ($3.60) for adults and 14 F ($2.50) for children.

Also try to visit the **Musée Jean-Peské,** route de Port-Vendres (tel. 68-52-05-66), with its collection of works by artists who migrated here to paint. Open June to September, daily from 3 to 8pm; October to May, Wednesday through Monday from 2 to 7pm. Admission is 15 F ($2.70).

The town's sloping and narrow streets, its charming and semi-fortified church, its antique lighthouse, and its eerily introverted culture make it worth an afternoon stopover.

WHERE TO STAY

LES CARANQUES, route de Port-Vendres, 66190 Cllioure. Tel. 68-82-06-68. 16 rms (14 with bath). TEL
$ Rates (including half board): 295 F ($53.10) single without bath, 380 F ($68.40) single with bath; 620 F ($111.60) double with bath. MC, V. **Parking:** Free. **Closed:** Oct 10–Mar.

Ⓢ Built in the 1960s in a low-slung, rustic format, this hotel is well scrubbed, comfortably furnished, personalized, and one of the best bargains in town. The terrace opens onto a view of the old port. The restaurant is for residents only, almost all of whom elect to stay here on the half-board plan.

CASA PAIRAL, impasse des Palmiers, 66190 Collioure. Tel. 68-82-05-81. Fax 68-82-52-10. 27 rms (all with bath). MINIBAR TV TEL
$ Rates: 350–795 F ($63–$143.10) single or double. Breakfast 40 F ($7.20) extra. AE, MC, V. **Parking:** 30 F ($5.40). **Closed:** Nov–Mar.

On sunny days the most alluring aspect of this 150-year-old house is an outdoor swimming pool in the shadows of century-old trees. Rooms are comfortable and large, filled with charming old furniture. Only breakfast is served, but many restaurants are nearby.

WHERE TO DINE

LA PEROUSE, 6, rue de la République. Tel. 68-82-05-60.
Cuisine: FRENCH. **Reservations:** Recommended.
$ Prices: Appetizers 45–90 F ($8.10–$16.20); main dishes 105–160 F ($18.90–$28.80); fixed-price menus 88–200 F ($15.80–$36). AE, MC, V.
Open: July–Sept, lunch daily noon–2pm; dinner daily 7–9:30pm. **Closed:** Tues Oct–June.

Ⓢ This restaurant occupies the whitewashed cellar of a building in the heart of town. Small windows illuminate the enormous antique barrels and the bullfighting accessories in back, although some visitors prefer a seat on the establishment's glassed-in (and sun-flooded) veranda instead. The kitchens make few concessions to modern cuisine. Instead, food is prepared with solid authenticity, following the traditions of the region. Menu items might include a salade catalán, a panaché of anchovies, spicy preparations of scallops, and a time-honored version of bouillabaisse. Dessert might be a simple but satisfying crème caramel.

8. CERET

580 miles SW of Paris, 19 miles SW of Perpignan

GETTING THERE   By Car   From Perpignan motorists can head south on the E4 express highway to Spain, turning west at the signposted junction with Route 115 toward Céret.

ESSENTIALS   Information   The Syndicat d'Initiative is on avenue Georges-Clemenceau (tel. 68-87-00-53).

Painters inspired by views here have covered the walls of museums around the world. Picasso and Braque made it the capital of cubism. Céret is one of the most vivid showcases of Catalán culture in the French Pyrénées. Irrigated orchards, thousands of acres of them, make this one of the most important fruit-harvesting regions in Europe. Cherries are especially important, making this region the biggest producer, in volume, in France. Rare for a country which severely prunes (some arborists say deforms) their plane trees, the soaring trees of the center of Céret tower high above the rooftops of the village—etching spidery lines against the sky and encouraging extended afternoon strolls through their shadows.

At the turn of the century a group of avant-garde painters were attracted here by the Catalonian sculptor Manolo (1873–1945). They lent to Céret the name "Mecca of Cubism." Later, French composer Deodat de Severac (who died in 1921) made Céret his vacation home. The monument to his memory stands near the chamber of commerce, bearing a bas-relief by Manolo.

You can visit the **Musée d'Art Moderne,** 8, bd. du Maréchal-Joffre (tel. 68-87-27-76), which is dedicated to the painters who have passed through. Works by Braque, Matisse, Maillol, Chagall, and Picasso, among others, are displayed. Admission is 20 F ($3.60), free for children 16 and under. Open in July and August, daily from 10am to 7pm; September to June, Wednesday through Monday from 10am to 6pm.

The town's monument to the fallen of World War I is by Aristide Maillol.

WHERE TO STAY & DINE

LES ARCADES, 1, place Picasso, 66400 Céret. Tel. 68-87-12-30. Fax 68-87-18-86. 26 rms (all with bath). TV TEL
$ Rates: 220–320 F ($39.60–$57.60) single or double. Breakfast 28 F ($5) extra. AE, DC, V. **Parking:** Free. **Closed:** Most of Nov.
This small, centrally located hotel is unpretentious and very French. Rooms are simply furnished. The bar is decorated with dozens of modern paintings, and there's a sun terrace. Only breakfast is served.

LA TERRASSE AU SOLEIL, route de Fontfrède, 66400 Céret. Tel. 68-87-01-94. Fax 68-87-39-24. 25 rms (all with bath or shower), 1 suite. MINIBAR TV TEL
$ Rates: 495–695 F ($89.10–$125.10) single or double; 1.095 F ($197.10) suite. Breakfast 60 F ($10.80) extra; half board 480–780 F ($86.40–$140.40) per person. MC, V. **Parking:** Free. **Closed:** Jan 2–Mar 7.
I recommend this "Relais de Silence" for its exceptional calm. Surrounded by wild scenery, it has as its star attraction a swimming pool. The hotel is also known for its restaurant, once a favorite of Salvador Dalí. The menu might include a filet of beef with shallots, lobster with poached eggs flavored with tarragon vinegar, and noisette

of veal flavored with citrus and served with a zucchini flan. The restaurant is open daily from 12:30 to 2pm and 7:30 to 9:30. Fixed-price menus cost 150 F ($27), 250 F ($45), and 350 F ($63).

9. PERPIGNAN

562 miles SW of Paris, 229 miles NW of Marseille

GETTING THERE   By Train   Six trains per day arrive from Paris (trip time: 10 hours) and 12 trains from Marseille (trip time: 4 hours). There are also five trains per day arriving from Nice (trip time: 7 hours).

By Car   If already on the French Riviera, motorists can continue west along the A9 to Perpignan.

ESSENTIALS   Orientation   Perpignan was built near the junction of the Têt River and its much smaller tributary, the Basse River. On the southern edge of the old town are massive fortifications around the Palais des Rois de Majorque. At the northern end of the old city is the Cathédrale de St-Jean, and a few blocks to the west, Le Castillet. Busy boulevards encircle the old town.

Information   Contact the Office Municipal du Tourisme, Palais des Congrès, place Armand-Lanoux (tel. 68-66-30-30).

At Perpignan you may think you've already crossed the border into Spain. Actually, Perpignan was once the second city of Catalonia, ranking after Barcelona. Even earlier it was the capital of that curiosity, the kingdom of Majorca. But when the Roussillon—the French part of Catalonia—was finally partitioned off, Perpignan became French forever, authenticated by the Treaty of the Pyrénées in 1659. However, Catalán is still spoken, especially among the country people. There is much traffic between Perpignan and Barcelona.

Perpignan derives its name from the legend of Père Pinya, a plowman who is said to have followed the Têt River down the mountain to the site of the town today, where he started cultivating the fertile soil, with the river carrying out its promise to water the fields.

WHAT TO SEE & DO

Among the chief things to see, the **Castillet** (castle) is a machicolated and crenellated building of red brick. It's a combination of a gateway and fortress, dating from the 14th century. If you ask the keeper, you can climb the tower for a good view of the town. The Castillet houses **La Casa Païral,** place de Verdun (tel. 68-35-42-05), which has exhibitions of Catalán regional artifacts and folkloric items, including typical dress. Admission is free. Open June to mid-September, Wednesday through Monday from 9:30 to 11:30am and 2:30 to 6:30pm; mid-September to May, Wednesday through Monday from 9am to noon and 2 to 6pm.

The **Cathédrale de St-Jean,** rue de l'Horloge (tel. 68-51-33-72), dates from the 14th and 15th centuries. It has an admirable nave and some interesting 17th-century retables. Leaving by way of the south door, you'll find a chapel on the left containing the Devot Christ, a magnificent wood carving depicting a Jesus contorted with pain and suffering—his head, crowned with thorns, drooping on his chest. Open daily from 7am to noon and 3 to 7pm.

At the top of the town, the Spanish citadel encloses the **Palais Rois de Marjorque (Palace of the Kings of Majorca),** rue des Archers (tel. 68-34-48-29). This structure from the 13th and 14th centuries has been restored by the government. It is built around a court encircled by arcades. You can see the old throne room with its large fireplaces and a square tower with a double gallery. From the tower there's a fine view of the Pyrénées. A guided tour—in French only—is mandatory, and one departs every 30 minutes, costing 10 F ($1.80) for adults, 5 F

(90¢) for students, free for children 7 and under. Open June through September, daily from 10am to 6pm; October to May, daily from 9am to 5pm.

WHERE TO STAY

HOTEL ATHENA, 1, rue Queya (Marché-République), 66000 Perpignan. Tel. 68-34-37-63. Fax 68-51-07-25. 39 rms (25 with bath or shower). MINIBAR TV TEL

$ **Rates:** 235–255 F ($42.30–$45.90) single with bath or shower; 140 F ($25.20) double without bath or showers, 290–310 F ($52.20–$55.80) double with bath or shower. Breakfast 30 F ($5.40) extra. AE, DC, MC, V. **Parking:** 30 F ($5.40).

Close to the major sights, the Athena is in a tranquil zone in the old part of town, near the cathedral. The building dates from the 14th century when it was a cloister, but has been considerably modernized. There's no restaurant, but a continental breakfast is offered. Garage parking is available.

HOTEL DE LA LOGE, place de la Loge, 66000 Perpignan. Tel. 68-34-41-02. Fax 68-34-25-13. 22 rms (all with bath). MINIBAR TV TEL

$ **Rates:** 275–350 F ($49.50–$63) single or double. Breakfast 35 F ($6.30) extra. AE, DC, MC, V.

This beguiling little hotel is modern, with a charming and tasteful interior. The location is right in the heart of town, near not only the Loge de Mer, from which it takes its name, but also the Castillet. It's also near a canal outlet of the Têt. Rooms are attractively furnished.

PARK HOTEL, 18, bd. Jean-Bourrat, 66000 Perpignan. Tel. 68-35-14-14. Fax 68-35-48-18. 67 rms (all with bath). A/C MINIBAR TV TEL

$ **Rates:** 260 F ($46.80) single; 550 F ($99) double. Breakfast 38 F ($6.80) extra. AE, DC, MC, V. **Parking:** 30 F ($5.40).

Favored by many travelers heading for Spain's Costa Brava, this hotel faces the Jardins de la Ville. Rooms are well furnished and soundproof. A first-class cuisine is served in the restaurant, Le Chapon Fin, which offers not only à la carte listings but also two fixed-price menus, at 180 F ($32.40) and 350 F ($63). The restaurant is open for lunch Monday through Saturday and for dinner Monday through Friday. Parking is provided in the basement.

WHERE TO DINE

The restaurant in the Park Hotel (see "Where to Stay," above) also offers fine dining.

FESTIN DE PIERRE, 7, rue du Théâtre. Tel. 68-51-28-74.
Cuisine: FRENCH. **Reservations:** Required.
$ **Prices:** Appetizers 45–85 F ($8.10–$15.30); main dishes 95–155 F ($17.10–$27.90); fixed-price menu 160 F ($28.80). AE, DC, MC, V.
Open: Lunch Thurs–Tues noon–2pm; dinner Thurs–Mon 7–9:30pm. **Closed:** Feb 8–28.

This restaurant attracts a conservative and socially prestigious clientele who dine under a Renaissance-era ceiling in a building with a 15th-century framework of exposed brick, wood paneling, and antiques. The excellent cuisine is traditional—no frivolity. In a clublike atmosphere, patrons enjoy such offerings as cutlets of red mullet with a watercress salad, filet of turbot in a champagne sauce, and veal kidneys in an aged sweet wine sauce.

MARINE, 40, rue de la Fusterie. Tel. 68-51-21-14.
Cuisine: FRENCH. **Reservations:** Required.
$ **Prices:** Appetizers 30–60 F ($5.40–$10.80); main dishes 56–110 F ($10.10–$19.80); fixed-price menus 69 F ($12.40), 110 F ($19.80), and 160 F ($28.80). AE, DC, MC, V.
Open: Lunch Tues–Sat noon–2pm; dinner Tues–Sat 7–11pm.

One of the best in town, this restaurant serves a sophisticated cuisine in an informal bistro setting. Chef and owner Jean-Pierre Mariné offers such dishes as basil-stuffed salmon, filet of trout with sorrel, and lamb cutlets in a garlic-cream sauce. Tournedos in a roquefort sauce is another well-prepared main dish.

LA VILLA DUFLOT, 109, av. Victot Dalbiez, 66000 Perpignan. Tel. 68-56-67-67. Fax 68-56-54-05.

Cuisine: FRENCH. **Reservations:** Required. **Directions:** Take the N9 from the town center, leading to the autoroute, and exit at Perpignan Sud (South) heading toward Argelès.

$ Prices: Appetizers 65–110 F ($11.70–$19.80); main dishes 110–175 F ($19.80–$31.50). AE, MC, V.

Open: Lunch daily noon–2:30pm; dinner daily 8–11pm.

Slightly removed from the city center, this restaurant/hotel is the most tranquil oasis in the area. The Mediterranean villa stands in its own tree-dotted park, with a swimming pool and a reflecting pool. André Duflot is a chef of remarkable skill and professionalism, and he offers a warm salad of squid, a platter of fresh anchovies marinated in vinegar, foie gras of duckling, and, for dessert, peaches in Banyuls wine. On the premises is an American bar and 18 handsomely furnished bedrooms and suites, each with air conditioning, minibar, TV, and phone. Rooms, either single or double, rent for 540–740 F ($97.20–$133.20) daily, plus 55 F ($9.90) for breakfast. Suites begin at 950 F ($171).

10. NARBONNE

525 miles SW of Paris, 38 miles E of Carcassonne

GETTING THERE Narbonne has rail, bus, and highway connections with other cities on the Mediterranean coast and with Toulouse. Rail travel is the most popular means of transport, with 14 trains per day arriving from Perpignan (trip time: 45 minutes), 13 trains per day from Toulouse (trip time: 1½ hours), and 12 trains per day from Montpellier (trip time: 55 minutes).

ESSENTIALS Orientation The city lies on either side of the canal de la Robine, 10 miles inland from the coast. The Basilique St-Just is in the center of town at the edge of the canal; it is the monument from which all distances in the old city are measured. To its south is a large parking lot.

Information The Office de Tourisme is on place Roger-Salengro (tel. 68-65-15-60).

A medieval city, Narbonne was a port to rival Marseille in Roman times, its "galleys laden with riches." It was the first town outside Italy to be colonized by the Romans. But the Mediterranean, now five miles away, left it high and dry. For that very reason it's an intriguing old place to visit, steeped as it is with antiquity.

WHAT TO SEE & DO

All the museums listed below sell a global ticket costing 10 F ($1.80) and entitling visitors to enter the museums over a period of 48 hours.

Construction of the **Basilique St-Just,** place de l'Hôtel-de-Ville (tel. 68-32-09-52), began in 1272, but it was never finished. Only the transept and a choir were completed; the choir is 130 feet high, built in the bold Gothic style of northern France. At each end of the transept, the towers, 194 feet high, are from 1480. There is an impressive collection of Flemish tapestries. The cloisters are from the 14th and 15th centuries, and they connect the cathedral with the **Palais des Archevêques** (Archbishops' Palace) (tel. 68-90-30-30). The attraction is open March to October, Tuesday through Sunday from 9:30am to 12:30pm and 3 to 7pm; November to February, Tuesday through Sunday from 10am to noon and 2 to 5pm.

The Archbishops' Palace is fortified, with three towers from the 13th and 14th centuries. The Old Palace on the right is from the 12th century and the so-called New Palace on the left dates from the 14th century. The Neo-Gothic **Hôtel de Ville,** part of the complex, was constructed by Viollet-le-Duc in 1845–50.

The archbishops of Narbonne lived elegantly in the **Palais Neuf (New Palace).** The archbishops' rooms are reached by climbing 88 steps up the monumental and impressive Louis XIII staircase. It's said that the old archbishops were hauled up the stairs on mules. Today these apartments have been converted into museums.

The **Musée Archéologique** (tel. 68-90-30-30) displays prehistoric artifacts, Bronze Age tools, 14th-century frescoes, and Greco-Roman amphorae. Several of the sarcophagi date from the 3rd century, and some of the mosaics are of pagan origin. It's open May to October, Tuesday through Sunday from 9:30am to 12:30pm and 3 to 7pm; November to April, Tues–Sun 10am to noon and 2 to 5pm.

The **Musée d'Art et d'Histoire** (tel. 68-90-30-30) is three floors above street level in the former private apartments of the archbishops. These are the rooms in which Louis XII stayed during his siege of Perpignan. The coffered ceilings are enhanced with panels depicting the nine Muses. A Roman mosaic floor and 17th-century portraits are on display. There's a collection of antique porcelain, enamels, and a portrait bust of Louis XIV. This museum keeps the same hours as the Musée Archéologique (see above).

The **Donjon Gilles-Aycelin,** dating from the late 13th century, has a lofty observation platform with a view of the cathedral, the surrounding plain, and the Pyrénées.

See Roman artifacts at the **Musée Lapidaire,** place Lamourguier (tel. 68-65-53-58), within the 13th-century Church of Lamourguier. The collection of broken sculptures, Roman inscriptions, and relics of medieval buildings is considered one of the largest such exhibits in France and one of the most important. It's open Monday through Saturday from 10 to 11:50am and 2 to 6pm.

The early Gothic **Basilique St-Paul-Serge,** rue de l'Hôtel-Dieu (tel. 68-41-09-82), was built on the site of a 4th-century necropolis. Inside, it has an elegantly decorated choir with fine Renaissance wood carving and some ancient Christian sarcophagi. The chancel from 1229 is admirable. The north door leads to the Paleo-Christian Cemetery, part of an early Christian burial ground. Open daily from 9am to 5pm.

WHERE TO STAY

LANGUEDOC, 22, bd. Gambetta, 11100 Narbonne. Tel. 68-65-14-74.
Fax 68-65-81-48. 42 rms (all with bath). TEL
$ Rates: 275 F ($49.50) single; 450 F ($81) double. Breakfast 40 F ($7.20) extra. AE, DC, MC, V. **Parking:** 30 F ($5.40).
This modernized hotel is near the canal de la Rhône. Owned by the Lion family, it offers well-equipped bedrooms. The restaurant serves regional specialties, with meals costing 90–220 F ($16.20–$39.60). Typical Languedoc specialties include grilled salmon with anchovy butter, fresh sole, tender lamb cooked with beans, veal liver provençal, and sautéed chicken chasseur. The hotel's English Pub is open daily from 6pm to 2am.

NOVOTEL NARBONNE SUD, quartier Plaisance, route d'Espagne, 11100 Narbonne. Tel. 68-42-72-00. Fax 68-42-72-10. 96 rms (all with bath). A/C MINIBAR TV TEL
$ Rates: 410 F ($73.80) single; 460 F ($82.80) double. Breakfast 50 F ($9) extra. AE, DC, MC, V. **Parking:** Free.
About a mile south of Narbonne, this hotel is a few hundred yards from the Narbonne Sud exit of the autoroute. Built in 1975 and renovated several years later, the hotel offers a restaurant, bar, swimming pool, and garden terrace. Each bedroom is simple but comfortable. Designed in a pattern proven successful dozens of times throughout Europe, each contains a double bed and a single bed (which converts into a sofa) and a long writing desk.

LA RESIDENCE, 6, rue de Ier-Mai, 11100 Narbonne. Tel. 68-32-19-41.
Fax 68-65-51-82. 26 rms (all with bath). A/C TV TEL
$ Rates: 350–390 F ($63–$70.20) single; 450–490 F ($81–$88.20) double. MC.
V. **Parking:** 50 F ($9).

My favorite hotel in Narbonne is near the Cathedral of St-Just and the
Archbishops' Palace. La Résidence is very comfortable and decorated with a
collection of antiques. The atmosphere will charm lovers of antiquity. The
hotel doesn't have a restaurant, but it offers breakfast.

WHERE TO DINE

L'ALSACE, 2, av. Pierre-Sémard. Tel. 68-65-10-24.
Cuisine: FRENCH. **Reservations:** Recommended.
$ Prices: Appetizers 70–160 F ($12.60–$28.80); main dishes 110–180 F
($19.80–$32.40); fixed-price menus 100–330 F ($18–$59.40). AE, DC, MC, V.
Open: Lunch Wed–Mon 12:30–2pm; dinner Wed–Sun 7:30–9:30pm.
Situated across from the rail station, this restaurant is one of the best in Narbonne.
The comfortable dining room is outfitted in an English style, with a long menu. In
spite of the name of the restaurant, the cuisine is not of Alsace-Lorraine in eastern
France, but more typical of the food of western France. The Sinfreu family, the
owners, offer a fry of red mullet, a savory kettle of bourride, and magrêt of duck with
flap mushrooms. One specialty is an assiette des pêcheurs, containing grilled portions
of many different kinds of fish, plus a lobster salad.

AUX 3 CAVES, 4, rue Benjamin. Tel. 68-65-28-60.
Cuisine: FRENCH. **Reservations:** Required.
$ Prices: 48–130 F ($8.60–$23.40); main dishes 96–195 F ($17.30–$35.10);
fixed-price menus 78 F ($14), 109 F ($19.60), 130 F ($23.40), 154 F ($27.70),
209 F ($37.60), and 310 F ($55.80). AE, DC, V.
Open: Lunch daily noon–2pm; dinner daily 7–9:30pm.
This excellent restaurant is installed in comfortably restored Romanesque cellars. The
owners offer a carefully orchestrated and elegant decor and also present a classic
menu, their repertoire focusing on popular platters from the region. They are known
for their traditional cassoulet, but they also prepare a confit of duckling with garlic,
platters of fresh sardines cooked in white wine, grilled turbot, and a gratin of snails.

11. MONTPELLIER

471 miles SW of Paris, 100 miles NW of Marseille

GETTING THERE Twenty trains per day arrive from Avignon (trip time: 1 hour),
eight from Marseille (trip time: 2 hours, 10 minutes), one per hour from Toulouse (trip
time: 3¼ hours), and 10 trains per day from Perpignan (trip time: 1 hour, 50 minutes).
Nine trains per day arrive from Paris, calling for a change in Lyon (trip time: 5 hours).
Two buses a day arrive from Nîmes (trip time: 1¾ hours). For motorists, Montpellier
lies off the A9 heading west.

ESSENTIALS Orientation The old town is bordered by busy boulevards on
all sides. To the east and west are parks, and near the town center is place Jean-Jaurès,
probably the centerpiece of the jumbled streets comprising the old town. Following
rue de la Loge to the southeast, you'll enter the café-lined place de la Comédie, where
you'll find the Théâtre de l'Opera.

Information The Office de Tourisme is at 78, av. du Pirée (tel. 67-22-06-16).

The capital of Mediterranean (or Lower) Languedoc, this ancient university city 31
miles southwest of Nîmes is still renowned for its medical school, founded in the
13th century. Nostradamus qualified as a doctor here, and even Rabelais studied at
the school. Petrarch also came to Montpellier in 1317, staying for seven years.

WHAT TO SEE & DO

Paul Valéry met André Gide in the **Jardin des Plantes,** and you might well begin your tour there, as it's the oldest such garden in France, dating from the 15th and 16th centuries. Reached from boulevard Henri-IV, this botanical garden, filled with exotic plants, was opened in 1593. Admission free, it's open daily from 9am to noon and 2 to 5pm.

Nearby is the **Cathédrale de St-Pierre,** on place St-Pierre (tel. 67-66-04-12), which was founded in 1364. Once the church of a Benedictine monastery, the cathedral suffered badly in religious wars. (After 1795 the monastery was occupied by the medical school.) The cathedral today has a somewhat bleak west front with two towers and a canopied porch.

Called "the Oxford of France," Montpellier is a city of young people, as you'll notice if you sit at a café opening onto the heartbeat **place de la Comédie,** admiring the Théâtre, the 18th-century Fountain of the Three Graces, or whatever else amuses you. It's the living room of Montpellier, the meeting place of students from all over the world who study here.

The **Musée Fabre,** boulevard Bonne Nouvelle (tel. 67-66-06-34), is one of the great provincial art galleries of France. It occupies the former Hôtel de Massilian, where Molière once played for a season. The origins of the collection were gleaned from an exhibition of the Royal Academy that was sent to Montpellier by Napoléon in 1803. The bulk and most important works of the collection, however, were given by François Fabre (1766–1837), a Montpellier painter, in 1825. Later, after Fabre's death, many other paintings from his collection were donated to the gallery. Several of these he painted himself, but the more important works were ones that he had acquired. These include Poussin's *Venus and Adonis,* and such Italian paintings as *The Mystical Marriage of Saint Catherine.* This generosity was followed by donations from other parties, notably Valedau, who in 1836 left his collection of Rubens, Gérard Dou, and Téniers.

Also in the collection, donated by yet other donors, are Zurbarán's *Angel Gabriel* and his *Saint Agatha* (these are actually fashionable Sevillana girls masquerading as saints). Delacroix's *Women of Algiers* is on display, and you'll also find *Female Bathers* and *The Meeting* by Courbet. There are also two large marble sculptures by Houdon, famed for his busts of the ancient régime (one is of Benjamin Franklin). Several of the lesser-known paintings are by native sons of Montpellier, and there are also ceramic vessels made in Montpellier.

The museum is open Tuesday through Friday from 9am to 5:30pm and on Saturday and Sunday from 9:30am to 5pm. Admission is 16 F ($2.90).

Before leaving town, everybody takes a stroll along the 17th-century **promenade du Peyrou,** a terraced park with views of the Cévennes and the Mediterranean. This is a broad esplanade constructed at the loftiest point of Montpellier. Opposite the entrance is an Arch of Triumph, erected in 1691 to celebrate the victories of Louis XIV. In the center of the promenade is an equestrian statue of Louis XIV, and at the end, the Château d'Eau, a monument to 18th-century classicism, a pavilion with Corinthian columns. Water is brought here by a conduit, nearly nine miles long, and an aqueduct. Montpellier was quite popular with British visitors in the 19th century, who strolled along this promenade admiring the splendid terraces and the neoclassic hotels adorned with wrought-iron balconies, a charming sight.

WHERE TO STAY
Expensive

METROPOLE, 3, rue Clos-René, 34000 Montpellier. Tel. 67-58-11-22.
Fax 67-92-13-02. 81 rms (all with bath or shower), 4 suites. A/C MINIBAR TV TEL **Bus:** 7 or 9.
$ Rates: 620 F ($111.60) single; 675 F ($121.50) double; from 850 F ($153) suite. Breakfast 55 F ($9.90) extra. AE, DC, MC, V. **Parking:** 50 F ($9).
Superior rooms in the heart of Montpellier can be found at the Métropole. The agreeably decorated rooms are well equipped and have marble baths. Ask for a room

overlooking the unusual interior garden, as these accommodations have a pleasant view and are quieter. The rooms are beautifully maintained by the polite staff.

Moderate

CHEVALIER D'ASSAS, 18, av. d'Assas, 34000 Montpellier. Tel. 67-52-02-02. Fax 67-04-18-02. 14 rms (all with bath). A/C MINIBAR TV TEL **Bus:** 7 or 9.

$ Rates: 460–560 F ($82.80–$100.80) single or double. Breakfast 56 F ($10.10) extra. AE, DC, MC, V. **Parking:** 45 F ($8.10).

Located next to the promenade du Peyrou, this turn-of-the-century hotel with a terra-cotta tile roof would be described as Edwardian if it had been built in England. Rooms are spacious with high ceilings, unique decor, and individual heating controls. The Bauer family welcomes guests with a platter of food.

HOTEL GEORGE-V, 42, av. St-Lazare, 34000 Montpellier. Tel. 67-72-35-91. Fax 67-72-53-33. 39 rms (all with bath). TV TEL **Bus:** 7 or 9.

$ Rates: 360 F ($64.80) single; 470 F ($84.60) double. Breakfast 36 F ($6.50) extra. AE, DC, MC, V. **Parking:** 30 F ($5.40).

Located near a park on the northern edge of the city, this well-managed hotel offers traditionally furnished bedrooms. There is a bar reserved for residents. Fixed-price menus cost 98–118 F ($17.60–$21.20).

HOTEL DE NOAILLES, 2, rue Ecoles-Centrales, 34000 Montpellier. Tel. 67-60-49-80. Fax 67-66-08-26. 30 rms (all with bath). TV TEL **Bus:** 7 or 9.

$ Rates: 280 F ($50.40) single; 480 F ($86.40) double. Breakfast 38 F ($6.80) extra. AE, DC, MC, V.

This is an attractive 17th-century building in the old part of the city, behind the Musée Fabre. You'll feel connected to the past here, near the Church of Notre-Dame des Tables and the esplanade with its small lake and rows of plane trees. The rooms are well furnished and handsomely kept. Breakfast is brought to your room if you wish, but no other meals are served.

Inexpensive

LES ARCEAUX, 33-35, bd. des Arceaux, 34000 Montpellier. Tel. 67-92-03-03. Fax 67-92-05-09. 18 rms (all with bath). TV TEL **Bus:** 9.

$ Rates: 240–310 F ($43.20–$55.80) single or double. Breakfast 32 F ($5.80) extra. MC, V. **Parking:** Free.

A hotel has survived in this location since the turn of the century. Its location is excellent, right off the renowned promenade du Peyrou. Rooms are pleasantly furnished, and there is a shady terrace adjoining the hotel. Breakfast is the only meal served.

WHERE TO DINE

LE CHANDELIER, 3, rue Leenhardt. Tel. 67-92-61-62.
Cuisine: FRENCH. **Reservations:** Required. **Bus:** 7 or 9.

$ Prices: Appetizers 85–120 F ($15.30–$21.60); main dishes 110–180 F ($19.80–$32.40); fixed-price menus 240 F ($43.20), 285 F ($51.30), and 360 F ($64.80). AE, DC, MC, V.

Open: Lunch Tues–Sat noon–1:30pm; dinner Mon–Sat 7:30–9:30pm.

This elegant restaurant is in a comfortably decorated house with Italian neoclassical decor. It's located on a not-so-chic street near the train station, but this doesn't mar the success of two long-established partners, Jean-Marc Forest and Gilbert Furlan. At round tables decorated with flowers and elegant porcelain, you can enjoy the day's array of super-fresh specialties. These change frequently, but might include mousse of smoked eel with mint-flavored mussels, sweetbreads of lamb with crayfish in a vinaigrette sauce, veal kidneys in basil, a mosaic of hare with foie gras, and breast of duckling with shallots en confit.

L'OLIVIER, 12, rue Aristide-Olivier. Tel. 67-92-86-28.
Cuisine: FRENCH. **Reservations:** Not required. **Bus:** 7 or 9.

$ Prices: Appetizers 60–98 F ($10.80–$17.60); main dishes 98–140 F ($17.60–$25.20); fixed-price menus 138 F ($24.80) and 176 F ($31.70). AE, DC, MC, V.
Open: Lunch Tues–Sat noon–1:30pm; dinner Tues–Sat 7:30–9:30pm. **Closed:** Aug 1–15.

This small restaurant, a short distance from the railroad station, is operated by Michel Breton of Paris. The limited number of menu items include fresh salmon with oysters, fricassée of lamb with thyme, warm terrine of monkfish, salad of lamb sweetbreads with extract of truffles, and sea bass with vegetables. The welcome you receive is warm-hearted and sincere.

LA RESERVE RIMBAUD, 820, av. St-Maur. Tel. 67-72-52-53.
Cuisine: FRENCH. **Reservations:** Required. **Bus:** 8 or 10.
$ Prices: Appetizers 70–130 F ($12.60–$23.40); main dishes 80–200 F ($14.40–$36). AE, DC, MC, V.
Open: Lunch Tues–Sun noon–2pm; dinner Tues–Sat 8–10pm. **Closed:** Mid-Jan to mid-Feb.

Located in the Quartier des Aubes, some two miles east of the city center, this restaurant offers gracious and elegant dining in an 1876 building. Meals are served on a terrace overlooking Le Lez, a river, or in the harmonious dining room, which is warmly decorated. Top-quality meat, seasonal seafood from the Mediterranean, local game, and fresh vegetables are expertly prepared. Trained by his father, who was also a distinguished chef, Jean Tarrit has earned a culinary reputation of his own. He is assisted by his wife, Catherine, who greets guests. Delicately conceived specialties include fricassée of sole with small vegetables and roast young pigeon.

NEARBY ACCOMMODATIONS

DEMEURE DES BROUSSES, route de Vauguières, 34000 Montpellier.
Tel. 67-65-77-66. Fax 67-22-22-17. 17 rms (all with bath). TV TEL **Directions:** Take the D172E about two miles out of town.
$ Rates: 400–630 F ($72–$113.40) single or double. Breakfast 50 F ($9) extra. AE, DC, MC, V. **Parking:** Free. **Closed:** Jan–Feb.

This 18th-century country house stands in an impressive park. The bedrooms are beautifully furnished. The hotel has been discreetly and tastefully converted, its public and private rooms agreeably decorated. The selection of furniture and decorative objects provides the intimate atmosphere of a gracious home. The country house is not far from the sea, about a 10-minute drive from the heart of Montpellier.

12. SETE

489 miles SW of Paris, 21 miles SW of Montpellier

GETTING THERE   By Train   Sète has rail connections from all other cities of the Mediterranean coastline, including Montpellier, from where 20 trains arrive per day (trip time: 20 minutes).

By Ferry   There's ferry service from major ports of Morocco and the Balearic Islands.

ESSENTIALS   Orientation   The city sprawls across two islands and a complicated series of estuaries, connected and crisscrossed by bridges.

Information   The Office de Tourisme is located at 60, Grand Rue Mario-Roustan (tel. 67-74-71-71).

Unlike any other city in France, Sète, the largest port for fish on the Mediterranean, has a heavy overlay of nostalgia today. Once it was the principal link to France's colonies in North Africa. A writer once said: "One feels that, when Marlene Dietrich boarded her ship in *Morocco,* she must have been sailing from Sète."

Built on the slopes and at the foot of Mont Saint-Clair, on a limestone rock connected to the rest of the mainland via two sandspits, Sète, a city of canals, evokes comparison to Venice. Its architecture is a blend of art deco and Second Empire.

Paul Valéry, best known for his *Le cimetière marin,* was born here and once claimed that "all my works imply and vibrate the place of my birth." Since 1666 the town has been famous for its aquatic jousts, where a combatant armed with a cudgel attempts to knock his counterpart in the opposing boat into the water.

Occupied since the Roman era, the city came into prominence in the 17th century when Colbert announced the construction of a port here at the place where the Canal du Midi dumped into the Canal des Deux-Mers. The 19th century, however, was the port's golden era, when it became the fifth busiest in France. This was helped by the colonization of Algeria. Even today a car-ferry deposits passengers with frequency from North Africa. It's worth a visit, as it is richly evocative of the type of exotic ports you see only in the movies.

WHERE TO STAY & DINE

LE GRAND HOTEL, 17, quai de Tassigny, 34200 Sète. Tel. 67-74-71-77.
Fax 67-74-29-27. 47 rms (all with bath), 4 suites. A/C MINIBAR TV TEL **Bus:** 1.
$ Rates: 285–480 F ($51.30–$86.40) single or double; 555–1,150 F ($99.90–$207) suite. Breakfast 33 F ($5.90) extra. AE, DC, MC, V. **Parking:** 32 F ($5.80).
This is the best and most interesting hotel in town, with a well-run restaurant. Because it's situated near the intersection of two canals, the moored boats and grand buildings might remind you of Venice. The limestone facade is accented with elaborate corbels and bas-reliefs, some of which are designed like the prows of boats. Its grandeur dates from the 1880s, when potted palms, a skylit atrium, and wicker armchairs were considered the necessary luxuries for a clientele growing rich from commerce with North Africa. Today the place retains much of its Beaux Arts charm. Many of its bedrooms have been modernized.

The restaurant, La Rotonde (tel. 67-46-12-20), takes up two impressive ground-floor rooms and is separately managed. Typical dishes are grilled fish with anchovy butter, roast lobster with tarragon, veal cutlet with basil-cream sauce, and a crêpe soufflé with raspberries. Meals run 145–215 F ($26.10–$38.70). The restaurant is open for lunch Sunday through Friday from noon to 2:30pm, and for dinner Monday through Saturday from 7 to 9:30pm.

13. AIGUES-MORTES

466 miles SW of Paris, 39 miles NE of Sète

GETTING THERE Five trains per day connect Aigues-Mortes and Nîmes (trip time: 40 minutes), and four buses per day arrive from Nîmes (trip time: 55 minutes).

ESSENTIALS Orientation Aigues-Mortes is divided by its surrounding ramparts dating from 1270. Walk along the top of the ramparts by climbing the Tour de Constance.

Information There's an Office du Tourisme at porte de la Gardette (tel. 66-53-73-00).

South of Nîmes you can explore a lot of the Camargue country by car. The most rewarding target in this curious landscape is Aigues-Mortes, the city of the "dead waters." In the middle of dismal swamps and melancholy lagoons, Aigues-Mortes is the most perfectly preserved walled town in France. Four miles from the sea, it stands on four navigable canals. Once Louis IX and his crusaders set forth from Aigues-Mortes, then a thriving port, the first in France to be built on the Mediterranean. The walls, which still enclose the town, were constructed between 1272 and 1300. The

Tour de Constance is a model castle of the Middle Ages, its stones looking out on the marshes today, perhaps recalling the former greatness of the port. At the top, which you can reach by elevator, a panoramic view unfolds.

Admission is 25 F ($4.50) for those 25 or older, 14 F ($2.50) for those 18–24, and 6 F ($1.10) for children under 18. The monument is open in July and August, daily from 9am to 7pm; April to June, daily from 9am to 6pm September to March, daily from 9:30am to noon and 2 to 5pm.

WHERE TO STAY

The Restaurant Les Arcades, recommended in "Where to Dine," below, also has rooms for rent.

HOSTELLERIE DES REMPARTS, 6, place d'Armes, 30220 Aigues-Mortes. Tel. 66-53-82-77. 19 rms (all with bath). TEL

$ Rates: 280–455 F ($50.40–$81.90) single or double. Breakfast 37 F ($6.70) extra. AE, DC, V. **Parking:** 15 F ($2.70). **Closed:** Nov–Mar 15.

Established around 300 years ago, this rustic and weather-worn inn lies at the foot of the Tower of Constance, adjacent to the town's medieval fortifications. Popular and often fully booked throughout the year (especially in summer), the establishment has a narrow stone staircase which winds up to the upper floor, and rooms with simple furniture; 10 contain TV sets. No meals other than breakfast are served here.

ST-LOUIS, 10, rue de l'Admiral-Courbet, 30220 Aigues-Mortes. Tel. 66-53-72-68. Fax 66-53-75-92. 22 rms (all with bath or shower). MINIBAR TV TEL

$ Rates: 380 F ($68.40) single; 450 F ($81) double. Breakfast 45 F ($8.10) extra. AE, DC, MC, V. **Parking:** 45 F ($8.10). **Closed:** Jan–Mar 14.

This small inn near place St-Louis offers rooms that are attractively furnished. The restaurant serves good regional food, with meals costing 100–180 F ($18–$32.40).

WHERE TO DINE

RESTAURANT LES ARCADES, 23, bd. Gambetta, 30220 Aigues-Mortes. Tel. 66-53-81-13. Fax 66-53-75-46.
Cuisine: FRENCH. **Reservations:** Recommended.

$ Prices: Appetizers 45–85 F ($8.10–$15.30); main dishes 88–150 F ($15.80–$27). AE, DC, MC, V.
Open: Lunch Tues–Sun noon–2pm; dinner Tues–Sun 7:30–9:30pm. **Closed:** Feb 15–Mar 15.

This restaurant has several formal sections with ancient beamed ceilings or intricately fitted stone vaults. Almost as old as the nearby fortifications surrounding the city, the place is especially charming on sultry days, when the thickness of the masonry keeps the interior cool. Good food is served at reasonable prices. Dishes are likely to include lobster fricassée, two kinds of bouillabaisse, and grilled duckling.

The owner also rents six comfortable rooms upstairs, each with private bath. Doubles cost 480 F ($86.40); three guests in the same room cost 550 F ($99). Breakfast is another 60 F ($10.80).

---

14. NIMES

440 miles S of Paris, 27 miles W of Avignon

GETTING THERE   By Train   Nîmes has bus and train service from the rest of France and is located near several autoroutes. Nîmes lies on the main rail line between Marseille and Bordeaux. Six trains a day arrive from Paris, taking 4½ hours.

ESSENTIALS   Orientation   The old town lies just north of the ancient Roman Amphitheater on place des Arènes, and encompasses the Maison Carrée and the Cathédrale de St-Castor at place aux Herbes. A major inner-city traffic artery west

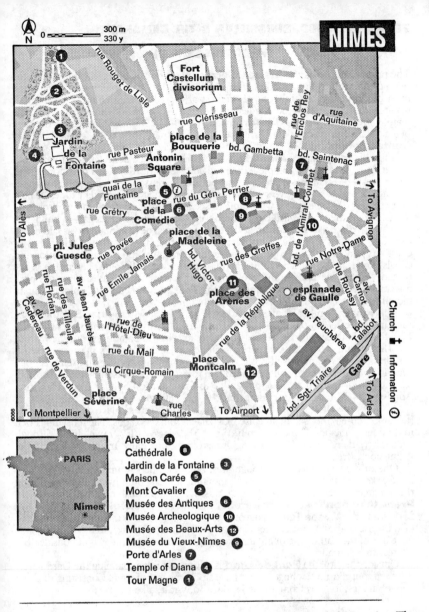

NIMES

0 300 m
   330 y

Fort Castellum divisorium

rue Rouget de Lisle

rue Clérisseau

rue de l'Enclos Rey

rue d'Aquitaine

place de la Bouquerie

bd. Gambetta

bd. Saintenac

Jardin de la Fontaine

rue Pasteur

Antonin Square

quai de la Fontaine

rue du Gén. Perrier

place de la Comédie

rue Grétry

place de la Madeleine

pl. Jules Guesde

rue Pavée

rue Emile Jamais

bd. Victor-Hugo

rue des Greffes

bd. de l'Amiral-Courbet

rue Notre-Dame

av. Jean Jaurès

rue des Tilleuls

rue Florian

av. du Cadereau

rue de Verdun

rue de l'Hôtel-Dieu

rue du Mail

rue du Cirque-Romain

place des Arènes

place de la République

esplanade de Gaulle

av. Feuchères

place Montcalm

place Séverine

rue Charles

To Montpellier ↓

To Airport ↓

rue de la République

bd. Sgt. Triaire

Gare

To Arles ↓

av. Carnot

rue Roussy

bd. Talabot

To Alès ←

To Avignon ↗

Church ✚
Information ⓘ

PARIS ★

Nîmes ▪

Arènes ⑪
Cathédrale ⑧
Jardin de la Fontaine ③
Maison Carée ⑤
Mont Cavalier ②
Musée des Antiques ⑥
Musée Archeologique ⑩
Musée des Beaux-Arts ⑫
Musée du Vieux-Nîmes ⑨
Porte d'Arles ⑦
Temple of Diana ④
Tour Magne ①

---

of the old town is avenue Jean-Jaurès, which leads to the Jardin de la Fontaine. The famous Pont du Gard, the Roman aqueduct, is 12 miles northeast of Nîmes, heading toward Avignon on the N86.

Information The Office de Tourisme is located at 6, rue Auguste (tel. 66-67-29-11).

Nîmes, the ancient Nemausus, is one of the finest places in the world for wandering among Roman relics. A busy industrial city today, about 27 miles southwest of Avignon, it is the gateway to the Rhône Valley and to Provence.

WHAT TO SEE & DO

The pride of Nîmes is the **Maison Carrée,** place de la Comédie, built during the reign of Augustus. On a raised platform with tall Corinthian columns, it's one of the most beautiful and certainly one of the best-preserved Roman temples of Europe. It inspired the builders of the Madeleine in Paris as well as Thomas Jefferson. The temple houses the **Musée des Antiques** (tel. 66-67-25-57), displaying, for the time being, paintings by Julian Schnabel. In front is the new **Musée d'Art Contemporain,** built by Norman Foster and opened in 1993.

The elliptically shaped **Amphithéâtre Romain,** place des Arènes, a twin to the one at Arles, is far more complete than the colosseum of Rome. It's two stories high and consists of 60 arches each, and was built of huge stones fitted together without mortar. One of the best preserved of the arenas existing from ancient times, it held more than 20,000 spectators who came to see gladiatorial combats and wolf or boar hunts. Today, the city of Nîmes uses it for everything from ballet recitals to bullfights.

The **Jardin de la Fontaine,** at the end of the quai de la Fontaine, was laid out in the 18th century, using the ruins of a Roman shrine. It was planted with rows of chestnuts and elms, adorned with statuary and urns, and intersected by grottos and canals—one of the most beautiful gardens of France. Adjoining the garden is the ruined **Temple of Diana** and the remains of some Roman baths. Over the park towers **Mont Cavalier,** surmounted by the **Tour Magne,** the city's oldest Roman monument, which you can climb for a panoramic view.

Nîmes has a number of museums. My favorite is the **Musée des Beaux-Arts,** rue Cité-Foulc (tel. 66-67-38-21), containing French paintings and sculptures from the 17th to the 20th century and Flemish, Dutch, and Italian paintings from the 15th to the 18th century. Seek out in particular one of G. B. Moroni's masterpieces, *La Calomnie d'Apelle* and a well-preserved Gallo-Roman mosaic. The museum is open June 15 to September 15, daily from 9:30am to 6:30pm; off-season, Monday through Saturday from 9:30am to 12:30pm and 2 to 6pm, and on Sunday from 2 to 6pm. Admission is 20 F ($3.60) for adults and 10 F ($1.80) for children.

Also, if time allows, visit the **Musée du Vieux-Nîmes,** place de la Cathédrale (tel. 66-36-00-64), housed in an episcopal palace from the 1600s. The museum is rich in antiques, including pieces from the 17th century. It's open June through September, daily from 10am to 6:30pm; off-season, daily from 10am to 6pm. Admission is free.

One of the city's busiest thoroughfares, boulevard de l'Amiral-Courbet, leads to the **Porte d'Arles**—the remains of a monumental gate built by the Romans during the reign of Augustus. Farther along this same boulevard lies the **Musée de Préhistoire et d'Histoire Naturelle,** the **Musée Archéologique** (tel. 66-67-25-57), and the **Musée Taurin,** devoted to bullfighting and its memorabilia. All three of these are housed in the former Collège des Jésuites, whose church (1673–78) was once one of the Catholic strongholds in the region, and which today is of considerable interest to historians.

Outside the city, the **Pont du Gard** is a Roman bridge spanning the Gard River. Built without mortar, its huge stones have stood the test of time. Consisting of three tiers of arches, it dates from about 19 B.C. To visit it, take the N86.

WHERE TO STAY

Expensive

IMPERATOR CONCORDE, quai de la Fontaine, 30900 Nîmes. Tel. 66-21-90-30. Fax 66-67-70-25. 65 rms (all with bath or shower), 3 suites. A/C MINIBAR TV TEL **Bus:** 3 or 5.

$ Rates: 530–850 F ($95.40–$153) single or double; 1,800 F ($324) suite. Breakfast 65 F ($11.70) extra. AE, DC, MC, V. **Parking:** 70 F ($12.60).

This leading hotel is near the city center and the Roman monuments, opposite the Jardin de la Fontaine. You can order lunch in the hotel's enticing rear gardens. The best rooms have Provençal pieces. Others have been renewed in a traditional way to preserve their character.

MERCURE NIMES-OUEST, Parc Hôtellier Ville Active, 30900 Nîmes. Tel. 66-84-14-55. Fax 66-38-01-44. 98 rms (all with bath). A/C MINIBAR TV TEL **Bus:** 4.
$ Rates: 330–550 F ($59.40–$99) single or double. Breakfast 50 F ($9) extra. AE, DC, MC, V. **Parking:** Free.
This hotel is outside the city but only a five-minute drive from the arena and Maison Carrée. The design is contemporary, and the furnishings are attractive. There are also an adjoining swimming-pool area, a sun terrace, and a tennis court. The hotel restaurant, Le Mazet, serves grilled meats and several regional dishes.

Moderate

CARRIERE, 6, rue Grizot, 3000 Nîmes. Tel. 66-67-24-89. Fax 66-67-28-08. 54 rms (all with bath). TV TEL **Bus:** 3 or 5.
$ Rates: 225 F ($40.50) single; 300 F ($54) double. Breakfast 30 F ($5.40). AE, DC, MC, V.
This recently modernized hotel has furnishings that are functional, not stylish. The Carrière's restaurant is good but not expensive, with fixed-price menus beginning at 87 F ($15.70).

LE CHEVAL BLANC, 1, place des Arènes, 30000 Nîmes. Tel. 66-67-32-32. Fax 66-76-32-33. 35 rms (all with bath or shower). A/C TV TEL **Bus:** 3 or 5.
$ Rates: 500 F ($90) single; 1,900 F ($342) double. Breakfast 70 F ($12.60) extra. AE, DC, V.
The city's most impressive hotel is opposite the arena. The large classical reception hall is furnished with Provençal pieces; the grandest dining room has fine furniture and plenty of silver and crystal. Most of the rooms are soundproof, and the furniture is mainly Directoire, with assorted murals and tapestries.
Many local critics claim that the hotel serves the finest food in Nîmes, especially when it's offered on a dining terrace overlooking the Roman amphitheater. Try such specialties as confit (preserved duck) and magrêt de canard (breast of duck). Many excellent fish dishes are also offered.

LE LOUVRE, 2, square de la Couronne, 30000 Nîmes. Tel. 66-67-22-75. Fax 66-36-07-27. 31 rms (all with bath or shower), 2 suites. TV TEL **Bus:** 3 or 5.
$ Rates: 380 F ($68.40) single; 420 F ($75.60) double; from 600 F ($108) suite. Breakfast 38 F ($6.80) extra. AE, DC, MC, V. **Parking:** 70 F ($12.60).
Le Louvre is a beautifully preserved 17th-century villa, which has functioned as an inn since almost anyone can remember. (One of its most prominent guests was Thomas Jefferson, who stayed here to sample the local wines during one of his many sojourns in France.) Bedrooms are well equipped and comfortable, some looking out over an inner courtyard lined with flowering plants. Set in the heart of town, near the Roman arenas, the hotel does not maintain a restaurant on the premises, but directs clients to one of several nearby choices.

NOVOTEL NIMES, chemin de l'Hostellerie, bd. Périphérique Sud, 30000 Nîmes. Tel. 66-84-60-20. Fax 66-38-02-31. 96 rms (all with bath). A/C TV TEL
$ Rates: 400 F ($72) single; 450 F ($81) double. Breakfast 48 F ($8.60) extra. AE, DC, MC, V.
This chain hotel is one of the city's best. It's easily accessible, only a few hundred feet from the Nîmes Sud exit of the autoroute. Each of its rooms contains a double bed, a single bed (which converts into a sofa), well-equipped bathrooms, and a wide writing desk. The hotel offers a bar and an attractive restaurant serving food daily from 6am to midnight, with meals beginning at 160 F ($28.80).

Inexpensive

HOTEL L'AMPHITHEATRE, 4, rue des Arènes, 30000 Nîmes. Tel. 66-67-28-51. Fax 66-67-07-79. 18 rms (all with bath or shower). TV TEL **Bus:** 3 or 5.

$ **Rates:** 155–210 F ($27.90–$37.80) single; 200–260 F ($36–$46.80) double; 250–280 F ($45–$50.40) triple or quad. Breakfast 33 F ($5.90) extra. MC, V.

Behind the Arènes, this hotel sits on a narrow, quiet street. The building dates from the 18th century. Each room has its own color scheme and is furnished with either antiques or modern pieces.

HOTEL MICHEL, 14, bd. de l'Amiral-Courbet, 30000 Nîmes. Tel. 66-67-26-23. Fax 66-21-13-00. 28 rms (all with bath or shower). TV TEL **Bus:** 3 or 5.
$ **Rates:** 150 F ($27) single with shower but no toilet; 200–230 F ($36–$41.40) single or double with bath or shower. Breakfast 30 F ($5.40) extra. MC, V.
Parking: 40 F ($7.20).

This traditional small French hotel close to the major monuments is well run and welcoming. Rooms are simply but comfortably furnished. A few do not have a toilet, but all have either a private bath or shower. Breakfast is the only meal served.

HOTEL MILAN, 17, av. Feuchères, 30000 Nîmes. Tel. 66-29-29-90. Fax 66-29-05-31. 33 rms (all with bath). TV TEL **Bus:** 3 or 5.
$ **Rates:** 200 F ($36) single; 300 F ($54) double. Breakfast 30 F ($5.40) extra. AE, MC, V.

The Hôtel Milan is near the train station and is especially good for Eurailpass holders arriving in Nîmes on a tight budget. Rooms are basic—no frills, but clean and decent. It serves breakfast only and has no restaurant, but some inexpensive restaurants are located nearby.

WHERE TO DINE

ALEXANDRE, route de l'Aéroport de Garons. Tel. 66-70-08-99.
Cuisine: FRENCH. **Reservations:** Required.
$ **Prices:** Appetizers 120–160 F ($21.60–$28.80); main dishes 135–170 F ($24.30–$30.60); fixed-price menus 255–320 F ($45.90–$57.60). AE, MC, V.
Open: Lunch Tues–Sat noon–1:30pm; dinner Tues–Sat 7:30–9:30pm. **Closed:** Feb 26–Mar 13 and Aug 24–Sept 7.

On the outskirts of Nîmes, near the local airport, is one of the region's finest restaurants. In a Provençal villa is the elegant and rustic domain of Michel Kayser, an exceptional chef. The dessert tray is one of the most delectable in the district. Menu choices might include rillette of home-smoked eel or flan of foie gras with truffle juice. Chef Kayser's version of tournedos Frédéric-Mistral has won culinary awards. Equally tempting is an ambrosia of gamecock with Chinese cabbage and a gallette of turbot with leeks and fresh truffles.

LE BISTROT DU CHAPON FIN, 3, rue du Château-Fadaise. Tel. 66-67-34-73.
Cuisine: FRENCH. **Reservations:** Required. **Bus:** 3 or 5.
$ **Prices:** Appetizers 29–54 F ($5.20–$9.70); main dishes 75–110 F ($13.50–$19.80); fixed-price lunch 68 F ($12.20). AE, MC, V.
Open: Lunch Wed–Sun noon–2pm; dinner Wed–Sat 7:30–10pm. **Closed:** Aug.

This tavern-restaurant is on a little square behind St. Paul's Church, and it's run by Monsieur and Madame Grangier. It has beamed ceilings, pictures on the walls, small lamps, and a white-and-black stone floor. The owner's wife is from Alsace, and the menu has many Alsatian specialties. From the à la carte menu you can order foie gras d'oie-truffé d'Alsace, coq au vin with riesling, and entrecôte flambé with morels. The proprietor makes his own confit d'oie from geese direct from Alsace. A *plat du jour* is featured.

SAN FRANCISCO STEAK HOUSE, 33, rue Roussy. Tel. 66-21-00-80.
Cuisine: FRENCH. **Reservations:** Required. **Bus:** 3 or 5.
$ **Prices:** Appetizers 25–85 F ($4.50–$15.30); main dishes 60–90 F ($10.80–$16.20). AE, DC, MC, V.
Open: Lunch Mon and Wed–Fri noon–1:30pm; dinner Wed–Mon 8pm–midnight.

This restaurant, near place de la Couronne, was founded by two young Frenchmen who have lived in America. They serve juicy steaks, chops, and filets in an informal decor guaranteed to make a visitor feel at home. Begin your meal with a shrimp-stuffed avocado or a tender salad of grapefruit and crayfish segments.

SAN FRANCISCO WINE BAR, 11, place de la Couronne. Tel. 66-76-19-59.

    Cuisine: FRENCH. **Reservations:** Not required. **Bus:** 3 or 5.

$ **Prices:** Appetizers 25–75 F ($4.50–$13.50); main dishes 35–130 F ($6.30–$23.40); fixed-price lunch 77 F ($13.90). AE, DC, MC, V.

    Open: Lunch Tues–Sat noon–2pm; dinner Tues–Sat 7pm–midnight.

The success of the San Francisco Steak House (above) spawned this restaurant, probably the most famous and creative American eatery in the south of France. The place is paneled with mahogany and has the same leather banquettes you might have found in a turn-of-the-century California saloon. An array of salads and platters are served, and at lunch you can order a quick menu, including an appetizer, a garnished main course, and two glasses of wine. Typical dishes include magrêt of duckling and contrefilet of steak with a roquefort sauce. There are more than 300 varieties of wine, served by the glass or pitcher, from the long copper-top bar.

15. UZES

425 miles S of Paris, 38 miles NW of Arles, 15 miles N of Nîmes

GETTING THERE   **By Bus**   Uzès has bus service from Avignon and Nîmes.

ESSENTIALS **Orientation**   The old town is surrounded by busy roads, which keeps traffic in the historic section to a minimum. Principal monuments include place aux Herbes, the medieval headquarters of the Duché d'Uzès, and the panoramic promenade Jean-Racine, which lies near the Cathédrale de St-Théodorit.

Information   The Office de Tourisme is on avenue de la Libération (tel. 66-22-68-88).

Called "a dream of the Middle Ages," Uzès is an ancient duchy in the Gard region. It has been praised by eminent visitors, such as André Gide, and classified as a *ville d'art* and a protected national monument. While the people of Uzès have mixed feelings about their town's discovery, today people from around the globe walk its cobbled streets and admire the facades of its houses, some almost five centuries old.

Uzès is important in French cultural history because of Jean Racine, who called it home for a time. Racine's theatrical ambitions horrified his family and he was sent to live with an uncle who was the "vicar general" of Uzès. Racine never did become a clergyman. Instead, he fled from his uncle and became France's foremost dramatist.

WHAT TO SEE & DO

The town was built in a circle behind its fortified walls. The medieval fortifications were eventually razed and replaced by encircling boulevards.

The proud family of Comte Jacques de Crussol d'Uzès has occupied **Le Duché d'Uzès** (tel. 66-22-43-56) for more than a thousand years. It stands in the center of Vielle-Ville, off rue Jacques-d'Uzès. The title duc d'Uzès is the premier ducal title in the country, second only to the pretender to the throne, the comte de Paris. A yellow-and-red-striped flag waves from the tower when ducal members are "at home." (The home is always called a duché, never a château.) The architectural styles are wide-ranging. This is one of the few private homes on view in France. In the courtyard is the **Square Dungeon** (sometimes called Bermonde Tower), dating from the 11th century. Viollet-le-Duc rebuilt the tower in the 19th century, as the original was destroyed in the Revolution. From its terrace, a panoramic view of the town unfolds. To the left of this tower is the **Tower of the Vicomte,** dating from the 14th century. The latter has an octagonal stairwell. Of the many towers within the ramparts, only one remains—the **Tower of Vigie,** built in the 14th century. The tower contains a handsome Renaissance staircase and a gallery of paintings. The duché is open June to September, Tuesday through Sunday from 9:30am to noon and 2:30 to 6pm; off-season, Tuesday through Sunday from 10:30am to noon and 2 to 4:30pm. Admission is 35 F ($6.30) for adults, 20 F ($3.60) for children.

Other sights include the **Cathédrale de St-Théodorit,** place de l'Evêché. Built in the 17th century and rebuilt in the 19th century, the cathedral has a beautiful and noteworthy organ from the era of Louis XV. Open daily from 9am to 5pm.

Connected to the cathedral is the **Tour Fenestrelle,** from the 12th century. This is the only remaining section of a Romanesque cathedral built in the 12th century that wasn't completely destroyed during the wars of religion. It has six different levels, each growing progressively smaller than the one below. Each level has windows shaped differently. The tower looks like the Leaning Tower of Pisa without the tilt.

WHERE TO STAY

HOTEL D'AGOULT/CHATEAU D'ARPAILLARGUES, Arpaillargues, 30700 Uzès. Tel. 66-22-14-48. Fax 66-22-56-10. 26 rms (all with bath or shower). TV TEL

$ Rates: 750–850 F ($135–$153) single or double. Breakfast 55 F ($9.90) extra. AE, DC, MC, V. **Parking:** Free. **Closed:** Nov 15–Mar 15.

The best accommodations and cuisine are outside of town (via the D982). Built in the 1400s, this manor house has been sensitively updated with furnishings and decorations that evoke the 17th century. The hotel has a courtyard garden for summer meals and a grill near the swimming pool. The cuisine served here is as elegant as the decor. Meals begin at 210 F ($37.80).

HOTEL D'ENTRAIGUES, 8, rue de la Calade, 30700 Uzès. Tel. 66-22-32-68. Fax 66-22-57-01. 19 rms (all with bath or shower). TEL

$ Rates: 320–450 F ($57.60–$81) single or double. Breakfast 40 F ($7.20) extra. AE, DC, MC, V. **Parking:** 50 F ($9).

Gérard and Isabelle Savry have transformed this hotel in the town center, overlooking place de l'Evêché, that was originally a 15th-century manor. Today it looks the way it did three centuries ago. Any room above the fourth floor has a good view of the Eute River. A good restaurant on the premises serves moderately priced meals. It's open for lunch Thursday through Monday and daily for dinner.

WHERE TO DINE

AUBERGE ST-MAXIMIN, St-Maximin. Tel. 66-22-26-41.

Cuisine: FRENCH. **Reservations:** Recommended in summer. **Directions:** In St-Maximin, outside town, via the D981.

$ Prices: Fixed-price menus 150–190 F ($27–$34.20). AE, DC, MC, V.

Open: Lunch Wed–Sun noon–2pm; dinner Wed–Sun 7–11pm. **Closed:** Nov–May 1.

Bruno Griffoul has successfully exploited the charms of a pretty village house, lying in a village of some 600 people. The agreeable dining room has a small courtyard garden ringed with a centuries-old stone wall. Monsieur Griffoul has a fresh culinary style, and typical of his dishes are filet of sardines marinated in coriander, monkfish in pistou (garlic, basil, and olive oil), and foie gras in muscat. Try his roast duck with figs. A dessert specialty is chocolate in puff pastry with your choice of fruit. In July and August, they are closed on Monday and Tuesday for lunch, but are open for dinner.

PROVENCE

Provence, in southeast France, has been called a bridge between the past and present. Yesterday blends with today in a quiet, often melancholy way.

The Greeks and Romans founded cities here, complete with Hellenic theaters, Roman baths, amphitheaters, and triumphal arches. Medieval man erected Romanesque fortresses and Gothic cathedrals. By the 19th century the light and landscapes of Provence were attracting such illustrious painters as Cézanne and van Gogh.

Despite changes over the years, withered black cypresses and dark-haired, hazel-eyed Provençal people remain. And the howling laughter of the mistral will forever be heard through broad-leaved plane trees.

Provence has its own language and its own customs. Naturally it has its own wines, ranging from elegant Châteauneuf-du-Pape to vins de pays, and its own dishes, such as ratatouille and bouillabaisse.

A part of Provence, the glittering Côte d'Azur, will be dealt with in the chapter on the French Riviera. Provence is bounded on the north by the Dauphiné, on the west by the Rhône, on the east by the Alps, and on the south by the Mediterranean.

SEEING PROVENCE

GETTING THERE Provence can be visited at any time of year. July and August tend to be a bit hot and crowded, but June, September, and October are ideal.

The fastest way to go is to fly Air Inter from Paris to Marseille, which takes an hour and a half. There are 12 daily departures from both Charles-de-Gaulle and Orly. The TGV leaves Paris (Gare de Lyon) for the five-hour trip to Marseille and stops in Avignon. If you depend on public transportation, make Avignon or Marseille your base.

If you're driving from Paris to Marseille, count on at least eight hours by car. The toll road from Paris, Autoroute du Soleil, takes you straight to Provence.

A SUGGESTED ROUTE The best way to tour the area is by car. Use Marseille as your gateway (Days 1 and 2), then proceed northeast along the autoroute to Aix-en-Provence (Day 3) for an overnight stop. Head west the following day for Arles (Day 4), then continue to Les Baux (Day 5).

Now continue along a secondary road to the ancient papal seat of Avignon (Days 6 and 7). I'd also suggest a side trip to Nîmes, at the doorway to Languedoc (see Chapter 25). Finally, to cap your tour, go north to Orange (Day 8) to see its Roman theater. Then you'll be ready to continue along the autoroute north to Lyon or Paris.

WHAT'S SPECIAL ABOUT PROVENCE

Beaches
☐ Ile de Porquerolles, off the coast, whose northern shore is made up of sandy, herb-bordered beaches.

Architectural Highlights
☐ Cours Mirabeau, the main street of Aix-en-Provence, considered one of the most beautiful in Europe.
☐ Pont St-Bénézet, at Avignon, the famous bridge of the ditty "Sur le Pont d'Avignon."

Great Towns/Villages
☐ Marseille, capital of Provence, the largest French seaport and the second-largest city of France.
☐ Avignon, "city of the popes," surrounded by nearly intact ramparts.
☐ Aix-en-Provence, a historic city of monuments, museums, and memories of famous painters.
☐ Arles, the former capital and a typical Roman city of Provence.
☐ Les Baux, the most spectacular village of Provence, "a nesting place for eagles."

Ancient Monuments
☐ Château d'If, off the coast of Marseille, an ancient fortress used as the setting for *The Count of Monte Cristo.*
☐ Roman Theater and Amphitheater, at Arles, two great classical monuments.
☐ Les Palais de Papes, at Avignon, the ancient seat of the popes during the "Babylonian captivity."
☐ Le Théâtre Antique, at Orange, an 8,000-seat theater from the days of Hadrian.

Events/Festivals
☐ Festival of Avignon, held from early June to early August, a month of great theater and cultural performances.
☐ Aix-en-Provence, in July and August, an International Music Festival, one of the best on the Continent.

1. ILES D'HYERES

24 miles ESE of Toulon, 74 miles SW of Cannes

GETTING THERE By Ferry There's ferry service to the Ile de Porquerolles from one of four ports along the Côte d'Azur. It's a 15-minute ride from the harbor of La Tour Fondue, on the peninsula of Gien, 20 miles east of Toulon, with 5–20 daily departures. For information, call the Transports Maritimes et Terrestres du Littoral Varois, in La Tour Fondue (tel. 94-58-21-81). Other, less frequent midsummer routes include a 50-minute boat ride from Le Lavandou, a 90-minute ride from Cavalaire, and a 50-minute ride from Toulon. For information on crossings from Toulon, call the Trans-Med 2000, quai Stalingrad, Toulon (tel. 94-92-96-82).

The most popular maritime route to the Ile de Port-Cros is the 30-minute crossing from Le Lavandou, which departs three to nine times daily. For information, call the Compagnie Maritime des Vedettes Iles d'Or et Le Corsaire, in Le Lavandou (tel. 94-71-01-02). There's also a one-hour crossing from Cavalaire and a 75-minute crossing from Hyères-Plage.

ESSENTIALS Orientation The Iles d'Hyères are an unspoiled Mediterranean archipelago a short boat ride from the Côte d'Azur. Its three largest islands are (from east to west) Ile de Porquerolles, Ile de Port-Cros, and Ile de Levant. The last island is the least developed, reserved exclusively for the French navy and a secluded nudist colony near Heliopolis. Large parts of the Ile de Port-Cros are designated as a nature preserve, with many walking paths. Ile de Porquerolles is the most frequently visited, especially in midsummer.

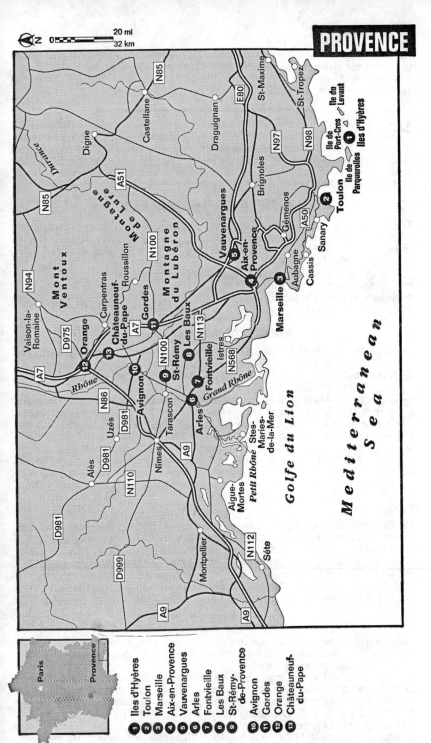

PROVENCE

20 ml
0 _____ 32 km
N

Mediterranean Sea

Golfe du Lion

❶ Iles d'Hyères	❿ Avignon
❷ Toulon	⓫ Gordes
❸ Marseille	⓬ Orange
❹ Aix-en-Provence	⓭ Châteauneuf-du-Pape
❺ Vauvenargues	
❻ Arles	
❼ Fontvieille	
❽ Les Baux	
❾ St-Rémy-de-Provence	

Paris · Provence

Information There are no tourist bureaus on the islands, but the tourist offices in Toulon and Hyères try to fill in the gaps. Contact the Office de Tourisme, Rotonde J-Salusse, avenue de Belgique, Hyères (tel. 94-65-33-40), or the Office de Tourisme, 8, av. Colbert, Toulon (tel. 94-22-08-22).

Lying off the Riviera in the Mediterranean is a little group of islands enclosing the southern boundary of the Hyères anchorage, from south of Le Lavandou westward to south of Hyères. During the Renaissance, they were called the Iles d'Or from a golden glow sometimes given off by the rocks in the sunlight. The tranquil islands today give no reflection of the periods of attacks by pirates and Turkish galleys, British fleet activity, and landing of Allied troops during World War II.

ILE DE PORQUEROLLES

This is the largest and westernmost of the Iles d'Hyères, with a rugged south coast, the north strand being made up of sandy beaches bordered by heather, scented myrtles, and pine trees. The island is about 5 miles long and 1¼ miles wide, and lies 3 miles from the mainland.

You can get here by ferryboat from many of the seaports along the Côte d'Azur. For example, between mid-June and October 1, two or three daily one-hour trips are made from Toulon. The fare for a round-trip is 80 F ($14.40). Information is available from Trans-Med 2000, quai Stalingrad, in Toulon (tel. 94-92-96-82).

WHERE TO STAY & DINE

LE MAS DU LANGOUSTIER, 83400 Porquerolles. Tel. 94-58-30-09. Fax 94-58-36-02. 60 rms (51 with bath). TV TEL
$ Rates (including full board): 779–1,305 F ($40.22–$234.90) per person. AE, DC, MC, V. **Closed:** Oct 18–Apr.

Located in a large park on the western tip of the island about 2¼ miles from the port, the Mas du Langoustier is a tranquil resort hotel with tennis courts and a view of a lovely bay ringed with pine trees. The hotel has a colorful past, and former guests have included Georges Simenon and Jean Giraudoux. During World War II it served a brief stint as headquarters for the U.S. Army and Gen. George Patton. Today, hotel employees greet guests in a covered wagon by the jetty. Should you visit only for a meal, prices begin at 300 F ($54). Try the loup (sea bass) with Noilly Prat in puff pastry. The house wine is an agreeable island rosé, probably from the very vineyards you passed on your ride to the Mas. You can drink and dine on the hotel's terraces.

LE RELAIS DE LA POSTE, place des Armes, 83540 Porquerolles. Tel. 94-58-30-26. Fax 94-58-33-57. 30 rms (all with bath or shower). TEL
$ Rates (including continental breakfast): 494–714 F ($88.90–$128.52) single or double. No credit cards. **Parking:** 27 F ($4.80). **Closed:** Late Sept to Apr.
Situated on a small square with a church, trees, café tables, and a boules ground, this pleasant little hotel offers Provençal-style bedrooms, with loggias. The hotel has a crêperie and mountain bicycle rentals.

ILE DE PORT-CROS

Lush subtropical vegetation reminiscent of an island in the Caribbean makes this little dot of land in the Mediterranean a green paradise, 3 miles long and 1¼ miles wide. No cars are allowed on the island.

To get here, take a ferry from one of three Côte d'Azur ports. From Le Lavandou, between Easter and October 20, there are 2–12 daily 50-minute crossings; from October 21 to Easter, there are only 3 trips per week. For information, contact Cie Maritime des Vedettes "Iles d'Or" in Le Lavandou (tel. 94-71-01-02). Between June 10 and September 15, there's one crossing per day from Cavalaire, taking an hour and 5 minutes; contact Cie Maritime des Vedettes "Iles d'Or" in Cavalaire (tel. 94-64-08-04). From Port de la Plage d'Hyères, up to four crossings per day are made, in 1¼ hours. For information in Port d'Hyères, contact Transports Maritimes et Terrestres du Littoral Varois (tel. 94-57-44-07).

WHERE TO STAY & DINE

LE MANOIR, 83400 Ile de Port-Cros. Tel. 94-05-90-52. Fax 94-05-90-89. 24 rms (all with bath or shower). TEL
$ Rates (including half board): 950–1,100 F ($171–$198) single; 1,000–1,200 F ($180–$216) double. DC, MC, V. **Closed:** Sept 27–May 14.

This 18th-century mansion, designed with cozy nooks and filled with attractive, sometimes antique furniture, is set in a park. The terrace overlooks the bay of Port-Cros, shaded by fronds of bamboo, eucalyptus, and oleander. The restaurant serves lobster and fish terrine, several kinds of seasoned meats, and fresh local fish with baby vegetables, as well as regional goat cheese and velvety smooth mousses. The Buffet family charges 250 F ($45) for a fixed-price menu. Dinner is served daily from 7 to 9pm.

ILE DU LEVANT

Another of the Iles d'Hyères, this one is five miles by three-quarters of a mile, mostly a long, narrow ridge. Monks once used this island as a granary and garden, but now it's occupied mostly by ruins and abandoned houses, except for the village of Heliopolis where nudists congregate in summer. The French navy also has installations on the island. Some ferries from Le Lavandou and Cavalaire make stops here en route to Port-Cros.

2. TOULON

519 miles S of Paris, 79 miles SW of Cannes, 42 miles E of Marseille

GETTING THERE From Marseille (see below), trains arrive about every 30 minutes in Toulon (trip time: 1 hour). If you're on the Riviera, frequent trains arrive from Nice (trip time: 2 hours) and from Cannes (trip time: 80 minutes). Three buses per day arrive from Aix-en-Provence (trip time: 75 minutes).

ESSENTIALS Orientation Midway between Marseille and Cannes, Toulon is focused around the complicated waterways of its industrial port. The old city is centered north of quai Stalingrad, around the Cathédrale de Ste-Marie-Majeure.

Information There's an Office de Tourisme at 8, av. Colbert (tel. 94-22-08-22).

This fortress and modern town is the principal naval base of France—the headquarters of the Mediterranean fleet. A beautiful harbor, it is surrounded by hills and crowned with forts. The place is protected on the east by a large breakwater and on the west by the great peninsula of Cap Sicié. Projecting from Sicié is Cap Cépet. Separated by the breakwater, the outer roads are known as the Grande Rade and the inner roads are called Petite Rade. On the outskirts is a winter resort colony.

WHAT TO SEE & DO

In Vieux Toulon, lying between the harbor and boulevard de Strasbourg (the main axis of town), there are many remains of the port's former days before it developed along more modern lines. Visit the **Poissonerie,** the typical Provençal covered market, which is busy and bustling in the morning with fishmongers and buyers. Another colorful market, the **Marché,** spills over onto the narrow streets around cours Lafayette. Go in the morning, when it is at its peak.

Also in old Toulon, the **Cathédrale de Ste-Marie-Majeure** (St. Mary Major) was built in the Romanesque style in the 11th and 12th centuries, then much expanded in the 17th century. Its badly lit nave is Gothic, and the belfry and facade are from a much later period, the 18th century. Open daily from 9am to 5pm.

In contrast to the cathedral, tall modern buildings line **quai Stalingrad,** opening onto Vieille d'Arse. On place Puget, look for the *atlantes* or caryatids, figures of men used as columns. These interesting figures support a balcony at the Hôtel de Ville and are also included in the facade of the naval museum.

The **Musée de la Marine,** place Monsenergue (tel. 94-02-02-01), contains many figureheads and ship models and is open daily from 10am to noon and 1:30 to 6pm; closed holidays. Admission costs 22 F ($3.90) for adults and 11 F ($1.90) for children.

An annex of the naval museum has been installed in the **Tour Royale,** Pointe de la Mître (tel. 94-24-91-00), built by Louis XII in the early 16th century. The seven circular pillboxes dug into the rock are exhibition rooms which present figureheads, telamons which formerly adorned vessels, and the guns that armor them. There is a very old, heavy, decorated Chinese gun in one room. The first French navy bathyscaphe is exhibited on the tower esplanade. Open June to September, Tuesday through Sunday from 10am to 6pm; mid-September to October and April and May, Tuesday through Sunday from 1 to 6pm; closed the rest of the year (except in the Christmas and New Year's season) and for holidays. Admission is 12 F ($2.10) for adults and 6 F ($1) for children.

Another museum, the **Musée de Toulon,** 113, bd. du Général-Maréchal-Leclerc (tel. 94-93-15-54), contains both old and contemporary works. The paintings range from the 16th century to the present day. There's a particularly good collection of Provençal and Italian paintings, as well as a collection of religious works. The latest acquisitions include New Realism pieces, as well as minimalist art. Open daily from 1 to 7pm, charging 8 F ($1.40) for adults and 4 F (70¢) for children.

Once you have exhausted the list of sites, I suggest taking a drive, an hour or two before sunset, along the **corniche du Mont-Faron.** It's a splendid boulevard along the lower slopes of Mont Faron, providing views of the busy port, the town, the cliffs, and, in the distance, the Mediterranean.

Earlier in the day, consider boarding a funicular near Altéa La Tour Blanche Hôtel. This **téléphérique (cable car)** operates daily from 9 to 11:45am and 2:15 to 6:30pm, costing 30 F ($5.40) for adults and 20 F ($3.60) for children for a round-trip. In addition to enjoying the view, once you get to the top, visit the **Memorial National du Débarquement,** Mont Faron (tel. 94-88-08-09), which documents, among other exhibits, the Allied landings in Provence in the summer of 1944. Open Tuesday through Sunday from 9 to 11:45am and 2 to 6:45pm in summer, from 9 to 11:30am and 2 to 5:45pm in winter. Admission is 20 F ($3.60) for adults, 8 F ($1.40) for children 5–12.

WHERE TO STAY

LA CORNICHE, 1, Littoral Frédéric-Mistral at Le Mourillon, 83000 Toulon. Tel. 94-41-35-12. Fax 94-41-24-58. 22 rms (all with bath), 4 suites. A/C MINIBAR TV TEL **Bus:** 3.

$ Rates: 350–370 F ($63–$66.60) single; 490–510 F ($88.20–$91.80) double; from 610 F ($109.80) suite. Breakfast 45 F ($8.10) extra. AE, DC, MC, V. **Parking:** 40 F ($7.20).

An attractive hotel with an interior garden, a café, and a restaurant, La Corniche contains exposed stonework, a raised fireplace accented with copper, patterned upholstery, and live tree trunks covered with ivy. Located across from Port St-Louis, this hotel offers some accommodations with sea views and loggias. The dining room, which has ivy extending through the ceiling, also offers a sea view.

MARITIMA, 9, rue Gimelli, 83000 Toulon. Tel. 94-92-39-33. 40 rms (21 with bath or shower). TEL **Bus:** 3.

$ Rates: 140 F ($25.20) single or double without bath, 220–240 F ($39.60–$43.20) single or double with bath. Breakfast 27 F ($4.80) extra. MC, V. **Parking:** 11 F ($1.90).

Near the railway station and the Jardin Alexandre-Ier, this hotel was built in the late 1800s, and has been slowly renovated bit by bit throughout recent years. Accommodations are modest but well maintained; 11 contain TVs. There's no restaurant, but breakfast is available.

MERCURE-ALTEA LA TOUR BLANCHE, bd. de l'Amiral-Vence, 83299
Toulon. Tel. 94-24-41-57. Fax 94-22-42-25. 92 rms (all with bath or shower).
A/C MINIBAR TV TEL **Bus:** 3.
$ Rates: 420 F ($75.60) single; 550–720 F ($99–$129.60) double. Breakfast 50 F
($9) extra. AE, DC, MC, V. **Parking:** 40 F ($7.20).

With excellent, modernized accommodations, attractive gardens with terraces, and a
swimming pool, this is the best hotel at the naval port. The restaurant with a
panoramic view serves a fixed-price menu costing 160 F ($28.80). The hotel is located
about 1½ miles north of the center of Toulon, at the foot of the cable car to Mont
Faron.

WHERE TO DINE

LA DAUPHIN, 21 bis, rue Jean-Jaurès. Tel. 94-93-12-07.
Cuisine: FRENCH. **Reservations:** Required. **Bus:** 3.
$ Prices: Appetizers 55–128 F ($9.90–$23); main dishes 86–128 F ($15.40–$23);
fixed-price menus 135–195 F ($24.30–$35.10). MC, V.
Open: Lunch Mon–Fri noon–1:45pm; dinner Mon–Sat 7:30–9:30pm. **Closed:**
Aug 1–15.

Le Dauphin serves some of the best food in Toulon. Chef Alain Biles has worked at
some of the most prestigious restaurants in Paris, including Lasserre, Lucas Carton,
and Jacques Cagna. His *cuisine moderne* is rich and varied and always includes the
freshest ingredients. Consider one of his suggestions du jour as well as one of the
wines from the well-stocked cellar. He always has a selection of fish, such as scallops,
filets of red mullet (often flavored with thyme, basil, and a fondue of tomatoes),
salmon, and poissons du jour. His meat selections range from duck breast to pigeon to
a filet of beef, which is often served with foie gras.

MADELEINE, 7, rue des Tombades. Tel. 94-92-67-85.
Cuisine: PROVENÇAL. **Reservations:** Recommended. **Bus:** 3.
$ Prices: Appetizers 42–50 F ($7.50–$9); main dishes 70–120 F ($12.60–
$21.60); fixed-price menus 90–170 F ($16.20–$30.60). DC, MC, V.
Open: Lunch Thurs–Tues 12:15–1:30pm; dinner Thurs–Mon 7:30–9:30pm.

Situated just a few steps from the cathedral in a building dating from the 13th
century, the Belloumeau family restaurant is almost always full. The restaurant
serves Provençal and Bordelaise dishes as well as other French specialties in its
Provençal dining room. Featured selections include escalope of fresh salmon with a
champagne sabayon, cassoulet of stuffed goose neck, confit of veal kidneys, and
tournedos béarnaise.

3. MARSEILLE

479 miles S of Paris, 116 miles SW of Nice

GETTING THERE   By Plane   The Marseille airport accepts international
flights from all over Europe and several weekly flights from New York.

By Train   Marseille has rail connections from hundreds of European cities, with
especially good connections to and from Italy. Marseille is also the terminus for the
TGV bullet train, which departs daily from Paris's Gare de Lyon. Local trains leave
Paris almost every hour, making a number of stops before reaching Marseille.

ESSENTIALS   Orientation   The heart of Marseille lies around the Vieux-
Port, originally colonized by the Greeks 2,600 years ago. Within walking distance to
the north lie the modern shipyards of the Gare Maritime. The main boulevard leading
from the northeast to the Vieux-Port is La Canebière, one of the seediest main streets
in France. Arm yourself with a good map, keep your sense of humor, and hold onto
your purse or wallet.

Information For information, contact the Office de Tourisme, 4, La Canebière (tel. 91-54-91-11).

Bustling Marseille is the second city of France in size but the premier port of the country. A crossroads of world traffic, the city is ancient, founded by Greeks from the city of Phocaea, near present-day Izmir, Turkey, in the 6th century B.C. The city is a place of unique sounds, smells, and sights. It has seen wars and much destruction, but trade has always been its raison d'être.

Perhaps its most common association is with the national anthem of France, "La Marseillaise." During the Revolution, 500 volunteers marched to Paris, singing this rousing song along the way. The rest is history.

GETTING TO KNOW MARSEILLE

Many visitors never bother to visit the museums, preferring to absorb the unique spirit of the city as reflected on its busy streets and at its sidewalk cafés, particularly those along the main street, **Canebière.** Known as "can of beer" to World War II GIs, it is the spine and soul of Marseille, but the seediest main street in France. The street, lined with hotels, shops, and restaurants, is filled with sailors of every nation and a wide range of foreigners, especially Algerians. In fact, some 100,000 North Africans live in the city and its tenement suburbs, often in souklike conditions. Some 1½ million others pass through every year. It winds down to the **Vieux-Port,** dominated by the massive neoclassic forts of **St-Jean** and **St-Nicholas.** The port is filled with fishing craft and yachts, and is ringed with seafood restaurants offering that specialty of Marseille, bouillabaisse. The Nazis blew up the old quarter in 1943, destroying the narrow streets and subterranean passages (and the houses of prostitution).

Throughout the world, Marseille has a seamy reputation. It is considered dangerous, the center of a rich crime empire, a seat of drug smuggling and prostitution. Remember *The French Connection?* Or the Bar du Téléphone massacre when a gang of 10 was wiped out? In other words, exercise caution.

Motorists can continue along to the **corniche Président-J-F-Kennedy,** a promenade running for about three miles along the sea. You pass villas and gardens along the way, and have a good view of the Mediterranean as well. To the north, the **Port Moderne,** the "gateway to the East," is man-made. Its construction began in 1844, and a century later the Germans destroyed it. Motorboat trips are conducted along the docks.

A Boat Ride to Château d'If From quai des Belges at Vieux-Port, you can take one of the motorboats on a 20-minute boatride to Château d'If (tel. 91-59-02-30), for 40 F ($7.20) round-trip. Boats leave about every 15 minutes. Contact GACM (tel. 91-55-50-09), whose office on quai des Belges is open daily from 7am to 7pm.

On the sparsely vegetated island of Château d'If, François I built a fortress to defend Marseille, the place later housing a state prison that sheltered such illustrious guests as Mirabeau. Carvings by Huguenot prisoners can still be seen inside some of the cells. Alexandre Dumas used the château as a setting for *The Count of Monte Cristo,* although the adventure he invented never took place here. Its most famous association—with the legendary *Man in the Iron Mask*—is also apocryphal. Open in summer from 8am to noon and 1:30pm to dusk; from October to May, it closes at 4pm. Entrance to the château is included in the boat fare.

Avant-Garde Housing The 17-story **Cité Radieuse,** boulevard Miche-let, was once an avant-garde housing development and a landmark in modern architecture designed by the late Corbusier, the Swiss architect who introduced influential concepts in functional architecture. Built between 1947 and 1952, and also known as Unité d'Habitation, it's considered the first structure of its kind. Its flawed units have been much criticized, but are credited with ushering in city planning in France.

WHAT TO SEE & DO

One of the most scenic oases in Marseille is the **Palais Longchamp,** place Bernex, with its spectacular fountain and colonnade, built in the era of the Second Empire.

Housed in a northern wing of the palace is the **Musée des Beaux-Arts** (tel. 91-62-21-17), displaying a vast array of paintings, both foreign and domestic, from the 16th through the 19th century. Some 80 sculptures and objets d'art were bequeathed to the museum and are displayed on two floors. The museum also shows works by Corot, Millet, Vuillard, Ingres, David, Courbet, Perugino, Philippe de Champaigne (*The Ascension*), Puget (*The Baptism of Clovis*), and Rubens (*Wild Boar Hunt*). Particularly interesting is a gallery of sculpture by Pierre Puget (1620–94). On the second floor are paintings by Monticelli (19th century), including his *Les Flamants*, plus works of other Provençal artists. One salon on the second floor is devoted entirely to the works of Honoré Daumier, the French caricaturist and painter who was born in Marseille in 1808. Displayed are satiric lithographs and 26 bronzes of the series known as the *The Parliamentarians*.

Open daily from 10am to 5pm. Admission is 12 F ($2.10) for adults, 6 F ($1) for children; seniors 65 or older are admitted free.

Nearby is the **Musée Grobet-Labadié**, 140, bd. Longchamp (tel. 91-62-21-82), housed in a mansion and containing what was once a private collection that was bequeathed to the city in 1923. It possesses exquisite Louis XV and Louis XVI furniture, as well as an outstanding collection of medieval Burgundian and Provençal sculpture, including capitals from Notre-Dame-des-Doms at Avignon. A music salon displays antique violins, bagpipes, and guitars, plus a letter from Beethoven. Paintings on view are by Monticelli, Corot, and Daubigny. Other exhibits include 17th-century Gobelins tapestries, 15th-century German and Flemish paintings, and 17th-century faïence. Open on Wednesday from 2 to 6:30pm and Thursday through Monday from 10am to noon and 2 to 6pm. Admission is 12 F ($2.10); children are admitted free.

At the **Musée Cantini**, 19, rue Grignan (tel. 91-54-77-75), the temporary exhibitions of contemporary art are often better than the permanent collection. Housed in what was once a private 17th-century mansion, this museum is devoted to modern international art with masterpieces by André Derain, Albert Marquet, Max Ernst, André Masson, Francis Bacon, Balthus, and others. The museum has an ever-growing collection, including masterpieces by Jean Dubuffet, Joseph Cornell, and Raoul Dufy. It also owns a good selection of important young international artists. Opening onto a beautiful courtyard, the museum may be visited Wednesday through Monday from noon to 7pm. The entrance fee is 17 F ($3) for adults, 10 F ($1.80) for students, free for seniors over 65 and children under 11.

The **Musée du Vieux-Marseille**, Maison Diamantée, 2, rue de la Prison (tel. 91-90-80-28), near the city hall, is a history and folklore museum known for its collection of *santons*—little statuettes made of colored clay representing characters associated with the Nativity. Santons are traditionally made by a few families living in the outskirts, the models and molds being passed down from generation to generation. The santons appear at a traditional fair in December in Marseille. Other exhibits include furniture, pottery, old maps, and engravings, 19th-century paintings by Provençal artists, antique costumes, a scale model of Marseille in 1848, and a costume room. Open Thursday through Monday from 10am to noon and 2 to 6pm. Admission is 12 F ($2.10) for adults, 6 F ($1) for children.

The **Musée des Docks Romains du Lacydon**, place Vivaux (tel. 91-91-24-62), is devoted to the remains of Roman docks unearthed in the old quarter of town. Some discoveries came to light as a result of the German bombings of the port in World War II. There are remnants from boats dating from the 6th century B.C. to the 4th century A.D., as well as a collection of urns and amphorae from ancient Marseille. The museum, charging an admission of 10 F ($1.80), is open daily from 10am to 5pm; children under 10 are admitted free.

The **Musée d'Histoire de Marseille**, Centre Bourse, square Belsunce (tel. 91-90-42-22), is an unusual museum. You're allowed to wander through an archeological garden where excavations are still going on, as scholars attempt to learn more about the ancient town of Massalia, which was founded by Greek sailors. Of course, many of the exhibits, such as old coins and fragments of pottery only suggest their former glory. To help you more fully realize the era, you're aided by audio-visual exhibits, and the museum has a free exhibition room and a library as well. You can also see what's left of a boat that was dug up on the site.

The museum is open Monday through Saturday from noon to 7pm. Admission is 12 F ($2.10) for adults, 6 F ($1) for children.

For a city as ancient as Marseille, antique ecclesiastical monuments are few. However, the seemingly fortified **Basilique St-Victor,** quai de Rive-Neuve (tel. 91-33-25-86), has a crypt that dates from the 5th century, when the church and abbey were founded by St. Cassianus. The crypt, which also reflects work done in the 10th and 11th centuries, may be visited from 10 to 11am and 3 to 6pm, and on Sunday from 3 to 6pm. Admission to the crypt is 6 F ($1). With its battlemented towers, the present church is from the 11th century. It's reached by going out the Quai de Rive-Neuve (near the Gare du Vieux-Port).

There are two cathedrals on place de la Major, near Old Marseille. Their domes and cupolas may remind you of Istanbul. (For information on both of these cathedrals, call 94-92-28-91.) The **Ancienne Cathédrale de la Major** dates chiefly from the 12th century, having been built on the ruins of a Temple of Diana. In its left aisle is the Chapel of St-Lazare, in the early Renaissance style. Nearby is a Lucca della Robbia bas relief. The Ancienne Cathédrale is open Wednesday through Monday from 9am to noon and 2 to 6:30pm. Admission is free.

The newer edifice, **Cathédrale de la Major,** was one of the largest churches built in Europe in the 19th century, some 450 feet long. Its interior is adorned with mosaic floors and red-and-white marble banners, and the exterior is in a bastardized Romanesque-Byzantine style. The Cathédrale de la Major is open Wednesday through Monday from 9am to noon and 2 to 6:30pm. Admission is free.

The landmark **Basilique Notre-Dame de la Garde,** place du Colonel-Edon (tel. 91-37-42-82), crowns a limestone rock overlooking the southern side of Vieux-Port. It was built in the Romanesque-Byzantine style popular in the 19th century, and was topped by a 30-foot-high gilded statue of the Virgin. The pilgrimage to this sanctuary dates from 1214. Visitors come here not so much for the church as for the panoramic vista—best seen at sunset—from its terrace. Spread out before you are the city, the islands, and the sea.

About 700 feet below Notre-Dame de la Garde, on the same hill, near where tour buses park, is a World War II tank, the *Jeanne d'Arc,* destroyed by a German shell on this very spot during the battle for the liberation of Marseille, August 25, 1944. Motorists can drive to the site, and pedestrians can take bus no. 60, which runs every half hour from the Vieux-Port. A restaurant here is open daily from 8am to 6pm in summer.

Another vantage point for those seeking a panoramic view is **Parc du Pharo,** a promontory facing the entrance to Vieux-Port. You stand on a terrace overlooking Château du Pharo, built by Napoleon III for his empress Eugénie. Fort Saint-Jean and the old and new cathedrals can be seen clearly.

WHERE TO STAY

Very Expensive

RESIDENCE LE PETIT NICE, corniche Président-J-F-Kennedy/Anse-de Maldormé, 13007 Marseille. Tel. 91-59-25-92. Fax 91-59-28-08. 17 rms (all with bath), 2 suites. A/C MINIBAR TV TEL **Bus:** 83.

$ **Rates:** 1,100 F ($198) single; 1,900 F ($342) double; from 3,500 F ($630) suite. Breakfast 100 F ($18) extra. AE, MC, V. **Parking:** Free.

Considered among the best hotels and restaurants in Marseille, the Résidence le Petit Nice has been in existence ever since 1917, when the Passédat family joined two suburban villas hidden behind a wrought-iron gate and high wall. The narrow approach to the establishment will take you past what looks like a row of totally private villas perched above the sea, in a secluded area below the busy street that parallels the beach. Bedrooms are either in the main building or in an annex, which looks out over the coastline, a statue-filled garden, and its P-shaped swimming pool.

The restaurant is beautifully furnished, with a sweeping view of the Marseille shore and the rocky islands off its coast. It is run by Jean-Paul Passédat and Gerald, his son, whose imaginative culinary successes include royal daurade with a confit of eggplant, vinaigrette of rascasse (hogfish), sea devil with saffron and garlic, and many other delectable dishes. Table d'hôte menus are offered at 650 F ($117), or you can dine à la carte for 450 F ($81) and up. The restaurant is open Tuesday through Sunday; from early October to the end of March, the restaurant is closed Sunday and on Monday at lunch.

Expensive

SOFITEL MARSEILLE VIEUX-PORT, 36, bd. Charles-Livon, 13007 Mar-seille. Tel. 91-52-90-19. Fax 91-31-46-52. 127 rms (all with bath), 3 suites. A/C MINIBAR TV TEL **Bus:** 83.

$ Rates: 780–960 F ($140.40–$172.80) single or double; from 1,750 F ($315) suite. Breakfast 70 F ($12.60) extra. AE, DC, MC, V. **Parking:** 40 F ($7.20).

This chain hotel was originally built in 1976, in one of the city's most desirable positions, close to the lighthouse that guards the eastern entrance of the Vieux-Port. The land it occupies is owned by the French navy, which granted a 99-year lease and technically can reclaim the land in the event of a military emergency. The building, with its many windows, looms above the massive embankments. Depending on the exposure, rooms may look out on the boulevard traffic or on one of the best panoramic views of the port of Old Marseille.

In 1987 its owner, France's hotel giant, Accor, decided to turn over 93 of its rooms to a newly created three-star Novotel. Today two separate entrances, two separate staffs, and separate dining and drinking facilities exist within the same stylish building. There are a swimming pool, an elegant bar, and Les Trois Forts, a restaurant with panoramic views of the harbor and its defenses. Meals, beginning at 185 F ($33.30) per person, are served daily from noon to 2pm and 7 to 9:30pm.

Moderate

LE CONCORDE PRADO, 11, av. de Mazargues, 13008 Marseille. Tel. 91-76-51-11. Fax 91-77-95-10. 100 rms (all with bath or shower), 1 suite. A/C MINIBAR TV TEL **Bus:** 83.

$ Rates: 595 F ($107.10) single; 660 F ($118.80) double; 850 F ($153) suite. Breakfast 60 F ($10.80) extra. AE, DC, MC, V. **Parking:** 40 F ($7.20).

Located away from the harbor in the newer section of town, Le Concorde Prado is the pace-setter in hotel design in Marseille. Created in the '70s, it has bronze elevators and six floors of gadget-filled accommodations. Beside each bed is a master electronic-control panel. You have a choice of rooms overlooking the busy street or the garden with its reflection ponds.

HOTEL CONCORDE–PALM BEACH, 2, promenade de la Plage, 13008 Marseille. Tel. 91-16-19-00. Fax 91-16-19-39. 145 rms (all with bath). A/C MINIBAR TV TEL **Bus:** 83.

$ Rates: 655 F ($117.90) single; 730 F ($131.40) double. Breakfast 60 F ($10.80) extra. AE, DC, MC, V. **Parking:** 40 F ($7.20).

Popular with commercial travelers, this modern hotel complex and seaside resort, located 1½ miles east of the town center, is one of the best and most sophisticated hotels in Marseille. The interior is a tasteful blend of big windows, soothing colors, expansive terraces, and unusual accessories. On the premises are a sauna, an outdoor pool, and modern, international bedrooms, the best of which have balconies opening onto the sea. Meals in the grill room, Les Voiliers, cost 140 F ($25.20); a more elegant meal at La Réserve begins at 175 F ($31.50).

MERCURE-CENTRE, rue Neuve-St-Martin, 13001 Marseille. Tel. 91-39-20-00. Fax 91-56-24-57. 198 rms (all with bath), 1 suite. A/C MINIBAR TV TEL **Métro:** Colbert.

$ Rates: 575–750 F ($103.50–$135) single or double; 1,200 F ($216) suite. Breakfast 60 F ($10.80) extra. AE, DC, MC, V. **Parking:** 40 F ($7.20).

One of the most modern hotels in town, this bronze building looks out over the

Greco-Roman ruins of the Jardin des Vestiges, a two-minute walk from the Old Port. Located near a collection of about 70 boutiques called the Centre Bourse, it contains both a formal and an informal restaurant and a bar where many of Marseille's shoppers go. Rooms are furnished in a functional modern style, comfortably appointed and well maintained. Many staff members speak English.

NOVOTEL MARSEILLE CENTRE, 36, bd. Charles-Livon, 13007 Marseille. Tel. 91-59-22-22. Fax 91-31-15-48. 90 rms (all with bath). A/C TV TEL
$ Rates: 500 F ($90) single; 560 F ($100.80) double. Breakfast 47 F ($8.40) extra. AE, DC, MC, V. **Parking:** 35 F ($6.30).

As mentioned above, this Novotel was created in 1987 when its owner, the multinational French-based Accor, took 90 spacious bedrooms out of the already-existing Sofitel Marseille Vieux-Port. Each was stylishly overhauled to the extent that many clients prefer these bedrooms to the better-rated (and more expensive) Sofitel, several floors away. The rooms with views of the Old Port tend to sell out first. In a time-tested Novotel format, the rooms do not receive the services offered at Sofitel (you wheel your own bags to your room on a cart, for instance), but if that doesn't bother you, this is one of the best and most reasonably priced hotels in town. Each unit contains a double bed and a single bed (which serves, thanks to bolster cushions, as a couch) and a desk. There is a garage in the basement, and the lattice-decorated restaurant serves basic, good meals—beginning at 160 F ($28.80)—every day from 6am to midnight.

PULLMAN BEAUVAU, 4, rue Beauvau, 13001 Marseille. Tel. 91-54-91-00. Fax 91-54-15-76. 71 rms (all with bath or shower). A/C MINIBAR TV TEL **Bus:** 83.
$ Rates: 620 F ($111.60) single; 830 F ($149.40) double. Breakfast 65 F ($11.70) extra. AE, DC, MC, V.
Located right at the Old Port, this traditional chain hotel is the most convenient place for tourists. The lobby has a Provençal decor. The good-sized rooms are often in the style of Louis-Philippe or Napoléon III. Breakfast is the only meal served.

Inexpensive

GRAND HOTEL GENEVE-VIEUX-PORT, 3 bis, rue Reine-Elisabeth, 13001 Marseille. Tel. 91-90-51-42. Fax 91-90-76-24. 43 rms (29 with bath, 14 with shower). A/C MINIBAR TV TEL **Bus:** 83.
$ Rates: 350–490 F ($63–$88.20) single or double. Breakfast 40 F ($7.20) extra. AE, DC, MC, V. **Parking:** 60 F ($10.80).
Located near the port, this stylish and comfortable hotel is a good value. The most expensive bedrooms open onto views of the port. There is no restaurant. Public parking is nearby.

NEW HOTEL BOMPARD, 2, rue des Flots-Bleus, 13007 Marseille. Tel. 91-52-10-93. Fax 91-31-02-14. 47 rms (all with bath). TV TEL **Bus:** 61 or 83.
$ Rates: 435 F ($78.30) single; 498 F ($89.10) double. Breakfast 48 F ($8.60) extra. AE, DC, MC, V. **Parking:** Free.
This tranquil retreat on a cliff along the corniche road is, with its Mediterranean garden, like an elegant home. Ideal for motorists, it's about a 10-minute drive from the town center. Bedrooms have balconies or terraces overlooking the grounds. The hotel serves breakfast only, but drinks are available in the Parisian atmosphere of the Lautrec bar.

LA RESIDENCE DU VIEUX-PORT, 18, quai du Port, 13001 Marseille. Tel. 91-91-91-22. Fax 91-56-60-88. 52 rms (all with bath or shower). A/C TV TEL **Bus:** 83.
$ Rates: 320–450 F ($57.60–$81) single; 350–500 F ($63–$90) double. Breakfast 30 F ($5.40) extra. AE, DC, MC, V. **Parking:** 50 F ($9).

Situated right on the port, this 1956 nine-story hotel is highly recommended for those who want to be in the center of Marseille's waterfront life. The entrance to the reception area is flanked by a pair of stone lions. Inside are antiques, old sculpture, a stone floor, and baroque columns dividing one of the many secluded seating areas. A café and a breakfast room are on the second floor, while a well-designed bar is behind the lobby. Rooms have loggia-style terraces opening onto the port.

WHERE TO DINE
Expensive

AU PESCADOU, 19, place Castellane. Tel. 91-78-36-01.
   Cuisine: SEAFOOD. **Reservations:** Recommended. **Bus:** 83.
$ Prices: Appetizers 48–70 F ($8.60–$12.60); main dishes 80–160 F ($14.40–$28.80); fixed-price menus 160–200 F ($28.80–$36). AE, MC, V.
   Open: Lunch daily noon–2pm; dinner Mon–Sat 7–11pm. **Closed:** July 15–Aug.

Established in 1946, and today maintained by three multilingual sons of the original owner (Barthélémy Mennella), this is one of the finest and best-recommended seafood restaurants in Marseille. Situated beside a busy traffic circle downtown, close to the freeway to Nice, it overlooks a fountain, an obelisk, and its own sidewalk display of fresh oysters. For appetizers, try the mussels stuffed with almonds, or the "hors d'oeuvres of the fisherman." Main-dish specialties include bouillabaisse de Marseille, gigot de lotte (monkfish stewed slowly in a cream sauce with fresh vegetables), and scallops cooked with morel mushrooms.

Adjacent to the main restaurant, and under the same administration, are two deliberately informal newcomers, both of which emphasize rapid service and low prices. Within **Le Bistro,** simple platters are served to a (for the most part) very youthful clientele at a price of around 65 F ($11.70) each. In another room, **La Brasserie,** simple platters of non-fish dishes are the norm. Menu items include blanquettes of veal, steak à la pizzaiola, and a variety of pastas, which are served rapidly and without fuss for around 100 F ($18) per meal per person. Despite these new additions, only the most formal original core of this establishment, Au Pescadou, receives the benefit of a Frommer star, so select your dining area within this complex appropriately.

LE CHAUDRON PROVENÇAL, 48, rue Caisserie. Tel. 91-91-02-37.
   Cuisine: SEAFOOD. **Reservations:** Recommended.
$ Prices: Appetizers 60–100 F ($10.80–$18); main dishes 85–235 F ($15.30–$42.30). AE, MC, V.
   Open: Lunch Mon–Fri noon–2pm; dinner Mon–Sat 8–10:30pm.

Set in the historic Panier district, this is one of the best-established fish restaurants in Marseille. Run by a local family, and decorated with copper pots and 19th-century utensils hanging from roughly textured ceiling beams, the restaurant sells portions of a wide array of fish by the gram, a system guaranteed to confuse North Americans. One of the most frequently ordered dishes is bouillabaisse at 190 F ($34.20) per person. Full meals, without wine, tend to cost upward from around 250 F ($45) per person, so be warned in advance that despite its rusticity, the meals here are not inexpensive, although many dine at moderate cost by ordering less expensive dishes. The day's catch, which many locals like to inspect, is displayed in baskets near the entrance to the cramped kitchen.

LE JAMBON DE PARME, 67, rue de La-Palud. Tel. 91-54-37-98.
   Cuisine: ITALIAN. **Reservations:** Not required. **Bus:** 83.
$ Prices: Appetizers 60–135 F ($10.80–$24.30); main dishes 70–180 F ($12.60–$32.40). AE, DC, MC, V.
   Open: Lunch Tues–Sun noon–2pm; dinner Tues–Sat 8–10:15pm. **Closed:** July–Sept 2.

Le Jambon de Parme is not only the best Italian restaurant in Marseille but also the best restaurant—period. The cuisine of Lucien Giravalli is both classic and original, and the wine list is extensive. The atmosphere is exquisite, with Louis XVI decor complemented by framed engravings of Italian towns. The fried scampi and the homemade ravioli are as good as any you'll find in Italy. The veal kidneys in a marsala sauce are exceptional. You might try the tortellini in a smooth cream sauce or filets of capon cooked with champagne. The soup with truffles is a masterpiece, and the sweetbreads with cream is another skillfully prepared dish. Naturally, there is ham from Parma.

RESTAURANT MICHEL [Brasserie des Catalans], 6, rue des Catalans. Tel. 91-52-30-63.

Cuisine: SEAFOOD. **Reservations:** Recommended. **Bus:** 83.

$ **Prices:** Appetizers 70 F ($12.60); main dishes 180–250 F ($32.40–$45). AE, MC, V.

Open: Lunch Thurs–Mon noon–2pm; dinner Thurs–Mon 8–10pm.

Established in 1931, and at its present address at the beginning of corniche Kennedy since 1946, this restaurant serves the most famous bouillabaisse in Marseille. At least 80% of the clientele wouldn't consider ordering anything else; priced at 240 F ($43.20) per person, the spicy fish stew is succulent, delicious, and appropriately laced with just the right amount of garlic. A selection of other fish, grilled simply, perhaps with lemon and herbs, and a flavorful seafood bourride, are also available. Since many of the fish dishes are priced per portion by the gram, it's useful to know that full meals, with wine, usually cost around 350 F ($63) per person. The decor here, lined with varnish-covered shells of lobster and starfish scattered amid local memorabilia, is one of the most-photographed scenes in Marseille.

Moderate

BRASSERIE NEW-YORK VIEUX-PORT, 33, quai des Belges. Tel. 91-33-91-79.

Cuisine: FRENCH/PROVENÇALE. **Reservations:** Recommended at lunch.

$ **Prices:** Appetizers 45–140 F ($8.10–$25.20); main dishes 80–110 F ($14.40–$19.80). AE, DC, MC, V.

Open: Brasserie, lunch daily noon–2:30pm; dinner daily 7:30–11:30pm. Bar and café, daily 6:30am–3:30am.

Established in 1932 by a Marseillais entrepreneur who greatly appreciated one of his business trips to New York, this time-honored brasserie sits directly on one of the quais overlooking the city's ancient harbor. Many local residents consider it their favorite café, taking advantage of its dawn-to-dusk hours for a glass of midmorning wine, afternoon coffee, or whatever.

At mealtime, amid a pleasantly battered art deco interior, you can enjoy a farci du jour (a stuffed vegetable of the day, either tomatoes, peppers, or onions, usually served as part of a main course), a wide selection of grilled fish, côte du boeuf with marrow sauce, bouillabaisse, and a wide array of grilled meats. Wines, as you'd expect, focus heavily on the vintages of Provence, and the accents of the clientele within are unmistakeably Marseillais.

Inexpensive

CHEZ ANGELE, 50, rue Caisserie. Tel. 91-90-63-35.

Cuisine: PROVENÇAL/ITALIAN. **Reservations:** Recommended. **Bus:** 83.

$ **Prices:** Appetizers 35–50 F ($6.30–$9); main dishes 55–100 F ($9.90–$18); fixed-price menu 85 F ($15.30). V.

Open: Lunch Tues–Sun noon–2:30pm; dinner Tues–Sun 7–11pm. **Closed:** Aug.

A local friend guided me here, and although most of Marseille's cheap eating places are not recommendable, this one is worthwhile if you're watching your francs. It's small, with a typical bistro ambience, and is usually filled with locals. You can come here for pizza or well-prepared varieties of ravioli, tagliatelle, osso buco, escargots provençals, and Marseille-style tripe.

NEARBY ACCOMMODATIONS & DINING

LE RELAIS DE LA MAGDELEINE, 13420 Gemenos. Tel. 42-32-20-16. Fax 42-32-02-26. 20 rms (all with bath), 3 suites. TV TEL **Directions:** Head east of Marseille for 14 miles along the A50.

$ **Rates:** 420–450 F ($75.60–$81) single; 580–710 F ($104.40–$127.80) double; 825–970 F ($148.50–$174.60) suite. Breakfast 65 F ($11.70) extra. MC, V.

Parking: Free. **Closed:** Jan 15–Mar 15.

Housed in a country mansion at the foot of the Sainte-Baume mountain range, Le Relais de la Magdeleine is surrounded by parks and woodlands, near the venerated spot where Mary Magdalene is believed to have died. The inn has pleasant architectural details, with an old carving of the Virgin and Child above the fireplace, antiques in the drawing room, and portraits and landscape paintings throughout. Bedrooms are pleasant and personal.

The relais also serves good meals. Lunches begin at 150 F ($27); dinner, at 250 F ($45). Specialties include such regional dishes as lamb cooked with the herbs of Provence and filet of sole Beau Manoir. There is a good-size swimming pool, tennis courts are 10 minutes away, golf is 20 minutes away, and the beach is 15 minutes away.

4. AIX-EN-PROVENCE

469 miles S of Paris, 50 miles SE of Avignon, 20 miles N of Marseille

GETTING THERE Set at a rail and highway junction, the city is easily accessible, with especially good connections from Marseille. Trains arrive hourly from Marseille, taking 40 minutes. Independent bus companies service Aix-en-Provence. SATAP (tel. 42-26-23-78) operates six buses a day to and from Avignon, taking 1½ hours, and SCAL (tel. 42-26-29-13) runs three buses a day between Nice and Aix-en-Provence, taking 2¼ hours.

ESSENTIALS Orientation The widest, most visible promenade in Aix is cours Mirabeau. To its north is the Hôtel de Ville, and even farther north is the Cathédrale de St-Sauveur, with its adjacent Archbishop's Palace and museums. Most of the town's streets are one way, making driving extremely difficult—it's easier to rely on walking.

Information The Office de Tourisme is at 2, place du Général-de-Gaulle (tel. 42-26-02-93).

SPECIAL EVENTS The highlight of the season is the annual music festival, one of the best on the Continent.

Founded in 122 B.C. by a Roman general, Caius Sextius Calvinus, who named it Aquae Sextiae in his own honor, Aix was successively a Roman military outpost and then a civilian colony, administrative capital of a province of the later Roman Empire, seat of an archbishop, official residence of the medieval counts of Provence, and thus its political capital. After the union of Provence with France, Aix remained until the French Revolution a judicial and administrative headquarters.

The celebrated son of this old capital city of Provence, Paul Cézanne, immortalized the countryside nearby. Just as he saw it, Montagne Sainte-Victoire still looms over the town, although a string of high-rises has now cropped up on the landscape. The most charming center in all of Provence, the faded university town was once a seat of aristocracy, its streets walked by counts and kings. Aix still contains much of the atmosphere acquired in the 17th and 18th centuries before losing its prestige to Marseille, 20 miles to the south. The highlight of the season is its annual music festival.

WHAT TO SEE & DO

Cours Mirabeau, the city's main street, is one of the most beautiful in Europe. Plane trees stretch their leafy branches across the top to shade it from the hot Provençal sun like an umbrella, filtering the light into shadows that play on the rococo fountains below. On one side are shops and sidewalk cafés, on the other richly embellished sandstone hôtels (mansions) from the 17th and 18th centuries. Honoring Mirabeau, the French revolutionist and statesman, the street begins at the 1860 landmark fountain on **place de la Libération.**

The **cathedral,** on place des Martyrs de la Résistance (tel. 42-23-45-65), is dedicated to Christ under the title Saint-Sauveur, that is, Holy Savior or Redeemer. Its Baptistery dates from the 4th and 5th centuries, but the architectural complex as a whole has seen many additions. The cathedral contains a brilliant triptych, *The Burning Bush,* a work of Nicolas Froment in the 15th century. One side depicts the Virgin and Child, the other Good King René and his second wife, Jeanne de Laval. Open Wednesday through Monday from 8am to noon and 2 to 6pm.

You might also visit the **Chapelle Penitents-Bleus,** 2 bis, rue du Bon-Pasteur. This 16th-century chapel was built in honor of St. Joseph on the ancient Roman Aurelian road linking Rome and Spain. The chapel was restored by Herbert Maza, founder and former president of the Institute for American Universities. Open Monday through Friday from 9am to noon and 2 to 6pm.

Nearby in a former archbishop's palace is the **Musée des Tapisseries,** 28, place des Martyrs de la Résistance (tel. 42-21-05-78). Lining its white and gilded walls are three series of tapestries of the 17th and 18th centuries collected by the archbishops to decorate the palace: *The History of Don Quixote* by Notoire, the *Russian Games* by Leprince, and *The Grotesques* by Monnoyer, who was inspired by the Berain style. In addition, the museum exhibits rare furnishings from the 17th and 18th centuries.

Charging 11 F ($1.90) for admission, it is open Wednesday through Monday from 9:30am to noon and 2:30 to 6pm in summer (to 5pm in winter); closed in January. Children under 12 are admitted free.

Up rue Cardinale is the **Musée des Beaux-Arts,** place St-Jean-de-Malte (tel. 42-38-14-70), also called the Musée Granet-Palais-de-Malte. The museum owns mainly sketches—not a very typical collection of the great artist's work. Matisse contributed a nude in 1941.

Housed in the former center of the Knights of Malta, the fine-arts gallery contains work by van Dyck, van Loo, Rigaud, Monticelli; portraits by Pierre and François Puget; and (the most interesting of all) a *Jupiter and Thetis* by Ingres. Ingres also did an 1807 portrait of the museum's namesake, François Marius Granet (1775–1849). Granet's own works abound, along with engravings, prints, paintings, and watercolors by Cézanne. Yet another salon contains Celto-Ligurian statuary discovered at the Roman town of Entremont, plus archeological discoveries that are Egyptian, Grecian, and Etruscan.

Open Wednesday through Monday from 10am to noon and 2 to 6pm; closed January. Admission is 14 F ($2.50) for adults and 7 F ($1.20) for children.

Outside town, at 9, av. Paul-Cézanne, is the **Atelier de Cézanne** (tel. 42-21-06-53), the studio of the painter who is considered to be the major forerunner of cubism. Surrounded by a wall, the house was restored by American admirers. Repaired again in 1970, it remains much as Cézanne left it in 1906, "his coat hanging on the wall, his easel with an unfinished picture waiting for a touch of the master's brush," as Thomas R. Parker wrote.

The atelier, where he "became one with my pictures," may be visited Wednesday through Monday from 10am to noon and 2 to 5pm (to 6pm June to September). Admission is 12 F ($2.10) for adults, 6 F ($1) for children.

Even more recommended than a visit to Cézanne's studio, and much more than the Musée Granet's Cézanne mementos, is a walk along the ✪ **route de Cézanne,** the D17, which winds eastward through the Provençal countryside toward the Sainte-Victoire. From the east end of cours Mirabeau, take rue du Maréchal-Joffre across boulevard Carnot to boulevard des Poilus, which becomes avenue des Ecoles-Militaires and finally the D17.

The stretch between Aix and the hamlet of Le Tholonet is full of twists and turns where Cézanne often set up his easel to paint. Although it's a longish hike (3½ miles), it's possible to do it at a leisurely pace by starting early in the morning. Le Tholonet has a café or two where you can rest and refresh yourself while waiting for one of the frequent buses back to Aix.

WHERE TO STAY
Expensive

MERCURE PAUL-CEZANNE, 40, av. Victor-Hugo, 13100 Aix-en-

Provence. Tel. 42-26-34-73. Fax 42-27-20-95. 55 rms (all with bath). A/C MINIBAR TV TEL **Bus:** 27, 42, or 51.
$ Rates: 520 F ($93.60) single; 950 F ($171) double. Breakfast 60 F ($10.80) extra. AE, DC, MC, V.

On a street of sycamores, the Paul Cézanne has an elegant and refined interior decorated like a private home, incorporating lots of antiques. The lounge seems more like a private sitting room than the lobby of a hotel. Accommodations may have mahogany Victorian furniture, Louis XVI chairs, marble-top fruitwood chests, gilt mirrors, and oil paintings. All bathrooms have hand-painted tiles. A small room, serving only breakfast, opens onto a rear courtyard.

LE PIGONNET, 5, av. du Pigonnet, 13090 Aix-en-Provence. Tel. 42-59-02-90. Fax 42-59-47-77. 49 rms (all with bath or shower). A/C MINIBAR TV TEL **Bus:** 27, 42, or 51.
$ Rates: 650 F ($117) single; 750–850 F ($135–$153) double. Breakfast 70 F ($12.60) extra. AE, DC, MC, V. **Parking:** Free.
Located at the edge of town, this pink Provençal villa is surrounded by gardens. The hotel has antique and reproduction provincial furnishings in its bedrooms, 80% of which are air-conditioned. Breakfast is served under the colonnaded veranda overlooking the courtyard reflecting pool. In summer, dinner is served outside or at the hotel's restaurant, Le Patio, which offers both a table d'hôte and an à la carte menu, with meals from 300 F ($54). There is also a swimming pool.

VILLA GALLICI, av. de la Violette (impasse des Grands Pins), 13100 Aix-en-Provence. Tel. 42-23-29-23. Fax 42-96-30-45. 15 rms (all with bath), 2 suites. A/C MINIBAR TV TEL
$ Rates: 800–1,500 F ($144–$270) single or double; 1,600–1,850 F ($288–$333) suite. Breakfast 90 F ($16.20) extra. AE, DC, MC, V. **Parking:** Free.

Established in 1992 in a villa originally built during the 1940s, this elegant inn is probably the most lavishly and stylishly decorated hotel in Aix. Created by a trio of architects and interior designers (Mssrs Dez, Montemarco, and Jouve, two of whom are affiliated with a prominent design firm nearby), the hotel is awash with silk brocades, regional antiques, artful accessories, and the 18th-century Italian/Provençale aesthetic for which Aix used to be famous. Until they know better, most newcomers would swear that even the building itself dates from the 18th century. Each room contains a private safe and an individualized decor of subtlety and charm, richly infused with the decorative traditions of Aix.

The villa sits in a large enclosed garden in the residential heart of town, close to one of the area's best restaurants, Le Clos de la Violette (see "Where to Dine," below). Simple meals can be ordered from this restaurant and served at lunchtime beside the Villa Gallici's swimming pool, in the shadow of figs, roses, and century-old cypress trees. *Plats du jour* begin at around 95 F ($17.10) each. On the premises are a limited array of spa facilities as well.

Moderate

HOTEL DES AUGUSTINS, 3, rue de la Masse, 13100 Aix-en-Provence. Tel. 42-27-28-59. Fax 42-26-74-87. 32 rms (all with bath). A/C MINIBAR TV TEL **Bus:** 27, 42, or 51.
$ Rates: 496–696 F ($89.20–$125.20) single; 592–792 F ($106.50–$142.50) double. Breakfast 50 F ($9) extra. AE, DC, MC, V. **Parking:** 50 F ($9).
Converted from the 12th-century Grands Augustins Convent, the Hôtel des Augustins has been beautifully restored, with ribbed-vault ceilings, stained-glass windows, stone walls, terra-cotta floors, and Louis XIII furnishings. The reception desk is in a chapel, and oil paintings and watercolors decorate the public rooms. The spacious, soundproof bedrooms—two of which have terraces—all have automatic alarm-call facilities. The hotel has a private garage on the other side of place de la Rotonde, where you can rent a space for your vehicle.

NEGRE COSTE HOTEL, 33, cours Mirabeau, 13100 Aix-en-Provence.

Tel. 42-27-74-22. Fax 42-26-80-93. 37 rms (all with bath or shower). TV TEL
Bus: 27, 42, or 51.
$ Rates: 400–700 F ($72–$126) single or double. Breakfast 55 F ($9.90) extra.
AE, DC, MC, V. **Parking:** 55 F ($9.90).

This hotel is so popular with the dozens of musicians who flock to Aix for the summer
music festivals that it's usually difficult to get a room at any price. Such popularity is
understandable at this elegant, white-shuttered hotel. Outside, flowers cascade from
jardinières and windows are surrounded with 18th-century carvings. Inside, there is a
wide staircase, marble portrait busts, and a Provençal armoire. The soundproof
bedrooms contain high ceilings and interesting antiques, and many are air-
conditioned. Higher floors overlook cours Mirabeau or the old city.

**NOVOTEL AIX-EN-PROVENCE SUD, périphérique Sud, arc de Méyran,
13100 Aix-en-Provence. Tel. 42-16-09-09.** Fax 42-26-00-09. 80 rms (all
with bath). A/C MINIBAR TV TEL **Directions:** Take the ring road two miles south
of the town center (exit at Aix-Est 3 Sautets).
$ Rates: 420 F ($75.60) single; 470 F ($84.60) double. Breakfast 48 F ($8.60)
extra. AE, DC, MC, V. **Parking:** Free.

Located at the end of a labyrinthine but well-marked route, this clean chain hotel
offers some of the largest accommodations in town. Bedrooms have been designed for
European business travelers, each with one single bed and one double bed and a fully
accessorized bathroom. Built in 1974, the hotel offers one of the most pleasant dining
rooms in the suburbs, with big windows overlooking Rivière arc de Méyran and an
ivy-covered forest.

If this hotel is full, which it often is, rooms are usually available at the slightly
newer Novotel Aix-Beaumanoir, périphérique Sud, 13100 Aix-en-Provence (tel.
42-27-47-50; fax 42-38-46-41). Accommodations are similar and cost exactly the
same.

**RESIDENCE ROTONDE, 15, av. des Belges, 13100 Aix-en-Provence. Tel.
42-26-29-88.** Fax 42-38-66-98. 42 rms (all with bath or shower). MINIBAR TV
TEL **Bus:** 27, 42, or 51.
$ Rates: 300 F ($54) single; 395 F ($71.10) double. Breakfast 40 F ($7.20) extra.
AE, DC, MC, V. **Closed:** Nov 25–Jan 5.

A contemporary hotel located in the town center, the Résidence Rotonde provides
cheerful, streamlined accommodations. Occupying part of a residential building, it
has an open spiral cantilevered staircase, with molded-plastic and chrome furniture.
The rooms have ornate wallpaper and Nordic-style beds. There is no restaurant, but
breakfast is served.

Inexpensive

**HOTEL CARDINAL, 24, rue Cardinale, 13100 Aix-en-Provence. Tel.
42-38-32-30.** Fax 42-21-52-48. 24 rms (all with bath), 6 suites. TV TEL
$ Rates: 220–280 F ($39.60–$50.40) single or double; 330–380 F ($59.40–
$70.20) suite. Breakfast 28 F ($5) extra. V. **Parking:** 40 F ($7.20).

Near the Musée Granet, this "small hotel" could have inspired the refrain from
Rodgers and Hart. Many frequent visitors to Aix-en-Provence consider it the
best value for the franc in town. Rooms are furnished in an old-fashioned way,
just like your Provençale grandmère might have done, providing you had such a
relative. The top rooms open onto the best views of the town. Filled with charm and
character, this hotel has been installed in an 18th-century building. The staff is helpful
in directing you to points of interest or nearby restaurants and cafés.

**HOTEL DE FRANCE, 63, rue Espariat, 13100 Aix-en-Provence. Tel.
42-27-90-15.** Fax 42-26-11-47. 27 rms (all with bath). MINIBAR TV TEL **Bus:**
27, 42, or 51.
$ Rates: 263–303 F ($47.30–$54.50) single; 276–376 F ($49.60–$67.60) double.
Breakfast 35 F ($6.30) extra. AE, DC.

Conveniently situated at place des Augustins, around the corner from cours

Mirabeau, this five-story, two-star 19th-century building has a glass-and-wrought-iron canopy and modernized bedrooms. Rooms with streetside exposure tend to be noisy.

HOTEL LA CARAVELLE, 29, bd. du Roi-René, 13100 Aix-en-Provence.
   Tel. 42-21-53-05. Fax 42-96-55-46. 32 rms (all with bath or shower). TV TEL
   Bus: 27, 42, or 51.
$ **Rates:** 250–390 F ($45–$70.20) single or double. Breakfast 32 F ($5.70) extra.
   AE, DC, MC, V.

Located three miles away from the center at cours Mirabeau is this conservatively furnished hotel with a bas-relief of a three-masted caravelle on the beige stucco facade. The hotel was opened in 1985 and is now run by M and Mme Henri Denis, who offer breakfast in the stone-floored lobby. Bedrooms are decorated in muted colors.

WHERE TO DINE
Expensive

LE CLOS DE LA VIOLETTE, 10, av. de la Violette. Tel. 42-23-30-71.
   Cuisine: FRENCH. **Reservations:** Required. **Bus:** 27, 42, or 51.
$ **Prices:** Appetizers 100–175 F ($18–$31.50); main dishes 130–230 F ($23.40–$41.40); fixed-price lunch 180 F ($32.40); fixed-price menus 300–420 F ($54–$75.60). AE, V.
   Open: Lunch Mon–Sat noon–1:30pm; dinner Tues–Sat 7:30–9:30pm. **Closed:** Jan 10–30.

Located in an elegant residential neighborhood, which most visitors reach by taxi, Le Clos de la Violette is the finest and most sophisticated restaurant in town. Enclosed within a high stone wall and garden, this imposing Provençal villa contains an octagonal reception area and several modern, peach-colored dining rooms. The food produced by Jean-Marc and Brigitte Banzo is absolutely superb. Typical dishes include an upside-down tart of snails with parsley juice, fricassée of sole with lobster, filet of pigeon with foie gras, and a sumptuous array of desserts.

Moderate

BRASSERIE ROYALE, 17, cours Mirabeau. Tel. 42-26-01-63.
   Cuisine: FRENCH. **Reservations:** Required. **Bus:** 27, 42, or 51.
$ **Prices:** Appetizers 35–70 F ($6.30–$12.50); main dishes 60–90 F ($10.80–$16.20); fixed-price meals 70 F ($12.60) at lunch, 100 F ($18) at dinner. MC, V.
   Open: Lunch daily noon–2pm; dinner daily 7pm–1am.

Located on a tree-lined boulevard, the informal Brasserie Royale offers excellent, unpretentious regional cooking at moderate prices. It's a modernized, animated, and invariably crowded restaurant with an interior dining room and a popular, glass-enclosed, canopied section on the sidewalk. You're served such hearty fare as tripe provençal, daube provençal (one of my favorite dishes here), and bourride provençale. The chef is known for his *plats du jour,* which on my last visit included lapin (rabbit) chasseur, paella, osso buco, and couscous. If you're dining light, you might enjoy one of four different kinds of omelets. Wines of Provence come by the half or full bottle. The brasserie is also a *glacier* during the afternoon, serving several different ice-cream specialties as well as milkshakes and Irish coffee.

   Note that one small section of the Brasserie Royal is identified as a "restaurant," where prices are a bit higher, but where the food quality and the ambience are not significantly different. Most diners hardly notice the difference because of the relatively fluid boundaries between the two areas.

CHEZ MAXIME, 12, place Ramus. Tel. 42-26-28-51.
   Cuisine: FRENCH. **Reservations:** Recommended.
$ **Prices:** Appetizers 40–75 F ($7.20–$13.50); main dishes 80–145 F ($14.40–$26.10); fixed-price menus 120–160 F ($21.60–$28.80).
   Open: Lunch Tues–Sat noon–2pm; dinner Mon–Sat 8–11pm. **Closed:** Feb.

Set in the pedestrian zone in the historic heart of town, in a neighborhood filled with several other less-recommendable restaurants, this establishment specializes in the regional dishes of Provence. There's an outdoor terrace on the sidewalk in front, suitable for people-watching, and an uncomplicated stone and wood-trimmed interior where the most important element is the cuisine. Specialties include a cassolette of mussels; côte de boeuf, served either with truffle juice or with bone marrow; salmon, sole, or filet of rascasse served with pistou; and several preparations of lamb cooked over an oakwood fire in the traditional style. (If you request it, a resident butcher will dress the lamb's carcass adjacent to your table, an experience which some local diners consider entertaining, but which I usually opt to avoid.)

RESTAURANT DE L'ABBAYE DES CORDELIERS, 21, rue Lieutaud. Tel. 42-27-29-47.
   Cuisine: FRENCH. **Reservations:** Required. **Bus:** 27, 42, or 51.
$ Prices: Appetizers 55–130 F ($9.90–$23.40); main dishes 79–130 F ($14.20–$23.40); fixed-price menus 128 F ($23) and 240 F ($43.20). AE, V.
   Open: Lunch daily noon–2:30pm; dinner daily 7:30–11:30pm.

The owners operate this excellent restaurant in an 11th-century cloister. You'll be impressed with the thick stone walls, the stucco accents, the high-timbered ceilings, and rows of copper pots. The chef specializes in various kinds of fresh fish, either grilled or with sauce. You might also sample beef with morels and many other fine dishes, which vary according to the season and the produce markets. In both summer and winter, 10 tables are placed on a veranda.

Inexpensive

LE BISTRO LATIN, 18, rue de la Couronne. Tel. 42-38-22-88.
   Cuisine: FRENCH. **Reservations:** Recommended. **Bus:** 27, 42, or 51.
$ Prices: Appetizers 60–70 F ($10.80–$12.60); main dishes 60–110 F ($10.80–$19.80); fixed-price menus 119 F ($21.42), 182 F ($32.70), and 245 F ($44.10). AE, DC, MC, V.
   Open: Lunch Tues–Sat noon–2pm; dinner Tues–Sat 7–10:30pm.

⑤ The best little bistro in Aix-en-Provence—for the price, that is—is run by Bruno Ungaro, who prides himself (with justification) on his fixed-price menus. Behind a blue entrance are two intimate dining rooms, decorated attractively with antiques. The staff is young and enthusiastic, and Provençal music plays in the background. Try the chartreuse of mussels, one of the meat dishes served with a spinach-and-saffron cream sauce, or a crêpe of hare with a basil sauce.

NEARBY ACCOMMODATIONS & DINING

MAS DE LA BERTRANDE, 13100 Beaurecueil. Tel. 42-66-90-09. Fax 42-66-82-01. 10 rms (all with bath). MINIBAR TV TEL **Directions:** Follow the A8 six miles east of Aix-en-Provence.
$ Rates: 320–520 F ($57.60–$93.60) single or double. Breakfast 45 F ($8.10) extra. AE, DC, V. **Parking:** Free. **Closed:** Feb 15–Mar 15.

This charming three-star hotel, created by Pierre Bertrand, is set in what looks like a canvas by Cézanne, at the foot of Montaigne Sainte-Victoire. About 4½ miles outside town near the hamlet of Beaurecueil, the former stable includes ceiling beams, a country fireplace, and plush furniture. The hotel has a very attentive staff.
   The cuisine is one of the primary reasons for a stopover here. The chef's innovative specialties are served either on the outdoor terrace or in the dining room, both of which are ringed with flowers. The cheese board has selections from all over France. Fixed-price menus cost 100 F ($18), 140 F ($25.20), and 190 F ($34.20). The restaurant is closed Sunday night and Monday.

5. VAUVENARGUES

471 miles S of Paris, 10 miles E of Aix-en-Provence

GETTING THERE From Aix-en-Provence, drive east on the D110. Three buses a day also make the run to Vauvenargues from Aix-en-Provence.

ESSENTIALS Orientation The château dominates the village, and the hotel is nearby.

Information The nearest tourist office is in Aix-en-Provence (see above).

In forbidding hill country 10 miles east of Aix-en-Provence the body of Pablo Picasso is buried. Here in this village of mainly retired people, the artist, who died at 91, painted his *Luncheon on the Grass* and did a portrait in red and black of his wife, the former Jacqueline Roque, who is also interred here.

The ocher stone walls of the turreted **château** date from the 14th century, and the buildings in the square style are from the 16th and 17th centuries. On top of the Louis XIII porch is the coat-of-arms of the Vauvenargues family, who were the owners from 1790 until 1947. The castle was purchased by antique dealers, who sold all the furnishings. Picasso acquired it in 1958 and lived here between 1959 and 1961. Visitors aren't allowed inside, but they can see some of his sculptures in the castle park during the day.

WHERE TO STAY & DINE

AU MOULIN DE PROVENCE, rue des Maquisards, 13126 Vauvenargues. Tel. 42-66-02-22. Fax 42-66-01-21. 12 rms (9 with bath). TEL

$ Rates: 120 F ($21.60) single without bath; 210 F ($37.80) double without bath, 250–280 F ($45–$50.40) double with bath. Breakfast 32 F ($5.70) extra. MC, V.

Closed: Early Jan to Mar 1.

Cozy and homelike, in the best tradition of a Provençal inn, Au Moulin de Provence is the town's only hotel. The English-speaking host, Magdeleine Yemenidjian, welcomes her guests, most of whom were attracted here by the Picasso legacy. Bedrooms have balconies with views of Mont Saint-Victoire, the mountain range that inspired many artists, such as Cézanne. The inn serves a good meal for 120 F ($21.60). You can also order a gastronomic menu at 180 F ($32.40). Guests are requested to take their meals at the hotel, and Madame is rather firm about this.

---

6. ARLES

450 miles S of Paris, 22 miles SW of Avignon, 55 miles NW of Marseille

GETTING THERE By Train Arles lies on the Paris–Marseille and the Bordeaux–St-Raphaël rail lines, so has frequent connections from most cities of France. Trains arrive about every hour from Avignon (trip time: 20 minutes) and 16 per day from Marseille (trip time: 1 hour). From Aix-en-Provence, 10 trains arrive per day (trip time: 1¾ hours).

By Bus There are about five buses per day from Aix-en-Provence (trip time: 1 hour, 50 minutes).

ESSENTIALS Orientation Arles lies on the eastern bank of the Rhône River, north of the marshy grasslands of the Camargue. The borders of the old town are the Rhône, boulevard Émile-Combes, and boulevard des Lices. Within these boundaries are the ancient Roman monuments, the medieval church of St-Trophime, and most of the town's museums.

Information The Office du Tourisme, where you can buy a *Billet Globale,* is on the esplanade des Lices (tel. 90-96-29-35).

It has been called "the soul of Provence." Art lovers, archeologists, and historians are attracted to this town on the Rhône. Many of its scenes, painted so luminously by van Gogh in his declining years, remain to delight. The great Dutch painter left Paris for Arles in 1888. It was in that same year that he cut off part of his left ear. But he was to paint some of his most celebrated works in the Provençal town, including *Starry Night, The Bridge at Arles, Sunflowers,* and *L'Arlésienne.*

The Greeks are said to have founded Arles in the 6th century B.C. Julius Caesar established a Roman colony here in 46 B.C. Under Roman rule Arles prospered. Constantine the Great named it the second capital in his empire in A.D. 306, when it was known as "the little Rome of the Gauls." It wasn't until 1481 that Arles, 55 miles northwest of Marseille by road, was incorporated into France.

WHAT TO SEE & DO

Before visiting the attractions, go to the tourist office (see "Essentials," above) where you can purchase one of three different passes, depending upon your time and interests. **Forfait 1** admits you to the town's museums, and costs 25 F ($4.50) for adults and 19 F ($3.40) for children. **Forfait 2** provides access only to the Roman monuments, costing 30 F ($5.40) for adults and 20 F ($3.60) for children, and **Forfait 3** admits you to all the city's major attractions, at a cost of 44 F ($7.90) for adults and 31 F ($5.50) for children.

The town is full of monuments from Roman times. The general vicinity of the old Roman forum is occupied by **place du Forum,** shaded by plane trees. Once van Gogh's *Café du Nuit* stood on this square. Two columns in the Corinthian style and pediment fragments from a temple can be viewed at the corner of the Hôtel Nord-Pinus.

South of this square lies **place de la République,** the principal plaza of Arles. A blue porphyry obelisk some 50 feet high dominates this square. On the north is the impressive **Hôtel de Ville,** the town hall from 1673, built to Mansart's plans. It is surmounted by a Renaissance belfry.

On the east side of the square is the **Eglise St-Trophime,** noted for its 12th-century portal, one of the finest achievements of the southern Romanesque style. In the pediment the figure of Christ is surrounded by the symbols of the Evangelists. Frederick Barbarossa was crowned king of Arles on this site in 1178. The cloister of Eglise St-Trophime is built in both the Gothic and Romanesque styles and is noted for its medieval carvings. The church is open daily from 8am to 7pm, free. The cloister hours are 9 to 11:30am and 2 to 4:30pm daily, with an admission charge of 18 F ($3.20) for adults, 10 F ($1.80) for students.

Slated to open in 1995, the **Institut de Recherche sur la Provence Antique,** avenue de la Première Division Française Libre, is housed in a building designed by Ciriani, lying between the Rhône and the Roman Circus. The museum will offer displays going back to prehistoric days. All the treasure trove was found at Arles, including mosaics, potteries, ancient coins, and the like. Among the attractions is a series of fine marble sculptures from the 1st century B.C. If you're in Arles in 1995, check with the tourist office (see "Essentials," above) about admission prices and opening times.

The **Museon Arlaten** (tel. 90-96-08-23) is entered at 29, rue de la République. (The museum name is written in the old Provençal style.) It was founded by Frédéric Mistral, the Provençal poet and leader of a movement to establish Modern Provençal as a literary language, using the money he received with his Nobel Prize for literature in 1904. He selected the 16th-century, former Hôtel Laval-Castellane for the setting. Collections illustrate the everyday life of Provence. It's really a folklore museum, with regional costumes, portraits, fans, furniture, dolls, a music salon, and one room devoted entirely to mementos of Mistral. Among its curiosities is a letter (in French) from Theodore Roosevelt to Mistral, bearing the letterhead of the "Maison Blanche" in Washington, D.C. Admission is 12 F ($2.10) for adults and 7 F ($1.20) for children. The museum is open April to October, daily from 9am to noon and 2 to 7pm; November to March, Tuesday through Sunday from 9am to noon and 2 to 5pm.

The two great classical monuments of Arles are the **Roman Theater** (tel. 90-96-93-30) and the **Amphitheater.** The Roman theater, begun by Augustus in the 1st century A.D., was mostly destroyed, and it was later used as a quarry. Only two marble Corinthian columns remain. Now rebuilt, the theater is the setting for an annual drama festival in July. The theater was also the site where the *Venus of Arles* was discovered in 1651. Take rue de la Calade from the town hall. The theater is open daily: June to September from 8:30am to 7pm; in March and October, from 9am to 12:30pm and 2 to 6pm; in April, from 9am to 12:30pm and 2 to 6:30pm; in May, from 9am to 12:30pm and 2 to 7pm; and November to February, from 9am to noon and 2 to 4:30pm. Admission is 12 F ($2.10) for adults and 6.50 F ($1.10) for children.

Nearby, the **Amphitheater** (tel. 90-96-03-70), or arena, also built in the 1st century A.D., seats almost 25,000 spectators and still hosts bullfights in summer. The arena is a huge, colonnaded, oval structure. The government warns you to visit the old monument at your own risk. For a good view, you can climb the three towers that remain from medieval times, when the amphitheater was turned into a fortress. It keeps the same hours as the Roman theater (see above). Admission is 17 F ($3) for adults and 8.50 F ($1.50) for children.

Perhaps the most memorable sight in Arles is **les Alyscamps,** rue Pierre-Renaudel, once a necropolis established by the Romans, converted into a Christian burial ground in the 4th century. As the latter, it became a setting for legends in epic poetry in medieval times. Today it's lined with poplars as well as any remaining sarcophagi. Arlesiens escape here to enjoy a respite from the heat.

Another ancient monument is the **Baths of Constantine,** rue Dominique-Maisto, near the banks of the Rhône. Today only the baths, or the thermae, remain of a once-grand imperial palace. Visiting hours are the same as at the Amphitheater. Admission is 12 F ($2.10) for adults and 6.50 F ($1.10) for children.

Nearby, with an entrance at 10, rue du Grand-Prieuré, is the **Musée Réattu** (tel. 90-96-37-68), containing the collection of Jacques Réattu (1760–1833), a local painter. The museum has been updated by more recent works, including etchings and drawings by Picasso, some depicting bullfighting scenes. Other works are by Gauguin, Dufy, Utrillo, and Léger. Note the Arras tapestries from the 16th century. Also, there is an entire salon devoted to Henri Rousseau. The museum is in the former Commandery of the Order of Malta from the 15th century. It's open June to September, daily from 9am to 12:30pm and 2 to 7pm; October to January, daily from 10am to 12:30pm and 2 to 5pm; February to May, daily from 10am to 12:30pm and 2 to 7pm. Admission is 15 F ($2.70) for adults and 8.50 F ($1.50) for children.

WHERE TO STAY

CALENDAL, 22, place Pomme, 13200 Arles. Tel. 90-96-11-89. 27 rms (all with shower). TEL **Bus:** 4.
$ Rates: 180 F ($32.40) single; 290 F ($52.20) double. Breakfast 29 F ($5.20) extra. AE, DC, MC, V. **Closed:** Nov 15–Feb 8.
On a quiet square not far from the arena, the Calendal offers bedrooms that have a Provençal decor and some antiques, most with views of the garden. Only breakfast is served.

HOTEL D'ARLATAN, 26, rue du Sauvage, 13631 Arles. Tel. 90-93-56-66. Fax 90-49-68-45. 42 rms (all with bath). MINIBAR TV TEL **Bus:** 4.
$ Rates: 385 F ($69.30) single; 680 F ($122.40) double. Breakfast 53 F ($9.50) extra. AE, DC, MC, V. **Parking:** 55 F ($9.90).
Created from the former residence of the comtes d'Arlatan de Beaumont, the Hôtel d'Arlatan has been managed by the same family since 1920. The hotel was built in the 15th century on the ruins of an old palace ordered by Constantine—in fact, there is still a wall dating from the 4th century. The rooms are furnished with authentic Provençal antiques, the walls covered with tapestries in the Louis XV and Louis XVI styles. Try to get a bedroom overlooking the garden with its palms, pond, and climbing vines; 25 rooms are air-conditioned.

HOTEL LE CLOITRE, 16, rue du Cloître, 13200 Arles. Tel. 90-96-29-50. Fax 90-96-02-88. 33 rms (all with bath or shower). TEL **Bus:** 4.
$ Rates: 220–295 F ($39.60–$53.10) single or double; 380 F ($68.40) triple. Breakfast 32 F ($5.70) extra. AE, MC, V. **Parking:** 50 F ($9).

S Situated between the ancient theater and the Cloister of St-Trophime, the Hôtel le Cloître is one of the best-value stopovers in Arles. The restored old house has a Provençal atmosphere, pleasant bedrooms, and a TV lounge, although 17 rooms have their own TVs. Parking is available nearby.

JULES CESAR ET RESTAURANT LOU MARQUES, 7, bd. des Lices, 13200 Arles. Tel. 90-93-43-20. Fax 90-93-33-47. 55 rms (all with bath or shower), 3 suites. A/C MINIBAR TV TEL **Bus:** 4.

$ Rates: 800 F ($144) single; 950 F ($171) double; 1,600 F ($288) suite. Breakfast 65 F ($11.70) extra. AE, DC, MC, V. **Parking:** 70 F ($12.60). **Closed:** Nov 2–Dec 22.

Located in the center of Arles, this 17th-century, former Carmelite convent has been skillfully transformed into a stately country hotel, with the best restaurant in Arles. Although this is a noisy neighborhood, most of the rooms face the quiet, unspoiled cloister. The decoration is luxurious, with antique Provençal furnishings that owner Michel Albagnac finds at auctions throughout the countryside. Guests wake to the scent of roses and the sounds of birds singing and can swim in an outside heated swimming pool.

The restaurant, Lou Marquès, has tables outside on the front terrace. The food is extremely fresh. On the à la carte menu, I recommend Arles lamb. Fixed-price menus cost 200–400 F ($36–$72), with à la carte dinners averaging 480 F ($86.40).

MAS DE LA CHAPELLE, petite route de Tarascon, 13200 Arles. Tel. 90-93-23-15. Fax 90-96-53-74. 15 rms (all with bath). MINIBAR TV TEL **Directions:** Head north from Arles for three miles on the D35.

$ Rates: 410 F ($73.80) single; 470–670 F ($84.60–$120.60) double. Breakfast 50 F ($9) extra. MC, V. **Parking:** Free. **Closed:** Feb.

Set on six acres of private land, the core of this charming inn was originally built during the 1500s by the Knights of Malta as a chapel. During the 1800s, a rambling Provençale farmhouse was erected nearby for the cultivation of olives and wheat. After World War II, the chapel was deconsecrated, the farmhouse transformed into a private residence, and in 1979, the entire complex became a sophisticated country hotel. Today, beamed ceilings, exposed stone, a massive fireplace capped with a neoclassical frieze, and Louis XIII furnishings create a warmly historic setting. Within the park are three tennis courts, two swimming pools, and masses of flowers.

The in-house restaurant is popular even for nonresidents passing through the region who telephone in advance. Fixed-price meals cost 145–280 F ($26.10–$50.40), appetizers are 90–130 F ($16.20–$23.40), and main courses run 100–130 F ($18–$23.40). Open for lunch and dinner every day, the restaurant serves Provençal specialties which include thigh of goat permeated with garlic and served with a herb, anchovy, and black-olive purée (une tapenade provençale). An excellent beginning to any meal might be a fondant of artichoke hearts served with warm foie gras and provençal herbs, and a Mediterranean seafish (le lieu) served with a confit of fennel.

WHERE TO DINE

LA COTE D'ADAM [Adam's Rib], 12, rue de la Liberté. Tel. 90-49-62-29. **Cuisine:** FRENCH. **Reservations:** Required in summer. **Bus:** 4.

$ Prices: Appetizers 28–40 F ($5–$7.20); main dishes 49–62 F ($8.80–$11.10); fixed-price menus 69 F ($12.40), 79 F ($14.20), and 99 F ($17.80). MC, V.

Open: Lunch Tues–Sun noon–2pm; dinner Tues–Sun 7:15–9:30pm.

S Located in the historic center of town near place du Forum, La Côte d'Adam has a rustic interior with a beamed ceiling and a very high carved-stone fireplace. The restaurant, which holds 40 customers, serves such dishes as fish filets with shellfish and duckling ragoût in white wine.

HOSTELLERIE DES ARENES, 62, rue du Refuge. Tel. 90-96-13-05. **Cuisine:** FRENCH. **Reservations:** Required. **Bus:** 4.

$ Prices: Appetizers 38–80 F ($6.80–$14.40); main dishes 59–80 F ($10.60–$14.40); fixed-price menus 75 F ($13.50) and 99 F ($17.80). MC, V.

Open: Lunch Wed–Mon noon–2pm; dinner Wed–Mon 7–9pm. **Closed:** Jan.

Ⓢ Close to the arenas, the Hostellerie des Arènes offers Provençal meals whose well-prepared specialties include seafood in puff pastry, braised duckling laced with green peppercorns, brochette of mussels with tartar sauce, and veal marengo. In warm weather, meals are served on the terrace. Owner and chef Maurice Naval offers inexpensive wines by the carafe or by the bottle.

LE VACCARES, place du Forum, 9, rue Favorin. Tel. 90-96-06-17.
   Cuisine: FRENCH. **Reservations:** Required. **Bus:** 4.
Ⓢ **Prices:** Appetizers 70–135 F ($12.60–$24.30); main dishes 95–155 F ($17.10–$27.90); fixed-price menus 165 F ($29.70), 225 F ($40.50), and 300 F ($54). MC, V.
   Open: Lunch Tues–Sat noon–2pm; dinner Tues–Sat 7:30–9:30pm. **Closed:** Jan 4–Feb 5.

Named after one of the saltwater ponds of the Camargue, Le Vaccarès offers southern French elegance and some of the finest food in Arles. Bernard Dumas uses unusual ingredients to create innovative Provençal dishes. Specialties include sauté of lamb with pistou, sucarello of mussels with herbs, sea-devil soup, Zander à la poutargne, steamed sea bass, and émincé of beef with Châteauneuf.

7. FONTVIEILLE

449 miles S of Paris, 6½ miles N of Arles

GETTING THERE   By Car   Motorists from Arles can head north for 6½ miles along D17.

ESSENTIALS   Orientation   The center of the village is place de la Mairie; and the area's most important monument, Le Moulin de Daudet, is two miles north.

Information   The Office de Tourisme, place de la Mairie (tel. 90-54-70-01), is open April through October.

Just 6½ miles from Arles, this sleepy little town in the foothills of the Alpilles enjoys associations with the 19th-century novelist Alphonse Daudet. Writing his first novel at the age of 14, this handsome young man in time became a member of the inner circle of the fashionable bohemian literary figures of his day. In 1884 he published the novel *Sappho*. He later became a patron of the young Marcel Proust. Daudet died in 1897, his health having been undermined by venereal disease.

On top of a small hill stands the mill that provided the title for Daudet's *Lettres de mon moulin*. The mill has been restored and turned into the **Musée Alphonse-Daudet,** avenue des Moulins (tel. 90-54-60-78), with memorabilia of the novelist in the basement. Open June to September, daily from 9am to noon and 1 to 7pm; October to May, daily from 2 to 6pm only. Admission costs 10 F ($1.80) per person.

WHERE TO STAY & DINE

AUBERGE LA REGALIDO, rue Frédéric-Mistral, 13990 Fontvieille. Tel. 90-54-60-22. Fax 90-54-64-29. 14 rms (all with bath or shower). A/C MINIBAR TV TEL
Ⓢ **Rates:** 600–1,350 F ($108–$243) single or double. Breakfast 78 F ($14) extra. AE, DC, MC, V. **Parking:** Free. **Closed:** Dec–Feb.

Converted from a 17th-century olive mill, this Relais & Châteaux is a charming Provençal manor, tastefully decorated by the Michel family. Bedrooms, named after regional spices and herbs, are furnished with antiques; the dining room has flower arrangements from Madame Michel's garden.

The Michel's son, Jean-Pierre, is a *maître-cuisinier,* following in the footsteps of his father, who was one of the leading chefs of France. The young chef specializes in gratin de moules aux épinards (tender Mediterranean mussels with spinach), pièce d'agneau en casserole et à l'ail (lamb delicately flavored with garlic and herbs), and canard farci au poivre vert (stuffed duckling with green peppercorns). Meals cost 280–400 F ($50.40–$72). The restaurant is open for lunch Wednesday through Sunday from 12:30 to 1:30pm, and for dinner Tuesday through Sunday from 7:30 to 9pm. Reservations are essential.

8. LES BAUX

444 miles S of Paris, 12 miles NE of Arles, 50 miles N of Marseille
and the Mediterranean

GETTING THERE   By Bus   There are local buses from Avignon.

ESSENTIALS   Orientation   Most motorists park outside the city walls (there are many parking lots, including one beside rue de Porte-Mage) and navigate the old town on foot. The Grand-Rue is the walled town's principal thoroughfare.

Information   There's an Office de Tourisme on the impasse du Château (tel. 90-54-34-39), open Easter through October.

Cardinal de Richelieu called this village a nesting place for eagles. In its lonely position high on a windswept plateau overlooking the southern flank of the Alpilles, Les Baux is a mere ghost of its former self. Once it was the citadel of the powerful seigneurs of Les Baux, who ruled with an iron fist and sent their conquering armies as far as Albania. They claimed descent from one of the Magi, Balthazar. The town lies just 50 miles north of Marseille and the Mediterranean, nestling in a valley surrounded by mysterious, shadowy rock formations. Hewn out of rock, Les Baux became a mighty fortress. In medieval times troubadours from all over Europe came to this "court of love." Here they recited western Europe's earliest-known vernacular poetry. When one ardent troubadour acted out his poetry with a married woman, her husband, a jealous knight, served the singer's heart in her stew that night. On learning of the ingredients of her supper, the errant woman threw herself off a cliff—or so the story goes.

Eventually, the notorious "Scourge of Provence" ruled Les Baux, sending his men throughout the land to kidnap people. If no one would pay ransom for one of his victims, the poor wretch was forced to walk a gangplank to death over the cliff's edge.

Fed up with the rebellions against Louis XIII in 1632, Richelieu commanded his armies to destroy Les Baux. Today the castle and ramparts are a mere shell, although remains of great Renaissance mansions are to be seen. The population of Les Baux, which once numbered in the thousands, is reduced to only a few hardy souls who endure the fierce sun of summer and the harsh winds of winter.

WHERE TO STAY
Expensive

L'OUSTAU DE BEAUMANIERE, Les Baux, 13520 Maussane-les-Alpilles. Tel. 90-54-33-07. Fax 90-54-40-46. 11 rms (all with bath), 13 suites. A/C MINIBAR TV TEL

$ Rates: 1,050 F ($189) single or double; from 1,600 F ($288) suite. Breakfast 95 F ($17.10) extra; half board 1,250–1,500 F ($225–$270) per person. AE, DC, MC, V. **Parking:** Free. **Closed:** Jan 15–Mar 2.

For years American travelers have been making gastronomic pilgrimages to this Relais & Châteaux in the valley at the foot of Les Baux de Provence. Opened by the late Raymond Thuilier after the war, it quickly developed a following. In the 1960s it was considered by many critics to be the finest country restaurant of France. Since its well-publicized early days under its since-departed founder, this establishment has provoked often lively discussion among both French and North Americans about whether its standards might have fallen somewhat. Despite that, it continues to draw a clientele under the direction of Jean-André Charial, son-in-law of Thuilier.

It consists of four separate houses, with guest rooms dating from the 16th and 17th centuries. Rooms open onto the pool, the gardens, or the Provence countryside.

In the stone-vaulted dining room, the chef serves such specialties as lobster soufflé, lamb with eggplant, mullet cooked in red wine and served on a bed of leeks, and pink gigot d'agneau (lamb) en croûte, followed by a soufflé of red fruits. He blends the best of traditional and regional cuisine, with an emphasis on what's fresh. Fixed-price menus cost 400 F ($72), 600 F ($108), and 690 F ($124.20). Service is daily from noon to 3pm and 7:30pm to midnight. The restaurant is closed on Wednesday and for Thursday lunch from November 1 to March 15. Reservations are essential.

Moderate

AUBERGE DE LA BENVENGUDO, Vallon de l'Arcoule, route d'Arles, 13520 Les Baux. Tel. 90-54-32-54. Fax 90-54-42-58. 17 rms (all with bath), 3 suites. TV TEL

$ Rates: 495–620 F ($89.10–$111.60) single or double; 720–158.40 F ($129.60–$158.60) suite. Breakfast 55 F ($9.90) extra. AE, MC, V. **Parking:** Free outside, 50 F ($9) inside. **Closed:** Nov 15–Feb 1.

Named for the Provençal word for "welcome," the Auberge de la Benvengudo is a tastefully converted 19th-century farmhouse surrounded by sculptured shrubbery, towering trees, vine-filled urns, and parasol pines. Just one mile from the village, this attractive hotel includes stone-walled and timbered salons and many 18th-century furnishings. Extra benefits include a swimming pool, a tennis court, and an expansive flagstone-covered terrace. An annex contains attractive modern bedrooms, some with antique four-poster beds, and each with large bathrooms, terraces, and views of either the garden or the village; 10 bedrooms are air-conditioned.

Owned and operated by members of the Rossi family, former employees of the nearby (and more expensive) Oustaù de Beaumanière, the inn serves a delectable cuisine. Menu items include a cassolette of snails with orange sauce, a fisherman's salad with basil, Mediterranean filet of sole fried with rosemary, and magrêt of duckling with pink peppercorns. At least some of the specialties are grilled over olive or vinewood branches in the Provençal style. The fixed-price menus change every day, according to whatever is seasonally available, and cost around 225 F ($40.50) each.

BAUTEZAR, rue Frédéric-Mistral, 13520 Les Baux. Tel. 90-54-32-09. 10 rms (all with bath), 1 suite. TEL

$ Rates: 350–500 F ($63–$90) single or double; 600 F ($108) suite. Breakfast 45 F ($8.10) extra. MC, V. **Parking:** 21 F ($2.10). **Closed:** Restaurant closed Mon year round. Hotel closed Jan 4–Mar 15.

The entrance of this inn takes you down a few steps and into the large medieval vaulted dining room, where you'll find Provençal furnishings and cloth tapestries hanging from the white stone walls. At the end of the dining room is a terrace with a view of Val d'Enfer. Bedrooms are decorated in the Louis XVI style. The food is good, with a fixed-price menu that begins at 145 F ($26.10).

MAS D'AIGRET, 13520 Les Baux. Tel. 90-54-33-54. Fax 90-54-41-37. 14 rms (all with bath), 1 suite. MINIBAR TV TEL

$ Rates: 450–800 F ($81–$144) single or double; 900 F ($162) suite. Breakfast 70 F ($12.60) extra. AE, DC, MC, V. **Parking:** Free.

Situated below the ruined fortress of Les Baux, this ancient but fully restored farmhouse offers spectacular terrace views over miles of Provence toward the Mediterranean. Tables are set among the pines, and its swimming pool is floodlit at night like the fortress. Your hosts are Englishman Pip Phillips and his French wife, Chantal. The fully equipped bedrooms and baths are attractive, with almost all rooms containing private terraces or balconies filled with flowers. Two of the larger bedrooms are partly built into natural rock and contain four-poster beds, one of which was made for Edward VII when he was Prince of Wales. The restaurant, carved out of a rock, serves excellent regional and traditional dishes, with menus priced at 130 F ($23.40) (lunch only), 190 F ($34.20), 280 F ($50.40), and 360 F ($64.80).

Inexpensive

HOSTELLERIE DE LA REINE-JEANNE, Grand-Rue, 13520 Les Baux. Tel. 90-54-32-06. Fax 90-54-32-33. 11 rms (all with bath or shower). TEL

$ Rates: 225–325 F ($40.50–$58.50) single or double. Breakfast 35 F ($6.30) extra. MC, V. **Closed:** Restaurant closed Tues mid-Oct to late Nov and Feb 2 to mid-Mar. Hotel closed late Nov–Feb 1.

S   This warm, immaculate inn is the best bargain at Les Baux. Guests enter through a typical provincial French bistro where they are welcomed by Alain Guilbard, standing behind a bar of waxed wood. All the bedrooms are very comfortable, and three have their own terraces with a view of Val d'Enfer. Fixed-price menus cost 85 F ($15.30), 98 F ($17.64), 100 F ($18), 110 F ($19.80), 120 F ($21.60), and 135 F ($24.30).

WHERE TO DINE

LA RIBOTO DE TAVEN, Le Val d'Enfer. Tel. 90-54-34-23.
Cuisine: FRENCH. **Reservations:** Required.
$ Prices: Appetizers 80–160 F ($14.40–$28.80); main dishes 130–200 F ($20.80–$36); fixed-price menus 220 F ($39.60) (lunch only), and 300–420 F ($54–$75.60). AE, DC, MC, V.
Open: Lunch Tues–Sun noon–2pm; dinner Tues–Sat 7:30–10pm. **Closed:** Feb–Mar 15.

★   This 1835 farmhouse, below the cliffs just outside the medieval section of town, is named for the good witch Taven, from a 9th-century Provençal fairy tale. The establishment has been owned by two generations of the Novi family, of which Christine and Philippe Theme are the English-speaking daughter and son-in-law. The inn has a manicured garden and a stone interior. The Provençal salon is a slope-roofed, timbered room with a vast fireplace and Louis XIII furniture. It's so elegant you'd never know that it was originally designed as a sleeping area for lambs. In summer, guests can sit outdoors at the beautifully laid tables, one of which is a millstone. Menu items are likely to include sea bass cooked in olive oil, fricassée of mussels flavored with basil, and lamb en croûte with olives—plus homemade desserts.

9. ST-REMY-DE-PROVENCE

438 miles S of Paris, 16 miles NE of Arles, 8 miles N of Les Baux

GETTING THERE **By Bus**   There are local buses from Avignon.

ESSENTIALS **Orientation**   Many hotels lie on the rural tracts set outside the town center. The old town is ringed by a boulevard that keeps traffic away from the heart of town. The Eglise St-Martin is the most visible monument, and the ancient Roman ruins of Glanum lie about a mile south of the center of town.

Information   For information, inquire at the Office de Tourisme, place Jean-Jaurès (tel. 90-92-05-22).

N ostradamus, the French physician and astrologer whose reputation is enjoying great vogue today, was born here in 1503. In 1922 Gertrude Stein and Alice B. Toklas found St-Rémy after "wandering around everywhere a bit," Ms. Stein wrote to Cocteau. But mainly St-Rémy is associated with van Gogh. He committed himself to an asylum here in 1889 after cutting off his ear. Between moods of despair, he painted such works as *Olive Trees* and *Cypresses*.

WHAT TO SEE & DO

The cloisters of the asylum that van Gogh made famous in his paintings can be visited at the 12th-century **Monastère de St-Paul-de-Mausolée** (tel. 90-92-02-31).

Now a psychiatric establishment, the former monastery lies east of the D5 highway, a short drive north of Glanum (see below). The cell in which this genius was confined is closed to the public, but it's still worth a visit to explore the Romanesque chapel and cloisters with their circular arches and columns, which have beautifully carved capitals.

The cloisters are open daily from 9am to noon and 2 to 6pm. On your way to the church you'll see a bust of van Gogh. You might also note that Dr. Albert Schweitzer was "detained" here in World War I. Admission is 12 F ($2.10).

In the center of St-Rémy, the **Musée Archéologique,** in the Hôtel de Sade, rue du Parage (tel. 90-92-08-10), displays both sculptures and bronzes excavated at Glanum. Open June through October, daily from 9am to noon and 2 to 6pm; in April and May, Monday through Friday from 3 to 6pm and on Saturday and Sunday from 10am to noon; closed November to March. Admission is 15 F ($2.70) for adults and 6 F ($1) for children.

WHERE TO STAY

In addition to the accommodations recommended below, the Bar/Hotel/Restaurant des Arts offers lodging (see "Where to Dine," below).

LES ANTIQUES, 15, av. Pasteur, 13210 St-Rémy-de-Provence. Tel. 90-92-03-02. Fax 90-92-50-40. 27 rms (all with bath or shower). MINIBAR TEL
$ Rates: 340–480 F ($61.20–$86.40) single or double. Breakfast 52 F ($9.30) extra. AE, DC, MC, V. **Parking:** Free. **Closed:** Oct 21–Apr 8.
This moderately priced, stylish 19th-century villa is set in a beautiful seven-acre park with a swimming pool. It contains a magnificent reception lounge, with marble floors and tapestries on the walls, which open onto several salons. All furnishings are Napoléon III. Some of the accommodations are in a private, modern pavilion, with direct access to the garden. The rooms are handsomely furnished, usually in pastels or rose. In summer, guests have breakfast in what used to be the Orangerie. There is no restaurant.

CHATEAU DE ROUSSAN, route de Tarascon, 13210 St-Rémy-de-Provence. Tel. 90-92-11-63. Fax 90-92-37-32. 21 rms (18 with bath or shower). TEL
$ Rates: 380 F ($68.40) single or double without bath or shower, 450–750 F ($81–$135) double with bath or shower. Breakfast 55 F ($9.90) extra. AE, MC, V. **Parking:** Free.
While this isn't the most glamorous of the château-hotels in the region, its overwhelming sense of history makes it a favorite with traditionalists. When it was first built, it was the envy of Europe. Its most famous resident, the Renaissance psychic Nostradamus, lived in a rustic outbuilding a few steps from the front door. The château was transformed into a hotel in 1954 when the owners needed funds to rebuild the place after it and the outlying 18th-century greenhouses had been destroyed by the Nazis. Today, guests pass beneath an archway of 100-year-old trees leading up to the neoclassical facade, which was constructed of softly colored local stone in 1701. As you wander around the grounds you will be absorbed in the history, especially when you come upon the baroque sculptures lining the basin, fed by a stream. A restaurant on the premises is open for dinner, plus a Sunday lunch; the restaurant is closed on Wednesday. Fixed-price menus begin at 135 F ($24.30).

HOTEL CHATEAU DES ALPILLES, ancienne route du Grès, 13210 St-Rémy-de-Provence. Tel. 90-92-03-33. Fax 90-92-45-17. 19 rms (all with bath), 4 suites. MINIBAR TV TEL
$ Rates: 760–810 F ($136.80–$145.80) single; 760–980 F ($136.80–$176.40) double; 1,154–1,460 F ($207–$262.80) suite. Breakfast 65 F ($11.70) extra. AE, DC, MC, V. **Parking:** Free. **Closed:** Jan 10 to mid-Mar and mid-Nov to Dec 11.
The philosophy that motivated Françoise Bon when she converted this mansion in 1980 was to create a "house for paying friends." When it was first built, in 1827, by the Pichot family, it housed Châteaubriand and a host of other French luminaries. To

reach it, you pass beneath the 300-year-old trees that surround the dignified and neoclassical exterior. The carefully decorated rooms have combined the best of an antique framework with plush upholsteries, rich carpeting, and vibrant colors. Each bedroom is spacious and filled with elegantly whimsical accessories, such as a pair of porcelain panthers flanking one of the carved mantelpieces. And all the accommodations have travertine-trimmed baths with large windows. During the renovations, Madame Bon installed an elevator, although you may prefer to descend the massive stone stairwell. In the garden, the château has an outdoor swimming pool, two tennis courts, a sauna, and a grill by the pool where you can order lunch in summer.

VALLON DE VALRUGUES, chemin Canto-Cigalo, 13210 St-Rémy-de-Provence. Tel. 90-92-04-40. Fax 90-92-44-01. 41 rms (all with bath), 8 suites. MINIBAR TV TEL

$ Rates: 750 F ($135) single; 960 F ($172.80) double; from 1,200 F ($216) suite. Breakfast 85 F ($15.30) extra. AE, DC, MC, V. **Parking:** Free.

⭐ Surrounded by a flowered park, this stylish Mediterranean hotel has the best accommodations and restaurant in town. The hotel is set on a hillside, and its designers incorporated pastel paneling, ceiling beams, and trompe-l'oeil murals. Constructed of limestone blocks and prefaced by a stone staircase, it has rows of French doors, an arched loggia, and a uniformed guard at the door. Owners Françoise and Jean-Michel Gallon offer beautifully furnished rooms and suites, all with built-in safes. The hotel's restaurant is one of the best in the area, and facilities include a heated swimming pool, tennis courts, a sauna, a gym, and horseback riding.

WHERE TO DINE

BAR/HOTEL/RESTAURANT DES ARTS, 32, bd. Victor Hugo, 13210 St-Rémy-de-Provence. Tel. 90-92-08-50.
Cuisine: FRENCH. **Reservations:** Recommended.
$ Prices: Appetizers 25–55 F ($4.50–$9.90); main dishes 80–140 F ($14.40–$25.20). AE, MC, V.
Open: Lunch daily noon–2pm; dinner daily 7:30–9:30pm. **Closed:** Feb, Nov 1–12, and Wed Oct–Mar 15.

💲 If the bohemian life still exists in St-Rémy, you'll probably find it at this old-style café-restaurant and hotel on the east side. The wait for dinner can be as long as 45 minutes, so you might want to spend some time at the smoke-stained bar, with its wooden tables and slightly faded decor. The restaurant itself is elegant, with pine paneling, masses of copper pots, and original paintings that the family has been collecting since 1947.

The menu lists such specialties as rabbit terrine, steak au poivre with champagne, tournedos with madeira and mushrooms, duckling in orange sauce, frogs' legs provençal, and trout served three different ways. By special order, the chef will serve crayfish, lobster, and game dishes.

If you want to spend the night, the 17 rooms upstairs are pleasantly decorated, some in Provençal style, with rustic ceiling beams and exposed timbers. Eight contain private baths. Rooms are rented as either singles or doubles. A room without bath costs 204 F ($36.72) daily, rising to 300 F ($54) with bath, plus 35 F ($6.30) for breakfast. Parking is free.

LE JARDEN DE FREDERIC, 8, bd. Gambetta. Tel. 90-92-27-76.
Cuisine: FRENCH. **Reservations:** Required.
$ Prices: Appetizers 70–110 F ($12.60–$19.80); main dishes 95–130 F ($17.10–$23.40); fixed-price menus 160–200 F ($28.80–$36). AE, DC, MC, V.
Open: Lunch Thurs–Tues noon–2pm; dinner Thurs–Tues 7:30–9:30pm. **Closed:** Feb.

Housed in a small villa close to the town center, this popular bistro is the best restaurant around. It was named after the Provençal poet Frédéric Mistral, whose garden once occupied this spot. The family-run restaurant offers rabbit with plums, terrine de canard, onion tart, gigot with roquefort, and poached turbot with sorrel. In summer guests can dine at tables in front of the house.

NEARBY ATTRACTIONS

A mile south of St-Rémy, along the D5, is **Ruines de Glanum** (tel. 90-92-23-79), a Gallo-Roman city (follow the road signs to Les Antiques). Its historical monuments include an **Arc Municipal,** a triumphal arch dating from the time of Julius Caesar, and a cenotaph called the **Mausolée des Jules.** Garlanded with sculptured fruits and flowers, the arch dates from 20 B.C. and is the oldest in Provence. It is also decorated with bas-reliefs representing chained prisoners. The mausoleum was raised to honor the grandsons of Augustus and is the only extant monument of its type. In the area are entire streets and the foundations of private residences from the 1st-century A.D. town. Some remains are from an even earlier Gallo-Greek town dating from the 2nd century B.C.

Admission is 28 F ($5) for adults, 16 F ($2.80) for ages 18–24 and over 60; free for children under 18. The excavations are open April to September, Wednesday through Monday from 9am to noon and 2 to 6pm; in other months, Thursday through Monday from 10am to noon and 2 to 5pm.

10. AVIGNON

425 miles S of Paris, 50 miles NW of Aix-en-Provence,
66 miles NW of Marseille

GETTING THERE   By Plane   The local airport, Avignon-Caumont, is four miles north of the city.

By Train and Bus   Avignon is a junction for bus routes throughout the region and train service from other towns is frequent. The fast TGV trains from Paris arrive 13 times per day (trip time: 4 hours), and 17 trains per day arrive from Marseille (trip time: 1¼ hours).

ESSENTIALS   Orientation   The city is set near the junction of two branches of the Rhône River. The old town is surrounded by 14th-century ramparts, which are paralleled by modern traffic arteries. Inside these walls, all distances are measured from the Palais des Papes. Nearby is the Cathédrale de Notre-Dame.

Information   There's an Office de Tourisme at 41, cours Jean-Jaurès (tel. 90-82-65-11).

In the 14th century Avignon was the capital of Christendom; the popes lived here during what the Romans called "the Babylonian Captivity." The legacy left by that "court of splendor and magnificence" makes Avignon even today one of the most interesting and beautiful of Europe's cities of the Middle Ages.

Papal History

In 1309 a sick man, nearing the end of his life, arrived in Avignon. His name was Clement V, and he was the leader of the Christian world. Lodged as a guest of the Dominicans, he died in the spring of 1314 and was succeeded by John XXII. The new pope, unlike the popes of Rome, lived modestly in the Episcopal Palace. When Benedict XII took over, he greatly enlarged and rebuilt the old palace. Clement VI, who followed, built an even more elaborate extension called the New Palace. After Innocent VI and Urban V, Pope Gregory XI did no building. Inspired by Catherine of Siena, he was intent upon returning the papacy to Rome, and he succeeded. In all, seven popes had reigned at Avignon. Under them, art and culture flourished, as did vice. Prostitutes blatantly went about peddling their wares in front of fat cardinals, rich merchants were robbed, and innocent pilgrims from the hinterlands were brutally tricked and swindled.

From 1378, during the Great Schism, one pope ruled in Avignon, another in Rome. The reign of the pope and the "antipope" continued, one following the other, until both rulers were dismissed by the election of Martin V in 1417. Rome continued to rule Avignon until it was joined to France at the time of the French Revolution.

The ramparts (still standing) around Avignon were built in the 14th century, and are characterized by their machicolated battlements, turrets, and old gates. Olga Carlisle called them "squat and very thick, like huge children's blocks placed there according to a playful up-and-down design."

WHAT TO SEE & DO

Even more famous than the papal residency is the ditty *"Sur le pont d'Avignon, l'on y danse, l'on y danse,"* echoing through every French nursery and around the world. Ironically, **pont St-Bénézet** was too narrow for the *danse* of the rhyme. It was all you could do to pass, much less dance. Spanning the Rhône and connecting Avignon with Villeneuve-lès-Avignon, the bridge is now only a fragmented ruin.

According to legend, the bridge was inspired by a vision a shepherd boy had while tending his flock in the field. His name was Bénézet. Actually, the bridge was built between 1117 and 1185, and it suffered various disasters from that time on. Finally, in 1669, half of the bridge toppled into the river. St. Nicholas Chapel stands on one of the piers. It's a two-story structure, one designed in the Romanesque style, the other in the Gothic.

The pont may be visited daily from 9am to noon and 2 to 7pm (to 6pm in winter). The bridge is open daily from 9am to 6:30pm in season; from October to March, daily from 9am to 5pm. Admission is 10 F ($1.80).

Dominating the city and standing on a hill is the **Palais des Papes,** place du Palais-des-Papes (tel. 90-86-03-32). You are shown through the palace on a guided tour, usually lasting 50 minutes. The long tour of the papal palace is somewhat monotonous, as the rooms for the most part have long been stripped of their finery. The exception is **St. John's Chapel,** which is known for its beautiful frescoes attributed to the school of Matteo Giovanetti and painted between 1345 and 1348. These frescoes present scenes from the life of St. John the Baptist and St. John the Evangelist. St. Martial's Chapel, however, was painted by Giovanetti himself. It is on the eastern wall, above St. John's Chapel. The Giovanetti frescoes depict the miracles of St. Martial, the patron saint of Limousin province.

The **Grand Tinel** or banquet hall is about 135 feet long and 30 feet wide. The pope's table stood on the southern side. The bedroom of the pope is on the first floor of the Tour des Anges. Its walls are entirely decorated in tempera with wide foliage on which birds and squirrels perch. Birdcages are painted in the recesses of the windows. In a secular vein, the **Stag Room**—the study of Clement VI—was frescoed in 1343 with hunting scenes. Added under the same Clement VI, who had a taste for grandeur, the **Great Audience Hall** contains frescoes of the prophets, also attributed to Giovanetti and painted in 1352.

The palace is open July to September, daily from 9am to 7pm; April to June and in October, daily from 9am to 12:15pm and 2 to 6pm; November to March, daily from 9am to noon and 2 to 5pm. Admission is 38 F ($6.80) for adults, 29 F ($5.20) for children and those over 65. Guided tours in English depart daily at 10am and 3pm, costing 46 F ($8.20) for adults and 37 F ($6.60) for children.

Near the palace is the 12th-century **Cathédrale de Notre-Dame,** place du Palais-des-Papes, containing the flamboyant Gothic tomb of John XXII, who died at the age of 90. Benedict XII is also buried here. Crowning the top is a gilded statue of the Virgin from the 19th century. Open daily from 11am to 6pm. Admission is free.

From the cathedral, enter the **promenade du Rocher-des-Doms** to stroll through its garden and enjoy the view across the Rhône to Villeneuve-lèz-Avignon.

The **Musée du Petit-Palais,** place du Palais-des-Papes (tel. 90-86-44-58), is housed in a palace dating from the 14th and 15th centuries. It contains an important collection of paintings from the Italian schools from the 13th through the 16th century, including works from Florence, Venice, Siena, and Lombardy. In addition, salons display 15th-century paintings done in Avignon. Several galleries are devoted to Roman and Gothic sculptures from the city. Open Wednesday through Monday from 9:30 to 11:50am and 2 to 6pm. Admission costs 18 F ($3.20) for adults, 9 F ($1.60) for children.

The **Musée Calvet,** 67, rue Joseph-Vernet (tel. 90-86-33-84), is housed in an 18th-century mansion with a courtyard once praised by Stendhal. It shelters a collection of prehistoric stoneware, Greek marbles, Egyptian monuments, and many paintings. My favorite oil is by Brueghel (the younger), *Le Cortège Nuptial* (The Bridal Procession). Look for a copy of Bosch's *Adoration of the Magi* as well. Other works are by Vasari, Mignard, Joseph Vernet, David, Manet, Delacroix, Daumier, Viullard, Renoir, Dufy, and Utrillo (his *Lapin Agile*). Open daily from 10am to noon and 2 to 6pm. Admission is 20 F ($3.60) for adults, 10 F ($1.80) for children.

The **Musée Lapidaire,** entered at 18, rue de la République (tel. 90-85-75-38), is in a 17th-century Jesuit church. It displays an important collection of Gallo-Roman sculptures. Open Wednesday through Monday from 10am to noon and 2 to 6pm. Admission is 15 F ($2.70) for adults, free for children.

Across the Rhône in Villeneuve-lèz-Avignon

The modern world is impinging on Avignon, but across the Rhône at Villeneuve-lèz-Avignon, the Middle Ages slumber on. When the popes lived in exile at Avignon, wealthy cardinals built palaces, or *livrées,* across the river. Many visitors prefer to live or dine there rather than in Avignon (see my recommendations, below).

However, even if you're staying at Avignon or just passing through, you'll want to visit Villeneuve, especially to see its Carthusian monastery, **Chartreuse du Val-de-Bénédiction,** 60, rue de la République, in the heart of town (tel. 90-25-05-46). The largest charterhouse in France, it's now a cultural center, where artistic events are organized.

Pope Innocent VI (whose tomb can be viewed) founded this charterhouse, which in time became the most powerful in the country. Inside, a remarkable *Coronation of the Virgin* by Enguerrand Charonton is enshrined. Painted in 1453, the masterpiece contains a fringed bottom that is Bosch-like in its horror, representing the denizens of hell. The 12th-century graveyard cloister is lined with cells where the former fathers prayed and meditated.

The charterhouse is open April to September, daily from 9 to 6:30pm; October to June, daily from 9:30am to 5:30pm. Admission is 24 F ($4.20) for adults, 5 F (90¢) for children.

Crowning the town is **Fort St-André** (tel. 90-25-55-95), founded in 1360 by Jean-le-Bon to serve as a symbol of might to the pontifical powers across the river. The Abbey of St. André, now owned privately, was installed in the 18th century. You can visit the formal garden encircling the mansion. The mood here is tranquil, with a rose-trellis colonnade, fountains, and flowers.

The grounds are open April to September, daily from 9am to noon and 2 to 6:30pm; October to March, daily from 10am to noon and 2 to 5pm. Admission costs 8 F ($1.40). You can also visit the twin towers, with their impressive rooms and even more impressive terraces with panoramic views. The towers are open April to September, daily from 9:30am to 12:30pm and 2 to 6:30pm; October to March, daily from 10am to noon and 2 to 5pm. Admission is 18 F ($3.20) for adults, 5 F (90¢) for children 7–17.

Try to visit the **Church of Notre-Dame,** place Meissonier, founded in 1333 by Cardinal Arnaud de Via, in the town center. Its proudest possession is a 14th-century *Virgin of Ivory,* considered one of the great French art treasures. Open April to September, Wednesday through Monday from 10am to noon and 3 to 7:30pm; October through March, Wednesday to Monday from 10am to noon and 2 to 5pm; closed in February. Admission is free.

WHERE TO STAY

Also see my recommendations under "Where to Stay & Dine in Villeneuve-lèz-Avignon," below.

Expensive

HOTEL D'EUROPE, 12, place Grillon, 84000 Avignon. Tel. 90-82-66-92.
Fax 90-85-43-66. 44 rms (all with bath or shower). A/C TV TEL

$ Rates: 610 F ($109.80) single; 610–1,300 F ($109.80–$234) double; 1,950 F ($351) suite. Breakfast 90 F ($16.20) extra. AE, DC, MC, V. **Parking:** 50 F ($9). Built in 1580 as a palace for the marquis de Gravezon, the Hôtel d'Europe has been in operation since 1799. You enter through a courtyard, where tables are set in the warmer months. Whether you go into the grand hall or any of the salons, you'll find tastefully arranged antiques and decorative elements, such as Aubusson tapestries, Empire consoles, gilt-framed paintings, and an especially fine assortment of Directoire pieces. The bedrooms also are tasteful, with handsome decorations and period furnishings; 24 have minibars. Its restaurant, La Vieille Fontaine, is the most distinguished in Avignon. Meals are served in elegant dining rooms or in a charming inner courtyard. Fixed-price menus cost 185–250 F ($33.30–$45).

Moderate

HOTEL BRISTOL, 44, cours Jean-Jaurès, 84009 Avignon. Tel. 90-82-21-21. Fax 90-86-22-72. 65 rms (all with bath). TV TEL **Bus:** 11.
$ Rates: 425 F ($76.50) single; 500 F ($90) double. Breakfast 38 F ($6.80) extra. AE, DC, MC, V. **Parking:** 50 F ($9).
Located in the center of Avignon on one of the principal streets leading to the landmark place de l'Horloge and the Papal Palace, the Hôtel Bristol is one of the better bets in town. A traditional establishment, it offers comfortably furnished bedrooms. Breakfast is the only meal served.

HOTEL CITE-DES-PAPES, 1, rue Jean-Vilar, 84000 Avignon. Tel. 90-86-22-45. Fax 90-27-39-21. 63 rms (all with bath). A/C MINIBAR TV TEL **Bus:** 11.
$ Rates: 375–410 F ($67.50–$72) single or double; 550 F ($99) triple; 750 F ($135) quad. Breakfast 60 F ($10.80) extra. AE, DC, MC, V. **Closed:** Dec 18–Jan 25.
At the foot of the Palace of the Popes, the most prominent place in Avignon, the Hôtel Cité-des-Papes offers you modern comfort in pleasant and restful surroundings. It's just 20 yards from the city's biggest parking lot and very close to the New Congress Palace. Breakfast is the only meal served.

MERCURE PALAIS-DES-PAPES, quartier de la Balance, rue Ferruce, 84000 Avignon. Tel. 90-85-91-23. Fax 90-85-32-40. 86 rms (all with bath or shower). A/C TV TEL **Bus:** 11.
$ Rates: 490–550 F ($88.20–$99) single or double. Breakfast 50 F ($9) extra. AE, DC, MC, V. **Parking:** 50 F ($9).
This chain hotel is one of the best in Avignon. It lies in the center of town, at the foot of the Palace of the Popes, next to the pont d'Avignon and place de l'Horloge. Bedrooms are well furnished. Breakfast is the only meal served, and there's a piano bar.

PRIMOTEL HORLOGE, 1, rue Félicien-David, 84000 Avignon. Tel. 90-86-88-61. Fax 90-82-17-32. 70 rms (all with bath). A/C MINIBAR TV TEL **Bus:** 11.
$ Rates: 400–490 F ($72–$88.20) double. Breakfast 40 F ($7.20) extra. AE, DC, MC, V. **Parking:** Free.
Situated in the heart of the city, overlooking the place de l'Horloge near the Palace of the Popes, this member of a nationwide chain opened in 1987 in a much-renovated older building. Today, it's considered one of the best in its price category. The soundproof accommodations each come with either bath or shower and, in some cases, a terrace. Breakfast is the only meal served.

Inexpensive

HOTEL D'ANGLETERRE, 29, bd. Raspail, 84000 Avignon. Tel. 90-86-34-31. Fax 90-86-86-74. 40 rms (35 with bath or shower). TEL **Bus:** 11.
$ Rates: 230 F ($41.40) single without bath; 240–350 F ($43.20–$63) double with bath. Breakfast 30 F ($5.40) extra. MC, V. **Parking:** Free. **Closed:** Dec 20–Jan 28.

Near the heart of Avignon, this classical structure is one of the best budget hotels in town. Bedrooms are comfortably furnished, 35 with TVs. Breakfast is the only meal served.

HOTEL DANIELI, 17, rue de la République, 84000 Avignon. Tel. 90-86-46-82. Fax 90-27-09-24. 29 rms (all with bath). TV TEL **Bus:** 11.

$ Rates: 350–450 F ($63–$81) single; 390–490 F ($70.20–$88.20) double. Breakfast 40 F ($7.20) extra. AE, DC, MC, V.

Centrally located, the Hôtel Danieli's Italian influence is evidenced by its arches, chiseled stone, tile floors, and baronial staircases. The hotel, possibly named after one of the great hotels of Venice, is small and informal. The peach-and-white bedrooms combine modern furnishings with touches of art deco styling. Breakfast is the only meal served.

WHERE TO DINE

BRUNEL, 46, rue de la Balance. Tel. 90-85-24-83.
   Cuisine: FRENCH. **Reservations:** Required. **Bus:** 11.
$ Prices: Appetizers 100–150 F ($18–$27); main dishes 130–180 F ($23.40–$32.40); fixed-price menus 180 F ($32.40), 230 F ($41.40), 285 F ($51.30), 330 F ($59.40) and 400 F ($72). AE, MC, V.
   Open: Lunch daily noon–1:30pm; dinner daily 7:45–9:15pm. **Closed:** July 15–Aug 15.

Located in the historic heart of Avignon, this is an elegant, modern, flower-filled restaurant with air conditioning, managed by the Brunel family. It offers such specialties as warm curried oysters, warm pâté of duckling, lambs' brains with caramelized lemon, and breast of duckling with apples. Desserts are excellent. Feel free to order house wines by the carafe.

CHRISTIAN ETIENNE, 10, rue Mons. Tel. 90-86-16-50.
   Cuisine: FRENCH. **Reservations:** Recommended.
$ Prices: Appetizers 100–220 F ($18–$39.60); main dishes 180–290 F ($32.40–$52.20); fixed-price menus 280–480 F ($50.40–$86.40). AE, MC, V.
   Open: July, lunch daily noon–2:30pm; dinner daily 8–10:30pm. Other months, lunch Mon–Sat noon–2:30pm; dinner Mon–Sat 8–10:30pm.

This is considered the best and probably the most unusual restaurant in Avignon. The stone house containing it was built just prior to the construction of the Palais des Papes (which lies next door), and was used as the office of the building supervisor during the palace's construction. You'll climb a few steps to reach the dining room, which contains very old ceiling and wall frescoes honoring the marriage of Anne of Brittany to the French king in 1491.

Several of the fixed-price menus here present specific themes: For example, the one at 290 F ($52.20) features only vegetables, the one at 400 F ($72) features different preparations of lobster, and the one at 480 F ($86.40) relies solely on the discretion of the chef (*un menu "confiance"*). A la carte specialties include fennel soup with sea barnacles, a terrine of foie gras cooked with sauterne, red snapper fried with a fricassée of artichokes and basil, roast pigeon served with an escalope of foie gras, and filet of sole cooked with dill and stuffed with a compôte of eggplant.

LA FOURCHETTE II, 7, rue Racine. Tel. 90-85-20-93.
   Cuisine: FRENCH. **Reservations:** Not required. **Bus:** 11.
$ Prices: Appetizers 40–60 F ($7.20–$10.80); main dishes 70–90 F ($12.60–$16.20); fixed-price menu 140 F ($25.20). MC, V.
   Open: Lunch Mon–Fri noon–2pm; dinner Mon–Fri 7:30–9:30pm; **Closed:** June 15–30.

This bistro offers creative cooking at a moderate price. There are two dining rooms, one like a summer house with walls of glass, the other more like a tavern with oak beams. Ladderback chairs, checked tablecloths, baskets of fresh cherries (in season), wooden kegs, ceramic jugs, and copper urns of trailing plants complete the ambience. Begin with a parfait of chicken liver with a spinach flan or a mousseline of fish in a saffron sauce. Fresh sardines marinated with citrus also are served. Two specialties are the daube of beef prepared in the Avignonnaise style with macaroni and the grilled lambs' liver with raisins.

HIELY, 5, rue de la République. Tel. 90-86-17-07.
   Cuisine: FRENCH. **Reservations:** Required. **Bus:** 11.
$ **Prices:** Fixed-price menus 195 F ($35.10) and 295 F ($53.10). AE, MC, V.
   Open: Lunch Wed–Sun noon–2pm; dinner Wed–Mon 7:30–9:30pm. **Closed:** Jan 6–30 and June 18–July 4.

This Relais Gourmand is one of the finest places to eat in Provence, with a devoted following. Chef Pierre Hiely prepares special appetizers, such as petite marmite du pêcheur, a savory fish soup ringed with black mussels. A main-dish specialty is pintadeau (young guinea hen) with peaches. The pièce de résistance is agneau des Alpilles grillé (alpine lamb) sur feu de bois. Carafe wines include Tavel Rosé and Châteauneuf-du-Pape.

LES TROIS CLEFS, 26, rue des Trois-Fauçons. Tel. 90-86-51-53.
   Cuisine: FRENCH. **Reservations:** Required. **Bus:** 11.
$ **Prices:** Appetizers 80–155 F ($14.40–$27.90); main dishes 118–212 F ($21.25–$38.16); fixed-price menus 140 F ($25.20) and 175 F ($31.50). AE, DC, MC, V.
   Open: July, lunch daily 12:15–1:30pm; dinner daily 7:30–9:30pm. Other months, lunch Mon–Sat 12:15–1:30pm; dinner Mon–Sat 7:30–9:30pm. **Closed:** Nov 15–30.

Located just behind the city ramparts and the Lapidary Museum, Les Trois Clefs is an attractively decorated, intimate, air-conditioned dining room—complete with lacquered paneling, flowers, well-chosen fabrics, and good prices. The restaurant's dishes change according to the availability of ingredients at the markets. Laurent and Martine Mergnac's specialties might include hot foie gras of duckling in a herbflavored sauce, brioche of eggs with truffles, and suprême of guinea fowl with crayfish.

WHERE TO STAY & DINE IN VILLENEUVE-LEZ-AVIGNON

HOTEL DE L'ATELIER, 5, rue de la Foire, 30400 Villeneuve-lèz-Avignon. Tel. 90-25-01-84. Fax 90-25-80-06. 19 rms (all with bath or shower). TV TEL
$ **Rates:** 260–400 F ($46.80–$72) single or double. Breakfast 38 F ($6.80) extra. AE, DC, MC, V. **Parking:** Free on street, 45 F ($8.10) in nearby garage.

Villeneuve's budget offering is this 16th-century village house that has preserved much of its original style. Inside is a tiny duplex lounge with a large stone fireplace. Outside, a sun-filled rear garden, with potted orange and fig trees, provides fruit for the breakfast. The immaculate accommodations are comfortable and informal. In the old bourgeois dining room, a continental breakfast is the only meal served.

LA MAGNANERAIE HOSTELLERIE, 37, rue Camp-Bataille, 30400 Villeneuve-lèz-Avignon. Tel. 90-25-11-11. Fax 90-25-46-37. 25 rms (all with bath or shower), 2 suites. A/C MINIBAR TV TEL
$ **Rates:** 400–600 F ($72–$108) single or double; 900 F ($162) suite. Breakfast 65 F ($11.70) extra. AE, DC, MC, V. **Parking:** Free.

One of the most charming accommodations in the region is set on two acres of exquisite gardens under the direction of Gérard and Eliane Prayal. Originally built in the 15th century as the country home of a local cardinal, the building later served as a wine-tasting center for owners of the surrounding vineyards. Tastefully renovated, and enlarged with an architecturally compatible new wing in the 1980s, the place is beautifully furnished with antiques and good-quality reproductions. Many guests here arrive for only one night but remain for many days, to enjoy the good food, the atmosphere, the garden, the tennis court, and the elegantly landscaped swimming pool.

In 1993, French tourist authorities increased the government-sponsored rating of this fine inn to four stars. Much of this was because of Mr. Prayal's excellent cuisine, which in summer is served on a flowering terrace. Fixed-price menus range from 170 F ($30.60) for a well-flavored celebration of traditional Provençal recipes to 330 F

($59.40) for a *menu dégustation*. Also available is a 10-course feast for serious eaters (with many hours to spare at table) priced at 450 F ($81). Menu items are original and sophisticated, and include zucchini flowers stuffed with a purée of mushrooms and cream, a petit feuilleté of foie gras and truffles, a marée de poissons served with a barigoule provençale, a croustillant of red snapper with basil and a local olive oil, and a rack of lamb roasted with fresh thyme. Dessert might be a gratin of seasonal fruits with a sabayon of lavender-flavored honey.

LE PRIEURE, place du Chapître, 30400 Villeneuve-lèz-Avignon. Tel. 90-25-18-20. Fax 90-25-45-39. 26 rms (all with bath), 10 suites. A/C MINIBAR TV TEL

$ Rates: 520 F ($93.60) single; 520–1,200 F ($93.60–$216) double; 1,400–1,750 F ($252–$315) suite. Breakfast 80 F ($14.40) extra. AE, DC, MC, V. **Parking:** Free. **Closed:** Early Nov to early Mar.

Built in the center of the village in 1322 as a residence for a cardinal (reportedly, the nephew of one of the antipopes in Avignon), this small and charming property was purchased in 1943 by the grandfather (Roger Mille) of the present owner, François Mille. Set adjacent to the village church, and laden with Provençal-provincial charm, the hotel has an ivy-covered stone exterior, green shutters, a tiled roof, and a series of plushly rustic public rooms similar to what you might find in a country estate. Fixed-price meals, served daily at both lunch and dinner, cost 195–420 F ($35.10–$75.60).

NEARBY ACCOMMODATIONS & DINING

Noves is 8½ miles from Avignon, via the D28. Le Pontet is 3 miles east of Avignon.

LES AGASSINS, 52, av. Charles-de-Gaulle, Le Pigeonnier, route d'Avignon, 84130 Le Pontet. Tel. 90-32-42-91. Fax 90-32-08-29. 24 rms (all with bath). A/C MINIBAR TV TEL **Directions:** Take the N7 three miles northeast of Avignon.

$ Rates: 500–600 F ($90–$108) single; 500–700 F ($90–$162) double. Half board 550–700 F ($99–$126) per person. AE, DC, V. **Parking:** Free. **Closed:** Jan–Mar 1.

Only a five-minute drive from Avignon, this Provençal house lies in the Pigeonnier (dovecote) part of Le Pontet. It takes its name from the chicks of the *agassins* (Provençal for magpies). The original house built here was constructed for Guillaume de Fargis, nephew of Pope Clement V. In the 1960s a Florentine family took over the site and built a hotel. The main house is filled with character, from its antique-filled lounges to its flower-filled balconies. Floors are covered with old-fashioned pottery tiles, and the family's collection of paintings decorates the walls. Guests can wander in the century-old park and gardens or relax by the open-air swimming pool. Accommodations are beautifully decorated and maintained, each spacious and with complete facilities such as private bath, radio, minibar, cable TV, phone, and even a flowery balcony. A special feature of the hotel is Le Florentin, a traditional French restaurant *gastronomique*, considered one of the finest in the area.

AUBERGE DE CASSAGNE, 450, allée de Cassagne, route de Vèdene (D62), Le Pontet, 84130 Avignon. Tel. 90-31-04-18. Fax 90-32-25-09. 23 rms (all with bath), 6 suites. A/C MINIBAR TV TEL

$ Rates: 420–580 F ($75.60–$104.40) single; 490–1,080 F ($88.20–$194.40) double; 1,380 F ($248.40) suite. Breakfast 80 F ($14.40) extra. AE, DC, MC, V. **Parking:** 20 F ($3.60).

This could be your best bet for food and lodging in the Avignon area. The hotel, set in a park with a swimming pool, is an enchanting little Provençal inn with country-style bedrooms.

The cuisine here is exceptionally good, much of it in the style of Paul Bocuse. You can enjoy your meals in a rustically decorated dining room or at a table in the garden. A trio of owners feature such dishes as sea bass, turbot, and deviled lamb. Meals, costing 210–440 F ($37.80–$79.20), are available to nonresidents who make reservations.

AUBERGE DE NOVES, 13550 Noves. Tel. 90-94-19-21. Fax 90-94-47-76.
23 rms (all with bath), 4 suites. A/C MINIBAR TV TEL
$ Rates (including half board): 2,150–2,750 F ($387–$495) for two. AE, DC, MC,
V. **Parking:** Free. **Closed:** Jan 3–Feb 15.

⭐ The Auberge de Noves is an elegant Relais & Châteaux run by the Lalleman
family, who offer modern and attractive rooms. On its own hilltop park, it's a
cross between a Riviera villa and a 1920s-style Beverly Hills mansion. When M
and Mme Lalleman purchased the auberge in 1950, it was a religious retreat, which
they transformed into one of the finest luxury country estates in Provence. The
bedchambers, each individually conceived, are furnished with period pieces. Some
have terraces, and most have exceptional views. During the day, guests enjoy the
tennis courts and swimming pool.

The food is among the best in the area, including duck cooked in a salt crust, red
snapper flavored with fresh tomatoes and garlic, and a garlic-flavored lentil soup that's
delectable. From the first-class wine cellar emerge such selections as Châteauneuf-du-
Pape and Lirac. The restaurant does not serve lunch on Wednesday, and reservations
are always required. Meals cost 260–475 F ($46.80–$85.50).

**LES FRENES, 645, av. Vertes-Rives, 84140 Avignon-Montfavet. Tel.
90-31-17-93.** Fax 90-23-95-03. 18 rms (all with bath), 4 suites. A/C TV TEL
Directions: Take the D53 three miles southeast of Avignon.
$ Rates: 595 F ($107.10) single; 1,800 F ($324) double; 2,500 F ($450) suite.
Breakfast 75 F ($13.50) extra. AE, DC, V. **Parking:** Free. **Closed:** Hotel, Nov
15–Mar 15; restaurant, Nov–Mar.

In an imposing garden surrounded by century-old trees, this is one of the most
impressive, tranquil, and charming stopovers in the Avignon area. The Biancone
family welcomes you as if you were a guest in their private home, which you are.
Around the original château, modern detached houses have been built, providing
more privacy. The bedrooms are each individually decorated, all with style and taste.
Such modern amenities have been added as whirlpool baths and multijet showers in
the bedrooms. Rooms also contain safe-deposit boxes. The food prepared under the
baton of the chef de cuisine, Antoine Biacone, is reason enough to visit. Menus cost
335 F ($60.30), 390 F ($70.20), and 490 F ($88.20). During the day, guests relax
around the outdoor swimming pool.

---

11. GORDES

444 miles S of Paris, 38 miles SE of Avignon, 60 miles N of Marseille

GETTING THERE   By Bus   There is some limited bus service from Avignon.

ESSENTIALS   Information   The Office de Tourisme, place du Château (tel.
90-72-02-75), is open all year.

To reach Gordes, take the winding road, past typical Provençal countryside, and
eventually you'll come across a village filled with stone huts called *bories*. These
windowless, beehive-shaped stone dwellings continue to puzzle archeologists. Some
have suggested that they predate Christ, while others maintain that they were built as
recently as the 16th century, possibly by residents fleeing the plague.

The **Château de Gordes** dominating the town was erected in the 11th century,
then later rebuilt during the first half of the 16th. The Renaissance château was really a
fortress with round towers in each of its four corners. A crenellated roof is supported
by the north walls. Ask the guard about visiting. Inside is the **Musée Vasarely** (tel.
90-72-02-89), named after painter Victor Vasarely, one of the founders of kinetic art.
He has a house nearby and has leased the château from the village for 35 years for a
rental of 1 F a year. On the first floor are brilliantly colored tapestries. Older works,

untouched by the influence of surrealism, are on the third floor. In all, the château houses 1,500 paintings. Open July and August, daily from 7am to 7pm; other months, Wednesday through Monday from 10am to noon and 2 to 6pm. Admission is 20 F ($3.60) for adults, 14 F ($2.50) for children.

WHERE TO STAY

BASTIDE DE GORDES, Le Village, 84220 Gordes. Tel. 90-72-12-12. Fax 90-72-05-20. 18 rms (all with bath). A/C TV TEL
$ Rates: 750 F ($135) single; 1,250 F ($225) double. Breakfast 75 F ($13.50) extra. AE, V. **Parking:** Free. **Closed:** Nov 3–Feb.

Considered the finest hotel or dining choice in Gordes, this agreeable hostelry stands 1,200 feet up in the foothills of the Plateau de Vaucluse. Attracting tranquility seekers from the Riviera, the hotel opens onto views of the Lubéron mountain range, a nature park.

At the end of the war, the Nazis shelled the property to bits, but it has risen from the ashes admirably. (Gordes was a hotbed of the French resistance.) Marble is used in profusion, and one commentator called the furnishings and decor "Louis Quelquechose" (Louis "something or other"). A time-worn beam or weathered stone remains to evoke the original building. The owners have installed an open-air swimming pool beside the reconstructed tower and loggia. Bedrooms are elegantly, tastefully furnished. The least expensive rooms open onto the village side.

Many visitors arrive just to patronize the restaurant, a worthy idea. Lunch is served on a shady terrace opening onto a view of olive trees and the vineyards below. You might begin with zucchini blossoms, hearts of artichoke filled with tapenade, or a basil-flavored tomato coulis. The fish *du pays* is likely to be a perfectly cooked daurade in a salt shell, followed by a salad of greens recently picked from the field. Dining is in an elegant vaulted restaurant. A fixed-price menu is served at lunch for 195 F ($35.10). Fixed-price dinners cost 345–450 F ($62.10–$81). The restaurant is closed on Monday and Tuesday at lunch.

DOMAINE DE L'ENCLOS, route de Sénanque, 84200 Gordes. Tel. 90-72-08-22. Fax 90-72-03-03. 14 rms (all with bath), 2 suites. A/C MINIBAR TV TEL
$ Rates: 650–1,150 F ($117–$207) double; 1,700 F ($306) suite. Half board 230 F ($41.40) per person. AE, DC, MC, V. **Parking:** Free.

One of the most charming hotels in the region, the Domain de l'Enclos sits on six acres of flowering terrain a short distance above the town center, opposite the nearby mountains. Surrounded by a manicured garden, the rooms, many with terraces, are in stone cottages or in the *mas,* or main building. A pool and tennis court also are available.

A superb cuisine is served in the panoramic dining room, featuring an array of creative, regional dishes with a creative twist. Specialties change frequently, based both on the availability of ingredients and the inspiration of the chef. Nonresidents must call for a reservation. Meals cost 260–410 F ($46.80–$73.80).

LA MAYANELLE, 6, rue Combe, 84220 Gordes. Tel. 90-72-00-28. Fax 90-72-06-99. 9 rms (all with bath). TEL
$ Rates (including half board): 420–520 F ($75.60–$93.60) per person. AE, DC, MC, V. **Parking:** Free. **Closed:** Jan 4–Mar 1.

This 12th-century stone mansion is owned by Eugène Mayard, who offers guests beautifully furnished, accessorized bedrooms. The vaulted dining room contains high ceilings, an informal terrace with a weeping willow, an open stone staircase, arched windows, and flower planters. You'll be served such regional specialties as roast guinea fowl, duck with olives, lamb flavored with the herbs of Provence, grilled salmon, and homemade fruit tarts. If you visit for a meal only, fixed-price menus cost 160 F ($28.80) and up. The small mansion, overlooking the rolling hill of Vaucluse, is closed for dining Monday night and on Tuesday.

NEARBY ATTRACTIONS

The **Village des Bories** (tel. 90-72-03-48) lies about two miles outside Gordes. Head out the D15, going right beyond a fork at the D2. A sign will indicate that you make a right turn onto an unpaved road. Park your car and walk for about 45 minutes to reach this museum, where several dwellings have been furnished with primitive tools, including some pottery excavated on the site. Open February to mid-November, daily from 9am to dusk; in mid-winter, 10am to dusk on Saturday and Sunday only. Admission is 16 F ($2.80) for adults, free for children.

In the neighborhood of Gordes is **Vénasque,** seven miles southeast of Carpentras on the way to Orange. In this village, a bapistry dates from the 6th century.

Even closer to Gordes is **Sénanque,** on the D15 and D177. The **Abbey de Sénanque** (tel. 90-72-05-72) is one of the three Cistercian abbeys of Provence. After nearly a 20-year hiatus, it became an abbey again in 1988. Founded in 1148, the abbey was abandoned during the French Revolution, when all church property was confiscated by the state. However, the monks came back in the 19th century and stayed until 1969. As you walk around and explore, it's possible to understand why Thomas Merton found peace here some 30 years ago. Open Monday through Saturday from 10am to noon and 2 to 6pm, and on Sunday from 2 to 6pm. Admission is 15 F ($2.70) for adults and 8 F ($1.40) for children.

---

12. ORANGE

409 miles S of Paris, 34 miles NE of Nîmes, 75 miles NW of Marseille, 16 miles S of Avignon

GETTING THERE Orange sits directly on some of the major French north-south rail and highway arteries, making arrivals by train, bus, or car convenient.

ESSENTIALS Orientation The historic center of town, Vieil Orange, developed between the Théâtre Antique and the Cathédrale de Notre-Dame. At the southern edge of the Théâtre Antique is the Park of the Hill of St-Europe. The Ancient Triumphal Arch lies across the banks of the town's narrow river, north of the center.

Information The Office de Tourisme is on cours Aristide-Briand (tel. 90-34-70-88).

SPECIAL EVENTS At the end of July, a drama, dance, and music festival called Les Chorégies d'Orange takes place at the Théâtre Antique. For information or tickets, call 90-34-15-52.

Orange gets its name from the days when it was a dependency of the Dutch House of Orange-Nassau. Overlooking the Valley of the Rhône, the city tempts visitors with the third-largest triumphal arch extant in Europe, and the best-preserved Roman theater in Europe. Louis XIV, who toyed with the idea of moving the theater to Versailles, said: "It is the finest wall in my kingdom."

WHAT TO SEE & DO

In the southern part of town, **O Le Théâtre Antique,** place des Frères-Mounet (tel. 90-51-80-06), dates from the days of Augustus. Built into the side of a hill, it once held 8,000 spectators in tiered seats divided into three sections based on class. Carefully restored, the nearly 350-foot-long and 125-foot-high theater is noted for its fine acoustics and is used today for outdoor entertainment. Open April to September, daily from 9am to 6:30pm; October to March, daily from 9am to noon and 1:30 to 5pm. Admission is 22 F ($3.90) for adults and 17 F ($3) for children.

To the west of the theater once stood one of the biggest temples in Gaul, which, combined with a gymnasium and the theater, formed one of the greatest buildings in the empire. Across the street at place des Frères-Mounet, the **Musée Municipal** d'Orange, place du Théâtre-Antique (tel. 90-51-80-06), displays fragments excavated in the arena. Your ticket to the ancient theater will also admit you to this museum, which is open April to September, Monday through Saturday from 9am to 6:30pm; October to March, Monday through Saturday from 9am to noon and 1:30 to 5:30pm.

Even older than the theater is the **Triumphal Arch** on avenue de l'Arc-de-Triomphe. It has decayed, but its sculptural decorations and other elements are still fairly well preserved. Built to honor the conquering legions of Caesar, it rises 72 feet and is nearly 70 feet wide. Composed of a trio of arches held up by Corinthian columns, it was used as a dungeon for prisoners in the Middle Ages.

Before leaving Orange, head for the hilltop park, the **Colline Saint-Eutrope,** for a view of the surrounding valley with its mulberry plantations.

WHERE TO STAY

HOTEL LOUVRE ET TERMINUS, 89, av. Frédéric-Mistral, 84100 Orange. Tel. 90-34-10-08. Fax 90-34-68-71. 32 rms (all with bath or shower), 2 suites. TEL

$ Rates: 260 F ($46.80) single; 320 F ($57.60) double; 380 F ($68.40) suite. Breakfast 38 F ($6.80) extra. AE, MC, V. **Parking:** 30 F ($5.40). **Closed:** Dec 20–Jan 5.

Surrounded by a garden terrace, this conservatively decorated hotel offers good value. Here, 12 rooms have minibars, 25 contain TVs, and 4 are air-conditioned. The hotel also has a good restaurant, serving meals daily beginning at 90 F ($16.20). It also has a swimming pool.

MERCURE ALTEA ORANGE, 80, route de Caderousse, 84100 Orange. Tel. 90-34-24-10. Fax 90-34-85-48. 99 rms (all with bath). MINIBAR TV TEL

$ Rates: 430 F ($77.40) single; 530 F ($95.40) double. Breakfast 52 F ($9.30) extra. AE, DC, MC, V. **Parking:** 30 F ($5.40).

This is a comfortable modern hotel outside the edge of the city. Its well-furnished rooms are arranged around a series of gardens, the largest of which contains an outdoor swimming pool. Fixed-price menus in the restaurant begin at 120 F ($21.60).

WHERE TO DINE

PARVIS, 3, cours Pourtoules. Tel. 90-34-82-00.
   Cuisine: FRENCH. **Reservations:** Required.

$ Prices: Appetizers 60–145 F ($10.80–$26.10); main dishes 60–115 F ($10.80–$20.70); fixed-price menus 98 F ($17.60) and 192 F ($34.50). AE, DC, MC, V.

Open: Lunch Tues–Sun noon–2:30pm; dinner Tues–Sat 7–9:30pm. **Closed:** Jan 16–Feb 1 and Nov 17–Dec 3.

Jean-Michel Berengier sets the best table in Orange. He bases his cuisine on the fresh products of the season, using not only well-selected vegetables but also the best ingredients from "mountain or sea." Try his escalope of braised sea bass with fennel or feuilleté of asparagus. Service is efficient and polite. A special children's menu is offered for 60 F ($10.80).

NEARBY ACCOMMODATIONS

CHATEAU DE ROCHEGUDE, 26790 Rochegude. Tel. 75-04-81-88. Fax 75-04-89-87. 25 rms (all with bath), 4 suites. A/C MINIBAR TV TEL **Directions:** Take the D976 toward Gap for nine miles.

$ Rates: 500–1,500 F ($90–$270) single; 650–1,500 F ($117–$270) double; 1,800–2,500 F ($324–$450) suite. Breakfast 80 F ($14.40) extra. AE, DC, MC, V. **Parking:** Free. **Closed:** Jan–Feb.

At Rochegude, a hamlet of 1,000 people, 21 miles north of Orange, this magnificent Relais & Châteaux stands in its own 20 acres of parkland. The stone castle is located at the edge of a hill, surrounded by Rhône vineyards. Throughout its history this 11th-century turreted residence has been renovated by a series of distinguished owners, ranging from the pope to the dauphin. The current owners have made many 20th-century additions as well, but ancient touches, such as the Roman dungeon, still survive.

The furnishings and decor throughout the hotel are outstanding. Each of the bedrooms is done in a period, such as Napoléon III or Louis XVI. Some rooms have tapestries, some are mirrored, and others are adorned with gilt, crystal, and fine carpeting. The bathrooms are deluxe as well.

Dining/Entertainment: The food and service are exceptional. You can enjoy meals surrounded by flowering plants in the stately dining room. There are also a barbecue by the swimming pool and sunny terraces where refreshments are served. In the restaurant, fixed-price menus cost 190 F ($34.20) at weekday lunches; other menus (available at both lunch and dinner) cost 250–450 F ($45–$81).

Facilities: Marble swimming pool, tennis courts.

HOSTELLERIE LE BEFFROI, rue de l'Evêché, 84110 Vaison-la-Romaine. Tel. 90-36-04-71. Fax 90-36-24-78. 20 rms (all with bath or shower). MINIBAR TEL

$ Rates: 300–500 F ($54–$90) single; 450–800 F ($81–$144) double. Breakfast 44 F ($7.90) extra. AE, DC, MC, V. **Parking:** Free. **Closed:** End of Nov to mid-Mar.

Located in the old medieval town of Vaison-la-Romaine, 15 miles northeast of Orange, is this charming 16th-century hotel with ocher walls and original detailing. To get to the hotel, you'll have to wind through the cobblestone streets of the old town. For your convenience, the hotel, across from the chiseled fountain in the Haute-Ville sector, maintains a limited number of parking spaces. The rustic interior contains flowered wallpaper, heavy ceiling beams, plaster detailing, and fireplaces. The bedrooms, most with TVs, display 19th-century antiques. There's a garden with a view of the town and a court where you can order meals under a giant fig tree. Fixed-price menus begin at 185 F ($33.30) at dinner or 98 F ($17.60) at lunch, and the restaurant is closed Monday, Tuesday, and on Friday at lunch.

---

13. CHATEAUNEUF-DU-PAPE

417 miles S of Paris, 12 miles N of Avignon, 8 miles S of Orange

GETTING THERE Buses run from Avignon. Most visitors arrive by car, however. Head north from Avignon along the Rhône, joining the N7. After passing through Sorgues, turn left onto the D17 toward Châteauneuf-du-Pape (there's a sign).

ESSENTIALS Orientation The center of the village is place du Portail, but the real attractions of the region are its vineyard, its wines, and its famous hotel (see below).

Information The Office de Tourisme is on place du Portail (tel. 90-83-71-08); it's closed in November.

Châteauneuf-du-Pape was built in the 14th century as the Castelgandolfo, or country seat, for the French popes of Avignon. Now in ruins, the "new castle of the pope" lies near the north border of Provence. The castle was built during the term of Pope John XXII, who also had acres and acres of vineyards planted, thereby initiating a regional wine industry. Today, some of the world's finest red wines, as well as a scarce but elegant white wine, still bear its name. Little except a magnificent view remains of the castle, but the cellars have been restored and are used as headquarters for the local wine society, Echansonnerie des Papes.

In the vicinity, there are **14 wineries** that can be visited for wine tastings. A map in **place de la Fontaine,** the main square of the little village of Châteauneuf-du-Pape, which lies below the castle ruins, shows how to find these wineries.

The museum of the **Caves du Père-Anselme** (tel. 90-83-70-07) contains a wine press from the 16th century, plows from the 17th and 18th centuries, an amphora from one century before Julius Caesar, winemakers' tools, barrelmaking equipment, and a tasting cellar. Open daily from 9am to noon and 2 to 6pm. Admission is free.

WHERE TO STAY & DINE

HOSTELLERIE DU CHATEAU DES FINES-ROCHES, route d'Avignon, 84230 Châteauneuf-du-Pape. Tel. 90-83-70-23. Fax 90-83-78-42. 7 rms (all with bath). MINIBAR TV TEL. **Directions:** Take the D17 for 6 miles south from Orange or 12 miles north from Avignon.

$ Rates: 650–850 F ($117–$153) single or double. Breakfast 65 F ($11.70) extra. MC, V. **Parking:** Free. **Closed:** Dec 23–Feb 5.

Set about two miles outside the village of Châteauneuf-du-Pape, this château was built late in the 19th century by local landowners who successfully added dozens of architectural features inspired by the Middle Ages. Named for the smooth rocks found in the soil of its vineyards, the château devotes its huge cellars to the storage of thousands of bottles of local wines and its upper floors to this charming hotel. Bedrooms are handsomely furnished with some antiques, but the restaurant of the establishment is its pièce de résistance. Two generations of the Estevenin family offer menu specialties which might include tournedos with truffles, an *assiette dégustation,* filets of red mullet with rosemary, aiguillette of duckling with peaches, or fisherman's salad with olive oil and lime juice. An impressive and reasonable wine list is offered, including local vintages that are so popular they are consumed here alone and cannot be found elsewhere. Fixed-price lunches cost 195 F ($35.10), 270 F ($48.60), and 330 F ($59.40), and fixed-price dinners go for 270 F ($48.60) and 330 F ($59.40). Food is served Tuesday through Sunday until 9pm. Seating is limited, so make a reservation.

CHAPTER 27

THE FRENCH RIVIERA

It's been called the world's most exciting stretch of beach. The towns, ports, and hamlets of the Riviera are best approached as if on a safari, going from chic St-Tropez in the west to sleepy Menton at the Italian frontier, climbing into the hill towns such as St-Paul-de-Vence when you tire of the sands.

Every habitué has a favorite oasis and will try to convince you of its merits. Some say "Nice is passé." Others maintain that "Cannes is queen." Still others shun both resorts in favor of Juan-les-Pins, and yet another discriminating crowd would winter only at St-Jean/Cap Ferrat. If you have a large bankroll you may prefer Cap d'Antibes, but if money is short you may find companions at the old port of Villefranche. Truth is, there is no best resort. Each place along the Riviera—Beaulieu by the sea or eagle's-nest Eze— offers its unique flavor and special merits. It's a question of taste, and the French Riviera—Stephen Liégeard's "Côte d'Azur" (Azure Coast)—is famous or infamous for catering to every taste.

The coast is steep and rocky in the main, but it's studded with harbors, ports, gambling casinos, and beach resorts. It's a sun-drenched land, with olive groves and vineyards, where if you're Harold Robbins, you can afford a villa. Cactus, eucalyptus, bougainvillea, lemons, almonds, mimosa, wild anemones, oranges, roses, and laurel grow in abundance, at the foot of the last spurs of the alpine chain.

A trail of modern artists attracted to the brilliant light and the setting of the Côte d'Azur have left a rich heritage: Matisse in his chapel at Vence, Cocteau at Menton and Villefranche, Picasso at Antibes (and seemingly everywhere else), Léger at Biot, Renoir at Cagnes, and Bonnard at Le Cannet. The best collection of all is at the Maeght Foundation at St-Paul-de-Vence.

The Riviera's high season used to be winter and spring. Fashion dictated that no one went in the summer. However, with changing tastes, July and August have long been the most crowded months, and reservations are imperative. In summer the average temperature is 75° Fahrenheit. In winter the temperature averages around 49° Fahrenheit, particularly in January, when Nice experiences its coldest weather.

In hotels the choice is perhaps the most varied in the world, ranging from a Belle Époque palace to a stone house in a grape-grower's vineyard in the hills.

WHAT'S SPECIAL ABOUT THE FRENCH RIVIERA

Outstanding Museums

☐ Musée Ile-de-France, at St-Jean, with the collection of the baronne de Rothschild.

☐ The Maeght Foundation, at St-Paul-de-Vence, a distinguished modern art collection.

☐ Matisse Chapel, not a museum, but the artist's final masterpiece, at age 77.

Great Towns/Villages

☐ Roquebrune, a restored medieval hill village.

☐ St-Paul-de-Vence, a fortified hill village favored by artists.

☐ Eze, on a rocky outcrop above the sea.

☐ St-Jean-Cap-Ferrat, a peninsula for the glitterati.

Great Resorts

☐ Monte Carlo/Monaco, the Côte d'Azur at its most glamorous and expensive—with casino action.

☐ Nice, still the reigning resort, but now a little tarnished.

☐ Cannes, for the trappings of high sophistication.

☐ St-Tropez, the *only* place to be if you look like Bardot when she filmed *Et Dieu créa la femme (And God Created Woman)* here.

Events/Festivals

☐ Monte Carlo Motor Rally, in mid- to late January, one of the world's most famous races.

☐ Carnival of Nice, mid- to late February, France's major carnival.

☐ Cannes Film Festival, mid- to late May, a parade of flesh, genius, and dashed hopes.

Beaches

☐ Cannes, with a magnificent sandy beach, at La Croisette; the Carlton Hôtel has the most fashionable strip.

☐ St-Tropez, with sandy beaches running for four miles—all topless, and some bottomless, where exotic hedonism reigns supreme.

The **Corniches of the Riviera,** as depicted in countless films, stretch from Nice to Menton. The Alps drop into the Mediterranean, and roads were carved along the way. The lower road, about 20 miles long, is called the **Corniche Inférieure.** Along this road you'll reach the port of Villefranche, the Cap Ferrat peninsula, Beaulieu, and Cap Martin.

Built between World War I and the beginning of World War II, the Middle Road, or **Moyenne Corniche,** 19 miles long, also runs from Nice to Menton. Winding in and out of tunnels and through mountains, it is spectacular. The highlight of the trip is at mountaintop Eze.

Finally, the **Grande Corniche**—the most spectacular of the roads from Nice to Menton—was ordered built on the ancient Aurelian Way by Napoleon in 1806. La Turbie and Le Vistaëro are the principal targets along the 20-mile stretch which reaches an altitude of more than 1,600 feet at Col d'Eze.

In this chapter we'll explore the Riviera beginning in Menton and ending in St-Tropez.

SEEING THE FRENCH RIVIERA

GETTING THERE   All roads in August, or so it seems, lead to the Riviera. In many ways, that's the worst time to visit, since the Riviera is its most expensive and overcrowded then. Nevertheless, summer remains the most popular time. Actually, the Côte d'Azur is a vacationland for all seasons—it can get cold in January and February, but there are still many sunny days, and fall and spring are ideal.

The quickest way to get there is to fly Air Inter from Paris; some 12 flights leave daily for Nice from Charles-de-Gaulle and Orly airports. There are also flights from London and New York to Nice. Six daily TGV bullet trains make the eight-hour run from Paris to Nice, and another six make the seven-hour journey from Paris to Cannes. There are also overnight trains to Cannes and Nice, with departures from Gare de Lyon in Paris.

At the airport and train terminals, you can rent a car to continue exploring on your own, since getting around the Riviera by train or bus is difficult. However, if you depend on public transportation, make Nice your center.

A SUGGESTED ROUTE Allow at least a week to see the major resorts and attractions. Make Nice your center for Days 1–3. On the second day, drive to St-Paul-de-Vence, taking a side trip to Vence to see the Matisse Chapel. Spend the final day taking in Nice itself. Go to Monte Carlo (Day 4) for the night, perhaps visiting its casino, taking in the villa-studded St-Jean-Cap-Ferrat peninsula scenery on the way. Then head west to Cannes (Days 5 and 6), perhaps spending a morning on the Lerins Islands.

Drive to St-Tropez (Day 7) for an afternoon on the beach and a sampling of its lively nighttime scene.

1. MENTON

596 miles S of Paris, 39 miles NE of Cannes, 5 miles E of Monaco

GETTING THERE By Bus and Train There are good bus and rail connections that make stops at each resort along the Mediterranean coast, including Menton. Many visitors arrive by car along one of the corniche roads. Two trains per hour arrive from Nice (trip time: only 35 minutes), and two trains per hour from Monte Carlo (trip time: only 10 minutes). A local company, Autocars Broch, also runs buses between Nice and Menton, one almost every hour. Likewise, the same frequent bus service is offered between Monte Carlo and Menton.

ESSENTIALS Orientation The main pedestrian walkway is the promenade du Soleil, which parallels the beach and a hysterically busy traffic artery. There's less congestion one block inland, where the grand 19th-century pomp is centered around the casino and the Palais de l'Europe, which contains the tourist office. The Cocteau museum lies beside the quai Napoléon-III, a short walk south of the Old Port. The Vieille-Ville, an old neighborhood of winding Provençal streets, is centered at the northeast end of town, around the parvis St-Michel and the Eglise St-Michel.

Information Contact the Office de Tourisme, Palais de l'Europe, 1, av. Boyer (tel. 93-57-57-00).

It's Italianate more than French. Right at the border of Italy, Menton marks the eastern frontier of the Côte d'Azur. Its climate, incidentally, is considered the warmest on the Mediterranean coast, a reputation that attracts a large, rather elderly British colony throughout the winter. Menton experiences a foggy day every ten years, or so they say. And it doesn't have one puddle of posh the way Cannes or Juan-les-Pins does. For that reason, it is sought out and widely praised by its habitués, many of whom are complaining that more and more visitors are discovering Menton's charms every year.

According to a local legend, Eve was the first to experience Menton's glorious climate. Expelled from the Garden of Eden along with Adam, she tucked a lemon in her bosom, planting it at Menton because it reminded her of her former stamping ground. The lemons still grow in profusion here, and the fruit of that tree is given a position of honor at the Lemon Festival in February. Actually, the oldest Menton visitor may have arrived 30,000 years ago. He's still around—or at least his skull is—in the Municipal Museum (see below).

Don't be misled by all those "palace-hotels" studding the hills. No longer open to

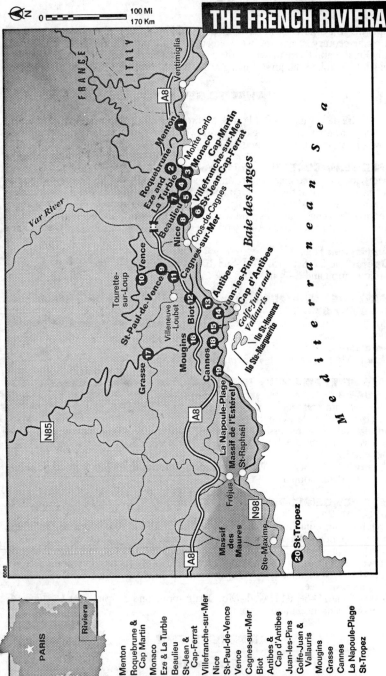

THE FRENCH RIVIERA

1. Menton
2. Roquebrune &
   Cap Martin
3. Monaco
4. Eze & La Turbie
5. Beaulieu
6. St-Jean &
   Cap-Ferrat
7. Villefranche-sur-Mer
8. Nice
9. St-Paul-de-Vence
10. Vence
11. Cagnes-sur-Mer
12. Biot
13. Antibes &
    Cap d'Antibes
14. Juan-les-Pins
15. Golfe-Juan &
    Vallauris
16. Mougins
17. Grasse
18. Cannes
19. La Napoule-Plage
20. St-Tropez

the public, they have been divided and sold as private flats. Many of these turn-of-the-century structures were erected to accommodate elderly Europeans, mainly English and German, who arrived carrying a book written by one Dr. Bennett in which he extolled the joys of living at Menton.

WHAT TO SEE & DO

On the Golfe de la Paix (Gulf of Peace), Menton, which used to belong to Monaco, is on a rocky promontory, dividing the bay in two. The fishing town, the older part with narrow streets, is in the east; the tourist zone and residential belt is in the west.

MUSEE JEAN-COCTEAU, quai Napoléon-III. Tel. 93-57-72-30.

Jean Cocteau liked this resort, and this museum, in a 17th-century fort near promenade du Soleil at the harbor, contains the death portrait of Cocteau sketched by MacAvoy, as well as MacAvoy's portrait of Cocteau. Some of the artist's memorabilia are here—stunning charcoals and watercolors, ceramics, signed letters, and 21 brightly colored pastels. Two Aubusson tapestries based on cartoons by Cocteau are also on display.

Admission: Free.
Open: June 15–Sept 15, Wed–Sun 10am–noon and 3–5pm; off-season, Wed–Sun 10am–noon and 2–6pm.

LA SALLE DES MARIAGES, at the Hôtel de Ville, rue de la République. Tel. 93-57-87-87.

Cocteau painted the frescoes here, which depict, among other things, the legend of Orpheus and Eurydice.

Admission: 10 F ($1.80).
Open: Mon–Fri 8:30am–12:30pm and 1:30–5pm.

MUSEE DE PREHISTOIRE REGIONALE, rue Lorédan-Larchey. Tel. 93-35-84-64.

This museum presents human evolution on the Côte d'Azur for the past million years. There's an emphasis on the prehistoric era, including the head of Grimaldi Man, found in 1884 in the Baousse-Rousse caves. Audiovisual aids, dioramas, and video-cassettes enhance the exhibition.

Admission: Free.
Open: June 15–Sept 15, Wed–Mon 10am–noon and 3–7pm; Sept 16–June 14, Wed–Mon 10am–noon and 2–6pm.

MUSEE DES BEAUX-ARTS, Palais Carnoles, 3, av. de la Madone. Tel. 93-35-49-71.

This museum contains a collection of 14th-, 16th-, and 17th-century paintings from Italy, Flanders, Holland, and the French schools, as well as an exhibition of modern paintings, including works by Dufy, Valadon, Derain, and Leprin—all of which were acquired by a British subject, Wakefield-Mori. Acquisitions of modern art also are displayed biannually.

Admission: Free.
Open: June 15–Sept 15, Wed–Mon 10am–noon and 3–7pm; Sept 16–June 14, Wed–Mon 10am–noon and 2–6pm.

WHERE TO STAY

Moderate

LE DAUPHIN, 28, av. du Général-de-Gaulle, 06500 Menton. Tel. 93-35-76-37. Fax 93-35-31-74. 30 rms (all with bath). TV TEL **Bus:** 3.
$ Rates (including continental breakfast): 240 F ($43.20) single; 490 F ($88.20) double. MC, V. **Parking:** 35 F ($6.30). **Closed:** Oct 20–Dec 20.

Totally rebuilt in 1967, this hotel is just off the beach and has balconies facing the sea. The glistening marble entry hall is inviting. The decor in the soundproof bedrooms is uncluttered, with white walls, floral draperies, and Louis XVI–style chairs and beds.

HOTEL CHAMBORD, 6, av. Boyer, 06500 Menton. Tel. 93-35-94-19. Fax 93-41-30-55. 40 rms (all with bath). A/C MINIBAR TV TEL **Bus:** 4.
$ Rates: 356–415 F ($64.10–$74.70) single; 382–560 F ($68.80–$100.80) double. Breakfast 35 F ($6.30) extra. AE, DC, MC, V. **Parking:** 35 F ($6.30).
Located on the main square next to the casino, this is a clean hotel with rows of balconies and awnings. The streamlined modern bedrooms are colorful. Breakfast is the only meal served.

HOTEL MEDITERRANEE, 5, rue de la République, 06500 Menton. Tel. 93-28-25-25. Fax 93-57-88-38. 90 rms (all with bath). MINIBAR TV TEL **Bus:** 4.
$ Rates: 460 F ($82.80) single; 500 F ($90) double. Breakfast 35 F ($6.30) extra. Children under 4 stay free in parents' room. AE, DC, MC, V. **Parking:** 35 F ($6.30).
This white-and-salmon-colored eight-story hotel, open all year, is three short blocks from the sea. A raised terrace with a view of the water, chaises longues, and potted plants are on the premises. The rooms are attractively decorated and include radios.

HOTEL NAPOLEON, 29, Porte de France, 06503 Menton. Tel. 93-35-89-50. Fax 93-35-49-22. 40 rms (all with bath). A/C MINIBAR TV TEL **Bus:** 4.
$ Rates (including half board): 420–520 F ($75.60–$93.60) per person. AE, DC, MC, V. **Parking:** 35 F ($6.30). **Closed:** Nov–Dec 18.
Built on a palm-tree-shaded avenue, this hotel has its own swimming pool set in a small garden and stone terrace. Furnished with 18th-century English and Italian pieces, the main lounge, which has a bar, is really like a large living room. The bedrooms, decorated in vivid colors, have mahogany furniture and balconies overlooking the sea and the old town. There are a rooftop terrace and an air-conditioned restaurant, entirely refurbished and redecorated. Nonresidents are welcome to visit for lunch or dinner in the hotel's panoramic restaurant on the sixth floor, where meals begin at 150 F ($27).

HOTEL PRINCESS ET RICHMOND, 32, av. du Général-de-Gaulle, 06500 Menton. Tel. 93-35-80-20. Fax 93-57-40-20. 44 rms (all with bath or shower). A/C MINIBAR TV TEL **Bus:** 3.
$ Rates (including continental breakfast): 435 F ($78.30) single; 540 F ($97.20) double. AE, DC, MC, V. **Parking:** 35 F ($6.30).
At the edge of the sea not far from the commercial center, this hotel has a vivid blue-and-white facade with a sunny garden terrace. The owner rents comfortable soundproof rooms with conservative furnishings and private balconies. Drinks are served on the roof's panoramic terrace, where a view of the curving shoreline can be enjoyed. The hotel minibus will pick you up at the train station or the airport, and the staff organizes sightseeing expeditions.

VIKING, 2, av. du Général-de-Gaulle, 06500 Menton. Tel. 93-57-95-85. Fax 93-35-89-57. 34 rms (all with bath). TV TEL **Bus:** 3.
$ Rates: 320–420 F ($57.60–$75.60) single; 370–540 F ($66.60–$97.20) double. Breakfast 40 F ($7.20) extra. AE, DC, MC, V. **Parking:** 45 F ($8.10). **Closed:** Nov–Dec 20.
This 1970s hotel, one block from the beach, offers contemporary Scandinavian comfort and style. Most rooms have tall, wide glass doors that open onto private balconies. Some rooms are air-conditioned but contain no minibar, whereas other rooms have a minibar but no air conditioning. Amenities include a sixth-floor sun terrace, a swimming pool, and a massage room with a sauna.

WHERE TO DINE

LA CALANQUE, 13, square Victoria. Tel. 93-35-83-15.
Cuisine: FRENCH/ITALIAN. **Reservations:** Not required. **Bus:** 4.

$ Prices: Appetizers 28–62 F ($5–$11.20); main dishes 76–138 F ($13.70–$24.80); fixed-price menu 120 F ($21.60). AE, DC, MC, V.
Open: Lunch Thurs–Tues noon–2pm; dinner Thurs–Mon 7:15–9:30pm.
Closed: Nov.

Of the restaurants along the port, this is the best for the budget. In fair weather, tables are set out under shade trees within full view of the harbor. Both French and Italian dishes are offered. I recommend the spaghetti napolitaine, tripe niçoise, soupe de poissons, and fresh sardines (grilled on charcoal and very savory). A specialty of the house is the bouillabaisse. Another delight is barba giuan, small biscuits cooked in olive oil after having been stuffed with a variety of local greens similar to spinach. If the weather forbids al fresco dining, find a table inside, where it's pleasantly decorated in the style of a provincial inn.

PETIT PORT, 1, place Fontana. Tel. 93-35-82-62.
   Cuisine: FRENCH. **Reservations:** Recommended.
$ Prices: Appetizers 30–55 F ($5.40–$9.90); main dishes 90–150 F ($16.20–$27); fixed-price menus 95–140 F ($17.10–$25.20). AE, MC, V.
   Open: Lunch Thurs–Tues noon–3pm; dinner Thurs–Tues 7pm–midnight.
Small and charming, cutting costs by employing many members of an extended family, this restaurant serves well-prepared portions of fresh fish in a century-old house near the medieval port of Menton (Le Vieux Port). Specialties include grilled sardines (succulent and increasingly difficult to find), fish soup, several different preparations of mussels, several kinds of grilled meats, and (in honor of the northern France origins of its owner), tripe in the style of Caen. The place prides itself on its location—less than a mile from the Italian border.

ROCAMADOUR, 1, square Victoria. Tel. 93-35-76-04.
   Cuisine: FRENCH. **Reservations:** Recommended. **Bus:** 4.
$ Prices: Appetizers 55–100 F ($9.90–$18); main dishes 95–115 F ($17.10–$20.70). AE, DC, MC, V.
   Open: Lunch Tues–Sun noon–2pm; dinner Tues–Sun 7–9:30pm. **Closed:** Nov.
This especially pleasant restaurant overlooks the port. You dine at tables set under a canopy where colored lights are turned on at night. Some specialties offered by the chef are from the Périgord region, including foie gras.

2. ROQUEBRUNE & CAP MARTIN

Roquebrune: 592 miles S of Paris, 3 miles W of Menton
Cap Martin: 3 miles W of Menton, 1½ miles W of Roquebrune

GETTING THERE   By Train and Bus   Cap Martin has train and bus connections from the other cities of the Mediterranean coast, including Nice and Menton. To reach Roquebrune, you'll have to take a taxi or bus from the station at Cap Martin or Menton.

ESSENTIALS   Information   The Office de Tourisme is located at 20, av. Paul-Doumer in Roquebrune (tel. 93-35-62-87).

Roquebrune, along the Grande Corniche, is a charming little mountain village with vaulted streets. The only one of its kind, the **Château de Roquebrune** (tel. 93-35-07-22) was originally a 10th-century Carolingian castle. The present structure dates in part from the 13th century. Characterized by two square towers, it houses a historical museum. From the towers, there's a spectacular view along the coast to Monaco. The castle gates are open every day from 10am to noon and 2 to 6pm; admission is 10 F ($1.80) for adults and 6 F ($1.10) for children.

Three miles west of Menton, **Cap Martin** is a satellite of the larger resort. It has long been associated with the wealthy and the famous, ever since the Empress Eugénie wintered here in the 19th century. In time, the resort was honored by the presence of

Sir Winston Churchill. Don't go there thinking you'll find a wide, sandy beach. You'll encounter plenty of rocks, against a backdrop of pine and olive trees.

WHERE TO STAY

HOTEL VICTORIA ET DE LA PLAGE, 7, promenade Cap-Martin, 06190 Roquebrune/Cap Martin. Tel. 93-35-65-90. Fax 93-28-27-02. 32 rms (all with bath). A/C TV TEL

$ **Rates:** 420 F ($75.60) single; 550 F ($99) double. Breakfast 35 F ($6.30) extra. AE, DC, MC, V. **Parking:** 50 F ($9). **Closed:** Jan 5–Feb 5.

This rectangular building constructed in the mid-'60s is set behind a garden across from the sea. The well-furnished bedrooms have air conditioning or ventilation and hairdryers. You can have a drink at the bar decorated with a sweeping mural of the Alps. Breakfast is the only meal served.

VISTA PALACE HOTEL, Grande Corniche, 06190 Roquebrune/Cap Martin. Tel. 92-10-40-00. Fax 93-35-18-94. 42 rms (all with bath), 26 suites. A/C MINIBAR TV TEL

$ **Rates:** 950–1,200 F ($171–$216) single; 1,100–1,500 F ($198–$270) double; 1,300–4,000 F ($234–$720) suite. Breakfast 100 F ($18) extra. AE, DC, MC, V. **Parking:** 90 F ($16.20).

For years, stopping here has been one of the highlights of driving along the Grande Corniche. This extraordinary hotel and restaurant stands on the outer ridge of the mountains that runs parallel to the coast. Featured in many films, the "airplane view" of Monaco is spectacular. Equally imposing is the design of the Vista Palace: Three levels are cantilevered out into space so that every room seems to float. Descending to the lower lounges and rooms, you reach a large reflecting pool surrounded by subtropical plants and flowers. Nearly all the bedrooms have balconies facing the Mediterranean, and all have individual safes. This deluxe hotel is 1,000 feet high.

Dining/Entertainment: If you don't want to stay here, at least consider stopping for lunch or dinner—it's expensive but worth it. Le Vistaero is open daily from 12:15 to 2:15pm and 8 to 10pm; three fixed-price menus are available, at 200 F ($36), 300 F ($54), and 550 F ($99).

Facilities: Swimming pool, Corniche Club, sauna, solarium, massage, Turkish bath, body-building equipment, indoor squash court, fitness center, free shuttle service to Monte Carlo.

WHERE TO DINE

AU GRAND INQUISITEUR, 18, rue du Château. Tel. 93-35-05-37.
    Cuisine: FRENCH. **Reservations:** Required.
$ **Prices:** Appetizers 50–105 F ($9–$18.90); main dishes 80–175 F ($14.40–$31.50); fixed-price menus 140 F ($25.20) and 230 F ($41.40). MC, V.
    Open: Mid-Oct to May, lunch Tues–Sun noon–1:30pm; dinner Tues–Sun 7:30–10pm. June to mid-Oct, dinner only, Tues–Sun 7:30–10pm. **Closed:** Early Nov to Dec 25 and two weeks in mid-Mar.

This culinary find is a miniature restaurant in a two-room cellar (actually an old converted sheep pen) near the top of the medieval mountaintop village of Roquebrune. On the steep, winding road to the château, this building is made of rough-cut stone, with large oak beams. Every nook is crammed with bric-a-brac, pewter plates, and copper utensils. Sixteenth-century music contributes to the atmosphere. The restaurant is run by a French couple; the husband has been a professional cook since he was 14 years old, and his English-speaking wife runs the dining room. The cuisine depends on the season, as they rely on fresh produce. For example, in summer they offer squash blossoms stuffed with morels.

HIPPOCAMPE, 44, av. Winston-Churchill. Tel. 93-35-81-91.
    Cuisine: FRENCH. **Reservations:** Required.
$ **Prices:** Appetizers 80–160 F ($14.40–$28.80); main dishes 120–150 F ($21.60–$27); fixed-price menus 180 F ($32.40) and 120 F ($21.60). AE, MC, V.

Open: Lunch Tues–Sun noon–1:45pm; dinner Tues–Wed and Fri–Sat 7:30–9:30pm. **Closed:** Jan 6–25, May 1–17, and Oct–Nov 1.

Built and established in 1963, this fine restaurant along the seafront has a full view of the bay and even the Italian coastline. Made safe by a thick stone wall, a terrace is shaded by five crooked pine trees. The "Sea Horse" is a stone-and-glass garden house with a tile roof and scarlet and pink potted geraniums. Specialties include filets de sole en brioche, coq au vin, terrine of salmon in a basil sauce, and duck with peaches.

---

3. MONACO

593 miles S of Paris, 11 miles E of Nice

GETTING THERE   Monaco has rail, bus, and highway connections from other coastal cities, especially from Nice. Trains arrive every 30 minutes from Cannes, Nice, Menton, and Antibes. There are no border formalities for anyone entering Monaco from mainland France.

ESSENTIALS Orientation   Monaco is divided into the ornate 19th-century neighborhood around the Grand Casino in Monte Carlo, and the medieval city of Monaco-Ville. They lie north and south, respectively, of the port and are linked by a complicated series of access roads. The seaside residential neighborhood between Monaco-Ville and Monte Carlo is La Condamine. Wherever you go within the principality, the roads will be steep, complicated, and filled with blind turns, so be careful when driving. Parking is almost impossible, so many visitors simply take taxis.

Information   Contact the Direction du Tourisme, 2A, bd. des Moulins, Monte Carlo (tel. 93-30-87-01).

SPECIAL EVENTS   For car-racing fans, there's the Rallye and Grand Prix in May.

The outspoken Katharine Hepburn once called it "a pimple on the chin of the south of France." She wasn't referring to the principality's lack of beauty but rather to the preposterous idea of having a little country, a feudal anomaly, taking up some of the choicest coastline along the Riviera. Hemmed in by France on three sides and facing the Mediterranean, Monaco staunchly maintains its independence. Even Charles de Gaulle couldn't force Prince Rainier to do away with his tax-free policy. As almost everybody in an overburdened world knows by now, the Monégasques do not pay taxes. Part of their country's revenue comes from tourism and gambling.

Monaco, or rather its capital of Monte Carlo, has for a century been a symbol of glamour. Its legend was further enhanced by the marriage in 1956 of the world's most eligible bachelor, Prince Rainier, to an American film star, Grace Kelly. She met the prince when she attended the Cannes Film Festival to promote the Hitchcock movie she made with Cary Grant, *To Catch a Thief*. A daughter, Caroline, was born to the royal couple in 1957; a son, Albert, in 1958; and finally a second daughter, Stephanie, in 1965. The Monégasques welcomed the birth of Caroline but went wild at the birth of Albert, a male heir. According to a treaty drawn up in 1918, Monaco would become an autonomous state under French protection should the ruling dynasty become extinct.

At the time of writing, there is speculation that Prince Rainier will turn his tiny realm over to his son, Albert, following the tragic accidental death of Princess Grace. Her sports car plunged over a cliff, killing her instantly, and the Monégasques still mourn her death.

Monaco became a property of the Grimaldi clan, a Genoese family, as early as 1297. With shifting loyalties, it has maintained something resembling independence ever since. In a fit of impatience, the French annexed it in 1793, but the ruling family

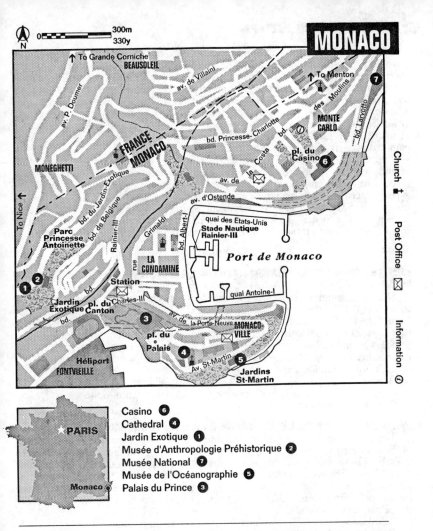

MONACO

Casino ⑥
Cathedral ④
Jardin Exotique ①
Musée d'Anthropologie Préhistorique ②
Musée National ⑦
Musée de l'Océanographie ⑤
Palais du Prince ③

recovered it in 1814, although the prince at the time couldn't bear to tear himself away from the pleasures of Paris for "dreary old Monaco."

WHAT TO SEE & DO

The second-smallest state in Europe (Vatican City is the tiniest), Monaco consists of the old town, **Monaco-Ville,** sitting on a promontory, the Rock, 200 feet high—the seat of the royal palace and the government building, as well as the Oceanographic Museum (see below). On the west of the bay, **La Condamine,** the home of the Monégasques, is at the foot of the old town, forming its harbor and port sector.

Up from the port (walking is steep in Monaco) is **Monte Carlo,** once the playground of European royalty and still the center for the wintering wealthy, the setting for the casino and its gardens and the deluxe hotels, such as the Hôtel de Paris. The fourth part of Monaco, **Fontvieille,** is an industrial suburb, surprisingly neat; but this entire principality is kept tidy.

Ironically, **Monte-Carlo Beach** (about which more below), at the far frontier, is on French soil. It attracts a chic, well-heeled crowd, including movie stars in bikinis so perishable they would disappear should they get wet. The resort consists of a freshwater swimming pool, an artificial beach, and a sea-bathing establishment.

No one—just no one—used to go to Monaco in the summer. That has totally changed now—in fact, July and August tend to be so crowded that it's hard to get a room. Further, with the decline of royalty and multimillionaires, Monaco is developing a broader base of tourism (you can live there moderately, as you'll see from some of my restaurant and hotel recommendations). But it is misleading to suggest that you can live there cheaply. The Monégasques very frankly court the affluent visitor. You can also lose your shirt. "Suicide Terrace" at the casino, although not used as frequently as in the old days, is still a real temptation to many who have foolishly gambled away family fortunes.

Life still focuses around the **casino,** which has been the subject of countless legends and the setting for many films. High drama is played to the fullest here. Depending on the era, you might have seen Mata Hari shooting a tsarist colonel with a jewel-encrusted revolver when he tried to slip his hand inside her brassiere to discover her secrets—military, not mammillary. Before his death, King Farouk, known as "The Swine," used to devour as many as eight roast guinea hens and 50 oysters before losing thousands of dollars at the table. *Chacun à son goût.*

Attractions

LES GRANDS APPARTEMENTS DU PALAIS, place du Palais. Tel. 93-25-18-31.

During the summer, most visitors—many over from Nice just for the day—want to see the Italian-style home of Monaco's royal family, dominating the principality from "The Rock." Visitors are shown the Throne Room and allowed to see some of the royal family's art collection, including works by Brueghel and Holbein. The palace was originally built in the 13th century, and part of it dates from the Renaissance era. The ideal time to arrive is at 11:55am to watch the changing of the guard; it's a 10-minute show.

Admission: 25 F ($4.50) adults, 12 F ($2.20) children.
Open: June–Sept, daily 9:30am–6:30pm; Oct, daily 10am–5pm.
Closed: Nov–May.

JARDIN EXOTIQUE, bd. du Jardin-Exotique. Tel. 93-30-33-65.

The Exotic Garden was built on the side of a rock and is known for its collection of cacti. The gardens were begun by Prince Albert I, who was both a naturalist and a scientist. He spotted some succulents growing in the palace gardens. Knowing that these plants were normally found only in Central America or Africa, he created the garden from them. You can also explore the **grottoes** in this garden, as well as a **Museum of Prehistoric Anthropology** (tel. 93-15-80-06). From here, the view of the principality is splendid.

Admission: 40 F ($7.20) adults, 28 F ($5) children 6–18.
Open: June–Sept, daily 9am–7pm; Oct–May, daily 9am–noon and 2–6pm.

MUSEE DE L'OCEANOGRAPHIE, av. St-Martin. Tel. 93-15-36-00.

This major attraction of Monaco was founded by Prince Albert, the great-grandfather of the present prince. In the main rotunda is a statue of Albert in his favorite costume—that of a sea captain. Displayed are specimens he collected during 30 years of expeditions aboard his oceanographic boats. The aquarium—one of the finest in Europe—contains more than 90 tanks.

Prince Albert's collection is exhibited in the zoology room. Some of the exotic life he brought up were unknown species before he captured them. You'll see models of the oceanographic ships, aboard which the prince directed his scientific cruises from 1885 to 1914. Prince Albert's last cruises were on board the *Hirondelle II.* The most important part of its laboratory has been preserved and reconstituted as closely as possible. The cupboards contain all the equipment and documentation necessary for a scientific expedition.

Skeletons of specimens are exhibited on the main floor, such as a giant whale that drifted ashore at Pietra Ligure in September 1896—it's believed to be the same that was harpooned by the prince in May of that year. The skeleton is remarkable for its healed fractures sustained when a vessel struck the animal as it was drifting asleep on the surface. An exhibition devoted to the "Discovery of the Ocean" is in the physical-oceanography room on the first floor. In addition, underwater movies are shown continuously in the lecture room.

Admission: 50 F ($9) adults, 25 F ($4.50) children 6–18.

Open: July–Aug, daily 9am–9pm; Sept–June daily 9am–7pm.

MUSEE DU PALAIS PRINCIER [Palace Museum] (Souvenirs Napoléoniens et Collection d'Archives), place du Palais. Tel. 93-25-18-31.

In a wing of the palace, the Palace Museum contains a collection of mementos of Napoléon and of Monaco itself. When the royal residence is closed, this museum is the only part of the palace that remains open to the public.

Admission: 18 F ($3.20) adults, 9 F ($1.60) children.

Open: Early June to Sept, daily 9:30am–6:30pm; first three weeks of Oct, daily 10am–5pm; early Dec to early June, Tues–Sun 10:30am–12:30pm and 2–5pm.

Closed: Nov.

MUSEE NATIONAL [National Museum], 17, av. Princesse-Grace. Tel. 93-30-91-26.

Another fun museum for children, this features "automatons and dolls of yesterday," along with sculptures in the rose garden. In a villa designed by Charles Garnier, this museum is said to house one of the world's greatest collections of mechanical toys and dolls. See especially the Neapolitan crib from the 18th century, which contains some 200 figures. This collection, assembled by Madame de Galea, was presented to the principality in 1972; it stemmed from the 18th- and 19th-century trend of displaying new fashions on doll models.

Admission: 26 F ($4.70) adults, 16 F ($2.90) children 6–16.

Open: Easter–Sept, daily 10am–6:30pm; Oct–Easter, daily 10am–12:15pm and 2:30–6:30pm.

Daytime Swimming

MONTE-CARLO BEACH HOTEL, av. Princesse-Grace, Monte-Carlo Beach. Tel. 93-78-21-40.

On French soil, Monte-Carlo Beach adjoins the Monte-Carlo Beach Hôtel. The beach club becomes an integral part of the social life of Monaco (especially for the international set). In addition to the artificial beach, there are two pools, one for children.

STADE NAUTIQUE RAINIER-III, quai Albert-Ier, at La Condamine. Tel. 93-15-28-75.

Built to overlook the yacht-clogged harbor, this stupendous pool frequented by Monégasques was a gift from the prince to his loyal subjects.

Admission: 20 F ($3.60).

Open: July–Aug, daily 9am–midnight; Mar–June and Sept–Nov daily 9am–6pm.

Closed: Dec–Feb.

WHERE TO STAY

Very Expensive

HERMITAGE, square Beaumarchais, 98005 Monaco CEDEX. Tel. 92-16-40-00. Fax 93-50-82-06. 240 rms (all with bath), 25 suites. A/C MINIBAR TV TEL

Bus: 1 or 2.

$ Rates: 1,100–2,300 F ($198–$414) single; 1,400–2,700 F ($252–$486) double; from 5,600 F ($1,008) suite. Breakfast 140 F ($25.20) extra. AE, DC, MC, V.

Parking: 140 F ($25.20).

Picture yourself sitting in a wicker armchair, being served drinks in a Belle Epoque rotunda under an ornate stained-glass dome with an encircling wrought-iron balcony of trailing ivy. This is the setting of the Hermitage. The "palace" was the creation of Jean Marquet (who created marquetry—wood inlaid with a different-colored wood, shell, or ivory). Just a few minutes from the casino, clinging to the edge of a clifftop, this hotel has views of the harbor of yachts and the royal palace. Large brass beds are in the bedrooms, where decoratively framed doors open onto balconies. High-season rates are charged during Christmas, New Year's, Easter, July, and August.

Dining/Entertainment: The stylish Belle Epoque dining room has Corinthian columns, potted palms, and glittering chandeliers. Fixed-price menus begin at 310 F ($55.80). The Bar Scorpion is a chic rendezvous spot that at night is a piano bar.

HOTEL DE PARIS, place du Casino, 98000 Monaco. Tel. 92-16-30-00. Fax 93-25-59-17. 206 rms (all with bath), 41 suites. A/C MINIBAR TV TEL **Bus:** 1 or 2.
$ Rates: 2,600 F ($468) single; 2,900 F ($522) double; from 5,600 F ($1,008) suite. Breakfast 140 F ($25.20) extra. AE, DC, MC, V. **Parking:** 120 F ($21.60).

Located on the main plaza of Monte Carlo, opposite the casino, this is one of the most famous hotels in the world. It opened in 1865. At least two dozen movie companies have used this lobby as a background.

The ornate facade has marble pillars, and the impressive lounge has an art nouveau rose window at the peak of the dome. The hotel is furnished with a dazzling decor of marble pillars, statues, crystal chandeliers, sumptuous carpets, Louis XVI chairs, and a wall-size fin-de-siècle mural. Bedrooms are stylish and fashionable and, in many cases, sumptuous.

Dining/Entertainment: The evening usually begins in the bar, which combines a paneled ceiling with a baroque gilt bas-relief carving. On top of the Hôtel de Paris, the Louis XIV royal-galley–style Le Grill has an impressive sliding roof. While dining you can watch the arrival and departure of the world's greatest yachts. In addition to the distinguished cuisine, the hotel has a collection of rare and fine wines kept in a dungeon chiseled out of the rocks—a honeycomb of passageways with racked bottles. In Le Grill, a complete meal begins at 500 F ($90). The elegant Le Louis XV is recommended under "Where to Dine," below.

Facilities: Boutiques, beauty parlor, natural-pine Finnish sauna; "Des Terrasses"—perhaps the most spectacular indoor swimming pool on the coast.

MONTE-CARLO BEACH MOTEL, av. Princesse-Grace, Monte-Carlo Beach, 06190 Roquebrune/Cap Martin. Tel. 93-28-66-66. Fax 93-78-14-18. 44 rms (all with bath). A/C MINIBAR TV TEL
$ Rates: 2,300–2,500 F ($414–$450) single or double. Breakfast 140 F ($25.20) extra. AE, DC, MC, V. **Parking:** 130 F ($23.40). **Closed:** Oct 11–May 18.
Despite its name, this hotel is located in France, not in Monaco. Built in 1928, it was known for years as the "Old Beach Hotel" until the Société des Bains de Mer decided that that was too unglamorous a title for such a luxury retreat. Tons of money later, it emerged with a new name and vastly improved rooms and facilities. The most pampered guest always asks for the most beautiful accommodation in the house, the spacious circular unit above the lobby. Eva Peron stayed here in 1947 during her infamous tour of Europe, and Princess Grace came here almost every day to paddle around the pool, a rendezvous point for the rich and beautiful people. The well-furnished bedrooms have radios. Although Roquebrune/Cap Martin is its postal address in France, the hotel is located not there but at the border of Monaco.

Expensive

HOTEL MIRABEAU, 1, av. Princesse-Grace, 98000 Monaco. Tel. 92-16-65-65. Fax 93-50-84-85. 99 rms (all with bath), 4 suites. A/C MINIBAR TV TEL **Bus:** 1 or 2.
$ Rates: 1,500 F ($270) single; 2,000 F ($360) double; from 4,000 F ($720) suite. Breakfast 135 F ($24.30) extra. AE, DC, MC, V. **Parking:** 115 F ($20.70).
This attractive hotel at the edge of the sea is next to the Monte Carlo Casino. It has a courtyard filled with plants, terraces, and well-decorated bedrooms. Because of its height, the hotel is a landmark in the area.

Dining/Entertainment: La Coupole, ranked as one of the best restaurants on the Côte d'Azur, is capped with a glass canopy and has a fashionable bar.

Facilities: Garage, swimming pool.

LOEWS MONTE-CARLO, 12, av. des Spélugues, 98007 Monaco CEDEX. Tel. 93-50-65-00. Fax 93-30-01-57. 600 rms (all with bath), 35 suites. A/C MINIBAR TV TEL **Bus:** 1 or 2.

$ Rates: 2,100 F ($378) single; 2,400 F ($432) double; from 3,500 F ($630) suite. Breakfast 115 F ($20.70) extra. AE, DC, MC, V. **Parking:** 100 F ($18).

Loews lies in the heart of Monte Carlo, directly below the terraces that support the resort's famous casino, on one of the most valuable pieces of real estate along the Côte d'Azur. Considered architecturally daring when it was completed in 1975 (some of its foundations were sunk directly into the seabed, and some of the principality's busiest highways roar beneath it) the resort is now viewed as an integral and much-appreciated enhancement of Monégasque life. It contains the highest concentration of restaurants, bars, and nightclubs in Monaco, with a flavor somewhat like that of Las Vegas with a Gallic accent. Many celebrities have been attracted to the hotel, including Walter Cronkite and Peter Ustinov. Even Prince Albert and Princess Stephanie show up for regular workouts in the seventh-floor health club. The rooms in this entertainment extravaganza are tastefully furnished and comfortable and have sweeping panoramic views. The cavernous casino, with its slot-machine "annex" on the seventh floor, has all any gambler could ask for.

Dining/Entertainment: The drinking facilities include a sunny Tahitian lobby bar with a view of the water and the more intimate Jockey Club. A pampas-type restaurant, L'Argentin, serves South American–style grilled meats and succulent fish. There is also a formal gourmet restaurant, Le Foie Gras, for cozy suppers. The informal and nautical Le Café de la Mer is for breakfasts, snacks, and light meals. Near the rooftop, Le Pistou re-creates the flavors of Provence. Guests also enjoy the regular cabaret.

Facilities: Tennis, golf, deep-sea fishing, sailing, and scuba diving are some of the sports that can be arranged at the Monte Carlo Country Club and the Monte Carlo Yacht Club.

LE METROPOLE PALACE, 4, av. de la Madone, 98000 Monaco. Tel. 93-15-15-15. Fax 93-25-24-44. 98 rms (all with bath), 30 suites. A/C MINIBAR TV TEL. **Bus:** 1 or 2.

$ Rates: 1,400 F ($252) single; 1,950 F ($351) double; 2,500 F ($450) suite. Breakfast 100 F ($18) extra. AE, DC, MC, V. **Parking:** 100 F ($18).

In the heart of Monaco near casino square, this hotel was rebuilt on the site of the original Metropole, on Monte Carlo's "golden square." The hotel is superb in every way and has an array of handsomely furnished and beautifully decorated bedrooms spread across six floors. Each room includes a radio, hypoallergenic pillows, a hairdryer, and a full line of toiletries.

Dining/Entertainment: The upscale restaurant is Les Ambassadeurs.

Services: Same-day and overnight laundry, valet service, babysitting, 24-hour room service.

Facilities: Heated seawater swimming pool.

Moderate

BALMORAL, 12, av. de la Costa, 98006 Monaco. Tel. 93-50-62-37. Fax 93-15-08-69. 77 rms (all with bath or shower), 2 suites. MINIBAR TV TEL **Bus:** 1 or 2.

$ Rates: 400–600 F ($72–$108) single; 550–850 F ($99–$153) double; 1,200–1,500 F ($216–$270) suite. Breakfast 55 F ($9.90) extra. AE, DC, MC, V. **Parking:** 70 F ($12.60).

This hotel was built in 1898 by the grandfather of the present owner, Jacques Ferreyrolles. Located on a cliff halfway between the casino and the Royal Palace, it overlooks the yacht harbor. There are eight floors of bedrooms and lounges with sea views. The little lounge has many family antiques as well as subtle additions that have been made over the years. The bedrooms, 50 of which are air-conditioned, are like the public rooms—homelike, immaculate, and quiet. The Balmoral is so inviting that guests often extend their stays.

HOTEL ALEXANDRA, 33, bd. Princesse-Charlotte, 98000 Monaco. Tel. 93-50-63-13. Fax 92-16-06-48. 56 rms (all with bath or shower). A/C TV TEL **Bus:** 1 or 2.
$ Rates: 650 F ($117) single; 780 F ($140.40) double. Breakfast 50 F ($9) extra. AE, DC, MC, V.

This Belle Epoque hotel is in the center of the business district. Set on a busy street corner, its 19th-century design includes an elegant lobby with high ceilings. The comfortably furnished rooms also have radios.

HOTEL DU LOUVRE, 16, bd. des Moulins, 98000 Monaco. Tel. 93-50-65-25. Fax 93-30-23-68. 34 rms (all with bath). A/C MINIBAR TV TEL **Bus:** 1 or 2.
$ Rates (including breakfast): 600–800 F ($108–$144) single; 750–950 F ($135–$171) double. AE, DC, MC, V. **Parking:** 50 F ($9).

Built like a traditional century-old mansion, this hotel is filled with antique furniture. The rooms are comfortable, carpeted, and unique. Expect to pay higher prices for rooms facing the sea. Breakfast is the only meal served.

Inexpensive

HOTEL COSMOPOLITE, 4, rue de la Turbie, 98000 Monaco. Tel. 93-30-16-95. 24 rms (none with bath). **Bus:** 1, 2, or 4.
$ Rates: 135–160 F ($24.30–$28.80) single; 170–270 F ($30.60–$48.60) double. Breakfast 30 F ($5.40) extra. No credit cards. **Parking:** Free on street, 37 F ($6.70) in the garage.

This 100-year-old hotel is down a set of steps from the train station. Madame Gay Angèle, the English-speaking owner, is proud of her "Old Monaco" establishment. Her more expensive rooms have showers, but the cheapest way to stay here is to request a room without shower—there are adequate facilities in the hallway.

HOTEL DE FRANCE, 6, rue de la Turbie, 98000 Monaco. Tel. 93-30-24-64. 26 rms (all with bath). TEL **Bus:** 1 or 2.
$ Rates: 265 F ($47.70) single; 330 F ($59.40) double; 390 F ($70.20) triple. Breakfast 30 F ($5.40) extra. V. **Parking:** 40 F ($7.20).

Not all Monégasques are rich, as a stroll along this street will convince you. Here is where you'll find some of the cheapest living and eating establishments in the high-priced principality. This 19th-century hotel, located three minutes from the station, has modest furnishings but is clean and comfortable.

WHERE TO DINE
Very Expensive

LE FOIE GRAS, in the Loews Monte-Carlo, 12, av. des Spélugues. Tel. 93-50-65-00.
Cuisine: FRENCH. **Reservation:** Recommended. **Bus:** 1 or 2.
$ Prices: Appetizers 105–315 F ($18.90–$56.70); main dishes 165–360 F ($29.70–$64.80); fixed-price menus 320 F ($57.60) and 390 F ($70.20). AE, DC, MC, V.
Open: Dinner only, daily 7:30–11:30pm.

Le Foie Gras serves exquisitely prepared French food in an elegant turn-of-the-century decor. Specialties include an array of dishes made with the delicately flavored foie gras, from which the restaurant takes its name, as well as sliced veal kidney prepared at tableside, roast turbot with small onions, and roast veal kidney with wild rice. Jackets and ties are mandatory for men.

LE GRILL DE L'HOTEL DE PARIS, place du Casino. Tel. 92-16-30-00.
Cuisine: FRENCH. **Reservations:** Required.
$ Prices: Appetizers 155–265 F ($27.90–$47.70); main dishes 195–385 F ($35.10–$69.30). AE, DC, MC, V.

Open: Lunch daily noon–2:30pm; dinner daily 7:30–10pm. **Closed:** Jan 10–Feb 9.

⭐ There is no more swank address to be seen having dinner than the rooftop of the previously recommended Hôtel de Paris. The view alone is worth the rather expensive food, with the turrets of the fabled casino on one side and the yacht-clogged harbor of Old Monaco on the other. Princess Grace can no longer be seen dining here, of course, but I recently spotted at least three women who looked almost exactly as she did in 1958.

In fair weather and in summer, the ceiling opens to reveal the starry sky. The fine cuisine is backed up with one of the Riviera's finest wine lists, with some 20,000 bottles; the wine cellar is carved out of a rock below. In a soft, elegant atmosphere, an array of temptations is presented to you. Les poissons de la Méditerranée feature the inevitable loup (sea bass) which can be grilled for one or two diners, as can the daurade. Lamb from the Alps is featured in a number of ways, and various beef dishes, such as côte de boeuf du Charolais, also tempt diners.

LE LOUIS XV, in the Hôtel de Paris, place du Casino. Tel. 93-30-23-11.
   Cuisine: FRENCH/ITALIAN. **Reservations:** Recommended. **Bus:** 1 or 2.
$ **Prices:** Appetizers 155–265 F ($27.90–$47.70); main dishes 240–345 F ($43.20–$62.10); fixed-price menus 680–740 F ($122.40–$133.20). AE, DC, MC, V.
   Open: July–Aug, lunch Thurs–Mon noon–2pm; dinner Wed–Mon 8–10pm. Sept–June, lunch Thurs–Mon noon–2pm; dinner Thurs–Mon 8–10pm.

⭐ The arrival of French culinary star Alain Ducasse in this restaurant's kitchen was greeted with enthusiastic acclaim. Located on the lobby level of this five-star hotel, Le Louis XV offers what one critic called "down-home Riviera cooking within a Fabergé egg." Despite the intensely regal trappings (or perhaps as a reaction against them), Ducasse creates a consciously simple cuisine. Everything is light, attuned to the seasons, with an intelligent and modern interpretation of both Provençal and northern Italian dishes. The superb service is known as some of the best in France. Jackets and ties for men are mandatory at dinner.

Expensive

L'ARGENTIN, in the Loews Monte-Carlo, 12, av. des Spélugues. Tel. 93-50-65-00.
   Cuisine: ARGENTINIAN. **Reservations:** Recommended. **Bus:** 1 or 2.
$ **Prices:** Appetizers 55–150 F ($9.90–$27); main dishes 95–175 F ($17.10–$31.50); fixed-price menu 310 F ($55.80). AE, DC, MC, V.
   Open: Dinner daily 7:30pm–1am; late supper daily 1–4:30am.

Conceived with panache by the developers of one of the most imaginative hotels on the Riviera, L'Argentin is unique. One of the largest restaurants in town, it is banked with rows of windows facing the sea and has the most impressive grills anywhere. A team of uniformed chefs tends three blazing fires, from which diners are protected by a thick sheet of glass. The decor was inspired by the Argentinian pampas and has gaucho accessories, such as cowskins draped over banquettes, a trio of South American musicians, and lots of exposed wood. Gamblers appreciate the late-night suppers (with a limited menu) from 1 to 4:30am. Much of the beef is imported from America; menu choices include Texas ribs of pork, a mixed grill called parillada Argentine, sizzling contrefilet or filet steaks, and a Spanish-inspired seafood zarzuela.

RAMPOLDI, 3, av. des Spélugues. Tel. 93-30-70-65.
   Cuisine: FRENCH/ITALIAN. **Reservations:** Required. **Bus:** 1 or 2.
$ **Prices:** Appetizers 55–160 F ($9.90–$28.80); main dishes 140–190 F ($25.20–$34.20). AE, DC, MC, V.
   Open: Lunch daily 12:15–2:30pm; dinner daily 7:30–11:30pm. **Closed:** Nov.

One of the leading independent restaurants, Rampoldi serves some of the finest cuisine in Monte Carlo. Its spirit is more Italian than French, although classic meats of both countries are served in an agreeable setting, at the edge of the Casino Gardens.

Although this is the eating club of "the great," its tabs are not dazzlingly high. First, try the soupe de poissons (fish soup), a house specialty. The fish dishes are universally good, including sole prepared in two different ways and grilled sea bass with fennel (for two people). All the meat dishes are well prepared, including veal kidneys in a madeira sauce. A spectacular finish is the crêpes Suzette.

Moderate

PIZZERIA MONEGASQUE, 4, rue Terrazzani. Tel. 93-30-16-38.

Cuisine: FRENCH/ITALIAN. **Reservations:** Not required. **Bus:** 1 or 2.

$ **Prices:** Appetizers 45–55 F ($8.10–$9.90); pizzas 45–55 F ($8.10–$9.90); main dishes 65–105 F ($11.70–$18.90). AE, MC, V.

Open: Dinner only, Tues–Sat 7:30pm–12:30am.

This luxurious pizzeria is considered the melting pot of Monte Carlo. Almost anyone might arrive—in a Bentley or on a bicycle—even members of the royal family. The owner has grown accustomed to seeing all the follies and vanities of this town pass through his door; he just serves pizzas, fish, and grilled meats to whomever shows up. Specialties include magrêt du canard (duckling), grilled scampi, carpaccio, and tartare of beef.

RESTAURANT DU PORT, quai Albert-Ier. Tel. 93-50-77-21.

Cuisine: ITALIAN. **Reservations:** Recommended.

$ **Prices:** Appetizers 50–140 F ($9–$25.20); main dishes 125–180 F ($22.50–$32.40); fixed-price menus 140 F ($25.50) (lunch Tues–Fri only), and 150–180 F ($27–$32.40). AE, DC, MC, V.

Open: July–Aug, lunch daily noon–2:30pm; dinner daily 8–11pm. Sept–Oct and Dec–June, lunch Tues–Sun noon–2:30pm; dinner Tues–Sun 8–11pm. **Closed:** Nov.

Set in a big-windowed restaurant directly on one of the quays overlooking the old port, this is a formal and elegant restaurant specializing in the cuisines of Italy. Menu items might include a selection of elegant pastas (tagliatelle with smoked salmon and spaghetti with lobster), antipasti, and such meat and fish dishes as filet of beef aux délices, mignon of veal in orange sauce, rack of lamb with Mediterranean herbs, and a full array of Italian and French wines. Dessert? Why not a cassata siciliana? In summer, the restaurant expands onto an outdoor terrace overlooking the yachts of the harbor.

SAM'S PLACE, in the Palais de la Scala, 1, av. Henri-Dunant. Tel. 93-50-89-33.

Cuisine: AMERICAN. **Reservations:** Not required. **Bus:** 1 or 2.

$ **Prices:** Appetizers 35–50 F ($6.30–$9); main dishes 50–90 F ($9–$16.20); fixed-price menu 97 F ($17.50). AE, DC, MC, V.

Open: Lunch Mon–Sat noon–3pm; dinner Mon–Sat 7pm–midnight.

Despite its convincing presentation of the American aesthetic, this place was established years ago by an Englishman. Today, this friendly restaurant/bar attracts those who prefer Texas-style chili con carne, good steaks, a super-hamburger, and french fries. Sam's is a gratifying stopover for lunch, but in the evening it almost turns into a social club, it's so informal. You can also order good, big drinks at the American-style bar.

Inexpensive

LE CAFE DE PARIS, place du Casino. Tel. 92-16-20-20.

Cuisine: INTERNATIONAL. **Reservations:** Not required. **Bus:** 1 or 2.

$ **Prices:** Appetizers: 42–150 F ($7.60–$27); main dishes 90–145 F ($16.20–$26.10). AE, DC, MC, V.

Open: Daily 8am–4am.

If you frequent the Café de la Paix in Paris, you'll gravitate to its counterpart in Monte Carlo. Everyone seems to drop in here at least once a day. Directly opposite the casino and the Hôtel de Paris, the Café de Paris provides a front-row seat to the never-ending spectacle in the "living room" of Monte Carlo. Owned by the Société des Bains de Mer, the café was completely rebuilt in the late 1980s, and a Belle Epoque–style brasserie was created. The Grand Café with its terrace and adjacent bar are still there, as are several boutiques and a Parisian-style "drugstore." One room is devoted to "one-armed bandits." Around six *plats du jour* are offered, and the cuisine is international. A limited supper menu is offered after 2am.

LE TEXAN, 4, rue Suffren-Reymond. Tel. 93-30-34-54.
Cuisine: TEX/MEX. **Reservations:** Recommended. **Bus:** 1 or 2.
$ Prices: Appetizers 25–38 F ($4.50–$6.80); main dishes 55–125 F ($9.90–$22.50); fixed-price lunch 75 F ($13.50). AE, DC, MC, V.
Open: Lunch Mon–Fri noon–2:30pm; dinner Mon–Thurs 7–10:30pm, Fri–Sat 7–11:30pm.

⑤ These Tex/Mex specialties have entertained even the most discriminating French taste buds. There's a handful of outdoor tables, a long bar, a roughly plastered dining room draped with the flag of the Lone Star State, and a scattering of Mexican artifacts. You'll find Le Texan on a sloping residential street leading down to the old harbor—a world away from the glittering casinos and nightlife of the resort's upper reaches. Menu choices include T-bone steak, barbecued ribs, pizzas, nachos, tacos, a Dallasburger (with guacamole), and the best margaritas in town.

EVENING ENTERTAINMENT
The Casinos

LOEWS CASINO, in the Loews Monte-Carlo, 12 av. des Spélugues. Tel. 93-50-65-00.
A huge room adjoining the lobby is filled with the one-armed bandits (slot machines). It features blackjack, craps, and American roulette. Additional slot machines are available on the roof starting at 11am—for those who want to gamble with a wider view of the sea. It's open daily from 4pm to 4am (to 5am for slot machines).
Admission: Free.

MONTE CARLO CASINO, place du Casino. Tel. 92-16-21-21.
★ A speculator, François Blanc, made the Monte Carlo Casino the most famous in the world, attracting Sarah Bernhardt, Mata Hari, Farouk, and Aly Khan (Onassis used to own a part-interest). The architect of the Paris Opéra, Charles Garnier, built the oldest part of the casino, and it remains a fascinating, extravagant example of period architecture. The nostalgia for the past has faded. The new grand dukes are fast-moving international businessmen on short-term vacations. Baccarat, roulette, and chemin-de-fer are the most popular games, although you can play "le craps" and blackjack as well.

Different parts of this famous building open at different times of day. The Salle Americaine, containing only Las Vegas–style slot machines, opens at noon, as do other doors for roulette and "trente-quarente." A section for roulette and chemin-de-fer opens at 3pm. The most sophisticated action begins at 4pm when the full casino swings into action, with more roulette, craps, and blackjack. The gambling continues until very late (or very early, depending on your point of view), the closing depending on the crowd. The casino classifies its "private rooms" those areas not reserved for slot machines. To enter this famous casino, you must carry a passport, be at least 21 years old, and pay an admission of 50–100 F ($9–$18) if you want to enter the private rooms. In lieu of a passport, an identity card or driver's license will suffice.

The foremost winter establishment, under the same ownership, is the **Cabaret in the Casino Gardens.** You can dance to the music of a smooth orchestra. A good cabaret is featured, sometimes with ballet numbers. It is open from mid-September until the end of June, but it's closed Tuesday. From 9pm you can enjoy dinner at a cost of 500–600 F ($90–$108). Drinks ordered separately begin at 150 F ($27). For reservations, call 92-16-36-36.

In the **Salle Garnier** of the casino, concerts are held periodically; for information, contact the tourist office (see "Essentials," above). The music is usually classical, featuring the Orchestre Philharmonique de Monte Carlo.

The casino also contains the **Opéra de Monte-Carlo,** whose patron is Prince

Rainier. This world-famous opera house, opened in 1879 by Sarah Bernhardt, presents a winter and spring repertoire that traditionally includes Puccini, Mozart, and Verdi. The famed Ballets Russes de Monte-Carlo was created here by Diaghilev. The national orchestra and ballet company of Monaco appear here. Tickets may be hard to come by; your best bet is to ask the concierge of your hotel. You can make inquiries about tickets on your own at the Atrium du Casino (tel. 92-16-22-99), which is open Tuesday through Sunday from 10am to 12:30pm and 2 to 5pm. Standard tickets generally cost 500–700 F ($90–$126) each.

Clubs and Bars

LA FOLIE RUSSE, in the Loews Monte-Carlo, 12, av. des Spélugues. Tel. 93-50-65-00.

This is a dinner-dance cabaret combination. Many viewers like its shows much more than those staged at the cabaret of the Monte Carlo casino. Vaudeville acts are thrown in to ease the "monotony" of all those nude dancers. There's a dinner-dance on Friday and Saturday with food served from 8:30 to 9:30pm, and a floor show, *La Folie Russe*, is presented Tuesday through Sunday at 11pm. Jackets for men are mandatory.

Admission: 550 F ($99) show with dinner, 250 F ($45) show only.

LE JOCKEY CLUB BAR, in the Loews Monte-Carlo, 12, av. des Spélugues. Tel. 93-50-65-00.

This elegantly appointed English bar contains a sculptured cherrywood ceiling and original paintings of the horseraces at Vincennes by the Parisian painter André Brasilier. Drinks begin at 60 F ($10.80). It's open daily from 6pm to midnight.

Admission: Free.

NEW JIMMY'S, Sporting d'Eté, av. Princesse-Grace. Tel. 93-25-14-14.

Associated with Régine's, this is the once-favorite see-and-be-seen hot-spot for the rich—and for those who wish they were. It requires the correct allure of dress, comportment, and class. Drinks cost 125 F ($22.50). Open daily from 11pm to 4am.

Admission: Free.

NOROC, rue du Portier. Tel. 93-25-09-25.

The decor glitters in a high-tech gloss, and the clientele is more than 30. Located near the Hôtel Mirabeau, Noroc plays disco music. Drinks begin at 125 F ($22.50). Open daily from 10pm to 4am.

Admission: Free.

---

4. EZE & LA TURBIE

585 miles S of Paris, 7 miles NE of Nice

GETTING THERE   Eze (also known as Eze-Village) is most easily reached by car via the Moyenne (Middle) Corniche road.

ESSENTIALS Orientation   Because many streets are pedestrians-only, park in the lower town and continue on foot. Eze, on the side of a rocky mountain, is not to be confused with Eze-Bord-de-Mer, its beachside suburb, or the Col d'Eze, a nearby mountaintop. La Turbie is 2½ miles northeast of Eze, accessible by a steep and winding road leading to the Upper (Grande) Corniche.

Information   For information, contact the Office de Tourisme, place du Général-de-Gaulle, Eze-Village (tel. 93-41-26-00), which is open March through October.

Reached via the Moyenne (Middle) Corniche, Eze occupies an eagle's-nest perch where once medieval villagers were safe from Corsairs raiding the coast and capturing the young girls for harem duty or the strong men for slaves. You park your car in the little square below, then scale the narrow medieval maze to the top, the streets becoming steps. Ancient stone houses, often occupied by artisans who have restored them to their natural beauty, line the way.

At the top of the hill is the cactus-filled **Jardin Exotique** (tel. 93-41-10-30). It has a spectacular view. It is open daily from 9am to 8pm (closes at dusk in winter). Admission is 10 F ($1.80).

After Eze, a road leads to La Turbie, on the Upper Corniche. At the highest point along the Grand Corniche, 1,500 feet above sea level, stands Emperor Augustus' **Trophy of the Alps.** At the base of the **Tête de Chien** (Head of a Dog), it was erected in 6 B.C. The monument, restored with funds donated by Edward Tuck, was erected by the Roman Senate to celebrate the subjugation of the people of the French Alps. You can visit the **Musée du Trophée des Alps** (tel. 93-41-10-11) from April through September, daily from 9am to 7pm; October through March, daily from 9am to noon and 2 to 4:30pm. Admission is 20 F ($3.60) for adults, 13 F ($2.30) for young people 18–24, and 6 F ($1.10) for children 7–17.

At the **Centre de Rapaces,** year-round bird demonstrations are given daily at 2:30, 3:30, and 4:30pm. Admission to see the trophy and the demonstrations costs 40 F ($7.20) for adults and 28 F ($5) for children. Guests can "get acquainted" with such species as the South American condor, the great African vultures, and several different kinds of eagles, among other feathered friends. At night, from June to September, the trophy is floodlit—it's a striking sight along the Upper Corniche. From the terraces, there's a panoramic view of Monaco.

WHERE TO STAY & DINE

AUBERGE LE SOLEIL, 44, av. de la Liberté, 06360 Eze-Bord-de-Mer. Tel. 93-01-51-46. Fax 93-01-58-40. 10 rms (all with bath). MINIBAR TEL
$ Rates (including half board): 340 F ($61.20) single; 560 F ($100.80) double. **Parking:** 50 F ($9). **Closed:** Mid-Nov to mid-Dec.

This pink stucco villa is a few steps from the Basse-Corniche. It has a quiet rear terrace, and the interior is filled with rattan chairs, exposed brick, and lots of brass. The simply furnished doubles draw mainly a summer crowd, although the inn is open all year. The half-board rate is a good price on the Riviera—especially because the meals are satisfying.

LE CAP ESTEL, 06380 Eze-Bord-de-Mer. Tel. 93-01-50-44. Fax 93-01-55-20. 31 rms (all with bath), 9 suites. A/C MINIBAR TV TEL
$ Rates (including half board): 1,250–1,700 F ($225–$306) per person. MC, V. **Parking:** 50 F ($9). **Closed:** Oct 26–Mar.

At one of the most dramatic points along the Côte d'Azur between Nice and Monte Carlo, Le Cap Estel is on a rocky promontory jutting out into the sea. Just two miles east of Beaulieu, reached along the Lower Corniche, this is a successful reincarnation of a turn-of-the-century seacoast villa built for a princess, now transformed into a luxurious hotel. Below the coast road, Le Cap Estel lies on five acres of terraced, landscaped gardens reached by a sweeping staircase. A heated indoor swimming pool projects out over the waves like the bow of a ship. Exotic birds are kept in cages, mauve petunias add color, and the reflection pool has a spraying fountain and is lit by colored lights at night. Because of its location, all the rooms overlook the sea, and each is near a terrace. Guests can dine inside, on an open-air terrace, or at umbrella tables under the trees. Occasional barbecues and chicken-on-the-spit dinners are featured.

HOSTELLERIE DU CHATEAU DE LA CHEVRE D'OR, rue du Barri, 06360 Eze-Village. Tel. 93-41-12-12. Fax 93-41-06-72. 15 rms (all with bath), 8 suites. A/C TV TEL
$ Rates: 1,200–1,400 F ($216–$252) single; 1,500 F ($270) double; 4,000 F ($720) suite. Breakfast 90 F ($16.20) extra. V. **Parking:** Free. **Closed:** Jan 3–Mar 1.

Not unlike a luxurious converted monastery, this is a miniature village retreat. On the side of a stone medieval village off the Moyenne Corniche, this Relais & Châteaux is a well-preserved complex of village houses, all with views of the coastline. The owner, Pierre de Daeniken, has had the interior of the "Golden Goat" flawlessly decorated to maintain its old character while adding modern comfort. Even if you don't stop in for a meal or a room, try to visit for a drink in the lounge, which has a great view. French doors open onto a terraced swimming pool, and some of the accommodations have private terraces.

Fresh salads and original fruit cocktails are served in the Café du Jardin, which overlooks the Mediterranean. Le Grill du Château is a more traditional French restaurant where you can enjoy grilled fish and meat. The main restaurant is closed Wednesday.

---

5. BEAULIEU

583 miles S of Paris, 6 miles E of Nice, 7 miles W of Monte Carlo

GETTING THERE **By Train** Rail service connects Beaulieu with Nice, Monaco, and the rest of the Côte d'Azur.

By Car Most visitors drive from Nice via the Moyenne Corniche or the coastal highway.

ESSENTIALS Orientation The waterfront is a large marina that berths many yachts. The center of town is place Georges-Clemenceau, and to the south, on the Baie des Fourmis (almost at the border of neighboring Cap Ferrat) is the town's most famous museum, the Villa Kérylos.

Information The Office de Tourisme is on place Georges-Clemenceau (tel. 93-01-02-21).

Protected from the cold north winds that blow down from the Alps, Beaulieu-sur-Mer is often referred to as "La Petite Afrique" (Little Africa). Like Menton, it has the mildest climate along the Côte d'Azur and is especially popular with the wintering wealthy—including, in days gone by, James Gordon Bennett, the founder and editor of the New York *Herald* (he sent Stanley to find Livingstone). Originally, English visitors staked it out, after an English industrialist founded a hotel here between the rock-studded slopes and the sea. Beaulieu is graced with lush vegetation, including oranges, lemons, and bananas, as well as palms.

WHAT TO SEE & DO

The **Beaulieu Casino** fronts **La Baie des Fourmis,** the beautiful gardens that attract the evening promenade crowd.

The **Villa Kérylos,** rue Gustave-Eiffel (tel. 93-01-01-44), is a replica of an ancient Greek residence. It was painstakingly designed and built by an archeologist, Theodore Reinach (1860–1928). Inside, the cabinets are filled with a collection of Greek figurines and ceramics. But most interesting is the reconstructed Greek furniture, much of which would be extremely fashionable today. One curious mosaic depicts the slaying of the minotaur and provides its own labyrinth (if you try to trace the path, expect to stay for weeks). Open in July and August, daily from 3 to 7pm; September to June, Tuesday through Sunday from 2 to 6pm; closed in November. Admission is 20 F ($3.60) for adults, 10 F ($1.80) for children and seniors over 65.

The **golf course** of Mont Agel is 10 minutes from the resort.

WHERE TO STAY

Very Expensive

LE METROPOLE, 15, bd. du Général-Leclerc, 06310 Beaulieu-sur-Mer. Tel. 93-01-00-08. Fax 93-01-18-51. 50 rms (all with bath), 3 suites. A/C TV TEL
$ Rates (including half board): 1,450–1,850 F ($261–$333) per person. AE, MC, V.
Parking: Free. **Closed:** Oct 20–Dec 20.

⭐ This fin-de-siècle private villa offers about the most luxurious living along the Côte d'Azur. It's classified as a Relais & Châteaux. The owners, among them Jean Badrutt, have constructed a large swimming pool at the edge of the rocky coastline and surrounded it with flagstones, palm trees, and parasols. Another part of the grounds contains a manicured grassy area so flat it looks like a putting green on a golf course. The accommodations are glamorously furnished.

LA RESERVE, 5, bd. du Général-Leclerc, 06310 Beaulieu-sur-Mer. Tel. 93-01-00-01. Fax 93-01-28-99. 40 rms (all with bath), 3 suites. A/C MINIBAR TV TEL

$ Rates: 600–1,600 F ($108–$288) single; 800–2,600 F ($144–$468) double; 3,600–5,200 F ($648–$936) suite. Breakfast 120 F ($21.60) extra. AE, DC, MC, V. **Parking:** Free. **Closed:** Nov 9–Dec 20.

⭐ One of the Riviera's most famous hotels, this pink-and-white palace is right on the Mediterranean. A number of the public lounges open onto a courtyard with bamboo chairs, grass borders, and urns of flowers. The social life centers around the main drawing room, which is much like the grand living room of a country estate. The hotel has been rebuilt in stages, so the bedrooms range widely in size and design; however, all rooms are deluxe and individually decorated, and each has a beautiful view of either the mountains or the sea. Half board is required from May to September.

Dining/Entertainment: La Réserve won its acclaim as a "rendezvous of queens and kings" when it was founded as a restaurant by the Lottier family in 1894. The dining room has a coved frescoed ceiling, parquet floors, crystal chandeliers, and picture windows facing the Mediterranean. Specialties include sea bass with thin slices of potatoes in a savory tomato sauce, sea bream stuffed with local vegetables, and roast rack of lamb.

Facilities: Private harbor for yachts, submarine fishing gear, sauna, thalasso-therapy, seawater swimming pool (heated October to May).

Expensive

HOTEL CARLTON RESIDENCE, 7, av. Edith-Cavell, 06310 Beaulieu-sur-Mer. Tel. 93-01-14-70. Fax 93-01-29-62. 33 rms (all with bath). MINIBAR TEL

$ Rates: 675–1,160 F ($121.50–$208.80) single or double. Breakfast 65 F ($11.70) extra. AE, DC, MC, V. **Parking:** 50 F ($9). **Closed:** Oct–Apr 7.

Guests staying here are within 200 yards of the beach and a three-minute walk from the town's tennis courts. This immaculate hotel was originally built in the early 1970s. Most rooms have private balconies or terraces, and all have radios. Twenty rooms are air-conditioned and contain TVs. There's a small garden in back. Breakfast is the only meal served, and there is a bar.

HOTEL FRISIA, bd. Eugène-Gauthier, 06310 Beaulieu-sur-Mer. Tel. 93-01-01-04. Fax 93-01-31-92. 35 rms (26 with bath or shower). MINIBAR TV TEL

$ Rates: 190–210 F ($34.20–$37.80) single without bath or shower; 210–270 F ($37.80–$48.60) double without bath or shower; 440–540 F ($79.20–$97.20) single or double with bath or shower. Breakfast 30 F ($5.40) extra. AE, V. **Closed:** Nov–Dec 20.

Lying just in front of the marina, this small hotel has been owned by the same family since 1907. Its well-furnished bedrooms, decorated in a modern style, most often open onto views of the harbor. English is spoken, and foreign guests are made especially welcome. The hotel has a sunny garden and comfortable, inviting lounges, furnished as in a private home in Provence. Breakfast is the only meal served, but many reasonably priced dining places are within walking distance.

HOTEL LE HAVRE BLEU, 29, bd. du Maréchal-Joffre, 06310 Beaulieu-sur-Mer. Tel. 93-01-01-40. Fax 93-01-29-92. 22 rms (all with bath). TEL

$ Rates: 280 F ($50.40) single; 300 F ($54) double. Breakfast 28 F ($5) extra. MC, V. **Parking:** Free.

This has one of the prettiest facades of any inexpensive hotel in town. Housed in what used to be a private Victorian villa, the hotel has a front garden dotted with flowering urns and arched ornate windows. The bedrooms are impeccable and functional. Breakfast is the only meal served.

HOTEL MARCELLIN, 18, av. Albert-ler, 06310 Beaulieu-sur-Mer. Tel. 93-01-01-69. Fax 93-01-37-43. 21 rms (15 with bath), 1 suite. TEL

$ Rates: 170 F ($30.60) single without bath; 240 F ($43.20) double without bath; 300 F ($54) double with bath; from 500 F ($90) suite. Breakfast 30 F ($5.40) extra. MC. **Parking:** Free.

A good budget selection in an otherwise high-priced resort, the Marcellin rents restored rooms with homelike amenities, each with a southern exposure. The hotel is well run and welcoming and has a little outside terrace. The government has given the Hôtel Marcellin two stars.

WHERE TO DINE

THE AFRICAN QUEEN, Port de Plaisance. Tel. 93-01-10-85.
Cuisine: INTERNATIONAL. **Reservations:** Recommended.
$ Prices: Appetizers 30–80 F ($5.40–$14.40); main dishes 78–200 F ($14–$36); pizzas 44–78 F ($7.90–$14). MC, V.
Open: Daily noon–11:30pm.

Named by its movie-loving founders after the Hollywood classic of the 1950s, this hip and popular restaurant is filled with posters of Hepburn and Bogart and has a jungle-inspired decor of orange and green. Much influenced by restaurants in the United States (its sophisticated maître d'hôtel lived in Miami for six years), it has welcomed such film stars as Jack Nicholson, Raymond Burr, Robert Wagner, and Diana Ross to its premises during their appearances at the nearby film festival in Cannes. Menu specialties include a *dégustation de bouillabaisse,* African curry made with lamb or beef and served like a rijstaffel with about a dozen different condiments, or any of an array of steaks, fish, or shellfish. Less expensive are the seven or eight kinds of pizza, which even visiting Italians claim are very very good. No one will mind if you stop into this place for a strawberry daquiri or a rum-based piña colada, priced at around 45 F ($8.10) each. When it's time to pay the bill, the check will be presented in a videocassette carrying case labeled as—what else?—*The African Queen.*

LA PIGNATELLE, 10, rue de Quincenet. Tel. 93-01-03-37.
Cuisine: FRENCH. **Reservations:** Recommended.
$ Prices: Appetizers 28–85 F ($5–$15.30); main dishes 65–135 F ($11.70–$24.30); fixed-price menus 128–185 F ($23–$33.30). MC, V.
Open: Lunch Thurs–Tues 12:15–1:30pm; dinner Thurs–Tues 7:15–9:30pm.
Closed: Mid-Oct to mid-Nov.

Even in this super-expensive resort, you can still find an excellent and affordable Niçois bistro—La Pignatelle. After all, the locals have to eat somewhere, and not all visitors can afford the high prices of La Réserve and the Métropole. This family-run restaurant, which has a rustic decor, is the most popular dining room in town, and it's usually crowded. Right in the center of Beaulieu, it has a small dining room with a garden. Specialties include the inevitable salade niçoise, soupe de poissons (fish), a cassolette of mussels, fresh lobster, daurade, three kinds of sole, scampi provençal, and tripe niçoise.

6. ST-JEAN & CAP FERRAT

583 miles S of Paris, 6 miles E of Nice

GETTING THERE Most visitors drive or take a taxi from the railway station at nearby Beaulieu. There is also bus service from Nice.

ESSENTIALS Orientation Cap Ferrat is a jagged peninsula jutting southward from the French mainland into the Mediterranean. Although carefully guarded villas and hotels lie scattered across its terrain, its only village is St-Jean, on the eastern edge.

Information The Office de Tourisme is on avenue Denis-Séméria (tel. 93-76-08-90).

It has been labeled Paradise Found. Of all the oases along the Côte d'Azur, no place has the snob appeal of Cap Ferrat. It is a nine-mile promontory sprinkled with luxurious villas, outlined by sheltered bays, beaches, and coves. Vegetation is lush. In the port of St-Jean, the harbor accommodates both yachts and fishing boats.

Somerset Maugham once lived at Cap Ferrat, quite grandly, receiving friends and confiding to them such tidbits as that he hadn't read *Of Human Bondage* since it was published or (in later years) that he longed for death. Leopold II of Belgium once had a villa here (now taken over by the owner of Grand Marnier). Today Brazilian millionaires as well as movie stars (Gregory Peck) own villas along the pine-studded peninsula.

The **Musée Île-de-France,** avenue Denis-Séméria (tel. 93-01-33-09), affords you a chance to visit one of the most legendary villas along the Côte d'Azur. It was built in the Italianate style by the Baroness Ephrussi, a Rothschild. She died in 1934, leaving the building and its magnificent gardens to the Institut de France on behalf of the Académie des Beaux-Arts. According to her reputation, "she pinched everything from all Europe." The wealth of her collection is preserved: 18th-century furniture; Tiepolo ceilings; Savonnerie carpets; screens and panels from the Far East; tapestries from the factories of Gobelins, Aubusson, and Beauvais; original drawings by Fragonard; canvases by Renoir, Sisley, and Boucher; and rare Sèvres porcelain. Covering 12 acres, the gardens contain fragments of statuary from churches, monasteries, and torn-down palaces. One entire section is planted with cacti.

The museum and its gardens are open in July and August, Tuesday through Saturday from 10am to noon and 3 to 7pm, and on Sunday from 2 to 6pm; in September and October and December to June, Tuesday through Saturday from 10am to noon and 2 to 6pm, and on Sunday from 2 to 6pm; closed in November. Admission to the museum and gardens is 30 F ($5.40) for adults and 20 F ($3.60) for children. To visit just the gardens costs 12 F ($2.20).

WHERE TO STAY

Very Expensive

HOTEL BEL AIR DU CAP-FERRAT, bd. du Général-de-Gaulle, 06290 St-Jean-Cap-Ferrat. Tel. 93-76-50-50. Fax 93-76-04-52. 59 rms (all with bath), 11 suites. A/C MINIBAR TV TEL

$ Rates (including continental breakfast): 1,300–4,700 F ($234–$846) single or double; from 4,750 F ($855) suite. AE, DC, MC, V. **Parking:** Free.

⭐ One of the best features of this turn-of-the-century palace is its location—at the tip of the peninsula in the midst of a 12-acre garden of semitropical trees and manicured lawns. Parts of the exterior are pierced with open loggias and big arched windows, and guests enjoy the views from the elaborately flowering terrace over the sea. The bedrooms are conservatively modern with dressing rooms, and rates include admission to the pool, Club Dauphin. The beach is accessible via funicular from the main building. The hotel is open year-round.

Dining/Entertainment: The hotel's indoor/outdoor restaurant serves *cuisine du marché,* which might include a salad of warm foie gras and chanterelles, nage of crayfish and lobster, or breast of duckling with honey-and-cider vinegar. A la carte meals cost 390–500 F ($70.20–$90). The American-style bar opens onto the garden.

Services: 24-hour room service, same-day laundry.

Facilities: Swimming pool, tennis courts.

LA VOILE D'OR, 31, av. Jean-Mermoz, St-Jean-Cap-Ferrat, 06230 Villefranche-sur-Mer. Tel. 93-01-13-13. Fax 93-76-11-17. 50 rms (all with bath), 5 suites. A/C MINIBAR TV TEL

$ Rates (including half board): 3,100–3,210 F ($558–$577.80) for two. No credit cards. **Parking:** Free. **Closed:** Nov–Mar 12.

⭐ "The Golden Sail" is a brilliant tour de force and offers intimate luxury. An antique collector turned hôtelier, Jean R. Lorenzi owns this hotel located at the edge of the little fishing port and yacht harbor, with a panoramic view of the coast. Living at La Voile d'Or is like being a guest at a house party. The bedrooms, the lounges, and the restaurant open onto terraces. The guest rooms are individually decorated with hand-painted reproductions of antiques, carved gilt headboards, baroque paneled doors, parquet floors, antique clocks, and paintings.

Dining/Entertainment: Guests gather on the canopied outer terrace for lunch, and in the evening they dine in the more formal and stately room with Spanish armchairs and white wrought-iron chandeliers. The sophisticated menu offers regional specialties and a few international dishes, as well as the classic French cuisine. The drawing room is richly decorated with hand-loomed fabric-covered sofas and armchairs, Iberian tables, Italian chests, and oil paintings. Most intimate is a little drinking bar, with Wedgwood-blue paneling and antique mirroring.

Facilities: Two swimming pools.

Moderate

BRISE MARINE, av. Jean-Mermoz, St-Jean-Cap-Ferrat, 06230 Ville-franche-sur-Mer. Tel. 93-76-04-36. Fax 93-76-11-49. 16 rms (all with bath). TV TEL

$ Rates: 600 F ($108) single; 655 F ($117.90) double. Breakfast 55 F ($9.90) extra. MC, V. **Closed:** Nov–Jan.

Ⓢ A bargain paradise for so chic a situation, this three-story villa with a front and rear terrace is located on a hillside. A long rose arbor, beds of subtropical flowers, palms, and pines provide an attractive setting. The atmosphere is casual and informal, and the bedrooms are comfortably furnished. Guests have breakfast either in the beamed lounge or under the rose trellis. There's a little corner bar for afternoon drinks.

HOTEL CLAIR LOGIS, 12, av. Centrale, 06230 St-Jean-Cap-Ferrat. Tel. 93-76-04-57. Fax 93-76-11-85. 18 rms (all with bath or shower). TEL

$ Rates: 260–380 F ($46.80–$68.40) single; 350–600 F ($63–$108) double. Breakfast 40 F ($7.20) extra. AE, DC, MC, V. **Parking:** Free. **Closed:** Nov–Dec 15.

Ⓢ A rare find among the various hostelries of Cap Ferrat, this hotel was established in 1950 in what had been a 19th-century villa surrounded by two acres of semitropical gardens. The pleasant bedrooms are scattered over three buildings within the confines of the garden. The hotel's most famous guest was General de Gaulle, who lived in a room called "Strelitzias" (Bird of Paradise) during many of his retreats from Paris. Each room is named after a flower. The most romantic and the most spacious accommodations are located in the main building; the rooms in the outlying annex are the most modern.

HOTEL PANORAMIC, 3, av. Albert-Ier, 06230 St-Jean-Cap-Ferrat. Tel. 93-76-00-37. Fax 93-76-15-78. 20 rms (all with bath or shower). TV TEL

$ Rates: 507–687 F ($91.30–$123.70) single or double. Breakfast 45 F ($8.10) extra. AE, DC, MC, V. **Parking:** Free. **Closed:** Nov 4–Dec 20.

The Hôtel Panoramic, built in 1958 with a red-tile roof and much style and glamour, is owned by Christiane Maiffret. You'll reach the hotel by passing over a raised bridge lined with colorful pansies. The well-furnished bedrooms have a sweeping view of the water and the forest leading down to it. Breakfast is the only meal served.

LES TOURTERELLES, 9, av. Denis-Séméria, 06230 St-Jean-Cap-Ferrat. Tel. 93-01-33-31. Fax 93-76-06-48. 17 rms (all with bath or shower). TV TEL

$ Rates: Oct–June, 420 F ($75.60) single or double. July–Sept, 630 F ($113.40) single or double. No credit cards.

This is a small hillside apartment house where you can live economically and independent of a hotel staff. It's a three-floor building, surrounded by a garden, reached via a lane with roses and geraniums. Guests gather to sunbathe in the garden and swim in the pool. The living space will amaze you: a private sun terrace, a living room, a dining area, a twin-bedded room, a private tile bath with shower, and a complete kitchen with all the necessary equipment to prepare a meal. Each apartment is named after a painter and contains reproductions of the artist's work—Rousseau, Utrillo, Gauguin, Degas. Most apartments accommodate one to three people—the rates remain the same, varying only according to the time of year. A minimum stay of one week is required. No food is served.

WHERE TO DINE

LE PROVENÇALE. 2, av. Denis-Séméria. Tel. 93-76-03-97.
  Cuisine: FRENCH. **Reservations:** Required.
$ Prices: Appetizers 130–200 F ($23.40–$36); main dishes 230–360 F ($41.40–$64.80); fixed-price menus 200–550 F ($36–$99) at lunch (except Sun), 350–550 F ($63–$99) at dinner.
  Open: Apr–Sept, lunch Thurs–Mon noon–2:30pm; dinner daily 7:30–9:30pm. Oct–Mar, lunch Tues–Sun noon–2:30pm; dinner Tues–Sat 7:30–9:30pm.
  Closed: Feb.

The building containing this restaurant was originally built around the turn of the century as a hotel. Today, from a position high above the village, with a sweeping panorama, it functions only as a restaurant. Inside the Provence-inspired dining room, you'll enjoy such dishes as the marinated hearts of purple artichokes served with half a lobster, John Dory roasted in fig leaves and served with fresh figs, roasted pigeon with cinnamon, a classic bourride provençal, and a choice of five "petits desserts" which might include macaroons with chocolate or crème brûlée.

LE SLOOP, au Nouveau Port. Tel. 93-01-48-83.
  Cuisine: FRENCH. **Reservations:** Recommended.
$ Prices: Appetizers 42–110 F ($7.60–$19.80); main dishes 110–155 F ($19.80–$27.90); fixed-price menu 155 F ($27.90). AE, DC, MC, V.
  Open: Oct–May, lunch Thurs–Tues noon–2:30pm; dinner Thurs–Tues 7–9:30pm. June–Sept, lunch Thurs–Tues noon–2:30pm; dinner daily 7–9:30pm.
  Closed: Nov 15–Dec 2.

This is the most popular, and one of the most reasonably priced, bistros in this very expensive area. Completely outfitted in marina-inspired colors of blue and white, it sits directly at the edge of the port, overlooking the yachts in the harbor. The best of regional produce is handled deftly by the chefs, who present such dishes as a tartare of salmon with baby onions; a warm salad of red mullet; a salad composed of fresh mozzarella, avocados, and lobster; John Dory with fresh pasta and basil; turbot with lobster sauce and calamari; and filet of veal with basil sauce.

7. VILLEFRANCHE-SUR-MER

581 miles S of Paris, 4 miles E of Nice

GETTING THERE Trains arrive from most towns on the Côte d'Azur, especially Nice, but most visitors drive via the Corniche Inférieure (Lower Corniche).

ESSENTIALS Orientation The harbor dominates the town; a short walk inland, the narrow streets of the old town are centered around the church of St-Michel.

Information The Office de Tourisme is on Jardin François-Binon (tel. 93-01-73-68).

According to legend, Hercules opened his arms and Villefranche was born. It sits on a big blue bay that looks like a gigantic bowl, large enough to attract U.S. Sixth

Fleet cruisers and destroyers. Quietly slumbering otherwise, Villefranche takes on the appearance of an exciting Mediterranean port when the fleet's in. Four miles from Nice, it is the first town reached along the Lower Corniche.

Once popular with such writers as Katherine Mansfield and Aldous Huxley, it is still a haven for artists, many of whom take over the little houses—reached by narrow alleyways—that climb the hillside. **Rue Obscure** is vaulted, one of the strangest streets in France (to get to it, take rue de l'Église). In spirit it belongs more to a North African casbah. People live in tiny houses on this street, totally protected from the elements. Occasionally, however, there's an open space, allowing for a tiny courtyard.

One artist who came to Villefranche left a memorial. His name was Jean Cocteau, and he decorated the 14th-century Romanesque **Chapel of St-Pierre,** quai de la Douane (tel. 93-80-73-68), presenting it to "the fishermen of Villefranche in homage to the Prince of Apostles, the patron of fishermen." One panel pays homage to the gypsies of the Saintes-Maries-de-la-Mer. In the apse is a depiction of the Miracle of St. Peter walking on the water, not knowing that he's supported by an angel. On the left side of the narthex Cocteau honored the young women of Villefranche in their regional costumes.

The chapel, which charges a 10-F ($1.80) admission, is open July to September, Tuesday through Sunday from 9:30am to noon and 2:30 to 7pm; October to March, Tuesday through Sunday from 9:30am to noon and 2 to 5pm; April to June, Tuesday through Sunday from 9:30am to noon and 2 to 6pm; closed mid-November to mid-December.

WHERE TO STAY

VERSAILLES, av. Princesse-Grace-de-Monaco, 06230 Villefranche-sur-Mer. Tel. 93-01-89-56. Fax 93-01-97-48. 46 rms (all with bath or shower), 3 suites. A/C MINIBAR TV TEL
$ Rates: 580 F ($104.40) single; 860 F ($154.80) double. Breakfast 50 F ($9) extra. AE, DC, MC, V. **Parking:** 50 F ($9). **Closed:** Nov–Dec.
Set back several blocks from the harbor and outside the main part of town, this location gives you a perspective of the entire coastal area. Constructed in the 1960s, the hotel offers comfortably furnished bedrooms with big windows for a good view. Guests congregate on the roof terrace, where they can order breakfast or lunch under an umbrella. In the panoramic dining room, meals begin at 170 F ($30.60). The swimming pool is surrounded by a terrace, palms, and bright flowers.

WELCOME, 1, quai Courbet, 06230 Villefranche-sur-Mer. Tel. 93-76-76-93. Fax 93-01-88-81. 32 rms (all with bath or shower). A/C MINIBAR TV TEL
$ Rates: 630 F ($113.40) single; 860 F ($154.80) double. Breakfast 50 F ($9) extra. AE, DC, MC, V. **Closed:** Nov 22–Dec 22.
Involving you instantly in Mediterranean port life, the Welcome was a favorite of Jean Cocteau. Within hailing distance of the fishing and motor boats, it's a six-floor villa hotel with shutters and balconies. Once Pope Paul III embarked from this site with Charles V, but nowadays the departures are much more casual—usually for fishing expeditions.

The sidewalk café is the focal point of town life. The lounge and the restaurant, St-Pierre, have open fireplaces and fruitwood furniture; meals begin at 170 F ($30.60).

WHERE TO DINE

LA MERE GERMAINE, quai Courbet. Tel. 93-01-71-39.
Cuisine: FRENCH. **Reservations:** Recommended.
$ Prices: Appetizers 65–135 F ($11.70–$24.30); main dishes 120–425 F ($21.60–$76.50). AE, MC, V.
Open: May–Oct, lunch daily noon–2pm; dinner daily 7–10pm. Off-season, lunch Thurs–Tues noon–2pm; dinner Thurs–Tues 7–10pm. **Closed:** Nov 22–Dec 24.

Plan to relax here over a long lunch while watching fishers repair their nets. One of the best of a string of restaurants directly on the port, this place is popular with U.S. Navy officers, who have discovered the bouillabaisse made with tasty morsels of freshly caught fish and mixed in a caldron with savory spices. I also recommend the grilled loup (bass) with fennel, salade niçoise, sole Tante Marie (stuffed with mushroom purée), and the beef filet with three different peppers. If two or more are dining, you can order the carré d'agneau (lamb).

LA TRINQUETTE, Port de la Darse. Tel. 93-01-71-41.
  Cuisine: FRENCH. **Reservations:** Recommended.
$ Prices: Appetizers 40–80 F ($7.20–$14.40); main dishes 80–150 F ($14.40–$27); fixed-price meals 125–145 F ($22.50–$26.10) at lunch, 185–245 F ($33.30–$44.10) at dinner. No credit cards.
  Open: Lunch Thurs–Tues noon–2:15pm; dinner Thurs–Tues 7:30–10pm.
  Closed: Dec–Jan.

Charming and traditional, this restaurant was established in 1938 on the site of what had functioned as a tavern since the days of Napoléon. Set a few steps from the harborfront, the establishment prides itself on its fish. Clients choose from among about 30 different kinds, all fresh, which are prepared any way a client specifies, with a wide variety of well-flavored sauces. One of these might be aïoli, the garlic-enriched mayonnaise of the region.

---

8. NICE

577 miles S of Paris; 20 miles NE of Cannes

GETTING THERE By Plane Visitors who arrive at the Aéroport Nice–Côte d'Azur (tel. 93-21-30-30) can take an airport bus departing every 20 minutes to the Station Centrale in the city center. Buses run from 6am to 10:30pm and cost 8 F ($1.40). For 25 F ($4.50) you can take a *navette*, or airport shuttle, that goes several times a day from the train station or the airport. A taxi ride into the city center will cost at least 180 F ($32.40).

By Train Trains arrive at Gare Nice-Ville, avenue Thiers (tel. 93-87-50-50). From here, you can take frequent trains to Cannes, Monaco, and Antibes, among other destinations. An information office at the station is open Monday through Saturday from 8am to 7pm and on Sunday from 8am to noon and 2 to 7pm. If you face a delay, you can take showers at the station and eat at the cafeteria. The *navette* travels several times a day from the train station to the city center for 25 F ($4.50).

GETTING AROUND By Bus Most buses in Nice leave from the Station Centrale, 10, av. Félix-Fauré (tel. 93-62-08-08), in the vicinity of place Masséna. Take bus no. 12 to the beach. To save money, purchase a *carnet* of five tickets for 30 F ($5.40) available at the tourist offices (see "Information" in "Fast Facts," below).

By Moped or Bicycle You can rent these at Nicea Rent, 9, av. Thiers (tel. 93-82-42-71), near the Station Centrale. From March to October, it's open daily; from November to April, Monday through Saturday from 9am to noon and 2 to 6pm. The cost begins at 120 F ($21.60) per day, plus a 2,000-F ($360) deposit.

SPECIAL EVENTS At certain times of the year, Nice is caught up in frenzied carnival activities. The **Nice Carnival** draws visitors from all over Europe and North America to this ancient spectacle. The **Mardi Gras of the Riviera** begins 12 days before Shrove Tuesday, celebrating the return of spring with parades, floats (*corsi*), masked balls (*veglioni*), confetti, and battles in which pretty girls toss flowers, and only the most wicked throw rotten eggs instead of carnations. Climaxing the event is a fireworks display on Shrove Tuesday, lighting up the Bay of Angels. King Carnival goes up in flames on his pyre, but rises from the ashes the following spring.

FAST FACTS   American Express   The American Express office is next to the Palais de la Méditerranée at 11, promenade des Anglais (tel. 93-87-29-82). It's open May to September, Monday through Friday from 9am to 6pm and on Saturday from 9am to noon; October to April, Monday through Friday from 9am to noon and 2 to 6pm. To use the company's mail-service department, you need either an American Express card or American Express traveler's checks.

Banks   Banks are generally open Monday through Friday from 9am to noon and 1 or 1:30 to 4:30pm. For currency exchange, go to Office Provençal, 17, av. Thiers (tel. 93-88-56-80), which is across from the train station and open daily from 7am to midnight. It's best to cash American Express traveler's checks at the American Express office (see above).

Bookstores   Try the Riviera Bookshop, 10, rue Chauvain (tel. 93-85-84-61), open Monday through Saturday from 9:30am to 12:30pm and 2 to 6:30pm.

Emergencies   The main hospital for Nice is the Hôpital Pasteur, 30, Voie Romaine (tel. 93-81-71-71). For police assistance, the station is at 13, rue St-François-de-Paule (tel. 93-13-20-00 during daytime hours, 93-53-53-53 at night). In a crisis, dial 17.

Information   Go to the Office de Tourisme, avenue Thiers at the Station Centrale (tel. 93-87-07-07), or 5, av. Gustave-V (tel. 93-87-60-60), near place Masséna, open Monday through Saturday from 8:45am to 12:30pm and 2 to 6pm. These offices will make you a hotel reservation; the fee depends on the classification of the hotel category.

Laundry   Try Laverie Self-Service, 18, rue de Belgique, open daily from 6am to 11pm.

Mail and Post Office   If you're a client of American Express (holder of a card or traveler's checks), you can have your mail sent to the local office (see above). If not, have your mail sent *Poste Restante* (General Delivery) to the post office at 23, av. Thiers, 06000 Nice (tel. 93-88-55-41), open Monday through Friday from 8am to 7pm and on Saturday from 8am to noon. You can purchase air letters and stamps there, but you'll need your passport to pick up mail.

Medical Services   Call SOS Medical Services (tel. 93-53-03-03) 24 hours a day.

Pharmacy   Nice has many pharmacies, but if you need one between 7:30pm and 8:30am, go to the Pharmacie at 7, rue Masséna (tel. 93-87-78-94).

The Victorian upper class and tsarist aristocrats loved Nice in the 19th century, but it is solidly middle class today. In fact, of all the major resorts of France, from Deauville to Biarritz to Cannes, Nice is the least expensive. It is also the best excursion center on the Riviera, especially if you're dependent on public transportation. For example, you can go to San Remo, the queen of the Italian Riviera, returning to Nice by nightfall. From the Nice Airport, the second largest in France, you can travel by bus along the entire coast to such other resorts as Juan-les-Pins and Cannes.

Nice is the capital of the Riviera, the largest city between Genoa and Marseille (also one of the most ancient, having been founded by the Greeks, who called it "Nike," or victory). Because of its brilliant sunshine and relaxed living, artists and writers have been attracted to Nice for years. Among them were Matisse, Dumas, Nietzsche, Apollinaire, Flaubert, Victor Hugo, Guy de Maupassant, George Sand, Stendhal, Chateaubriand, and Mistral.

WHAT TO SEE & DO

In 1822 the orange crop at Nice was bad and the workers faced a lean time. The English residents put them to work building the **boulevard des Anglais,** which today remains a wide boulevard fronting the bay and, split by "islands" of palms and flowers, stretching for a distance of about four miles. Fronting the beach are rows of grand cafés, the Musée Masséna, villas, and hotels—some good, others decaying.

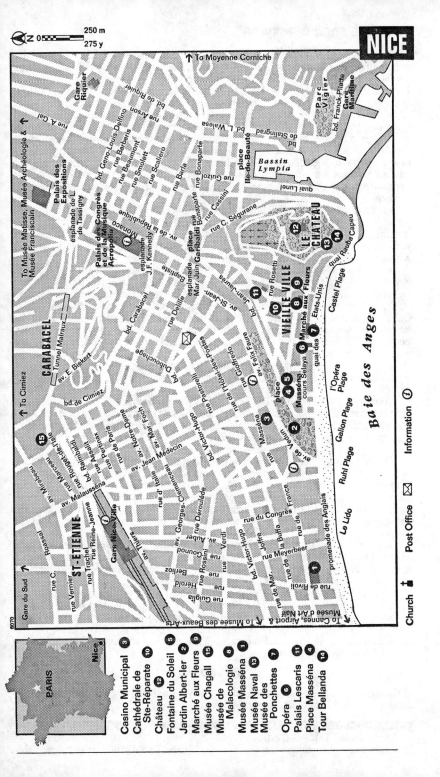

NICE

Baie des Anges

Church ✝ Post Office ⊠ Information ⓘ

Casino Municipal ❸
Cathédrale de Ste-Réparate ❿
Château ⓬
Fontaine du Soleil ❺
Jardin Albert-Ier ❷
Marché aux Fleurs ❾
Musée Chagall ⓯
Musée de Malacologie ❽
Musée Masséna ❶
Musée Naval ⓭
Musée des Ponchettes ❼
Opéra ❻
Palais Lescaris ⓫
Place Masséna ❹
Tour Bellanda ⓮

Crossing this boulevard in the briefest of bikinis are some of the most attractive people in the world, who come all the way from Israel or Minnesota. They're heading for the beach—"on the rocks," as it is called here. Tough on tender feet, the beach at Nice is shingled, one of the least attractive (and least publicized) aspects of the cosmopolitan resort city. Many bathhouses provide mattresses for a charge.

In the east, the promenade becomes the **quai des États-Unis,** the original boulevard, lined today with some of the best restaurants in Nice, each of which specializes in bouillabaisse. Rising sharply on a rock is the **château,** the spot where the dukes of Savoy built their castle, which was torn down in 1706. The steep hill has been turned into a garden of pines and exotic flowers. To reach the château, you can take an elevator. Actually, many prefer to take the elevator up, then walk down. The park is open May through August, daily from 10am to 7:30pm; off-season, it closes at 4:30pm.

At the north end of Castle Hill is the famous old graveyard of Nice, which is visited primarily for its lavishly sculpted monuments that form their own enduring art statement. It is the largest one in France and the fourth largest in Europe. To reach it, you can take a small canopied "toy train," which will take you to the Bar du Donjon where you can enjoy a drink or a meal.

In the **Tour Bellanda** is the **Musée Naval** (Naval Museum), Parc du Château (tel. 93-80-47-61), sitting on "The Rock." The tower stands on a precariously perched belvedere overlooking the beach, the bay, the old town, and even the terraces of some of the nearby villas. Of the museum's old battle prints, one depicts the exploits of Caterina Segurana, the Joan of Arc of the Niçois. During the 1543 siege by Barbarossa, she ran along the ramparts, raising her skirts and showing her shapely bottom to the Turks as a sign of contempt, although the soldiers were reported to have been more excited than insulted.

The Naval Museum is open May through September, Wednesday to Monday from 10am to noon and 2 to 7pm; off-season, it closes at 5pm; and it is closed entirely from November 15 to December 15.

Continuing east from the Rock one reaches the **harbor,** where the restaurants are even cheaper and the bouillabaisse just as good. While sitting here over an apéritif at a sidewalk café, you can watch the boats depart for Corsica (perhaps take one yourself). The port was excavated between 1750 and 1830. Since that time an outer harbor—protected by two jetties—has also been created.

The "authentic" Niçois live in **Vieille Ville,** the old town, beginning at the foot of the Rock. Under sienna-tiled roofs, many of the Italianate façades suggest 17th-century Genoese palaces. The old town is a maze of narrow streets, teeming with local life and studded with the least expensive restaurants in Nice. Buy an onion pizza (*la pissaladière*) from one of the local vendors. Many of the old buildings are painted a faded Roman gold, and their banners are multicolored laundry flapping in the sea breezes.

While there, try to visit the **Marché aux Fleurs,** the flower market at Cours Saleya. The vendors start setting up their stalls at noon. The market opens between 2 and 4pm. A flamboyant array of carnations, violets, jonquils, roses, and birds of paradise is wheeled in on carts.

The center of Nice is the **place Masséna,** with its pink buildings in the 17th-century Genoese style and a **Fontaine du Soleil** (Fountain of the Sun) by Janoit, dating from 1956. The **Municipal Casino,** now closed, was built in 1883. Stretching from the main square to the promenade is the **Jardin Albert-Ier,** with an open-air terrace and a **Triton Fountain.** With its palms and exotic flowers, it is the most relaxing oasis at the resort.

Museums

If the pebbles of the beach are too sharp for your tender toes, you can escape into some of the finest museums along the Riviera.

GALERIE-MUSEE ALEXIS ET GUSTAV-ADOLF MOSSA, 59, quai des Etats-Unis. Tel. 93-62-37-11.
Considered the partner of the Galerie-Musée Raoul Dufy (see below), this

museum was inaugurated in 1990. Here, admire the dynamic lines of a veritable family dynasty of Nice-born artists. Among them is Alexis Mossa (1844–1926), famous for local landscapes and scenes of the Nice carnival. He is considered one of the early symbolist painters, a representative of a movement that brought a definitive end to the romantic movement of the late 19th century and an early harbinger of surrealism.

Also sharing gallery space are the works of Alexis's son, Gustav-Adolf Mossa (1883–1971), who continued his father's work. One series of works exhibited, executed between 1903 and 1919, gracefully serves as a precursor to surrealism.

Admission: Free.

Open: Tues–Sat 10am–noon and 3–6pm, Sun 3–6pm. **Bus:** 8.

GALERIE-MUSEE RAOUL-DUFY, 77, quai des Etats-Unis. Tel. 93-62-31-24.

La Galerie des Ponchettes, inaugurated in 1950 by Matisse, became, in 1990, the Galerie-Musée Raoul-Dufy, which is contained in an annex of the Musée des Beaux-Arts (see below). It presents one of the most beautiful collections of works by the "Havrais" artist (that means he comes from Le Havre) who lived from 1877 to 1953. Most of the collection was bequeathed to the museum by his widow. The extremely diversified collection includes 28 oil paintings, 15 watercolors, 88 drawings, three ceramics, one tapestry, and 15 proposals for fabric designs commissioned for Dufy by the legendary couturier Paul Poiret. In its new setting, Dufy is immortalized, facing the waters of the Baie des Anges, which his works helped to immortalize.

Admission: Free.

Open: Tues–Sat 10am–noon and 2–6pm, Sun 3–6pm. **Bus:** 8.

MUSEE DES BEAUX-ARTS, 33, av. des Baumettes. Tel. 93-44-50-72.

The fine-arts museum is housed in the former private residence of the Ukrainian Princess Kotchubey. Its construction began in 1878 and was completed by a later owner, the American James Thompson. It has an important gallery devoted to the masters of the Second Empire and the Belle Epoque, with an extensive collection of the 19th-century French experts, including Besnard, Blanche, Cabanel, Constant, Flameng, Marie Bashkirtseff and her friends, Bastein-Lepage and Breslau, and many others. The gallery of sculptures includes works by J. B. Carpeaux, Rude, and Rodin. There are also 17th- and 18th-century works by such European artists as Fragonard, Hubert Robert, and Natoire. Note the important collection by a dynasty of painters, the Dutch Vanloo family. One of its best-known members, Carle Vanloo, born in Nice in 1705, was Louis XV's "Premier Peintre."

Works by Jules Chéret also can be seen. A contemporary of Toulouse-Lautrec, he died in Nice and left a series of posters, drawings, and paintings. In a way, he was the inventor, before Toulouse-Lautrec, of modern poster art.

A fine collection of 19th- and 20th-century art is displayed, including works by Ziem, Raffaelli, Boudin, Renoir, Monet, Guillaumin, and Sisley. Paintings by Bonnard, Seyssaud, and some early Fauve painters round out the collection.

Admission: Free.

Open: May–Sept, Tues–Sun 10am–noon and 3–6pm; Oct–Apr, Tues–Sun 10am–noon and 2–5pm. **Closed:** Three weeks in Nov. **Bus:** 3, 7, 12, 18, or 38.

MUSEE INTERNATIONAL D'ART NAÏF ANATOLE-JAKOVSKY [Museum of Naïve Art], av. Val-Marie. Tel. 93-71-78-33.

This museum is housed in the beautifully restored Château Ste-Hélène, on avenue Val-Marie in the Fabron district. The collection was once owned by the namesake of the museum, for years one of the world's leading art critics. His donation of some 600 drawings and canvases was turned over to the institution and made accessible to the public. Artists from more than two dozen countries are represented in the exhibition, which ranges from primitive painting to contemporary 20th-century works.

Admission: Free.

Open: May–Sept, Wed–Mon 10am–noon and 2–6pm; Oct–Apr, Wed–Mon 10am–noon and 2–5pm. **Bus:** 9, 10, or 12.

MUSEE MASSENA, 65, rue de France. Tel. 93-88-11-34.

This fabulous villa was built in 1900 in the style of the First Empire as a private residence for Victor Masséna, the Prince of Essling and grandson of Napoléon's marshal. The city of Nice has converted the villa, next door to the deluxe Negresco Hôtel, into a museum of local history and regional art.

A remarkable First Empire drawing room completely furnished in the opulent taste of that era, with mahogany-veneer pieces and ormolu mounts, is on the ground floor. Of course there's the representation of Napoléon as a Roman Caesar and a bust by Canova of Marshal Masséna.

The large gallery on the first floor exhibits a collection of Niçois primitives, including works by such 15th-century painters as Brea and Durandy. It also has a display of 14th- and 15th-century painters, as well as a collection of 13th-century masterpieces of plates and jewelry decorated with enamel (school of Limoges). See also the 15th- and 17th-century sculptures. There are art galleries devoted to the history of Nice and the memories of Masséna and Garibaldi. Yet another gallery is reserved for a display of views of Nice during the 19th century. Folklore and the ethnographia of the County of Nice are presented in three other galleries, together with examples of the history of "the Carnival" in Nice.

Admission: Free.

Open: June–Sept, Tues–Sun 10am–noon and 3–6pm; Oct–May, Tues–Sun 10am–noon and 2–5pm. **Closed:** Holidays. **Bus:** 3, 7, 8, 9, 10, 12, 14, or 22.

More Attractions

LA CATHEDRALE ORTHODOXE RUSSE ST-NICHOLAS A NICE, av. Nicolas-II (off bd. du Tzarewitch). Tel. 93-96-88-02.

Ordered built by none other than Tsar Nicholas II, this cathedral is considered the most beautiful religious edifice of the Orthodoxy outside Russia and is the most perfect expression of Russian religious art abroad. It dates from the Belle Epoque, when some of the Romanovs and their entourage turned Nice and parts of the Riviera into a stamping ground. Everyone from grand dukes to ballerinas walked the promenade. The cathedral is richly ornamented and decorated with lots of icons. You'll easily spot the building from afar because of its collection of ornate onion domes. Church services are held on Sunday morning.

Admission: 12 F ($2.20).

Open: June–Sept, daily 9am–noon and 2:30–6pm; Oct–May, daily 9:30am–noon and 2:30–5pm. **Directions:** From the central rail station along avenue Thiers, head west to boulevard Gambetta; then go north to avenue Nicolas-II.

PALAIS LASCARIS, 15, rue Droite. Tel. 93-62-05-54.

This baroque palace is intimately linked to the Lascaris-Vintimille family, whose recorded history predates the year 1261. Constructed in the 17th-century, it contains elaborately detailed ornaments. An intensive restoration undertaken by the city of Nice in 1946 brought back its original beauty, and the palace is now classified as a historic monument. The most elaborate floor is the *étage noble,* which still retains many of its 18th-century panels and plaster embellishments. A circa-1738 pharmacy, complete with many of the original Delftware accessories, is on the premises.

Admission: Free.

Open: Tues–Sun 9:30am–noon and 2:30–6pm. **Closed:** Nov. **Bus:** 1, 2, 3, 5, 6, 14, 16, or 17.

PARC DES MINIATURES, bd. de l'Impératrice-Eugénie. Tel. 93-97-02-02.

The Park of Miniatures, set on six acres, overlooks Nice and the Baie des Anges. A $5-million project, it consists of hundreds of well-crafted miniature buildings, monuments, and people illustrating the history of Nice from prehistoric times to the present. The park is filled with fountains, waterfalls, and lakes. Automated and animated models use the latest technologies; there's even an automated perfume factory.

Admission: 47 F ($8.50) adults, 27 F ($4.90) children 4–12.

Open: Daily 9am–5pm. **Bus:** 22.

Nearby Attractions in Villa des Arènes

In the once-aristocratic hilltop quarter of Cimiez, Queen Victoria wintered at the Hôtel Excelsior and brought half the court of England with her. Founded by the Romans, who called it Cemenelum, Cimiez was the capital of their province of the Maritime Alps. To reach this suburb, take bus no. 15, 17, or 22 at place Masséna. Recent excavations uncovered the ruins of a Roman town, and you can wander among the diggings. The arena was big enough to hold at least 5,000 spectators, who watched contests between gladiators and wild beasts shipped in from Africa.

MONASTERE DE CIMIEZ (Cimiez Convent), place du Monastère. Tel. 93-81-00-04.

This convent embraces a church that owns three of the most important works from the primitive painting school of Nice by the Brea brothers. See the carved and gilded wooden main altarpiece. In the sacristy, frescoes are of a most peculiar style, with symbolic and esoteric pictures. Most of these works are in the sacristy, and many other works can be seen only on guided tours.

In a restored part of the convent, the **Musée Franciscain** is decorated with 17th-century frescoes and has been called "historical and spiritual." Some 350 documents and works of art from the 15th to the 18th century are displayed, and a monk's cell has been re-created. See also the 17th-century chapel.

In the **gardens** you can get a magnificent view of Nice and the Bay of Angels. Matisse and Dufy are buried in the cemetery.

Admission: Free.

Open: Mon–Sat 10am–noon and 3–6pm. Tours given Mon–Fri at 10 and 11am and 3, 4, and 5pm.

MUSEE MATISSE, 164, av. des Arènes-de-Cimiez. Tel. 93-81-08-08.

This museum honors the great artist, who spent the last years of his life in Nice; he died here in 1954. Even in his final years he continued to develop his technique of bright colors and flattened perspective. Seeing his nude sketches today, you wonder how early critics could denounce them as "the female animal in all her shame and horror." The museum occupies the 17th-century Villa des Arènes-de-Cimiez, one of the most venerable mansions in town.

The museum has several permanent collections, most of which were painted in Nice and many were donated by Henri Matisse and his heirs. These include *Nude in an Armchair with a Green Plant* (1937), *Nymph in the Forest* (1935/1942), and a chronologically arranged series of paintings from 1890 to 1919. The most famous of these might be *Portrait of Madame Matisse* (1905), which is usually displayed near another portrait of the artist's wife, by Marquet, painted in 1900.

There is also an ensemble of drawings and designs (*Flowers and Fruits*) he prepared as practice sketches for the Matisse Chapel at Vence. Probably the most famous of all include *The Créole Dancer* (1951), *Blue Nude IV* (1952), and around 50 dance-related sketches he did between 1930 and 1931. An array of his personal possessions, including furniture, plants, birds, and goldfish, are exhibited on each of the stairwell landings.

Admission: Free.

Open: Apr–Sept Wed–Mon 11am–7pm; Oct–Mar Wed–Mon 10am–5pm.

MUSEE NATIONAL MESSAGE BIBLIQUE MARC-CHAGALL (Chagall Museum), av. du Docteur-Ménard. Tel. 93-81-75-75.

In the hills of Cimiez above Nice, this single-story museum is devoted to Marc Chagall's treatment of biblical themes. The handsome museum is surrounded by shallow pools and a garden planted with thyme, lavender, and olive trees.

Born in Russia in 1887, Chagall became a French citizen in 1937. The artist and his wife donated the works—considered the most important collection of Chagall ever assembled—to the French state in 1966 and 1972. Displayed are 450 of his oil paintings, gouaches, drawings, pastels, lithographs, sculptures, and ceramics; a mosaic; three stained-glass windows; and a tapestry. A splendid concert room was especially decorated by Chagall with outstanding stained-glass windows.

Temporary exhibitions are organized each summer about great periods and artists of all times. Special lectures in the rooms are available in both French and English (call for an appointment). The advantages to its members include signed posters by Chagall.

Admission: 20 F ($3.60) adults, 10 F ($1.80) ages 18–24 and over 60, free for children under 18. Fees may be higher for special exhibitions.

Open: July–Sept, Wed–Mon 10am–7pm; Oct–June, Wed–Mon 10am–12:30pm and 2–5:30pm.

WHERE TO STAY
Very Expensive

NEGRESCO, 37, promenade des Anglais, 06007 Nice CEDEX. Tel. 93-88-39-51. Fax 93-88-35-68. 132 rms (all with bath), 18 suites. A/C MINIBAR TV TEL **Bus:** 8.

$ Rates: 1,250–2,250 F ($225–$405) single or double; from 3,750 F ($675) suite. Breakfast 110 F ($19.80) extra. AE, DC, MC, V. **Parking:** Free.

The Négresco is one of the many super-glamorous Belle Epoque hotels strung along the French Riviera. Jeanne Augier took over the hotel, and because of her taste, imagination, and money, she triumphed. The hotel is named after its founder, who died without a franc in Paris in 1920. Some say that the original glamour has been restored, while others maintain that even in its heyday the Négresco wasn't as good as it is today. The deluxe hotel was built right on the seafront, in the "French château" style, with a mansard roof and a domed tower. The interior design was inspired by the châteaux and museums of France.

The decorators of the bedrooms scoured Europe to gather antiques, tapestries, paintings, and art. Some of the rooms have personality themes, such as the Louis XIV chamber, which has a green-velvet bed set under a brocaded rose canopy. The "Chambre Impératrice Joséphine 1810" regally re-creates the Empire bedroom, with a huge rosewood "swan bed" set in a fleur-de-lis–draped recess. The Napoléon III bedroom has swagged walls and a half-crowned canopy in pink, with a leopard-skin carpet. The most expensive rooms face the Mediterranean. The staff wears 18th-century costumes.

Dining/Entertainment: Less expensive meals are served in La Rotonde, although the featured restaurant—one of the greatest on the Riviera—is Chantecler (see "Where to Dine," below).

PALAIS MAETERLINCK, Basse Corniche, 06300 Nice. Tel. 90-00-72-00. Fax 92-00-72-10. 22 rms (all with bath), 6 suites. A/C MINIBAR TV TEL **Directions:** Drive four miles east of Nice along the Basse Corniche.

$ Rates: 1,800–3,500 F ($324–$630) single or double; from 3,800 F ($684) suite. AE, V. **Parking:** Free. **Closed:** Jan 3–Feb 16.

Set on nine acres of landscaped grounds east of Nice, this deluxe hotel—called "the jewel of the Côte d'Azur"—is a sumptuous palace. It was originally constructed as a private villa for Maurice Maeterlinck, the Belgian writer and winner of the Nobel Prize for literature. In a garden setting, filled with banana trees, olive trees, and cypresses, the writer lived between the two world wars. From the lofty grounds of the hotel, guests can take a funicular down to the rock-strewn beach, complete with a marina.

The elegantly furnished bedrooms, one with mirrored walls, have terraces opening onto views of such chic enclaves as Cap d'Antibes, so beloved by F. Scott Fitzgerald, or Cap Ferrat, so beloved of Gen. Charles de Gaulle. The hotel's restaurant offers an excellent French and international cuisine, with Provençal specialties. Meals go for 220–370 F ($39.60–$66.60), and there's no restaurant service on Sunday night or Monday. A buffet lunch is served on the terrace. The hotel has many neoclassical touches, as evoked by the Ionic pillars ringing the swimming pool.

ELYSEE-PALACE, 59, promenade des Anglais, 06000 Nice. Tel. 93-86-06-06. Fax 93-44-50-40. 143 rms (all with bath), 22 suites. A/C MINIBAR TV TEL **Bus:** 8.

$ Rates: 1,000–1,200 F ($180–$216) single; 1,100–1,300 F ($198–$234) double;

from 1,650 F ($297) suite. Breakfast 95 F ($17.10) extra. AE, DC, MC, V. **Parking:** 70 F ($12.60).

This modern hotel with a sweeping view of the sea was built on the site of a demolished 19th-century hotel with the same name. The decor is contemporary. Guests are admitted to the private beach on the Beau Rivage (see below), which is under the same management.

Dining/Entertainment: The hotel has a gastronomic restaurant and a bar. Gourmet Italian cuisine is a specialty. There's also a barbecue restaurant on the rooftop.

Facilities: Rooftop swimming pool, hairdresser, health club, sauna.

Expensive

HOTEL ABELA, 223, promenade des Anglais, 06200 Nice. Tel. 93-37-17-17. Fax 93-71-21-71. 321 rms (all with bath), 12 suites. A/C MINIBAR TV TEL **Bus:** 8.

$ Rates: 945–1,295 F ($170.10–$233.10) single; 1,045–1,395 F ($188.10–$251.10) double; from 2,800 F ($504) suite. Breakfast 85 F ($15.30) extra. AE, DC, MC, V. **Parking:** 100 F ($18).

Set alongside the major beachside thoroughfare of Nice, this streamlined and tastefully contemporary hotel was built in 1973 as the Beach Regency Hotel and remains today one of the most alluring modern palaces in town. In 1992, it was acquired by a consortium of Lebanese and French investors who renamed it, but who maintain its original high standards. A discreet portico leads into the sun-flooded, elegantly simple lobby. Most of the attractive bedrooms open onto the promenade des Anglais, with balconies fronting the sea.

Dining/Entertainment: Visitors enjoy soft piano music in the sophisticated piano bar in the lobby. Les Mosaïques offers a gastronomic French cuisine with full meals priced from around 300 F ($54) per person, without wine. At lunchtime, between June and September, one of the most sumptuous buffets in Nice is served beside the swimming pool at a price of 195 F ($35.10) per person.

Services: 24-hour concierge, same-day laundry and valet.

Facilities: Rooftop swimming pool with bar, boutiques, beauty salon, sauna, fitness center, underground garage.

HOTEL BEAU RIVAGE, 24, rue St-François-de-Paule, 06300 Nice. Tel. 93-80-80-70. Fax 93-80-55-77. 98 rms (all with bath), 10 suites. A/C MINIBAR TV TEL **Bus:** 1, 2, 5, 12, or 22.

$ Rates: 850–950 F ($153–$171) single; 950–1,050 F ($171–$189) double; from 1,800 F ($324) suite. Breakfast 89 F ($16) extra. AE, DC, MC, V.

This Belle Epoque hotel is famous for having housed both Matisse and Chekhov. It closed in the early 1980s for elaborate restorations, and today the interior has a tasteful modern decor. Large and rambling, the hotel contains soundproof rooms that are small but elegant and filled with art deco furniture.

Dining/Entertainment: The restaurant in a beachfront dining spot offers salads and light meals from May to September. The street-level Le Relais Beau Rivage is more formal and prepares quality cuts of meats on a large grill.

Facilities: Private beach.

HOTEL MERIDIEN, 1, promenade des Anglais, 06000 Nice. Tel. 93-82-25-25. Fax 93-16-08-90. 314 rms (all with bath). A/C MINIBAR TV TEL **Bus:** 8.

$ Rates: 1,130–3,300 F ($203.40–$594) single or double. Breakfast 95 F ($17.10) extra. AE, DC, V.

The Méridien occupies one of the most desirable positions in Nice—the angle of the resort's famous seaside promenade and a flowering park, Le Jardin Albert-Ier. Two escalators carry visitors to the reception area. The bedrooms are comfortably modern.

Dining/Entertainment: In the marble-floored lobby is a small restaurant, Café-Jardin. One of my favorite spots is the piano bar, which has a view of the water. The charmingly elegant La Terrasse offers excellent cuisine, with meals beginning at 200 F ($36).

Facilities: Health center with spa and hydrotherapy, rooftop pool and sun deck.

SPLENDID-SOFITEL, 50, bd. Victor-Hugo, 06048 Nice. Tel. 93-16-41-00. Fax 93-87-02-46. 116 rms (all with bath), 14 suites. A/C MINIBAR TV TEL **Bus:** 8.

$ Rates: 690–790 F ($124.20–$142.20) single or double; from 1,500 F ($270) suite. Breakfast 75 F ($13.50) extra. AE, DC, MC, V. **Parking:** 62 F ($11.20).

One of the best modern hotels of Nice, the Splendid is on the corner of a wide boulevard lined with large shade trees—just four blocks from the beach. The hotel was built in 1964 on the site of the 1881 Splendid, which was the residence of the King of Wurtenberg. Rooms are equipped with hairdryers and radios, and most open onto balconies or good-sized terraces. One floor has no-smoking rooms. Swimmers in the pool enjoy the panoramic view of the city, the sea, and the surrounding hills.

Dining/Entertainment: The hotel's restaurant, Le Concerto, features classic French cooking, with a three-course lunch or dinner offered for 140 F ($25.20). The eighth-floor Topsail Bar offers a terrace where you can order light meals and snacks or patronize the salad bar.

Facilities: Hairdresser, currency exchange, garage, boutiques, open-air solar-heated swimming pool (plus a wading pool for children).

WESTMINSTER CONCORDE, 27, promenade des Anglais, 06000 Nice. Tel. 93-88-29-44. Fax 93-82-45-35. 105 rms (all with bath), 8 suites. A/C MINIBAR TV TEL **Bus:** 8.

$ Rates: 750–1,050 F ($135–$189) single; 850–1,250 F ($153–$225) double; from 1,300 F ($234) suite. Breakfast 75 F ($13.50) extra. AE, DC, MC, V. **Parking:** 70 F ($12.60).

This hotel, standing prominently along the famous promenade, is a reminder of the grandest Belle Epoque era of Nice. Its elaborate facade was recently restored to its former grandeur, and many renovations were made. The contemporary bedrooms are comfortable and have soundproof windows. Dining and drinking facilities include plant-ringed terraces with a view of the water and Le Farniente restaurant, where a fixed-price lunch or dinner begins at 220 F ($39.60). Despite the modernization of this landmark, it's still "old world."

Moderate

BUSBY, 36–38, rue du Maréchal-Joffre, 06000 Nice. Tel. 93-88-19-41. Fax 93-87-73-53. 80 rms (all with bath). TV TEL **Bus:** 9, 10, 12, or 22.

$ Rates: 475–525 F ($85.50–$94.50) single; 550–650 F ($99 $117) double. Breakfast 30 F ($5.40) extra. AE, DC, MC, V. **Closed:** Nov 15–Dec 20.

This one should please you if you want an elegant, centrally located hotel that has all the modern amenities. Totally renovated, the hotel has kept its old Niçois facade, with balconies and shutters at its tall windows. The rooms are dignified yet colorful, and some contain pairs of mahogany twin beds and two white-and-gold wardrobes. The bar is cozy, and the long dining room has marble columns, mirrors, and ladderback fruitwood chairs. The restaurant is open from December 15 through May, with meals costing 120 F ($21.60) and up.

GRAND HOTEL ASTON, 12, av. Félix-Fauré, 06000 Nice. Tel. 93-80-62-52. Fax 93-80-40-02. 156 rms (all with bath).

$ Rates: 600–820 F ($108–$147.60) single; 900–1,050 F ($162–$189) double. Breakfast 70 F ($12.60) extra. AE, DC, MC, V. **Parking:** 70 F ($12.60).

One of the most alluring in its price bracket, this elegantly detailed 19th-century hotel has been radically renovated. Most rooms overlook the splashing fountains of the city's showcase, the Espace Masséna, a few blocks from the water. The rooftop garden offers dance music and a bar on summer evenings and has a panoramic view of the coastline.

HOTEL GOUNOD, 3, rue Gounod, 06000 Nice. Tel. 93-88-26-20. Fax 93-88-23-84. 45 rms (all with bath or shower), 6 suites. A/C MINIBAR TV TEL **Bus:** 8.

$ Rates (including continental breakfast): 490 F ($88.20) single; 590 F ($106.20) double; from 800 F ($144) suite. AE, DC, MC, V. **Parking:** 70 F ($12.60).

A few minutes from the sea, the Gounod stands next to the Splendid-Sofitel. Although it has been entirely modernized, it retains its old Niçois exterior, with ornate balconies and a domed roof. The attractive lobby and adjoining lounge are festive, with Boussac cloth on the walls, old prints, and copper pots with flowers. Most of the well-furnished rooms are quiet and overlook the gardens of private homes on both sides. Guests have free use of the Splendid-Sofitel's pool next door.

HOTEL VICTORIA, 33, bd. Victor-Hugo, 06000 Nice. Tel. 93-88-39-60, or toll free 800/528-1234 in the U.S. Fax 93-88-39-60. 39 rms (all with bath or shower). MINIBAR TV TEL **Bus:** 8.
$ Rates (including continental breakfast): 570 F ($102.60) single; 660 F ($118.80) double. AE, DC, MC, V.

Part of the Best Western chain, the Hôtel Victoria is about five blocks from the seafront and faces one of the major boulevards of Nice. The classic facade has balconies and shutters on the wide French windows. The best of all is the quiet, rear garden and lawn studded with trees. A living room opens onto the garden, and the interior is stylishly decorated. The immaculate bedrooms are of good size and have soundproof windows.

HOTEL WEST-END, 31, promenade des Anglais, 06000 Nice. Tel. 93-88-79-91. Fax 93-88-85-07. 130 rms (all with bath), 3 suites. A/C MINIBAR TV TEL **Bus:** 8.
$ Rates: 500 F ($90) single; 1,350 F ($243) double; from 1,750 F ($315) suite. Breakfast 80 F ($14.40) extra. AE, DC, MC, V.

While this hotel is traditional and stately, it has been completely renovated. The Hôtel West-End enjoys a prime location—on the promenade fronting the sea in the city center. Many of the modern, functional bedrooms offer views of the sea, and all are soundproof and have hairdryers. Guests can enjoy drinks on the terrace at Le Shaker Bar and first-class meals at L'Orangerie, the hotel's restaurant. Facilities include a sauna and a solarium, and the hotel has a private beach and offers water sports.

LA PEROUSE, 11, quai Raube-Capéu, 06300 Nice. Tel. 93-62-34-63. Fax 93-62-59-41. 63 rms (all with bath or shower), 3 suites. A/C MINIBAR TV TEL **Bus:** 1, 2, 5, 12, or 22.
$ Rates: 565–1,150 F ($101.70–$207) single or double; from 1,400 F ($252) suite. Breakfast 75 F ($13.50) extra. AE, DC, MC, V. **Parking:** 70 F ($12.60).

Once a prison, La Pérouse has been reconstructed and is now a unique Riviera hotel. Set on a cliff, this establishment overlooks the sea and is entered through a lower-level lobby, where an elevator takes you up to the gardens and a pool. In fact, La Pérouse is built right into the gardens of an ancient château-fort. Inside, the hotel is like an old Provençal home, with low ceilings, white walls, and antiques. Most of the well-furnished rooms have loggias overlooking the bay.

WINDSOR, 11, rue Dalpozzo, 06000 Nice. Tel. 93-88-59-35. Fax 93-88-94-57. 60 rms (all with bath or shower). A/C MINIBAR TV TEL **Bus:** 8.
$ Rates: 405–515 F ($72.90–$92.70) single; 530–650 F ($95.40–$117) double. Breakfast 40 F ($7.20) extra. AE, DC, MC, V.

A short walk from the promenade des Anglais, right in the heart of Nice, the Windsor seems more like a stone villa than a hotel. It's a charmer, and the rooms, all of which have radios, are excellently kept. Many of the French windows open onto a rear garden with a swimming pool. The intimate drawing room has a fireplace, and the hotel's fitness center contains a sauna and a Turkish bath. Shiatsu massages are offered.

Inexpensive

HOTEL ALIZE, 65, rue Buffa, 06000 Nice. Tel. 93-88-99-46. 11 rms (all with bath or shower). A/C TEL **Bus:** 8.
$ Rates: 200–220 F ($36–$39.60) single; 250–260 F ($45–$46.80) double; 320–350 F ($57.60–$63) triple. Breakfast 30 F ($5.40) extra. V.

Right off the promenade des Anglais and boulevard Gambetta, this is a modest hotel, but one that's completely well maintained. Bedrooms are comfortably furnished, often in bright, inviting colors. Near the chic Négresco Hôtel, this hotel is a bargain.

Breakfast is the only meal served, but the rooms are mercifully air-conditioned and each has a private bath or shower with a direct-dial phone.

HOTEL CANADA, 8, rue Halévy, 06000 Nice. Tel. 93-87-98-94. Fax 93-87-17-12. 18 rms (all with shower). TV TEL **Bus:** 12 from the train station to Grimaldi.
$ Rates: 210–330 F ($37.80–$59.40) single or double with shower, 270–360 F ($48.60–$64.80) single or double with shower and kitchenette. Breakfast 25 F ($4.50) extra. AE, DC, MC, V.

⑤ Nearby are some fancy and expensive neighbors, but the Canada is a bargain, and it's also popular with families who like to reserve one of the rooms with kitchenettes. This cuts down on the rising food costs of having to eat out all the time while vacationing in Nice. Near the sea, the Hôtel Canada is in a pedestrian zone. Many Canadians are attracted to it because of its name, although it's French run. Each bedroom is comfortably furnished, containing small baths—coated in tiles—and TV sets. Little decorative touches abound, including, for example, an occasional brass headboard on a bed. The most expensive rooms, those with the kitchenettes, are also air-conditioned. The hotel is well known for being a bargain, so reservations in summer—as far in advance as possible—are needed.

HOTEL DE LA MER, 4, place Masséna, 06000 Nice. Tel. 93-92-09-10. Fax 93-85-00-64. 12 rms (all with bath or shower). MINIBAR TV TEL **Bus:** 1, 2, 5, 12, or 22.
$ Rates: 250–300 F ($45–$54) single; 280–320 F ($50.40–$57.60) double. Breakfast 25 F ($4.50) extra. AE, MC, V. **Parking:** Free.
In the very center of the heartbeat square of Old Nice, this hotel has been renovated in a major way, yet it keeps its prices low. Ms. Feri Forouzan, the owner, welcomes visitors to her little two-star pension. Each room is of good size and has such items as a minibar and TV, not often found in inexpensive Nice hotels. From the hotel it's possible to walk to the promenade des Anglais and the seafront. Breakfast will be delivered to your room.

HOTEL DURANTE, 16, av. Durante, 06000 Nice. Tel. 93-88-84-40. Fax 93-87-77-76. 26 rms (all with bath or shower). TV TEL **Bus:** 1, 2, 5, 12, 18, 23, or 24.
$ Rates: 230 F ($41.40) single; 390 F ($70.20) double. Breakfast 40 F ($7.20) extra. MC, V. **Parking:** Free.
This hotel is very popular with producers, actors, and directors during the nearby Cannes Film Festival. Many bedrooms face a quiet courtyard and all have a kitchenette and refrigerator. All rooms have been recently furnished. The owner, Mme Dufaure de Citres, dispenses both charm and information about local cinematic events and has installed an elevator. There is also a private garden.

HOTEL EXCELSIOR, 19, av. Durante, 06000 Nice. Tel. 93-88-18-05. Fax 93-88-38-69. 45 rms (40 with bath). TV TEL **Bus:** 1, 2, 5, 12, 18, 23, or 24.
$ Rates: 195 F ($35.10) single without bath; 400 F ($72) double with bath. Breakfast 30 F ($5.40) extra. AE, MC, V.
Its ornate corbels and chiseled stone pediments rise grandly a few steps from the railway station. This 19th-century hotel has a pleasantly modern decor with comfortably upholstered armchairs. There's a reflecting pool in the large lobby, and the high-ceilinged bedrooms, some with private showers or baths, are cozy. The beach is a 20-minute walk from the hotel through the residential and commercial center of Nice.

HOTEL MAGNAN, square du Général-Ferrié, 06200 Nice. Tel. 93-86-76-00. Fax 93-44-48-31. 25 rms (all with bath or shower). TV TEL **Bus:** 12 or 24.
$ Rates: 270–420 F ($48.60–$75.60) double. Breakfast 25 F ($4.50) extra. MC, V.
This good, little, well-run, modern hotel is a 10-minute bus ride into the heart of town but only a minute or so from the promenade des Anglais and the bay. Many of the

bedrooms in this six-story building have balconies facing the sea, and some have minibars. Breakfast is served in the rooms.

LE PETIT PALAIS, 10, av. Emile-Bieckert. Tel. 93-62-19-11. Fax 93-62-53-60. 25 rms (all with bath or shower). TV TEL **Bus:** 15 or 15A.
$ Rates: 480–680 F ($86.40–$122.40) single or double. Breakfast 50 F ($9) extra. AE, DC, V.

A Belle Epoque mansion, this hotel lies about a 10-minute drive from the city center in the Carabacel residential district. Much of its old architectural grace remains, as evoked by the Italianate furnishings and the Florentine moldings and friezes. The preferred rooms, and the most expensive, have balconies for sea views during the day and sunset watching at dusk. Management is friendly and helpful. Breakfast is the only meal served.

SUISSE, 15, quai Raube-Capéu, 06300 Nice. Tel. 93-62-33-00. Fax 93-85-30-70. 41 rms (all with bath), 1 suite. A/C MINIBAR TV TEL **Bus:** 1, 2, 5, 12, or 22.
$ Rates: 360–490 F ($64.80–$88.20) single; 400–490 F ($72–$88.20) double; 750 F ($135) suite. Breakfast 45 F ($8.10) extra. AE, DC, V. **Parking:** 60 F ($10.80).

In the heart of the Old Town, the building containing this hotel was built early in the 20th century directly against the rocky outcrop that supports the medieval château of Nice, which rises above it. Completely renovated in 1991, the hotel's interior is more modern than you might have at first suspected. Bedrooms are comfortable and clean, and on the premises is a likable restaurant, where meals begin at around 125 F ($22.50).

VILLA EDEN, 99 bis, promenade des Anglais, 06000 Nice. Tel. 93-86-53-70. 10 rms (6 with shower). TEL **Bus:** 8.
$ Rates (including breakfast): 195 F ($35.10) single without shower, 325 F ($58.50) single with shower; 350 F ($63) double with shower. MC, V. **Parking:** Free.

In 1925, an exiled Russian countess built this art deco villa on the seafront near the Hôtel Négresco, surrounded it with a wall, and planted a tiny garden. Today, the villa remains, despite the construction on both sides of much-taller modern buildings. Today, guests enjoy the ivy and roses in the garden, and live in old-fashioned, partially modernized bedrooms whose size varies greatly from one to another. The owner maintains a wry sense of humor, and greets guests at breakfast, which is the only meal served.

WHERE TO DINE
Very Expensive

ANE ROUGE, 7, quai Deux-Emmanuel. Tel. 93-89-49-63.
Cuisine: FRENCH. **Reservations:** Required. **Bus:** 1 or 2.
$ Prices: Appetizers 95–170 F ($17.10–$30.60); main dishes 180–270 F ($32.40–$48.60). AE, DC, MC, V.
Open: Lunch Mon–Fri noon–2pm; dinner Mon–Fri 7:30–9:30pm. **Closed:** Sept 1–20.

Facing the Old Port, this Niçois institution is one of the best-known and -established restaurants in the city. Didier and Paule Vidalot have many admirers of their cuisine, which is devoted to seafood. There is a satisfying choice of traditional dishes and an array of house specialties. You might try the seawolf stew flavored with champagne, salmon with spinach, or the house-style lobster. The Louis XIII dining room is elegant, and the service is commendable.

CHANTECLER, in the Hôtel Négresco, 37, promenade des Anglais. Tel. 93-88-39-51.
Cuisine: FRENCH. **Reservations:** Required. **Bus:** 8.
$ Prices: Appetizers 90–200 F ($16.20–$36); main dishes 160–250 F ($28.80–$45); fixed-price menus 390 F ($70.20), 490 F ($88.20), and 550 F ($99). AE, DC, MC, V.

Open: Lunch daily 12:30–2:30pm; dinner daily 7:30–10:30pm. **Closed:** Mid-Nov to mid-Dec.

⭐ Of all the great palace hotels of France (and there are many), none has a chef to equal Dominique Le Stanc—the growing fame of this talented culinary genius in the kitchen merits such high praise. Beautifully restored and redecorated, in part with wood paneling from the 1600s, this restaurant is a delight to behold. In peak season guests dine on the terrace. You know you're in for a treat when the waiter comes around with a dozen different homemade breads for your selection.

Monsieur Le Stanc's cuisine is excellent and attractively presented. To begin, try one of his special dishes: ravioli stuffed with small lobster, asparagus, and artichokes. Don't expect it to be buried under a sauce—Monsieur Le Stanc is not Escoffier. "My kitchen is without sauces," he tells reporters. He also does a "symphony" of truffles, scallops, potatos, and leeks in a feathery-thin "potato hamburger," as one food critic called it. Try his fricassée of sweetbreads with morels—in fact, try almost anything. This is one of the few restaurants on the Riviera where every dish is likely to be good, especially the desserts.

Moderate

BARALE, 39, rue Beaumont. Tel. 93-89-17-94.
 Cuisine: FRENCH/ITALIAN. **Reservations:** Required. **Bus:** 14 or 17.
$ **Prices:** Appetizers 38–65 F ($6.80–$11.70); main dishes 75–180 F ($13.50–$32.40); fixed-price menu 210 F ($37.80). No credit cards.
 Open: Dinner only, Tues–Sat 8:15–9pm. **Closed:** Aug.
Barale is presided over by Catherine-Hélène Barale, who believes in preserving a "Nissarda" cuisine—a unique Riviera blend of Italian and French. Her charmingly rustic restaurant—filled with antiques—is usually crowded with diners who know that they can enjoy one of their most memorable Côte d'Azur meals here. Madame Barale was born here, and she has learned the family secrets well. Her wares are listed on a blackboard menu hung with garlic pigtails, and her menu depends on her whim—or shopping. However, she almost always sells squares of the Nice pizza called pissaladière and, of course, the classic salade niçoise. For a second course, try gnocchi or green lasagne. Main courses often include pieche—poached veal stuffed with fresh Swiss chard, cheese, ham, eggs, and rice—which is superb. I recommend the fresh fruit tart for dessert.

CHEZ MICHEL [Le Grand Pavois], 11, rue Meyerbeer. Tel. 93-88-77-42.
 Cuisine: SEAFOOD. **Reservations:** Required. **Bus:** 8.
$ **Prices:** Appetizers 45–95 F ($8.10–$17.10); main dishes 110–160 F ($19.80–$28.80); fixed-price menus 195–250 F ($35.10–$45). AE, DC, MC, V.
 Open: Lunch Tues–Sun noon–2:30pm; dinner Tues–Sun 7–11pm.
Chez Michel is nestled under an art deco apartment building near the water. The brass-trimmed ship's steering wheel adds to the nautical decor—as you'd expect, this is a seafood restaurant. One of the partners, Jacques Marquise, is from Golfe Juan, where he managed the famous fish restaurant Tetou for 25 years. Tetou is known for its bouillabaisse, which Monsieur Marquise now prepares at Chez Michel. Other delectable specialties are baked sea bass in white wine, herbs, and lemon sauce and also grilled flambé lobster.

DON CAMILLO, 5, rue Ponchettes. Tel. 93-85-67-95.
 Cuisine: FRENCH/ITALIAN. **Reservations:** Required. **Bus:** 1, 2, or 5.
$ **Prices:** Appetizers 60–100 F ($10.80–$18); main dishes 85–155 F ($15.30–$27.90). MC, V.
 Open: Lunch Tues–Sat noon–2:30pm; dinner Tues–Sat 7–10pm.
This restaurant, set back from the coastal road near the foot of the château and the Naval Museum, is run like a country inn. The long, narrow dining room has a decorative clutter of paintings and plates set in niches, and the cuisine is generally considered some of the tastiest in Nice. Begin with those violet-colored artichokes of

Provence, served with olive oil, fresh thyme, and a vinaigrette sauce; then follow with ravioli or red mullet as a main course. The chef also does an excellent bouillabaisse.

FLORIAN, 22, rue Alphonse Karr. Tel. 93-88-66-60.

Cuisine: FRENCH. **Reservations:** Recommended. **Bus:** 9, 10, or 12.
$ Prices: Appetizers 80–150 F ($14.40–$27); main dishes 100–210 F ($18–$37.80); fixed-price menus 250–350 F ($45–$63). MC, V.
Open: Lunch Mon–Fri noon–2pm; dinner Mon–Sat 7:30–10pm. **Closed:** Jul–Aug.

This elegant art deco restaurant occupies half the ground floor of a turn-of-the-century apartment building in the commercial heart of Nice. It produces a conservatively elegant French cuisine which is only moderately influenced by the Niçois cuisine of the region. Amid mahogany paneling and a vivid sense of the 1930s, chef Claude Gillon prepares such dishes as ravioli stuffed with shellfish and served with a lobster bouillon and cream sauce, oxtail with foie-gras sauce, stuffed pigs' feet, suckling lamb with lima beans, and Challons duckling with red wine sauce. Restrained and dignified, the restaurant is sometimes confused with its less formal partner, Le Bistrot du Florian, which lies next door and which is recommended separately.

LA TOQUE BLANCHE, 40, rue de la Buffa. Tel. 93-88-38-18.

Cuisine: FRENCH. **Reservations:** Not required. **Bus:** 8.
$ Prices: Appetizers 85–140 F ($15.30–$25.20); main dishes 120–160 F ($21.60–$28.80); fixed-price menus 130 F ($23.40), 160 F ($28.80), and 280 F ($50.40). AE, MC, V.
Open: Lunch Tues–Sun 12:30–2pm; dinner Tues–Sat 7:30–9:30pm. **Closed:** Sept 1–15.

La Toque Blanche has only about a dozen tables amid its winter-garden decor. Owners Denise and Alain Sandelion pay particular attention to their shopping and buy only very fresh ingredients. The cuisine is skillfully prepared—try their sea bass roasted with citrus juice, sautéed version of sweetbreads with crayfish, or salmon prepared with fresh shrimp. Their fish dishes, all of which seemed to be handled with care, are particularly good.

Inexpensive

ALBERT'S BAR, 1, rue Maurice-Jaubert. Tel. 93-16-27-69.

Cuisine: FRENCH. **Reservations:** Recommended. **Bus:** 7, 8, 9, 12, or 22.
$ Prices: Appetizers 40–60 F ($7.20–$10.80); 80–180 F ($14.40–$32.40); fixed-price menu 78 F ($14). AE, DC, MC, V.
Open: Lunch Mon–Sat noon–2:30pm; dinner daily 7–9:30pm.

This bar and restaurant brings a touch of Britain to the Riviera. It's a friendly, inviting oasis known for its English atmosphere but French food that, although it is familiar fare, is always reliably prepared. Order a classic French dish such as sole meunière, a pot-au-feu of the sea (with scallops, monkfish, lobster, and sea bass), grilled John Dory with fennel, a cassolette of sweetbreads and scallops with spinach in a port wine sauce, or steak tartare. The hors d'oeuvres are excellent, including stuffed mushrooms and salmon blinis. Two diners can order crêpes Suzette for dessert; otherwise, just settle for a velvety chocolate mousse.

LE BISTROT DU FLORIAN, 22, rue Alphonse-Karr. Tel. 93-16-08-49.

Cuisine: FRENCH. **Reservations:** Not accepted. **Bus:** 9, 10, or 12.
$ Prices: Appetizers 40–80 F ($7.20–$14.40); main dishes 70–100 F ($12.60–$18). MC, V.
Open: Lunch Mon–Fri noon–2pm; dinner Mon–Sat 7:30–10:30pm.

This is the boisterous and informal cousin to the previously recommended Restaurant Florian, which occupies the street level of the same apartment building, in the commercial heart of Nice. Amid a consciously rustic background inspired by the great brasseries of Lyon, typical dishes from the old-fashioned French traditions are served and consumed with gusto. Menu items include assiettes de charcuterie, tripe, tête de veau ravigote, steaks au poivre, warm sausages with lentils, and several kinds of fish, including sole meunière. During the cold-weather months, a typical feature is sauerkraut.

FLO, 2-4, rue Sacha-Guitry. Tel. 93-13-38-38.
   Cuisine: FRENCH. **Reservations:** Recommended. **Bus:** 1, 2, or 5.
$ Prices: Appetizers 20–80 F ($3.60–$14.40); main dishes 50–125 F ($9–$22.50); fixed-price menus 99–145 F ($17.80–$26.10). AE, DC, MC, V.
   Open: Lunch daily noon–3pm; dinner daily 7pm–12:30am.

In 1991, one of the most successful chains of historic brasseries in France bought the premises of a bankrupt, once-stylish restaurant and transformed it into this brasserie. Modeled after its namesake in Paris (the Brasserie Flo), it occupies what was built in the 19th century as a theater for plays and comic opera, and which later served as a casino. The original very high ceilings remain today covered with their original Belle Epoque frescoes, but the venue is brisk, stylish, and fun. Menu items include an array of freshly grilled fish, choucroute (sauerkraut) in the Alsatian style, steaks with a brandied pepper sauce, and many other dishes from the brasserie tradition.

LA NISSARDA, 17, rue Gubernatis. Tel. 93-85-26-29.
   Cuisine: NIÇOIS. **Reservations:** Recommended.
$ Prices: Appetizers 35–45 F ($6.30–$8.10); main dishes 60–85 F ($10.80–$15.30); fixed-price menus 78–138 F ($14–$24.80). AE, DC, MC, V.
   Open: Lunch Mon–Sat noon–2pm; dinner Mon–Sat 7–10pm. **Closed:** Aug.

Set in the heart of town, about a 10-minute walk from place Masséna, this restaurant is maintained by a Normandy-born family (the Adam Pruniers) who work hard to maintain the aura and (some of) the culinary traditions of Nice. In an intimate (40-seat) setting lined with old engravings and photographs of the city, the place serves local versions of ravioli, spaghetti carbonara, lasagne, and fresh-grilled salmon with herbs. A handful of Norman-based specialties also manage to creep into the menu, much to the appreciation of diners lonely for northern France, including escalopes of veal with cream sauce and apples. Ceiling fans spin overhead as you dine.

L'OLIVIER, 2, place Garibaldi. Tel. 93-26-89-09.
   Cuisine: PROVENÇAL/SICILIAN. **Reservations:** Recommended.
$ Prices: Appetizers 45–70 F ($8.10–$12.60); main dishes 60–130 F ($10.80–$23.40); fixed-price menus 140 F ($25.20) (lunch only) and 170 F ($12.60). AE, DC, MC, V.
   Open: Lunch Tues–Sat noon–2:30pm; dinner Mon–Sat 7:45–10pm. **Closed:** One week in Aug.

Established in 1989 by Nice-born Franck Musso, this charming restaurant lies beneath the arcades of place Garibaldi, in the heart of Old Nice, just in back of the Museum of Modern Art. Named in honor of the premises' former occupant, an old-style shop selling olives, olive oil, and anchovies, the restaurant serves an original and sometimes unique cuisine based on modern versions of local culinary traditions. Menu items include smoked slices of foie gras, deboned sea bass stuffed with shellfish and herbs and served with a crabmeat sauce, lasagne made with a daube joues de boeuf, and a Sicilian-inspired medley of eggplant, olives, olive oil, and herbs combined into a southern Italian ratatouille. Dessert might be a gratin of frozen and caramelized lemons, or black-chocolate truffles.

PATIN COUFFIN, 1, rue Francis-Gallo. Tel. 93-92-00-92.
   Cuisine: NIÇOIS. **Reservations:** Recommended. **Bus:** 12.
$ Prices: Appetizers 35–68 F ($6.30–$12.20); main dishes 70–105 F ($12.60–$18.90); pastas 48–58 F ($8.60–$10.40); fixed-price menus 79–120 F ($14.20–$21.60). DC, MC, V.
   Open: Lunch daily 11:30am–3pm; dinner daily 6–11pm.

Richly attuned to its Provençal origins, this restaurant occupies a 200-year-old house near La Porte Fosse and place Masséna. In a dining room capped with beams and stone vaults, you can enjoy the specialties of longtime Nice resident Patricia Boschiazzo, who prepares such dishes as pissaladière (a kind of onion- and herb-enriched pizza), rack of lamb with Provençal herbs, beignets of vegetables, stuffed socca (a kind of crêpe), ratatouilles, and several kinds of grilled fish. The most impressive appetizer might be a farandole des spécialités niçoises, loaded with a variety of traditional regional specialties, including beignets of squid. The staff tends to be charming. In case you're wondering what the name of this establishment means, it translates from the Provençal as "et cetera, et cetera."

RESTAURANT L'ESTOCAFICADA, 2, rue de l'Hôtel-de-Ville. Tel. 93-80-21-64.
   Cuisine: NIÇOIS. **Reservations:** Recommended. **Bus:** 1, 2, or 5.
$ Prices: Appetizers 28–45 F ($5–$8.10); main dishes 55–200 F ($9.90–$36); pizzas 31–47 F ($5.60–$8.50). AE, MC, V.
   Open: Lunch Mon–Sat noon–2pm; dinner Mon–Sat 7–10pm. **Closed:** Two weeks in Nov.

Estocaficada is the Provençal word for stockfish, the ugliest fish in Europe. You can see one for yourself—there might be a dried-out, balloon-shaped version of one on display in the cozy dining room of this typically local restaurant in Old Nice. Brigitte Autier is the owner-chef, whose busy kitchens are visible from virtually anywhere in the dining room. Descended from a matriarchal line (since 1958) of mother-daughter teams who managed this place, she's one of the most devoted adherents of the preservation of recipes prepared long ago by her Niçois grandmother.

Examples of her cuisine are simple and robust, and include gnocchis, petits fritures of tiny seafish, beignets, several types of farcies (tomatoes, peppers, or onions stuffed with herbed fillings), grilled sardines, bouillabaisse served either as a main course or as a mini-version of its usual copious size, and faux-filets either with black pepper or with Calvados. As a concession to popular demand, the place also serves pizzas and pastas.

EVENING ENTERTAINMENT

Nice has some of the most active nightlife along the Riviera, with evenings usually beginning at one's favorite café. A quarterly booklet, *L'Infor,* available free at the tourist office, lists the city's cultural attractions. You can also pick up a copy of *La Semaine des Spectacles,* outlining the week's nighttime diversions.

The Performing Arts

OPERA DE NICE, 4, rue St-François-de-Paule. Tel. 93-85-67-31.
   The major cultural center along the Riviera, this institution has a busy season in winter. A full repertoire is presented, including both operas and the popular French Opéra Comique. In one season alone you might see *La Bohème, Tristan und Isolde,* and *Carmen,* as well as a *saison symphonique,* dominated by the Orchestre Philharmonique de Nice. The opera hall is also the major venue for concerts and recitals. The box office is open Tuesday through Saturday from 11am to 7pm.
   Admission: Tickets, 35–240 F ($6.30–$43.20).

Dance Clubs

JOK CLUB, in the Casino Roule, 1, promenade des Anglais. Tel. 93-87-95-87.
   This disco is connected to the town's casino, and attracts an over-25 crowd. Small, intimate, and glittering, it has its own entrance from one side of the casino. Drinks cost 70 F ($12.60). Open daily from 11pm to 4am.
   Admission: 120 F ($21.60).

LE MISSISSIPPI, 5, promenade des Anglais. Tel. 93-82-06-61.
   The atmosphere at this two-story establishment changes throughout the day. Its street level opens at 8am as a tea room and café, then changes at dusk into a piano bar. But it's best to come here after 10pm, when there is live music as often as four nights a week. The second-floor disco is open from 9pm to 3am. Drinks begin at 50 F ($9). The club is open Wednesday through Sunday from 8am to 3am.
   Admission: Disco, 100 F ($18); women admitted free Wed–Sun.

The Bar Scene

THE PIANO BAR, Hôtel Abela, 223, promenade des Anglais. Tel. 92-37-17-17.

Many nonresidents come to this piano bar for the sophisticated conviviality, and for the streamlined simplicity of its spartan but elegant setting. In a corner of the lobby, where a piano is set up almost like a piece of sculpture, a pianist will perform most evenings after 6pm. Beginning around 10:30pm, a musical trio will sometimes continue to perform. Drinks start at 65 F ($11.70). Open daily from 11am to 1am.

LE RELAIS AMERICAN BAR, in the Hôtel Négresco, 37, promenade des Anglais. Tel. 93-88-39-51.

This is the most beautiful bar in Nice, filled with white columns, an oxblood-red ceiling, Oriental carpets, English paneling, Italianate chairs, and large tapestries. It was once a haunt of actress Lillie Langtry, who would silently sit here, swathed in veils to hide her advancing age. With its piano music and white-jacketed waiters, the bar still attracts a chic clientele. Drinks go for 62 F ($11.20), and beer starts at 37 F ($6.70). It's open daily from 11am to midnight.

EN ROUTE TO LEVENS

Levens is an attractive residential town guarding the Vallée de la Vésubie. Fifteen miles from Nice on the D19, it's at an altitude of 1,800 feet. Tourists come this way to see some of the most beautiful spots in the mountains. I recommend taking a trip to the **Saut des Français (Frenchmen's Leap),** at the exit from the village of Duranus. In 1793, French Republican soldiers were tossed over this belvedere by guerrilla bands from Nice, called Barbets. The fall—without a parachute—was some 1,200 feet down to the Vésubie. Fifteen miles farther, **La Madone d'Utelle,** at an altitude of 3,900 feet, offers a panoramic view of the Maritime Alps.

WHERE TO STAY & DINE

MALAUSSENA, place de l'Hôtel-de-Ville, Levens, 06670 St-Martin-du-Var. Tel. 93-79-70-06. Fax 93-79-85-89. 14 rms (10 with bath or shower). TEL
$ Rates: 280 F ($50.40) single or double without bath or shower, 330 F ($59.40) single or double with bath or shower. Breakfast 25 F ($4.50) extra. MC, V.
Parking: Free. **Closed:** Nov–Dec 15.
This centrally located two-story hotel offers clean, comfortable bedrooms—some of which have first-rate plumbing. Although the inn is fairly simple, the welcome is definitely first-class. The food is excellent but not recommended for dieters. Two fixed-price menus are offered: A substantial dinner costs only 110 F ($19.80), while a larger repast costs 135 F ($24.30). Dinner is served at 7:30pm. The restaurant is closed to nonresidents except in July and August, when the general public is welcome, with reservations.

---

9. ST-PAUL-DE-VENCE

575 miles S of Paris, 14 miles E of Grasse,
17 miles E of Cannes, 19 miles N of Nice

GETTING THERE   By Bus   A bus makes infrequent runs from Nice to Vence, stopping off in St-Paul-de-Vence along the way.

ESSENTIALS   Orientation   The town's main street is rue Grande; an important square is place du Général-de-Gaulle. The Fondation Maeght, set in its own grounds a short walk from the center of town, is clearly indicated with signs.

Information   The Office de Tourisme, Maison Tour, rue Grande (tel. 93-32-86-95), is closed from November 15 to December 15.

Of all the perched villages of the Riviera, St-Paul-de-Vence is the best known. It was popularized in the 1920s when many noted artists lived there, occupying the little 16th-century houses that flank the narrow cobblestone streets. The hill town was originally built to protect its inhabitants from Saracens raiding the coast. The feudal hamlet grew up on a bastion of rock, almost blending into it. Its ramparts (allow about 30 minutes to encircle them) overlook a peaceful setting of flowers and olive and orange trees. As you make your way through the warren of streets you'll pass endless souvenir shops, a charming old fountain carved in the form of an urn, and a Gothic church from the 13th century.

WHAT TO SEE & DO

The most important attraction of St-Paul lies outside the walls at **✪ Fondation Maeght** (tel. 93-32-81-63). It's one of the most modern art museums in all of Europe. On the slope of a hill in pine-studded woods, the Maeght Foundation is like a Shangri-la. Not only is the architecture avant-garde, but the building houses one of the finest collections of contemporary art on the Riviera. Nature and the creations of men and women blend harmoniously in this unique achievement of the architect José Luís Sert. Its white concrete arcs give the impression of a giant pagoda.

A stark Calder rises like some futuristic monster on the grassy lawns. In a courtyard, the elongated bronze works of Giacometti (one of the finest collections of his works in the world) form a surrealistic garden, creating a hallucinatory mood. Sculpture is also displayed inside, but it's at its best in a naturalistic setting of surrounding terraces and gardens. The museum is built on several levels, its many glass walls providing an indoor-outdoor vista.

The foundation, a gift "to the people" from Aimé and Marguerite Maeght, also provides a showcase for new talent. Exhibitions are always changing. Everywhere you look, you see 20th-century art: mosaics by Chagall and Braque, Miró ceramics in the "labyrinth," and Ubac and Braque stained glass in the chapel. Bonnard, Kandinsky, Léger, Matisse, Barbara Hepworth, and many other artists are well represented.

There are a library, a cinema, and a cafeteria. In one showroom you can buy original lithographs by such artists as Chagall and Giacometti and limited-edition prints. Admission is 45 F ($8.10) for adults and 30 F ($5.40) for children. Open July through September, daily from 10am to 7pm; October through June, daily from 10am to 12:30pm and 2:30 to 6pm.

WHERE TO STAY
Very Expensive

LA COLOMBE D'OR [The Golden Dove], 1, place du Général-de-Gaulle, 16570 St-Paul-de-Vence. Tel. 96-32-80-02. Fax 93-32-77-18. 15 rms (all with bath), 11 suites. A/C TV TEL

$ Rates (including half board): 1,255 F ($225.90) single; 1,450 F ($261) double; from 1,600 F ($288) suite for two. AE, DC, MC, V. **Parking:** Free. **Closed:** Nov 5–Dec 20.

A stay here is like a visit to the museum of contemporary art. You'll see works by Chagall, Rouault, Dufy, Braque, Picasso, and Miró. According to a Riviera legend, many of the paintings were left in the 1920s by artists who "painted for their supper." High walls surround this hotel and its garden, terrace, and pool. The rooms are full of fine antiques. Reservations are required for accommodations as well as for meals.

Dining/Entertainment: You may dine on the garden patio or in the more informal dining rooms inside. A la carte meals average 300–400 F ($54–$72). Enjoy an after-dinner drink before the fireplace in the lower "pit lounge."

Facilities: Swimming pool, sauna.

LE MAS D'ARTIGNY, route de la Colle et des Hauts de St-Paul, 06570 St-Paul-de-Vence. Tel. 93-32-84-54. Fax 93-32-95-36. 53 rms (all with bath), 29 suites. A/C MINIBAR TV TEL

$ Rates: 850–1,830 F ($153–$329.40) single or double; from 2,680 F ($482.40) suite. Breakfast 115 F ($20.70) extra; half board 840–1,310 F ($151.20–$235.80) per person. MC, V. **Parking:** 70 F ($12.60).

⭐ This hotel might remind you of a sprawling Provençal homestead. It's about two miles from St-Paul, at the end of a winding road lined with pines and laurels. Semitropical plants surround the outside. In the lobby, there's a constantly changing exhibition of art. Former French president Giscard d'Estaing and Germany's Helmut Schmidt are two of the illustrious former guests of this Relais & Châteaux.

Each of the comfortably large bedrooms has its own terrace or balcony. Private suites (with a private pool) are on a slope below the blue-tile pool of the hotel, with hedges for privacy.

Dining/Entertainment: There's a bar and restaurant on the premises.
Facilities: Swimming pool.

Expensive

HOTEL LE ST-PAUL, 86, rue Grande, 06570 St-Paul-de-Vence. Tel. 93-32-65-25. Fax 93-32-52-94. 18 rms (all with bath), 3 suites. A/C MINIBAR TV TEL

$ Rates: 700–1,200 F ($126–$216) single or double; 1,100–1,900 F ($198–$342) suite. Breakfast 85 F ($15.30) extra; half board 385 F ($69.30) per person extra. AE, DC, MC, V.

⭐ Converted from an authentic 16th-century private residence and retaining many original features, this four-star Relais & Châteaux hotel is in the heart of the medieval village of Saint-Paul-de-Vence between Cannes and Monaco. Rooms, decorated in a sophisticated yet Provençal style, have safe-deposit boxes, satellite TV, and many extra touches. Prices vary according to the season and the view. Many rooms enjoy a sweeping view of the valley of Saint-Paul with the Mediterranean in the distance.

Dining/Entertainment: The hotel restaurant has a flower-bedecked terrace sheltered by the 16th-century ramparts of Saint-Paul as well as a superb dining room with vaulted ceilings. The menus might include such locally inspired dishes as homemade crab ravioli served with a creamy broth, filets of red mullet and fresh spinach in a crispy rosette and decorated with tomatoes cooked in saffron, filet of lamb from Sisteron served "rosé" and garnished with an eggplant and lamb pie, crispy strawberry millefeuille with a light Grand Marnier cream, or a fine apple and fig tart with vanilla ice-cream. Menus change with the season, according to local produce. Fixed-price lunches cost 190 F ($34.20) and fixed-price dinners are 290 F ($52.20) or 420 F ($75.60). The restaurant is open for lunch from noon to 2pm and for dinner from 7:30 to 10pm; closed for lunch on Wednesday and all day Thursday.

Moderate

AUBERGE LE HAMEAU, 528, route de la Colle, 06570 St-Paul-de-Vence. Tel. 93-32-80-24. Fax 93-32-55-75. 16 rms (all with bath or shower), 3 suites. MINIBAR TEL

$ Rates: 295–400 F ($53.10–$72) single; 340–400 F ($61.20–$72) double; from 600 F ($108) suite. Breakfast 43 F ($7.70) extra. AE, MC, V. **Parking:** Free. **Closed:** Jan 7–Feb 15 and Nov 16–Dec 22.

This romantic Mediterranean villa is on a hilltop on the outskirts of St-Paul-de-Vence, on the road to Colle at Hauts-de-St-Paul. There's a remarkable view of the surrounding hills and valleys, and most of the comfortable whitewashed bedrooms overlook a vineyard. There also are a sunny terrace with fruit trees, flowers, and a swimming pool.

HOTEL CLIMAT-DE-FRANCE, quartier des Fumerates, 06570 St-Paul-de-Vence. Tel. 93-32-94-24. Fax 93-32-91-07. 19 rms (all with bath). TV TEL

$ Rates: 500–600 F ($90–$108) single or double. Breakfast 55 F ($9.90) extra. AE, MC, V. **Parking:** Free.

Built in 1975, this hotel lies half a mile from the town center. This complex of low-slung, tile-roofed town houses is at the end of a steep driveway. While reclining in a chair by a pool, you can survey the countryside. Each room has its own small salon, balcony, or terrace. There's a restaurant near the reception desk where fixed-price menus cost 108–190 F ($19.40–$34.20).

LES ORANGERS, chemin des Fumerates, route de la Colle (D107), 06570 St-Paul-de-Vence. Tel. 93-32-80-95. Fax 93-32-00-32. 7 rms (all with bath), 2 suites. TEL

$ Rates: 380 F ($68.40) single; 490–580 F ($88.20–$104.40) double; 690 F ($124.20) suite. Breakfast 40 F ($7.20) extra. MC, V. **Parking:** Free.

Monsieur Franklin has created a beautiful "living oasis" in his villa less than half a mile from the village in a residential and commercial neighborhood beside the highway. The scents of roses, oranges, and lemons waft through the air. The main lounge is impeccably decorated with original oil paintings and furnished in a provincial style. Expect to be treated like a guest in a private home here. Rooms, decorated with antiques and Oriental carpets, have great views. On the sun terrace are banana trees, flowerbeds, and climbing geraniums.

Inexpensive

LES BASTIDES ST-PAUL, 880, route des Blaquières (route de Vence), 06570 St-Paul-de-Vence. Tel. 92-02-08-07. FAX 92-20-50-41. 17 rms (all with bath). MINIBAR TEL

$ Rates: 450–550 F ($81–$99) single or double. Breakfast 45 F ($8.10) extra. AE, DC, MC, V. **Parking:** Free.

This hotel was built in 1992 in the hills outside town, a mile south of St-Paul and 2½ miles south of Vence, in a style evocative of a tile-roofed, white-walled Provençal village. Divided into three separate buildings, it offers clean and comfortably carpeted accommodations, each accented with regional artifacts and designed in the regional style. On the premises is a swimming pool shaped like a cloverleaf, a cozy breakfast area, and a sensitive management staff headed by long-time hoteliers Marie José and Maurice Giraudet. Breakfast is served virtually anytime a client wants it.

WHERE TO DINE

LA COLOMBE D'OR, 1, place du Général-de-Gaulle. Tel. 96-32-80-02.
Cuisine: FRENCH. **Reservations:** Required.
$ Prices: Appetizers 52–410 F ($9.40–$73.80); main dishes 92–225 F ($16.60–$40.50). AE, DC, MC, V.
Open: Lunch daily noon–2:30pm; dinner daily 7–10:30pm. **Closed:** Nov 5–Dec 20.

"The Golden Dove," for decades the most celebrated restaurant in St-Paul, always seems to appear as a setting on virtually every film ever shot on the Riviera. Famous for its remarkable art collection, it offers sumptuous dining to guests who can also enjoy Miró, Picasso, Klee, Dufy, Utrillo, and Calder. In fair weather, everyone tries for a seat on the terrace so they can soak up the view.

You might begin with smoked salmon or a plate of foie gras from the Landes if you've recently won at the casino. Otherwise, you can generally count on a good-tasting soup made with the fresh vegetables of the season. One of the best fish dishes is poached sea bass, served with a mousseline sauce. You can also order daurade grilled to your specifications. Delectable tender beef comes with a side order of gratin dauphinois (potatoes), or you may prefer the delectable lamb from Sisteron. A spectacular finish to any meal is a soufflé flambé au Grand-Marnier.

10. VENCE

575 miles S of Paris, 19 miles N of Cannes, 15 miles NW of Nice

GETTING THERE   There's bus service from Nice, but most visitors drive.

ESSENTIALS Orientation Most of the village's narrow streets end at the Vieille Fontaine (Old Fountain) on place du Peyra, the geographic center of town.

Information The Office du Tourisme is on place Grand-Jardin (tel. 93-58-06-38).

Travel up into the hills 15 miles northwest of Nice—across country studded with cypresses, olive trees, and pines, where bright flowers, especially carnations, roses, and oleanders, grow in profusion—and Vence comes into view. Outside the town, along Boulevard Paul-André, two old olive presses carry on with their age-old duties. But the charm lies in the **Vieille Ville** (Old Town). Visitors invariably have themselves photographed on **Place du Peyra** in front of the urn-shaped **Vieille Fontaine** (Old Fountain), a background shot in several motion pictures. The 15th-century **square tower** is also a curiosity.

If you're wearing the right kind of shoes, the narrow, steep streets of the old town are worth exploring. Dating from the 10th century, the **cathedral** on Place Godeau is unremarkable except for some 15th-century Gothic choir stalls. But if it's the right day of the week, most visitors quickly pass through the narrow gates of this once-fortified walled town to where the sun shines more brightly, at the—

MATISSE CHAPEL It was a beautiful golden autumn along the Côte d'Azur. The great Henri Matisse was 77 years old, and after a turbulent personal search, he set out to create his masterpiece, or to quote the artist, "the culmination of a whole life dedicated to the search for truth." Just outside Vence, Matisse created the **Chapelle du Rosaire**, avenue Henri-Matisse (tel. 93-58-03-25), for the Dominican nuns of Monteils. From the front you might find it unremarkable and pass it by—until you spot a 40-foot crescent-adorned cross rising from a blue-tile roof.

Matisse wrote: "What I have done in the chapel is to create a religious space . . . in an enclosed area of very reduced proportions and to give it, solely by the play of colors and lines, the dimensions of infinity." The light picks up the subtle coloring in the simply rendered leaf forms and abstract patterns: sapphire-blue, aquamarine, and lemon-yellow. In black-and-white ceramics, St. Dominic is depicted in only a few lines. The most remarkable design is in the black-and-white-tile Stations of the Cross with Matisse's self-styled "tormented and passionate" figures. The bishop of Nice came to bless the chapel in the late spring of 1951. The artist's work was completed. He died three years later.

The chapel is open December 13 through October, only on Tuesday and Thursday from 10 to 11am and 2:30 to 5:30pm. Admission is free, but donations are welcomed.

WHERE TO STAY

Very Expensive

LE CHATEAU DU DOMAINE ST-MARTIN, route de Coursegoules, 06140 Vence. Tel. 93-58-02-02. Fax 93-24-08-91. 14 rms (all with bath), 10 suites. MINIBAR TV TEL
$ Rates: 1,560–2,250 F ($280.80–$405) single or double; from 2,900 F ($522) suite. Breakfast 105 F ($18.90) extra. AE, DC, MC, V. **Parking:** Free. **Closed:** Nov 15–Mar 15.

⭐ This château is in a 35-acre park on the crest of a high hill two miles outside Vence. It was built in 1936 on the grounds where the "Golden Goat treasury" was reputedly buried. When the Genève family purchased the estate, they had to sign a bill of sale agreeing to share the treasure, if found, with the previous owners. The rambling hacienda has spacious courtyards, twin rooms, and terraces—an idyllic retreat. A complex of tile-roofed villas with suites was built in the surrounding terraced gardens. You can walk through the gardens on winding paths lined with tall cypresses, past the ruined chapel and olive trees. Tall arched windows let in the coastal sunlight in the hand-tiled loggia, a gallery with antiques. The main drawing room, which faces the sea, has attracted such guests as Harry Truman, Isaac Stern, and

Konrad Adenauer, who called the château "the anteroom of paradise." The bedrooms are finely furnished.

Dining/Entertainment: The glass-enclosed restaurant has a view of the coast. Nonguests who make reservations are welcome. Fixed-price menus range from 250 F ($45) at lunch to 390–450 F ($70.20–$81) at dinner.

Facilities: Heart-shaped swimming pool.

Moderate

LE FLOREAL, av. Rhin-et-Danube, 06140 Vence. Tel. 93-58-64-40. Fax 93-58-79-69. 43 rms (all with bath), 2 suites. A/C MINIBAR TV TEL

$ Rates: 500 F ($90) single; 610 F ($109.80) double; from 910 F ($163.80) suite. Breakfast 50 F ($9) extra. MC, V. **Parking:** Free.

On the road to Grasse is this pleasant, comfortable hotel with a view of the mountains. Many of the well-furnished rooms look out on the large swimming pool in the well-kept garden, where orange trees and mimosa add fragrance to the breezes. The hotel has parking, air-conditioned lounges, and a bar.

Inexpensive

AUBERGE DES SEIGNEURS [Inn of the Noblemen], place du Friene, 06140 Vence. Tel. 93-58-04-24. Fax 93-24-08-01. 8 rms (all with shower). TEL

$ Rates: 300–320 F ($54–$57.60) single or double. Breakfast 50 F ($9) extra. AE, DC, MC, V. **Parking:** Free. **Closed:** Hotel closed mid-Oct to Nov. 30. Restaurant closed Mon year round and Sun for dinner Dec–Mar.

⑤ This 400-year-old stone hostelry in the old part of town lets you experience Old France. The inn is shaded by one of the largest trees on the Côte d'Azur; hence the plaza is called "Ash Square." Inside is a long wooden dining table, in view of an open fireplace with a row of hanging copper pots and pans. The cuisine of François I is served in the antique atmosphere of corner cupboards, ladderback chairs, wooden casks of flowers, dark beams, and an open spit for roasting and grilling. Fascinating decorative objects and antiques are everywhere. The food is superb, with fixed-price menus costing 200–230 F ($36–$41.40).

LA ROSERAIE, av. Henri-Giraud, route de Coursegoules, 06140 Vence. Tel. 93-58-02-20. Fax 93-58-99-31. 12 rms (all with shower or bath). TV TEL

$ Rates: 320 F ($57.60) single; 390 F ($70.20) double. Breakfast 45 F ($8.10) extra. AE, MC, V. **Parking:** Free. **Closed:** Jan.

This 19th-century manor house is on the road to Col-de-Vence. The Belle Epoque architecture is framed by a tropical landscape of trees, including kumquat, banana, orange, and a giant magnolia and cedar. Some of the newer rooms are spacious, with a private garden and terrace. Maurice and Josette Ganier have a reputation for good food and hospitality.

A restaurant terrace overlooks the spotlighted pool and gardens. On fair nights you can enjoy a romantic meal by candlelight. The cuisine of southwestern France is served, including ducks from Landes and the Dordogne. I especially recommend the duck-liver terrine. Armagnac flavors many dishes. Fixed-price menus run 180–200 F ($32.40–$36).

WHERE TO DINE

LA FARIGOULE, 15, rue Henri-Isnard. Tel. 93-58-01-27.
Cuisine: FRENCH. **Reservations:** Recommended.

$ Prices: Fixed-price menus 115–140 F ($20.70–$25.20). AE, MC, V.
Open: June–Sept, lunch Sat–Thurs 12:30–2pm; dinner Sat–Thurs 7–10pm. Off-season, lunch Sat–Thurs 12:30–2pm; dinner Sat–Thurs 7–9pm. **Closed:** Mid-Nov to mid-Dec.

⑤ During the summer you can enjoy regional cuisine in the garden under a rose arbor. The chef, Georgette Gastaud, grills much of the food on an open fire. A long line forms on Sunday afternoon. The least expensive fixed-price menu might include fish soup, trout meunière, a vegetable, and cheese or dessert—with service and drinks extra. The most expensive fixed-price menu is far more enticing and might include asparagus vinaigrette, mussels marinara, a tender rabbit with seasonal vegetables, cheese and dessert—with drinks and service extra.

11. CAGNES-SUR-MER

570 miles S of Paris; 13 miles NE of Cannes

GETTING THERE   By Bus   Buses from Nice and Cannes stop at Cagnes-Ville and at Béal/Les Collettes, within walking distance of Cros-de-Cagne. The climb from Cagnes-Ville to Le-Haut-de-Cagnes is very strenuous, so there's a minibus running about every 45 minutes from place de Gaulle, in the center of Cagnes-Ville to Le-Haut-de-Cagnes.

ESSENTIALS   Orientation   Divided into three distinct sections, the municipality includes the seafront resort of Cros-de-Cagnes, the commercial center of Cagnes-Ville, and the hilltop fortress of Le-Haut-de-Cagnes.

Information   The Office de Tourisme is located at 6, bd. Maréchal-Juin, Cagnes-Ville (tel. 93-20-61-64).

SPECIAL EVENTS   The International Festival of Painting is presented by the Musée d'Art Moderne Méditerranéen from July to September; 40 nations participate. For information, call 93-20-85-57.

Cagnes-sur-Mer, like the Roman god Janus, shows two faces. Perched on a hill in the "hinterlands" of Nice, **Le Haut-de-Cagnes** is one of the most charming spots on the Riviera. Naomi Barry wrote that it "crowns the top of a blue-cypressed hill like a village in an Italian Renaissance painting." At the foot of the hill is an old fishing port and rapidly developing beach resort called **Cros-de-Cagnes,** between Nice and Antibes.

For years Le Haut-de-Cagnes attracted the French literati, including Simone de Beauvoir, who wrote *Les Mandarins* here. A colony of painters also settled here; Renoir said the village was "the place where I want to paint until the last day of my life." Today the **racecourse** is considered one of the finest in France.

WHAT TO SEE & DO

The orange groves and fields of carnations of the upper village provide a beautiful setting for the narrow cobblestone streets and 17th- and 18th-century homes. Drive your car to the top, where you can enjoy the view from place du Château and have lunch or a drink at a sidewalk café.

While in Le Haut-de-Cagnes, visit the **fortress** on place Grimaldi. It was built in 1301 by Rainier Grimaldi, a lord of Monaco and a French admiral (see the portrait inside). Charts reveal how the defenses were organized. In the early 17th century the dank castle was converted into a more gracious Louis XIII château.

The château contains the **Musée de l'Olivier (Museum of the Olive Tree)** and a **Musée d'Art Moderne Méditerranéen (Museum of Modern Mediterranean Art),** 7, place Grimaldi (tel. 93-20-87-29). The ethnographical museum shows the steps involved in the cultivation and processing of the olive. The modern-art gallery displays work by Kisling, Carzou, Dufy, Cocteau, and Seyssaud, among other painters, along with temporary exhibitions. In one salon is an interesting trompe-l'oeil fresco depicting *La Chute de Phaeton* by Carlone, an Italian. From the tower you get a spectacular view of the Côte d'Azur. Open June 15 to September, Wednesday through Monday from 10am to noon and 2 to 6pm; October to June 14, Wednesday through Monday from 10am to noon and 2 to 5pm; closed from October 15 to November 15. Admission is 6 F ($1.10) for adults, 3 F (50¢) for children. The International Festival of Painting takes place here (see "Special Events," above).

Cagnes-sur-Mer offers several options for dining and accommodations: You can stay and dine either in Le Haut-de-Cagnes, the hilltop town, or on the water at Cros-de-Cagnes. You can also find food and lodging nearby at La Colle-sur-Loup.

WHERE TO STAY

In Le Haut-de-Cagnes

LE CAGNARD, rue du Pontis-Long, le Haut-de-Cagnes, 06800 Cagnes-sur-Mer. Tel. 93-20-73-21. Fax 93-22-06-39. 18 rms (all with bath), 10 suites. MINIBAR TV TEL

$ Rates: 500 F ($90) single; 650–900 F ($117–$162) double; 1,100–1,500 F ($198–$270) suite. Breakfast 70 F ($12.60) extra. AE, DC, MC, V. **Parking:** Free. **Closed:** Nov–Dec 19.

This 18th-century inn has attracted such outstanding members of the French literary and art worlds as Simone de Beauvoir, Renoir, Chagall, Soutine, and Modigliani. Several village houses have been joined to form the handsome hostelry owned by Felix Barel. The dining room is covered with frescoes, and there is also a vine-draped terrace. The bedrooms and salons are furnished with family antiques, such as fruitwood provincial chests, armoires, Louis XV chairs, and copper lavabos. Each room has its own style; some are in a duplex, and others have private terraces and views of the countryside.

The restaurant features Sisteron lamb (carré d'agneau), spit-roasted with Provençal herbs, served only for two. The côte de boeuf is good and tender. For dessert, the pièce de résistance is the extravagantly prepared mousseline de glace aux charmeuses de bois. Fixed-price menus begin at 400 F ($72); à la carte meals average 530 F ($95.40).

In Cros-de-Cagnes

HOTEL LE MINARET, av. Serre, 06800 Cros-de-Cagnes. Tel. 93-20-16-52. 20 rms (all with bath or shower). TV TEL

$ Rates: 200 F ($36) single; 280 F ($50.40) double. Breakfast 25 F ($4.50) extra. MC, V.

Across from the post office, this two-star hotel has a courtyard with café tables in the front and a hard-working staff. Built in 1958, it once sported a decorative minaret in the North African style. Although it was later removed in a restoration, the name has remained. Fifty yards from the beach, Le Minaret also has a shaded garden filled with mimosa, orange trees, and palms. Some rooms have terraces or balconies and small kitchenettes. There's a bar on the premises, but no restaurant, although several lie within walking distance.

WHERE TO DINE

In Le Haut-de-Cagnes

LE GRIMALDI, 6, place du Château, le Haut-de-Cagnes, 06800 Cagnes-sur-Mer. Tel. 93-20-60-24.
Cuisine: FRENCH. **Reservations:** Recommended.

$ Prices: Appetizers 38–55 F ($6.80–$9.90); main dishes 60–150 F ($10.80–$27); fixed-price menus 110 F ($19.80) and 180 F ($32.40). AE, DC, MC, V.
Open: Wed–Mon lunch daily noon–3pm; dinner Wed–Mon 7:30–11pm.
Closed: Jan 15–Feb 15.

At Le Grimaldi, you can dine either under bright umbrellas on the town's main square or in a dining room whose walls were built during the Middle Ages. Run by the same hard-working family since 1963, the restaurant serves succulent specialties which include salade niçoise, lapin (rabbit) chasseur, a savory version of bouillabaisse, mussels provençal, or trout with almonds.

The hotel also offers six simply furnished rooms, usually with their original, roughly hewn ceiling beams, a wash basin, and a bidet. The price is 200 F ($36) for single or double occupancy, plus 30 F ($5.40) for breakfast and 30 F ($5.40) for overnight parking.

JOSY-JO, 8, place du Planastel. Tel. 93-20-68-76.
   Cuisine: FRENCH. **Reservations:** Required.
$ **Prices:** Appetizers 55–120 F ($9.90–$21.60); main dishes 130–160 F ($23.40–$28.80). MC, V.
   Open: Lunch Mon–Fri noon–2pm; dinner Mon–Sat 7:30–10pm. **Closed:** July 14–Aug 15.

The best restaurant outside the hotels of Cagnes-sur-Mer is on the main road leading to the château. Sheltered behind masses of vines and flowers, it used to be the home and studio of Modigliani and Soutine during their hungriest years. Today it belongs to the charming and cheerful Bandecchi family, who have lined the dining room with art. Their cuisine is simple, fresh, and excellent. You can enjoy a brochette of gigot of lamb with kidneys, four succulent varieties of steak, calves' liver, a homemade terrine of foie gras of duckling, an array of salads, and Irish coffee. Meats are roasted over an open grill flaming with Portuguese charcoal; other dishes are prepared in the modern kitchen.

In Cros-de-Cagnes

LOULOU [La Réserve], 91, bd. de la Plage. Tel. 93-31-00-17.
   Cuisine: FRENCH. **Reservations:** Recommended.
$ **Prices:** Appetizers 80–130 F ($14.40–$23.40); main dishes 135–320 F ($24.30–$57.60). MC, V.
   Open: Sept–July 14, lunch Mon–Fri noon–2:30pm; dinner Mon–Sat 7–9:45pm. July 15–Aug, dinner only, Mon–Sat 7–9:45pm.

Named after a famous, long-departed chef named Loulou, this restaurant occupies a three-story 19th-century building across the street from the sea. In front is a glassed-in veranda which many guests find suitable for people-watching. Chef Eric Campo is noted for his fresh fish dishes, as well as for a soup of rockfish (in season), aiguillettes of duckling with herbs, and a selection of grilled meats.

NEARBY ACCOMMODATIONS & DINING

In La Colle-sur-Loup

HOSTELLERIE DE L'ABBAYE, av. de la Libération (route de Grasse), 06480 La Colle-sur-Loup. Tel. 93-32-66-77. Fax 93-32-61-28. 13 rms (all with bath). MINIBAR TV TEL **Directions:** Take the D6 1½ miles northwest of Cagnes-sur-Mer.
$ **Rates:** 520–740 F ($93.60–$133.20) single; 610–800 F ($109.80–$144) double. Breakfast 55 F ($9.90) extra. AE, DC, MC, V. **Parking:** Free. **Closed:** Jan.

This charming and unusual hotel, just off the D6 between Grasse and Cagnes-sur-Mer, was installed in a 10th-century abbey. It's surrounded by old trees. One of the salons was formerly a stable for horses; today it's comfortably furnished with a fireplace and wrought-iron chandeliers. The rooms are beautifully furnished. Meals are served in the garden near the fountain or in the timbered dining room, with fixed-price menus costing 220 F ($39.60), 300 F ($54), and 400 F ($72). There's a heated swimming pool in the garden.

NEARBY ATTRACTIONS

LES COLLETTES, 19, chemin des Collettes. Tel. 93-20-61-07.
   This museum has been restored to what it looked like when Renoir lived here from 1908 until his death in 1919. He continued to sculpt here, even though he was crippled by arthritis and had to be helped in and out of a wheelchair. He also

continued to paint, with a brush tied to his hand and with the help of assistants. One of his last paintings, *Rest After Bathing,* is owned by the Louvre.

The house was built in 1907 in an olive and orange grove. There's a bust of Madame Renoir in the entrance room. You can explore the drawing room and dining room on your own before going upstairs to the artist's bedroom. In his atelier are his wheelchair, easel, and brushes. From the terrace of Madame Renoir's bedroom is a stunning view of Cap d'Antibes and Le Haut-de-Cagnes. The museum owns only three paintings, but it has 12 sculptures. On a wall hangs a photograph of one of Renoir's sons, Pierre, as he appeared in the 1932 film *Madame Bovary.*

Admission: 20 F ($3.60) adults, 10 F ($1.80) children.
Open: Wed–Mon 11–11:30am and 2–5:30pm.

LE MUSÉE DE L'ART CULINAIRE, Villeneuve-Loubet, Foundation Escoffier, rue Escoffier. Tel. 93-20-80-51.

This culinary center honoring Escoffier, the world's greatest chef, was created in 1956 by Joseph Donon, his former apprentice. The international museum preserves mementos of great chefs from the 16th to the 20th century, including many sugar creations by French pastry cooks. The focus of the museum, however, is on memorabilia from "the king of chefs and the chef of kings," Escoffier, who was born here in 1846, in Villeneuve-Loubet in the Alps-Maritimes. His career began in 1859 at the age of 13 and he became the world-famous chef of the Savoy in London in the 1890s. He worked until he retired from London's Carlton in 1920. He died in 1935 at Monte Carlo at the age of 89.

Admission: 12 F ($2.20) adults, 8 F ($1.40) children.
Open: June–Sept, Tues–Sun 2–7pm; Oct and Dec–May, Tues–Sat 2–6pm.
Closed: Nov.

---

12. BIOT

570 miles S of Paris; 6 miles E of Cagnes-sur-Mer; 4 miles NW of Antibes

GETTING THERE   By Train   The train station is two miles from the town center. There is frequent service from Nice and Antibes.

By Bus   The bus from Antibes is even more convenient than the train.

ESSENTIALS   Orientation   An important square in the old city is place de la Chapelle. The famous Léger museum lies a short walk southeast from the center of town.

Information   For information, contact the Office de Tourisme, place de la Chapelle (tel. 93-65-05-85).

Biot has been famous for its pottery ever since merchants began to ship earthenware jars to Phoenicia and destinations throughout the Mediterranean. Biot was originally settled by Gallo-Romans and has had a long war-torn history. Somehow the potters still manage to work at their ancient craft. Biot is also the place Fernand Léger (1881–1955) chose to paint until the day he died. The greatest collection of his work is on display at a museum here.

In the late 1940s glassmakers created a bubble-flecked glass known as *verre rustique.* It comes in brilliant colors such as cobalt and emerald and is displayed in many store windows on the main shopping street. The town also is known for its carnations and roses, which are sold on the town's arcaded square. Flowers also are flown to the capitals of northern Europe.

WHAT TO SEE & DO

The most popular attraction in town is the ✪ **Musée National Fernand-Léger,** chemin du Val-de-Pome (tel. 93-65-63-61), inaugurated in 1960. The collection was assembled by his widow, Mme Nadia Léger. The stone-and-marble facade of the museum is enhanced by Léger's mosaic and ceramic mural. On the grounds is a polychrome ceramic sculpture, *Le Jardin d'Enfant*. Inside are two floors of geometrical forms in pure, flat colors. The collection includes gouaches, paintings, ceramics, tapestries, and sculptures—showing the development of the artist from 1905 until his death. His paintings abound with cranes, acrobats, scaffolding, railroad signals, buxom nudes, casings, and crankshafts. From his first cubist paintings, Léger was dubbed a "Tubist." Perhaps the most unusual work depicts a Léger *Mona Lisa* contemplating a set of monumental keys, a wide-mouthed fish dangling at an angle over her head.

One critic wrote that "Léger has been attacked by several varieties of 'humanists' for 'dehumanizing' art by mechanizing his figures; but has he not at the same time helped to humanize the machine by integrating it in the painting?" During World War II Léger lived in the United States, most of the time in New York.

The museum is open Wednesday through Monday from 10am to noon and 2 to 6pm (to 5pm in winter). Admission is 30 F ($5.40) for adults, 20 F ($3.60) for ages 18–24 and over 60.

WHERE TO DINE

LES TERRAILLERS, 11, route du Chemin-Neuf. Tel. 93-65-01-59.
  Cuisine: FRENCH. **Reservations:** Required, as far in advance as possible.
$ Prices: Appetizers 98–135 F ($17.60–$24.30); main dishes 125–310 F ($22.50–$55.80); fixed-price menus 160 F ($28.80), 200 F ($36), 230 F ($41.40), 290 F ($52.20), and 340 F ($61.20). AE, V.
  Open: Lunch Thurs–Tues noon–2pm; dinner Thurs–Tues 7–10pm. **Closed:** Nov.

★ This 16th-century studio that produced clay pots and ceramics has been transformed into a restaurant. Today the specialties coming from the ovens are far more succulent. The menu might include a terrine of foie gras flavored with Armagnac, ravioli stuffed with lobster, and rabbit with wild mushrooms. You might prefer the well-decorated dining room if the noise of the passing cars might spoil a meal for you on the terrace.

---

13. ANTIBES & CAP D'ANTIBES

567 miles S of Paris; 13 miles SW of Nice

GETTING THERE By Train   Antibes is about a 20-minute train ride from Nice.

ESSENTIALS Orientation   The town of Antibes lies on the northeastern boundary of a rocky jagged peninsula called Le Cap d'Antibes, full of glamorous private homes, hotels, and restaurants. In the town, the **Vieille-Ville** lies between Port Vauban, Vieux Port, the rocky coastline, and the busy traffic arteries west of boulevard du Président-Wilson.

Information   For information, inquire at the Office de Tourisme, place du Général-de-Gaulle (tel. 93-33-95-64).

On the other side of the Bay of Angels, across from Nice, is the port of Antibes. This old Mediterranean town has a quiet charm, unique on the Côte d'Azur. Its little harbor is filled with fishing boats and pleasure yachts. The marketplaces are full of flowers, mostly roses and carnations. When the Bonaparte family was here in 1794, the future princesses reportedly stole artichokes and figs from the nearby farms. If you're in Antibes in the evening, you can watch fishermen playing the popular Riviera game of boule.

Spiritually, Antibes is totally divorced from Cap d'Antibes, a peninsula studded with the villas and swimming pools of the wealthy. Long a playground of the rich, it was described in F. Scott Fitzgerald's *Tender Is the Night* as "old villas rotted like water lilies among the massed pines." Photographs of film stars lounging at the Eden Roc have appeared in countless Sunday supplements.

WHAT TO SEE & DO

On the ramparts above the port of Antibes is the **Château Grimaldi,** place du Château, which contains the ✪ **Picasso Museum** (tel. 93-34-91-91). Once the home of the princes of Antibes of the Grimaldi family, who ruled the city from 1385 to 1608, today it houses one of the greatest Picasso collections in the world. He came to the small town after his bitter war years in Paris and stayed in a small hotel room at Golfe-Juan until the museum director at Antibes invited the great Spaniard to work and live at the museum. Picasso agreed and spent 1946 painting at the museum. When he departed he gave the museum all the work he'd done at Antibes that year—two dozen paintings, nearly 80 pieces of ceramics, 44 drawings, 32 lithographs, 11 oils on paper, two pieces of sculpture, and five tapestries. All are on display. In addition, a gallery of contemporary art exhibits works by Léger, Miró, Ernst, de Staël, and Calder, among others. For contrast there's an exhibit of Ligurian, Greek, and Roman artifacts. Open July to September, daily from 10am to noon and 3 to 7pm; off-season, daily from 10am to noon and 2 to 6pm. Admission is 22 F ($4) for adults, 12 F ($2.20) for ages 18–24 and over 60; free for children under 18.

Cap d'Antibes has the **Musée Naval et Napoléonien,** Batterie du Grillon, boulevard du Maréchal-Juin (tel. 93-61-45-32). This ancient military tower contains an interesting collection of Napoleonic memorabilia, naval models, paintings, and army mementos. A toy-soldier collection depicts various uniforms, including one used by Napoléon in the Marengo campaign. A wall painting on wood shows Napoléon's entrance into Grenoble; another tableau shows him disembarking at Golfe-Juan on March 1, 1815. In contrast to Canova's Greek-god image of Napoléon, a miniature pendant by Barrault reveals the Corsican general as he really looked, with pudgy cheeks and a receding hairline. In the rear rotunda is one of the many hats worn by the emperor. You can climb to the top of the tower for a view of the coast that's worth the price of admission, including a wide sweep of Juan-les-Pins and the harbor dotted with sailboats. The museum is open Monday through Friday from 9:30am to noon and 2 to 5pm; and on Saturday from 9:30am to noon; closed in October. Admission is 10 F ($1.80) for adults and 5 F (90¢) for children under 10.

WHERE TO STAY

Very Expensive

HOTEL DU CAP-EDEN ROC, bd. J-F-Kennedy, 06600 Cap d'Antibes. Tel. 93-61-39-01. Fax 93-67-76-04. 130 rms (all with bath), 10 suites. A/C TEL **Bus:** A2.

$ **Rates:** 1,500–2,300 F ($270–$414) single; 2,300–3,000 F ($414–$540) double; from 4,000 F ($720) suite. Breakfast 120 F ($21.60) extra. No credit cards. **Parking:** Free. **Closed:** Mid-Oct to mid-April.

✪ This palatial Second Empire hotel, opened in 1870, is surrounded by 22 splendid acres of gardens. In Fitzgerald's words, "the notable and fashionable people" lounge around the swimming pool built in the rugged rocks next to the lapping waves of the Mediterranean. The celebrities change with the years but have included Lloyd George, Anatole France, Bernard Shaw, Somerset Maugham, Chaplin, Fairbanks, Gable, Bogart, Orson Welles, Marlene Dietrich, Johnny Carson, Mary Pickford, Sophia Loren, Picasso, Chagall, Gary Cooper, and the Ford, Kennedy, and du Pont families. Today you might see Madonna. The hotel is like a great country estate, with spacious, well-decorated public rooms, marble fireplaces, scenic paneling, crystal chandeliers, and clusters of richly upholstered armchairs. Some rooms and suites have regal and luxurious period furnishings.

Dining/Entertainment: The world-famous Pavillon Eden Roc is near a rock garden apart from the hotel. It has a magnificent view of the Mediterranean. Venetian chandeliers, Louis XV chairs, and elegant draperies add to the dramatic setting. Lunch is served on an outer terrace, under umbrellas and an arbor. Dinner specialties include bouillabaisse, lobster Thermidor, and sea bass with fennel. Meals cost 500–700 F ($90–$126).

Moderate

AUBERGE DE LA GARDIOLE, chemin de la Garoupe, 06600 Cap d'Antibes. Tel. 93-61-35-03. Fax 93-67-61-87. 21 rms (all with bath or shower). MINIBAR TV TEL **Bus:** A2.

$ Rates (including half board): 480–500 F ($86.40–$90) per person. AE, DC, MC, V. **Closed:** Nov 4–Dec 10.

Anne Marie Arama runs this country inn with a delightful personal touch. The large villa is surrounded by gardens and pergola and is located in an area of private estates. The charming bedrooms, on the upper floors of the inn and in the little buildings in the garden, contain personal safes, and 15 are air-conditioned.

Anne Marie buys the food and supervises its preparation; the cuisine is French and Provençal. The cheerful dining room has a fireplace and hanging pots and pans. In good weather you can dine under a trellis covered with a wisteria vine. Fixed-price menus cost 140–280 F ($25.20–$50.40) for nonguests.

BEAU SITE, 141, bd. J-F-Kennedy, 06600 Cap d'Antibes. Tel. 93-61-53-43. Fax 93-67-78-16. 26 rms (all with bath). TV TEL **Bus:** A2.

$ Rates: 430–470 F ($77.40–$84.60) single; 450–490 F ($81–$88.20) double. Breakfast 48 F ($8.60) extra; additional bed 150 F ($27) per person. AE, MC, V. **Parking:** Free.

This white stucco villa with a tile roof and heavy shutters is surrounded by eucalyptus trees, pines, and palms. Located off the main road, a seven-minute walk from the beach, it has a low wall of flower urns and wrought-iron gates. The interior is like a country inn, with oak beams and antiques. Bedrooms are comfortable and well maintained.

HOTEL ROYAL, bd. du Maréchal-Leclerc, 06600 Antibes. Tel. 93-34-03-09. Fax 93-34-23-31. 38 rms (all with bath). TEL **Bus:** A2.

$ Rates (including half board): 390–490 F ($70.20–$88.20) per person. AE, DC, MC, V. **Parking:** 40 F ($7.20). **Closed:** Nov 5–Dec 15.

Built 80 years ago, this is the oldest hotel in Antibes. Former guests include Bing Crosby and novelist Graham Greene. The Royal has its own private beach, a café terrace in front, two restaurants, and an English bar just off the lobby. Even if you're not a guest at the hotel, you can enjoy a meal at Le Dauphin—open for lunch daily from noon to 2:30pm and for dinner daily from 7 to 10pm. Fixed-price menus run 145–185 F ($26.10–$33.30). The most expensive menu is a seafood specialty.

MANOIR CASTEL GAROUPE AXA, 959, bd. de la Garoupe, 06600 Antibes. Tel. 93-61-36-51. Fax 93-67-74-88. 25 apts (all with bath or shower). MINIBAR TV TEL **Bus:** A2.

$ Rates (including continental breakfast): 670 F ($120.60) single; 720–1,000 F ($129.60–$180) double. MC, V. **Parking:** Free. **Closed:** Nov 15–Mar 15.

I highly recommend this Mediterranean villa because it offers apartments for the price of hotel rooms elsewhere. It has a tile roof, private balconies, arches, and shuttered windows. It's located on a private lane in the center of the cape and has a tranquil, shady garden. Facilities include a freshwater swimming pool and a tennis court amid gnarled olive trees. The rooms are nicely appointed.

Inexpensive

LE CAMEO, place Nationale, 06600 Antibes. Tel. 93-34-24-17. 8 rms (3 with shower but no toilet, 5 with bath and toilet). TEL **Bus:** A2.

$ Rates (including breakfast): 215 F ($38.70) single or double with shower but no toilet, 275 F ($49.50) single or double with bath and toilet. DC, MC, V. **Closed:** Jan–Feb.

Located on a historic square with large trees, this 19th-century Provençal villa is the best-known inn in the center of town. Local residents gather every afternoon and evening in the bar, perhaps taking a meal in the adjacent home-style dining room. Amid bouquets of flowers and crowded tables, you'll enjoy local fish dishes, stuffed mussels, fish soup, bouillabaisse, and fried scampi. Fixed-price menus are offered for 120–160 F ($21.60–$28.80). The restaurant is open for lunch Wednesday through Monday from noon to 2pm and for dinner Monday and Wednesday through Saturday from 7 to 10:30pm.

WHERE TO DINE

LA BONNE AUBERGE, quartier de Brague, route N7. Tel. 93-33-36-65.
   Cuisine: FRENCH. **Reservations:** Required. **Directions:** Take the coastal highway (N7) 2½ miles from Antibes.
$ Prices: Fixed-price menu 175 F ($31.50). MC, V.
   Open: Oct–Nov 14 and Dec 16–Apr, lunch Tues–Sun noon–2pm; dinner Tues–Sun 7–10:30pm. May–Sept, lunch daily noon–2pm; dinner daily 7–10:30pm. **Closed:** Nov 15–Dec 15.

For many years following its establishment in 1975 by Jo Rostang, this was one of the most famous restaurants on the French Riviera. In 1992, following the death of its famous founder, the culinary heir, Philippe Rostang, wisely limited its scope and transformed it into a worthwhile but less ambitious restaurant. Today, you'll approach the ivy-covered premises of a villa built in 1945, passing an impressive crescent-shaped driveway and long rows of arbors and arches.

   The menu offers a wide selection of food items at a single fixed price of 175 F ($31.50) per person, plus wine. Menu items vary with the seasons and the availability of fresh ingredients, but might include a Basque-inspired pipérade with poached eggs, a savory swordfish tart, chicken with vinegar and garlic, and quenelles de brochet Jo Rostang. Dessert might be a truly enchanting peach soufflé.

RESTAURANT DE BACON, bd. de Bacon. Tel. 93-61-50-02.
   Cuisine: FRENCH. **Reservations:** Required.
$ Prices: Appetizers 55–320 F ($9.90–$57.60); main dishes 250–500 F ($45–$90). AE, DC, MC, V.
   Open: Lunch Tues–Sun 12:30–2pm; dinner Tues–Sun 8–10pm. **Closed:** Nov 15–Jan.

This restaurant occupies an airy postwar building on a rocky peninsula extending seaward from Cap d'Antibes. Set among some of the most expensive private residences in the world, it has a panoramic view of the Nice coastline. Bouillabaisse aficionados claim that Bacon's offers the consistently best version in all of France. Bouillabaisse, which was originally conceived centuries ago as a simple fisherman's supper, is now one of the great dishes of the world. In its deluxe version, saltwater crayfish float atop the savory brew; I prefer the simple version—a waiter adds the finishing touches at your table. Don't expect a wide array of meats here, but there is plenty of Mediterranean fish. If bouillabaisse is not to your liking, try a fish soup with the traditional garlic-laden rouille sauce, a fish terrine, sea bass, John Dory, or something from an exotic collection of fish unknown in North American waters. These include sar, pageot, and denti, prepared in several different ways. If you order one of the messier dishes (such as lobster), someone will tie an enormous bib around your neck.

   Many North American visitors are confused by the way fish courses are priced by the gram. A guideline to remember is that light lunches here cost around 350–450 F ($63–$81); substantial dinners go for 410–700 F ($73.80–$126).

LES VIEUX MURS, promenade de l'avenue de l'Amiral-de-Grasse. Tel. 93-34-06-73.
   Cuisine: FRENCH/SEAFOOD. **Reservations:** Recommended.
$ Prices: Appetizers 100–160 F ($18–$28.80); main dishes 130–220 F ($23.40–$39.60); fixed-price menu 200 F ($36). AE, MC, V.
   Open: Lunch daily noon–2pm; dinner daily 7:30–10pm.

This charming Provençal tavern occupies a room inside the 17th-century ramparts that used to fortify the old seaport of Antibes. Designed, like the rest of the fortress, by the military architect Vauban, the space contains soaring stone vaults and a simple decor painted for the most part in white. There's also a glassed-in front terrace which offers a pleasant view of the water. Menu specialties include a warm salad of mullet, oysters baked in champagne sauce, and very fresh filets of such fish as daurade, rascasse, sole, salmon, and rougeot, prepared in dozens of different ways.

14. JUAN-LES-PINS

567 miles S of Paris, 6 miles S of Cannes

GETTING THERE Juan-les-Pins is connected by rail and bus to most other Mediterranean coastal resorts, especially Nice, from which frequent trains arrive throughout the day (trip time: 30 minutes).

ESSENTIALS Orientation The seacoast promenades are paralleled by the busy boulevard Charles-Guillaumont. The casino is close to the beach, a few blocks south of the railway station.

Information The Office de Tourisme is at 51, bd. Charles-Guillaumont (tel. 93-61-04-98).

SPECIAL EVENTS There is a jazz festival in July. The tourist office (see above) will supply the details, which change from year to year.

This suburb of Antibes is a resort that was developed in the 1920s by Frank Jay Gould. At that time, people flocked to "John of the Pines" to escape the "crassness" of nearby Cannes. In the 1930s Juan-les-Pins drew a chic, wealthy crowd during the winter. Today it attracts young Europeans from many economic backgrounds.

Juan-les-Pins is often called a honky-tonk town or the "Coney Island of the Riviera," but anyone who calls it that hasn't seen Coney Island in a long time. One newspaper writer called it "a pop-art Monte Carlo, with burlesque shows and nude beaches"—a description much too enticing or provocative for such a middle-class resort.

Juan-les-Pins offers some of the best **nightlife** on the Riviera. The action reaches its frenzied height during the jazz festival in July. Many revelers stay up all night in the smoky jazz joints, then sleep it off the next day on the beach. The **casino,** in the center of town, offers cabaret entertainment, sometimes until daybreak. During the day, skin-diving and waterskiing predominate. The pines sweep down to a good **beach,** crowded with summer sunbathers.

WHERE TO STAY

In addition to the following recommendations, the Auberge de l'Esterel (see "Where to Dine," below) has rooms to rent.

Expensive

BELLES-RIVES, bd. Baudoin, 06160 Juan-les-Pins. Tel. 93-61-02-79. Fax 93-67-43-51. 41 rms (all with bath), 4 suites. A/C MINIBAR TV TEL

$ Rates (including half board): 1,260–1,675 F ($226.80–$301.50) per person. AE, MC, V. **Closed:** Oct 5–Mar.

This bayside hotel has rooms with a subdued and elegant decor. It's one of the most tranquil oases along the coast.

Dining/Entertainment: The lower terraces are devoted to garden dining rooms, and a waterside aquatic club with a snack bar/lounge and a jetty extending into the water. Dinners are served in a romantic setting on the terrace with a panoramic view of the bay. Meals begin at 360 F ($64.80).

Facilities: Boating, waterskiing, sailing, fishing, private beach.

HOTEL JUANA, La Pinède, av. Gallice, 06160 Juan-les-Pins. Tel. 93-61-08-70. Fax 93-61-76-70. 45 rms (all with bath or shower), 5 suites. A/C TV TEL

$ Rates: 500–900 F ($90–$162) single; 700–1,600 F ($126–$288) double; 1,800 F ($324) suite. Breakfast 90 F ($16.20) extra; half board 390 F ($70.20) per person extra. No credit cards.

This oasis of chic sophistication, owned by the Barache family since 1931, is separated from the sea by the park of pines that gave Juan-les-Pins its name. The hotel has a private swimming club where hotel guests can rent a "parasol and pad" on the sandy beach at reduced rates and an art deco facade much admired by architectural enthusiasts. Nearby is a park with umbrella tables and shady palms.

Dining/Entertainment: La Terrasse restaurant is recommended under "Where to Dine," below. There is also a bar in the poolhouse.

Services: 24-hour room service.

Facilities: Heated outdoor swimming pool, solarium.

Moderate

HOTEL DES MIMOSAS, rue Pauline, 06160 Juan-les-Pins. Tel. 93-61-04-16. 36 rms (all with bath). MINIBAR TEL

$ Rates: 395–630 F ($71.10–$113.40) single or double. Breakfast 48 F ($8.60) extra. No credit cards. **Parking:** Free. **Closed:** Oct–Mar.

Five minutes from the town center, this elegant 1870s-style villa sprawls in a tropical garden on a hilltop. Michel and Raymonde Sauret redesigned the interior in 1976 with the help of an architect who was trained in the United States. The decor is a mix of high-tech and Italian-style comfort, with antique and modern furniture. There's a bar, but no restaurant. Ten of the rooms have private terraces. A swimming pool is set, California style, amid huge palm trees. The hotel is fully booked in the summer, so reserve far in advance.

HOTEL LE PRE CATELAN, 22, av. des Palmiers, 06160 Juan-les-Pins. Tel. 93-61-05-11. Fax 93-67-83-11. 18 rms (all with bath or shower) TEL

$ Rates: 350–500 F ($63–$90) single or double. Breakfast 35 F ($6.30) extra. AE, MC, V. **Parking:** Free.

Located in a residential area near the town park and the sea, this Provençal villa has a garden with rock terraces, towering palms, lemon and orange trees, large pots of pink geraniums, trimmed hedges, and outdoor furniture. The atmosphere is casual. The more expensive rooms have private terraces. The hotel and restaurant are open all year.

LE PASSY, 15, av. Louis-Gallet, 06160 Juan-les-Pins. Tel. 93-61-11-09. Fax 93-67-91-78. 35 rms (all with bath). TV TEL

$ Rates: 420 F ($75.60) single; 460–580 F ($82.80–$104.40) double. Breakfast 35 F ($6.30) extra. AE, DC, MC, V.

Centrally located, Le Passy opens onto a small garden with palm trees and a wide flagstone terrace. The other side faces the sea and coastal boulevard. Furnishings are Nordic modern, and the newer rooms have their own little balconies.

Inexpensive

HOTEL CECIL, rue Jonnard, 06160 Juan-les-Pins. Tel. 93-61-05-12. Fax 93-67-09-14. 21 rms (all with shower). TV TEL

$ Rates: 220–245 F ($39.60–$44.10) single; 280–380 F ($50.40–$68.40) double. Breakfast 30 F ($5.40) extra. MC, V. **Parking:** 50 F ($9). **Closed:** Oct 15–Jan 15.

Located 50 yards from the beach, this well-kept hotel is considered one of the best bargains in Juan-les-Pins. Owner and chef Michel Courtois provides a courteous welcome and good meals. In summer, guests may dine on a patio.

WHERE TO DINE

AUBERGE DE L'ESTEREL, 21, rue des Iles, 06160 Juan-les-Pins. Tel. 93-61-86-55.
  Cuisine: FRENCH. **Reservations:** Recommended.
$ Prices: Fixed-price menus 150–200 F ($27–$36). AE, MC, DC, V.

Open: July–Aug, lunch daily 12:30–2pm; dinner daily 7:30–9:30pm. Sept–Oct and Dec–June, lunch Tues–Sun 12:30–2pm; dinner Tues–Sat 7:30–9:30pm. **Closed:** Nov

The dining room of this hotel combines charm with simplicity and good food. There's a beautiful garden set up with tables for outdoor dining during clement weather. Prices, considering the neighborhood and the demand, are reasonable. Everything is ordered as part of fixed-price meals which, at press time, did not exceed 200 F ($36) per person, plus wine and service. Specific dishes might include a brouillade of eggs with truffles and foie gras, a platter of varied hors d'oeuvres which reflect the culinary breadth of the chefs, an osso buco of lotte with fresh spaghetti, and a rack of lamb with Provençal herbs.

The inn rents 14 comfortably furnished bedrooms, all with telephones and 6 with private baths or showers. Almost everyone who occupies them opts for half board. With half board included, rooms without private bath cost 345 F ($62.10) for a single and 525 F ($94.50) for a double; rooms with private bath cost 380–480 F ($68.40–$86.40) for a single and 560–660 F ($100.80–$118.80) for a double. Rooms with bath contain TV sets and, in some cases, private balconies or terraces.

LA TERRASSE, in the Hôtel Juana, La Pinède, av. Gallice. Tel. 93-61-20-37.
Cuisine: FRENCH. **Reservations:** Required.
$ **Prices:** Appetizers 155–320 F ($27.90–$57.60); main dishes 230–340 F ($41.40–$61.20); fixed-price menus 390 F ($70.20), 480 F ($86.40), and 590 F ($106.20). No credit cards.
Open: July–Aug, lunch daily 12:30–2pm; dinner daily 7:30–10:30pm. Sept–Oct and Apr–June, lunch Thurs–Tues 12:30–2pm; dinner Thurs–Tues 7:30–10:30pm. **Closed:** Nov–Mar.

Bill Cosby loves this gourmet restaurant so much that he sometimes flies chef Christian Morisset to New York to prepare dinner for him. Morisset, who trained with Verger and Lenotre, cooks with a light, precise, and creative hand. His cuisine is the best in Juan-les-Pins. The ideal place to dine in summer is the terrace, among a lively, sophisticated crowd. The chef interprets traditional dishes and creates his own. His specialties include a terrine of pigeon with Landes foie gras and truffles, cannelloni made with small lobsters, and alpine lamb with stuffed zucchini flowers. Desserts, both classic and imaginative, are made with the fresh fruit of the season. Order à la carte or select a *menu méditerranéen*.

15. GOLFE-JUAN & VALLAURIS

Golfe-Juan: 567 miles S of Paris, 4 miles E of Cannes
Vallauris: 565 miles S of Paris, 4 miles E of Cannes

GETTING THERE   By Bus   Buses travel to both Vallauris and Golfe-Juan from Cannes, and other buses connect the two towns.

ESSENTIALS   Orientation   The towns are within a mile of each other; Golfe-Juan is on the seacoast, Vallauris in the hills. Both can easily be explored on foot. Focal points of Vallauris include place Paul-Isnard and square 8-Mai. An important street in Golfe-Juan is avenue de la Liberté.

Information   There's an Office de Tourisme at 84, av. de la Liberté in Golfe-Juan (tel. 93-63-73-12) and another on square 8-Mai in Vallauris (tel. 93-63-82-58).

Napoléon and 800 men landed at Golfe-Juan in 1815 to begin his Hundred Days. Protected by hills, Golfe-Juan was also the favored port for the American navy, although it's primarily a family resort known for its sandy beaches. It contains one notable restaurant, Chez Tétou (see below). A short road leads from Golfe-Juan to Vallauris. Once merely a stopover along the Riviera, Vallauris (noted for its pottery) owes its reputation to Picasso, who "discovered" it. The master came to Vallauris after

World War II and occupied an unattractive little villa known as "The Woman from Wales."

WHAT TO SEE & DO

Ceramics and souvenirs—many the color of rich burgundy—line the street. Frankly, most of the ware displayed in shops is in poor taste. One notable exception is at **Galerie Madoura** (tel. 93-64-66-39), the only shop licensed to sell reproductions of Picasso's works. The master knew and admired the work of the Ramie family, who founded Madoura. It's open Monday through Friday from 9:30am to 12:30pm and 2:30 to 7pm. Some of the Picasso reproductions are limited to 25–500 copies.

Picasso's *Homme et Mouton (Man and Sheep)* is the outdoor statue where Aly Kahn and Rita Hayworth were married. The council of Vallauris had intended to ensconce this statue in a museum, but Picasso insisted that it remain on the square "where the children could climb over it and the dogs water it unhindered."

At place de la Libération stands a chapel of rough stone shaped like a Quonset hut. It houses the **Musée National Picasso,** Chapelle du Château (tel. 93-64-18-05). Picasso decorated the chapel with two paintings: *La Paix (Peace)* and *La Guerre (War)*. The paintings offer contrasting images of love and peace on the one hand and violence and conflict on the other. In 1970 a house painter gained illegal entrance to the museum one night and substituted one of his own designs, after whitewashing a portion of the Picasso original. When the aging master inspected the damage, he said, "Not bad at all." Open June to September, daily from 10am to noon and 2 to 6pm; off-season, daily from 10am to noon and 2 to 5pm. Admission is 8 F ($1.40) for adults, 4 F (70¢) for children.

WHERE TO DINE

CHEZ TETOU, av. des Frères-Roustand, sur la Plage. Tel. 93-63-71-16.
 Cuisine: FRENCH. **Reservations:** Required.
$ **Prices:** Appetizers all 100 F ($18); main dishes 390–460 F ($70.20–$82.80). No credit cards.
 Open: Lunch Thurs–Tues noon–2:30pm; dinner Thurs–Tues 8–10pm. **Closed:** Oct 15–Dec 20.

In its own raffish and amusing way, this might be one of the most famous restaurants along the Côte d'Azur, capitalizing richly upon the glittering *beau monde* who frequented it during the 1950s and 1960s. Retaining its Provençal earthiness despite its high prices, it has thrived in a white-sided beach cottage for more than 65 years. Although, like much of the rest of the Côte d'Azur, it's a bit more "touristy" than in years gone by, it still serves a bouillabaisse which is often remembered years later by non-French visitors who consider it superb. Other items on the deliberately limited menu include grilled sea bass with tomatoes provençal, sole meunière, and several different preparations of lobster. The list of appetizers is extremely limited (platters of charcuterie, or perhaps several almost-perfect slices of fresh melon), because most diners head immediately for the house specialty, bouillabaisse. Dessert might be a special powdered and chewy croissant with grandmother's jams (in winter), or homemade raspberry and strawberry tarts (in summer).

16. MOUGINS

561 miles S of Paris, 7 miles S of Grasse, 5 miles N of Cannes

GETTING THERE   There is limited daily bus service from Cannes. The bus from Cannes to Grasse stops one mile from Mougins.

ESSENTIALS Orientation   Within Mougins, the most central squares are place du Commandant-Lamy and place de la Mairie. The town is so small, though, that most addresses are listed as simply "au village" (within the village).

Information   The Syndicat d'Initiative (tourist office) is at 15, av. Jean-Charles-Mallet (tel. 93-75-87-67).

This once-fortified town on the crest of a hill provides an alternative for those who want to be near the excitement of Cannes but not in the midst of it. Picasso and other artists appreciated the rugged, sun-drenched hills covered with gnarled olive trees. Gentle streams flow in the little valleys. Mougins is the perfect haven for those who feel the Riviera is overrun, spoiled, and overbuilt.

Mougins preserves the quiet life very close to the international resort. The wealthy come from Cannes to **golf** here.

WHERE TO STAY

In addition to the following moderately priced recommendations, the very expensive Moulin de Mougins (see "Where to Dine," below) has five apartments for rent.

MANOIR DE L'ETANG, aux Bois de Font-Merle, allée du Manoir, 06250 Mougins. Tel. 93-90-01-07. Fax 92-92-20-70. 15 rms (all with bath). TV TEL
$ Rates: 500–950 F ($90–$171) single or double. Breakfast 50 F ($9) extra. AE, V.
Parking: Free. **Closed:** Nov 15–Dec 15.
In a historic setting, in the midst of olive trees and cypresses, this is one of the choice places to stay on the Riviera. It has all the romantic ingredients associated with some Riviera properties, including "love goddess" statuary in the garden and candlelit dinners around a swimming pool, but it charges reasonable tariffs for these pleasures. Bedrooms are bright and modern, each comfortable, almost as if you were staying in a private home—which this place virtually is. In winter, meals are served around a wood-burning Provence fireplace. The chef bases his menu on the freshest ingredients available in any season. Fixed-price menus cost 145 F ($26.10), 190 F ($34.20), and 250 F ($45), and diners can also order à la carte.

MAS CANDILLE, bd. Rebuffel, 06250 Mougins. Tel. 93-90-00-85. Fax 92-92-85-56. 21 rms (all with bath). A/C TEL
$ Rates: 900–1,100 F ($162–$198) single or double. Breakfast 65 F ($11.70) extra. AE, DC, MC, V. **Parking:** Free.
This 200-year-old Provençal farmhouse was renovated in 1982. The public rooms contain many 19th-century furnishings, and some open onto the gardens. The dining room has elegant stone detailing and a massive fireplace with a timbered mantelpiece. The food is exceptional. Typical dishes include soupe de poissons (fish), stuffed zucchini flowers, and braised sweetbreads with mushrooms. Fresh salads and light meals are available throughout the day. In good weather lunch is served on the terrace; dinner is served on the terrace in summer only. Menus cost 215–300 F ($38.70–$54).

WHERE TO DINE

L'AMANDIER DE MOUGINS CAFE-RESTAURANT, place du Commandant-Lamy. Tel. 93-90-00-91.
Cuisine: FRENCH. **Reservations:** Recommended.
$ Prices: Appetizers 35–60 F ($6.30–$10.80); main dishes 65–88 F ($11.70–$15.80). AE, DC, MC, V.
Open: Lunch daily noon–2:15pm; dinner daily 8–10pm. **Closed:** Feb.
The illustrious founder of this relatively inexpensive bistro is the world-famous Roger Vergé, whose much more expensive Moulin de Mougins is described below. Conceived as a mass-market satellite to its exclusive neighbor, the restaurant serves wholesome, relatively simple platters of food in a pleasant setting of vaulted ceilings, antiques, and masses of flowers, in an airy stone house in the center of the village. Specialties are usually based on traditional Niçois and Provençal recipes, and might include salmon carpaccio; tagliatelli with olives; a michette of tomatoes, zucchini, and mozzarella; a stouffi of duckling; grilled skewers of chicken with local herbs; and John Dory with lime sauce.

LE FEU FOLLET, place de la Mairie. Tel. 93-90-15-78.
   Cuisine: FRENCH. **Reservations:** Required.
$ **Prices:** Appetizers 90–110 F ($16.20–$19.80); main dishes 120–145 F ($21.60–$26.10); fixed-price menus 160–210 F ($28.80–$37.80). MC, V.
   Open: Lunch Tues–Sun noon–2pm; dinner Tues–Sat 7:30–10pm. **Closed:** Mar 8–21.

Located beside the square in the old village, this good-value restaurant has two roughly plastered rooms that always seem full of enthusiastic diners. It's managed by Jean-Paul and Micheline Battaglia, who serve excellent meals. Typical dishes include fish soup with rouille, ravioli with foie gras and morels, magrêt of duckling with tarragon, and veal kidneys in a mustard sauce.

LE MOULIN DE MOUGINS, Notre-Dame-de Vie, 06250 Mougins. Tel. 93-75-78-24. Fax 93-90-18-55.
   Cuisine: FRENCH. **Reservations:** Required.
$ **Prices:** Appetizers 180–480 F ($32.40–$86.40); main dishes 210–390 F ($37.80–$70.20); fixed-price menus 550–700 F ($99–$126). AE, DC, MC, V.
   Open: Mid-July to Aug, lunch daily noon–2:15pm; dinner daily 8–10pm. Apr to mid-July and Sept–Jan, lunch Wed and Fri–Mon noon–2:15pm; dinner Tues–Sun 8–10pm. **Closed:** Feb–Mar.

This 16th-century olive-oil mill is a restaurant that serves one of the finest, most imaginative cuisines in France. A 10-foot-wide stone oil vat, complete with a wooden turnscrew and a grinding wheel, is near the entrance. This culinary kingdom belongs to Roger Vergé, the "maître cuisinier de France." His specialties include poupeton de truffe au fumet de champignons, filets de rougets (red mullet) de roche en barigoule d'artichaut, and noisettes d'agneau (lamb) de Sisteron with eggplant cake in a thyme-flavored sauce. His particular forte is fish from the Mediterranean, bought locally each morning fresh. Monsieur Vergé has a lot of fantastic, even historic wines, but there's also a good selection of local vintages at reasonable prices.

The old mill offers five beautifully decorated, air-conditioned suites, honeymoon lairs with provincial beds, Louis XVI chairs and chests, bay windows, and matching flowered toile coverings for furniture and beds. All contain minibars, TVs, and phones. A double costs 800–1,300 F ($144–$234) plus 75 F ($13.50) for breakfast.

LE RELAIS A MOUGINS, place de la Mairie. Tel. 93-90-03-47.
   Cuisine: FRENCH. **Reservations:** Recommended.
$ **Prices:** Appetizers 35–45 F ($6.30–$8.10); main dishes 58–88 F ($10.40–$15.80); fixed-price menus 250–500 F ($45–$90) MC, V.
   Open: Lunch Wed–Sun noon–2:15pm; dinner Wed–Sun 7:30–10:30pm.

This is one of the best restaurants in the village, attracting a celebrity clientele from both sides of the Atlantic. Opened in 1977, it is housed in a beautifully proportioned Provençal building, with a black-and-white marble floor and a vaulted ceiling. Photographs of Picasso are part of the decor. The restaurant fronts one of the most perfect village squares in Provence, with three graceful fountains and flowering shrubs. Many clients prefer the outdoor terrace with a canopy and a nearby plane tree. Owner André Surmain, who founded Lutèce in New York, has had a colorful, adventurous life. Born in Cairo, he was a member of the French Resistance and, for a time, a member of the OSS in the U.S. Army. His menu embraces light and creative dishes, although the chef is most proud of his *menu dégustation*. Specialties include salade oasis (lobster, apples, and endive), saddle of baby lamb en chemise (boned and served in thin pancakes with fresh tarragon), and Bresse pigeon en croûte (baked in a thin potato crust).

17. GRASSE

563 miles S of Paris, 11 miles N of Cannes

GETTING THERE   By Bus   Grasse has bus service from Cannes and other neighboring resorts; the bus terminal is at the northern end of town, near the tourist office.

ESSENTIALS **Orientation** Situated between sea and mountains, Grasse is the capital of perfume. At its center are the Hôtel de Ville and the cathedral.

Information The Office de Tourisme is on place de la Foux (tel. 93-36-03-56).

Grasse is the most fragrant town on the Riviera. Surrounded by jasmine and roses, it has been the capital of the perfume industry since the 19th century. It was once a famous resort, attracting such royalty as Queen Victoria and Princess Pauline Borghese.

WHAT TO SEE & DO

One of the best-known perfume factories is the **Parfumerie Fragonard,** 20, bd. Fragonard (tel. 93-36-44-65), named after the French painter of the 18th century. An English-speaking guide will show you how "the soul of the flower" is extracted. After the tour, you can explore the museum of perfumery, which displays bottles and vases that trace the industry back to ancient times. Open daily, including holidays, from 8:30am to 6:30pm.

The **Musée d'Art et d'Histoire de Provence,** 2, rue Mirabeau (tel. 93-36-01-61), is in the Hôtel de Clapiers-Cabris. The building was constructed in 1771 by Louise de Mirabeau, the marquise de Cabris and sister of Mirabeau. The collection includes paintings, four-poster beds, marquetry, ceramics, brasses, kitchenware, pottery, urns, even archeological finds. Open June to September, daily from 10am to noon and 2 to 7pm; in October and December to June, Wednesday through Sunday from 10am to noon and 2 to 5pm; closed in November. Admission is 12.60 F ($2.30) for adults, 6.30 F ($1.10) for children.

Nearby is the **Villa Fragonard,** 23, bd. Fragonard (tel. 93-36-01-61). The collection includes the paintings of Jean-Honoré Fragonard; his sister-in-law, Marguerite Gérard; his son, Alexandre; and his grandson, Théophile. Fragonard was born at Grasse in 1732. The grand staircase was decorated by Alexandre. Open June to September, Wednesday through Sunday from 10am to noon and 2 to 6pm; in October and December to June, Wednesday through Sunday from 10am to noon and 2 to 5pm; closed in November. Admission is 10 F ($1.80) for adults, free for children.

Another popular place to visit is the **Parfumerie Molinard,** 60, bd. Victor-Hugo (tel. 93-36-01-62). The firm is well known in the United States and its products are sold at Saks, Neiman-Marcus, and Bloomingdales. In the factory, you can witness the extraction of the essence of the flowers. The process of converting flowers into essential oils is explained in detail. You'll discover why turning flowers into perfume has been called a "work of art." You can also admire a collection of antique perfume-bottle labels as well as see a rare collection of Baccarat and Lalique, plus Provençal furniture from the 16th through the 18th century. It's open April to June, daily from 9am to noon and 2 to 6pm; July to September 15, daily from 9am to 6:30pm; and September 16 to March, Monday through Saturday from 9am to noon and 2 to 6pm.

WHERE TO STAY

LES ARÔMES, route de Cannes, 06130 Grasse. Tel. 93-70-42-01. 7 rms (all with bath). TV TEL
$ Rates (including half board): 380 F ($68.40) single; 480 F ($86.40) double. Breakfast 25 F ($4.50) extra. AE, MC, V. **Parking:** Free.

S Although Les Arômes is near a noisy highway between Grasse and Cannes, privacy and calm are guaranteed by the surrounding wall and gravel-covered courtyard. Half a mile south of the center of Grasse, this modern building was designed in a Provençal style, with beige stone, pink stucco, and terra-cotta tiles. The dining room, with three large arched windows overlooking the courtyard, is open daily except Saturday lunch from noon to 2pm and 7:30 to 9:30pm. It's open to nonresidents, who pay 90–130 F ($16.20–$23.40) for a fixed-price menu.

HOTEL PANORAMA, 2, place du Cours, 06130 Grasse. Tel. 93-36-80-80. Fax 93-36-92-04. 36 rms (all with bath). MINIBAR TV TEL

$ Rates: 310 F ($55.80) single; 395–460 F ($71.10–$82.80) double. Breakfast 37 F ($6.70) extra. AE, DC, MC, V. **Parking:** 30 F ($5.40).

Built in 1984, this centrally located hotel has a facade in a sienna hue that its owners call "Garibaldi red." The more expensive rooms have balconies, southern exposure, and views of the faraway sea. Twenty rooms contain air conditioning. There's no bar or restaurant, but food is brought to your room on request.

WHERE TO DINE

RESTAURANT AMPHITRYON, 16, bd. Victor-Hugo. Tel. 93-36-58-73.
Cuisine: FRENCH. **Reservations:** Recommended.

$ Prices: Appetizers 58–109 F ($10.40–$19.60); main dishes 88–188 F ($15.80–$33.80); fixed-price menus 125 F ($22.50), 162 F ($29.20), and 242 F ($43.60). AE, DC, MC, V.

Open: Lunch Mon–Sat noon–1:30pm; dinner Mon–Sat 7:30–9pm. **Closed:** Aug.

The buildings that line this street, including this restaurant, were stables in the 19th century. Today, in a modern ambience of fabric-covered walls, you can enjoy the cuisine of Michel André, who serves the best food in Grasse. The fixed-price menus are a bargain. The cuisine is inspired by southwestern France, including plenty of foie gras and duckling, as well as lamb from the alpine foothills roasted with thyme. You might also try the Mediterranean fish soup with a Provençal rouille.

18. CANNES

562 miles S of Paris, 101 miles E of Marseille, 16 miles SW of Nice

GETTING THERE Cannes is connected to each of the Mediterranean resorts, to Paris, and to the rest of France by rail and bus lines. Cannes lies on the major coastal rail line along the Riviera, with trains arriving frequently throughout the day. From Antibes to Cannes by rail takes only 15 minutes, or 35 minutes from Nice. The fast TGV from Paris going via Marseille also services Cannes. Buses pick up passengers at the Nice Airport every 40 minutes during the day, delivering them to Cannes, and service is also available from Antibes at one bus every half hour. The international airport at Nice is only 20 minutes northeast.

ESSENTIALS Orientation Cannes revolves around La Croisette, its seaside promenade, and the ports (Port I and Port II) at either end of it. Much of the city's architecture is 19th-century Belle Epoque style, except the medieval Vieille-Ville, north of Port I, on the hill of Le Suquet.

Information The Office de Tourisme is in the Palais du Festival, 1, bd. de la Croisette (tel. 93-39-24-53).

SPECIAL EVENTS The world-famous International Film Festival is in April or May.

When Coco Chanel went there and got a suntan, returning to Paris bronzed, she startled ladies of society. Nonetheless they quickly began copying her, abandoning their heretofore fashionable peach complexions. Today the bronzed bodies—in the briefest of bikinis—that line the sandy beaches of this chic resort continue the late fashion designer's long-ago example.

Popular with celebrities, Cannes is at its most frenzied during the **International Film Festival** at the **Palais des Festivals** on the Promenade de la Croisette. Held in either April or May, it attracts not only film stars but those with similar aspirations. On the seafront boulevards flashbulbs pop as the starlets emerge—usually wearing what women will be wearing in 1999. International regattas, galas, *concours d'élégance,* even a Mimosa Festival in February—something is always happening at Cannes, except in November, which is traditionally a dead month.

Sixteen miles southwest of Nice, Cannes is sheltered by hills. For many it consists of only one street, the **Promenade de la Croisette,** curving along the coast and split by islands of palms and flowers. It is said that the Prince of Wales (before he became Edward VII) contributed to its original cost. But he was a Johnny-come-lately to Cannes. Setting out for Nice in 1834, Lord Brougham, a lord chancellor of England, was turned away because of an outbreak of cholera. He landed at Cannes and liked it so much he decided to build a villa there. Returning every winter until his death in 1868, he proselytized it in London, drawing a long line of British visitors. In the 1890s Cannes became popular with Russian grand dukes (it is said that more caviar was consumed there than in all of Moscow). One French writer claimed that when the Russians returned as refugees in the 1920s, they were given the garbage-collection franchise.

A port of call for cruise liners, the seafront of Cannes is lined with hotels, apartment houses, and chic boutiques. Many of the bigger hotels, some dating from the 19th century, claim part of the beaches for the private use of their guests. But there are public areas.

WHAT TO SEE & DO

Above the harbor, the old town of Cannes sits on Suquet Hill, where you'll see a 14th-century tower, which the English dubbed the "Lord's Tower."

Nearby is the **Musée de la Castre,** Château de la Castre, Le Suquet (tel. 93-68-91-91), housing a museum of fine arts with a section on ethnography. The latter includes relics and objects from everywhere from the Pacific islands to Southeast Asia, including both Peruvian and Mayan pottery. There's also a gallery devoted to relics of ancient Mediterranean civilizations, ranging from the Greeks to the Romans, from the Cypriots to the Egyptians. Five rooms are devoted to 19th-century paintings.

The museum is open April to June, Wednesday through Monday from 10am to noon and 2 to 6pm; July to September, Wednesday through Monday from 10am to noon and 3 to 7pm; and October to March, Wednesday through Monday from 10am to noon and 2 to 5pm. Admission is 10 F ($1.80) per person.

Another museum of note, the **Musée de la Mer,** Fort Royal (tel. 93-38-55-26), displays artifacts from Ligurian, Roman, and Arab civilizations, including paintings, mosaics, and ceramics. You can also see the jail where the prisoner in the Iron Mask was incarcerated. Temporary exhibitions of photography are also shown here.

Open June to September only, the museum can be visited daily from 10am to noon and 2 to 6pm. Admission is 10 F ($1.80) per person.

WHERE TO STAY

Very Expensive

CARLTON INTERCONTINENTAL HOTEL, 58, bd. de la Croisette, 06400 Cannes. Tel. 93-68-91-68, or toll free 800/327-0200 in the U.S. 326 rms (all with bath), 28 suites. A/C MINIBAR TV TEL **Bus:** 11.

$ **Rates:** 2,000 F ($360) single; 3,350 F ($603) double; from 5,000 F ($900) suite. Breakfast 145 F ($26.10) extra. AE, DC, MC, V. **Parking:** 120 F ($21.60).

Cynics say that one of the most amusing sights in Cannes is the view from under the vaguely art deco and very grand gate of the Carlton. There you'll see vehicles of every description pulling up to drop off huge amounts of baggage and vast numbers of fashionable guests who have made this one of the most colorful hotels in Cannes. It has become such a part of the heartbeat of the city that to ignore it would be to miss the spirit of the resort. The twin gray domes at either end of the facade are often the first thing to be recognized by the various starlets planning their grand entrances, grand exits, and grand scenes in the hotel's public and private rooms.

Shortly after its construction in 1912, the Carlton attracted the most prominent members of the *haut monde* of Europe, including members of royal families. They were followed decades later by the most important screen personalities of the cinematic golden age. Today the property accepts both industrial conventions and tour groups. Nonetheless, during summer, and especially during the film festival, the ornate public rooms still are filled with all the voyeuristic and exhibitionistic fervor that seems so much a part of the Riviera.

Dining/Entertainment: The Carlton Casino Club is an eighth-floor casino that opened in 1989. La Côte restaurant is considered one of the most distinguished along the French Riviera.

Facilities: Private beach, health club with many spa facilities.

HOTEL MARTINEZ, 73, bd. de la Croisette, 06400 Cannes. Tel. 92-98-73-00. Fax 93-39-67-82. 418 rms (all with bath), 12 suites. A/C MINIBAR TV TEL **Bus:** 1.

$ Rates: 1,300 F ($234) single; 3,250 F ($585) double; from 5,500 F ($990) suite. Breakfast 100 F ($18) extra. AE, DC, MC, V. **Parking:** 120 F ($21.60). **Closed:** Mid-Nov to mid-Jan.

When this landmark art deco hotel was built in the 1930s, it rivaled any other hotel along the coast in sheer size alone. Over the years, however, this waterfront hotel has fallen into disrepair and has closed and reopened several times. But in 1982 the Concorde chain returned the hotel and its restaurants to their former luster. Today, bedrooms have conservative modern furniture and are immaculately kept.

Dining/Entertainment: La Palme d'Or, among the finest restaurants in Cannes, is recommended under "Where to Dine," below. The poolside restaurant, l'Orangerie, serves light, low-calorie meals in a decor of azure and white lattices.

Services: 24-hour room service, same-day laundry and valet.

Facilities: Private beach, waterskiing school, cabañas, octagonal swimming pool.

LE MAJESTIC, 14, bd. de la Croisette, 06400 Cannes. Tel. 92-98-77-00. Fax 93-38-97-90. 263 rms (all with bath), 24 suites. A/C MINIBAR TV TEL **Bus:** 1.

$ Rates: 1,150–1,800 F ($207–$324) single; 3,500 F ($630) double; from 4,000 F ($720) suite. Breakfast 110 F ($19.80) extra. AE, DC, MC, V. **Parking:** 120 F ($21.60). **Closed:** Nov 10–Dec 20.

Le Majestic has long stood for glamour. Open since 1926, this hotel is located at the west end of La Croisette. Like the Carlton, it's a favorite with celebrities during the annual film festival. Constructed around an overscale front patio with a swimming pool, the hotel opens directly onto the esplanade and the sea. Under tall palms and flowering orange and fig trees, it draws some of the chicest suntans in Europe.

Inside, the setting is one of shiny marble, clusters of "dripping" crystal chandeliers, tapestries, seasoned antiques and reproductions, salons with Oriental carpets, Louis XV silk furniture, and potted palms. The bedrooms are furnished with antiques and reproductions, offset by Oriental rugs and marble tables.

Dining/Entertainment: There's a classic restaurant, serving haute cuisine, and a grill with tables placed around the pool. There's also a restaurant and bar on the beach.

Services: Hairdresser, 24-hour room service, same-day laundry and valet service.

Facilities: Parking, swimming pool.

Expensive

LE GRAND HOTEL, 45, bd. de la Croisette, 06400 Cannes. Tel. 93-38-15-45. 76 rms (all with bath), 2 junior suites. A/C MINIBAR TV TEL **Bus:** 1.

$ Rates: 550–1,110 F ($99–$199.80) single; 660–1,460 F ($118.80–$262.80) double; 2,600 F ($468) suite. Breakfast 60 F ($10.80) extra. AE, MC, V. **Parking:** 100 F ($18).

This is one of the five leading hotels in Cannes. It has a garden with tall date palms and a lawn sweeping down to the waterfront esplanade. A splendid structure of glass and marble, it's part of a complex of adjoining apartment-house wings and encircling boutiques. Eleven floors of bedrooms—each with wall-to-wall picture windows—

open onto tile terraces. Vibrant colors are used throughout: sea blue, olive, sunburst red, and banana gold. The baths are lined with colored checkerboard tiles, with matching towels and rows of decorative bottles. Rooms with sea views are the most expensive.

HOTEL GRAY-D'ALBION, 38, rue des Serbes, 06400 Cannes. Tel. 92-99-79-79. Fax 93-99-26-10. 172 rms (all with bath), 14 suites. A/C MINIBAR TV TEL **Bus:** 1.
$ Rates: 1,200–1,350 F ($216–$243) single; 1,550 F ($279) double; 2,400–5,800 F ($432–$1,044) suite. Breakfast 85 F ($15.30) extra. AE, DC, MC, V.

The smallest of the major hotels in Cannes contains pastel-colored rooms, each outfitted with all the luxury that a modern hotel can offer—some critics consider the Gray-d'Albion among the most luxurious hotels in France. It's between the Croisette and the popular shopping street rue d'Antibes. Some of the in-house restaurants, as well as a disco, are described below. Each room comes with video and private balcony. The hotel is open all year.

NOVOTEL MONTFLEURY, 25, av. Beauséjovr, 06400 Cannes. Tel. 93-68-91-50. Fax 93-38-37-08. 181 rms (all with bath). A/C MINIBAR TV TEL **Bus:** 1.
$ Rates: 650 F ($117) single; 1,150 F ($207) double. Breakfast 60 F ($10.80) extra. AE, DC, MC, V. **Parking:** 100 F ($18).

Although this hotel seems distant from the crush of Cannes, it's actually only a short, but winding, drive away. The modern palace is set in a 10-acre park that it shares with an up-to-date sports complex. The magnificent, curved swimming pool is covered with a sliding roof and surrounded by palms. Other facilities include tennis courts (many lit for night play), a volleyball court, sauna, massage facilities, and a gymnasium, plus two restaurants. The comfortable bedrooms are stylishly filled with all the modern conveniences, including radios and private entrances.

SOFITEL MEDITERRANEE, 2, bd. Jean-Hibert, 06400 Cannes. Tel. 93-99-22-75. Fax 93-39-68-36. 150 rms (all with bath), 5 suites. **Bus:** 1.
$ Rates: 940 F ($169.20) single; 1,360 F ($244.80) double; from 1,960 F ($352.80) suite. Breakfast 100 F ($18) extra. AE, DC, MC, V. **Parking:** 90 F ($16.20). **Closed:** Nov 21–Dec 21.

The favorite of the international yachting set, this Sofitel stands directly on the harbor, with surrounding balconies and an open-air rooftop swimming pool. This hostelry, which is a remake of an older hotel, has a well-designed, bright interior, offsetting muted tones with warm colors. The best rooms have balconies with views of the sea and yacht harbor. A delectable cuisine is served in the Mediterranean restaurant, Le Palmyre.

Moderate

CANBERRA, 120, rue d'Antibes, 06400 Cannes. Tel. 93-38-20-70. Fax 92-98-03-47. 45 rms (all with bath or shower). A/C MINIBAR TV TEL **Bus:** 1.
$ Rates: 390 F ($70.20) single; 540 F ($97.20) double. Breakfast 40 F ($7.20) extra. AE, DC, MC, V. **Parking:** Free.

This is another wonderful little hotel, lying between the Carlton and the Festival Palace. The Canberra is a mellower remake of an older hotel. The overall effect is a mixture of modern and traditional. Limited parking is available by the hotel's small garden.

HOTEL LE FOUQUET'S, 2, rond-point Duboys-d'Angers, 06400 Cannes. Tel. 93-38-75-81. Fax 92-98-03-39. 10 rms (all with bath). A/C MINIBAR TV TEL **Bus:** 1.
$ Rates: 1,100 F ($198) single; 1,300 F ($234) double. Breakfast 60 F ($10.80) extra. AE, DC, MC, V. **Parking:** 90 F ($16.20). **Closed:** Nov–Dec 26.

This is an intimate, select hotel. Very "Riviera French" in design and decor, it lies several blocks from the beach. The hotel is built on a circular street surrounded by several other hotels. Each of its attractive, airy rooms is decorated in bold colors, containing a loggia, a dressing room, and a hairdryer.

HOTEL SPLENDID, allée de la Liberté (4 et 6, rue Félix-Fauré), 06400 Cannes. Tel. 93-99-53-11. Fax 93-99-55-02. 64 rms (all with bath), 2 suites. A/C TV TEL
$ Rates (including continental breakfast): 570–650 F ($102.60–$117) single; 650–930 F ($117–$167.40) double; from 1,300 F ($234) suite. AE, DC, MC, V.
This is a good, conservative hotel—a favorite of academicians, politicians, actors, and musicians. Opened in 1871, it's one of the oldest hotels at the resort. An ornate white building with sinuous wrought-iron accents, the Hôtel Splendid looks out onto the sea, the old port, and a park. There's a small reception area. Rooms contain antique furniture, paintings, and videos; 40 are equipped with kitchenettes. The more expensive rooms have sea views.

VICTORIA, rond-point Duboys-d'Angers, 06400 Cannes. Tel. 93-99-36-36. Fax 93-38-03-91. 25 rms (all with bath). A/C MINIBAR TV TEL **Bus:** 1.
$ Rates: 1,200 F ($216) single or double. Breakfast 50 F ($9) extra. AE, DC, MC, V. **Parking:** 60 F ($10.80). **Closed:** Nov–Dec.
A stylish, modern hotel in the heart of Cannes, the Victoria offers accommodations with period reproductions and refrigerators. Nearly half the rooms have balconies overlooking the small park and the hotel's swimming pool. Bedspreads of silk and padded headboards evoke a boudoir quality. The accommodations facing the park cost a little more, but are well worth it. The best rooms have terraces. After a day on the beach, guests congregate in the paneled bar and sink comfortably into the couches and armchairs.

Inexpensive

ATHENEE, 6, rue Lecerf, 06400 Cannes. Tel. 93-38-69-54. Fax 92-98-68-30. 15 rms (all with bath). A/C MINIBAR TV TEL **Bus:** 1.
$ Rates: 350 F ($63) single; 450 F ($81) double. Breakfast 35 F ($6.30) extra. AE, DC, MC, V. **Parking:** Free.
Situated on a quiet business street about four blocks from the seafront, this small hotel occupies the first floor of a modern, five-story apartment building. Owner Jean-Pierre Challer, who lives on the premises, offers comfortable, unpretentious bedrooms that are clean and relatively affordable. No meals are served other than breakfast, although three neighborhood bistros offer inexpensive fixed-price meals to residents who want them. Priced at 70–80 F ($12.60–$14.40) each, they offer good value in an otherwise relatively expensive neighborhood.

HOTEL DE FRANCE, 85, rue d'Antibes, 06400 Cannes. Tel. 93-39-23-34. Fax 93-68-53-43. 34 rms (all with bath or shower). A/C TV TEL **Bus:** 1.
$ Rates: 250–390 F ($45–$70.20) single; 290–430 F ($52.20–$77.40) double. Breakfast 35 F ($6.30) extra. AE, DC, MC, V.
This centrally located hotel is only two blocks from the sea. Rooms are large and contain radios. Guests can sunbathe on the rooftop.

HOTEL DE PROVENCE, 9, rue Molière, 06400 Cannes. Tel. 93-38-44-35. Fax 93-39-63-14. 30 rms (all with bath). A/C MINIBAR TV TEL **Bus:** 1.
$ Rates: 290–450 F ($52.20–$81) single; 390–480 F ($70.20–$86.40) double. Breakfast 33 F ($5.90) extra. AE, MC, V. **Parking:** 30 F ($5.40).
This family-owned hotel was established in 1966 in a villa originally built in the 1890s. In 1992, the rooms were renovated into a comfortably uncluttered format of well-scrubbed convenience. Most have private balconies, and many overlook the garden. The hotel stands in its own walled garden of palms and flowering shrubs on a

quiet inner street lined with angular apartment buildings and 19th-century tile-roofed houses, a short walk from the beaches and casinos of La Croisette. In warm weather, breakfast is served outside under the vines and flowers of an arbor, and *plats du jour* are usually available at mealtime, to residents only, for 60–75 F ($10.80–$13.50) each.

HOTEL TOBOSO, 7, allée des Olivers (blvd. Montfleury), 06400 Cannes. Tel. 93-38-20-05. Fax 93-68-09-32. 15 rms (all with bath). A/C MINIBAR TV TEL. **Bus:** 1.
$ Rates: 250–600 F ($45–$108) single or double. Breakfast 35 F ($6.30) extra. MC, V. **Parking:** Free.
Set adjacent to the largest sports center in Cannes, this former private villa has been transformed into a small, homey, and tranquil hotel. (In a romantic outburst, the former owner named it after the city in Spain where Cervantes' Don Quixote is said to have met Dulcinea for the first time.) The main lounge—formerly the family salon—has a concert piano. Dancers from the neighboring Rosella Hightower School often frequent this hotel. Most of the personalized rooms have windows facing the gardens, and some have terraces and kitchens. There's a swimming pool in the garden. Families will be interested to know that some units are large enough for six.

MONDIAL, 77, rue d'Antibes, and 1, rue Teïsseire, 06400 Cannes. Tel. 93-68-70-00. Fax 93-99-39-11. 56 rms (all with bath). TV TEL **Bus:** 1.
$ Rates: 530 F ($95.40) single; 740 F ($133.20) double. Breakfast 40 F ($7.20) extra. AE, DC, MC, V.
This is a modern, six-floor hotel on a commercial street, with stores on its lower floor. The hotel is about a three-minute walk from the beach; three-quarters of its rooms have views of the water, while the others overlook the mountains and a street. The soft Devonshire-cream facade has a few small balconies. The attractive rooms are the draw here, with matching fabric on the beds and drapes and sliding mirror doors for wardrobes.

LE SAINT-YVES, 49, bd. d'Alsace, 06400 Cannes. Tel. 93-38-65-29. Fax 93-68-50-67. 10 rms (all with bath), 2 suites. TV TEL **Bus:** 1.
$ Rates: 290 F ($52.20) single; 430–470 F ($77.40–$84.60) double; from 650 F ($117) suite. Breakfast 35 F ($6.30) extra. DC. **Parking:** Free.
Set back from the busy coastal boulevard by a front garden and a grove of palm trees, this genuine, old villa is a historical monument. It's only a five-minute stroll from the seafront, although the garden of the villa is so enjoyable that many guests spend a good part of their day at the hotel. English-speaking Marylene Camplo owns the villa, part of which she has converted into private apartments that can be rented by the week or by the month. However, she has kept some rooms to rent for short periods. The bedrooms differ in size and are pleasantly furnished, mainly with odds and ends. Breakfast includes fresh croissants, country butter, and rich jam.

WHERE TO DINE
Expensive

HOTEL GRAY RESTAURANT, in the Hôtel Gray-d'Albion, 38, rue des Serbes. Tel. 93-68-54-54.
Cuisine: FRENCH. **Reservations:** Required. **Bus:** 1.
$ Prices: Appetizers 88–135 F ($15.80–$24.30); main dishes 150–250 F ($27–$45); fixed-price menus 380 F ($68.40) and 520 F ($93.60). AE, DC, MC, V.
Open: Oct–May, lunch Tues–Sat noon–2pm; dinner Tues–Sat 8–10:30pm. June–Sept, lunch Tues–Sat noon–2pm; dinner Mon–Sat 8–10:30pm. **Closed:** Feb.
Thanks to chef Jacques Chibois, this elegant place is one of the best in Cannes. The restaurant is furnished with Belle Epoque details in shades of peach, oxblood, maroon, and ocher. A faithful follower of Michel Guérard, Monsieur Chibois offers such specialties as crayfish salad with orange-flavored vinaigrette, basil, and baby spinach; fricassée of lobster; pigeon cooked en papillote; suprême of chicken

with crayfish; stuffed eggplant with morels; and suprême of daurade. Dessert is usually an award-winning concoction.

LA PALME D'OR, in the Hôtel Martinez, 73, bd. de la Croisette. Tel. 92-98-74-14.

Cuisine: FRENCH. **Reservations:** Required. **Bus:** 1.

$ Prices: Appetizers 95–380 F ($17.10–$68.40); main dishes 135–240 F ($24.30–$43.20); fixed-price menus 280–550 F ($50.40–$99). AE, DC, MC, V.

Open: Lunch Wed–Sun 12:30–2pm; dinner Tues–Sun 7:30–10:30pm. **Closed:** Nov 20–Jan 20.

When this hotel was renovated by members of the champagne-based Taittinger family, one of their primary concerns was to establish a restaurant that could rival the tough competition in Cannes. The result was a light-wood-paneled, art deco marvel overlooking the swimming pool and the sandy expanse of La Croisette. Alsatian-born chef Christian Willer has worked at some of the greatest restaurants in France. Here his sublime specialties include warm foie gras with a fondue of rhubarb, nage of sole with Bellet wine, slightly warm salad of monkfish with a hint of pepper, and salmon served with a caviar-cream sauce. Many diners find it hard to pass up the bouillon of lobster with basil and fresh vegetables or the palate-cleansing sorbet flavored with white cheese. Service is excellent.

Moderate

LE FESTIVAL, 55, bd. de la Croisette. Tel. 93-38-04-81.

Cuisine: FRENCH. **Reservations:** Required. **Bus:** 1.

$ Prices: Appetizers 80–160 F ($14.40–$28.80); main dishes 130–370 F ($23.40–$66.60); fixed-price menu 240 F ($43.20). AE, DC, V.

Open: Lunch daily 11:30am–3pm; dinner daily 7:30–10pm. **Closed:** Nov 15–Dec 10, and Mon Oct–Mar.

Screen idols and sex symbols flood the front terrace of this place during the film festival. There, where almost every chair is emblazoned with the name of a different movie star (who may or may not have graced it with their bottoms), tables are among the most sought-after entity in town. Diners gravitate to either the Restaurant or the somewhat less formal Grill Room. Meals in the Restaurant might include bourride provençale, soupe des poissons with rouille, a selection of simply grilled fresh fish (perhaps with aïoli), bouillabaisse with lobster, pepper steak, and sea bass flambéed with fennel. Items in the Grill are more in the style of an elegant brasserie, served a bit more rapidly and without as much fuss. An appropriate finish in either section might be a smoothly textured peach Melba—invented by Escoffier.

GASTON-GASTOUNETTE, 7, quai St-Pierre. Tel. 93-39-49-44.

Cuisine: FRENCH. **Reservations:** Required. **Bus:** 1.

$ Prices: Appetizers 70–125 F ($12.60–$22.50); main dishes 130–200 F ($23.40–$36); fixed-price meals 120–165 F ($21.60–$29.70) at lunch, 190 F ($34.20) at dinner. AE, DC, MC, V.

Open: Lunch daily noon–2pm; dinner daily 7–11pm. **Closed:** Jan.

This is the best restaurant to offer views of the marina. Located in the old port, the restaurant has a stucco exterior with oak moldings and big windows and a sidewalk terrace that's surrounded by flowers. Inside you'll be served bouillabaisse, breast of duckling in a garlic-cream sauce, grilled sea bass with herbs, fish soup, stuffed mussels, pot-au-feu de la mer, and such fish platters as turbot and sole. Sorbet, after all that savory Mediterranean food, is an appropriate choice for dessert.

LA MERE BESSON, 13, rue des Frères-Pradignac. Tel. 93-39-59-24.

Cuisine: FRENCH. **Reservations:** Required. **Bus:** 1.

$ Prices: Appetizers 40–70 F ($7.20–$12.60); main dishes 75–140 F ($13.50–$25.20). AE, DC, MC, V.

Open: Lunch Mon–Sat 12:15–2pm; dinner Mon–Sat 7:30–10:30pm.

The culinary traditions of Mère Besson are carried on in one of Cannes's favorite restaurants, in business since 1969. All the recommended specialties are prepared with consummate skill, especially the different Provençal dishes featured daily. The most delectable offering is estouffade provençale—beef braised with red wine and a rich country stock flavored with garlic, onions, herbs, and mushrooms. Specialties include soupe au pistou and soupe de poissons. Every Wednesday you can order lou piech, a Niçois name for veal brisket stuffed with white-stemmed vegetables, peas, ham, eggs, rice, grated cheese, and herbs. The meat is cooked in salted water with vinegar, carrots, and onions, like a stockpot, then served with a thick tomato sauce known as coulis.

LE RELAIS DES SEMAILLES, 9, rue St-Antoine. Tel. 93-39-22-32.

Cuisine: FRENCH. **Reservations:** Required.

$ Prices: Appetizers 90–160 F ($16.20–$28.80); main dishes 130–160 F ($23.40–$28.80); fixed-price menus 135 F ($24.30), 220 F ($39.60), and 280 F ($50.40). AE, MC, V.

Open: Dinner only, daily 7–11:30pm. **Closed:** Nov.

This restaurant is reason enough to visit Le Suquet, Canne's Old Town neighborhood. The casual atmosphere is complemented by the food, which is *cuisine du marché*, based on available local ingredients. Stuffed pigeon is a typical dish. The vegetables are always beautifully prepared.

LA VILLA, 7, rue Marceau. Tel. 93-38-79-73.

Cuisine: FRENCH. **Reservations:** Recommended.

$ Prices: Appetizers 50–65 F ($9–$11.70); main dishes 80–120 F ($14.40–$21.60). AE, DC, MC, V.

Open: June–Aug, dinner only, daily 9pm–midnight (bar, daily 8:30pm–1:30am). Sept–May, dinner only, Tues–Sat 9pm–midnight (bar, Tues–Sat 8:30pm–1:30am).

Best described as a supper club where the clientele seems equally divided between drinkers and diners, this establishment is housed in what appears at first like a small palace built in the Italianate style. Originally a private home, it lies a few steps from the very important rue d'Antibes. The flowering terrace has painted columns; the interior is decorated with trompe l'oeil and ornate plaster ceilings. Food items are conservative, uncomplicated, and a suitable foil for the conviviality which sometimes develops within. Examples include avocadoes stuffed with shrimp, tomato-mozzarella salads with fresh basil, salade paysanne with croûtons and lardons, rack of lamb with gratin of zucchini, tournedos, salmon, and filets of sole meunière. If you stop in just for a drink, a whisky with soda costs around 50 F ($9).

Inexpensive

AU BEC FIN, 12, rue du 24-Août. Tel. 93-38-35-86.

Cuisine: FRENCH. **Reservations:** Required. **Bus:** 1.

$ Prices: Appetizers 30–40 F ($5.40–$7.20); main dishes 85–120 F ($15.30–$21.60); fixed-price menus 95–115 F ($17.10–$20.70). AE, DC, MC, V.

Open: Lunch Mon–Sat noon–2:30pm; dinner Mon–Fri 7–10pm. **Closed:** Dec 20–Jan 20.

On a street halfway between the train station and the beach, this 1880s bistro has little decor but offers especially good meals. Sometimes red carnations are brought in from the fields to brighten the tables. A typical meal might include salade niçoise, the house specialty; then caneton (duckling) with cèpes (flap mushrooms); and finally a choice of cheese and dessert.

AU MAL ASSIS, 15, quai St-Pierre. Tel. 93-39-13-38.

Cuisine: FRENCH. **Reservations:** Required. **Bus:** 1.

$ Prices: Appetizers 50–75 F ($9–$13.50); main dishes 120–250 F ($21.60–$45); fixed-price menus 120–180 F ($21.60–$32.40). AE, MC, V.

Open: June–Sept, lunch daily noon–2:30pm; dinner daily 7–10:30pm. Oct and Dec 16–May, lunch Tues–Sun noon–2:30pm; dinner Tues–Sat 7–10:30pm. **Closed:** Late Oct to Dec 15.

For unpretentious and appealingly earthy Provençal charm, this is my choice. Relatively moderate in its pricing, especially when compared to many of the resort's more expensive choices, it was established in 1949 and has done a thriving business ever since. You can order moules (mussels) provençales, sole meunière, bourride, a wide array of fresh fish, several versions of lobster, and a succulent version of bouillabaisse prepared for two diners. Its deliberately ambiguous name is a source of endless local humor, because it translates either as "at the place where guests are badly seated" or "at the place where men [but not women] are seated." The fixed-price menu at 180 F ($32.40) is an especially good value, considering what it contains.

LE CAVEAU 30, 45, rue Félix-Fauré. Tel. 93-39-06-33.

Cuisine: FRENCH. **Reservations:** Required. **Bus:** 1.

$ Prices: Appetizers 55–120 F ($9.90–$21.60); main dishes 65–120 F ($11.70–$21.60); fixed-price menus 105–160 F ($18.90–$28.80). AE, DC, MC, V.

Open: Lunch daily noon–2pm; dinner daily 7–11pm.

This restaurant, specializing in fine cuisine, emphasizes seafood. Begin with a seafood platter and follow with one of the chef's classic dishes, a pot-au-feu "from the sea" or a shellfish paella. Bouillabaisse is the classic dish to order, but you may prefer a côte de boeuf (beef) or even fresh pasta. The 1930s decor, the air conditioning, and the terrace all make dining a pleasant experience.

LE MONACO, 15, rue du 24-Août. Tel. 93-38-37-76.

Cuisine: FRENCH/ITALIAN. **Reservations:** Required. **Bus:** 1.

$ Prices: Appetizers 35–42 F ($6.30–$7.60); main dishes 50–70 F ($9–$12.60); fixed-price menus 78–98 F ($14–$17.60). No credit cards.

Open: Lunch Mon–Sat noon–2pm; dinner Mon–Sat 7–10pm. **Closed:** Nov 10–Dec 15.

This working person's favorite eatery, crowded but always cheap, is located conveniently near the train station. The likable ambience features closely placed tables, clean napery, and a staff dressed in bistro-inspired uniforms of black and white. Dishes include generous portions of osso buco with sauerkraut, spaghetti bolognese, trout with almonds, and minestrone with basil. Paella and couscous are very popular. Another specialty is that local favorite, grilled sardines, which many restaurants won't serve any more, considering them too messy and too old-fashioned.

EVENING ENTERTAINMENT

LE CASINO DU CARLTON, in the Carlton Intercontinental Hôtel, 58, bd. de la Croisette. Tel. 93-68-91-68.

On the eighth floor (seventh in France), this casino was established in 1988 as part of one of the resort's most legendary hotels. Considerably smaller than its major competitor (the Casino Municipale; see below), its modern decor nonetheless draws its share of devotees. Jackets are required for men, and a passport or government-issued identity card is required for admission. Open daily from 4pm to 4am.

Admission: 65 F ($11.70)

CASINO MUNICIPALE, 1, jetée Albert-Edouard (near bd. de la Croisette). Tel. 93-38-12-11.

The largest and most legendary casino in Cannes moved into a new building set on piers over the old port in 1983. Within its glittering confines, you'll find all the gaming tables you'd expect—open daily from 5pm to 4 or 5am—and one of the best nightclubs in town, Jimmy's, which is completely outfitted in shades of red. Jimmy's is open Wednesday through Sunday from 11pm until dawn; drinks begin at 70 F ($12.60). You must present your passport to enter the gambling room.

A glamorous restaurant, Le Restaurant des Jeux, occupies one semicircular end of the gaming floor, a format that successfully combines classic French cuisine with casino-watching. Dinner begins at around 350 F ($63) per person, and jackets for men are requested. The restaurant is open daily from 8pm to 3am, and AE, DC, MC, and V are accepted.

Admission: Gambling areas, 70 F ($12.60); Jimmy's, 130 F ($23.40), which includes one drink.

CLUB LA CHUNGA, 72, bd. de la Croisette. Tel. 93-94-11-29.

Club La Chunga is a restaurant and international piano bar; typical entertainment includes a South American trio. The panoramic terrace makes it especially appealing in summer as an elegant Côte d'Azur rendezvous for show-business people. The restaurant serves à la carte menus daily from 8pm to 12:30am for an average of 300 F ($54). Drinks run 120 F ($21.60). The club is open daily from 9pm to 5am.

JANE'S PIANO BAR/DISCO, in the Hôtel Gray-d'Albion, 38, rue des Serbes. Tel. 93-68-54-54.

This place has a sophisticated ambience of colored lights and warm tints. The restaurant features a fixed-price menu at 280 F ($50.40). Drinks cost 105 F ($18.90). Open daily from 8:30pm to 2am.

L'OPERA, rue des Cerfs. Tel. 93-99-09-01.

Modern and racy, this is the favorite disco for those in their early 20s. The place pulsates with life, noise, and activity. Drinks start at 35 F ($6.30). Open daily from 11pm to 3am.

Admission: 100 F ($18).

WHISKY A GO-GO, 115, av. de Lérins. Tel. 93-43-20-63.

This is a favorite spot for the young—or the young at heart. Facing the shut-down Palm Beach Casino, this two-level nightclub has comfortable armchairs and a dance floor. Seating 700, Whisky is the biggest club of its kind on the French Riviera. Guests are treated to a light show with colored lasers, smoke, and fog, as a disc jockey spins the latest dance music. Changing color patterns are projected on the mirrored back wall. Drinks cost 55 F ($9.90). Open daily from 10:30pm to 6am.

Admission: 100 F ($18) Mon–Fri, 120 F ($21.60) Sat–Sun.

EASY EXCURSION TO THE ILES DE LERINS

Across the bay from Cannes, the Lérins Islands are the most interesting excursion from the port. A boat leaves frequently from the harbor, taking 15 minutes to reach Ile Ste-Marguerite and 30 minutes to Ile St-Honorat. For information about departures, call 93-99-62-01. The round-trip fare to Ile Ste-Marguerite is 40 F ($7.20); to St-Honorat, 45 F ($8.10); or 60 F ($10.80) round-trip to both islands.

Ile Ste-Marguerite

The first island is named after St. Honorat's sister, St. Marguerite, who lived here with a group of nuns in the 5th century. Today the island is a youth center whose members—when they aren't sailing and diving—are dedicated to the restoration of the fort. From the dock where the boat lands, you can stroll along the island (signs point the way) to the **Fort de l'Ile**, built by Spanish troops from 1635 to 1637. Below is the 1st-century B.C. **Roman town** where the unlucky man immortalized in *The Man in the Iron Mask* was imprisoned.

One of French history's most perplexing mysteries is the identity of the man who wore the *masque du fer,* a prisoner of Louis XIV who arrived at Ste-Marguerite in 1698. Dumas fanned the legend that he was a brother of Louis XIV, and it has even been suggested that the prisoner and a mysterious woman had a son who went to Corsica and "founded" the Bonaparte family. However, the most common theory is that the prisoner was a servant of the superintendent, Fouquet, named Eustache Dauger. At any rate, he died in the Bastille in Paris in 1703.

You can visit his cell at Ste-Marguerite, in which every visitor seemingly has written his or her name. As you stand listening to the sound of the sea, you realize what a forlorn outpost this was.

The **Musée de la Mer,** Fort Royal (tel. 93-38-55-26), traces the history of the island, displaying artifacts of Ligurian, Roman, and Arab civilizations, plus the remains discovered by excavations. These include paintings, mosaics, and ceramics. Open June to September, daily from 10am to noon and 2 to 6pm (to 5pm off-season). Admission is 10 F ($1.80). Hours vary, depending on the arrival of the boats.

Ile St-Honorat

Only a mile long, Ile St-Honorat is even lonelier. St. Honorat founded a monastery here in the 5th century. Since the 1860s the Cistercians have owned the ecclesiastical complex, consisting of both an old fortified monastery and a contemporary one. You can spend the entire day wandering through the pine forests on the west side of the island, the other part being reserved for silent prayer.

19. LA NAPOULE-PLAGE

560 miles S of Paris, 5 miles W of Cannes

GETTING THERE   La Napoule lies on the bus and train routes between Cannes and St-Raphael.

ESSENTIALS Orientation   Most of the townspeople live near the busy coastal highway. The most-visited monument, the Château de la Napoule/Musée Henry-Clews, lies on a rocky summit between the sea and the coastal road, a short walk from the Royal Hôtel and the marina.

Information   For information, contact the Office de Tourisme, 274, bd. Henry-Clews (tel. 93-49-95-31).

This secluded resort is on the sandy beaches of the Golfe de la Napoule. In 1919 the once-obscure fishing village was a paradise for eccentric sculptor Henry Clews and his wife, who was an architect. Fleeing America's "charlatans," whom he believed had profited from World War I, the New York banker's son emphasized the fairy-tale qualities of his new home. His house is now the **Musée Henry-Clews;** an inscription over the entrance reads "Once upon a time."

The **Château de la Napoule,** bd. Henry-Clews (tel. 93-49-95-05), was rebuilt from the ruins of a medieval château. Clews covered the capitals and lintels with his own private, grotesque menagerie—scorpions, pelicans, gnomes, monkeys, lizards— the revelations of a tortured mind. The sculptor was once described as "the greatest America has ever produced." Women, feminism, and old age are recurring themes in the sculptor's work, as exemplified by the distorted suffragette depicted in his *Cat Woman.* The artist was preoccupied with old age in both men and women, and greatly admired chivalry and dignity in man as represented by Don Quixote—whom he likened to himself.

Clews died in Switzerland in 1937, and his body was returned to La Napoule-Plage for burial. Mrs. Clews later opened the château to the public. Open in July and August, Wednesday through Monday from 3 to 6pm; February to June and September to late November, Wednesday through Monday from 3 to 5pm; closed late November through January. Admission is 25 F ($4.50) for adults, 20 F ($3.60) for children.

WHERE TO STAY

LA CALANQUE, bd. Henry-Clews, 06210 La Napoule. Tel. 93-49-95-11.
   17 rms (all with bath or shower). TEL
$ Rates (including half board): 280–295 F ($50.40–$53.10) per person. MC, V.
   Parking: Free. **Closed:** Nov–Mar.
   The foundations of this charming hotel date from the Roman Empire, when an aristocrat built a villa here. The present hotel was built in 1942 and looks like a hacienda, with pink stucco walls and shutters. Register in the bar in the rear (through the dining room). The restaurant is garden style, with an outdoor terrace. It offers the cheapest fixed-price meal in La Napoule, for 99 F ($17.80). Nonresidents are welcome. The bar has a fireplace.

ERMITAGE DU RIOU, bd. Henry-Clews, 06210 La Napoule. Tel. 93-49-95-56. Fax 92-97-69-05. 42 rms (all with bath). A/C TV TEL

$ Rates (including breakfast): 810 F ($145.80) single; 1,340 F ($241.20) double. AE, DC, V. **Closed:** Nov 3–Dec 22.

This old Provençal house was turned into a seaside hotel in 1952. It borders the Riou River and the Cannes-Mandelieu international golf club. The bedrooms are furnished in Provençal style with genuine furniture of the area and ancient paintings. The most expensive rooms have private safes. Views are of either the sea or the golf course.

Dining/Entertainment: The restaurant has a wood ceiling with beams. Seafood is featured and meals begin at 185 F ($33.30).

Facilities: Swimming pool, solarium, garden.

LE ROYAL HOTEL, bd. Henry-Clews, 06210 Mandelieu La Napoule. Tel. 92-97-70-00. Fax 93-49-51-50. 185 rms (all with bath). 26 suites. A/C MINIBAR TV TEL

$ Rates: 980 F ($176.40) single; 1,850 F ($333) double; from 2,500 F ($450) suite. Breakfast 100 F ($18) extra. AE, DC, MC, V. **Parking:** Free.

This Las Vegas–style hotel is on the beach near an artificial harbor, about five miles from Cannes. It was the first hotel in France to include a casino and the last establishment (just before the building codes changed) to be allowed to have a casino directly on the beach. The hotel has one of the most contemporary designs on the Côte d'Azur, making it a major contender in the competitive world of Riviera palace hotels.

The interior is dramatically contemporary, filled with plush touches, warm shades, and lots of marble. Most of the attractive, modern rooms are angled toward a view of the sea. Rooms contain videos and hairdryers.

Dining/Entertainment: Le Féréol is recommended under "Where to Dine," below. The casino offers blackjack, craps, and roulette. It's open daily from 8pm to 4am. In the bar lounge, a show is presented at 10pm and another at 1am. The entertainment mingles nudity with music, feathers, glitter, plumes, and Nevada-style choreography, making for a glamorous extravaganza.

Services: 24-hour room service, same-day laundry and valet.

Facilities: Swimming pool, tennis courts, 27-hole golf course.

WHERE TO DINE

LE FEREOL, in Le Royal Hôtel & Casino, bd. Henry-Clews. Tel. 92-97-70-00.

Cuisine: FRENCH. **Reservations:** Recommended.

$ Prices: Appetizers 80–120 F ($14.40–$21.60); main dishes 90–130 F ($16.20–$23.40); buffet lunch 180 F ($32.40). AE, DC, MC, V.

Open: Lunch daily noon–3:30pm; dinner daily 7:30pm–1am.

This well-designed restaurant services all the culinary needs for the largest hotel (and the only casino) in town. Expanded in 1991 with the addition of a large outdoor terrace, it offers one of the most impressive lunchtime buffets in the neighborhood, with an usually large selection of hors d'oeuvres. If you don't want the buffet, a limited list of *plats du jour* is also offered for 70–90 F ($12.60–$16.20) each.

At night, the place becomes candlelit, more formal, and more elegant. Menu items include a filet of beef gourmandine, served with a filling of duck liver and a fricassée of flap mushrooms; a traditional version of bourride provençale; noisettes of lamb with an olive sauce; and a wide array of grilled meats and fish.

L'OASIS, rue Honoré-Carle. Tel. 93-49-95-52.

Cuisine: FRENCH. **Reservations:** Required.

$ Prices: Appetizers 160–220 F ($28.80–$39.60); main dishes 190–240 F ($34.20–$43.20); fixed-price menus 190–240 F ($34.20–$43.20). AE, DC, MC, V.

Open: July 14–Sept 14, lunch Sun only, noon–1:30pm; dinner daily 8–10pm. Sept 15–July 13, lunch Tues–Sun noon–1:30pm; dinner Tues–Sat 8–10pm.

Set directly at the entrance to the harbor of La Napoule, in a 40-year-old house with a lovely garden and an unusual re-creation of a mock-medieval cloister, this restaurant became world-famous under the tutelage of Louis Outhier during the 1960s and '70s. Mr. Outhier, half retired, now serves as a consultant to the new master chef, Stephane Raimbault, who prepares the most sophisticated cuisine in La Napoule. In summer, meals are served beneath the shade of the plane trees in the garden, in a setting which evokes the most glamorous days of the Côte d'Azur's heyday.

Menu specialties include a taboulette of crayfish with tamarind juice, warm foie gras of duckling with verdure de blettes (a Provençal vegetable similar to spinach), turbot en meunière with beets and capers, sea bass en croûte, filet of pork with sage oil, and John Dory roasted with herbs in the traditional style. The wine cellar houses one of the most sophisticated collections of Provençal wines anywhere.

---

20. ST-TROPEZ

543 miles S of Paris, 47 miles SW of Cannes

GETTING THERE **By Train** The nearest railway station is in St-Raphael, a neighboring resort; from there, you can take a taxi to St-Tropez or catch one of the local buses.

By Bus Buses run directly to St-Tropez from Toulon or Hyères.

By Car If you drive, you'll have to squeeze your car into impossibly small parking spaces wherever you can find them. One large parking lot lies just south of place des Lices/place du XVᵉ Corps, several blocks inland from the port.

ESSENTIALS **Orientation** Originally built on a rocky promontory, the city expanded over the centuries to include the lowlands beside the port. Today, covering the town on foot requires a lot of climbing on steep and winding streets. Except for the outlying beaches, anywhere from 2½ to 4 miles outside town, most of St-Tropez lies between three important sights or locations: place des Lices, in the south; the citadel, in the northeast; and the port, in the northwestern town.

Information The Office de Tourisme is on quai Jean-Jaurès (tel. 94-97-45-21).

Lasciviousness is rampant in this carnival town, but a true Tropezian resents the fact that the port has such a bad reputation. "We can be classy too," insisted one native. Creative people in the lively arts along with ordinary folk create a volatile mixture. One observer said that St-Tropez "has replaced Naples for those who accept the principle of dying after seeing it. It is a unique fate for a place to have made its reputation on the certainty of happiness."

St-Tropez was greatly popularized by Bardot in *And God Created Woman,* but it's been known for a long time. Colette lived here for many years. Even the late diarist Anaïs Nin, confidante of Henry Miller, posed for a little cheesecake on the beach here in 1939 in a Dorothy Lamour bathing suit. Composer Ned Rorem bought a canary-yellow shirt at Vachon, to go, as related in his famous diary, with "my golden legs in khaki shorts, my tan sandals, and my orange hair." Earlier, St-Tropez was known to Guy de Maupassant, Signac, Matisse, and Bonnard.

Artists, composers, novelists, and the film colony are attracted to St-Tropez in summer. Trailing them is a line of humanity unmatched anywhere else on the Riviera for sheer flamboyance. Some of the most fashionable yachts bringing the chicest people anchor here in summer, disappearing long before the dreaded mistral of winter.

WHAT TO SEE & DO

Near the harbor is the **Musée de l'Annonciade,** at the Place Georges-Grammont (tel. 94-97-04-01), installed in the former chapel of the Annonciade. As a legacy from the artists who loved St-Tropez, the museum shelters one of the finest modern-art collections on the Riviera. Many of the artists, including Paul Signac, depicted the port of St-Tropez. Opened in 1955, the collection includes such works as Kees Van Dongen's yellow-faced *Women of the Balustrade,* and paintings and sculpture by Bonnard, Matisse, Rouault, Braque, Vuillard, Dufy, Utrillo, Seurat, Dunoyer de Segonzac, Vlaminck, Derain, Despiau, and Maillol. It is closed in November.

The museum is open June through September, Wednesday through Monday from 10am to noon and 4 to 8pm; October and December through May, Wednesday through Monday from 10am to noon and 2 to 6pm; closed in November. Admission is 25 F ($4.50).

On the outskirts of St-Tropez, at a distance of two miles, **Port Grimaud** makes for an interesting outing. If you approach the village at dusk when it is softly bathed in Riviera pastels (much like Portofino, Italy), it will look like some old hamlet, perhaps from the 16th century. But this is a mirage. Port Grimaud is the dream-fulfillment of its promoter, François Spoerry, who carved it out of marshland and dug canals. Flanking these canals, fingers of land extend from the main square to the sea. The homes are Provençal style, many with Italianate window arches. The owners of boats can anchor right at their doorsteps. One newspaper called the port "the most magnificent fake since Disneyland." One of its promoters has described it as "a village as it would have been if architects did not exist."

WHERE TO STAY

Very Expensive

BYBLOS, av. Paul-Signac, 83990 St-Tropez. Tel. 94-97-00-04. Fax 94-97-40-52. 60 rms (all with bath), 47 suites. A/C MINIBAR TV TEL
$ Rates: 1,700–2,730 F ($306–$491.40) single or double; from 4,000 F ($720) suite. Breakfast 100 F ($18) extra. AE, DC, MC, V. **Parking:** Free. **Closed:** Nov–Mar.

⭐ The builder said he created "an anti-hotel, a place like home." That's true if your home resembles a palace in Beirut with salons decorated with Phoenician gold statues from 3000 B.C. On a hill above the harbor, this deluxe complex has intimate patios and courtyards. There are seductive retreats filled with antiques and rare decorative objects, many brought from Lebanon, including polychrome carved woodwork on the walls, marquetry floors, and a Persian-rug ceiling.

Every bedroom is unique. In one, for example, there's a fireplace on a raised hearth, paneled blue-and-gold doors, and a bed recess on a dais. Le Hameau contains 10 individual duplex apartments built around a small courtyard with an outdoor spa. Some rooms have balconies overlooking an inner courtyard; others open onto a terrace of flowers.

Dining/Entertainment: You may dine in the restaurant, Les Arcades. Later in the evening you can dance on a circular floor surrounded by bas-relief columns in the hotel's nightclub. There are also two bars.

Services: 24-hour room service, same-day laundry and valet service, beauty salon.

Facilities: "High-fashion" swimming pool, sauna.

RESIDENCE DE LA PINEDE, plage de la Bouillabaisse, 83900 St-Tropez. Tel. 94-97-04-21. Fax 94-97-73-64. 35 rms (all with bath), 6 suites. A/C MINIBAR TV TEL
$ Rates: 550–1,815 F ($99–$326.70) single; 800–2,915 F ($144–$524.70) double; 2,050–7,150 F ($369–$1,287) suite. Breakfast 100 F ($18) extra. AE, DC, MC, V. **Parking:** Free. **Closed:** Oct 16–Mar.

⭐ This four-star luxury hotel was constructed in 1952 around an existing tower once used to store olives. Jean-Clause Delion owns this seaside Relais & Châteaux, which has housed many celebrities, including Raquel Welch. The airy, spacious rooms are decorated in pastels; amenities include video. Rooms open onto balconies or terraces with a view over the bay of St-Tropez. The hotel is considered the finest in St-Tropez after the Byblos (see above).

Dining/Entertainment: Excellent food, especially seafood, is served in the dining room or on the terrace under the pine trees.

Services: 24-hour room service, same-day laundry and valet service.

Facilities: Swimming pool, beach.

VILLA DE BELIEU, 83580 Gassin, Presqu'Ile de Saint-Tropez. Tel. 94-56-16-83. Fax 94-43-43-34. 12 rms (all with bath), 5 suites. A/C MINIBAR TV TEL

$ Rates: 1,800–4,000 F ($324–$720); from 4,400 F ($792) suite. Breakfast 95 F ($17.10) extra. AE, V.

A short drive from the center of St-Tropez, this villa lies in the heart of the wine-growing estate of Bertaud-Belieu on the peninsula of St-Tropez, a land that has produced grapes for wine for more than 2,000 years. The villa is Italianesque and the decor is pure Provence. Everything, under the direction of its owner, Carole Gourmelon, is old-world charm. Each beautifully furnished room or suite has a different name, ranging from "Exotique" (with a canopy bed and a private garden) to "And God Created Woman," a reference to Bardot's most fabled film with a St-Tropez setting. The most provocative suite is named "Kamasutra" and is for lovers only.

Dining/Entertainment: In a romantic setting, ranging from outside under the stars to a candlelit wood-beamed restaurant, dinners are served with French porcelain and antique silverware. Traditional and modern dishes are featured, each accompanied by the estate's best wines.

Services: 24-hour room service, hairdresser.

Facilities: Tennis, wine cellar visits, nearby golf, and a spa complete with sauna, Hammam, Jacuzzi, and gym.

Expensive

LA BASTIDE DE ST-TROPEZ, route des Caries, 83990 St-Tropez. Tel. 94-97-58-16. Fax 94-97-21-71. 20 rms (all with bath), 6 suites. A/C MINIBAR TV TEL

$ Rates: 1,200–1,950 F ($216–$351) single or double; 2,250–3,300 F ($405–$594) suite. Breakfast 105 F ($18.90) extra. AE, DC, MC, V. **Parking:** Free. **Closed:** Jan 3–Feb 5.

Located near the landmark place des Lices, this tile-roofed manor looks deliberately severe, but the interior is far more opulent. A grand staircase leads from a sun-filled living room to the upper floors. The rooms are named according to their unique decor, including "rose of Bengal" and "tangerine dawn." Each room has a terrace or private garden, and some have Jacuzzis.

Dining/Entertainment: The hotel is noted for its restaurant, l'Olivier, offering meals for 210–480 F ($37.80–$86.40).

Services: 24-hour room service.

Facilities: Outdoor swimming pool.

HOTEL DE LEVANT, route des Salins, 83990 St-Tropez. Tel. 94-97-33-33. Fax 94-97-76-13. 28 rms (all with bath). MINIBAR TV TEL

$ Rates: 595–825 F ($107.10–$148.50) single or double. Breakfast 52 F ($9.40) extra. AE, DC, MC, V. **Parking:** Free. **Closed:** Mid-Oct to Mar 15.

Located on the road leading from the old town of St-Tropez to the beach at Les Salins, this hotel is behind a screen of cypresses and palmettos. It was designed like a low-slung Provençal farmhouse, with thick stucco walls and a tile roof. The rooms are decorated with Provençal motifs, with big windows and white walls, as well as private entrances overlooking the garden, which has a swimming pool.

HOTEL LA MANDARINE, route de Tahiti, 83990 St-Tropez. Tel. 94-97-06-66. Fax 94-97-33-67. 38 rms (all with bath), 4 suites. A/C MINIBAR TV TEL

$ Rates (including continental breakfast): 850–1,050 F ($153–$189) single; 890–1,800 F ($160.20–$324) double; from 2,000 F ($360) suite. AE, DC, MC, V. **Parking:** Free. **Closed:** Mid-Oct to mid-Mar.

One of the finest hotels in the area, La Mandarine is built in the Provençal style with strong angles, thick stucco walls, tile roof, and patios. It's located half a mile southeast of the center and just off the road leading to the famous Tahiti beach. Rooms in the complex are luxuriously furnished and open onto one or more terraces. Some of the suites offer as many as three separate terraces. You definitely get glamour here.

Dining/Entertainment: The restaurant specializes in *cuisine moderne* recipes using fish and shellfish; meals start at 255 F ($45.90).

Facilities: Heated swimming pool.

HOTEL RESIDENCE DES LICES, 135, av. Augustin-Grangeon, 83900 St-Tropez. Tel. 94-97-28-28. 41 rms (all with bath). A/C TV TEL

$ Rates: 540–1,050 F ($97.20–$189) single or double. Breakfast 55 F ($9.90) extra. MC, V. **Parking:** Free. **Closed:** Nov 3–Mar 24.

One consistently reliable bet for lodgings in St-Tropez is this modern hotel, built in the 1970s, which lies in its own small garden close to the place des Lices. The price of bedrooms varies widely according to their view and size. No meals are served other than breakfast, although afternoon snacks are served beside the swimming pool.

LE YACA, 1, bd. d'Aumale, 83900 St-Tropez. Tel. 94-97-11-79. Fax 94-97-58-50. 22 rms (all with bath). A/C TV TEL

$ Rates: 1,000–2,000 F ($180–$360) single or double. Breakfast 70 F ($12.60) extra. AE, DC, MC, V. **Closed:** Oct 16–Mar.

Built in 1722, Le Yaca was the first hotel in St-Tropez. Colette lived here in 1927, and before that it was the home of pre-impressionist painters, including Paul Signac. The unpretentious facade is off a narrow street in the old part of town. Inside is a reception area with a high ceiling and a view of an inner courtyard filled with flowers. Many of the rooms also have views of the quiet courtyard of the hotel. Many rooms are on the upper floor, with handmade terra-cotta floor tiles and massive ceiling timbers. There is a swimming pool.

Moderate

HOTEL ERMITAGE, av. Paul-Signac, 83990 St-Tropez. Tel. 94-97-52-33. Fax 94-97-10-43. 29 rms (all with bath), 2 suites. MINIBAR TEL

$ Rates: 590–790 F ($106.20–$142.20) single or double; 990 F ($178.20) suite. Breakfast 55 F ($9.90) extra. AE, DC, MC, V. **Parking:** Free.

Attractively isolated amid the rocky upper heights of St-Tropez, near the base of the Citadelle, this three-story hotel was originally built during the 19th century as a private villa. Today, its red-tile roof and green shutters shelter a plushly comfortable hideaway. A walled garden is romantically illuminated at night, and a cozy corner bar near a wood-burning fireplace takes the chill off blustery winter evenings. Rooms are pleasantly furnished, and the staff can be charming. Breakfast is the only meal served.

HOTEL LA TARTANE, route des Salins, 83990 St-Tropez. Tel. 94-97-21-23. Fax 94-97-09-16. 14 rms (all with bath). A/C TV TEL

$ Rates: 690–900 F ($124.20–$162) single or double. Breakfast 68 F ($12.20) extra. AE, V. **Parking:** Free. **Closed:** Nov 5–Mar 15.

This hotel is located midway between the center of St-Tropez and the Plage des Salins, about a three-minute drive from each. There's a stone-rimmed pool set into the garden and attractively furnished public rooms with terra-cotta floors. The rooms are well-furnished bungalows centered around the pool. Facilities include a Jacuzzi. Breakfasts are elaborate and attractive, and lunch is offered between 1 and 3pm; dinner is not served.

LA PONCHE, 3, place Révelin, 83990 St-Tropez. Tel. 94-97-02-53. Fax 94-97-78-61. 20 rms (all with bath). A/C TV TEL

$ Rates: 750–2,050 F ($135–$369) single or double. Breakfast 60 F ($10.80) extra. AE, MC, V. **Closed:** Oct 16–Mar 14.

This hotel is a cluster of remodeled fishermen's houses, with a little plaza and a tiny beach where a club atmosphere prevails. It's in a secluded and relatively unknown part of central St-Tropez. It was originally a pub also called La Ponche, and Picasso came here for his pastis. The little plaza becomes a social center in the evening. Most rooms are charmingly furnished; a few face the beach. A glass-walled lounge in the main building and the two dining rooms are furnished with antiques and original paintings. The food is *cuisine moderne,* and grilled fish from the Mediterranean has always been featured. Specialties are stuffed fish and savory bouillabaisse.

SUBE, 15, quai Suffren, 83900 St-Tropez. Tel. 94-97-30-04. Fax 94-54-89-08. 30 rms (all with bath). A/C TV TEL
$ Rates: 590–1,500 F ($106.20–$270) single or double. Breakfast 40 F ($7.20) extra. AE, DC, MC, V.
If you want to be right on the port, this should be your first choice. It's directly over the Café de Paris in the center of a shopping arcade. The two-story lounge has a beamed ceiling and a glass front, allowing a great view of the harbor activity. The lounge is furnished with a 10-foot-high fireplace, a wall torchère, and provincial chairs. The bedrooms are very small and decorated in a provincial style. The beds are soft, and the maids keep everything tidy.

Inexpensive

LOU CAGNARD, av. Paul-Roussel, route de Ramatuelle, 83990 St-Tropez. Tel. 94-97-04-24. 19 rms (all with bath or shower). TEL
$ Rates: 250–400 F ($45–$72) single or double. Breakfast 35 F ($6.30) extra. No credit cards. **Closed:** Nov 15–Jan 4.

This pleasant roadside inn, with a tile roof and green shutters, has quiet rooms in the rear overlooking the garden. Madame Rul doesn't speak English, but somehow she manages to assist her North American guests. Continental breakfast is available.

WHERE TO DINE

Expensive

LE BISTROT DES LICES, 3, place des Lices. Tel. 94-97-29-00.
  Cuisine: FRENCH. **Reservations:** Required in summer.
$ Prices: Appetizers 50–190 F ($9–$34.20); main dishes 110–230 F ($19.80–$41.40). MC, V.
  Open: July–Aug, dinner only, daily 7:30pm–midnight. Mid-Apr to June and Sept–Oct 14, lunch daily noon–2pm; dinner daily 7:30pm–midnight. **Closed:** Oct 15 to early Apr.
This informal bistro with a pleasant decor attracts a glamorous clientele, especially on sunny days, when the lace curtains filter the light. There's a glass-enclosed outdoor café, and a piano bar and café in the outer room. In summer there are tables in the rear garden. The menu changes every month. Typical dishes include sole sautéed with morels and the juice of truffles, grilled fresh fish, gigot of sea bass, a bourride of white seafish, and filets of duckling with peach juice.

LEI MOUSCARDINS, 16, rue Portalet. Tel. 94-97-01-53.
  Cuisine: FRENCH. **Reservations:** Required.
$ Prices: Appetizers 40–130 F ($7.20–$23.40); main dishes 135–380 F ($24.30–$68.40); fixed-price menu 180 F ($32.40). AE, MC, V.
  Open: Lunch daily noon–2:30; dinner daily 7:30–11:30pm. **Closed:** Nov–Mar 15.
Located at the end of the harbor, this restaurant has won awards for culinary perfection. It's upstairs and has picture windows with harbor views. The dining room is formal Provençal with an adjoining sun room under a canopy. The menu includes superb classic Mediterranean dishes. For an appetizer, I recommend moules (mussels) marinières. The two celebrated fish stews of the Côte d'Azur are offered here: a bourride provençale and a bouillabaisse. The fish dishes are especially good, particularly the loup (sea bass). If you're not in the mood for fish, try the grilled, tender entrecôte. The chef prepares two dessert specialties—soufflés made with Grand Marnier or Cointreau.

Moderate

L'ECHALOTTE, 35, rue Allard. Tel. 94-54-83-26.
Cuisine: FRENCH. **Reservations:** Recommended in summer.
$ Prices: Appetizers 35–120 F ($6.30–$21.60); main dishes 80–160 F ($14.40–$28.80); fixed-price menu 160 F ($28.80). AE, MC, V.
Open: Lunch daily 12:30–2pm; dinner daily 8–11:30pm. **Closed:** Nov 15–Dec 15.

This charming restaurant, with a tiny garden and clean dining room, serves consistently good food for moderate prices. You can enjoy lunch on the veranda or dinner indoors. Tables are difficult to get, especially in peak summer weeks. The cuisine is solidly bourgeois, including grilled veal kidneys, crayfish with a drawn-butter sauce, and filet of turbot with truffles. The major specialty is several kinds of fish, especially sea bass and daurade royale cooked in a salt crust.

LE GIRELIER, quai Jean-Jaurès. Tel. 94-97-03-87.
Cuisine: FRENCH. **Reservations:** Not required.
$ Prices: Appetizers 50–145 F ($9–$26.10); main dishes 70–480 F ($12.60–$86.40); fixed-price menu 170 F ($30.60). AE, DC, MC, V.
Open: Lunch daily noon–2:30pm; dinner daily 7–11:30pm.

The Rouets, an old family of St-Tropez, own this portside restaurant whose blue-and-white color scheme has become its own kind of trademark. Filled with rattan furniture, with a large glassed-in veranda, it serves well-prepared grilled fish in many different manifestations, as well as bouillabaisse, priced at 540 F ($97.20) and served only to two diners. Also available is a brochette of monkfish, a kettle of mussels, or perhaps a pipérade (a Basque omelet with pimento, garlic, and tomatoes).

Inexpensive

BOEUF SUR LA PLACE, 3, place des Lices. Tel. 94-97-60-50.
Cuisine: STEAKS. **Reservations:** Not required.
$ Prices: Appetizers 35–55 F ($6.30–$9.90); main dishes 80–190 F ($14.40–$34.20). MC, V.
Open: Lunch daily noon–2:30pm; dinner daily 7–10:30pm.

A recent newcomer to the historic place des Lices lies adjacent to the previously recommended Bistro des Lices, and is owned by the same management. Specializing only in flavorful cuts of meat, it offers well-prepared steaks and chops which are best consumed with one of the bottles of hearty red wine that the staff makes readily available. Menu choices include carpaccio (thinly sliced raw marinated beef laden with garlic and herbs), "brochettes of the butcher," filets and faux-filets prepared in several carefully seasoned styles, and a wide array of desserts. Unlike many other restaurants in town, this one remains open throughout the entire year.

EVENING ENTERTAINMENT

LE BAL, Résidence du Port. Tel. 94-97-14-70.
The white-tile walls prompted one writer to describe this club as "like a ballroom-sized bathroom." It's very chic and sophisticated, and you might even see Elton John here. It's located above several boutiques. Open daily from 11pm to dawn.
Admission: 110 F ($19.80), including one drink.

CAFE DE PARIS, sur le Port. Tel. 94-97-00-56.
Located below the Hôtel Sube, this is one of the most consistently popular hangouts in town. An attempt has been made to glorify a fairly utilitarian room with turn-of-the-century globe lights, an occasional 19th-century bronze, masses of artificial flowers, and a long zinc bar. The crowd is irreverent and animated. It's busy even in winter, after the yachting crowd departs. Café crème goes for 9–20 F ($1.60–$3.60); whisky, 60 F ($10.80). Open June to September, daily from 8am to 3am; off-season, daily from 8am to 7pm.

CAFE DES ARTS, place des Lices. Tel. 94-97-02-25.

This local blue-collar hangout occasionally gets rowdy. Many of the residents interrupt a game of boules on the square outside to come in for a glass or two of wine. Designed with a low ceiling and stone columns, the café entertains regulars and tourists as well. The restaurant serves dinner only and is open Easter through mid-October daily from 8:30 to 11:15pm. Drinks begin at 52 F ($9.40); meals, at 200 F ($36). Open June to September, daily from 8am to 3am; off-season, daily from 8am to 8:30pm.

CAFE SENEQUIER, sur le Port. Tel. 94-97-00-90.

Reporter Leslie Maitland once described the kind of clientele attracted here at cocktail hour: "What else can one do but gawk at a tall, well-dressed young woman who appears *comme il faut* at Sénéquier's with a large white rat perched upon her shoulder, with which she occasionally exchanges little kisses, while casually chatting with her friends?" This is one of many oddities at this anything-goes café.

All the tables, chairs, and stools are red. There is a great view of the port from under the canopy. During summer, yacht-watching is a favorite pastime here. Whisky costs 66 F ($11.90); coffee, 13 F ($2.30). Open June to September, daily from 8am to 1am; off-season, daily from 8am to 7pm; closed November 11 to December 20.

LES CAVES DU ROY, in the Hôtel Byblos, av. Paul-Signac. Tel. 94-97-00-04.

Considered the choicest disco along the French Riviera, Les Caves du Roy certainly provides the most romantic background for dancing. It also features the best live entertainment in St-Tropez. Members of the 25-and-older set dance to the latest music on the circular dance floor, surrounded by decorative bas-relief columns amid a Provençal and Lebanese decor. The dress code is elegant but casual. Drinks cost 130 F ($23.40). Open June to September only, daily from 11pm to 5am.

Admission: Free.

HILARIOS, quai Jean-Jaurès. Tel. 94-97-02-44.

This piano bar is decorated like the interior of a classic yacht. Live bands frequently play jazz here. Drinks run 60 F ($10.80). Open daily from 4:30pm to dawn.

Admission: Free.

MENU SAVVY

A la "In the manner of" or "accompanied with"

Alsacien/a l'alsacienne Alsace-style (usually with sauerkraut, foie gras, or sausage)

A l'Ancienne Old-fashioned, "in the style of grandmother"

A point Medium rare

Aiguillettes Long thin slivers, usually of duck

Aïoli Garlic-laced mayonnaise

Amuse-gueule A pre-appetizer

Andouillette Chitterling or tripe sausage

Apéritif Before-dinner libation said to "awaken" the appetite

Assiette du pêcheur Mixed seafood plate

Baguette The famous long loaf of French bread

Ballottine Deboned, stuffed, and rolled poultry

Basquais/à la basquaise Basque-style, usually with tomatoes, red peppers, and ham

Béarnaise Sauce made with egg yolks, shallots, white wine, vinegar, butter, and tarragon

Béchamel Buttery white flour sauce flavored with onion and herbs

Beurre blanc "White butter" sauce with white wine, butter, and shallots

Bigarade Bitter orange sauce, often served with duck

Blanc de volaille Breast of hen

Blanquette Stewed meat with white sauce, enriched with cream and eggs

Boeuf à la môde Marinated beef braised with red wine and served with vegetables

Boeuf en Daube Beef stew with red wine

Bordelais/à la bordelaise Bordeaux-style; usually accompanied with a wine-laced brown sauce flavored with shallots, tarragon, and bone marrow

Boudin noir Blood sausage

Bouillabaisse Mediterranean fish soup, made with tomatoes, garlic, saffron, and olive oil

Bourguignon/à la bourguignonne Burgundy-style, usually with red wine, mushrooms, bacon, and onions

Bourride Mediterranean fish soup with aïoli, served over slices of bread

Breton/à la bretonne Brittany-style, often with white beans

Brunoise Tiny cut-up vegetables

Canard à la presse Duck killed by suffocation, then pressed to extract the blood and juices, which are simmered with cognac and red wine

Canard sauvage Wild duck

Carbonnade Beef stew, originally from Flanders, often cooked with beer

Carré d'agneau Crown roast or loin of lamb

Cassolette Dish served in a small casserole

Cassoulet Toulousien specialty of white beans cooked with preserved goose or duck, pig's trotters, sausages, carrots, and onions

Céleri rémoulade Shredded celery root with a tangy mayonnaise

Cèpes à la bordelaise Large, meaty wild boletus mushrooms cooked with oil, shallots, and herbs

Choucroute garni Alsatian sauerkraut garnished with pork products and boiled potatoes

Cochon de lait Roast suckling pig

Confit Meat (usually duck or goose) cooked and preserved in its own fat

Coq au vin Chicken stewed with mushrooms and red wine

Côte d'agneau Lamb chop

Côte de boeuf Rib steak

Court bouillon A broth with white wine, herbs, carrots, and soup greens in which poultry, fish, or meat is cooked

Crème brûlée Thick custard dessert with a caramelized topping

Crème chantilly Sugared whipped cream

Crème fraîche Sour heavy cream

Crème pâtissière Custard filling for cakes

Croque-monsieur Toasted sandwich containing cheese and ham; if prepared with a fried egg on top, its called a *croque-madame*

Darne A slice of fish steak, usually salmon

Daurade Prized sea bream (similar to porgy)

Desmoiselles de Cherbourg Small Norman lobsters in court bouillon

Diable Deviled and peppery

Digestif Any after-dinner liqueur (e.g., Armagnac) that is presumed to aid the digestive processes

Dijonnais/à la dijonnaise Denotes the presence in a dish of mustard, usually Dijon

Duxelles Chopped shallots and mushrooms sautéed and mixed with rich cream

Eau-de-vie "Water of life"—brandy distilled from fruit or herbs; usually has a very high alcohol percentage and is usually consumed at the end of a meal

Ecrevisse Freshwater crayfish

Escabèche Provençale dish of small fish (often sardines) browned in olive oil, marinated, and served cold

Escargot de Bourgogne Land snail prepared with garlic, parsley, and butter

Estoficado Purée of dried codfish, tomatoes, olive oil, onions, and herbs; a specialty of Nice

Faisan Pheasant

Farci Stuffed

Feu de bois, au Cooked over a wood fire

Fraise des bois Wild strawberry

Française, à la Garnish of peas with lettuce, pearl onions, and herbs

Fricassée Braised meat or poultry stew; any medley of meat, even fish, that is stewed or sautéed

Friture Fried food

Fromage blanc White cheese (like cottage cheese)

Fumet Fish-based stock

Galantine Classic dish of cooked meat or fowl, served cold in jelly aspic

Garni Garnished

Gelée Jelly or aspic

Galette Flat round cake or pastry; in Brittany, a crêpe of buckwheat flour

Gâteau Cake

Gibelotte Rabbit fricassée in wine sauce

Gigot Haunch (or leg) of an animal, almost always that of lamb or mutton

Glaces Ice in general; ice cream in particular

Glaçons Ice cubes

Gratin Brown crust that forms on top of a dish when it's oven-browned; a dish that is covered with bread crumbs and melted cheese

Grenouilles Frogs' legs

Grillé Grilled

Herbes de Provence A medley of rosemary, summer savory, bay leaf, and thyme

Hollandaise Yellow sauce of egg yolk, butter, and lemon juice whipped into a smooth blend

Homard à l'armoricaine Lobster browned and simmered with shallots, cognac, white wine, and onions

Hors d'oeuvres Appetizers

Huile d'olive Olive oil

Ile Flottante "Floating Island," a rich dessert of a kirsch-soaked biscuit dressed with maraschino cherries and whipped cream

Jambon de Bayonne Salt-cured ham from the Basque region

Jardinière Garnish of freshly cooked vegetables

Julienne Cut into thin strips

Jus Juice; *"au jus"* means, with natural, unthickened gravy

Landais/à la landaise Landes-style—a garnish of goose fat, pine nuts, and garlic

Langouste Clawless spiny lobster or rock lobster

Langoustine Clawed crustacean (in Britain, a prawn)

Lardons Cubes of bacon, often served with soups and salads

Léger/légère Light in texture, flavor, and calories

Legume Vegetable

Limande Lemon sole

Lotte Monkfish or angler fish

Lou magrêt Breast of fattened duck

Loup de mer Wolf-fish, a Mediterranean sea bass

Lyonnais/à la lyonnaise White wine sauce with shredded and sautéed onions

Macédoine Medley of diced vegetables or fruits

Marchand de vins Wine-merchant; it also implies a rich sauce made from shallots and red wine

Marmite A thick soup made from beef and vegetables, simmered for hours on a low fire; the pot in which the soup is cooked. A *marmite des pêcheurs* refers to a fish soup, or stew, prepared in a marmite

Ménagère, à la "Housewife style"—accompanied with potatoes, onions, and carrots

Meunière, à la "In the style of the miller's wife"—rolled in flour and sautéed in butter

Meurette A red wine sauce, often served with poached eggs and freshwater fish; any wine sauce

Mignonette A substance (usually beef) cut into small cubes

Millefeuille A napoleon

Mirepoix Minced onions, ham, and carrots sautéed in butter and flavored with herbs

Mornay Béchamel sauce flavored with cheese

Moules à la marinière Mussels in herb-flavored white wine with shallots

Nage, à la An aromatic court bouillon used for poaching

Nantua Pink sauce made of white wine, crayfish, and tomatoes

Navarin Mutton prepared with potatoes and turnips

Normande Sauce of eggs, cream, and mushrooms, Normain style; meat or fish flavored with Calvados

Oeufs à la neige "Eggs in snow"—beaten egg whites poached in milk and served with a vanilla-flavored custard

Omelette norvegienne Baked Alaska à la française

Pain Bread

Palourde Clamlike mollusk, most often stuffed

Pamplemousse Grapefruit

Panaché Any mixture

Papillote, en Cooked in parchment paper

Parfait Layered ice-cream dessert

Parisienne, à la With leeks and potatoes

Parmentier A dish with potatoes

Pâté Minced meat that is spiced and baked in a mold and served either hot or cold; sometimes made from fish or vegetables

Pâté feuilletée Puff pastry

Paysanne Chicken or meat braised and garnished with vegetables

Périgourdine, à la Sauce usually made with foie gras and truffles

Pipérade Classic Basque dish of scrambled eggs with onions, tomatoes, peppers, and ham

Piquante Tangy sauce made with shallots, vinegar, herbs, small pickles, and white wine

Pistou Sauce of garlic, fresh basil, and olive oil, from Provence

Plat du jour The daily special

Poêlé Pan-fried

Poisson Fish—*de mer* is from the ocean; *de lac* from the lake; *de rivière* from the river

Poivrade Peppery brown sauce made with wine and vinegar

Pomme Apple

Pommes de Terre Potato; *pommes de terre* is frequently shortened to *pommes,* as in *pommes frites* (french fries)

Porc Pork; *porc salé* is salt pork

Pot-au-feu "Pot on the fire"—meat stew cooked in an earthenware pot

Poulet, Poularde Chicken—*poulet fermier* is free-range; *poussin* is a chick

Pré salé Seaside meadow whose grasses are said to be especially beneficial for the pasturing of lambs or sheep; flesh from lambs raised in these meadows is especially succulent

Pressé Pressed or squeezed, as in fresh orange juice

Prix fixe A set meal with a fixed price

Profiteroles Small cream puffs of chou pastry with a filling of whipped cream or custard

Provençal/à la provençale In the style of Provence, most often with garlic, tomatoes, onion

Purée Mashed or forced through a sieve

Quenelles Rolls of pounded and baked fish, often pike, usually served warm; can also be made from chicken or veal

Ragoût Stew, usually made from beef

Rascasse A scorpion fish in Mediterranean bouillabaisse

Ratatouille A Mediterranean medley of peppers, tomato, eggplant, garlic, and onions

Ravigote Sauce made with vinegar, lemon sauce, white wine, shallot butter, and herbs

Rémoulade Cold mayonnaise flavored with mustard

Rillettes Minced pork spread popular in Tours

Rognons Kidneys, usually veal

Ris de veau Veal sweetbreads

Rosé Meat or poultry cooked rare

Rôti Roasted

Rouennaise (canard à la . . .) Duck stuffed with its liver in a blood-thickened sauce

Rouille Olive-oil based mayonnaise, with peppers, garlic, and fish broth, served with bouillabaisse in Provence

Roulade Meat or fish roll, most often stuffed

Sabayon Egg custard flavored with marsala wine

Saignant/saignante "Bleeding"— referring to anything cooked rare, especially roast beef

Salade lyonnaise Green salad flavored with cubed bacon and soft-boiled eggs

Salade niçoise Made with tomatoes, green beans, tuna, black olives, potatoes, artichokes, and capers

Salade verte Green salad

Sandre Pickerel; a perchlike river fish

Saucisse French pork sausage

Sole cardinal Poached filet of sole with a crayfish-flavored cream sauce

Sommelier Wine steward

Sorbet Sherbet, usually flavored with fresh fruit

Soubise A béchamel sauce with onion

Soufflé A "blown up" fluffy baked egg dish flavored with almost anything, from cheese to Grand Marnier

Steak au poivre Pepper steak, covered with fresh peppercorns, with a cognac flambé

Suprême White sauce made with heavy cream

Table d'hôte A fixed-price, pre-selected meal, usually offering a limited (if any) choice of the specific dishes that comprise it

Tartare Any preparation of cold chopped raw meat flavored with piquant sauces and spices (including capers and onions)

Tartare (sauce) Cold mayonnaise spiced with herbs, vinegar, and mustard

Tarte tatin Caramelized upside-down apple pie

Tartine Open-face sandwich, or bread slathered with jam and butter

Terrine Potted meat in a crock

Timbale Fish or meat dishes cooked in a casserole

Tournedos Rossini Beef filet sautéed in butter with pan juices, served with a foie gras garnish

Tripes à la môde de Caen Beef tripe cooked in Calvados with carrots, leeks, onions, herbs, and spices

Truite au bleu Fish that is gutted moments before being plunged into a mixture of boiling vinegar and water, which turns the flesh blue

Vacherin Ice cream in a meringue shell; a rich cheese from eastern France

Velouté Classic velvety sauce, thickened with a roux of flour and butter

Véronique, à la Garnished with peeled white grapes; usually applies to filet of sole

Vichy With glazed carrots

Vichyssoise Cold creamy potato-and-leek soup

Vinaigrette Oil-and-vinegar dressing flavored with herbs and perhaps a hint of mustard

Vol-au-vent Puff pastry shell

Xérès, vinaigre de Sherry-flavored vinegar

Zeste Citrus peel without its white pith, twisted and used to flavor drinks, such as vermouth

INDEX

GENERAL INFORMATION

DESTINATIONS

Key to abbreviations * = Author's favorite; $ = Super-value choice; B = Budget; E = Expensive; I = Inexpensive; M = Moderately priced; VE = Very expensive.

Please Send Me the Books Checked Below:

FROMMER'S COMPREHENSIVE GUIDES
(Guides listing facilities from budget to deluxe,
with emphasis on the medium-priced)

	Retail Price	Code		Retail Price	Code
☐ Acapulco/Ixtapa/Taxco 1993–94	$15.00	C120	☐ Jamaica/Barbados 1993–94	$15.00	C105
☐ Alaska 1994–95	$17.00	C130	☐ Japan 1992–93	$19.00	C020
☐ Arizona 1993–94	$18.00	C101	☐ Morocco 1992–93	$18.00	C021
☐ Australia 1992–93	$18.00	C002	☐ Nepal 1994–95	$18.00	C126
☐ Austria 1993–94	$19.00	C119	☐ New England 1993	$17.00	C114
☐ Belgium/Holland/ Luxembourg 1993–94	$18.00	C106	☐ New Mexico 1993–94	$15.00	C117
☐ Bahamas 1994–95	$17.00	C121	☐ New York State 1994–95	$19.00	C132
☐ Bermuda 1994–95	$15.00	C122	☐ Northwest 1991–92	$17.00	C026
☐ Brazil 1993–94	$20.00	C111	☐ Portugal 1992–93	$16.00	C027
☐ California 1993	$18.00	C112	☐ Puerto Rico 1993–94	$15.00	C103
☐ Canada 1992–93	$18.00	C009	☐ Puerto Vallarta/Manzanillo/ Guadalajara 1992–93	$14.00	C028
☐ Caribbean 1994	$18.00	C123	☐ Scandinavia 1993–94	$19.00	C118
☐ Carolinas/Georgia 1994–95	$17.00	C128	☐ Scotland 1992–93	$16.00	C040
☐ Colorado 1993–94	$16.00	C100	☐ Skiing Europe 1989–90	$15.00	C030
☐ Cruises 1993–94	$19.00	C107	☐ South Pacific 1992–93	$20.00	C031
☐ DE/MD/PA & NJ Shore 1992–93	$19.00	C012	☐ Spain 1993–94	$19.00	C115
☐ Egypt 1990–91	$17.00	C013	☐ Switzerland/Liechtenstein 1992–93	$19.00	C032
☐ England 1994	$18.00	C129	☐ Thailand 1992–93	$20.00	C033
☐ Florida 1994	$18.00	C124	☐ U.S.A. 1993–94	$19.00	C116
☐ France 1994–95	$20.00	C131	☐ Virgin Islands 1994–95	$13.00	C127
☐ Germany 1994	$19.00	C125	☐ Virginia 1992–93	$14.00	C037
☐ Italy 1994	$19.00	C130	☐ Yucatán 1993–94	$18.00	C110

FROMMER'S $-A-DAY GUIDES
(Guides to low-cost tourist accommodations and facilities)

	Retail Price	Code		Retail Price	Code
☐ Australia on $45 1993–94	$18.00	D102	☐ Mexico on $45 1994	$19.00	D116
☐ Costa Rica/Guatemala/ Belize on $35 1993–94	$17.00	D108	☐ New York on $70 1992–93	$16.00	D016
☐ Eastern Europe on $30 1993–94	$18.00	D110	☐ New Zealand on $45 1993–94	$18.00	D103
☐ England on $60 1994	$18.00	D112	☐ Scotland/Wales on $50 1992–93	$18.00	D019
☐ Europe on $50 1994	$19.00	D115	☐ South America on $40 1993–94	$19.00	D109
☐ Greece on $45 1993–94	$19.00	D100			
☐ Hawaii on $75 1994	$19.00	D113	☐ Turkey on $40 1992–93	$22.00	D023
☐ India on $40 1992–93	$20.00	D010	☐ Washington, D.C. on $40 1992–93	$17.00	D024
☐ Ireland on $40 1992–93	$17.00	D011			
☐ Israel on $45 1993–94	$18.00	D101			

FROMMER'S CITY $-A-DAY GUIDES
(Pocket-size guides with an emphasis on low-cost tourist accommodations and facilities)

	Retail Price	Code		Retail Price	Code
☐ Berlin on $40 1994–95	$12.00	D111	☐ Madrid on $50 1992–93	$13.00	D014
☐ Copenhagen on $50 1992–93	$12.00	D003	☐ Paris on $45 1994–95	$12.00	D117
☐ London on $45 1994–95	$12.00	D114	☐ Stockholm on $50 1992–93	$13.00	D022

FROMMER'S WALKING TOURS
(With routes and detailed maps, these companion guides point out the places and pleasures that make a city unique)

	Retail Price	Code		Retail Price	Code
☐ Berlin	$12.00	W100	☐ Paris	$12.00	W103
☐ London	$12.00	W101	☐ San Francisco	$12.00	W104
☐ New York	$12.00	W102	☐ Washington, D.C.	$12.00	W105

FROMMER'S TOURING GUIDES
(Color-illustrated guides that include walking tours, cultural and historic sites, and practical information)

	Retail Price	Code		Retail Price	Code
☐ Amsterdam	$11.00	T001	☐ New York	$11.00	T008
☐ Barcelona	$14.00	T015	☐ Rome	$11.00	T010
☐ Brazil	$11.00	T003	☐ Scotland	$10.00	T011
☐ Florence	$ 9.00	T005	☐ Sicily	$15.00	T017
☐ Hong Kong/Singapore/			☐ Tokyo	$15.00	T016
Macau	$11.00	T006	☐ Turkey	$11.00	T013
☐ Kenya	$14.00	T018	☐ Venice	$ 9.00	T014
☐ London	$13.00	T007			

FROMMER'S FAMILY GUIDES

	Retail Price	Code		Retail Price	Code
☐ California with Kids	$18.00	F100	☐ San Francisco with Kids	$17.00	F004
☐ Los Angeles with Kids	$17.00	F002	☐ Washington, D.C. with Kids	$17.00	F005
☐ New York City with Kids	$18.00	F003			

FROMMER'S CITY GUIDES
(Pocket-size guides to sightseeing and tourist accommodations and facilities in all price ranges)

	Retail Price	Code		Retail Price	Code
☐ Amsterdam 1993–94	$13.00	S110	☐ Montreál/Québec		
☐ Athens 1993–94	$13.00	S114	City 1993–94	$13.00	S125
☐ Atlanta 1993–94	$13.00	S112	☐ New Orleans 1993–94	$13.00	S103
☐ Atlantic City/Cape			☐ New York 1993	$13.00	S120
May 1993–94	$13.00	S130	☐ Orlando 1994	$13.00	S135
☐ Bangkok 1992–93	$13.00	S005	☐ Paris 1993–94	$13.00	S109
☐ Barcelona/Majorca/			☐ Philadelphia 1993–94	$13.00	S113
Minorca/Ibiza 1993–94	$13.00	S115	☐ Rio 1991–92	$ 9.00	S029
☐ Berlin 1993–94	$13.00	S116	☐ Rome 1993–94	$13.00	S111
☐ Boston 1993–94	$13.00	S117	☐ Salt Lake City 1991–92	$ 9.00	S031
☐ Cancún/Cozumel 1991–			☐ San Diego 1993–94	$13.00	S107
92	$ 9.00	S010	☐ San Francisco 1994	$13.00	S133
☐ Chicago 1993–94	$13.00	S122	☐ Santa Fe/Taos/		
☐ Denver/Boulder/Colorado			Albuquerque 1993–94	$13.00	S108
Springs 1993–94	$13.00	S131	☐ Seattle/Portland 1992–93	$12.00	S035
☐ Dublin 1993–94	$13.00	S128	☐ St. Louis/Kansas		
☐ Hawaii 1992	$12.00	S014	City 1993–94	$13.00	S127
☐ Hong Kong 1992–93	$12.00	S015	☐ Sydney 1993–94	$13.00	S129
☐ Honolulu/Oahu 1994	$13.00	S134	☐ Tampa/St.		
☐ Las Vegas 1993–94	$13.00	S121	Petersburg 1993–94	$13.00	S105
☐ London 1994	$13.00	S132	☐ Tokyo 1992–93	$13.00	S039
☐ Los Angeles 1993–94	$13.00	S123	☐ Toronto 1993–94	$13.00	S126
☐ Madrid/Costa del			☐ Vancouver/Victoria 1990–		
Sol 1993–94	$13.00	S124	91	$ 8.00	S041
☐ Miami 1993–94	$13.00	S118	☐ Washington, D.C. 1993	$13.00	S102
☐ Minneapolis/St.					
Paul 1993–94	$13.00	S119			

Other Titles Available at Membership Prices

SPECIAL EDITIONS

	Retail Price	Code		Retail Price	Code
☐ Bed & Breakfast North America	$15.00	P002	☐ Marilyn Wood's Wonderful Weekends (within a 250-mile radius of NYC)	$12.00	P017
☐ Bed & Breakfast Southwest	$16.00	P100	☐ National Park Guide 1993	$15.00	P101
☐ Caribbean Hideaways	$16.00	P103	☐ Where to Stay U.S.A.	$15.00	P102

GAULT MILLAU'S "BEST OF" GUIDES
(The only guides that distinguish the truly superlative from the merely overrated)

	Retail Price	Code		Retail Price	Code
☐ Chicago	$16.00	G002	☐ New England	$16.00	G010
☐ Florida	$17.00	G003	☐ New Orleans	$17.00	G011
☐ France	$17.00	G004	☐ New York	$17.00	G012
☐ Germany	$18.00	G018	☐ Paris	$17.00	G013
☐ Hawaii	$17.00	G006	☐ San Francisco	$17.00	G014
☐ Hong Kong	$17.00	G007	☐ Thailand	$18.00	G019
☐ London	$17.00	G009	☐ Toronto	$17.00	G020
☐ Los Angeles	$17.00	G005	☐ Washington, D.C.	$17.00	G017

THE REAL GUIDES
(Opinionated, politically aware guides for youthful budget-minded travelers)

	Retail Price	Code		Retail Price	Code
☐ Able to Travel	$20.00	R112	☐ Kenya	$12.95	R015
☐ Amsterdam	$13.00	R100	☐ Mexico	$11.95	R128
☐ Barcelona	$13.00	R101	☐ Morocco	$14.00	R129
☐ Belgium/Holland/ Luxembourg	$16.00	R031	☐ Nepal	$14.00	R018
☐ Berlin	$13.00	R123	☐ New York	$13.00	R019
☐ Brazil	$13.95	R003	☐ Paris	$13.00	R130
☐ California & the West Coast	$17.00	R121	☐ Peru	$12.95	R021
☐ Canada	$15.00	R103	☐ Poland	$13.95	R131
☐ Czechoslovakia	$15.00	R124	☐ Portugal	$16.00	R126
☐ Egypt	$19.00	R105	☐ Prague	$15.00	R113
☐ Europe	$18.00	R122	☐ San Francisco & the Bay Area	$11.95	R024
☐ Florida	$14.00	R006	☐ Scandinavia	$14.95	R025
☐ France	$18.00	R106	☐ Spain	$16.00	R026
☐ Germany	$18.00	R107	☐ Thailand	$17.00	R119
☐ Greece	$18.00	R108	☐ Tunisia	$17.00	R115
☐ Guatemala/Belize	$14.00	R127	☐ Turkey	$13.95	R027
☐ Hong Kong/Macau	$11.95	R011	☐ U.S.A.	$18.00	R117
☐ Hungary	$14.95	R118	☐ Venice	$11.95	R028
☐ Ireland	$17.00	R120	☐ Women Travel	$12.95	R029
☐ Italy	$18.00	R125	☐ Yugoslavia	$12.95	R030